MW01078270

# PREACHING WITH SACRED FIRE

Also edited by Martha Simmons and Frank A. Thomas

*9.11.01: African American Leaders Respond to an American Tragedy*

# PREACHING WITH SACRED FIRE

*An Anthology of African American Sermons, 1750 to the Present*

EDITED BY MARTHA SIMMONS AND FRANK A. THOMAS

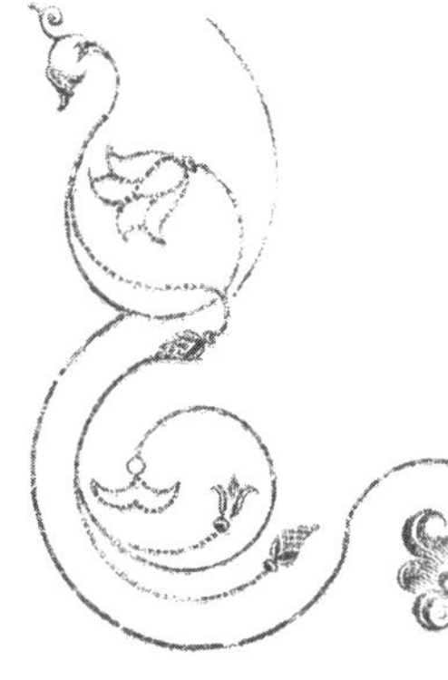

W. W. NORTON & COMPANY
NEW YORK LONDON

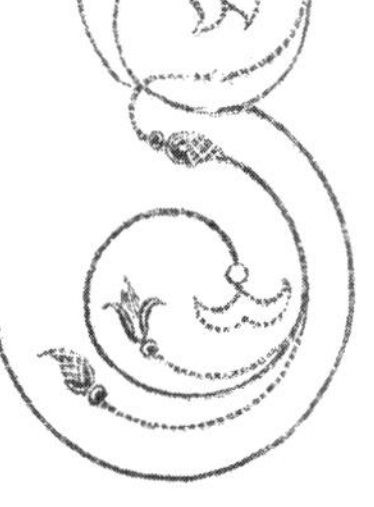

Printed in the United States of America
First Edition



Manufacturing by RR Donnelley Harrisonburg
Book design by Lovedog Studio
Production manager: Julia Druskin

Library of Congress Cataloging-in-Publication Data

Preaching with sacred fire : an anthology of African American sermons, 1750 to the present / edited by Martha Simmons and Frank A. Thomas. — 1st ed.
p. cm.
Includes bibliographical references.
ISBN 978-0-393-05831-4 (hardcover)
1. Sermons, American—African American authors.
I. Simmons, Martha J. II. Thomas, Frank A. (Frank Anthony), 1955–
BV4241.5.P75 2010
252.0089'96073—dc22

2010025164

W. W. Norton & Company, Inc.
500 Fifth Avenue, New York, N.Y. 10110
www.wwnorton.com

W. W. Norton & Company Ltd.
Castle House, 75/76 Wells Street, London W1T 3QT

1 2 3 4 5 6 7 8 9 0

James Earl Massey
*Anderson School of Theology (Retired)*

Marvin A. McMickle
*Pastor, Antioch Baptist Church, Cleveland, Ohio, and Ashland Theological Seminary*

Henry H. Mitchell
*Interdenominational Theological Center (Retired)*

Anthony B. Pinn
*Rice University*

Cheryl Sanders
*Howard Divinity School*

Elton Weaver
*University of Memphis*

*To all of our griots, diviners, seers, imams,*
*mystics, conjurers, priests, exhorters, ecclesiasts, bishops,*
*apostles, evangelists, priestesses,*
*preachers, pulpiteers, prophets, gospel pushers, heralds,*
*holy mothers,*
*divine fathers, sermonizers,*
*and those who tell the story . . .*

*those whose words and deeds*
*the Spirit called forth*
*out of mourning*
*the dawning of this morning*

—Martha Simmons

# CONTENTS

# FOREWORD

It is, perhaps, a truism to say that the preaching that gets closest to the throbbing heart of God is preaching that rises out of circumstances touched and tinged with heartbreak, heartbreak that sees and senses and says something of the heartbreak of God, which is undaunted by resistance and opposition, and which marches resolutely by way of a cross on a hill to shout in a cemetery.

And so it is with great pride and expectation that I introduce the long overdue *Preaching with Sacred Fire: An Anthology of African American Sermons, 1750 to the Present*. This volume makes available to the world that fiery preaching born of holy fire that characterizes African American pulpit discourse at its best. Here we have centuries of such preaching rising out of the tears and travails and triumphs of a people, "not many wise, not many mighty, not many noble" (1 Corinthians 1:26), who have seen the ways of God in their "weary years" and in their "silent tears."

Who can forget the great New Testament preaching of John the Baptist, in the desert preaching a baptism of repentance for the forgiveness of sin and yet able to speak to Herod that his morals were not pleasing to God. John's preaching got him beheaded, and yet he marched resolutely by way of a cross on a hill to shout in a cemetery. Who can forget Peter preaching on the day of Pentecost, and three thousand came to God, and yet Peter marched resolutely by way of a cross on a hill to shout in a cemetery.

The august poet James Weldon Johnson penned these words in his song of legendary hope for African Americans: "Sing a song full of the faith that the dark past has taught us." Preaching is a way that African Americans have sung the faith that the dark past has taught us. Specifically, preaching with sacred fire is the way that we extracted hope from the lessons of faith that years of slavery, segregation, and racism have taught us.

All true preaching is singed with sadness, heartbreak, and opposition, and yet it marches resolutely by way of a cross on a hill to shout in a cemetery and then moves to release its message of victory to the countryside and the city. As Christians, we believe that God was in Christ reconciling the world based upon a life and a resurrection after crucifixion, and therefore Jesus sets the paradigmatic example in word and deed of the preacher that experiences the heartbreak of God and yet in his or her preaching and his or her body, and yet . . .

*—Gardner C. Taylor*

# PREFACE

GIVEN THE SPAN AND SCOPE OF THE TRAGIC, TORTUOUS, AND YET TRIUMPHANT history of blacks in North America, it is legitimate to ask this question: What has sustained and liberated blacks during more than four hundred years of systemic slavery, racism, hatred, violence, and second-class citizenship? The answer is, of course, as complex and varied as black people. Yet, by all accounts, black religion and religious institutions (brush harbors, storefronts, churches, mosques, and denominational assemblages) have been the most important and vital instruments of black survival and liberation during their four-hundred-year history in North America. In addition to being the spiritual foundation of the black community, these institutions have also been the initiators of freedom movements for black people.

These institutions have been led by some of the most imaginative and skilled leaders, orators, and preachers in history. Throughout this anthology, the term *preacher* is used to refer to ordained and non-ordained persons, regardless of the orientation of their faiths or their denominational affiliations or lack of denominational affiliations. We also include those who serve as imams, conjurers, and exhorters.

Even during the most difficult and oppressive times, the delivery, creativity, charisma, expressivity, fervor, forcefulness, passion, persuasiveness, poise, power, rhetoric, spirit, style, and vision of black preaching gave and gives hope to a community under siege. It is also noteworthy that the homiletical skills of many preachers were obtained with little or no formal academic training.

Preaching has been the most celebrated method used by blacks to communicate their spirituality, culture, history, victories, visions, and vicissitudes to each other and to the world. Unfortunately, up and until the last twenty-five years or so, even the black community failed to systematically document and record much of this genius for future generations. This failure says more about the oral nature of black culture than it does about how much it values the preached word.

Preaching has been so significant to black culture that the sermonic style and the ethos of the griot, the brush harbor storyteller, the imam, and the folk and urban preacher have become embedded in and/or helped to spawn the birth of musical genres: spirituals, gospel, blues, jazz, and rap. Black preaching has been choreographed in dance, memorialized in movies and documentaries, and immortalized in folklore. Black preaching and religious oratory has also provided the impetus for numerous books, novels, and other forms of American literature, including James Weldon Johnson's *God's Trombones*, James Baldwin's *Go Tell It on the Mountain* and *The Amen Corner*, Zora Neale Hurston's *The Sanctified Church* and *Their Eyes Were Watching God*, and Toni Morrison's *Beloved*.

Historically, in the literature, black preachers have been lumped as one homogenous group. Even though a great deal has been written about black religion and religious institutions in general in the last fifty years, there has been inadequate attention paid to the homiletical genius of individual preachers within the black community, with the exception of three or four select preachers. Most of what has been written suffers from at least two shortcomings.

First, there has not been enough said about the genius of women in the black preaching tradition. Accordingly, we have included in this anthology known and unknown women preachers to show their varying approaches to texts and cultural issues. We have also paid homage to the women sermonette-singers in an extended fashion in the introduction to section five (Civil Rights and Direct Action, 1951–1968). These women were brave forerunners of many of today's best women preachers. They found a method—singing—through which God could speak through them and through which they could gain a hearing.

Second, because of its historical significance in the black church, we included a section on whooping. Though greatly loved and admired by those who are familiar with this preaching art form, it has rarely been properly chronicled by scholars or by whoopers themselves. Whooping is a style of melody used during preaching which is most often defined by a series of cohesive pitches which have continuity, tonality, quasi-metrical phraseology, and formulaic cadence.[1]

We have put together this collection to address these shortcomings and provide a more expansive presentation of black preaching. However, this anthology is not without its own shortcomings. First, there were many whom we did not include due to space constraints or our inability to obtain material. Second, time and space did not allow us to give adequate attention to non-Christian preachers who were and are an important part of the black faith community. We hope that future projects will tackle this important task. Third, this is clearly a North American perspective. Although we pay homage to the role of our African ancestors in many instances, we are clear that a much larger role could have been given to that continent.

## PREACHING WITH SACRED FIRE: AN ANTHOLOGY OF AFRICAN AMERICAN SERMONS, 1750 TO THE PRESENT

The phrase *sacred fire* is representative of the fact that ministers and those to whom they minister know that for souls to be fed, healed, and liberated, the Holy Spirit in Christian churches, the spirit of beneficence and mercy in Muslim mosques, and the ever-abiding spirit of the ancestors in African Traditional Religion must be present. The phrase acknowledges that something more than the skills or wisdom of the preacher is at hand. Indeed, the very power and wisdom of the universe and all of life is speaking, manifesting, and communicating, channeled through the preacher directly to those who have "ears to hear."

### *How We Decided Whom to Include*

Given the finite realities of time and space, we were faced with difficult choices as to whose sermons would be included. Because of this, we have included in a section titled "Other Notable Preachers" brief sketches of other preachers who should be studied. We hope this section will help future researchers pick up the mantle where we stopped.

There were thousands of sermons and messages from which to select and even more for which we could not obtain permission, such as material for Elijah Muhammad, George Baker Jr. (aka Father Divine), and Charles Manuel Grace (aka Sweet Daddy Grace). We know that other anthologists may have made different choices. We used the following criteria:

- **The preacher's oratorical prowess is undisputed by his or her peers and the wider community.** Each generation produces a small cadre of preachers whose gifts and talents are unquestioned and well known. Most of the preachers featured in this anthology fall into this category.
- **A literary trail attests to his or her gifts and genius.** Because black preaching culture has historically been oral and has had few scribes, many messages have been lost or were not recorded. So, while history shows us the footprints of many outstanding black preachers, written indications of their presence in sermonic form have been lost. Thank goodness for those who did leave an accessible literary trail.
- **The emergence of his or her voice signaled a new homiletical and/or oratorical movement.** These particular preachers reinvented old stylistic and rhetorical devices that opened up the language of the black pulpit and or provided entirely new homiletical approaches.
- **He or she produced generations of imitators.** If imitation is the highest form of flattery, then there have long been black preachers who have been highly flattered, even across racial and ethnic lines. Moreover, the imitators, in many instances, gave extended life to preaching styles that would otherwise have had a shorter life span because of the black community's strong reliance on orality.
- **His or her oratory spoke decisively to a historical moment and often was coupled with action.** From Reverend Frederick Douglass to Sojourner Truth to Martin Luther King Jr. to Malcolm X: part of what made their oratory so powerful was the creative and imaginative way that these preachers were able to name a significant current flowing wide and deep in the hearts and minds of black people, and *all* people, during challenging historical moments.

In addition, these speakers gained notoriety by coupling their voices with important movements of their day. In instances when their oratory may have been overlooked, or at least minimized, it instead grew in stature and acclaim because it was combined with significant deeds. This was especially true of leaders who established educational institutions, headed newspapers, led protest movements, developed community-based programs for the poor, advocated against unjust laws, and stood up to violence.

## The Scope of the Anthology

This anthology does not purport to be a homiletical instruction manual. Instead, it was our desire that academicians and nonacademicians, blacks and non-blacks, persons with religious proclivities and those without could gain a glimpse of the heart and sinew of black preaching—its vocabulary, its methodologies, its shifts, and what makes it distinctive. We have also endeavored to include materials that would provide students in undergraduate and graduate programs a basic understanding of black preaching.

In producing this anthology, we hope to achieve at least four things: First, we wanted to place a record of several hundred years of black preaching in one volume, to preserve and maintain for posterity a reader on black preaching. Second, we wished to document the richness and variety of the preaching that has been produced by black Americans. The black faith community is not monolithic. It includes preachers whose messages are practical, holy, prophetic, contemplative, eclectic, social, dynamic, and so much more. Third, we wanted to expand the world's understanding of black preaching and show how it has provided orators whose words and lives have so enhanced the human landscape that they deserve much further study. And finally, we wanted to extend a clarion call to African American universities, colleges, seminaries, and libraries, urging them to establish permanent facilities, to collect, house, analyze, interpret, and preserve the preaching legacy of our faith community so that future generations of preachers, students, scholars, congregants, and all others so interested will have access to this supreme treasure.

## A Word about Terminology

Throughout this anthology, the word *slave* is used sparingly, because the word in its familiar and common currency masks the full humanity of those who were brought captive from Africa and prohibits serious, scholarly inquiry into identity questions that reveal who these men, women, and children were, as well as their hopes, dreams, and fears. Through the word *slave*, the captured became nameless, faceless, and cultureless cargo, beasts of burden. We prefer the phrases *forced immigrants* or *the enslaved*, because these terms give human identity and dignity to the great civilization of the human beings who were forced into servitude and exile in the Americas.[2]

This anthology is not immune from the age-old quandary of what terms to use when speaking of those born in America to American-born parents whose ancestors are of African origin. We have used the word *Negro* in sections of the anthology that concern the eighteenth through mid-twentieth centuries. In many instances, we have also used *black*, a term that grew out of the social movements of the 1960s and is still commonly used. Often, we use *African American*, especially when referring to persons and events in the twentieth century and beyond. This term is not used to identify immigrants from African nations, the Caribbean islands, or Central and South America. It identifies those who are descendants of Africans brought to the Americas as slaves between the sixteenth and nineteenth centuries. No additional determinations were made concerning the use of the terms black or African American, other than a desire for consistency when possible.

—Martha Simmons
Atlanta, Georgia

—Frank A. Thomas
Memphis, Tennessee
March 2009

### *Notes*

1. Jon Michael Spencer, *Sacred Symphony: The Chanted Sermon of the Black Preacher* (New York: Greenwood Press, 1987), 9.
2. Michael Mason, "Captive and Client Labor and the Economy of the Bida Emirate, 1857–1901," *Journal of African History* 14, no. 3 (1973), 459–60.

# INTRODUCTION

THIS ANTHOLOGY RESTS FIRST UPON THE PREMISE THAT THE MAIN initiators of freedom and emancipation for black people have been their religious faith, the religious communities and institutions, and the souls that house that faith. The second premise is that the role of preaching to that religious faith and those religious communities, institutions, and souls has been paramount. Black preaching has sustained and liberated black people in the sweltering heat of servitude and American oppression. This anthology seeks to delineate the liberating, transformative, and celebratory role of preaching. But before we further expand upon black preaching's role, we turn to the significant connection between black preaching and Africa.

## THE AFRICAN ROOTS OF BLACK PREACHING

The black preaching tradition is rooted in the religions of the foreparents of the Africans who were forcefully brought to the Americas. From the moment they were removed from their home village and tribal lands and chained in ships' holds, their traditional belief systems and rituals of communication were all they had to depend on. After they arrived in North America, they did not know how to make sense of life once separated from their tribal religions' supreme being. For instance, the Yorubas of

Nigeria came here believing in a high god named Olodumare, the Yoruba term for omnipotent.[1] While they originally turned to their god for meaning and comfort, life in the Americas was so cruel and chaotic that they searched for the reigning local deity and sought to learn how that deity operated. Out of this spiritual necessity grew the slow and tedious process of creating black North American religions out of the common practices of many African belief systems. Because they were seeking to meet real needs, the enslaved created a spiritual orientation and functional faith on their own terms, as opposed to what their enslavers tried to teach them.

The process of establishing the religions of black folk on North American shores was slow, in part, because there were Africans from many tribes, with different languages, belief systems, and worship practices. It took time to develop makeshift languages in which they could communicate with one another. Yet, the enslaved used their last drop of energy to satisfy the universal human hunger for dignity and honor, including through religious expression. They had enough commonality among their various tribal traditions to extract core beliefs and develop "one Neo-African consciousness—basically similar yet already significantly different from West African understandings of traditional African religion."[2]

There were many aspects of Traditional African Religion that were easily adaptable into the Christian-based North American cosmology; there were major overlaps between Traditional African Religion and the Old Testament. As historian Carter G. Woodson wrote, "it was easy for the Negro to accept a faith which differed little from the one he had in Africa."[3] Examples of the similarity between the two include the African concept of the "living dead" and the Christian concept of the afterlife; the African Law of Identical Harvest and the Bible's "you reap what you sow" (Galatians 6:8); the prayer offered to the Supreme Being as the creator spirit with access to extraordinary power and as the giver of health and medicine, and the Christian concept of God's ability to heal through prayer.[4] Also, the water rites of religious rebirth in African religious practices were similar to Christian baptism.[5]

Even more to our purpose in this anthology, Traditional African Religion had a great respect for the power of words, illustrated by certain folktales and myths. The Bible in Western culture was held in much this same esteem, though in Africa oral telling held sway over written text. African religion contributed to black preaching the necessity of a serious verbal engagement with the audience in order to pass on holy wisdom (proverbs and other forms) and, most importantly, the presence of the unspeakable Presence.

In fact, black religion in North America began with combinations of

Bible stories told in English mixed with African retellings and interpretations, primarily in African folk styles. The most important elements were vivid narration and call-and-response. The indigenous renditions in the motherland had been at once entertaining and spiritually instructive, essentially intended to inform and teach the young in the traditions of African society. All of this served well the goals of preaching on North American shores.

Eventually, perhaps around the mid-eighteenth century, the English Bible replaced much of the indigenous wisdom tradition of the enslaved. It was chosen primarily for content, to fill the role of the holy wisdom once couched in the African languages; by this time English had become the only commonly understood language. But the Bible was also seen as a means of access to the power wielded by the deity worshiped by the masters. It was natural, after that, to add African culture's emphasis on oratory, imagery, drama, and tonality to what became black preaching in America. This was especially true after the Africans saw and heard white preachers like George Whitefield use such strategies during the First Great Awakening, a colonies-wide revival in the mid-eighteenth century.

It is not known precisely when authentic black preaching of the Christian faith began to take shape, but it is likely that the tradition formally surfaced toward the end of the First Great Awakening. Very few written records of preaching by enslaved Africans exists prior to that time. Preaching from the outset was done without notes, often without the ability to read. It is tragic that we have no record of how it sounded or what preachers said when black preaching began in what became America.

## FAITHS BEYOND CHRISTIANITY

While the majority of blacks in America are part of the Christian church, from the time that Africans were first brought to the Americas and the Caribbean during the transatlantic slave trade until the present, blacks have embraced religious traditions other than Christianity.

The practice of these observances is, in large part, a reaction to social and political issues, particularly racism, that have confronted blacks over the past four hundred years, but most especially from the eighteenth to the twentieth century. The most notable and oldest of these traditions have been various forms of Islam. Finding the exact number of Muslims who landed in North America as captives is an extremely difficult task. There are no precision documents relative to the religion of human cargo noted by slavetraders and slave dealers. Therefore, suggesting numbers and figures is highly problematic and risky. Allan Austin asserts that between 5 and 10 percent of all slaves from ports between Senegal and the Bight of Benin (from which half of all Africans were sent to North America) were Muslims. If the total number of enslaved was twelve million and roughly 6 or 7 percent arrived in North America, then there may have been forty thousand Muslims in colonial and pre–Civil War America. Austin admits that future systematic gathering of records on slave trading ports on both sides of the Atlantic as well as other scholarly studies will lead to "better figures and descriptions."[6] Though many African slaves were Muslim, and a number of them continued to practice Islam once in North America, African Muslim captives never formed into a sizeable American community of faith that passed on its traditions from one generation to the next.[7] The Muslim community diminishes until what Edward E. Curtis calls "the English speaking black theorists of Islam," especially Noble Drew Ali and Elijah Muhammad, define Islam in America.[8] However, blacks have also embraced other non-Christian religions, such as Judaism and Buddhism, and created Santeria, Vodun, and Rastafarianism using West African and other principles.

It is important to note that in most of these religions, there is nothing that compares exactly to the form of the sermon or the homiletical techniques and traditions of preaching discussed most often in this anthology. The Bible is not an authoritative text in most of these non-Christian traditions. Rituals, dietary customs, distinctive forms of worship, special readings, and prayers have often taken the place of preaching or made it secondary, though not unimportant.

Many significant non-Christian leaders have emerged within the black community during the years considered in this anthology, but few if any have ever enjoyed the reputation of being a "great preacher." They have been compelling orators on matters of social policy, race relations, and moral conduct. They have been masterful teachers and interpreters of the texts of their religions. However, because they did not base their speech or orations on texts taken from the Bible, which many blacks continue to view as the normative text for religious worship, the ability of these non-Christian leaders to appeal to a large cross-section of the black community has been limited. Also, because the numbers of such persons have remained relatively small in comparison to the number of Christian clergy, there are many within the Christian community who still do not have an awareness of or an appreciation for the non-Christian religious traditions and religious leaders that emerged around them. For example, though there is a tradition of at least three hundred years of Muslim preaching in North America, little is known about the continent's Muslim faith community prior to Elijah Muhammad's ascendance as the leader of the most well-known black Muslim group (the Nation of Islam) in the 1950s.

Given the general absence of the sermon in most non-Christian traditions, the entire approach to worship, and for other reasons, the work of spiritual formation, is quite different from those that are employed by most black Christians. Most black Christians are familiar with observing such occasions as Christmas and Easter, but they are less familiar with Ramadan and other Islamic festivals and holy days. They are generally familiar with the Bible as a book of religious instruction, but less familiar with how parts of that book are interpreted by black Jews.

Jesus Christ as the perfect sacrifice that takes away the sins of the world is a well-known doctrine among African American Christians, but animal sacrifice as practiced by the devotees of Santeria or Vodun is much less understood or appreciated. Similarly, spirit possession is frequently seen and experienced in many African American Christian settings, most notably among many of the Holiness-Pentecostal, Apostolic, and Baptist groups. However, the actions that can result in spirit possession and the reasons for seeking spiritual possession in the first place are very different among some of the black non-Christian and African-based religious groups.

Given the dominance of Christianity within the United States from the country's inception, and given the central role that the African American church has played within the lives of so many within the African American community, the question must be asked: Why or how do African Americans come to the decision to practice faiths other than Christianity? The first answer, as briefly mentioned earlier, is that the Africans who were brought to this country during the slave trade brought much of their cultural heritage with them during the Middle Passage journey from Senegal, Ghana, Angola, and other places in Africa to Brazil, Haiti, Cuba, the United States, and settlements in the Americas and Caribbean. As early as the 1730s, observants of Islam were among those from throughout West Africa who were captured and brought as slaves to North America. Islam, along with various aspects of the Yoruba religion from West Africa, was among those cultural mementos that survived the journey and continued to survive in the spirit and behavior of African people in the diaspora.

Second, African captives continued earlier African practices under the guise of Christianity, what Elizabeth McAlister calls "a creolized system" of religion or "code-switching" between some form of Christianity, usually Roman Catholicism, and traditional African religions.[9] New religions such as Santeria, in Cuba, Vodun, in Haiti, and Candomble, in

Brazil, took root as a result of that process of creolization. Leonard Barrett refers to the newer religious traditions as "black redemption cults," inferring that African people turned to these created religious practices as a way to cope with and in some ways to actually resist their lives as slaves.[10] Over time, the practitioners of Santeria and Vodun, in particular, made permanent homes in the United States, especially in cities such as Miami, New Orleans, and New York.

Third, African captives practiced non-Christian religions as a protest against Christianity and white society. Some of the most charismatic and controversial figures to emerge from within the African American faith community were those who urged their followers to reject Christianity and embrace other religious traditions. They largely based their argument on the facts that Christianity had been imposed upon black people, and, to make matters worse, leaders within the white Christian church continued to support the oppression and second-class status of their black Christian brothers and sisters. The non-Christian leaders believed that the black community needed to reclaim their original, authentic, African faith and identity. This approach would include such men and movements as Noble Drew Ali and the Moorish Science Temple, Rabbi Wentworth A. Matthew and the Black Jews of Harlem, and W.D. Fard, who was followed by Elijah Muhammad and the Nation of Islam.[11]

Any discussion of the practice of non-Christian traditions in black religion would have to include the personality movements that emerged in urban centers during the Great Migration, when millions of blacks moved from the rural South to the cities of the North during World War I and into the 1920s, which was followed by the cataclysmic Depression of the 1930s. Social dislocation and harsh economic forces made the messages of some groups very appealing.

George "Father Divine" Baker of the Peace Mission Movement and Charles Manuel "Sweet Daddy" Grace of the United House of Prayer for All People founded the most prominent of these movements. In addition to religious identity, these groups also provided people with a social community and even basic needs, such as food, clothing, and minimal employment during the hard times of the Great Depression. They were providing a level of service that most Christian churches, with a few exceptions, could not or would not provide. Seiger and Singer describe these urban movements as "a variant of African American nationalism that combines religious belief with the ultimate objective of achieving some degree of political, social, cultural and/or economic autonomy."[12]

Lastly, blacks adopt non-Christian traditions of religious observance because they find those traditions fulfilling in their search for spiritual identity. As the twenty-first century dawns, there are many within the African American community who have voluntarily turned to a wide variety of non-Christian religions. In many cases, their search for spiritual identity is unrelated to any of the protest issues or the inclusion of African rituals that may have been the impetus to join or create earlier non-Christian religions. With the resurgence of African pride and the phenomenal popularity of the Jamaican singer Bob Marley, some African Americans have embraced Rastafarianism, and others, such as R&B singer Tina Turner, have turned to Buddhism in one of its many forms. Some adhere to the Baha'i faith or to another of the world's religions as a way to embrace what they view as their relevant messages and worldviews. Having briefly noted the role and nature of the main non-Christian sectors of the African American faith community, we now turn to the principles that underline African American Christian preaching.

## PRINCIPLES OF BLACK CHRISTIAN PREACHING

When we consider the black (primarily Christian) preaching tradition, several principles emerge. The first is the centrality of the Bible. This is not to be mistaken for rigid literalism; the Bible is seen as an inspired and dynamic source for understanding the world and as a wise guide for life's decisions. Homiletican Cleophus J. LaRue has stated it thus: "Indeed, it is no secret that the Bible occupies a central place in the religious life of black Americans. More than a mere source for texts, in black preaching the Bible is the single most important source of language, imagery, and story for the sermon."[13]

The second principle of black preaching is that the Bible is made to come literally alive by means of an eyewitness style of picture painting and narration. The preacher has studied and meditated on the Bible to a point where the Bible is not only ideas, but visual images. These images can be easily remembered and delivered, without notes, to an audience, which then shares in the preacher's experience. Faith is transmitted holistically, viscerally rather than only intellectually, as art rather than as argument. The preachers strive for sincere faith based upon religious experience, moving hearers to a relationship with the Divine.

Third, a reason for such profound sermonic insights is the cultural habit of the close observation of life, which yields a rich storehouse of interesting, true stories illustrative of biblical precepts with which the hearer may identify. This method could be termed *existential exegesis*. It was practiced by the best slave preachers and continues to this day.

Not to be overlooked is the preacher's desire for relevance. The preacher prays that his or her sermons will help the hearer at points of need, not just reach them as abstract doctrine. The Western notion held by many of sermons as primarily offered to God is supplemented by a traditional African notion of sermons as a vehicle to give useful instruction. If it glorified God, then it had to help people. Even the sermon's eloquence was not for mere decoration, but was and is seen as lending power to the Word, and fostering its purposes.

Black preaching fosters an aptitude of thinking deeply and learning wherever possible, in formal academic settings and in the classroom of life. This is in relation to all of life, not just for preaching purposes and shapes the "cultural habit of the perceptive observation of life" as expressed in principle three. This explains why the homiletical quality of sermons by the best of the self-educated preachers have not been in the least inferior to those by preachers with formal training. Indeed, it is likely that the response of the hearers to the self-educated is often better because there is a strong suspicion they have not been educated away from their own culture.

Next, the black preaching tradition is aware of dependence on a power beyond the preacher's power. It can be called transcendence, divine beneficence, the Holy Spirit, the Holy Ghost, or the Spirit. Preachers believe that beyond their best abilities and preparation, their sermons are controlled, enriched, and guided by the Spirit. Preachers believe that their words ultimately come from the Creator and Sustainer of the Universe, who has shaped them and delivers messages through the preacher's careful and thorough discipline. The glory then belongs to the Divine and not to the preacher.

A final underlying principle of much of black preaching is the use of suspense followed by a powerful and uplifting conclusion (also known as the sermon celebration or close). The timing within the art of preaching is like the timing of a great drama or symphony. Suspense is built in stages, resolved, and then concluded in a focused, emotionally powerful ending. The typical black sermon ends in a joyful celebration, not a challenge for hearers to do this or that. The admonition to do, to change, to serve, and so forth is reserved for the body of the message. The close is reserved for pure celebration. The conclusion gives reinforcement to the text and primary purpose of the sermon, or message in the case of the Koran. The weight that the black faith community places upon a good conclusion to a message or sermon is unparalleled. It is not matched by other faith communities, though there is evidence that this is slowly changing with the increase of "praise and worship" and neo-Pentecostal-styled worship services.

## THE DIVISIONS OF THIS ANTHOLOGY

This anthology is divided into six periods or eras:

THE BEGINNINGS OF AFRICAN AMERICAN PREACHING:
1750–1789

SOCIAL AND RELIGIOUS EMANCIPATION:
1790–1865

FROM RECONSTRUCTION TO DECONSTRUCTION:
1866–1917

WORLD WARS, FREEDOM STRUGGLES, AND RENAISSANCE:
1918–1950

CIVIL RIGHTS AND DIRECT ACTION:
1951–1968

FROM BLACK TO AFRICAN AMERICAN AND BEYOND:
1969 TO THE PRESENT

Each section begins with a brief historical overview of the period, followed by a discussion of the preaching and then brief biographies of some of the distinguished personalities whose preaching and methods made significant impacts upon the period. Their sermons follow. Sermons have not been placed in periods using a scientific method. Rather, their placement is most often an attempt to place a preacher with his or her contemporaries and within the period in which they were most active.

## CATEGORIES OF BLACK PREACHING

Detailed and careful attention to the powerful and liberating black preaching tradition reveals four classifications that serve as a homiletical umbrella: *social activist preaching*, which provides the spiritual, moral, and cultural underpinnings for liberation struggles; *black identity preaching*, which seeks to reconstruct blacks' humanity, dignity, and self-esteem; *cultural survival preaching*, which constructs and maintains black culture; and *empowerment preaching*, which provides an unequivocal message of wealth and success through change in consciousness as a liberation strategy. All black preaching falls within at least one of these classifications; some overlaps into one or more categories.

*Social activist preaching* aims to induce social activism by providing the spiritual, political, and cultural underpinnings for liberation struggles, including the prophetic voice of social critique and redress. It is principally projected to a wider American culture and world, but also serves as an inner critique of the black church and black culture. The social activist preaching agenda includes poverty alleviation, racial and gender equality, and all peace, justice, and economic struggles.

*Preaching for black identity* is preaching to construct and reconstruct humanity and dignity, and to enhance the self-esteem of blacks. The experience of slavery and its ideological justifications functioned to assault black identity and personhood. This category encompasses so much black preaching that an eminent authority on preaching, Gardner C. Taylor, has stated that the essence of *all* black preaching is raising the self-esteem of black people.[14] Though we can agree with Taylor, there are important, obvious distinctions that are blurred if we subsume all other black preaching classifications under this heading. For example, preaching for black identity is closely related to social activist preaching, in that the social activist sermon attempts to raise the esteem of hearers in order to encourage them to act. But the critical difference is that preaching for black identity usually does not feature a political program.

*Preaching for cultural survival* is preaching for the construction and maintenance of black culture that helps blacks endure in their average, day-to-day, week-to-week living. In addition to systemic oppression, blacks still contend with the nodal events of human life—birth, death, sickness, disease, marriage, school, financial crisis, birthdays, job loss, and so forth. The experience of oppression has often been writ so large that we can forget that much of black preaching concerned the maintenance and development of everyday survival skills. This culture of survival was forged Sunday after Sunday, prayer meeting after prayer meeting, even funeral after funeral, in the lives of religious adherents. Preaching for cultural survival often resembles preaching for black identity. It too encourages persons to endure for another week, despite the highs and lows of life. Preaching for cultural survival is the largest area of black preaching; in all of its manifestations it seeks to give stability to hearers and order to their everyday lives. It contains four subareas: the regular Sunday-morning sermon (typically concerning biblical and theological doctrines, denomination polity, local issues, and in-house church issues), the revival sermon, the funeral sermon, and the annual-day sermon (for occasions such as Men's Day, Mother's Day, Choir Anniversary, Usher's Day, and so forth).

*Empowerment preaching* provides an unequivocal message of black power, a belief in entrepreneurism, wealth, and success where individuals primarily find liberation through changing their consciousness and through hard work, and less through social reform movements. Empowerment preaching is a liberation strategy. For most empowerment sermons the homiletical focus is not social protest, but individual initiative buttressed by one's familial, and in some instances community, unit. For some in the black community, it is only acceptable to combine individual achievements with social movements that aid the entire black race. Empowerment preaching asserts that the American Dream is real—everyone has the opportunity to move up if they work hard and are talented. While empowerment preaching acknowledges structural barriers that limit individual wealth and success, it does not view them as forces that cannot be overcome. The message of empowerment preaching not only includes financial well-being, it also stresses the need for blacks to be political leaders and controllers of their own destiny. Being empowered to control one's destiny is the overriding concern of empowerment preaching.

Although it gained prominence among blacks in the late 1900s, by the 1930s some advocates of empowerment preaching, through white preachers who taught that faith was rewarded with wealth and health, shifted its focus to individual wealth, as opposed to communal wealth. The focus was no longer the advancement of persons so that they and their communities would thrive, nor was the focus tied to increasing appreciation of one's ethnic heritage. The focus shifted so sharply to individual wealth that it became clear by the 1980s that a segment of black preaching had adopted *prosperity preaching*. Prosperity preaching places its greatest emphasis on the achievement of financial wealth by individuals. While it may purport to have other concerns, they are all treated as secondary or insignificant. The most important thing is that individuals prosper financially. Often, such prospering occurs after preachers ask hearers to sow seeds that will result in the hearer achieving a financial and physical blessing (or healing).

With the strands of black preaching now presented, we begin the journey through the liberating, salvific, and celebratory messages of centuries of black preaching in North America. While blacks were the direct beneficiaries of this preaching, all of America and indeed the world benefited greatly from it. From Jarena Lee to John Jasper to Noble Drew Ali and Vernon Johns, the African American preaching tradition has at its highest and best always had as its ultimate concern the spiritual and social liberation of all persons. This anthology salutes those

*whose words and deeds*
*the Spirit called forth*
*out of mourning*
*the dawning of this morning.*

## *Notes*

1. E. Bolaji Idowu, *Olodumare: God in Yoruba Belief* (London: Longman Group, 1962), 30–37.
2. Mechal Sobel, *Trabelin' On: The Slave Journey to an Afro-Baptist Faith* (Westport, CT: Greenwood Press, 1979), xvii.
3. Carter G. Woodson, *African Background Outlined* (New York: Negro University Press, 1936), 359.
4. Kofi Asare Opoku, *West African Traditional Religion* (Accra, Ghana: FEP International Private, 1979), 137–39.
5. Ibid., 60ff.
6. Allan Austin, *African Muslims in Antebellum America: Transatlantic Stories and Spiritual Struggles* (New York: Routledge, 1997), 22, 23.
7. Edward E. Curtis IV, *Islam in Black America: Identity, Liberation, and Difference in African American Islamic Thought* (Albany: State University of New York Press, 2002), 7.
8. Ibid., 7.
9. Elizabeth McAlister, "The Madonna of 115th Street Revisited: Vodou and Haitian Catholicism in the Age of Transnationalism," in *African American Religious Thought*, ed. Cornel West and Eddie Glaude Jr. (Louisville, KY: Westminster John Knox Press, 2003), 942–77.
10. Leonard Barrett, *Soul Force: African Heritage in Afro-American Religion* (Garden City, NY: Anchor Books, 1974), 96.
11. Entries on each of these men can be found in Marvin A. McMickle's *An Encyclopedia of African American Christian Heritage* (Valley Forge, PA: Judson Press, 2002), as well as in the *Encyclopedia of African American Religions*, ed. Larry Murphy, Gordon Melton, and Gary L. Ward (New York: Garland, 1993).
12. Hans Seiger and Merrill Singer, "Religious Diversification During the Era of Advanced Industrial Capitalism," in *African American Religious Thought*, 525.
13. Cleophus J. LaRue, *The Heart of Black Preaching* (Louisville, KY: Westminster John Knox Press, 2000), 10.
14. An informal 2003 conversation between Martha Simmons and Gardner C. Taylor at the Hampton University Ministers' Conference.

# I

# THE BEGINNINGS OF AFRICAN AMERICAN PREACHING: *1750–1789*

# INTRODUCTION

By 1650, more than a million Africans had been forced to migrate to the Americas. By the end of the colonial era, almost seven million Africans had been brought to the Americas against their will.[1] This number does not include those who died in Africa rather than be captured, those who died during the more than two hundred slave ship revolts between 1650–1789,[2] nor those who committed suicide on slave ships or died due to the barbaric conditions of the Middle Passage, the popular name given to the treacherous three- to twelve-week voyage to the Americas.

When the need grew for cheap labor to plant and strip the sugar canes of the West Indies and to work in the tobacco, cotton, and rice fields in the British North American colonies, history changed forever. As Lerone Bennett points out in *Before the Mayflower*, Africans provided the perfect labor source that Native Americans did not. Africans proved strong, they could not blend in if they tried to run away, they had no monarchy to protect them, they did not know the countryside and therefore could not easily escape, and they could be purchased cheaply. Cheap and free labor solved a pressing problem for white landowners and businessmen.[3] The transatlantic slave trade exploded with the increased demand for labor in the New World.

Africans were enslaved because in the minds of slaveholders they were viewed as being only a little more advanced than apes; they were dehumanized hewers of wood and drawers of water. Much of the white church, with the exception of a large number of Quakers, Mennonites, and Amish, joined with the merchants, colonists, and political authorities in endorsing African slave labor. According to church logic, it gave the church a means to pursue the religious conversion of Africa. This evangelistic emphasis provided a justification that was used for hundreds of years: forced migrants were better off as Christian captives in the New World than they would be as free pagans in Africa.[4]

The carriers of the human captives flew the flag of virtually every European nation, including Portugal, Spain, France, Holland, Britain, and Denmark.[5] The enslaved came principally from the west coast of Africa: from Senegambia (present-day Senegal, Gambia, Guinea, and Guinea-Bissau), the Gold Coast (present-day Ghana), Sierra Leone (a part of which became present-day Liberia), the Windward Coast (which is the present-day Ivory Coast), and the Bight of Benin (Togo, Benin, and west Nigeria). Smaller numbers came from southeast Africa (Madagascar and Mozambique), the Bight of Biafra (the southern part of Nigeria, Cameroon, and Equatorial Guinea), and central Africa (Gabon, Angola, and the Democratic Republic of the Congo).[6] People from different African locations were known for specific skills in agriculture, farming, and mining. The Africans of Ghana were noted for smelting iron ore, and the Benins were famous for their cast bronze artwork.[7] These captives spoke Hausa, Nupe, Yoruba, French, Portuguese, and Arabic, as well as other languages.[8] All captives were removed from the land they called home and forced to live in a land that was foreign—foreign customs, foreign food, foreign religions, foreign languages, and foreign people, many of whom were also new to the Americas. A continent, not a country, was pillaged of its most valuable asset: its youngest and healthiest, along with some of its most talented people.

## BLACKS IN THE COLONIES

This brief synopsis of black life in the colonies begins with the southern colonies, given that the South is historically known as the area where blacks received the most severe treatment during slavery. John Hope Franklin writes that from 1650 to 1789 the still-developing colonies of Virginia, the Carolinas, Georgia, and Maryland needed to augment their labor forces; use of indentured servants had failed.[9] Blacks as forced laborers were the solution.

Jamestown, Virginia, bears the ignominious distinction of being the landing point for sixteen slaves in 1619, the beginning of involuntary servitude that would last for more than two hundred years. Slavery was legalized in Virginia by 1661, although blacks had actually been forced to serve without indentured status for twenty years by the time their status as slaves was legalized.[10] There were approximately twelve thousand blacks and eighteen thousand whites in Virginia in 1708; by 1756, the number was 120,156 blacks and 173,316 whites.[11] Because white Virginians feared insurrections by blacks, they implemented codes that controlled the movement and behavior of blacks toward whites. The codes addressed issues such as when, where, and in what numbers blacks could assemble, as well as penalties for failing to adhere to the codes. In Virginia, a slave could have his or her ears cut off for stealing from a store or home.[12] Many slaves in Virginia worked on tobacco plantations. Over time, those who owned large numbers of slaves and profited greatly from their labor became the state's powerbrokers. Eventually, those slave owners who had gained positions of power and wealth from slavery used their influence to prolong slavery and adversely impact the republic for their self-interests.[13]

In Maryland, when slavery was legalized in 1663, there were one hundred thousand whites and almost forty thousand blacks.[14] As in Virginia, the state enacted slave codes with punishments that ranged from branding to death. Those enslaved in Maryland worked mainly in the tobacco fields. "Production of tobacco was very labor intensive, and as the number and size of plantations/farms increased, so did the number of slaves: from 15 percent of the population in 1690, to 26 percent in 1710, to 38 percent in 1755, and by 1760, 46 percent of the residents of Maryland were slaves."[15]

In the colonial era, North Carolina had fewer slaves, and its plantation economy was not as vital as that of Virginia and South Carolina, yet the colony remained primarily rural throughout the period.[16] Many plantations were small; by the end of the colonial era, most North Carolina plantations had one to four slaves.[17] However, its economy was more diversified, so its export trade was greater than several of the other colonies.[18] Lumber production was important; blacks also worked on plantations growing corn and rice.[19] North Carolina enacted harsh laws regarding runaway slaves, which applied even to those who were manumitted. Under a 1715 law, those who had been freed for whatever reason and had remained in North Carolina for six months after their manumission could be reinslaved for seven years. This same law levied a fine against whites who married blacks and against any minister who performed the ceremony. In 1741, a new law referred to interracial marriage as an "abominable Mixture."[20] By 1775, blacks were a primary part of North Carolina colony life and likely totaled almost 30 percent of its population; the heaviest concentration of blacks lived in the Lower Cape Fear area.[21]

In colonial-era South Carolina, because of, or perhaps in spite of, its strong plantation system, blacks fared no better than their counterparts in North Carolina. Their daily lives were as arduous and as prescribed. However, the numbers of blacks in South Carolina, compared to the number of whites, may have exacerbated their plight. As historian John Hope Franklin writes:

> No other colony experienced quite the threat that sheer numbers brought to South Carolina; and the colony did not wait for any demonstration of the Negroes' ungovernable temper to erect a slave code that became a model for the mainland in severity and scope. Beginning in 1686 the colonial legislature passed laws to insure the domination of white masters over their slaves. . . . In 1740 a plot involving roughly 200 Negroes in the Charleston area was uncovered. On the appointed day one hundred and fifty unarmed Negroes were attacked. Fifty were captured and hanged at the rate of ten per day. In the same year, fire swept through the city. . . . Slaves were immediately suspected. . . . These disturbances led to a revision of the slave code. More stringent provisions were enacted against the assembling of slaves and against other situations which might lead to insurrections.[22]

The mid-Atlantic colonies—New York, New Jersey, Pennsylvania, and Delaware—obtained Negroes from Dutch Curaçao, and later Jamaica, Barbados, and even other North American colonies. The last was preferable to obtaining Africans directly, because the harsh weather in the middle colonies could result in their deaths. Those already in North America had experienced at least one climate change.[23] However, slaves from Africa were also accepted. The middle colonies contained large numbers of white immigrants. They had manufacturing centers, and farming was also part of the economy. Many blacks worked as servants, not as farm laborers. The middle colonies were also filled with numerous religious denominations. Blacks appear on the rolls of most white churches in New Jersey and New York, where blacks were fifteen to twenty percent of the population. However, those colonies passed legislation indicating that baptism did not make slaves free.[24] Other codes were also enacted, and treatment of blacks, while perhaps not as physically brutal as in the southern colonies, was still merciless and cruel. For example, New York enacted a law that allowed slaves to be beaten for gambling; in 1705 another law allowed a slave to be killed if he or she was caught traveling forty miles north of Albany (likely seeking freedom in Canada). The colony also increased the number of crimes that were punishable by death.[25]

Many Quakers settled the mid-Atlantic colony of Pennsylvania. Although some owned slaves, as early as 1688, the colony's Quakers were objecting to slavery. However, slavery had existed in Philadelphia for almost a quarter century before the Quakers arrived. This gave Pennsylvania perhaps the most back-and-forth struggle for and against slavery in the colonies. According to historian Philip Foner, slaves were 19 percent of the population of Philadelphia at the opening of the eighteenth century.[26] After an economic depression in the 1720s, the need for slaves decreased. However, by the 1730s slavery had expanded in Pennsylvania.

Slaves in Pennsylvania's urban areas were used as craftsmen, and some farmed. Those who lived in the rural areas were subjected to more severe labor and treatment. By 1779, Pennsylvania passed the first abolition law in America. Slavery had been greatly weakened through a series of laws and economic factors. In spite of this, "rural slavery grew almost eightfold in the 1780s and 1790s."[27] It was not until 1847 that Pennsylvania totally outlawed the practice.

Slavery expanded in the middle colony of Delaware in the early eighteenth century as the corn and tobacco economy increased. At one point, Delaware had one of the highest percentages of slaves in the mid-Atlantic and New England colonies.[28] Black codes were passed, and blacks were treated poorly throughout the reign of slavery in Delaware. Even though slave trading had drastically subsided in the colony by the end of the colonial era and abolition societies were well established, slavery was fixed deep in its core. Delaware did not ratify the Thirteenth Amendment (which abolished slavery in 1865), the Fourteenth (which established due process before depriving persons of life, liberty, or property in 1868), or the Fifteenth (which in 1870 granted persons the right to vote regardless of race, color, or previous servitude) until 1901.[29]

In the New England colonies—Massachusetts, New Hampshire, Connecticut, and Rhode Island—slavery abounded. Massachusetts was the first American colony to legalize slavery, doing so in 1641. Connecticut legalized slavery in 1650. New England's diverse economy made it necessary for slaves to learn trades, but slave masters did little to help slaves become literate. Education was sometimes allowed for children and to aid one in learning to read the Bible.[30] Concerning the day-to-day life of blacks in the New England colonies, William Piersen writes: "In work habits and labor skills, in culinary and musical arts, as in dress, entertainment, and folklore, slave immigrants maintained their own traditions or blended them with Yankee ways to create a truly Afro-American folk culture."[31] Further insight into the daily lives of blacks in the New England colonies can be seen through some of Connecticut's codes and statutes, which are representative of those enacted throughout the region. A 1708 statute prohibited whites from purchasing items from slaves. A 1723 law made it illegal for slaves to be on the street after 9 P.M. without a certificate from their masters; if one was, he or she was picked up, given ten lashes, and incarcerated until the master paid to have him or her released. A 1730 statute fined a free person if a slave was in the person's home after 9 P.M. without a certificate from the slave's master.[32]

By the end of the colonial era, all New England colonies had abolished the slave trade. Although many of those colonies are now famous for abolition societies and for opposing slavery, the vestiges of slavery lingered there for many years. In Connecticut it continued in unlegalized form until 1848.[33]

## THE INVISIBLE INSTITUTION BLACKS FORGED IN THE COLONIES

Black preaching did not begin in white- or black-led denominations. The history of the American black preaching tradition has its roots in Africa and is refashioned in the cultural context of the slave and free communities of the early American colonies. Consequently, black preaching and communication belong on a cultural continuum that begins in Africa, not the American colonies.

Africans and white colonists shared some religious commonalities that allowed for a synergy of certain beliefs and cultural practices. However, as we have earlier stated, enslaved Africans held on to some aspects of engaging the world that were developed in their motherland. They also retained some of their religious rituals, music, folktales, foods, herbs or roots, and their dances, even though on a different continent.[34] Their African religions, conceptions of the world, and cultural distinctiveness did not wilt under the scorching heat of chattel slavery.

The tenacity with which Africans held on to their culture, along with other factors, made it difficult for white denominations in the colonies to greatly impact the enslaved for more than one hundred and fifty years. In fact, the efforts of groups such as The Society for the Propagation of the Gospel in Foreign Parts, which was organized in London in 1701 with the primary goal of "evangelizing" the "heathen" Indians and Africans in the colonies, were abject failures before the 1770s.[35]

While we posit that the lack of conversion among the early enslaved black population was due to their retaining aspects of their African heritage, as well as other known and unknown factors, others have posited that very little was retained from Africa.[36] However, instead of simply searching for specific cultural elements that Africans retained in the colonies, many scholars now realize that Africans both retained and reconfigured their cultural heritages—especially their religious practices—based on social exigencies. This reconfiguration of cultural distinctiveness was not a rejection, but instead a powerful articulation of the importance of their indigenous cultural artifacts in a new world. Those cultural artifacts were too valuable to be discarded. So Africans re-tooled them for service in new circumstances.

As black Africans moved from their motherland to the colonies, their recalcitrant yet malleable religious faith intersected with that of white colonists and was buoyed in secret meetings in brush arbors, barns, sugar cane fields, and sheds, behind rocks, under trees, down by rivers and in any place that was relatively safe.[37] These meetings can be thought of as gatherings of the invisible institution. This institution is the religious precursor to black churches and source of black preachers' pulpits for proclamation. Here they honed their skills long before there were formal structures. Delores Williams defines the invisible institution in this manner:

> The black church is invisible, but we know it when we see it: our daughters and sons rising up from death and addiction recovering and recovered; our mothers in poverty raising their children alone, with God's help, making a way out of no way and succeeding; Harriet Tubman leading hundreds of slaves into freedom; Isabel, the former African-American slave, with God's help transforming destiny to become Sojourner Truth. . . . The black church is invisible, but we know it when we see oppressed people rising up in freedom.
>
> It has neither hands nor feet nor form, but we know it when we feel it in our communities. . . . It is invisible, but we know when we see, hear and feel it quickening the heart, measuring the soul and bathing life with the spirit in time.[38]

By *invisible institution*, we also mean the cultural context—blacks participating in social and religious practices from preaching to conjuring to rebellion-hatching, to mourning, to moaning, to calling on Jesus as they knew him, all of which was done—allowed blacks to establish a cultural shelter for a new black identity in a strange land. This invisible institution existed alongside the churches that blacks attended with whites and alongside the gospel that was preached by whites who advocated submission and docility among slaves. Later it continued to exist alongside churches formed by blacks and for blacks that began with white preachers, and those black churches that were more attentive to the espousal of white social and biblical doctrines than they were to black liberation. It is this invisible institution that helped refashion the black preacher, who became the storyteller, prophet, underground railroad conductor, and hope-igniter in the Americas.

## THE NATURE OF EARLY BLACK PREACHING

A great deal of preaching by blacks and whites in the mid to late 1700s can be referred to as *folk preaching*. This term is used to describe the type of sermons that are given by clergy who pastor blue-collar or poorer congregations and who have little or no formal education. Some black folk preachers used what has been termed *black vernacular English*,[39] and also used tonality or *whooped* (a term explained in detail later in this anthology) during their sermons. The term folk preaching is often used to devalue early, later, and current black preaching, most often by those who do not understand or appreciate its nature. Some blacks were and are ashamed of it. They associate it with the illiterate, the poor, and the overly emotional.[40]

As the early folk messages in this anthology by preachers such as Brother Carper, John Jasper, and Sojourner Truth show, one need not be ashamed of folk preaching. The best early folk preaching is filled with literary and homiletical devices that today's preachers would do well to emulate. They lead listeners into biblical and cultural scenarios as few have been able to do since. This preaching resonates with vivid colors, concrete images, dazzling metaphors, and sounds that ring in the ear in a welcomed fashion.

Those who are unfamiliar with folk preaching are likely thrown by what they may see as a lack of logical organization in the sermons. However, these critics are most often looking for logically designed deductive sermons—those in which a preacher indicates a destination for a sermon and then gives logical reasons or a defense for choosing that destination. Also, black folk sermons may be organized around a central image, such as an eagle or a train or a valley of dry bones, or a familiar black cultural image.[41] Finally, those unfamiliar with black folk preaching may be startled by black folk sermons as they often conclude with a cathartic emotional explosion.

Because black preaching has never been homogenous (although many have lumped all black preaching into one basket), there were also black preachers from the period 1750–1789 who did not produce folk sermons: Lemuel Haynes, John Chavis, Absalom Jones, and Hosea Easton, to name a few. Additionally, one need not be a folk preacher to understand folk religion, which is the religion of all the people, for all the people, and in which all people can participate without regard to social status or formal literacy level.

## THE FOCUS OF EARLY BLACK PREACHING

The small sample of black preaching recorded in the sixteenth and seventeenth centuries focused primarily on three areas: Enabling blacks to survive the hardships of life, church doctrine and instructing persons relative to behavior or conduct, and abolishing slavery. As can be seen in the sermons of the nineteenth and twentieth century included later in this anthology and in other collections of black oratory, these categories still exist, with slight alterations in focus prompted by changes in laws and the educational and economic gains of blacks.[42] These categories are to be expected because the early black preacher had to be all of these things (hope provider, teacher of doctrine, and activist) to the community he (rarely she) served. (Although there were female griots and priests in Africa, the patriarchy of the colonies made it difficult for women to overtly serve as religious leaders in the seventeenth and eighteenth centuries.)

Whether on plantations, in brush arbors, in churches with whites, or in churches that belonged to blacks, the preacher had to offer survival sermons. Those suffering from the trauma of having family members sold away, lynched, raped, or beaten, and the depression wrought by everyday drudgery and poverty, had to be given tools to hold on to their sanity and fight.

Preaching on biblical doctrines and Christian conduct was also a primary concern of the black preacher. It made sense to many leaders and preachers to try to convince enslavers and bigoted whites who did not own slaves that blacks were good Christians and did not engage in behavior that could harm whites. This was particularly important in areas where black insurrections occurred. Preachers also had to teach biblical doctrines, for some of the same reasons. Some brave preachers taught biblical doctrines that refuted those being taught by slave masters and race mongers, such as the idea that all blacks are cursed because of Ham, or that Apostle Paul was right when he told slaves to return to their masters.[43]

Finally antislavery preaching was needed to apply pressure to those who would not relent from racist beliefs and violence. It also provided hope and empowerment for the young who would have to carry on the fight of their foreparents. Most often, antislavery preaching was recorded in the early days of black preaching because the best and most well-known antislavery preachers were often also connected to other social efforts. Many had high levels of education, some economic stability, owned or co-owned newspapers, or had white associates who would help them get sermons and speeches published. Some of these black preachers were legally free; others were not. Many did not reside in the South, where the cruelties of slavery and racism were the most visible and, some would say, the most vicious.

## TRENDS IN WHITE PREACHING FROM 1750 TO 1789

Black preaching impacted Christianity practiced by whites in the colonies, a fact rarely written about during the colonial era. White preaching likewise affected black preaching. One instance that is often noted is the onset of Revivalism in the 1700s. Beginning in approximately 1720, Theodore J. Frelinghuysen (1787–1862) began preaching a Dutch Reformed gospel that was considered emotive, and it caused controversy among most Dutch Reformed congregations. Nevertheless, Revivalism spread from the Dutch Reformed churches to the Presbyterians, where "Log College" graduates picked up the mantle and spread it further.[44] Jonathan Edwards (1703–1758), a white Puritan in Northampton, Massachusetts, who was not a Revivalist, did sympathize with the Revivalists and preached some of their themes. His pamphlet *A Faithful Narrative of the Surprising Work of God in the Conversion of Many Hundred Souls in Northampton and the Neighbouring Towns and Villages of New Hampshire, in New England: in a Letter to the Rev. Colman of Boston* (1736) caused a great stir in the Protestant world. For some, it was the first classic of Revivalism; crowds lined up to hear its author.[45]

The Wesleyan Revivals of the late 1700s, led by John Wesley (1703–1791) and his brother Charles (1707–1788), a great hymn writer, helped transform England's religious landscape. The Wesleys were likely also captivated by the Edwards pamphlet, which went through several printings and was produced in several countries. In the late 1700s the Wesleys brought Methodism to America. Their itinerant preachers traveled circuits to reach believers that many denominations did not, and Methodism quickly took hold and began to emerge as a stable, predominant denomination in the early 1800s.[46]

In 1740, George Whitefield (1714–1770), a friend of the Wesley brothers, took the first Great Awakening to new heights, or through its second stage. Whitefield was not an educated man, but he possessed extraordinary oratorical skills. During a seventy-five-day period in 1740, Whitefield delivered more than 175 sermons to thousands.[47] His fame rapidly spread, even among free blacks and those who were enslaved, who would have heard about Whitefield because many attended religious gatherings with their masters, and given the very religious nature of much of the early colonies, events such as Whitefield tent meetings were big news.[48]

Whitefield's sermons were fiery and vivid, which certainly reminded some slaves of African griots and priests. His sonorous delivery would have appealed to the tonal language roots of many of the enslaved. Whitefield spoke extemporaneously and urged all other preachers to do the same. This was important for those who could not read. Some suggest that Whitefield's methods, along with the Great Awakening, are directly responsible for the increased acceptance of Christianity by blacks.[49]

## THE COLONISTS MARCH TOWARD INDEPENDENCE

While religious fires flared, another type of revolution had commenced. In 1770, the Boston Massacre occurred as colonists fought with British soldiers patrolling Boston. Crispus Attucks, a runaway slave, was the first to fall for freedom.[50] In April 1775, the first battles of the Revolutionary War were waged between British and Colonial armies at Lexington and Concord, in Massachusetts, and black minutemen participated in the fighting. Later, however, General George Washington only agreed to allow blacks to fight against the British after the British said in 1775 that they would free all Negroes who served on their side.[51] John Hope Franklin writes, "Hardly a military action between 1775 and 1781 was without some Negro participants. They were at Lexington, Concord, Ticonderoga, Bunker Hill, Long Island, White Plains, Trenton, Princeton, Bennington, Brandywine, Stillwater, Bemis Heights, Saratoga, Red

Bank, Monmouth, Rhode Island, Savannah, Stony Point, Ft. Griswold, Eutaw Springs and Yorktown."[52]

After numerous skirmishes with the British, on July 4, 1776, the Second Continental Congress declared the independence of the United States in the Declaration of Independence, written primarily by Thomas Jefferson. The United States was at war with Britain until the Treaty of Paris was ratified in 1783. Shortly thereafter, a constitutional convention was held in 1787. During this convention, the newly formed United States had an opportunity to end slavery. However, its leaders lacked the necessary courage and will. Instead, provisions against even granting liberty to runaway slaves were approved.[53] Technically, the Constitution of the United States went into effect when last-needed New Hampshire ratified it in 1788. Steps were then taken for the first national election; George Washington was chosen as the first president and inaugurated in 1789.

Though blacks such as Crispus Attucks, Reverend Lemuel Haynes, and Reverend John Chavis fought valiantly against the French, the Native Americans, and the British in a long list of battles that helped what would become the United States earn its freedom, and black preachers aided the cause as well, the new era of independence for the United States would, sadly, not prove to be an era of independence for those who gave so much and received so little—its black citizenry.

## THE EARLY BLACK CHURCHES

In the second half of the colonial era, under threat of persecution coupled with the missionary zeal of Christian proselytizers, Africans began accepting those aspects of Christianity that addressed their plight and resembled some of their African religious beliefs and their African worldviews. Those practicing Islam won converts as well, but not nearly as many as their Christian counterparts.[54]

From the 1750s through 1789, as enslaved and free Africans were slowly fashioning their religious roots and new lives in America, the earliest black congregations were begun with the aid of whites; in most instances blacks could not own land. Many early black churches had white pastors.[55] Some of the earliest black churches include the African Baptist or Bluestone Church, founded in Mecklenberg County, Virginia, in 1758 on the plantation of William Byrd III, a wealthy white landowner who was an abolitionist; the Silver Bluff Baptist church in Silver Bluff, South Carolina, formed around 1773; the church at Petersburgh, Virginia, in 1776; and the Baptist church founded by George Liele around 1779 in Savannah, Georgia.[56] Religious associations founded by blacks such as Prince Hall, who formed the first black society of Masons in 1787 in Boston, also met some black religious needs (such as space for worship services and funerals) as did black societies.[57]

By 1789, the black church as a formal institution was established in America, though still in grave danger from those who fought against any assertion of the humanity of Africans or any of their descendants. Black preachers such as Absalom Jones, Gullah Jack Pritchett, John Chavis, and Hosea Easton were among the strongest voices of the era. All addressed the issue of slavery, some as abolitionist preachers, some in quiet ways, some while pastors and some as itinerants traveling from one place to another. Each used remnants of their African heritage, the gospel, and more to urge America to provide freedom and basic rights for its black citizens. This would allow the country to live up to the words of its recently written Declaration of Independence, "all men are created equal."

## Notes

1. For the most current information on the number of slaves who came to the Americas see: Stephen Behrendt, David Eltis, David Richardson, and Herbert S. Klein, eds., *The Trans-Atlantic Slave Trade: A Database on CD-ROM* (Cambridge: Cambridge University Press, 2000); Paul Lovejoy, "The Impact of the Atlantic Slave Trade on Africa: A Review of the Literature," *Journal of African History* 30 (1989): 365–94; Paul Lovejoy, *Transformations in Slavery: A History of Slavery in Africa* (Cambridge: Cambridge University Press, 1983); Hugh Thomas, *The Slave Trade: The Story of the Atlantic Slave Trade: 1440–1870* (New York: Simon and Schuster, 1999); and Herbert S. Klein and Stuart Swartz, *The Atlantic Slave Trade: New Approaches to the Americas* (Cambridge: Cambridge University Press, 1999).
2. The *Trans-Atlantic Slave Trade* CD-ROM also contains the records of 27,233 transatlantic slave ship voyages made between 1596 and 1866 and addresses slave ship revolts and the death of slaves en route to the Americas. See also John Hope Franklin's *From Slavery to Freedom*, 3rd ed. (New York: Alfred A. Knopf, 1967), 56–58; and Antonio T. Bly, "Crossing the Lake of Fire: Slave Resistance During the Middle Passage, 1720–1842," *The Journal of Negro History* 83, no. 3 (1998), 178–86.
3. Lerone Bennett, *Before the Mayflower: A History of Black America*, 6th ed. (New York: Penguin Books, 1993), 34–46.
4. Marcus W. Jernegan, "Slavery and Conversion in the American Colonies," *American Historical Review* 21, no. 3 (Apr 1916), 504–27.
5. For information on the nationality of the slavers who transported slaves to the Americas, see *The Trans-Atlantic Slave Trade: A Database on CD-ROM*.
6. For additional information on the past and current locations in Africa from which Africans emanated before they were enslaved, see *The Trans-Atlantic Slave Trade* database.

7. For additional information on the trades and talents of persons brought to the Americas during the Atlantic slave trade, see John Hope Franklin's *From Slavery to Freedom*, 25–28, and *The Trans-Atlantic Slave Trade* database.
8. For additional information concerning the languages spoken by enslaved blacks in the colonies, see Paul Lovejoy, "The African Diaspora: Revisionist Interpretations of Ethnicity, Culture and Religion under Slavery," *Studies in the World History of Slavery, Abolition and Emancipation* 2 (1997).
9. For information on indentured servitude see David W. Galenson, "The Rise and Fall of Indentured Servitude in the Americas: An Economic Analysis," *Journal of Economic History*, March 1984, 1–26; and Edward S. Morgan's *American Slavery, American Freedom: The Ordeal of Virginia* (New York: W. W. Norton, 1975), especially pages 236–40.
10. *From Slavery to Freedom*, 72.
11. Ibid., 73.
12. Ibid., 74.
13. For information on the impact of plantation owners on the rise of the republic, see *American Slavery, American Freedom*, especially chapters 15, 16, and 18.
14. *From Slavery to Freedom*, 76.
15. C. Aubrey Land, *Colonial Maryland: A History of the American Colonies* (New York: Kraus International Publishing, 1981), 166–67.
16. Marvin Mckay and Lorin Lee Cary, *Slavery in North Carolina 1748–1775* (Chapel Hill: University of North Carolina Press, 1996), 11.
17. Ibid., 33.
18. Ibid., 11.
19. Ibid., 43.
20. Ibid., 67; also see Walter Clark, ed., *The State Records of North Carolina*, vol. 23 (North Carolina: Winston and Goldsboro, 1895–1906), 65.
21. Ibid., 22.
22. *From Slavery to Freedom*, 79.
23. For information on slaves in the middle colonies being sent from the West Indies and other colonies and the concept of "seasoning" (the preparation of slaves through work in one location of the Americas to make them more suited to work in other locations), see William D. Piersen's *Black Yankees: The Development of an Afro-American Subculture in Eighteenth-Century New England* (Amherst: The University of Massachusetts Press, 1988), 1–5.
24. *From Slavery to Freedom*, 91.
25. Ibid., 91–92.
26. Philip Foner, *Northern Labor and Antislavery: A Documentary History* (Westport, CT: Greenwood Press, 1994), 189.
27. *Northern Labor and Antislavery*, 214.
28. William H. Williams, *Slavery and Freedom in Delaware 1639–1865* (Lanham, MD: SR Books, 1999), 17.
29. Ibid., 243.
30. *Black Yankees*, 44–45.
31. Ibid., 96.
32. Slavery in America, "Connecticut Slave Law Summary and Record," http:// www

.slaveryinamerica.org/geography/slave_laws_CT.htm (accessed January 20, 2004). For additional information on black codes in Connecticut and other colonies, see Helen T. Catterall, ed., *Judicial Cases Concerning American Slavery and the Negro*, vol. 4, *Cases from the Courts of New England, the Middle States and the District of Columbia* (Washington, DC: The Carnegie Institution, 1936). For information on Connecticut specifically, see pages 413–47.

33. "Connecticut Slave Law Summary."

34. For information on African retentions in America, see the anthropological research of Melville J. Herskovits, *The Myth of the Negro Past* (Boston: Beacon Press, 1990). Also see Roger Bastide, *African Civilizations in the New World* (New York: Harper and Row, 1971); Joseph E. Holloway, ed., *Africanisms in American Culture* (Bloomington: Indiana University Press, 1990); Albert Robateau, *Slave Religion: The Invisible Institution in the Antebellum South* (New York: Oxford University Press, 1980); and Mechal Sobel, *Trabelin' On: The Slave Journey to an Afro-Baptist Faith* (Westport, CT: Greenwood Press, 1979).

35. This information concerning the achievements of The Society for the Propagation of the Gospel in Foreign Parts from 1701 to 1786 was obtained from copies of its records that are located in the Billy Graham Center Evangelism Library located at Wheaton College, Wheaton, Illinois. For a list of other groups who also attempted to convert enslaved Africans before 1790 and failed, see Carter G. Woodson's *The History of the Negro Church*, 2nd ed., 1945, especially chapters 1 and 2.

36. For more on those who have posited that Africans retained very little of their cultural heritage shortly after their arrival in America, see E. Franklin Frazier's seminal work, *The Negro Church in America* (Liverpool: Liverpool University Press, 1964).

37. For information on the religious faith of blacks in the colonies, see Sobel's *Trabelin' On* and Timothy Fulop and Albert Raboteau, *African-American Religion: Interpretive Essays in History and Culture* (New York: Routledge, 1997).

38. Delores S. Williams, *Sisters in the Wilderness: The Challenge of Womanist God-Talk* (Maryknoll, NY: Orbis, 1993), 205–6.

39. For information on use of black vernacular English by folk preachers, see Walter Pitts, "West African Poetics in Black Preaching Style," *American Speech* 64, no. 2 (1989) 137–49.

40. For instances of folk preaching being devalued, see Richard Allen's *The Life, Experience and Gospel Labors of the Rt. Rev. Richard Allen* (Philadelphia: Lee and Yeocum, 1888), 64; William Pipes, *Say Amen, Brother! Old-Time Negro Preaching: A Study in American Frustration* (Detroit: Wayne State University Press, 1992), especially page 158. Pipes refers to folk preaching as "old-time Black preaching." Also, see Bruce Rosenberg, *Can These Bones Live: The Art of the American Folk Sermon* (Urbana: University of Illinois Press, 1988), specifically page 4, where Rosenberg, who attempts to flatter the folk preacher in some instances, reveals his real feelings by referring to the work of the folk preacher as "transmissions of illiteratures."

41. See Gary Layne Hatch, "Logic in the Black Folk Sermon: The Sermons of C.L. Franklin," *Journal of Black Studies* 26, no. 3. (Jan 1996), 227–44, for more on the analogical sermon centered around images.

42. Significant collections of black oratory that include sermons are: Dorothy Porter, *Early Negro Writing, 1760–1837* (Boston: Beacon Press [republished 1995]); Philip

Foner, ed., *The Voice of Black America: Major Speeches by Negroes in the United States, 1797–1973* (Wiltshire, England: Capricorn Books, 1975); and Philip Foner and Robert James Branham, eds., *Lift Every Voice: African American Oratory 1787–1900* (Tuscaloosa: University of Alabama Press, 1998).

43. For instances of early sermons that refute that blacks were cursed and teach that the Bible did not ordain slavery, see in this anthology John Marrant's "You Stand Among the Greatest Kings on Earth," preached June 24, 1789, and Maria Stewart's "Why Sit Ye Here and Die," preached in September 1832.

44. For information on Revivalism in the colonies see Samuel E. Morrison's *The Oxford History of the American People* (New York: Penguin Press, 1965), 150–53, and see Frank Lambert's *Inventing the "Great Awakening"* (Princeton, NJ: Princeton University Press, 1999). For information on Edwards, Whitefield, and the Wesleys, see Mark A. Nolls, *The Rise of Evangelicalism: The Age of Edwards, Whitfield and the Wesleys* (Westmont, IL: Intervarsity Press, 2004).

45. George Mardsen, *Jonathan Edwards: A Life* (New Haven, CT: Yale University Press, 2003), 171–73.

46. For information on Methodism, see John H. Wigger and Nathan O. Hatch, eds., *Methodism and the Shaping of American Culture* (Nashville, TN: Abingdon Press, 2001); and John H. Wigger, *Taking Heaven by Storm: Methodism and the Rise of Popular Christianity in America* (New York: Oxford, 1998).

47. For information on the many sermons delivered by Whitefield, see Harry S. Stout, *The New England Soul: Preaching and Religious Culture in Colonial New England* (New York: Oxford, 1986), 185–89.

48. For information on Whitefield's tent meetings, see John W. Blassingame, *The Slave Community: Plantation Life in the Antebellum South* (New York: Oxford, 1972), 61; and also Harry S. Stout, *The Divine Dramatist: George Whitefield and the Rise of Modern Evangelicalism, Library of Religious Biography Series* (Grand Rapids, MI: Eerdmans, 1991).

49. For those who suggest that Whitefield's methods are tied to increased acceptance of Christianity by blacks, see Henry H. Mitchell, "Preaching and the Preacher in African American Religion" in *The Encyclopedia of African American Religions*, ed. Larry G. Murphy, J. Gordon Melton, and Gary L. Ward (New York: Garland Publishing, 1993), 607–8; and Mitchell's *Black Preaching: The Recovery of a Powerful Art* (Nashville, TN: Abingdon, 1990), especially chapter 2. For an insightful article on Whitefield and blacks, see Frank Lambert, "'I Saw the Book Talk': Slave Readings of the First Great Awakening," *Journal of African American History* 87, no. 1 (2002), 12–25.

50. *From Slavery to Freedom*, 128.

51. Ibid., 133.

52. Ibid., 137.

53. Ibid., 143.

54. For additional information on Islam in the colonies and in antebellum America, see Allan D. Austin, *African Muslims in Antebellum America: Transatlantic Stories and Spiritual Struggles*, rev. ed. (New York: Routledge, 1997); Sylviane A. Diouf, *Servants of Allah: African Muslims Enslaved in the Americas* (New York: New York University Press, 1998); and Sulayman S. Nyang, "Islam in America: A Historical Perspective," *American Muslim Quarterly* 2, no. 1, 7–38.

55. For information on black churches with white pastors, see Henry H. Mitchell, *Black Church Beginnings: The Long-Hidden Realities of the First Years* (Grand Rapids, MI: Eerdmans, 2004), 46–69.
56. Ibid., 46–70.
57. *From Slavery to Freedom*, 164–65.

# JOHN CHAVIS

*(ca. 1763–1838)*

John Chavis was born a free man in approximately 1763, in or around Granville County, North Carolina, to William Chavis and Sarah (or Lottie) Chavis. His father and his grandfather, whose name was also William, were among the largest landowners in the colonies prior to the Revolutionary War. Reverend Chavis was of mixed heritage: African, Indian, and Caucasian.

Reverend Chavis served in the Revolutionary War and fought with the Colonists; studied at Princeton from 1792 to 1795,[1] and completed his studies at Washington College (now known as Washington and Lee University) in 1802. He was the first ordained African American Presbyterian preacher. To become a minister in the Presbyterian church, Chavis completed an exegesis in Latin on the theme *in quo consistat salvation ab pecato* (What is necessary for salvation from sin?) and a sermon on the Decree of Election.[2] He was married to Sarah Frances Anderson and to this union no children were born.

Sometime around 1805, Chavis opened a school in Raleigh where he taught black and, initially, white students. Some of his white students went on to hold national offices. He also operated schools in Chatham, Wake, and Granville counties. The insurrection of Nat Turner in 1831 and the appeal of David Walker, urging blacks to spiritually and physically battle for their freedom, occurred when Chavis was a member of the Orange Presbytery in North Carolina. Chavis courageously defended Turner and other blacks who had been killed.[3] After 1831, a state law was passed that made it illegal for anyone to teach blacks. In 1832, numerous southern states, including North Carolina, enacted laws to keep blacks from teaching or preaching. By 1831, whites had stopped sending their children to Chavis's school. The actions of white citizens in response to Nat Turner's insurrection and others basically ended Chavis's career as a teacher and sharply curtailed his preaching career.

Some scholars have called Chavis conservative and not an abolitionist. However, the great historian John Hope Franklin said of him, "The effect which he had upon its [North Carolina's] intellectual development was far reaching and was doubtless salutary on both whites and Free Negroes."[4] From his service as a patriot, to his gifts as a scholar, teacher, and preacher, Chavis was one of the most remarkable men in the early church in America. He died in 1838. John Chavis was the great-great-grandfather of Benjamin Chavis Jr. (also known as Benjamin Chavis Muhammad). Benjamin briefly served as president of the National Association for the Advancement of Colored People (NAACP) and in 1997 became a minister with the Nation of Islam.

• • •

*John Chavis wrote that he did not understand the doctrine of the atonement of Christ as his teachers and books had explained it. They covered it in mystery. Having had his living as a preacher and teacher taken away from him in 1832, Chavis decided to write a sermon on the atonement and publish it as a pamphlet, since the doctrine was a hot topic of debate among Presbyterians in his day. Chavis sided with the New School Presbyterians, who wanted to offer the grace of being saved to all people. Chavis, though thought by some to be an accommodationist, leaves no doubt in this message that God died for all and that salvation is available to all. Without saying it specifically, it was clear that blacks were included in his understanding of the atonement. The Orange Presbytery refused to publish the message and Chavis ultimately left for the Roanoke Presbytery, where he remained until his death. He had the sermon published in 1837 by J. Gales and Son in Raleigh, North Carolina.*

## Letter Upon the Doctrine of the Extent of the Atonement of Christ (1833)

To the Moderator of the Orange Presbytery of N. Carolina

Revd. Sir: From Reading the Minutes of the last General Assembly of the Presbyterian Church and other Religious publications, I find that the Redeemer's kingdom is advancing in an astonishing manner; and, it is my unshaken belief, that much of this glorious work may be attributed to the increasing belief, which appears to prevail, of the extent of the doctrine of the Atonement of Christ. Such a belief expands the mind of the Christian, and, in prayer, the desire of his heart grasps in one view the whole world of mankind and leaves the event to God, who hears and grants the blessing.

The time was, when I was a firm believer in a limited atonement, and I do believe, that it was God alone that convinced me of my mistake, and that, in an almost miraculous manner.

In the early part of my Ministry, after Preaching, I could nearly recollect my Sermon verbatim. And it was my usual custom, after Preaching, to review my Sermon, to see if I had not advanced some false doctrine or said something improperly.

At a certain time I preached to a large congregation, and my subject led me to treat the fall of man, and of the remedy that was provided for his recovery, and I invited my congregation with all the pathetic zeal of which I was capable, to come and believe on the Lord Jesus Christ, that they might be saved; that he was the only Saviour of sinners and the only way to eternal life; that unless they were regenerated and born again of the spirit, they could not enter the kingdom of heaven; yea, I felt as though I was standing on the brink of eternity and my congregation ready to be precipitated into utter destruction. After Preaching, I got upon my horse, and as usual began to review my Sermon, and it was suddenly impressed upon my mind, as though some person had spoken to me: What? you believe in a limited atonement, and yet you have been inviting all mankind to believe on the Lord Jesus Christ for life and salvation! How is this? Such was the shock, that it appeared as if I rebounded from my saddle, and certain I am, from my feelings, that my whole frame must have been in a tremour; and I rode on, one of the most miserable of men, and found no peace of mind until I became satisfactorily convinced that the atonement which our Saviour had made was commensurate to the spiritual wants of the WHOLE HUMAN FAMILY; that he had made it possible for each individual to be saved.

At the door of my investigation, I met with much difficulty. I knew that if I reasoned from false premises, my conclusions would be false. To contrast the moral perfections of God with the moral law, and reason from the moral law being a transcript of God's moral perfections, did not appear to me would be conclusive. Here I was at a loss for some time, not knowing what theory to adopt to reason from, that would be conclusive. At length, it occurred to me that I must have recourse to God's natural perfections, and of these his infinity would best answer my purpose, for it appeared plain, that the sin which Adam and his posterity had committed by violating the law of an infinite God, carried in it an infinite evil; because it was committed in the violation of a law of an infinite God, and therefore required infinite satisfaction and none but an infinite God could render that satisfaction. At this discovery my burden was removed, and I felt comforted because I conceived that I had got upon safe ground—that the Apostle had said, that Christ came to redeem those that were under the Law, to satisfy the Law and make it honorable that God might be just and justify the sinner that believeth. Then, as all Adam's posterity were under the curse of one and the same Law, all doomed to eternal destruction, it appeared evident that he could not die to satisfy the demands of that very same and express law for a part and not for the whole; that when he addressed his Father and when he expired upon the cross, and cried "it is finished" and the veil of the temple was rent from the top to the bottom, which signified that the middle wall of partition was broken down between Jew and Gentile, that all mankind individually, might enter into the holy of holies, and have access to a throne of grace through a Redeemer and a Mediator. This laid the foundation upon which the extent of the atonement was built, and which gave authority for such free and unbounded invitations and promises, which are recorded both in the Old and New Testament. "Look unto me and be ye saved all the ends of the earth, for I am God and there is none else. Ho [Lo], every one that thirsteth, come ye to the waters, and he that hath no money come ye, buy and eat, yea come buy wine and milk without money and without price. Seek and ye shall find, knock and it shall be opened unto you. And the spirit and the bride say come. And, let him that is athirst, come. And whosoever will, let him take of the water of life freely." Now it is plain that those invitations and promises are made to the whole human family without limitation, and whatever may be their import or meaning, that they are intended for and do embrace the spiritual wants of the whole human family individually, is a truth which cannot be denied nor disproved. Let me be permitted further to remark, that if Jesus Christ did not die to make atonement for the sins of the whole human family individually, where I would ask, the propriety of complaining, "Ye will not come unto me that ye might have life." Of whom does he complain? Undoubtedly, both of Jew and Gentile, or in other words, of all the disobedient of the whole human family individually. Surely no person will be so presumptuous as to charge the Saviour of mankind with folly, or that he would complain without a just cause. For it must or ought to be supposed, that his complaint is founded upon his death and suffering. Permit me further to remark, that as death ever has, and ever will make the dying man tell the truth, I ask, whoever read or heard tell of any person on a death bed ascribe his lost state to God, but in every instance they ascribe it to their own disobedience? Now if Jesus Christ did not die to make atonement for the whole human family individually, would not the dying man set up a defense for himself and plead that Jesus Christ did not die for him, and therefore he could not be saved? And, as he does not set up any such defense, does it not prove plainly that he believes that Jesus Christ died for him and that he might have been saved, provided he had complied with the terms of the Gospel; and as he did not, is it not, at least, a tacit confession that his damnation is just? Now as this is the experience of the dying all over the word, does it not prove that the doctrine of the extent of the atonement is true?

To put the proof of the doctrine beyond all question, permit me to state that express emphatic command of the Saviour himself to all his Ministers of every nation, tongue and language: "Go ye into all the world and preach the Gospel to every creature, and he that believeth and is baptised shall be saved, and he that believeth not, shall be damned." What language could be more explicit to prove the doctrine of the extent of the atonement which makes provision for the whole human family, individually? Moreover, if Jesus Christ did not die to make atonement for each individual, why preach to each individual? Can it possibly be believed that the Saviour would send his Ministers to preach to any part of the human family for whom he did not die, when he knew from the nature of their situation they could not believe on him (for without the shedding of blood there could be no remission of sin) and to add to the awful curse of damnation upon them for their unbelief? The character of the Saviour, the plan of Redemption, reason and common sense forbid such a belief.

I might go on and quote more Scripture, and illustrate the subject more fully by familiar examples, but I think it quite unnecessary, because the language of the Saviour just quoted defies contradiction; but more of this hereafter. But notwithstanding the proof of the doctrine of the extent of the atonement appears to be so plain, explicit and unequivocal, yet another difficulty presented itself. How were all mankind individually to have the opportunity of partaking of the blessings contained in the blood of the atonement? To remove this difficulty was a matter of anxious solicitude. At length, it occurred to me that the atonement made must be one thing, and the application of it another; that there was blood enough in the Saviour to save all, and that if any were lost, it must be for the want of application; and here another difficulty presented itself. Why did not all make application? To remove this, was a matter of the utmost importance. Here I had to make a solemn pause, and to look into the broad fields of theories, to see if I could find any of their number from which I could so reason as to make the subject plain and intelligible to all capacities.

And here I discovered that I must adopt as theories, the doctrine of motives, the freedom of the will, and the object of choice. And should I be asked, what is a motive, I answer, it is that something, whatever it may be, that excites or prompts to action; and should I be asked also, what it is that gives the will, I answer, it is the object of choice. And lest I should be charged with too much tautology, let it be understood, that whenever I may use the word motive, the freedom of the will and the object of choice is to be understood in every instance.

In my explanation, I shall pass unnoticed the ignorance of those who say they have done many things contrary to their wills, and take with me the Philosopher and the experience of mankind, as witness, to prove that no person ever did nor ever will act contrary to their will. That action which any person performs contrary to their will is compulsory, and therefore it is not their action at all.

It cannot be readily supposed, that any person can be willing to be punished for committing a crime, though they may acknowledge that they ought to be punished; but to be heartily willing, is not a supposable case . . .

For instance, suppose a servant disobeys his master, who calls him to account for his disobedience, and orders him to strip himself, that he intends to chastise him for his disobedience. The servant at first hesitates, being unwilling to be chastised, but presently obeys and strips himself; and why does he do it? It must be, because he knows that his master has him completely under his power and authority, and therefore he becomes willing to obey him; and his motive is to induce his master to be merciful in his punishment. And so it is in all other cases of the actions of mankind; they have motives and objects of choice for all they do.

From this short definition of the doctrine of motives, which I believe will accord with the experience of all mankind, I hope I shall be able to give a satisfactory reason why some men are saved, and some lost.

By the death and suffering of the Saviour, a free and unbounded fountain is opened for sin and uncleanness, and all mankind, individually, are freely invited to come to this fountain and partake of its cleansing and healing influences, and be made whole from the pollution of sin; and we find that a part of mankind do obey the call and invitation, and do come and partake of the benefits of this fountain and are made whole. Ask them why they acted thus, and they will answer that it was because it pleased God by the light of his Holy Spirit, to set life and death before them; that they saw that they were wholly polluted with sin and corruption; that unless they were cleansed and made whole by the blood of Christ, they were eternally lost; that the motive of their actions was that they were willing to be saved upon the terms of the Gospel of Jesus Christ; that they had acted freely and willingly, from motives of choice, and not from compulsion.

We find that those others who have had life and death set before them by the Holy Spirit of God, had it made known to them that they were wholly polluted with sin and corruption; that they were freely invited to come to this fountain and be cleansed and made whole; but they shut their eyes, and hardened their hearts, and refused to obey the call and invitation so freely offered. Ask them why they acted thus, and they will answer that it was because they were unwilling to obey the call and invitation of the Gospel; that they had other motives of gratification, and therefore were unwilling to come; that in so doing, they had acted freely and willingly, and from motives of choice and not from compulsion.

Thus we have a true and plain definition, why it is that some men are saved and some lost. This definition also makes the road which mankind travels to heaven and to hell as plain as two and two make four.

But here I saw that I should be met with the Calvinistic doctrine, or the doctrine of God's decrees; for they are built upon the Atonement of Christ.

The opposers of this doctrine say that if God did from all eternity foreordain or decree whatsoever comes to pass, then everything is unalterably fixed, and mankind cannot act otherwise than they do—and beside, this doctrine makes God the author of sin, which cannot be admitted.

If the opposers of this doctrine understand it to mean that God as it were, put his hand upon one man and pushes him up into heaven, and upon another man, and pushes him down into hell, irresistibly, they are grossly mistaken. This would indeed be making God the author of sin, which I say with them, cannot be admitted.

Whatever the Westminster Divines meant by God's foreordination or decrees was simply this: that God did certainly foreknow from all eternity whatsoever would come to pass, but there was to be no compulsion in the case. It is plain then, God's foreordination or decree is nothing more nor less than his foreknowledge. Rob God of his foreknowledge, and you at once say there is no God; and who that looks upon the works of creation, can possibly deny the being of a God? Here I must appeal to the experience of the opposers of this doctrine themselves, that God's foreordination or decree has no compulsion or influence upon the actions of mankind at all. And here I ask them to go back to their infancy, and carefully examine all their actions, and the motives of their actions, and say whether they conscientiously believe that God's foreknowing what they did or intended to do, had compulsive influence at all upon their actions; or whether in all they ever did or intended to do, in any single instance, they first looked forward to see whether God foreknew or had any knowledge of what they were about to do, or intended to do? If not, in what does their opposition to the Calvinistic doctrine consist? For here they must acknowledge that all they ever did was done freely and willingly, and from motives of choice, however, righteously or unrighteously they might have acted; and that God's foreknowing what they would do or intended to do had no compulsion or influence upon their actions at all; therefore God is not the author of sin. Then it is plain and put beyond all contradiction, that God's foreknowledge or decree has no compulsion or influence upon the actions of mankind at all.

Witness the crucifixion of the Saviour. The Scriptures inform us that this transaction was foreordained by God from all eternity; yet Jews have ever been blamed and ever will be blamed for their conduct. And for why? Because they acted from wicked motives and that freely and willingly, and that of choice and not from compulsion, and even Judas, for the part he acted in the cruel transaction, did not pretend to set up a defense for himself that he was compelled to do what he did; so far from it, such was his conviction to the horrid deed, that he could not bear the sight of man, nor the light of the sun, and therefore hurried himself out of the world by hanging himself.

Again, the opposers of this doctrine raise another objection to show its inconsistency. They say that according to this doctrine, there can be no possible use for preaching; for let a man do what he will, he will be saved, and let him do what he will, he will be damned, and yet we see from the explanation given of the doctrine of motives, of the freedom of the will and the object of choice, that it is emphatically true, that let a man do what he will, he will be saved, and let a man do what he will, he will be damned, and it is because he wills all his actions, and in so doing, acts freely, willingly and from motives of gratification, and not from motives of compulsion.

Thus we have a demonstrative evidence of the fatal and dangerous effects of prejudice—that it blinds the mind and forbids free and open investigation after truth. Whereas, if the opposers of this doctrine would lay aside prejudice and reason calmly and dispassionately, and that upon Philosophical principles, how easy it would be to determine that there is no bugbear in the doctrine at all; but that it is perfectly consistent with the character of God and the state and condition of all mankind.

It is plain also from the explanation given of the Calvinistic doctrine, that the faith and practice of consistent Calvinists and consistent Armenians when rightly understood are one and the same thing. Both preach and believe that man has a will to choose and refuse and that he acts accordingly. Both believe and practice that faith that works by love and purifies the heart and which is always productive of good works, by which we are to be judged at the last day; upon the whole, the only difficulty before us, is to reconcile God's decrees with moral agency, which is a secret which must be left alone for God to reveal.

Here I saw again that I should be met with the doctrine of election, which is also founded upon the atonement of Christ. If I understand the opposers of this doctrine right, they say, that the doctrine of election makes God a partial God, and therefore an unjust God. For say they, if all Adam's posterity are under the condemnatory sentence of God's righteous law and liable to eternal punishment, equally guilty and helpless and have no power or method of their own to extricate themselves, then for God to choose or elect a part to eternal life, and part to eternal death, must undoubtedly make him a partial God, and therefore an unjust God.

To obviate this objection, I must again bring to my assistance the doctrine of motives, the freedom of the will, and the object of choice.

Upon the foundation of the doctrine of the extent of the atonement of Christ, I do believe that God did from all eternity, according to his foreknowledge and foreordination, and his eternal purpose, determine or decree to elect, raise and build up a Church and people, to love and to serve him through all succeeding generations and ages of the world; that his name should be put upon them; that they should be called his people; that they should fill all the various stations in his Church, whether Ministers, Bishops, Elders, Deacons or lay members; all for the purpose of his own glory, and for the good and prosperity of his Church and people. But how did he elect them? Contrary to their will? No. How then? Why, according to their own free will and choice, and from love to God and to his Church and people and the salvation of their own souls. Then it is plain that their election was of their own choosing according to the foreknowledge and purpose of God (for they acted precisely as he foreknew they would do, by repentance and faith in his blood). All of which did not proceed from compulsions at all, but from their own free will and choice. For the truth of this I must appeal to the experience of all the professors of Christianity in the church at the present day, of every grade, to say whether their standing and spheres of action in the church, did not proceed from their own free will and choice, and whether, in all they ever did, in and for the church did not proceed from the motives of love to God and to his church and people? If so, where can there be any possible ground for supposing that the doctrine of election makes God a partial God, and therefore an unjust God. For it is plain and put beyond all contradiction, that from the same parity of reasoning which has already been given, that those who are lost, choose their own election of damnation. Upon the same principles of motives, the freedom of the will, and the object of choice, that instead of their choosing a life of salvation and eternal happiness, they have chosen a life of damnation and eternal misery.

It is now time for me to say to the opposers of the doctrine of God's decrees and election, that I do believe that those doctrines are perfectly consistent with the character of the sovereign Ruler and Governor of the world, and as perfectly consistent with the present fallen state and condition of the whole human family individually. For I find that it is the belief of all those who are well instructed in the fundamental doctrines of Christianity, that, after the fall of man, God was under no obligation to save a single individual of the whole human family. Then it certainly is or ought to be comforting and consoling consideration for us to know, that God has in mercy determined or decreed to elect a church and people to love and to serve him. And for that glorious purpose, laid the plan of redemption, and executed it by or through the death and suffering of his son, to give them the opportunity of being restored to their primitive state of rectitude, and to make their way to heaven and eternal happiness. And because it is found that some refuse to accept of the offered mercy and are lost, then for God to be charged with partiality and injustice is language too insolent and heaven-daring for mortals to use; and all those who use it, ought to fall prostrate before him, and repent of their sins and lay in the depths of humility to the end of their day. And why? Because God's ways and dealings with his creatures are merciful and full of compassion in the plan of redemption, and perfectly consistent with their present state and condition.

In a word, my opinion is this, that wherever the word election is mentioned in the New Testament, it is intended to be adapted to the various capacities of mankind, to give them to understand that there is such a thing as an election of grace to eternal life through our Lord Jesus Christ and that it is a matter of the utmost importance for them to earnestly endeavor to make use of all the means which God has ordained, or put in their power to attain to that blessed inheritance. That there is some agency in this affair, cannot be doubted; but how or by whom, or in what manner it is put into operation, or how the operation is affected is a matter not so easily to be understood. However, on the one hand, God by the enlightening influences of his holy spirit, may touch, at least, one of the cogs and put the wheel in motion, and on the other hand, when we take into consideration the faculties of the mind of man, and begin and reason from philosophical principles founded upon the Bible, and take with us the doctrine of motives, the freedom of the will and the object of choice, we are enabled to arrive at the fair conclusion, that man himself is one of the prime agents in the operation, which proves I think satisfactorily (if I may be allowed to adopt a course of reasoning which may be called the splitting of a hair) that God ought to be charged neither with partiality nor with impartiality, neither with justice nor with injustice; for at the great day of accounts, the books are to be opened, in which the actions and transactions of the whole human family individually are recorded, and out of those books they are to be judged according to the deeds done in the body, whether they be good, or whether they be evil; and when the final sentence of the judge is pronounced, each individual will have to say Amen, either to their salvation or to their damnation, and will then and there be constrained to acknowledge that all those records were true, and proceeded from motives of gratification, and not from compulsion. This I think ends and puts the capstone upon the whole affair, from the beginning to the end, and leaves the opposers of those doctrines which I have been investigating wrapped up in a mantle of something, which I shall leave themselves to give a name. For it is plain and put beyond contradiction, that God never did nor never will compel any man to be saved, or to be damned.

But to return to the proof of the doctrine of the atonement. Perhaps it may be thought by some that I have not sufficiently established the proof of the doctrine. If so, it cannot be amiss for me to ratify it, and put a seal upon it, from the oracles of the records of the court of heaven. John, in the Isle of Patmos, informs us that, in one of his visions, "he beheld and lo a great multitude which no man could number, of all nations and kindreds and people and tongues, stood before the throne and before the Lamb, clothed with white robes, and palms in their hands, and cried with a loud voice, saying, salvation to our God which sitteth upon the throne, and unto the lamb, and all the angels stood round about the throne, and about the elders, and the four beasts fell before the throne on their faces, and worshipped God saying, Amen, blessing, and glory, and wisdom, and thanksgiving, and honor, and power, and might, be to our God, for ever and ever, Amen. And one of the Elders, answered, saying unto me, what are those which are arrayed in white robes? And whence come they? And I said unto him, sir thou knowest. And he said unto me, these are they which come out of great tribulation, and have washed their robes and made them white in the blood of the lamb, therefore are they before the throne of God, and serve him day and night in the temple. And he that sitteth upon the throne shall dwell among them. And they shall hunger no more, neither thirst any more, neither shall the sun light upon them nor any heat. For the lamb, which is in the midst of the throne; shall feed them and shall lead them unto living fountains of water, and God shall wipe away all tears from their eyes" (Rev. 7:9–17, KJV).

Now if Jesus Christ did not die to make atonement for the sins of the whole human family individually, how comes it to pass that this glorious vision should be made known to John; that he should be instructed by one of the elders of the heavenly court or church, that this great multitude, which no man could number, had come out of great tribulation and had washed their robes and made them white in the blood of the lamb. What a remarkable and striking coincidence is it, that from the days of John in the Isle of Patmos, to the present day, that wherever Jesus Christ has sent his ministers to preach the gospel to any nation, tongue, or language of people, that some of these more or less, have embraced religion, and have become humble followers of the meek and lowly Jesus, and have manifested by their manner of worship and adoration that they possessed kindred spirits with the heavenly host, and serve God day and night in the temple. What an astonishing proof of the doctrine of the extent of the atonement of Christ, and the fulfillment of the promise of the Father to the son, that "he would give him the heathen for his inheritance, and the utmost parts of the earth for his possession."

And here let me ask, does this vision of John, taken in connection with all the concurring circumstances which have taken place through all the stages of the church, put a seal upon the doctrine that cannot be broken?

And here I am constrained to ask boldly and fearlessly, who is it, in this enlightened day of the gospel, that will come forward and undertake to prove positively, absolutely and unequivocally, that Jesus Christ did not die for the sins of the whole human family individually. So certain am I that he did, that I would ask, who it is that would not thank God for a bible? No wonder that a society should be instituted for the purpose of sending the bible to the houses of all the families throughout Christendom, yea to the houses and families of all nations of the earth, that God may be glorified and sinners saved.

That my letter may not be too lengthy and weary your patience too much, your revered body will readily perceive that I have purposely omitted to mention and to comment on a number of those scripture texts upon which the fundamental doctrines of Christianity are founded, because I conceive that these and their practical use and application, are as familiar to you as the drops from your fingers over your wash-basins. Therefore, I shall content myself with giving concise answers to a few of your questions. What is faith? It is the assent and consent of the mind: I agree that Jesus Christ is the only saviour of sinners, and I consent to take my part and lot in him and to trust to him alone for life and salvation. What is true and genuine faith? It is the faith that works by love and purifies the heart, and which is always productive of good works by which we are to be judged at the last day. What is saving faith? Saving faith has, what I shall take the liberty to call, a golden chain with three links, the holiness of God, the justice of God and the truth of God. Therefore, whosoever can freely, conscientiously and unreservedly make Peter's appeal, Lord thou knowest all things, thou knowest that I love thee, because thou art a holy God of untainted truth, may take it for granted that they have saving faith. Can this appeal be made perpetually? No it cannot. It can only be made periodically, and then only, when grace is in lively exercise in the soul.

Thus sir, you have my letter before you. It is an original child of my weak brain and I would with much humility ask your reverend body to cast your charitable garments over its deformities. I have written it for the purpose of letting you know some of the doctrines, in my private and fireside conversations with my neighbors. And if I have been in an error, I know it is a duty incumbent on you to reprove me, which, I trust, I shall receive with humility and Christian kindness.

That God may bless you in your deliberations to promote the best interests of the Redeemer's kingdom, is the prayer of your unworthy licentiate and beneficiary.

P.S. I have had the doctrine of the Atonement of Christ of God's decrees and of election, under investigation for about forty years. And although upon those subjects, I have read the writings of some of the greatest men the world has produced, yet they left those doctrines wrapped up in so much mystery that I could not be satisfied with their investigations.

Nor could I be satisfied with my own investigations, until I adopted as theories the doctrine of motives, the freedom of the will and object of choice, and for these I am indebted to Edwards on the Will.[5] He says that the will is produced from the last dictate of the understanding, which enabled me to come to the conclusion, that it is produced from the object of choice; which, I think, will accord with the experience of every person who will carefully examine the motives of their actions. Having adopted and reasoned from these theories, those doctrines are no longer a mystery, but are as plain to me as the letters A B C, and although I said, when treating on the doctrine of the decrees, that the only difficulty was to reconcile God's decrees with moral agency, yet I do humbly conceive that by this method of reasoning that those doctrines are stripped of all mystery, and stand clothed in as brilliant colours as the shining of the sun's rays at noon-day.

To conclude my Postscript, permit me to observe, that I believe it is acknowledged on all hands that the doctrine of the Atonement and the doctrine of God's decrees, and the doctrine of election, are three of the most mysterious doctrines belonging to the fundamental doctrines of Christianity. And that there is no other method of explaining them satisfactorily, but the philosophical reasoning, and although such kind of reasoning is not so easily comprehended by common readers, yet those doctrines ought not to be left wrapped up in mystery, because of their want of comprehension. Such characters must do, as others have done, go to the school of Philosophy, for instruction, which has the Bible for its foundation.

J.C.

## *Notes*

*Sermon source:* Helen Chavis Othow, *John Chavis, African American Patriot, Preacher, Teacher and Mentor (1763–1838)* (Jefferson, NC: McFarland and Company, 2001), 13–32.

1. Carter G. Woodson, *The Education of the Negro Prior to 1861*, 2nd ed. (Washington, DC: Association for the Study of Negro Life and History, 1919), 181–82.

2. See the minutes of the Lexington Presbytery, October 23–25, 1800, Presbyterian Study Center, Montreat, NC.

3. See the letter from John Chavis to Willie P. Mangum, September 3, 1831, Willie Person Mangum Collection, The Library of Congress.

4. John Hope Franklin, *The Free Negro in North Carolina, 1790–1860* (Chapel Hill: University of North Carolina Press, 1943), 173.

5. The reference here is to Jonathan Edwards. In 1754, Edwards wrote an essay that was originally titled "A Careful and Strict Enquiry into the Modern Prevailing Notions of that Freedom of Will which is Supposed to be Essential to Moral Agency, Virtue and Vice, Reward and Punishment, Praise and Blame." It came to be known as "Freedom of the Will." For additional information on this essay, see Allen C. Guelzo's *Edwards on the Will: A Century of American Theological Debate* (Lebanon, NH: University Press of New England, 1989).

## *Bibliographical Sources*

Eaton, Clement. *The Mind of the Old South*, rev. ed. Baton Rouge: Louisiana State University Press, 1967.

Franklin, John Hope. *The Free Negro in North Carolina, 1790–1860*. Chapel Hill: University of North Carolina Press, 1943.

Hudson, Gossie. "John Chavis, 1763–1838: A Social-Psychological Study." *Journal of Negro History* 64, no. 2 (Spring 1979): 142–56.

Knight, Edgar W. "Notes on John Chavis." *The North Carolina Historical Review* 7, no. 3 (July 1930): 336.

Othow, Helen Chavis. *John Chavis, African American Patriot, Preacher, Teacher and Mentor (1763–1838)*. Jefferson, NC: McFarland and Company, 2001.

Shaw, G.C. *John Chavis 1763–1838*. Binghamton, NY: Vail-Ballou Press, 1931.

Weeks, Stephen. "John Chavis, Antebellum Negro Preacher and Teacher." *Southern Workman*, February 1914: 101–6.

## HOSEA EASTON

*(1798–1837)*

Hosea Easton was born free in 1798, the son of James and Sarah Easton. Evidence suggests that Hosea's father was part Wampanoag and part Narragansett Indian, and that his mother Sarah (Dunbar) was the daughter of a mulatto. Given this mixed heritage, perhaps it is not as surprising that Hosea's brother, Caleb, married into one of North Bridgewater (now Brockton) Massachusetts's well-to-do white families. Hosea was the youngest of seven children (Joshua and Sarah, who became abolitionists; James, who became a physician; Caleb and Sulvanus, manufacturers; and Mary).

Easton's parents fought resolutely against racism in Boston. When their church, the Fourth Church of Christ of Bridgewater, constructed a porch for Negroes, the Eastons remained on the main floor and were ultimately bodily removed from the church. When they joined a Baptist church in Stoughton Corner and purchased a pew, it was tarred. The next Sunday the Eastons returned with chairs. Eventually they were formally banished from this church as well. All of these actions undoubtedly had a strong impact on the Easton children.

The Eastons were among the black elite of Massachusetts. Hosea's father served in the American Revolution under George Washington as a fortification engineer and later opened an iron foundry, and attached to it a manual labor school for promising black youth. It soon closed for lack of funding—racism again.

The record is scant on the dates and means by which Easton received his schooling. However, by 1828 he was educated and already receiving great praise for his work as a minister. He was married to Louisa (Matrick), and they had two children. Around 1830, they moved to Boston, where Easton quickly became a community leader. At a meeting of the National Colored Convention in 1831, he joined with William Garrison and others in attempting to open a manual labor college in New Haven, Connecticut, for young black men. For Hosea, this was a way of reviving what his father had tried earlier. However, it was not to be, due to the racism that did not allow students to attend in safety or sufficient funding to be raised. The school closed after about ten years. In 1833, Easton became the pastor of the black Talcott Congregational Church in Hartford. A white mob burned the church to the ground in 1836. Understandably, having watched his father's dream be destroyed by hate and now seeing his church dissipated by the same sentiment, Easton became defeated and depressed. In his fifty-eight-page pamphlet, *Treatise on the Intellectual Character, and Civil and Political Condition of the Colored People of the U. States; and the Prejudice Exercised towards Them: With a Sermon on the Duty of the Church to Them*, he writes that white racism is intractable and that there is nothing that blacks can do to alleviate it. Whites themselves must defeat it. Tied to this belief was his sense that racist acts by whites had so injured blacks that they had been made inferior and would never be whole. Easton understood how deeply embedded racism was in the fabric of America. In 1837 in Massachusetts before the Anti-Slavery Society, he said, "The spirit of slavery will survive in the form of racial prejudice, long after the system of slavery is overturned. Our warfare ought not to be against slavery alone, but against the spirit which makes color a mark of degradation."[1] Hosea Easton died at age forty-one in Hartford, Connecticut. He and his wife were buried in the Old North Cemetery.

• • •

*Easton gave the following address in 1828. In it he criticizes in the harshest manner possible the evils wrought by white men against blacks (including "beating them with clubs, roasting them alive, dissecting them limb by limb or starving them to death").[2] While much of the address is directed toward cruel white behavior, he gives particular attention to encouraging black uplift. Easton also attacks the American Colonization Society, which some blacks thought was a great abolitionist group. However, Easton saw it as another means by which whites could get rid of the most vocal blacks by sending them into exile to places such as Liberia, doing so in the name of helping blacks to begin anew in a land where they could exert their rights and humanity.*

## An Address: Delivered Before the COLOURED POPULATION, of Providence Rhode Island on Thanksgiving Day, November 27, 1828 (November 27, 1828)

Men and Brethren—This is a day set apart by our Rulers as a day of rejoicing for the many blessings enjoyed, while greater prospects of plenty and happiness are enjoyed, while greater prospects of plenty and happiness are continually heaving in view. We, as a nation, have great reason to rejoice, that by the great wheel of Providence, prosperity has graced our train while marching up the hill of popularity and honor. Let the expanding mind reflect for a moment, the rapid growth of this Nation, from the time a little handful held their council upon Plymouth Beach, until the present time. And if their hearts are not under the influence of a sordid disposition, they will today tune them in anthems of praise and thanksgiving to God, for thus rearing us from nothing, to a great and mighty nation.

I repeat again, that prosperity has graced our train. Prosperity has opened the door of the forest for the reception of our forefathers; granting them an opportunity to display their superior knowledge in the use of firearms above that of the natives: by which means the latter were drove out before them, being slain by thousands, thus, leaving them in peaceable possession of the soil. Again, Prosperity did attend their endeavours to introduce agriculture, the mechanic arts, and scientific knowledge. Prosperity did also aid their labours while propagating religious principles through our Republic, insomuch, that there is not a city, town, or hardly a neighborhood, but in which you will not find a temple of worship, said to be erected to the worship of God. In a word, whatever course we have taken, the wheel of providence has led us into a field of prosperity. The memorable fourth of July, brings into our view, that important era of our country, when her liberties were threatened by England's pride. But methinks, I hear, a brave Washington, standing on his dignified eminence, exclaiming, Liberty! Liberty! Liberty! Or death. His valiant confederates rejoin'd the theme, and ere long, every heart burned with the fire of Liberty. The Ensign of Liberty was hoisted, and manfully defended. A Constitution was wisely framed, declaring all men to be free and equal. Who can say that our constitution is not founded on the principles of liberty and equality! We are indebted, then to divine providence for thus prospering our march as a nation. Many other blessings that we enjoy, might be brought into notice. But time will not permit us even to contemplate one out of ten thousand of the blessings we enjoy daily. How animating then is the celubrious [salubrious] sound of Liberty. The voice of Liberty calls the energies of the human soul to emerge out of nature's darkness, and to explore divine spiritual principles; from thence to angelic. How admirable it is, that the higher the soul arises by being expanded by intelligent perception, the more it breathes forth praise and thanksgiving to God, still beholding momentarily new delights in the vast field of Liberty, which God has given it for an inheritance, it bursts forth in the inspired language of the Psalmist. "It is a good thing to give thanks unto the Lord, and to sing praises to thy name, O, most high. For thou Lord hast made me glad through thy work. I will triumph in the work of thy hands." Again—If we follow the same train of reflection in natural intelligence, we shall find that liberty has proportionably the same effect and proffers the same reward. In this, our country, how soon do we see the infant grow to a stature which qualifies him to fill the highest seat of honour among our rulers? And thus be able to rejoice to see the expanded wings of Liberty, brooding over her votaries, sheltering them from slavery and oppression. But while I have endeavored to inspire your hearts with thankfulness to God, there has reflections forced themselves into my mind which has caused me to tremble for the fate of this country. O, America! Listen to your subjects. Allied to you by birth and blood. Shut out from all slavery which you have riveted on their necks. Look at Virginia! Look at Washington! See droves of your subjects coupled together by pairs, while others are administering the laws of Liberty. And to fill out the file, we see those, who have received the dignified appellation of "Negro Drivers," inflicting merciless stripes upon their fellow subjects; drawing forth that sacred blood which God has forbidden to be shed; forcing their march, some from wives, some from parents, some from children, others from all that is near and dear to them. And for what? To gratify the avarice of proud America. O, Liberty, where art thou! Is this all? No! We will pass on. Leaving behind thought the barbarous cruelty imposed upon the natives, and as to the hellish practice of importing a foreign nation to a country of liberty, to be sold in slavery; it were better to be buried in oblivion and remembered no more forever. There are about five hundred thousand of the above-named degraded sufferers, who are said to be free, which assertion I deny. It is true, we live under a milder State Administration at present. It is also true, that we are in some respects exalted to heaven, in point of Liberty, above that of our fellow subjects, who are under the immediate scourge of avarice. Their awful situation, doubtless, many of you have experienced, who compose this respectable auditory—while others of you have been eyewitnesses to the bloody scenes of cruelty and murder. Bretheren, what was the sensation of your minds, when you beheld many of the female sex, pregnant with their young, tied to a tree or stake, and whipt by their masters, until nature gave way, and both mother and infant yielded up the ghost, while bearing the hellish scourge of these candidates for hell? What were they, when you saw your bretheren shot or beat with clubs? When you saw their master vent his rage, by murdering them by degrees, either, by roasting them alive, dissecting them limb by limb, or starving them to death for not complying with their unjust requirements? What were they, when you beheld the youth massacred for the smallest misdemeanor, and their affectionate parents not daring to make the least resistance for fear of falling victims to the same fate? What were they, when you saw the disciples of Christ, denied the privilege of meeting in groves and bylots, to worship their God as guided by his spirit? What were they, I would ask, when you saw these things and many more, in the very heart of our country—A country of Liberty—Near the very seat of Government? Did not the spirit of Liberty cry within you, for vengeance to fall upon this country, which has so falsified the principles of Liberty, and trampled justice under foot. Now as we compose a part of the number who are said to be free, of course it becomes our duty to consider how far our liberty extends. The first enquiry is, Are we eligible to an office? No.—Are we considered subjects of the government? No.—Are we initiated into free schools for mental improvement? No.—Are we patronised as salary men in any public business whatever? No.—Are we taken into social compact with Society at large? No.—Are we patronised in any branch of business which is sufficiently lucrative to raise us to any material state of honour and respectability among men, and this, qualify us to demand respect from the higher order of Society? No.—But to the contrary. Everything is withheld from us that is calculated to promote the aggrandizement and popularity of that part of the community who are said to be the descendants of Africa. I am sensible the white population will deny the fact above stated. But to confirm the fact, let us notice our ordinary course since the American Independence.

We will notice, first, our march in religious improvement. God has raised up some able ambassadors of truth among our population; and though they are held in contempt among the whites, yet God has caused his light to shine through them, to the great shame of our oppressors; and has decided the question, respecting the natural intelligence of the sable race, which has so long employed the pen of learned interrogators. But where are their privileges? Where even they can embody a little handful of coloured people together, there they can display their respective talents, as long as the means of subsistence is left them, but when that is exhausted, they are compelled to appeal to day labour for support. Or should they obey the heavenly command to "go into all the world and preach the gospel to every creature," they would often be treated with contempt by those that ought to be their patrons. Should one enter a town or city, with his credentials, and offer them to the minister of the church, it is more than probable, that the best appointments the minister would make for him, to discharge his duty, would be at a private house on a weekday. Should he stop over the Sabbath, he would be introduced into the most remote part of the house of God, that is too demeaning to have the beasts for its occupants. How does he fare on his journey from place to place? I am bold to say that he cannot purchase a seat in the public stage, only by sufferance. I have known men of that profession, to be detained in towns and cities, not far distant from this place, ten days, before they could prosecute their journey; and then be under the necessity of getting some white man as an intercessor to the driver or owners for a passage on the outside of the carriage, by paying full price for fare. I know of an occurrence which took place in a stage passing from New Bedford to Fall River. It appears that two coloured men paid their passage upon the above named rout, they being the only passengers, occupied the back seat. When they arrived at Westport village, there was a white sailor of low grade, and a young girl that worked in the factory, that made application for a passage to Fall River. They were immediately gallanted to the stage, the door was thrown open, and orders given by the driver, for the coloured men to take the forward seats, which were complied with; when the two genteels got into the carriage and took the highest seat. One of these coloured gentlemen, was a minister of the gospel, of no mean standing; and what must have been his feelings, God only knows.

We will now notice our means of acquiring literary information. It is true, that in our northern States, the laws have made provisions for us without distinction. But though we claim our right lawfully, yet, like all our other rights, we are denied enjoyment of them. We send our children to primary schools among white children; and if there is any demeaning place of contempt, to be found in any part of the School Room, there is the place for our children to get their information; while the little flax-headed boys and girls, are learnt by their parents to place a reproach upon them, by calling them Negroes, and the place where they are destined to sit, negro seats. Thus, our poor youth are discouraged, disheartened, and grow up in ignorance; fitted only to be an object of ridicule and contempt through life, by the higher order of Society. Some, doubtless, will be ready to say, that our liberty is above this. In answer to whom I will acknowledge that there is an exception in States and Cities. In New York and Connecticut, the coloured population are brought more into public notice, as well as in the cities of New York and Boston; also, in many other places, public support for schools is set apart for the coloured population. In those schools, we have youths well qualified for the common business of life; but when they have obtained their education, they know enough only to feel sensible of their misery. Their minds being expanded, their perception brightened, their zeal ardent for promotion; they look around for business, they find that custom cuts them off from all advantages. They apply to merchants to patronise them as Clerks, they are rejected. They apply to attornies at law to receive them into their office, they are rejected. They apply to the mariner, they are rejected, except, to go before the mast, cook, or steward. They apply to Mechanics of different occupations, here, too, they are rejected. And for what? Because it is customary. Leaving law, justice, and equity altogether out [of] the question. And should it become customary to cut off a black man's head (as it is already at the south), then of course we must lose our head, if custom says it is right. We see then the situation of our youth, turned out of doors without the least encouragement whatever. Now let us notice the consequence. Those bright minds enlarged by education, being under the necessity of taking up some low calling, which is not calculated to satisfy the extension of them, they become like the starving man, who, for the want of wholesome food, partakes of that which is poisonous and destructive. So it is with our youth, for the want of those encouragements set up before them, that is calculated to draw their attention to the pursuits of honour, respectability, virtue and industry, their expanded minds relapse into sordid dissipation, and fall victim to all the vices and folly incident to discouraged minds; and thus, the more education they have, under such circumstances, the more artful they are in following the haunt of dissipated principles. O, shocking! Is America to answer for all this? When then does justice sleep? It is true, that many of our population survive the struggle, so far as to arise to a degree of respectability. But with what respect are they treated? Let the man of business travel through the northern States. And I am ready to prove to you, that he will not pass ten miles, without meeting with insults almost sufficient to enrage a saint. If he hires his passage in the stage, he must be posted up with the driver to suffer the severity of the weather. When the passengers stop to dine, he must take his fare in the cook room, with the cook. And for a sitting parlour, he must take the bar-room; to have his feelings injured by tavern haunters and drunkards. If you look for his lodging chamber, you will find it in the garret, or back clutter chamber. These are fine places for men of business. Under these, and other disadvantages, we see the man is not calculated to do business, for the want of society. Society is the very mother who supplies men of business with useful knowledge; for the want of which, the poor man lays out his money at seventy-five percent, disadvantage; and to discourage and depress his mind still further, the question is asked by the whites: Why is it that Negroes cannot do business like other people? Again—Should any one become religious, and feel desirous to follow the precepts of his Lord and Master, by having his name enrolled in the Church Militant, he is there treated more like a beast than in any other course of life. How say you? I answer—The coloured "brother," however able to provide for himself, must have a place provided for him. And where is it? In some remote part of the Meeting-House, or in a box built above the gallery. When the Church is called to partake of the sacred elements, the black communicants must come down, stand or sit in some remote part of the lower floor, until the white bretheren have eaten what they want of the Lord's body, and drank what they want of his blood; then cries the minister, "Come coloured bretheren, now come and partake of the broken body of Christ. It is free for all without any distinction." And it is a chance if he does not, while thus officiating, offer an insult to their feelings, by saluting them as Africans or Ethiopians. While in fact they are Americans, and perhaps distantly related to some of the white members, by reason of the brutal conduct of their fathers. Now these are facts. There is not a church in the circle of my knowledge but what, must bear the character above asserted. And can rational beings, believe that God is a fool, that he is well pleased with such idolatry? We will follow this subject a little further, and see if we cannot find other things that gives character to a Christian nation. It is an obvious fact, that the white population are alarmed at the rapid growth of the coloured people; insomuch, that there is not a soul, that has any forecast, but that is troubled; and I would to God, that they might be confounded in their own craft, until, brought to experience true repentance, and are willing to deal justly with their neighbors.

The *Colonizing Craft* is a diabolical pursuit, which a great part of our Christian community are engaged in. Now bretheren, I need not enlarge, on this point. You that have been observing, have already seen the trap under the bait; and although some of our population, have been foolish enough to sell their birthright for a mess of pottage, yet I doubt, whether the Colonization Society will entrap many more. It is too barefaced, and contrary to all reason, to suppose, that there is any good design in this project. If they are willing to restore four-fold for what they have taken by false accusation, they can do it to better advantage in the bosom of our country, than at several thousand miles off. How would you do, bretheren, if your object was really to benefit the poor? Would you send them into a neighboring forest, and there deal out that food which they were famishing for? Now we stand different from beggars. Our ancestors were stolen property, and property which belonged to God. This is well known by our religious community; and they find that the owner is about to detect them. Now if they can slip away these stolen goods, by smuggling all those out of the country, which God would be likely to make an instrument of, in bringing them to justice, and keeping the rest in ignorance; by such means, things would go on well with them, and they would appease their consciences by telling what great things they are doing for the coloured population and God's cause. But we understand better how it is. The deception is not so well practised, but that we can discover the mark of the beast. They will steal the sons of Africa, bring them to America, keep them and their posterity in bondage for centuries, letting them have what education they can pick up of themselves; then transport them back to Africa; by which means America gets all her drudgery done at little expense, and endeavor to flatter [the] Deity, by making him a sacrifice of good works of this kind. But to the awful disappointment of all such blasphemers, they will meet the justice of God, which will be to them a devouring sword.

## TO CONCLUDE.

BRETHEREN—My heart is filled with sorrow for this nation. I am far from being envious, and I would caution you against any revengeful or malignant passions; but stand still and see the salvation of God. Stand still did I say? Yes, so far as it respects the providence of God; we are to stand still, look, wonder, and adore. But as it respects the great labour and ardent zeal which involves upon us at the present day; there is no time to stand still. The time has come, when our necessities calls aloud for our exertions, to prepare ourselves for the great events which are about heaving in view. Bretheren, the dreary night of darkness, which our fathers passed through, is about to disperse. And notwithstanding we are a divided people, tossed to and fro, and hunted like the partridge upon the mountain, yet the glorious rays of rational intelligence and literary acquirements, are beginning to backen the chaos darkness, which has so long pervaded the minds of our population. Yes, bretheren, let a theme of praise and thanksgiving to God, thrill through every heart, in silent accents; for the sunbeams of Liberty are casting forth their glorious rays through the eastern atmosphere; and we may rationally entertain the hope, that God, in his wise Providence, will cause this glorious sun to arise to its meridian, and burst those fetters with which we are bound, and unlock the prison doors of prejudice; granting us Liberty to enjoy the blessings of life like other men. But we must not suppose that we shall obtain those blessings without our cooperation with divine order; for, inasmuch as mankind are created intelligent beings, and recipient forms, it follows, that every principle, whether natural or spiritual, is obtained by the rational principle which is always found with man; that turning itself toward divine order, they join hands as companions, cooperate with each other, and thus, they become the parents which begets understanding to recipient man. What I wish to be understood by divine order, are those principles or attributes of light, which, in the order of providence flow to man. Now all persons that have arrived to the years of discretion, have already a degree of understanding, which enables them to perceive the duty that is set before them. Then as it respects our community, it is plain to see, by the foregoing statements, respecting our oppresst community, what is necessary. It is evident that we ought to turn our attention to moral improvement. A principle of jealousy one towards another, has become almost hereditary; which prevents any combined operation among us. The first thing necessary, is, to cultivate the principles of concord and unanimity among ourselves, that we may become aids to each other; for the prosecution of which, we ought to introduce operations that is accordant with the object in pursuit. In all cases of improvement, there must be an object set up with way-marks, that are calculated to attract the mind from a low state to higher attainments. If then, we can combine our ability, and bend it [to] this course, it will open a field of labour for the reception of our youth, who are coming upon the stage of action, and give them an opportunity of displaying their intellectual talents; which will give a character to our community, and take away our reproach. When our operations become united, that the voice of our community, may be heard as the voice of one man; then shall we be able to control the principles of indolence and immorality of every species, and inculcate those of industry and virtue, with all qualifications necessary to enable us to control the effects of our own labour, and make it subservient to the benefit of our own community. We may look abroad and see sufficient to induce us to become active in our own interest. You, that are the fathers of our community, ought to use your feeble efforts to the establishment of the temple of Liberty; and when your sun shall hide itself beyond the western region, it shall leave a principle enstampt upon rising generations, which will embellish our bright prospects, and entail honours to your name while time shall last. Mothers, you have something to do with this important undertaking. Your virtuous council to your daughters, will qualify them to become useful in their circles. By which means, the haunt of the dance-hall will be broken. Bretheren, the time has come, when you, that are in the meridian of life, ought to raise the voice of Liberty and equality: truth and justice: virtue and industry, both by example and precept. I would also encourage the female part of our community, in the language of the people of Israel to Boaz, "The Lord make the woman that is come into thy house, like Rachel and Leah; which two, did build the house of Israel; and do thou worthily in Ephratah, and be famous in Bethlehem. And let thy house, be like the house of Pharez, whom Tamar bare unto Judah, of the seed which the Lord shall give thee of this young woman." So let it be concerning you. The Lord make you to our community, like Rachel and Leah; which two, did build the house of Israel; and do thou worthily in Ephratah, and be famous in Bethlehem. And let thy house, be like the house of Pharez, whom Tamar bare unto Judah, of the seed which the Lord shall give thee of this young woman. But my dear youth what shall I say to you? Can I make use of any language that will detach your minds from delusive pleasures, and cause you to look to the great object of your interest. Remember, my young friends, that your fathers were deprived the opportunity you now enjoy; and while I am addressing you, methinks I hear a voice from the graves of our fathers! And what is the language? It calls on you to forsake those foolish practices, which are so common amongst us; and apply your hearts to wisdom.

It is no time, my young friends, to spend your time in the dance-hall. It is no time to exercise your ability in gambling. But you must lay aside all unnecessary diversion, and alter your courses; Come out of this degrading course of life; Distinguish yourselves as pious, industrious, and intelligent men and women. This will demand respect from those who exalt themselves above you. I must now leave this subject with you, hoping that this day's labour will not be in vain; for I assure you my heart mourns daily, while beholding the clouds of evil thickening over this Republic. The awful consequences are plain to be seen, by the aid of both ancient and modern history. Let him that readeth understand. But, O, for a Gideon, with his three hundred men, chosen of God, to go up against the towering walls of evil, and cause them to fall, forever fall, to rise no more.

### *Notes*

*Sermon source: To Heal the Scourge of Prejudice: The Life and Writings of Hosea Easton.*

1. *The Liberator*, February 11, 1837.
2. *To Heal the Scourge*, 53.

### *Bibliographical Sources*

Easton, Hosea. *To Heal the Scourge of Prejudice: The Life and Writings of Hosea Easton*, edited with an introduction by George Price and James Brewer Stewart. Amherst: University of Massachusetts Press, 1999.

Price, George R., and James Brewer Stewart. "The Roberts Case, the Easton Family, and the Dynamics of the Abolition Movement in Massachusetts, 1776–1870." *Massachusetts Historical Review* 4 (2002), 89.

# LEMUEL HAYNES

*(1753–1833)*

Lemuel Haynes was the son of an African American father and a white mother. Unwanted, he grew up without the presence of either; he lived with the Rose family in Granville, Massachusetts, as an indentured servant until he was twenty-one.

After serving as a Minuteman in the Revolutionary War, Haynes studied privately for the ministry and learned Latin and Greek. In 1780 he became a licensed preacher; he was ordained in 1785 as a Congregationalist minister. In 1783 he married Elizabeth Babbit, a white woman, and they had ten children. Erudite and popular in New England, Haynes is believed to have been the first black pastor of a white church in the United States, serving in Torrington, Connecticut. He later served other white congregations in New Hampshire, Vermont, and New York. In 1788, he became the pastor of the West Rutland Congregational Church in Rutland, Vermont, where he remained for thirty-four years. Well known and well regarded, Haynes was honored in 1804 by Middlebury College with an honorary degree, a master of arts, the first black so honored in America.

Lemuel Haynes was an exemplar of the little-written-about black contemplative preacher.[1] He has become the subject of considerable research because of his contribution to early New England history: as a Minuteman, as a pastor of several white Congregational churches, as a forward-thinking essayist who left a considerable canon of works on human liberty, written years before the abolitionist movement fully began, and as a thoughtful and highly regarded preacher. *Black Preacher to White America: The Collected Writings of Lemuel Haynes*, edited by the late Richard Newman, shows some of the depth and breadth of Haynes's thought and indicates to some extent his spirit and tone as a preacher. Haynes's oratory contains the elements of all great and relevant preaching as described by Reverend Gardner Taylor: the majesty of life, the glory of its possibilities, and the greatness and glory of God.[2]

Despite more than thirty years of service, in 1818 the church did not renew his contract. Anecdotal evidence suggests that this was because his congregation no longer wanted to be pastored by a black man.[3] Lemuel Haynes died in Vermont in 1833.

• • •

*This sermon was delivered by Haynes in Rutland, Vermont, following a sermon delivered by Reverend Hosea Ballou, a white Universalist preacher. Haynes, a Calvinist, believed in predestination and personal election. Ballou believed that salvation was universal and that people gained it by living according to the Gospel. Their disagreement on this issue was widely known, and the encounter between them had long been awaited and encouraged. Reverend Ballou preached first, and after he finished speaking he asked for comments. Haynes rose and delivered his message without notes. It was reprinted in more than seventy editions during the first sixty years after its delivery.*

## Universal Salvation: A very eminent doctrine; with some Account of the Life and Character of its Author. A Sermon Delivered at Rutland, West Parish in the Year 1805, by Lemuel Haynes (1805)

*And the serpent said unto the woman, Ye shall not surely die.*

—Genesis 3:4

The holy scriptures are a peculiar fund of instruction. They inform us of the origin of creation; of the primitive state of man; of his fall, or apostacy from God. It appears that he was placed in the garden of Eden, with full liberty to regale himself with all the delicious fruits that were to be found, except what grew on one tree—if he eat of that, that he *should surely die*, was the declaration of the Most High God.

Happy were the human pair amidst this delightful Paradise, until a certain preacher, in his journey, came that way, and disturbed their peace and tranquility, by endeavoring to reverse the prohibition of the Almighty, as in our text, Ye shall not surely die.

*She pluck'd, she ate,*
*Earth felt the wound; nature from her seat,*
*Sighing through all her works, gave signs of woe,*
*That all was lost.*[4]

We may attend—To the character of the preacher, to the doctrines inculcated; to the hearer addressed; to the medium or instrument of the preaching.

I. As to the preacher, I would observe, he has many names given him in the sacred writings; the most common is the devil. That it was he that disturbed the felicity of our first parents, is evident from Second Corinthians 11:3, and many other passages of Scripture. He was once an angel of light and knew better than to preach such doctrine: he did violence to his own reason.

But to be a little more particular, let it be observed,

1. He is an old preacher. He lived above one thousand seven hundred years before Abraham; above two thousand four hundred and thirty years before Moses; four thousand and four years before Christ. It is now five thousand eight hundred and nine years since he commenced preaching. By this time he must have acquired great skill in the art.
2. He is a very cunning, artful preacher. When Elymas the sorcerer came to turn away people from the faith, he is said to be full of all subtlety, and a child of the devil, not only because he was an enemy to all righteousness, but on account of his carnal cunning and craftiness.
3. He is a very laborious, unwearied preacher. He has been in the ministry (a minister of sin) almost six thousand years; and yet his zeal is not in the least abated. The apostle Peter compares him to a roaring lion, walking about seeking whom he may devour. When God inquired of this preserving preacher, Job

2:2, *From whence comest thou?* He answered and said, From going to and fro in the earth, and from walking up and down in it. He is far from being circumscribed within the narrow limits of parish, state, or continental lines; but his haunt and travel is very large and extensive.

4. He is a heterogeneous preacher, if I may so express myself. He makes use of a Bible when he holds forth, as in his sermon to our Savior, Matthew 4:6.—He mixes truth with error, in order to make it go well, or to carry his point, in ruining souls.
5. He is a very presumptuous preacher. Notwithstanding God had declared, in the most plain and positive terms, Thou shalt surely die, or in dying, thou shalt die; yet this audacious wretch had the impudence to confront Omnipotence, and say, *ye shall not surely die!*
6. He is a very successful preacher. He draws a great number after him. No preacher can command hearers like him. He was successful with our first parents, and with the old world. Noah once preached to those spirits who are now in the prison of hell; and told them from God, that they should surely die; but this preacher came along and declared the contrary, *Ye shall not surely die.* The greater part, it seems, believed him, and went to destruction. So it was with Sodom and Gomorrah. Lot preached to them; the substance of which was, *Up, get ye out of this place, for the Lord will destroy this city.*—Genesis 19:14. But this old declaimer told them, *No danger, no danger, ye shall not surely die.* To which they generally gave heed, and Lot seemed to them as one who mocked; they believed the universal preacher, and were consumed agreeable to the declaration of the apostle Jude, *Sodom and Gomorrah and the cities about them, suffering the vengeance of eternal fire.*

II. Let us attend to the doctrine inculcated by this preacher, *Ye shall not surely die.* Bold assertion! Without a single argument to support it. The death contained in the threatening was doubtless eternal death—as nothing but this would express God's feelings towards sin, or render an infinite atonement necessary. To suppose it to be spiritual death, is to blend crime and punishment together; to suppose temporal death to be the curse of the law, then believers are not delivered from it, according to Galatians 3:13. What Satan meant to preach, was that there is no hell, and that the wages of sin is not death, but eternal life.

III. We shall now take notice of the hearer addressed by the preacher. This we have in the text, *And the serpent said unto the woman, et cetera.* That Eve had not so much experience as Adam, is evident; and so was not equally able to withstand temptation. This doubtless was the reason why the devil chose her, with whom he might hope to be successful. Doubtless he took a time when she was separated from her husband.

That this preacher has had the greatest success in the dark and ignorant parts of the earth, is evident: His kingdom is a kingdom of darkness. He is a great enemy to light. St. Paul gives us some account of him in his day, Second Timothy 3:6.—*For of this sort are they which creep into houses, and lead captive silly women, laden with sin led away with divers lusts.* The same apostle observes, Romans 16:17, 18—*Now I beseech you, brethren, mark them which cause divisions and offences, contrary to the doctrine which ye have learned, and avoid them. For they that are such serve not the Lord Jesus Christ, but their own bell; and by good words and fair speeches deceive the hearts of the simple.*

IV. The instrument or medium made use of by the preacher will now be considered. This we have in the text, *And the serpent said, et cetera.* But how came the devil to preach through the serpent?

1. To save his own character, and the better to carry his point. Had the devil come to our first parents personally and unmasked, they would have more easily seen the deception. The reality of a future punishment is at times so clearly impressed on the human mind, that even Satan is constrained to own that there is a hell; although at other times he denies it. He does not wish to have it known that he is a liar; therefore he conceals himself, that he may the better accomplish his designs, and save his own character.
2. The devil is an enemy to all good, to all happiness and excellence. He is opposed to the felicity of the brutes. He took delight in tormenting the swine. The serpent, before he set up preaching universal salvation, was a cunning, beautiful, and happy creature; but now his glory is departed; *for the Lord said unto the serpent, Because thou hast done this, thou art cursed above all cattle, and above every beast of the field; upon thy belly shalt thou go, and dust shalt thou eat all the days of thy life.*[5] There is therefore, a kind of duplicate cunning in the matter, Satan gets the preacher and hearers also.

*And is not this triumphant flattery,*
*And more than simple conquest in the foe!*
—*Young*

3. Another reason why Satan employs instruments in his service is, because his empire is large and he cannot be every where himself.
4. He has a large number at his command, that love and approve of his work, delight in building up his kingdom, and stand ready to go at his call.

*Inferences*

1. The devil is not dead, but still lives; and is able to preach as well as ever, *Ye shall not surely die.*
2. Universal Salvation is no newfangled scheme, but can boast of great antiquity.
3. See a reason why it ought to be rejected, because it is an ancient devilish doctrine.
4. See one reason why it is that Satan is such an enemy to the Bible, and to all who preach the gospel, because of that injunction—*And he said unto them, go ye into all the world, and preach the gospel to every creature. He that believeth and is baptized shall be saved; but he that believeth not shall be damned.*[6]
5. See whence it was that Satan exerted himself so much to convince our first parents that there was no hell! Because the denunciation of the Almighty was true, and he was afraid they would continue in the belief of it. Was there no truth in future punishments, or was it only a temporary evil, Satan would not be so busy, in trying to convince men that there is none. It is his nature and element to lie. *When he speaketh a lie, he speaketh of his own; for he is a liar, and the father of it.*
6. We infer that ministers should not be proud of their preaching. If they preach the true gospel, they only, in substance, repeat Christ's sermons. But if they preach *ye shall not surely die*, they only make use of the devil's old notes, that he delivered almost six thousand years ago.
7. It is probable that the doctrine of Universal Salvation will still prevail, since this preacher is yet alive, and not in the least superannuated; and every effort against him only enrages him more

> and more, and excites him to new inventions and exertions to build up his cause.

To close the subject: As the author of the foregoing discourse has confined himself wholly to the character of Satan, he trusts no one will feel himself personally injured by this short sermon; but should any imbibe a degree of friendship for this aged divine, and think that I have not treated this Universal Preacher with that respect and veneration which he justly deserves, let them be so kind as to point it out, and I will most cheerfully retract; for it has ever been a maxim with me—RENDER UNTO ALL THEIR DUES.

## *Notes*

*Sermon source:* Phillip S. Foner and Robert James Branham, eds., *Lift Every Voice: African American Oratory 1787–1900* (Tuscaloosa: University of Alabama Press, 1998), 59–64.

1. Contemplation, as explained in the *Confessions* (7.16), was Augustine's way of looking at life with "the eye of the soul." He was concerned to see above and beyond what is mental, which is to gain illumination, and to hear with "the ears of the heart," which is to gain discernment. This is the path and approach of the contemplative preacher. Barbara Holmes further clarifies the definition of contemplation in *Joy Unspeakable: Contemplative Practices of the Black Church* (Minneapolis: Fortress Press, 2004, 45): "Some who study contemplation have assumed that the difference between European and Africana approaches to contemplation is based on the presence or lack of silence. This distinction could only be made during the modern era, as historically silence was interwoven in both traditions. Although silence is not necessarily the focus of contemplation in Africana contexts, it is always a part of the human experience."

2. This statement was made by Reverend Taylor in a lecture he gave at Pacific School of Religion, Berkeley, California, in 1984.

3. The source of the best-known story concerning Reverend Haynes's dismissal comes from the Fitch Manuscript History of Washington County, New York. This collection was prepared by Dr. Asa Fitch from 1847 to 1878; it contains articles, bits of transcribed oral history, and pieces of genealogy, mostly of Washington County. Fitch died before the manuscript was published. The Vermont Historical Society has a copy. Dr. Fitch heard about the story from Captain Donald McDonald, of Salem, New York, in about 1848, which would be about thirty years after the dismissal. Captain McDonald said, "They found out he was a nigger and turned him away." The quote is McDonald's, not Haynes's. Ebenezer Baldwin, *Observations on the Intellectual, and Moral Qualities of Our Colored Population: With Remarks on the Subject of Emancipation and Colonization* (New Haven, CT: L.H. Young, 1834, 46) relates the same incident but uses the phrase "a colored man."

4. John Milton, *Paradise Lost*, bk. 8, lines 781–84.

5. Genesis 3:14 (King James Version)

6. Mark 16:15 (KJV).

### *Bibliographical Sources*

Berry, Mary Frances, and John Blassingame. *Long Memory: The Black Experience in America.* New York: Oxford University Press, 1982, 296–97.

Bogin, Ruth. "Liberty Further Extended: A 1776 Antislavery Manuscript by Lemuel Haynes," *William and Mary Quarterly* 40, no. 1 (Jan. 1983): 85–105.

Cooley, Timothy Mather. *Sketches of the Life and Character of the Rev. Lemuel Haynes, A.M., for Many years Pastor of a Church in Rutland, Vt., and in Granville, New York.* New York: Harper and Brothers, 1837.

Franklin, John Hope, and Alfred A. Moss Jr., *From Slavery to Freedom: A History of African Americans*, 8th ed. New York: Alfred A. Knopf, 2002, 89, 178.

George, Carol V.R. *Segregated Sabbaths: Richard Allen and the Emergence of Independent Black Churches, 1760–1840.* New York: Oxford University Press, 1973, 169–72.

Newman, Richard. *Black Apostles at Home and Abroad: Afro-Americans and the Christian Mission from the Revolution to Reconstruction.* Boston: G. K. Hall, 1982.

———, ed. *Black Preacher to White America: The Collected Writings of Lemuel Haynes, 1774–1833.* Brooklyn, NY: Carlson Publishing Inc., 1990.

Newman, Richard, and David W. Wills, eds. *Lemuel Haynes: A Bio-Bibliography.* New York: Lambeth Press, 1984.

Richardson, Harry V. *Dark Salvation.* Garden City, NY: Anchor Press, 1976, 170.

Woodson, Carter G. *The Negro in Our History.* Washington, DC: The Associated Publishers, Inc., 1931, 157–58.

## JOHN JEA

*(1773–ca. 1817)*

According to the first page of his autobiography, John Jea was born in the well-known slave port of Old Callabar, in southern Nigeria in 1773. Jea's father, Hambleton Robert Jea, his mother, Margaret Jea, and their children, including two-and-one-half-year-old John, came to America in a slave ship and were sold to the New York Dutch family of Oliver and Angelika Triehuen. Jea relates the cruelness of his owners: "often they treated the slaves in such a manner as caused their death, shooting them with a gun, or beating their brains out with some weapon, . . ." Jea was heavily influenced by John Wesley's theology and music, and included many of Wesley's hymns in his own hymnal.

According to Jea, he underwent a bitter conversion process. He developed deep depression, characteristic of the conversions of some Africans into Christianity. Mr. Triehuen sought to instill docility in John by sending him to a church school, which Jea strongly rejected. Jea came to grips with his faith by praying in a secret place in the woods; his master responded by beating him unmercifully. Unable to deter Jea's piety, which was not really desired by his master, he was eventually sold to the first of three other masters. Jea accepted Christianity sufficiently to be baptized by a Presbyterian minister, without permission from his fourth owner. Furious, this owner took Jea before magistrates, and Jea gave confession in the name of Jesus. When he did not go to jail, he thought the magistrates had freed him. In reality the magistrates had only validated his conversion and baptism. Later, after a vision, Jea claimed he became literate miraculously. He read the entire Bible, and this time, after proving his literacy before the magistrates, Jea received his freedom at the age of sixteen. Literacy was a multifaceted sign of liberty; many slaves connected Bible reading and literacy with physical, as well as spiritual, emancipation. In many states, it was still illegal for slaves to read, but not in New York.

Jea began his ministry in 1788. He traveled through rural New York and eastern New Jersey as an itinerant preacher and conducted major preaching rallies on the East Coast. Holding all-night vigils in New York's rural environs, Jea skirted laws against unlicensed assemblages by blacks. As a roving preacher, Jea signed up as a cook for the first of his many ocean voyages. He traveled to Europe, South America, and Asia preaching the gospel.

Throughout his autobiography, Jea preaches against slavery as a grievous sin. For him, true Christianity required the abolition of slavery. This belief led to his spending a great deal of time preaching abroad. In addition to black liberationist Christianity, he preached on the themes of holiness and rebirth. His preaching showed that he knew how to discern the essence of God, which he believed to be love. He was not fooled by whites who claimed to be Christians while enslaving others. Jea, among many Africans, understood how to reinterpret the Gospel for its liberative power.

Jea was married on three occasions, first to an American Indian, Elizabeth; next to a Maltese woman, Charity; and lastly to an Irish woman, Mary. In his autobiography he states that he had several children, all of whom were deceased by the time he married for the third time.

In 1811, John Jea wrote about his life in *The Life, History, and Unparalleled Sufferings of John Jea, the African Preacher.* In 1816, a collection of more than three hundred hymns in a songbook, which included approximately twenty-nine of his own, was published.

• • •

*No entire sermons from John Jea have survived; it was common for preaching in the antebellum period to be summarized and not fully written out. Although only snatches of a sermon are available, we include them because his preaching is among the earliest recorded by a black forced from Africa to the New World. In his autobiography, Jea provides the backdrop for one of his overseas sermons, along with part of that sermon.*

## Excerpts of Sermons by John Jea (1811)

### The Backdrop for the Sermon

Thus the Lord blessed and prospered my ways, even until I got to Sunderland, and there I preached, and had great success. The Lord owning and blessing my ministry in this manner, caused great hatred to spring up among the brethren, so that they desired the people not to follow me, for they said that they could not get a congregation to preach unto, worth speaking of. This was the case with one of the preachers with whom I travelled; while the other was my friend, and desired me to continue preaching in the name of the Lord. His name was Mr. John Booth, about forty years of age. The other's name, who was my enemy, was Mr. Chittle; he was of rich parents, and for the sake of his father he was offended with me: for I and his father preached together in one meetinghouse, his father first, and I afterwards. His father being an old man he did not preach very often, only on particular occasions; for this reason he was to preach the same evening as I did, for he wished to convince the people that they should not follow after a man, but after Christ. He compared me to poor Lazarus; because wherever I went to preach the meetinghouses could not hold the people, but wherever the other preachers went to preach, they had plenty of room, having scarcely any congregation; which caused him to preach on this part of the gospel: "*Now a certain man was sick, named Lazarus, of Bethany, the town of Mary and her sister Martha. (It was that Mary which anointed the Lord with ointment, and wiped his feet with her hair, whose brother Lazarus was sick . . .*"

According to Jea, the preacher read and briefly expounded upon John 11:1–11; 17–25; 32–46, and Luke 12:8–11.

Jea continues:

During which time I was sitting in the pulpit behind him, for I was to preach after him. He then began to explain who Lazarus was, and said that he was a poor man, a porter, of no reputation, and making out that scarcely any notice was taken of him, because he was a poor stinking man. He then exclaimed to the people, that they were all running after a poor dead Lazarus, and that they did not come to see Jesus; and told the people that they might as well throw their bibles and books away, as to be always running after a poor dead man, nothing but a poor wounded Lazarus.

Thus he preached to the people, and told them he was sorry to say that they had been running to see and hear a poor dead Lazarus, that was risen from the dead, and that they were not then come to see Jesus, but Lazarus. This was his discourse to the congregation, and then he closed the subject; and said, "Our friend, our black brother, will speak a few words unto you."

## The Lazarus Sermon

I then stood up and addressed the congregation, saying, "Men and brethren, I shall not take a text, but only make a few remarks, by God's assistance, on what our brother has spoken unto you concerning poor Lazarus." I then said unto the congregation, "Spiritually speaking, who is this Lazarus? Yea," said I, "every sinner is as Lazarus; for we were all born in sin, and brought forth in iniquity, dead in trespasses and sins, laying in the grave of sin and wickedness, and stinking in the nostrils of the Almighty God."

Jea then focuses on readers of his autobiography.

My dear reader, are you laying in the grave of sin and wickedness? For many have been laying in that state ten, twenty, thirty, yea, and some fifty years, stinking in the nostrils of the Almighty God; and indeed, so are all sinners, who sin against God, and disbelieve his blessed word; it therefore becomes you to enquire and examine whether you have been raised from this awful state or not.

The Jews did not only come to see Lazarus, because of the miracle which was wrought by Jesus Christ on him, but that they might be enabled to lay hands upon him, and kill him, even as they wanted to kill Jesus Christ; for, they said, if they let him alone, his life and conduct, wherever he went, would shew that he was that dead stinking Lazarus, whom Jesus had raised from the grave. So it is with every one, whether they be men or women, that confesses Jesus Christ before man on earth, being an evident proof that they are risen from the grave of sin and wickedness by the resurrection of the Lord Jesus Christ from the dead, even as Jesus Christ himself confesseth.

I told them, our brother that had preached against me, had not always been a preacher, but was once like other men, for he was born in sin, and brought forth in iniquity, and going astray from the womb, telling lies, and was laying in the grave of sin and wickedness, and stinking in the nostrils of the Almighty. But God, in his infinite goodness and mercy, was pleased to send his only begotten Son into the world, to save all such as should not perish, who lay in the grave of sin and wickedness: Jesus Christ being troubled in the spirit for poor sinners, wept over him as he did over Jerusalem, and rolled the stone of unbelief from his heart, and cried with a loud voice, and said unto him, "Awake, thou that sleepest, and arise from the dead, and Christ shall give thee light." Thus the grave of sin and wickedness opened, and the dead sinner arose from it, by the Spirit of God, bound with the grave clothes of lust, and his face bound up with a napkin of speechlessness, but God said unto the Spirit, Loose him and let him go.

Thus, I said God had done to our brother that preached against me, and that he had opened his grave in which he had once lain stinking in the nostrils of God; and that Jesus had risen him from the grave, and had loosened him by his Spirit, to let him go to the gospel feast, to shew himself unto all men, that he was the stinking sinner Christ had risen by his Spirit, to preach the gospel to every creature. On hearing this the congregation clapt their hands and shouted.

## NOTES

*Sermon source:* These excerpts are taken from John Jea's *The Life, History, and Unparalleled Sufferings of John Jea, the African Preacher*, at Documenting the American South, University of North Carolina at Chapel Hill Digitization Project, at http://www.docsouth.unc.edu/neh/jeajohn/jeajohn.html (accessed January 13, 2004).

1. *Life, History, and Unparalleled Sufferings*, 4.
2. Ibid., 10.
3. Ibid., 32–33.
4. Ibid., 35–38.

### *Bibliographical Sources*

Bolster, W. Jeffrey. *Black Jacks: African American Seamen in the Age of Sail.* Cambridge, MA: Harvard University Press, 1997, 38, 40, 77–78, 87–88, 95.

Hodges, Graham Russell, ed., *Black Itinerants of the Gospel: The Narratives of John Jea and George White.* Madison, WI: Madison House Publishers, 1993.

Jea, John. *A Collection of Hymns Compiled and Selected by John Jea, African Preacher of the Gospel.* Portsea, England, 1816.

———. *The Life, History, and Unparalleled Sufferings of John Jea, the African Preacher.* Documenting the American South, University of North Carolina at Chapel Hill Digitization Project, www.docsouth.unc.edu/neh/jeajohn/jeajohn.html (accessed January 13, 2004).

# ABSALOM JONES

*(1746–1818)*

In 1746, Absalom Jones was born in slavery in Sussex, Delaware, on a plantation known as Cedar Town. No information concerning his parents is known. He learned to read in the home of the family that enslaved him, the Wynkoops. Jones moved with the Wynkoops to Philadelphia when he was sixteen. He continued his education at a night school for blacks while working in Benjamin Wynkoop's store. In 1770 he married Mary King, purchasing her freedom by 1778 and his own in 1784 at the age of thirty-eight.

The membership of St. George's Methodist Episcopal Church in Philadelphia, which fellow black lay preacher Richard Allen (1760–1831) attended, included both blacks and whites. In 1787, the white members decided black members should not pray at the same time as whites. Jones, along with Allen, learned of the decision when Jones and others were pulled from their knees during prayer. Jones, Allen, and the other black members left the church.

Seven months later Jones and Allen formed the Free African Society. They started holding services in 1791 at a temporary site and began planning to build a church. When the time came for members to vote for denominational affiliation most wanted to be Episcopal (Church of England). Absalom Jones and Richard Allen voted for Methodist affiliation. The majority prevailed. In July 1794 the church was dedicated with the name St. Thomas African Episcopal Church. Twelve days later Bethel Church with Richard Allen as its leader was dedicated by Methodist Bishop Asbury.

Jones became one of the major freedom fighters of his day. In 1799, along with seventy-three others, he helped draft and present a historic petition to revise the Fugitive Slave Act and abolish slavery to President John Adams and the United States Congress. Jones died in 1818 in Philadelphia.

• • •

*Jones's sermons matched his works: they often focused on justice and equal rights. Jones preached the following sermon at the African Episcopal Church in Philadelphia in celebration of the abolition of the slave trade by the U.S. Congress. This sermon uses a motif in which black preachers draw parallels between the suffering of the Jews in the Bible and that of contemporary blacks. This motif is still prevalent in many black churches today.*

## A Thanksgiving Sermon, Preached January 1, 1808, In St. Thomas's or the African Episcopal, Church, Philadelphia: on Account of The Abolition of the African Slave Trade, on That Day, By the Congress of the United States (1808)

> *And the Lord said, I have surely seen the affliction of my people which are in Egypt, and have heard their sorrows; and I am come down to deliver them out of the hand of the Egyptians.*
>
> —Exodus 3:7–8

These words, my brethren, contain a short account of some of the circumstances which preceded the deliverance of the children of Israel from their captivity and bondage in Egypt.

They mention, in the first place, their affliction. This consisted in their privation of liberty: they were slaves to the kings of Egypt, in common with their other subjects; and they were slaves to their fellow slaves. They were compelled to work in the open air, in one of the hottest climates in the world; and, probably, without a covering from the burning rays of the sun. Their work was of a laborious kind: it consisted of making bricks, and traveling, perhaps to a great distance, for the straw, or stubble, that was a component part of them. Their work was dealt out to them in tasks, and performed under the eye of vigilant and rigorous masters, who constantly upbraided them with idleness. The least deficiency, in the product of their labour, was punished by beating. Nor was this all. Their food was of the cheapest kind, and contained but little nourishment: it consisted only of leeks and onions, which grew almost spontaneously in the land of Egypt. Painful and distressing as these sufferings were, they constituted the smallest part of their misery. While the fields resounded with their cries in the day, their huts and hamlets were vocal at night with their lamentations over their sons; who were dragged from the arms of their mothers, and put to death by drowning, in order to prevent such an increase in their population, as to endanger the safety of the state by an insurrection. In this condition, thus degraded and oppressed, they passed nearly four hundred years. Ah! Who can conceive of the measure of their sufferings, during that time? What tongue, or pen, can compute the number of their sorrows? To them no morning or evening sun ever disclosed a single charm: to them, the beauties of spring, and the plenty of autumn had no attractions: even domestic endearments were scarcely known to them: all was misery; all was grief; all was despair.

Our text mentions, in the second place, that, in this situation, they were not forgotten by the God of their fathers, and the Father of the human race. Though, for wise reasons, he delayed to appear in their behalf for several hundred years; yet he was not indifferent to their sufferings. Our text tells us, that he saw their affliction, and heard their cry: his eye and his ear were constantly open to their complaint: every tear they shed was preserved, and every groan they uttered was recorded, in order to testify, at a future day, against the authors of their oppressions. But our text goes further: it describes the Judge of the world to be so much moved, with what he saw and what he heard, that he rises from his throne—not to issue a command to the armies of angels that surrounded him to fly to the relief of his suffering children—but to come down from heaven, in his own person, in order to deliver them out of the hands of the Egyptians. Glory to God for this precious record of his power and goodness: let all the nations of the earth praise him. Clouds and darkness are round about him, but righteousness and judgment are the habitation of his throne. O sing unto the Lord a new song, for he hath done marvelous things: his right hand and his holy arm hath gotten him the victory. He hath remembered his mercy amid truth toward the house of Israel, and all the ends of the earth shall see the salvation of God.

The history of the world shows us, that the deliverance of the children of Israel from their bondage is not the only instance in which it has pleased God to appear in behalf of oppressed and distressed nations, as the deliverer of the innocent, and of those who call upon his name. He is as unchangeable in his nature and character, as he is in his wisdom and power. The great and blessed event, which we have this day met to celebrate, is a striking proof, that the God of heaven and earth is the same, yesterday, and today, and forever. Yes, my brethren, the nations from which most of us have descended, and the country in which some of us were born, have been visited by the tender mercy of the Common Father of the human race. He has seen the affliction of our countrymen, with an eye of pity. He has seen the wicked arts, by which wars have been fomented among the different tribes of the Africans, in order to procure captives, for the purpose of selling them for slaves. He has seen ships fitted out from different ports in Europe and America, and freighted with trinkets to be exchanged for the bodies and souls of men. He has seen the anguish which has taken place, when parents have been torn from their children, and children from their parents, and conveyed, with their hands and feet bound in fetters, on board of ships prepared to receive them. He has seen them thrust in crowds into the holds of those ships, where many of them have perished from the want of air. He has seen such of them as have escaped from that noxious place of confinement, leap into the ocean, with a faint hope of swimming back to their native shore, or a determination to seek an early retreat from their impending misery, in a watery grave. He has seen them exposed for sale, like horses and cattle, upon the wharves, or, like bales of goods, in warehouses of West India and American sea ports. He has seen the pangs of separation between members of the same family. He has seen them driven into the sugar, the rice, and the tobacco fields, and compelled to work—in spite of the habits of ease which they derived from the natural fertility of their own country—in the open air, beneath a burning sun, with scarcely as much clothing upon them as modesty required.

He has seen them faint beneath the pressure of their labors. He has seen them return to their smoky huts in the evening, with nothing to satisfy their hunger but a scanty allowance of roots; and these, cultivated for themselves, on that day only, which God ordained as a day of rest for man and beast. He has seen the neglect with which their masters have treated their immortal souls; not only in withholding religious instruction from them, but, in some instances, depriving them of access to the means of obtaining it. He has seen all the different modes of torture, by means of the whip, the screw, the pincers, and the red hot iron, which have been exercised upon their bodies, by inhuman overseers: overseers, did I say? Yes: but not by these only. Our God has seen masters and mistresses, educated in fashionable life, sometimes take the instruments of torture into their own hands, and, deaf to the cries and shrieks of their agonizing slaves, exceed even their overseers in cruelty. Inhuman wretches! though You have been deaf to their cries and shrieks, they have been heard in Heaven. The *ears* of Jehovah have been constantly open to them: He has heard the prayers that have ascended from the hearts of his people; and he has, as in the case of his ancient and chosen people the Jews, come down to deliver our suffering countrymen from the hands of their oppressors. He came down into the United States, when they declared, in the constitution which they framed in 1788, that the trade in our African fellowmen, should cease in the year 1808: He came down into the British Parliament, when they passed a law to put an end to the same iniquitous trade in May, 1807. He came down into the Congress of the United States, the last winter, when they passed a similar law, the operation of which commences on this happy day. Dear land of our ancestors! thou shall no more be stained with the blood of thy children, shed by British and American hands: the ocean shall no more afford a refuge to their bodies, from impending slavery: nor shall the shores of the British West India islands, and of the United States, any more witness the anguish of families, parted forever by a public sale. For this signal interposition of the God of mercies, in behalf of our brethren, it becomes us this day to offer up our united thanks. Let the song of angels, which was first heard in the air at the birth of our Saviour, be heard this day in our assembly: Glory to God in the highest, for these first fruits of peace upon earth, and good-will to man: O! let us give thanks unto the Lord: let us call upon his name, and make known his deeds among the people. Let us sing psalms unto him and talk of all his wondrous works.

Having enumerated the mercies of God to our people, it becomes us to ask, What shall we render unto the Lord for them: Sacrifices and burnt offerings are no longer pleasing to him: the pomp of public worship, and the ceremonies of a festive day, will find no acceptance with him, unless they are accompanied with actions that correspond with them. The duties which are inculcated upon us, by the event we are now celebrating, divide themselves into five heads.

In the first place, let not our expressions of gratitude to God for his late goodness and mercy to our countrymen, be confined to this day, nor to this house: let us carry grateful hearts with us to our places of abode, and to our daily occupations; and let praise and thanksgivings ascend daily to the throne of grace, in our families, and in our closets, for what God has done for our African brethren. Let us not forget to praise him for his mercies to such of our colour as are inhabitants of this country; particularly, for disposing the hearts of the rulers of many of the zeal of the friends he has raised up to plead our cause; and for the privileges we enjoy, of worshiping God, agreeably to our consciences, in churches of our own. This comely building, erected chiefly by the generosity of our friends, is a monument of God's goodness to us, and calls for our gratitude with all the other blessings that have been mentioned.

Secondly, let us unite, with our thanksgiving prayer to Almighty God, for the completion of his begun goodness to our brethren in Africa. Let us beseech him to extend to all the nations in Europe, the same humane and just spirit towards them, which he has imparted to the British and American nations. Let us, further, implore the influence of his divine and holy Spirit, to dispose the hearts of our legislatures to pass laws, to ameliorate the condition of our brethren who are still in bondage; also, to dispose their masters to treat them with kindness and humanity; and, above all things, to favour them with the means of acquiring such parts of human knowledge, as will enable them to read the holy scriptures, and understand the doctrines of the Christian religion, whereby they may become, even while they are the slaves of men, the freemen of the Lord.

Thirdly, let us conduct ourselves in such a manner as to furnish no cause of regret to the deliverers of our nation, for their kindness to us. Let us constantly remember the rock whence we were hewn, and the pit whence we were digged. Pride was not made for man, in any situation; and, still less, for persons who have recently emerged from bondage. The Jews, after they entered the promised land, were commanded, when they offered sacrifices to the Lord, never to forget their humble origin; and hence, part of the worship that accompanied their sacrifices consisted in acknowledging, that a Syrian, ready to perish, was their father, in like manner, it becomes us, publicly and privately, to acknowledge, that an African slave, ready to perish, was our father or our grandfather. Let our conduct be regulated by the precepts of the gospel; let us be sober minded, humble, peaceable, temperate in our meats and drinks, frugal in our apparel and in the furniture of our houses, industrious in our occupations, just in all our dealings, and ever ready to honor all men. Let us teach our children the rudiments of the English language, in order to enable them to acquire a knowledge of useful trades, and, above all things, let us instruct them in the principles of the gospel of Jesus

Christ, whereby they may become raised unto salvation. It has always been a mystery, why the impartial Father of the human race should have permitted the transportation of so many millions of our fellow creatures to this country, to endure all the miseries of slavery. Perhaps his design was, that a knowledge of the gospel might be acquired by some of their descendants, in order that they might become qualified to be the messengers of it, to the land of their fathers. Let this thought animate us, when we are teaching our children to love and adore the name of our Redeemer. Who knows but that a Joseph may rise up among them, who shall be the instrument of feeding the African nations with the bread of life, and of saving them, not from earthly bondage, but from the more galling yoke of sin and Satan.

Fourthly, let us be grateful to our benefactors, who, by enlightening the minds of the rulers of the earth, by means of their publications and remonstrances against the trade in our countrymen, have produced the great event we are this day celebrating. Abolition societies and individuals have equal claims to our gratitude. It would be difficult to mention the names of any of our benefactors, without offending many whom we do not know. Some of them are gone to heaven, to receive the reward of their labours of love towards us; and the kindness and benevolence of the survivors, we hope, are recorded in the book of life, to be mentioned with honor when our Lord shall come to reward his faithful servants before an assembled world.

Fifthly, and lastly, let the first of January, the day of the abolition of the slave trade in our country, be set apart in every year, as a day of public thanksgiving for that mercy. Let the history of the sufferings of our brethren, and of their deliverance, descend by this means to our children, to the remotest generations; and when they shall ask, in time to come, saying, What mean the lessons, the psalms, the prayers and the praises in the worship of this day? let us answer them, by saying, the Lord, on the day of which this is the anniversary, abolished the trade which dragged your fathers from their native country, and sold them as bondmen in the United States of America.

Oh thou God of all the nations upon the earth! We thank thee, that thou art no respecter of persons, and that thou hast made of one blood all nations of men. We thank thee, that thou hast appeared, in the fullness of time, in behalf of the nation from which most of the worshiping people, now before thee, are descended. We thank thee, that the sun of righteousness has at last shed his morning beams upon them. Rend thy heavens, O Lord, and come down upon the earth; and grant that the mountains, which now obstruct the perfect day of thy goodness and mercy towards them, may flow down at thy presence. Send thy gospel, we beseech thee, among them. May the nations, which now sit in darkness, behold and rejoice in its light. May Ethiopia soon stretch out her hands unto thee, and lay hold of the gracious promise of thy everlasting covenant. Destroy, we beseech thee, all the false religions which now prevail among them; and grant, that they may soon cast their idols, to the moles and the vats of the wilderness.

O, hasten that glorious time, when the knowledge of the gospel of Jesus Christ, shall cover the earth, as the waters cover the sea; when the wolf shall dwell with the lamb, and the leopard shall lie down with the kid and the calf and the young lion and the fatling together, and a little child shall lead them; and, when, instead of the thorn, shall come up the fir tree, and, instead of the brier, shall come up the myrtle tree: and it shall be to the Lord for a name and for an everlasting sign that shall not be cut off. We pray, O God, for all our friends and benefactors, in Great Britain, as well as in the United States: reward them, we beseech thee, with blessings upon earth, and prepare them to enjoy the fruits of their kindness to us, in thy everlasting kingdom in heaven: and dispose us, who are assembled in thy presence, to be always thankful for thy mercies, and to act as becomes a people who owe so much to thy goodness. We implore thy blessing, O God, upon the President, and all who are in authority in the United States. Direct them by thy wisdom, in all their deliberations, and O save thy people from the calamities of war. Give peace in our day, we beseech thee, O thou God of peace! and grant, that this highly favored country may continue to afford a safe and peaceful retreat from the calamities of war and slavery, for ages yet to come. We implore all these blessings and mercies, only in the name of thy beloved Son, Jesus Christ, our Lord. And now, O Lord, we desire, with angels and arch-angels, and all the company of heaven, evermore to praise thee, saying, Holy, holy, holy, Lord God Almighty: the whole earth is full of thy glory. Amen.

## *Note*

*Sermon source:* Dorothy Porter, *Early Negro Writing, 1760–1837* (Boston: Beacon Press, 1971), 335.

## *Bibliographical Sources*

Christian, Charles M. *Black Saga: The African American Experience: A Chronology*. Boston: Houghton Mifflin, 1995.

Kaplan, Sidney, and Emma Nogrady Kaplan. *The Black Presence in the Era of the American Revolution*, rev. ed. Amherst: University of Massachusetts Press, 1989.
Murphy, Larry G., J. Gordon Melton, and Gary L. Ward, eds. *Encyclopedia of African American Religion*. New York: Garland Publishing, 1993, 404.

# JOHN MARRANT

*(1755–1791)*

John Marrant is one of the first two African American preachers for whom there is a written record; the other is Jupiter Hammond (1720–?). It is believed that Marrant may have been the first ordained black minister to preach in the United States. Born free in New York City in 1755, his father died when John was four. He and his mother moved briefly to St. Augustine, Florida, and then settled in Georgia. Marrant learned to read and write and left school around age eleven. He also played two instruments, the violin and French horn.

At thirteen, after conversion under the preaching of the Great Awakening preacher George Whitefield, Marrant wrote that he ran away from home and ended up on Indian land. He was held by the Cherokees for two years. After torturing him, they decided to kill him. Marrant said that his life was spared after praying in the Cherokee language and converting their chief.

Marrant eventually returned home to his family, who thought that he had died. In 1774, he enlisted as a soldier for the British, and served with them during the Revolutionary War. He was injured in the Battle of Charleston and discharged from the navy in 1782. He then worked in London, where he realized his call to preach and was ordained by a Calvinist Methodist preacher in 1785. That fall, he was persuaded by his brother to come as a missionary to Nova Scotia, where numerous blacks had settled. Marrant embarked on an almost four-year mission among the blacks, poor whites, and Micmac Indians of southeastern Nova Scotia. Birchtown, a refuge for black Loyalists and liberated slaves, became the seat of his ministry. There he founded a church and appointed pastoral assistants. Fueled by Marrant's love for Africa as the black homeland, after his departure his Nova Scotia congregation immigrated to Sierra Leone under the guidance of Marrant's successor, Cato Perkins. Writers have speculated as to why Marrant did not join the congregation in Africa.

Before Marrant left Nova Scotia, he published and sold the diary of his missionary years: *A Journal of the Rev. John Marrant, From August the 18th, 1785, to the 16th of March, 1790. To which are attached Two Sermons; One Preached on Ragged Island on Sabbath Day, the 27th Day of October 1787; the Other at Boston in New England, on Thursday, the 24th of June, 1789.* The volume includes Marrant's seventy-five-page account of his North American mission, a list of subscribers, letters he received from church officials and others during his time in Nova Scotia, and two sermons—one delivered at a 1787 funeral, the other at a 1789 gathering of Boston's African Lodge. The book is the most extensive published account of black evangelism and community life in the eighteenth century; in its time it was a best seller. By 1835, it had gone through twenty printings, though Marrant received very little of the proceeds. Marrant had been sent to Nova Scotia with the financial assistance and backing of Lady Selina Huntingdon who, after problems with the Anglican church, had founded the "Countess of Huntingdon's Connexion." This was a Calvinistic movement within the Methodist church.

Marrant left Nova Scotia and returned to London, where he was met with rumors that he had squandered the Connexion's money. Although those in London did not know it, Marrant had been "reduced so low" by the amount he earned as a preacher that at times he sold his clothes; he wrote that he did this four times. Although these hardships ultimately accrue to "the glory of God," Marrant observed that no "preacher belonging to the Connection could have suffered more than I have."[1]

In 1789, he moved to New England, where he became friends with Prince Hall, founder of the African Masonic Lodge, the first black lodge. His eloquent sermons won him the post of chaplain.

Marrant returned to London in 1791, where he died of an unknown cause at the age of thirty-five.

• • •

*In Boston, before returning to London for his last year of life, Marrant preached a lengthy sermon for a special occasion of the Masonic Lodge. The sermon focuses on the building of Solomon's temple and masonry. It also extols Africans as masters of "architecture, art and science," rails against the mistreatment of blacks, and argues vehemently for their civil rights. The sermon was given shortly after the Massachusetts Commonwealth's court voted to require that blacks produce a certificate of citizenship from any state in which they had previously resided. Those who did not produce these certificates could be deported or jailed.*

## A Sermon Preached on the 24th Day of June 1789, Being the Festival of St. John the Baptist, at the Request of the Right Worshipful the Grand Master Prince Hall, and the Rest of the Brethren of the African Lodge of the Honorable Society of Free and Accepted Masons in Boston (June 24, 1789)

*Be kindly affectioned one to another, with brotherly love, in honour preferring one another.* —Romans 12:10

In this chapter, from whence my text is taken, we find the Apostle Paul labouring with the Romans to press on them the great duties of Brotherly Love.

By an entire submission and conformity to the will of God, whereby are given to us exceeding great and precious promises, that by these we might be made partakers of the divine nature, having escaped the corruption that is in the world through lust—That being all members of the body of Christ with the Church, we ought to apply the gifts we have received to the advantage of our brethren, those of us especially who are called to any office in the church, by discharging it with zeal and integrity and benevolence, which is the most important duty, and comprehends all the rest, and particularly the following—which the apostle here sets down—which are to love one another sincerely, to be ready to all good offices—to sympathize in the good or evil that befalls our brethren, to comfort and assist those that are in affliction, and to live together in a spirit of humility, peace and unity. Benevolence does yet further oblige Christians to love and bless those who hate them and injure them, to endeavour to have peace with all men, to abstain from revenge, and to render them good for evil; these are the most essential duties of the religion we profess; and we deserve the name of Christians no further than we sincerely practise them to the glory of God and the good of our own souls and bodies, and the good of all mankind.

But first, my Brethren, let us learn to pray to God through our Lord Jesus Christ for understanding, that we may know ourselves; for without this we can never be fit for the society of man, we must learn to guide ourselves before we can guide others, and when we have done this we shall understand the apostle [in] Romans 12:16. "Be not wise in your own conceits," for when we get wise in ourselves we are then too wise for God, and consequently not fit for the society of man—I mean the Christian part of mankind. Let all my brethren Masons consider what they are called to—May God grant you an humble heart to fear God and love his commandments; then and only then you will in sincerity love your brethren: And you will be enabled, as in the words of my text, to be kindly affectioned one to another, with brotherly love in honour preferring one another. Therefore, with the Apostle Paul, I beseech you therefore brethren, by the mercies of God, that ye present your bodies a living sacrifice, holy, acceptable unto God, which is your reasonable service—let love be without dissimulation, abhor that which is evil, cleave to that which is good. These and many other duties are required of us as Christians, every one of which are like so many links of a chain, which when joined together make one complete member of Christ; this we profess to believe as Christians and as Masons—I shall stop here with the introduction, which brings me to the points I shall endeavour to prove.

First, the anciency of Masonry, that being done, will endeavour to prove all other titles we have a just right as Masons to claim—namely, honourable, free and accepted: To do this I must have recourse to the creation of this our world—After the Grand Architect of the Universe had framed the heavens for beauty and delight for the beings he was then about to make, he then called the earth to appear out of darkness, saying, let there be light, and it was so; he also set the sun, moon and stars in the firmament of heaven, for the delight of his creatures—he then created the fishes of the sea, the fowls of the air, then the beasts of the earth after their various kinds, and God blessed them.

Thus all things were in their order prepared for the most excellent accomplished piece of the visible creation, Man.—The forming [of] this most excellent creature Man, was the close of the creation, so it was peculiar to him to have a solemn consultation and decree about his making, and God said, let us make Man.—Seneca says, that man is not a work huddled over in haste, and done without fore-thinking and great consideration, for man is the greatest and most stupendous work of God—Man hath not only a body in common with all inferior animals, but into his body was infused a soul of a far more noble nature and make—a rational principle to act according to the designs of his creation; that is, to contemplate the works of God, to admire his perfections, to worship Him, to live as becomes one who received his excellent being from him, to converse with his fellow creatures that are of his own order, to maintain mutual love and society, and to serve God in consort. Man is a wonderful creature, and not undevedly [*sic*] said to be a little world, a world within himself, and containing whatever is found in the Creator.

In him is the spiritual and material nature of God, the reasonableness of Angels, the sensitive power of brutes, the vegetative life of plants, and the virtue of all the elements he holds converse within both worlds. . . . Thus man is crowned with glory and honour, he is the most remarkable workmanship of God. And is man such a noble creature and made to converse with his fellow men that are of his own order, to maintain mutual love and society, and to serve God in consort with each other?—then what can these God-provoking wretches think, who despise their fellow men, as tho' they were not of the same species with themselves, and would if in their power deprive them of the blessings and comforts of this life, which God in His bountiful goodness, hath freely given to All his creatures to improve and enjoy? Surely such monsters never came out of the hand of God in such a forlorn condition.

Which brings me to consider the fall of man; and the Lord God took the man and put him into the garden of Eden, to dress it and to keep it, and freely to eat of every tree of the garden; here was his delightful employ and bountiful wages, and but one tree out of all that vast number he was forbidden to eat of. Concerning this garden, there have been different opinions about it by the learned, where it was, but the most of them agree that the four rivers parted or divided the four quarters of the world. The first was Pison, that was it which compasseth the land of Havilah; this river Pison is called by some the Phasis, or Phasi Tigris, it runs (they say) by that Havilah whither the Amalekites fled, see First Samuel 15:7, and divides it from the country of Susianna, and at last falls into the Persian Gulf, saith Galtruchius and others; but from the opinions of Christian writers, who hold, that Havilah is India, and Pison the river Ganges. This was first asserted by Josephus, and from him Eustubius, Jerom, and most of the fathers received it, and not without good reason; for Moses here adds, as a mark to know the place by, that there is gold, and the gold of that land is good; now it is confessed by all, that India is the most noted for gold, and of the best sort. It is added again, a note whereby to discover that place, that there is bdellium and the onyx stone—and India is famous for precious stones and pearls.—The name of the second river is Gihon, the same is it which compasseth the whole land of Ethiopia (or Cush as it is in the original) there is reason to believe that this Gihon is the river of Nile, as the forenamed Josephus and most of the ancient writers of the church hold, and by the help of the river Nile, Paradise did as it were border upon Egypt, which is the principal part of the African Ethiopia, which the ancient writers hold is meant there: The name of the third river is Hiddekel, that is it which goeth toward the east of Assyria, verse 14. That it was a river belonging to Babylon is clear from Daniel 10:4; this is concluded to be the river Tygris, which divides Mesopotamia from Assyria, and goeth along with Euphrates, this being the great middle channel that ran through Edom or Babylon, and may be thought to take its name from its fructifying quality. These are the four grand landmarks which the all-wise and gracious God pleased to draw as the bounds and habitation of all nations which he was about to settle in this world; if so, what nation or people dare, without highly displeasing and provoking that God to pour down his judgments upon them.—I say dare to despise or tyrannize over their lives or liberties, or encroach on their lands, or to enslave their bodies? God hath and ever will visit such a nation or people as this.—Envy and pride are the leading lines to all the miseries that mankind have suffered from the beginning of the world to this present day. What was it but these that turned the devil out of heaven into a hell of misery, but envy and pride?—Was it not the same spirit that moved him to tempt our first parents to sin against so holy and just a God, who had but just (if I may use the expression) turned his back from crowning Adam with honour and glory?—But envy at his prosperity hath taken the crown of glory from his head, and hath made us his posterity miserable.—What was it but this that made Cain murder his brother, whence is it but from these that our modern Cains call us Africans the sons of Cain? (We admit it if you please) and we will find from him and his sons Masonry began, after the fall of his father. Altho, Adam, when placed in the garden, God would not suffer him to be idle and unemployed in that happy state of innocence, but set him to dress and to keep that choice piece of earth; here he was to employ his mind as well as exercise his body; here he was to contemplate and study God's work; here he was to enjoy God, himself and the whole world, to submit himself wholly to his divine conduct, to conform all his actions to the will of his Maker; but by his sudden fall he lost that good will that he owed to his God, and for some time lost the study of God's works; but no doubt he afterwards taught his sons the art of Masonry; for how else could Cain after so much trouble and perplexity have time to study the art of building a city, as he did on the east of Eden, Genesis 4:17, and without doubt he teached his sons the art, verses 20, 21.

But to return, bad as Cain was, yet God took not from him his faculty of studying architecture, arts and sciences—his sons also were endowed with the same spirit, and in some convenient place no doubt they met and communed with each other for instruction. It seems that the all-wise God put this into the hearts of Cain's family thus to employ themselves, to divert their minds from musing on their father's murder and the woeful curse God had pronounced on him, as we don't find any more of Cain's complaints after this.

Similar to this we have in Genesis 6:12 and 13, that God saw that all men had corrupted their way, and that their hearts were only evil continually; and 14, 15, 16 verses, the great Architect of the universe gives Noah a complete plan of the ark and sets him to work, and his sons as assistants, like deputy and two grand wardens. One thing is well known, our enemies themselves being judges, that in whatsoever nation or kingdom in the whole world where Masonry abounds most, there hath been and still are the most peaceable subjects, cheerfully conforming to the laws of that country in which they reside, always willing to submit to their magistrates and rulers, and where Masonry most abounds, arts and sciences, whether mechanical or liberal, all of them have a mighty tendency to the delight and benefit of mankind; therefore we need not question but the all-wise God by putting this into our hearts intended, as another end of our creation, that we should not only live happily ourselves, but be likewise mutually assisting to each other. Again, it is not only good and beneficial in a time of peace, in a nation or kingdom, but in a time of war, for that brotherly love that cements us together by the bonds of friendship, no wars or tumults can separate; for in the heat of war if a brother sees another in distress he will relieve him some way or other, and kindly receive him as a brother, preferring him before all others, according to the Apostle's exhortation in my text, as also a similar instance you have First Kings 10, from 31st to 38th verse, where you find Benhadad in great distress, having lost a numerous army in two battles, after his great boasting, and he himself forced to hide himself in a chamber, and sends a message to Ahab king of Israel to request only his life as a captive; but behold the brotherly love of a Mason! No sooner was the message delivered, but he cries out in a rapture—is he alive—he is my brother! Every Mason knows that they were both of the craft, and also the messengers. Thus far may suffice for the anciency of this grand art; as for the honor of it—it is a society which God himself has been pleased to honor ever since he breathed into Adam the breath of life, and hath from generation to generation inspired men with wisdom, and planned out and given directions how they should build, and with what materials. And first, Noah in building the ark wherein he was saved, while God in his justice was pleased to destroy the unbelieving world of mankind. The first thing Noah did upon his landing was to build an altar to offer sacrifice to that great God which had delivered him out of so great a deluge; God accepted the sacrifice and blessed him, and as they journey from the east towards the west, they found a plain in the land of Shinar and dwelt there, and his sons.

Nimrod the son of Cush, the son of Ham, first founded the Babylonian monarchy, and kept possession of the plains, and founded the first great empire at Babylon, and became grand master of all Masons, he built many splendid cities in Shinar, and under him flourished those learned mathematicians, whose successors were styled in the book of Daniel, Magi, or wise men, for their superior knowledge. The migration from Shinar commenced fifty-three years after they began to build the tower, and one hundred and fifty-four years after the flood, and they went off at various times and traveled east, west, north and south, with their mighty skill, and found the use of it in settling their colonies; and from Shinar the arts were carried to distant parts of the earth, notwithstanding the confusion of languages, which gave rise to Masons faculty and universal practice of conversing without speaking, and of knowing each other by signs and tokens; they settled the dispersion in case any of them should meet in distant parts of the world who had been before in Shinar. Thus the earth was again planted and replenished with Masons the second son of Ham carried into Egypt; there he built the city of Heliopolis—Thebes with an hundred gates—they built also the statue of Sphynx, whose head was 120 feet round, being reckoned the first or earliest of the seven wonders of arts. Shem the second son of Noah remained at Ur of the Chaldes in Shinar, with his father and his great-grandson Heber, where they lived in private and died in peace: But Shem's offspring traveled into the south and east of Asia, and their offspring propagated the science and the art as far as China and Japan.

While Noah, Shem and Heber diverted themselves at Ur in mathematical studies, teaching Peleg the father of Rehu, of Sereg, Nachor, and Terah, father of Abram, a learned race of mathematicians and geometricians; thus Abram, born two years after the death of Noah, had learned well the science and the art before the God of glory called him to travel from Ur of the Chaldes, but a famine soon forced him down to Egypt; the descendants of Abram sojourned in Egypt, as shepherds still lived in tents, practiced very little of the art of architecture till about eighty years before their Exodus, when by the overruling hand of providence they were trained up to the building with stone and brick, in order to make them expert Masons before they possessed the promised land; after Abram left Charran 430 years, Moses marched out of Egypt at the head of six hundred thousand Hebrews, males, for whose sakes God divided the Red Sea to let them pass through Arabia to Canaan. God was pleased to inspire their grand master Moses, and Joshua his deputy, with wisdom of heart; so the next year they raised the curious tabernacle or tent; God having called Moses up into the mount and gave him an exact pattern of it, and charges him to make it exactly to that pattern, and withal gave him the two tables of stone; these he broke at the foot of the mount; God gave him orders to hew two more himself, after the likeness of the former. God did not only inspire Moses with wisdom to undertake the oversight of the great work, but he also inspired Bezaleel with knowledge to do all manner of cunning workmanship for it.—Having entered upon the Jewish dispensation, I must beg leave still to take a little notice of the Gentile nations, for we have but these two nations now to speak upon, namely, the Gentiles and the Jews, till I come to the Christian era.

The Canaanites, Phoenicians and Sidonians, were very expert in the sacred architecture of stone, who being a people of a happy genius and frame of mind, made many great discoveries and improvements of the sciences, as well as in point of learning. The glass of Sidon, the purple of Tyre, and the exceeding fine linen they wove, were the product of their own country and their own invention; and for their extraordinary skill in working of metals, in hewing of timber and stone; in a word, for their perfect knowledge of what was solid in architecture, it need but be remembered that they had in erecting and decorating of the temple at Jerusalem, than which nothing can more redound to their honor, or give a clearer idea of what this one building must have been.—Their fame was such for their just taste, design, and ingenious inventions, that whatever was elegant, great or pleasing, was distinguished by way of excellence with the epithet of Sidonian.—The famous temple of Jupiter Hammon, in Libian Africa, was erected, that stood till demolished by the first Christians in those parts; but I must pass over many other cities and temples built by the Gentiles.

God having inspired Solomon with wisdom and understanding, he as grand master and undertaker, under God the great architect, sends to Hiram king of Tyre, and after acquainting him of his purpose of building a house unto the name of the Lord his God, he sends to him for some of his people to go with some of his, to Mount Lebanon, to cut down and hew cedar trees, as his servants understood it better than his own, and moreover he requested him to send him a man that was cunning, to work in gold and in silver, and in brass, iron, purple, crimson and in blue, and that had skill to engrave with the cunning men, and he sent him Hiram, his namesake; this Hiram, God was pleased to inspire with wisdom and understanding to undertake, and strength to go through the most curious piece of workmanship that was ever done on earth.—Thus Solomon as grand master, and Hiram as his deputy, carried on and finished that great work of the temple of the living God, the inside work of which, in many instances as well as the tabernacle, resembles men's bodies; but this is better explained in a well-filled lodge; but this much I may venture to say, that our blessed Saviour compared his sacred body to a temple, when he said, John 2:19. Destroy this temple and I will raise it up again in three days; and the Apostle, First Peter, 1:14 says, that shortly he should put off this tabernacle. I could show also that one grand end and design of Masonry is to build up the temple that Adam destroyed in Paradise—but I forbear. Thus hath God honored the Craft, or Masons, by inspiring men with wisdom to carry on his stupendous works.

It is worthy of our notice to consider the number of Masons employed in the work of the Temple: Exclusive of the two Grand Masters, there were 300 princes, or rulers, 3,300 overseers of the work, 80,000 stone squarers, setters, layers or builders, being able and ingenious Crafts, and 30,000 appointed to work in Lebanon, 10,000 of which every month, under Adoniram, who was the Grand Warden; all the free Masons employed in the work of the Temple was 119,600, besides 70,000 men who carried burdens, who were not numbered among Masons; these were partitioned into certain Lodges, although they were of different nations and different colors, yet were they in perfect harmony among themselves, and strongly cemented in brotherly love and friendship, till the glorious Temple of Jehovah was finished, and the cape-stone was celebrated with great joy—Having finished all that Solomon had to do, they departed unto their several homes, and carried with them the high taste of architecture to the different parts of the world, and built many other temples and cities in the Gentile nations, under the direction of many wise and learned and royal Grand Masters, as Nebuchadnezar over Babylon—Cyrus over the Medes and Persians—Alexander over the Macedonians—Julius Caesar over Rome, and a great number more I might mention of crowned heads of the Gentile nations who were of the Craft, but this may suffice.—I must just mention Herod the Great, before I come to the state of Masonry from the birth of our Saviour Jesus Christ.—This Herod was the greatest builder of his day, the patron and Grand Master of many Lodges; he being in the full enjoyment of peace and plenty, formed a design of new building of the Temple of Jerusalem. The Temple built by the Jews after the captivity was greatly decayed, being five hundred years standing, he proposed to the people that he would not take it down till he had all the materials ready for the new, and accordingly he did so, then he took down the old one and built a new one.—Josephus describes this Temple as a most admirable and magnificent fabric of marble, and the finest building upon earth.—Tiberius having attained the imperial throne, became an encourager of the fraternity.

Which brings me to consider their freedom, and that will appear not only from their being free when accepted, but they have a free intercourse with all Lodges over the whole terrestrial globe; wherever arts flourish, a man hath a free right (having a recommendation) to visit his brethren, and they are bound to accept him; these are the laudable bonds that unite Free Masons together in one indissoluble fraternity—thus in every nation he finds a friend, and in every climate he may find a house—this it is to be kindly affectioned one to another, with brotherly love, in honor preferring one another.

Which brings me to answer some objections which are raised against the Masons, and the first is the irregular lives of the professors of it.—It must be admitted there are some persons who, careless of their own reputation, will consequently disregard the most instructive lessons.—Some, I am sorry to say, are sometimes to be found among us; many by yielding to vice and intemperance, frequently not only disgrace themselves, but reflect dishonor on Masonry in general; but let it be known that these apostates are unworthy of their trust, and that whatever name or designation they assume, they are in reality no Masons: But if the wicked lives of men were admitted as an argument against the religion which they profess, Christianity itself, with all its divine beauties, would be exposed to censure; but they say there can be no good in Masonry because we keep it a secret, and at the same time these very men themselves will not admit an apprentice into their craft whatever, without enjoining secrecy on him, before they receive him as an apprentice; and yet blame us for not revealing ours—Solomon says, Proverbs 11:12, 13, He that is void of wisdom despiseth his neighbour, but a man of understanding holdeth his peace; a tale-bearer revealeth secrets, but he that is of a faithful spirit concealeth the matter. Thus I think I have answered these objections. I shall conclude the whole by addressing the Brethren of the African Lodge.

Dear and beloved Brethren, I don't know how I can address you better than in the words of Nehemiah (who had just received liberty from the king Artaxerxes, letters and a commission, or charter, to return to Jerusalem) that thro' the good hand of our God upon us we are here this day to celebrate the festival of St. John—as members of that honorable society of free and accepted Masons as by charter we have a right to do—remember your obligations you are under to the great God, and to the whole family of mankind in the world—do all that in you lies to relieve the needy, support the weak, mourn with your fellow men in distress, do good to all men as far as God shall give you ability, for they are all your brethren, and stand in need of your help more or less—for he that loves everybody need fear nobody: But you must remember you are under a double obligation to the brethren of the craft of all nations on the face of the earth, for there is no party spirit in Masonry; let them make parties who will, and despise those they would make, if they could, a species below them, and as not made of the same clay with themselves; but if you study the holy book of God, you will there find that you stand on the level not only with them, but with the greatest kings on the earth, as men and as Masons and these truly great men are not ashamed of the meanest of their brethren. Ancient history will produce some of the Africans who were truly good, wise, and learned men, and as eloquent as any other nation whatever though at present many of them in slavery, which is not a just cause of our being despised; for if we search history, we shall not find a nation on earth but has at some period or other of their existence been in slavery, from the Jews down to the English Nation, under many Emperors, Kings and Princes; for we find in the life of Gregory, about the year 580, a man famous for his charity, that on a time when many merchants were met to sell their commodities at Rome, it happened that he passing by saw many young boys with white bodies, fair faces, beautiful countenances and lovely hair, set forth for sale; he went to the merchant, their owner and asked him from what country he brought them; he answered from Britain, where the inhabitants were generally so beautiful. Gregory (sighing) said, alas! for grief, that such fair faces should be under the power of the prince of darkness, and that such bodies should have their souls void of the grace of God.

I shall endeavour to draw a few inferences on this discourse by way of application.

My dear Brethren, let us pray to God for a benevolent heart, that we may be enabled to pass through the various stages of this life with reputation, and that great and infinite Jehovah, who overrules the grand fabric of nature, will enable us to look backward with pleasure, and forward with confidence and in the hour of death, and in the day of judgment, the well grounded hope of meeting with that mercy from our Maker which we have ever been ready to show to others, will refresh us with the most solid comfort, and fill us with the most unspeakable joy.

And should not this learn us that new and glorious commandment of our Lord Jesus Christ to his disciples, when he urges it to them in these words—Love the Lord thy God with all thy heart, and thy neighbor as thyself.—Our Lord repeats and recommends this as the most indispensable duty and necessary qualification of his disciples, saying, hereby shall all men know that ye are my disciples, if ye have love one to another. And we are expressly told by the Apostle, that charity, or universal love and friendship, is the end of the commandment.

Shall this noble and unparalleled example fail of its due influence upon us—shall it not animate our hearts with a like disposition of benevolence and mercy, shall it not raise our emulation and provoke our ambition—to go and do likewise.

Let us then beware of such a selfishness as pursues pleasure at the expense of our neighbor's happiness, and renders us indifferent to his peace and welfare; and such a self-love is the parent of disorder and the source of all those evils that divide the world and destroy the peace of mankind; whereas Christian charity—universal love and friendship—benevolent affections and social feelings, unite and knit men together, render them happy in themselves and useful to one another, and recommend them to the esteem of a gracious God, through our Lord Jesus Christ.

The few inferences that have been made on this head must be to you, my worthy brethren, of great comfort, that every one may see the propriety of a discourse on brotherly love before a society of free Masons—who knows their engagements as men and as Christians, have superadded the bonds of this ancient and honourable society—a society founded upon such friendly and comprehensive principles, that men of all nations and languages, or sects of religion, are and may be admitted and received as members, being recommended as persons of a virtuous character.

Religion and virtue, and the continuance and standing of this excellent society in the world—its proof of the wisdom of its plan—and the force of its principles and conduct has, on many occasions, been not a little remarkable—as well among persons of this, as among those of different countries, who go down to the sea and occupy their business in the great waters, they know how readily people of this institution can open a passage to the heart of a brother; and in the midst of war, like a universal language, is understood by men of all countries—and no wonder.—If the foundation has been thus laid in wisdom by the great God, then let us go on with united hearts and hands to build and improve upon this noble foundation—let love and sincere friendship in necessity instruct our ignorance, conceal our infirmities, reprove our errors, reclaim us from our faults—let us rejoice with them that rejoice, and weep with those that weep—share with each other in our joys, and sympathize in our troubles.

And let the character of our enemies be to resent affronts—but ours to generously remit and forgive the greatest; theirs to blacken the reputation and blast the credit of their brethren—but ours to be tender of their good name, and to cast a veil over all their failings; theirs to blow the coals of contention and sow the seeds of strife among men—but ours to compose their differences and heal up their breaches.

In a word, let us join with the words of the Apostle John in the nineteenth chapter of Revelations, and after these things I heard a great voice of much people in heaven, saying, Alleluia, salvation and glory, and honour, and power, unto the Lord our God; for true and righteous are his judgments—and the four and twenty elders, and the four beasts, fell down and worshipped God that sat on the throne, saying, Amen; Alleluia; and a voice came out of the throne, saying, praise our God, all ye his servants, and ye that fear him, both small and great.

To conclude the whole, let it be remembered, that all that is outward, whether opinions, rites or ceremonies, cannot be of importance in regard to eternal salvation, any further than they have a tendency to produce inward righteousness and goodness—pure, holy, spiritual and benevolent affections can only fit us for the kingdom of heaven; and therefore the cultivation of such must needs be the essence of Christ's religion—God of his infinite mercy grant that we may make this true use of it. Unhappily, too many Christians, so called, take their religion not from the declarations of Christ and his apostles, but from the writings of those they esteem learned.—But, I am to say, it is from the New Testament only, not from any books whatsoever, however piously wrote, that we ought to seek what is the essence of Christ's religion; and it is from this fountain I have endeavoured to give my hearers the idea of Christianity in its spiritual dress, free from any human mixtures—if we have done this wisely we may expect to enjoy our God in the world that *is* above—in which happy place, my dear brethren, we shall all, I hope, meet at that great day, when our great Grand Master shall sit at the head of the great and glorious Lodge in heaven—where we shall all meet to part no more for ever and ever—Amen.

## NOTES

*Sermon source:* See *Black Atlantic Writers* for an explanation concerning the authorship of the sermon, especially see page 74. This version of the sermon comes from that book, pages 106–118.

1. Brooks, "John Marrant's Journal," 1.
2. *Black Atlantic Writers*, 79–88.
3. Ibid., 69.

## BIBLIOGRAPHICAL SOURCES

Brooks, Joanna. "John Marrant's Journal: Providence and Prophecy in the Eighteenth-Century Black Atlanta," *The North Star Journal* 3, no. 1 (Fall 1999).

Brown, Wallace, and Hereward Senior. *Victorious in Defeat: The Loyalists in Canada*. Toronto: Methuen Publications, 1984.

Carretta, Vincent, ed. *Unchained Voices: An Anthology of Black Authors in the English Speaking World of the Eighteenth Century.* Lexington: University of Kentucky Press, 1996.

Gates, Henry Louis, Jr. *The Signifying Money.* New York: Oxford University Press, 1988.

Marrant, John. *A Journal of the Rev. John Marrant, From August the 18th, 1785, to the 16th of March 1790. To which are attached Two Sermons; One Preached on Ragged Island on Sabbath Day, the 27th Day of October, 1787; the Other at Boston, in New England, on Thursday, the 24th of June, 1789.* London: J. Taylor and Company at the Royal Exchange, and Mr. Marrant, No. 2, Black Horse Court, in Aldersgate-street, 1791.

———. *A Narrative of the Life of John Marrant, of New York, in North America, Giving an Account of His Conversion.* Halifax: J. Nicholson Press, 1812.

Potkay, Adam, and Sandra Burr, eds., *Black Atlantic Writers of the Eighteenth Century: Living the New Exodus in England and the Americas.* New York: St. Martin's Press, 1995.

Salliant, John, "'Wipe Away All Tears from Their Eye': John Marrant's Theology in the Black Atlantic 1785–1808," *Journal of Millennial Studies* 1, no. 2 (Winter 1999).

Schomburg, Arthur. "Two Negro Missionaries to the American Indians, John Marrant and John Stewart." *Journal of Negro History* 21, no. 4 (October 1936): 394–410.

## GEORGE WHITE

*(1764–1836)*

George White was born in slavery in Accomack, Virginia, and had been sold twice by the age of six. After he was released from bondage by a dying slaveholder in the early 1780s, White spent several years in a futile search for his mother. He then moved north to New York City. He converted to Methodism but was incensed by the church's segregationist practices. With other black Methodists, he left to build a separate church. In 1804, he felt the call to preach and served as an itinerant exhorter for black camp meetings in New Jersey and on Long Island. He was repeatedly denied a license to preach by the white Methodist elders, but was finally approved in 1807 and appointed a deacon (the highest office then open to a black Methodist) in 1815. In 1820, he joined the African Methodist Episcopal Church.

• • •

*Black preachers delivered tens of thousands of funeral sermons in the early republic, but the texts of only a few have survived. In his autobiography, one of the first published by an African American, White wrote of returning from a preaching tour of Long Island in 1809 to discover that Mary Henery, an enslaved twenty-year-old whom he had converted at a New York camp meeting, was deathly ill and calling for him. He included in his memoir the following text of the sermon he delivered at her funeral.*

## THE FUNERAL SERMON OF MARY HENERY (1809)

From "Strive to enter in at the strait gate, for many, I say unto you, shall seek to enter in, and shall not be able." Luke 13:24.

The occasion on which we are assembled this day, is truly solemn, interesting and alarming; being met together to pay our last respects to the remains of our departed sister, who but recently filled her usual seat in this house; and rejoiced, on all religious occasions, to unite with you, my brethren, in chanting the songs of Zion, with an heart filled with the love of Christ, and exulting in the joys of his salvation.

But she is now no more: and though called to lament the loss of so worthy a member of the Church of Christ; yet we do not mourn as those without hope, for, "Them that sleep in Jesus, God will bring with him," at the last day; and our Saviour says, he "came to seek and save that which was lost": and in the chapter of which our text is a part, he intimates, that the chief of sinners may be saved who will repent; by preaching the doctrine of repentance, from the circumstance of the Gallaleans, whose blood Pilate mingled with their sacrifices; and that without repentance, none can be saved. But this blessing our departed sister had no doubt attained, with whom we hope to join in strains of immortal praise hereafter, when our bodies shall have endured the original sentence denounced against us for sin, "Dust thou art, and unto dust shalt thou return." For like her, through Jesus Christ we may obtain victory over death, hell and the grave, by complying with the terms of our text, which says "Strive to enter in at the strait gate, for many, I say unto you, shall seek to enter in, and shall not be able."

From which I shall take the liberty briefly to shew,

First, what we are to understand by the strait gate, and how we are to enter in thereat. *Secondly,* why it is called strait. And, *thirdly,* who they are that shall seek to enter in, and shall not be able.

I. I am to shew what we are to understand by the strait gate, and how we are to enter in thereat. By the strait gate we are undoubtedly to understand, Jesus Christ himself, who has said, "I am the way, and the truth, and the life; no man cometh unto the Father but by me."[1] And again: "Strait is the gate and narrow is the way that leadeth to life, and few there be that find it."[2] "I am," says he, "the door, by me if any man enter in he shall be saved, and go in and out and find pasture."[3]

Christ then being "the strait gate," and his doctrines the narrow way, and himself the only door of admission to the favour of God, and salvation; the scripture directs us how we are to enter in thereat, that is, by repentance, and faith in the merits of the atonement he has made for sinners, by the once offering of himself to God without spot.

By faith, then, we are to enter in at this gate: for although it is said, "strive to enter in at the strait gate," yet we are to place no dependence upon our labours or strivings; for we can do nothing effectual in our own salvation, only as far as we are assisted by the all-sufficient grace of God; for it is written, "By grace are ye saved, through faith, and that not of yourselves, it is the gift of God."[4]

Yet although our strivings alone cannot prove effectual to our salvation, in this way, however, we must come to Christ, and receive him into our hearts. Therefore, "Strive to enter in at the strait gate, for many, I say unto you, shall seek to enter in, and shall not be able."[5] But,

II. Why is this gate called strait? I answer: from the example Christ has left us, that we should follow his steps, which is directly contrary to the corruptions of our own natures; and because repentance and faith, by which we must enter in thereat, are crossing, humbling and self-renouncing; in the attainment of which, the soul is brought into great inward straits of fear, terror and difficulty, but is always accompanied with hope of mercy, and followed with a revelation of Jesus Christ, as the all-sufficient Savior, to such as commit the care of their souls to him, trusting in his mercy alone for pardon and eternal salvation; and if adhered to, will lead to that eternal rest of glory, which our departed sister this day enjoys, in the presence of God and the Lamb. Therefore, "Strive to enter in at the strait gate, for many, I say unto you, shall seek to enter in, and shall not be able."

I am thirdly, and lastly to shew, who they are that shall seek to enter in, and shall not be able.

There is no impediment to our entering in at the strait gate, but what originates in ourselves; for Christ has said, "He that cometh unto me, I will no wise cast out":[6] and assigns it as the only reason why men are not saved, that they will not come unto him, that they might have life. And they do not come to Christ, because their hearts are opposed to his government, and his ways too crossing to their carnal inclinations.

But says, the text, "Many shall seek to enter in, and shall not be able:" either because they do not seek aright, or in good earnest, by forsaking all their sins, resisting evil of every kind and degree; and by an agonizing, wrestling spirit, which refuses to be comforted, till Christ is formed in the heart the hope of glory.

Or lastly, because they seek too late; which is the reason Christ assigns in the words immediately following the text, "Strive to enter in at the strait gate, for many, I say unto you, shall seek to enter in, and shall not be able"; for, "When once the master of the house is risen up, and hath shut to the door, and ye begin to stand without, and to knock at the door, saying, Lord, Lord, open unto us; and he shall answer and say unto you, I know you not whence you are, depart from me all ye workers of iniquity."[7] How sad the disappointment, to seek for mercy too late to find it; even at the hand of him, who now says, "Behold, I stand at the door and knock; if any man hear my voice, and will open the door, I will come in to him, and will sup with him, and he with me."[8]

## Improvement

Whoever would go to heaven then, must repent, and believe in Jesus Christ, who is the only door of salvation, the way, the truth, and the life; and as our Lord said to Nichodemus, must be born again, or they cannot see the kingdom of God: for except renewed by the grace of God, in the very nature of things, no man can be happy; for the very nature of sin prevents the enjoyment of God, the only source and fountain of all happiness; so that, whoever dies without being renewed, must meet the just reward of their ungodliness, in the awful day of judgment, when the secret of all hearts shall be revealed.

As this change of heart is called entering in at the strait gate, because it implies self-denial, mortification, self-renunciation, conviction and contrition for sin; and as all this is directly contrary to the dispositions of corrupt nature, it requires great and constant exertions, and mighty struggles of soul, under the influence of divine grace, to attain the blessing. For let none vainly imagine, that barely wiping their mouth will excuse them from damnation, or answer as a substitute for inward and outward holiness, in the great day of the wrath of God Almighty, when he shall come to judge the world in righteousness: therefore, "Seek ye the

Lord while he may be found, call ye upon him while he is near: let the wicked forsake his way, and the unrighteous man his thoughts, and let him turn unto the Lord, who will have mercy upon him, and to our God, for he will abundantly pardon."[9]

And in this great and important work there is no time for delay; for life, the utmost extent of the day of grace, is uncertain; which is not only proved by the common occurrences of every day, but particularly by the instance of mortality which has occasioned our convention at this time; which speaks to you in the most pathetic language: "Be ye also ready, for in such an hour as ye think not the Son of man is risen up, and shut the door, and ye begin to stand without, and to knock, saying, Lord, Lord, open unto us"; you will be only be answered with "depart from me all ye that work iniquity":[10] therefore now return unto the Lord from whom you have departed, by sincere repentance, that your souls may live. Secure a supply of the oil of grace; trim your lamps, and prepare to meet the bridegroom at his coming, that ye may enter in to the marriage supper of the Lamb, before the door of mercy is forever shut.

I see before me a large number of mourners, whose showering tears bespeak the anguish of heart excited by the death of her, whose relics we have so recently followed to the house appointed for all the living. But hush the heaving sigh, and dry the briny tear, for your deceased relative, and our much-loved Christian sister, has, no doubt, found a safe passage through the strait and narrow gate to the blissful regions of eternal day; where she now joins the Church triumphant, around the dazzling throne of God, in songs of praise and shouts of victory.

And while you, with the rest of the congregation, have the offers of mercy yet held out to you in the name of Jesus Christ, who stands knocking at the door of your hearts for entrance; embrace it, and bid him welcome, that you may be prepared when death shall call you hence, to join the jubilant throng with our departed sister, and chant the wonders of redeeming grace forever.

But to you, especially, who are in the bloom of youth, this instance of mortality calls aloud to prepare for death; remember your all is at stake; death is at your door, and will shortly summon you to appear at the bar of God, who will assuredly bring you into judgment for living after the desires of your own wicked hearts. Reflect then for a moment, how awful it will be to die in your sins, strangers to God, and meet the awful Judge of quick and dead, to hear the sentence pronounced upon your guilty souls, "Depart ye cursed into everlasting fire, prepared for the devil and his angels."[11] To avert this dreadful doom delay no longer; but now, even now, embrace the offers of mercy tendered to you by the gospel of Jesus Christ, and experience his great salvation.

And finally, brethren, let us all consider our ways, turn to the Lord, and strive to enter in at the strait gate, that we may not be found among the number of those, who by seeking too late, shall not be able to enter in; that when we are called to lie upon our death bed, we may have the same ravishing views of heaven, our departed sister had two days before her death, who said, she "saw heaven opened, and heard the saints in glory sing": and like her, leave the world, crying glory! glory! glory! even so, Lord Jesus. Amen! and Amen!

## *Notes*

*Sermon source: Black Itinerants of the Gospel*, see especially pages 1–88.

1. John 14:6 (King James Version).
2. Matthew 7:14 (KJV).
3. John 10:9 (KJV).
4. Ephesians 2:8 (KJV).
5. Luke 13:24 (KJV).
6. John 6:37 (KJV), paraphrased.
7. Luke 13:27 (KJV).
8. Revelations 3:20 (KJV).
9. Isaiah 55:6–7 (KJV).
10. Luke 13:27 (KJV).
11. Matthew 25:41 (KJV).

## *Bibliographical Sources*

Hodges, Graham Russell, ed. *Black Itinerants of the Gospel: The Narratives of John Jea and George White.* Madison, WI: Madison House, 1993, see especially the introduction.

White, George. *A Brief Account of the Life, Experience, Travels and Gospel Labours of George White, An African.* New York: John C. Totten Press, 1810.

# 2

# SOCIAL AND RELIGIOUS EMANCIPATION: *1790–1865*

# INTRODUCTION

FROM THE SMOKE AND ASHES OF THE REVOLUTIONARY WAR EMERGED A fledgling nation, the United States of America. While reveling in its newfound freedom from Britain, the U.S. also had to respond to the challenges of governance and of nation building. At the beginning of the nineteenth century, an abundance of dilemmas and opportunities confronted the United States. Three salient issues that dramatically shaped this period included the unresolved slavery question, the territorial expansion of the country, and the divide between North and South that would eventuate in the Civil War.

While the rhetoric of independence and democracy had buttressed the war effort, the United States was unwilling to grant freedom to all its inhabitants. Slavery was a prevalent and accepted feature in the American colonies. However, the debate concerning the political feasibility and morality of slavery that simmered during the war surfaced again as the founders forged the country's constitution. The U.S. could have outlawed slavery, but "Constitutional compromises" were enacted to appease the southern states: no rights were given to slaves, and a slave counted as three-fifths of a person when determining a state's population, which increased the political representation of southern slave-holding states in the House of Representatives. Slavery was now officially embedded in the Constitution.

The prospect of slavery's abolition decreased as the geographical size of the United States increased. In the Louisiana Purchase of 1803, the United States bought an immense swath of land formerly owned by France, expanding the borders by more than eight hundred thousand square miles. Much of this newly acquired land was conducive to growing cotton and sugar cane—crops that the U.S. often exported at enormous profit. Eli Whitney's cotton gin, a device that rapidly removed the seeds from cotton, greatly increased that crop's profitability. Thus, in the early to mid-1800s, large cotton and sugar cane plantations sprang up across the Deep South, and slaves provided a cheap, abundant, and indispensable supply of labor. From 1820–1830, more than a quarter million human beings were sold into the Deep South.[1] By definition, slavery was dehumanizing, but the treatment of the enslaved on large plantations in the Deep South was especially brutal.

March 25, 1807, the Abolition of the Slave Trade Act was passed by the British Parliament. However, it was not until August 23, 1833, that slavery was outlawed in the British colonies. From 1807–1860 the British Royal Navy seized more than sixteen hundred ships and freed Africans. Unfortunately, still more than two million enslaved Africans were brought to the Americas (including Cuba and Brazil) during this period.[2] The entrenchment of slavery in the United States did not go unchallenged; many free blacks in the North formed antislavery organizations and black mutual aid societies, such as the Free African Society and black Masonic organizations. These organizations often spawned black churches or worked in tandem with black churches to meet the spiritual, social, and economic needs of blacks and to advocate for slavery's abolition.

The American Colonization Society, a group founded in 1817 by prominent white political leaders in the United States, addressed the slavery dilemma by promoting emigration of blacks to Africa. While many blacks remained skeptical about the society's aims, some notable black church leaders supported colonization. For instance, Daniel Coker, an African Methodist Episcopal minister, led a group of blacks supported by the American Colonization Society to form the West African colony of Liberia.

Also in this period, antislavery advocates established the Underground Railroad—a complex social system by which slaves escaped to freedom in the North and Canada, aided by abolitionists who hid them along the way and moved them North to the next "conductor" on the line. Harriet Tubman, the most celebrated conductor, led over seventy slaves to freedom and helped countless hundreds find their own roads to freedom.[3]

# PREACHING, 1790–1865

The black churches that emerged during this period grew out of, and in some cases in response to, the eighteenth-century evangelical revivals. This connection made much of the preaching theologically and ecclesiologically pietistic.[4] Yet preachers such as Richard Allen, Alexander Crummell, and J.W.C. Pennington still espoused a gospel that subverted the teachings and preaching of those who enslaved blacks. Whether in church or in other forums, when asked to speak, these clergy often used the opportunity to speak of a God who was on the side of the slave and the oppressed. The most noted clergy of the era demanded full emancipation for all God's children.

Abolitionist David Walker's tract *Appeal to Colored Citizens of the World* continued to challenge the religious and theological underpinnings that supported and maintained slavery. One such belief was the Ham Doctrine, conjured up by whites using incorrect exegesis of Genesis 9:20–27. Ham, who was dark, was cursed along with his descendants. Blacks, who were also dark, were the descendants of Ham and therefore cursed and therefore rightfully enslaved. African American preaching countered with the prophetic word in Psalm 68:31, "Princes shall come out of Egypt and Ethiopia shall stretch forth her hand to God." This response was indicative of the belief by Africans that they were not a cursed people; they knew that they were capable and a blessing to America. Walker's sentiment could be found in much of the published black preaching of the period.

Most black preachers of the era were not as famous as Crummell, Pennington, and Allen. They were not well-known evangelists, nor were they known for their social activism. They were esteemed for providing encouragement and hope Sunday after Sunday to those to whom they preached and pastored. They were men and a few women of whom little is known and written, but theirs was some of the most potent preaching within the black community because it was a consistent, verbally and metaphorically appealing gospel of hope. Their ranks included such preachers as Brother Carper and Alexander Campbell Vinegar. Although sermons by Vinegar have not survived, a sermon by Brother Carper is included in this anthology.

## PIONEERING PREACHING WOMEN, 1790–1865

Notable black women who challenged the racial and gender oppression of this period included the Reverends Jarena Lee, Zilpha Elaw, Sojourner Truth, Julia Foote, and Maria Stewart. Although it would be unseemly to suggest a hierarchy of suffering, one is not needed to substantiate the historical maltreatment of black women in the larger society and in their own faith communities. Were it not for the "black church invisible," which theologian Deloris Williams in *Sisters in the Wilderness* defines as "a Godforce for justice healing and resistance," black women would not have survived the treacherous wilderness that was and is America visible and the black male-dominated church. These pioneering women all preached during the height of American patriarchy and racism. The hostility that was entrenched in those who supported either or both of these life-confiscating prejudices meant that black women preachers faced an almost unbearable existence. They were hated for something they could not change, their skin color, and for something that they should not have had to change, their belief that God called them to proclaim good news to the captive and oppressed. The "Godforce" was indeed upon and with these sisters. From brush arbors (also called hush arbors) to national and in some cases international stages, they took their stout courage and sanctified imaginations and put forth some of the earliest known sermons and religious messages from women preachers.

Many women preachers used aspects of their lives as the basis for their sermons. These preaching women, who had to fight to enter pulpits or find other places to preach, used their autobiographies to introduce texts and to explain those texts in terms of the needs of their community (primarily justice for black people and for women). Their sermons typically concluded enthusiastically, sometimes with a song. By drawing upon their autobiographies, they have securely placed themselves in homiletical, theological, and literary history.

We need to add a word of caution regarding the biographies of Jarena Lee, Zilpha Elaw, Sojourner Truth, and other black women preachers whose sermons are included in this anthology: They were either written by white women and men or strongly influenced by white women and men. Although these biographers and publishers must have believed the women worthy of biographies, one must remember that racist assumptions often lurked beneath the good intentions of even the most open-minded whites. For example, historian Nell Painter points out concerning Sojourner Truth:

> The author of the text is the knower and speaker, while the person who writes down the words is the amanuensis. Sojourner Truth used writing in this way when she dictated her autobiography to Olive Gilbert in Northampton in the late 1840s. Gilbert interposed her own ear and by dint of having taken down a third-person narrative acquired citation as the author of the *Narrative of Sojourner Truth*. . . . What is known of Sojourner Truth in print comes mainly from the pens of four educated white women (Olive Gilbert, Harriet Beecher Stowe, Frances Dana Gage and Frances Titus) who were fascinated by Truth.[5]

Painter also points out that Titus listed herself as the author of Truth's republished narratives in the 1870s and 1880s.

## THE MOVEMENTS TOWARD FREEDOM

Likely the most famous ex-slave then and now, Reverend Frederick Douglass was the silver-tongued black orator of the period and a primary precursor to other preachers who would begin in the church and then take their message of God's love and God's desire for justice for blacks beyond to international audiences; Douglass traveled throughout the British Isles. This model of a preacher who made the world his or her pulpit would much later be seen in the noted work of preachers such as Adam Clayton Powell Jr., Dr. Martin Luther King Jr., and Rev. Jesse Louis Jackson.

The question of how to achieve freedom was ever present from 1790 to 1865. The slave rebellion in Haiti in the late 1700s, which resulted in the first independent black nation in the Western Hemisphere, inspired many blacks in the United States to resist slavery through force. Thus, in the 1800s, several slave rebellions occurred in the U.S., including those led by Gabriel Prosser, Denmark Vesey, and Nat Turner. Abolitionism was propelled to a new and more militant phase.[6]

The use of violence expanded beyond limited slave revolts to engulf the entire nation as the Civil War erupted in 1861. At the heart of the war was the divide between slave-holding southern states and emancipated northern states. Initially, the United States prevented black soldiers from fighting with the Union against the rebelling Confederacy. However, in

1862 the Union began enlisting black soldiers, who proved to be a decisive factor in its war efforts.[7]

On January 1, 1863, President Lincoln's Emancipation Proclamation became effective, thereby freeing the slaves in the Confederacy. This did little to ameliorate the wretched condition of the majority of blacks. Nevertheless, the antislavery sentiment of the proclamation provided a new rallying point for the Union. The U.S. victory against the Confederacy in 1865 heralded a new future for the country. Finally in December 1865, through the Thirteenth Amendment, chattel slavery was ended in the United States.

## *Notes*

1. James Oliver Horton and Lois E. Horton, *Hard Road to Freedom: The Story of African America* (New Brunswick, NJ: Rutgers University Press, 2001), 92.
2. Thomas Clarkson, *The History of the Rise, Progress and Accomplishment of the Abolition of the African Slave-Trade by the British Parliament* (1808; repr., London: Frank Cass, 1968), 611–12.
3. Catherine Clinton, *Harriet Tubman: The Road to Freedom* (New York, NY: Little, Brown, 2004), 216.
4. Milton C. Sernett, *Black Religion and American Evangelicalism: White Protestants, Plantation Missions and the Flowering of Negro Christianity (1787–1865)* (Lanham, MD: Scarecrow Press, 1975), 211, 326.
5. Nell Irvin Painter, "Representing Truth: Sojourner Truth's Knowing and Becoming Known," *Journal of American History* 81, no. 2 (September 1994), 465, 471.
6. *Hard Road*, 150–75.
7. John Hope Franklin, *From Slavery to Freedom*, 3rd ed. (New York: Alfred A. Knopf Press, 1967), 290–94.

## *Bibliographical Sources*

Ambrose, Stephen E. *Undaunted Courage: Meriwether Lewis, Thomas Jefferson and the Opening of the American West.* New York: Touchstone Books, 1997.

Emancipation Proclamation and the Louisiana Purchase Treaty, www.archives.gov/exhibits (accessed November 4, 2004).

Hinks, Peter P. *To Awaken My Afflicted Brethren: David Walker and the Problem of Antebellum Slave Resistance.* University Park: Pennsylvania State University Press, 1996.

Miller, Hunter. *Treaties and Other International Acts of the United States*, vol. 2. Washington, DC: Government Printing Office, 1931.

Still, William. *The Underground Railroad: A Record of Facts, Authentic Narratives, & Letters, Narrating the Hardships, Hair-Breadth Escapes and Death Struggles of the Slaves in Their Efforts for Freedom, As Related by Themselves and Others, or Witnessed by the Author.* Philadelphia: People's Publishing Co., 1879.

Walker, David. *David Walker's Appeal: To the Coloured Citizens of the World, but in particular, and very expressly, to those of The United States of America*, rev. ed. Introduction by Sean Wilentz. New York: Hill and Wang, Inc., 1995.

Williams, Delores S. *Sisters in the Wilderness: The Challenge of Womanist God-Talk*. Maryknoll, NY: Orbis, 1993.

# RICHARD ALLEN

*(1760–1831)*

Richard Allen was born in 1760 in Philadelphia to enslaved parents. He was converted by a Methodist preacher at age seventeen in 1777. Allen soon began preaching and even converted the man from whom he purchased his freedom. Illiterate and without funds, Allen began his amazing career on the Methodist preaching circuit. It is not known if Allen ever really learned to read. It is known that his grandson, who was literate, often accompanied him after Allen was elected bishop of the African Methodist Episcopal Church and took notes of meetings.[1]

Allen worked hauling supplies for General Washington's army and preached along the way. He was a bi-vocational preacher, also operating a successful boot and shoe business, along with other enterprises.

When he returned to Philadelphia, his preaching attracted many blacks. He attended St. George Methodist Church, along with many other blacks who attended because of him. When the church's white membership demanded segregated seating, Allen and several of his friends, including Reverend Absalom Jones (later to become the first black priest in the Episcopal church), left the church and founded the Free African Society, which provided aid to blacks and advocated for abolition. In 1794, Allen established Bethel Church and was ordained as the first AME bishop in 1816. After legal battles with the Methodist Episcopal Church, which tried to claim ownership of the Bethel building, the AME Church became a separate legal entity in 1816. This was the first of three main black Methodist denominations that were formed, each of which followed a polity similar to that of the white Methodist Church. Under Allen's leadership, the AME denomination grew rapidly, especially in the mid-Atlantic states and on the East Coast.

Throughout his life, Allen used his voice to aid black and abolitionist causes. He and Absalom Jones had founded the African Masonic Lodge in 1798. In 1804, Allen began the Society of Free People of Color, which promoted the instruction and education of children of African descent.

The first hymnal compiled expressly for a black congregation was published in 1801. Entitled *A Collection of Spiritual Songs and Hymns, Selected from Various Authors*, it was printed for Richard Allen, who compiled it, and is identified on the title page as "African Minister." According to musicologist Eileen Southern, "As a 'folk-selected' anthology, it indicates which hymns were popular among black Methodists at the beginning of the nineteenth century. . . . Many of these hymns served as source material for the spirituals of the slaves, the so-called Negro spirituals." Southern asserts that Allen's hymnal is apparently the earliest source in history that includes hymns to which "wandering" choruses or refrains are attached; that is, choruses that are freely added to any hymn rather than affixed permanently to specific hymns.

The first edition of Allen's hymnal contains fifty-four hymns; the second adds ten more. Some of the hymns most certainly were written by Allen himself, judging by their similarity to hymns he published in other places; others have all the earmarks of folk hymns and may have been penned by Allen's church associates.[2]

Allen was married twice. His first wife, Flora, died in 1801. Sarah Bass Allen, his second wife, was one of the principal reasons that Allen enjoyed much of his success. She was known for her work in assisting runaway slaves and also organized the Daughters of the Conference, which assisted AME ministers, many of whom were poor. The couple had six children.

Richard Allen died in 1831. Richard and Sarah Allen are interred on the lower level of what is now Bethel AME Church in Philadelphia. A lengthy inscription on the tomb includes the following: "He was instrumental in the hands of the lord in enlightening many thousands of his brethren, the descendants of Africa, and was the founder of the first African Church in America."

• • •

*In this message Allen takes direct aim at slaveholders and proponents of slavery, using scripture as his basis for condemning the practice as ungodly. In the second part of the message, directed "to those who have no helper," Allen exhorts blacks not to become what they hate. Although inhumanely treated, he pleads for his people to remember that their actions are also viewed by God and that not all whites have stood against blacks, that some have worked mightily for their liberation. Additionally, he encourages those who have been freed to live respectful lives and to fight for the cause of freedom.*

## An Address
## to those who keep slaves and approve the practice
## (ca. 1820)

The judicious part of mankind, will think it unreasonable, that a superior good conduct is looked for from our race, by those who stigmatize us as men, whose baseness is incurable, and may therefore be held in a state of servitude, that a merciful man would not doom a beast to; yet you try what you can, to prevent our rising from a state of barbarism you represent us to be in, but we can tell you from a degree of experience, that a black man, although reduced to the most abject state human nature is capable of, short of real madness, can think, reflect, and feel injuries, although it may not be with the same degree of keen resentment and revenge, that you who have been, and are our great oppressors would manifest, if reduced to the pitiable condition of a slave. We believe if you would try the experiment of taking a few black children, and cultivate their minds with the same care, and let them have the same prospect in view as to living in the world, as you would wish for your own children, you would find upon the trial, they were not inferior in mental endowments. I do not wish to make you angry, but excite attention to consider how hateful slavery is, in the sight of that God who hath destroyed kings and princes, for their oppression of the poor slaves. Pharaoh and his princes with the posterity of King Saul were destroyed by the protector and avenger of slaves. Would you not suppose the Israelites to be utterly unfit for freedom, and that it was impossible for them, to obtain to any degree of excellence? Their history shews how slavery had debased their spirits. Men must be willfully blind, and extremely partial, that cannot see the contrary effects of liberty and slavery upon the mind of man; I truly confess the vile habits often acquired in a state of servitude, are not easily thrown off; the example of the Israelites shews, who with all that Moses could do to reclaim them from it, still continued in their habits more or less; and why will you look for better from us, why will you look for grapes from thorns, or figs from thistles? It is in our posterity enjoying the same priviledges with your own, that you ought to look for better things.

When you are pleaded with, do not you reply as Pharaoh did, "Wherefore do ye Moses and Aaron let the people from their work, behold the people of the land now are many, and you make them rest from their burthens [burdens]." We wish you to consider, that God himself was the first pleader of the cause of slaves.

That God who knows the hearts of all men, and the propensity of a slave to hate his oppressor, hath strictly forbidden it to his chosen people, "Thou shalt not abhor an Egyptian, because thou wast a stranger in his land."[3] The meek and humble Jesus, the great pattern of humanity, and every other virtue that can adorn and dignify men, hath commanded to love our enemies, to do good to them that hate and despitefully use us. I feel the obligations, I wish to impress them on the minds of our colored brethren, and that we may all forgive you, as we wish to be forgiven, we think it a great mercy to have all anger and bitterness removed from our minds; I appeal to your own feelings, if it is not very disquieting to feel yourselves under dominion of wrathful disposition. If you love your children, if you love your country, if you love the God of love, clear your hands from slaves, burthen [burden] not your children or your country with them, my heart has been sorry for the blood shed of the oppressors, as well as the oppressed, both appear guilty of each others blood, in the sight of him who hath said, he that sheddeth man's blood, by man shall his blood be shed.

Will you, because you have reduced us to the unhappy condition our color is in, plead our incapacity for freedom, and our contented condition under oppression, as a sufficient cause for keeping us under the grevious yoke. I have shown the cause,—I will also shew why they appear contented as they can in your sight, but the dreadful insurrections they have made when opportunity has offered, is enough to convince a reasonable man, that great uneasiness and not contentment, is the inhabitant of their hearts. God himself hath pleaded their cause, he hath from time to time raised up instruments for that purpose, sometimes mean and contemptible in your sight, at other times he hath used such as it hath pleased him, with whom you have not thought it beneath your dignity to contend. Many have been convinced of their error, condemned their former conduct, and become zealous advocates for the cause of those, whom you will not suffer to plead for themselves.

## To the People of Colour

Feeling an engagement of mind for your welfare, I address you with an affectionate sympathy, having been a slave, and as desirous of freedom as any of you; yet the bands of bondage were so strong that no way appeared for my release; yet at times a hope arose in my heart that a way would open for it; and when my mind was mercifully visited with the feeling of the love of God, then these hopes increased, and a confidence arose that he would make way for my enlargement; and as a patient waiting was necessary, I was sometimes favoured with it; at other times I was very impatient. Then the prospect of liberty almost vanished away, and I was in darkness and perplexity.

I mention experience to you, that your hearts may not sink at the discouraging prospects you may have, and that you may put your trust in God, who sees your condition; and as a merciful father pitieth his children, so doth God pity them that love him; and as your hearts are inclined to serve God, you will feel an affectionate regard towards your masters and mistresses, so called, and the whole family in which you live. This will be seen by them, and tend to promote your liberty, especially with such as have feeling masters; and if they are otherwise, you will have the favour and love of God dwelling in your hearts, which you will value more than anything else, which will be a consolation in the worst condition you can be in, and no master can deprive you of it, and as life is short and uncertain, and the chief end of our having a being in this world is to be prepared for a better, I wish you to think of this more than anything else; then you will have a view of that freedom which the sons of God enjoy; and if the troubles of your condition end with your lives, you will be admitted to the freedom which God hath prepared for those of all colours that love him. Here the power of the roost cruel master ends, and all sorrow and fears are wiped away.

To you who are favoured with freedom—let your conduct manifest your gratitude toward the compassionate masters who have set you free; and let no rancour or ill will lodge in your breast for any bad treatment you may have received from any. If you do, you transgress against God, who will not hold you guiltless. He would not suffer it even in his beloved people Israel; and you think he will allow it unto us? Many of the white people have been instruments in the hands of God for our good; even such as have held us in captivity, are now pleading our cause with earnestness and zeal; and I am sorry to say, that too many think more of the evil than of the good they have received, and instead of taking the advice of their friends, turn from it with indifference. Much depends upon us for the help of our colour—more than many are aware. If we are lazy and idle, the enemies of freedom plead it as a cause why we ought not to be free, and say we are better in a state of servitude, and that giving us our liberty would be an injury to us, and by such conduct we strengthen the bands of oppression, and keep many in bondage who are more worthy than ourselves. I entreat you to consider the obligations we lie under to help forward the cause of freedom. We who know how bitter the cup is of which the slave hath to drink, O how ought we to feel for those who yet remain in bondage! will even our friends excuse—will God pardon us—for the part we act in making strong the hands of the enemies of our colour?

## A Short Address to the Friends of Him Who Hath No Helper

I FEEL an inexpressible gratitude towards you who have engaged in the cause of the African race; you have wrought a deliverance for many from more than Egyptian bondage; your labours are unremitted for their complete redemption from the cruel subjection they are in. You feel our afflictions—you sympathize with us in the heartrending distress, when the husband is separated from the wife, and the parents from the children, who are never more to meet in this world. The tear of sensibility trickles from your eye to see the sufferings that keep us from increasing. Your righteous indignation is roused at the means taken to supply the place of the murdered babe; you see our race more effectually destroyed than was in Pharaoh's power to effect upon Israel's sons; you blow the trumpet against the mighty evil; you make the tyrants tremble; you strive to raise the slave to the dignity of a man; you take our children by the hand to lead them in the path of virtue, by your care of our education; you are not ashamed to call the most abject of our race brethren, children of one Father, who hath made of one blood all the nations of the earth. You ask for this, nothing for yourselves, nothing but what is worthy [worth] the cause you are engaged in; nothing but that we would be friends to ourselves, and not strengthen the bands of oppression by an evil conduct, when led out of the house of bondage. May He who hath arisen to plead our cause, and engaged you as volunteers in the service, add to your numbers, until the princes shall come forth from Egypt, and Ethiopia stretch out her hands unto God.

### *Notes*

*Sermon source:* Richard Allen, "The Life, Experiences, and Gospel Labours of the Rt. Rev. Richard Allen," 45–60, at Documenting the American South, University of North Carolina at Chapel Hill Digitization Project, http://docsouth.unc.edu/neh/allen/menu.html (accessed August 15, 2009).

1. For additional information on Allen's grandson attending meetings with Allen and providing secretarial services, see Daniel H. Payne, ed., *History of the African Methodist Episcopal Church*, vol. 1 (1891; repr., New York: Arno Press, 1969), and Henry H. Mitchell's *Black Church Beginnings: The Long Hidden Realities of the First Years* (Grand Rapids, MI: Eerdmans, 2004), 105.

2. Allen's autobiography, *The Life Experience and Gospel Labours of the Right*

*Reverend Richard Allen,* includes two hymns, "The God of Bethel Heard Her Cries" and "Ye Ministers That Are Called to Preaching." A third song, "Spiritual Song," is published in Dorothy Porter's *Early Negro Writing, 1760–1837* (Boston: Beacon Press, 1971).

3. Deuteronomy 23:7 (King James Version).

### *Bibliographical Sources*

Allen, Richard. *The Life, Experience, and Gospel Labors of the Right Reverend Richard Allen.* 1793. Reprint, Philadelphia: Martin & Boden, 1833.

Jones, Absalom, and Richard Allen. *A Narrative of the Proceedings of the Black People During the Late Awful Calamity in Philadelphia in 1793, and a Refutation of Some Censures, Thrown Upon Them in Some Late Publications.* Philadelphia: William W. Woodward, 1794.

Southern, Eileen, ed. *Readings in Black American Music*, 2nd ed. New York: W. W. Norton & Company, 1983, 52.

Wesley, H. Charles. *Richard Allen: Apostles of Freedom.* 1935. 2nd ed., Washington, DC: Associated Publishers, 1969.

# BROTHER CARPER

*(?–1850s?)*

Unfortunately, very little biographical information exists concerning the masterful folk preacher known to us only as Brother Carper. Knowledge of his extraordinary ability as a Baptist preacher comes to us through the white Methodist preacher, James V. Watson (1814–1856), editor of the *Northwestern Christian Advocate*, the Chicago-based edition of the official paper of the Methodist Episcopal Church.[1] From memory, and perhaps an interview that he conducted with Carper, Watson wrote down parts of two sermons, giving "a sketch of some of their most eloquent passages."[2] While Watson was not black, he was said to have a "rare subtlety of perception, and transparency of imagination."[3] These traits would explain his ability to understand and record the folk preaching of Carper in a manner that, for the most part, appears to be in keeping with the black folk preaching idiom, although caution must always accompany the writings of whites who record blacks, especially when the recorders are of different denominations and cultural backgrounds.

Brother Carper was born in Kentucky and was the son of his white plantation owner and a black mother who was said to be "distinguished for her intelligence."[4] After the death of his father, Carper was enslaved by his half-brother, at which point Carper learned of his own paternity. According to Watson, Carper purchased his freedom, and planned to do the same for his wife and two children. However, before he could do so, his family was killed by cholera. In adulthood, Carper moved to Tennessee, joined the Baptist church, and was allowed to preach to blacks. Poor all of his life, but beloved, a grave was purchased for Carper on the banks of the St. Francis River, and there he was buried.

• • •

*The following sermon is written in dialect as recorded by James V. Watson in* Tales and Takings, Sketches and Incidents, From the Itinerant and Editorial Budget of Rev. J.V. Watson. *For ease of reading, the formal English version of certain words has been placed in brackets. Brackets have also been used to indicate the notes of the recorder, Watson, and to indicate the call-and-response [CR] of those present during the sermon. It is not known when this sermon was preached or recorded, but is assumed to have been preached and recorded in either the 1840s or early 1850s. The sermon contains vivid metaphors and what is termed in black preaching an eyewitness account: A preacher is said to have given an eyewitness account if they discuss a biblical occurrence in a manner that makes listeners believe that the preacher was actually present during the event.*

## The Shadow of a Great Rock in a Weary Land (ca. 1840–1854)

> *And a man shall be as an hiding-place from the wind, and a covert from the tempest; as rivers of water in a dry place, as the shadow of a great rock in a weary land.* —Isaiah 32:2

Dare be two kinds ob language, de literal and de figerative. De one expresses de tought [thought] plainly but not passionately; de oder passionately, but not always so plainly. De Bible abounds wid bof dese mode[s] ob talk. De text is an enample of dat lubly stile of speech de figerative. De prophet's mind was as clear as de sea ob glass in Rebalations and mingled wid fire. He seed away down de riber ob ages[,] glorious coming events. He held his ear to de harp ob prophecy, and heard its fainter cadences, loudening as he listened, de birf [birth] song ob de multitude ob de hebenly host on de meadows ob Bethlehem. He seed the hills ob Judea tipped wid hebenly light; de fust sermun mountin, and de transfigeration mountin, and de crucivixion mountin, and, de mountin ob ascension, clapped dare hands in de prophet's wision [vision] ob gladness. Gray-bearded Time stretched his brawny sinews to hasten on de fullness of latter-day glory.

Brederen, de text am as full ob latter-day glory as am de sun ob light. It am as full ob Christ as de body ob heben am ob God. De sinner's danger and his certain destruction; Christ's sabin lub; his sheltering grace and his feasting goodness am brought to view in de text, and impressed in de language ob comparison.

"And a man shall be as a hiding place from de wind." Many parts ob de ancient countries (and it still am de case) was desert; wild wastes ob dreary regions ob fine blistering sands; just as it was leff when de flood went away, and which has not been suffered to cool since de fust sunshine that succeed[ed] dat event. No grass, no flower, no tree dare be pleasant to de sight. A scene of unrelebed waste; an ocean made of powder, into which de curse ob angered heben had ground a portion ob earth. Now and den, a huge rock, like shattered shafts and fallen monuments in a neglected graveyard, and big enof to be de tombstone ob millions, would liff its mossless [muscles] 'bove de 'cumulating sands. No poisnous sarpint or venemous beast here await dare prey, for death here has ended his work and dwells mid silence. But de traveler here, who adventures, or necessity may have made a bold wanderer, finds foes in de elements fatal and resistless. De long heated earth here at places sends up all kinds ob poisnous gases from de many minerals ob its mysterious bosom; dese tings [things] take fire, and dey dare be a tempest ob fire, and woe be to de traveler dat be obertaken in dis fire ob de Lord widout a shelter. Again, dem gases be poison, and dare be de poison winds, as well as de fire[y] winds. Dey can be seen a coming, and look green and yeller, and coppery, spotted snake-like, and float and wave in de air, like poison coats on water, and look like de wing ob de death angel; fly as swift as de cloud shadow ober de cotton field, and when dey obertake the flying traveler dey am sure to prove [end up being] his winding sheet; de drifting sands do dare [there] rest, and 'bliterate de faintest traces ob his footsteps. Dis be death in de desert, 'mid de wind's loud scream in your sand-filling ears for a funeral sermun, and your grave [will be] hidden foreber. No sweet spring here to weave her hangings ob green [a]bout your lub-guarded dust. De dews ob night shall shed no tears 'pon your famined grave. De resurrection angel alone can find ye.

But agin dis fire wind and dis tempest ob poison dat widthers [withers] wid a bref, and mummifies whole caravans and armies in dare [their] march, dare is one breastwork, one "hiding-place," one protectin' "shadow" in de dreaded desert. It am "de shadow ob a great rock in dis weary land." Often has de weary traveler seen death in de distance, pursuing him on de wings of de wind, and felt de certainty ob his fate in de darkness ob de furnace-like air around him. A drowsiness stronger 'most dan de lub ob life creeps ober him, and de jaded camel reels in de heby [heavy] sand-road under him. A shout ob danger from de more resolute captin ob de caravan am sent along de ranks, prolonged by a thousand thirst-blistered tongues, commingled in one ceaseless howl ob woe, varied by ebery tone ob distress and despair. "To de great rock," shouts de leader as 'pon his Arab hoss he heads dis "flight to de Refuge." Behind dem at a great distance, but yet fearfully near for safety, is seen a dark bell bending ober de horizon, and sparkling in its waby windings like a great sarpint, air hung at a little distance from de ground, and advancing wid de swiftness ob an arrow. Before dem, in de distance, a mighty great rock spreads out its broad and all-resisting sides, lifting its narrowing pint [point] 'bove the clouds, tipped wid de sun's fiery blaze, which had burnt 'pon it since infant creation 'woke from de cradle ob kaos at de call ob its Fader.

[Watson: Here our sable orator pointed away to some of the spurs of the Ozark Mountains seen off to the northwest through a forest opening, at a distance of from ten to fifteen miles, and whose summits of barren granite blazed in the strength of a clear June sun, like sheeted domes on distant cathedrals.]

Dat light be de light ob hope, and dat rock be de rock ob hope to de now flyin', weepin', faintin', and famishin' hundreds. De captin' has arrived dare. [Watson: Here a suppressed cry of "Thank God," escaped from many in the audience.] See, he has disappeared behind it, perhaps to explore its cavern converts. But see, he has soon reappeared, and wid joy dancing in his eye, he stands shoutin' and beckonin', "Onward, onward, ONWARD, ONWARD," when one reels from weariness and falls in behind de rock. Onward dey rush, men, women, husbands, wives, parents, children, broders and sisters, like doves to de windows, and disappear behind dis rampart ob salvation. Some faint just as dey 'rive at de great rock, and dare [their] friends run out and drag dem to de "hidin' place," when wakin' up in safety, like dat sister dare, dat lose her strength in de prayer-meetin', dey shout loud for joy. [Watson: Here many voices at once shouted "Glory."] De darknin' sand-plain ober which dese fled for life, now lies strewed wid beast, giben out in the struggle, and all useless burdens was trowed [throwed] 'side. De waby sheet ob destruction, skimmin' the surface wid de swiftness ob a shadow, now be very near and yet, a few feeble stragglers and lubbed friends ob dis sheltered multitude are yet a great way off. [Watson: Here words were uttered in a choked accent, the speaker seeming unable to resist the thrilling character of the analogy.] Yes, a great way off. But see, moders and broders from behind de rock are shoutin' to dem to hasten. Dey come, dey come. A few steps more, and dey are sabed. But O, de pison wind is just behind dem, and its choke [choking] mist already round dem! Dare [There] one falls, and dare is a scream. No, he rises and am sabed. But one still is exposed. It be de fader ob dat little nest of sweet-eyed children for which he had fled to de rear to hurry on. Dey have passed forward and are safe. He am but a little distance from de rock, and not a head dares to peep to him encouragement from behind it. Already de wings ob de death angel am on de haunches ob his strong dromedary. His beast falls, but 'pon de moment ob him falling, de rider leaps out ob his saddle into dis [this] hiding-place from de wind. His little boy crouched in a hole ob de rock into which he thrusts his head, entwines his neck with his little arms and says, "Papa, you hab come, and we be all here." [Watson: Here the shouts of "Salvation Salvation," seemed to shake the place in which we were assembled.]

Now, de burnin' winds and de pison winds blow and beat 'pon dat rock, but dose who hab taken refuge behind it, in its overhanging precipices, are safe until de tempest am ober and gone.

And now, brederen, what does all dis represent in a figure? Dat rock am Christ; dem winds be de wrath ob God rabealed [revealed] against de children ob disobedience. Dem that he sabed be dem dat hab fled to de refuge, to de hope set before dem, Christ Jesus de Lord. De desert am de vast howling wilderness ob dis world, where dare be so little ob lub, and so much ob hate; so little ob sincerity, and so much ob hypocrisy; so little ob good, and so much ob sin; so little ob heben, and so much ob hell. It seem to poor me, dat dis world am de battle-ground ob de debil and his angels against Christ and his elect, and if de debil hab not gained de victory, he hold possession because every sinner am a Tory.[5] God ob de Gospel, open the batteries [balconies] of heben to-day! [Watson: Here a volley of hearty "Amens."] Sinner, de wrath ob God am gathering against you for de great decisive battle. I already sees in de light ob Zina's lightnings a long embankment ob dark cloud down on de sky. De tall thunder heads nod wid dare plumes of fire in dare onward march. De day of vengeance am at hand. Mercy, dat has pleaded long for you wid tears of blood, will soon dry her eyes and hush her prayers in your behalf. Death and hell hang on your track wid de swiftness ob de tempest. Before you am de "hiding-place." Fly, *fly*, I beseeches you, from de wrath to come!

But, brederen, de joy ob de belieber in Jesus am set forth in a figerative manner in de text. It am compared to water to dem what be dying ob thirst. O, how sweet to de taste ob de desert traveler sweltering under a burning sun, as if creation was a great furnace! Water, sweet, sparklin', livin', bubblin', silvery water, how does his languid eye brighten as he suddenly sees it gushing up at his feet like milk from de fountain ob lub, or leaping from de sides ob de mountain rock like a relief angel from heben. He drinks long and gratefully, and feels again de blessed pulsations ob being. And so wid de soul dat experience joy in beliebing; de sweets ob pardon; de raptures ob peace; de witnessin' Spirit's communing, and de quiet awe ob adoption. Such a soul be obershadowed wid de Almighty; he linger in de shady retreats ob de garden ob God; he feed in de pastures ob his lub, and am led by still waters, and often visits de land ob Beulah, whare it always am light. But, my brederen, all comparison be too dispassionate, and an angel's words am too cold to describe de raptures ob salvation! It am unspeakable and full ob glory. De life ob innocence and prayer; de sweet, childlike smile and de swimmin' eye; de countenance so glorious in death, dat but for decay, de body ob de gone-home saint might be kept as a breathin' statue of peace and patience, smiling in victory ober all de sorrows ob life and de terrors ob death, are de natural language ob dis holy passion. O, glory to God! I feels it today like fire in my bones! Like a chained eagle my soul rises toward her native heben, but she can only fly just so high. But de fetters ob flesh shall fall off soon, and den,

*I shall bathe my weary soul*
*In seas ob hebenly rest,*
*And not a wabe ob trouble roll*
*Across my peaceful breast.*[6]

✦ ✦ ✦

*An African American sentiment frequently expressed in preaching—that life will make sense in heaven, by and by—has often been referred to as escapism. But this sermon by Carper and others like it show that by-and-by theology is a practical hermeneutic for coping with suffering. It is grounded in the experience of oppression, committed to liberation, and draws on a transcendent vision of reality that is critical of the status quo and the slave master's religion. In this sermon, Carper refers to the ultimate River of Life, which is beyond the earth plane. However, as he paints the picture of this magnificent river, he does not fail to subtly malign slavery and slaveholders as he describes a better place (Heaven) as well as a better life on earth for black people.*[7]

## The River of the Water of Life (ca. 1840–1854)

*And he showed me a pure river of water of life, clear as crystal, proceeding out of the throne of God and of the Lamb.*

—Revelation 22:1

Brederen, we all knows what a ribber [river] am. It am a mighty pretty ting, an' looks to me like a ribbin [ribbon] danglin' from de bosom ob old moder earth. Dere be White Ribber[s], an' dere be Black Ribber[s]; de Mississippi Ribber, an' de Ohio Ribber; Tennessee an' old Tombigbee, which we used to see way down in old Alabama. How ofen hab we stood on de banks ob some ob dese here ribbers, an' seed dere blue or creamy waters move along dotted an' dented wid eddies an' ripples, like de great dent corn ob de big bottoms; an' dese eddies whirling an' gamboling, an' den melting out into each oder, like de smile ob welcome on de face ob a friend, afore he do you a favor, an' seemin' to say ob de ribbers, whose waters dey adorn, We flow for all, an' flow on, on, foreber. What would we do in dis world widout ribbers! Dey be de servants ob de sea, an' as dat great water press itself up fru [through] de earth, an' as de sun an' de cloud, as de larnt men tell us, lift its waters up fru de air, to descend in sparklin' showers on de hill an' de vale [valley], de corn, cotton, tobacca, fillin' men's hearts wid joy an' gladness; an' dese ribbers gedder [gather] de sea-born springs an' de cloud-born rains, an' return dem again to dere home in de sea, to repeat dere mission ob mercy to man! De waters, brederen, are like circuit-riders, gwine [going] all de while round an' round, doing good.

O, how we lub our preacher! when he come round here to dis 'pointment [this appointment], an' preach once a Sunday to us poor black people, telling us how Jesus died for all, an' how dat we shall be as white as any ob dem in hebben, an' sweep de gold-paved streets ob de new Jerusalem wid our muslin robes ob linen, white an' clean, which be de righteousness ob de saints. Sister, instead dere ob leanin' ober de cotton-hill in de hot day, wid the great drops ob sweat drippin' down on the hoe-handle, an' castin' a wishful eye now an' den at your shortenin' shadder [shadow], which am your watch to tell you when it is noon, instead ob wishin, in your weariness, dat de row was hoed out, de hoe-cake dun, an' dat de horn would blow, you shall bend wid an angel form ober de harp of Judea, an' wake its strings to close notes [Watson: Here the old man's voice became very tremulous, and a big tear trembled in his eye.] which has sounded down de ages so sweet in de ears of all de saints, an' which notes in hebben are as much sweeter in dere music den dey eber can be on earth, as de notes ob a fiddle ober yer gourd banjoes. [Watson: Here a loud shout of hallelujahs was raised, and the sable audience seemed to perfectly appreciate the illustration.]

But I'se speakin' ob ribbers. Dey are God's great turnpike roads from the Nort to de Sout, from de East to de West, an' de big steamboats jus walk in dem, not like de giants 'fore de flood to do no good, but to bear our cotton, an' rice, an' sugar to de market, an' make de hearts ob our massrs [masters] laugh. Dey also float de "broad horn" [a flat-bottom boat] from de upper country, bringin' down de pig, de beans, de bacon, an' de chick'ns, widout which our moufs at de sugar-house, in de cotton fields, de rice swamp an' tobacca field, would seldom be blessed with greasy victuals [vittles/food], which poor slave like as much as old Isaac like de savory meat ob de deceivin' Jacob. When we get to hebben, brederen, we shall hunger an' thirst no more. We shall lib just as well dere, in de quarters, as massrs and missns [masters and misses] in de mansion. Dere be no quarters in hebben; all be mansions. We read ob many mansions, but ob no quarters; ob saints an' angels, so many dat no man can number dem, an' yet ob no white folks nor black folks. [Watson: Here a volley of "Amens" and "Glories" momentarily drowned the voice of the speaker.] Ribbers begin wid leetle [little] creeks, which a leetle kitten might wade, an' swell to a greatness on which de commerce ob de nations may trabel. Dey come widenin' an' widenin', an' growin' an' bilin', [building] from old Chimborazo,[8] de Mountains ob de Moon, de Rocky Mountains, or some oder region unknown to yer speaker's geography. Dere distant trabel, an' mighty grof, takin' de leetle streams an' lesser ribbers in dere bosom as dey flow, as a hen gaddereth her chick'ns under her wings, am one ob de tings which I like to tink about, as dey makes me tink of Him who makes all tings bery good, an' who did not consider de garden ob Eden as finished till he had made a ribber to water it. De tree ob life, in de garden, no doubt, soaked its roots in de water ob dis ribber.

But de tex speak ob de ribber ob life. Dis, brederen, be de ribber ob salvation. De world be bad off widout de great an' mighty ribbers which encircle it, like girdles ob silver an' purity, but much wuse off widout dis one great ribber ob life, proceedin' out of de trone [throne] of God an' de Lamb. In dis tex, salvation be compared to waters, an' its course in de world to a flowing ribber. Let us notice de last fac fust, trace de fountain head ob dis ribber, an' take a trip down it in de old ship Zion.

Dis ribber flow out ob de trone of God; dat is, it flow out ob God himself. God can hab no trone, an' when de Bible speak ob him sitting on de trone like a king, it only speak in de language ob figure to help our idees [ideas]. God am too great to hab a trone; he fill eberywhar himself. Larnt men tell us dat dis earth be mighty big, eight thousand miles fru it, an' twenty-four thousand miles around it; an' 'stronomers tell us dat dere be millions ob worlds all 'bout us, dancin' in nofin'ness, many hundred times greater den dis, an' yet if all dese worlds were put togedder to make a seat for God to sit upon, dey wouldn't answer de purpose any more den a pin's head would hab done for Jacob's pillar at Bethel, when he seen de angels comin' down an' goin' up agin to hebben, as it were on a ladder. Sister, don't you nebber tink dat yer leetle child who die in your arms, a long time ago, down in old Alabama, does not come down here in de night seasons, an', in de form of an angel, spread its wing ober yer piller, or nestle in yer busum! O! when I lost my sweet, darlin' boy, dat belong to Judge Noble, way down in Georgia, de third night after I buried him under de yellow clay, it seem as dough I seen him in de quarters, a lookin' right at me, an' pointin' away up in de sky, sayin', Daddy, I lib up yender! [Watson: Here a large, fat sister fetched a scream, and commenced jumping toward heaven, with streaming eyes exclaiming, "Dere's my home an' portion fair," etc. But after this temporary episode and agreeable interruption the speaker slowly and eloquently proceeded.] God am great, too great to sit down, too great to stand, too great to take form; he be widout body or parts. God am a spirit, an' his ribber ob life head in dis infinite fountain. It am de Spirit dat quickeneth our dead souls; it be de Spirit dat beget us anew in Christ Jesus; it be de Spirit dat make us happy. When we be filled wid de Spirit, we be filled wid de new wine ob de kingdom. De Holy Ghost be one ob de authors ob salvation. Den there be de Lamb; O, de precious, bleedin', Calvary Lamb! God, trone, Lamb! Dis brederen, teach de doctrine ob de holy Trinity. As de ribber dat watered Paradise. So de ribber ob salvation, dat water de world, rise in tree springs, and yet are dese springs but one. Dere be tree dat bear record in hebben, but dese trees are one.

But now ob de ribber. An', fust, like all de ribbers, it begin in a little spring branch. Dere be what I call de ribber ob promise. When Adam fell, an' de debbel tought [thought] he had outdone God, an' was about to run away wid de world, God appeared amid de glories ob him shameful victory, an' promised to bruise his head wid de seed ob de bery woman he had deceived. Dis, brederen, must hab humbled, 'stonished, an' alarmed de debbel terribly, as we do not s'pose he know what war comin'. His hell was bery hot before, but he had now 'creased it by an attempt to 'stinguish [extinguish] de flames dat tortured him. Adam an' Eve sorry for what dey had done, an' fully believin' dis promise ob de Lord, hung up dere blasted hopes on dis golden chain let down from hebben, an' waterin' it wid de tears ob dere penitence, it soon bloomed agin like de orange blossoms on de coast in de spring ob de year. Here war [was] de beginnin' ob dis ribber. It flowed out ob Eden, an' our fust parents were compelled to follow its course, an' to find in drinkin' ob its waters dere only consolation. Abel drinked as dem as he lifted up his bleedin' lamb upon his altar. Enoch always dwelt near the brink of its waters. An' by invitation ob de angels, one day, who were guidin' its infant channel, he went home wid dem to hebben. He war not, for God took him; took to show in de 'ginnin' ob de world's history, dat body as well as soul war [was] to go up to hebben. De tree ob life, which would hab kept it from bein' sick or dyin', Adam war removed from, so dat now our souls an' bodies must be sep'rated by death; but dey are to be put togeder agin in the resurrection. Oder patriarchs, an' Noah an' him sons, seated upon de bank of dis ribber, drank ob its waters, an' lib foreber. After de flood, Abraham war called from Ur ob de Chaldees to nestle upon its widenin' banks, an' teach him children after him de efficacy ob its waters. But time would fail us to speak of Melchizedek, ob Isaac, ob Jacob, ob Joseph an' Moses, ob Aaron an' Dabid, ob the lawgibbers, priests an' kings, all who libbed along on de banks ob dis ribber, like de beautiful houses dat peep from orange groves, from behind de levee, along de mighty Mississippi. All dese libbed on de ribber ob promise. Den dere were prophets who declared dat de ribber war flowin' on, and dat it would break forth in a mighty flood, an' spread ober de whole earth; dat reeds an' rushes should spring up 'mid rocks an' sands; an' dat harvests should wave, an' beauty should blush whar total barrenness had reigned sobereign for six thousand years. Here old Isaiah, who tuned his harp by holdin' his ear up to hebben, an' catchin' de keynote ob dis new an' strange moosic, which de angels invented 'mid dere rapturous 'stonishment, when dere war silence up dere for de space ob half an hour: "De wilderness an' de sol'tary place shall be glad for dem, an' de desert shall rejoice an' blossom as de rose. It shall blossom 'bundantly, an' de glory ob Lebanon, ob Carmel, an' ob Sharon shall be gib'n [given] it. De parched ground shall become a pool, an' de tirsty land springs ob water; an de hab'tation ob dragons, whar each lay, shall become green an' grassy, wid reeds an' rushes. A 'ighway shall be dere"; dat be dis ribber, [Audience call and response (CR): Amen.] It shall be called de way ob holiness; dat be dis ribber [CR: Amen] "de unclean shall not pass ober it [CR: Glory!] but it shall be for dose [those]"—us poor, unlarnt people ob color—"de wayfarin' men, dough [the] fools, shall not err [enter] derein." [CR: Glory! Halleluiah!] O, brederen; how sweet to float down dis ribber! Ofn, when I hab floated down de Mississippi, on one ob massa's boats, an' set down on de deck in de ebenin', when all be still, an' de pale silbery moon show eberyting in de hazy, mellow light; an' I'd hear de boat-horn from afar, 'bove us, fillin' de whole air wid sweet, sad music, seemin' to say, We are comin', wid de voice ob song, an', like you, hastenin' down de ribber to obtain de treasures: ofn [often], den, hab I tought ob dis ribber ob salvation; and I tink ob dis fact, now, when I hear Isaiah's windin' horn away up de ribber ob life in tones ob joy an' gladness. But de stream ob ages, floatin' down de waters ob dis ribber ob promise an' ob prophecy, break forth into de ribber of redemption and fulfillment, when, instead ob prophet's harps, or smokin' types, a light is seen upon de plains ob Bethlehem, which smote pious shepherds to de ground, followed by a multitude ob de hebbenly host, singin' togeder in de midnight sky, old Adam himself, p'raps [perhaps], pourin' out his voice in bass, "Glory to God in de highest, on earth peace, an' good-will to man." Ob de 'istory, ob de birf ob Jesus, ob his life ob miracles an' mercy, ob his death on Calvary, his resurrection de third day, an' ob his gwine up into hebben, we hab no time now to speak. But, O! how sweet de story, an' what a mighty rise here in dis ribber ob salvation! It has been risin' ebber since; ebery shower cause it to oberflow its banks, widin [within] which, de old Jews always tought dey would keep it—de banks ob de law, brederen, dat is, de law ob carnal ordinances, which neider we nor our faders were able to bear.

De fust great shower dat produced de fust great freshet [freshness] in dis ribber, came to pass on de day ob Pentecost. Tree tousand here drinked ob its waters, an' ebber after took passage in de old ship Zion. Dey be 'rived safely on t' other shore. But de shower dat turn away dis ancient ribber for eber from its old channel, and send it forth to water de earth wherebber it was tirsty, took place at de home ob Cornelius de Gentile. He war dry, and knew not what to drink. His alms an' prayers went up to God, but Christ come not into his heart, de hope ob glory. To be good, an' to do good, brederen, is not to hab religion. Yet du hab religion will always be good an' do good. An angel reliebed Cornelius, an' might hab pointed his thirsty soul to de exhaustless waters ob de ribber of life. But angels may sing ebbery time far-off Omnipotence make a new world to break de blank ob emptiness; dey may eben be jurymen, an' help to judge de world in de day ob judgment; but dey shall not fill de exalted office ob preachin' to man. Dis office has been reserved alone for frail flesh, and even poor, despised "nigger" am permitted to fill dis princely station. Dis be to show de honor which God put upon our flesh when he came down to dis earth. Dis show, too, dat dis frail body, which crawlin' worms will consume, has been tak'n into de keepin' ob God, an' dat he will keep it, dough the lightnins may sport wid it, de alligators chaw it up, as dey did my breder, or de plow turn up our bones to bleach in de cotton-fields, as it has some ob people 'fore [before] us. For I be persuaded dat He will keep dat which I hab committed unto Him against dat day.

An' now, brederen, a word about de waters ob salvation. Dey be pure, clear as crystal. Dis be intended to show de word ob God, or de truth ob God, in which dere be no mixture ob error. Just tink how clear an' nothing like, and yet it be somefin' [something]. De pure waters gurgle up in your spring house, so dat you can see de bottom ob de spring just as easy as if nothin' war dere. An' yet, when de day am hot an' you be dry, how you lub to take de gourd dat hang up there, an' lift to yer lip dat pure substance, which, when you hab drunk, you feel strong agin, an' good all ober. Now, brederen, it be so wid de truth ob God to dat weepin', penitent, despairin' sinner. When he drink ob dese pure waters, clear as crystal, dey make bof soul an' body happy. O, sinner, come to dis flowin' ribber! its waters murmur at yer feet; its billers kneel beseech'n'ly to you, cryin', "Ho, ebbery one dat tirsts, come ye to de waters, an' him dat hab no money; come ye, buy wine an' milk, widout money an' widout price." Yes, tank God, dis ribber be water, or milk, or wine to us, accordin' to our faith; a continual feast to de poor, as well as to de rich. Hallelujah! Bless God dat he ebber let loose dis ribber! How rapidly we glide today upon its movin' waters! It will open in de ocean ob eternity, right at de entrance on which am an island, called the land ob Beulah whar dere am always light, life, an' love, ah' whar de ransomed ob de Lord shall be near him, and go way from him into sin an' sorrow no more foreber an' eber. May we land safely dere, is de prayer ob yer unwordy [unworthy] speaker.

## *Notes*

*Sermon source:* Both sermons are from James V. Watson's *Tales and Takings, Sketches and Incidents, from the Itinerant and Editorial Budget of Rev. J.V. Watson.*

1. Neither the date of birth nor the date of death is known for Brother Carper. Given that Reverend James Watson, who published Carper's sermons, died in 1856 and that in his book he discussed Carper's death, it is safe to assume that Brother Carper died in the late 1840s or early 1850s.
2. J.V. Watson, *Tales and Takings, Sketches and Incidents, from the Itinerant and Editorial Budget of Rev. J.V. Watson* (New York: Carlton and Porter, 1857), 98.
3. *Methodist Quarterly Review* 39 (1857), 138.
4. *Tales and Takings*, 107–8.
5. The word *Tory* here likely means outlaw or one not supportive of God, as Tories opposed the United States and favored Britain during the American Revolution.

6. The conclusion of this sermon is the last stanza of the song "When I Can Read My Title Clear," written by Isaac Watts (1674–1748).
7. For additional information on the preaching of Carper see H. Dean Trulear and Russell E. Richey, "Two Sermons By Brother Carper: 'The Eloquent Preacher' " *American Baptist Quarterly* 6, no. 1 (March 1987): 3–11.
8. Chimborazo, a mountain in Ecuador, was for a long time thought to be the tallest mountain in existence.

### *Bibliographical Source*

Warner, Michael, ed. *American Sermons: The Pilgrims to Martin Luther King, Jr.* New York: Literary Classics of the United States, Inc., 1999, 640.

# ALEXANDER CRUMMELL

*(1819–1898)*

Alexander Crummell, born to the son of an African prince and a free mother, attended an interracial school in Canaan, New Hampshire, then an institute in Whitesboro, New York, that was run by abolitionists. Alexander's father helped ensure his son's academic success by hiring private tutors. When he was denied admission to the General Theological Seminary of the Episcopal church in 1839 because of his race, Crummell studied privately and became an ordained Episcopalian minister in the Diocese of Massachusetts in 1844 at the age of twenty-five. About four years later, he went to England and raised funds for a church for poor blacks and soon began studies at Queen's College, Cambridge, earning an Artium Baccalaureus (now known as the Bachelor of Arts) in 1853.

After graduation, Crummell went to Liberia as a missionary, spending almost twenty years there as a parish rector, a professor of intellectual and moral science at Liberia College, and a public figure. Crummell hoped that Liberia would establish a black Christian republic, combining the best of African and European culture, led by a Western-educated black bishop. Differences with the administration led to his being dismissed from his professorship at Liberia College. During political unrest in 1871, which was partly aimed at Americans whom some Liberians saw as interlopers, Crummell received death threats and was assaulted on the streets of Monrovia. He safely returned to the United States with his family shortly after the coup d'etat of 1871.

In 1873 he returned to Washington, D.C., where he founded St. Luke's

Episcopal Church. After the death of his first wife in the 1870s, he married Jennie Simpson in 1880. Following his retirement from the ministry in 1894, he taught at Howard University (1895–97) and founded the American Negro Academy, the first major intellectual society for black Americans, which promoted the publication of scholarly work dealing with African American culture and history. As a religious leader and an intellectual, he cultivated scholarship and leadership among young blacks. W.E.B. DuBois saw Crummell as one of the brightest men he knew and saluted him in *The Souls of Black Folk.*

Crummell refashioned sermons originally written to extol Liberian nationalism and "recast them as American loyalist manifestos,"[1] abandoning appeals for African American efforts to establish a separate black nation. Nevertheless, Crummell's American sermons retain powerful elements of Pan-Africanism.

• • •

*In this homiletical tour de force, Crummell makes clear his Pan-African leanings and his learnedness. He sternly rebukes those who have harmed blacks and, unfortunately, also belittles those whose cultures and religions he likely did not understand, such as that of the American Indian. Even with its failings, this sermon stands tall as one that is designed to uplift and increase the self-esteem of blacks; it makes scripture relevant and shows how Crummell's theological knowledge affected his sociological view of the world.*

## The Destined Superiority of the Negro (1877)

*For your shame ye shall have double, and for confusion they shall rejoice in their portion.* —Isaiah 61:7

The promise contained in the text is a variation from the ordinary rule of the divine government. In that government, as declared in the Holy Scriptures, shame signifies the hopeless confusion and the utter destruction of the wicked. But in this passage we see an extraordinary display of God's forbearance and mercy. Shame, here, is less intense than in other places. In this case it stands, indeed, for trial and punishment, but for punishment and trial which may correct and purify character.

The allusion is supposed to refer to the Jews after their restoration, and the passage is regarded as teaching that, for all their long-continued servitude and suffering, God, in the end, would make them abundant recompenses. Great shame and reproach He had given them, through long centuries; but when discipline and trial had corrected and purified them, He promises them double honor and reward.

As thus explained, the text opens before us some interesting features of God's dealing with nations; by the light of which we may, perchance, somewhat determine the destiny of the race with which we are connected. My purpose is to attempt, this morning, an investigation of God's disciplinary and retributive economy in races and nations; with the hope of arriving at some clear conclusions concerning the destiny of the Negro race.

1. Some peoples God does not merely correct; He destroys them. He visits them with deep and abiding shame. He brings upon them utter confusion. This is a painful but a certain fact of Providence. The history of the world is, in one view, a history of national destructions. The wrecks of nations lie everywhere upon the shores of time. Real aboriginal life is rarely found. People after people, in rapid succession, have come into constructive being, and as rapidly gone down; lost forever from sight beneath the waves of a relentless destiny. We read in our histories of the great empires of the old world; but when the traveller goes abroad, and looks for Nineveh and Babylon, for Pompeii and Herculaneum, he finds nought but the outstretched graveyards which occupy the sites of departed nations. On the American continent, tribe after tribe have passed from existence; yea, there are Bibles in Indian tongues which no living man is now able to read. Their peoples have all perished!

When I am called upon to account for all this loss of national and tribal life, I say that God destroyed them. And the declaration is made on the strength of a principle attested by numerous facts in sacred and profane history; that when the sins of a people reach a state of hateful maturity, then God sends upon them sudden destruction.

Depravity prepares some races of men for destruction. Every element of good has gone out of them. Even the most primitive virtues seem to have departed. A putrescent virus has entered into and vitiated their whole nature. They stand up columnar ruins! Such a people is doomed. It cannot live. Like the tree "whose root is rottenness," it stands awaiting the inevitable fall. That fall is its property. No fierce thunder-bolt is needed, no complicated apparatus of ethereal artillery. Let the angry breath of an Archangel but feebly strike it, and, tottering, it sinks into death and oblivion!

Such was the condition of the American Indian at the time of the discovery of America by Columbus. The historical fact abides, that when the white man first reached the shores of this continent he met the tradition of a decaying population.

The New Zealand population of our own day presents a parallel case. By a universal disregard of the social and sanitary conditions which pertain to health and longevity, their physical constitution has fallen into absolute decay; and ere long it also must become extinct.

Indeed, the gross paganism of these two peoples was both moral and physical stagnation; was domestic and family ruin; and has resulted in national suicide! It came to them as the effect, the direct consequence of great penal laws established by the Almighty, in which are wrapped the punishment of sin. Hence, if you reject the idea of direct interference in the affairs of peoples, and take up the idea of law and penalty, or that of cause and effect, it amounts to the same thing. Whether through God's fixed law, or directly, by His personal, direful visitation, the admission is the same. The punishment and the ruin come from the throne of God!

The most striking instances of the working of this principle of ruin are set before us in the word of God. The case of Egypt is a signal one. For centuries this nation was addicted to the vilest sins and the grossest corruption. There was no lack of genius among them, no imbecility of intellect. It was a case of wanton, high-headed moral rebellion. As generations followed each other, they heaped up abominations upon the impurities of their ancestors, until they well-nigh reached the heavens. Then the heavens became darkened with direful wrath! The earth quaked and trembled with God's fearful anger; and judgment upon judgment swept, like lava, over the doomed people, assuring them of the awful destruction which always waits upon sin. And the death of the first-born at the Passover, and the catastrophe of the Red Sea, showed that the crisis of their fate had come.

In precisely the same manner God dealt with the wicked people of Assyria, Babylon, Tyre, and Persia. Read the prophecies concerning these nations, and it seems as though you could see an august judge sitting upon the judgment-seat, and, of a sudden, putting on his black cap, and, with solemn gesture and a choked utterance, pronouncing the sentence of death upon the doomed criminals before him!

2. Turn now to the more gracious aspects of God's economy. As there are people whom He destroys, so on the other hand there are those whom, while indeed He chastises, yet at the same time He preserves. He gives them shame, but not perpetual shame. He disciplines; but when discipline has worked out its remedial benefits, he recompenses them for their former ignominy, and gives them honor and prosperity.

The merciful aspect of God's economy shines out in human history as clearly as His justice and judgment. The Almighty seizes upon superior nations and, by mingled chastisement and blessings, gradually leads them on to greatness. That this discipline of nations is carried on in the world is evident. Probation, that is, as designed to teach self-restraint, and to carry on improvement, is imposed upon them, as well as upon individuals. It is part of the history of all nations and all races; only some will not take it; seem to have no moral discernment to use it; and they, just like willful men, are broken to pieces. Some, again, fit themselves to it, and gain all its advantages. What was the servile sojourn of the children of Israel, four hundred years, in Egypt, but a process of painful preparation for a coming national and ecclesiastical responsibility? What, at a later period, the Babylonish captivity, but a corrective ordeal, to eliminate from them every element of idolatry? What was the feudality of Europe, but a system of training for a high and grand civilization?

Now it seems to me that these several experiments were not simply judicial and retributive. For vengeance crushes and annihilates; but chastisement, however severe, saves, and at the same time corrects and restores. We may infer, therefore, that these several providences were a mode of divine schooling, carried on by the Almighty for great ends which He wished to show in human history.

But how! in what way does God carry on His system of restorative discipline? The universal principle which regulates this feature of the Divine system is set forth very clearly in the Eighteenth Psalm: "With the merciful thou wilt shew thyself merciful; with an upright man thou wilt shew thyself upright; with the pure thou wilt shew thyself pure; and with the froward thou wilt shew thyself froward." These words show the principles by which God carries on His government. And they apply as well to organic society as to single persons.

We have already seen that with the froward God showed Himself froward; that is, those who resist Him, God resists, to their utter shame and confusion. Their miseries were not corrective or disciplinary. They were the blows of avenging justice; the thunder-bolts of final and retributive wrath! In their case, moreover, there was a constitutional fitness to destruction, brought upon them by their own immoral perverseness. So, too, on the other hand, we may see qualities which God favors, albeit He does put the peoples manifesting them to trial and endurance. He sees in them cultivated elements of character, which, when brought out and trained, are capable of raising them to superiority. He does not see merit; and it is not because of desert [*sic*] that He bestows His blessings. But when the Almighty sees in a nation or people latent germs of virtues, he seizes upon and schools them by trial and discipline; so that by the processes of divers correctives, these virtues may bud and blossom into beautiful and healthful maturity.

Now, when the Psalmist speaks of the merciful, the upright, and the pure, he does not use these terms in an absolute sense, for in that sense no such persons exist. He speaks of men comparatively pure, upright, and merciful. Some of the nations, as I have already pointed out, were at the lowest grade of moral turpitude. On the other hand, there are and ever have been heathen peoples less gross and barbarous than others; peoples with great hardihood of soul; peoples retaining the high principle of right and justice; peoples with rude but strong virtues, clinging to the simple ideas of truth and honor; peoples who guarded jealously the purity of their wives and the chastity of their daughters; peoples who, even with a false worship, showed reluctance to part with the gleams which came, though but dimly, from the face of the one true God of heaven!

Now the providence of God intervenes for the training and preservation of such peoples. Thus we read in Genesis that, because of man's universal wickedness, "it repented the Lord that he had made man"; but immediately it says that He approved "just Noah, and entered into covenant with him." So, after the deluge, God saw, amid universal degeneracy, the conspicuous piety of one man; for obedience and faith were, without doubt, original though simple elements of Abraham's character. To these germinal roots God brought the discipline of trial; and by them, through this one man, educated up a people who, despite their faults, shed forth the clearest religion light of all antiquity, and to whom were committed the oracles of God.

The ancient Greeks and Romans were rude and sanguinary Pagans; and so, too, the Germans and the Scandinavian tribes. Yet they had great, sterling virtues. The Greeks were a people severely just; the Spartans, especially, rigidly simple and religious. The Romans were unequalled for reverence for law and subjection to legitimate authority. Tacitus, himself a heathen, extols the noble and beneficent traits of German character, and celebrates their hospitality and politeness. The Saxons, even in a state of rudeness, were brave, though fierce; truthful; with strong family virtues, and great love of liberty. Added to these peculiarities we find the following characteristics common to each and all these people—common, indeed, to all strong races; wanting in the low and degraded. The masterful nations are all, more or less, distinguished for vitality, plasticity, receptivity, imitation, family feeling, veracity, and the sentiment of devotion. These qualities may have been crude and unbalanced. They existed perchance right beside most decided and repulsive vices; but they were deeply imbedded in the constitution of these people; and served as a basis on which could be built up a character fitted to great ends.

Archbishop Trench,[2] in his comment upon the words of the "Parable of the Sower,"—that is, that "They on the good ground are they who, in an honest and good heart, having heard the word, keep it"—says, "that no heart can be said to be absolutely good; but there are conditions of heart in which the truth finds readier entrance than in others." So we maintain that there are conditions of character and of society, to which the divine purposes of grace and civilization are more especially fitted, and adapt themselves. Such, it is evident, is the explanation of the providential spread of early civilization. It passed by the more inane peoples, and fastened itself to the strong and masculine. Such, too, was the spontaneous flow of early Christianity from Jerusalem. It sought, as by a law of affinity, the strong colonies of Asia Minor, and the powerful states along the Mediterranean; and so spread abroad through the then civilized Europe.

Does God then despise the weak? Nay, but the weak and miserable peoples of the earth have misused their prerogatives, and so unfitted themselves to feel after God. And because they have thus perverted the gifts of God, and brought imbecility upon their being, they perish. The iniquity of the Amorites in Joshua's day was full—as you may see in Leviticus 18—full of lust and incest and cruelty and other unspeakable abominations; and they were swept from the face of the earth! They perished by the sword; but the sword is not an absolute necessity to the annihilation of any corrupt and ruined people. Their sins, of themselves, eat out their life. With a touch they go. It was because of the deep and utter demoralization of Bois Gilbert that he fell before the feeble lance of Ivanhoe; for, in the world of morals, weakness and death are ofttimes correlative of baseness and infamy.

On the other hand the simplest seeds of goodness are pleasing to the Almighty, and He sends down the sunshine of His favor and the dews of His conserving care into the darkest rubbish, to nourish and vivify such seeds, and to "give them body as it pleaseth Him; and to every seed his own body." And the greatness of the grand nations has always sprung from the seeds of simple virtues which God has graciously preserved in them; which virtues have been cultured by gracious providences or expanded by Divine grace, into true holiness.

3. Let us not apply the train of thought thus presented to the history and condition of the Negro; to ascertain, if possible, whether we can draw there from expectation of a future for this race.

At once the question arises: Is this a race doomed to destruction? Or is it one possessed of those qualities, and so morally disciplined by trial, as to augur a vital destiny, and high moral uses, in the future?

To the first of these questions I reply that there is not a fact, pertinent to this subject, that does not give a most decisive negative. The Negro race, nowhere on the globe, is a doomed race!

It is now five hundred years since the breath of the civilized world touched, powerfully, for the first time, the mighty masses of the Pagan world in America, Africa, and the isles of the sea. And we see, almost everywhere, that the weak, heathen tribes of the earth have gone down before the civilized European. Nation after nation has departed before his presence, tribe after tribe! In America the catalogue of these disastrous eclipses overruns, not only dozens, but even scores of cases. Gone, never again to take rank among the tribes of men, are the Iroquois and the Mohegans, the Pequods and the Manhattans, the Algonquins and the brave Mohawks, the gentle Caribs, and the once refined Aztecs!

In the Pacific seas, islands are scattered abroad like stars in the heavens; but the sad fact remains that from many of them their population has departed, like the morning mist. In other cases, as in the Sandwich Islands, they have long since begun their "funeral marches to the grave!"[3] Just the reverse with the Negro! Wave after wave of a destructive tempest has swept over his head, without impairing in the least his peculiar vitality. Indeed, the Negro, in certain localities, is a superior man, to-day, to what he was three hundred years ago. With an elasticity rarely paralleled, he has risen superior to the dread inflictions of a prolonged servitude, and stands, to-day, in all the lands of his thraldom, taller, more erect, more intelligent, and more aspiring than any of his ancestors for more than two thousand years of a previous era. And while in other lands, as in cultivated India, the native has been subjected to a foreign yoke, the negro races of Africa still retain, for the most part, their original birthright. Their soil has not passed into the possession of foreign people. Many of the native kingdoms stand this day, upon the same basis of power which they held long centuries ago. The adventurous traveler, as he passes farther and farther into the interior, sends us reports of populous cities, superior people, and vast kingdoms; given to enterprise, and engaged in manufactures, agriculture, and commerce.

Even this falls short of the full reality. For civilization, at numerous places, as well in the interior as on the coast, has displaced ancestral heathenism; and the standard of the Cross, uplifted on the banks of its great rivers, at large and important cities, and in the great seats of commercial activity, shows that the Heralds of the Cross have begun the conquest of the continent for their glorious King. Vital power, then, is a property of the Negro family.

But has this race any of those other qualities, and such a number of them, as warrants the expectation of superiority? Are plasticity, receptivity, and assimilation among his constitutional elements of character?

So far as the first of these is concerned there can be no doubt. The flexibility of the negro character is not only universally admitted; it is often formulated into a slur. The race is possessed of a nature more easily moulded than any other class of men. Unlike the stolid Indian, the Negro yields to circumstances, and flows with the current of events. Hence the most terrible afflictions have failed to crush him. His facile nature wards off, or else, through the inspiration of hope, neutralizes their influences. Hence, likewise, the pliancy with which, and without losing his distinctiveness, he runs into the character of other people; and thus bends adverse circumstances to his own convenience; thus, also, in a measurable degree, linking the fortunes of his superiors to his own fate and destiny.

These peculiarities imply another prime quality, anticipating future superiority; I mean imitation. This is also universally conceded, with, however, a contemptuous fling, as though it were an evidence of inferiority. But Burke tells us that "imitation is the second passion belonging to society; and this passion," he says, "arises from much the same cause as sympathy." This forms our manners, our opinions, our lives. It is one of the strongest links of society. Indeed, all civilization is carried down from generation to generation, or handed over from the superior to the inferior, by the means of this principle. A people devoid of imitation are incapable of improvement, and must go down; for stagnation of necessity brings with it decay and ruin.

On the other hand, the Negro, with a mobile and plastic nature, with a strong receptive faculty, seizes upon and makes over to himself, by imitation, the better qualities of others. First of all, observe that, by a strong assimilative tendency, he reduplicates himself, by attaining both the likeness of and an affinity to the race with which he dwells; and then, while retaining his characteristic peculiarities, he glides more or less into the traits of his neighbor. Among Frenchmen, he becomes, somewhat, the lively Frenchman; among Americans, the keen, enterprising American; among Spaniards, the stately, solemn Spaniard; among Englishmen, the solid, phlegmatic Englishman.

This peculiarity of the Negro is often sneered at. It is decried as the simulation of a well-known and grotesque animal. But the traducers of the Negro forget that "the entire Grecian civilization is stratified with the elements of imitation; and that Roman culture is but a copy of a foreign and alien civilization." These great nations laid the whole world under contribution to gain superiority. They seized upon all the spoils of time. They became cosmopolitan thieves. They stole from every quarter. They pounced, with eagle eye, upon excellence wherever discovered, and seized upon it with rapacity. In the Negro character resides, though crudely, precisely the same eclectic quality which characterized those two great, classic nations; and he is thus found in the very best company. The ridicule which visits him goes back directly to them. The advantage, however, is his own. Give him time and opportunity, and in all imitative art he will rival them both.

This quality of imitation has been the grand preservative of the Negro in all the lands of his thraldom. Its bearing upon his future distinction in Art is not germain to this discussion; but one can clearly see that this quality of imitation, allied to the receptivity of the race, gives promise of great fitness for Christian training, and for the higher processes of civilization.

But observe, again, that the imitative disposition of the negro race leads to aspiration. Its tendency runs to the higher and the nobler qualities presented to observation. Placed in juxtaposition with both the Indian and the Caucasian, as in Brazil and in this land, the race turns away from the downward, unprogressive Indian, and reaches forth for all the acquisitions of the Caucasian or the Spaniard. And hence wherever the Negro family has been in a servile position, however severe may have been their condition, without one single exception their native capacity has always glinted forth Amid the storm; preserving the captive exiles of Africa from utter annihilation; stimulating them to enterprise and aspiration; and, in every case, producing men who have shown respectable talent as mechanics and artisans; as soldiers, in armies; as citizens of great commonwealths; not unfrequently as artists; not seldom as scholars; frequently as ministers of the Gospel; and at times as scientific men, and men of letters.

I referred, at the beginning, and as one of the conditions of a Divine and merciful preservation of a people—for future uses, to the probation of discipline and trial, for the cultivation of definite moral qualities. Is there any such large fact in the history of this race? What else, I ask, can be the significance of the African slave trade? What is the meaning of our deep thraldom since 1620? Terrible as it has been, it has not been the deadly hurricane portending death. During its long periods, although great cruelty and widespread death have been large features in the history of the Negro, nevertheless they have been overshadowed by the merciful facts of great natural increase, much intellectual progress, the gravitation of an unexampled and world-wide philanthropy to the race, singular religious susceptibility and progress, and generous, wholesale emancipations, inclusive of millions of men, women, and children.

This history, then, does not signify retribution; does not forecast extinction. It is most plainly disciplinary and preparative. It is the education which comes from trial and endurance; for with it has been allied, more or less, the grand moral training of the religious tendencies of the race.

Here, then are the several conditions, the characteristic marks which, in all history, have served to indicate the permanency and the progress of races. In all other cases they have been taken as forecasting greatness. Is there any reason for rejecting their teachings, and refusing their encouragements and inspirations, when discovered in the Negro?

I feel fortified, moreover, in the principles I have today set forth, by the opinions of great, scrutinizing thinkers. In his treatise on Emancipation, written in 1840, Dr. Channing says: "The Negro is one of the best races of the human family. He is among the mildest and gentlest of men. He is singularly susceptible of improvement."

Alexander Kinmont, in his "Lectures on Man," declares that "the sweet graces of the Christian religion appear almost too tropical and tender plants to grow in the soil of the Caucasian mind; they require a character of human nature of which you can see the rude lineaments in the Ethiopian, to be implanted in, and grow naturally and beautifully withal." Adamson, the traveller who visited Senegal, in 1754, said: "The Negroes are sociable, humane, obliging, and hospitable; and they have generally preserved an estimable simplicity of domestic manners. They are distinguished by their tenderness for their parents, and great respect for the aged—a patriarchal virtue which, in our day, is too little known." Dr. Raleigh, also, at a recent meeting in London, said: "There is in these people a hitherto undiscovered mine of love, the development of which will be for the amazing welfare of the world. . . . Greece gave us beauty; Rome gave us power; the Anglo-Saxon race united and mingles these; but in the African people there is the great, gushing wealth of love which will develop wonders for the world."[4]

1. We have seen, today, the great truth, that when God does not destroy a people, but, on the contrary, trains and disciplines it, it is an indication that He intends to make something of them, and to do something for them. It signifies that He is graciously interested in such a people. In a sense, not equal, indeed, to the case of the Jews, but parallel, in a lower degree, such a people are a "chosen people" of the Lord. There is, so to

speak, a covenant relation which God has established between Himself and them; dim and partial, at first, in its manifestations; but which is sure to come to the sight of men and angels, clear, distinct, and luminous. You may take it as a sure and undoubted fact that God presides, with sovereign care, over such people; and will surely preserve, educate, and build them up.

2. The discussion of this morning teaches us that the Negro race, of which we are a part, and which, as yet, in great simplicity and with vast difficulties, is struggling for place and position in this land, discovers, most exactly, in its history, the principle I have stated. And we have in this fact the assurance that the Almighty is interested in all the great problems of civilization and of grace carrying on among us. All this is God's work. He has brought this race through a wilderness of disasters; and at last put them in the large, open place of liberty; but not, you may be assured, for eventual decline and final ruin. You need not entertain the shadow of a doubt that the work which God has begun and is now carrying on, is for the elevation and success of the Negro. This is the significance and the worth of all effort and all achievement, of every signal providence, in this cause; or, otherwise, all the labors of men and all the mightiness of God is vanity! Nothing, believe me, on earth; nothing brought from perdition, can keep back this destined advance of the Negro race. No conspiracies of men nor of devils! The slave trade could not crush them out. Slavery, dread, direful, and malignant, could only stay it for a time. But now it is coming, coming, I grant, through dark and trying events, but surely coming. The Negro—black, curly-headed, despised, repulsed, sneered at—is, nevertheless, a vital being, and irrepressible. Everywhere on earth has been given him, by the Almighty, assurance, self-assertion, and influence. The rise of two Negro States within a century, feeble though they be, has a bearing upon this subject. The numerous emancipations, which now leave not more than a chain or two to be unfastened, have, likewise, a deep, moral significance. Thus, too, the rise in the world of illustrious Negroes, as Touissant [Toussaint] L'Ouverture, Henry Christopher, Benjamin Banneker, Eustace the Philanthropist, Stephen Allan Benson, and Bishop Crowther.

With all these providential indications in our favor, let us bless God and take courage. Casting aside everything trifling and frivolous, let us lay hold of every element of power, in the brain; in literature, art, and science; in industrial pursuits; in the soil; in cooperative association; in mechanical ingenuity; and above all, in the religion of our God; and so march on in the pathway of progress to that superiority and eminence which is our rightful heritage, and which is evidently the promise of our God!

### NOTES

*Sermon source:* Alexander Crummell, *The Greatness of Christ and Other Sermons* (New York: Thomas Whittaker Publishing, 1882), 332–52.

1. Philip S. Foner and Robert James Branham, eds., *Lift Every Voice: African American Oratory 1787–1900* (Tuscaloosa: University of Alabama Press, 1998), 589.
2. Richard C. Trench (1807–1886) was the Archbishop of Dublin.
3. "Funeral marches to the grave" reportedly refers to Hawaiian newspapers of 1866 that report the problem of leprosy in Hawaii on the Sandwich Islands. For more on this quote and the subject matter see William Tebb, *Leprosy and Vaccination* (London: Swan Sonnenschein and Company, 1893).
4. William E. Channing (1780–1842) published the book *Emancipation* in 1840. Alexander Kinmont (1799–1838) wrote *Twelve Lectures on the Natural History of Man and the Rise of and Progress of Philosophy* (Cincinnati: U.P. James, 1839). Alexander Raleigh (1817–1880) was a Congregationalist minister lauded for his pulpit oratory. He published numerous books; most contained his sermons.

### BIBLIOGRAPHICAL SOURCES

Crummell, Alexander. *Civilization and Black Progress: Selected Writings of Alexander Crummell on the South*, ed. J.R. Oldfield. Charlottesville: University of Virginia Press, 1995.

———. *Destiny and Race: Selected Writings, 1840–1898,* ed. Wilson Jeremiah Moses. Amherst: University of Massachusetts Press, 1992.

———. *The Future of Africa: Being addresses, sermons . . . Delivered in the Republic of Liberia.* New York: Charles Scribner and Sons, 1863.

———. *Jubilate: The Shades and the Lights of a Fifty Years' Ministry.* Washington, DC: R.L. Pendleton Printer, 1894.

Rigsby, Gregory U. *Alexander Crummell: Pioneer in Nineteenth-Century Pan African Thought (Contributions in Afro-American and African Studies).* Westport, CT: Greenwood Press, 1987.

Scruggs, Otey M. *We the Children of Africa in This Land.* Washington, DC: Howard University Department of History, 1972.

## FREDERICK DOUGLASS

*(1818–1895)*

Much has been made of whether Frederick Douglass, best known as the ultimate fiery abolitionist, was a preacher. He is included in this anthology because the record clearly indicates that he was. Douglass also merits inclusion in this anthology as an early exemplar of a black preacher whose pulpit was the world. Born in 1818, he was given the name Frederick Augustus Washington Bailey in Tuckahoe, Talbot County, Maryland. His mother, Harriet Bailey, was a slave, and died in 1826; his father was a white man and rumored to be his master. Douglass was principally reared by his grandmother. He had three older siblings (Perry, Sarah, and Eliza) and two younger siblings (Kitty and Arianna).

Douglass was taught to read in a limited way by Sophia Auld, the wife of one of his owners, Hugh Auld, and by white playmates. At thirteen, Douglass writes in *My Bondage and My Freedom* (1855), he copied from the Bible, a Methodist hymnbook, a speller, and other books that he had accumulated. At that time he was told by Father Lawson, an older black man to whom he was "deeply attached" that he "must preach the gospel."[1] Douglass became a Sunday school teacher and had fond memories of the experience years later. By 1838 he had escaped slavery and in the same year married Anna Murray. The following year they had a daughter, Rosetta. They would eventually have another daughter (Annie) and three sons (Lewis, Frederick, and Charles).

After Douglass escaped, he and Anna traveled to New Bedford, Massachusetts, where they stayed in the home of the well-to-do black family of Nathan Johnson. To go along with his new life, Frederick decided to change his name so as to make it more difficult for slave catchers to trace him. Nathan Johnson was at the time reading *The Lady of the Lake*, a novel by Scottish author Sir Walter Scott, and he suggested that Frederick name himself after a character in the book. Frederick Bailey thus became Frederick Douglass.

He joined a group of black Methodists known as the Zion Methodists and was made a class leader and then local preacher. This public speaking experience helped prepare him for all of the stages and all of the groups he would address over the years. In "Frederick Douglass, Preacher," William Andrews points out that African Methodist Episcopal Zion (AMEZ) bishop James Walker Hood, the earliest AMEZ historian, gained from Douglass in 1894 a letter in which Douglass talked about having worked with the AMEZ church in New Bedford. The letter is published in Hood's *One Hundred Years of the African Methodist Episcopal Zion Church*. The letter says in part:

> It is impossible for me to tell how far my connection with these devoted men (Reverend William Serrington, Reverend Peter Ross, Reverend Jehill Beman, Dempsy Kennedy, John P. Thomson, Leven Smith and Bishop Christopher Rush) influenced my career. As early as 1839 I obtained a license from the Quarterly Conference

as a local preacher, and often occupied the pulpit by request of the preacher in charge.[2]

Douglass began to preach at anti-slavery meetings in 1840 and was hired by the Massachusetts Anti-Slavery Society. By 1845, Douglass had built a reputation as a stout abolitionist and published *Narrative of the Life of Frederick Douglass*. While touring in Great Britain and Ireland and speaking on slavery with abolitionist William Lloyd Garrison, friends helped raise money to purchase Douglass's freedom from Hugh Auld in 1846 for $710.96. In 1847, Douglass began publishing the weekly abolition newspaper *The North Star* and continued it until 1851.

By 1855, Douglass had published his second autobiography, *My Bondage and My Freedom*. He continued to publish antislavery papers and journals. Following the legal end of slavery and the death of Abraham Lincoln, Douglass continued to work for equal rights for blacks. In 1877 he was appointed U.S. Marshal of the District of Columbia by President Hayes. He published his third and final autobiography, *The Life and Times of Frederick Douglass*, in 1881. Anna, his wife of forty-four years, died in 1882, and in January 1884 he married Helen Pitts, a white woman who had been his secretary. Douglass was made the consul general to the Republic of Haiti in 1889. On February 20, 1895, at age seventy-seven, Frederick Douglass died of heart failure.

• • •

*In this now-famous message, Douglass, as did many black preachers of his day, exegetes scriptures to make plain the evils of slavery and shame those who used the Bible as their authority for the practice. He makes clear his theological and historical acumen, as well as furiously attacks American republicanism.*

## What, to the Slave, is the Fourth of July? (July 5, 1852)

Friends and Fellow citizens: He who could address this audience without a quailing sensation, has stronger nerves than I have. I do not remember ever to have appeared as a speaker before any assembly more shrinkingly, nor with greater distrust of my ability, than I do this day. A feeling has crept over me, quite unfavorable to the exercise of my limited powers of speech. The task before me is one which requires much previous thought and study for its proper performance. I know that apologies of this sort are generally considered flat and unmeaning. I trust, however, that mine will not be so considered. Should I seem at ease, my appearance would much misrepresent me. The little experience I have had in addressing public meetings, in country schoolhouses, avails me nothing on the present occasion.

The papers and placards say, that I am to deliver a Fourth of July oration. This certainly sounds large, and out of the common way, for it is true that I have often had the privilege to speak in this beautiful Hall, and to address many who now honor me with their presence. But neither their familiar faces, nor the perfect gage I think I have of Corinthian Hall, seems to free me from embarrassment.

The fact is, ladies and gentlemen, the distance between this platform and the slave plantation, from which I escaped, is considerable—and the difficulties to be overcome in getting from the latter to the former, are by no means slight. That I am here to-day is, to me, a matter of astonishment as well as of gratitude. You will not, therefore, be surprised, if in what I have to say I evince no elaborate preparation, nor grace my speech with any high sounding exordium. With little experience and with less learning, I have been able to throw my thoughts hastily and imperfectly together; and trusting to your patient and generous indulgence, I will proceed to lay them before you.

This, for the purpose of this celebration, is the Fourth of July. It is the birthday of your National Independence, and of your political freedom. This, to you, is what the Passover was to the emancipated people of God. It carries your minds back to the day, and to the act of your great deliverance; and to the signs, and to the wonders, associated with that act, and that day. This celebration also marks the beginning of another year of your national life; and reminds you that the Republic of America is now seventy-six years old. I am glad, fellow-citizens, that your nation is so young. Seventy-six years, though a good old age for a man, is but a mere speck in the life of a nation. Three score years and ten is the allotted time for individual men; but nations number their years by thousands.

According to this fact, you are, even now, only in the beginning of your national career, still lingering in the period of childhood. I repeat, I am glad this is so. There is hope in the thought, and hope is much needed, under the dark clouds which lower above the horizon. The eye of the reformer is met with angry flashes, portending disastrous times; but his heart may well beat lighter at the thought that America is young, and that she is still in the impressible stage of her existence. May he not hope that high lessons of wisdom, of justice and of truth, will yet give direction to her destiny? Were the nation older, the patriot's heart might be sadder, and the reformer's brow heavier. Its future might be shrouded in gloom, and the hope of its prophets go out in sorrow. There is consolation in the thought that America is young. Great streams are not easily turned from channels, worn deep in the course of ages. They may sometimes rise in quiet and stately majesty, and inundate the land, refreshing and fertilizing the earth with their mysterious properties. They may also rise in wrath and fury, and bear away, on their angry waves, the accumulated wealth of years of toil and hardship. They, however, gradually flow back to the same old channel, and flow on as serenely as ever. But, while the river may not be turned aside, it may dry up, and leave nothing behind but the withered branch, and the unsightly rock, to howl in the abyss-sweeping wind, the sad tale of departed glory. As with rivers so with nations.

Fellow citizens, I shall not presume to dwell at length on the associations that cluster about this day. The simple story of it is that, seventy-six years ago, the people of this country were British subjects. The style and title of your "sovereign people" (in which you now glory) was not then born. You were under the British Crown. Your fathers esteemed the English Government as the home government; and England as the fatherland. This home government, you know, although a considerable distance from your home, did, in the exercise of its parental prerogatives, impose upon its colonial children, such restraints, burdens and limitations, as, in its mature judgment, it deemed wise, right and proper.

But, your fathers, who had not adopted the fashionable idea of this day, of the infallibility of government, and the absolute character of its acts, presumed to differ from the home government in respect to the wisdom and the justice of some of those burdens and restraints. They went so far in their excitement as to pronounce the measures of government unjust, unreasonable, and oppressive, and altogether such as ought not to be quietly submitted to. I scarcely need say, fellow-citizens, that my opinion of those measures fully accords with that of your fathers. Such a declaration of agreement on my part would not be worth much to anybody. It would, certainly, prove nothing, as to what part I might have taken, had I lived during the great controversy of 1776. To say now that America was right, and England wrong, is exceedingly easy. Everybody can say it; the dastard, not less than the noble brave, can flippantly discant on the tyranny of England towards the American Colonies. It is fashionable to do so; but there was a time when to pronounce against England, and in favor of the cause of the colonies, tried men's souls. They who did so were accounted in their day plotters of mischief, agitators and rebels, dangerous men. To side with the right against the wrong, with the weak against the strong, and with the oppressed against the oppressor! here lies the merit, and the one which, of all others, seems unfashionable in our day. The cause of liberty may be stabbed by the men who glory in the deeds of your fathers. But, to proceed.

Feeling themselves harshly and unjustly treated by the home government, your fathers, like men of honesty, and men of spirit, earnestly sought redress. They petitioned and remonstrated; they did so in a decorous, respectful, and loyal manner. Their conduct was wholly unexceptionable. This, however, did not answer the purpose. They saw themselves treated with sovereign indifference, coldness and scorn. Yet they persevered. They were not men to look back.

As the sheet anchor takes a firmer hold, when the ship is tossed by the storm, so did the cause of your fathers grow stronger, as it breasted the chilling blasts of kingly displeasure. The greatest and best of British statesmen admitted its justice, and the loftiest eloquence of the British Senate came to its support. But, with that blindness which seems to be the unvarying characteristic of tyrants, since Pharaoh and his hosts were drowned in the Red Sea, the British Government persisted in the exactions complained of.

The madness of this course, we believe, is admitted now, even by England; but we fear the lesson is wholly lost on our present ruler.

Oppression makes a wise man mad. Your fathers were wise men, and if they did not go mad, they became restive under this treatment. They felt themselves the victims of grievous wrongs, wholly incurable in their colonial capacity. With brave men there is always a remedy for oppression. Just here, the idea of a total separation of the colonies from the crown was born! It was a startling idea, much more so, than we, at this distance of time, regard it. The timid and the prudent (as has been intimated) of that day, were, of course, shocked and alarmed by it.

Such people lived then, had lived before, and will, probably, ever have a place on this planet; and their course, in respect to any great change (no matter how great the good to be attained, or the wrong to be redressed by it), may be calculated with as much precision as can be the course of the stars. They hate all changes, but silver, gold and copper change! Of this sort of change they are always strongly in favor.

These people were called Tories in the days of your fathers; and the appellation, probably, conveyed the same idea that is meant by a more modern, though a somewhat less euphonious term, which we often find in our papers, applied to some of our old politicians.

Their opposition to the then dangerous thought was earnest and powerful; but, amid all their terror and affrighted vociferations against it, the alarming and revolutionary idea moved on, and the country with it.

On the 2nd of July, 1776, the old Continental Congress, to the dismay of the lovers of ease, and the worshipers of property, clothed that dreadful idea with all the authority of national sanction. They did so in the form of a resolution; and as we seldom hit upon resolutions, drawn up in our day whose transparency is at all equal to this, it may refresh your minds and help my story if I read it.

> [We] solemnly publish and declare, That these united colonies are, and of right, ought to be free and Independent States; that they are absolved from all allegiance to the British Crown; and that all political connection between them and the State of Great Britain is, and ought to be, dissolved.

Citizens, your fathers made good that resolution. They succeeded; and to-day you reap the fruits of their success. The freedom gained is yours; and you, therefore, may properly celebrate this anniversary. The Fourth of July is the first great fact in your nation's history—the very ring-bolt in the chain of your yet undeveloped destiny.

Pride and patriotism, not less than gratitude, prompt you to celebrate and to hold it in perpetual remembrance. I have said that the Declaration of Independence is the ring-bolt to the chain of your nation's destiny; so, indeed, I regard it. The principles contained in that instrument are saving principles. Stand by those principles, be true to them on all occasions, in all places, against all foes, and at whatever cost.

From the round top of your ship of state, dark and threatening clouds may be seen. Heavy billows, like mountains in the distance, disclose to the leeward huge forms of flinty rocks! That bolt drawn, that chain broken, and all is lost. Cling to this day—cling to it, and to its principles, with the grasp of a storm-tossed mariner to a spar at midnight.

The coming into being of a nation, in any circumstances, is an interesting event. But, besides general considerations, there were peculiar circumstances which make the advent of this republic an event of special attractiveness.

The whole scene, as I look back to it, was simple, dignified and sublime. The population of the country, at the time, stood at the insignificant number of three millions. The country was poor in the munitions of war. The population was weak and scattered, and the country a wilderness unsubdued. There were then no means of concert and combination, such as exist now. Neither steam nor lightning had then been reduced to order and discipline. From the Potomac to the Delaware was a journey of many days. Under these, and innumerable other disadvantages, your fathers declared for liberty and independence and triumphed.

Fellow citizens, I am not wanting in respect for the fathers of this republic. The signers of the Declaration of Independence were brave men. They were great men, too—great enough to give fame to a great age. It does not often happen to a nation to raise, at one time, such a number of truly great men. The point from which I am compelled to view them is not, certainly, the most favorable; and yet I cannot contemplate their great deeds with less than admiration. They were statesmen, patriots and heroes, and for the good they did, and the principles they contended for, I will unite with you to honor their memory.

They loved their country better than their own private interests; and, though this is not the highest form of human excellence, all will concede that it is a rare virtue, and that when it is exhibited, it ought to command respect. He who will, intelligently, lay down his life for his country, is a man whom it is not in human nature to despise. Your fathers staked their lives, their fortunes, and their sacred honor, on the cause of their country. In their admiration of liberty, they lost sight of all other interests.

They were peace men; but they preferred revolution to peaceful submission to bondage. They were quiet men; but they did not shrink from agitating against oppression. They showed forbearance; but that they knew its limits. They believed in order; but not in the order of tyranny. With them, nothing was "settled" that was not right. With them, justice, liberty and humanity were "final," not slavery and oppression. You may well cherish the memory of such men. They were great in their day and generation. Their solid manhood stands out the more as we contrast it with these degenerate times.

How circumspect, exact and proportionate were all their movements! How unlike the politicians of an hour! Their statesmanship looked beyond the passing moment, and stretched away in strength into the distant future. They seized upon eternal principles, and set a glorious example in their defense. Mark them!

Fully appreciating the hardship to be encountered, firmly believing in the right of their cause, honorably inviting the scrutiny of an on-looking world, reverently appealing to heaven to attest their sincerity, soundly comprehending the solemn responsibility they were about to assume, wisely measuring the terrible odds against them, your fathers, the fathers of this republic, did, most deliberately, under the inspiration of a glorious patriotism, and with a sublime faith in the great principles of justice and freedom, lay deep the corner-stone of the national superstructure, which has risen and still rises in grandeur around you.

Of this fundamental work, this day is the anniversary. Our eyes are met with demonstrations of joyous enthusiasm. Banners and pennants wave exultingly on the breeze. The din of business, too, is hushed. Even mammon seems to have quieted his grasp on this day. The ear-piercing fife and the stirring drum unite their accents with the ascending peal of a thousand church bells. Prayers are made, hymns are sung, and sermons are preached in honor of this day; while the quick martial tramp of a great and multitudinous nation, echoed back by all the hills, valleys and mountains of a vast continent, bespeak the occasion one of thrilling and universal interests nation's jubilee.

Friends and citizens, I need not enter further into the causes which led to this anniversary. Many of you understand them better than I do. You could instruct me in regard to them. That is a branch of knowledge in which you feel, perhaps, a much deeper interest than your speaker. The causes which led to the separation of the colonies from the British crown have never lacked for a tongue. They have all been taught in your common schools, narrated at your firesides, unfolded from your pulpits, and thundered from your legislative halls, and are as familiar to you as household words. They form the staple of your national poetry and eloquence.

I remember, also, that, as a people, Americans are remarkably familiar with all facts which make in their own favor. This is esteemed by some as a national trait—perhaps a national weakness. It is a fact, that whatever makes for the wealth or for the reputation of Americans, and can be had cheap will be found by Americans. I shall not be charged with slandering Americans, if I say I think the American side of any question may be safely left in American hands.

I leave, therefore, the great deeds of your fathers to other gentlemen whose claim to have been regularly descended will be less likely to be disputed than mine! My business, if I have any here to-day, is with the present. The accepted time with God and his cause is the ever-living now.

*Trust no future, however pleasant,*
*Let the dead past bury its dead;*
*Act, act in the living present,*
*Heart within, and God overhead.*[3]

We have to do with the past only as we can make it useful to the present and to the future. To all inspiring motives, to noble deeds which can be gained from the past, we are welcome. But now is the time, the important time. Your fathers have lived, died, and have done their work, and have done much of it well. You live and must die, and you must do your work. You have no right to enjoy a child's share in the labor of your fathers, unless your children are to be blest by your labors. You have no right to wear out and waste the hard-earned fame of your fathers to cover your indolence. Sydney Smith tells us that men seldom eulogize the wisdom and virtues of their fathers, but to excuse some folly or wickedness of their own. This truth is not a doubtful one. There are illustrations of it near and remote, ancient and modern. It was fashionable, hundreds of years ago, for the children of Jacob to boast, we have "Abraham to our father," when they had long lost Abraham's faith and spirit. That people contented themselves under the shadow of Abraham's great name, while they repudiated the deeds which made his name great. Need I remind you that a similar thing is being done all over this country to-day? Need I tell you that the Jews are not the only people who built the tombs of the prophets, and garnished the sepulchres of the righteous? Washington could not die till he had broken the chains of his slaves. Yet his monument is built up by the price of human blood, and the traders in the bodies and souls of men, shout—"We have Washington to our father."—Alas! that it should be so; yet so it is.

*The evil that men do, lives after them,*
*The good is oft interred with their bones.*[4]

Fellow citizens, pardon me, allow me to ask, why am I called upon to speak here to-day? What have I, or those I represent, to do with your national independence? Are the great principles of political freedom and of natural justice, embodied in that Declaration of Independence, extended to us? and am I, therefore, called upon to bring our humble offering to the national altar, and to confess the benefits and express devout gratitude for the blessings resulting from your independence to us?

Would to God, both for your sakes and ours, that an affirmative answer could be truthfully returned to these questions! Then would my task be light and my burden easy and delightful. For who is there so cold, that a nation's sympathy could not warm him? Who so obdurate and dead to the claims of gratitude that would not thankfully acknowledge such priceless benefits? Who so stolid and selfish, that would not give his voice to swell the hallelujahs of a nation's jubilee, when the chains of servitude had been torn from his limbs? I am not that man. In a case like that, the dumb might eloquently speak, and the "lame man leap as an hart."

But, such is not the state of the case. I say it with a sad sense of the disparity between us. I am not included within the pale of this glorious anniversary! Your high independence only reveals the immeasurable distance between us. The blessings in which you, this day, rejoice, are not enjoyed in common. The rich inheritance of justice, liberty, prosperity and independence, bequeathed by your fathers, is shared by you, not by me. The sunlight that brought life and healing to you, has brought stripes and death to me. This Fourth of July is yours, not mine. You may rejoice, I must mourn. To drag a man in fetters into the grand illuminated temple of liberty, and call upon him to join you in joyous anthems, were inhuman mockery and sacrilegious irony. Do you mean, citizens, to mock me, by asking me to speak today? If so, there is a parallel to your conduct. And let me warn you that it is dangerous to copy the example of a nation whose crimes, lowering up to heaven, were thrown down by the breath of the Almighty, burying that nation in irrecoverable ruin! I can to-day take up the plaintive lament of a peeled and woe-smitten people!

> By the rivers of Babylon, there we sat down. Yea! we wept when we remembered Zion. We hanged our harps upon the willows in the midst thereof. For there, they that carried us away captive, required of us a song; and they who wasted us required of us mirth, saying, Sing us one of the songs of Zion. How can we sing the Lord's song in a strange land? If I forget thee, O Jerusalem, let my right hand forget her cunning. If I do not remember thee, let my tongue cleave to the roof of my mouth.[5]

Fellow citizens, above your national, tumultuous joy, I hear the mournful wail of millions! whose chains, heavy and grievous yesterday, are, to-day, rendered more intolerable by the jubilee shouts that reach them. If I do forget, if I do not faithfully remember those bleeding children of sorrow this day, "may my right hand forget her cunning, and may my tongue cleave to the roof of my mouth!" To forget them, to pass lightly over their wrongs, and to chime in with the popular theme, would be treason most scandalous and shocking, and would make me a reproach before God and the world. My subject, then fellow citizens, is American slavery. I shall see this day and its popular characteristics, from the slave's point of view. Standing, there, identified with the American bondman, making his wrongs mine, I do not hesitate to declare, with all my soul, that the character and conduct of this nation never looked blacker to me than on this Fourth of July! Whether we turn to the declarations of the past, or to the professions of the present, the conduct of the nation seems equally hideous and revolting. America is false to the past, false to the present, and solemnly binds herself to be false to the future. Standing with God and the crushed and bleeding slave on this occasion, I will, in the name of humanity which is outraged, in the name of liberty which is fettered, in the name of the Constitution and the Bible, which are disregarded and trampled upon, dare to call in question and to denounce, with all the emphasis I can command, everything that serves to perpetuate slavery—the great sin and shame of America! "I will not equivocate; I will not excuse;"[6] I will use the severest language I can command; and yet not one word shall escape me that any man, whose judgment is not blinded by prejudice, or who is not at heart a slaveholder, shall not confess to be right and just.

But I fancy I hear some one of my audience say, "It is just in this circumstance that you and your brother abolitionists fail to make a favorable impression on the public mind. Would you argue more, and denounce less, would you persuade more, and rebuke less, your cause would be much more likely to succeed." But, I submit, where all is plain there is nothing to be argued. What point in the antislavery creed would you have me argue? On what branch of the subject do the people of this country need light? Must I undertake to prove that the slave is a man? That point is conceded already. Nobody doubts it. The slaveholders themselves acknowledge it in the enactment of laws for their government. They acknowledge it when they punish disobedience on the part of the slave. There are seventy-two crimes in the State of Virginia, which, if committed by a black man, (no matter how ignorant he be), subject him to the punishment of death; while only two of the same crimes will subject a white man to the like punishment. What is this but the acknowledgement that the slave is a moral, intellectual and responsible being? The manhood of the slave is conceded. It is admitted in the fact that Southern statute books are covered with enactments forbidding, under severe fines and penalties, the teaching of the slave to read or to write. When you can point to any such laws, in reference to the beasts of the field, then I may consent to argue the manhood of the slave. When the dogs in your streets, when the fowls of the air, when the cattle on your hills, when the fish of the sea, and the reptiles that crawl, shall be unable to distinguish the slave from a brute, then will I argue with you that the slave is a man!

For the present, it is enough to affirm the equal manhood of the Negro race. Is it not astonishing that, while we are ploughing, planting and reaping, using all kinds of mechanical tools, erecting houses, constructing bridges, building ships, working in metals of brass, iron, copper, silver and gold; that, while we are reading, writing and ciphering, acting as clerks, merchants and secretaries, having among us lawyers, doctors, ministers, poets, authors, editors, orators and teachers; that, while we are engaged in all manner of enterprises common to other men, digging gold in California, capturing the whale in the Pacific, feeding sheep and cattle on the hill-side, living, moving, acting, thinking, planning, living in families as husbands, wives and children, and, above all, confessing and worshipping the Christians' God, and looking hopefully for life and immortality beyond the grave, we are called upon to prove that we are men!

Would you have me argue that man is entitled to liberty? that he is the rightful owner of his own body? You have already declared it. Must I argue the wrongfulness of slavery? Is that a question for republicans? Is it to be settled by the rules of logic and argumentation, as a matter beset with great difficulty, involving a doubtful application of the principle of justice, hard to be understood? How should I look to-day, in the presence of Americans, dividing, and subdividing a discourse, to show that men have a natural right to freedom, speaking of it relatively, and positively, negatively, and affirmatively? To do so, would be to make myself ridiculous and to offer an insult to your understanding. There is not a man beneath the canopy of heaven that does not know that slavery is wrong for him.

What, am I to argue that it is wrong to make men brutes, to rob them of their liberty, to work them without wages, to keep them ignorant of their relations to their fellow men, to beat them with sticks, to flay their flesh with the lash, to load their limbs with irons, to hunt them with dogs, to sell them at auction, to sunder their families, to knock out their teeth, to burn their flesh, to starve them into obedience and submission to their masters? Must I argue that a system thus marked with blood, and stained with pollution, is wrong? No! I will not. I have better employments for my time and strength than such arguments would imply.

What, then, remains to be argued? Is it that slavery is not divine; that God did not establish it; that our doctors of divinity are mistaken? There is blasphemy in the thought. That which is inhuman, cannot be divine! Who can reason on such a proposition? They that can, may; I cannot. The time for such argument is past.

At a time like this, scorching irony, not convincing argument, is needed. O! had I the ability, and could I reach the nation's ear, I would, to-day, pour out a fiery stream of biting ridicule, blasting reproach, withering sarcasm, and stern rebuke. For it is not light that is needed, but fire; it is not the gentle shower, but thunder. We need the storm, the whirlwind, and the earthquake. The feeling of the nation must be quickened; the conscience of the nation must be roused; the propriety of the nation must be startled; the hypocrisy of the nation must be exposed; and its crimes against God and man must be proclaimed and denounced.

What, to the American slave, is your Fourth of July? I answer: a day that reveals to him, more than all other days in the year, the gross injustice and cruelty to which he is the constant victim. To him, your celebration is a sham; your boasted liberty, an unholy license; your national greatness, swelling vanity; your sounds of rejoicing are empty and heartless; your denunciations of tyrants, brass fronted impudence; your shouts of liberty and equality, hollow mockery; your prayers and hymns, your sermons and thanksgivings, with all your religious parade, and solemnity, are, to him, mere bombast, fraud, deception, impiety, and hypocrisy—a thin veil to cover up crimes which would disgrace a nation of savages. There is not a nation on the earth guilty of practices, more shocking and bloody, than are the people of these United States, at this very hour.

Go where you may, search where you will, roam through all the monarchies and despotisms of the Old World, travel through South America, search out every abuse, and when you have found the last, lay your facts by the side of the everyday practices of this nation, and you will say with me, that, for revolting barbarity and shameless hypocrisy, America reigns without a rival.

Take the American slave trade, which, we are told by the papers, is especially prosperous just now. Ex-Senator Benton tells us that the price of men was never higher than now. He mentions the fact to show that slavery is in no danger. This trade is one of the peculiarities of American institutions. It is carried on in all the large towns and cities in one-half of this confederacy; and millions are pocketed every year, by dealers in this horrid traffic. In several states, this trade is a chief source of wealth. It is called (in contradistinction to the foreign slave trade) "the internal *slave trade*." It is, probably, called so, too, in order to divert from it the horror with which the foreign slave trade is contemplated. That trade has long since been denounced by this government, as piracy. It has been denounced with burning words, from the high places of the nation, as an execrable traffic. To arrest it, to put an end to it, this nation keeps a squadron, at immense cost, on the coast of Africa. Everywhere, in this country, it is safe to speak of this foreign slave trade, as a most inhuman traffic, opposed alike to the laws of God and of man. The duty to extirpate and destroy it, is admitted even by our doctors of divinity. In order to put an end to it, some of these last have consented that their colored brethren (nominally free) should leave this country, and establish themselves on the western coast of Africa! It is, however, a notable fact that, while so much execration is poured out by Americans upon those engaged in the foreign slave trade, the men engaged in the slave trade between the states pass without condemnation, and their business is deemed honorable.

Behold the practical operation of this internal slave trade, the American slave trade, sustained by American politics and America religion. Here you will see men and women reared like swine for the market. You know what is a swine-drover? I will show you a man-drover. They inhabit all our Southern States. They perambulate the country, and crowd the highways of the nation, with droves of human stock. You will see one of these human flesh-jobbers, armed with pistol, whip and bowie-knife, driving a company of a hundred men, women, and children, from the Potomac to the slave market at New Orleans. These wretched people are to be sold singly, or in lots, to suit purchasers. They are food for the cotton-field, and the deadly sugar-mill. Mark the sad procession, as it moves wearily along, and the inhuman wretch who drives them. Hear his savage yells and his blood-chilling oaths, as he hurries on his affrighted captives! There, see the old man, with locks thinned and gray. Cast one glance, if you please, upon that young mother, whose shoulders are bare to the scorching sun, her briny tears falling on the brow of the babe in her arms. See, too, that girl of thirteen, weeping, yes! weeping, as she thinks of the mother from whom she has been torn! The drove moves tardily. Heat and sorrow have nearly consumed their strength; suddenly you hear a quick snap, like the discharge of a rifle; the fetters clank, and the chain rattles simultaneously; your ears are saluted with a scream, that seems to have torn its way to the center of your soul! The crack you heard, was the sound of the slave whip; the scream you heard, was from the woman you saw with the babe. Her speed had faltered under the weight of her child and her chains! that gash on her shoulder tells her to move on. Follow the drove to New Orleans. Attend the auction; see men examined like horses; see the forms of women rudely and brutally exposed to the shocking gaze of American slave buyers. See this drove sold and separated forever; and never forget the deep, sad sobs that arose from that scattered multitude. Tell me citizens, where, under the sun, you can witness a spectacle more fiendish and shocking. Yet this is but a glance at the American slave trade, as it exists, at this moment, in the ruling part of the United States.

I was born amid such sights and scenes. To me the American slave trade is a terrible reality. When a child, my soul was often pierced with a sense of its horrors. I lived on Philpot Street, Fell's Point, Baltimore, and have watched from the wharves, the slave ships in the Basin, anchored from the shore, with their cargoes of human flesh, waiting for favorable winds to waft them down the Chesapeake. There was, at that time, a grand slave mart kept at the head of Pratt Street, by Austin Woldfolk.

His agents were sent into every town and county in Maryland, announcing their arrival, through the papers, and on flaming handbills, headed "Cash for Negroes." These men were generally well dressed men, and very captivating in their manners. Ever ready to drink, to treat, and to gamble. The fate of many a slave has depended upon the turn of a single card; and many a child has been snatched from the arms of its mother by bargains arranged in a state of brutal drunkenness.

The flesh-mongers gather up their victims by dozens, and drive them, chained, to the general depot at Baltimore. When a sufficient number have been collected here, a ship is chartered, for the purpose of conveying the forlorn crew to Mobile, or to New Orleans. From the slave prison to the ship, they are usually driven in the darkness of night; for since the antislavery agitation, a certain caution is observed.

In the deep still darkness of midnight, I have been often aroused by the dead heavy footsteps, and the piteous cries of the chained gangs that passed our door. The anguish of my boyish heart was intense; and I was often consoled, when speaking to my mistress in the morning, to hear her say that the custom was very wicked; that she hated to hear the rattle of the chains, and the heart-rending cries. I was glad to find one who sympathized with me in my horror.

Fellow citizens, this murderous traffic is today in active operation in this boasted republic. In the solitude of my spirit, I see clouds of dust raised on the highways of the South; I see the bleeding footsteps; I hear the doleful wail of fettered humanity, on the way to the slave markets, where the victims are to be sold like horses, sheep, and swine, knocked off to the highest bidder. There I see the tenderest ties ruthlessly broken, to gratify the lust, caprice and rapacity of the buyers and sellers of men. My soul sickens at the sight.

*Is this the land your Fathers loved,*
*The freedom which they toiled to win?*
*Is this the earth whereon they moved?*
*Are these the graves they slumber in?*[7]

But a still more inhuman, disgraceful, and scandalous state of things remains to be presented. By an act of the American Congress, not yet two years old, slavery has been nationalized in its most horrible and revolting form. By that act, Mason and Dixon's line has been obliterated; New York has become as Virginia; and the power to hold, hunt, and sell men, women, and children as slaves remains no longer a mere state institution, but is now an institution of the whole United States. The power is coextensive with the Star-Spangled Banner and American Christianity. Where these go, may also go the merciless slave hunter. Where these are, man is not sacred. He is a bird for the sportsman's gun. By that most foul and fiendish of all human decrees, the liberty and person of every man are put in peril. Your broad republican domain is hunting ground for men. Not for thieves and robbers, enemies of society, merely, but for men guilty of no crime. Your lawmakers have commanded all good citizens to engage in this hellish sport. Your President, your Secretary of State, your lords, nobles, and ecclesiastics, enforce, as a duty you owe to your free and glorious country, and to your God, that you do this accursed thing. Not fewer than forty Americans have, within the past two years, been hunted down and, without a moment's warning, hurried away in chains, and consigned to slavery and excruciating torture. Some of these have had wives and children, dependent on them for bread; but of this, no account was made. The right of the hunter to his prey stands superior to the right of marriage, and to all rights in this republic, the rights of God included! For black men there are neither law, justice, humanity, nor religion. The Fugitive Slave Law makes mercy to them a crime; and bribes the judge who tries them. An American judge gets ten dollars for every victim he consigns to slavery, and five, when he fails to do so. The oath of any two villains is sufficient, under this hell-black enactment, to send the most pious and exemplary black man into the remorseless jaws of slavery! His own testimony is nothing. He can bring no witnesses for himself. The minister of American justice is bound by the law to hear but one side; and that side, is the side of the oppressor. Let this damning fact be perpetually told. Let it be thundered around the world, that, in tyrant-killing, king-hating, people-loving, democratic, Christian America, the seats of justice are filled with judges, who hold their offices under an open and palpable bribe, and are bound, in deciding in the case of a man's liberty, hear only his accusers!

In glaring violation of justice, in shameless disregard of the forms of administering law, in cunning arrangement to entrap the defenseless, and in diabolical intent, this Fugitive Slave Law stands alone in the annals of tyrannical legislation. I doubt if there be another nation on the globe, having the brass and the baseness to put such a law on the statute-book. If any man in this assembly thinks differently from me in this matter, and feels able to disprove my statements, I will gladly confront him at any suitable time and place he may select.

I take this law to be one of the grossest infringements of Christian Liberty, and, if the churches and ministers of our country were not stupidly blind, or most wickedly indifferent, they, too, would so regard it.

At the very moment that they are thanking God for the enjoyment of civil and religious liberty, and for the right to worship God according to the dictates of their own consciences, they are utterly silent in respect to a law which robs religion of its chief significance, and makes it utterly worthless to a world lying in wickedness. Did this law concern the mint, anise and cumin, abridge the right to sing psalms, to partake of the sacrament, or to engage in any of the ceremonies of religion, it would be smitten by the thunder of a thousand pulpits. A general shout would go up from the church, demanding repeal, repeal, instant repeal! And it would go hard with that politician who presumed to solicit the votes of the people without inscribing this motto on his banner. Further, if this demand were not complied with, another Scotland would be added to the history of religious liberty, and the stern old Covenanters would be thrown into the shade. A John Knox would be seen at every church door, and heard from every pulpit, and Fillmore would have no more quarter than was shown by Knox, to the beautiful, but treacherous queen Mary of Scotland. The fact that the church of our country (with fractional exceptions) does not esteem "the Fugitive Slave Law" as a declaration of war against religious liberty, implies that that church regards religion simply as a form of worship, an empty ceremony, and not a vital principle, requiring active benevolence, justice, love and good will towards man. It esteems sacrifice above mercy; psalm-singing above right doing; solemn meetings above practical righteousness. A worship that can be conducted by persons who refuse to give shelter to the houseless, to give bread to the hungry, clothing to the naked, and who enjoin obedience to a law forbidding these acts of mercy, is a curse, not a blessing to mankind. The Bible addresses all such persons as "scribes, Pharisees, hypocrites, who pay tithe of mint, anise, and cumin, and have omitted the weightier matters of the law, judgment, mercy and faith."[8]

But the church of this country is not only indifferent to the wrongs of the slave, it actually takes sides with the oppressors. It has made itself the bulwark of American slavery, and the shield of American slave hunters. Many of its most eloquent Divines. who stand as the very lights of the church, have shamelessly given the sanction of religion and the Bible to the whole slave system. They have taught that man may, properly, be a slave; that the relation of master and slave is ordained of God; that to send back an escaped bondman to his master is clearly the duty of all the followers of the Lord Jesus Christ; and this horrible blasphemy is palmed off upon the world for Christianity.

For my part, I would say, Welcome infidelity! welcome atheism! welcome anything! in preference to the gospel, as preached by those divines!

They convert the very name of religion into an engine of tyranny, and barbarous cruelty, and serve to confirm more infidels, in this age, than all the infidel writings of Thomas Paine, Voltaire, and Bolingbroke, put together, have done! These ministers make religion a cold and flinty-hearted thing, having neither principles of right action, nor bowels of compassion. They strip the love of God of its beauty, and leave the throng of religion a huge, horrible, repulsive form. It is a religion for oppressors, tyrants, man stealers, and thugs. It is not that "pure and undefiled religion" which is from above, and which is "first pure, then peaceable, easy to be entreated, full of mercy and good fruits, without partiality, and without hypocrisy."[9] But a religion which favors the rich against the poor; which exalts the proud above the humble; which divides mankind into two classes, tyrants and slaves; which says to the man in chains, stay there; and to the oppressor, oppress on; it is a religion which may be professed and enjoyed by all the robbers and enslavers of mankind; it makes God a respecter of persons, denies his fatherhood of the race, and tramples in the dust the great truth of the brotherhood of man. All this we affirm to be true of the popular church, and the popular worship of our land and nation—a religion, a church, and a worship which, on the authority of inspired wisdom, we pronounce to be an abomination in the sight of God. In the language of Isaiah, the American church might be well addressed, "Bring no more vain oblations; incense is an abomination unto me: the new moons and Sabbaths, the calling of assemblies, I cannot away with; it is iniquity even the solemn meeting. Your new moons and your appointed feasts my soul hateth. They are a trouble to me; I am weary to bear them; and when ye spread forth your hands I will hide mine eyes from you. Yea! when ye make many prayers, I will not hear: Your hands are full of blood; cease to do evil, learn to do well; seek judgment; relieve the oppressed; judge for the fatherless; plead for the widow."[10]

The American church is guilty, when viewed in connection with what it is doing to uphold slavery; but it is superlatively guilty when viewed in connection with its ability to abolish slavery.

The sin of which it is guilty is one of omission as well as of commission. Albert Barnes but uttered what the common sense of every man at all observant of the actual state of the case will receive as truth, when he declared that "There is no power out of the church that could sustain slavery an hour, if it were not sustained in it."[11]

Let the religious press, the pulpit, the Sunday school, the conference meeting, the great ecclesiastical, missionary, Bible and tract associations of the land array their immense powers against slavery and slaveholding; and the whole system of crime and blood would be scattered to the winds;

and that they do not do this involves them in the most awful responsibility of which the mind can conceive.

In prosecuting the antislavery enterprise, we have been asked to spare the church, to spare the ministry; but how, we ask, could such a thing be done? We are met on the threshold of our efforts for the redemption of the slave, by the church and ministry of the country, in battle arrayed against us; and we are compelled to fight or flee. From what quarter, I beg to know, has proceeded a fire so deadly upon our ranks, during the last two years, as from the Northern pulpit? As the champions of oppressors, the chosen men of American theology have appeared—men honored for their so-called piety, and their real learning. The Lords of Buffalo, the Springs of New York, the Lathrops of Auburn, the Coxes and Spencers of Brooklyn, the Gannets and Sharps of Boston, the Deweys of Washington, and other great religious lights of the land have, in utter denial of the authority of Him by whom they professed to be called to the ministry, deliberately taught us, against the example of the Hebrews and against the remonstrance of the Apostles, they teach that we ought to obey man's law before the law of God.

My spirit wearies of such blasphemy; and how such men can be supported, as the "standing types and representatives of Jesus Christ" is a mystery which I leave others to penetrate. In speaking of the American church, however, let it be distinctly understood that I mean the great mass of the religious organizations of our land. There are exceptions, and I thank God that there are. Noble men may be found, scattered all over these Northern States, of whom Henry Ward Beecher of Brooklyn, Samuel J. May of Syracuse, and my esteemed friend on the platform,[12] are shining examples; and let me say further, that upon these men lies the duty to inspire our ranks with high religious faith and zeal, and to cheer us on in the great mission of the slave's redemption from his chains.

One is struck with the difference between the attitude of the American church towards the antislavery movement, and that occupied by the churches in England towards a similar movement in that country. There, the church, true to its mission of ameliorating, elevating, and improving the condition of mankind, came forward promptly, bound up the wounds of the West Indian slave, and restored him to his liberty. There, the question of emancipation was a high religious question. It was demanded, in the name of humanity, and according to the law of the living God. The Sharps, the Clarksons, the Wilberforces, the Buxtons, and Burchells and the Knibbs, were alike famous for their piety, and for their philanthropy. The antislavery movement there was not an antichurch movement, for the reason that the church took its full share in prosecuting that movement:

and the antislavery movement in this country will cease to be an anti-church movement when the church of this country shall assume a favorable instead of a hostile position towards that movement.

Americans! your republican politics, not less than your republican religion, are flagrantly inconsistent. You boast of your love of liberty, your superior civilization, and your pure Christianity, while the whole political power of the nation (as embodied in the two great political parties), is solemnly pledged to support and perpetuate the enslavement of three millions of your countrymen. You hurl your anathemas at the crowned headed tyrants of Russia and Austria, and pride yourselves on your Democratic institutions, while you yourselves consent to be the mere tools and bodyguards of the tyrants of Virginia and Carolina. You invite to your shores fugitives of oppression from abroad, honor them with banquets, greet them with ovations, cheer them, toast them, salute them, protect them, and pour out your money to them like water; but the fugitives from your own land you advertise, hunt, arrest, shoot and kill. You glory in your refinement and your universal education yet you maintain a system as barbarous and dreadful as ever stained the character of a nation—a system begun in avarice, supported in pride, and perpetuated in cruelty. You shed tears over fallen Hungary, and make the sad story of her wrongs the theme of your poets, statesmen and orators, till your gallant sons are ready to fly to arms to vindicate her cause against her oppressors; but, in regard to the ten thousand wrongs of the American slave, you would enforce the strictest silence, and would hail him as an enemy of the nation who dares to make those wrongs the subject of public discourse! You are all on fire at the mention of liberty for France or for Ireland; but are as cold as an iceberg at the thought of liberty for the enslaved of America. You discourse eloquently on the dignity of labor; yet, you sustain a system which, in its very essence, casts a stigma upon labor. You can bare your bosom to the storm of British artillery to throw off a three penny tax on tea; and yet wring the last hard-earned farthing from the grasp of the black laborers of your country. You profess to believe "that, of one blood, God made all nations of men to dwell on the face of all the earth,"[13] and hath commanded all men, everywhere to love one another; yet you notoriously hate (and glory in your hatred), all men whose skins are not colored like your own. You declare, before the world, and are understood by the world to declare, that you "hold these truths to be self-evident, that all men are created equal; and are endowed by their Creator with certain inalienable rights; and that, among these are life, liberty, and the pursuit of happiness;" and yet, you hold securely, in a bondage which, according to your own Thomas Jefferson, "is worse than ages of that which your fathers rose in rebellion to oppose," a seventh part of the inhabitants of your country.

Fellow citizens, I will not enlarge further on your national inconsistencies. The existence of slavery in this country brands your republicanism as a sham, your humanity as a base pretence, and your Christianity as a lie. It destroys your moral power abroad; it corrupts your politicians at home. It saps the foundation of religion; it makes your name a hissing, and a byword to a mocking earth. It is the antagonistic force in your government, the only thing that seriously disturbs and endangers your Union. It fetters your progress; it is the enemy of improvement, the deadly foe of education; it fosters pride; it breeds insolence; it promotes vice; it shelters crime; it is a curse to the earth that supports it; and yet, you cling to it, as if it were the sheet anchor of all your hopes. Oh! be warned! Be warned! A horrible reptile is coiled up in your nation's bosom; the venomous creature is nursing at the tender breast of your youthful republic; for the love of God, tear away, and fling from you the hideous monster, and let the weight of twenty million crush and destroy it forever!

But it is answered in reply to all this, that precisely what I have now denounced is, in fact, guaranteed and sanctioned by the Constitution of the United States; that the right to hold and to hunt slaves is a part of that Constitution framed by the illustrious Fathers of this Republic.

Then, I dare to affirm, notwithstanding all I have said before, your fathers stooped, basely stooped

*To palter with us in a double sense:*
*And keep the word of promise to the ear,*
*But break it to the heart.*[14]

And instead of being the honest men I have before declared them to be, they were the veriest imposters that ever practiced on mankind. This is the inevitable conclusion, and from it there is no escape. But I differ from those who charge this baseness on the framers of the Constitution of the United States. It is a slander upon their memory, at least, so I believe. There is not time now to argue the constitutional question at length—nor have I the ability to discuss it as it ought to be discussed. The subject has been handled with masterly power by Lysander Spooner, Esq., by William Goodell, by Samuel E. Sewall, Esq., and last, though not least, by Gerritt Smith, Esq. These gentlemen have, as I think, fully and clearly vindicated the Constitution from any design to support slavery for an hour.

Fellow citizens, there is no matter in respect to which, the people of the North have allowed themselves to be so ruinously imposed upon, as that of the proslavery character of the Constitution. In that instrument I hold there is neither warrant, license, nor sanction of the hateful thing; but, interpreted as it ought to be interpreted, the Constitution is a glorious liberty document. Read its preamble, consider its purposes. Is slavery among them? Is it at the gateway? Or is it in the temple? It is neither. While I do not intend to argue this question on the present occasion, let me ask, if it be not somewhat singular that, if the Constitution were intended to be, by its framers and adopters, a slaveholding instrument, why neither slavery, slaveholding, nor slave can anywhere be found in it. What would be thought of an instrument, drawn up, legally drawn up, for the purpose of entitling the city of Rochester to a tract of land, in which no mention of land was made? Now, there are certain rules of interpretation, for the proper understanding of all legal instruments. These rules are well established. They are plain, common-sense rules, such as you and I, and all of us, can understand and apply, without having passed years in the study of law. I scout the idea that the question of the constitutionality or unconstitutionality of slavery is not a question for the people. I hold that every American citizen has a right to form an opinion of the Constitution, and to propagate that opinion, and to use all honorable means to make his opinion the prevailing one. Without this right, the liberty of an American citizen would be as insecure as that of a Frenchman. Ex-Vice President Dallas tells us that the Constitution is an object to which no American mind can be too attentive, and no American heart too devoted. He further says, the Constitution, in its words, is plain and intelligible, and is meant for the home-bred, unsophisticated understandings of our fellow citizens. Senator Berrien tell us that the Constitution is the fundamental law, that which controls all others. The charter of our liberties, which every citizen has a personal interest in understanding thoroughly. The testimony of Senator Breese, Lewis Cass, and many others that might be named, who are everywhere esteemed as sound lawyers, so regard the Constitution. I take it, therefore, that it is not presumption in a private citizen to form an opinion of that instrument.

Now, take the Constitution according to its plain reading, and I defy the presentation of a single pro-slavery clause in it. On the other hand it will be found to contain principles and purposes, entirely hostile to the existence of slavery.

I have detained my audience entirely too long already. At some future period I will gladly avail myself of an opportunity to give this subject a full and fair discussion.

Allow me to say, in conclusion, notwithstanding the dark picture I have this day presented, of the state of the nation, I do not despair of this country. There are forces in operation, which must inevitably work the downfall of slavery. "The arm of the Lord is not shortened,"[15] and the doom of slavery is certain. I, therefore, leave off where I began, with hope. While drawing encouragement from the Declaration of Independence, the great principles it contains, and the genius of American Institutions, my spirit is also cheered by the obvious tendencies of the age. Nations do not now stand in the same relation to each other that they did ages ago. No nation can now shut itself up from the surrounding world, and trot round in the same old path of its fathers without interference. The time was when such could be done. Long established customs of hurtful character could formerly fence themselves in, and do their evil work with social impunity. Knowledge was then confined and enjoyed by the privileged few, and the multitude walked on in mental darkness. But a change has now come over the affairs of mankind. Walled cities and empires have become unfashionable. The arm of commerce has borne away the gates of the strong city. Intelligence is penetrating the darkest corners of the globe. It makes its pathway over and under the sea, as well as on the earth. Wind, steam, and lightning are its chartered agents. Oceans no longer divide, but link nations together. From Boston to London is now a holiday excursion. Space is comparatively annihilated. Thoughts expressed on one side of the Atlantic are distinctly heard on the other. The far-off and almost fabulous Pacific rolls in grandeur at our feet. The Celestial Empire, the mystery of ages, is being solved. The fiat of the Almighty, "Let there be Light," has not yet spent its force. No abuse, no outrage whether in taste, sport or avarice, can now hide itself from the all-pervading light. The iron shoe, and crippled foot of China must be seen, in contrast with nature. Africa must rise and put on her yet unwoven garment. "Ethiopia shall stretch out her hand unto God." In the fervent aspirations of William Lloyd Garrison, I say, and let every heart join in saying it:

*God speed the year of jubilee*
*The wide world o'er*
*When from their galling chains set free,*
*Th' oppress'd shall vilely bend the knee,*
*And wear the yoke of tyranny*
*Like brutes no more.*
*That year will come, and freedom's reign,*
*To man his plundered fights again*
*Restore.*

*God speed the day when human blood*
*Shall cease to flow!*
*In every clime be understood,*
*The claims of human brotherhood,*
*And each return for evil, good,*
*Not blow for blow;*
*That day will come all feuds to end.*
*And change into a faithful friend*
*Each foe.*

*God speed the hour, the glorious hour,*
*When none on earth*
*Shall exercise a lordly power,*
*Nor in a tyrant's presence cower;*
*But all to manhood's stature tower,*
*By equal birth!*
*That hour will come, to each, to all,*
*And from his prison-house, the thrall*
*Go forth.*

*Until that year, day, hour, arrive,*
*With head, and heart, and hand I'll strive,*
*To break the rod, and rend the gyve,*
*The spoiler of his prey deprive—*
*So witness Heaven!*
*And never from my chosen post,*
*Whate'er the peril or the cost,*
*Be driven.*[16]

## NOTES

*Sermon source:* Phillip S. Foner and Robert James, eds., *Lift Every Voice: African American Oratory 1787–1900* (Branham: University of Alabama Press, 1988), 246–68.

1. Frederick Douglass, *My Bondage and My Freedom* (New York: Miller, Orton and Mulligan, 1855; reprinted by New York: Dover Publishing, 1969), 168.
2. James Walker Hood, *One Hundred Years of the African Methodist Episcopal Zion Church* (New York: AME Zion Book Concern, 1895), 541.
3. Henry Wadsworth Longfellow, "A Psalm of Life."
4. Shakespeare, *Julius Caesar*, act 3, scene 2.
5. Psalm 137:1–6 (King James Version).
6. These words were used by William Lloyd Garrison in the first issue of *The Liberator*, January 1, 1831.

7. From John Greenleaf Whittier, "Stanzas for the Times."
8. Matthew 23:23 (KJV).
9. James 1:27, 3:17 (KJV).
10. Isaiah 1:13–17 (KJV).
11. Albert Barnes, *An Inquiry into the Scriptural Views of Slavery* (Philadelphia: Perkins & Purves, 1846), 383.
12. The reference here is to Rev. R.R. Raymond, an antislavery advocate.
13. Acts 17:26 (KJV).
14. Shakespeare, *Macbeth*, act 5, scene 8, lines 20–22.
15. Isaiah 59:1 (KJV).
16. William Lloyd Garrison, "The Triumph of Freedom," *The Liberator*, January 10, 1845.

### *Bibliographical Sources*

Andrews, William L., ed. *Critical Essays on Frederick Douglass.* Boston: G.K. Hall, 1991.

———. *The Oxford Frederick Douglas Reader.* New York: Oxford University Press, 1996.

Douglass, Frederick. *My Bondage and My Freedom.* New York: Miller, Orton and Mulligan, 1855; reprint New York: Dover Publishing, 1969.

Foner, Philip S., ed. *Frederick Douglass on Women's Rights.* Westport, CT: Greenwood Press, 1976.

Huggins, Nathan Irvin. *Slave and Citizen: The Life of Frederick Douglass.* Boston: Little, Brown, 1980.

Martin, Waldo E. *The Mind of Frederick Douglass.* Chapel Hill: University of North Carolina Press, 1985.

McFeely, William S. *Frederick Douglass.* New York: W. W. Norton, 1991.

Quarles, Benjamin. *Frederick Douglass.* Englewood Cliffs, NJ: Prentice-Hall, 1968.

Weiner, Eric. *The Story of Frederick Douglass: Voice of Freedom.* New York: Dell, 1992.

## JARENA LEE

*(1783–ca. 1850)*

One of the first African American women known to have preached the gospel in the thirteen colonies was Jarena Lee. Her call came in 1811, before the official formation of the African Methodist Episcopal Church in 1816. Although she was never ordained, she is now highly regarded as not only a pioneer and trailblazer for women in ministry but also a preacher of uncommon courage.

Reverend Jarena Lee, whose maiden name is not known, was born probably a free woman in Cape May, New Jersey, on February 11, 1783, to poor parents. At the age of seven, she was separated from her parents when they sent her to be a maid to the Sharp family, some sixty miles away. She remained there for fourteen years. She does not note her age when she was later taken to Philadelphia, where she moved from family to family. She was so depressed she twice attempted suicide. Her lowest period was when she lived with a Roman Catholic family; her mistress hid her Bible and gave her a novel to read instead. After this Lee moved closer to the center of Philadelphia and began to attend one of the first Methodist meetings there.

In 1804, at age twenty-one, she was profoundly moved by a Presbyterian missionary. However, she was also distraught by her new spiritual experience and again contemplated suicide. In Philadelphia she felt drawn to the meetings of Richard Allen of the African Methodist Episcopal church. She reported that "three or four weeks from that day, my soul was gloriously converted to God."[1] Yet, for four years after that she was depressed and again contemplated suicide. In 1807, Lee had a vision and perceived an urgent call to preach. When she told Bishop Allen, he told her of a woman leading cottage prayer meetings, but indicated that the Methodist Discipline made no mention of women preaching. She never fully believed the verdict of the Discipline and wrote a pointed warning against the possible evils of such denominational doings. Allen's serious obedience to the white Discipline was indeed strange, since he had been breaking ties with the white Methodists since 1787. Was Reverend Allen really being faithful to the Discipline, or was he using it to disguise a culture-bound bias against women preachers? Lee harbored a suspicion that it was the latter, but did not express it directly in public. Years later, she accepted Allen's belated recognition of her as an unordained traveling exhorter. With that she preached wherever she could, first mostly in homes, and saw people saved, many of whom had been resistant to the faith as preached by established male clergy.

In 1811, Jarena married Reverend Joseph Lee, pastor of the AME Society congregation at Snow Hill, New Jersey (now known as Lawnside), where she did not know anyone and was not able to preach as much as she desired. Six years later Joseph Lee died, and Jarena was left with one child two years old and one infant six months old.

Lee writes that eight years after her initial request to preach she renewed her request, and Allen, now a bishop, granted her permission to hold prayer meetings and preach in her home, as well as in other homes wherever she was invited. From the beginning, her ministry included many impressive experiences of spiritual power. The responses of her audiences were remarkable. Lee wrote, "the Lord scattered fire among them of his own kindling, as people mourned and cried out."[2] In addition to her meetings in homes, she also began to hold forth in schoolhouses and other public places. She drew a wide variety of people, black and white, including lawyers, doctors, and magistrates.

Given her vocal opposition to slavery, Lee was willing to risk preaching in slave states and spent considerable time in places like Maryland's eastern shore. Her travel was daring, with such trips as a sixteen-mile one-day walk to New Hope, Pennsylvania. One of her reports says, "I have traveled, in four years, sixteen hundred miles and of that I walked two hundred and eleven miles."[3] In a summary written in 1835, she writes that she had preached ninety-two sermons and traveled two thousand miles by coach and boat. As her ministry enlarged, it carried her as far north as Canada, as far west as the Northwest Territory. In light of her chronic ill health and the great expense of coach travel, her wide-ranging ministries were amazing. Her son, when grown, helped greatly with her expenses, and her impressively large network of loyal and supportive friends testify to her gifts as a preacher and spiritual leader.

Lee became known for memorable sermons. In about 1819, as she sat in Bethel Church in Philadelphia, the well-known Rev. Richard Williams stood to give a sermon based on Jonah 2:9. The subject was "Salvation is of the Lord." Lee reported, "As he proceeded to explain, he seemed to have lost the spirit; when in the same instant, I sprang, as by altogether supernatural impulse, to my feet, when I was aided from above to give an exhortation on the very text which brother Williams had taken."[4] It was Jonah's confession from the belly of the whale, which fitted her experience well, since she had fled from her call not wanting to endure the obvious persecution that women preachers of her day suffered. She was pleased by the way God's power was manifest, but she was afraid "that for this indecorum . . . I should be expelled from the church." Instead, she spoke so well and so linked the text to her life and call that Bishop Allen arose and admitted that she had requested license eight years before, and he had put her off. "But now he believed that I was as much called to that work as any of the preachers present."[5] However, he never formally ordained Jarena Lee. Scholars are not certain of the date of her death. It is only known that she died in the 1850s. She published her autobiography in 1836 and revised it in 1849.

• • •

*It is expected that at some point a preacher will provide testimony of their experience of receiving salvation and likely their experience of being called to preach. In this passage, Lee offers vivid, personal testimony of her call to preach and goes on to offer an apologetic for all women preachers. She uses Mary, the mother of Jesus, to suggest that God can use women for any purposes and has, including proclaiming the Word.*

## Receiving the Call to Preach (1833)

Between four and five years after my sanctification, on a certain time, an impressive silence fell upon me, and I stood as if someone was about to speak to me, yet I had no such thought in my heart. But to my utter surprise there seemed to sound a voice which I thought I distinctly heard, and most certainly understood, which said to me, "Go preach the Gospel!" I immediately replied aloud, "No one will believe me." Again I listened, and again the same voice seemed to say, "Preach the Gospel; I will put words in your mouth, and will turn your enemies to become your friends."

At first I supposed that Satan had spoken to me, for I had read that he could transform himself into an angel of light, for the purpose of deception. Immediately I went into a secret place, and called upon the Lord to know if he had called me to preach, and whether I was deceived or not; when there appeared to my view the form and figure of a pulpit, with a Bible lying thereon, the back of which was presented to me as plainly as if it had been a literal fact.

In consequence of this, my mind became so exercised that during the night following, I took a text and preached in my sleep. I thought there stood before me a great multitude, while I expounded to them the things of religion. So violent were my exertions, and so loud were my exclamations, that I awoke from the sound of my own voice, which also awoke the family of the house where I resided. Two days after, I went to see the preacher in charge of the African Society, who was the Rev. Richard Allen (the same before named in these pages) to tell him that I felt it my duty to preach the gospel.

But as I drew near the street in which his house was, which was in the city of Philadelphia, my courage began to fail me; so terrible did the cross appear, it seemed that I should not be able to bear it. Previous to my setting out to go to see him, so agitated was my mind that my appetite for my daily food failed me entirely. Several times on my way there, I turned back again; but as often I felt my strength again renewed, and I soon found that the nearer I approached to the house of the minister, the less was my fear. Accordingly, as soon as I came to the door, my fears subsided, the cross was removed, all things appeared pleasant—I was tranquil.

I now told him that the Lord had revealed it to me that I must preach the Gospel. He replied by asking, in what sphere I wished to move in? I said, among the Methodists. He then replied, that a Mrs. Cook, a Methodist lady, had also some time before requested the same privilege, who it was believed, had done much good in the way of exhortation, and holding prayer meetings, and who had been permitted to do so by the verbal license of the preacher in charge at the time. But as to women preaching, he said that our Discipline knew nothing at all about it—that it did not call for women preachers. This I was glad to hear, because it removed the fear of the cross—but no sooner did this feeling cross my mind, than I found that a love of souls had in a measure departed from me; that holy energy which burned within me as a fire, began to be smothered. This I soon perceived.

O how careful ought we to be, lest through our bylaws of church government and discipline, we bring into disrepute even the word of life. For as unseemly as it may appear nowadays for a woman to preach, it should be remembered that nothing is impossible with God. And why should it be thought impossible, heterodox, or improper for a woman to preach, seeing the Saviour died for the woman as well as the man? If the man may preach, because the Saviour died for him, why not the woman, seeing he died for her also? Is he not a whole Saviour, instead of a half one, as those who hold it wrong for a woman to preach, would seem to make it appear?

Did not Mary *first* preach the risen Saviour, and is not the doctrine of the resurrection the very climax of Christianity—hangs not all our hope on this, as argued by St. Paul? Then did not Mary, a woman, preach the Gospel? For she preached the resurrection of the crucified Son of God.

But some will say that Mary did not expound the Scripture, therefore she did not preach, in the proper sense of the term. To this I reply, it may be that the term *preach*, in those primitive times, did not mean exactly what it is now *made* to mean; perhaps it was a great deal more simple then, than it is now; if it were not, the unlearned fishermen could not have preached the Gospel at all, as they had no learning.

To this it may be replied by those who are determined not to believe that it is right for a woman to preach, that the disciples, though they were fishermen, and ignorant of letters too, were inspired so to do. To which I would reply, that though they were inspired, yet that inspiration did not save them from showing their ignorance of letters, and of man's wisdom; this the multitude soon found out, by listening to the remarks of the envious Jewish priests. If then, to preach the Gospel, by the gift of heaven, comes by inspiration solely, is God straitened; must he take the man exclusively? May he not, did he not, and can he not inspire a female to preach the simple story of the birth, life, death, and resurrection of our Lord, and accompany it too, with power to the sinner's heart. As for me, I am fully persuaded that the Lord called me to labour according to what I have received, in his vineyard. If he has not, how could he consistently bear testimony in favour of my poor labours, in awakening and converting sinners?

In my wanderings up and down among men, preaching according to my ability, I have frequently found families who told me that they had not for several years been to a meeting, and yet, while listening to hear what God would say by his poor colored female instrument, have believed with trembling, tears rolling down their cheeks—the signs of contrition and repentance towards God. I firmly believe that I have sown seed in the name of the Lord, which shall appear with its increase at the great day of accounts, when Christ shall come to make up his jewels.

At a certain time I was beset with the idea that soon or late I should fall from grace, and lose my soul at last. I was frequently called to the throne of grace about this matter, but found no relief; the temptation pursued me still. Being more and more afflicted with it, till at a certain time when the spirit strongly impressed it on my mind to enter into my closet, and carry my case once more to the Lord; the Lord enabled me to draw nigh to him, and to his mercy seat, at this time, in an extraordinary manner; for while I wrestled with him for the victory over this disposition to doubt whether I should persevere, there appeared a form of fire, about the size of a man's hand, as I was on my knees; at the same moment, there appeared to the eye of faith a man robed in a white garment, from the shoulders down to the feet; from him a voice proceeded, saying: "Thou shalt never return from the cross." Since that time I have never doubted, but believe that God will keep me until the day of redemption. Now I could adopt the very language of St. Paul and say that nothing could have separated my soul from the love of God, which is in Christ Jesus. From that time, 1807, until the present, 1833, I have not yet doubted the power and goodness of God to keep me from falling, through sanctification of the spirit and belief of the truth.

### NOTES

*Sermon source:* Jarena Lee, "The Life and Religious Experience of Jarena Lee, A Coloured Lady, Giving an Account of her Call to Preach the Gospel: Revised and Corrected from the Original Manuscript Written by Herself" (Philadelphia: Printed and published for the author, 1836). Microfilm at Emory University (Candler School of Theology).

1. Jarena Lee, "The Life and Religious Experience of Jarena Lee, A Coloured Lady, Giving an Account of her Call to Preach the Gospel: Revised and Corrected from the Original Manuscript, Written by Herself." Reprinted in *Sisters of the Spirit: Three Black Women's Autobiographies of the Nineteenth Century*, ed. William L. Andrews (Bloomington: Indiana University Press, 1986), 29.
2. *Sisters of the Spirit*, 46.
3. Jarena Lee, "The Life and Religious Experience of Jarena Lee, A Coloured Lady, Giving an Account of her Call to Preach the Gospel: Revised and Corrected from the Original Manuscript Written by Herself," 36.
4. *Sisters of the Spirit*, 44–45.
5. Ibid., 45.

### BIBLIOGRAPHICAL SOURCES

Andrews, William L., ed. *Sisters of the Spirit: Three Black Women's Autobiographies of the Nineteenth Century*. Bloomington: Indiana University Press, 1986.

Grammer, Elizabeth Elkin. *Some Wild Visions: Autobiographies by Itinerant Female Preachers in Nineteenth-Century America*. New York: Oxford, 2003.

Moody, Jocelyn. *Sentimental Confessions: Spiritual Narratives of Nineteenth-Century African American Women*. Athens: University of Georgia Press, 2001.

Peterson, Carla L. *Doers of the Word: African-American Women Speakers and Writers in the North (1830–1880)*. New York: Oxford University Press, 1995.

Richey, Russell E., Kenneth E. Rowe, and Jennifer Miller Schmidt. *Perspectives on American Methodism: Interpretive Essays*. Nashville, TN: Kingswood Books, 1993.

*Spiritual Narratives*. Introduction by Sue E. Houchins. New York: Oxford University Press, 1988.

## ZILPHA ELAW

*(ca. 1790–ca. 1840s)*

Zilpha Elaw's work was not sponsored or sanctioned by a denomination or a society or board. Elaw was a bold, black woman. Her visits into the slave states, in which she could have been killed or sold into bondage, to preach the gospel single her out as a heroine. She was one of a group of women preachers (the others being Jarena Lee and Sojourner Truth) who were firmly resolved to let no man hinder them, to let their voices be heard, and to let their lives be a rich legacy of spirituality and activism. All three were contemporaries; Elaw and Lee even shared the pulpit on at least one occasion.

Zilpha Elaw was born around 1790 near Philadelphia, Pennsylvania. Her mother died when she was twelve years old, after giving birth to a twenty-second child. Only Zilpha, an older brother, and a younger sister survived childhood. After her mother's death, Elaw was sent to live with Pierson and Rebecca Mitchell, a white Quaker family, until age eighteen. Her father died when she was about fourteen. While she was with the Mitchell family she experienced conversion and saw a vision of Jesus. In 1808, she joined the Methodist Episcopal Church. In 1810, she married Joseph Elaw, a fuller by trade, with whom she had a daughter, Rebecca, in 1812 in Burlington, New Jersey.

In 1817, Elaw attended the first of many camp meetings and in the course of one gave her first public prayer. She spent the next five years on "the errands and services of the Lord," attending meetings and being approached by persons and asked to pray for them. In 1819, when she was deathly ill she had a vision of future health and was directed in that vision to go to a camp meeting. About a year later she attended a camp meeting and felt the divine word telling her to preach. This followed a message from her sister, Hannah. Hannah told Zilpha that she had received a vision that told her that Zilpha was to preach. Zilpha subsequently received the approval of the Methodist Church elders, but she was still ostracized in her church community for stepping into what was thought of as a man's role. Her husband was not pleased with her preaching, but she continued. On January 27, 1823, after a decline in health, he passed away.

After her husband's death, Elaw became a domestic, as did her eleven-year-old daughter. Later she opened a school for black children in her home, which slowly grew with the help of Quaker friends. In 1827 she returned to Philadelphia to preach, arriving back in Burlington in April 1828 with enough money to pay all the debts amassed from running a school and taking care of a child as the only bread-earner. After a few days she began a preaching tour of Maryland, Washington, D.C., and the South. The power of her preaching combined with the novelty of a black woman as a public speaker made her a sensation wherever she went.

In 1830 she made her way to the northeastern states, where she continued to win over congregations and individuals, even hostile ones. She was known to criticize white Christians whose racism and immorality was hidden behind a veil of piety. She wrote: "The Almighty accounts not the black races of men either in the order of nature or spiritual capacity as inferior to the white; for He bestows his Holy Spirit on, and dwells in them as readily as in persons of whiter complexion."[1] She answered critics of women preachers by referring to biblical figures, such as Phoebe and Priscilla, and by discussing the sometimes "extraordinary directions" of the Holy Spirit. In 1837 she had a vision that confirmed a previous intimation that she would someday go to England. She sailed from New York in July 1840, and spent at least six years in Britain as an evangelist, preaching more than one thousand sermons. In 1846 she published her autobiography, *Memoirs of the Life, Religious Experience, Ministerial Travels and Labours of Mrs. Zilpha Elaw, an American Female of Colour: Together with Some Account of the Great Religious Revivals in America*. After 1846 additional information concerning Elaw is not known.

• • •

*Although Elaw preached thousands of sermons, none have survived. In this brief but extremely frank assessment of marriage between Christians and non-Christians, Elaw offers us a glimpse of her courage and her outspokenness. Although aspects of the message suggest a subservient role for women, Elaw is wise enough to also give women the type of counsel that is liberating. These words from her autobiography also provide a view into the type of preaching that Elaw likely did. Her words are straightforward, show personal transparency, are practical and filled with scripture.*

## On Christian Marriage
## (ca. 1840s)

Oh! let me affectionately warn my dear unmarried sisters in Christ, against being thus unequally yoked with unbelievers. In general your lot would be better, if a millstone were hung about your necks, and you were drowned in the depths of the sea, than that you should disobey the law of Jesus,[2] and plunge yourselves into all the sorrows, sins, and anomalies involved in a matrimonial alliance with an unbeliever. This mischief frequently emanates from the delusive sentiments in which the female portion of the Christian community is steeped. Young ladies imagine themselves their own mistresses before they are able to shift for themselves; and especially when they attain the legal maturity fixed by the civil law. Pride, consequential haughtiness, and independent arrogance in females, are the worst vices in humanity, and are denounced in Scriptures as insuring the severest retributions of God.[3]

The laws of Scripture invest parents with the trust and control of their daughter, until the time, be it early or late in life, when her father surrenders her in marriage to the care and government of her husband; then and not till then, the guardianship and government of her father over her ceases; and then formed as she is by nature for subordination, she becomes the endowment and is subject to the authority of her husband.

The boastful speeches too often vented by young females against either the paternal yoke or the government of a husband, is both indecent and impious—conveying a wanton disrespect to the regulations of Scripture: the fancied independence and self-control in which they indulge, has no foundation either in nature or Scripture, and is prolific with the worst results both to religion and society. That woman is dependent on and subject to man, is the dictate of nature; that the man is not created for the woman, but the woman for the man, is that of Scripture.[4] These principles lie at the foundation of the family and social systems, and their violation is a very immoral and guilty act. These remarks will not, I trust be out of place here. I now observe, in reference to the marriage of a Christian with an unbeliever, that there is not, there cannot be in it, that mutual sympathy and affectionate accordance which exists in marriage lives of devoted Christians, when both parties are cordially progressing on the King's highway. How discordant are the sentiments, tastes, and feelings of the Christian and unbeliever, when unequally, and I may say, wickedly allied together in the marriage state. The worldly man displays his settled aversion to the things of religion, and especially against the sincerity and tenacity with which his believing partner adheres to them; and on the other hand, the believer displays his settled abhorrence of the things of the world, to which he is crucified and dead: nor can the strength of any carnal attachment betwixt the parties, or the utmost stretch of courtesy on both sides, ever reconcile the radical opposition of their principles. If the saint winks at the worldly course pursued by his partner, he evidences the weakness of Christian principle in himself, is unfaithful to his profession, and perfidious to the King of Kings; if he reproves it, he involves the household in strife, his own soul in vexation, and perils it by wrath. Besides, the wife is destined to be the help-meet of her husband; but if he be a worldly man, she cannot, she dare not be either his instrument or abettor in worldly lusts and sinful pursuits; if he be a saint, and she a child of wrath, she is not his help-meet, but his drawback and curse; and in either case she possesses the title or name of a wife without the qualification, namely, that of a help-meet. By the Jewish law, the marriage of a Jew with a woman of a prohibited nation, was not accounted marriage, but fornication,[5] and it is a very serious impropriety also under the Christian dispensation. I am aware that when once the carnal courtship is commenced, the ensnared Christian fondly imagines that he shall soon be able to persuade his unregenerate companion to think as he does, and also to love and serve God with him; and on the other hand, the carnal suitor accounts religion as mere whimsy and pretence, and flatters himself that he shall soon divert the object of his desire from so melancholy and superstitious pursuit; and thus both of them are miserably deceived, and miss of that happiness they so fallaciously had dreamt of. I am sorry to say, I know something of this by experience.

## *Notes*

*Sermon source:* Zilpha Elaw, *Memoirs of the Life, Religious Experience, Ministerial Travels, and Labours of Mrs. Zilpha Elaw, an American Female of Colour* (London: Charter-House Lane, 1846). Reprinted in *Sisters of the Spirit: Three Black Women's Autobiographies of the Nineteenth Century*, ed. William L. Andrews (Bloomington: Indiana University Press, 1986), 61–62.

1. *Sisters of the Spirit,* 85.
2. Matthew 18:6 (King James Version).
3. Isaiah 3:16–24 (KJV).
4. 1 Corinthians 11:9 (KJV).
5. Ezra 10:11 and Hebrews 12:16 (KJV).

## *Bibliographical Sources*

Andrews, William L., ed. *Sisters of the Spirit: Three Black Women's Autobiographies of the Nineteenth Century.* Bloomington: Indiana University Press, 1986.

Goode, Gloria. "African-American Women in Nineteenth-Century Nantucket: Wives, Modists and Visionaries," *Historic Nantucket* 40 (Winter 1992): 76–78.

Haynes, Rosetta. "Radical Spiritual Motherhood: The Construction of Black Female Subjectivity in Nineteenth-Century African-American Women's Spiritual Autobiographies," Ph.D. diss., Cornell University, 1996.

Riggs, Marcia Y., ed. *Can I Get A Witness? Prophetic Religious Voices of African American Women: An Anthology.* Maryknoll, NY: Orbis, 1997.

# JULIA A.J. FOOTE

*(1823–1900)*

Julia A.J. Foote was born in 1823 in Schenectady, New York. Her father was born a free man and later kidnapped and enslaved. Her mother was born a slave. Her family name is not known and she is referred to in the literature only by her married name. She had four siblings of whom we know very little. She did come upon, in a marine hospital before he died, one brother with whom she had lost touch early in life. At age ten Foote was sent to live in the country and work for the Primes family. She left the Primes and returned to her parents at age twelve. At fifteen she experienced conversion after her family had moved to Albany and felt herself grateful that God saved her, as she saw herself as a greatly fallen sinner. At approximately age eighteen Julia married George Foote, a sailor, and they moved to Boston.

Convinced of her calling and attracted to many of the doctrines of the Holiness movement, Foote went against custom and her husband, because she was certain that God had "plucked her out of the burning" pathway to hell to preach and teach.[1] Foote was cast out of the Boston African Methodist Episcopal Zion Church by Rev. Jehiel C. Beman (variously spelled *Jehill* and *Jehial*), who had a reputation as an abolitionist and freedom fighter. It has been said that Beman was bothered that Foote was female and bold, but was more irritated that she mixed Holiness Methodism ways and conventions with her sermons and teachings. Apparently, Foote had been religiously impacted by her earlier involvement with the Holiness Church and her context. According to historian William Andrews, "Foote grew up in New York's notorious 'Burned Over District,' where waves of revivalism had left . . . numerous sects devoted to the attainment of Christian perfection. Believers in the perfectionist doctrines of sanctification launched a 'Holiness' movement within and without Methodism in New York and Ohio during the 1830s and 1840s."[2] Some practices of the Holiness faith apparently bothered Beman. In her autobiography, Foote recalled Beman forbidding her to preach her "holiness stuff" to the flock, despite the requests of some "elder sisters" to give her a hearing.[3] So Foote began preaching in small house meetings to disaffected members of the congregation. For this, Beman excommunicated her. Foote then began preaching as an itinerant and did so for almost four decades. Her father, whom she cared for in his final days, died in 1849. Her husband died while at sea in the 1850s; her mother also died during this period.

While Foote clearly believed that she was blessed and fortunate to have been called by God, she also endured a heavy burden for her courage and her willingness to present the gospel. Having the call to preach be a blessing and a severe burden is a theme that runs through each of the lives and writings of the pioneer preaching women.

In 1884, Foote became the first woman to be ordained a deacon in the African Methodist Episcopal Zion denomination. The next, Mary J. Small, was ordained eleven years later. In 1900, the year she died, Foote was the second woman to be ordained an AMEZ elder.

Foote, like Sojourner Truth and other women preachers, argued strenuously and continuously for her right to preach.

• • •

*This message is featured in Foote's autobiography,* A Brand Plucked from the Fire: An AutoBiographical Sketch. *It stands as one of the earliest statements by an African American woman advocating a woman's right to preach.*

## Women in the Gospel (ca. 1887)

Thirty years ago there could scarcely a person be found, in the churches, to sympathize with any one who talked of Holiness. But, in my simplicity, I did think that a body of Christian ministers would understand my case and judge righteously. I was, however, disappointed.

It is no little thing to feel that every man's hand is against us, and ours against every man, as seemed to be the case with me at this time; yet how precious, if Jesus but be with us. In this severe trial I had constant access to God, and a clear consciousness that he heard me; yet I did not seem to have that plenitude of the Spirit that I had before. I realized most keenly that the closer the communion that may have existed, the keener the suffering of the slightest departure from God. Unbroken communion can only be retained by a constant application of the blood which cleanseth.

Though I did not wish to pain any one, neither could I please any one only as I was led by the Holy Spirit. I saw, as never before, that the best men were liable to err, and that the only safe way was to fall on Christ, even though censure and reproach fell upon me for obeying his voice. Man's opinion weighed nothing with me, for my commission was from heaven, and my reward was with the Most High.

I could not believe that it was a short-lived impulse or spasmodic influence that impelled me to preach. I read that on the day of Pentecost was the Scripture fulfilled as found in Joel 2:28, 29; and it certainly will not be denied that women as well as men were at that time pulled with the Holy Ghost, because it is expressly stated that women were among those who continued in prayer and supplication, waiting for the fulfillment of the promise. Women and men are classed together, and if the power to preach the Gospel is short-lived and spasmodic in the case of women, it must be equally so in that of men; and if women have lost the gift of prophecy, so have men.

We are sometimes told that if a woman pretends to a Divine call, and thereon grounds the right to plead the cause of a crucified Redeemer in public, she will be believed when she shows credentials from heaven; that is, when she works a miracle. If it be necessary to prove one's right to preach the Gospel, I ask of my brethren to show me their credentials, or I can not believe in the propriety of their ministry.

But the Bible puts an end to this strife when it says: "There is neither male nor female in Christ Jesus." Philip had four daughters that prophesied, or preached. Paul called Priscilla, as well as Aquila, his "helper," or, as in the Greek, his "fellow-laborer" (Romans 15:3; 2 Corinthians 8:23; Philippians 2:5; 1 Thessalonians 3:2). The same word, which, in our common translation, is now rendered a "servant of the church," in speaking of Phoebe (Romans 19:1), is rendered "minister" when applied to Titychus (Ephesians 6:21). When Paul said, "Help those women who labor with me in the Gospel," he certainly meant that they did more than to pour out tea. In the eleventh chapter of First Corinthians Paul gives directions, to men and women, how they should appear when they prophesy or pray in public assemblies; and he defines prophesying to be speaking to edification, exhortation and comfort.

I may further remark that the conduct of holy women is recorded in scripture as an example to others of their sex. And in the early ages of Christianity many women were happy and glorious in martyrdom. How nobly, how heroically, too, in later ages, have women suffered persecution and death for the name of the Lord Jesus.

In looking over these facts, I could see no miracle wrought for those women more than in myself.

Though opposed, I went forth laboring for God, and he owned and blessed my labors, and has done so wherever I have been until this day. And while I walk obediently, I know he will, though hell may rage and vent its spite.

✦ ✦ ✦

*This sermon, also found in Foote's autobiography, was preached during her travels in Ohio, and according to Foote was given to her by a man in Detroit who was a sinner when he told her to preach from Micah 4:13, but later accepted Christ. The sermon includes the use of a powerful metaphor. The frequent use of metaphors by Foote shows her clear understanding of the black preaching tradition.*

## A Threshing Sermon (1851)

One day, quite an influential man in the community, though a sinner, called on me and appeared deeply concerned about his soul's welfare. He urged me to speak from Micah 4:13: "Arise and thresh, O daughter of Zion," etc. I took his desire to the Lord, and was permitted to speak from that passage after this manner:

[In] 710 B.C. corn was threshed among the Orientals by means of oxen or horses, which were driven round an area filled with loose sheaves. By their continued tramping the corn was separated from the straw. That this might be done the more effectually, the text promised an addition to the natural horny substance on the feet of these animals, by making the horn iron and the hoof brass.

Corn is not threshed in this manner by us, but by means of flails, so that I feel I am doing no injury to the sentiment of the text by changing a few of the terms into those which are the most familiar to us now. The passage portrays the Gospel times, though in a more restricted sense it applies to the preachers of the word. Yet it has a direct reference to all God's people, who were and are commanded to arise and thresh. Glory to Jesus! now is this prophecy fulfilled—Joel 2:28 and 29. They are also commanded to go to God, who alone is able to qualify them for their labors by making their horns iron and their hoofs brass. The Lord was desirous of imparting stability and perpetuity to his own divine work, by granting supernatural aid to the faithful that they might perform for him those services for which their own feeble and unassisted powers were totally inadequate. More than this, it is encouraging to the saints to know that they are provided with weapons both offensive and defensive.

The threshing instrument is of the former description. It is of the same quality as that which is quick and powerful and sharper than any two-edged sword. "For this purpose the Son of God was manifested, that he might destroy the works of the devil," and this is one of the weapons which he employs in the hands of his people to carry his gracious designs into execution, together with the promise that they shall beat in pieces many people (Isaiah 23:18; 9:6–9).

There are many instances of the successful application of the Gospel flail, by which means the devil is threshed out of sinners. With the help of God, I am resolved, O sinner, to try what effect the smart strokes of this threshing instrument will produce on thy unhumbled soul. This is called the sword of the Spirit, and is in reality the word of God.

Such a weapon may seem contemptible in the eyes of the natural man; yet, when it is powerfully wielded, the consequences are invariably potent and salutary. Bless God! the Regulator says: "They overcame by the blood of the Lamb and by the word of their testimony; and they loved not their lives unto the death." The atonement is the greatest weapon. In making trial of its efficacy, little children have caused the parent to cry aloud for mercy; but, in every case, much of its heavenly charm and virtue depends upon the mode in which it is applied.

This Gospel flail should be lifted up in a kind and loving spirit. Many shrink at sight of the flail, and some of us know, by blessed experience, that when its smart strokes are applied in the power and demonstration of the Holy Spirit, it causes the very heart to feel sore and painful. Penitent soul, receive the castigation, and you will feel, after it, like saying: "Now let me be crucified, and this work of the devil, inbred sin, put to death, that Christ may live and reign in me without a rival."[4]

To the glory of God I wish to say, that the unconverted man, who gave me the text for the above discourse, gave his heart to God, together with many others, before we left Detroit. In after years I was informed of his happy death. Praise the Lord for full and free salvation! Reader, have you this salvation—an ever-flowing fountain—in your soul? God grant it. Amen!

✦ ✦ ✦

*In "A Word to My Christian Sisters," Foote makes one of the strongest appeals by a woman of her time to urge women to do what God has called them to do regardless of the opposition from men. She also testifies of her many difficulties in ministry and in her personal life (the death of her spouse, throat problems, and more) to let readers know that even when facing hardship, one must not relent from the work of God. Ultimately, the majority of the message is concerned with living a holy and righteous life, a theme throughout Foote's autobiography.*

## A Word to My Christian Sisters (ca. 1861)

Dear Sisters: I would that I could tell you a hundredth part of what God has revealed to me of his glory, especially on that never-to-be-forgotten night when I received my high and holy calling. The songs I heard I think were those which Job, David and Isaiah speak of hearing at night upon their beds, or the one of which the Revelator says "no man could learn." Certain it is, I have not been able to sing it since, though at times I have seemed to hear the distant echo of the music. When I tried to repeat it, it vanished in the direct distance. Glory! glory! glory to the Most High!

Sisters, shall not you and I unite with the heavenly host in the grand chorus? If so, you will not let what man may say or do, keep you from doing the will of the Lord or using the gifts you have for the good of others. How much easier to bear the reproach of men than to live at a distance from God. Be not kept in bondage by those who say, "We suffer not a woman to teach," thus quoting Paul's words, but not rightly applying them. What though we are called to pass through deep waters, so our anchor is cast within the veil, both sure and steadfast? Blessed experience! I have had to weep because this was not my constant experience. At times, a cloud of heaviness has covered my mind, and disobedience has caused me to lose the clear witness of perfect love.

One time I allowed my mind to dwell too much on my physical condition. I was suffering severely from throat difficulty, and took the advice of friends, and sought a cure from earthly physicians, instead of applying to the Great Physician. For this reason my joy was checked, and I was obliged to cease my public labors for several years. During all this time I was less spiritual, less zealous, yet I was not willing to accept the suggestion of Satan, that I had forfeited the blessing of holiness. But alas! the witness was not clear, and God suffered me to pass through close trials, tossed by the billows of temptation.

Losing my loving husband just at this time, I had much of the world to struggle with and against.

Those who are wholly sanctified need not fear that God will hide his face, if they continue to walk in the light even as Christ is in the light. Then they have fellowship with the Father and the Son, and become of one spirit with the Lord. I do not believe God ever withdraws himself from a soul which does not first withdraw itself from him, though such may abide under cloud for a season, and have to cry: "My God! my God! why hast thou forsaken me?"

Glory to God, who giveth us the victory through our Lord Jesus Christ! His blood meets all the demands of the law against us. It is the blood of Christ that sues for the fulfillment of his last will and testament, and brings down every blessing into the soul.

When I had well nigh despaired of a cure from my bodily infirmities, I cried from the depths of my soul for the blood of Jesus to be applied to my throat. My faith laid hold of the precious promises—John 14:14; Mark 2:23; 11:24. At once I ceased trying to join the iron and the clay—the truth of God with the sayings and advice of men. I looked to my God for a fresh act of his sanctifying power. Bless his name! Deliverance did come, with the balm, and my throat has troubled me but little since. This was ten years ago. Praise the Lord for that holy fire which many waters of trial and temptation cannot quench.

Dear sisters in Christ, are any of you also without understanding and slow of heart to believe, as were the disciples? Although they had seen their Master do many mighty works, yet, with change of place or circumstances, they would go back upon the old ground of carnal reasoning and unbelieving fears. The darkness and ignorance of our natures are such, that, even after we have embraced the Saviour and received his teaching, we are ready to stumble at the plainest truths! Blind unbelief is always sure to err; it can neither trace God nor trust him. Unbelief is ever alive to distrust and fear. So long as this evil root has a place in us, our fears cannot be removed nor our hopes confirmed.

Not till the day of Pentecost did Christ's chosen ones see clearly, or have their understandings opened; and nothing short of a full baptism of the Spirit will dispel our unbelief. Without this, we are but babes—all our lives are often carried away by our carnal natures and kept in bondage; whereas, if we are wholly saved and live under the full sanctifying influence of the Holy Ghost, we cannot be tossed about with every wind, but, like an iron pillar or a house built upon a rock, prove immovable. Our minds will then be fully illuminated, our hearts purified, and our souls filled with the pure love of God, bringing forth fruit to his glory.

✦ ✦ ✦

*Foote preached during a time when Holiness Methodism fervor gripped Ohio and much of the eastern seaboard. Perfection was a key belief that she espoused, and she suggested that much more attention should be accorded to it in preaching. According to Foote the sanctified Christian gains spiritual perfection, which she termed "Holiness," and this is shown by outward acts of right living. According to William Andrews, who reprinted Foote's 1879 biography, "This kind of perfection does not prevent the sanctified Christian from making mistakes, nor does sanctification obviate the Christian's obligation always to seek greater growth in grace and in the knowledge and love of God. What the experience of sanctification confers on the believer is the sense of being in total harmony with the will of God, of being perfectly pure in intention and action insofar as his or her acts are determined by individual intention."*[5] *According to cultural historian Bettye Collier-Thomas, "It was of utmost importance to preaching women such as Foote to ensure that the doctrine of Christian perfection did not fall into disrepute among the Methodists and other prominent denominations, for it was this doctrine—that all may be sanctified in order to do God's work of love—that legitimized the ministry of preaching women."*[6]

## Christian Perfection
## (1894)

Dear Editor of the *Star*:

Because I have but *one* talent I don't see why I should give it to your contributors that have ten. The Lord helping me I shall use it in offering a few thoughts on the all important subject of "Christian Perfection," etc.

(Matthew 5:48). "If a minister were as faithful in speaking the truth in these days, and in denouncing sin as Christ was in His day, he would sacrifice his life"—Dr. Parker, London, Eng.

The duty of a true preacher:—"Warning every man and teaching every man in all wisdom, that we may present every man perfect in Christ Jesus" (Colossians 1:28).

"Every man's work shall be made manifest, for the day shall declare it because it shall be realized by fire and the fire shall try every man's work, of what sort it is" (1 Corinthians 3:13).

The great object of the ministry of the Apostle Paul was to present every man perfect in Christ Jesus; this master purpose was the secret of his wonderful success.

I know it is said the Gospel is not adapted to the nineteenth century; men are different now from what they were. Yes, they may be different externally but essentially they are the same. What man was, man is; what man needed he needs still.

No, the Gospel is not adapted to any century; it wasn't intended to be. It was intended that the nineteenth century should be adapted to the Gospel. Our work is not to make the truths of the Bible fit into all the crooks and crevices of the lives and beliefs of men. We are to stamp, not overlay; to coin, not gild. There are peculiarities of the times that will require special methods of delivering the truth and special truth. We may be debarred entrance to many pulpits (as some of us now are) and stand at the door or on the street corner in order to preach to men and women. No difference when or where, we must preach a whole Gospel.

I think the words of the text are the greatest words that the Lord Jesus ever uttered: "Be ye therefore perfect, even as your Father in heaven is perfect." I think we may [emphasize] the word "ye"; every Greek scholar knows that is the emphatic word, for where the pronouns are used emphasis is always meant.

The revised version reads, "Ye shall be perfect." So perfection is not a privilege only, it is mandatory. There are two ways of commanding; one is to say "Do!" and the other "Thou shalt do." It is a little stronger to say, "John, you shall go to school!" than "John, go to school."

Most of the commandments use the emphatic "Thou shalt!" Jesus revised the law and put Himself on a par with the lawgiver: "I came not to destroy but to fulfill." He came to fill it full of meaning, to show its height and depth and breadth and length.

The "ye" must be put in contrast to what goes before, namely the usages of the publicans and worldly men. The publicans are represented as loving those who love them. We conclude that the "therefore" is confined to the exposition of the law of love and hatred.

What is the meaning of perfect? It is a great word. We ought honestly to inquire what is meant by it. It is used very frequently in the New Testament, also in the Old, and is used more times in the Revised New Testament than in the King [James] version. Regeneration is used only twice in the New Testament, and only once with reference to the reconstruction of human character; the second being used with reference to the reconstruction of human society. If preachers would observe the same proportions in preaching that the Scriptures do, they would preach twenty-five sermons on Perfection to one on Regeneration, but if a man today reverses the order and preaches every twenty-fifth sermon on Christian Perfection, people call him a hobbyist.

We are tempted to omit the use of the word perfection; then we turn to the Bible and read the thirty-eighth verse of the eighth chapter of Mark.

The life blood of Jesus is in His words; cut them and they will bleed; neglect them and you neglect Him. We are to find out their meaning as well as we can by study and prayer, but not to reject or neglect them. Behind every word of Jesus is a doctrine—a meaning deep and high.

Preachers have been tempted to skip this word because it has been abused. We notice some sources of abuse.

First. The Human Conscience seems to rise up and object to the use of this word. We feel so imperfect.

Second. Because it has been treated as a specialty; special meetings have been held and special periodicals issued to promote it. I believe it is a better way for every pulpit to preach the whole gospel. But if this doctrine drops out of the pulpit, what is to be done? Dr. Curry says a doctrine dropped out of the pulpit is lost in a generation. Preachers had better be specialists than go to judgement having neglected this doctrine.

Third. The word has been brought into disrepute by various parties. There was a people in Western New York who professed to get so near God that they had no need of prayer; their whole life was a prayer. They did not use the sacraments or the Bible; every meal was a sacrament, the Holy Spirit was their teacher.

Then there were the Oneida Perfectionists. They became so perfect that they invented the monstrous idea of complex marriages. By such means the word perfection has been brought into disrepute.

The Roman Catholics have helped to make the word unpopular. They teach that we should withdraw from society to monasteries and nunneries if we would attain perfection; we must take the vows of poverty, chastity and obedience to superiors.

The devil is a good climber; brick and mortar can not keep him out.

Thank God when Martin Luther began he did not throw overboard the idea of perfection, but insisted that it did not consist in celibacy, beggary and filthy clothing, but in utter self abnegation and love.

John Wesley afterwards did better. Luther's idea of ardent love was not quite up to Wesley's perfect love.

Calvin threw the whole doctrine overboard by putting it off till death. His followers have been against the doctrine as attainable in the present life. Arminius taught (article 6) that every believer may be certain or assured of his own salvation, and (7) it is possible for a regenerate man to live without sin.

The Westminster Catechism taught that in the moment of death men are sanctified. Their only proof text is "The spirits of just men made perfect." But the men, and not the spirits, were made perfect, and the time is not named in the proof text.

### *Notes*

*Sermon source:* "Women in the Gospel" and "A Threshing Sermon" were published in Foote's autobiography, "A Brand Plucked from the Fire." The letter "Christian Perfection" was published in *The Star of Zion* in 1894.

1. Julia A.J. Foote, "A Brand Plucked from the Fire: An AutoBiographical Sketch." Reprinted in *Sisters of the Spirit: Three Black Women's Autobiographies of the Nineteenth Century*, ed. William L. Andrews (Bloomington: Indiana University Press, 1986), 9, 181, 202–4.
2. *Sisters of the Spirit*, 4.
3. Ibid., 205.
4. The exact source of this quote is not known. Phrases contained in the quote can be found in songs of the period and in the founder of Methodism, John Wesley's, *A Plain Account of Christian Perfection* and in the book *Lessons for Seekers of Holiness* by Harmon A. Baldwin (1907), which contains, among other material, numerous quotes by Wesley and John Fletcher (1729–1785). Fletcher was a key interpreter of Wesleyan theology in the 1800s.
5. *Sisters of the Spirit*, 15.
6. Bettye Collier-Thomas. *Daughters of Thunder: Black Women Preachers and Their Sermons.* (San Francisco: Jossey Bass Publisher, 1998), 63.

### *Bibliographical Sources*

Andrews, William L., ed. *Sisters of the Spirit: Three Black Women's Autobiographies of the Nineteenth Century.* Bloomington: Indiana University Press, 1986.

Robinson, Marilyn. *Black Women and Religion: A Bibliography.* Boston: G.K. Hall and Co., 1980.

# NATHANIEL PAUL

*(1793–1839)*

Nathaniel Paul was born in Exeter, New Hampshire. His father was a veteran of the Revolutionary War. Paul likely attended Free Will Academy in Hollis, New Hampshire, which was an integrated school that trained ministers. He, along with his two brothers (Shadrach and Thomas), became Baptist ministers. Reverend Thomas Paul was notable for his abolitionist activities and his skill as a preacher. Nathaniel was married to a woman known only as Eliza; she died in 1827.

Nathaniel Paul became the founding pastor of First African Baptist Church in Albany, New York, in 1822. His abolitionist efforts gained him broad attention in the Northeast. He then became a member of the organizing committee of *Freedom's Journal* in 1827. The journal was one of the forums in which Paul was particularly critical of the American Colonization Society, which he accused of trying to wrongfully remove blacks from America. Paul spoke against the society during visits to England with William Lloyd Garrison, the publisher of *The Liberator.* During his travels in England, Paul helped form abolitionist societies and married his second wife, a white English woman of whom we only know her first name, Ann.

Growing tired of the lack of justice afforded blacks in the United States, in around 1830 he moved to Canada near what is now Lucan, Ontario, and established a church. While there he also started the Wilberforce School, which served as the only educational facility for black youth there for almost twelve years.

He eventually returned to Albany and resumed his pastorate, spending the remainder of his life there.

• • •

*Paul delivered this message in Exeter Hall in London. In it he describes the horrors of slavery and, in keeping with those black preachers who are master storytellers, even asks the waters in which slaves were drowned to comment on the pain and cruelty of slavery.*

## An Address on the Occasion of the Abolition of Slavery in New-York (July 5, 1827)

Through the lapse of ages, it has been common for nations to record whatever was peculiar or interesting in the course of their history. Thus when Heaven, provoked by the iniquities of man, has visited the earth, with the pestilence which moves in darkness or destruction, that wasteth at noonday, and has swept from existence, by thousands, its numerous inhabitants; or when the milder terms of mercy have been dispensed in rich abundance, and the goodness of God has crowned the efforts of any people with peace and prosperity; they have been placed upon their annals, and handed down to future ages, both for their amusement and profit. And as the nations which have already passed away, have been careful to select the most important events, peculiar to themselves, and have recorded them for the good of the people that should succeed them, so will we place it upon our history; and we will tell the good story to our children and to our children's children, down to the latest posterity, that on the fourth day of July, in the year of our Lord 1827, slavery was abolished in the state of New-York.

Seldom, if ever, was there an occasion which required a public acknowledgment, or that deserved to be retained with gratitude of heart to the all-wise disposer of events, more than the present on which we have assembled.

It is not the mere gratification of the pride of the heart, or any vain ambitious notion, that has influenced us to make our appearance in the public streets of our city, or to assemble in the sanctuary of the Most High this morning; but we have met to offer our tribute of thanksgiving and praise to almighty God for his goodness; to retrace the acts and express our gratitude to our public benefactors, and to stimulate each other to the performance of every good and virtuous act, which now does, or hereafter may devolve as a duty upon us, as freemen and citizens, in common with the rest of community.

And if ever it were necessary for me to offer an apology to an audience for my absolute inability to perform a task assigned me, I feel that the present is the period. However, relying, for support on the hand of Him who has said, "I will never leave nor forsake;"[1] and confiding in your charity for every necessary allowance, I venture to engage in the arduous undertaking.

In contemplating the subject before us, in connection with the means by which so glorious an event has been accomplished, we find much which requires our deep humiliation and our most exalted praises. We are permitted to behold one of the most pernicious and abominable of all enterprises, in which the depravity of human nature ever led man to engage, entirely eradicated. The power of the tyrant is subdued, the heart of the oppressed is cheered, liberty is proclaimed to the captive, and the opening of the prison to those who were bound, and he who had long been the miserable victim of cruelty and degradation, is elevated to the common rank in which our benevolent Creator first designed, that man should move—all of which have been effected by means the most simple, yet perfectly efficient: Not by those fearful judgments of the almighty, which have so often fell upon the different parts of the earth; which have overturned nations and kingdoms; scattered thrones and scepters; nor is the glory of the achievement, tarnished with the horrors of the field of battle. We hear not the cries of the widow and the fatherless; nor are our hearts affected with the sight of garments rolled in blood; but all has been done by the diffusion and influence of the pure, yet powerful principles of benevolence, before which the pitiful impotency of tyranny and oppression, is scattered and dispersed, like the chaff before the rage of the whirlwind.

I will not, on this occasion, attempt fully to detail the abominations of the traffic to which we have already alluded. Slavery, with its concomitants and consequences, in the best attire in which it can possibly be presented, is but a hateful monster, the very demon of avarice and oppression, from its first introduction to the present time; it has been among all nations the scourge of heaven, and the curse of the earth. It is so contrary to the laws which the God of nature has laid down as the rule of action by which the conduct of man is to be regulated towards his fellow man, which binds him to love his neighbour as himself, that it ever has, and ever will meet the decided disapprobation of heaven.

In whatever form we behold it, its visage is satanic, its origin the very offspring of hell, and in all cases its effects are grievous.

On the shores of Africa, the horror of the scene commences; here, the merciless tyrant, divested of every thing human, except the form, begins the action. The laws of God and the tears of the oppressed are alike disregarded; and with more than savage barbarity, husbands and wives, parents and children, are parted to meet no more: and, if not doomed to an untimely death, while on the passage, yet are they for life consigned to a captivity still more terrible; a captivity, at the very thought of which, every heart, not already biased with unhallowed prejudices, or callous to every tender impression, pauses and revolts; exposed to the caprice of those whose tender mercies are cruel; unprotected by the laws of the land, and doomed to drag out miserable existence, without the remotest shadow of a hope of deliverence, until the king of terrors shall have executed his office, and consigned them to the kinder slumbers of death. But its pernicious tendency may be traced still farther: not only are its effects of the most disastrous character, in relation to the slave, but it extends its influence to the slave holder; and in many instances it is hard to say which is most wretched, the slave or the master.

After the fall of man, it would seem that God, foreseeing that pride and arrogance would be the necessary consequences of the apostacy, and that man would seek to usurp undue authority over his fellow, wisely ordained that he should obtain his bread by the sweat of his brow; but contrary to this sacred mandate of heaven, slavery has been introduced, supporting the one in all the absurd luxuries of life, at the expense of the liberty and independence of the other. Point me to any section of the earth where slavery, to any considerable extent exists, and I will point you to a people whose morals are corrupted; and when pride, vanity and profusion are permitted to reign unrestrained in all their desolating effects, and thereby idleness and luxury are promoted, under the influence of which, man, becoming insensible of his duty to his God and his fellow creature; and indulging in all the pride and vanity of his own heart, says to his soul, thou hast much goods laid up for many years. But while thus sporting, can it be done with impunity? Has conscience ceased to be active? Are there no forebodings of a future day of punishment, and of meeting the merited avenger? Can he retire after the business of the day and repose in safety? Let the guards around his mansion, the barred doors of his sleeping room, and the loaded instruments of death beneath his pillow, answer the question.—And if this were all, it would become us, perhaps, to cease to murmur, and bow in silent submission to that providence which had ordained this present state of existence, to be but a life of degradation and suffering.

Since affliction is but the common lot of men, this life, at best, is but a vapor that ariseth and soon passeth away. Man, said the inspired sage, that is born of a woman, is of few days and full of trouble; and in a certain sense, it is not material what our present situation may be, for short is the period that humbles all to the dust, and places the monarch and the beggar, the slave and the master, upon equal thrones. But although this life is short, and attended with one entire scene of anxious perplexity, and few and evil are the days of our pilgrimage; yet man is advancing to another state of existence, bounded only by the vast duration of eternity! in which happiness or misery await us all. The great author of our existence has marked out the way that leads to the glories of the upper world, and through the redemption which is in Christ Jesus, salvation is offered to all. But slavery forbids even the approach of mercy; it stands as a barrier in the way to ward off the influence of divine grace; it shuts up the avenues of the soul, and prevents its receiving divine instruction; and scarce does it permit its miserable captives to know that there is a God, a Heaven or a Hell!

Its more than detestable picture has been attempted to be portrayed by the learned, and the wise, but all have fallen short, and acknowledged their inadequacy to the task, and have been compelled to submit, by merely giving an imperfect shadow of its reality. Even the immortal Wilberforce, a name that can never die while Africa lives, after exerting his ingenuity, and exhausting the strength of his masterly mind, resigns the effort, and calmly submits by saying, never was there, indeed, a system so replete with wickedness and cruelty to whatever part of it we turn our eyes; we could find no comfort, no satisfaction, no relief. It was the gracious ordinance of providence, both in the natural and moral world, that good should often arise out of evil. Hurricanes clear the air; and the propagation of truth was promoted by persecution, pride, vanity, and profusion contributed often, in their remoter consequences, to the happiness of mankind. In common, what was in itself evil and vicious, was permitted to carry along with it some circumstances of palliation. The Arab was hospitable, the robber brave; we did not necessarily find cruelty associated with fraud or meanness with injustice. But here the case was far otherwise. It was the prerogative of this detestable traffic, to separate from evil its concomitant good, and to reconcile discordant mischief. It robbed war of its generosity, it deprived peace of its security. We saw in it the vices of polished society, without its knowledge or its comforts, and the evils of barbarism without its simplicity; no age, no sex, no rank, no condition, was exempt from the fatal influence of this wide wasting calamity. Thus it attained to the fullest measure of its pure, unmixed, unsophisticated wickedness; and scorning all competition or comparison, it stood without a rival in the secure and undisputed possession of its detestable pre-eminence.

Such were the views which this truly great and good man, together with his fellow philanthropists, took of this subject, and such are the strong terms in which he has seen fit to express his utter abhorrence of its origin and effects. Thus have we hinted at some of the miseries connected with slavery. And while I turn my thoughts back and survey what is past, I see our forefathers seized by the hand of the rude ruffian, and torn from their native homes and all that they held dear or sacred. I follow them down the lonesome way, until I see each safely placed on board the gloomy slave ship; I hear the passive groan, and the clanking of the chains which bind them. I see the tears which follow each other in quick succession down the dusky cheek.

I view them casting the last and longing look towards the land which gave them birth, until at length the ponderous anchor is weighed, and the canvass [*sic*] spread to catch the favored breeze; I view them wafted onward until they arrive at the destined port; I behold those who have been so unfortunate as to survive the passage, emerging from their loathsome prison, and landing amidst the noisy rattling of the massy fetters which confine them; I see the crowd of trafficers in human flesh gathering, each anxious to seize the favored opportunity of enriching himself with their toils, their tears and their blood. I view them doomed to the most abject state of degraded misery, and exposed to suffer all that unrestrained tyranny can inflict, or that human nature is capable of sustaining.

Tell me, ye mighty waters, why did ye sustain the ponderous load of misery? or speak, ye winds, and say why it was that ye executed your office to waft them onward to the still more dismal state; and ye proud waves, why did you refuse to lend your aid and to have overwhelmed them with your billows? Then should they have slept sweetly in the bosom of the great deep, and so have been hid from sorrow. And, oh thou immaculate God, be not angry with us, while we come into this thy sanctuary, and make the bold inquiry in this thy holy temple, why it was that thou didst look on with the calm indifference of an unconcerned spectator, when thy holy law was violated, thy divine authority despised and a portion of thine own creatures reduced to a state of mere vassalage and misery? Hark! while he answers from on high: hear him proclaiming from the skies—Be still, and know that I am God! Clouds and darkness are round about me; yet righteousness and judgment are the habitation of my throne. I do my will and pleasure in the heavens above, and in the earth beneath; it is my sovereign prerogative to bring good out of evil, and cause the wrath of man to praise me, and the remainder of that wrath I will restrain.

Strange, indeed, is the idea, that such a system, fraught with such consummate wickedness, should ever have found a place in this the otherwise happiest of all countries,—a country, the very soil of which is said to be consecrated to liberty, and its fruits the equal rights of man. But strange as the idea may seem, or paradoxical as it may appear to those acquainted with the constitution of the government, or who have read the bold declaration of this nation's independence; yet it is a fact that can neither be denied or controverted, that in the United States of America, at the expiration of fifty years after its becoming a free and independent nation, there are no less than fifteen hundred thousand human beings still in a state of unconditional vassalage.

Yet America is first in the profession of the love of liberty, and loudest in proclaiming liberal sentiments towards all other nations, and feels herself insulted, to be branded with any thing bearing the appearance of tyranny or oppression. Such are the palpable inconsistencies that abound among us and such is the medley of contradictions which stain the national character, and renders the American republic a byword, even among despotic nations. But while we pause and wonder at the contradictory sentiments held forth by the nation, and contrast its profession and practice, we are happy to have it in our power to render an apology for the existence of the evil, and to offer an excuse for the framers of the constitution. It was before the sons of Columbia felt the yoke of their oppressors, and rose in their strength to put it off that this land become [*sic*] contaminated with slavery. Had this not been the case, led by the spirit of pure republicanism, that then possessed the souls of those patriots who were struggling for liberty, this soil would have been sufficiently guarded against its intrusion, and the people of these United States to this day, would have been strangers to so great a curse. It was by the permission of the British parliament, that the human species first became an article of merchandize among them, and as they were accessory to its introduction, it well becomes them to be first, as a nation, in arresting its progress and effecting its expulsion. It was the immortal Clarkson, a name that will be associated with all that is sublime in mercy, until the final consummation of all things, who first looking abroad, beheld the sufferings of Africa, and looking at home, he saw his country stained with her blood. He threw aside the vestments of the priesthood, and consecrated himself to the holy purpose of rescuing a continent from rapine and murder, and of erasing this one sin from the book of his nation's iniquities. Many were the difficulties to be encountered, many were the hardships to be endured, many were the persecutions to be met with; formidable, indeed, was the opposing party. The sensibility of the slave merchants and planters was raised to the highest pitch of resentment. Influenced by the love of money, every scheme was devised, every measure was adopted, every plan was executed, that might throw the least barrier in the way of the holy cause of the abolition of this traffic. The consequences of such a measure were placed in the most appalling light that ingenious falsehood could invent; the destruction of commerce, the ruin of the merchants, the rebellion of the slaves, the massacre of the planters, were all artfully and fancifully pictured, and reduced to a certainty in the minds of many of the members of parliament, and a large proportion of the community. But the cause of justice and humanity were not to be deserted by him and his fellow philanthropists, on account of difficulties. We have seen them for twenty years persevering against all opposition, and surmounting every obstacle they found in their way. Nor did they relax aught of their exertions, until the cries of the oppressed having roused the sensibility of the nation, the island empress rose in her strength, and said to this foul traffic, "thus far hast thou gone, but thou shalt go no farther." Happy for us, my brethren, that the principles of benevolence were not exclusively confined to the isle of Great Britain. There have lived, and there still do live, men in this country, who are patriots and philanthropists, not merely in name, but in heart and practice; men whose compassions have long since led them to pity the poor and despised sons of Africa. They have heard their groans, and have seen their blood, and have looked with an holy indignation upon the oppressor: nor was there any thing wanting except the power to have crushed the tyrant and liberated the captive.

Through their instrumentality, the blessings of freedom have long since been enjoyed by all classes of people throughout New-England, and through their influence, under the Almighty, we are enabled to recognize the fourth day of the present month, as the day in which the cause of justice and humanity have triumphed over tyranny and oppression, and slavery is forever banished from the state of New-York.

### *Notes*

*Sermon source: An Address Delivered on the Occasion of the Abolition of Slavery in the State of New-York, July 5, 1827. By Nathaniel Paul, Pastor of the First African Baptist Society in the City of Albany* (Albany: Trustees of the First African Baptist Society of Albany, 1827). Printed by John B. Van Steenbergh.

1. Paraphrase of Hebrews 13:5 (King James Version).

### *Bibliographical Sources*

Levine, Robert S. *Fifth of July: Nathaniel Paul and the Construction of Black Nationalism in Genius and Bondage,* ed. Vincent Carretta and Philip Gould. Lexington: University Press of Kentucky, 2001, 242–60.

Murphy, Larry G., J. Gordon Melton, and Gary L. Ward, eds. *Encyclopedia of African American Religions.* New York: Garland Publishing Inc., 1993, 573–74.

Pinn, Anthony. *Moral Evil and Redemptive Suffering: A History of Theodicy in African American Religious Thought.* Gainesville: University Press of Florida, 2002.

# JAMES WILLIAM CHARLES PENNINGTON

*(1809?–1870)*

James William Charles Pennington was born a slave in Maryland. He was nicknamed the "fugitive blacksmith," being a blacksmith by trade and a fugitive slave for much of his life. Pennington had no opportunities for early education. After his escape from bondage at approximately age twenty-one, he was taken in by a Quaker, William Wright, in Pennsylvania for about six months; Wright provided Pennington basic educational instruction. Pennington moved to New York in 1829, where he paid for night classes and tutoring. In future years, Pennington so applied himself to the study of languages, history, literature, and theology that he became a proficient and highly regarded preacher. He also audited classes at Yale

Divinity School. By 1831, he was already a good orator and antislavery advocate, and condemned the American Colonization Society.

Pennington felt a call to ministry around 1833 and was ordained in 1839. He spent most of his ministerial life as a Presbyterian. He served several Presbyterian churches, including the famous Shiloh Presbyterian Church in New York. In 1853 he was elected moderator of the presbytery of New York City. His personal and religious quests were joined: As late as the 1840s he was fighting to gain the release of his parents and siblings from their slave masters. He was able to help two of his brothers and his father escape to Canada; he was not able to secure the release of his mother and sister.

Pennington believed that the Bible was the best place to look for an answer to slavery, adamantly preaching that the Bible was the most solid ground on which to stand and protest the practice. Pennington's theology (his view of God, salvation, man, ethics, and eschatology) was geared toward the abolition of slavery and the emancipation of blacks.

Pennington made several trips to London as a delegate to the World Antislavery Society. On these occasions he was invited to preach and speak before some of the most aristocratic audiences in Europe. In recognition of his scholarship and other contributions, the University of Heidelberg conferred upon him the degree of Doctor of Divinity.

In 1841, he published his autobiography, *The Fugitive Blacksmith: or Events in the History of James W.C. Pennington*. He also wrote *A Text Book of the Origin and History of the Colored People* and *The Past and Present Condition, and the Destiny of the Colored Race*, both published in 1841.

Very little is known about his first wife, other than that her name was Harriet. She died in 1846 while Pennington was doing a seven-month-long missionary project in Jamaica. In 1851 Pennington's freedom was purchased from his former master. By 1855 Pennington had adopted a son, Thomas (Sands) Pennington, and had remarried. His second wife's name was Almira Way. With his family, he left New York and returned as pastor of his former church in Hartford, Connecticut, where he had pastored in the early 1840s. This was a Congregational Church. This was a brief return; he then became the pastor of the Second Colored Presbyterian Church in New Town, Long Island.

Pennington preached in the pulpits of the leading churches and was classed with the leading theologians and freedom-fighters of his day. It was Pennington who in 1859 penned the article "Pray for John Brown" after Brown's conviction for the events at Harpers Ferry. It was Pennington who sued New York City's trolley company to make it provide transportation to all New Yorkers. He ultimately won that case. Pennington presided at the marriage of Frederick Douglass to Douglass's first wife and worked closely with Douglass and William Lloyd Garrison to defeat slavery.

In 1865, after being left penniless from buying his brothers' freedom and from suing the New York Trolley Company, in declining health, possibly due to alcoholism, and declining reputation, likely due to his continued association with a denomination that was doing little to end slavery, Pennington left the Congregationalists and moved to New Orleans, where he was ordained for work by the Missouri Conference of the AME Church. He also taught and preached in Mississippi. In 1867 he returned to the Congregationalist church and pastored in Portland, Maine. He moved to Jacksonville, Florida, and on behalf of the Presbyterian Committee of Missions for Freedmen, founded a Presbyterian church and school there one year before his death in 1870.

• • •

*Pennington's message as presented here is taken from* The National Principia, *a New York newspaper, January 7 and 14, 1864. It was published after five days of riots by whites, primarily Irish and German immigrants. Following the presidential election in 1860, the Democratic Party warned New York's Irish and German residents to prepare for the emancipation of slaves and the competition for work when southern blacks moved north. To these New Yorkers, the Emancipation Proclamation was confirmation of their worst fears. In March 1863, fuel was added to the fire in the form of a stricter federal draft law. All male citizens between ages twenty and thirty-five and all unmarried men between ages thirty-five and forty-five were subject to military duty. The federal government entered all eligible men into a lottery. Those who could afford to hire a substitute or pay the government three hundred dollars might avoid enlistment. Blacks, who were not considered citizens, were exempt from the draft. On Sunday, July 12, the names of the draftees drawn the day before by the provost marshal were published in newspapers. Within hours, groups of irate citizens, many of them immigrants, banded together across the city; they began rioting that Monday. Eventually numbering some fifty thousand people, the mob terrorized neighborhoods on the East Side looting scores of stores. Blacks were the targets of most attacks on citizens; several lynchings and beatings occurred. In addition, a black church and orphanage were burned to the ground. All in all, the* *mob caused more than $1.5 million in damages. It is estimated that at least one hundred people died and more than three hundred were injured during the riot.*[1] *Blacks held meetings to discuss the riots and Pennington gave the following speech in August 1863, during one of these gatherings.*

## The Position and Duties of the Colored People (1863)

The mob against the colored people of New York in July 1863 was not the first of its kind, and it may not be the last. In the year 1740, when New York was a British, and a slaveholding city, it was the scene of one of the most curious and malignant attacks upon the colored people to be found on record. At that time the white population of the city was ten thousand; and the colored population was two thousand. By a wicked trick of some evil minded persons, combined with the fears of the timid, a report was gotten up that the negroes of the city, along with a few whites, had entered into a conspiracy to burn the city, and murder all the white inhabitants, except a few of the females. It was charged that this scheme embraced Long Island—then called "Nassau"—and extended even to South Carolina. The result was a legalised mob or public persecution which lasted for more than a year, during which time the entire colored population were subject to the most cruel and unheard of insults, abuses and injuries. There were a hundred and sixty trials on charge of conspiracy with intent to commit arson and murder. Seventy-one were condemned to banishment, or to be sold to the West Indies, eighteen were branded; and thirteen were burned at the stake. The remaining fifty-eight being the slaves of influential owners were acquitted. The volume containing the account of this affair covers nearly four hundred pages. It was compiled by the Supreme Court where the trials were held, and is falsely styled, "The Negro Plot."

Shame has blushed the book out of print. But the records of the old Provincial Supreme Court in the archives in the City Hall, contain all the facts, consisting of the indictment against Caesar, Quack, Cuffeo, &c., &c. Proclamations of the Governor, charges to juries, addresses to the prisoners, when sentenced, altogether forming a cabinet of curiosities. Time corrected the tongue of slander. It fully transpired, that instead of its being a plot of the negroes against the lives and property of the whites, it was a plot of the whites against the lives and liberties of the negroes.

## The Mob of 1863

And, now, after the lapse of more than a hundred and twenty years, we are called to witness a similar, but far more diabolical conspiracy and riotous outrage against the lives and liberties of the descendants of the same people, in the same city.

What shall we call the mob of July 1863? Although I am not now assuming the responsible task of giving it a full designation; yet, I may remark in passing, that intelligent colored men of studious minds, owe it to themselves to record this mob in history by its right name. We should let no mere considerations of present relief deter us from bringing out all the facts, that will fasten the weight of responsibility where it belongs.

If it is an Irish Catholic mob prompted by American Protestant demagogues and negro haters, let it be hereafter known as such in history. If it was a desperate effort to resurrect the old rabid and hateful spirit of colonization, so let it be known to be. If it was an attempt of the southern rebels to plant the black flag of the slavery propagandist on the banks of the Hudson, let future generations so read it. Ye living historians, record the truth, the whole truth and nothing but the truth.

## Its Antecedents

The elements of this mob have been centering and gathering strength in New York, for more than two years. And, as soon as the rebellion broke out, prominent colored men in passing the streets, were often hailed as "Old Abe," or "Jeff. Davis," evidently to feel their loyal pulse, and as it become evident that our sympathies were with the Federal government, we became objects of more marked abuse and insult. From many of the grocery corners, stones, potatoes, and pieces of coal, would often be hurled, by idle young loafers, standing about, with the consent of the keepers of those places, and very often by persons in their employ. The language addressed to colored men, not seemly to record on paper, became the common language of the street, and even of some of the fashionable avenues. The streets were made to ring with words, and sayings, the most filthy, and yet no effort was made by magistrates, the press, or authorities, to suppress these ebulitions of barbarism. In no other country in the world would the streets of refined cities be allowed to be polluted, as those of New York have been, with foul and indecent language, without a word of the rebuke from the press, the pulpit, or the authorities. Every loafer, from the little rebel, who could but just tussle over the curb stone, up to the lusty mutton fisted scamp who could throw a stone of half a pound's weight, across the street at a colored man's head, might anywhere about the city, on any day, and at any hour, salute colored persons with indecent language, using words surcharged with filth, malice, and brutal insult. And what has been the result? Why, just what we might have expected,—the engendering of a public feeling unfriendly toward colored people. This feeling, once created, might at any moment be intensified into an outbreak against its unoffending objects. We have, in this way, been made the victims of certain antagonisms.

## Opposition to the Draft

The opposition to the draft comes largely from that class of men of foreign birth who have declared their intention to become citizens, but who have not done so. They have been duly notified that they could leave the country within sixty days, or submit to the draft. As soon as the President's proclamation containing this notice was made public, men of foreign birth, of this class, began to speak openly against the draft. And for obvious cause. They do not wish to leave the country, and they do not wish to fight. They came to make money, and so far as the war interferes with their schemes, they oppose it.

Now, dishonest politicians aim to make these men believe that the war has been undertaken to abolish slavery; and so far as they believe so, their feelings are against colored people, of course.

From this class, there has been a very considerable mob element. Many of them are a little too shame-faced to be seen with a stone or brick-bat in their hands in the streets; but they have, in large numbers encouraged the mobbing of the colored people. It is known that they have allowed loafers to congregate in their places of business and concoct their plans. Yea, not a few of these men are among your grocerymen, and others that you deal with, and are extremely malignant in their feelings. They are fair to your face, and will take your money, but behind your back, it is "*nigger.*" These men know perfectly well, that in the countries from which they come, conscription laws, of a far more strict, and severe character exist, and they also know that they would not dare to resist those laws, if they were there; and hence their opposition to the draft is ungrateful and revolutionary. Many of this class of men are not so ignorant as to believe that the war is carried on by the President to abolish slavery. They have other objects in view. They fall in with the cry against the negro, only for effect.

## Catholicism and Protestantism

The next point of antagonism which has developed itself in the recent attack upon us, is that between Catholicism and Protestantism.

Why have Irish Catholics led the way in the late murderous attack upon the colored Protestants? It is not known that a single colored Catholic family or individual suffered during the late riots, at the hands of the Irish, except by mistake. If the colored people, as a body, were Roman Catholics, there would be no attacks made upon them by Irish Catholics. During the Sabbaths of the riots, while colored Protestant churches were closed; and colored Protestant ministers had to take shelter out of the city of New York, colored members of Catholic churches were quietly worshipping in Catholic churches without insult, or molestation.

As to the color of the skin. Everybody knows, that Catholics consist of all colors in the known world. In other countries, black priests, officials, and members, are as common as the sun that shines.

As to the labor question. If colored mechanics, and laborers; and all our women and youth who earn wages, were Catholics, we should hear no objection from the Irish Catholics about their employment, because the wages would be good Catholic money, and would go to extend that church.

The Irish objection to us is then, not as colored laborers; but as colored Protestant laborers. The American people may take a lesson from this, and judge what may come next.

## The Labor Question

Let us look at the labor question a little more closely, and see what must be the greed of those who would have us believe that there is not room and labor enough in this country for the citizens of foreign birth, and the colored people of native growth. The legitimate territory of these United States, is about 3,306,863 acres. That is ten times larger than Great Britain and France together. Three times larger than Britain, France, Austria, Prussia, Spain, Portugal and Denmark; and only one-sixth less, in extent, than the fifty-nine, or sixty republics and empires of Europe put together. And yet there are those who would teach the British and other foreigners the selfish and greedy idea that there is not room enough in this country for them and the colored man. Such a notion is ridiculous.

## Lessons of Duty

The foregoing state of fact suggests some lessons of duty.

1st. We must study the use of arms, for *self-defense*. There is no principle of civil, or religious obligation, that requires us to live on, in hazard, and leave our persons, property, and our wives and children at the mercy of barbarians. Self-defense is the first law of nature.

2nd. We must enter into a solemn free colored Protestant industrial or labor league. Let the greedy foreigner know that a part of this country belongs to us; and that we assert the right to live and labor here: That in New York and other cities, we claim the right to buy, hire, occupy and use houses and tenements, for legal considerations; to pass and repass on the streets, lanes, avenues, and all public ways. Our fathers have fought for this country, and helped to free it from the British yoke. We are now fighting to help to free it from the combined conspiracy of Jeff. Davis and Co.; we are doing so with the distinct understanding, that we are to have all our rights as men and as citizens, and that there are to be no side issues, no reservations, either political, civil, or religious. In this struggle we know nothing but God, Manhood, and American Nationality, full and unimpaired.

The right to labor, earn wages, and dispose of our earnings for the support of our families, the education of our children, and to support religious institutions of our free choice, is inherent. No party, or power, in politics, or religion, can alienate this right. No part of our influence has been used to prevent foreigners from coming to this country and enjoying its benefits. We have done them no wrong. What we ask in return is, nonintervention. Let us alone.

3rd. Let us place our daughters, and younger sons in industrial positions, however humble; and secure openings where they may be usefully employed. Every father, and every mother may be of service, not only to their own children, but also to those of others. You will have many applications for "colored help." Be useful to applicants. Prepare your sons and daughters for usefulness, in all the branches of domestic labor and service.

4th. Let our able bodied men go into the United States service. There is no better place for them. If I had a dozen sons, I would rather have them in the United States army and navy, than to have them among our loose population. The army of the United States must, hereafter, be the great bulwark of our life, as a nation. The rebellion has rendered it necessary that we should have a powerful standing army. Colored men should enter the army in force, for the sake of the strength it will give them, the education they will obtain, the pay they will get; and the good service they will do for God, the country, and the race.

### Colonization Influences—Education

5th. We should reconstruct our Union against the insidious influences of colonization. It is a fact, that the time our present troubles began, colored men were very much divided, on the question of our continuance in the country. Hardly any two of our leading men were agreed about the matter. Some had squarely gone over to colonization, adopting the views of those who hold that a black man can never be a man, in this country. Many angry discussions had taken place. Old friendships were broken up, and a bitter spirit had been engendered among us. All this is to be traced to the insidious influences of colonizationists. It is a fact that, for several years past, any prominent colored man in the city of New York who would not cave in, on "*the colored car*" system, and go for some modified scheme of colonization, was sure to be marked; and special effort made to break him down. This influence has been most deadly. Years will not redeem us from its effects. At this moment, while the great and glorious southern field of usefulness *is* spreading and widening before us, there is no adequate plan, or movement on foot among us, for raising up proper agents to occupy the field. Why is this the case? What are we, ministers and teachers, doing? Why is there not some great movement going on, to bring forward young men and women of color for the southern field? These questions are to the point, and call for action, on the part of our ministers and teachers, who are in positions of influence.

We have no right to leave it to the government entirely, nor to any one denomination of whites, to supply this vast field, which is opening before us. Evil always grows out of monopoly. With the exception of what the Zion AME, and the AME churches have done in the way of supplying ministers and teachers for the South, the colored churches North, are doing nothing. Some years ago it was found that eighty, or one hundred thousand of the southern slaves were held as Presbyterian property. Doubtless the great mass of those are now on the freedman's list; but what are the northern Presbyterians doing for their freed brethren? Is there a single colored Congregational or Presbyterian Church in New England, New York, New Jersey, or Pennsylvania, that has a young man in course of training for a teacher, or minister, with reference to the southern field? And echo answers, is there one? Thirty years hard and self-denying labors among the Congregational and Presbyterian churches of color, entitles me to speak, at least to them, upon this subject of religious and educational commissions to the South. These two wealthy bodies have a few semi-mission churches scattered about, in the North—for really not one of them is self-sustaining—but they have no plan for supplying the race with a sufficient number of instructors in this country. Would not some of our influential colored men do well to use an influence with a view to advance this cause or, will they continue to let the colonization influence neutralize their zeal for the advancement of home interests! It is painful to notice, that among the most indifferent to the cause of education, are some, who in former years, have, themselves been the recipients of liberal aid, when they were seeking education; and who now, since they have got into position, seem to be actuated by a jealousy, lest they should encourage too much competition.

I have recently heard of the case of a young man who applied to a colored Presbyterian clergyman for counsel and aid to enable him to obtain an education for the ministry, and was advised to go and join a body where it would require less education to be a minister. The young man was a member of that minister's church, and that church is under the care of one of the wealthiest Presbyteries in the city of New York. Now, it is known that that colored minister is strongly under the influence of prominent men of the colonization school. Hence the tree is known by its fruit. It has been part of the deep laid plan to divide the councils of colored men, and beset the government to unite colonization with emancipation. But God be thanked, that while emancipation is going on well, the unseemly colonization scheme which the President was induced to hitch on to his plan, has proved a failure. This fact should open the eyes of colored men who have been deluded by colonization emissaries.

About a year and a half ago, an official of the colonization society in New York remarked to me, with an appearance of satisfaction, that there was no doubt that the government would appropriate a large amount of money for colonization purposes. But as I said, thank God, it has failed. It is now evident that the country has no colored men to spare to people foreign countries; and no money to spare for expatriating them. The old colonization scheme has been buried so deep, that a century will not give it a resurrection.

## Spirit of Patriotism—Faith in God

Lastly, we should remember that emancipation was resorted to, as a purely military necessity imposed upon this Government in the Providence of an all wise God. The President has no alternative but to fall into the powerful current of events which God had put in motion.

This view of the subject is essential to the cultivation of a true and lofty spirit of patriotism. A true patriot must always feel that he owns and contends for property which God gave him, whether it be life, or liberty, or the pursuit of happiness. His greatest strength will be in the firm conviction that God is transacting his business, so to speak; even though he be called to pass through bitter waters of adversity, he feels that God has not undertaken for him in vain.

When the hand of God is with us, we are strong, and when he shows us his will, in regard to our duties, we should be in earnest to do it.

## A Terrible Contingency

An intelligent view of the history of God's providential dealings with slavery, leave no room to doubt that its doom is sealed in this country; but let us not forget that there is yet a terrible contingency before us. We may have to face, in the field, an army of our own colored brethren of the South! Already it is known that the southern commanders have made use of slaves in battle. And already it is rumored that the Confederate Government thinks seriously of arming the slaves as a retaliative military necessity. It is admitted, that from 1,750,000 to 2,000,000 out of the 4,000,000 of the slaves are yet in the possession of the rebels; of this number they can spare for arms at least 300,000 able bodied men. These men armed and so used, certainly cannot be expected to exercise any more liberty of choice than the poor white union men. So that if those men remain beyond our reach, and are armed and commanded by the Confederates to fight us, they will be obliged to do so. If we take them prisoners, I suppose they will have to be exchanged as others. If they desert and come to us, the case will be different. It is presumed they will do so, when the opportunity presents itself—but, how much mischief they may be compelled to do, in the meantime, it is impossible to foresee.

In my opinion, nothing is more likely to take place, under French influence, than this arming of the slaves by the rebels with the promise of freedom. It would be but a reproduction of the French plan in St. Domingo in 1794, to be followed by the same treachery by the Confederates, should they use the slaves successfully.

I have no doubt that Louis Napoleon is advising Jeff. Davis to this plan. Every week's delay in crushing out this rebellion increases the danger that the slaves may be brought into the field against us. I confess I am not of the number of those who covet such an event, with the expectation that the slaves would come to us *en masse*. It is not to be expected that, in the event of the rebels arming the slaves they would neglect also to present them with every possible allurement to fight hard; and at the same time, to surround them with every imaginable obstacle to their desertion. On our side, the only wise and safe course is to press rapidly into the heart of the slave country, and work out the problem of the Proclamation of freedom. We must prove to the slaves that we have both the will and the power to give effect to the proclamation, and that it is not a mere sound, reaching their ears, upon the wings of the wind. Here is where our danger lies. The President is right. The proclamation is the word of God's holy Providence, so to speak; but the great North is slow to repent of slavery. There is yet a great deal of wicked, angry, and unrighteous feeling in the heart of the Northern people. It may be that God intends to use the sword as a lance to bleed the whole nation, until she begins to faint, for very loss of blood, and then to swathe up the opened vein, and apply restoratives.

Let us, then, not flatter ourselves that we shall escape. Let us not be deceived by those who would persuade us that there is any destiny for us, as an integral part of this American nation, separate from the nation, as a whole. If the slaves are brought into the field by the Confederates, it will be a sad and awful day for us.

We conclude, then, that those who, in the late riots undertook to expel by murder, fire, and persecution, the colored people for the accomplishment, either of sham democratic, or Roman Catholic propagandism, have undertaken a heavy and dangerous task, a task in which all the plans and purposes of a just God are against them. And it now remains to be seen whether intelligent colored men among us who have suffered in the late riots will allow the history of that outrageous scheme to pass unrecorded. Shall a few thousand dollars of relief money, and a few words of good counsel, and consolation, be a sufficient inducement to neglect our own history? Remember, that one of the great tests of civilization, is that a people should be able to record their own annals, by the pens of their own historians.

How does the matter sum up? It sums up thus; for more than a year, the riot spirit had been culminating, before it burst forth. The police authorities were frequently applied to, by respectable colored persons, without being able to obtain any redress when assaulted and abused in the streets. We have sometimes pointed to the aggressors but no arrests have been made. We have appealed to them for protection and apprised them of the fact that we had good reason to believe that a general attack was about to be made upon us, under false pretenses. We have pointed to the street corners, and to the rowdies who stand at them, and in open day light assaulted colored persons, in passing. We have presented proof sufficient to indict houses where rioters assembled. We have named men who hired idle boys to throw stones at colored men, and offered to prove it. The hand of the ruffian has done its work, in sending to the bar of God, a number of swift witnesses against the perpetrators of the deeds of July, 1863. The better class of people of New York City would doubtless feel relief, could these departed spirits be called back to their earthly homes, and their testimony, now recorded on the book of God against the bloody city, be erased. But as now, no power can restore those valuable members of society, so the full history of the riot must stand in all its painful bearings.

The loss of life and property make only a small part of the damage. The breaking up of families; and business relations just beginning to prosper: the blasting of hopes just dawning; the loss of precious harvest time which will never again return; the feeling of insecurity engendered; the confidence destroyed; the reaction; and lastly, the gross insult offered to our character as a people, sum up a weight of injury which can only be realized by the most enlightened and sensitive minds among us.

The injury extends to our churches, schools, societies for mutual aid and improvement, as well as to the various branches of industry. And amidst the most honest, trustworthy, useful laborious, pious, and respected, none have suffered more than the sisters of the laundry. These excellent women are the support of our churches, ministers, and the encouragement of our school teachers. In these worthy women, New York landlords have found their best tenants. Many of them are the only support of orphan children. Many of them, the wives of absent seamen, and some of coasting men, and others who are absent during the week, but spend their Sabbaths in the city. The nature of the business of these women is such, that they are entrusted by their customers with large quantities of valuable clothing, from Monday morning until Saturday evening, when they are expected to return them, to a piece, in perfect order. The attack made upon the houses of the colored people has had the effect to render it extra hazardous to have valuable articles be looked upon as common plunder.

The pretense, therefore, that there was no intention, on the part of the rioters, to injure our women is false. The severest blow was aimed at them.

There was not only an attempt to murder, *en masse*, their only male protectors, but it was the design of the rioters also to render their homes dangerous and insecure, both for life and business.

For all the purposes, therefore, of social, civil, and religious enjoyment, and right, we hold New York solemnly bound to insure us, as citizens, permanent security in our homes. Relief, and damage money, is well enough. But it cannot atone, fully, for evils done by riots. It cannot bring back our murdered dead. It cannot remove the insults we feel; and finally, it gives no proof that the people have really changed their minds for the better, towards us.

During the late riots, my wife, and other lone females in the same tenement house, were repeatedly annoyed and threatened with mob law and violence. When there was not a man about the house, by night or by day, the rioters prowled about, watching for the return of absent marked victims. Failing to secure those, the defenseless women were repeatedly ordered, or mobishly advised to leave the house, and told that they "*must not be seen to carry a parcel away in their hands!*" Such was the treatment which our females received at the hands of the New York mobites, in the absence of their male protectors, which leaves no manner of doubt that a part of the hellish scheme was to mob and otherwise maltreat our women. Read this, and judge of its design: "The mob will come to this house, soon. You nigger wenches must leave here, and you must not carry away a bundle, or anything, with you." Such is a copy of a paper stuck under the door.

### *Notes*

*Sermon source:* Black Abolitionist Archives, Doc. No. 27335, at the University of Detroit's Mercy Library Web site, http://udmercy.edu/BAA/Pennington_27335spe.pdf (accessed August 15, 2009).

1. Iver Bernstein, *The New York City Draft Riots: Their Significance for American Society and Politics in the Age of Civil War* (New York: Oxford University Press, 1990).
2. Larry G. Murphy, J. Gordon Melton, and Gary L. Ward, eds., *Encyclopedia of African American Religions*, 582.
3. Ibid.
4. Ibid.

### *Bibliographical Sources*

Ellis, Robb Edward. *The Epic of New York City: A Narrative History.* New York: Kodansha International, 1966.

McPherson, J.M. *Ordeal by Fire: The Civil War and Reconstruction*, 2nd ed. New York: McGraw-Hill, Inc., 1992.

Murphy, Larry G., J. Gordon Melton, and Gary L. Ward, eds. *Encyclopedia of African American Religions.* New York: Garland Publishing, 1993.

Murray, Andrew E. *Presbyterians and the Negro: A History.* Philadelphia: Presbyterian Historical Society, 1966.

Washington, Joseph R., Jr. *The Fugitive Foreign and Domestic Doctor of Divinity.* Lewiston, NY: Edwin Mellon Press, 1990.
Young, Henry H. *Major Black Religious Leaders 1755–1940.* Nashville, TN: Abingdon Press, 1977.

# MARIA W. STEWART

*(1803–1879)*

Maria (Miller) Stewart was born free in 1803 in Hartford, Connecticut. According to Stewart, at age five she was orphaned and given in service to a clergyman's family. At fifteen, she left and studied the Bible in a sabbath school until age twenty. She married James W. Stewart in 1826 in Boston. He was a shipping agent and had been a seaman in the War of 1812. They became activists and members of Boston's black middle class under the tutelage of David Walker, who in 1829 wrote the provocative black empowerment manifesto *David Walker's Appeal in Four Articles Together with a Preamble to the Colored Citizens of the World, But in Particular and Very Expressly, to Those of the United States of America*, published in the anti-slavery newspaper, *The Liberator.* Maria Stewart was militant, a black nationalist who believed religion and black self-determination would lift blacks from degradation. She considered herself a voice of God for liberation. She believed in self-defense, and focused on black women's survival, moral purity, and social advancement.

She was widowed, only three years after marrying. She did not have children. The death of her husband and of Walker in 1830 brought on the search that was followed by her religious conversion. She ministered in Baptist, Methodist, and Episcopal churches. Stewart believed that God ordained her career as a preacher. Her meditation, "What If I Am a Woman," also known as her farewell address to Boston, was her apologetics for women preachers. In it she appealed to biblical women who were leaders and preachers. She was bold and fearless; some believed that she expected to be killed or die an early death because of her prophetic voice.

Her sermons and writings are peppered with songs, directly addressed to the listener, and prayers to God. She is confrontational and calls for acknowledgement of sin by white America, with the assurance of judgment from God to come for the abuse and degradation that America has foisted on the children of Africa. She chides her people for their lack of activism and demands leadership and moral uprightness as requisites for the coming freedom of blacks, especially black men. She often addressed her work to "ye daughters of Africa," confirming her call especially, but not limited to, women. She exhorted black women to collaborate with one another, start businesses, and lift the race. She detested slavery, and believed that ignorance was a form of slavery. She preached salvation in Christ alone, and believed this salvation to be her authority for preaching hope and self-determination for blacks. Her rhetoric was fierce, direct, and unequivocal. Also, she preached about Africa and encouraged blacks to be proud of their African heritage.

Stewart embarked on antislavery and women's rights lecture circuits in the 1830s. Her address in Boston's Franklin Hall on September 21, 1832, was the first public lecture by an American woman before a mixed audience of whites and blacks, males and females, and preceded by more than five years the famous antislavery speeches made by the Grimke sisters. Her public speaking career in Boston lasted just under three years. She moved to New York in 1833 and began to teach. In 1853, she moved to Maryland and there taught private students. Sometime between 1861 and 1863 she helped found a school for black children in Washington, D.C. She succeeded Sojourner Truth as the head of housekeeping services at the Freemen's Hospital at Howard University in the early 1870s. She died in 1879.

Her collected works, *Productions of Mrs. Maria Stewart*, were first published in 1835; an enlarged edition was published in 1879 under the title *Meditations from the Pen of Mrs. Maria W. Stewart*. Stewart funded the publications with the pension she received as a war widow.

• • •

*This message was delivered in Boston at Franklin Hall, the meeting place of the New England Anti-Slavery Society. In it, Stewart argues forcefully for the rights of women and poignantly articulates the third-class treatment that black women are receiving in America. She exhorts women and men to immediately and courageously stand up against the forces that dehumanize black women and men, and argues forcefully that blacks have all the talents and abilities of whites, but have not been allowed to flourish.*

## Why Sit Ye Here and Die?
## (September 21, 1832)

Why sit ye here and die? If we say we will go to a foreign land, the famine and the pestilence are there, and there we shall die. If we sit here, we shall die. Come let us plead our cause before the whites: if they save us alive, we shall live—and if they kill us, we shall but die.[1]

Methinks I heard a spiritual interrogation—"Who shall go forward, and take off the reproach that is cast upon the people of color? Shall it be a woman?" And my heart made this reply—"If it is thy will, be it even so, Lord Jesus!"

I have heard much respecting the horrors of slavery; but may Heaven forbid that the generality of my color throughout these United States should experience any more of its horrors than to be a servant of servants, or hewers of wood and drawers of water! Tell us no more of southern slavery; for with few exceptions, although I may be very erroneous in my opinion, yet I consider our condition but little better than that. Yet, after all, methinks there are no chains so galling as those that bind the soul, and exclude it from the vast field of useful and scientific knowledge. O, had I received the advantages of early education, my ideas would, ere now, have expanded far and wide; but, alas! I possess nothing but moral capability—no teachings but the teachings of the Holy Spirit.

I have asked several individuals of my sex, who transact business for themselves, if providing our girls were to give them the most satisfactory references, they would not be willing to grant them an equal opportunity with others? Their reply has been for their own part, they had no objection; but as it was not the custom, were they to take them into their employ, they would be in danger of losing the public patronage.

And such is the powerful force of prejudice. Let our girls possess what amiable qualities of soul they may; let their characters be fair and spotless as innocence itself; let their natural taste and ingenuity be what they may; it is impossible for scarce an individual of them to rise above the condition of servants. Ah! why is this cruel and unfeeling distinction? Is it merely because God has made our complexion to vary? If it be, O shame to soft, relenting humanity! "Tell it not in Gath! publish it not in the streets of Askelon!"[2] Yet, after all, methinks were the American free people of color to turn their attention more assiduously to moral worth and intellectual improvement, this would be the result: prejudice would gradually diminish, and the whites would be compelled to say, unloose those fetters!

*Though black their skins as shades of night,*
*Their hearts are pure, their souls are white.*

Few white persons of either sex, who are calculated for any thing else, are willing to spend their lives and bury their talents in performing mean, servile labor. And such is the horrible idea that I entertain respecting a life of servitude, that if I conceived of there being no possibility of my rising above the condition of a servant, I would gladly hail death as a welcome messenger. O, horrible idea, indeed! to possess noble souls aspiring after high and honorable acquirements, yet confined by the chains of ignorance and poverty to lives of continual drudgery and toil. Neither do I know of any who have enriched themselves by spending their lives as house-domestics, washing windows, shaking carpets, brushing boots, or tending upon gentlemen's tables. I can but die for expressing my sentiments; and I am as willing to die by the sword as the pestilence; for I am a true born American; your blood flows in my veins, and your spirit fires my breast.

I observed a piece in the *Liberator* a few months since, stating that the colonizationists had published a work respecting us, asserting that we were lazy and idle. I confute them on that point. Take us generally as a people, we are neither lazy nor idle; and considering how little we have to excite or stimulate us, I am almost astonished that there are so many industrious and ambitious ones to be found; although I acknowledge, with extreme sorrow, that there are some who never were and never will be serviceable to society. And have you not a similar class among yourselves?

Again. It was asserted that we were "a ragged set, crying for liberty."[3] I reply to it, the whites have so long and so loudly proclaimed the theme of equal rights and privileges, that our souls have caught the flame also, ragged as we are. As far as our merit deserves, we feel a common desire to rise above the condition of servants and drudges. I have learnt, by bitter experience, that continual hard labor deadens the energies of the soul, and benumbs the faculties of the mind; the ideas become confined, the mind barren, and, like the scorching sands of Arabia, produces nothing; or, like the uncultivated soil, brings forth thorns and thistles.

Again, continual hard labor irritates our tempers and sours our dispositions; the whole system becomes worn out with toil and failure; nature herself becomes almost exhausted, and we care but little whether we live or die. It is true, that the free people of color throughout these United States are neither bought nor sold, nor under the lash of the cruel driver; many obtain a comfortable support; but few, if any, have an opportunity of becoming rich and independent; and the employments we most pursue are as unprofitable to us as the spider's web or the floating bubbles that vanish into air. As servants, we are respected; but let us presume to aspire any higher, our employer regards us no longer. And were it not that the King eternal has declared that Ethiopia shall stretch forth her hands unto God, I should indeed despair.

I do not consider it derogatory, my friends, for persons to live out to service. There are many whose inclination leads them to aspire no higher;

and I would highly commend the performance of almost any thing for an honest livelihood; but where constitutional strength is wanting, labor of this kind, in its mildest form, is painful. And doubtless many are the prayers that have ascended to Heaven from Africa's daughters for strength to perform their work. O, many are the tears that have been shed for the want of that strength! Most of our color have dragged out a miserable existence of servitude from the cradle to the grave. And what literary acquirements can be made, or useful knowledge derived, from either maps, books or charts, by those who continually drudge from Monday morning until Sunday noon? O, ye fairer sisters, whose hands are never soiled, whose nerves and muscles are never strained, go learn by experience! Had we had the opportunity that you have had, to improve our moral and mental faculties, what would have hindered our intellects from being as bright, and our manners from being as dignified as yours? Had it been our lot to have been nursed in the lap of affluence and ease, and to have basked beneath the smiles and sunshine of fortune, should we not have naturally supposed that we were never made to toil? And why are not our forms as delicate, and our constitutions as slender, as yours? Is not the workmanship as curious and complete? Have pity upon us, have pity upon us, O ye who have hearts to feel for other's woes; for the hand of God has touched us. Owing to the disadvantages under which we labor, there are many flowers among us that are

*. . . born to bloom unseen*
*And waste their fragrance on the desert air.*[4]

My beloved brethren, as Christ has died in vain for those who will not accept of offered mercy, so will it be vain for the advocates of freedom to spend their breath in our behalf, unless with united hearts and souls you make some mighty efforts to raise your sons and daughters from the horrible state of servitude and degradation in which they are placed. It is upon you that woman depends; she can do but little besides using her influence; and it is for her sake and yours that I have come forward and made myself a hissing and a reproach among the people; for I am also one of the wretched and miserable daughters of the descendants of fallen Africa. Do you ask, why are you wretched and miserable? I reply, look at many of the most worthy and interesting of us doomed to spend our lives in gentlemen's kitchens. Look at our young men, smart, active and energetic, with souls filled with ambitious fire; if they look forward, alas! what are their prospects? They can be nothing but the humblest laborers, on account of their dark complexions; hence many of them lose their ambition, and become worthless. Look at our middle-aged men, clad in their rusty plaids and coats; in winter, every cent they earn goes to buy their wood and pay their rents; their poor wives also toil beyond their strength, to help support their families. Look at our aged sires, whose heads are whitened with the front of seventy winters, with their old wood-saws on their backs. Alas, what keeps us so? Prejudice, ignorance and poverty.

But ah! methinks our oppression is soon to come to an end; yea, before the Majesty of heaven, our groans and cries have reached the ears of the Lord of Sabaoth. As the prayers and tears of Christians will avail the finally impenitent nothing; neither will the prayers and tears of the friends of humanity avail us any thing, unless we possess a spirit of virtuous emulation within our breasts. Did the pilgrims, when they first landed on these shores, quietly compose themselves, and say, "the Britons have all the money and all the power, and we must continue their servants forever?" Did they sluggishly sigh and say, "our lot is hard, the Indians own the soil, and we cannot cultivate it?" No; they first made powerful efforts to raise themselves and then God raised up those illustrious patriots Washington and Lafayette to assist and defend them. And, my brethren, have you made a powerful effort? Have you prayed the legislature for mercy's sake to grant you all the rights and privileges of free citizens, that your daughters may raise to that degree of respectability which true merit deserves, and your sons above the servile situations which most of them fill?

✦ ✦ ✦

*In this message Stewart gives the reasons that black women should participate in politics and be change agents. She encourages and chides women to act. In the former speech in 1832 in Boston's Franklin Hall, she spoke strongly to a mixed audience of the need for justice for women. In this speech, she makes the case for her right to fight for women who need justice.*

## What If I Am a Woman?
## (September 21, 1833)

*Is this vile world a friend to grace,*
*To help me on to God? Ah, no![5]*

*For it is with great tribulation that any shall enter through the gates of the holy city.* —Acts 14:22

My Respected Friends,
You have heard me observe that the shortness of time, the certainty of death, and the instability of all things here, induce me to turn my thoughts from earth to heaven. Borne down with a heavy load of sin and shame, my conscience filled with remorse; considering the throne of God forever guiltless, and my own eternal condemnation as just, I was at last brought to accept of salvation as a free gift, in and through the merits of a crucified Redeemer. Here I was brought to see,

*Tis not by works of righteousness*
*That our own hands have done,*
*But we are saved by grace alone,*
*Abounding through the Son.*[6]

After these convictions, in imagination I found myself sitting at the feet of Jesus, clothed in my right mind. For I had been like a ship tossed to and fro, in a storm at sea. Then was I glad when I realized the dangers I had escaped; and then I consecrated my soul and body, and all the powers of my mind to his service, and from that time henceforth; yea, even for evermore, amen.

I found that religion was full of benevolence; I found there was joy and peace in believing, and I felt as though I was commanded to come out from the world and be separate; to go forward and be baptized. Methought I heard a spiritual interrogation, are you able to drink of that cup that I have drank of? And to be baptized with the baptism that I have been baptized with?[7] And my heart made this reply: Yea, Lord, I am able. Yet amid these bright hopes, I was filled with apprehensive fears, lest they were false. I found that sin still lurked within; it was hard for me to renounce all for Christ, when I saw my earthly prospects blasted. O, how bitter was that cup. Yet I drank it to its very dregs. It was hard for me to say, thy will be done; yet I was made to bend and kiss the rod. I was at last made willing to be anything or nothing, for my Redeemer's sake. Like many, I was anxious to retain the world in one hand, and religion in the other. "Ye cannot serve and God and mammon,"[8] sounded in my ear, and with giant-strength, I cut off my right hand, as it were, and plucked out my right eye, and cast them from me, thinking it better to enter life halt and maimed, rather than having two hands or eyes to be cast into hell.[9] Thus ended these mighty conflicts, and I received this heart-cheering promise, "That neither death, nor life, nor principalities, nor powers, nor things present, nor things to come, should be able to separate me from the love of Christ Jesus, our Lord."[10]

And truly, I can say with St. Paul that at my conversion I came to the people in the fullness of the gospel of grace.[11] Having spent a few months in the city of ——, previous, I saw the flourishing condition of their churches, and the progress they were making in their Sabbath Schools. I visited their Bible classes, and heard of the union that existed in their Female Associations. On my arrival here, not finding scarce an individual who felt interested in these subjects, and but few of the whites, except Mr. Garrison, and his friend, Mr. Knapp; and hearing that those gentlemen had observed that female influence was powerful, my soul became fired with a holy zeal for your cause; every nerve and muscle in me was engaged in your behalf. I felt that I had a great work to perform; and was in haste to make a profession of my faith in Christ, that I might be about my Father's business.[12] Soon after I made this profession, The Spirit of God came before me, and I spake before many. When going home, reflecting on what I had said, I felt ashamed, and knew not where I should hide myself. A something said within my breast, "Press forward, I will be with thee." And my heart made this reply, Lord, if thou wilt be with me, then I will speak for thee as long as I live. And thus far I have every reason to believe that it is the divine influence of the Holy Spirit operating upon my heart that could possibly induce me to make the feeble and unworthy efforts that I have.

But to begin my subject: "Ye have heard that it hath been said, whoso is angry with his brother without a cause, shall be in danger of the judgment; and whoso shall say to his brother, Raca, shall be in danger of the council. But whosoever shall say, thou fool, shall be in danger of hell-fire."[13] For several years my heart was in continual sorrow. And I believe that the Almighty beheld from his holy habitation, the affliction wherewith I was afflicted, and heard the false misrepresentations wherewith I was misrepresented, and there was none to help. Then I cried unto the Lord in my troubles. And thus for wise and holy purposes, best known to himself, he has raised me in the midst of my enemies, to vindicate my wrongs before this people; and to reprove them from sin, as I have reasoned to them of righteousness and judgment to come. "For as the heavens are higher than the earth, so are his ways above our ways, and his thoughts above our thoughts."[14] I believe, that for wise and holy purposes, best known to himself, he hath unloosed my tongue, and put his word into my mouth, in order to confound and put all those to shame that have rose up against me. For he hath clothed my face with steel, and lined my forehead with brass. He hath put his testimony within me and engraved his seal on my forehead. And with these weapons I have indeed set the fiends of earth and hell at defiance.

What if I am a woman; is not the God of ancient times the God to these modern days? Did he not raise up Deborah to be a mother and judge in Israel? Did not Queen Esther save the lives of the Jews? And Mary Magdalene first declare the resurrection of Christ from the dead? Come, said the woman of Samaria, and see a man that hath told me all things that ever I did; is it not this the Christ? St. Paul declared that it was a shame for a woman to speak in public, yet our great High Priest and Advocate did not condemn the woman for a more notorious offense than this; neither will he condemn this worthless worm. The bruised reed he will not break, and the smoking flax he will not quench till he send forth judgment unto victory. Did St. Paul but know of our wrongs and deprivations, I presume he would make no objection to our pleading in public for our rights.

Again: Holy women ministered unto Christ and the apostles; and women of refinement in all ages, more or less, have had a voice in moral religious and political subjects. Again: Why the Almighty hath imparted unto me the power of speaking thus I cannot tell. "And Jesus lifted up his voice and said, I thank thee, O Father, Lord of heaven and earth, that thou hast hid these things from the wise and prudent and hast revealed them unto babes: even so, Father, for so it seemed good in thy sight."[15]

But to convince you of the high opinion that was formed of the capacity and ability of woman by the ancients, I would refer you to "Sketches of the Fair Sex."[16] Read to the fifty-first page, and you will find that several of the northern nations imagined that women could look into futurity, and that they had about them an inconceivable something approaching to divinity. Perhaps the idea was only the effect of the sagacity common to the sex, and the advantages which their natural address gave them over rough and simple warriors. Perhaps, also, those barbarians, surprised at the influence which beauty has over force, were led to ascribe to the supernatural attraction a charm which they could not comprehend. A belief, however, that the Deity more readily communicates himself to women, has at one time or other prevailed in every quarter of the earth: nor only among the Germans and the Britons, but all the people of Scandinavia were possessed of it. Among the Greeks, women delivered the oracles. The respect the Romans paid to the Sybils is well known. The Jews had their prophetesses. The prediction of the Egyptian women obtained much credit at Rome, even unto the emperors. And in most barbarous nations all things that have the appearance of being supernatural, the mysteries of religion, the secrets of physic, and the rights of magic, were in the possession of women.

If such women as are here described have once existed, be no longer astonished, then, my brethren and friends, that God at this eventful period should raise up your own females to strive by their example, both in public and private, to assist those who are endeavoring to stop the strong current of prejudice that flows so profusely against us at present. No longer ridicule their efforts, it will be counted for sin. For God makes use of feeble means sometimes to bring about his most exalted purposes.

In the fifteenth century, the general spirit of this period is worthy of observation. We might then have seen women preaching and mixing themselves in controversies. Women occupying the chair of Philosophy and Justice; women haranguing in Latin before the Pope; women writing in Greek and studying in Hebrew; nuns were poetesses and women of quality divines; and young girls who had studied eloquence would, with the sweetest countenances and the most plaintiff voices, pathetically exhort the Pope and the Christian princes to declare war against the Turks. Women in those days devoted their leisure hours to contemplation and study. The religious spirit which has animated women in all ages showed itself at this time. It has made them, by turns, martyrs, apostles, warriors, and concluded in making them divines and scholars.[17]

Why cannot a religious spirit animate us now? Why cannot we become divines and scholars? Although learning is somewhat requisite, yet recollect that those great apostles, Peter and James, were ignorant and unlearned. They were taken from a fishing-boat, and made fishers of men.

In the thirteenth century, a young lady of Bologne devoted herself to the study of the Latin language and of the laws. At the age of twenty-three she pronounced a funeral oration in Latin in the great church of Bologne; and to be admitted as an orator, she had neither need of indulgence on account of her youth or of her sex. At the age of twenty-six she took the degree of doctor of laws, and began publicly to expound the Institutes of Justinian. At the age of thirty, her great reputation raised her to a chair, where she taught the law to a prodigious concourse of scholars from all nations. She joined the charms and accomplishments of a woman to all the knowledge of a man. And such was the power of her eloquence, that her beauty was only admired when her tongue was silent.

What if such women as are here described should rise among our sable race? And it is not impossible; for it is not the color of the skin that makes the man or the woman, but the principle formed in the soul. Brilliant wit will shine, come from whence it will; and genius and talent will not hide the brightness of its luster.

But to return to my subject. The mighty work of reformation has begun among this people. The dark clouds of ignorance are dispersing. The light of science is bursting forth. Knowledge is beginning to flow; nor will its moral influence be extinguished till its refulgent rays have spread over us from East to West and from North to South. Thus far is this mighty work begun, but not as yet accomplished. Christians must awake from their slumbers. Religion must flourish among them before the church will be built up in its purity or immorality be suppressed.

Yet, notwithstanding your prospects are thus fair and bright, I am about to leave you, perhaps never more to return; for I find it is no use for me, as an individual, to try to make myself useful among my color in this city. It was contempt for my moral and religious opinions in private that drove me thus before a public. Had experience more plainly shown me that it was the nature of man to crush his fellow, I should not have thought it so hard. Wherefore, my respected friends, let us no longer talk of prejudice till prejudice becomes extinct at home. Let us no longer talk of opposition till we cease to oppose our own. For while these evils exist, to talk is like giving breath to the air and labor to the wind. Though wealth is far more highly prized than humble merit, yet none of these things move me. Having God for my friend and portion, what have I to fear? Promotion cometh neither from the East or West; and as long as it is the will of God, I rejoice that I am as I am; for man in his best estate is altogether vanity. Men of eminence have mostly risen from obscurity, nor will I, although a female of a darker hue, and far more obscure than they, bend my head or hang my harp upon willows; for though poor, I will virtuous prove. And if it is the will of my Heavenly Father to reduce me to penury and want, I am ready to say: Amen, even so be it. "The foxes have holes, and the birds of the air have nests, but the Son of man hath not where to lay his head."[18]

During the short period of my Christian warfare, I have indeed had to contend against the fiery darts of the devil. And was it not that the righteous are kept by the mighty power of God through faith unto salvation, long before this I should have proved to be like the seed by the wayside; for it has actually appeared to me, at different periods, as though the powers of earth and hell had combined against me, to prove my overthrow. Yet amidst their dire attempts, I found the Almighty to be "a friend that sticketh closer than a brother."[19] He never will forsake the soul that leans on him; though he chastens and corrects, it is for the soul's best interest. "And as a father pitieth his children, so the Lord pitieth them that fear him."[20]

But some of you said: "Do not talk so much about religion; the people do not wish to hear you. We know these things; tell us something we do not know." If you know these things, my dear friends, and have performed them, far happier and more prosperous would you now have been. "He that knoweth his Lord's will, and obeyeth it not, shall be beaten with many stripes."[21] Sensible of this, I have, regardless of the frowns and scoffs of a guilty world, plead up religion and the pure principles of morality among you. Religion is the most glorious theme that mortals can converse upon. The older it grows the more new beauties it displays. Earth, with its brilliant attractions, appears mean and sordid when compared to it. It is that fountain that has no end, and those that drink thereof shall never thirst; for it is, indeed, a well of water springing up in the soul unto everlasting life.

Again: Those ideas of greatness which are held forth to us are vain delusions—are airy visions which we shall never realize. All that man can say or do can never elevate us; it is a work that must be effected between God and ourselves. And how? By dropping all political discussions in our behalf; for these, in my opinion, sow the seed of discord and strengthen the cord of prejudice. A spirit of animosity is already risen, and unless it is quenched, a fire will burst forth and devour us, and our young will be slain by the sword. It is the sovereign will of God that our condition should be thus and so. "For he hath formed one vessel for honor and another for dishonor." And shall the clay say to him that formed it: Why hast Thou formed me thus? It is high time for us to drop political discussions; and when our day of deliverance comes, God will provide a way for us to escape, and fight his own battles.

Finally, my brethren, let us follow after godliness, and the things which make for peace. Cultivate your own minds and morals: real merit will elevate you. Pure religion will burst your fetters. Turn your attention to industry. Strive to please your employers. Lay up what you earn. And remember that the grave distinction withers and the high and low are alike renowned.

But I draw to a conclusion. Long will the kind sympathy of some much-loved friend be written on the table of my memory, especially those kind of individuals who have stood by me like pitying angels and befriended me when in the midst of difficulty, many blessings rest on them. Gratitude is all the tribute I can offer. A rich reward awaits them.

To my unconverted friends, one and all, I would say, shortly this frail tenement of mine will be dissolved and lie mouldering in ruins. O, solemn thought! Yet why should I revolt, for it is the glorious hope of a blessed immorality beyond the grave that has supported me thus far through this vale of tears. Who among you will strive to meet me at the right hand of

Christ? For the great day of retribution is fast approaching; and who shall be able to abide his coming? You are forming characters for eternity. As you live, so you will die; as death leaves you, so judgment will find you. Then shall we receive the glorious welcome: "Come, ye blessed of my Father, inherit the kingdom prepared for you from before the foundation of the world."[22] Or hear the heartrending sentence: "Depart, ye cursed, into everlasting fire prepared for the devil and his angels."[23] When thrice ten thousand years have rolled away, eternity will be but just begun. Your ideas will but just begin to expand. O, eternity, who can unfathom thine end or comprehend thy beginning?

Dearly beloved, I have made myself contemptible in the eyes of many, that I might win some. But it has been like labor in vain. "Paul may plant and Apollos water, but God alone giveth the increase."[24]

To my brethren and sisters in the church I would say, be ye clothed with the breast-plate of righteousness, having your loins girt about you with truth, prepared to meet the bridegroom at his coming: for blessed are those servants that are found watching.

Farewell! In a few short years from now we shall meet in those upper regions where parting will be no more. There we shall sing and shout, and shout and sing, and make heaven's high arches ring. There we shall range in rich pastures and partake of those living streams that never dry. O, blissful thought! Hatred and contention shall cease, and we shall join with redeemed millions in ascribing glory and honor and riches and power and blessing to the Lamb that was slain and to Him that sitteth upon the throne. Nor eye hath seen nor ear heard, neither hath it entered into the heart of man to conceive of the joys that are prepared for them that love God. Thus far, has my life been almost a life of complete disappointment. God has tried me as by fire. Well was I aware that if I contended boldly for his cause I must suffer. Yet I chose rather to suffer affliction with his people than to enjoy the pleasures of sin for a season. And I believe that the glorious declaration was about to be made applicable to me that was made to God's ancient convent people by the prophet: "Comfort ye, comfort ye, my people; say unto her that her warfare is accomplished, and that her inequities are pardoned."[25] I believe that a rich reward awaits me, if not in this world, in the world to come. O, blessed reflection. The bitterness of my soul has departed from those who endeavor to discourage and hinder me in my Christian progress, and I can now forgive my enemies, bless those who have hated me, and cheerfully pray for those who have despitefully used and persecuted me. Fare ye well! Farewell!

## NOTES

*Sermon source:* "Why Sit Ye Here and Die?" is reprinted from Marilyn Richardson, ed., *Maria W. Stewart, America's First Black Woman Political Writer: Essays and Speeches* (Bloomington: Indiana University Press, 1987), 45–49. "What If I Am a Woman?" is from Maria W. Stewart, *Productions of Mrs. Maria W. Stewart, Presented to the First African Baptist Church & Society of the City of Boston. Boston: Published by Friends of Freedom and Virture, 1835*, reprinted in *Lift Every Voice: African American Oratory, 1787–1900*, ed. Philip S. Foner and Robert Branham (Tuscaloosa: University of Alabama Press, 1998), 135–42.

1. The beginning lines of this speech are likely a paraphrase of 2 Kings 7:4. Stewart often quoted scriptures; she was reared by a clergyman's family from age five to fifteen and attended sabbath schools for five years.
2. 2 Samuel 1:20 (King James Version).
3. The author of this quote is not indicated by the writings of Stewart. It is a general quote that almost anyone could have given regarding the state of Negroes during Stewart's time.
4. These lines are a paraphrase from "Elegy Written in a Country Churchyard," by Thomas Gray.
5. This quote is a line from the song, "Am I a Soldier of the Cross," written by Isaac Watts in 1709.
6. This quote is likely from the song "Salvation by Grace," written by Isaac Watts.
7. Matthew 20:22 (KJV).
8. Matthew 6:24 (KJV).
9. Mark 9:43 (KJV).
10. Romans 8:38, 39 (KJV).
11. Romans 15:29 (KJV).
12. Luke 2:49 (KJV).
13. Matthew 5:22 (KJV).
14. Isaiah 55:9 (KJV).
15. Matthew 11:24–26 (KJV).
16. This reference is to a book by John Adams, *Woman, Sketches of the History, Genius, Disposition, Accomplishments, Employment, Customs and Importance of the Fair Sex, in all Parts of the World. Interspersed with Many Singular and Entertaining Anecdotes. By A Friend to the* Sex (London: Printed for G. Kearsley, 1790).
17. According to Marilyn Richardson, Stewart is also reporting information here from the book by John Adams. See Marilyn Richardson, "'What If I Am A Woman?'": Maria W. Stewart's Defense of Black Women's Political Activism," in Donald M. Jacobs, ed., *Courage and Conscience: Black and White Abolitionists in Boston* (Bloomington: Indiana University Press, 1993), 201–3.
18. Matthew 8:20 and Luke 9:58 (KJV).
19. Proverbs 18:24 (KJV).
20. Psalm 103:13 (KJV).
21. Paraphrase of St. Luke 12:47 (KJV).
22. Matthew 25:34 (KJV).
23. Matthew 25:41 (KJV).

24. Paraphrase of 1 Corinthians 3:6 (KJV).
25. Paraphrase of Isaiah 40:2 (KJV).

### *Bibliographical Sources*

Flexner, Eleanor. *Century of Struggle: The Women's Rights Movement in the United States*. Cambridge, MA: Belknap Press, 1959.

Loewenberg, Bert James, and Ruth Bogin, eds. *Black Women in Nineteenth-Century American Life*. University Park: Pennsylvania State University Press, 1991.

Martin, Clarice J. "Biblical Theodicy and Black Women's Spiritual Autobiography: 'The Miry Bog, the Desolate Pit, a New Song in My Mouth,'" in *A Troubling in My Soul*, ed. Emilie Townes. Maryknoll, NY: Orbis Books, 1993.

Richardson, Marilyn, ed. *Maria W. Stewart, America's First Black Woman Political Writer: Essays and Speeches*. Bloomington: Indiana University Press, 1987.

Smith, Jessie Carney, ed. *Notable Black American Women*. Detroit: Gale Research, 1992, 1083–87.

Yee, Shirley. *Black Women Abolitionists: A Study in Activism, 1828–1860*. Knoxville: University of Tennessee Press, 1992, 112–16.

## SOJOURNER TRUTH

*(ca. 1797–1883)*

Isabella Bomefree (also spelled Baumfree) was born into slavery in the Hudson River county of Ulster, New York, around 1797. Her parents, James and Betsy, were enslaved by a Colonel Charles Hardenbergh.

Around 1814, Isabella married a fellow slave named Thomas. This may have been a marriage forced upon Truth by her third slave owner, John J. Dumont, who also raped her. She ran away from Dumont in 1827 when slavery was declared illegal in New York; she left Thomas as well. Although mythic stories indicate that Sojourner had thirteen children, she had only five: Diana, Peter, Elizabeth, Sophia, and one whose name is not known. Historians are uncertain whether all five were fathered by Thomas. In 1827, her son Peter was stolen from her and sold into slavery in Alabama. Truth went to court and regained her son with the help of the Van Wagener family to whose home she had escaped in 1827. She was also aided in this legal battle by some of her Quaker friends.

According to her writings, the Holy Spirit first struck her in 1827. In later years, it was this same spirit that she would depend on most for her preaching, as well as her abolitionist and women's rights work.

In 1829 she moved to New York and was employed as a domestic servant, becoming deeply involved with mystic cults and evangelical religions. One such cult, the Zion Hill communal group, was formally established in 1833. It was led by a white man, Robert Matthews, who called himself Matthias. His group believed in wife swapping and physical healing through spiritual cleansing; furthermore, members of the group turned over their worldly possessions to Matthews. The group lasted a little more than two years. After standing trial for murder and being found not guilty, Matthews left town. Truth suffered from her involvement with Matthews and spent several years defending herself, to the point of filing a libel suit. After that, she joined the African Methodist Episcopal Zion denomination and lived quietly in New York with two of her children.

In June 1843 Sojourner Truth adopted the name we know her by today and increased her work in ministry, although she had been preaching since the 1820s. Rev. Truth was without formal training, direct and no-nonsense. Her life experiences provided her with more education and training than the average white man of her day. In addition to what she learned while working in households and living and working with Quakers, she learned a great deal by traveling with her grandson, who could read and write. Truth read people, not books. Biographer Nell Painter writes: "Obviously, illiteracy did not separate Truth from wisdom. Isabella/Sojourner Truth employed three main ways of knowing: observation as practice, divine inspiration, and in a special sense of the word, reading. . . . As a preacher Truth learned through rehearsal. She preached to herself while working, one letter shows. She preached regularly at camp meetings in the 1820s, and in the 1830s she preached regularly around New York. By the time she joined the antislavery feminist lecture circuit in the 1840s, Sojourner Truth was a well-practiced public speaker."

Working well into her older years, Truth continued to preach, and even spoke before Congress. In 1881, in Michigan, where she died, Truth spoke against capital punishment and helped defeat the Wycoff Bill, which was designed to institute capital punishment by hanging. She also worked to help blacks in the army and was noted for traveling to obtain clothing and supplies for black regiments. She was received by Presidents Lincoln and Grant at the White House as reward for her work.

Nell Painter also writes: "As a symbol of race and gender, Sojourner Truth is usually summed up in a series of public speech acts, the most famous of which is 'Ar'n't I a Woman?' which Frances Dana Gage reported that Truth uttered at a women's rights convention in Akron, Ohio, in 1851. This phrase is sometimes rendered more authentically Negro as 'Ain't I a Woman?' "

• • •

*This message was delivered at the first anniversary meeting of the American Equal Rights Association at the Church of the Puritans in New York City. The AERA was formed in 1866 by Elizabeth Cady Stanton and Susan B. Anthony to work toward universal suffrage for all men and women.*

## Keeping the Thing Going While Things Are Stirring (May 9, 1867)

My friends, I am rejoiced that you are glad, but I don't know how you will feel when I get through. I come from another field—the country of the slave. They have got their liberty—so much good luck to have slavery partly destroyed; not entirely. I want it root and branch destroyed. Then we will all be free indeed. I feel that if I have to answer for the deeds done in my body just as much as a man, I have a right to have just as much as a man. There is a great stir about colored men getting their rights, but not a word about the colored women; and if colored men get their rights, and not colored women theirs, you see the colored men will be masters over the women, and it will be just as bad as it was before. So I am for keeping the thing going while things are stirring; because if we wait till it is still, it will take a great while to get it going again. White women are a great deal smarter, and know more than colored women, while colored women do not know scarcely anything. They go out washing, which is about as high as a colored woman gets, and their men go about idle, strutting up and down; and take it all, and then scold because there is no food. I want you to consider on that, chil'n. I call you chil'n; you are somebody's chil'n, and I am old enough to be mother of all that is here. I want women to have their rights. In the courts women have no right, no voice; nobody speaks for them. I wish woman to have her voice there among the pettifoggers. If it is not a fit place for women, it is unfit for men to be there.

I am above eighty years old;[1] it is about time for me to be going. I have been forty years a slave and forty years free and would be here forty years more to have equal rights for all. I suppose I am kept here because something remains for me to do; I suppose I am yet to help to break the chain. I have done a great deal of work; as much as a man, but did not get so much pay. I used to work in the field and bind grain, keeping up with the cradler; but men doing no more, got twice as much pay; so with the German women. They work in the field and do as much work, but do not get the pay. We do as much, we eat as much, we want as much. I suppose I am about the only colored woman that goes about to speak for the rights of colored women. I want to keep the thing stirring, now that the ice is cracked. What we want is a little money. You men know that you get as much again as women when you write or for what you do. When we get our rights we shall not have to come to you for money, for then we shall have money enough in our own pockets; and maybe you will ask us for money. But help us now until we get it. It is a good consolation to know that when we have got this battle once fought we shall not be coming to you any more. You have been having our rights so long, that you think, like a slave-holder, that you own us. I know that is hard for one who has held the reins for so long to give up; it cuts like a knife. It will feel all the better when it closes up again. I have been in Washington about three years, seeing about these colored people. Now colored men have the right to vote. There ought to be equal rights now more than ever, since colored people have got their freedom. I am going to talk several times while I am here; so now I will do a little singing. I have not heard any singing since I came here.

✦ ✦ ✦

*Reverend Truth delivered her most famous message in December 1851 at the Women's Convention in Akron, Ohio. The speech has become famous because it portrays a strong woman who had the courage to stand up for women's rights and for the rights of her race. This version of the speech made at the Women's Convention is from a letter that Frances Dana Gage sent to* The Independent, *a newspaper, on April 23, 1863. The letter was reprinted and edited; papers cut the lines that mentioned Sojourner Truth being whipped. This letter can be found in archives of* The Independent *in the collections of the American Antiquarian Society, Worcester, Massachusetts; it has also been digitized by the Library of Congress. Scholars such as Carleton Mabee, Susan Mabee Newhouse, and Nell Painter believe that Truth did not utter the phrase "Ar'n't I a woman," and that it was likely interjected by Frances Gage. The comments by Gage have been placed in brackets.*

## AR'N'T I A WOMAN?
## (APRIL 23, 1863)

Well, chilern, whar dar's so much racket dar must be som'ting out o' kilter. I tink dat, 'twixt the niggers of de Souf and de women at de Norf, all a talkin' 'bout rights, de white men will be in a fix pretty soon. But what's all dis here talkin' 'bout? Dat man ober dar say dat woman needs to be helped into carriages, and lifted ober ditches, and to have de best place every whar. Nobody eber help me into carriages, or ober mud puddles, or gives me any best place [and, raising herself to her full height, and her voice to a pitch like rolling thunder, she asked], And ar'n't I a woman? Look at me. Look at my arm! [and she bared her right arm to the shoulder, showing its tremendous muscular power.] I have plowed, and planted, and gathered into barns, and no man could head me—and ar'n't I a woman? I could work as much and eat as much as a man, (when I could get it,) and bear de lash as well—and ar'n't I a woman? I have borne chilern, and seen 'em mos' all sold off into slavery, and when I cried out with a mother's grief, none but Jesus heard—and ar'n't I a woman? When dey talks 'bout dis ting in de head—what dis dey call it? ["Intellect," whispered some one near.] Dat's it, honey. What's dat got to do with women's rights or niggers' rights? If my cup won't hold but a pint and yourn holds a quart, wouldn't ye be mean not to let me have my little half-measure full? [And she pointed her significant finger and sent a keen glance at the minister who had made the argument. The cheering was long and loud.]

Den dat little man in black dar, he say woman can't have as much right as man 'cause Christ wa'n't a woman. *Whar did your Christ come from?*

[Rolling thunder could not have stilled that crowd as did those deep, wonderful tones, as she stood there with outstretched arms and eye of fire. Raising her voice still louder, she repeated,] Whar did your Christ come from? From God and a woman. Man had noting to do with him. [Oh! what a rebuke she gave the little man.]

[Turning again to another objector, she took up the defense of Mother Eve. I cannot follow her through it all. It was pointed and witty and solemn; eliciting at almost every sentence deafening applause; and she ended by asserting that] if de fust woman God ever made was strong enough to turn de world upside down all 'lone, all dese togedder [and she glanced her eye over us], ought to be able to turn it back an git it right side up again, and now dey is asking to do it, de men better let 'em. [Long continued cheering.] 'Bleeged to ye for hearin' from me, and now ole Sojourner ha'n't got nothin' more to say.

## *Notes*

*Sermon source:* "Keeping the Thing Going While Things Are Stirring" is available at http://memory.loc.gov/cgi-bin/query/r?ammem/now:@field (accessed December 9, 2004). "Ar'n't I a Woman?" is available at University of Detroit Mercy Library's Black Abolitionist Archive at http://image.udmercy.edu/BAATruth_11639spe.pdf (accessed August 15, 2009).

1. Most biographers indicate that Truth was born in or around 1797. The date for this speech has been definitely determined as 1867. This would mean that she would have been around seventy, not eighty, as she claimed in the speech. Two possibilities explain this discrepancy. First, many slaves were uncertain of their date of birth since it was not noted in any formal fashion (birth certificates, church confirmations, in family Bibles, etc.) given that slaves were viewed as property by their owners, not persons whose lives were to be celebrated in any fashion. Second, given that the early biographers of Truth often exaggerated and fabricated areas of her life, it stands to reason that discrepancies concerning her age would also arise in print.

## *Bibliographical Sources*


Mabee, Carleton, and Susan Mabee Newhouse. *Sojourner Truth: Slave, Prophet, Legend.* New York: New York University Press, 1995.

Olive, Gilbert, ed. *Narrative of Sojourner Truth: A Bondswoman of Olden Time.* Boston: For the Author, 1875.

Ortiz, Victoria. *Sojourner Truth: A Self-Made Woman.* Philadelphia: Lippincot, 1974.

Painter, Nell. "Representing Truth: Sojourner Truth's Knowing and Becoming Known," *Journal of American History* 81, no. 2 (September 1994): 466–67.

———. *Sojourner Truth: A Life, A Symbol.* New York: W. W. Norton, 1996.

Stetson, Erlene, and Linda David. *Glorying in Tribulation: The Lifework of Sojourner Truth.* East Lansing: Michigan State University Press, 1994.

Vale, Gilbert. *Fanaticism, Its Source and Influence: Illustrated by the Simple Narrative of Isabella, In the Case of Matthias, Mr. and Mrs. B. Folger, Mr. Pierson, Mr. Mills, Catherine, Isabella, etc.*, 2 vols. New York: Published by the author, 1835.

# 3

# FROM RECONSTRUCTION TO DECONSTRUCTION:

## *1866–1917*

# INTRODUCTION

As the Civil War concluded, many blacks hailed President Abraham Lincoln as the Great Emancipator. Yet some southern whites interpreted Lincoln's growing support for racial justice as an intolerable violation of the southern white power structure. The South had lost the war, but a southerner, John Wilkes Booth, would wage a private battle for the continuation of the status quo.

Booth assassinated President Lincoln a few days after the fall of the Confederate capital in Richmond, Virginia, and the surrender of Confederate forces in Appomattox. Booth's bullet struck down a president, but it could not assassinate the desire for freedom and democracy surging in the hearts of countless blacks during this period.

Just as the nation faced pressing dilemmas after the Revolutionary War, the mending of a nation fractured by the Civil War was an equally daunting challenge. The nation needed reconstruction.

Of more than half a million black soldiers, thirty-seven thousand lost their lives in the Civil War.[1] In addition to providing assistance for families decimated by the war, the country had to integrate formerly enslaved blacks more fully into the political and economic mainstream. To facilitate this work, the federal government created the Freedmen's Bureau, a national relief agency charged with providing subsistence necessities and education for blacks.

Aiding the efforts of the Freedmen's Bureau was the migration of black and white teachers and missionaries from the North. These teachers and missionaries believed that education was a solid foundation upon which to reconstruct the black community and, indeed, the nation. During this period, venerable black colleges and universities such as Fisk University in Tennessee, Morehouse College in Georgia, Morgan College in Maryland, Howard University in Washington, D.C., and Tuskegee University in Alabama emerged to educate a new generation of blacks reveling in the emancipation of their bodies and minds.

During Reconstruction, blacks enjoyed unprecedented access to and involvement in national, state, and local electoral politics. For example, in 1870, Hiram Revels became the first black U.S. Senator. Revels, an African Methodist Episcopal minister, also served as the first president of Alcorn College in Mississippi. Blanche K. Bruce was sent to Washington in 1874 and served in the Senate. In 1870 blacks also occupied seats in the U.S. House of Representatives. Rev. Henry McNeal Turner became the first black postmaster. Constitutional amendments ratified in 1870 abolished slavery and ended the racial restrictions on United States citizenship and voting, which greatly facilitated black political activity.

Black denominations also flourished during this era. The African Methodist Episcopal Church continued to grow, as did black Baptist churches. The Colored (now Christian) Methodist Episcopal Church organized in Tennessee and elected William H. Miles and Richard Vanderhorst as bishops. James A. Healy was appointed the first black Roman Catholic bishop in 1875. St. Paul Colored Lutheran Church, the first black Lutheran church, was established in 1878 in Arkansas.

Blacks were also given the right to vote through the Fifteenth Amendment, but some Southern states added grandfather clauses to their state constitutions which countered this new right. Typical clauses stated that the right to vote extended only to citizens who had the right to vote prior to 1866 or 1867 and their descendants. While many white politicians, missionaries, and teachers assisted Reconstruction efforts, other whites violently opposed the economic and political advancement of blacks. To thwart the progression of civil rights, white supremacist groups such as the Ku Klux Klan emerged in the late nineteenth century. These groups unleashed a fury of lynchings and other acts of terrorism against blacks and those supporting black causes.

In the infamous 1896 decision *Plessy v. Ferguson*, the U.S. Supreme Court sanctioned segregation, thereby bolstering the discrimination and violent treatment of blacks. In the middle of the nineteenth century, hope—for fuller black participation in American democracy—burned intensely. By the close of the nineteenth century, hope was smoldering.

In this crucial period, several notable black leaders fanned the embers of freedom; Ida B. Wells Barnett, Mary McLeod Bethune, Booker T. Washington, and W.E.B. DuBois re-ignited the belief that fair treatment for blacks was obtainable.

Other notable preachers during this period included those who organized the Azusa Street Revival in 1906, which lasted for three years and from which Pentecostalism was spread around the world. In 1907, Charles H. Mason reorganized the Church of God in Christ as a Pentecostal denomination. Mary Lena Tate formed the Church of the Living God, the Pillar and Ground of Truth, another early Pentecostal body in Alabama in 1908. Noble Drew Ali launched the Moorish Science Temple of America in 1913.

Rev. Henry McNeal Turner, a bishop of the African Methodist Episcopal Church, offered a radical alternative to the loss of black civil rights in the late nineteenth and early twentieth century: Fueled by his black nationalist perspectives, Turner advocated the return of blacks to Africa.[2]

While Bishop Turner's initiative did not meet with wide acceptance among blacks, many migrated—not to the African continent—but to the northern United States. In the Great Migration of the 1910s and 1920s, thousands of blacks left the South for northern industrial centers, such as Chicago and New York. Furthermore, instead of migrating to Africa, some three hundred seventy thousand blacks traveled to Europe as soldiers to aid U.S. efforts in World War I. To its discredit, the United States failed to defend the civil rights of those soldiers and other blacks during and after the war.[3]

## NOTES

1. James Oliver Horton and Lois E. Horton, *Hard Road to Freedom: The Story of African America* (New Brunswick, NJ: Rutgers University Press, 2001), 181.
2. Anne H. Pinn and Anthony B. Pinn, *Fortress Introduction to Black Church History* (Minneapolis: Fortress Press, 2002), 38–42.
3. *Hard Road to Freedom*, 221.

## BIBLIOGRAPHICAL SOURCES

Berlin, Ira, Barbara J. Fields, Thavolia Glymph, Joseph P. Reidy, and Leslie S. Rowland, eds. *Freedom: A Documentary History of Emancipation, 1861–1867.* New York: Cambridge University Press, 1985.

Billings, Dwight B. *Planters and the Making of a "New South": Class, Politics, and Development in North Carolina, 1865–1900.* Chapel Hill: University of North Carolina Press, 1979.

Blassingame, John W. *The Slave Community: Plantation Life in the Antebellum South.* New York: Oxford University Press, 1979.

Blight, David. *Race and Reunion: The Civil War in American Memory*. Cambridge, MA: Belknap Press, 2002.

Litwack, Leon F. *Been in the Storm So Long: The Aftermath of Slavery*. New York: Knopf, 1979.

Montgomery, William E. *Under Their Own Vine and Fig Tree: The African-American Church in the South, 1865–1900*. Baton Rouge: University of Louisiana Press, 1993.

Nieman, Donald. *Black Southerners and the Law, 1865–1900*. New York: Garland, 1994.

———. *The Day of the Jubilee: The Civil War Experience of Black Southerners*. New York: Garland, 1994.

# HARRIET A. COLE BAKER

*(1829–ca. 1913)*

Harriet A. Cole was born in 1829 as a free person in Havre de Grace, Maryland. Her parents were William and Harriet Cole. She was one of seven children. Harriet's father died when she was eleven. At sixteen she married William Baker, a fugitive slave, and they escaped, leaving Maryland for Pennsylvania with their seven-month-old child. However, William was later captured and Harriet and their friends had to raise money to purchase his freedom.

In 1872 Baker announced her calling as a preacher. Her husband said that he would not forgive her if she went off to preach and something happened to the children. Less than twelve months later the two children became ill and died. Baker later had three more children.

According to her biography, the African Methodist Episcopal Church authorized her to preach sometime in 1875. For more than fifteen years Baker preached at camp meetings and led revivals. Because of her skill level and the fact that she was received as a preacher by blacks and whites, in 1889 the Philadelphia Conference of the AME church appointed her pastor of St. Paul's Church in Lebanon, Pennsylvania, after the denomination voted to license evangelists. Of course the church had few members and massive debt (then and now, black and white Methodist denominations most often appoint women to small, financially poor, churches).[1] It is quite unlikely that Baker was the first black woman pastor, but she appears to be the first appointed by an AME Conference.

Rev. Baker's autobiography, *The Colored Lady Evangelist*, was published in 1892. By 1897 Baker was well known on the East Coast. She settled in Allentown, Pennsylvania, and formed the Bethel Mission. Rev. Harriet Ann Cole Baker died in 1913.

• • •

*This sermon concerns the meekness of Jesus and his struggles to carry out his mission to redeem humanity. Knowing much about struggle as a woman preacher and a black living constantly in death-dealing circumstances, Baker skillfully describes the difficulties encountered by Jesus but is certain to make clear that Jesus did not yield to the pressures that he faced. Just as Jesus held out, Baker makes clear that she too will hold out.*

## Behold the Man
## (ca. 1880)

> *Then came Jesus forth, wearing the crown of thorns, and the purple robe. And Pilate said unto them, Behold the man!* —John 19:5

I repeat the text "Behold the Man," and in order to give you an idea of what gave rise to it, it is necessary to read the foregoing chapter.

I now call attention to this man, mentioned in the text, and I wish you all to give special attention, as the constant labor of five months has almost broken me down. But a cry for help came from Macedonia, and here I am in response to that cry. I ask you all to pray. Do pray now as there is hard work to be done. Pray now if ever. Look to Jesus, and not to me; see him by faith as he hangs on the cross in the last act of atonement, and get the blessing of Jesus, the man of my text. I think of myself as resembling a horn; as nothing but a horn. You all know what a horn is and the uses that are made of it. The horn talks the sentiments of the person blowing it; it may sound the alarm of fire, of murder, or of danger; or it may give the glad sound of invitation to dinner to some half-starved soul who is hungering for the richness of the Master's table, where all may freely partake of the bread of everlasting life.

I will consider my text from three principal points:

1st. Jesus in his power and might. 2nd. Jesus in his meekness. 3rd. Jesus in his humiliation.

Jesus was the Immaculate Son of God. Look at him as he was before the world was. When the wonders of creation were taking place, Jesus was there. When the Lord divided the waters from the dry land, and gave to the ocean its "metes and bounds," Jesus was there. When the darkness was driven away, and the glorious light beamed forth upon a new born world, Jesus was there. When the stars and planets were given their positions, and orbits, in the immensity of space, Jesus was there. When God said "Let us make man in, our image, after our likeness," Jesus was there. When God created the fishes which swim in the mighty ocean, and the beautiful lakes, and the winding rivers, and the mountain streams, Jesus was there. When the beasts of the field were made, and the birds of the air sent forth their first notes of praise, Jesus was there.

And dear friends I want you to hear to-day of his atonement for the sins of the world, and his ascension to heaven, where he has prepared a home for all his people. Glory to God for the atonement and for the resurrection.

On the sixth day of creation man was made in the image of God, male and female, and given the injunction to be fruitful, multiply, and replenish the earth. Upon the empty air this earth was well balanced, and with joy Jesus saw the mansion where the sons of men should dwell. Yes, this same Jesus was with the Father at the foundation of the world, and shall be with him until the last, for he is the first and the last. Truly when the morning stars sang together and the sons of God shouted for joy, this great Saviour of mine was there, and he was yet there when God made man, and when man fell from that happy state of purity, and was driven from that beautiful garden, he was yet there with man in his unhappy condition, and promised him salvation. And when the angels made the search in heaven to find one that could open the book, and read the contents thereof, this same Jesus came forth as a lamb from under the altar. And when the question was asked "who is worthy to open the book?" Jesus was there, and as the angels listened, and John wept at the revelation, a voice was heard saying "weep not!" and the four and twenty elders sang a new song, saying, "Thou art worthy to take the book, and to open the seal thereof: for thou wast slain, and hast redeemed us to God by the blood, out of every kindred, and tongue, and people, and nation." And thank God, Jesus came, and redeemed us, and he has been with his church ever since, and he fights for her to-day.

Oh! how I do thank the Lord for the gift of his Son, and for the gift of the Holy Ghost, how he taught me to pray, and to read and understand his holy word. And as the poet says,

*Grace led my roving feet,*
*To tread the heavenly road,*
*And new supplies each hour I meet*
*While pressing on to God.*

*Grace found me when I was in my sins,*
*and I was led to realize, and*
*Know that the Lord is God alone:*
*He can create, and He [can] destroy.*[2]

He is the foundation of all wisdom, upon the plain of wisdom this world was founded, and by the wisdom of God the sun, and moon, and stars, were made, and keep their regular course, and do not run one against the other. It is by the wisdom of God that the sun revolves in his place. It is by the wisdom of God that we move and live. Oh! how I do thank him for his grace, and for his wisdom, that he has given unto me. I can say in truth, all glory belongs to him. Wisdom cried aloud. It is the voice of God's eternal Son. And deserves it no regard? I hear the voice of Jesus saying,

*I was my Father's chief delight,*
*His everlasting Son,*
*Before the first of all his works,*
*Or creation was begun;*

*Before the flying clouds,*
*Before the solid land,*
*Before the fields, before the flood:*
*I dwelt at his right hand.*

*When he adorned the skies,*
*and built them;*
*when he ordained the time*
*for the sun to rise and set,*
*and when he marshalled every star, I was there.*

*When he poured out the sea,*
*And spread the roaring deep,*
*He gave the flood a firm decree,*
*And its own bounds to keep.*[3]

But I want to speak of Jesus in his meekness. Driven from Bethlehem by the wrath of a king, expelled from Nazareth by the violence of the people, received at Capernaum at first, only to be rejected at last, denied the protection of the three homes which was his by birth, by residence, and by adoption.

Jesus comes to Jerusalem to be betrayed, and to Calvary to die. Thirty years of retirement, and three years of public ministry, and yet all that the world will endure of its Messiah is not enough to secure him acceptance. It is not enough that he heals the sick, and feeds the hungry, and raises the dead. It is not enough that he speaks as never a man spake, and does the works which never a man did. It is not enough that he endures the contradiction of sinners with the meekness and majesty of infinite love. He must go down to a still lower depth of humiliation. He must take upon his soul the burden of a great agony, he must give his very life in sacrifice, before the strong walls of prejudice, and hatred, and unbelief will yield, and give him access to the hearts of men. We have something to learn from every step which he takes, as he approaches the great sacrifice of Calvary.

He had returned to Bethany for the night, the first decisive step towards the great sacrifice had been taken; he had showed himself the object of supreme interest to the multitude: and so had excited the envy and hatred of the customary leaders to the highest degree; he had come once more within their reach, they had already entered upon new plans to destroy him, it will take them yet four days to complete their dark counsel, and then when they demand the victim he will hold himself ready for the sacrifice.

Monday he comes back to the city, and made a still more striking exhibition of the power of his presence over men, by causing all that bought and sold in the temple to leave the holy place and take their tables and merchandise with them. At his command, hardened, selfish and calculating as they were, they could not withstand the authority with which he spake. The blind, the sick, and the lame, were brought to him in great numbers, and he healed them. The populace had been induced by threats or persuasions to hold their peace, but the children in the temple took up the songs and cries of the previous day, and sang [hosannas] to the son of David; When the priests and the scribes demanded his authority for what he did, he put them to shame before all the people by the wisdom of his reply. And when evening was come he went back to Bethany leaving them still more enraged, and intent upon seeking his life.

Tuesday he comes again to the city; this was the third and last successive day of his public teaching. His enemies assailed him in greater numbers, and with greater subtlety than ever before, when one was silenced, another would renew the assault, all alike endeavour to ensnare him in his words, and to draw from him some expression which could be used as an accusation against him, before the magistrate; But all in vain, they only induce him to set before the people by new parables, and in a more awful light, the dreadful doom which they would bring on themselves on the temple, and the holy city, by thus rejecting the Messiah, He pronounced in their hearing the most fearful woes upon the blind and bigoted leaders of the people, and then left them.

This is enough, the priests and scribes will see to it that the dreaded voice of their reprover shall not be heard in the courts of the temple, or in the streets any more. To-night the great council will meet in secret session, at the palace of their high priest, and the betrayer will be there to bargain for the reward of his iniquity in delivering Jesus into their hands.

On his way out to Bethany Jesus paused before passing the ridge of Olives, and sat down with his disciples over against the temple, to look back upon Jerusalem for the last time. The sun was setting and the whole city, with the surrounding [valleys], and the hill-sides which were covered with camps of pilgrims, lay beneath him. In the evening light, the history of a thousand years, the divine oracles speaking by a thousand voices, the monuments of prophets, patriarchs, and Kings, the visitation of Angels, the [miraculous] interposition in judgement, and in blessing, by the offering of [Isaac], and the building of the temple, was presented to him, as he looked upon Moriah and Zion; and as he heard the murmur, and the evening song of a million people gathered within, and around the walls of the whole city.

Now my hearers, was it possible here on earth to find another scene of such commanding interest, as that which lay [before] the eyes of Jesus, when he turned to look upon Jerusalem for the last time[?] There he sat until the sun went down, and the stars shone, and the already risen moon grows bright over the mountain. There he poured forth in the most solemn and touching words, prophecy, and warning, and [instruction], concerning the desolation of Jerusalem, the depression of the Jewish people, the preaching of the gospel to all nations, and his own final coming to judge the world in righteousness. And he closes this the most awful, and sublime of all his discourses with [a] distinct and solemn declaration that after two days he should be betrayed, and crucified. Then he resumes his walk to Bethany, and rested for the night.

The whole of the following day, Wednesday, he spent in retirement, at his chosen and quiet home in Bethany, his public work was done, and while his enemies [were] completing their plans, for his destruction, he would take a little time to gird up his soul for the trial of mockery and scourging, and for the crowning agony of the cross. He would need the repose of two quiet days to prepare himself for the last sleepless night, and for the long tortures of the last dreadful day. When he leaves the quiet village for the last time on Thursday, he goes to be betrayed and crucified. His whole body, and soul, and spirit will be [taxed] with the most exhausting intensity, until he bows his head in death at the ninth hour on Friday afternoon.

As the evening of Thursday draws near, Jesus sets forth upon his last walk with his disciples, before his passover. We do not know what words of farewell were spoken when he parted with his beloved friends at Bethany, they fondly hoping to see him return to lodge with them as before, and he well knowing that his next resting place would be the grave. We are not told what he said to his disciples as he walked with them up the same steep, or down the same descent of Olives, where the multitudes hailed his coming with [hosannas], four days before. We do not know whether in silence, or with weeping, or with comfortable words. He passed Gethsemanie, and across the brook Kidron, and climb[ed] up the ascent to what is now called St. Stephen's gate. And for the moment of his arrival at the upper chamber in the city, where the passover was prepared, we may well imagine that his countenance wore an unwonted tenderness and solemnity, and that the wondering disciples saw the foreshadowing signs of the final agony upon him. The awful history of this last night, and the following day, will be studied with wonder and adoration, by angels and redeemed men forever. We can now only recite its most familiar facts, as a preparation for the lesson of the cross.

I want now to speak of Jesus in his humiliation. He was just about to complete his earthly humiliation, and to return to the throne of heaven, with all power in his name, and all glory upon his head. Jesus teaches his disciples the greatest lesson of humiliation. While they were contending with each other for the promise of the highest place in his kingdom, he girded himself as a servant, and washed the feet of them that called him Lord.

He was just about to offer himself, the pure and spotless Lamb of God, in the great and only sacrifice for sin; He finished the sacrifice of four thousand years, as he [ate] the passover with his [disciples]. This was one of the national festivals which the Jewish people observed from the days of Moses.

Jesus started a new dispensation and instituted a memorial service, to be kept by his followers of every nation, to the end of time. As he looks around upon the chosen company of his disciples, the dark shadow of coming treachery over shadows and troubles his soul, and groaning within himself, he nerves his heart, to make the sad declaration, "Verily, verily, I say unto you that one of you shall betray me." The disclosure makes the company of the disciples, and the presence of the Master, intolerable to the traitor, and he goes immediately out.

It is night in the streets of blinded and abandoned Jerusalem, night in the councils of the enemies of Jesus, night in the soul of the betrayer, night upon the path which he must tread, for no sooner had the dark shadow of the traitor left the room, than the troubled cloud passed from the face of Jesus, and he turns to his remaining disciples with the light of heaven in his look, and he pours forth his soul in words of love, of counsel, and of prayer, which shall outlive the languish of earth, and shall be sung by happy voices to the music of heaven. He himself joins with his disciples in singing the great Hallelujah song, with which Israel had closed the Passover for a thousand years. Praise the Lord, all ye nations: praise him all ye people; for his merciful kindness is great towards us, his mercy endures forever.

He knows where the betrayer will expect to meet him, at the midnight hour, and there he goes that he may be ready, when the officers and soldiers come with Judas for their guide, to take him once more through their silent streets, and out of their eastern gate, and across the Kidron Valley, beneath the shadows of the olive trees which are cast in the full light of the moon. Jesus goes to his place of prayer, the betrayer knows the spot, for Jesus had often been there before with his disciples.

To this day in spite of all intervening changes, the scene can be identified with reasonable accuracy. And it is the most solemn and affecting of all the holy places in Palestine. The aged olive trees, with gnarled and distorted trunks, appearing as if bent and twisted by the [tortures] of centuries, are undoubtedly the most fitting monuments, if any be needed to make the ground sacred.

Whilst waiting for the armed band to appear, Jesus is again troubled in spirit, and his soul is bowed down under the weight of a more awful and mysterious agony than had ever come upon him before. He is overcome with a strange amazement, an inexplicable and shuddering dread, a horror of great darkness, and an exceeding great sorrow, embittered with more than the bitterness of death; the sweat wrung out by the inward torture, falls in blood drops to the ground. Thrice he prays in the same words, that the cup may pass from him.

When the armed band appears, and he goes forth to give himself up, his troubled countenance at once assumes so much of its serene and godlike majesty that the hardened soldiers, are struck to the ground with awe, but the delay is only momentary, he offers himself again, and they bind him, and lead him away. It is now past midnight, and from this time forward the course of the events in this awful history, ran swiftly on the closing scene on the cross.

Walking painfully with bound hands, amidst the rude and merciless mob, Jesus was hurried up the steep pass, through the city gates to the house of Annas, not for a formal trial did they bring him there, but only that the old father-in-law of the high priest[,] the man whose counsel was of the highest authority in the nation, might have the dreadful satisfaction of seeing Jesus of [Nazareth] a prisoner.

Then out again, into the dark, narrow streets, finding their way, only, by the uncertain light of lanterns and torches, they hurry their unresisting victim, with insult and mockery to the palace of Caiaphas. There he is questioned by the high priest, testified against by false witnesses, smitten by the officers, reviled by the whole assembly, condemned to death by the counsel, and still after the decision kept exposed to every form of [contemptuous] speech, and personal abuse, till the breaking of the day.

The morning of Friday breaks, a day to be recognized as the greatest of all the days of time, a day to be remembered as long as redeemed souls can remember the sacrifice which purchased for them a blessed immortality. The sentence of the Sanhedrin must now be confirmed and executed by the civil power, or it will be of no effect, and the enemies of Jesus hurry on their dreadful work, with such malignant and impetuous zeal, that the prisoner, who was seized in Gethsemanie, without the city, at midnight, has been led to and fro, through many streets, to four different places of tribunals, has been arranged before the high priest, twice before the Sanhedrin, twice before Pilate, once before Herod, once robed and crowned in mockery, twice scourged, everywhere mocked and condemned, led outside of the city wall, and by nine o'clock, when the sun is looking over the ridge of Olives, in the deep valley of Kidron, he is already nailed to the cross. In six hours more, the most momentous hours in the world's history, the awful tragedy is finished, and the Incarnate Son of God bows his head in death. It is all one act, one mysterious and [infinite] passion, from the agony in Gethsemanie, to the last bitter cry upon Calvary.

The betrayal, the arrest, the arraignment, the false accusation, the mockery, the denial, the scourging, the final sentence, and its execution, must all unite to make up the meaning of that most sacred and awful mystery, the cross of Christ. The most sorrowful procession that ever moved on this earth, was that in which Jesus was led out of the city, to be crucified, amidst the wails of the daughters of Jerusalem, and the mockery of the multitude who clamored for his death.

## NOTES

*Sermon source:* Bettye Collier-Thomas, ed., *Daughters of Thunder: Black Women Preachers and Their Sermons, 1850–1979* (San Francisco: Jossey Bass Publishers, 1998). All bracketed insertions are those of Collier-Thomas.

1. For information on the pay and placement of female clergy, see *The Journal for the Scientific Study of Religion* 36, no. 4 (December 1997), articles by Patricia Chang,

Joy Charlton, Mark Chaves, James Cavendish, and Paula Nesbit. Although they contain research that concerns the period 1970 to approximately 2005, they provide information that suggests that pay and placement of women clergy during the lifetime of Harriet Baker would have been more abysmal. Also see "Clergy Women: An Uphill Calling," a study carried out by the Hartford Institute of Religion Research, at http://hirr.hartsem.edu/bookshelf/clergywomen_abstract.html (accessed January 19, 2006).

2. The first stanza is from the poem "Grace 'tis a Charming Sound"; this verse of the song was written by Philip Doddridge in 1740. The second stanza is a mixture of song lyrics most likely from a hymn by Isaac Watts (1674–1748).

3. This is a slight paraphrase of the poem, later a song, "Christ the Wisdom of God," by Isaac Watts.

### *Bibliographical Sources*

Alcornley, John H., ed. *The Colored Lady Evangelist: Being the Life, Labors and Experiences of Mrs. Harriet A. Baker.* Brooklyn, NY: 1892.

Collier-Thomas, Bettye, ed. *Daughters of Thunder: Black Women Preachers and Their Sermons, 1850–1979.* San Francisco: Jossey Bass Publishers, 1998.

# RICHARD HARVEY CAIN

*(1825–1887)*

Richard Harvey Cain was one of the most gifted preachers, social activists, orators, politicians, pastors, and churchmen of his time. Because few of his writings remained after his death, he has not received much attention in spite of his tremendous contributions. Henry Highland Garnett said of Cain, he is a "distinguished man whose forceful name is as a hundred-pound parrot gun in the Church."[1]

Richard Harvey Cain was born free in Greenbriar County, Virginia, on April 12, 1825. His parents relocated to Ohio, where Cain attended school and worked on steamboats along the Ohio River. Cain moved to Missouri and entered the ministry, joining the Methodist Church, which licensed him in 1844. In 1848, dissatisfied with the Methodist Church, he joined the African Methodist Episcopal Church.

After Cain's wife Laura died in 1859, Bishop Daniel Payne sent him to Wilberforce University to study. He then became a pastor in New York, working with leading organizations supporting black civil rights and uplift. These included the African Civilization Society, which promoted emigration to Africa, and most importantly, the betterment of Africa.

The society also operated Freedmen schools in various states, and at one point had more than ten schools with a total of one thousand students. Cain was also heavily involved in enhancing the stature of Wilberforce, and raising substantial amounts of money to keep the school open. He served on its board of trustees.

In 1865 Cain moved to Charleston, South Carolina, and began organizing churches for the AME denomination. He organized Emmanuel AME Church in Charleston in 1865 and shortly thereafter the church had more than two thousand members. Cain saw the need for blacks to speak for themselves in the press, so in 1866 he purchased the *South Carolina Leader* newspaper, which was renamed the *Missionary Record*. Cain also entered the political fray and was a delegate to the constitutional convention of South Carolina after the enactment of black codes to restrict the movement of black Carolinians. By 1868 Cain had been elected as one of two black Carolina state senators and had gained a national reputation for his strong support of black civil rights. He was elected representative from South Carolina to the Forty-third and Forty-fifth Congresses. Ever the churchman, Cain continued to work for the AME church, becoming a bishop in 1880.

• • •

*A complete sermon by Cain suitable for use in this anthology was not obtainable. To at least give readers a sense of his oratory, we have included the following message. In it Cain shows his unbending fight for the rights of blacks. The speech was given in Congress, and Cain speaks amid numerous attempts to change the subject and to deride him. Although Cain addresses the subject of equal rights for blacks several times in this session of Congress, the message provided here picks up the second half of his remarks, which are among some of the most memorable that he gave on January 24, 1874.*

## All We Ask Is Equal Laws, Equal Legislation, and Equal Rights (January 24, 1874)

Mr. Speaker, I feel called upon more particularly by the remarks of the gentleman from North Carolina (Mr. Vance) on civil rights to express my views. For a number of days this question has been discussed, and various have been the opinions expressed as to whether or not the pending bill should be passed in its present form or whether it should be modified to meet the objections entertained by a number of gentlemen whose duty it will be to give their votes for or against its passage. It has been assumed that to pass this bill in its present form Congress would manifest a tendency to override the Constitution of the country and violate the rights of the States.

Whether it be true or false is yet to be seen. I take it, so far as the constitutional question is concerned, if the colored people under the law, under the amendments to the Constitution, have become invested with all the rights of citizenship, then they carry with them all rights and immunities accruing to and belonging to a citizen of the United States. If four, or nearly five, million people have been lifted from the thralldom of slavery and made free; if the Government by its amendments to the Constitution has guaranteed to them all rights and immunities, as to other citizens, they must necessarily therefore carry along with them all the privileges enjoyed by all other citizens of the Republic.

Sir, the gentleman from North Carolina (Mr. Vance) who spoke on the question stated some objections, to which I desire to address a few words of reply. He said it would enforce social rights, and therefore would be detrimental to the interests of both the whites and the blacks of the country. My conception of the effect of this bill, if it be passed into law, will be simply to place the colored men of this country upon the same footing with every other citizen under the law, and will not at all enforce social relationship with any other class of persons in the country whatsoever. It is merely a matter of law. What we desire is that our civil rights shall be guaranteed by law as they are guaranteed to every other class of persons; and when that is done all other things will come in as a necessary sequence, the enforcement of the rights following the enactment of the law.

Sir, social equality is a right which every man, every woman, and every class of persons have within their own control. They have a right to form their own acquaintances, to establish their own social relationships. Its establishment and regulation is not within the province of legislation. No laws enacted by legislators can compel social equality. Now, what is it we desire? What we desire is this: inasmuch as we have been raised to the dignity, to the honor, to the position of our manhood, we ask that the laws of this country should guarantee all the rights and immunities belonging to that proud position, to be enforced all over this broad land.

Sir, the gentleman states that in the State of North Carolina the colored people enjoy all their rights as far as the highways are concerned; that in the hotels, and in the railroad cars, and in the various public places of resort, they have all the rights and all the immunities accorded to any other class of citizens of the United States. Now, it may not have come under his observation, but it has under mine, that such really is not the case; and the reason why I know and feel it more than he does is because my face is painted black and his is painted white. We who have the color—I may say the objectionable color—know and feel all this. A few days ago, in passing from South Carolina to this city, I entered a place of public resort where hungry men are fed, but I did not dare—I could not without trouble—sit down to the table. I could not sit down at Wilmington or at Weldon without entering into a contest, which I did not desire to do. My colleague, the gentleman who so eloquently spoke on this subject the other day, (Mr. Elliott), a few months ago entered a restaurant at Wilmington and sat down to be served, and while there a gentleman stepped up to him and said, "You cannot eat here." All the other gentlemen upon the railroad as passengers were eating there; he had only twenty minutes, and was compelled to leave the restaurant or have a fight for it. He showed fight, however, and got his dinner; but has never been back there since. Coming here last week I felt we did not desire to draw revolvers and present the bold front of warriors, and therefore; we ordered our dinners to be brought into the cars, but even there we found the existence of this feeling; for, although we had paid a dollar apiece for our meals, to be brought by the servants into the cars, still there was objection on the part of the railroad people to our eating our meals in the cars, because they said we were putting on airs. They refused us in the restaurant, and then did not desire that we should eat our meals in the cars, although we paid for them. Yet this was in the noble State of North Carolina.

Mr. Speaker, the colored men of the South do not want the adoption of any force measure. No; they do not want anything by force. All they ask is that you will give them, by statutory enactment, under the fundamental law, the right to enjoy precisely the same privileges accorded to every other class of citizens.

The gentlemen, moreover, has told us that if we pass this civil rights bill we will thereby rob the colored men of the South of the friendship of the whites. Now, I am at a loss to see how the friendship of our white friends can be lost to us by simply saying we should be permitted to enjoy the rights enjoyed by other citizens. I have a higher opinion of the friendship of the southern men than to suppose any such thing. I know them too well. I know their friendship will not be lost by the passage of this bill. For eight years I have been in South Carolina, and I have found this to be the fact, that the higher class, comprising gentlemen of learning and refinement, are less opposed to this measure than are those who do not occupy so high a position in the social scale.

Sir, I think that there will be no difficulty. But I do think this, that there will be more trouble if we do not have those rights. I regard it important, therefore, that we should make the law so strong that no man can infringe those rights.

But, says the gentleman from North Carolina, some ambitious colored man will, when this law is passed, enter a hotel or railroad car, and thus create disturbance. If it be his right, then there is no vaulting ambition in his enjoying that right. And if he can pay for his seat in a first-class car or his room in a hotel, I see no objection to his enjoying it. But the gentleman says more. He cited, on the school question, the evidence of South Carolina, and says the South Carolina University has been destroyed by virtue of bringing into contact the white students with the colored. I think not. It is true that a small number of students left the institution, but the institution still remains. The buildings are there as erect as ever; the faculty are there as attentive to their duties as ever they were; the students are coming in as they did before. It is true, sir, that there is a mixture of students now; that there are colored and white students of law and medicine sitting side by side; it is true, sir, that the prejudice of some of the professors was so strong that it drove them out of the institution; but the philanthropy and good sense of others were such that they remained; and thus we have still the institution going on, and because some students have left, it cannot be reasonably argued that the usefulness of the institution has been destroyed. The University of South Carolina has not been destroyed.

But this gentleman says more. The colored man cannot stand, he says, where this antagonism exists, and he deprecates the idea of antagonizing the races. The gentleman says there is no antagonism on his part. I think there is no antagonism as far as the country is concerned. So far as my observation extends, it goes to prove this: that, there is a general acceptance upon the part of the larger and better class of the whites of the South of the situation, and that they regard the education and the development of the colored people as essential to their welfare, and the peace, happiness, and prosperity of the whole country. Many of them, including the best minds of the South, are earnestly engaged in seeking to make this great system of education permanent in all the States. I do not believe, therefore, that it is possible there can be such an antagonism. Why, sir, in Massachusetts there is no such antagonism. There the colored, and the white children go to school side by side. In Rhode Island there is not that antagonism. There they are educated side by side in the high schools. In New York, in the highest schools, are to be found, of late; colored men and colored women. Even old democratic New York does not refuse to give the colored people their rights, and there is no antagonism. A few days ago, when in New York, I made it my business to find out what was the position of matters there in this respect. I ascertained that there are, I think, seven colored ladies in the highest school in New York, and I believe they stand No. 1 in their class, side by side with members of the best and most refined families of the citizens of New York, and without any objection to their presence.

I cannot understand how it is that our southern friends, or a certain class of them, always bring back this old ghost of prejudice and of antagonism. There was a time, not very far distant in the past, when this antagonism was not recognized, when a feeling of fraternization between the white and the colored races existed that made them kindred to each other. But since our emancipation, since liberty has come, and only since—only since we have stood up clothed in our manhood, only since we have proceeded to take hold and help advance the civilization of this nation—it is only since then that this bugbear is brought up against us again. Sir, the progress of the age demands that the colored man of this country shall be lifted by law into the enjoyment of every right, and that every appliance which is accorded to the German, to the Irishman, to the Englishman, and every foreigner, shall be given to him; find I shall give some reasons why I demand this in the name of justice.

For two hundred years the colored men of this nation have assisted in building up its commercial interest. There are in this country nearly five millions of us, and for a space of two hundred and forty-seven years we have been hewers of wood and drawers of water; but we have been with you in promoting all the interests of the country. My distinguished colleague, who defended the civil rights of our race the other day on this floor, set this forth so clearly that I need not dwell upon it at this time.

I propose to state just this: that we have been identified with the interests of this country from its very foundation. The cotton crop of this country has been raised and its rice-fields have been tilled by the hands of our race. All along as the march of progress, as the march of commerce, as the development of your resources has been widening and expanding and spreading, as your vessels have gone on every sea, with the stars and stripes waving over them, and carried your commerce everywhere, there the black man's labor has gone to enrich your country and to augment the grandeur of your nationality. This was done in the time of slavery. And, if for the space of time I have noted, we have been hewers of wood and drawers of water; if we have made your cotton-fields blossom as the rose; if we have made your rice-fields wave with luxuriant harvests; if we have made your corn-fields rejoice; if we have sweated and toiled to build up the prosperity of the whole country by the production of our labor,

I submit, now that the war has made a change, now that we are free—I submit to the nation whether it is not fair and right that we should come in and enjoy to the fullest extent our freedom and liberty.

A word now as to the question of education. Sir, I know that, indeed, some of our republican friends are even a little weak on the school clause of this bill; but sir, the education of the race, the education of the nation, is paramount to all other considerations. I regard it important, therefore, that the colored people should take place in the educational march of this nation, and I would suggest that there should be no discrimination. It is against discrimination in this particular that we complain.

Sir, if you look over the reports of the superintendents of schools in the several States, you will find, I think, evidences sufficient to warrant Congress in passing the civil-rights bill as it now stands. The report of the commissioner of education of California shows that under the operation of law and of prejudice, the colored children of that State are practically excluded from schooling. Here is a case where a large class of children are growing up in our midst in a state of ignorance and semi-barbarism. Take the report of the superintendent of education of Indiana, and you will find that while efforts have been made in some places to educate the colored children, yet the prejudice is so great that it debars the colored children from enjoying all the rights which they ought to enjoy under the law. In Illinois, too the superintendent of education makes this statement: that, while the law guarantees education to every child, yet such are the operations among the school trustees that they almost ignore, in some places, the education of colored children.

All we ask is that you, the legislators of the nation, shall pass a law so strong and so powerful that no one shall be able to elude it and destroy the rights under the Constitution and laws of our country. That is all we ask.

But, Mr. Speaker, the gentleman from North Carolina (Mr. Vance) asks that the colored man shall place himself in an attitude to receive his rights. I ask, what attitude can we assume? We have tilled your soil, and during the rude shock of war, until our hour came, we were docile during the long, dark night, waiting patiently the coming day. In the Southern States during that war our men and women stood behind their masters; they tilled the soil; and there were no insurrections in all the broad lands of the South; the wives and daughters of the slaveholders were as scared then as they were before; and the history of the war does not record a single event, a single instance, in which the colored people were unfaithful, even in slavery; nor does the history of the war record the fact that on the other side, on the side of the Union, there were any colored men who were not willing at all times to give their lives for their country. Sir, upon both sides we waited patiently. I was a student at Wilberforce University, in Ohio, when the tocsin of war was sounded, when Fort Sumter was fired upon, and I never shall forget the thrill that ran through my soul when I thought of the coming consequences of that shot. There were one hundred and fifteen of us, students at that university, who, anxious to vindicate the stars and stripes, made up a company, and offered our services to the governor of Ohio; and, sir, we were told that this was a white man's war and that the negro had nothing to do with it. Sir, we returned—docile, patient, waiting, casting our eyes to the heavens whence help always comes. We knew that there would come a period in the history of the nation when our strong black arms would be needed. We waited patiently; we waited until Massachusetts, through her noble governor, sounded the alarm, and we hastened then to hear the summons and obey it.

Sir, as I before remarked, we were peaceful on both sides. When the call was made on the side of the Union we were ready; when the call was made for us to obey orders on the other side, in the confederacy, we humbly performed our tasks, and waited patiently. But, sir, the time came when we were called for; and, I ask, who can say that when that call was made, the colored men did not respond as readily and as rapidly as did any other class of your citizens? Sir, I need not speak of the history of this bloody war. It will carry down to coming generations the valor of our soldiers on the battle-field. Fort Wagner will stand forever as a monument of that valor, and until Vicksburgh shall be wiped from the galaxy of battles in the great contest for human liberty that valor will be recognized.

And for what, Mr. Spencer and gentlemen, was the great war made? The gentleman from North Carolina (Mr. Vance) announced before he sat down, in answer to an interrogatory by a gentleman on this side of the House, that they went into the war conscientiously before God. So be it. Then we simply come and plead conscientiously before God that these are our rights, and we want them. We plead conscientiously before God, believing that these are our rights by inheritance, and by the inexorable decree of Almighty God.

We believe in the Declaration of Independence, that all men are born free and equal, and are endowed by their Creator with certain inalienable rights, among which are life, liberty, and the pursuit of happiness. And we further believe that to secure these rights governments are instituted. And we further believe that when governments cease to subserve those ends the people should change them.

I have been astonished at the course which gentlemen on the other side have taken in discussing this bill. They plant themselves right behind the Constitution, and declare that the rights of the State ought not to be invaded. Now, if you will take the history of the war of the rebellion, as published by the Clerk of this House, you will see that in 1860 the whole country, each side, was earnest in seeking to make such amendments to the Constitution as would forever secure slavery and keep the Union together under the circumstances. The resolutions passed, and the sentiments expressed in speeches at that time, if examined by gentlemen, will be found to bear out all that I have indicated. It was felt in 1860 that anything that would keep the "wayward sisters" from going astray was desirable. They were then ready and willing to make any amendments.

And now, when the civil rights of our race are hanging upon the issue, they on the other side are not willing to concede to us such amendments as will guarantee them; indeed, they seek to impair the force of existing amendments to the Constitution of the United States, which would carry out the purpose.

I think it is proper and just that the civil-rights bill should be passed. Some think it would be better to modify it, to strike out the school clause, or to so modify it that some of the State constitutions should not be infringed. I regard it essential to us and the people of this country that we should be secured in this if in nothing else. I can not regard that our rights will be secured until the jury-box and the school-room, those great palladiums of our liberty, shall have been opened to us. Then we will be willing to take our chances with other men.

We do not want any discrimination to be made. If discriminations are made in regard to schools, then there will be accomplished just what we are fighting against. If you say that the schools in the State of Georgia, for instance, shall be allowed to discriminate against colored people, then you will have discriminations made against us. We do not want any discriminations. I do not ask any legislation for the colored people of this country that is not applied to the white people. All that we ask is equal laws, equal legislation, and rights throughout the length and breadth of this land.

The gentleman from North Carolina (Mr. Vance) also says that the colored men should not come here begging at the doors of Congress for their rights. I agree with him. I want to say that we do not come here begging for our rights. We come here clothed in the garb of American citizenship. We come demanding our rights in the name of justice. We come, with no arrogance on our part, asking that this great nation, which laid the foundations of civilization and progress more deeply and more securely than any other nation on the face of the earth, guarantee us protection from outrage. We come here, five millions of people—more than composed this whole nation when it had its great tea-party in Boston Harbor, and demanded its rights at the point of the bayonet—asking that unjust discriminations against us be forbidden. We come here in the name of justice, equity, and law, in the name of children, in the name of our country, petitioning for our rights.

Our rights will yet be accorded to us, I believe, from the feeling that has been exhibited on this floor of the growing sentiment of the country. Rapid as the weaver's shuttle, swift as the lightning's flash, such progress is being made that our rights will be accorded to us ere long. I believe the nation is perfectly willing to accord this measure of justice, if only those who represent the people here would say the word. Let it be proclaimed that henceforth all the children of this land shall be free; that the stars and stripes, waving over all, shall secure to every one equal rights, and the nation will say "amen."

Let the civil rights bill be passed this day, and five million black men, women, and children, all over the land, will begin a new song of rejoicing, and the thirty-five millions of noble-hearted Anglo-Saxons will join in the shout of joy. Thus will the great mission be fulfilled of giving to all the people equal rights.

Inasmuch as we have toiled with you in building up this nation; inasmuch as we have suffered side by side with you in the war; inasmuch as we have together passed through affliction and pestilence, let there be now a fulfillment of the sublime thought of our fathers—let all men enjoy equal liberty and equal rights.

In this hour, when you are about to put the cap-stone on the mighty structure of government, I ask you to grant us this measure, because it is right. Grant this, and we shall go home with our hearts filled with gladness. I want to "shake hands over the bloody chasm." The gentleman from North Carolina has said he desires to have forever buried the memory of the recent war. I agree with him. Representing a South Carolina constituency, I desire to bury forever the tomahawk. I have voted in this House with a free heart to declare universal amnesty. Inasmuch as general amnesty has been proclaimed, I would hardly have expected there would be any objection on this floor to the civil-rights bill, giving to all men the equal rights of citizens. There should be no more contest. Amnesty and civil rights should go together. Gentlemen on the other side will admit that we have been faithful; and now, when we propose to bury the hatchet, let us shake hands upon this measure of justice; and if heretofore we have been enemies, let us be friends now and forever.

Our wives and our children have high hopes and aspirations; their longings for manhood and womanhood are equal to those of any other race. The same sentiment of patriotism and of gratitude, the same spirit of national pride that animates the hearts of other citizens, animates theirs. In the name of the dead soldiers of our race, whose bodies lie at Petersburgh and other battle-fields of the South; in the name of the widows and orphans they have left behind; in the name of the widows of the confederate soldiers who fell upon the same fields, I conjure you let this righteous act be done. I appeal to you in the name of God and humanity to give us our rights, for we ask nothing more. [Loud applause.]

### *Notes*

*Source:* This speech, which has never been given a title, is taken from the *Congressional Record*, 43rd Congress, 1st session (January 10, 1874),: 565–67, where it is identified as the Civil Rights Bill. We have titled it "All We Ask Is Equal Laws, Equal Legislation, and Equal Rights" because it sums up what Cain was seeking for blacks when he made the speech.

1. Garnett is quoted in Bernard E. Powers Jr., "'I Go To Set the Captives Free': The Activism of Richard Harvey Cain, Nationalist, Churchman, Reconstruction Era Leader," in *The Southern Elite and Social Change: Essays in Honor of Willard B. Gatewood Jr.*, ed. Randy Finley and Thomas DeBlack (Fayetteville: University of Arkansas Press, 2002), 34.

### *Bibliographical Sources*

Lewis, Ronald L. "Cultural Pluralism and Black Reconstruction: The Public Career of Richard H. Cain." *Crisis* 85 (February 1978): 57–60.

Mann, Kenneth E. "Richard Harvey Cain, Congressman, Minister and Champion for Civil Rights." *Negro History Bulletin* 35 (March 1972): 64–6.

Middleton, Stephen. *Black Congressmen During Reconstruction: A Documentary Sourcebook*. Westport, CT: Praeger, 2002.

"Richard Harvey Cain" in *Black Americans in Congress, 1870–1989*, ed. Bruce A. Ragsdale and Joel D. Trees. Prepared under the direction of the Commission on the Bicentenary by the Office of the Historian, U.S. House of Representatives. Washington, DC: Government Printing Office, 1990.

# RICHARD R. DEBAPTISTE

*(1831–1901)*

Richard R. DeBaptiste was born in 1831 in Fredericksburg, Virginia. Carter G. Woodson included DeBaptiste among the "distinguished Negroes who impressed the world as preachers of power." Woodson wrote: "They not only built imposing edifices and pastored large congregations, but went from place to place in the State and country impressing the world with the power of God unto salvation."[1] Richard's father, William, jointly owned a construction company with other relatives. Richard was first educated by his father in the family residence, along with several other children. But it had to be done in secret, since it was still illegal to teach Negroes to read and write in Virginia in the 1830s and 1840s, and police officers were watching the premises.

DeBaptiste was ordained for ministry in Mount Pleasant, Ohio, after which he taught school for three years in Mount Pleasant. He married Georgiana Brische in 1855, and they had three children together. In 1863 he became the pastor of the Olivet Baptist Church of Chicago, where he remained until 1882. While there Olivet grew from a small struggling congregation to one that built two church edifices, one that would seat eight hundred and the other one thousand two hundred. During this time the church received over one thousand seven hundred persons as members, almost half by baptism. During his tenure at Olivet, DeBaptiste was one of the strongest voices in America. He was the first of what could be termed "the fabulous four" black Baptist leaders from Olivet; the others were Revs. Elijah Fisher, Lacey Kirk Williams, and Joseph Harrison Jackson. Williams and Jackson, like DeBaptiste, headed national Baptist bodies.

Rev. DeBaptiste was elected president of the Consolidated American Baptist Missionary Convention at its first meeting in 1869 and thereafter for all but two years until 1877. In 1870 he was elected president of the white American Baptist Free Mission Society.

DeBaptiste's first wife died in 1872, and in 1885 he remarried. He wrote numerous articles for secular and religious journals and also served as an editor of a journal and coeditor of two others. The state university of Louisville conferred upon him the Doctor of Divinity degree in 1887. After leaving Olivet, he worked as a pastor at several small churches and as a journalist. He died in 1901.

• • •

*The following is excerpted from a sermon by DeBaptiste that is included in a collection of sermons. E.M. Brawley edited the collection; it was first published in 1890 by the American Baptist Publication Society of Philadelphia in* The Negro Baptist Pulpit: A Collection of Sermon and Papers on Baptist Doctrine and Missionary and Educational Work by Colored Baptist Ministers. *This sermon is representative of a teaching sermon prepared for publication.*

## A Gospel Church (ca. 1889)

*And when they were come to Jerusalem, they were received of the church, and of the apostles and elders, and they declared all things that God had done with them.* —Acts 15:4

In translating this passage from the original Greek, the words, "of the church," are used to give the meaning of a word which in the common use of the Greek language signifies an "assembly." Coming from a word meaning to call together, it describes an assembly of citizens called together, usually by a herald, the members of which were therefore the elect—the called. Liddell and Scott define the word "ecclesia" as an assembly of citizens summoned by the crier; the legislative assembly. In ecclesiastical usage the church: 1. The body. 2. The place.

The ecclesiastical meaning of the word in the New Testament is closely allied to the term "congregation" in the Old Testament, where the word means the body assembled for religious worship, as distinguished from the whole congregation of Israel or any general assembly of the same. "At the bottom lies the idea that the congregation is called together by God himself."

The idea that Christ intended to found a visible organization or church, in distinction from what is by ecclesiastical writers called "the Jewish Church," has been called in question. Some who concur in the view that under Christ and the apostles a visible church or churches were established, assert "that the existence of the church does not depend upon the apostolic forms," while the Roman Catholic idea is, that the Roman hierarchy is "the development of the church of the New Testament."

These theories are at some points in conflict with one another, and both are opposed to the view which we regard as Scriptural—that the New Testament furnishes a true and perfect standard for the constitution and doctrines of a gospel church.

### I. Its organic form.

In the text "the church" is understood as denoting the collective body or assembly of believers or disciples of Christ in Jerusalem. The writers in the New Testament have generally (ninety-two times) employed the word *ecclesia*, with its grammatical modifications, in the sense of a local body or assembly for religious worship when speaking of the disciples of Christ in other cities as well as those at Jerusalem: as "the church that was at Antioch"; "the church of God which is at Corinth"; "the churches throughout Syria and Cilicia"; "the churches of the Gentiles." (Acts 13:1; Romans 16:1; 1 Corinthians 1:2; Acts 15:41; Romans 16:4)

But by the word "church" we are also, in some few instances, to understand the whole body of God's true people, without restriction as to place or time, as in Hebrews 12:23, "To the general assembly and church of the first born which are written in heaven," and Ephesians 3:21, "Unto him be glory in the church by Christ Jesus throughout all ages, world without end." In some instances it denotes the entire company of believers in the world, as in Ephesians 1:22–23, "And hath put all things under his feet, and gave him to be the head over all things to the church, which is his body, the fullness of him that filleth all in all," and Ephesians 3:10, "To the intent that now unto the principalities and powers in heavenly places, might be known by the church the manifold wisdom of God." In these instances its meaning cannot be restricted to any one congregation of believers, or local organization of the disciples of Christ, but evidently embraces all that are truly Christians. The church in the sense indicated by this use of the word is but one universal body. In this amplified sense its meaning is analogous to the term, "Kingdom of God," in John 3:3, 5, and consists of all who become "fellow-citizens with the saints, and of the household of God, and are built upon the foundation of the apostles and prophets, Jesus Christ himself being the chief corner stone." (Ephesians 2:19, 20) But the inspired writings nowhere speak of this universal church as having a visible organization in the world under any one earthly head. It is one body and is of one Spirit, "For by one Spirit we are all baptized into one body, whether we be Jews or Gentiles, whether we be bond or free; and have been all made to drink into one Spirit." (1 Corinthians 12:13) But this unity is in no way the result of a form of outward government under the control of a central earthly head, be that head a pope, a bench of bishops, or college of presbyters; nor could it be made more manifest by such a head. Its unity is of the Spirit, its bond is love, which bond of union is formed in the regeneration of the soul through the exercise of faith, in the one Lord, uniting him and the members of the body in fellowship. So we being many are one body in Christ and members in particular. Christ also is head of the church, being himself the Saviour of the body.

The form of the visible churches planted by the inspired men called and commissioned by Christ was local—companies spiritual, parts of the one spiritual body. Such were the church at Jerusalem, the church at Antioch, and the church at Corinth.

## II. Of whom composed.

1. These churches were composed of persons who had been baptized upon a profession of their faith in Jesus as the Christ. The disciples won by the preaching of Christ—the "twelve" and the "seventy"—were baptized. "And after these things came Jesus and his disciples into the land of Judea; and there he tarried with them and baptized." "When therefore the Lord knew how that the Pharisees had heard that Jesus was making and baptizing more disciples than John (although Jesus himself baptized not, but his disciples)." (John 4:1, 2) Of these about an hundred and twenty assembled with the apostles in the "upper chamber" after the ascension of the Lord to wait for the promise of the Father, for he had taught them that they should be baptized with the Holy Ghost "not many days hence." (Acts 1:4, 5) Into this church at Jerusalem, when the Holy Spirit came upon the disciples on the day of Pentecost, "they that gladly received his (Peter's) word were baptized: and the same day there were added unto them about three thousand souls." Paul, writing to the churches he had established among the Gentiles, refers to their union with Christ and baptism in his name. "Is Christ divided? was Paul crucified for you? or were you baptized in the name of Paul?" (1 Corinthians 1:13) "To the beloved of God, called to be saints" in Rome, he says, "Therefore we are buried with him by baptism into death." (Romans 6:4)

2. It is evident that they associated themselves voluntarily together under this covenant of faith in Christ and fellowship of the gospel.

They had exercised intelligence in the reception of gospel truth that was strongly opposed by the adherents of conflicting doctrines and systems. Paul says of them: "But first they gave their own selves to the Lord, and unto us by the will of God." (2 Corinthians 8:5) They were by that very choice compelled to sever long and dearly cherished social as well as religious ties, and often subject themselves to the severest persecutions. To profess faith in Jesus at that early period of the gospel history, whether among Jews or Gentiles, and become the followers of the despised Nazarene, required intelligence, courage, and character. No others could join themselves to the church and endure the tests, both from within and without, by which they were tried. National incorporation into church membership was incompatible with the teachings of Christ, who had said, "My kingdom is not of this world"; and, in fact, impossible in that age, for all the nations opposed Christ and his religion; and hereditary or infant membership formed no part of the teachings of either Christ or the apostles. Baptism and faith were always united in their preaching. "Hence, as at first, all who acknowledged Jesus as the Messiah withdrew from the mass of the Jewish people, and formed themselves into a distinct community, so all who acknowledged Jesus as the Messiah were alike baptized."[2]

3. They were persons whose moral and spiritual life gave evidence of spiritual regeneration. Christ had taught: "Except a man be born of water and of the Spirit, he cannot enter into the kingdom of God." "Except ye be converted and become as little children, ye shall not enter into the kingdom of heaven." (John 3:5; Matthew 18:3) Peter preached repentance, faith, and baptism at Pentecost. Paul testifies of the members of the Church at Corinth: "But ye are washed, but ye are sanctified, but ye are justified in the name of the Lord Jesus and by the Spirit of our God" (1 Corinthians 6:11); and of the members of the church at Thessalonica: "In every place your faith to God-ward is spread abroad; so that we need not speak anything." (1 Thessalonians 1:8) John, in his Second Epistle, says: "The elder unto the elect lady and her children" testifies (ver. 4): "I rejoiced greatly that I found of thy children walking in truth, as we have received a commandment from the Father"; and in his Third Epistle: "Unto the well-beloved Gaius" (ver. 3): "For I rejoiced greatly when the brethren came and testified of the truth that is in thee, even as thou walkest in the truth." Luke, in Acts 2:47, says of the church in Jerusalem: "And the Lord added to the church daily such as should be saved."

## III. The ordinances and worship of a gospel church.

1. The ordinances of the gospel were established by Christ. He delivered them to his disciples, and commanded their observance. He alone has this right. The church was founded by him, and it is a natural sequence that he alone should determine its ordinances, "as Christ the head of the church and Saviour of the body." The ordinances recognized and observed by the apostles and the churches under their guidance, as of continual obligation for all time, are two—baptism and the Lord's Supper. These were committed by the apostles to the churches. Paul, addressing the Corinthian Church, said: "Now I praise you, brethren, that ye remember me in all things, and keep the ordinances as I delivered them to you. . . . For I received of the Lord that which also I delivered unto you, That the Lord Jesus the same night in which he was betrayed took bread: and when he had given thanks, he brake it, and said, Take, eat: this is my body, which is broken for you: this do in remembrance of me. After the same manner also he took the cup, when he had supped, saying," etc. (1 Corinthians 11:2, 23–26)

Baptism is a specific act commanded by Jesus Christ. It is not, therefore, a thing of " modes" to choose between. "We who died to sin, how shall we any longer live therein? Or are ye ignorant that all we who were baptized into Jesus Christ were baptized into his death? We were buried therefore with him through baptism into death, that like as Christ was raised from the dead through the glory of the Father, so we also might walk in newness of life." (Romans 6:2–4, Revised Version) We are given here by the inspired apostle, who is certainly as competent to explain the matter as any uninspired exegete, patristic, mediaeval, or modern, what the specific command of Christ comprehends—namely, a symbolical burial in water and resurrection from it, as setting forth our death to sin and rising into new life, through the operation of the Spirit in our conversion.

2. The worship of a gospel church is a thing of very vital importance. It is a part of the organic life of the church. It is the proper exercise of the inward spiritual functions of its organic life. The charisms or gifts spoken of in Ephesians 4:8, 11, 12; 1 Corinthians 12:4–31, should be regarded, and their proper exercise provided for in the worship and work of the church.

The worship of the church does much toward determining the kind of religious character that will be developed in its members. It was the ground of an impressive address by Paul to the Philippian Church. (Philippians 3:1–3) There are no prescribed forms, or ritual, given to the churches in the New Testament for their invariable observance; but there are references to the exercises in which the disciples with devout spirit engaged when together in assembly for worship. Of these, singing, praying, reading the Scriptures, exhortation, preaching, and the administration of the ordinances are mentioned.

## IV. THE GOVERNMENT, LAWS, AND OFFICERS OF A GOSPEL CHURCH.

1. The government of the churches established by the apostles was lodged in the members of each congregation or church. It was therefore in the strictest sense a democratic form of government, in which all the members of the church participated, and had an equal voice. The majority voting upon any question settled it. This appears (1) from the fact that the churches were composed of members who were voluntarily associated together under a covenant with the Lord and one another, upon terms of mutual love and equality, though not equal in talents, or spiritual attainments, or in the possession of this world's goods. In all these

things there was diversity, but all had an equal right to enjoy the exercise of what gift or grace they possessed, and a voice in the decision of whatever came before the body. It would appear also (2) from the instruction given by Jesus to the apostles, that they should neither be "lords," nor have "authority" over one another, as the lords of the Gentiles did, who ruled over them; for one is your Master, even Christ, and all ye are brethren. This was also taught by Paul to the Gentiles, among whom he established churches. "Ye are all the children of God by faith in Christ Jesus," and "there is neither Jew nor Greek, there is neither male nor female, for ye are all one man in Christ Jesus." (Galatians 3:28, Revised Version) Recognizing the headship of Christ alone over the body, the members exercised their governing power under him.

(a) In the reception of members. "Him that is weak in the faith receive ye, but not to doubtful disputations." (Romans 14:1) On this, commentators say that "receive ye" means to cordial Christian fellowship—the communion of the church.

(b) In the discipline of members. They were so instructed by Christ. (Matthew 18:17) "Tell it to the church." "If he will not hear the church let him be unto thee as an heathen man and a publican." They were so instructed by Paul (1 Corinthians 5:4, 5, 9), to discipline the violators of moral purity among them, and "not to keep company with fornicators"; and at Thessalonica to withdraw from every brother that walked disorderly.

(c) In the election of an apostle in the place of Judas. (Acts 1:25, 26) "This was the first assembly convened to transact the business of the church; and the vote in so important a matter as electing an apostle was by the entire church. It settles the question that the election of a minister and pastor should be by the church, and that he should not be imposed on them by any right of presentation by individuals, or by any ecclesiastical body." (Barnes on Acts 1:25, 26)

(d) In the election of deacons. (Acts 6:2–6) "Then the twelve called the multitude of the disciples unto them and said, '. . . Wherefore, brethren, look ye out among you for seven men . . .' They chose 'seven,' whom they set before the apostles: and when they had prayed, they laid their hands on them."

(e) In the ordination of elders. "Ordained them elders in every church." (Acts 14:23) The word rendered here "ordained" is also rendered "chosen" elsewhere, denoting primarily to vote with uplifted hands. Alford says: "There is no good reason for departing from the usual meaning of electing by show of hands." . . .

2. The laws of a gospel church are those given by Christ and the apos-

tles, and found in the New Testament. No church has a right to alter, or add to any ordinance or law for the constitution, government, or doctrines of a church, that may be found in the New Testament. . . . A gospel church has no legislative authority in itself as to matters established by Christ; its prerogatives are executive only, and it must govern itself by the laws which Christ gave. . . .

3. The officers of a gospel church must be determined by the New Testament. The apostles completed the organization of the church, and they have left us in their writings all the necessary information on the subject. The permanent officers are only two, pastor, variously called bishop and elder, and deacon.

(a) The apostles are the first named in the earliest history of the church; but they had a special work for which they were called, endowed, and sent. The apostles' office ceased at their death. No successors were appointed; nor from the nature of the qualifications as indicated in Acts 1:21, 22, could any be appointed. The other seventy (Luke 10:1) appear as evangelists.

(b) The "seven" who were deacons are the first permanent officers. (Acts 6:2–6)

(c) Bishops or elders are named as permanent officers, who, with the deacons, are spoken of as such in connection with each other. (Philippians 1:1; 1 Timothy 3:1, 2, 8) Bishop and elder are used interchangeably in Acts 20:17, 28; Titus 1:5, 7. From these and 1 Peter 5:1, 2, it is quite evident that both names refer to one and the same office—elder expressing the dignity, and bishop the duty of the office. From Ephesians 4:11, and from the meaning of the word (Jeremiah 3:15), pastors are regarded as permanent officers in the church, and identical with elders and bishops. The various other ministerial gifts bestowed upon the church as "prophets," "evangelists," "teachers," "governments," do not necessarily represent officers, but ministerial endowments.

## NOTES

*Sermon source:* Edward MacKnight Brawley, ed., *The Negro Baptist Pulpit: A Collection of Sermons and Papers on Baptist Doctrine and Missionary and Education Work by Colored Baptist Ministers* (Philadelphia: American Baptist Publication Society, 1890).

1. Carter G. Woodson, *The History of the Negro Church*, electronic edition (Washington: Associated Publishers, 1921; placed online by University of North Carolina at Chapel Hill, 2000), 241.

2. The quote is from Johann August Wilhelm Neander (1789–1850), a German theologian and church historian.

### *Bibliographical Sources*

Jordan, Lewis G. *Negro Baptist History U.S.A., 1750–1930*, rev. ed., vol. 2. Nashville, TN: Townsend Press Sunday School Publishing Board National Baptist U.S.A. Inc., 1995.

Logan, Rayford W., and Michael R. Winston, eds. *Dictionary of American Negro Biography*. New York: W. W. Norton and Company, 1982.

Murphy, Larry G., J. Gordon Melton, and Gary L. Ward. *Encyclopedia of African American Religions*. New York: Garland Publishing, 1993.

Sernett, Milton, C. *Black Religion and American Evangelicalism: White Protestants, Plantation Missions and the Flowering of Negro Christianity, 1787–1865*. Metuchen, NJ: Scarecrow Press, 1975.

Simmons, William J. *Men of Mark: Eminent, Progressive and Rising*. 1887. Reprint, Chicago: Johnson Publishing Company, 1970.

# WILLIAM BENJAMIN DERRICK

*(1843–1913)*

William Benjamin Derrick was born on the island of Antigua in the British West Indies in 1843 to parents of means. His father, Thomas, was a planter from Scotland; his mother Eliza a West Indian. William's natural talent for oratory gained him applause from his classmates beginning in high school. He studied blacksmithing and, in 1861, began working as a sailor for the U.S. government during the Civil War. After marriage to Mary White, who died shortly afterward, he joined the African Methodist Episcopal Church. In 1868 he was ordained a deacon. Subsequently, he was elected an elder and ordained by Bishop Jabez Campbell. He married a woman named Lillian, and their marriage lasted until her death twenty-five years later. In 1909 he married Clara Henderson Jones.

After ordination, he was appointed pastor and presiding elder of the Staunton church and district. He served and was reappointed presiding elder, pastor, and conference secretary at the annual conferences held from 1870 to 1879. His political involvements led him to leave the South and take a trip to the West Indies. He returned to the United States and went on to enjoy a long tenure in New York City at the Sullivan Street Church. Wilberforce University conferred upon him the title Doctor of Divinity in 1885. In addition to using his oratorical powers to save souls, he was an advocate for education and greatly supported the work of all

AME schools, especially Wilberforce. Derrick also served as the missions secretary for the AME Church.

Derrick, a Republican, was always politically active. His voice was considered rich and his personality magnetic, adding to his power as an orator. Derrick was noted for his command of language, providing parishioners with metaphors and illustrations that were clear and thought provoking. His preaching was straightforward and formal when necessary. His sermons and speeches were printed in the *New York Tribune*, the *New York Times, The Sun*, and the *New York Herald*. The Sullivan Street Church was regularly filled to capacity even though the building seated one thousand five hundred. Derrick was elected on the first ballot to the bishopric of the AME Church in 1896. He died in Flushing, New York, in 1913.

• • •

*When sixty-five years of age, Derrick addressed the Twenty-third Annual Conference of the AME Church in Norfolk, Virginia. The message focused on the achievements of the denomination and the tasks that lay ahead. However, Derrick also used the occasion to address a wide range of issues, from the lack of unity among the five black Methodist bodies, to advocating against those who wanted to open certain types of establishments on Sunday, to the need for the church to protest mob rule.*

## Address to Twenty-third General Conference of the AME Church (1908)

As ministers and laymen, our devotion to Christ should be expressed in the most absolute manner. We should enter most energetically into His service, should manifest a high degree of reverence for His name and be deeply interested in the extension of His kingdom upon earth. Our renunciation of the foibles of the world should become more apparent and complete as the years roll by, and a clear conception of the spirit of self-denial be more strictly held. We should act with greater resolution and thus be enabled to act with greater firmness in the cause of our Lord and Master. Our devotion should increase to a higher pitch than most Christians are willing to believe is attainable in this life. Our attitude should be as having no interests to serve, no inclinations to gratify, nor any connections to maintain, but such as are entirely conformable to the nature of our union with our Lord and Master Jesus Christ. Wherever we go let us breathe the spirit of devotion, and wherever we are familiarly known let the fervor, the resolution, and the constancy of that devotion be universally apparent. We should daily feel and act in conformity to the powerful obligations by which we are bound to the King of kings, who is the Author and Finisher of our faith. Our vows of genuine affection and fidelity should be prayerfully and solemnly renewed, as occasion offers, both in public and in private. Let this line of conduct be followed through all the vicissitudes of our Christian warfare. We are aware that to reach this stage in our attainment will call for much patience in afflictions, in necessities, in distresses, in labors, in watching, in fasting, in knowledge, and in long suffering. But armed with the power of God, and protected by the armor of righteousness, we will conquer every stronghold of sin and put under foot every prompting of evil.

Time flies. Years of plenty and of scarcity, of peace and of war, fade and blend with eternity. Our prayer is that we may appreciate the value of the present hour and the opportunities that God offers, and may serve our day and generation with faithfulness and diligence, remembering that soon the night cometh.

The rapid numerical growth of our Church, and the vast area over which it is swiftly expanding; the various countries and governments in which our work is being carried on; the constantly changing social and economic condition surrounding those for whom and with whom we labor, all combine to increase both the number and the gravity of the questions, and the problems which must be confronted and dealt with in the task of directing her complex and numerous activities.

We stand in the dawn of the twentieth century surrounded by the blessings which have come to us from the heroic and wise labors of the departed fathers, and there open before us new tasks to be executed under new conditions. We must give due consideration to the fact that our ministry must be especially prepared to meet the demands that will be made upon it by the new generation that is so rapidly filling our pews. Our schools and colleges and the educational institutions everywhere open to our youth are each year sending forth multitudes of cultured young men and women, whose advent into our pews emphasizes the demand for a steadily advancing standard in the qualifications of our clergy. The future hope of our Church largely centers about Payne and Morris Brown Theological Seminaries, and these two schools should be considered the theological centers from which will go forth a trained ministry. There is imperative need for a thorough awakening to this truth. If proper endeavors are not put forth there is great and impending danger of the respectability and influence of our Church being seriously lessened. The constant advancement of culture in the pew renders absolutely imperative the demand for equal advancement of culture in the pulpit.

There are numbers of pious youths throughout the Church who might be serviceable in preaching the gospel, but through the want of sufficient financial aid are unable to obtain an education. It should be the intention as well as the desire of the Annual Conferences to have the ministers in their respective charges seek out such, so that after being examined and approved by the Annual Conferences, they may be encouraged to go to some theological seminary and receive final training. The expenses should be shared by the Annual Conferences within the bounds of the Episcopal district where such youths may reside.

In that memorable prayer which our Lord addressed to the Father previous to the consummation of his sufferings, we find this petition in behalf of his followers: "That they all may be one; as thou Father *art* in me, and I in thee, that they may be one in us: that the world may believe that thou hast sent me." Unhappily the Church of Christ is at present divided into a great variety of distinct organizations, from which it results that instead of marching forward with a united front *against* a common foe, much of the time and strength of the different denominations are wasted in opposing each other; and not infrequently has the world beheld the strange spectacle of different portions of the same Church opposing each other. Over this state of things the Church has long had occasion to mourn, and it seems to be time that some systematic effort should be made to bring into fellowship the different portions of the household of faith. In our country, there now exist five distinct branches of Colored Methodists, whose views of evangelical truth, as exhibited in their different standards, are substantially one and the same, and whose form of government is the same. Could these bodies be brought more closely together so as to act in concert, it is easy to see that much more might be accomplished in advancing the interests of the common faith and in promoting its more universal diffusion than is practicable in our present divided state. We consider that the Church of Christ constitutes one body, of which He is the Divine Head, and it should, therefore, be so organized as to exhibit to the view of the world the appearance as well as the reality of unity.

This government founded on the divine ideas of liberty and equality must continue to be the defender and propagator of all that constitutes true national greatness. The conduct of national affairs in the main is just and progressive, and tends to secure the highest good of the country; and there is much that promises the growth and perpetuity of her institutions. It is also true that there are forces at work which threaten the overthrow of this great temple of freedom. We are not pessimistic in our view and yet we must acknowledge the existence of gigantic forces inimical to liberty, law, righteousness, and truth. The political world is not wholly free from false political ideas, anti-Christian sentiments, corrupt practices, and conscienceless legislation. Efforts have constantly been made by the legislators of the country to pass laws which would open the places of drunkenness and crime on the Lord's day; and likewise laws which would discriminate against a certain class of helpless individuals, debarring them from enjoying certain rights and privileges to which they are entitled. We enter our vigorous protest against any legislation that would in any measure deprive men and women of their ordinary rights. The foes of our Christian Sabbath are still active in their efforts to abrogate it or to convert it into a day of merriment and sin. Intemperance, with all the evils that it entails, is on the increase. During the past four years the illegal butchery of American citizens has taken place,[1] which is not flattering to our civilization nor government, until sometimes we are led to inquire, "Has justice returned to heaven, that mob-law must reign to execute her behests?" The Church of God must set her seal of condemnation on all lawlessness and the taking of life without the legal process which a righteous government has instituted for the trial of the guilty.

The very existence and value of any people are involved in their economic features. We emphasize that this feature of a people's character is, to our mind, essential to their existence and to the determination of their comparative value. There is nothing of which we can conceive that is capable, by its harrowing privations leading to numerous temptations, of so thoroughly lowering a people and bringing them into utter contempt as the misfortune of poverty; and there is nothing, in our opinion, which is surer to lead to poverty than the utter disregard for the laws and principles of economy, domestic or otherwise, which ought to govern and regulate the use of money—laws and principles which are in some degree natural for every man to know. It is our candid conviction that the misfortune of poverty arises in the majority of instances not so much from utter recklessness, as from want of forethought and due reflection which must, as a natural result, lead to waste. There are persons—and not a few—who do not realize that they have misspent their money until some casual circumstance has brought them to a sorrowful sense of the fact. This could certainly have been averted by thought and reflection.

The political standing of any section of the population of a country has so close a bearing on its material progress, and is indeed of so much consequence in enabling thoughtful and observant persons to form a proper opinion of the form of government under which it is their lot to live, that it is not without some essential value here to ascertain and examine the political status and advise the necessity of exercising with the greatest care the boon of suffrage. Too much concern cannot be manifested in our efforts to assist in the maintenance of good government. "The worth of a State," says John Stuart Mill, "is the worth of the individuals composing it; they are the elements which constitute the State." It is true that we were once an empty space on the political map, but things have changed and we are now citizens with rights—citizens who recognize the fact that if the material, industrial, moral, intellectual, and religious conditions are of a healthful nature, all the inhabitants are benefited; and if things are contrary, all suffer. We would advise you to be peaceful and law-abiding citizens, regardless of what may be said as to your passiveness. . . .

## *Notes*

*Sermon source:* This message is taken from Charles Spencer Smith's *A History of the African Methodist Episcopal Church, Being a Volume Supplemental to a History of the African Methodist Episcopal Church, by Daniel Alexander Payne, D.D., LL.D., Late One of Its Bishops: Chronicling the Principal Events in the Advance of the African Methodist Episcopal Church From 1856 to 1922* (Philadelphia: Book Concern of the AME Church, 1922). Electronic edition at Documenting the American South, University of North Carolina at Chapel Hill Digitization Project, http://docsouth.unc.edu/church/csmith/wright.html (accessed February 9, 2004), 247–51.

1. One can not definitively determine the event(s) to which Derrick makes reference; so many heinous acts had been visited upon blacks during the course of Derrick's life. He is likely referencing the numerous lynchings that had taken place in and around New York and elsewhere after the establishment of the Klu Klux Klan in 1867. On March 15, 1904, the *New York Times* ran the following headline: "Lynchings Too Much for Bishop Derrick—Colored Divine, Tired of America Yearns for Africa. Says Negroes are Oppressed."

## *Bibliographical Sources*

Murphy, Larry G., J. J. Gordon Melton, and Gary L. Ward. *Encyclopedia of African American Religions.* New York: Garland Publishing, 1993, 233.

Simmons, William J. *Men of Mark: Eminent, Progressive and Rising.* 1887. Reprint, Chicago: Johnson Publishing Company, 1970, 37.

Smith, Charles Spencer. *History of the African Methodist Episcopal Church*, vol 2. Philadelphia: Book Concern of the AME Church, 1922.

Talbert, Horace. *The Sons of Allen: Together With a Sketch of the Rise and Progress of Wilberforce University, Wilberforce Ohio.* Xenia, Ohio: Aldine Press, 1906.

Wright, Richard R., Jr. *Centennial Encyclopaedia of the African Methodist Episcopal Church Containing Principally the Biographies of the Men and Women,*

*Both Ministers and Laymen, Whose Labors during a Hundred Years, Helped Make the A. M. E. Church What It Is; Also Short Historical Sketches of Annual Conferences, Educational Institutions, General Departments, Missionary Societies of the A. M. E. Church, and General Information about African Methodism and the Christian Church in General; Being a Literary Contribution to the Celebration of the One Hundredth Anniversary of the Formation of the African Methodist Episcopal Church Denomination by Richard Allen and others, at Philadelphia, Penna., in 1816*. Philadelphia: Book Concern of the AME Church, 1916. Electronic edition at Documenting the American South, University of North Carolina at Chapel Hill Digitization Project, http://docsouth.unc.edu/church/wright/wright.html (accessed February 9, 2004), 83.

# ELIJAH JOHN FISHER

*(1858–1915)*

Elijah John Fisher was a preacher of the last generation of black slaves. Born August 2, 1858, in LaGrange, Georgia, Fisher was one of seventeen siblings and next to the youngest of the eight boys born to Miles and Charlotte Fisher.

A great orator whose words rang with eloquence, Fisher was tall, as was his mother, who stood six feet. He heard his father, unlettered and untrained, preach in the brush arbors, and sometimes in church buildings when whites gave permission.

In 1877 Fisher married Florida Neely. Fisher and Florida had five children: two daughters, Gertrude and Shepherd Mattie, and three sons, Elijah John Jr., James Edward, and the noted historian Miles Mark.

Fisher studied grammar and arithmetic at Atlanta Baptist Seminary, where his call to preach was made clear to him. He was licensed to preach in 1879 by the first Baptist Church of LaGrange.

In 1880, Fisher boarded a train for Long Cane, Georgia, on his way to teach a class and then to preach. White conductors were known for not coming to complete stops in some of the smaller stations, and they did so this day. As Fisher reached the steps, his overcoat was caught and he was thrown on the track. "The train acted as a skilled surgeon, amputating his left leg about a foot above the knee, also his second toe on his right foot and his third finger on his right hand."[1] It was a ten-mile ride to the nearest hospital. Fisher lived the rest of his life on crutches.

In 1882, he was ordained by a council that included Revs. E.R. Carter, C.T. Walker (who would one day help eulogize Fisher), D.J. Wimbish,

J.A. Walker, and P.M. Mobley. His first pastorate was in Georgia. In 1889 he moved to Atlanta, accepting a pastorate there and attending school at the Atlanta Baptist Seminary (now Morehouse College). After gaining permission to enter in the senior class and after completing all necessary exams, he graduated in 1890. In the late 1890s, Fisher served as an editor for the *Atlanta Tribune*, a black newspaper.

Rev. Fisher believed that the more unprepared the people, the more prepared their leaders ought to be. But he also believed that a religion that could not be felt was no religion and a discourse that appealed only to the intellect and did not pull on the heartstrings was not a sermon. Fisher was an "all-around evangelist, giving his message both in song and in sermon. Crowds thronged, some likely out of curiosity, to hear this one-legged preacher."[2] But once they heard him, his plain, outspoken messages led many to turn to God. A 1911 flier advertising that Fisher would be preaching at Wheat Street Baptist Church in Atlanta said: "Doctor Fisher is preaching the gospel in a simple, convincing and unanswerable manner. His clarion voice in gospel and song is like trumpet-blasts, then like a mighty cyclone, and then again akin to the dove and nightingale."[3] At a ten-day revival in Pittsburgh, one hundred were converted. Fisher preached in almost every state in the United States where blacks were numerous.

He became the pastor of Olivet in Chicago in 1902. Prior to his arrival, the five hundred members of Olivet had suffered financial difficulties and soon after Fisher became their pastor, the church treasurer was jailed for being part of a scam that cost the church six thousand dollars, and they could not pay the church mortgage. Less than four years later, the church was back in its old space, had been enlarged to seat one thousand eight hundred and was full. Olivet became the best-known Baptist church and Fisher the best-known black pastor in not just Chicago and the Midwest, but the Northeast as well.

Elijah John Fisher's preaching was matched by social action, which is what made him such a major figure. By 1910, Olivet had three thousand one hundred members, an Athletic Club and Girls' Twilight League for the community, twenty-three church clubs that helped the public, an employment bureau, benevolent societies, a Woman's Christian Temperance Union, and two mission stations for the poor and homeless. He worked with local clergy to purchase a cemetery for blacks and worked with countless other business ventures. Reverend Fisher served as vice president of the National Baptist Convention and was one of the incorporators of the National Baptist Publishing Board.

He wrote *The Influence of Baptist Principles on Other Denominations* and *A Regenerated Church Membership and Why*. Morehouse conferred upon him an honorary Doctor of Divinity in 1912. That same year, he founded a seminary, which in two years had two hundred students. He died in 1915.

• • •

*In addition to being a pastor and teacher, Fisher was greatly involved in mission work with the National Baptist Convention. In this brief message, Fisher pleads with an audience of preachers to make real the Baptist commitment to mission by adequately funding it. He hails mission works as one of the most important things that Baptists must do.*

## The Duty of Baptists to Home Missions (ca. 1886)

Mr. President and Brethren composing the One Hundredth Anniversary of the Negro Baptists of Georgia:

It affords me no small degree of happiness to have the pleasure of even appearing before this intelligent, heaven-bound denomination, for the purpose of speaking a word. There have been many important subjects under discussion, which were handled with ability, and others to be discussed, among which there is one appearing on the programme with vital import: "The Duty of Baptists to Home Missions," and among the other names, I find E. J. Fisher, of LaGrange, and that happens to be my name.

Therefore, allow me to quote you a passage of scripture, which can be found in Joshua 3:1, where the Lord said unto him: "Thou art old and stricken in years, and there remaineth yet very much land to be possessed." He was a man of obedience. God sustained and blessed his efforts. He was also about one hundred years old. Nothwithstanding he had taken many cities and lands, still there were many more to conquer: the southland, governed by five lords, and westward, as far as Sardonia. It was his duty to go, because God sent him. In like manner, Jesus, after he had arisen from the dead, and was about to make His ascension back to heaven, told His disciples to "Go ye therefore and disciple all nations."

Looking this commission in the face, seeing it comes to us as to them, since we claim that we are keeping pace with His teaching and the practice of His disciples, it becomes more imperatively the duty of the Baptists to do mission work than any other denomination, for our message is of God and of His Christ. Therefore, the saving of the world is upon us. And, as the disciples were to begin at Jerusalem, ours is to begin in

Georgia, and continue throughout these United States. For no other can stand as do the Missionary Baptist, and cry, "One Lord, one faith, and one baptism." And, as we are the sent of God, the duty is not a small one. Hence, this army is to go on crying until Georgia is saved totally, and then reach out to save the world.

Since the Baptists believe the whole counsel of God, and that counsel is truth, and as the world is to be saved by the same, it follows that the Missionary Baptist is to do this home mission work; for they are better prepared to do it than any other, because they have what is necessary for its accomplishment, save the money which we are making great efforts to get. May the Lord assist us in getting the needed amount of money to carry it out. Since we have the men and the food we only need the train. Let each of us see that it is supplied. Now, I appeal to every Baptist, since it becomes our duty to do the mission work. As we are called of the Lord to do this work, I ask, shall we have the train for conveyance, which is money, since we can not do without it?

Listen. Before the birth of Christ, at the call, when the prophet said he saw an angel with six wings flying from the altar with a live coal in a pair of tongs, which he took therefrom, and came and touched his tongue, then there was a voice heard saying, "Who will go for us, or whom shall we send?" Isaiah answered and said, "Here am I, send me." In like manner when God called about one hundred years ago this army under the leadership of Revs. Leile and Bryan answered the same, and to-day we are still declaring one Lord, one faith and one baptism.

## *Notes*

*Sermon source:* The electronic edition of E.K. Love, ed., *History of the First African Baptist Church, From Its Organization, January 20th, 1788, to July 1st, 1888. Including the Centennial Celebration, Addresses, Sermons, Etc.* (Savannah, GA: The Morning News Print, 1888), 276. Electronic edition at Documenting the American South, University of North Carolina at Chapel Hill Digitization Project, http://docsouth.unc.edu/church/love/love.html (accessed March 15, 2005).

1. Miles Mark Fisher, *The Master's Slave: Elijah John Fisher A Biography* (Philadelphia: Judson Press, 1922), 21.
2. Ibid., 52.
3. Ibid., 123.

## *Bibliographical Sources*

Fisher, Miles Mark. "History of the Olivet Baptist Church." Thesis, University of Chicago. 1922.

———. *The Master's Slave: Elijah John Fisher A Biography*. Philadelphia: Judson Press, 1922.

Love, E.K., ed. *History of First African Baptist Church, From Its Organization, January 20th, 1788 to July 1st, 1888. Including the Centennial Celebration, Addresses, Sermons, Etc.* Savannah, GA: The Morning News Print, 1888. Electronic edition at Documenting the American South, University of North Carolina at Chapel Hill Digitization Project, http://docsouth.unc.edu/church/love/love.html (accessed March 15, 2005).

# GARFIELD T. HAYWOOD

*(1880–1931)*

Garfield Thomas Haywood was born in Green Castle, Indiana, on July 15, 1880, and reared in Indianapolis. He was the third of eight children born to Benjamin and Penny Ann Haywood. At an early age, he developed his talent for cartooning and sketching and after finishing only two years of high school worked for two weeklies that served the black community.

He began his religious training in the Methodist Church and then worked in a Baptist church. In 1902 he married Ida Howard; they had one child. By 1908 Haywood had become a member of the Apostolic Faith Assembly (a small interracial Pentecostal group) shortly after the foundation for Pentecostalism had been laid. Apostolics reject the doctrine of the Trinity, adhering instead to belief in the "oneness of God" as revealed in Jesus Christ. They do not use the Trinitarian formula (that is, "in the name of the Father, the Son, and the Holy Ghost") for baptism, as is characteristic of other Christian churches; they baptize in Jesus' name alone. Hence, the Apostolics are occasionally referred to as "Jesus only" or "Jesus name" churches. The term "Sanctified Church" also includes some Apostolic churches.

Ultimately Haywood began pastoring and in 1910 began publishing *Voice in the Wilderness* out of his home. He used dramatic drawings and charts to drive home his biblical messages. Haywood also published *The Bridegroom Cometh*, a hymnal that contained many of his own songs.

The Pentecostal Assemblies of the World (PAW) had its beginnings as a product of the Azusa Street Revival, which is to say, as a Pentecostal body, but took on the Apostolic doctrine and identity in 1914 after the rebaptism of G.T. Haywood and his followers "in Jesus' name." In 1916 PAW was formally established by members who, along with Haywood, had left another Apostolic denomination. Of the five original groups in black Holiness-Pentecostalism, the Pentecostal Assemblies of the World began last. First was the United Holy Church of America (1886), second the Church of Christ Holiness, U.S.A. (1895), third the Church of God in Christ (1895–97), and fourth the Fire Baptized Holiness Church of God in the Americas (1889).[1] PAW named G.T. Haywood their general secretary and the editor of their publication, the *Christian Outlook*, an office he held until 1930.

In 1924 Haywood renamed his church Christ Temple and moved into a twelve-hundred-seat building. At the time, this was the largest PAW church in the country. In 1924, many whites left PAW, which then reorganized and named Haywood as their first bishop. He pastored Christ Temple until his death.

• • •

*This sermon was delivered by Haywood at the Apostolic Faith Assembly in Indianapolis during a Sunday morning service. In the sermon, as an Apostolic believer, Haywood emphasizes spiritual power. He also preaches and promotes an ascetic ethic forbidding the use of alcohol. In other messages, he forbid gambling, secular dancing, and tobacco and other addictive substances. Haywood also does not fail to indicate a central tenet of his denomination, that people should be baptized in Jesus' name and baptized in the same fashion (submerged in water).*

## A Gospel Message of Hope (1922)

We wish to call your attention to the third chapter of Romans, beginning at verse 1, "What advantage then hath the Jew? or what profit is there of circumcision? Much every way: chiefly, because that unto them were committed the oracles of God." That is, the first opportunity to know God. The law of the ten commandments was given to them. God had committed unto their trust the oracles of God, and gave them that they might bring the light of God to the world. And although they failed their God, yet His purpose went forward. Even though some did not believe, "shall their unbelief make the faith of God without effect?" Man's unbelief does not change God's word, nor stop Him from working out His purpose.

The word of God is true whether the people believe it or not. God will bring Salvation near. It makes no difference what you say, or what

I may say, "God hath said." Our God can work while we are sleeping. And when we are folded away like a garment in our graves, God will still be working. If one man or one people fails God, He will take up another and move on. God brought Israel out and made them a great people, through a man who was only a shepherd of the plains of Midian and not a warrior, but could speak words of wisdom by the spirit of God—words which even to this day have astonished the world, God sent His Word from heaven unto this people, and walked in the midst of them with mighty signs and wonders showing His mighty arm. And yet they failed God through their unbelief.

The Lord had no people He could trust. So He declared He would "take a people who are not a people and make them a people of God." He did this to prove that He does not have to depend on any nation or individual. God Himself never failed and could not fail. Even the prophets He ordained became weak along the line and were filled with fear, or took honor to themselves. "The priest and the prophet have erred through strong drink, they are swallowed up of wine, they are out of the way through strong drink; they err in vision, they stumble in judgement" (Isaiah 28:7).

What if man does not believe the Gospel as it is laid down in the Book? The Gospel is true regardless of his unbelief. I believe in the Blood of Jesus Christ, and that without shedding of blood there is no remission of sins. But the question is: how shall I get the remission? One may say, "I will just believe." But to "believe" means more than to just say "I believe," Matthew 26:28 says.

If any people start out with the power of God in their midst and become full of pride and lose their spirituality, God will put them aside and take up another. And if the latter fails, He will set them aside and take up still another. I am satisfied that God does not depend upon any of us to carry His work through, but we are compelled to depend upon Him for without Him we can do nothing.

"For this is My blood of the New Testament, which is shed for many for the remission of sins." Jesus was the greatest preacher the world has ever known, and turned the preaching of the Gospel over to Peter as though He said, "You are next, Peter. You shall begin where I leave off." And that preacher in Acts 2:38 said: "Repent, and be baptized, every one of you, in the name of Jesus Christ, for the remission of sins and ye shall receive the gift of the Holy Ghost." That is the way the Holy Spirit gave it out on the day of Pentecost. In those days the people were always baptized in the name of Jesus Christ for the remission of sins that they might receive the Holy Spirit, which was God's witness to their faith.

What is the Holy Ghost? He is a witness to your having received remission of sins. That is what the Apostle said: "There are three that bear witness in the earth, the Spirit, the water and the blood." He did not say one was any greater than the other. All three of them are required to make one witness. Many people look at water alone, but the proper thing to do is to see the name in which it is administered. Take away the blood, and you have nothing but faith. Take away the water and you make Jesus a liar. The Bible, in the first epistle of John, tells us plainly that "this is He which came by water and blood; not by water only, but by water and blood." And that, "it is the Spirit that beareth witness." I do take notice of this much: there was so much authority in the command of Jesus to baptize, that nearly all the churches (with a few exceptions) try in some way to administer it, if it only be dipping the finger in the water. But if it is worth doing at all, it is worth doing rightly. However, a man's failure to believe does not change the Word of God. You can scarcely join a church in the city without some mode of baptism. There are about as many ways as there are human minds, and all for the lack of following the mind of the Spirit.

The reason some people do not live holy is because they have not been taught it and have been brought up wrongly. But you start a man or woman believing the Word of God, and you can bring them out on the Word. Our experiences are so varied that it does not pay to attempt to tell others about it, for they will try to get our experience instead of what is written in the Book. I do not want anybody to be able to rise and say the Word of God is not true. There has always been somebody filled with the Spirit, ever since the day of Pentecost. God has never left Himself without witness. No doubt some did not know just what they had. Luther had it. Wesley, Finney and Fox had it; and they had a hard, severe trial in their days.

We want God to be justified. We have not a thing to boast of this day. There is false holiness and true holiness. The true, is the Holy Ghost in you; and the false, is human efforts without God; self-righteousness. If we acknowledge our own failures God will give us His power to overcome day by day. God does not get behind a man with a whip and drive him to heaven, but He fixes it up so you "will" follow Him because you love Him.

Who is it that never did sin? Paul shows the whole human family had sinned, and if all sinned, all were condemned. But God had mercy. We could not help but sin. We were born that way. But God said, "You must be born again." And no new-born child walks perfectly at once. First they crawl, then they totter and fall. But they do not keep falling. By this

I mean that a man or woman who is filled with the Holy Ghost and starts out to walk with Jesus Christ, may stumble and fall at first, but don't get discouraged if the devil tries to trip you up. God will help you. He is able to keep you from falling, says Jude. I am talking about those who have it in their hearts to live for Christ. Do not let any failure daunt your courage. You know God is able to carry you through. Many have found it to be so.

If God brings judgment upon a sinner for his wrong doing, some will charge Him with injustice. But how can God then judge the world? God said He would give us a light for our path, and put His angels around us, and give us a pattern in Jesus, and place His Spirit within us. Brother, I would be ashamed to tell God I could not live right with all that help! And then folks will try to tell you, "You can't make it, Brother!" So we are going to commend the righteousness of God, by acknowledging—"O Lord, we are all failures."

It is the grace of God that is able to sustain and uphold any man or woman who desires to be kept by the Power of God. There are people who desire to boast of themselves and never have had a change of heart. And some even go so far as to say, "I am all right. I am good enough. I don't need that Holy Ghost." I don't care if you did not steal, drink, or commit adultery—it is in your *heart* anyhow! Everybody needs the power of God. Good works never did save anybody. It takes the "power of God unto salvation." I am not telling a moral man to get worse in order to get saved. No! I am telling him there is no condition so bad but that God does not have grace to save us from it.

You cannot make men righteous by legislation. "Ye must be born again." God says to the church "preach the word" and make a fertile spot in the terrible desert of sin, that men may see the water of life along the side of the road. No law can make you live right. God Almighty tried it Himself with the children of Israel, and the Word says, "What the law could not do, Christ did" (Romans 8:3). But do you know when a man becomes saved he will keep the spirit of the law? There is no law against attending to your own business, paying all your debts, and no law against praying—yet! Do right, and bless God, and pray without ceasing. No law is against doing that which is just and good (Galatians 5:22, 23).

Many homes have been torn asunder. Sorrow and mourning drapes the human heart because of sin. I dislike to hear some people talk because of their disgraceful utterances. But let God get into their hearts and then note the change. Everybody without Christ is guilty. Had God Almighty demanded justice, every living person would have been dead, and brought before the judgment bar to give an account of their misspent lives. The only thing that is going to save a man is the power of God. I am talking about genuine salvation, too! You can go any place and hear everything else but the Gospel of salvation. But men shall be saved. That is our whole service—to "save men." The church was ordained for that purpose.

God sums up the whole human family and declares that it is "full of wounds, bruises and putrefying sores." To tell a man he should not steal, or covet, or commit adultery is not enough. Tell him how to get saved so he will not do those things. The power of God can save anybody that will believe. The god of carnality has certainly got some folks fast. But O, I am so glad I am saved! Saved by the power of God! It is wonderful to be God's free man, delivered from the power of the pride of life, the lusts of the eye, and the lusts of the flesh. It does not make any difference whether a man is old or young, rich or poor, black or white or brown, just so he believes. If you have never been to school to learn a letter, you can "believe." I am satisfied that you do not have to have eyes to believe. You do not have to be able to speak to "believe." You may have both hands cut off, but still you can "believe." If you cannot hear, somebody will write, or make signs and you can "believe." You do not have to weigh so many hundred pounds or write letters, or understand the Bible to get saved. All God said was to "believe." Why, Jesus paid it all! The people that are saved today are people that "believed" the Gospel. And you do not believe God if you do not obey Him! I will prove it to you, too. "Show me your faith without your works, and I will show you my faith (without saying a word) by my works!" It is not merely *saying* "I believe"; it is *proving* your belief. If you actually believe then you know what Jesus was talking about when He said "He that believeth and is baptized shall be saved," and prove it by your actions. Jesus declared that "except a man be born of water and the Spirit he cannot enter into the Kingdom of God" (John 3:5–7). If you do not obey, then you do not believe.

God has fixed the matter so you need make no mistake about it, either. Too many jump over the fifth verse of the third chapter of John's Gospel. Moreover, Jesus stated emphatically that He "testified of that which He had seen; and spake that which He did know" (John 3:11), and this is what He spoke: "I know that if a man be not born of water and the Spirit, he cannot enter into the Kingdom of God." If you have never been baptized in the name of Jesus Christ, you have never been immersed properly. This is the only name under heaven given among men whereby they must be saved. If you repent deeply enough in your heart, and be baptized in the name of Jesus Christ, I will guarantee that you shall receive the baptism of the Holy Ghost as you "come up out of the water." If people do not believe God's Word they never get His best. Even if you do not understand, you must believe, before you can "see" the Glory of God.

### *Notes*

*Sermon source: The Life and Writings of Elder G.T. Haywood*, ed. Paul Dugas (Portland, OR: Apostolic Book Publishers, 1968).

1. Leonard Lovett, *Black Holiness-Pentecostalism: Implications for Ethics and Social Transformation* (Ph.D. diss., Emory University, 1978), 13.

### *Bibliographical Sources*

Foster, Fred J. *Their Story: 20th Century Pentecostals.* St. Louis, MO: World Aflame Press, 1983.

Golder, Morris E. *The Bishops of the Pentecostal Assemblies of the World.* Indianapolis: self-published, 1980.

———. *The Life and Works of Bishop Garfield Thomas Haywood.* Indianapolis: self-published, 1977.

Haywood, Garfield Thomas. *The Birth of the Spirit in the Days of the Apostles.* Indianapolis: Christ Temple Book Store, n.d.

Murphy, Larry G., J. Gordon Melton, and Gary L. Ward, eds. *Encyclopedia of African American Religions.* New York: Garland Publishing, 1993.

Sanders, Cheryl. *Saints in Exile: The Holiness-Pentecostal Experience in African American Culture and Religion.* New York: Oxford University Press, 1996.

Synan, Vinson. *The Holiness-Pentecostal Tradition: Charismatic Movements in the Twentieth Century.* Grand Rapids, MI: William B. Eerdmans, 1997.

# LUCIUS H. HOLSEY

*(1842–1920)*

Lucius H. Holsey was born near Columbus, Georgia, in 1842 to an enslaved woman and her master, James Holsey. His father died when Lucius was seven. Lucius then became the property of a white cousin, T.L. Wynn, who lived in Sparta, Hancock County, Georgia. He never again lived with his mother. The light-skinned redhead grew up among distant white relations, some of whom taught him to read. With his death approaching, Holsey's second master allowed Holsey to choose his next owner, the planter and educator Richard Malcolm Johnston.

While attending a Methodist plantation mission revival led by the black exhorter Henry McNeal Turner, Holsey converted to Methodism. When the Civil War suspended classes at the University of Georgia, where Richard Johnston worked, the Johnston family returned to Hancock County. There Johnston opened Rockby Academy and Holsey met his future wife, a slave named Harriett Turner.

During Reconstruction the white Methodist Episcopal Church, South, decided to separate its black members into a "colored conference" that could evolve into a distinct denomination. Organized in 1869, the Colored Methodist Episcopal (CME) Church attracted many of the black Methodists still attending white churches in the South. Holsey participated in the organizational meeting and received an appointment to Trinity CME Church in Augusta. When one of the black bishops died in 1873, Bishop George Foster Pierce joined other white Methodists and the remaining black bishops in the laying on of hands that signified the elevation of Holsey to the bishopric at the young age of thirty-one. He was the youngest man ever appointed to the bishopric at that time.

As a leader of the fledging denomination, Holsey buttressed it and increased its membership among black Methodists in Georgia. He founded a number of congregations, including Butler Street CME Church in Atlanta. He revised religious tracts, including a *Manual of Discipline*, and a hymnal for use in the CME Church entitled *Songs of Love and Mercy*, which contained 198 hymns. He promoted collaboration between black and white southern Methodists, which resulted in a number of successes, such as Paine College (also known as Paine Institute) in Augusta. He traveled extensively for this work and raised a large sum of money for the new school. He was also crucial in founding Lane College in Jackson, Tennessee. Holsey continued to influence the black community as a racial diplomat and bishop of the CME Church until his death in 1920.

• • •

*Holsey was widely praised for this sermon, in which he uses the subject of music (song) to discuss theological beliefs and the journey of every Christian believer. The version printed here has been shortened for inclusion in this anthology.*

## THE SONG OF BELIEVERS
## (CA. 1896)

*I will sing of mercy and judgment: unto thee, O Lord, will I sing.*
—Psalm 101:1

Whoever reads the history of man, weighs his sorrows and measures his joy, will read the history of songs and anthems of his days. Indeed, his pilgrimage through life's thorny mazes is a pilgrimage of song inspired by the lights and shadows that ever shine and shade his pathway. Age or nation, clime or condition, cannot take from him this plaintive or joyous melody that permeates his individuality, and fills his moments with this God-given and heavenly flame. There is in man a golden harp of a thousand sympathetic chords whose deep and resonant tones evolve from the golden strings which vibrate to the music of the spheres and the melodies of the heart. Whether plodding the lower walks of tears and sorrow, or on the joyful wing of prosperity, or hearing the dull thud of the funeral dirge, the carol of the sweetest note will stir the soul, revolutionize the heart and lift the drooping spirit to the altitude of God and the sunny plains of heaven.

Song is an antidote of the burdened heart, the laboring soul and the broken spirit. But the song of redemption is preeminently "the song." It is the song of songs. It is the sweetest note on angels lips, and the sweetest anthem of the skies. Indeed, the song of redemption is the thrilling cry that has stirred the ages, ramified the centuries, filled the decades, inspired the prophets, fired the tongues of bards, poets and seers and cheered the millions with the music of God and of his Christ. Touched by the omnific finger of God's love, and set to the dulcet strains of joy, the song of redemption shall go ringing through the nations, down the declivities of time, thread the centers of civilizations, cross the howling sea of death, and ring on up to God and heaven through countless ages and evolving cycles of endless duration.

*But what is song?*

Song is the music of the soul, the harmonious vibrations of the deep chords of the heart and the melodies of the spirit life. It involves the elevation of the affections and the utterances of the lips by which some theme, doctrine, or topic is proclaimed aloud and exultingly in the presence of others. In a broader sense, it is the vibration of the musical harmonies, of the empire of God, agitated and active. It is the effort of a kindred spark to return to its native sun, and be rehabilitated in its native clime. It is the divinity in man rising to God its source and parent head from whom it came to earth. It is the better and higher nature of man springing forward and leaping heavenward. It is the soul flying through the deep blue ether upon its fiery pinions in search after God its "maker who giveth songs in the night." Song implies harmony in sentiment and strain. Strain is the vehicle—the chariot wheels of song, but sentiment and doctrine are the life and spirit.

But song is more. It is a spiritual animation, a flame that stimulates, revives and quickens the moral, mental and spiritual manhood. It is true, song, like speech, may be greatly improved by the processes of culture and practice, and should be cultivated by the whole human race; for no system of training can be complete without it. Yet there is in man an innate attribute of song, an attribute which, when touched by the hand of sorrow or joy makes the chambers of the soul resonant with the symphonies of angels and the euphonies of heaven. It is an essential quality of his spiritual and religious instinct—a part of his organic spiritual constituency. It is organic and God-given. It is a part of his individual and indestructible selfhood.

Music is harmonies expressed, song is the vehement act of expression. This attribute of song in man has its counterpart in creation. Creation is a system of musical harmonies combining in a common unity, and that common unity is the unit of all units—God. He is the grand total of all the totalities in the universe. All the threads and lines of days and years, of events, acts, facts, natures, beings, agencies, entities, and things, center in his will and power, glory and majesty. The millenniums, with their creative acts and facts, with their mighty ponderable and imponderable realities, are yoked and linked together by the indissoluble bands and bonds of his high and majestic authority. At his command, angels fly, devils fall, comets flash, suns burn, stars twinkle, and systems live. Around him, all things dance and fly in the inimitable beauties of magnificent harmony, or dash their splintered shafts and shattered spears at his feet, and tremble at his voice.

Man is most in harmony with the universe and the music of the spheres when the deep and dulcet tones of the octachords of the soul are attuned and set to the music of God "and of his Christ" by the Holy Spirit.

Thus song is the golden sunlight that gilds the horizon of the ages with the gladness of the day of Christ, making every flower of hope bloom, the hills smile, and every lily, rose and violet blush in maiden sweetness amid the universal gush of joys.

*But song is old.* It is older than our physical earth, and was used in heaven before used on earth. Long anterior to the heavens and the earth that rose out of chaos, it was pressed into the service of the eldest children of eternity who tuned their golden lutes in the empyrean of the heavens and sang glorious anthems to the all powerful and all glorious God. Long before a ray of light had pierced the primeval darkness that covered earth and sky, when, as yet, the morning star had not been hung as a pendant lamp in the orient, nor the silvery goddess of the evening had snuffed her candle on the occident's setting sun, eternal beings were singing the praises of God.

Yea, there was song when as yet our earth and heavens were held, by the iron grip and sable bands of king Darkness who had reigned for myriads of millenniums, but was finally exiled by the Almighty's irrevocable fiat of his power.

*Ye shades dispel, the Eternal said,*
*At once the involving darkness fled,*
*And nature sprung to light.*[1]

Darkness fled "and nature sprung to light," while mighty and majestic systems rushed on the immortal paths of their burning orbits as if blazing around the throne of God. Where once all was dark and void, there was glory and beauty and the displays of almighty power and everlasting joy. Then it was that "The morning stars sang together and all the sons of God shouted for joy."

*But song is Universal and is inherent in nature.*

Creation is God's great harp of countless living strings that join the universal harmonies in one grand chorus. Creation sings of God, the Creator—the ages sing of his eternity, the Heavens sing of his glory, the earth of his power, and hell of his justice. From the burning lips of the lost to the enchanting melodies of blazing seraphs, song rises to God without stint or limit from every part of creation. All nature sings, especially when its golden chords are struck and vibrated by the plenipotent finger of God. There is music around us, above us, and beneath us. The mighty orchestra with rocking chimes sends its thrills through the ages, stirs and stimulates the nations with hope, joy and faith.

But man must die. The doleful song of death lulls the nations to long and sound repose, only to be broken by the funeral dirge of time, when the stentorian lays of the archangel in measured verse and solemn strains shall revivify all that have fallen in sleep. Go, take your stand upon some high rocky promontory by the raging sea, and listen to the great bass drum of God—the winds blowing, the sea roaring and spitting froth of its anger into the murky clouds above, and agitating its own deep and pebbly bed as if stirred by the fiery blasts of hell. The plenipotent finger of the omnipotent God strikes the combustible elements of the air, and his red lightnings flash along on their burning cables, sending their soprano anthems to hiss and howl and join the bass strains from the sea below.

High above all the sounds just mentioned are the screaking, hissing and crashing of the angry storms, with, as it were, its mottled, scarred and dusky-faced triumphant King rolling upon wheels of torrid amber mixed with fire and blood, and in his wake lay the shattered greatness of nature's might and virgin strength. His thundering chariot rolls in the clouds, while from his burning brazen car incandescent forked tongues leap out. A thousand golden cymbals are being simultaneously struck by the hands of a thousand archangels in heaven's aerial sea. The bosom of the clouds are recharged with electricity—the subtle vitality of nature—and their sable bands yield and in sunder break, baptizing herb, sea and land with the blessing of heaven. When the harsher notes of the storm have flown away upon the wings of the cloud, then nature, in sweeter and softer music of praise and joyful lays, is still heard striking the silver strings of her golden lute, emitting harmonious melodies which dance through the multiplex octaves of the spheres.

Blow, ye heavenly zephyrs, blow, agitate, oscillate and vibrate your grand old octachords until oceanic isles and rock-ribbed hills and smiling plains join in the mighty chorus and the gush of thrilling joys.

*But song is sentiment and doctrine, and has its heroes.* The song of creation has God for its hero, and the song of redemption has Christ for its hero, the charming embodiment of all melodies. In creation the harmonies of the spheres sing of God, the Hero of its preservation and the Master of its magnificent parts, forces, properties and powers. Every part is filled with God and instinct with music. "The whole earth is crammed with heaven, and every common bush afire with God."[2] "The heavens declare his glory, and the firmament his power." "All thy works shall praise thee, O Lord," says the sweet singer of Israel. Again, he says, "Praise the Lord from the earth, ye dragons, and all deeps: Fire, and hail; snow, and vapors; stormy winds fulfilling his word: Mountains, and all his hills; fruitful trees, and all cedars; beasts, and all cattle; creeping things, and flying fowl; Kings of the earth, and all people; princes, and all judges of the earth. Both young men, and maidens; old men and children; Let them praise the name of the Lord."[3] Here God is the Hero of creation's song, the vital Center in which all of creation's melodies, anthems and choruses meet in eternal celebration and forever pour their orchestral thunders at his feet.

Christianity is the ethical system, the high moral code of the universe and has Christ for its Head, its Song and its Hero. He is the ransoming and heroic "prince of peace" of which the ages have sung. The song is old and long, but sweet, soft, inspiring and thrilling. "Of him who did salvation bring," the first archangels sang. Living coals of heavenly fire dropped from the golden censers of angels, and started David's harp afresh with deeper notes and softer tunes descriptive of [the] Messiah and his triumphs. Indeed, the Old Testament Scriptures were largely written in verse, the whole of which was a part of the mighty anthem of redemption. The Christ of the prophets is the Christ of the ages. He is the life and subject of all their song and the joy of our salvation. He cheered the hearts, fired the tongues of bards and poets, and dwelt in sweetest strains upon the lips of priest and prophet, prince and king, while the rough seers and shepherds in the wild and weird desert took up the thrilling cry, and sent back to the walled city, its gleeful notes up to heaven and its joys on to God.

While the ages were pouring their verses on the templed hills of God[,] angels heard and awaited "the day star from on high." It is night. Shepherds are in the plains watching their flocks. An angelic legate from heaven's high arch appears. A halo of splendor encircles his dazzling face and his voice, wrapt in the soft accents of peace and love, was thrown out upon the wing of a heavenly carol. His theme is the culmination of the long and hoary decades of waiting. "And the angel said unto them, Fear not, for behold I bring you good tidings of great joy, which shall be to all people. . . . And suddenly there was with the angel a multitude of the heavenly hosts, praising God, and saying, 'Glory to God in the highest, and on earth peace, and good will toward men.'"[4] How glorious is this song. What impulses does it awaken in the heart of man! "Glory to God in the highest, and on earth peace, and good will toward men."

But the text says, "I will sing of mercy and judgment; unto thee, O Lord, will I sing."

*But what is mercy?* Mercy is a compound of goodness, patience and kindness to a lost and sinning race, to whom it is extended as a method of escape. God is good to all, to men, angels and inferior creatures. But to man his goodness is extended until it becomes more than mere goodness—it is *mercy*. It is melting pity borne away from God on the wings of his love and goodness to all the sinning race of Adam. It is an invention of Deity to reach and rescue that which could not be reached and saved by other methods. It presents to the world of man the only gateway of redemption from punishment and eternal "banishment from the presence of the Lord and the Glory of his power."

Mercy has no existence except in its exercise, and therefore is not an attribute or perfection of Deity. Now, an attribute is an essential quality or part of the eternal mind of God without which God would not be God. Eternity, self-existence, all-power, all-knowledge, immortality, fore-knowledge, infinite wisdom, et cetera, are attributes of God, because they are essential parts and elements of his character. Without these, or any one of them, he could not be what he is—the only and eternal Jehovah. We can conceive of God without the existence of mercy, but we cannot conceive him to be the Eternal Mind without those natural perfections that we call attributes. Could his power be taken away, he would cease to be God. Take away his wisdom, or goodness, or his eternity, and he ceases to be what he is, what he always was, and what he always will be—the eternal Jehovah. But take away his mercy and he is still "the same yesterday and to-day and forever." . . .

The attributes of God hold their respective functions and operate their several and wonderful offices, but none of them, and all of them could not, and do not save one guilty sinner. No, the complex government of God needed a provision of softer terms to reach and save the sinning and the lost. It needed the invention of Deity, and an assemblage and combination of attributes so adjusted and balanced as to harmonize with the nature, plan and the whole government of God. Man is to be saved. How shall it be done? All the attributes of God were silent, and profound muteness sat on every tongue. All the wheels of divine government stood still amid the dying echoes of receding centuries, as if the clattering machinery of the universe had unhinged its spindles and ungeared its pulleys and stopped every rolling belt and whizzing wheel, and had broken every bar and bolt that united them together in one harmonious whole.

But Mercy, like an archangel, wrapped in the seven colors of the rainbow, stood before God with pacification written on her brow. A tablet of solid carbuncle fringed with purest gold covered her heart, and in bold letters set with diamonds and engraved with the signet of love, was written "Melting Pity." Around her golden-crowned head flashed a halo of heavenly light, as if the graces of a thousand queens had gathered about her to beautify her glorious self. Her feet were covered with amber sandals as if electrified by the affinity of powers that continued to move while she stood. Her wings of fire were outspread, ready to fly at God's command. The thunders of wrath are hushed. Justice half sheathes her bloody sword. Angels and all the ranks and files of the heavenly world crowd about her to wonder and admire. There stood Mercy. Who is she? She is the queen of heaven, the gift of God to man, the grandest contrivance and the crowning conception of Deity. Slowly, but surely, through all the sinful ages of man she has gathered up the tears, the woes and sighs of men, and carries them to heaven, and to God.

The whole earth with its crowded intelligences once cried and travailed in pain to be delivered and saved. Through all the arteries of the human heart and soul, death, eternal death, pulsated in every flowing current, played on every string, gnawed asunder every silver cable and golden thread that ramified and cemented the entities and eternity of man with God. The night of the world was long, dreary and dark. A heavy leaden cloud in which the slow, dull mutterings of wrath were heard threw its dark shade of death and ashy penumbra athwart the space in which revolved the mental and moral hemisphered globe. Now and then, a red current of flame would leap from the darker center and flash across the leaden zones only to exhibit the stronger and sabler bands that held in awful solitude the pent-up wrath of the angry storm. Should God touch one wire, or send a flash of fire through the whole, like a cloudburst, his wrath would deluge the moral sphere and sink the sinning race to ruin.

But Mercy stands before the throne of God and waves the white flag of peace and a truce intervenes. Then stretching her golden pinions she views the leaden cloud of wrath, and death, as with steeds of flame and chariots of fire, she sweeps on and down from the throne of the great king. But in mid-air she seems to pause for a moment to survey the continents and islands, to count the slain millions and the dying thousands, to measure the depths of sorrows, and the exceeding sinfulness of sin. Her chariot wheels roll along the defiles of blood and death, where the prisoner dragged his chain, where mothers wept for their slain sons and daughters, and starving children cried for bread because their fathers and brothers fell in battle. She stands by dying man and his ruined race. Over his bleeding corpse she spreads her mantle of grace, recovers him from his sins, and establishes him in the Eternal, reconciled, sanctified and saved.

## *Notes*

*Sermon source:* Lucius H. Holsey, *Autobiography, Sermons, Addresses and Essays of Bishop L.H. Holsey* (Atlanta: Franklin Printing and Publishing Company, 1898).

1. This quote concerns Psalm 148:5 and is taken from George Horne's *A Commentary on the Book of Psalms . . .*, U.S. ed. (n.p.: 1792).
2. This quote is from Book VII in Elizabeth Barrett Browning, *Aurora Leigh* (London: J. Miller Publishing, 1864).
3. Psalm 148:7–13a (King James Version).
4. Luke 2:10, 13–14 (KJV).

## *Bibliographical Sources*

Cade, John B. *Holsey, The Incomparable*. New York: Pageant, 1963.

Duncan, Sarah J. *Progressive Missions in the South and Addresses with Illustrations and Sketches of Missionary Workers and Ministers and Bishops' Wives*. Atlanta: The Franklin Printing and Publishing Company, 1906.

Holsey, Lucius Henry. *The Autobiography of Bishop L. H. Holsey*, reprinted with an introduction by George E. Clary Jr. Keysville, GA: Brier Creek Press, 1988.

Murphy, Larry G., J. Gordon Melton, and Gary L. Ward. *Encyclopedia of African American Religions*. New York: Garland Publishing, 1993.

Phillips, Charles Henry. *The History of the Colored Methodist Episcopal Church*

*in America: Comprising Its Organization, Subsequent Development and Present Status*, 3rd ed. Jackson, TN: Publishing House C.M.E. Church, 1925.
Woodson, Carter Godwin. *The History of the Negro Church*. Washington, DC: The Associated Publishers, 1921.

# JOHN JASPER

*(1812–1901)*

John Jasper was born in slavery in Virginia's Fluvanna County in 1812, the last of twenty-four children. According to Jasper biographer Richard E. Day, John's mother's name was Tina and his father, who also was a preacher and who died before John was born, was named Philip. After several placements as a child servant, John was put to work in a tobacco factory in Richmond. His first marriage, to Elvy Weaden, was crushed by his master's refusal to allow him to visit his wife. After that, he lived in a mode of rebellion for five years before he was saved and called to preach. He ultimately remarried and had a daughter, Mary Elizabeth.

He began preaching immediately after his baptism, and his first sermons were extremely well received. He served as supply pastor for several churches. In 1867, soon after the Civil War, at almost age fifty-five, he organized the Sixth Mount Zion Baptist Church in Richmond, with a congregation of nine members. He served there for thirty-three years, and the membership grew to many hundreds, requiring major reconstruction of the church building.

Jasper studied constantly and was aided by William Eldridge Hatcher, a white pastor of the nearby Grace Street Baptist Church. Hatcher was a great admirer of Jasper, whom he saw as a brilliant, eloquent preacher. Jasper drew large numbers of whites as well as blacks to his services.

Jasper, history has shown, was erroneously typecast by many whites and some blacks for the folk dialect he used in his sermon "De Sun Do Move," printed in this volume. Much as Rev. Jonathan Edwards was misrepresented by a single sermon, "Sinners in the Hands of an Angry God," so was Jasper by his Sun sermon. Yet the sermon was so popular that Jasper was asked to deliver it before the Virginia legislature. Jasper died in 1901 and has since become one of the most written about folk preachers in history.

• • •

*Jasper's gift of vivid picture-painting and storytelling was not an end in itself, nor a mere means of preaching as entertainment. Even Jasper's flat-earth theory from "De Sun Do Move" was seriously embraced, both as a result of biblical literalism and the limited understanding of the earth's surface by many of his day. This issue first arose from Jasper's effort to settle an argument between two men at his church. He agreed with and quoted the Zetetic School of thought, a group insisting on a planet whose gravity demanded a flat earth; they believed that otherwise objects in the Southern Hemisphere would fall off into space. At the very least, this showed Jasper to be a reader of scientific works, with a laudable breadth and depth of interests. The version of the "De Sun Do Move" printed below maintains some of the dialect that was spoken by John Jasper and blacks and whites in the latter part of the nineteenth century and varied by region. However, much of the so-called folk dialect (dialect used by whites and blacks who were not formally educated) applied to this sermon by William Hatcher and others has been removed. Hatcher says in his book about Jasper that the preacher could turn the dialect off and on.[1] Accordingly, this sermon has been transcribed most often in standard English, but with traces of the dialect that Jasper was likely to slip into when speaking before a group with which he was familiar and comfortable, such as his congregation.*

## De Sun Do Move (ca. 1878)

'Low me to say, that when I was a young man and a slave, I knowed nothin' worth talkin' about consernin' books. They was sealed mysteries to me, but I tell you I longed to break the seal. I thirsted for the bread of learnin'. When I saw books, I ached to get into them, for I knew that they had the stuff for me, and I wanted to taste the contents, but most of the time they was barred against me.

By the mercy of the Lord a thing happened. I got a room-feller, he was a slave too, and he had learned to read. In the dead of the night, he give me lessons outta the New York spellin' book. It was hard pullin', I tell yah; harder on him, for he knew just a little, and it made him sweat to try to beat somethin' into my hard head. It was worse with me. Up the hill ever' night, but when I got the lesson in to my noodle, I fairly shouted; but I knew I was no scholar.

The consequence was, I crept along mighty tejus gettin' a crumb here and there, until I could read the Bible by skippin' the hard words tolerably well. That was the start of my education—that is, what little I got. I make mention of that young man. The years have fled away since then, but I ain't forgot my teacher and I never shall. I thank the Lord for him, and I carry his memory in my heart.

About seven months after my gettin' to readin', the first and main thing that I begged the Lord to give me, I got it: the power to understand his Word. I ain't braggin' and I hates self-praise, but I am bound to speak a thankful word. I believes that my prayer to understand the Scripture was heard. Since that time, I ain't cared about nothin' except to study and preach the Word of God.

Not, my brethren that I am a fool to think I know it all. No! Far from it! I don't hardly understand myself, nor half of the things around me, and there is millions of things in the Bible too deep for Jasper, and some of them too deep for everybody. I don't carry the keys to the Lord's closet, and He ain't tell me to peek in, and if I did, I'm so stupid, I wouldn't know what when I sees it. No, friends, I know my place at the feet of my masta' and there I stay.

But I can read the Bible and get the things what lay on the top of the soil. . . . Outside the Bible, I know nothin' extry about the sun. I sees its courses as he rides up there so grand and mighty; but there is heaps about that flamin' orbit that is too much for me. I know that the sun shines powerfully and powes down its light in floods, and yet that is nothin' compared with the light that flashes in my mind from the pages of God's book.

But you know all of that. I know that the sun burns—oh, how it did burn in those July days. I tell you he cooked the skin on my back many a day when I was hoein' in the cornfield. But you know all of that, and yet that is nothin' to the divine fire that burns in the souls of God's children. Can't you feel it, brethren?

But, 'bout the course of the sun, I got that all pat and safe. I have ranged [through] the whole blessed book and score the last thing the Bible has to say about its movements. . . . And if I don't tell the truth, march up on these steps and tell me I am a liar, and I will beg pardon. But God don't lie, and He ain't put no lie in His Book. I gives you what the Bible says and I am bound to tell the truth.

I got to takes you on a excursion to a great battl'field. Most folks like to see fights, and some is mighty quick to run down the back alley when there is a battl' goin' on for the right.

This battle is a curious battle. It took place soon after Isrel got in the Promise Land. The people of Gibyun made friends with God's people when they first entered Canaan, and they was mighty smart to do it. But just the same, it got them into an awful fuss. The cities round 'bout there flared up at that. And they all joined their forces and said they was goin' to mop the Gibyun people off of the ground, and they bunched all dere armies together and went up to do it. When they come up so bold and brave the Giby'nites was scared outta their senses, and they sent word to Joshua that they was in trouble and he must run up dere and git them out.

Joshua had the heart of a lion and he was up there direckly. They had an awful fight, sharp and bitter, but you might know that General Joshua was not up there to get whipped. He prayed and he fought, and the hours got away too fast for him, and so he asked the Lord to issue a special order that the sun hold up awhile and that the moon furnish plenty of moonshine down on the lower part of the fightin' grounds.

As a matter of fact, Joshua was so drunk with the battle, so thirsty for the blood of the enemies of the Lord, and so wild with the vict'ry that he told the sun to stand still til he could finish the job. What did the sun do? Did he glare down in fiery wrath and say: "What you talkin' about my stoppin' for, Joshua? I ain't never started yet. Been here all the time, and it would smash up ever'thing if I was to start"?

No, he ain't say that. But what the Bible say? That is what I ask to know. It says that it was at the voice of Joshua that it stopped. I don't say it stopped. Ain't for Jasper to say that. But the Bible, the book of God, say so.

But I say this, nothin' can stop until it has first started. So, I knows what I'm talkin' about. The sun was travelin' long dere through the sky when the order come. He hitched his red ponies and made quite a call on the land of Gibyun. He perched up dere in the skies just as friendly as a neighbor who comes to borrer somethin', and he stood up dere and he look like he enjoyed the way Joshua waxed them wicked armies. And the moon, she waited down in the low grounds there, and poured out her light, and looked just as calm and happy as if she was waitin' for her escort. They never budged, neither of them long as the Lord's army needed a light to carry on the battle.

I don't read when it was that Joshua hitched up and drove on, but I spose it was when the Lord told him to go. Anybody knows that the sun didn't stay there all the time. It stopped for business, and went on when it got through. This is about all that I has to do with this particlar case. I done showed you that this part of the Lord's Word teaches you that the sun stopped; which shows that he was movin' before that, and that he went on afterward. I told yah that I would prove this, and I have done it! I defy anybody to say that my point ain't made!

I tol' you in the first part of this discourse that the Lord God is a man of war. I 'spec by now you begin to see it is so. Why don't you admit it? When the Lord came to see Joshua in the day of his fears and warfare, and actually made the sun stop stone still in the heavens, so the fight could rage on till all the foes was slain, you obliged to understand that the God of peace is also the man of war. He can use both peace and war to help the righteous, and to scatter the host of the ailyuns.

A man talked to me las' week about the laws of nature, and he said they can't poss'bly be upset. And I had to laugh right in his face. As if the laws of anything was greater than my God, who is the lawgiver for ever'thing. My Lord is great; He rules in the heavens, and the earth, and down under the groun'. He is great, and greatly to be praised. Let all the people bow down and worship befo' Him!

But let us get along, for there is quite a lot mo' comin' on. Let us take next the case of Hezekiah. He was one of the kings of Judah. A mighty sorry lot, I mus' say, those kings were for the mos' part. I inclines to think Hezekiah was about the highes' in the general average, but he was no mighty man hisself.

Well, Hezekiah, he got sick. I must say that a king when he gets his crown and finery off, and when he is posterated with mortal sickness, he gets about as common lookin', and grunts and rolls, and is about as scary as the rest of us poe mortals! We know that Hezekiah was in a low state of min'; full of fears, and in ter'ble trouble. The fact is, the Lord stripped him of all his glory and landed him in the dust. He tol' him that his hour had come, and that he had bettah square up his affairs, for death was at the [door]. It was then that the king fell low befo' God; he turned his face to the wall; he cried, he moaned, he begged the Lord not to take him outta' the worl' yet. Oh, how good is our God! The cry of the king moved His heart, and He tell him he is going to give him another stay.

Ain't only the kings that the Lord hears. The cry of the pris'ner, the wail of the bondsman, the tears of the dyin' robber, the prayers of the backslider, the sobs of the woman that was a sinner, are mighty apt to touch the heart of the Lord. It look like its hard for the sinner to git so far off or so far down in the pit that his cry can't reach the ear of the merciful Savior.

But the Lord do even better then this for Hezekiah. He tell him He gone to give him a sign by which he know that what He said was comin' to pass. I ain't acquainted with them sundials that the Lord tol' Hezekiah 'bout, but anybody that has got a grain of sense knows that they was the clocks of them ol' times and they marked the travels of the sun by them dials. When, therefo', God tol' the king that He would make the shadow go backward, it mus' have been just' like puttin' the hands of the clock back; but, mark you, Isaiah expressly say that the sun return ten degrees. There you are! Ain't that the movement of the sun? Bless my soul! Hezekiah's case beats Joshua. Joshua stop the sun, but here the Lord make the sun walk back ten degrees; and yet they say that the sun stand stone still and never move a peg!

It look to me like he move around mighty brisk, and is ready to go anyway that the Lord orders him to go. I wonder if any of them philosophers is round here this afternoon? I'd like to take a square look at one of them, and ask him to explain this matter. He can't do it, my brethren. The philosophers knows a heap about books, maps, figures and long distances, but I defy him to take up Hezekiah's case and explain it off. He can't do it. The Word of the Lord is my defense and bulwark, and I fears not what men can say or do; my God gives me the vict'ry.

Allow me, my friends, to put myself square about this movement of the sun. It ain't no business of mine whether the sun move or stand still, or whether it stop or go back, or rise or set. All that is out of my hands entirely, and I got nothin' to say. I got no theory on the subject. All I ask is that we will take what the Lord say about it and let His will be done 'bout everything. What that will is, I can't know except He whisper into my soul or write it in a book. Here's the Book. This is enough for me, and with it to pilot me, I can't git far astray.

But I ain't done with you yet. As the song say, "There's more to follow." I invite you to hear the first verse in the seventh chapter of the book of Revelation. What do John, under the power of the Spirit, say? He say he saw four angels standing on the four corners of the earth, holdin' the four winds of the earth, and so forth. Allow me to ask if the earth is round, where does it keep its corners? A flat, square thing has corners; but tell me where is the corner of an apple, of a cannon ball, of a silver dollar? If there is anyone of them philosophers about here, what's been taking so many cracks at my old head, he is cordially invited to step forward and square up this vexin' business. I here tell you that you can't square a circle; but it looks like these great scholars done learned how to circle the square. If they can do it, let them step to the front and do the trick.

But, my brethren, in my po' judgment, they can't do it; ain't in them to do it. They is on the wrong side of the Bible; that's on the outside, and that's where the trouble comes in with them. They done got out of the breast works of the truth, and as long as they stay there, the light of the Lord will not shine on their path. I ain't carin' so much 'bout the sun, though its mighty convenient to have it; but my trust is in the Word of the Lord. Long as my feet is flat on the solid rock, no man can move me. I'm gettin' my orders from the God of my salvation.

The other day a man with a high collar and side whiskers come to my house. He was one of them nice North'rn gentlemen what think a heap of us "colored people" in the South. They is lovely folks and I honors them very much. But he seem from the start kinda strict and cross with me, and after while, he broke out furi'us and he said: "Allow me, Mister Jasper, to give you some plain advice. This nonsense 'bout the sun movin' is disgracin' your race all over the country, and as a friend of your people, I come to say it got to stop!"

Ha! Ha! Ha! Mastah Sam Hardgrove never smash me that way. That North'rn gentleman was equal to one of them ol' overseers way back yonder. I tell him that if he'll show me I'm wrong, I will give it all up.

My! My! Ha! Ha! He sailed in on me in such a storm about science, new discoveries, and the Lord only knows what all. Then he tell me my race is against me and po' ole Jasper must shut up his fool mouf.

When he got through—and it look like he nevah would—I tell the philosopher, I ain't tryin' to hurt my people, but is workin' day and night to lift them up. But Jasper's foot is on the rock of eternal truth. There he stand and there he is goin' to stand 'til Gabriel sounds the judgment note.

So I say to the gentleman what scol'd me so, that I hear him make his remarks, but I ain't hear where he get his Scripture from; and that between him and the Word of the Lord, I take my stand by the Word of God ever' time.

Jasper ain't mad; he ain't fightin' nobody; he ain't been appointed janitor to run the sun! He nothing but the servant of God and a lover of the Everlastin' Word. What I care 'bout the sun? The day [will] come when the sun will be called from his race track, and his light squinched out forever! The moon shall turn to blood, and this earth be consumed with fire! Let them go; that won't scare me nor trouble God's elect'd people! But the Word of the Lord shall endure forever, and on that Solid Rock we stand, and shall not be moved!

Is I got you satisfied yet? Is I proven my point? Oh, ye whose hearts is full of unbelief! Is you still holdin' out? I reckon the reason you say the sun don't move is 'cause you are so hard to move yourself. You is a real trial to me; but, nevah mind. I ain't giv'n you up yet, and nevah will. Truth is mighty; it can break the heart of stone, and I must fire another arrow of truth out of the quiver of the Lord. If you has a copy of God's Word about your person, please turn to that minor prophet Malachi who wrote the las' book in the Ol' Bible, and look at the first chaptah, verse eleven. What do it say? I bettah read it, for I got a notion you critics don't carry any Bible in those pockets. Here is what it says: "For from the risin' of the sun even until the goin' down of the same my name shall be great among the Gentiles."

"My name shall be great among the Gentiles," says the Lord of hosts. How do that suit yah? It look like that ought to fix it. This time it is the Lord of hosts Hisse'f that is doin' the talkin', and He is talkin' on a wonderful and glorious subject. He is tellin' of the spreadin' of His Gospel, of the coming of His last vict'ry over the Gentiles, and the world-wide glories that at the last He is to get.

Oh, my brethren, what a time that will be! My soul takes wings as I anticipate with joy that millen'um day! The glories of that day shines befo' my eyes and blinds me; and I forgets the sun and moon and stars. I just remember that long about those last days the sun and moon will go out of business; for they won't be needed no mo'. Then will King Jesus come back to see His people, and He will be the sufficient light of the world. Joshua's battle will be over. Hezekiah won't need no sun dial; and the sun and moon will fade out befo' the glorious splendor of the New Jerusalem.

But what is the matter with Jasper? I almost forget my business, and almost got to shoutin' over the far away glories of the second comin' of my Lord. I beg pardon, and will try to get back to my subject. I have to do as the sun in Hezekiah's case—fall back a few degrees. In that part of the Word that I give you, from Malachi—that the Lord Hisse'f spoke—He declare that His glory is goin' to spread. Spread? Where? "From the rising of the sun." What? Don't say that does it? That's exactly what it do say. Ain't that clear enough for you? The Lord pity these doubtin' Thomases. Here is enough to settle it all, and cure the worst cases. Walk up here, wise folks, and get your medicine. Where is them high collar'd philosophers now? What they sulkin' roun' in the bush for? Why don't you get out in the broad aftahnoon light and fight for your colors? Ah! I understand it; you got no answer. The Bible is against you, and in yoe conscience you is convicted.

But I hears you back there! What you whisperin' 'bout? I know you say you sent me some papers and I never answered them. Ha! Ha! Ha! I got 'em. The difficulty about them papers you sent me is that they don't answer me. They never mention the Bible one time. You think so much of yourse'f and so little of the Lord God, and thinks what you say is so smart, that you can't even speak of the Word of the Lord. If you ain't got yah feet on the Word of God, the devil will get you sure, just like he's got the philosophers. When you ask me to stop believin' in the Lord's Word and to put my faith in your words, I ain't 'bout to do it. I take my stand by the Bible and rest my case on what it says. I take what the Lord says 'bout my sins, 'bout my Savior, 'bout life, 'bout death, 'bout the world to come; and I take what the Lord says 'bout the sun and moon, and I cares little what the haters of my God choose to say. Think that I will forsake the Bible? It is my only Book, my hope, the arsenal of my soul's supplies, and I wants nothin' else.

But I got another word for you yet. I done worked over them papers that you sent me widout date, and widout your name. You deals in figgers and thinks you bigger than the archangels. Lemme see what you done said. You set yoese'f up to tell me how far it is from here to the sun. You think you got it down to a nice point. You say it is 3,339,002 miles from the earth to the sun. That's what you say. Another one say that the distance is 12,000,000; 'nuther got it to 27,000,000. I hear that the great Isaac Newton worked it up to 28,000,000, and later on the philosophers give another rippin' raise it to 50,000,000. The last one gets it bigger then all the others—up to 90,000,000. Don't any of 'em agree exactly! And so they runs a guess[ing] game, and the last guess is always the bigges'.

Now, when these guessers kin have a convention in Richmond and all agree upon the same thing, I'd be glad to hear from you agin, and I does hope that by that time you won't be 'shamed of your name.

Heaps of railroads has been built since I saw the fus' one when I was fifteen years ol'. But I ain't hear tell of a railroad built yet to the sun. I don't see, if they can measure the distance to the sun, why they might not get up a railroad or a telegraph and enable us to find something else 'bout it than merely how far off the sun is.

They tell me that a cannon ball could make the trip to the sun in twelve years. Why don't they send it? It might be rigged up with quarters for a few philosophers on the inside, and fixed up for a comfortable ride. They would need twelve years rations and a heap of changes of raiments—mighty thick ones when they start and mighty thin ones when they get there.

Oh! my brethren, these things make you laugh, and I don't blame you for laughin', 'cept it's always sad to laugh at the follies of fools. If we could laugh 'em out in count'in, we might well laugh day and night. What cuts into my soul is, that all these men is hittin' at the Bible. That is what stirs my soul and fills me with right'ous wrath. Little cares I what they say 'bout the sun, provided they let the Word of the Lord alone. But nevah mind, "Let the heathen rage and the people imagine a vain thing."[2] Our King shall break 'em in pieces and dash 'em down. Blessed be the name of our God, the Word of the Lord endureth forever! Stars may fall; moons may turn to blood; and the sun set to rise no more! But Thy kingdom, O Lord, is from everlastin' to everlastin'.

But I has a word this afternoon for my own brethren. They is the people for whose souls I got to watch—for them I got to stand and report at the last. They is my sheep and I is the shepherd, and my soul is knit to them forever. Ain't for me to be troublin' you wid these questions 'bout them heavenly bodies. Our eyes goes far beyon' the smaller stars; our home is clean out of sight of them twinklin' orbs. The chariot that will come to take us to our Father's mansion will sweep out them flickerin' lights and never halt til it brings us in clear view of the throne of the Lamb.

Don't you hitch yah hopes to no sun or stars! Your home is got Jesus for its light, and yah hopes mus' travel up that way. I preach this sermon just for to settle the minds of a few of my bruthr'n, and repeats it 'cause kind friends wish to hear it. I hopes it will do honor to the Lord's Word. But nothin' short of the pearly gates can satisfy me, and I charge you, my people, fix yah feet on the solid Rock, your heart on Calv'ry! These strifes and griefs soon be over; we shall see the King in His glory and be at ease in Zion. Go on! Go on! Ye ransom' of the Lord! Shout His praises as yah go, an' I'll meet yah in the city of the New Jerusalem, where we shall not need the light of the sun! The Lamb of the Lord is the light of the saints!

## *Notes*

*Sermon source:* This sermon is compiled from a number of accounts, but chiefly from the *Richmond Times-Dispatch* and *Rhapsody in Black: The Life Story of John Jasper.*

1. See pages 166–67 of the electronic edition of William Eldridge Hatcher's *John Jasper: The Unmatched Negro Philosopher and Preacher* at Documenting the American South, University of North Carolina at Chapel Hill Digitization Project, http://docsouth.unc.edu/church/hatcher/menu.html (accessed January 13, 2004).
2. Paraphrase of Psalm 2:1 (King James Version).

## *Bibliographical Sources*

Day, Richard Ellsworth. *Rhapsody in Black: The Life Story of John Jasper.* Valley Forge, PA: Judson Press, 1953.

Harlan, Howard H. *John Jasper: A Case History in Leadership.* Charlottesville: University of Virginia, 1936.

Hatcher, William E. *John Jasper: The Unmatched Negro Philosopher and Preacher.* New York: Fleming H. Revell Co., 1908.

Isaac, James. *"The Sun Do Move": The Life of John Jasper.* Richmond, VA: Whittet & Shepperson, 1954.

Randolph, Edwin Archer. *The Life of Rev. John Jasper, Pastor of Sixth Mt. Zion Baptist Church, Richmond, Va., from His Birth to the Present Time, with His Theory on the Rotation of the Sun.* Richmond, VA: R.T. Hill, 1884.

Smith, Timothy L. "Slavery and Theology: The Emergence of Black Christian Consciousness in Nineteenth-Century America," *Journal of the American Society of Church History* 1972: 497–512.

Watkins, Rees L. *Faith Stories: When Faith Prevailed: Stories in the Lives of Ten Virginia Baptist Men and Women of Great Faith.* Richmond, VA: Virginia Historical Society, 1997.

# EMILY CHRISTMAS KINCH

*(?–1932)*

Emily Christmas Kinch was born in Orange, New Jersey, the daughter of Rev. Jordan C. H. Christmas, who was an African Methodist Episcopal preacher. She was a graduate of the Institute for Colored Youth, in Philadelphia. Kinch was a pioneer in the African Methodist Episcopal (AME) Sunday school, the first degreed black Sunday school teacher in New Jersey, and founder and first president of the New Jersey AME conference Sunday School Institute. In 1905, Kinch was the only black delegate elected to represent New Jersey, along with forty-eight whites, to the International Sunday School Convention in Toronto. Rev. Kinch was the first woman to be elected permanent chairman of the lay electoral college of the AME Church.

In December 1908 she sailed as a missionary to West Africa and began the work of the Eliza Turner Primary School in Monrovia with twenty pupils; the school "grew to be one of the acknowledged educational forces of the Liberian Republic."[1] She was a trained musician, popular speaker, correspondent, and contributor to various church periodicals.

After her return from Africa she wrote "West Africa: An Open Door" (1917), a pamphlet that detailed the mission work in Africa by the AME Church and in which she pleaded for greater assistance for Africa.

Kinch was often featured in the AME newspaper the *Christian Recorder*, with her comments almost always couched by the male publishers as being from a missionary or educator. Although Kinch was both, she was also a preacher. Like all women of her time, Kinch was rarely spoken of as a preacher or even as an evangelist. However, the truth does eventually surface. In the *Christian Recorder* on October 21, 1926, a woman speaks of the rousing sermons given by Kinch during a revival Kinch conducted in Burlington, New Jersey: "To those of you who do not know Burlington, the writer wishes to say this town is like unto Sodom and Gomorrah, the majority of the church membership have but very little time for things spiritual. May this woman of God live long to give such Gospel as she has given here."

• • •

*This speech by Kinch was printed in the* Negro World *newspaper on June 26, 1920. It was delivered at a gathering of the Universal Negro Improvement Association (UNIA), led by Marcus Garvey. The UNIA flourished in the United States from 1919–27. In this message Kinch speaks boldly of her support for blacks returning to Africa and for Marcus Garvey. She chastises blacks for their lack of support of Garvey and black nationalism.*

## Speech Delivered in Liberty Hall (1920)

I am sure you know I am very happy to be here tonight, for whenever Africa is discussed it is my great fortune and pleasure to be present. And yet I never felt happier in all my life than I do tonight, for it is one of my great ambitions, especially since returning from Africa, to meet a group of people who have an idealism similar to my own, and that is—Back to Africa. And somehow, in my travels throughout the United States I feared the people had lost the vision of their opportunity of going back to Africa and possessing the land. Is it time? Is the time ripe? Yes, it is time. It is quite time. This is the noon hour of our opportunity. First of all, because Africa never was in a more susceptible, receptive mood for the UNIA than today. Before the world-wide war practically every door was closed to the Negroes of America. But God has mysteriously moved on the heart of the world, and everywhere there is unrest; and because of conditions brought about through the Belgians and Germans and other nations who had a strong and powerful grip on Africa. Today that grip has been gradually loosened, and everywhere the African wants to know why we in America do not come home.

### Back to Africa

I have never had very much use for the man or woman who said they have lost nothing in Africa. It has been a great pleasure for me to tell them they found nothing here. [Cheers.] If lynching and burning and disfranchisement, and Jim Crow law has given you a disposition to remain here, then remain. But there is a land that flows with milk and honey. There is a land that would receive you gladly—a land that you have turned your back on, a land to which men have gone over and come back bringing the joyful tidings that we are fully able to go up and possess the land. Let us go forward in His name and take it.

Now if there are men of vision and men of brains and men of character and men who will gladly die for this cause, then I want you to know that there are women also who will join you and will gladly die with you that Africa might be redeemed. [Cheers.] I want you men to remember that while you are the stronger part of the great whole that the larger numbers in this great group are the women, and the African womanhood is the one object of pity that stands out preeminently in all these deplorable conditions. The missionaries, for instance, have been gathering the boys and the men for many years around them, and this womanhood that has been crushed has been the object of the unscrupulous practices of the white man. They look today to the American Negro and to the men and women of this particular organization for redemption.

I was speaking to a friend of mine who has recently returned from her first trip abroad, and she told me that in Sierra Leone every other man was changing his name to Marcus Garvey. [Applause.] She told me that two weeks ago in the city of New York. And if the men of Africa have been so enthused and have caught the spirit of this man whom they have never seen, what about the men and women who are privileged with contact with this man of vision? "Where there is no vision the people perish,"[2] and "who knows but what we are come to the kingdom for such a time as this?"[3]

## Liberia Receives Our Delegates

Talk about the resources of Africa, I want to tell you just this one thing: There is enough mahogany burned in Liberia alone to furnish every family in the United States with three pieces of furniture. They do not need chimneys. All they need is just a little fire to cook, and they burn mahogany to cook with. Now then, if you want to grind out your life over the washtub, if you wish to spend the rest of your days upon the cooking table, if you are satisfied with these conditions, why, you can do nothing better than to remain here. But those of you who believe, who know that what I have said is the truth—Africa wants you. How I should have liked to be in Monrovia when the delegation arrived there, and seen the welcome which they received.[4] The Africans waited long and patiently for the delegation that would come from the descendants of the men and women who were slaves, and they have often said to us: "Why have you stayed so long? What has civilization and freedom meant to you if not to come back and give your life . . . [you have moved] mountains, bridged the rivers, thrown up skyscrapers for America, and yet you cannot go into a first-class hotel because you are black. You cannot ride in the Pullmans if you are tired, but must sit up or do the next best thing. Why not come back to Africa and make this a great country for ourselves, our children and our children's children?"

This friend of mine told me that the young men of Sierra Leone are giving up first-class jobs and waiting for the Black Star Line to touch the shores. This friend is a woman of integrity, and I believe every word she has said, and she says that the day a ship comes into the harbor of Sierra Leone there would not be an English army large enough to keep back the Sierra Leonians, for they are determined that having gone to the trenches of Europe to die for the white man, if needs be they will die that Africa might be redeemed.

You think it is a wonderful thing to be in Harlem, but you have never enjoyed your manhood until you have walked in Liberia and have come in contact with the black President of that country and received invitations to come to the banquet that is prepared in the State House. You surely cannot go to Washington to one. And so, after all, I would rather be in Liberia tonight, all things being equal, without her trolley cars, without her subways, without her elevated system, and to feel and know that I am a woman for all of that. Black skin or short hair, money or no money, you are a man and have the opportunity of being the greatest person in that republic; for the only requirement of Liberia is that you are black. Let us therefore join hands and back up the man who is leading us out of this wilderness into the Promised Land. [Applause.]

## NOTES

*Sermon source:* This version of the Kinch message is taken from Randall K. Burkett, *Black Redemption: Churchmen Speak for the Garvey Movement* (Philadelphia: Temple University Press, 1978), 47–49.

1. See page 144 of the electronic edition of Richard Robert Wright's *Centennial Encyclopaedia of the African Methodist Episcopal Church Containing Principally the Biographies of the Men and Women, Both Ministers and Laymen, Whose Labors during a Hundred Years, Helped Make the A. M. E. Church What It Is; Also Short Historical Sketches of Annual Conferences, Educational Institutions, General Departments, Missionary Societies of the A. M. E. Church, and General Information about African Methodism and the Christian Church in General; Being a Literary Contribution to the Celebration of the One Hundredth Anniversary of the*

*Formation of the African Methodist Episcopal Church Denomination by Richard Allen and others, at Philadelphia, Penna., in 1816* (Philadelphia: Book Concern of the AME Church, 1916) at Documenting the American South, University of North Carolina at Chapel Hill Digitization Project, http://docsouth.unc.edu/church/wright/menu.html (accessed March 12, 2006).

2. Proverbs 29:18a (King James Version).

3. Paraphrase of Esther 4:14b (KJV).

4. According to Burkett in *Black Redemption*, in early June 1920 a UNIA representative, Elie Garcia, met with Liberian president C.D.B. King concerning the feasibility of colonization in Africa by American blacks.

### *Bibliographical Sources*

Burkett, Randall K. *Black Redemption: Churchmen Speak for the Garvey Movement*. Philadelphia: Temple University Press, 1978.

Kinch, Emily Christmas. *West Africa: An Open Door*. Philadelphia: Book Concern of the AME Church, 1917.

## EMANUEL KING LOVE

*(1850–1900)*

Emanuel King Love was born in slavery near Marion, Perry County, Alabama, to Cumby Jarrett and Maria Antoinette Love. He was baptized in 1868 and licensed to preach soon after. He attended Lincoln University in 1871, but left after six months because he believed that he had learned everything that the school's curriculum could offer. He enrolled in August Institute in Georgia the following year and graduated in 1877.

Upon graduation, he was appointed missionary for Georgia under the joint supervision of the American Baptist Home Mission Board and the Georgia Mission Board (both white groups). In 1879 he resigned the former position and became pastor of the First African Baptist Church in Thomasville, Georgia. The church flourished under his leadership. In 1879 he also married Josephine Leeks.

In 1885 he became the pastor of the First African Baptist Church of Savannah, where he remained until he died. At its height, it is said that Love increased the membership to more than six thousand, making the church the largest black Baptist congregation of its time.

An ardent advocate of education and black uplift, he was considered a preacher's preacher. His sermons were prophetic and often liberationist in tone. Love was a well-read orator. When he was not preaching he was putting his ideas into print. He served as editor of the *Georgia Sentinel*, a Baptist newspaper in Augusta, and as editor of the *Baptist Truth*, the newspaper of the Georgia Negro Baptist Convention, for which Love also served as president.

Love was one of the founders of the Baptist Foreign Mission Convention and served as its president on four occasions. In 1895 this organization joined with others to form the National Baptist Convention, U.S.A., Inc. Love also helped found Central City College in Savannah.

• • •

*This message was delivered at the emancipation celebration in Augusta, Georgia, in January 1891. In it Love shows his prowess as a well-read voice of his people. In this sermon he addresses such important issues as the continued lynchings of blacks, stereotyped portrayals of blacks as shiftless and lazy, the need for blacks in politics, and the importance of blacks owning land and amassing economic power. Further, he extols the history of blacks and helps them remember the wonders and achievements of Africa. Love also reveals his sentiments concerning America as he tells blacks to remain patriotic even in the face of their poor treatment. Importantly, he uses his position to encourage blacks to remain hopeful until their situation changes: "However high the proud Caucasians may stand upon the hill and however vociferously they may extol their superiority and greatness, the Negroes are in the next valley just ahead of them and eternal fate has decreed that the Negroes shall make the grand stand first."*

## Emancipation Oration
## (1891)

Fellow Citizens:

I esteem it an honor for which I have no language to adequately express my gratitude to you for being invited to address you on this auspicious occasion. The emancipation of more than four million souls from the most cruel and diabolical system of slavery that ever disgraced this or any other country is no ordinary occurrence; and we should celebrate it with befitting ceremonies, characterized with the profoundest sense of gratitude, thanksgiving and patriotism, as often as that memorable day rolls around until time shall wane and be no more. Indeed this should be a great day among us. It marks the day when the mighty arm of Jehovah was moved in our defense, and effected eternally our deliverance. Embittered by no feeling of the injustices, indignities and the numberless indescribable injuries we have suffered in this land, we meet here to-day to thank God for deliverance, and to pledge with all our hearts, our love, patriotism and support of every interest of our common country.

We had no choice in selecting America as our home. We were decoyed from our father-land, and forced to serve as slaves in this country. In the Providence of God, this dungeon of the most ruthless prison was powdered, blasted and washed clean in the blood of America's noblest sons and made our home. But there are signs of the old disease developed and developing in a far more malignant form in the shape of murdering and lynching, and lawless mobs and the burning of human beings alive and many other Godless outrages which this country is morally bound to remedy. God, humanity and the onward march of civilization demand that an everlasting stop be put to these things—For be it understood by all who hear me this day: Revolutions do not go backward; God has begun this work, and He will complete the work begun and grace in glory ends. *The Negroes were not and will not always be as they are.* It was a plant of Africa that furnished the sublimely graphic picture and the wonderfully accurate illustration of the Messianic office of Jesus Christ, that called forth from Isaiah in charming eloquence, and in the profoundest sweetness these words "For he shall grow up before him as a tender plant and as a root out of dry ground."[1] This plant of the Prophet's vision grew in the North-Eastern part of Africa where it did not rain more than once in twenty-five years—But so peculiar was this plant that it furnished its own water by means of its large succulent roots, and thus moistured it was enabled to defy the severest and longest drought. So it is with the sable descendants of that dark, neglected and unfortunate Continent. Though they have been enslaved in this land and subjected to the most trying hardships, they are endued with such peculiar vitality that they cannot be lawed out, starved out, murdered out, lynched out, burned out, migrated out and if the Force bill is passed they will not much longer be counted out.

Much ado is made of Tom Reed's count in the present Congress: this is the clearest proof that the white folks North, and the white folks South view mathematics through different kaleidoscopes. When they were present, Reed counted them present. When we were present, they counted us absent. When they were in Reed counted them in, when we were in, they counted us out. Much eloquence and learning has been spent to show that the Negroes [are] dying out and that they are not capable of self government and unworthy of the sacred franchise. John C. Calhoun went down into his grave saying "keep the Negroes down." The lamented Henry W. Grady, Georgia's proud son, spent the energies of a gifted mind trying to prove the inferiority of the Negroes, and that they should not aspire to any position in this government. But Grady is dead and gone and the Negroes still live and yet will come. There was another mighty man in Georgia—He was a scholar and a logician of the first order—He was an able writer and editor of a powerful Religious Journal—He believed, preached, taught and wrote that the Negroes were an inferior race and must die out in the midst of a superior race. That man's pen is palsied and his voice hushed in death; but the Negroes are here yet. That man was the distinguished Dr. Henry Holcombe Tucker of the *Christian Index* of Atlanta. There was another man more bitter still—Of us he published many ills—But he is dead and beneath the clouds he sleeps—Yet the Negroes walk upon Macon's streets—That man was Editor Lamar of the *Macon Telegraph*. There was another mighty man who wielded an immense influence against us—His paper was bitter indeed—But a bullet from a pistol in the hands of a man of his own race pierced him and he fell mortally wounded: weltering in his blood, he died, and Negroes acquitted the man who slew him. That man was the able editor of the *News and Courier* of Charleston. Notwithstanding the alarming figures in the mortuary reports which come to us annually, and add to this number many thousands of murdered and lynched Negroes, yet their number has swollen to nearly eight million in a quarter of a century. This is double the number we had twenty-five years ago—This is a happy dying out.

In spite of men and devils the Negroes will rise. Their night has been dark and long; but from Piscah's lofty heights I see the day is breaking—Pilgrims rejoice! the glorious sun is coming out of his fiery chambers and the clouds and the darkness are breaking away.

Africa was once the glory of the world; there was no learning so enviable as that of Egypt; for in painting, sculpturing and architecture we excelled. The art of printing is traced to Africa, and we gave the world its first idea of banking. During a famine in Canaan, we gave Abraham, the Father of the faithful, shelter and food; when starvation threatened the extinction of the Jews in Canaan, we gave Jacob and his family a home surrounded with plenty. Moses, the greatest legislator the world has ever produced, was born upon our soil. When the treacherous Herod was flooding Bethlehem with the blood of babies seeking the Holy Child Jesus, our Lord found refuge in our cultured home; and when he went fainting and bleeding and falling to Calvary, scorned and derided by every other nation, a Negro helped him bear his cross.

The nations of earth are like men traveling over hills and valleys to a great city. When those ahead would be in the valley, those behind would be on a hill. It would be silly for those behind to boast that they were above those who were before—For those who are now in the valley were once on that same hill, and those who are behind must go down in that same valley. When they will be going down into that valley, those ahead will be going up the next hill. The Negroes, in the awful wake of moral courage, sweetness of disposition, loving spirit of forgiveness, meekness, humbleness, tenderness of heart, devotion to God and physical discipline, which demonstrate the development of true manhood, which is heaven's idea of greatness, are in advance of any other nation under heaven. However high the proud Caucasians may stand upon the hill and however vociferously they may extol their superiority and greatness, the Negroes are in the next valley just ahead of them and eternal fate has decreed that the Negroes shall make the grand stand first. Let the world hear the news—let the rising Sun as he comes out of his sacred chamber and unfolds his golden mantle declare it; let the stars as they dance in their diamond sockets, repeat it; let the Moon, the Queen of night, as she rides in her silvery chariot, proclaim it; let the whistling winds sound it; let the flying clouds reveal it; let the awful thunders publish it; let the angry lightnings dispatch it; let it be written in burning letters upon the cerulean skies; yea, let Africa's sons and daughters in every land sing it; that as we are, we were not, and as we are, we will not remain. Up yonder hill we will go, it matters not what it may cost—for to remain below we will be lost.

The vexed and intricate Negro Problem has received the attention of the civilized world. Volumes have been written upon it and yet its solution is a profound mystery. Why is the Negro problem any more difficult of solution than any other problem? Has America gone at this solution in an earnest practical common sense way? The weak, poor, oppressed, ignorant and enslaved in every age of the world have presented a problem and whenever statesmen and liberty loving people have gone earnestly and practically at its solution, "fading away as the stars of the morning, losing their light in the glorious dawn,"[2] so have these difficulties and intricacies passed away gently and lovingly, only remembered by what they have done. For more than four hundred years the Jews presented a serious problem to the Egyptians—in Africa, too, remember. We held the Jews as our slaves in Africa until God wrung them from our tenacious grasp. He solved that problem and rescued the Jews. In Babylon and Assyria the Jews presented a serious problem. In Great Britain the cultured Anglo-Saxons of to-day presented a serious problem. It might have been thought that they would have been so impressed by the oppression and hardships they endured that they would learn never to oppress, not even the beast—but alas! How soon do men forget the lessons which God in affliction teaches them. The Irishmen in Ireland present a serious problem to-day. America is wonderfully interested in fair play and home rule for Ireland, but is totally blind and indifferent to the murdering, lynching, injustices, outrages and the countless atrocious crimes at its own door. Much is said about ignorant Negro domination. What different an ignorant Negro from an ignorant Irishman or an ignorant anybody else? If education be the basis of recognition, then it would be consistent to rule out the ignorant of every race and turn in the educated of every race. If this rule was faithfully carried out, the Negroes would have more rights than they can now boast of. Of all the race problems to which I have referred, the Negro problem is the easiest of solution. This problem has an advantage over any other problem in several ways.

First, We think in writing and speaking the same language; there is no trouble of misunderstanding each other. Second, We embrace the same Christian Religion, accept the same God as our common Father, washed in the same hallowed blood of Christ and are journeying to the same heaven.

Third, We are not lazy. We are tillers of the same soil. We are mingled in the families of this people. We cook their food, nurse their children and many of them are our fathers, brothers, sisters, aunts, uncles and cousins. Surely these pleasant relations should, at least, serve as a key to the solution of this great problem. The Negroes are not foreign born—they have been subjects of no other government—they are patient, meek, humble, forgiving, kind hearted, good natured and religious: hence, the simple rule of fairness and common justice will throw a flood of light upon this great problem. If half the sympathy and money that is spent on Ireland were spent on the Negroes, the Negro problem would be as clear as the noon day sun at high meridian in a cloudless sky.

The Negroes have been made to feel that their votes were of paramount importance, and that the primary object of their emancipation was to clothe them with the right to vote. Hence, when they were first emancipated, they threw all of their souls into the ballot to the sad neglect of their brains and bodies. They were simply the tools of wicked designing politicians who did them more harm than good. I entertain the opinion that if at first, the Negroes had been urged to get an education, homes, land and money, even to the exclusion of the ballot, they would have been infinitely better off and farther up the hill of prosperity. It is not unreasonable to suppose that the political inspiration with which we were enthused twenty-five years left but little room for anything else, and, hence, the greatest things have received the least attention. If the political teachers who came among us directly after the war had taught the necessity of getting homes and money while we were docile and in our formative state, they would have done us far more good; and would have erected to themselves a monument more lasting than brass, higher than the regal sights of Pyramids which the voracious winds nor the innumerable series of years could destroy. Do not understand me to denounce in total what they did. Much of what they taught was right—but this they should have done and not have left the other undone. I judge it will not be denied that a man can do better without the right to vote and the protection of his ballot than he can without the right to live and the protection of his life. This government is far more anxious to throw around the ballot of the Negroes the mighty arm of its protection, and find it far more Constitutional to secure the ballot than to protect and secure their lives. I take it for granted that it will be admitted that the Negroes, of the two, would be better off without the ballot than without food, raiment, money and homes. They need these worse and should secure them first. Doubtless we all see this mistake. Let us set to work and correct it, as far as power in us lies. Success is in no other direction. Politicians may disagree with me, but if you will turn to the great Historical Dictionary of politics for the last twenty-five years, you will find that a politician means "one who wants an office that will pay well, and will usually do all in his power to get it, even at the expense of the best interest of the people, if there is no other road to the goal of his ambition." Hence they could not be expected to agree with me.

Education is that which develops the powers which nature has furnished us in their embryonal [*sic*] form. It is that which draws out the latent faculties and unties them in a pleasing symmetrical activity for the truest interest of a people. It is that which creates the desire for, and makes a people great. It lifts a people above low things, makes them better citizens, better neighbors, purifies and dignifies their homes. It begets the dispositions for virtue, thrift, frugality, justice and fair-play. It arms a people with the weapons with which to battle for their rights and to defend them when won. The ignorant people of every age have been and always will be in every age to come the servants of the *Educated*. To this rule there is no exception and from this decree there is no appeal. It is God's plan that intelligence—righteous intelligence—should rule. An ignorant man should not be placed in authority even though it be myself. If the ignorant rule the land groaneth just as truly as if the wicked ruled. The result would be the same if a doctor killed the patient because of wickedness or because of ignorance. One of the most pressing needs of the Negroes is education. It is past strange that the Negroes all over this broad land did not hold Educational Mass Meetings and urge, with all their might, the passage of the Blair Educational Bill. Senator Blair, in his efforts to pass this bill, is entitled to the everlasting gratitude and eternal support of every Negro in this land. I would rather see him President of this nation than any living man, and if Georgia's delegates to the next National Convention would hear me, they would vote for Blair first, last and all the time. This government ought to do something to remove the vast amount of illiteracy that drapes with a pall its National escutcheon. Is it more important to protect our ballot, and to secure our rights than to secure our intelligence? If Education is power, ignorance is weakness, and the more ignorance this government has, the weaker it is.

If we would help control the country, we must help own it. I fear that the day is not far distant when those who own nothing shall control nothing. Mississippi has led the way, and I shall not be surprised if other States follow right along in the line of disenfranchising, by their State Constitutions, the greater part of the Negroes, by property or educational qualifications. I warn you to get ready for it. A homeless people are a weak dependent people. A people without homes or money raises their families as by chance. Their virtue is as banks without vaults or locks; it might be safe, but then it mightn't. It is every man's duty, yea, it is his privilege to bring up his family under his own vine and fig tree. Our homes must be the foundation of our greatness. We cannot be collectively great if we are not first individually great—and be it understood, that we are just what we make ourselves. We cannot be made by laws nor Constitutions—we must carve our own destiny.

We were made of the dust and we should take peculiar pride in owning some of Mother Earth. If we had bought up the lands in the country and on the suburbs of the city of the cities and towns directly after the war when we could have done so for a song, we would be much better off to-day. I still advise the Negroes to buy land. Buy it anywhere you can get it. Be a free holder, and no powers on earth can keep you down. If the Negroes do not give this subject attention very soon they will see their mistake when it will be too late. This country is being rapidly flooded with foreigners of the poorest class of white people, and by and by they will buy up this land that is to-day lying idle and can be bought for a pittance, and the Negroes cannot then buy a foot of it for any price. This country bids fair to be the most wonderful theater of activity upon the Globe. I look forward to the day when the entire Continent will be cut up into little flourishing farms. I urge the Negroes to get ready to move off in the mighty march. Get land and cultivate farms—the farmer is a freeman indeed. He is lord of all he surveys. The Yankees did not give us that forty acres of land and the old mules, but we must not be discouraged—we must have them.

### *Notes*

*Sermon source:* The Library of Congress Web site American Memory Collection, http://memory.loc.gov/cgi-bin/query/r?ammem/murray:efield(DOCID+@lit(lcrbmrpt0608div2)) (accessed January 2008).

1. Isaiah 53:2a (King James Version).
2. This is the first line of the song "Only Remembered," written by Horatius Bonar with music by Ira D. Sankey.

### *Bibliographical Sources*

Carter, E.R. *Biographical Sketches of Our Pulpit.* 1888. Reprint, Chicago: Afro-American Press, 1969.

Fitts, Leroy. *A History of Black Baptists.* Nashville, TN: Broadman Press, 1985.

Love, Emanuel King. *History of the First African Baptist Church, from its Organization, January 20, 1788 to July 1, 1888.* Savannah, GA: The Morning News Print, 1888.

Martin, Sandy D. *Black Baptists and African Missions: The Origins of a Movement, 1880–1915.* Macon, GA: Mercer University Press, 1989.

Murphy, Larry G., J. Gordon Melton, and Gary L. Ward. *Encyclopedia of African American Religions.* New York: Garland Publishing, 1993, 461.

Simmons, William J. *Men of Mark: Eminent, Progressive and Rising.* 1887. Reprint, Chicago: Johnson Publishing Company, 1970.

## WILLIAM HENRY MOSES

*(1872–1940)*

William Henry Moses was born and reared in Charlotte County, Virginia, the eldest son of Thomas and Sarah Moses. His grandfather, a man of means, instilled in him a drive for education and interest in religion. Through hard work as overseer on his grandfather's plantation, Moses was able to save enough money by 1892 to pay his tuition to the recently opened Virginia Seminary and College at Lynchburg.

Moses's talents stood out early in the Baptist church. His first pastorate was the prestigious Mt. Zion Baptist Church in Staunton, Virginia, where he served for a decade. He then accepted a call from Metropolitan Baptist Church in Pittsburgh. While pastoring Metropolitan, the amount of money that Moses raised for foreign missions caught the attention of national Baptist leaders. He became field secretary for the National Baptist Convention, U.S.A., Inc. Foreign Mission Board. During and after his term as field secretary he served various churches, one in Newberry, South Carolina, another in Knoxville, Tennessee, and yet another in New York.

By the early 1900s black Baptist leaders knew Moses well. His name became know to the rank-and-file membership after he was a mediator in the split between factions of the National Baptist Convention over who owned their publishing board, then operated by Richard Boyd. Moses served as the spokesperson for the 1918 Peace Commission designed to find an amicable solution concerning the issue. The commission's efforts did not succeed.

Moses wrote *The White Peril*, which was used as a tract for missionary classes in the Baptist Church. In the preface Moses stated, "The White Peril is, that the darker races in general, and the black race in particular, is in danger of political, industrial, social, and economic slavery or extermination by the white Christian nations of the world." Written in 1919, when lynchings were still common, in this book Moses showed his courage and his defiant stance against racism.

Another of his achievements included cofounding, with R.R. Wright Jr., the Colored Protective Association, which, among other things, worked to lessen violence perpetrated against blacks by whites. In 1919, Moses became the pastor of National Baptist Church, one of the largest Baptist churches in New York. After the death of E.C. Morris in 1922, *The Negro World* newspaper endorsed Moses for president of the National Baptist Convention, although he didn't win. The warm support he had received from *The Negro World*, the official press organ of the Universal Negro Improvement Association (UNIA), led by Marcus Garvey, left him favorably disposed to Garvey. Thus, when Garvey found himself in serious legal trouble with federal authorities over a charge of mail fraud, Moses was one of the first of a number of prominent clergymen to defend him.

• • •

*This sermon was delivered in Liberty Hall in Harlem at a UNIA community meeting to help Garvey gain release from prison. Moses's biblical texts were drawn from the Old Testament books of 1 Chronicles 12:32 and Joel 2:28–29. The passage in Chronicles concerns knowing what to do in the midst of trouble, and the Joel Scripture focused on the spirit of God being poured out on men and women who would prophesy. Moses sought to portray Garvey as a prophet for black peo-*

*ple. In the course of his speech he touched on all the major issues under discussion in the debate over Garvey's program. Most importantly, he urged the audience to unite to have Garvey released from jail. Even when only reading the speech, one cannot help but feel the power of the oratorical ability that Moses possessed.*

## Understanding the Times and Knowing What to Do (July 1923)

Mr. Chairman, Sisters and Brothers:

I am one of that large group of sympathizers with this organization who has not become an active member. It is my privilege, in addition to being a pastor in the city of New York, to be the field representative of the National Baptist Convention of the United States, representing my denominational group of nearly four million Christians, the largest group of Negro Christians in the world. In the last sixty days I have been in some twenty States and everywhere throughout this country where I have been, North and South, East and West, during the trial of the Honorable Marcus Garvey I have not heard a single criticism even from those who used to criticize him and disagree with him throughout the length and breadth of this country. [Applause.] Sometimes we colored folks are like folks in a family. We quarrel until it gets serious. Whether you think it or not, don't let anybody fool you or fool themselves that the Negroes in this country or throughout the world want anybody to put Marcus Garvey in jail. Whether we are members or not, we want Marcus Garvey out. Because as long as Mr. Garvey is in, you and I are on the way in. He must come out.

I want to congratulate New York and America. There are some mean white folks in the world, but America has sense enough of fair play that, if you state your case fairly, America, white America, has enough fair play to hear the truth and liberate Mr. Garvey. Don't you fool yourself. Don't let folks fool you. England and France may treat us pretty well, but Garvey went all around the world and he found that Harlem was the best place to have a Liberty Hall. [Applause.] Under God you got to hand it to old New York. More folks say what they want to say in New York than anywhere else on God's earth, and when you want a judge to work on your case you had better go out of the district, to Chicago or somewhere else, because these folks around here have a kind of spirit to do right. Liberty Hall is in big New York. There is nothing bigger than this, no one city that God has made. We are in New York. [Laughter.] But I am a preacher. I take a text, and I am going to take it now, because I preach every problem from the angle of Jesus of Nazareth.

I want to call your attention to this passage that is found in the First Chronicles, the twelfth chapter, thirty-second verse: "The men of Issachar had understandings of the times to know what Israel ought to do." I want to talk a little while about understanding the times and knowing what to do. We have taken up the collection. Now let us sit here and understand it. I want to remark in the first place that this passage of Scripture is a practical definition of prophecy. Prophecy is understanding a time to know what to do. And it is not something that is confined to fortune-telling, it is not the foretelling, it is the telling forth what God is doing in your day and generation. It is to feel the thrill of what Jehovah has on His program for your times and your generation. The men of Issachar, back yonder in David's time, understood the times. They understood that they were in a pivotal period upon which centuries and decades turned. And we are in a pivotal period upon which centuries and decades will turn. The whole world is getting ready to move on another world-wide, universal cycle that is to go for many hundreds of years, and whatever you are going to do, do now, and whatever your program is, get it in now. [Applause.] If you don't get it in now, you need not try to put it in afterwards.

Everybody in the world is telling what they want, while the world is in a position to straighten out things, and we are not the only folks with a protest. White folks are not satisfied. A whole lot of us have grievances. We are kind of clubbing them up and adjusting ourselves, and all of us, white and black and everybody else, are throwing them in and coming to a common understanding as to what we should do. Now I am talking about preaching. I know a lot of you kind of feel that we preachers are responsible for much. [Laughter.] But I am saying that the man who understands his time is the man upon whom God has poured out His spirit. And He said this, this matchless Leader of men: "And it shall come to pass in the last days," saith God, "that I will pour out my spirit upon all flesh."[1] (Not on some; on all flesh, sons and daughters, preachers and laymen—upon all flesh.) "The young men shall see visions."[2] (That is to say, they shall have a clear grasp of master ideas.) "Your old men shall dream dreams."[3] (Things that they saw in the realm of dreamland years ago are about to come into the realm of reality.) The reason we do not believe in this Spirit of the Lord—and, brothers, if the Spirit of God is not on Marcus Garvey, it is not on anybody else. [Loud applause.] Mr. Garvey can truly say: "The Spirit of the Lord is upon me. He hath anointed me to open the eyes of the blind and preach the acceptable word of the Lord."[4] Today is this Scripture fulfilled. Right here today I want to say this, that God's spirit is poured out in a simple way on the world.

You know, we preachers have been talking about revivals. We want a revival of religion. Well, most of us preachers would not know the Holy Spirit if we met it in the road. I mean to say that we talk about a revival of religion. Most of us do not know our Bible when we see it. You know, among colored folks especially—for white folk do not pay much attention to their conditions; now and then a preacher rings true and they follow him, but they aren't that kind—the average man expects the Holy Spirit. Don't think that God runs nothing but churches. Don't think that the Lord is in business, just taking up collections and ordaining preachers. Don't think that a revival consists in nothing but a "Glory Hallelujah." How the Spirit expresses Himself depends altogether on the circumstances. If the conditions are not such as would justify rejoicing but protest, then the Spirit expresses Itself or Himself in the spirit of protest. The Spirit of God spoke to Samuel, and Samuel smote Agag in the presence of the Lord, hewed him into pieces.

There comes a time when the Spirit of God takes the form of protest, and anything besides protest is a mockery of God and a mockery of justice. What are you going to say Glory Hallelujah for, when somebody is beating your boy? That is the spirit of the devil. Somebody has taken your homeland and is dominating the whole earth, and is not associating with you and do not want you to associate with yourself. And you stand grinning. Any spirit that makes you submit to that is the spirit of cowardice and the spirit of the devil. There comes a time when the Spirit pours Himself out and expresses Himself in protest and in war, if you please. What did we risk our lives for in the recent war if the Spirit of God was not on the battlefield to beat down wrong and lift up the banner of righteousness? We have got to get a new kind of Holy Spirit here. That is all. I mean the spirit of protest. There is a spirit of love, there is a spirit of justice, there is a spirit of protest; and the man who stands for that, the Spirit of God is upon him, and he has proclaimed the era of opportunity. He will pour out His Spirit upon all flesh. Everybody will see, will find out what is right, and what is wrong, and what is truth. And you have never seen so many folks in your life trying to straighten out the world as now. I mean white folks and black folks. I mean all sorts of folks. The world knows this world is not running right. Hardly anything is running right. Talk about great cities like New York, London and Paris; and men living like devils in hell, can hardly get bread. Working from dawn to sunset, and cannot get a decent livelihood! That is not right. You need not think that the smart Negroes and the smart white folks are the only real reformers in this world. Those folks down in Mississippi and the people in every corner of the world know it is not running right, and under God the people of the earth are beginning to see what's wrong and are going to fix it. There is more religion than you think. I mean, there are more forces at work for God than you have folks baptized.

One of the hopeful signs of the times is that folks are cursing preachers. That is the hopeful sign. If you think folks are not cursing preachers you don't know the news. And do you think that folks are disloyal to the program of Jesus Christ? No. But they do not think that we are carrying out the principles of Jesus Christ. We are preaching and capering like children and are not practicing the opposite principles of the devil, and they say you don't represent what you say you do. Let me tell you something. Here in this country we have some five million Negroes organized in the churches. England and France and some white folks, who don't mean to be fair, are no more studying about you and your churches than they are about the winds that blow. And you know why? Because we are not going to do anything but say "Hallelujah." They are not paying any attention. No matter what anybody will tell you, the whole world wakes up to hear more what Marcus Garvey has to say than all the Negro preachers in the world. [Loud applause.] And why? Because the average preacher is not preaching anything worthwhile. For two thousand years we have been perverting this gospel that Jesus left here and have been preaching lies.

You talk about your Universal Negro Improvement Association. It is a fine thing. But as fine as it is your biggest asset is in "G." Don't let anybody fool you. Some may say; "But he has done so many things wrong; he has made mistakes." I tell you he is the biggest asset you have. I do not care how well others can do it. Whatever you may say about Mr. Garvey, his is the voice in the wilderness. When he cries they answer from everywhere in this land. And if you think you are a bigger man than Mr. Garvey, get you something like this. You may talk about you come from Harvard and "I am from Yale" and "I am from Cornell," but the man that speaks to the multitude must come from Heaven. He is not born in a day. No man can make him. He comes out of the groaning and travail of ages. Mr. Garvey is the pent-up feeling of the race that has been in the region of the shadow of death for ages. He did not come yesterday. You all talk about getting him out. Get him out if you want to. He will do more in jail than he will out. But I want to state the case to the judgment of mankind. They have all the machinery. The Jews have more pull than you and I can get in one hundred years. But you must state the case. There is something about the truth. It will get into your brain. It will sink down into your system, whether black or white, and when you find yourself you will feel like Marcus Garvey feels and moving according to his will. Know the truth and the truth will make you free.

I said that a hopeful sign of the times is that Christian folks are cursing preachers. That is the hopeful sign. They will make us carry the real truth. They will make these churches stand up for common righteousness and for economic uplift, and for salvation here now, or they are going to take the kingdom away from us. You hear people cursing. They believe we are not doing our duty. The average preacher is wasting money, white or black. He is wasting money. I will give you an idea. Most of us have taught our race to be without hope in the world. We have plenty hope hereafter, but not much here. That is the trouble with our salvation plan. The average colored man has lost hope. The average colored man is not praying about anything. He is asking for nothing. He does not believe He is going to do anything. We preachers are responsible. You go to prayer meeting, and there is nobody there but one or two folks who are ready to die. You know why he does not go to the prayer meeting until then, he does not believe God is going to do anything. If people thought God was going to give them clothes to wear and food to eat, they would serve Him some. The average man feels that God has to function here or not at all.

Listen to the average man pray. He prays like he is going to ask God for the whole world: "Aye, Lord! Say Jesus! Aye, my Father! Thy servant has come to thee in pain and trembling this morning. Yea, Lord! Oh, King, my Lord! You have been our help in ages past, our hope for years to come. Have mercy, my Lord. You have been my stay in days past and gone. I want You to pull back the curtains tonight and look down upon the Baptist Church for Jesus' sake." Fifteen minutes gone. Ain't asked for nothing yet. And by and by listen to his petition: "Have mercy, Lord. Have mercy. (You think he is going to pray for somebody in trouble.) Have mercy, Lord. Oh, Jesus. Save the choir. Have mercy on the Deacon Board for Jesus' sake." [Laughter.] A race in trouble, a race going to hell, a race suffering, and you praying about a choir. He does not expect God is going to do anything now. Hear him when he comes to the close: "Aye, Lord. When I come to the still waters of death . . ." [Laughter.] And everybody says this is the time. That is not the time at all. The time is out. My friends, we have been preaching for men to get ready when it comes to die. Jesus said the kingdom was at hand. Pray that it come on earth.

And what is prayer? Prayer is the soul's sincere desire. Prayer is the dynamo of the soul. Prayer is the creating capacity for enjoying the blessings that life promises. Prayer is not only the creating desire but the dynamo that starts the wheel turning to work out the salvation and get the thing you want. The trouble is we do not ask for anything. Negroes did not ask for anything until Mr. Garvey came. Here we are in this country. Up and down Harlem thousands and thousands of colored people. Shoe stores, grocery stores, hardware stores, drug stores, all sorts of manufacturing concerns. Not only here, but in Washington and Chicago and Philadelphia, miles of mills and mills, miles of factories, all owned by white folks. Thousands of ships in the sea, all owned by the white folks. Thousands of railroads in the world, all owned by white folks. Put you out of business in the morning and your business would not affect the world two hours outside of your own labor. That is true in the West Indies, in Africa and everywhere. You and I are dead broke, and our ministers and our leaders—the pity of it is not that it is the truth, but our pulpits, our politicians and public men are willing to stand for it. If a man really gets the desire, he will achieve. Brother, whether you think it or not, if the spirit of God enters in, you will go on. Say to yourself, I am tired living like a dog. I want to be a man like other men. I want to have the privileges that others have. I want to lift my head up and walk with the king's children. I want to have my own buildings, I want to have my own home, I want to have my own government. And if you don't want it, God ought to send you to the uttermost depths of hell. [Applause.]

Garvey! Garvey means to tell you that the hour has struck, and it is high noon and it was time our race was rising and getting up and wanting something like other folks. I defy anybody on God's earth to say that Garvey is disloyal to the black people of the world. I defy anybody on earth to say that he is disloyal to the white people of the earth. He is only asking for the black people the same thing that white folks are willing to die for, and any Negro who does not believe it ought to be sent down to the depths of hell. No matter what you say, you may have noticed that since Mr. Garvey has been on the scene we preachers have been waking up. Why? My friends, you are making more disciples than will ever join your lodge. These people in their churches and other organizations are going to make their leaders do what you are doing or take them out. I used to hold revivals and stretch a long face and say: "Where will you spend eternity?" A Negro brought me to my senses, just a plain Negro out of the alley. [Laughter.] I was saying, "Where will you spend eternity?" That Negro said to me, "I am interested in where I am going to spend the night." Whether you think it or not, the average black man wants to know where he is going to spend the night, and not only that, but where I am going to spend the day, and he wants to know not only where I am going to spend the day, but where my race is going to spend it. [Tremendous applause.]

Garvey may not expect to live in Africa, but his spirit will carry on the work that will be done. I hear a lot of fool people talk about going to Africa. How did Ireland get a measure of freedom? Ireland came here. The Irishmen in Boston, New York, Chicago, and everywhere, they organized and began to create public sentiment that they could not express on British territory, and they made this great America unlock the doors and bring more liberty to Ireland than she has ever had. And just as she was the base of preparations for Irishmen, so God has chosen this America of ours to lay the keel for the ship that shall bring success to the black peoples of the world. America has to stand by. American sentiment has to be loyal to this thing. Do it or deny the faith on which the Government was founded.

I told you the hopeful sign of the world was from people cursing preachers. That is because we preachers are such cowards. The average preacher is educated in college where the rule is, the more he knows, the worse off he is. He does not want to hurt anybody's feelings. They teach him to throw curves. That is, take ten thousand people and state one principle and throw one curve right round everybody and not hit anybody. Don't have no fuss. Don't disturb. And yet, Jesus said, "You shall hear of wars and rumors of wars. You shall be brought before kings and governors for my sake,"[5] and for the testimony of truth, and for the brotherhood of man. And when you ring that bell, they don't want to come. There are a few devils in the world that want to gobble up everything. But the spirit of God is upon all flesh. . . .

. . . Justice is not only in the hearts of black men; there are thousands of white men willing to give you justice. The English and the French pest everybody knows. The policy of the world is to hold the black man as the slave of society for time immemorial, but under God I would rather die and go to hell than to live like this. The spirit of the Lord is upon all flesh. Don't you know that we have no guns or anything? The District Attorney prosecuting Garvey said that we have guns, but we haven't a pistol. What we have is truth. And we will be heard. And God Almighty will change this world because Jehovah has said truth will be heard. We cannot do anything at this stage by fighting, but we will convince the world. The British Government has more black subjects than white ones. The British Empire has got less than one hundred million. We have two or three hundred million. And if it be their Empire or if there be any umpiring in the Empire, we will be heard. France. A fine nation. God bless the French! Bigger than anybody else. Gives us lots of liberty. France has more black Frenchmen than white. And from now on we want the President to know there are more black ones, than white ones. Belgium has more black citizens than she has white citizens. And we have got some scattered all over the world. Not only in our homeland, but everywhere in the world. And not only the black folks of the world are waking up, but in India, too. They may have no guns, but they are saying "Let's go." [Loud applause.] In India and Japan and China and in Australia and in the islands of the sea they are waking up and saying: "We are scattered around, and we want to come together. You don't want to live with us. We propose to lay the foundation for our coming together, so that if you don't want to be with us you can come over and visit us sometimes. [Applause.] I am just as sure that it is coming as I am living today. The Negroes here are just Negroes in quarters. The Negroes are out yonder. Tall sons and daughters, broad shoulders, men that can eat men alive." [Laughter.] . . .

. . . Talk about the Black Star Line![6] What have the white folks to do with our Black Star Line anyway? Wasting the people's money! Well, come back. Who wanted the Government's money? The harbor of Philadelphia is blocked with ships, ships are rotting in Brooklyn, in Galveston and Charleston—the merchant marine is not functioning. The Shipping Board is not doing anything. You had one thousand years and you could not do it. We want to see how our ships look now. And under God we are going to get some ships. [Loud applause.] It may not pay. But automobiles do not pay, yet we ride in them sometimes. We are going to get some ships and ride in them. Your protest is to keep the organization together. Raise more money and make more fuss and the country is going to rise. I believe the spirit is on you.

And do you think we are going to let them divide Africa now? Just as we did then, we are going to stand in the days to come. We are going to hurt nobody unless you get between us and the promised land. I see a time when black people everywhere are going to rise and shine, for the lie is given and the Light of God is shining on the books. I see a larger day. I see a city of schools and churches. I see cities everywhere, extending from the Cape of Good Hope to Cairo in Egypt. I see a crowd yonder extending from the Zambesi to the Niger River. I see this race of mine waking up, hand in hand, American and what not, pressing on together, having a home together. Let nobody deceive you. It may take a year. It may take ten thousand years. But under God the hour will come when Ethiopia shall stretch forth her hand unto God and black men shall hold their heads high, and the name of Marcus Garvey shall be embalmed in our memories and our children's through long ages. For, if in the future, as in the past, men continue to prize ennobling gifts used for the higher purpose and the advancement of a race, then at Marcus Garvey's tomb generations yet unborn shall pay homage till the stars sink at the day of Judgment. [Prolonged applause.]

### NOTES

*Sermon source:* This message is excerpted from *Black Redemption: Churchmen Speak for the Garvey Movement.*

1. Joel 2:28a (King James Version).
2. Joel 2:28b (KJV).
3. Joel 2:28b (KJV).
4. See Luke 4:18 (KJV).
5. See Mark 13:7–9 (KJV).
6. The Black Star Line was the steamship company operated by Marcus Garvey and the Universal Negro Improvement Association from 1919 to 1922. Due to mismanagement, theft and sabotage by the Bureau of Investigation (now the FBI), the steamship company lost a large sum of money and failed. In spite of its short run, many blacks viewed the Black Star Line as symbolic of the ability of blacks to surmount any challenge, even a business challenge, if given the training and opportunity.

### BIBLIOGRAPHICAL SOURCES

Burkett, Randall K. *Black Redemption: Churchmen Speak for the Garvey Movement*. Philadelphia: Temple University Press, 1978.

Moses, William Henry. *The Colored Baptists' Family Tree: A Compendium of organized Negro Baptists Church History showing the colored American Baptist family normally united in the one national Baptist Convention of the U.S.A.* Nashville, TN: The Sunday School Publishing Board of the National Baptist Convention of the United States of America, 1925.

——— *The Life of Our Lord: The Four Gospels Interwoven in one continuous narrative in the exact words of Matthew, Mark, Luke and John, arranged in chronological order, into chapters, sections and topics for historical and devotional study*. Nashville, TN: National Baptist Publishing Board, 1913.

———. *The White Peril*. Philadelphia: Lisle-Carey Press, 1919.

## ELIAS CAMP MORRIS

*(1855–1922)*

Elias Camp Morris was born in May 1855 near the small town of Springplace, Georgia, the son of the slaves James and Cora C. Morris, who lived on separate farms. Morris's father, who was a literate craftsman, taught his children to read and write when he came for his twice weekly visit. After the Civil War, Elias and his family moved to Tennessee and then to Alabama. After both parents died when he was fourteen, he worked as an apprentice to his cousin, who was a local shoemaker and a preacher. After three years, Morris began his own shoe repair business. This spirit of entrepreneurship continued throughout Morris's life, and at his death, he held a considerable financial portfolio. He was licensed to preach while in Alabama and attended the Nashville Institute for a year.

At the age of twenty-two, Morris moved to Helena, Arkansas, where, three years later, he was appointed to his first pastorate at the Centennial Baptist Church. He remained there for the rest of his life. He eventually became politically active with the Republican Party in Arkansas. In 1884, he married Fannie Austin, and to this union five children were born.

For many years, Morris struggled for parity for blacks in the Republican Party and was a delegate to the Republican National Convention. Eventually, Morris urged blacks to leave the Republican Party, which had been the party of Lincoln. He also served as president of the Arkansas State National Baptist Convention for more than thirty years and during his tenure began a denominational newspaper (the *Baptist Vanguard*) and helped establish the Arkansas Baptist College in Little Rock.

In 1895, Morris became the president of the National Baptist Convention, U.S.A., a new organization that combined three black Baptist conventions. He remained as president for twenty-seven years. During his tenure the Baptist Youth Department, the Women's Auxiliary, a retirement fund for preachers, and a publishing house were created. After a denominational battle over ownership of the publishing house, the convention was restructured and became the National Baptist Convention, U.S.A., Inc. At the time of his death, the organization for which he served as the first president and led for nearly thirty years was the largest black denomination in America with more than two million members and an extensive foreign mission program. E.C. Morris helped lead Baptists to denominational stability.

As the president of the united body, Morris weathered numerous storms. By all accounts, from friends and foes, much of the success that Morris was able to achieve and his long tenure as leader was due to his management and negotiation skills and, importantly, to his great ability as an orator. His eulogist, Washington Monroe Taylor, said, "He preached the gospel with the Holy Ghost sent down from heaven. The unction that attended his word was not merely like the oil that ran down Aaron's beard; it was like the anointing of the Spirit that penetrates the heart. He preached with his soul full of glory."[1]

In addition to leading a convention and business ventures, in the early 1900s, Morris was appointed as minister to the Belgian Congo—at the time a dictatorship—by President Theodore Roosevelt. Morris reported cruel treatment of the Belgians by their leaders and urged the President to intervene.

• • •

*At its 1899 convention, President Morris addressed the parent body in Nashville. Parts of that speech are reprinted here. In it, Morris shows not only his keen understanding of the workings of the convention, but also uses his platform as president to explain why he urges Negroes to build their own businesses and schools and communities. The speech also encourages the 1.7 million member group to take action on behalf of the Negro race.*

## Presidential Address to the National Baptist Convention (1899)

Brethren of the Convention, Ladies, and Gentlemen:

Again, by permission of a kind Providence, I have the honor of coming before you to deliver my annual address as President of your great Convention. I congratulate you upon the wonderful record and unparalleled progress made by the Baptists since the organization of this Convention. It came into existence at the right time and for the very purposes it has so ably served—namely, to save this wing of our great and invincible denomination from disgrace; to show that in the onward movement of the great army of God in the world Negro Baptists are a potent factor. Until thrown into a separate organization, such as this, it was not known what part those of our race in Baptist churches were bearing in the mighty conquest against the kingdom of darkness and in the upbuilding of the Master's kingdom on earth.

The wisdom which dictated such an organization was, in my opinion, divine. Had it not been divine, the strong and well-organized forces which have conspired to overthrow every enterprise put on foot by this Convention would have succeeded. But I am glad to say that instead of being overthrown, the Convention and its enterprises are stronger to-day than at any time before, and it has, by its peerless record, drawn to it many who once stood in open rebellion against its objects. It has been my opinion for some time that the leaders in this Convention have been for many years misunderstood, and, therefore, misrepresented, and that when the real objects and policy of the leaders are fully known all opposition will cease, and we will have the encouragement and cooperation of all the great Baptist societies in the country.

I wish to repeat what I have said on several occasions: that this Society entertains no ill will toward any other Christian organization in the world. It seeks to be on friendly terms with all, and the charge that this organization means to draw the color line, and thereby create prejudice in "Negro" Christians against "white" Christians, is without foundation. We admit, however, that practically, and not constitutionally, the color line has been drawn by the establishment of churches and schools for the "colored people" and the employment of missionaries, colporteurs, et cetera, to the colored people, which has resulted in the organization of associations and conventions by the Negroes in more than half of the States in the Union. And since these organizations exist, it is the duty of all to do everything in their power to build up the cause of Christ in and through these agencies.

But if these separate organizations did not exist, there is a reason for the existence of a National Baptist Convention, because, owing to the agitation of the slavery question, the white Baptists of the North and South had divided into two societies, represented respectively by Northern Baptists and Southern Baptists and when the cause of the division had been removed, the Northern Baptists went immediately to work to educate and evangelize the emancipated. The Southern white people soon fell in line and began by a system of taxation to aid the emancipated in acquiring a common school education, and many of the Southern white ministers lent their aid in church work. But their organizations remained separate and are separate to-day. Hence, it was one of the prime objects of the promoters of this Convention to obliterate all sectional lines among Baptists and have one grand national society, which would know no North, no South, no East, no West; and in this we have been successful. From Maine to California we are one, notwithstanding the efforts of designing men to disrupt the Convention by making false publications concerning it. If you will pardon the particular reference, I will say that one of our number who for three years held official position in this Convention had published in a little paper out in North Carolina the startling statement that the "Convention has departed from the New Testament standard and has turned into an ecclesiastical body; and that it exists for political purposes, the President exercising his powers the year round, attempting to dictate the policy for one million seven hundred thousand Baptists." Others of our ranks have styled us ingrates—all because we

*Dare to be a Daniel,*
*Dare to stand alone! Dare to have a purpose firm!*
*Dare to make it known!*[2]

But against all we have marched steadily on, and disproved all that has been said, until we have enlisted the cooperation of the most thoughtful Negro Baptists throughout the civilized world. We have endeavored to avoid any entangling alliances with other Baptist organizations, but have prayed for and sought to maintain friendly relations with all. I cannot account for the apparent disposition of some of our Baptist societies to ignore utterly the existence of the National Baptist Convention. Since the Negro Baptists in all the States of this great Union are in harmony with the work of this Convention and are contributors to its objects, there can be no good reason why any organization should attempt to form alliances with the respective States to do the very work which the Convention is endeavoring to do. In the matter of Cuban missions, notwithstanding the fact that this Convention has declared its purpose to do mission work in Cuba, other Baptist societies which had a similar purpose in view, consulted and even had correspondence with persons not officially connected with the National Convention upon the matter of cooperation. This breach of fraternal courtesy is not understood, except it be that others think that they can more easily handle our people by having them divided than by recognizing an organization with an official Board or Boards empowered by the constitution to act for the whole body. That the time will come when all the Baptist societies in America will recognize the existence of this Society, I have not the slightest doubt; but for reasons known only to themselves they have not done so yet.

A prominent minister of our denomination told me a few weeks ago at Greenville, Mississippi, that he had opposed the work of the National Baptist Convention because he did not think it possible to get the Negro Baptists of this country organized, and that their notions of church independence and church sovereignty were such as to preclude any such thing as a national organization. "But," says he, "I see you are about to get them together." I was a bit modest in giving a reply at that time, but I will assure you, my brethren, that the time is not far away when our organization will be so systematic that at the pressing of a button the Baptists from Maine to California and from the Canadian border to the Gulf of Mexico will spring to action as one man, and there will be a oneness of faith, a oneness of purpose in holding forth the truths of that Book which teaches that there is but one God.

I stated that the Convention had declared its purpose to do mission work in Cuba. And it did, at the meeting held in Kansas City one year ago, appoint a commission to visit the island with a view of ascertaining the moral, religious, and educational status of the Cuban people. An appeal was made to the churches to send up money to pay the expenses of the commissioners, and I am glad to say that many churches responded to the appeal and sent money to the Treasurer of our Convention. The commission, owing to the unsettled state of affairs, thought it would be a useless expenditure of money to go there at the time designated by the Convention; hence, the money sent is now in the treasury subject to the orders of the Convention. The principal points in Cuba had been entered through the agency of our Foreign Mission Board and other Baptist societies before the time had come for the committee to go out, so that we may say, Baptist missions are already under way in Cuba. Providence seems to have favored us in that Rev. Campbell and wife were secured by our Board, and that Dr. C.T. Walker and Rev. Richard Carroll were given chaplaincies in the army. Dr. Walker succeeded in gaining one hundred conversions while there, and you may surmise the rest. We are in duty bound to aid in carrying the Gospel to the Cuban people. Like the black troopers who went up El Caney and saved the lives of their white comrades from destruction, so must the Negro Baptists of this country join their white brethren in carrying the Gospel of the Son of God to that people.

## The Philippine Affair

. . . The policy of our government in the prosecution of the Philippine war has been severely criticised, and even now, many are openly opposing the further prosecution of the war. Necessarily, Christians are opposed to armed conflicts and bloodshed. And we contend that all international questions can and should be settled by arbitration. The war which is now upon us has divided our country into two strong factions—Expansionists and Anti-Expansionists, and the contention growing out of the points of this division makes the horizon dark with commotion, and calls to Christians everywhere to appeal to that God who holds the reins of governments, that he might intervene and establish peace among the nations. . . .

## Law and Order Versus a Race Problem

In our domestic relations to this country, many of our people feel that they have a just cause to complain of the treatment they receive at the hands of the people among whom they live. And the man is indeed blind who cannot see that the race feeling in this country has grown continually for the last two decades. But since the organic law of the land stands unimpeached, there is room left to inquire, is it only race hatred, or is it not the out-growth of a lawless spirit which has taken possession of many of the people in this country? Perhaps it appeared when this spirit of anarchy first took hold in this country that it was directed to a particular class or race of people. But that can no longer be said. For, indeed, it is evident that those who will forget themselves so far as to take the laws into their own hands and hang, shoot down, and burn helpless Negroes, will ere long turn and slaughter one another. Indeed, such is the case now. Mob violence is not confined to any particular section of our country. The same disregard for law and order which exists in the South when a Negro is involved, exists in the North when the miners or other laborers are involved. The people have become crazed and have lost their respect for the law and the administrators of the law, and unless there is a change no man will be secure in life or property. The apologies which are being given for the mob's shameful work, by no means remove the fact that there is a growing disregard for the laws of our country. I would counsel my people everywhere to be law-abiding, no matter how much they may suffer thereby. It does not stand to reason that the whole race is a set of cowards because the inhuman treatment administered to members of our race is not resented. But one thing is true: the men who will take the laws into their own hands and thereby prevent the piercing rays of the letter and spirit of the law from shining through the courts upon the crimes committed, are themselves a set of cowards. Ministers of the Gospel and good people everywhere should lift their voices against all classes of crime which is blackening the record of our country. The man who will not lift his voice in defense of the sacredness of the home and the chastity of the women in this country, is unworthy to be called a man. It is but right that the man who breaks open the sacred precincts of the home and perpetrates a dastardly deed—it is but right that he be made to pay the penalty of the inhuman act. But let all such be done by and through the law. The wisest and most prudent men of our country foresee the evils which threaten the perpetuity of our republican institutions if the present disregard for law and order be kept up. The agitations which are going on will soon bring a reaction. Reason will again be enthroned; the laws of the country, like the laws of God will be supreme; and from the least to the greatest, the people will "submit to every ordinance of man, for the Lord's sake."

Those who are inclined to the opinion that there is a great "Race Problem" confronting us, are asked to look beyond racial lines for a moment and behold the civil strife in many of the States in the Union where the State militia, United States marshals and sheriffs with strong guard, are called upon to protect life and property, to stand and guarantee the moving of the wheels of commerce, while the cries of hungry women and children force husbands, fathers, and brothers to wage open conflict with the administrators of the law, and then they will modify their opinion as to a race problem and agree that a serious law and order problem confronts the people of this country.

## A Look Ahead

Thirty-six years have passed since the shackles of slavery were broken from the limbs of our people in this country. And these have been years of trial and conflict of which the Negro Baptists have borne no little part. In this brief period they have succeeded in building more schools and colleges than any other denomination of Negro Christians, and have enrolled as members of their churches more than all the rest combined. For this glorious heritage we sincerely thank God, and have a heart full of love for all who have aided in any way to bring about such a condition. But the fact that such a vast army has volunteered to follow the lead of those who contend for the principles enunciated at Olivet and for which the Apostles suffered and died; for which Bunyan, Hall, Roger Williams, Spurgeon, and an innumerable host of others battled to uphold, it is but meet that we pause to ask: What of the future? A very large number of the one million seven hundred thousand Negro Baptists are crude and undeveloped. They know but little of the practical side of Christianity. The work of developing these that they may become the safe guardians of the undying principles which have distinguished our Church in all ages of the Christian era, is no small task. But I assure you, my brethren, that we have the men and means to keep our organization abreast of the times. And we will keep it so if we will only be united and submit to proper leadership, I have no doubt that the census of 1900 will show nearly two million Negro Baptists in this country. Can you as leaders trust that host to support the present and future enterprises as you trusted them in the past to build and support churches all over this land? The charge of mutiny seldom ever comes against a Baptist; and as they have been loyal and true to their local organizations, so will they be to this Convention and every enterprise put in motion by it.

We are nearing the close of the present century, the most remarkable in many respects of all the centuries since the dawn of creation. And, without reference to the wonderful achievements in steam, printing, and electricity, and many more unparalleled discoveries and inventions, I come to say that when the light from the eternal hills announced the birth of the nineteenth century, our race—our fathers and mothers—groaned in the grasp of slavery, and held the place of goods and chattels. But by the direction of an unerring providence, when a little past the meridian of the century, a decree was handed down that the "slaves are and henceforth shall be free." Hence, I conclude that one of the marvels of the century will be that although it opened and looked for sixty-three years on a race of slaves, it closes with that same race a happy, free people, having built more churches and school houses, in proportion to their numbers, than any people dwelling beneath the sun. While the flickering light and agonizing groans of the nineteenth century are being lost in the misty and retreating past, let us look ahead. A little less than sixteen months from now that tireless steed, Time, will come forth and announce the birth of the twentieth century. Already in the distance can be heard the thunder of his neck and the fury of his nostrils, and the inhabitants of the world are preparing to greet his coming. Many of the great Christian societies are planning to make the opening year the most important and aggressive in Christian missions since the beginning of the New Dispensation. Some are asking for a million dollars, some for half a million, and some for still less. And as I see these great societies line up as if on dress parade and call for more men and means to go more strongly against the power of darkness, I am forced to ask: What is the duty of the Negro Baptists? The answer comes back that as the nineteenth century opened upon us as slaves and closed upon us as freemen, so may the Gospel, borne on the tongues of the liberated, set at liberty during the twentieth century, the millions bound in heathen darkness. . . .

## NOTES

*Sermon source:* E.C. Morris's *Sermons, Addresses and Reminiscences and Important Correspondence, with a Picture Gallery of Eminent Ministers and Scholars* (Nashville, TN: National Baptist Publishing Board, 1901). Electronic edition at Documenting the American South, University of North Carolina at Chapel Hill Digitization Project, http://docsouth.unc.edu/church/morris/menu.html (accessed March 11, 2003).

1. Washington Monroe Taylor, "The Eulogy of E.C. Morris," *The African American Pulpit* 5, no. 4 (Fall 2002).

2. These lines are taken from the song "Dare to Be a Daniel," written in 1873 by Philip P. Bliss.

### *Bibliographical Sources*

Brawley, Edward M., ed. *The Negro Baptist Pulpit.* 1890. Reprint, Freeport, NY: Books for Libraries Press, 1971.

Griffin, Marvin C., ed. *The President Speaks: Annual Addresses Delivered to the National Baptist Convention of America, 1898–1986.* Nashville, TN: National Baptist Convention, 1989.

Jackson, Joseph Harrison. *A Story of Christian Activism: The History of the National Baptist Convention, U.S.A. Inc.* Nashville, TN: Townsend Press, 1980, chapter 2.

Morris, E.C. *Sermons, Addresses and Reminiscences and Important Correspondence, with a Picture Gallery of Eminent Ministers and Scholars.* Nashville, TN: National Baptist Publishing Board, 1901.

Murphy, Larry G., J. Gordon Melton, and Gary L. Ward. *Encyclopedia of African American Religions.* New York: Garland Publishing, 1993.

## JAMES PRESTON POINDEXTER

*(1819–1907)*

James Poindexter was born in 1819 in Richmond, Virginia, to Evelina Poindexter, a black woman with Cherokee blood; she died when James was four. Little is known of his father, except that his name was Joseph Poindexter and that he was a white man who worked for a newspaper and may have been the brother of George Poindexter, the second governor of Mississippi. At age ten James Poindexter was already fending for himself as a barber's assistant, working for a relative. He educated himself, learning as he served some of Richmond's aristocracy. He moved to Ohio, settling in Columbus, where he was baptized at the Second Baptist Church. He was married in the early 1840s, ordained in 1849, and in 1862 became pastor of Second Baptist Church, where he remained for almost forty years.

By appointment of the governor, he served for four years as a trustee of the Institute for the Blind of Ohio. He also served for four years as a member of the Columbus city council and was its vice president. He was a member of the city's school board, a position he won over a Democratic opponent. He became noted for his charged advocacy of equal education for black students. Poindexter said in one school board meeting, "The white youth of Ohio are reaping a rich harvest from our public schools; the colored youth are gleaning but little. . . . No people ever attached greater value to education than do the colored people. They are more worried about their ignorance than about their poverty; they feel that slavery, in depriving them of the means of education, inflicted upon them greater wrong than it did in working them two hundred years without pay."[1]

In addition to being a proponent of equal education for blacks, Poindexter was a celebrated antislavery advocate, serving as one of the leaders of one of the strongest stations of the Underground Railroad and of an antislavery group. Poindexter was also the first black man in Ohio nominated by the Republican Party to run for a seat in the House of Representatives, but he was defeated at the polls. He was also appointed a trustee of Ohio University at Athens, but the state senate would not confirm it. He did get to serve as the first black foreman of an Ohio grand jury. The first public housing project built in Columbus (Poindexter Village) was named for him.

• • •

*Poindexter's preaching was thoughtful, yet blunt. His theology was often conservative. The first excerpt addresses the subject of "pulpit and politics" in a message delivered by Poindexter before the Ohio Baptist Pastor's Union, of which he was the only black member.*

## Speech Before the Ohio Baptist Pastor's Union (1889)

Nor can the preacher more than any other citizen plead his religious work or the sacredness of that work as an exemption from duty. Going to the Bible to learn the relation of the pulpit to politics, and accepting the prophets, Christ and the apostles and the pulpit of their times, and their precepts and examples as the guide of the pulpit to-day, I think that the conclusion will be that wherever there is a sin to be rebuked, no matter by whom committed, and ill to be averted or good to be achieved by our country or mankind, there is a place for the pulpit to make itself felt and heard. The truth is, all the help the preachers and all other good and worthy citizens can give by taking hold of politics is needed in order to keep the government out of bad hands and secure the ends for which governments are formed.

Now it is a fact worthy of note in this connection that objections to preachers holding with politics generally comes from the thing assailed. Advocates of slavery never objected to the preachers who, in or out of the pulpit, maintained that the Bible sanctions slavery, or preached often from the text "Servants be obedient to your masters." Men who gave their sympathy to the rebellion never scolded the preacher who argued that the Constitution conferred no authority on the government to coerce a State or one who justified the legislator who said, "not a dollar and not a man to whip the South," nor would man pecuniarily interested in the whiskey and beer traffic utter a note of dissent if all preachers would unite in denouncing legislative intervention to control that traffic as a sumptuary legislation. It will not be denied that some good persons deprecate the presence of the pulpit in politics; that it is so unclean a thing that it cannot be touched without taint, unfitting one for spiritual usefulness. Such persons are deceived, as a careful perusal of the Bible with careful inspection of the lives, private and public, of the preachers referred to, will show.

✦ ✦ ✦

*Poindexter thundered this sermon against electoral corruption from his pulpit in vehement and powerful language on October 5, 1885. He held up to scorn and ridicule those who bought votes as well as those who sold them. He raised in 1885 a subject which is still explored in African American churches during elections.*

## The Crime of Buying and Selling Votes (October 5, 1885)

. . . that our votes are not ours in any such sense that we *may* dispose of them as we choose for our own pleasure *or* profit, as we may any other kind of property. They belong to the whole people; they are ours in trust to be conscientiously used by us to promote the safety, peace and prosperity of the whole. The trust itself is the highest, most important, most sacred ever vouchsafed by the Almighty God to a free self-governing people; in the exercise of it, it is the primary duty of the voter to see to it that the individual for whom he votes is an honest, capable man, one who knows how to discharge the duties of the office and has the integrity to discharge those duties in the light of an all-wise God. . . .

When the bad men of the South wanted to defeat all the results of the war, they brought to bear on the colored people the persuasiveness of the revolver, bowie knife, shotgun and halter, and when the world stood aghast and cried shame, shame, the South responded, "No, no, not at all, not at all; if the North was in our place it would do as we do;

it would be compelled to do as we do. The Negro is ignorant and as a consequence he is vicious, cannot tell the truth, steals everything he puts his hands upon, and must be scourged to his work, is insulting to white people; our women shudder when they meet him on the highway and have a right to; and above all and worse than all, he won't vote with his old masters." . . .

This self-evident damning lie was exhibited *as* a true bill against the Southern people by too many good people of the North, and as a consequence they were left to the tender mercies of the men whom they had helped to defeat in their cherished object, and that to destroy the only free government on the earth. I denounce this charge against the colored people of the South. A self-evident lie, because the men most entitled to be believed—men, who, when the fight was over, accepted the situation and went to work to rebuild their prostrate South—say it is a lie: say the Negro is a good citizen: say that when the strong men of the Confederacy were in the army, their women and children were undisturbed and safe in the hands of the Negro, and no single case of the outrages now so lavishly attributed to them, and so readily believed in the North, was known to occur. I denounce the charge as a damning lie on the colored man, because it does not present him as he is, but does present him as the monster two and a half centuries of barbarous oppression would seem calculated to make him, and thus obtained that credence in the North, which, to its shame, leaves the poor creature in a condition worse than when he was a slave.

## *Notes*

*Sermon source:* Both sermons from William J. Simmons's *Men of Mark*, 261–64.

1. Myron Seifert, *Early Black History in the Columbus Public Schools*, 13, found in the Columbus, Ohio, Board of Education Archives.

## *Bibliographical Sources*

Arnett, Benjamin William. *The Centennial Jubilee of Freedom at Columbus, Ohio, Saturday, September 22, 1888: Orations, Poems, and Addresses.* Xenia, OH: The Aldine Printing House, 1888.

Minor, Richard Clyde. "James Preston Poindexter, Elder Statesman of Columbus." *Journal of the Ohio Historical Society* 56, no. 3 (July 1947): 266–86.

Simmons, William J. *Men of Mark: Eminent, Progressive and Rising.* 1887. Reprint, Chicago: Johnson Publishing Company, 1970.

Woodson, Carter G. *The History of the Negro Church.* Washington, DC: Associated Publishers, 1921.

# JOSEPH CHARLES PRICE

*(1854–1893)*

All historical records attest that one of the greatest voices of the nineteenth century was Joseph C. Price. Price was born an only child in Elizabeth City, North Carolina, in 1854. His father, Charles Dozier, was a slave, but his mother, Emily Pailin, was a free woman and because the laws conveyed status through the mother, Joseph was born free. Joseph's father was sold off and his mother married David Price, whose last name Joseph took.

As a child, Joseph attended the St. Cyprian Episcopal School, which was also attended by the likes of Alexander Crummel and Henry Highland Garnett. Price became a teacher and principal in North Carolina. He went on to briefly attend Shaw University, and after accepting the call to ministry, attended Lincoln University in Pennsylvania. He received oratorical awards throughout his educational career. Price's biography said that "by powers of speech he gained for himself the sobriquet of 'Lion of the Lyceum.'"[1] Theodore Cuyler said of Price in the *New York Evangelist* in 1887, "J.C. Price of North Carolina is a fair match for [Frederick] Douglass in eloquence and culture. He has a style peculiarly his own; but his first sentences pleasingly captivate his audience, and his 'wit and wisdom' with a combination of rhetoric and logic, poured forth in such masterly strains of eloquence, claims his hearers as influenced by magic."[2]

Price was licensed to preach in 1876 by the AMEZ Church. In 1881, Price gained national and international fame for the speech he gave during the World Methodist Conference in London. After it, the London *Times* called him "The World's Orator."[3] Price was the first black preacher to stand in the pulpit of the famous Brooklyn minister and brother of Harriet Beecher Stowe, Henry Ward Beecher. He also preached for Charles Spurgeon while in London. He married Jennie Smallwood and they had five children: William, Louise, Alma, Joseph, and Josie. Despite being nominated for the bishopric and offered many other jobs, including Minister Plenipotentiary to Liberia by President Grover Cleveland, his heart and main energies belonged to Livingston College in North Carolina, of which he was cofounder and first president. He also supported the temperance movement and delivered many speeches for this cause. Price never became a pastor. Unfortunately, he died of Bright's disease at the young age of thirty-nine. Price was so beloved and missed that newspapers around the country noted his passing. George C. Rowe even penned a poem. It said in part:

*A star arose at close of night:*
*'tis dark before the dawn;*
*A brilliant star, a righteous light, Foretoken of the morn—*
*The day when the oppressor's hand should palsied be throughout the land.*
*A man of influence and power, Who laid himself with grace,*
*Upon the altar of his God, An offering for his race.*
*E'er prodigal of strength and thought,*
*And from his race withholding nought.*
*He cried: "If I'd a thousand tongues, And each a thunderbolt;*
*I'd turn them on in mighty power, Like an electric volt;*
*I'd send them forth with lightning pace—To help and elevate my race!"*

• • •

*Although Price gave many sermons and speeches, he is best known for his speech before the National Education Association in 1890, lines from which are included in the Rowe poem above. Price addressed those who wanted to segregate the National Education Association.*

## Education and the Race Problem (1890)

If I had a thousand tongues and each tongue were a thousand thunderbolts and each thunderbolt had a thousand voices, I would use them all today to help you understand a loyal and misrepresented and misjudged people.

The real question implied in this subject, as I understand it, is, Will education solve the race problem? With such an idea in view, it is but proper that we have some conception of what the problem is, in order that we may select the best means for its solution; for it is evident that all remedies, whether for the removal of disorders in the body, or in the social state—whether in physianthropy or sociology—must be in proportion to their affected parts or abnormal conditions.

It is further observable that the length of time a malady is allowed to grow, or an evil condition is permitted to exist and develop baneful results, has much to do with the nature of the forces that will neutralize the growth or destroy the evil. It is not infrequently the case that the age of a complaint or an undesirable state of affairs has to determine, to a very large degree, the means of resistance, or the remedies which will effect the cure. More is true. As it is admitted that time is a large element in the stubbornness of a condition or evil, so it is also true that time, coupled with the highest wisdom of administration, becomes an indispensable element in producing the healthier and more desirable conditions. It is further patent to every thoughtful mind that there are complex irregularities in the human system, as well as in the body politic, that no single remedy or manner of procedure can regulate. In such cases we have to proceed step by step, and take only one phase of the complaint at a time; and the remedies that are efficient in one stage are totally inadequate to the other. Each stage has its peculiar prescription—some requiring milder, and others severer antidotes; and whenever these antidotes are used substitutionally, we are thwarted in our desired end, and our purposes often miscarry.

The negro problem is different from the Indian or Chinese question. In the negro, we find a commendable absence of all the stubborn and discordant characteristics which are peculiar to the Indian or the Chinaman; and yet the negro problem, together with its solution, is the all-absorbing topic of the country, and the negro, in the opinion of some, is the only destructive element, and least acceptable member of the body politic of America.

The race problem, as now understood, had its beginning in 1620, when the negroes were forced to accept this country as their home. So, in one form or another, the negro question has been before the country for two hundred and seventy years, and this question, with its constant and incident dangers, has been a source of anxiety and vexation, and rock of offense, during all those years.

Now if the difficulties involved in the problem inhere in the negro as a race, it is but natural that we should seek to change, not his color, but his character, under reasonable and fair encouragements to do so, and if they are the results of preconceived opinions, or even conscientious convictions, produced by unfavorable and misleading environments, these opinions and convictions must change—all other things being equal—with a change of the environments.

The "peculiar institution" continued to grow, with all its attendant evils, until it threatened the very life of the republic; so much so, until it was declared by one of the wisest men the country ever produced, that the nation could not live half free and half slave. Every means possible was called into requisition to solve this phase of the negro question in America, and it was only solved permanently and effectively by the bloody arbitrament of arms. Slavery is no more, and can never exist again in this country, simply because it was settled right. But this does not argue that every phase of this question must be settled in the same manner, or by the same means.

## What Do We Mean By the Solution of the Problem?

The solution of the race problem means the satisfactory and harmonious adjustment of the racial relation in the South and in the country as well, on the principles of humanity and justice. In other words, it is the concession to the negro of all the inalienable rights that belong to him as a man and as a member of that family of which God is the common Father; and the granting to him all the civil immunities and political privileges guaranteed to every other citizen by the authority and power of the Constitution of the American Government. To do this solves the problem; not to do it is to leave it unsolved; and to leave it unsolved, in the face of the growing numbers and increasing intelligence of the negro, is to intensify the bitterness between the races, and to involve both in a conflict more destructive and widespread than the country has hitherto witnessed.

## Slavery at the Bottom of It All

Slavery, as a system, degraded the negro to the level of the brute, because it denied him the untrammeled exercise of all the instincts of a higher and better manhood. It recognized no moral sensibility in man or woman, regarded no sacred and inviolable relation between husband and wife, sundered at will or caprice the tenderest ties that the human heart is capable of forming or the mind is able to conceive. Such a system had the support of the highest tribunal of men, and even the representatives of the church of God came to its rescue and defense, with all the weight of its divine authority and power. From the maternal knee, the table, the family altar, the forum, and the pulpit was the lesson taught that the person of sable hue and curly hair was a doomed, and therefore an inferior, race—not entitled to a place in the brotherhood of men. This impression, made on childhood's plastic nature, grew with his growth, and strengthened with the power of increasing years. To deepen the blot, and intensify the damning heresy, the law of the land wrote him down as a chattel, that is, cattle, and forbade the training of the mind and the culture of the heart, by making learning on his part, and teaching on the part of others, a crime. It is not surprising, then, that men brought up in the face of such a system for two hundred and fifty years should be skeptical as to the real manhood of the negro, and hesitate to give him a place in the one-blood family.

The feeling against the negro, which helps to make our race problem, is called prejudice, and is not without some grounds. For two hundred and fifty years the white man of the South saw only the animal, or mechanical, side of the negro. Wherever he looked, there was degradation, ignorance, superstition, darkness there, and nothing more, as he thought. The man was overshadowed and concealed by the debasing appetites and destructive and avaricious passions of the animal; therefore the race problem of to-day is not an anomaly—it is the natural and logical product of an environment of centuries. I am no pessimist. I do not believe we are approaching a race war in the South. I entertain an impression, which is rapidly deepening into a conviction, that the problem can and will be solved peaceably; but this can only be done by changing the character of the environment which has produced it. It is an unfavorable condition which has given the country a race problem, and it will never be solved until we put at work the forces that will give us a changed condition. This does not argue nor imply the removal of the environment, as is suggested by colonization, deportation, or amalgamation; but it does mean a transformation of the same environment.

## The Real Element of Power in the Race Problem

What is the great element of power in the race problem? It is opposition to the claims of manhood and constitutional rights as made by the negro or his friends, because it is thought that he is not in all things a man like other men. It is an avowed determination to resist the full exercise of his inalienable and God-given rights. It is a premeditated purpose not to give him justice. In some portions of the country this spirit is more violent than in others; but it manifests itself, in one form or another, the land over. Sometimes it denies to the man of the negro race the exercise of his elective franchise; refuses to accord him first-class accommodations in public highways of travel, on land or sea, when he pays for the same; denies him, however competent and qualified, an opportunity to earn an honest living, simply because he belongs to a different race; and seeks to organize a Southern Educational Association, because it is said that the National Educational Association "has some ways that do not at all accord with the conditions of Southern society," or "for obvious reasons"; and, as one has said, "to be out of smelling distance of the sable brother." When it is asked, Why this opposition, this determination, and this premeditated purpose against the human and constitutional rights of a man and citizen? we are told, directly and indirectly, that while there are rare and commendable exceptions, the race, as such, is ignorant, poverty-stricken, and degraded. Now if ignorance, poverty, and moral degradation are the grounds of objection against the negro, it is not difficult to discover that the knotty elements of the race problem are the intellectual, moral, and material conditions of the negro race. It is reasonable, therefore, to suppose that if we can find the means that will change these conditions, we have found a key to the problem, and gone a great distance toward its satisfactory solution. Of course none of us would argue that intelligence, or even education, is a panacea for all the ills of mankind; for, even when educated, a Nero, a Robespierre, a Benedict Arnold, an absconding state treasurer, or a New York sneak-thief, would not necessarily be impossibilities. I do not argue that increased intelligence, or multiplied facilities for education, will, by some magic spell, transform the negro into the symmetry, grace, and beauty of a Grecian embodiment of excellence. It is certainly not my humble task to attempt to prove that education will, in a day, or a decade, or a century, rid the black man of all the physical peculiarities and deformities, moral perversions and intellectual distortions which are the debasing and logical heritage of more than two and a half centuries of enslavement. It is, nevertheless, reasonable to assume that, admitting the ordinary human capabilities of the race, which no sane and fair-minded man will deny, it can be readily and justly predicated that if the same forces applied to other races are applied to the negro, and these forces are governed by the same eternal and incontrovertible principles, they will produce corresponding results and make the negro as acceptable to the brotherhood of men as any other race laying claims to the instincts of our common humanity. I believe that education, in the full sense of the term, is the most efficient and comprehensive means to this end, because in its results an answer is to be found to all the leading objections against the negro which enter into the make-up of the so-called race problem.

Let us examine more minutely these elements of the problem, in order to justify the reasonableness of our position. The Southern problem shows its intense forms most in those sections and States where the negroes are in the majority. This is because the whites, as they say, fear negro supremacy. This supremacy is feared on account of the ignorance of the negro voter. It is concluded that the majority of voters being ignorant, they would put ignorant or illiterate men in charge of the affairs of the county, State, or section; and this would work to the bankruptcy or destruction of the county, State or section thus governed or controlled. Hence, it is claimed that opposition to the exercise of negro franchise, by whatever means, is a patriotic duty—a matter of self-preservation. Now it is evident that so far as this objection is concerned, education or increased intelligence among those representing the majority is the remedy. Ignorance being the ground of objection, if this cause is removed (and it can be by widespread intelligence), the objection must disappear as the darkness recedes at the approach of the light of the sun. None of us, even negroes, desire to be officered by ignorant or incompetent men. It is the patriotic duty of every man to bring about such reforms as will put only the duly qualified in positions of responsibility and power. But this ought only to be done by lawful means and by forces that are acknowledged to be in every way legitimate and in harmony with the humane spirit of our times. Dr. T.T. Eaton, writing on the Southern problem, in the *Christian Union*, June 5, says: "It does seem a great outrage to practically deprive American citizens of the right to vote; but it is a greater outrage to destroy all the ends of government by putting an inferior and semi-barbarous race in control of a superior race who own the property and have the intelligence." It not only seems but is a great outrage to deprive American citizens of the right to vote, except on the conditions sustained by law, and not by mobs and the caprices of men. Such mob violence is the more reprehensible, when it is taken for granted that these outrages are the only way of escape from the conditions confronting us.

## What Ought To Be Done?

If the voter is unprepared to exercise his franchise aright, then prepare him for its intelligent use, or deprive him of it by constitutional enactments. The latter cannot now be done, but the former can and ought to be done, and by doing so we will save the negro from unlawful oppression and outrage simply because he claims his rights, and save the nation from the disgrace and burning shame because it denies him these rights. Intelligence is universally admitted to be the prime requisite for good-citizenship. Whenever this condition of things obtains there will be no necessity or fear of "destroying all the ends of government by putting a semi-barbarous race in control of a superior race who own the property and have the intelligence." For it is true and unalterable as expressed by Dr. A.G. Haygood, of Georgia, in his "Pleas for Progress," when he says: "Good government implies intelligence, and universal suffrage demands universal education." It cannot now be said, as it was stated fifty years ago, that a negro cannot be educated. The history of education among the colored people for a quarter of a century does not confirm the statement. The noble men and women who went into the South as missionaries, and felt their way through the smoke of battle and stepped over crimson battle-fields and among the wounded and the dying to bring intelligence to the negroes, were taunted as going on a fool's errand. But the tens of thousands of young men and women in the schools of high grade established by Northern service and philanthropy—a million negro children in the public schools of the South—are an imperishable monument to the wisdom of their action. I *again* quote from Dr. Haygood, who is an authority on this subject: "All told, fully fifty millions of dollars have gone into the work of their education since 1865. Of this fifty millions, more than half has been Southern money." The negroes have made more progress in elementary and other education during these twenty-three years than any other illiterate people in the world, and they have justified the philanthropy and public policy that made the expenditure.

## Whites Must Be Educated, As Well

It must be remembered, however, that there is more to be done than the education of the blacks, as a solution to the race problem; for much of the stubbornness of the question is involved in the ignorant, lawless and vicious whites of the South, who need education worse than many of the blacks. To educate one race and neglect the other, is to leave the problem half solved, for there is a class of whites in the South, to some extent, more degraded and hopeless in their mental and moral condition than the negro. This is the class to which many of the actual outrages are more attributable than to any other class. Educate these, as well as the blacks, and our problem is shorn of its strength. When we call to mind the fact that seventy per cent of the colored vote in the South is illiterate, and thirty per cent of the white vote in the same condition, it is not difficult for one to discern that education of the blacks and whites, as well, is not only necessary for the solution of the race problem and for good government, but for the progress and prosperity of that section where such illiteracy obtains. For the safety of the republic, the perpetuity of its glory and the stability of its institutions are commensurate, with the intelligence and morality of its citizens, whether they be black men or white men.

## The Poverty of the Negro

The poverty of the negro is another stubborn element of the problem. It is urged that the wealth and intelligence of the South must not suffer a man, if he is poor and black, to exercise the prerogatives of American citizenship. Strange doctrine this, in a republic which is a refuge for the oppressed from all lands under the sun, and the so-called land of the free! But will education help to remove this objectionable element in the negro? It is the object of all education to aid man in becoming a producer as well as a consumer. To enable men and women to make their way in life and contribute to the material wealth of their community or country, to develop the resources of their land, is the mainspring in the work of all our schools and public or private systems of training. From a material point of view we find that one of the great differences—in fact, contrasts—between the North and the South, is a difference of widespread intelligence. Labor, skilled or intelligent, coupled with the impetus arising from capital, will touch the South as with a magnetic hand, and that region with marvelous resources and immeasurable capabilities will blossom as the rose. It is a matter of observation and history that a section or country that seeks to keep its labor-producing class ignorant, keeps itself poor; and the nation or state that fails to provide for the education of its whole people, especially its industrial forces, is considered woefully lacking in statesmanship and devoid of the essential elements in material progress and prosperity. To this general rule the negro is no exception. To educate him, then, makes him an industrial factor of the state, and argues his own changed condition from repulsive property to more acceptable conditions of wealth. Whatever strengthens the negro of the South adds to the strength and wealth of that section; and nothing militates against the negro but militates against the South as well. Even in his present condition of illiteracy, the negro is evidently the backbone of the labor element of the South. He is, therefore, a wealth-producer now. Whether he reaps all the benefit of his labor or not, it is clear that he is the prime element in its growing and boasted prosperity. The late Henry W. Grady said, just before his death, that the negroes in his State [Georgia] paid taxes on twenty million dollars' worth of property, and that the negroes in the South contribute a billion dollars' worth of products every year to the material prosperity of that section. The Atlanta *Constitution*, speaking of the negroes in Texas, said recently that they own a million acres of land and pay taxes on twenty million dollars' worth of property, have two thousand churches, two thousand benevolent associations, ten high schools, three thousand teachers, twenty-three doctors, fifteen lawyers, one hundred merchants, five hundred mechanics, fifteen newspapers, hundreds of farmers and stockmen, and several inventors. Now these two States are but samples of the wealth-producing results of twenty-five years of labor. If this has been their progress when it is admitted they have been under the hampering influence of ignorance, not to speak of other disadvantages, it is fair to assume that under the stimulus of intelligence they will do a hundred-fold more, and year by year and decade by decade change their poverty-stricken state, and thus remove another element in the problem, and thereby hasten its solution.

But it is not necessary for me to stand in this intelligent and representative presence and argue the advantages of education to alter the material condition of countries or races. Intelligence and industry have always demanded the respectful consideration of men, no matter how intense their opinions to the contrary; and it has been their universal opinion that these forces have been the leverage to lift their less-fortunate fellows to their proper place on the plane of political and civil equality. These industrial forces are the things that must enter as a key into the solution of the problem. It will be as impossible to deny to a people thus gifted with intelligence and exercising it in wise and consistent efforts in the accumulation of wealth, their inalienable and constitutional rights, as it is to keep back the sweep of the cyclone with a wave of the hand, or hinder the swell of the sea by stamping on its shore.

## The Moral Condition of the Race

But it is further argued that the negro is not entitled to his rights in the human brotherhood, and under the constitution of his country, because his standard of morality is low. Now the question that at once presents itself, is this: Does education help to improve the moral condition of a people? If this be granted, it is not hard to conclude that such a means will be a long step toward the removal of this element of the problem. We will not assume, however, that education is a synonym for morality, for it is clear that many persons and some races claiming a superiority of intelligence are not always models of moral purity. But, while this is true, it is an unusual position for one to hold that intelligence is a hinderance to the development of virtuous tendencies. It is, rather, conceded that ignorance is a great source of immorality; and this is made emphatic when we take into consideration the fact that conscience, enlightened or unenlightened, determines to a large degree the moral acts of men. It cannot be denied that what may be termed an innate moral consciousness is subject to education in order to make it a safe guide in the realm of moral obligation. I think it is Dr. Buchner, who says in his "Treatise on Man": "It is a generally recognized fact, and moreover sufficiently proved by history, that the idea of morality in the general, as in the particular, becomes further and more strongly developed in proportion as culture, intelligence and knowledge of the necessary laws of the common weal increase." The negro's moral condition, against which objection is raised, is the result of his training in the peculiar institution. It taught him no moral obligations of the home, for it recognized no home in the civilized sense of the term; it rather encouraged him to violate the sacred bonds of husband and wife, because, in so doing, he was taught the advancement of the interest of his master in adding to the number and value of his human stock for the plantation or the market. He was prompted, under scanty provisions for physical sustenance, to appropriate his master's hog or chicken to his own strength and comfort, on the principle and argument that he was simply improving his master's property. When a woman was made to feel that her honor, which is the glory of every true woman, was not her right, but subject to the carnal caprice of a master, it is not strange that an impression thus deepened by centuries of outrage should make her rather lightly regard this honor just after escape from such a school and from under such a system of instruction. It is certainly apparent, in the light of what has already been done for the moral improvement of the negro, that education will undo much of that which slavery has done to him.

Hear what Dr. Haygood says: "No theory of universal education entertained by a rational people proposes knowledge as a substitute for virtue, or virtue as a substitute for knowledge. Both are necessary. Without virtue, knowledge is unreliable and dangerous; without knowledge, virtue is blind and impotent." . . . "I must say a word in defense," says this same authority, "of the negroes, particularly those living in the Southern States. Considering the antecedents of the race in Africa, in those States before the emancipation, and their condition to-day, the real surprise is that there is so much virtue and purity among them." . . . "Above all things," says Dr. Haygood, "let the white people set them better examples." Since progress has already been made in this direction, we are permitted to hope that education will continue its beneficent work in the moral reformation of the people. Education will certainly afford a better knowledge of the duties of the home, a keener appreciation of the obligations of the marriage state, a more consistent regard for the rights and the property of others, and a clearer conception of what virtue in womanhood signifies, and, therefore, a more determined purpose and means of defending that honor from the assaults of any man, even at the very risk of their lives.

### The Great Work To Be Done

The great work of education among negroes consists in leading them out of the errors which centuries of a debasing servitude fastened upon them;

but even when this is done, the negro will not be an embodiment of every moral excellence, but he will at least stand on the same plane of morals with the other representatives of our common and fallen humanity, and whatever is the possibility and hope of one will be the possibility and hope of the other, so far as education is concerned; for under it, we believe that the negro can be and do what any other race can do, from the tickling of the soil with his hoe and plow, to make it burst forth into life-giving fruitage, to the lifting of world upon world upon the lever of his thought, that they may instruct and entertain him as they pass his vision in grandeur in the heavens.

But do we find in the negro exclusively all the immorality involved in the solution of the race problem? Not by any means. After the necessary evidence is given which entitles a man to the recognition of his rights, and these rights are still denied, then, the one denying them becomes the moral law-breaker; for morality, according to a scholarly authority (and he is not writing on the race problem in America), may be defined as a law of mutual respect for the general and private equal rights of man for the purpose of securing general human happiness. Everything that injures or undermines this happiness and this respect, is evil; everything that advances them, is good. "The greatest sinners, therefore," says this authority, "are egoists, or those who place their own I higher than the interests and the lives of the common weal, and endeavor to satisfy it at the cost and to the injury of those possessing equal rights."

## Christian Education

We have said nothing of Christian education; but it is reasonable to conclude that white or black men, under the influence of Christian intelligence, are prepared to solve all the problems peculiar to our earthly state, for Christianity levels all the distinctions of race. It is this spirit that struck the conceit of the Jew and broke down the middle wall of cruel separation between him and the Gentile world. It taught the Greek that humanity was a term for the wide brotherhood of all races, which he did not realize before; for all other races were regarded and despised as barbarians by him until Paul, from Mars Hill, thundered in the eager eyes and anxious ears of the Athenian the new doctrine that God had made of one blood all nations of men to dwell on all the face of the earth. The Roman, according to Geike, considered all who did not belong to his own state, as hosts or enemies, and held that the only law between them and those who were not Romans was that of the strong to subjugate such races, if they could, plunder their possessions, and make the people slaves.

"It was left to Christ," says this authority, "to proclaim the brotherhood of all nations by revealing God as their common Father in Heaven." If Christian education or a full knowledge of the principles of Christianity will not solve our relations with men, we are seriously at fault in our professed religion, and deplorable in our spiritual condition. For a people imbued with the spirit of the Christ idea cannot defraud a brother of a penny, nor rob him of his labor, nor deny him the rights which he has in common with other men; for by these principles we are taught to

*"Evince your ardent love for God By the kind deeds ye do for men."*

Dr. Chapin well says: "The great doctrine of human brotherhood, of the worth of a man, that he is not to be trod upon as a footstool or dashed in pieces as a worthless vessel, and the doctrines of popular liberty, education, and reform—all these have become active and every-day truths under the influence of Christianity." If Christian education is not to produce these results, the country and the race have a dark and uninviting future, for one has truly said, "There are mysteries which, if not solved by the truths of Christianity, darken the universe."

But I do not despair of the solution of the problem under Christian intelligence, as it radiates from the indiscriminating Cross of Calvary. For the principles of this grand system, both in the hearts and in the dominion of men, are all-conquering, either sooner or later, in their onward sweep around the world. No error can forever withstand their power. It may be stubborn and even violent for awhile, but it must eventually give way to truth for it is unalterable, as declared by Dr. Chapin, that "before the love which is in God, all things are sure to come around to His standard, and the most gigantic iniquity of earth strikes its head at last against the beam of God's providence and goes down."

## NOTES

*Sermon source:* The speech was published in *The National Education Association Journal of Proceedings and Addresses* (Topeka: Kansas Publishing, 1890). The first verse of the speech is not contained in the NEA materials but was indicated in Walls, *Joseph Charles Price, Educator and Race Leader,* 267–76. This version of the speech is taken from Philip S. Foner and Robert James Branham, eds., *Lift Every Voice: African American Oratory 1787–1900* (Tuscaloosa: University of Alabama Press, 1998).

1. Walls, *Joseph Charles Price, Educator and Race Leader,* 42.
2. Ibid., 309.
3. Ibid., 338.

### *Bibliographical Sources*

Foggie, Charles Herbert. *The Social Significance of Joseph Charles Price and His Times (1854–1893).* M.A. thesis, Boston University, 1939.

Jewell, James William. *Praise in Verse of the Leader of Our Race, Joseph Charles Price.* Salisbury, NC: n.p., 1894.

———. *I Am Looking Down on Your Proceedings; An Interpretation of the Life of Joseph Charles Price.* Salisbury, NC: n.p., n.d.

Rountree, Louise M. *An Annotated Bibliography on Joseph Charles Price, 1882–1893, Founder of Livingston College.* Salisbury, NC: n.p., 1963 (revised edition).

Walls, William Jacob. *Joseph Charles Price, Educator and Race Leader.* Boston: Christopher, 1943.

Yandle, Paul David. *Joseph Charles Price and the Southern Problem.* M.A. Thesis, Wake Forest University, 1990.

———. "Joseph Charles Price and His 'Peculiar Work.'" *North Carolina Historical Review* 70, no. 1 (January 1993): 40–56; 70, no. 2 (April 1993): 130–52.

# MARY LENA LEWIS TATE
*(1871–1930)*

Mary Lena (later also called Mary Magdalena) Street was born January 5, 1871, in Steel Springs, Tennessee, to Belfield Street and Nancy (Hall) Street. She was one of nine children. Both of her parents had children from previous marriages; Belfield and Nancy had four children from their union: Mary, Martha, Dora, and Queen Esther.

Slavery had been found unconstitutional, but racism and lynching had in no way ended. Mary Lena spent most of her early life in the rural South. Her mother made sure that she and her sisters learned to read and write. In 1888, Mary Street married David Lewis, and they had two sons, Walter and Felix, both of whom joined her in the ministry.

"The unique combination of factors—a woman, black, formally untrained, the ministry, and the period (early 1900s)—even by today's comparatively liberal standards would strongly mitigate against Mary Tate" becoming the organizer of a faith community, stated Meharry Lewis, the senior editor of the Lewis-Tate Archives.[1] Her vision was not just for the approval of men through recognized ordination, but to demonstrate the approval of Jesus Christ as evidenced through her works. She surmounted the hurdles of education and transportation (walking, using barges, steamships, mule-drawn wagons, decrepit automobiles, and Jim Crow trains) to prevail.

Mary Lena Lewis earned the nickname Ms. Do Right because she always tried to do the right thing. Around 1895 she informally established a group of religious adherents that she called "The Do Rights," and they began purchasing property. Lewis began her work in Tennessee, but also preached in Paducah, Kentucky; Brooklyn, Illinois; St. Louis; Greenville, Alabama; Waycross, Georgia; and throughout many other cities and states in the eastern United States. Crowds came to hear her preach and sing. She also wrote spiritual ballads. According to one of her biographers, the songs were even sung on the radio and ultimately "usurped by others."[2]

In 1908, Lewis became seriously ill and was given little hope of being cured. She was suddenly healed, however, and experienced speaking in tongues, the Pentecostal baptism of the Holy Spirit. In June 1908 the Church of the Living God, The Pillar and Ground of The Truth was formally established from the Do Rights. Lewis was ordained a bishop by the board of trustees and served as general overseer until her death. She ordained the first ministers for the church in Georgia; the denomination quickly spread to the surrounding southern states. By 1918 the Church of the Living God, The Pillar and Ground of the Truth reached into almost twenty states.

In 1914 (after having divorced at least two husbands some years earlier) Lewis married Robert Tate. She then raised up four bishops for the growing church, including her two sons, Walter Curtis Lewis and Felix Early Lewis. Her two sisters, Queen Esther Edwards and Doral Louvenia O'Neal, also became bishops. In 1919 a schism occurred, which led to the founding of the House of God, Which is the Church of the Living God, the Pillar and Ground of Truth, Inc., in Philadelphia. The denomination survived and in 1923, Bishop Mary Lena Tate opened the New and Living Way Publishing House in Nashville, Tennessee. She wrote much of the early literature of the church, including the *First Decree Book* (1914) and the *Constitution, Government, and General Decree Book* (1923), with subsequent revisions.

Tate's last preaching tour ended in the winter in Philadelphia; she died of complications from frostbite, gangrene, and diabetes. The church was then reorganized by the three general overseers: F.E. Lewis, M.F.L. Keith (the widow of W.C. Lewis), and B.L. McLeod.

• • •

*This sermon offering from Bishop Tate shows her preaching style and that of numerous Holiness preachers of the 1920s, 1930s, and today. Note the use of numerous scriptures from a variety of books of the Bible. This approach makes for a less-focused sermon. However, those with this preaching style (especially those in the Holiness-Pentecostal faith community), attribute it to their being open to the movement of the Holy Spirit. If the Spirit gives one a thought during the sermonic moment, this is to be added to the sermon.*

*Delivered in the early 1900s and printed toward the end of her life, this sermon appears shorter than most preached by Bishop Tate because it does not include the additional thirty-three scriptures upon which she may have expounded.*

## If We Work Six Days, the Seventh Is the Sabbath (ca. 1928)

This is a true fact and cannot be denied, that is this as follows: Now, all who expect to be ready to meet Jesus when He comes to earth again must keep God's commandments in recognizing the Sabbath day by remembering of it and keeping it holy as God has taught through His precious words and His Word shall never pass away. Read Isaiah, chapter 40 and verse 35; St. Mark, chapter 13, verse 31; St. Matthew, chapter 24, verse 33. Certainly, the carnal mind is not subject to the Law of God, neither indeed can be (Romans, chapter 8 and verse 7). Therefore, it is for the people of God to fully remember the Sabbath day to keep it holy and to recognize six days to be workdays, and the seventh day to be a day of rest. Of course, it is good and moral for any person upon earth to obey God in keeping the Sabbath and to do just and right in doing as nearly like the real people of God as they can in all things than they would otherwise do, no doubt, on the Sabbath, as was the case of the man whom Jesus, beholding him, loved because he had observed so many good things from his youth (see St. Mark, chapter 10, verses 20 and 21). Now, we see plainly according to these words of Jesus Christ that it may cause Jesus to love you if you live a good moral life and follow after that which is good, even if you are lacking in some things as it makes a chance for you to have treasures in heaven, that is, if you will take up the cross and follow Jesus. I shall herein further say concerning the keeping of the Sabbath that God so loved the word Sabbath that He saw fit and necessary to give a Sabbath in the land. Now it does seem reasonable that the increase of our land would be so much more bountiful and progressive if it could have a time in which it is not to be worked, and whatsoever, grass or weeds, or whatever grew upon it would be plowed under and be allowed to enrich the earth. Meanwhile, it would be a blessing to such land and those who owned it (see Leviticus, chapter 25, verses 1 to 4; Exodus, chapter 23, verses 10 to 12).

Now, if six years working the earth and the seventh year rest from working it would make the earth more progressive in bringing forth its increase, how much more would the blessings of God come to the souls of men for keeping the Sabbath day by working six days and resting on the seventh which is the holy Sabbath of the Lord. Note the acts of Jesus Christ and the Apostles and the saying of Jesus Christ as shown in Scriptures as follows: St. Matthew, chapter 12, verse 1; St. Luke, chapter 6, verses 1 to 5, also verse 9; St. Mark, chapter 2, verse 27. It is plain and true to be seen that this has no meaning whatever to show that Jesus meant not to recognize the keeping of the Sabbath, but it shows and explains the privilege that the sons of God have in doing good on the Sabbath day by saving life rather than destroying it for as many as are led by the Spirit of God, they are the sons of God and if children, then heirs—heirs of God and joint heirs with Christ (see Romans, chapter 8, verses 14 and 17). Therefore, they who are led by the Spirit of God are also lords of the Sabbath, not to seek causes to break the Sabbath neither encourage others to do so. The *lord* of anything is to care for whatever he or she is *lord* over or of, and to see that others do the same. So the saints and Apostles in times past were mindful of the Sabbath. Jesus even showed that God allows man to have mercy even on the beast, his ox, and should loose him on the Sabbath and give him water. So let us ever seek to see God's will plainly in all things and not seek and hunt occasion to frame up excuses and stumbling stones, for there is no excuse for breaking the least one of God's commandments or to teach others to do so, but Jesus came to obey God's commandments and He wants us to do the same (see St. Matthew, chapter 5, verses 17 and 18; Romans, chapter 8, verses 1 to 4).

Now, the day before the Sabbath is the day of *preparation* (St. John, chapter 19, verses 14 and 42), therefore, all who keep the Sabbath should prepare everything on the day of preparation. Prepare food and everything necessary for yourselves and beasts if you have them, for the Lord showed to the Children of Israel plainly that He did not want any gathering and preparing on the Sabbath at all. Brother Paul knew that the saints at Corinth should not do this when he came, for he no doubt arrived among the saints on time to keep the Sabbath with them in most of his visits and the next day was the first day of the week. So, he would have them gather and lay aside whatever they wanted to give to him before the Sabbath so that they would have it ready and would not have to go about gathering for him on the Sabbath day; but rather, they could just hand it to him (see 1 Corinthians, chapter 15, verse 2; St. Matthew, chapter 27, verse 62; St. Mark, chapter 15, verse 42; St. Luke, chapter 23, verse 54; St. John, chapter 19, verse 14; Exodus, chapter 16, verses 26 to 35).

Now, in case of such things as the ox being in the pit and all such similar happenings, if the people of God should, in doing good, break the Sabbath, they are not guilty at all (see St. Luke, chapter 14, verses 1 to 5). The first day of the week is the first working day, it is the first day of the seven days God gave to man. Out of seven days, He allowed six days for man to work and labor in order to make a carnal living for sustenance of his natural body and also to care for the ones who deliver the spiritual things of God as taught in 1 Corinthians, chapter 9, verse 11. For further study on the subject, please see some real true facts in Holy Scripture, Old and New Testaments. [Here, Tate proceeded to talk through a series of scriptures.]

"And in that day ye shall ask me nothing. Verily, verily I say unto you, whatsoever ye shall ask the father in my name, he will give it you" (St. John, chapter 16, verse 23). Dearly beloved, did you ever wonder why sometimes your prayers seemed not to be answered? Perhaps what I shall say herein might help you once considered. Do you always ask the Father in Jesus' name? If so, you should not fail to receive it unless you ask amiss, that is, that you may consume it upon your lusts (St. James, chapter 4, verse 3). According to God's Will, He heareth us. It could be that it is not in His Will to hear us at times, but a surer way of knowing He will answer according to His Will when we ask of the Father in Jesus' name (St. John, chapter 16, verses 23 to 27). We have a sure promise of receiving just what we ask for as Jesus plainly explains in the Gospel according to St. John. Praise the Lord. Amen.

## Notes

*Sermon source:* This sermon was provided by the Lewis-Tate Foundation and Archives, Nashville, TN. According to the archives, there were thirty-two additional scriptures mentioned in the sermon: Genesis 2:2; Deuteronomy 5:12–14; Exodus 16:23; Nehemiah 10:1–23; Exodus 20:8–11; Nehemiah 13:15–17; Exodus 23:12; Nehemiah 9:13–14; Exodus 31:13–16; Isaiah 5:13–14; Exodus 34:21; Isaiah 56:1–5; Exodus 35:2; Jeremiah 17:21–22; Leviticus 16:31; Ezekiel 46:1; Leviticus 25:3–4; Ezekiel 20:12–13; Leviticus 23:3; Amos 8:11; Matthew 12:1; Luke 6:5; Matthew

12:11; Mark 2:23–28; Luke 6:5; Luke 13:13, 14; Luke 13:15; St. John 20:1, 19, 26; Hebrew 4:4; Acts 13:27–28; Acts 28:14; Acts 18:4; and Revelation 1:10.

1. This information is taken from Meharry H. Lewis's *Mary Lena Lewis Tate: Vision! A Biography of the Founder and History of the Church of the Living God, the Pillar and Ground of the Truth, Inc.* (Nashville, TN: The New and Living Way Publishing Company, 2005), 26. This information can also be found at http://clgpgt.org/ORG/founder1.html (accessed February 30, 2004).

2. Meharry H. Lewis, *Mary Lena Lewis Tate: "A Street Called Straight" The Ten Most Dynamic and Productive Black Female Holiness Preachers of the Twentieth Century* (Nashville, TN: The New and Living Way Publishing Company, 2002), 17.

### *Bibliographical Sources*

Lewis, Helen M., and Meharry H. Lewis. *Seventy-fifth anniversary yearbook of the Church of the Living God, the Pillar and Ground of the Truth, Inc., 1903–1978, Mary Magdalena Tate, revivor and first chief overseer, Felix Early Lewis, co-revivor and second chief overseer, Walter Curtis Lewis, co-revivor and Bishop.* Nashville, TN: Church of the Living God, the Pillar and the Ground of the Truth, 1978.

Lewis, Meharry H., ed. *Mary Lena Lewis Tate: Collected Letters and Manuscripts.* Nashville, TN: New and Living Way Publishing Company, 2002.

Lewis, Meharry H., and Helen M. Lewis. *The Church of the Living God, The Pillar and Ground of the Truth, Inc: Eighty-fifth Anniversary Yearbook, 1903–1988: one in a series of anniversary yearbooks that commemorate the history, establishment, growth and development of the organization founded by Mary Lena Lewis Tate.* Nashville, TN: New and Living Way Publishing Company, 2002.

Mendiola, Kelly. *The Hand of Woman: Four Holiness-Pentecostal Evangelists and American Culture, 1840–1930.* Ph.D. diss., University of Texas, Austin, 2002.

Tate, Mary Lena Lewis. *The Constitution, Government, and General Decree Book of the Church of the Living God, the Pillar and Ground of Truth Incorporated: St. Mary Magdalena, first chief Overseer.* Nashville, TN: New and Living Way Publishing Company, 1924.

# HENRY McNEAL TURNER

*(1834–1915)*

Henry McNeal Turner was born in Abbeville, South Carolina, in 1834 of free black parents. His father died when he was young. Turner worked beside slaves in cotton fields on plantations. After running away from that work, he labored as a janitor in a law office in Abbeville, where he learned to read and write, and also probably acquired his first political ambitions. Because the field of politics was closed to blacks in the 1850s, Turner became a preacher. As a traveling evangelist for the Southern Methodist Church, he attracted large audiences of whites and blacks throughout the southeast. He married Eliza Peacher in 1856, and they had fourteen children. Two survived to adulthood. In 1857, he visited New Orleans and learned of the existence of a church controlled exclusively by black men—the African Methodist Episcopal (AME) church. He joined it on the spot and was soon in Baltimore studying and preparing for ordination. He was assigned to Israel Church on Capitol Hill, in Washington, D.C., in 1862, where his flamboyant preaching was heard not only by blacks but by government officials as well.

Turner was known as the Black Spurgeon (the reference is to the famous English sermonizer Charles H. Spurgeon). When President Abraham Lincoln decided to enlist black soldiers, Turner helped recruit them and was rewarded by being appointed the first black chaplain in the U.S. Armed Forces.

When the war ended, he was assigned to the Freedmen's Bureau in Georgia, but he soon resigned from the army because of the racial snubs he received. Entering politics, he helped recruit black voters in Georgia for the Republican Party and was elected as a delegate to the 1868 constitutional convention as well as a representative to the 1868 Georgia legislature. After he and other black representatives were refused their seats, he was appointed postmaster in Macon and then a customs official in Savannah.

During the later years of Reconstruction, when politics was generally closed to him, Turner concentrated his efforts entirely on the church. He worked strenuously to build the membership of the AME Church in Georgia, wooing black Methodists away from the white-dominated Southern Methodist Church. By 1876 he was well known and popular enough to be elected to a national AME office. In 1880 he was elected one of twelve bishops of the denomination and for the next thirty-five years exercised considerable influence in the AME Church.

After the failure of northern whites to follow through on their promises of protection and aid for the freed slaves, Turner became disillusioned with the United States and became the most outspoken American advocate of militant black nationalism during his lifetime. His writings and speeches provide a stinging criticism of American racism and a strong rebuke to blacks who were afraid to take radical action against their oppression. Turner urged blacks to leave the United States and to emigrate to Africa, where their manhood and their human rights would be recognized, where they could find equality and power. There, he predicted, black Americans could build a great and powerful nation that would win respect not only for its own citizens, but for black men everywhere.

In the grim years of Afro-American history between Reconstruction and World War I—years of lynching, disenfranchisement, riots, and general oppression—Turner proclaimed an alternative to the accommodationists. His rejection of the United States struck a responsive chord in the minds of many blacks who might have been afraid to speak such words themselves and offered an alternative that appealed to many of those neglected by Booker T. Washington and W.E.B. DuBois.

After his first wife died Turner married Martha DeWitt in 1893. He married Harriet Wyman in 1900 and Laura Pearle in 1907. Turner visited Africa four times—in 1891, 1893, 1895, and 1898—but never planned to move there permanently, unless he could convince thousands of blacks to immigrate as well. Those thousands never materialized; although interest was great, opposition was also great and money was not available for transportation and black nation-building.

Bishop Turner was highly critical of African Americans who disagreed with his black nationalist ideas. Although his strong attacks on his opponents made him many enemies, his assaults on American racism won him many supporters, especially among southern black farmers. Even so, Turner frequently cooperated openly with white segregationists who agreed that blacks should leave the country. At the same time, he devoted great energy and intelligence to his church work, especially its missionary efforts. He was a complex man, but the dominant feature of his thought and action was his desire to have the black man stand proud and assert his independence and masculinity.

Turner also wrote and spoke frequently and vigorously on church problems. He wrote regularly for the AME weekly newspaper, the *Christian Recorder*. He also founded and edited the following newspapers: *The Southern Recorder* (1886–88), *The Voice of Missions* (1893–1900), and *The Voice of the People* (1901–07). Turner organized four conferences in Africa in Sierra Leone, Liberia, Transvaal, and South Africa. He wrote an African Methodist Episcopal hymnal in 1876, an African Methodist Episcopal catechism in 1877, and a book on Methodist polity in 1889. He died in Windsor, Ontario, in 1915.

• • •

*"God Is a Negro" reveals Turner's vigorous approach to the race problem, his strong personality, his fascination with Africa, and his style of lead-*

*ership. After Turner remarked in the newspaper the* Observer *that God is a Negro, the white press reacted strongly and ridiculed him. Turner answered the criticism with this editorial in* The Voice of Missions.

## God Is a Negro (1898)

We have as much right biblically and otherwise to believe that God is a Negro, as you buckra, or white, people have to believe that God is a fine looking, symmetrical and ornamented white man. For the bulk of you, and all the fool Negroes of the country, believe that God is white-skinned, blue-eyed, straight-haired, projecting-nosed, compressed-lipped and finely-robed *white* gentleman, sitting upon a throne somewhere in the heavens. Every race of people since time began who have attempted to describe their God by words, or by paintings, or by carvings, or by any other form or figure, have conveyed the idea that the God who made them and shaped their destinies was symbolized in themselves, and why should not the Negro believe that he resembles God as much so as other people? We do not believe that there is any hope for a race of people who do not believe that they look like God.

Demented though we be, whenever we reach the conclusion that God or even that Jesus Christ, while in the flesh, was a white man, we shall hang our gospel trumpet upon the willow and cease to preach.

We had rather be an atheist and believe in no God, or a pantheist and believe that all nature is God, than to believe in the personality of a God and not to believe that He is a Negro. Blackness is much older than whiteness, for black was here before white, if the Hebrew word, coshach, or chasack, has *any* meaning. We do not believe in the eternity of matter, but we do believe that chaos floated in infinite darkness or blackness, millions, billions, quintillions and eons of years before God said, "Let there be light," and that during that time God had no material light Himself and was shrouded in darkness, so far as *human* comprehension is able to grasp the situation.

Yet we are no stickler as to God's color, anyway, but if He has any we would prefer to believe that it is nearer symbolized in the blue sky above us and the blue water of the seas and oceans: but we certainly protest against God being a white man or against God being white at all; abstract as this theme must forever remain while we are in the flesh. This is one of the reasons we favor African emigration, or Negro nationalization, wherever we can find a domain, for as long as we remain among the whites, the Negro will believe that the devil is black and that he (the Negro) favors the devil, and that God is white and that he (the Negro) bears no resemblance to Him, and the effect of such a sentiment is contemptuous and degrading, and one-half of the Negro race will be trying to get white and the other half will spend their days trying to be white men's scullions in order to please the whites; and the time they should be giving to the study of such things as will dignify and make our race great will be devoted to studying about how unfortunate they are in not being white.

We conclude these remarks by repeating for the information of the *Observer* what it adjudged us demented for—*God is a Negro.*

## *Note*

*Sermon source:* See the AME's *Voice of Missions*, 1898, for additional information concerning this message. It can be found online at http://godisanegro.wordpress.com/2006/03/16/god-is-a-negro-1898/.

## *Bibliographical Sources*

Batten, J. Minton. "Henry M. Turner, Negro Bishop Extraordinary," *Church History* 7 (Sept. 1938): 231–46.

Coulter, E. Merton. "Henry M. Turner: Georgia Negro Preacher-Politician During the Reconstruction Era," *Georgia Historical Quarterly* 48 (Dec. 1964): 371–410.

Cummings, Melborne S. "The Rhetoric of Bishop Henry McNeal Turner." *Journal of Black Studies* 12, no. 4 (June 1982): 457–67.

Malone, Dumas, ed. *Dictionary of American Biography.* New York: Charles Scribner's Sons, 1928–36, 19: 65–66.

Murphy, Larry G., J. Gordon Melton, and Gary L. Ward. *Encyclopedia of African American Religions.* New York: Garland Publishing, 1993.

Ponton, Mungo M. *The Life and Times of Henry M. Turner.* Atlanta: A.B. Caldwell Publishing Company, 1917.

Redkey, Edwin S. "Bishop Turner's African Dream," *Journal of American History,* 54, no. 2 (Sept. 1967): 271–90.

———. *Black Exodus: Black Nationalist and Back-to-Africa Movements, 1890–1910.* New Haven, CT: Yale University Press, 1969.

———, ed. *Respect Black: The Writings and Speeches of Henry McNeal Turner.* New York: Arno Press, 1971.

Turner, Henry McNeal. *Civil Rights, The Outrage of the Supreme Court of the United States Upon the Black Man. Reviewed in a Reply to the New York "Voice," The Great Temperance Paper of the United States.* Philadelphia: Publication Department AME Church, 1889.

## SAMUEL RINGGOLD WARD

*(1817–ca. 1866)*

Samuel Ringgold Ward was brought to New York when he was nine, along with his two siblings. His parents, William and Ann, were escaped slaves. Ward attended the Mulburry Street School in New York. He became a schoolteacher in Newark, New Jersey. He also attended the Oneida Institute in Whitesboro, New York, to gain additional training and to enhance his writing and oratorical skills. In 1838 he married a woman named Reynolds; her first name is unknown. In the same year they had the first of several children.

In 1839 Ward became an agent for the American Anti-Slavery Society. In the same year he was licensed to preach by the New York Congregationalist Society. In 1841 he became the pastor of a white church in South Butler, New York. It is said he left the church two years later for medical reasons. For the next five years he worked with antislavery campaigns and antislavery newspapers. In 1846 he became the pastor of another white church in Cortland Village, New York. Ward was often called "the Black Daniel Webster" and considered as a speaker second only to Frederick Douglass. Douglass also spoke highly of Ward. He founded newspapers and was active in raising funds, even abroad, for antislavery efforts. He ultimately had to flee to Canada to avoid imprisonment or death because of his fierce antislavery pronouncements and his participation in the freeing of a slave from the Syracuse County Courthouse.

In Canada, Ward continued his work as an agent for the Anti-Slavery Society of Canada. In 1855 he penned his life story in *Autobiography of a Fugitive Slave*. Given land in Jamaica as a gift, he moved there to farm. He continued his church and antislavery efforts, writing *Reflections Upon the Gordon Rebellion* in or around 1866, shortly before his death.

• • •

*In a speech before the U.S. Senate on March 7, 1850, noted attorney and future Secretary of State Daniel Webster supported the Compromise of 1850, speaking against Southern threats of secession but asking that the North give stronger support for the recovery of fugitive slaves. In a speech at Faneuil Hall in Boston, Samuel Ringgold Ward responded to Webster's speech and all who supported the Fugitive Slave Bill, which called for, among other things, returning to their masters slaves who fled to northern states.*

## The Fugitive Slave Bill Speech (April 3, 1850)

I am here tonight simply as a guest. You have met here to speak of the sentiments of a Senator of your state whose remarks you have the honor to repudiate. In the course of the remarks from the gentleman who preceded me, he has done us the favor to make honorable mention of a Senator of my own State—William H. Seward.

I thank you for this manifestation of approbation of a man who has always stood head and shoulders above his party, and who has never receded from his position on the question of slavery. It was my happiness to receive a letter from him a few days since, in which he said he would never swerve from his position as the friend of freedom.

To be sure, I agree not with Senator Seward in politics, but when an individual stands up for the rights of man against slaveholders, I care not for party distinctions. He is my brother.

We have here much of common cause and interest in this matter. That infamous bill of Mr. Mason, of Virginia, proves itself to be like all other propositions presented by Southern men. It finds just enough of Northern dough-faces who are willing to pledge themselves, if you will pardon the uncouth language of a backwoodsman, to lick up the spittle of the slavocrats, and swear it is delicious.

You of the old Bay State—a State to which many of us are accustomed to look as to our fatherland, just as well look back to England as our mother country—you have a Daniel who has deserted the cause of freedom. We, too, in New York, have a "Daniel who has come to judgment," only he don't come quite fast enough to the right kind of judgment. Daniel S. Dickinson represents someone, I suppose, in the state of New York; God knows he doesn't represent me. I can pledge you that our Daniel will stand cheek to jowl with your Daniel. He was never known to surrender slavery, but always to surrender liberty.

The bill of which you most justly complain, concerning the surrender of fugitive slaves, is to apply alike to your State and to our State, if it shall ever apply at all. [*sic*] but we have come here to make a common oath upon a common altar, that bill shall never take effect. Honorable Senators may record their names in its behalf, and it may have the sanction of the House of Representatives; but we, the people, who are Superior to both Houses and the Executive, too (hear! hear!), we, the people, will never be human bipeds, to howl upon the track of the fugitive slave, even though led by the corrupt Daniel of your State, or the degraded one of ours.

Though there are many attempts to get up compromises—and there is no term which I detest more than this, it is always the term which makes right yield to wrong; it has always been accursed since Eve made the first compromise with the devil. I was saying, sir, that it is somewhat singular, and yet historically true, that when ever these compromises are proposed, there are men of the North who seem to foresee that Northern men, who think their constituency will not look into these matters, will seek to do more than the South demands. They seek to prove to Northern men that all is right and all is fair; and this is the game Webster is attempting to play.

"Oh," says Webster, "the will of God has fixed that matter, we will not re-enact the will of God." Sir, you remember the time in 1841, '42, '43 and '44, when it was said that Texas could never be annexed. The design of such dealing was that you should believe it, and then, when you thought yourselves secure, they would spring the trap upon you. And now it is their wish to seduce you into their belief that slavery never will go there, and then the slave holders will drive slavery there as fast as possible. I think that this is the most contemptible proposition of the whole, except the support of that bill which would attempt to make the whole North the slavecatchers of the South.

You will remember that the bill of Mr. Mason says nothing about color. Mr. Phillips, a man whom I will always love, a man who taught me my horn-book on this subject of slavery, when I was a poor boy, has referred to Marshfield. There is a man who sometimes lives in Marshfield, and who has the reputation of having an honorable dark skin. Who knows that some postmaster may have to sit upon the very gentleman whose character you have been discussing tonight? "What is sauce for the goose is sauce for the gander." If this bill is to relieve grievances, why not make an application to the immortal Daniel of Marshfield? There is no such thing as complexion mentioned. It is not only true that the colored man of Massachusetts—it is not only true that the fifty thousand colored men of New York may be taken—though I pledge you there is one, whose name is Sam Ward, who will never be taken alive! Not only is it true that the fifty thousand black men in New York may be taken, but anyone else also can be captured. My friend Theodore Parker alluded to Ellen Craft. I had the pleasure of taking tea with her, and accompanied her here tonight. She is far whiter than any who come here slave-catching. This line of distinction is so nice that you cannot tell who is white or black. As Alexander Pope used to say, "White and black soften and blend in so many thousand ways, that it is neither white nor black."

This is the question, Whether a man has a right to himself and his children, his hopes and his happiness, for this world and the world to come. That is a question which, according to this bill, may be decided by any backwoods postmaster in this State or any other. Oh, this is a monstrous proposition; and I do thank God that if the Slave Power has such demands to make on us, that the proposition has come now—now, that the people know what is being done—now that the public mind is turned toward this subject—now that they are trying to find out what is the truth on this subject!

Sir, what must be the moral influence of this speech of Mr. Webster on the minds of young men, lawyers and others, here in the North? They turn their eyes toward Daniel Webster as towards a superior mind, and a legal and constitutional oracle. If they shall catch the spirit of this speech, its influence upon them and upon following generations will be so deeply corrupting that it never can be wiped out or purged.

I am thankful that this, my first entrance into Boston, and my first introduction to Faneuil Hall, gives me the pleasure and privilege of uniting with you in uttering my humble voice against the two Daniel's [*sic*], and of declaring, in behalf of our people, that if the fugitive slave is traced to our part of New York State, he shall have the law of Almighty God to protect him, the law which says, "*Thou shall not return to the master the servant that has escaped unto thee, but he shall dwell with thee in thy gates, where it liketh him best.*" And if our postmasters cannot maintain their constitutional oaths, and cannot live without playing the pander to the slave-hunter, they need not live at all. Such crises as these leave us to the right of Revolution, and if need be, that right we will, at whatever cost, most sacredly maintain.

✦ ✦ ✦

*This next message by Ward shows the breadth of his oratory. He is just as at home talking to youth about the issue of character as discussing the Fugitive Slave Bill. Ultimately, Ward suggests that the character to be emulated is that of the Man from Nazareth, Jesus Christ. The speech was delivered at the Cortlandville Academy Lyceum. These are excerpts of the speech.*

## CHARACTER
## (1849)

. . . Youth is, emphatically, the season of hope. Standing midway between childhood and maturity, it is buoyant with the recollection of the former, while unacquainted with the experience of the latter. The lights and shades, the joys and sorrows, which are interspersed amid the scenes; the thorns and flowers which are scattered along the pathway of manhood, are, to those in this interesting stage of life, like a *terra incognita*. And, as we are in our youth, unacquainted with what lies before us in the next stage of life, so we are too apt to pay but little attention to, what shall prepare us to act the part of men. All our prospects are painted upon the retina or our imagination's eye, in the greatest and most fascinating colors. We are our future selves, in the full enjoyment of all that is desirable, in human relations and positions. If letters is our chosen pursuit, we fancy that we shall not only enjoy, all the rights, immunities and privileges of *citizens* of the Republic, of letters, but we persuade ourselves that we shall be chosen Umpires in and over that Republic, writing upon our vestments the insignia of its highest honors. If our attention be turned to the acquisition of wealth, we feel perfectly confident of success, and we suffer ourselves to entertain no other ideas than those connected with pomp and state, honors and obeisance as to the earning and homage of such a distinguished position as we shall occupy among ourselves.

Now, the steps by which we shall reach those towering ascents, the obstacles to be overcome, the rugged toils to which we shall be obliged to submit, the frowning face of adversity which we shall have to encounter are matters not very intimately connected with, much less are they parts and parcels of the manhood, described in the poetry of our youth.

Yet an important, an immensely important, stage of our existence in youth—youth with its inexperience, its flowers, its fancies, its day-dreams, and its facility of giving to Airy nothing a local habitation and a name with all its faults and follies *incalculably* important is this budding, blooming, hopeful season of youth.

For in youth, we lay the foundation of our future weal or woe. Not only the unreal and imaginary is entertained in the youthful mind; solid and substantial acquisitions are now and here made, which from their nature must be among the elements, if indeed they are not the chief elements of the future man, I mean not that youth is the season allotted to the acquirement of wealth, for, as a general thing, this is not true, nor do I refer simply to what is more important, the acquisitions of learning; but

I speak of what is most important of all, the purposes to which youth is naturally devoted—the formation of Character.

As was intimated at an early day, I solicit your attention to this, as the subject for this evening's contemplation. My arrangement includes the following points, viz: CHARACTER—ITS ELEMENTS—ITS IMPORTANCE, AND ITS TRUE STANDARD.

I. Of course I allude alone to good, correct, upright character. That which is worthy of the approval of the good, and which indeed, like Pollock's Virtue, in the midst of hell, challenges the admiration of the most depraved.—That which maintains its virgin-like purity, when surrounded and offended by the vicious, as well as when associated with the chosen and the faithful of the earth. That which can afford to repose on its own consciousness of rectitude, whether it meets the smiles or frowns of the multitude, that which can feel itself supported alike, when arising to the surface of the social circle, or when depressed beneath it; brilliant alike in the rough and homely garb of poverty, so arrayed in the "purple and fine linen" of some modern Dives.

Character, so defined and described, may be said to be but a rare plant among us. This point I do not purpose to discuss. Sufficient is its forms now to repeat that the beautiful and interesting season of life which is yours, gentlemen of the Lyceum, is the season when more is done to form, acquire, and develope [*sic*] character, than at any other; and that what is now done, and well done, will leave [word unclear] traces upon your future selves not only, but lay broad and deep the basis of your happiness in this life, and that beyond the grave. At the same time, if from thoughtlessness or whatever cause, this stage of your experience be so neglected or perverted, as that an unhappy inclination be given you now, lasting in time, and ceaseless beyond time, must be the fruits—the bitter fruits thereof.

## What are among the most essential elements of upright character?

In a most conspicuous position among them stands—indeed, at the very basis of them lies—that bright, rare, precious, corner-stone, integrity, a happier apparel which never adorned the character of an Angel. It is on almost every page of the inspired volume ascribed to the Deity as the grand and glorious testing ground of the Christian's faith. It is a trait, too, as indispensable as it is brilliant, in the character of any earthly or celestial intelligence. It is that unswerving, immovable, appreciation and choice of the right, which causes the *wrong* to be seen, in all its hideous monstrosity; which makes it impossible for vice to array herself in a garb so attractive, to utter words so suasive, in sounds so musical as to captivate and seduce. If this be regarded as saying too much, sure I am that even profane history furnishes most admirable examples of it. It was this incorruptible trait, which has made the moral firmness in the character of a Roman proverbial down to this day.

But witness it in the character of "Urrean Job." Behold him when stripped of his vast possessions, bereft of his children, and subjected to the evil councils of the wife of his bosom, while about his hearthstone were friends—pseudo-friends—who in their infatuation of misanthropy, or both, loaded him with reproaches unswerved by the astounding suddenness of his reverses, undismayed at the "selfish council of those hangers-on," "unshaken" in the near face to face view, into which he had been thrown with stern visaged adversity—unseduced by the appeal made to his impatient impulses by his wife, and unterrified by the fierce assaults of Satan, like a bold rock in the mid-ocean which defies the surge, yields not to the wave and says aha! to the billow—he stands erect and looking his God in the face, exclaims—"Until I die mine integrity shall not depart from me!"

Behold it in that bright star of Israelitish [*sic*] integrity, the young Daniel at the court of Nebbuchadnezzar; Daniel, whom no place, power, threats, or what not, could swerve from his principles, but who, in spite of all these, opened his windows toward Jerusalem, and poured forth his adoration to Israel's God. Nor could the starved lion into whose dreadful den he was thrown, awe him into a dishonoring of himself as the price of the royal favor. His *integrity* he must maintain, and his integrity he did maintain, and the God whom he honored thus, closed the voracious jaws of the terrible beast, and made him as harmless as a suckling lamb.

I might mention that splendid constellation of young men, whose names and deeds are furnished to our hands by the inspired writers, beginning with Abel, pausing to admire Joseph, paying a merited tribute to the three Hebrew children, and so sweeping along the moral heavens, we might take in the range of our view Saul and Timothy, and a host of others, of equal glory and brilliancy.

But above them all the great central Sun of our moral system, shines in infinite splendor and effulgence, *Jesus, the Model Man*. And shall I attempt to tell you amid reproach and scorn, and hate and contumely [*sic*] subject to poverty, and all its long-train of inconveniences, privations and exposures, He bore himself aloft above the incidents of his condition, how He put His enemies to the pains and expense of exhausting their every malice in the invention of plots, plans and pretexts, for his destruction, and the overthrow of His system of atonement! No, gentlemen, I will content myself with pointing you to the simple, and ample story of his life, and character, and death, as written by his immediate friends and followers. There shall you learn what is more valuable, more reliable, more exemplary, in respect to integrity of character, than is to be found in all the biographies of all the men of whom pens have ever written.

Another, and an analogous element of good character, is decision. No appreciation of the virtuous and commendable, however high-toned and thorough—no more approval of the right—no more preference for that which is intrinsically good, can be of very great importance, if it be not stable. A man needs not only to choose goodness, for its own sake, but he needs the moral nerve, to abide his choice in the storm as well as in the sun shine, under frowns and reproaches, as well as when met by courteous homage.

Not unfrequently, in these times, are we called upon to embrace truths emanating from God's own heart, of whose origin and character, we have no more doubt than we have of the being of Jehovah, of the authenticity of his word. And yet the very recognition of the divine authority, which we find in such truths, will expose us to circumstances anything else than pleasant and desirable. Now the acknowledgment and embracement of truth is one of the lowest conditions upon which we can maintain our integrity. Nay, more, the avowal and the defense of truth is not unfrequently altogether vital to one's maintenance of integrity; and if integrity be wanting, good character cannot exist.—When one is places where he must conceal, disavow, or deny his principles, (which is but another name for denying his God), or lose the favor of some powerful benefactor, and incur the reproaches of those whose opinions are generally esteemed, he must make his election as to which course he shall pursue. If he lacks the decision to tread the path, in which, according to his convictions, truth leads, as she smiles and beckons him onward, then there is that deficiency in his character which is nothing less than a destitution of one of its keystones and corner-stones.—A Joseph, a Daniel, he never can be, and what is worse, a follower of Jesus he can scarcely be, for the *cross bearing element* his character does not contain;—And any transforming or regenerating process through which he thinks he has passed has done but very little good, if it has not supplied this deficiency. A practically, and a reliably good character, *without decision*, is a moral phenomenon which is yet to be witnessed.

Prominent among the sparkling traits of all the men whose names have come down to us on the historic page, who were great on account of their goodness, is Simplicity. To the shame of our civilization be it spoken, we find this admirable trait more frequent among the untutored sons of nature than in the halls of refinement. Where nature unadorned, and unsophisticated, he left unspoiled by this and that form of fashionable duplicity; there we see this important element of character in its native power and brilliancy. Society is too frequent a refinement of deceit; its sentiments a bundle of prejudices; its commerce a set of measures for reciprocal deception and overreaching simplicity, straight forwardness, open handed honesty, therefore, in not so much a matter of fashion among us as it ought to be. Yet the very rareness with which it is to be found, makes it the more precious. That a man cannot trade without being constantly exposed to the varied forms of penny-wise knavery is indeed deplorable. But that he should suffer himself to become fraudulent and deceptive, like too many of his neighbors, is still more deplorable. That a man should find so little of the reliable in the coined expression, and honed professions of his neighbors is grievous indeed. But that he should become one in heart, and practice, with them, is much more grievous. In truth, the more subtle, the more ambiguous, the more deceptive, is the state of society around us, the more *simplicity* of character do we need to counter act to overcome it. If we allow men in this particular, to impress upon us their own image we are "overcome of evil" instead of "overcoming evil with good." . . .

God has ordained—most wisely ordained—that character, to be good must be under the containment of reason and conscience, and that they both shall bow in meek and complacent subjection to the moral law. That law not only comes to us under the most sacred sanctions, as an emanation from the Supreme legislative power of the Universe, but it comes in perfect adaptation to our circumstances in general, and especially to that important stage of our life which is peculiarly allotted to the formation of character. . . .

But if reason is suffered to maintain the control of passion, and conscience shall sit always as reason's umpire, and the divine law shall rule supreme over all, we shall, in spite of evil examples without, and evil tendencies within, be enabled to form and to secure that greatest of all blessings in this world and that to come—a good character.

II. My second point is the importance of character. I shall make but a very small draft upon your patience in the discussion of this and the remaining portions of the subject: man thinks himself wisely employed, and his followers in the main give him credit for wisdom, when he devotes his early risings, his late retirings, his sweaty toil, or his brain's most laborious exercise, to the gathering up of wealth. If success crown his efforts, after many years of alteration of hope and fear, the wisdom of his devotion to his favorite good but few will venture to question. But does he ever realize the objects of his highest hopes? Does he ever make his deeds and title papers cover so many broad acres as to satisfy his cravings? Do his coffers ever contain enough of gold to still and hush his longings for more? Has he when most successful found that amount of this world's goods which fills up the desires of an immortal spirit? In fine, has he acquired *a permanent possession!* No! No! His riches may take wings and fly away. The curling crackling flame, the mighty tempest, the flood, the wave, may the next moment dash to earth the tenure by which he holds his boasted goods. *Not so with character. . . .*

In countries where poverty passes from generation to generation, by a sort of entail, or where certain *external peculiarities* mark out some men, as according to certain *high authority*, "doomed men," or "doomed races," not unfrequently do you see some of these very same "doomed men," through the force of their uprightness and energy of character, arise superior to the influences which crush them, and extort from those who "doomed" them, the well earned credit of an upright character.

Politicians have addled their brains, at one time and another, to produce, and to prevent to their fellow citizens, such a system of legislation as should most, or best, conduce to what is called a "credit system." When I became twenty-one, this was one of the most exciting, difficult, and strife engendering of all the family of political *questions vexiate*. But the plain truth is, legislation is as impotent as the infant of yesterday, to make a basis or system of credit. That matter lies altogether in another direction. *The only real and true basis of* CREDIT is CHARACTER. Wealth is but *ability* to pay an honest demand. Law may force the unwillingly able to pay what he would not, otherwise. But neither wealth nor law gives a man credit. A man's credit depends, among men of sense, among men of real discernment, upon the character he possesses, whether rich or poor. When you trust wealth, or trust law, you trust not man. But when you trust a man for what he is, for what his character is, you trust him. *This basis of true credit*, whatever may be done by, or whatever may become of legislation, is character. . . .

We have seen in a meeting of Quakers, the words of one man, a small man, a poor man he might be, a young man, (sometimes a woman) outweigh the words of a whole meeting, in one of their religious discussions. Now, that person, so far from being the most eloquent member of the body, is often the least gifted as an orator. But still, his voice controls.— To him all pay deference; and the grave members feel no doubt, that their decision receives the sanction of the Great Head of the Church. Now, what is the secret of this man's power? The coolness and strength of his judgment, has much to do with it, be sure, but that is only an element of the controlling attributes: it is the influence of his UPRIGHT CHARACTER.

The same fact, in another form, was noticed by a traveller, who happened to be present at an Indian council, the most eloquent member of which made, to the stranger's mind, a most thrilling speech, without receiving the least apparent attention, and resumed his seat unnoticed. In all their deliberations, not so much as an allusion was made to the oration of the gifted, young chief. Astonished at this apparently unwarranted neglect, the stranger asked the reason of it. He was told that *a falsehood* had once escaped those eloquent lips; he had thus lost his *character,* and with it his influence. Quakers and Indians are not the only men among whom one's influence depends upon his character. Poverty, ignorance, nothing can, in the long run, deprive the man of probity of character of that influence which belongs to moral worth. CHARACTER is the best ground, the only true ground of MORAL INFLUENCE.

But gentlemen, there is one more method of estimating the value of character, to which I will now ask your attention. It is a view of what *God does to promote it,* and a consideration of the *rewards* which He confers upon it. That we may form a correct character, he placed before us the best possible model, the highest possible standard, and the most moving inducement, and the happiest facilities, the model He gave us is Himself, the standard is His Word, as contained in the Law and the Gospel. The inducements, are the internal satisfaction arising from doing right, and the good influences we may exert upon our fellow men; and the rewards of an everlasting life, in which is to be enjoyed the completest, most perfect felicity. The facilities referred to, are the aids and encouragements He, in infinite grace, bestows upon us, to enlighten and cheer us in the rugged labors to which we are called, not the least of which is the overcoming of the obstacles *within ourselves* which is in the way of forming a good character.

It is not possible too frequently or too strongly to urge upon your attention, the fact, that character to be *correct* must be Christian; while the Christianity which does not embody integrity, decision, and a complete, invariable, universal subjection to the Divine Law of Rectitude, is without a Bible warrant, destitute of a likeness to Christ, unfit for life, and unsafe for death. The rewards, therefore, which God holds out to the hope of the Christian, are but rewards for the formation and maintenance of good, upright, and Christian character. Such is God's estimate of it.

### My method includes as its third particular, the True Standard of Character

To this allusion has been made. And now, to speak at the same time with brevity and fullness, let me say, THAT STANDARD is the young man—the poor YOUNG MAN OF NAZARETH . . . The very best I can do, is to hold up for your admiring gaze the Man Jesus Christ, as the true standard of moral character and excellence. I do so, gentlemen, in full remembrance of the fact, that whether in realms of endless and indescribable bliss, we shall be welcomed to seas of unalloyed, unfading, and increasing felicity, by the God Jesus Christ; depends upon our appreciation, of our assimilation, to the Man Jesus Christ. . . .

Follow Him from His manger-cradle to His [word unclear] cross, till His image shall be impressed [sentence missing] of the Lyceum; allow me to wish you the most abundant success in the noble and mind magnifying objects which engage your attention, and occupy your time, in this, your collective capacity. And may God grant, that in intimate connexion—indeed, a very apposite connexion—with your literary pursuits, you may be blessed with that wisdom, that humility, which shall induce you practically to appreciate, the great and glorious end of books, letters, law, time, education,—life itself: THE ACQUIREMENT AND DEVELOPMENT OF A CHRIST-LIKE CHARACTER.

## *Note*

*Sermon source:* Ward's speeches in Faneuil Hall and at the Cortlandville Academy Lyceum were taken from Ronald Burke's *Samuel Ringgold Ward: Christian Abolitionist* (New York: Garland Publishing, 1995).

## *Bibliographical Sources*

Blackett, R.J.M. *Building an Anti-Slavery Wall: Black Americans in the Atlantic Abolitionist Movement, 1830–1860.* Baton Rouge: Louisiana State University Press, 2002.

Douglass, Frederick. *Life and Times of Frederick Douglass. Written by Himself. His Early Life as a Slave, His Escape from Bondage, and His Complete History to the Present Time, Including His Connection with the Anti-Slavery Movement; His Labors in Great Britain as well as in His Own Country; His Experience in the Conduct of an Influential Newspaper; His Connection with the Underground Railroad; His Relations with John Brown and the Harper's Ferry Raid; His Recruiting the 54th and 55th Mass. Colored Regiments; His Interviews with Presidents Lincoln and Johnson: His Appointment by Gen. Grant to Accompany *the Santo Domingo Commission—Also to a Seat in the Council of the District of Columbia: His Appointment as United States Marshal by President J.A. Garfield; With Many Other Interesting and Important Events of His Most Eventful Life* (Boston: DeWolfe & Fiske Co., 1892). Electronic edition at Documenting the American South, University of North Carolina at Chapel Hill Digitization Project, http://docsouth.un.edu/neh/dougl92/menu.html (accessed January 23, 2009).

Quarles, Benjamin. *Black Abolitionists*. New York: Oxford University Press, 1969.

Ripley, Peter, and Jeffrey Rossbach, eds. *The Black Abolition Papers, Volume I: The British Isles 1830–1865*. Chapel Hill: University of North Carolina Press, 1985.

Ward, Samuel Ringgold. *Autobiography of a Fugitive Negro: His Anti-Slavery Labors in the United States, Canada, and England*. London: John Snow, 1855.

# 4

# WORLD WARS, FREEDOM STRUGGLES, AND RENAISSANCE: *1918–1950*

# INTRODUCTION

After the conclusion of World War I, many white Americans enjoyed the postwar prosperity of the Roaring Twenties, while many African Americans continued to suffer the indignities of second-class citizenship. Protesting these gross social indignities and inequities, African Americans in the North began forming mass movements to assert their racial pride.

Marcus Garvey, the charismatic, Jamaican-born black nationalist, founded the most celebrated of these movements. He called his group the Universal Negro Improvement Association (UNIA). The UNIA appealed especially to blacks in lower economic strata who felt that civil rights organizations such as the National Association for the Advancement of Colored People (NAACP) catered to elite blacks.[1]

Garvey encouraged blacks to identify with and celebrate their noble African past. He founded numerous black-owned businesses and mesmerized masses of black people across the United States with his elaborate costumes and fiery rhetoric denouncing white supremacy. A central tenet of his movement was that black people would only achieve genuine freedom if they fled the United States and returned to Africa. Garvey once declared, "If Europe is for the Europeans, then Africa shall be for the black people of the world, we say it; we mean it."[2]

Garvey's exhortation for migration was not novel. Various leaders, black and white, in the previous century had urged similar action. Yet Garvey's reformulation of this century-old idea resonated deeply with

African Americans exasperated with racial discrimination. Although Garvey's 1923 conviction on mail fraud and subsequent imprisonment derailed his movement, he blazed a new trail for black racial solidarity and political organization. The sermons in this anthology by Emily Christmas Kinch and William Henry Moses (see part 3) were delivered during UNIA meetings. Baptist and Methodist leaders often spoke at UNIA meetings.

As Marcus Garvey elevated the political aspirations of the black community, the artistic genius of African Americans reached full bloom during the famed Harlem Renaissance of the 1920s. In the clubs and dance halls of Harlem and in other northern cities, black musicians such as Duke Ellington, Cab Calloway, and Count Basie thrilled black and white audiences with their swinging jazz tunes. Southern African American blues singers such as Bessie Smith and Gertrude "Ma" Rainey also captivated crowds in all parts of the United States with their sultry tones and risqué lyrics. Music did not exhaust the cultural creativity of the Harlem Renaissance. Renaissance virtuosos such as Paul Robeson, Zora Neale Hurston, and Langston Hughes forged new frontiers in theater and literature.

While black political aspirations and artistic creativity surged during this period, countless blacks, especially those in urban settings, still suffered under the scourge of poverty. The population explosion in many northern cities resulting from the Great Migration depleted already scarce financial resources. The stock market crash of 1929 and the ensuing Great Depression only exacerbated the financial degradation of many blacks.

During this period, many black churches addressed financial needs and ministered to the spirits of disenfranchised African Americans. For instance, the pioneering African American Baptist missionary Nannie Helen Burroughs advocated vigorously for churches to alleviate the social plight of African Americans who had migrated to northern cities. In her 1920 report to the National Baptist Convention, she presented a thoroughgoing program by which churches could ameliorate the bleak living conditions of blacks and challenge the patriarchy that was rampant both in the country and in black churches.[3]

In addition, black churches continued to exercise their influence on higher education, as several historically black colleges elected clergypersons as their presidents. Notable examples included the Reverend Doctor Mordecai Johnson, president of Howard University; the Reverend Doctor Benjamin Mays, president of Morehouse College; and the Reverend Doctor John Ellison, president of Virginia Union University.

Since the days of the Civil War, many blacks had sided politically with the Republican Party—the party of Abraham Lincoln, the so-called Great Emancipator. In the 1930s, black political allegiance shifted to the Democratic Party, because many blacks considered Democratic president Franklin D. Roosevelt and his wife, Eleanor, to be socially progressive, and allies for black causes. Black political support enabled Roosevelt to be elected to an unprecedented four terms.

As President Roosevelt pulled the country from the mire of economic depression, a menace to world peace emerged in Europe. Adolf Hitler led Nazi Germany into a clash with the rest of the world. Before the end of World War II, the Japanese had attacked Pearl Harbor, Hitler had massacred more than six millions Jews and millions of other people, and the United States had unleashed the devastating power of atomic annihilation.

Nearly one million blacks served in the U.S. military during World War II.[4] Once again, the historical and social irony of black patriotism was inescapable. In this war, black soldiers fought valiantly to end the genocidal oppression of a European dictator. By 1945, Eisenhower allowed blacks to integrate the combat infantry.[5] Yet these black soldiers wore the uniforms of a country that had participated in the genocidal oppression of Native Americans and African Americans. World War II had toppled Hitler's Nazism in Europe, but the regime of Jim Crow segregation remained as tenacious as ever in the United States. Postwar investigations led to the complete integration of the U.S. military, which then had a trickle-down effect into other areas of North American culture in the 1950s and 1960s.[6]

## THE SANCTIFIED CHURCH: 1918–1950

One of the most important movements in American religious history is the rise of black Holiness and Pentecostal churches in the late nineteenth and early twentieth centuries. Their distinguishing mark was adherence to the traditions of oral music and ecstatic praise associated with slave religion. The label "Sanctified Church" emerged within the black community to distinguish congregations of "the saints" from those of other black Christians, especially the black Baptists and Methodists, who assimilated and imitated the cultural and organizational models of European-Americans.[7] William C. Turner Jr. cites Leonard Lovett's list of the five original groups in black Holiness-Pentecostalism, shown here in order of date founded: United Holy Church of America (1886); Church of Christ Holiness, U.S.A. (1894–96); Church of God in Christ (1895–97); Fire Baptized Holiness Church of God in the Americas (1889); and Pentecostal Assemblies of the World (1914–24).[8]

What the Holiness-Pentecostal churches all have in common is an emphasis upon the experience of Spirit baptism, some form of doctrine and practice of speaking in tongues (glossolalia), and the belief in sanctification, or "holiness."[9] Historically, these churches have been known to preach and promote an ascetic ethic and forbid the use of alcohol, tobacco, and other addictive substances; gambling; secular dancing; and the wearing of immodest apparel. The saints follow the mandate of holiness in their worship, in their personal morality, and in their relationship to society, based upon their religious tradition to be "in the world, but not of the world."

Folklorist and novelist Zora Neale Hurston addressed the distinctiveness of Holiness-Pentecostals in a collection of essays, *The Sanctified Church*, published in 1981, more than twenty years after her death.[10] Hurston rejected the widely held view that the emergence of the Sanctified Church in the early twentieth century represented a new religious movement among blacks. Instead, she saw it as representing "older forms of Negro religious expression asserting themselves against the new."[11] She sets this re-emerging tradition in opposition to Negro Protestantism on the one hand, and against white protest Protestantism (whose adherents she called "Holy Rollers") on the other. Hurston's belief that "the Sanctified Church is a protest against the highbrow tendency in Negro Protestant congregations as the Negroes gain more education and wealth" reveals her profound contempt for Negro Protestantism, which she viewed as an inauthentic imitation of white religion.

The Sanctified Church is distinctly African-influenced, and her essay identifies these features and practices with particular attention to music and dance. Hurston's assessment of the Sanctified Church as a manifestation of lowbrow religion asserting itself against highbrow religion is revealing in terms of its identification of the critical tensions in African American life, which are the questions of cultural impact, racial awareness, and class consciousness in African Americans as they gain more wealth and status.

## PREACHING FORMS: 1918–1950

Black-led religious movements during this period took several significant directions, including Elijah Muhummad's Nation of Islam and Noble

Drew Ali's Moorish Science Temple.[12] But of critical interest is folk preaching, and what might be considered a subgroup of folk preaching, Pentecostal-Holiness preaching. Both forms, as Zora Neale Hurston suggests, adhere to their African roots and resist imitating white Protestant practices.

### *The Folk Preaching Tradition*

Historically, black preachers generally come out of either a grassroots, folk approach (folk preaching), or an academic, including seminary, approach (educated preaching). Anthropologist Walter Pitts provides a commonly held, although too narrow, description of the black folk preacher and sermon:

> The term *black folk sermon* refers to the Sunday verbal performance of the black folk preacher who is not seminary-trained but called to the ministry by some visionary experience and whose congregation consists principally of black working-class worshipers.[13]

Based upon lack of educational attainment by blacks and whites, and the number of working-class people in their congregations, most eighteenth- and nineteenth-century sermons could be labeled "folk," but the term only came to be applied after a corpus of more learned preachers began to develop prominently during the early twentieth century. Then and since, the term has been most often applied to black preaching.

Until very recently, the sermons of the folk tradition have been more often recorded by scholars of folklore and other fields than of preaching and religion.[14] One of the best known chroniclers of black folk preaching and folk culture was Zora Neale Hurston. Though not a preacher, Hurston had an uncanny ability to tap into the nuances and emotions of the black church. She based her writings on interviews with preachers or sermons given in authentic folk settings. We have included in this anthology "The Wounds of Jesus" as an example of Hurston's recording of folk preaching. By the beginning of the twentieth century, the folk tradition had evolved to the extent that it paralleled the folklore and epic poetry of other continents and centuries, which extend as far back as *Homer.* A sermon by another non-preacher, James Weldon Johnson, is also included. One of Johnson's now legendary "seven Negro sermons in verse," titled the "Creation," has achieved the status of not only great poetry, but because it so resonated in the hearts and with the dramatic sensibilities of black religious adherents, it has been regular fare for recitation and use in sermons in black churches for almost seventy-five years.[15]

Now, some final remarks on folk preaching. Folk preaching affirmed the power of narration and metaphor. It also emphasized the use of intonation, or whooping. (See the article on page 864 by Martha Simmons for a fuller analysis of whooping.) In addition to the sermons recorded by Zora Neale Hurston and James Weldon Johnson, the sermons in this anthology by C.L. Franklin, J.M. Gates, Calvin P. Dixon, A.W. Nix, Caesar Clark, and Jasper Williams are excellent examples of this important aspect of folk preaching, which has not been sufficiently celebrated in scholarly literature.

### *Pentecostal-Holiness Preaching*

Pentecostal and Holiness preachers saw their role as keepers of the folk tradition and as advocates for the causes and concerns of the poor, even as the "lowbrow-highbrow" debate continued to rage in churches. The distinctive offerings of Holiness and Pentecostal preaching includes: energetic performance, expression of emotion, evocation and response, experienced spirituality, and a mandate of holy living.

The energy of the Sanctified preacher is not as readily discernible in the pages of manuscripts as it is in live or taped preaching. A high level of energy is exerted in a concerted manner by the preacher in order to engage both the spiritual and aesthetic sensibilities of the audience. Preachers point to the Holy Spirit as the source of this energy. The preaching event itself becomes a choreography of bodily movement, animated gesture, vocal modulation, and the like, with the goal of bringing a palpable exclamation point to what might otherwise be a mundane monologue. Holy dancing, drama, song, poetry, and humor may be employed to add depth and range to the sermon.

This dramatic event is often fueled by the expression of emotion (as opposed to the suppression of emotion and movement in preaching that characterizes most white Protestant denominations and the Catholic faith). The preacher in the Holiness-Pentecostal tradition has at hand a full palette of emotions for use in coloring the presentation of the preached message, with feelings such as anger, outrage, sorrow, regret, disappointment, contentment, joy, exhilaration, and exasperation all used to convey the sermon's message more deeply. Emotion, physical movement, and vocal modulation are employed to bring the worshipping audience to some form of active participation—shouting, tears, praise, repentance, tongues-speaking—all toward the end of demonstrating openly the manifestation of the Holy Spirit.

Evocation and response, also known as call and response, is a key component of the African and African American religious heritage. The expression "call and response" comes from a style of singing in which a soloist or lead singer performs a line or melody that is responded to by other singers. Call and response is certainly applicable in the context of preaching, where the preacher's words elicit a verbal response from the listeners in an ongoing dialogue. However, the term "evocation and response" is offered here as a more appropriate designation for what happens between the preacher and the congregation. Evocation connotes the creation of something new through the power of the imagination and the summoning of supernatural forces. So, the conversation proceeds between preacher and listener, and there is the added dimension of a three-way conversation with God, who calls preachers to preach then uses them to call saints and sinners to repentance.

The spiritual experience is the major theme and content of many of these sermons, and the focus of the application and interpretation of Scripture. For Holiness and Pentecostal churches especially, the desired outcome of preaching and worship is the replication of the New Testament day of Pentecost, when the people were drawn together "on one accord" and "they were all filled with the Holy Ghost, and began to speak with other tongues, as the Spirit gave them utterance" (Acts 2:4).

Throughout the first half of the twentieth century, the theme of holy living was the dominant focus of the preacher's exhortation. As the century progressed, the mutual influences of Holiness and Pentecostal churches and black Protestant churches on each other were such that the lifestyles and worship practices of Holiness and Pentecostal believers became more closely identified with those of other black Protestants.

## NOTES

1. John Hope Franklin and Alfred A. Moss Jr., *From Slavery to Freedom: A History of Negro Americans*, 6th ed. (New York: Alfred A. Knopf, 1988).
2. James Oliver Horton and Lois E. Horton, *Hard Road to Freedom: The Story of African America* (New Brunswick, NJ: Rutgers University Press, 2001), 228.
3. Nannie H. Burroughs, "Report of the Work of Baptist Women," in *African American Religious History: A Documentary Witness*, ed. Milton C. Sernett (Durham, NC: Duke University Press, 1999), 376–402.
4. *Hard Road to Freedom*, 263.
5. Rich Anderson, "The United States Army in World War II: Manpower, Replacements,

and The Segregated Army" in Military History Online, http://www.militaryhistory online.com/wwii/usarmy/manpower.aspx. (accessed January 18, 2004).
6. Ibid.
7. "Saint" is a euphemism that identifies adherents to a religious tradition where the emphasis is on "sanctification," or personal holiness in daily living, hence the term "sanctified" church. These extremely virtuous individuals maintain membership in the sanctified church.
8. Leonard Lovett, "Black Holiness-Pentecostalism: Implications for Ethics and Social Transformation" (Ph.D. diss., Emory University, 1978), 13.
9. "Tongues" or "glossolalia" is a form of ecstatic utterance solely between the individual and the Divine. The voice or gift of communication, which has natural and physical use, is consecrated for a spiritual or liturgical purpose and then utilized as a sacrificial offering unto God. "Tongues" or "glossolalia" is often referred to as being in the spirit—some make it akin to spirit possession or a trance in which the Divine controls one's speech. See Apostle Paul, 1 Corinthians 14:18–19.
10. Zora Neale Hurston, *The Sanctified Church* (Berkeley, CA: Turtle Island Press, 1981), 103.
11. Ibid.
12. See in this volume the personal biography of Noble Drew Ali (in part 4).
13. Walter Pitts, "West African Poetics in the Black Preaching Style," *American Speech* 64, no. 2 (Summer 1989), 137–49.
14. Gerald L. Davis, *I Got the Word in Me and I Can Sing It, You Know: A Study of the Performed African-American Sermon* (Philadelphia: University of Pennsylvania Press, 1985); see William H. Pipes, *Say Amen, Brother! Old Time Negro Preaching: A Study in American Frustration* (Westport, CT: Negro University Press, 1951); see Bruce A. Rosenberg, *Can These Bones Live? The Art of the American Folk Preacher*, rev. ed. (1970; Chicago: University of Illinois Press, 1988).
15. James Weldon Johnson, *God's Trombones: Seven Negro Sermons in Verse* (New York: Viking Press, 1955), 17–20.

# WILLIAM JOSEPH SEYMOUR

*(1870–1922)*

From 1906 to 1909, William Joseph Seymour established and led the historically interracial, multicultural Azusa Street Revival Mission. Seymour envisioned an interracial Pentecostal movement that preached and practiced love for all humanity. Biographer Douglas Nelson declared, "Bishop Seymour championed one law above all others: there shall be no color line, or discrimination, of any kind in the church of Jesus Christ because God is no respecter of persons."[1]

Seymour was born on May 2, 1870, in Centerville, Louisiana. A son of emancipated slaves Simon and Phillis Seymour, he grew up in the ambiance of southern African American Baptist Christianity. As a child, Seymour was given to visions and divine dreams, and as a young adult sought a fuller revelation of God. Seymour's quest for truth, divine power, and a much-needed solution to the racial horrors that plagued African Americans who lived during the late nineteenth and early twentieth centuries caused him to travel throughout the country in search of a social cure. In 1895, Seymour left the South and settled in Indianapolis, Indiana. There he worked odd jobs and became a minister in the African Methodist Episcopal Church.

In 1900, he left Indianapolis and traveled to Cincinnati, Ohio, and embraced the Holiness movement's doctrine of entire sanctification. He was influenced by Martin Wells Knapp's God's Revivalist movement and joined Daniel S. Warner's Church of God Reformation movement/Evening Light Saints (also known as Church of God). Warner's organization taught that a great spiritual revival would occur before the rapture of the church. While traveling, Seymour contracted smallpox, which rendered his left eye impaired. During his near-death ordeal, Seymour is believed to have received ministerial licensure through the Evening Light Saints movement.

Sometime between 1903 and 1905, Seymour, in search of lost relatives, moved to Houston, Texas, where he met Holiness pastor Lucy Farrow and began pastoring a black Holiness church. Seymour also met Charles Fox Parham, a white Methodist preacher who had embraced the Holiness movement and had founded a Pentecostal Bible school in Topeka, Kansas, in 1901. His travels among blacks in the Holiness movement brought him in contact with C.P. Jones and C.H. Mason in Mississippi. In 1905, Parham established a satellite location in Houston. Seymour investigated Parham's school, and his "initial evidence" theory that receiving the baptism of the Holy Spirit was first accompanied by glossolalia.

Parham endorsed racist views and uncompromisingly upheld the racial segregation laws of the South. Seymour was segregated to the hall, where he could only hear the instructor's voice; he could not see any faces and was not allowed to participate in discussions or theological debates. Although Seymour would initially use Parham's Apostolic Faith label as the official name of his Azusa mission, he would later break all ties with Parham's movement. Cognizant of segregation and racism, Seymour taught that love for all humanity accompanied tongues and was the true evidence that a person was filled with the Spirit of God. In fact, Seymour believed that the power of love outweighed glossolalia. Nelson believed that Seymour's theology was revolutionary during the early twentieth century because it stressed "interracial inclusiveness" as the mark of the true church, and that love transcended the separation of humanity.[2] For Seymour, as Nelson explains, "The primary work of the Holy Spirit is not to produce glossolalia, but to make all races and nations into one common family. White people misunderstood Seymour's accomplishment, taking glossolalia as the distinctive mark of Pentecostal fellowship. He saw it differently."[3] For Seymour and other early twentieth-century African American Pentecostals, baptism in the Holy Spirit enabled humanity to overcome the sickness of racism, classism, sexism, and empowered those who believed with strength to love their enemies.

In the spring of 1906, Pastor Julia W. Hutchins invited Seymour to preach at her Holiness church in Los Angeles. Hutchins's church was affiliated with the California Holiness Association. After Seymour preached "Receive Ye the Holy Ghost" from Acts 2:4, he was locked out of the church, and forced to take up residence with the Asberry family on Bonnie Brae Street. After conducting several weeks of prayer meetings in the Asberry home, Seymour and the Asberrys were filled with the Holy Spirit, and afterward the revival spread into the street outside the home where Seymour preached to crowds of whites and blacks. In an attempt to accommodate the enormous gathering, a building at 312 Azusa Street was secured to hold services. After conducting weeks of revival, news of the Azusa Street Mission echoed throughout the world. Within the first few years of operation, Azusa attracted thousands of whites, blacks, and Latin Americans. In fact, many of the early leaders of the Pentecostal movement received their transformation while attending Seymour's revival, including William H. Durham, John C. Sinclair, G.B. Cashwell, and C.H. Mason. In 1906, Seymour also began publishing and distributing *The Apostolic Faith* newspaper, and by the middle of Azusa's revival years *The Apostolic Faith* periodical had gained between fifty and sixty thousand national subscribers.

The Azusa revival was ultimately crushed by racial pressures from without and undermined by some of its white members from within. Scholar Cecil M. Robeck explained how racism undermined the movement: "Many of the white congregants, though by no means all of them, had not submitted fully to the blood which was washing away the color line. The seeds of racial dissatisfaction were clearly present."[4] For example, in 1908 disaster struck the Azusa Street Mission when Clara Lum, Seymour's white mission secretary, betrayed his trust and stole the mission's national and international mailing lists and carried them to Portland, Oregon, where she and a former Azusa Street associate, Florence Crawford, began publishing Seymour's influential *Apostolic Newspaper.* Nelson asserts, "With the passing of the newspaper from Seymour and Azusa Mission an era ended at Los Angeles. The Pentecostal movement changed decisively from one of interracial equality characterized by unity to one of white domination separated into divisions."[5] Impaired by internal and external conflict and the loss of the mission's organ, Seymour's influence and leadership declined. The Pentecostal movement split along racial lines and "his supreme desire for love between Christians . . . [was] increasingly unwelcome and neglected."[6] Racial attacks severed the phenomenal interracial Azusa Street Revival. Robeck summarized Seymour's impact, "Clearly, Seymour may be credited with providing the vision of a truly 'color blind' congregation. His was a radical experiment that ultimately failed because of the inability of whites to allow for a sustained role for black leadership."[7]

On September 28, 1922, William Joseph Seymour died of a heart attack at the age of fifty-two. The association Seymour founded in 1907 as the Azusa Street Mission Churches is now known as the Apostolic Faith Churches of God, Inc. and is based in Franklin, Virginia.

• • •

*"Receive Ye the Holy Ghost" is the sermon that resulted in Seymour being locked out of the Los Angeles Holiness Church, which led to the eventual establishment of the Azusa Mission. The sermon served as a deep source of inspiration for C.H. Mason and many others for the powerful Pentecostal and Holiness movements that have developed within African American culture.*

## Receive Ye the Holy Ghost (Spring 1906)

The first step in seeking the baptism with the Holy Ghost is to have a clear knowledge of the new birth in our souls, which is the first work of grace and brings everlasting life to our souls. "Therefore, being justified by faith, we have peace with God." Every one of us that repents of our sins and turns to the Lord Jesus with faith in Him, receives forgiveness of sins. Justification and regeneration are simultaneous. The pardoned sinner becomes a child of God in justification.

The next step for us is to have a clear knowledge, by the Holy Spirit, of the second work of grace wrought in our hearts by the power of the blood and the Holy Ghost. "For by one offering, He hath perfected forever them that are sanctified, whereof the Holy Ghost also is a witness to us" (Hebrews 10:14, 15). The Scripture also teaches, "For both He that sanctifieth and they who are sanctified are all of one; for which cause He is not ashamed to call them brethren" (Hebrews 2:11). So we have Christ crowned and enthroned in our heart, "the tree of life." We have the brooks and streams of salvation flowing in our souls, but praise God, we can have the rivers. For the Lord Jesus says, "He that believeth on me as the Scripture hath saith, out of his innermost being shall flow rivers of living water. This spake He of the Spirit, for the Holy Ghost was not yet given."[8] But, praise our God, He is now given and being poured out upon all flesh. All races, nations and tongues are receiving the baptism with the Holy Ghost and fire, according to the prophecy of Joel.

When we have a clear knowledge of justification and sanctification, through the precious blood of Jesus Christ in our hearts, then we can be a recipient of the baptism with the Holy Ghost. Many people today are sanctified, cleansed from all sin and perfectly consecrated to God, but they have never obeyed the Lord according to Acts 1, 4, 5, 8, and Luke 24:39, for their real personal Pentecost, the enduement of power for service and work and for sealing unto the day of redemption. The baptism with the Holy Ghost is a free gift without repentance upon the sanctified, cleansed vessel. "Now He which establish us with you in Christ, and hath anointed us, is God, who hath also sealed us, and given the earnest of the Spirit in our hearts" (2 Corinthians 1:21–22). I praise our God for the sealing of the Holy Spirit unto the day of redemption.

Dearly beloved, the only people that will meet our Lord and Savior Jesus Christ and go with Him into the marriage supper of the Lamb, are the wise virgins—not only saved and sanctified, with pure and clean hearts, but having the baptism with the Holy Ghost. The others we find will not be prepared. They have some oil in their lamps but they have not the double portion of His Spirit.

Before Pentecost, the disciples were filled with the unction of the Holy Spirit that sustained them until they received the Holy Ghost baptism. Many people today are filled with joy and gladness, but they are far from the enduement of power. Sanctification brings rest and sweetness and quietness to our souls, for we are one with the Lord Jesus and are able to obey His precious Word that "Man shall not live by bread alone but by every word that proceedeth out of the mouth of God," and we are feeding upon Christ.

But let us wait for the promise of the Father upon our souls, according to Jesus' word, "John truly baptized with water, but ye shall receive the Holy Ghost not many days hence. . . . Ye shall receive power after that that the Holy Ghost is come upon you: and ye shall be witnesses into me, both in Jerusalem and in all Judea, and in Samaria, and unto the uttermost part of the earth" (Acts 1:5, 8). Glory! Glory! Hallelujah! O worship, get down on your knees and ask the Holy Ghost to come in, and you will find Him right at your hearts door, and He will come in. Prove Him now. Amen.

## NOTES

*Sermon source: The Apostolic Faith* 1, no. 5 (January 4, 1907), 2.

1. Nelson, "For Such a Time as This," 13.
2. Ibid., 13–14.
3. Ibid., 204. Cf. Ithiel Clemmons, "True Koinonia: Pentecostal Hopes and Historical Realities," *Pneuma: The Journal of the Society for Pentecostal Studies* 4 (Spring 1982), 46–56.
4. Robeck, "The Past," 19.
5. Nelson, "For Such a Time as This," 218.
6. Nelson, "For Such a Time as This," 266.
7. Cecil M. Robeck, "Azusa Street Revival," in Stanley M. Burgess and Gary B. McGee, eds., *Dictionary of Pentecostal and Charismatic Movements* (Grand Rapids, MI: Zondervan Publishing, 1988), 33.
8. See John 7:38.

## BIBLIOGRAPHICAL SOURCES

Daniels, David D. "They Had a Dream: Racial Harmony Broke Down, but the Hope Did Not." *Christian History* 17, no. 2, issue 58 (Spring 1998).

Nelson, Douglas. "The Black Face of Church Renewal: The Meaning of a Charismatic Explosion (1901–1985)," in *Faces of Renewal: Studies in Honor of Stanley M. Horton*, ed. Paul Elbert. Peabody, MA: Hendrickson Publishers, 1998.

———. "For Such a Time as This: The Story of Bishop William J. Seymour and the Azusa Street Revival." Ph.D. diss., University of Birmingham, England, 1981.

———. "William Joseph Seymour," in *Encyclopedia of Religion in the South*, ed. Samuel S. Hill and Samuel Hill. Reprint, Macon, GA: Mercer University Press, 1998.

Robeck, Cecil M., Jr. "The Past: Historical Roots of Racial Unity and Division in American Pentecostalism." Paper presented at "Pentecostal Partners: A Reconciliation Strategy for a 21st-Century Ministry," October 17–24, 1994, Memphis, TN.

Sanders, Rufus G.W. *William Joseph Seymour: Black Father of the 20th Century Pentecostal/Charismatic Movement.* Sandusky, OH: Alexandria Publications, 2001.

Synan, Vinson. "William Joseph Seymour," in *Dictionary of Pentecostal and Charismatic Movements*, ed. Stanley M. Burgess and Gary B. McGee. Grand Rapids, MI: Zondervan Press, 1988.

Tinney, James S. "William J. Seymour: Father of Modern Day Pentecostalism." *The Journal of the Interdenominational Theological Seminary* 4, no. 1 (1976).

# NOBLE DREW ALI

*(1886–1929)*

In the year 1886, Noble Drew Ali was born in the state of North Carolina. He identified himself as a prophet of Islam, sent to save the Moors of America, who were commonly called Negroes, from the wrath of Allah. In 1913, Ali founded the first African American Islamic Society (The Canaanite Temple) in Newark, New Jersey. The movement spread across the country as the Moorish Holy Temple of Science, and by 1920 there were twenty-five thousand Moorish Scientists spread across temples in Pittsburgh, New York, Philadelphia, Detroit, and some southern cities. Ali instilled racial pride, and his appointment of women to leadership positions within the organization was remarkably progressive.

In 1925, wearing a flaming red fez, Ali appeared on the street corners of Chicago's South Side, exhorting listeners to reject the appellation of *negro*, that African Americans were properly referred to as *Moors* (people of Moroccan descent) and had an Islamic heritage rather than a Christian one. In 1928, the movement was incorporated as The Moorish Science Temple of America, Inc.

Claiming Marcus Garvey as his forerunner, Ali eloquently defined a new sense of identity for his followers and developed Black Nationalism into a confession of faith. One of his disciples was Elijah Muhammad, who became the major force behind the Nation of Islam. Ali preached racial harmony, urging Americans of all races to reject hate and embrace love, and published his basic beliefs in *The Holy Koran of the Moorish Science Temple* (1927). In the last chapter, Prophet Noble Drew Ali wrote the following, which sums up his movement and life:

> Come all ye Asiatics of America and hear the truth about your nationality and birthrights, because you are not Negroes. Learn of your forefathers ancient and Divine Creed that you will learn to love instead of hate. We are trying to uplift fallen humanity. Come and link yourselves with the families of nations. We honor all true and divine prophets.[1]

Noble Drew Ali died in 1929.

• • •

*"Divine Warning" is a brief but illustrative message that encapsulates several of Noble Drew Ali's core beliefs: that Ali believed that he was a prophet, that Allah was the judge of the world, and that Ali and his followers were under attack by social forces and would ultimately be blessed by Allah if they remained faithful. Ali had reason to remind his followers that they were under attack, given that the group was surveilled by police and harassed by the federal Bureau of Investigation for several years. The message is printed as it exists in the files of the Moorish Science Temple, located at the Schomburg Center for Research in Black Culture, with the exception of capitalization having been provided for the name of a deity.*

## Divine Warning
## (October 17, 1928)

### The Prophet's Instruction

ISLAM?

To the members of the Moorish Science Temple of America this is the instruction from your prophet noble drew ali, be faithful to your forefathers divine and national creed that you will be blessed for your good deeds that you sow in the flesh. Allah is the one that judges the world; and his judgement is now on, but they can comprehend it not, the end of time is drawing near, so says Allah through his prophet 1' [one] noble drew ali and that is why many hearts have been turned to stone, and many have eyes to see the ears to hear, but can not hear, least they be confounded by their sin, these are the trying hours now dear moors, the evil spirits is moving; and they are trying every way [illegible words] to over throw, and drag out the true foundation of Allah [that] has been laid, and to cause confusion in the life of the ones that do believe, but if you [illegible] the favor of Allah and spirit of your forefathers, you know what you hear or see, [illegible] will sacrifice. [illegible] You will give your life to protect your movement and you [illegible] watch your enemies dear moors, your enemies are great and speak against your prophet and ridicule him to the very lowest, and the ones that speak against your divine Moorish national principles of your temple act according to [illegible]. Allah will bless your for your good works.

✦ ✦ ✦

*The following are excerpts from the teachings of Noble Drew Ali from the opening page and chapter forty-eight of his pamphlet published in 1927,* The Divine Instructions from the Holy Prophet. *This text came to be known as* The Holy Koran of the Moorish Science Temple of America, *and is referred to as the "uniting of the Holy Koran of Mecca." Sometimes the title is shorthanded as the Circle Seven Koran, because of the design on its cover. These teachings reveal Ali's basic beliefs in a form of Islam that also contains a large mixture of Christianity.*

## Excerpts from *The Divine Instructions from the Holy Prophet* (1927)

### Opening Page

The genealogy of Jesus with eighteen years of the events, life work and teachings in India, Europe, and Africa. These events occurred before He was thirty years of age. These secret lessons are full [illegible] of those who love Jesus and desire to know about His life and teaching.

Dear readers, do not falsely use these lessons. They are for good, peace, and happiness for all those who love Jesus.

Dear mothers, teach these lessons to your little ones, that they may learn to love instead of hate.

Dear fathers, by these lessons you can set your house in order and your children will learn to love instead of hate.

The lessons of this pamphlet are not for sale, but for the sake of humanity, as I am a prophet and the servant is worthy of his hire, you can receive this pamphlet for expenses. The reason these lessons have not been known is because the Moslems of India, Egypt and Palestine had these secrets and kept them back from the outside world, and when the time appointed by Allah they loosened the keys and [illegible] these secrets, and for the first time in ages have these secrets been delivered in the hands of Moslems of America. All authority and rights of publishing this pamphlet of 1927.

The industrious acts of the Moslems of northwest and southwest Africa. These are the Moabites, Hamathites, Canaanites, who were driven out of the land of Canaan, by Joshua, and recieved permission from the Pharoahs of Egyot to settle in that portion of Egypt. In later years they formed themselves kingdoms. These kingdoms are called this day Morocco, Algiers, Tunis, Tripoli, etc.

By the Prophet NOBLE DREW ALI

## Chapter XLVIII
## The End of Time and the Fulfilling of the Prophesies

1. The last Prophet in these days is Noble Drew Ali, who was prepared divinely in due time by Allah to redeem men from their sinful ways; and to warn them of the great wrath which is sure to come upon the earth.

2. John the Baptist was the forerunner of Jesus in those days, to warn and stir up the nation and prepare them to receive the divine creed which was to be taught by Jesus.

3. In these modern days there came a forerunner, who was divinely prepared by the great God-Allah and his name is Marcus Garvey, who did teach and warn the nations of the earth to prepare to meet the coming Prophet; who was to bring the true and divine Creed of Islam, and his name is Noble Drew Ali: who was prepared and sent to this earth by Allah, to teach the old time religion and the everlasting gospel to the sons of men. That every nation shall and must worship under their own vine and fig tree, and return to their own and be one with their Father God-Allah.

4. The Moorish Science Temple of America is lawfully chartered and incorporated. Any subordinate Temple that desires to receive a charter; the prophet has them to issue to every state throughout the United States, etc.

5. That the world may hear and know the truth, that among the descendants of Africa there is still much wisdom to be learned in these days for the redemption of the sons of men under Love, Truth, Peace, Freedom, and Justice.

6. We, as a clean and pure nation descended from the inhabitants of Africa, do not desire to amalgamate or marry into the families of the pale skin nations of Europe. Neither serve the gods of their religion, because our forefathers are the true and divine founders of the first religious creed, for the redemption and salvation of mankind on earth.

7. Therefore we are returning the Church and Christianity back to the European Nations, as it was prepared by their forefathers for their earthly salvation.

8. While we, the Moorish Americans are returning to Islam, which was founded by our forefathers for our earthly and divine salvation.

9. The covenant of the great God-Allah: "Honor they father and they mother that they days may be longer upon the earth land, which the Lord thy God, Allah hath given thee!"

10. Come all ye Asiatics of America and hear the truth about your nationality and birthrights, because you are not negroes. Learn of your forefathers ancient and divine Creed. That you will learn to love instead of hate.

11. We are trying to uplift fallen humanity. Come and link yourselves with the families of nations. We honor all the true and divine prophets.

## *Notes*

*Sermon source:* "Divine Warning" is from the files of the Moorish Science Temple, Schomburg Center for Research in Black Culture. Excerpts from *The Divine Instructions from the Holy Prophet*, also known as *The Holy Koran of the Moorish Science Temple of America* (1927), are contained in Federal Bureau of Investigation, Moorish Science Temple of America (Noble Drew Ali) BUFILE: 62-25889, http://foia.fbi.gov/moortemp/moortempla.pdf (accessed April 9, 2007), part 1a, page 82.

1. Johnson-Bey, "Noble Drew Ali and the M.S.T. of A."

## *Bibliographical Sources*

Appiah, Kwame Anthony, and Henry L. Gates Jr., eds. *Africana: The Encyclopedia of the African and African American Experience*, 5 vols. New York: Oxford University Press, 2005.

Essien-Udom, Essien Udosen. *Black Nationalism: The Search for an Identity.* Chicago: University of Chicago Press, 1995.

Gates, Henry Louis, Jr., and E. Higginbotham. *African American Lives.* New York: Oxford University Press, 2004.

Gomez, Michael A. *Black Crescent: The Experience and Legacy of African Muslims in the Americas.* Cambridge: Cambridge University Press, 2005.

Johnson-Bey, Susan D. "Noble Drew Ali and the M.S.T. of A." 3rd ed. Moorish Science Temple of America, 1999.

Pleasant-Bey, Elihu. *The Biography of Noble Drew Ali: The Exhuming of a Nation.* Charleston, SC: BookSurge Publishing, 2004.

# CALVIN P. DIXON

*(birth and death dates unknown)*

Calvin P. Dixon was the first black preacher to record a sermon, doing so in 1925. His recordings are quite somber compared to those of the spirited whooping preachers who would soon follow him. However, Dixon was admired by black and white audiences. In fact, whites who heard him nicknamed him Black Billy Sunday after the famous white evangelist, William Ashley Sunday (1862–1935).

As Dixon's recordings show, his preaching was theologically conservative and simple for hearers to understand. Dixon is representative of the nineteenth-century black folk preacher who, with more opportunities for education and travel, began to lose much of the dialect that so clearly marked preachers from the South. However, he, like other recorded preachers such as A.W. Nix, maintained their ability to relate to the "folk" and the everyman, including the poor, as shown by his record sales. Dixon was the first to record "As an Eagle Stirreth Up Her Nest," the sermon which would later make C.L. Franklin, father of soul singer Aretha Franklin, a household name in the black religious community.

• • •

*In this message, Dixon retells the well-known story of the prophet Elijah, who goes head to head with Ahab and the prophets of Baal. The sermon is straightforward and no-frills, a Dixon trademark. His message is that those who are on God's side will win and those who are not will lose.*

## Who Is Your God
## (1925)

You will find my text this morning the eighteenth chapter of First Kings and the twenty-first verse. "How long halt ye between two opinions."

Let us go to Mount Carmel for few a minutes. King Ahab had forsaken God and all of the coast of Israel and all the upper kingdom had fallen into shambles. There was an old prophet out in the mountains who God has told to go to Ahab and tell him that he was going to lock up the heavens. God locked up the heavens and gave the prophet the keys. He burst upon him like a clap of thunder. Give him the message and hurry that way. I suppose Ahab laughed at him. What? No more rain. Why you must be crazy. There were 850 priests and Baal altogether and pretty soon the weather gets dry and the earth parches and the cracks open. The rivers have but a little water in them and the brooks dry up all together. The grass begins to perish and the cattle begin to die too. There was famine and death in the land. If it doesn't rain pretty soon, there will not be rain nor land at all. One day the king was talking to the Prophet Obadiah. He had one good man near him among the false prophets of Baal. Most every man likes to have a good person near him even if he's bad himself. He may be walking in a hurry some time. See here, Obadiah, you go one way and I'll go another and see if we can find some water and grass somewhere.

So all this time, God has Elijah hid to let Ahab know that there was a shelter in the time of confusion. God fed Elijah with angel food by a raven. The Bible said that God will give us water and bread is sure. But God fed Elijah with bread and water. The heavens is locked because of sin and they was unlocked because of obedience. Elijah is found. Is that you? says Obadiah. Ahab has been hunting for you in all of the kingdom for me to fetch you up if you were alive. Yes. I am here, said Elijah. You go and tell Ahab that I want to see him. I dare not do that, said Obadiah. For just as soon as I tell him that you are here, the spirit will catch you away and take you somewheres else. Then the king will be angry and maybe he will kill me. No, said Elijah. As the Lord liveth and I will meet Ahab face to face this day. Go Obadiah hurry and find Ahab and tell him you have seen the prophet.

What? Elijah? Yes. Why didn't you bring him along? He will not come. He said he wants to come to you. Ahab was not used to having people talk that way to him. But he is anxious to see the man of God. So, when he sees Elijah he is angry and says, aren't thou he that troubleth Israel?

And Elijah answered and said, thou art the man that has been giving Israel so much trouble. We have enough of this sort of stuff.

Some people are praying to God and some are praying to Baal and this question must be settled. You just bring all of your prophets and your praying upon Mount Carmel and I'll also come. We'll build an altar and offer sacrifice on it and the God that answers by fire, let him be God. I agree said Ahab, oh yes. And away he went and told the prophets to get ready for the triumph.

All the places of business were closed and everybody was going up to Mount Carmel. There were 850 prophets, the priest of Baal all together. The king in his chariot, at the head. Elijah marched all alone clad in the skin of wild beasts with a staff in his hand. No banner. No possessions. No great men in his train, but he could hold the keys of heaven in his hand for three years and six months. He was all alone. Now Elijah says to the people: How long halt ye between two opinions? Let the priests of Baal, build them an altar and offer sacrifice but put no fire under it and I'll do the same. The God that answers by fire let him be God. So the priest built their altar. I'm sure if God would have let him, Satan would have brought a spark of fire and set the altar on fire. But God would not let him. Well they began to pray. Oh, hear us Baal. Oh, hear us Baal. Elijah might have said, why haven't you prayed for water wiith this dry weather? You might as well have prayed for water as to pray for fire. After a long time, they begin to get hoarse. You must pray louder. Maybe if you want Baal to hear, pray loud. Maybe he's asleep. Poor fellows. They haven't any voice left. So they began to pray and grunt. Then they cut themselves with knives, lifting up their streaming arms to Baal. But no fire came down.

It is getting towards sundown and the prophet of the Lord built an altar. Mind you, he does not have anything to do with the altar of Baal. He builds an entirely different one on the ruins of the Lord's altar that had been broken down. We'll not have any trick about this thing, said the prophet. So they began with twelve barrels of water and poured it on the altar. I do not know how they managed to get so much water; but they did it. Elijah prayed, ahhhh God of Abraham, Isaac and Jacob, let it be known this day that thou art God in Israel. He did not have to pray very loud. God heard him at once and the fire came down. First on the cypress, burnt up the wood, burnt up the stone and the altar. Jehovah is God. Nobody can talk any longer; he's God. Calvary is more wonderful than Mount Carmel. The sacrifice of Christ on the cross is more than the burnt sacrifice on the altar. Glory to God. Amen.

### NOTE

*Sermon source: Preachers and Congregations: Complete Recorded Works—Volume 3, 1925–1929* (Austria: Document Records, 1997).

### BIBLIOGRAPHICAL SOURCE

Oliver, Paul. *Songsters and Saints: Vocal Traditions on Race Records.* Cambridge: Cambridge University Press, 1984.

## J.M. GATES

*(1884–1945)*

J.M. Gates is likely the most prolific black sermonizer of the early 1900s who has had very little written about him. He was born on July 14, 1884, in Georgia to George Gates and Minnie Gates (Harris). J.M. Gates was married to his first wife, Nellie, in 1924, and to his second wife, Lydia, in 1937. He began preaching in his early twenties. In 1914, he became the pastor of Mount Calvary Church in Rockdale Park, Georgia. As his recording career waned, due to disagreements between Gates and church leaders, Gates was voted out as pastor in 1941 after twenty-seven years as pastor of Mount Calvary.

The sheer number of Gates' recordings is still unparalleled (two hundred between 1926 and 1941). He made his debut in 1926, recording for Columbia Records. Not anticipating how well-received Gates would be, Columbia did not sign him to a contract. Talent scout Polk Brockman signed Gates, and he then recorded ninety-three sides by the end of 1926. Brockman had Gates record for Banner Records, Pathe, Victor Records, Vocalion, Paramount, and Gannett. It is amazing to note that Gates recorded one quarter of all the sermons released in the country up to 1943, although he sometimes recorded the same sermon for more than one label. His popularity was unquestionable. When "Death's Black Train Is Coming" was released in 1926, it sold more than fifty thousand copies.

Gates had a unique preaching and recording style. Gospel scholar Tony Heilbut notes, "Reverend Gates, the most celebrated folk preacher, would usually preach a brief sermonette to hieratic encouragement from the sisters. Then everything climaxed in a rhythmic shout accompanied by syncopated hand-clapping and quasi-Dixieland instrumentation, much resembling the Sunday services still broadcast from many sanctified churches."[1] Adding to Gates's popularity was the fact that he produced recordings that had the titles of blues songs or were very provocative: "Kinky Hair Is No Disgrace," "Will the Coffin Be Your Santa Claus?" "Hitler and Hell," "To All You Negro Haters," "The Woman and the Snake," and "Mannish Women."

What also made his recordings unique was the presence of Sister Norman, Sister Bell, and Deacon Leon Davis, who often served as the congregation. They, along with Gates, also sang on many of his recordings. They gave Gates's sermons a sound that was typical of that heard in black Baptist and Holiness churches of the time, where listeners might respond to the preaching by saying, "Amen," "Yes, Lord," "Say it," and "Go 'head preacher," in the call-and-response nature of the black church. However, in atypical fashion during some of the Gates recordings Norman, Bell, and Davis can be heard actually talking back to Gates in entire sentences. Gates was part of a group of early recordings by African American preachers that included Calvin P. Dixon, Mose Doolittle, William McKinley Dawkins, P.C. Edmonds, and J.F. Forest. Their work is a rich legacy of black folk preaching.

Gates died in 1945 in Atlanta of an acute cerebral hemorrhage. According to professor and folklorist of African American culture Pete Lowry, Gates was so popular that his funeral lasted almost four hours and was the largest held in Atlanta prior to that of Martin Luther King Jr.

• • •

*Long before the days of the "big box" stores, Gates advocates boycotting chain stores that close down local and neighborhood merchants and do not extend credit to poor people. This sermon is presented in a story-telling, conversational form. It is atypical of black preaching of this period, and its uniqueness, along with the relevant subject matter, likely account for it being a top-seller.*

## Goodbye to Chain Stores, Part I (April 1930)

I think the password of this country should be on today, *Stay Out of the Chain Stores* or *Goodbye Chain Store*. I tell you when I hear and see so much evil being done through the chain store—my people particularly—you just as well open your eye and look on the field. Because, it means to you no job—number one.

Number two—it means to you—no credit. You spend a hundred dollars a week; you get no credit. When you become sick [and] out of a job, you gets no credit. I'm thinking of a good old deacon of mine who used to spend his money in this church, but now he don't even attend the church.

BELL: Yes, sir, I tell you the truth, Brother Pastor, the place I's working at, you see, the white folk went out of business 'cause the chain store ruint them. And that's why you ain't been seeing me to church. If things keep on like they is right now, Brother Pastor, you won't see me soon. But, I hope it'll change.

GATES: Ah, it'll never change so long as you stay in the chain store. I'm going to tell you this thing means to you what it meant to me when I cut the limb off between me and the tree. It meant a fall. And, you're going to get a fall if you keep it up. You just as well to patronize the independent merchant; patronize the hometown merchant because you have a reason.

The first reason is this: who is going to credit you? Second reason—who's buying the mules for the country people when they come to town to spend their cash money? Who's going to let you have a mule on a credit? Who's going to let you have a wagon on a credit? Who's going to let you have an automobile or help you to get one and let you pay for it when you can? Who's going to put up with the boll weevils eating up everything you're trying to make and then crediting you and feeding you? Is the chain store people going to do it? Nah! They never have done it and never will.

So, Sister Bell, I don't see you now much.

BELL: Well, I don't know why!

GATES: I saw you with a bundle coming from some store.

BELL: Where you thought I's coming from?

GATES: Chain store is what I thought.

BELL: Well you must saw . . . not me. I trade right round the corner there with that man that gives me my credit any time.

GATES: That's what you ought to do.

BELL: Oh yes, if it's raining and I can't carry my clothes, I gets my credit right on and if I carry in my clothes and pay him off, it's just the same thing. No, not me with the chain store.

GATES: Well, you got good sense and now I'm thinking about Sister Jordan who is a good cook and said to be one of the best cooks. But, I don't see her now at the job and neither is she in the big house she used to live in.

BELL: Yes, Bro' Pastor, those people are cooking, but they're cooking for their self now.

GATES: Yes, that's it. A man that used to come by my home driving one of those big red trucks, he, too, used to boast about his job. But, the man that he was working for then is driving a little Ford and he's walking now. His boss man was in the Cadillac. So, these chain stores have got one man that's going up and down these highways that don't help pave these highways and these streets and don't pay for nothing in town. Stay outta these chain stores.

✦ ✦ ✦

*Faced again with a relevant, everyday issue, Gates admonishes church members to pay for their burials in advance.*

## PAY YOUR POLICY MAN (DECEMBER 1930)

I want to talk to you on an important subject: *Pay Your Policy Man.* And, pay him at the door. You hear me? Pay him at the door.

WOMAN IN CONGREGATION: I know I ain't got to pay this week at nowhere.

GATES: You know I'm getting tired of begging the church to bury your dead. You should pay your policy man.

WOMAN: I know but the thing what gets on my nerve—you worry us 'bout paying the policy man, but you never do say anything about the policy man paying us when somebody dies.

GATES: You know but no longer than this morning I heard a woman muddling about the insurance company not paying her when I heard her say the funeral man is always at my door and she didn't pay her policy man and she's expecting the company to pay her. But, you should pay your policy man.

WOMAN: Well, I paid mine in September. Mine's all set.

GATES: Why don't you take out a five or ten cents, fifteen or twenty-five cents policy and pay by the week or by the month or by the year?

MAN IN CONGREGATION: Ah, I takes out policies every week but I ain't got nothing to pay 'em.

GATES: That's the very thing I want to talk to you about. Why don't you stop taking out policies and pay them you have?

MAN: They keep on a running me down. I don' told them I don't have nothing.

GATES: Well, you ought to have sense enough to know if you expect to get anything out of a policy, you must pay your policy man. That's all.

MAN: One just left my house this morning, Brother Pastor—just worrying me. I turned around and joined it but I know good and well I ain't got anything to pay.

GATES: Some people will try to take a new policy each month in the year and pay one week in each month and then die and somebody else have to bury them.

WOMAN: Um huh, I don't take out no new ones, though. I've got policies I've had for years. I mean I did have 'em, but since it's got so tight like that, you see, I done got out of it.

GATES: If you want the companies to pay off like the contract said, then you must pay your policy man.

MAN: Well, I'll tell you about me. I don't know if I die I don't know what will come of me but I'm gon' sho have it fixed so the church can take care of me some way; may have to beg. I don't know what they have to do 'cause I can't pay no policy.

GATES: Yeah, but some men won't pay their policy because they're afraid that when they die somebody else will get up in it. But, I'm going to tell you whatever you have in this world; you're going to leave it in this world. You hear me?

MAN: Oh, I ain't worried about dying, now. Far as that's concerned 'cause I know I've got to die.

GATES: Yes, but you should pay your policy man. You hear me? You owe it and you should pay it if you expect somebody to take care of you. And then, you ought to pay it because a policy when you're dead wipes away tears from many widows.

WOMAN: That's right, Brother Pastor. I believe I'll pay mine tomorrow 'cause it's been due ever since September when I paid it. Well, what do you mean by this wiping away tears business?

GATES: Well, I'll tell you what I mean—I mean just what I saw. I saw a widow go up in the health insurance company—up there weeping, but when they paid her off, she come down smiling. Pay your policy man.

WOMAN: That's what I thought.

✦ ✦ ✦

*In this sermon, Gates encourages parishioners not to follow gamblers, drunkards, robbers, and the like because they are all traveling on an express train bound for hell. Unlike "Goodbye to Chain Stores," "Hell Bound Express Train" was a sermon that Gates whooped almost from beginning to end. Its popularity spawned sermons by others that contained similar titles and ideas.*

## Hell Bound Express Train (October 1927)

All aboard for the hell bound express train. It makes some stops. I heard a man say she made fourteen stops and pulled out one hour and a half behind time. I don't believe it. My Bible tells me when the rich man died; he lifted up his eyes in hell. So all you've got to do is die at the hell bound station and the hell bound train is leaving from all the stations at all times. Not only leaving, but persons getting on board.

I can hear the damnation bell ringing. I hear it moving through the land. All persons getting on board. Lawyers getting on board. Gamblers getting on board. Drunkards getting on board. Highway robbers—they getting on board. Those who don' smoked getting on board.

Some getting on from round Fourth Street in New Orleans. Some getting on up on Beale Street in Memphis, Tennessee. Some getting on board from Eighteenth Street, Birmingham, Alabama. Street singer, gambler is getting on board up on Decatur Street, Atlanta, Georgia. The midnight rambler getting on board from Church Street in Norfolk, Virginia.

Some are getting on board on an express hell bound train. She's going lightning speed through State Street in Chicago, Illinois, and down Taylor Street in Detroit, Michigan, and onto Harlem, New York, through Harris up to the burning city of hell. I can hear the damnation passengers when they cry: *Woe is me.* The hot fire of eternal damnation awaiting them in the burning city of hell. I see black smoke rushing as she is moving down the road. I can hear them when they cry: [singing] *Lord, have mercy! Lord, have mercy! Lord, have mercy!*

### Notes

*Sermon source:* The sermons are transcribed from *Reverend J.M. Gates (Volume I) Sermons with Responses Assisted by His Congregation.*

1. Cohn, introduction to compact disc notes for J.M. Gates, *The Best of Reverend J.M. Gates.*

### *Bibliographical Sources*

Cohn, Lawrence. Introduction to compact disc notes for J.M. Gates, *The Best of Reverend J.M. Gates.* Sony Music International, 2004.

Gates, J.M. *Reverend J.M. Gates (Volume I) Sermons with Responses, Assisted by His Congregation.* Originally released 1927–1940; re-released on compact disc by Sony Music International Inc./Columbia—Legacy and Okeh Electric, 2004.

*Preachers and Congregations, Vol. 3: 1925–1929.* Austria: Document Records DOCD-5547, 1997.

Werner, Craig. *Higher Ground: Stevie Wonder, Aretha Franklin, Curtis Mayfield and the Rise and Fall of American Soul.* New York: Crown Publishers, 2004, 17.

## ZORA NEALE HURSTON

*(1891–1960)*

Folklorist, novelist, autobiographer, essayist, and anthropologist Zora Neale Hurston was born in Eatonville, Florida, one of eight children of John Hurston, a Baptist minister, and Lucy Ann Hurston (Potts), a schoolteacher. Eatonville was the first incorporated black community in America. John Hurston was elected as mayor of the town on three occasions. Zora's mother died when Zora was thirteen. Zora went to live with various relatives after her father remarried. She left Eatonville soon after and, though underage, worked as a seamstress with a traveling theater troupe.

She left the troupe and went back to high school, graduating in 1918 at age twenty-three. She then attended Howard University, where she began to write and had her first story published in the Howard newspaper in 1921. At age thirty she moved to New York and became part of the Harlem Renaissance. Her writing skill gained her a scholarship to Barnard College in 1925. After Barnard she did graduate work at Columbia. She used her talents as a writer and anthropologist to distinctively capture the diversities of black folklore in the United States as well as in Bermuda, Haiti, and Jamaica. *Their Eyes Were Watching God*, considered Hurston's greatest novel, was published in 1937. Her stories and articles appeared in several notable magazines, and she published three additional novels: *Jonah's Gourd Vine* (1934), *Moses, Man of the Mountain*

(1939), and *Seraph on the Suwanee* (1948). She gained two Guggenheim fellowships for her research of black culture.

Hurston married twice: once in 1927 and again in 1939. She was well known during the 1920s and 1930s, but was virtually forgotten by the 1950s. Years after she died in poverty and obscurity, Hurston's writings were "found" by white and African American writers, notably Alice Walker, who claims her as an early feminist and literary ancestor.

• • •

*Hurston recorded the following sermon by Rev. C.C. Lovelace in Eau Gallie, Florida, and it is contained in her book,* The Sanctified Church. *No additional historical information is known concerning Rev. Lovelace. However, those who love great preaching, especially folk preaching, are grateful to Hurston, because through her recording, she has placed Lovelace securely in history as the author of one of the best whooped folk sermons of the twentieth century. The sermon exemplifies the powerfully imaginative use of metaphors and the vivid details that make a sermon come alive. The presence of the "ha!" in the sermon indicates words that were intoned. Intonation is also indicated by the spelling out of words as they were spoken (i.e., see-eee-ee). "Ah!" is the breath that the preacher takes in the preaching art form known as "whooping."*

## The Wounds of Jesus (May 3, 1929)

Our theme this morning is the wounds of Jesus. When the Father shall ask "What are these wounds in thine hand?" He shall answer, "Those are they with which I was wounded in the house of my friends" (Zachariah 8:6).

We read in the fifty-third chapter of Isaiah where He was wounded for our transgressions and bruised for our iniquities; and the apostle Peter affirms that His blood was spilt from before the foundation of the world.

I have seen gamblers wounded. I have seen desperadoes wounded; thieves and robbers and every other kind of characters, law-breakers, and each one had a reason for his wounds. Some of them was unthoughtful, and some for being overbearing, some by the doctor's knife. But, all wounds disfigures a person.

Jesus was not unthoughtful. He was not overbearing. He was never a bully. He was never sick. He was never a criminal before the law and yet

He was wounded. Now a man usually gets wounded in the midst of his enemies; but this man was wounded, says the text, in the house of His friends. It is not your enemies that harm you all the time. Watch that close friend, and every sin we commit is a wound to Jesus. The blues we play in our homes is a club to beat up Jesus; and these social card parties. . . .

Jesus have always loved us from the foundation of the world.
When God
Stood out on the apex of His power
Before the hammers of creation
Fell upon the anvils of Time and hammered out the ribs of the earth
Before he made ropes
By the breath of fire
And set the boundaries of the ocean by gravity of His power
When God said, ha!
Let us make man
And the elders upon the altar cried, ha!
If you make man, ha!
He will sin.
God my master, ha!
Christ, yo' friend said?
Father!! Ha-aa!
I am the teeth of Time.

That comprehended de dust of de earth
And weighed de hills in scales
Painted de rainbow dat marks de end of de parting storm
Measured de seas in de holler of my hand
Held de elements in a unbroken chain of controllment.
De Moon, Ha!
Grabbed up de reins of de tides
And dragged a thousand seas behind her
As she walked around de throne—
Ah-h, please make man after me
But God said, No.
De stars bust out from their diamond sockets
And circled de glitterin throne cryin'
A-aah! Make man after me.

God said, No!
I'll make man in my own image, ha

I'll put him in de garden
And Jesus said, ha!
And if he sin,
I'll go his bond before yo' mighty throne
Ah, He was yo' friend
He made us all, ha!
Delegates to de judgment convention
Ah!
Faith hasn't got no eyes, but she's long-legged
But take de spy-glass of Faith
And look into dat upper room
When you are alone to yourself
When yo' heart is burnt with fire, ha!
When de blood is lopin thru yo' veins
Make man, ha!
If he sin, I will redeem him
I'll break de chasm of hell
Where de fire's never quenched
I'll go into de grave
Where de worm never dies, Ah!
So God A'mighty, ha!
Got His stuff together
He dipped some water out of de mighty deep
He got Him a handful of dirt, ha!
From de foundation sills of de earth.
He seized a thimble full of breath, ha!
From de drums of de wind, ha!
God my master!

Now I'm ready to make man
Aa-aah!
Who shall I make him after? Ha!
Worlds within worlds begin to wheel and roll.

God said, No!
I'll make man in my own image, ha
I'll put him in de garden
And Jesus said, ha!
And if he sin,
I'll go his bond before yo' mighty throne
Ah, He was yo' friend

He made us all, ha!
Delegates to de judgment convention
Ah!
Faith hasn't got no eyes, but she's long-legged
But take de spy-glass of Faith
And look into dat upper room
When you are alone to yourself
When yo' heart is burnt with fire, ha!
When de blood is lopin thru yo' veins
Make man, ha!
If he sin, I will redeem him
I'll break de chasm of hell
Where de fire's never quenched
I'll go into de grave
Where de worms never dies, Ah!
So God A'mighty, ha!
Got His stuff together
He dipped some water out of de mighty deep
He got Him a handful of dirt, ha!
From de foundation sills of de earth.
He seized a thimble full of breath, ha!
From de drums of de wind, ha!
God my master!
Now I'm ready to make man
Aa-aah!
Who shall I make him after? Ha!
Worlds within worlds begin to wheel and roll.

De Sun, Ah!
Gethered up de fiery skirts of her garments
And wheeled around de throne, Ah!
Saying, Ah, make man after me, Ah!
God gazed upon the sun
And sent her back to her blood-red socket
And shook His head, ha!
Like de iron monsters on de rail
Look into dat upper chamber, ha!
We notice at de supper table
As He gazed upon His friends, ha!
His eyes flowin wid tears, ha!
"My soul is exceedingly sorrowful unto death, ha!

For this night, ha!
One of you shall betray me, ha!
It were not a Roman officer, ha!
It were not a centurion soldier
But one of you
Who I have chosen my bosom friend
That sops in the dish with me shall betray me."
I want to draw a parable.
I see Jesus
Leaving heben with all of His grandeur
Disrobin Hisself of His matchless honor
Yieldin up de scepter of revolvin worlds
Clothing Hisself in de garment of humanity
Coming into de world to rescue His friends
Two thousand years have went by on their rusty ankles
But with the eye of faith I can see Him
Look down from His high towers of elevation
I can hear Him when He walks about the golden streets
I can hear em ring under His footsteps
Sol me—e-e, Sol do.
Sol me—e-e, Sol do.

I can see Him step out upon the rim bones of nothing
Crying I am de way
De truth and de light.
Ah!
God A'mighty!
I see Him grab de throttle
Of de well ordered train of mercy.
I see kingdoms crush and crumble
Whilst de angels held de winds in de corner chambers.
I see Him arrive on His earth
And walk de streets thirty and three years.
Oh-h-hhh!
I see Him walking beside de sea of Galilee wid his disciples
this declaration gendered on His lips,
"Let us go on the other side."
God A'mighty!

Dey entered de boat,
Wid their oarus [oars] stuck in de back.

Sails unfurled to de evenin breeze
And de ship was now sailin.
As she reached de center of de lake
Jesus was 'sleep on a pillow in de rear of de boat
And de dynamic powers of nature become disturbed
And de mad winds broke de heads of de western drums
And fell down on de Lake of Galilee
And buried themselves behind de gallopin waves
And de white-caps marbilized themselves like an army
And walked out like soldiers goin to battle
And de zig-zag lightning
Licked out her fiery tongue
And de flying clouds
Threw their wings in the channels of the deep
And bedded de waters like a road-plow
And faced de current of de chargin billows.

And de terrific bolts of thunder—they bust in de clouds
And de ship begin to reel and rock.
God A'mighty!
And one of de disciples called Jesus
"Master!! Carest thou not that we perish?"
And He arose
And de storm was in its pitch
And de lightin played on His raiments as He stood on the prow of the boat
And placed His foot upon the neck of the storm
And spoke to the howlin winds
And de sea fell at His feet like a marble floor
And de thunders went back in their vault
Then He set down on de rim of de ship
And took de hooks of His power
And lifted de billows in His lap
And rocked de winds to sleep on His arm
And said, "Peace be still."
And de Bible says there was a calm.
I can see Him wid de eye of faith
When He went from Pilate's house
Wid the crown of seventy-two wounds upon His head
I can see Him as He mounted Calvary and hung upon de cross for our Sins.
I can see-eee-ee
De mountains fall to their rocky knees when He cried

"My God, my God! Why hast thou forsaken me?"
The mountains fell to their rocky knees and trembled like a beast
From the stroke of the master's axe.

One angel took the flinches of God's eternal power
And bled the veins of the earth
One angel that stood at the gate with a flaming sword
Was so well pleased with his power
Until he pierced the moon with his sword
And she ran down in blood
And de sun
Batted her fiery eyes and put on her judgment robe
And laid down in de cradle of eternity
And rocked herself into sleep and slumber.
He died until the great belt in the wheel of time
And de geological strata fell aloose
And a thousand angels rushed to de canopy of heben
With flamin swords in their hands
And placed their feet upon blue ether's bosom and looked
back at de dazzlin throne
And de arc angels [archangels] had veiled their faces
And de throne was draped in mournin
And de orchestra had struck silence for the space of half an hour
Angels had lifted their harps to de weepin willows
And God had looked off to-wards immensity
And blazin worlds fell off His teeth
And about that time Jesus groaned on de cross and said,
"It is finished."
And then de chambers of hell explode
And de damnable spirits
Come up from de Sodomistic world and rushed into de
smoky camps of eternal night
And cried, "Woe! Woe! Woe!"
And then de Centurion cried out
"Surely this is the Son of God."
And about dat time
De angel of Justice unsheathed his flamin sword and
ripped de veil of de temple
And de High Priest vacated his office
And then de sacrificial energy penetrated de mighty strata
And quickened de bones of de prophets.

And they arose from their graves and walked about in de streets of
Jerusalem.
I heard de whistle of de damnation train
Dat pulled out from Garden of Eden loaded wid cargo goin to hell
Ran at break-neck speed all de way thru de law
All de way thru de prophetic age
All de way thru de reign of kings and judges
Plowed her way thru de Jordan
And on her way to Calvary when she blew for de switch
Jesus stood out on her track like a rough-backed mountain
And she threw her cow-catcher in His side and His blood
ditched de train.

He died for our Sins.
Wounded in the house of His friends.
That's where I got off de damnation train
And dats where you must get off, ha!
For in dat mor-ornin', ha!
To dat judgment convention, ha!
When de two trains of Time shall meet on de trestle
And wreck de burning axles of de unformed ether
And de mountains shall skip like lambs
When Jesus shall place one foot on de neck of de sea, ha!
One foot on dry land
When His chariot wheels shall be running hub-deep in fire
He shall take His friends thru the open bosom of a unclouded sky
And place in their hands de hosanna fan
And they shall stand round and round His beatific throne
And praise His name forever.
Amen.

### *Note*

*Sermon source:* Zora Neale Hurston, *The Sanctified Church* (Berkeley, CA: Turtle Island Press, 1981).

### *Bibliographical Sources*

Gates, Henry Louis, Jr., and Evelyn Brooks Higginbotham, eds. *African American Lives*. New York: Oxford University Press, 2004, 425–27.

Gilyard, Keith, and Anissa Wardi, eds. *African American Literature*. New York: Pearson Longman, 2004.

Logan, Rayford W., and Michael R. Winston, eds. *Dictionary of American Negro Biography*. New York: W. W. Norton, 1992, 340–43.

# VERNON JOHNS

*(1892–1965)*

Vernon Napoleon Johns was born on April 22, 1892, in Darlington Heights, Prince Edward County, Virginia, to William Branch and Sally Price Branch. His father was a Baptist preacher. When at the age of ten, his family no longer had money to send him to school, Johns educated himself while working in the fields. He taught himself Latin, Greek, German, and Hebrew. Johns would later use his farming experiences as inspiration for moving sermons about the value of hard work and the sacredness of nature. Educated at Union University, Oberlin College, and Virginia Seminary, with later studies at the University of Chicago, he was ordained to the Baptist ministry in 1918. Eight years later, Johns became the first African American preacher to have a sermon, "Transfigured Moments," (presented here) published in *Best Sermons of the Year*. In 1927 he married Altona Trent, the daughter of the president of Livingston College in North Carolina, and they had six children (three boys and three girls). After launching a pamphlet series, *Negro Pulpit Opinion*, Johns left Lynchburg early in 1927 to succeed Mordecai Johnson as pastor of First Baptist Church in Charleston, West Virginia. In 1929 he became the president of Virginia Seminary. After four years at Virginia Seminary he left the school and pastored several churches in various states.

Later in his career, Johns developed his sermons into fiery speeches against the "separate but equal" system of segregation, criticizing both blacks and whites for failing to work in earnest for complete equality for blacks. He became the minister of Dexter Avenue Baptist Church in Montgomery, Alabama, in 1948 and often upset its conservative congregation with his unique sermons on racial pride and societal justice. Throughout his career Johns influenced a generation of preachers and future civil rights leaders. Johns also preached that African Americans should support each other economically and demonstrated this by selling fresh produce on the streets of Montgomery, an embarrassment to Dexter's mainly middle-class congregation. Although Johns' message was not always well received, he laid the groundwork for the civil rights movement of the 1960s. Not only did Johns' congregation reel from some of his sermons, he also upset local white Birmingham preachers by protesting on a bus in Montgomery and by preaching sermons such as "Segregation After Death," "It's Safe to Murder Negroes in Montgomery," and "When the Rapist is White." Also while at Dexter his essay, "Civilized Interiors," was published in Herman Dreer's *American Literature by Negro Authors* in 1950. Johns resigned from Dexter in 1953 and moved back to Virginia, and Dexter Avenue Baptist church appointed their new preacher, a young man by the name of Martin Luther King Jr. Vernon Johns spent the rest of his life farming and touring as a preacher and lecturer.

• • •

*The following sermon was preached while Johns was pastor at Court Street Baptist Church in Lynchburg, Virginia, around 1925. Publication of the sermon in 1926 in Joseph Fort Newton's* Best Sermons, *along with the sermons of great white preachers such as Reinhold Neibuhr, Harry Emerson Fosdick, and Henry Sloane Coffin, increased Johns' already growing stature among blacks; his preaching genius coupled with his vociferous fight for social justice led some of the future leaders of the civil rights movement to seek out Johns as a mentor. The sermon also made whites aware of the preaching prowess of Vernon Johns. In this message Johns takes yet another opportunity to present his lifelong message that humanity ought to daily be faithful to God and seek justice. He implores every man to speak truth to power as did Moses in one age, Elijah the Tisbite in another, and Jesus and Lincoln in others. John thunders "We enthrone Justice in places where there is no serious objection to it. We practice brotherhood within carefully restricted areas. We forgive other people's enemies. We carry a Bible but not a cross. Instead of the Second Mile, we go a few yards of the first and then wonder that Christian goals are not realized. 'O fools and slow of heart to believe all that the prophets have spoken!' "*

## Transfigured Moments
## (ca. 1925)

*Then answered Peter, and said unto Jesus, Lord, it is good for us to be here: if thou wilt, let us make here three tabernacles; one for thee, and one for Moses, and one for Elijah.*

—Matthew 17:4 (King James Version)

Peter, James and John, who had already gone with the Master to the death bed in the house of Jairus, and would very soon come closer to his agony in Gethsemane than the other disciples, were now with him in "a place apart," somewhere on the slopes of Hermon. Strange things were happening there: things difficult for people to believe until they have felt the unfathomed mystery of life, and learned that "there are more things in heaven and earth than we have dreamed in our philosophy."[1] As the Divine man prayed that night, on the snow-capped mountain, with the weight of humanity's sin and humanity's hope upon his heart, his disciples beheld his body suddenly overcast with an unfamiliar luster. His pure soul had overflowed and clothed his figure with a wonderful radiance. His face shone as the sun, and his garments became glistening-white such "as no fuller on earth could white them;" the glory of Jesus, already attested by a few fine and sensitive souls, was now apparent to the very eyes of men. And, Moses and Elijah, venerable pioneers of law and prophecy, had come through the intervening mystery which separates the living from the dead, and were talking with Jesus, within sight and hearing of the disciples. Then a voice broke forth from the luminous clouds: "This is my beloved son: hear ye him!"[2]

Anyone acquainted with Simon Peter will not be surprised if he speaks now. He is the type of man who can be depended on to say what others must need think and feel, but dare not utter. He was a valuable man to Jesus: a rock foundation man, for this very reason he revealed his thoughts and made it possible for Jesus to give them direction. Bishop McConnell says that Peter asked many foolish questions, but those questions brought from Jesus very wise answers. It would be difficult for us to sojourn with Simon and dodge sensitive questions; covering up grave issues that so nearly concern us, and trying to hide them from ourselves as though they did not exist. The blundering genius for expression, which was the virtue of Simon Peter, would save us from the folly of applying ostrich wisdom to vital problems. If we had the courage to talk frankly concerning our problems, there would be less occasion to fight about them. In grave moral and social situations where the spokesmen of Jesus, so-called, keep dependably mute, Simon Peter would certainly have something to say or at least ask some embarrassing questions. Peter was a true disciple of the one who came to earth "That thoughts out of many hearts might be revealed."[3]

So on the Mount of Transfiguration, while experiencing was rife, James reflected deeply, John thrilled with awe, and Peter spoke! Peter felt the tides running high in his soul: and he said so: "Lord it is good to be here." When Peter has a weighty idea or a generous impulse, it is likely to get expression. No matter what celebrities are present, no matter how delicate the situation, no matter if he breaks down short of the goal which he sets for himself; at least his Master may count on him to give honest expression to the best that he knows and feels. This is the man whom Jesus commissions to feed his sheep and lambs. This is the foundation man, on whose God-inspired utterance the Kingdom will be built against, which the gates of hell shall not prevail. One of the biographers of Jesus felt it necessary to apologize for Peter's speech during the Transfiguration. "He knew not what to say, for he was sore afraid."[4] There are always disciples, more cautious, but less valuable than Peter, who guard their words very zealously in tense situations, and for fear they may say something indiscreet will almost certainly be silent. They talk most when there is but little need to say anything, and the topic of their conversation is not likely to be material, which will spread fire in the earth, or set a father against his son, or make a man's enemies those of his own household. Who can doubt that it was good to be there, high upon Hermon, in those Transfigured Moments! The experience was so rich and lasting that it went to record, many years later, in three of the Gospels and one New Testament epistle: and the glory, which shone that night, in "a mountain place apart," lingers after two thousand years on every continent and over every sea.

*It is good to be the possessor of some mountain-top experience.* Not to know life on the heights, is to suffer an impoverishing incompleteness. To be sure, there is better opportunity for practical pursuits in the valley regions, and life is easier and safer there: but views are possible from the mountain-top which are not to be had in the vale. A missionary in the Balkans once took a small boy, who lived at the base of a mountain, on a journey up its side. When they gained the summit, the little climber looked this way and that, and then said with astonishment: "My! What a wonderful world. I never dreamed it was so large."

Horizons broaden when we stand on the heights. There is always the danger that we will make of life too much of a dead-level existence; that we will make of life a slavish following of the water courses; a monotonous tread of beaten paths; a matter of absorbing, spiritless, deadening routine. There is the danger that we will drop our lives into the passing current to be kept steadily going we hardly know where or why. Crowded in the throngs that traverse the common ways, we proceed through life with much motion and little vision.

The late President Wilson, in a wonderful essay, spoke of the man who allows his duties to rise about him like a flood. Such a man goes on through the years "swimming with sturdy stroke, his eyes level with the surface, never seeing any clouds or any passing ships." We can pay such regular tribute to motion that all valid sense of direction is lost; so that all our hurrying activities may prove but the rush to ruin. In view of this, it is good for us, occasionally at least, to clamber up from the levels of our set habits of thought, our artificial actions and our settled prejudices, to some loftier plane which affords a more commanding view than we have from the crowded thoroughfare, the low familiar ways. From some mountain eminence let us have occasionally a quiet look upon life, to reflect what it means and whither it is carrying us. The luminaries of humanity were familiar with elevated ground. Moses, Elijah, Mohammed and Jesus all had mountain traditions. It is said, by a well-known Old Testament interpreter, that the religious history of the Hebrew people is inseparable from the topography of their country. The mountains round about Jerusalem are tied up with the vision of God and the vision of life, which Israel gave to mankind.

Who of all the contemporaries of Jesus, busy in marketplace fields and thoroughfares, dreamed that the next great strides of history would take their direction from the visions of one who was praying in the midst of three unheralded fishermen, far above sea level and the level of life! So, it was. So, it may ever be. How many people in high and lofty moments, when they have taken the time and pains to climb above the dingy, foggy levels of incorporated thinking and living, have struck out for themselves and others new and better courses! "I thought on my ways, and turned my feet . . ." "And he taketh them up into an exceeding high mountain."[5] These passages belong to the experience of epoch makers. On the heights is the location for moral discovery. It is a slower process and requires stouter gear to do the mountain road than to run along the shining speedways of the valley. But, woe to the world when there are no visitors on the heights!

*It is good to be present when the ordinary is transformed*; when the dull plain garments of a peasant becoming shining white, and the obscure "mountain place, apart," comes into the gaze of centuries. It is good to see the commonplace illumined and the glory of the common people revealed. On the Mount of Transfiguration, there is no representative of wealth, social rank, or official position. The place could boast in the way of population only four poor men, members of a despised race, and of the remnant of a subjected and broken nation. But, it is here, instead of Jerusalem or Rome, that the voice of God is heard. It is here, instead of Mount Moriah, where the mighty temple stands, that the cloud of glory hovers. Out there, where a carpenter and three fishermen kept vigil with the promise of a new day, God is a living Reality and life is charged with meaning and radiance. Out there in a deserted place, the meek and lowly are enabled.

There is no recounting the instances where the things that are excellent have blossomed in unexpected places. "He giveth power to the faint; and to them that have not might He increaseth strength."[6] A man who is not a prophet, neither a prophet's son, is called by the Lord from following the sheep, to prophesy to the House of Israel. In the heyday of Egyptian civilization, God visits the wilderness of Midian and commissions a shepherd for the most significant work of the age: "In the fifteenth year of the reign of Tiberius Caesar, Pontius Pilate being governor of Judaea, and Herod tetrarch of Galilee, and his brother Philip tetrach of Iturea and the region of Trachonitis, and Lysanias the tetrach of Abilene; in the high priesthood of Annas and Caiphas, the word of the Lord came to John the son of Zacharias, in the wilderness."[7] "Who is this man that is answering Douglas in your State?" wrote prominent statesman of the East, to the editor of a Chicago paper, concerning the unheralded Lincoln. "Do you realize that his knowledge of the most important question before the American people is complete and profound; that his logic is unanswerable and his style inimitable?" It is the illumination of the commonplace, the transfiguring of the ordinary, the glistening radiance of a peasant's seamless robe!

There are two ways in which this transfiguring of the ordinary is specially needed. The lowly ones of earth need to experience this transformation. The great majority of our lives must be lived apart from any elaborate or jeweled settings; must plod along without any spectacular achievements. We ordinary people, then, must learn how to set the scraggy bushes of the wilderness ablaze with glory and make the paths that we tread, under the pressure of duty, like Holy Ground. In the humblest routine, we must discover our task as a part of the transforming enterprise of the Heavenly Father. The laborer that toils on a country road must know himself as the builder of a highway to a Christian civilization. The cobbler may be a mere cobbler, or he may transform his occupation and be a foundation man in the Kingdom of Christ. Make tents if we must, but we will illumine the old task with a radiant new heart, and, with our tent making, make a shining new earth. If toil be confined to the same old field, keep a land of promise shining in the distance and call down angels to sing until the drab turns golden. "My garden is very small," said an old German, "but it's wondrous high." Let us light up the commonplace and make the ordinary radiant. Let us make seamless peasant garments shine like the sun.

Again, those who think themselves the favored ones of earth need a transforming vision of life among the lowly. There is no warrant in the theory and practice of Jesus for dull and frigid doctrines of "lesser breeds within the law." If the life of Jesus means anything, it means implicit faith in the universal capacity of man for the highest character and worth. To this end, the doors of the kingdom of the best are thrown open to all the points of the compass that men may "come from the North and the South, the East and the West to sit down with Abraham and Isaac, in the Kingdom of God."[8]

A low theory, a despicable view of a given group must usually be thrown ahead like a barrage before we can follow with the outrage and mistreatment of that group. We make them hydra-headed in theory so that we may be inhuman in our practice toward them. The validity for such judgment crops out unawares at times, as when masters avow their slaves' inability to learn and at the same time penalize them if caught with a book. Humanity that has climbed to places of social and economic authority must learn how to trace the rainbow tint over the life of the lowly, and to interpret the swelling and ferment at the bottom of society as a healthy and beautiful essay of one's fellowmen in the direction of fuller life. It is a heart strangely unChrist-like that cannot thrill with joy when the least of men begin to pull in the direction of the stars.

*It is good to be in the presence of persons who can kindle us for fine, heroic living.* The population on the Mount of Transfiguration was very small, but it was tremendously significant. Jesus, Moses and Elijah! In the presence of personality like this, men can kindle their torches and go forth in life as bearers of light and heat. Humanity needs the contagion of lofty spirits. Humanity needs contact with persons who are aglow with the good life. All too frequently, our righteousness is sufficiently meager to go to waste: it is not vital enough to communicate itself. Mr. Roosevelt's criticism of his progressive party was that it meant well, but meant it feebly. That is often the trouble with our righteousness. It lacks intensity. It does not make itself felt. We are trying to grind great mills with a quart of water; we would set great masses of cold and slimy material aglow with a wet match. We have our hands full of half-way measures. We scrap a part of our navies. We enthrone Justice in places where there is no serious objection to it. We practice brotherhood within carefully restricted areas. We forgive other people's enemies. We carry a Bible but not a cross. Instead of the Second Mile, we go a few yards of the first and then wonder that Christian goals are not realized. "O fools and slow of heart to believe all that the prophets have spoken!"[9] When we lift ourselves, at least from the ruin and entanglements of our diluted and piecemeal righteousness, it will be under the leadership of persons for whom righteousness was a consuming and holy fire, instead of a mere lukewarm and foggy something. It is such leadership, such righteous dynamics as this that we find in the presence of Jesus and Moses and Elijah. "We beheld his glory, glory as of the only begotten of the Father, full of grace and truth. And of his fullness we have all received." You can kindle at a flame like that! It is the full receptacle that overflows, spreading its content to neighboring borders. It is a flame vital enough not to be extinguished by a slight jostle at which men can kindle. "I have come to set a fire in the earth."[10]

We need power for renunciation. In the service of social progress, justice and brotherhood there are views and possessions of which one must have power to let go. Nothing short of power will work the transformation. But, we are apt to hang on to our self-love, our vantage points, our place with the strong, our purpose of self-advancement. And, we get no strength for the demands laid upon us from the weaklings on our level. But, here, on the mountain-top is personality in which the power of renunciation rises to white heat!

"By faith, Moses when he was come to years, refused to be called the son of Pharaoh's daughter, choosing rather to suffer affliction with the people of God than to enjoy the pleasures of sin for a season; esteeming the reproach of Christ greater riches than the treasure of Egypt."[11] When this ancient Hero exchanged a princely existence at court for exile in Midian, and defied the oppressor in the interest of the oppressed, he lighted a flame at which humanity through thousands of years has kindled power of heroic renunciation. It is good to sit in the presence of Moses if one is to live the life of heroic self-denial.

And, there is a power on the Mount of Transfiguration which kindles tongues and sends forth in evil times for the service of justice. Ahab the king has lifted his bloody hand against a weak subject. He has killed Naboth and taken his patch of land to fill out a nook in one of the royal estates. It is a dastardly act, but Naboth is weak and Ahab mighty, so the voices of justice are not heard. Tyranny broods restfully over the face of the nation. Murder and robbery issue from the very sea of law—and all is well. Thank God, here comes a loud, clear note of discord in the evil harmony! Ahab has gone down to his ill-gotten vineyard and Elijah meets him there. No one can stand with Elijah in that garden without feeling the thrill of manhood: it is a fine place to kindle holy courage. Mighty is Ahab in Israel, but mighty also is Elijah in the service of truth. The Tishbite, in his camel's hair, rubs against the purple of a king mighty in war and peace. He does not wait for royal permission. One listening to that conversation without seeing the participants would have mistaken peasant for king and king for peasant. "Hast thou killed and also taken possession? Hast thou found me, O mine enemy?" And Elijah answered, "I have found thee; and thus saith the Lord, in the spot where dogs licked the blood of Naboth, shall dogs lick thy blood."[12]

The courage of Elijah is a glowing flame at which humanity has kindled power to shake the foundations of a thousand despotisms! And how Jesus could kindle people for courageous, loving and lofty living! Here is Zacchaeus hovering at zero! His malady is not emotional, passionate weakness, but cold-blooded guile. He is a professional trader in the political misfortunes of his nation. His business is to sell the helplessness of his own race to the Roman overlord, and he has made the business pay. With Zacchaeus "business is business." The trouble with Zacchaeus is that he has never been shown a pattern of selflessness as large as his own selfishness. There have been little sputters of righteousness here and there, but nothing dramatic in that line. Zacchaeus feels some serious lack in connection with his own life and method, but he has never seen character the opposite of his own that was sufficiently large or radiant to be attractive. In the flaming proximity of Jesus, the lost son of Israel finds himself. His frigidity thaws up: a new found sense of justice and generosity blazes out: "Half of my goods I give to the poor, and if I have wronged any man by false accusation I will restore unto him fourfold."[13] At the flaming soul of Jesus the frigid soul of Zacchaeus is set aglow.

Here is a woman who is a victim of a great primal emotion. Her name has dishonorable associations; her respect is buried deep beneath the ashes of excess. Each day finds her more shameless and deeper lost; each person passing throws a few more ashes upon the tiny spark of virtue left amid the embers. A lustful suggestion from this man, a contemptuous look from that woman, and the dim inner vision of something wholesome and pure fades rapidly toward extinction. But, Jesus comes along! In the atmosphere about him every slumbering impulse of love and purity begins to quicken. He discovers the faint spark in the ashes and embers and warms it to life. He is so pure himself that this poor woman, sunk to the depths, feels the contagion of his character pulling her toward the stars. A touch of shame mounts the throne in her cheek where a calloused indifference had sat: it turns to penitence and then to hope. "Can I become a worthy person in spite of all that is?" her heart is asking the Master. And the Master, who understands the language of hearts and listens for it, answers: "Verily, I say unto you, wherever this gospel is preached in all the earth, your name and character shall attend it like the fragrance of precious ointment."[14] Again, the strength of a Personality, radiant with truth and love, had lifted a life from shame to sainthood.

Jesus kindled the consciousness of human brotherhood in the most self-conscious and provincial of all races. His character was so dramatically free from all class and national and racial hatreds and prejudices that no follower could long mistake him. To mistake him would have been to cease following! "There is no difference between Jew and Greek, barbarian, Scythian, bond or free, but all are one in Christ Jesus."[15] "I perceive that God is no respecter of persons, but in every nation they that fear God and work righteousness are acceptable with him."[16] "Out of one blood hath God created all nations to dwell upon the face of the earth."[17] This is the language of men who had kindled their lives at the feet of Jesus for the wise and noble adventure in human brotherhood.

*It is good to be present when the great, distant peaks of history join hands to point the way of life*: when seers, standing in different ages and places, one on Sinai another on Carmel and another on Olivet come together to speak to us out of the wisdom of the ages concerning the way and the meaning of life. All this is the privilege of those who frequent the heights! Up there we can read history with our eyes instead of our prejudices. Up there we do not hear the clamor of time-servers and self-servers; and as we look down from the heights, it is too far to descry the hue of faces or the peculiarity of skulls. All we can see is the forms of men, toiling or contending in the valleys—swayed by the same hopes and fears, the same joys and sorrows. The whole creation groaning in travail and pain, together, and waiting for deliverance—one in need, one in destiny. "If drunk with sight of Power" we incline to boastings and vauntings, the seers on the heights say to us out of the wealth of the ages: "Not by might; not by power; but by My Spirit saith the Lord."[18]

And they have wide inductions from the debris of many civilizations as warrant for the utterance. On the heights, too, there is hope for the world! Too often, history strikes us as a medley of blind and futile ramblings. "A tale told by an idiot amid great sound and fury, signifying nothing."[19] The drift of the Maker is dark.[20]

*Into this Universe and why not knowing;*
*Now whence, like water willy-nilly flowing*
*And out of it, like wind along the waste*
*I go, I know not whither! Willy-nilly blowing.*

But on the mountain-top, perspective is possible; above the confusion of the plains, the visitant beholds Moses in one age, Elijah in another, Jesus, Luther and Lincoln, each in another; all joining hands across the Ages and moving humanity in the direction of that "one far off, divine event to which the whole creation moves." "It is good for us to be here."[21]

## NOTES

*Sermon source: Best Sermons* is online at http://www.bestsermons.net/1926/Transfigured_Moments.html (accessed June 1, 2007); the site is the source for the sermon reprinted here.

1. William Shakespeare, *The Yale Shakespeare: The Tragedy of Hamlet Prince of Denmark*, ed. Tucker Brooke and Jack Randall Crawford, rev. ed. (1917; reprint, New Haven, CT: Yale University Press, 1947), 1.5, 165–66.
2. Matthew 17:5 (King James Version).
3. Luke 2:35 (KJV).
4. Mark 9:6 (KJV).
5. See Matthew 17:1.
6. See Isaiah 40:31.
7. Luke 3:1–2 (KJV).
8. See Luke 13:29.
9. Luke 24:25 (KJV).
10. See Luke 12:49.
11. Hebrews 11:24 (KJV).
12. See 1 Kings 21:19.
13. See Luke 19:8.
14. See Luke 7:37–50.
15. See Romans 10:12.
16. See Acts 10:34–35.
17. Acts 17:26 (KJV).
18. Zechariah 4:6 (KJV).
19. William Shakespeare, *Macbeth*, ed. Kenneth Muir (Cambridge: Cambridge University Press, 1968), 5.5, 27–28.
20. See Thomas Bulfinch, *Bulfinch's Mythology: The Age of Fable* (Cambridge, MA: Allen & Farnham, 1855; reprint, Philadelphia: Running Press, 1987), 224.
21. Mark 9:5 (KJV).

## BIBLIOGRAPHICAL SOURCES

Branch, Taylor. *Parting the Waters: America in the King Years*. New York: Simon & Schuster, 1988.

Dexter Avenue Baptist Church. "Reverend Vernon Johns, 1947–1952, the Church's Nineteenth Pastor." *Dexter Echo Centennial Souvenir Program*, 1997.

Luker, Ralph E. "Murder and Biblical Memory: The Legend of Vernon Johns." *Virginia Magazine of History and Biography* 112. http://www.vahistorical.org/publications/abstract_luker.htm (accessed Jan 14, 2005).

# JAMES WELDON JOHNSON

(1871–1938)

Poet, fiction writer, diplomat, and historian of African American culture, James Weldon Johnson was born in 1871 in Jacksonville, Florida, and educated by his mother, a schoolteacher. Johnson's parents sent him to both high school and college at Atlanta University, from which he graduated in 1894. After graduation, Johnson returned to Jacksonville as principal of his old elementary school. During this period, he read law and became the first African American to be admitted to the Florida bar in 1897.

Johnson and his brother, John Rosamond Johnson (1873–1954), a talented composer, also wrote songs, including "Lift Every Voice and Sing," which has been called the black national anthem. They also wrote for the Broadway stage. Continuing his studies at Columbia University, Johnson met other African American artists and helped nurture a distinct literary community in the years leading up to the Harlem Renaissance.

Johnson wrote *Autobiography of an Ex-Colored Man*, which was published anonymously in 1912. He was also a leader in the National Association for the Advancement of Colored People. He edited three anthologies in the 1920s: *The Book of Negro American Poetry* (1922) and *American Negro Spirituals* (two volumes, in 1925 and 1926). Johnson's introductions to his anthologies contain some of the most insightful assessments ever made of black contributions to American culture.

His best-known work, *God's Trombones*, a collection of seven sermons in verse, appeared in 1927. A collection of poetry, *St. Peter Relates an Incident: Collected Poems* was written in 1935. *God's Trombones* and several other of Johnson's writings reveal his abiding interest in the black church.

• • •

*In "The Creation," Johnson channels, though in the erudite fashion of a man of his schooling, the black folk preacher's voice as a grand mixture of majestic King James English, vibrant folk idioms, and insightful metaphor. The sonorous sermonic prose of the black folk preacher falls easily and comfortably into poetic verse and maintains the narrative and dramatic movement of the sermon and the lyrical quality of the black preacher. As a result, this piece has become one of the most oft recited in the black church. In the preface to* God's Trombones, *Johnson wrote:*

> *In a general way, these poems were suggested by the rather vague memories of sermons I heard preached in my childhood; but the immediate stimulus for setting them down came quite definitely at a comparatively recent date. I was speaking on a Sunday in Kansas City, addressing meetings in various colored churches. When I had finished my fourth talk it was after nine o'clock at night, but the committee told me there was still another meeting to address. I demurred, making the quotation about the willingness of the spirit and the weakness of the flesh, for I was dead tired. I also protested the lateness of the hour, but I was informed that for the meeting at this church we were in good time.*
>
> *When we reached the church an "exhorter" was just concluding a dull sermon. After his there were two other short sermons. These sermons proved to be preliminaries, mere curtain-raisers for a famed visiting preacher. At last, he arose. He was a dark-brown man, handsome in his gigantic proportions. He appeared to be a bit self-conscious, perhaps impressed by the presence of the "distinguished visitor" on the platform, and started in to preach a formal sermon from a formal text. The congregation sat apathetic and dozing. He sensed that he was losing his audience and his opportunity.*
>
> *Suddenly he closed the Bible, stepped out from behind the pulpit and began to preach. He started intoning the old folk-sermon that begins with the creation of the world and ends with Judgment Day. He was at once a changed man, free, at ease and masterful. The change in the congregation was instantaneous. An electric current ran through the crowd. It was in a moment alive and quivering; and all the while the preacher held it in the palm of his hand. He was wonderful in the way he employed his conscious and unconscious art. He strode the pulpit up and down in what was actually a very rhythmic dance, and he brought into play the full gamut of his wonderful voice, a voice—what shall I say?—not of an organ or a trumpet, but rather of a trombone, the instrument possessing above all others the power to express the wide and varied range of emotions encompassed by the human voice—and with greater amplitude. He intoned, he moaned, he pleaded—he blared, he crashed, he thundered. I sat fascinated; and more, I was, perhaps against my will, deeply moved; the emo-*

*tional effect upon me was irresistible. Before he had finished I took a slip of paper and somewhat surreptitiously jotted down some ideas for the first poem, "The Creation. . . ."*

## The Creation
(1927)

And God stepped out on space,
And he looked around and said:
I'm lonely—
I'll make me a world.

And far as the eye of God could see
Darkness covered everything,
Blacker than a hundred midnights
Down in a cypress swamp.

Then God smiled,
And the light broke,
And the darkness rolled up on one side,
And the light stood shining on the other,
And God said: That's good!

Then God reached out and took the light in his hands,
And God rolled the light around in his hands
Until he made the sun;
And he set that sun a-blazing in the heavens.
And the light that was left from making the sun
God gathered it up in a shining ball
And flung it against the darkness,
Spangling the night with the moon and stars.
Then down between
The darkness and the light
He hurled the world;
And God said: That's good!

Then God himself stepped down—
And the sun was on his right hand,
And the moon was on his left;
The stars were clustered about his head,

And the earth was under his feet.
And God walked, and where he trod His footsteps hollowed the valleys out
And bulged the mountains up.

Then he stopped and looked and saw
That the earth was hot and barren.
So God stepped over to the edge of the world
And he spat out the seven seas—
He batted his eyes, and the lightning flashed—
He clapped his hands, and the thunders rolled—
And the waters above the earth came down,
The cooling waters came down.

Then the green grass sprouted,
And the little red flowers blossomed,
The pine tree pointed his finger to the sky,
And the oak spread out his arms,
The lakes cuddled down in the hollows of the ground,
And the rivers ran down to the sea;
And God smiled again,
And the rainbow appeared,
And curled itself around his shoulder.

Then God raised his arm and he waved his hand
Over the sea and over the land,
And he said: Bring forth! Bring forth!
And quicker than God could drop his hand,
Fishes and fowls
And beasts and birds
Swam the rivers and the seas,
Roamed the forests and the woods,
And split the air with their wings.
And God said: That's good!

Then God walked around,
And God looked around
On all that he had made.
He looked at his sun,
And he looked at his moon,
And he looked at his little stars;

He looked on his world
With all its living things,
And God said: I'm lonely still.

Then God sat down—
On the side of a hill where he could think;
By a deep, wide river he sat down;
With his head in his hands,
God thought and thought,
Till he thought: I'll make me a man!

Up from the bed of the river
God scooped the clay;
And by the bank of the river
He kneeled him down;
And there the great God Almighty
Who lit the sun and fixed it in the sky,
Who flung the stars to the most far corner of the night,
Who rounded the earth in the middle of his hand;
This Great God,
Like a mammy bending over her baby,
Kneeled down in the dust
Toiling over a lump of clay
Till he shaped it in his own image;

Then into it he blew the breath of life,
And man became a living soul.
Amen. Amen.

## NOTE

*Sermon source:* James Weldon Johnson, *God's Trombones: Seven Negro Sermons in Verse* (New York: Viking Press, 1955), 17–20.

## BIBLIOGRAPHICAL SOURCES

Andrews, William L., ed. *Oxford Companion to African American Literature.* London: Oxford University Press, 1997.

Appiah, Kwame Anthony, and Henry Louis Gates Jr., eds. *Africana: The Encyclopedia of the African and African American Experience.* New York: Oxford University Press, 2005, 1053–54.

# MORDECAI WYATT JOHNSON

*(1890–1976)*

Mordecai Wyatt Johnson was born in Paris, Tennessee, on January 12, 1890, the only child of the Reverend Wyatt J. Johnson, a former slave, pastor of Mount Zion Baptist Church, and his wife Carolyn (Freeman).

Johnson completed his college degree at Atlanta Baptist College (now Morehouse College). He obtained a second baccalaureate degree at the University of Chicago (1913), and graduated in 1916 from Rochester Theological Seminary, where he was influenced by the teaching, writings, and ministry of Walter Rauschenbusch (1861–1918), the prophetic white social reformer. Following graduation he accepted the pastorate of First Baptist Church, Charleston, West Virginia. In 1916 he married Anna Gardner, with whom he had five children.

During his years at First Baptist Church, Johnson earned his master of sacred theology degree at Harvard (1922), and like the legendary W.E.B. DuBois, won the competition to represent all the graduate schools at the commencement exercises as a presenter. He delivered "The Faith of the American Negro," a speech which garnered for him considerable praise, some influential allies in high places, and many open doors for speaking engagements throughout the nation. In 1923, Howard University acknowledged his evident prowess and exemplary ministries by conferring on him the degree of Doctor of Divinity, *honoris caus*; at age thirty-three, he was one of the youngest persons to receive that honor from the university.

In 1926, he left his Charleston pastorate after being elected president of Howard University, a post he held for thirty-four years, and from which he retired in 1960.

In addition to his fame as a progressive long-term president of a national university, Mordecai Wyatt Johnson was acclaimed as one of the nation's most eloquent and charismatic speakers. A man of sharp intellect and a compelling platform presence, he always prepared well and usually spoke without a manuscript. True to the spirit and concerns of a moral and spiritual leader, he was especially attentive to the relation between religion and society, and he spoke about it in many of his sermons and addresses, always with intellectual power, strategic words, practical illustrations, and spiritual depth. In 1954 *Ebony* listed him one of America's top ten black preachers. He died in 1976.

• • •

*The following sermon illustrates Johnson's controlled and creative tone, his devotional demeanor, accented logic, and grand vision of a healthy relationship between religion and society. Johnson was known for his intellect, practical illustrations, and spiritual depth. He would in future years come to be known as a contemplative African American preacher. The original sermon is much longer and a condensed version is used here.*

## WORK, BUSINESS, AND RELIGION (AUGUST 10, 1924)

> *What, know ye not that your body is the temple of the Holy Ghost, which is in you, which ye have of God and ye are not your own?*
> —1 Corinthians 6:19

> *And let the beauty of the Lord our God be upon us; and establish thou the work of our hands upon us; yea, the work of our hands establish thou it.*
> —Psalms 90:17

I [am using] two texts this morning. One of them states a fact in the form of a question, and the other is a prayer. You can see from these two texts the substance of what I want to say this morning. . . . I hope to say two things that are of the essence of the Gospel and the truth of religion: A man's work is the expression of his religion; the relationship between a man's work and his religion is analogous to the relationship between a man's spirit and his body. The next thing I want to say is, to put it negatively, "No man can establish the validity of his own work." To put it positively, "No work is fit and enduring except God establishes it by his spirit." Or, to put it even more positively, "Wherever the spirit of God is expressed in a man's work, that work is holy and is itself a religious act wherein a man is in direct touch with the living God."

Now among public men of high character, there is a decided tendency to separate and distinguish the fields of religion and business, and to work just as clearly as a church building is separated from a bank building; holding that they do not have anything to do with one another, and that when one of them offers an opinion on the other, he goes out of his province.

Now, is that a true position? Does it stand that way? Are the two fields separate? Oh, there is a lot in human nature that would love for it to be that way. Just see what happens when men make them separate. Look what happens on the business side (I have seen it happen many a time). Then I will tell you what happens on the religious side.

As soon as a certain type of man comes to the conclusion there is a direct and thorough cleavage between business and religion, he begins to think, "Let me see: Six days for most of my working hours I am busy working; getting bread, meat, and clothes; paying rent; or buying my house. I do not need a preacher or anybody else to tell me how necessary that is. That is perfectly manifest. One day a week and two hours on that day I go to church, and the preacher talks to me about things that I cannot see. Sometimes he gets a grip on me but most of the time he does not. Now it looks to me as if this working side of my life, this business side of my life, is overwhelmingly important and absolutely necessary, while this religious side of my life does not matter much. Anyhow, it is just about one-seventh as important as the other side. It is a kind of distant, far-off dream. Here is a man over here who says there is nothing to it. I just conclude there is nothing to it, and I will just attend to my business and carry on my work." That is a legitimate issue and a legitimate conclusion from the separation of religion and business.

See what has happened in the world whenever religion feels it has nothing to do with the bank and politics and with the man who works out in the ditch. Several times in history, the world has become decidedly corrupt in its business and in its social and political relationships. Several times in history, religious men have felt that the claims of God upon the soul were so strong that in all probability they did not have anything to do with business, with social life, or with politics. So they have withdrawn from the world—those "hermit souls" that you read about. They have gone into the desert places living alone, eating figs off the trees or anything they could pick up, begging from day to day, and withdrawing themselves entirely from business and social relationships and political life. What always happens?

You can read the literature of such a movement as that. . . . In other words, I am saying to you that, as a matter of history, wherever religion and business and work have consented to a separation, both business and work have suffered on the one hand, and religion has suffered on the other.

Again the first doctrine I want to preach to you out of the Gospel of Jesus Christ is that there cannot be any separation between business and work and religion, and for this simple and perfectly commonsense reason: The same man who sits in the pew on Sunday morning and listens to the sermon is the same man who is behind the bank counter yonder, the same man who works in the ditch, the same man who organizes politics, the same man who attends to the labor union yonder. There cannot be any separation between his business and his religion because it is the same man who has both the business and the religion.

That is a perfectly commonsense reason. There is no such thing as a man being a scoundrel in religion and a saint in business. There is no such thing as a man being a saint in religion and a scoundrel in business. It is absolutely impossible.

As I stated to you in the beginning of my remarks, the whole matter is analogous to the relationship between the mind and the body, or, to put it better, the soul and the body. . . . When you look at Jesus Christ, is that not what you see? You see a human body radiated and made beautiful by the spirit dwelling in it. I imagine the hands of Jesus Christ were beautiful to look at as they touched the blind man's eyes. I imagine the eyes of Jesus Christ were things of sparkling beauty that one would have stood a long time and looked at with delightful affection because out of those eyes there shone the spirit that was from above. I imagine that the feet of Jesus Christ as he trod on to Jerusalem—facing the cross with certainty, dignity, and confidence in the living God—were stronger and more courageous than the feet of each one of those soldiers marching along by that body that was filled with the spirit of the living God.

The Gospel about your body is this: The good news about it is that this body of yours—even in the case of some of us who have been slaves, who have been beaten and whipped and scourged—may shine with the glory of God. God may take hold of this black hand that has slaved and say, "I will use you to bless some little children." God can take these crude lips and bring out of them words that will make men tremble. That is the good news about the body.

The good news about your work is that your work and your business may become God's temple when you take Him along with you in your work. That is the reason Jesus Christ said, "I have come to preach good news to the poor."[1] He meant us, to the poor men.

You do not have to go to the temple on the mount to worship God; you do not have to go to the temple at Jerusalem to worship God. You can worship God in this ditch where you are working in the slime and mud. You can worship God in this hospital where you stand with your instruments in your hands as an efficient nurse tending some soul at death's door. You can worship God, doctor, by the way you hold your scalpel while helping some soul who begs to live. You can worship God by the way you work in your kitchen and attend to the region of your kitchen so one walking in there and seeing how you work will know that God has made a temple of your kitchen.

That is the Gospel and that is the good news about work. My friends, it is such good news that slaves who have been living under the worst conditions in the world have discovered it, and many of them have been content to suffer in slavery by seeing the glory of hard work.

There is nothing wrong about common work—the truest end of work and not the accidental end of it—because God made everyday work and business. That is the fundamental reason the religious man must continually cry against all kinds of base work, all kinds of base methods, all kinds of harmful activities in connection with men's work and men's business. The religious man is just as sure to cry out against them as he lives. He cannot help it to save his life. . . . When he sees his whole vision degraded, he has to cry out.

It is of the very nature of the wicked and perverse generation not to want to hear the truth about its work and business because it is right there that the issues are. When a man criticizes work and business, a group of men always arises with the cry, "He is fighting business." They know they are liars. He is fighting corruption and unrighteous business.

There is no conflict among work and business and religion, for the fundamental reason that God himself can dwell in a good man's work and in a good man's business.

Religion is not in this world to sanctify laziness, slothfulness, the possession of nothing, and the want of nothing. Religion is not in this world to sanctify that. Religion is in this world for ability and genius, which are needed in the building of this world. But, religion is bound to cry out against all of those parasites and hucksters who would take the whole fabric of work and chuck it to the dogs.

So we have a kind of watchword in our day, and you hear a man speaking of sharp practices in a business transaction with another. You call his attention to the fact that certain things should not be done in connection with business transactions, and he may argue with you for a while until he sees he cannot get out. Then he will hump his shoulders and say, "Oh, it is a matter of business with me."

The answer of religion is that "there are several kinds of business." There are several kinds of business. There is a business in which a man's word is his honor. There is another kind of business in which a man gives his word only to deceive. He agrees to give you oak lumber, and he gives you wallboard. He agrees to give you brass, and he gives you some stuff scrubbed over with brass. He agrees to give you one kind of foundation, and he puts in it something that will send your house down in ruins. He agrees to give you the best kind of carpentry and hires a "jackleg" and instructs him to swindle you.

That kind of business has no right to exist. When people realize their rights, that man will suffer worse than would a horse thief in the West. When men's laws were not so well developed and a man in the West stole a horse, he was hanged. Now a man will sell a poorly constructed house, beat his neighbor out of money by doing it, and go about "nigger-rich." When men were strong, hanging would not have been too good. Yet such men call on the present generation to worship them as gods. I would rather be a man feeding on rancid hot dogs, the lowest of my race, or any race, than dependent upon that kind of crookedness.

So let the issue be made clear. What the church is after is not a world in which there is no business, no toil, no money, no wealth, no leisure, no beauty, but it is after a world in which money, toil, work, and business will be sanctified because the men who toil and work and conduct business will do it by putting the spirit of God in the foreground. They are bound to express God in their business.

It is a comfort, and I want to make it reach the majority of us that there are only three things, my beloved, that, in the case of ordinary people like you and me, will keep our business from being religious.

The first of them is that the business itself is destructive of the higher human values. If it is, God cannot and will not come into it. . . . The first thing that faces men's work is that God cannot have anything to do with it, whatever its nature, if it hurts the human race or keeps the human race from growing toward God. In the very nature of the case, no Christian man with a conscience can engage in it. He will leave it as a child leaves hot stuff when he first puts his hand on it. The first endeavor of every Christian man and woman will be to engage in the kind of work and in the kind of business that is in itself connected with the fundamental needs of the human race.

The second thing that vitiates good work—even though the work be good itself—is the way you do it . . . however holy work may be in itself, when you do it slovenly or so lazily or so neglectfully or in any manner whatsoever as to hide defects and not bring out excellence, then your work is degrading and discouraging to others.

Whatever kind of work you are in, if it is decent work, put your best intelligence and mind into it; put your honor into it. A man may be in the workshop and God himself is there. He honors and loves you and calls you His children. You can lay down your wrench and say, "God has fixed this automobile. Blessed be His name." If I carry an automobile to a man's shop and there is something the matter with it that I do not know, the man comes and with his intelligence divines the situation, conceals nothing from me, and puts everything in right and says, "Here is the car. My honor is in that. If it is not straight, then bring it back to me." I feel like saying to that man, "I thank you for discovering a man who fixes automobiles with his soul as well as with his hands."

The third and last thing that degrades work is the use of the proceeds therefrom for purposes destructive of human life and its powers. . . . Conversely, the one who will dignify his work is the one who will take the proceeds of it and put the money into something his soul approves of.

Beloved, you may say what you please, but the spirit of God tells me that every legitimate human business is capable of being conducted just like that workingman's business, just like he conducts his life. Every legitimate human business is capable of being a straight-out, honest, and above-board business that will offer itself for the inspection of any man.

Every legitimate business is a business that can be done with honor. There are no circumstances in this world that will justify a Christian man in doing any business with dishonor. Every legitimate business in this world is capable of bringing a man such proceeds that he can use those proceeds for the development of some high spiritual quality. Every legitimate business is like that.

. . . [The] time will come when every business on this earth will be shot through with an invisible dignity and religion, and men will not have to go to church and say to the preacher, "Tell us about God," for every man will know God himself.

There is no occupation in the world in which God is not at work, in which people do not have an influence that, expressed, will reach the heart of common humanity. The Church will never be able to work out the technique of a bank. It will never be able to work out the technique of the medical profession. It will never be able to work out the technique of cooking. But, the Church is always here to tell men that it has the final word on the morality of all businesses and that it will never cease—until its presence has been made unnecessary by the living presence of God Himself—to speak to each man's individual soul.

May the Lord bless you and make His face to shine upon you—make it shine in that kitchen, that grocery store, that real estate business, that banking business, that dentist's office, that house where you are painting. Whenever you go, may men somehow be made to feel that "God Almighty has something to do with this work that I have done in this place."

### *Notes*

*Sermon source:* Richard I. McKinney, *Mordecai: The Man and His Message: The Story of Mordecai Wyatt Johnson* (Washington, DC: Howard University Press, 1997).

1. Luke 4:18 (King James Version).

### *Bibliographical Sources*

Embree, Edwin R. *13 Against the Odds.* New York: Viking Press, 1944, 175–95.

Howard University. *Education For Freedom: A Documentary Tribute to Celebrate the Fiftieth Anniversary of the Election of Mordecai W. Johnson as President of Howard University.* Washington, DC: Howard University Archives, Moorland-Spingarn Research Center, 1976.

# CHARLES PRICE JONES

*(1865–1949)*

Preacher, denominational leader, songwriter, and composer Charles Price Jones was born in Texas Valley near Rome, Georgia, on December 9, 1865. He was taught to read and write and developed a love of books at an early age. At age seventeen, after his mother's death in 1882, he traveled through Tennessee and Kentucky looking for work as a laborer. In October 1884 Jones was converted at Cat Island along the Mississippi River in Arkansas, a scene of mass baptisms. Soon thereafter he began teaching Sunday School and preaching in the local Baptist church.

In 1888, Jones enrolled at Arkansas Baptist College to pursue his calling to be a missionary in Africa. Charles Lewis Fisher, academic dean of the college, ordained Jones in October of that same year. Jones pastored two Baptist churches while continuing his college studies. He graduated from Arkansas Baptist College in 1891. After graduation he accepted a call to pastor Bethlehem Baptist Church in Searcy, Arkansas, and became editor of the *Arkansas Baptist Vanguard.* Having impressed Baptist denominational leaders with his gifts and abilities, Jones was elected corresponding secretary of the Arkansas Baptist State Convention and trustee of the Arkansas Baptist College. Ithiel Clemmons notes a report of the impact of Jones' preaching on the occasion of his departure from Arkansas to accept a pastorate in Selma, Alabama:

> Just how powerful was Jones' preaching? His final message to the Arkansas State Convention, after he accepted the call to Tabernacle Baptist Church at Selma, Alabama, made a deep impression. He preached with such conviction that men in that great assembly wept, sobbed, and cried, "Stop him, stop him."[1]

Jones' popularity increased as a preacher, evangelist and singer during his years as pastor of Tabernacle Baptist Church.

In 1895, Jones accepted the call to Mt. Helm Missionary Baptist Church in Jackson, Mississippi, and began preaching with emphasis on holiness and sanctification. Jones "gave himself to the Lord to be sanctified" in Selma in 1894, and the conviction that he needed to be holier "ate him up."[2] Although still Baptist, he convened a Holiness convocation at the church in June 1897 and began producing a bimonthly publication entitled *Truth*. Jones described some of his experiences during this period: "Our movement was entirely interdenominational and in spirit anti-sectarian. The sick were healed, the blind were made to see, the afflicted were blessed . . . Black and white, Jew and gentile sought God together."[3] The convocation and the newsletter formed the nucleus for organization of the Church of God in Christ and later the Church of Christ Holiness, U.S.A.

Following the lead of the Holiness movement, Jones strongly emphasized the work of the Holy Spirit in preaching and worship, and linked sanctification to the goal of realizing the unity of the church. Both views threatened the Baptists' sense of denominational identity. When Jones found no scriptural support for having the word "Baptist" as part of the name of the church, he attempted to change the name of Mt. Helm Missionary Baptist Church to the Church of Christ. Some members of the congregation sued in court to block the change on the basis of the church's charter. The lower court decided in Jones' favor, but the decision was reversed by the Mississippi Supreme Court in 1901. Jones and his followers were ordered to vacate the premises, and they left to start the Christ Temple Church in Jackson, Mississippi. They erected a building in 1903, which served as the meeting place for their Holiness convocation. An association was formed with Jones as general overseer, C.H. Mason as overseer of Tennessee, and J.A. Jeter as overseer of Arkansas. Jones and Mason were expelled by the National Baptist Convention U.S.A. in 1899, "because of their zeal for Wesleyan perfectionism and their militant defense of slave worship practices the rest of the black church sought to forget."[4] However, for the remainder of his life Jones maintained a close relationship with the National Baptist Publishing Board in Nashville, Tennessee.

After Mason experienced the "third blessing" of speaking in tongues at the Azusa Street Revival in 1907, he and Jones parted ways. In 1909, when Mason organized a new convocation under the name Church of God in Christ, Jones was using the same name. When Mason incorporated, Jones reorganized the churches and pastors that remained with him as the Church of Christ Holiness U.S.A.

Another significant aspect of Jones' legacy was his hymn writing. He wrote over one thousand hymns and gospel songs, many of which were published in his hymnal *His Fullness* in 1906. Among his best-known hymns are "All I Need," "Deeper, Deeper," "I Will Make the Darkness Light," and "I'm Happy in Jesus Alone."

Jones relocated to Los Angeles in 1917, where he established a new congregation. He died in Los Angeles on January 19, 1949, and was laid to rest at Evergreen Cemetery less than 100 feet from the burial place of William J. Seymour.

• • •

*This sermon is from Jones's annual address as president of the Church of Christ Holiness U.S.A. Convention, delivered at Bethel Church of Christ in Los Angeles, California. His teaching stressed the themes of spiritual cleansing, intellectual advancement, and moral betterment. For Jones, holiness was empowerment for living; it enabled resistance to the forces of oppression that confronted African Americans. The Church of Christ (Holiness) is often viewed through the stereotype of being separatist. The following sermon underscores Jones's clarion call for humility and respect for all denominations.*

## The Battle Royal: A Contention for the Faith Once Delivered to the Saints (Jude 25) (August 24, 1930)

To the Bishops and Deacons, Elders and Servants, and Fathers and Mothers in Israel; to the pastors and teachers, prophets and evangelists, constituting the Holiness Convention and Convocation of the Churches of Christ; to the Saints and Faithful Brethren, blood-washed, Spirit-filled, sanctified by God the Father and called; sons and daughters of the truth as it is in Christ Jesus; heroes of the faith that takes up the cross and walk, as strength is supplied by an indwelling Savior, the way called *The Way of Holiness*; saved by grace so as to exclude boasting; living, standing, and walking by the faith of Christ, who loved us and gave Himself for us; living and yet not living, since Christ liveth in us; citizens of the Kingdom of Heaven; children of the Most High God; members of the Royal Household of God; Kings and priests; princes and judges; witnesses to the Eternal One; the new creation in Christ Jesus who have tasted the power of the age to come: I greet you this day in the Name of God our Savior; in the Name of Jehovah, the God of Abram, Isaac and Jacob; in the Name of our Lord Jesus Christ, who gave Himself for the church that He might sanctify it, having cleansed it with the washing of water by the Word; in the name of the One God, Father, Son and Holy Ghost (Ephesians 5:1–33; 2 Corinthians 13:14).

Nor is it with enticing words of men's wisdom that I would speak to you; but repudiating all human eloquence and strength, I would speak in the demonstration of the Spirit and power, holy words of truth and of soberness, peace, and purity, God and salvation; words that are pregnant with grace and scintillating with the holy brilliance of heavenly wisdom; words that chime with heavenly music like the bells that jingled on the High Priest's robes; words that are redolent with odor of the Holy Anointing that was on the High Priest's head.

## Convention Thirty-four

This is our thirty-fourth annual session, our first session having been called in 1897. Not to form a new church was this convention called, but to establish a new fellowship, yet as old as Pentecost.

The world was cursed with denominational conceit, the braggadocio, the bravado, the blindness, the ignorance, the vanity, the hatred, the false worship of "our-crowdism." The fellowship of the Spirit spoken of in 1 Corinthians 16:16 was unknown, practically. People no longer made their boast in the Lord (Psalms 34:2), rather they boasted in their sect.

They no longer received one another or blessed one another in the name of the Lord (Matthew 23:28); they received one another as members of this or that denomination. If you belonged to the other denomination you were wrong, and being wrong you were-well-maybe not on your way to hell, but it was doubtful about your going to heaven.

There were decent people in those days as now, nice people, in the churches, but such was their doctrine that the very word holiness produced an unbelieving protest in their hearts. The idea of living holy was scorned and nobody tried to understand the meaning of the *call to Holiness*. And God is holy. He who hates holiness hates God. This they did not know (1 Peter 1:14–16; Hebrews 12:1–14).

The idea of religious benefit did not include the presence of God nor the Kingdom of God within you, but a resting place after you were dead: a land that flowed with milk and honey, inhabited by beautiful angels, dead mothers and dead babies and saints of old, for whom God did things that He would not do for anybody now. That was the dominant notion. The attitude was taken and the doctrine taught even by those who professed strenuously to believe and preach *all* the Bible and *only* the Bible, *that this Age of Miracles* was passed. The doctrine they taught insistently; and one who believed otherwise was a fanatic and a heretic and a full fledged fool. Christians were tobacco users, snuff dippers and whiskey drinkers, and married as often as they pleased and quit when they wished; nor cared, many of them, to go to the trouble to get a license to marry. Spiritual darkness and gloominess filled the churches and though religion was popular, "darkness covered the earth," as said Isaiah, "and gross darkness the people" (Isaiah 60:2).

## The Hungry Few

But God has always had a *few* saints, a few hearts hungering and thirsting after righteousness. And the cry of these went up into the ears of the Lord of Sabaoth that more light shine from glory above. And so it came to pass that God had this convention called that "the people who sat in darkness might see a great light," and that "to those who sat in the region and shadow of death light might spring up" (Matthew 4:16).

People when they were instructed in the Scriptures as to conduct, answered, "Yes, the Bible says so and so, but who is doing it?" And they said that as a dismissal of obligation to take up the cross and follow Jesus. His word was made a dead letter. As Jeremiah said, "In vain made He it."

But when this convention was called and the indwelling Christ began to be preached; when the Spirit of truth began guiding His ministers into truth; when we began to teach the Bible to the people and preach the "gospel of the Kingdom," people bought Bibles and began to read. They no longer joined lodges to be popular, for they became obsessed with a desire to be popular in heaven; they wanted their names written there. Not all, but a vast number awoke, and all the churches were helped. They themselves have confessed this again and again.

## Not Church Destroyers

We have never sought to overthrow the churches—we knew that the earth was the Lord's and the fullness thereof; we knew the denominations were themselves the result of efforts at holiness or a greater spirituality or stricter scripturalness of doctrine; or greater faithfulness of public practice.

The Methodists and Quakers were once Holiness people. The *Quakers and some of the Methodists* are now. The Baptists stood for a regenerated church standing in the liberty of the Spirit and the literalness of New Testament authority and for immersion alone as scriptural baptism. The Baptists were Calvinists contending that a person once converted to Christ and baptized could never be lost. A very comforting doctrine, this, and it has considerable scripture and deep logic for its foundation. But as the doctrine was being put to the people, it was robbing them of the fear of God and of all incentive for holy Christian living; and consequently ministers and people were "burning their candles at both ends." A religion without the fear of God is a sad and destructive thing. Not worse than no religion, perhaps, but bad indeed. They were trying to serve God with an evil conscience. This cannot be done. We can *hope* in God. We can serve a *sect*. We can "serve our *own bellies*," as the apostle so bluntly put it in Romans 16, but we can not serve God. We can organize churches and build church houses, but they will be seared with selfishness, smeared with moral filth, and shot through with sin and unbelief. We cannot serve God till we know Him (John 17; Galatians 4:8, 9). We can not know Him without keeping His commandments (1 John 2; John 7:17). And though we be as moral as the Pharisee that insulted God and the Publican in the temple, and as blameless as Paul when he persecuted the church, or as popular and generous as Nicodemus, or as high in authority as Annas and Caiaphas, we *cannot* serve God with an evil conscience. We must be washed in regeneration, renewed in the Holy Ghost and kept by the power of God. The blood of Jesus must do a real work in us, and that daily, as well as for us (Hebrews 13; 1 Peter 1).

## The Church a Priesthood

The church constitutes a royal priesthood, a holy nation and a peculiar people (1 Peter 2:9). A priest is holy by divine decree in the very appointment and attitude he sustains toward God. *All priests are holy* and therefore *all believers are saints.*

The Bible does not know God's people as Catholics, Episcopalians, Lutherans, Presbyterians, Campbellites, Adventists, Methodists, Baptists, Congregationalists, Nazarenes nor Holiness people; Evening Lights nor Pentecostals. These are manmade names and stand for division and sectarian contention; for the conceit of doctrinal superiority; for a religious pride that obscures the face of that God who is our salvation, of Him whom Jesus His Son only Begotten lived and died to reveal. "This is life eternal that they might know Thee, the Only True God and Jesus Christ, whom Thou hast sent" (John 17:3).

## More About Final Perseverance

I spoke of the distressing effect of the overemphasis and incorrect interpretation of the beautiful and consoling doctrine of the final perseverance of the saints, or the final *preservation* of the saints as some theologians put it. They both mean the same thing, for no saint can persevere unless kept by the power of God (1 Peter 1:9). Our salvation is altogether of grace and entirely divine.

The Methodists contended that we had to work our way, and they had lots of scripture to back up that contention, and the natural mind itself understands a salvation on personal merit much better than it understands election, predestination, and salvation by faith in the merits of another. Also the Methodists differed with the Baptists on what was meant by baptism, and there was much contention over that, sometimes sincere, strenuous, and enthusiastic contention, that ran into hatred.

The Presbyterians and Congregationalists agreed with the Baptists on Calvinism, that is predestination and election, but disagreed with them on what constituted baptism and who should receive the ordinance. The Campbellites agreed with the Baptists in the mode of baptism, but with the Methodists in their Armenian attitude that salvation demanded good works. About these things there was much contention. But I am sorry to say that they all lived about alike and the call to holiness was ignored.

## Honorable Exceptions

Now understand that there have always been honorable exceptions as to moral conduct and religious faithfulness. But the churches were not *called to holiness* (1 Thessalonians 4:1–8). It was ignored, even flouted.

There were religious works; there was a sort of religious heroism, in some, that fought whiskey and tobacco and the ballroom and the circus and the theater, but nobody called the people to holiness. Nobody was expected to be perfect. Holiness was in the creeds, in the declarations of faith, and whatnot. But there it lay dormant. To call people to it, to urge it upon the conscience, to make it a daily thought, a daily aim, a goal, a faith, an experience, a life so as to give it room in all manner of conversation was accounted supreme folly and heresy; a very presumptuous and disagreeable fanaticism. The honorable exceptions in this matter were regarded as rank hypocrites or as Pharisees of the most disagreeable type.

## The Adventist Et Al

The Catholics and Episcopalians regarded themselves as historically and ceremonially holy and regarded everybody else as wrong, accursed, and on his way to hell, and let it go at that. They had apostolic succession, whatever that could be; and while we could not charge them with blasphemously saying "To hell with the rest of the world," they regarded the rest of the world as deludedly on its way there and seemed to regard the matter contemptuously.

The Adventists had a sort of holiness that centered in the law and stood heroically around the glory of the two tables of stone (2 Corinthians 3). *They served a day* which was fulfilled in the Christ who said, "Come unto *me*, all ye that labor and are heavy laden, and I will give you rest." They did not serve Christ at all, for they deny His salvation. They mixed the law and gospel, which the Savior plainly showed could not savingly be done. He taketh away the first that He may establish the second. Would you mind when you are alone, reading a few scriptures with this thought in view? Take Matthew 11:25–30; then Matthew 12:1–14 as a closely related chain of thought. Then take Mark 3:1–6 and 15–28; Matthew 9:14–17; Luke 5:37, 38. These people explain away plain statements of the New Testament in which life and immortality are brought to light and base their doctrines on the Old. . . .

## Evening Venting Light and the Lamb's Book

The Evening Light people were doing a beautiful work in a few rare places, but withdrew themselves with a "holier-than-thou" attitude that made them worse sectarians than those they designated as sects; for truly the Spirit saith, "that not he that commendeth himself is approved, but he whom the Lord commendeth" (2 Corinthians 10:18). Surely he that glorieth must glory in the Lord (1 Corinthians 1:30, 31; 1 Corinthians 3:21–23). The foundation of God standeth sure, having this seal, "The Lord knoweth them that are His." It is the *lamb's book* of Life that contains our names in heaven, not some sect's book of life, nor yet some crowd of men. Nor does affiliating with any set of men, whether with a church roll or without one, assure us that our names are written in heaven. "The Lord knoweth them that are His" (2 Timothy 2:19). The approval of no set of men, however self-approved they may presume to be, nor what their apparent power, is required to assure you of a home in heaven. You are bought with a price, and the Spirit beareth witness with *your* spirit that you are the children of God; and He saith, "Be not the servants of men."

## Proclaim Liberty

The Spirit hath said unto me for years, "Proclaim liberty! Proclaim liberty!" Yet we have been meeting for years now binding God's people under rules and laws and constitutions (Jeremiah 34:17).

There are helps and governments, according to 1 Corinthians, twelfth chapter, and one form of government may fit a condition or purpose that another may not, but in every case we must be careful not to lean to the human understanding, but rather we must commit our works to God that our thoughts may be established (Proverbs 16:3; Psalms 37:6). Our thoughts can not save men. Law condemns but can not give life. Salvation belongs to God. In His presence alone is salvation and deliverance. In His right arm is the power of victory. He gives us our faculties. We may use them assumptuously and even presumptuously, but we will reap small satisfaction and poor fruit, if any. But if, like the boy who had five loaves and two fishes, we give them to Him, He can use them to bless, feed and satisfy the multitude. O for Jesus!

To proclaim liberty does not mean that we must ignore rules made to work by; but that the rule of love, the rule of kindness, the rule of forbearance, the rule of peace, the rule of the fruit of the Spirit, must not be supplanted by the rigid, frowning and dry appeal to some man-made mode. Where the spirit of man is there is impatience, fretfulness, faultfinding and whatnot, till the hearts and spirits of the people, longing after God as they may be, are worn out with discouragement. Where the Spirit of the Lord is there is Liberty! Liberty! Liberty!

## The People Want to Go

Brethren, the people want to go with us. If they did not they have but to drift away to other churches that let them do as they please. But they need help. It was said of the disciples, "Then were their hearts glad when they saw the Lord." And the elect are always glad when they see the Lord. Shall we lift Him up? Even Peter was glad when he saw the Lord, though he had denied Him, and cursed and sworn. It is a vision of the Lord that heals the bite of the serpent of sin; that sends the leper to his knees in supplication and raises him up clean and whole; that restores the widow's dead son to her arms and Mary's and Martha's brother to a lonely home. O the vision of the Lord! O the fullness of the Spirit! If the clouds be full of rain they empty themselves upon the earth. God has blessed us and made us a blessing. We do not begin to know how much. It is Jesus. *He* works our works in us (Isaiah 26).

## The Call

Now this was what we longed to carry to the churches, even thirty-six years ago, that resulted in the calling of the first holiness convention at Jackson, Mississippi, thirty-four years ago.

And the people came, and night and day *we studied the Word* and prayed. The people wanted to go to heaven; we put before them *Christ, the Way*, and they fell before Him (Psalms 45). We only wanted to carry the message to the churches. We did not want another denomination. We are not sectarians. But the churches rejected us. So we had to build for the Lord. We rejected every name but His. . . .

### Notes

*Sermon source*: Charles Price Jones, *The Battle Royal: A Contention for the Faith Once Delivered to the Saints* (The Annual Address of Bishop C.P. Jones, President of the General Holiness Convention, 1930), published as a pamphlet by General Holiness Convention, Los Angeles, California, 1930.

1. Ithiel C. Clemmons, *Bishop C.H. Mason and the Roots of the Church of God in Christ, Centennial Edition* (Bakersfield, CA: Pneuma Life Publishing, 1996), 7.
2. Cobbins, *History of the Church of Christ (Holiness) U.S.A. 1895–1965*, 23–24.
3. Clemmons, *Bishop C.H. Mason*, 9.
4. Ibid, 21.

### Bibliographical Sources

Cobbins, O.B., ed. *History of the Church of Christ (Holiness) U.S.A. 1895–1965*. New York: Vantage Press, 1966.

Cyber Hymnal. "Charles Price Jones." http://www.cyberhymnal.org/bio/j/o/jones_cp.htm (accessed April 19, 2005).

Daniels, David Douglas, III. "The Cultural Renewal of Slave Religion: Charles Price Jones and the Emergence of the Holiness Movement in Mississippi." Ph.D. diss., Union Theological Seminary, 1992.

Irvin, Dale T. "Charles Price Jones: Image of Holiness," in *Portraits of a Generation: Early Pentecostal Leaders*, ed. James R. Goff Jr. and Grant Wacker. Fayetteville: University of Arkansas Press, 2002.

Jones, Charles Edwin. *Black Holiness: A Guide to the Study of Black Participation in Wesleyan Perfectionist and Glossolalic Pentecostal Movements.* Metuchen, NJ: American Theological Library Association/Scarecrow Press, 1987.

Turner, William C., Jr. "Movements in the Spirit: A Review of African American Holiness/Pentecostal/Apostolics," in *Directory of African American Religious Bodies*, ed. Wardell J. Payne. Washington, DC: Howard University Press, 1991.

Williams, Juan, and Quinton Dixie. *This Far by Faith: Stories from the African American Religious Experience.* New York: Blackside, Inc., 2003, 156.

# CHARLES HARRISON MASON

*(1866–1961)*

In the late nineteenth and early twentieth centuries, the mainline African American churches sought respectability in white society; they distanced themselves from the practices of the old "underground church" of slavery, banned ecstatic liturgical worship, and banned speaking in tongues (glossolalia). Mason, on the other hand, along with his diverse constituency, preached and practiced a wide-ranging freedom of expression that flowed throughout the national Church of God in Christ (COGIC) organization. Mason dared to be different and as a result preserved the roots of African American Christianity.

A son of emancipated slaves Jeremiah and Eliza Mason, Charles Harrison Mason was born on September 8, 1866 near Shelby County, Tennessee, and raised in the African American Baptist church. In 1878, after a devastating yellow fever epidemic hit Shelby County, Mason's family moved to Plumersville, Arkansas. Mason fell sick with tuberculosis. That same year he was miraculously healed, and afterward dedicated his life to the service of God. At age fourteen, Mason was baptized, ordained, and licensed to preach in the black Baptist church by his half-brother, Rev. Israel Nelson, a Baptist preacher.

In 1895, Mason met pastor Charles Price Jones, and after both were ousted from the black Baptist church for preaching sanctification and holiness, which emphasized baptism by the Holy Spirit and the belief in personal holiness, they later established the Church of God in Christ Fellowship of churches. Mason later wrote that the name of the organization was given to him through divine revelation while he was in Little Rock, Arkansas. In 1897, Mason established Lexington, Mississippi's first COGIC church.

In March 1907, Mason traveled to Los Angeles to investigate the famed interracial, multicultural Azusa Street Revival, led by the African American preacher William Joseph Seymour. Mason was filled with the Holy Ghost and began to speak in tongues. At that point, his ministry underwent a fundamental transformation. When he returned to Memphis, his Wellington Street church embraced the new phenomenon of spiritual baptism—the internal recognition of new life in Christ Jesus upon the acceptance of the Holy Spirit and the outward display of spiritual gifts, such as speaking in tongues. However, the issue of speaking in tongues caused Mason and C.P. Jones to part ways. Mason kept the name COGIC, and all of the churches in the organization that believed Mason's message of spiritual transformation elected him as the new general overseer, with the *Whole Truth* as the COGIC official publication and Memphis as its headquarters. Mason's movement immediately experienced interracial growth. Future leaders of the Assemblies of God, E.N. Bell and Howard Goss, came to Memphis and asked Mason for permission to use his church's ecclesiastical powers. Mason allowed the white Pentecostal ministers access to the COGIC charter to conduct marriages, license white Pentecostals to preach, and to ride the trains at a discounted price, as his ministers did. Bishop Ithiel Clemmons claimed that from 1907 to 1914 Mason ordained more than three hundred fifty white Pentecostals. However, in 1914 in a Hot Springs organizational meeting, the white members of the Church of God in Christ pulled away from Mason's church and formed their own, exclusively white, Assemblies of God organization.

Mason preached a message of hope, despite racial and economic despair. He allowed anyone from any walk of life and social class to become a member of the COGIC, whether educated or illiterate. In the 1920s and 1930s Mason's church experienced astronomical growth throughout the country. As working-class southern blacks migrated north, east, and west, they took Mason's African American Pentecostal teachings with them. When Mason's movement reached the cities, it immediately took root and over time became an urban phenomenon.

Between 1917 and 1918, the federal Bureau of Investigation probed Bishop Mason. Referring to his pacifistic teachings and the COGIC's early doctrinal statement against the shedding of blood, the bureau accused him of subverting the draft and encouraging black men in the south not to fight in World War I. On June 23, 1918, Mason preached the sermon "The Kaiser in the Light of the Scriptures" at an outdoor service in Memphis. As the reader will see, he made clear his objection to German policy and stressed his commitment to the war's Liberty Bond drive.

On November 17, 1961, Bishop Charles Harrison Mason died at age ninety-five in a Detroit hospital. His body was enshrined in a marble vault located in the lobby of Memphis's historic Mason Temple. At the time of his death, the COGIC church had established fifty-five hundred congregations and had 482,679 members. As of 2009 the COGIC reports an estimated membership of over seven and a half million in the United States alone; it may be the nation's largest African American denomination.

• • •

*Bishop Mason published the COGIC's doctrinal statement in 1918. In a section entitled "Political Governments," Mason said: "We believe that the shedding of human blood or the taking of human life to be contrary to the teachings of our Lord and Savior, and as a body we are averse to war in all its various forms." This statement was adopted by COGIC's General Assembly in 1895, thereby forbidding its members to take up arms or to shed human blood in any form. "We herewith offer our services to the President for any service that will not conflict with our conscientious scruples in this respect, with love to all, with malice toward none, and with due respect to all who differ from us in our interpretation of the Scriptures."[1] As a result of Mason's opposition to war, he and many of his associates were arrested and charged with subverting the draft; one of his associates was tarred and feathered by a mob in Arkansas for distributing COGIC literature against the war. Some say to allay fears that he was against the American government and not patriotic, Mason preached "The Kaiser in the Light of the Scriptures."*

*Mason's first general secretary, a German American named William B. Holt, recorded "The Kaiser in the Light of the Scriptures," inserting his comments into the sermon. It was preached to a vast throng that gathered to hear Mason in North Memphis, Tennessee.*

## The Kaiser in the Light of the Scriptures (June 1918)

According to Secretary Holt:

The Overseer was led to speak of the German Kaiser in the light of the Scriptures, basing his remarks on the vision of the prophet as recorded in the second chapter of Habakkuk 2:2: "The Lord answered me and said write the vision and make it plain."

[Bishop Mason said] They tell me the Kaiser went into prayer and came out and lifted up his hands and prayed, and afterwards declared war.[2]

Let us see, what did he pray and for what did he pray? Surely he did not pray thy Kingdom come, because the Kingdom of God is righteousness, peace and joy in the Holy Ghost (Romans 14:17).

If he had been praying for peace he would not have declared war. The Apostle Paul declared in 1 Timothy 2:1–2 "I exhort therefore that, first of all, supplications, prayers, intercessions and giving of thanks be made for all men—for kings and for all who are in authority—that we may lead a quiet and peaceful life in all Godliness and honesty." If he had the spirit of this prayer he himself would have endeavored to live a peaceful life.

In 1 Timothy 2:8, the apostle again says, I will that men pray everywhere, lifting up holy hands, without wrath and doubting. This is the attitude to be in while praying with uplifted hands. The Kaiser prayed in wrath, with the purpose to work wrath, which was a vain prayer, as he had not the spirit of Christ, or the authority of the Scriptures. Thus, the prayer of the Kaiser was unscriptural.

Secretary Holt noted: He [Bishop Mason] complimented the president, and showed he was in harmony with the scriptures, as recorded in 1 Kings 8:33–45.

He [Bishop Mason] called the American people to a day of fasting and prayer, that they might confess their sins and shortcomings and humble themselves before the Lord, in order that they might find favor with Him, who causes wars to cease and maketh bare His holy arm in defense of a righteous nation, and was in harmony with Him who taught us to pray, Thy kingdom come, thy will be done, on earth as it is in heaven.

The Lord declared by the mouth of Isaiah, the prophet: "Open ye the gates that the righteous nation that keepeth the truth might enter in" (Isaiah 26:24).

He [Bishop Mason] now called attention of his vast audience to the spirit of the Christ that prayed. He quoted from the prayer of the savior founded in the gospel of John 17:15. I pray not that thou should take them out of the world, but that thou should keep them from the evil.

The Kaiser is praying to the end, that evil might come into the world; the savior prayed that men should not be killed, but that God would keep them from evil.

He [Bishop Mason] declared the Kaiser appeared to be the war beast of Revelations thirteenth chapter, causing the entire world to wander after the beast, and that his power came not from God, but from the dragon.

He [Bishop Mason] now again referred to the vision of the prophet Habakkuk, saying the vision was for an appointed time, but at the end of it should speak. He declared that prophesies were being fast fulfilled, and that present events proved that we are living in the last days and the end was near.

Quoting the fourth verse: Behold, his soul which is lifted up is not upright in him.

He [Bishop Mason] declared the events of the present war proved that the soul of the Kaiser was lifted up in him, and in his estimation he was not of God.

Quoting the fifth verse: He is a proud man; neither keepeth at home; he enlarges his desire as hell, and is as death, and cannot be satisfied, but gathereth unto him all nations and heapeth unto him all peoples with the Kaiser's ambition to rule the world and the spirit of militarism that possesses him. He fittingly described [the] condition, thus. He does not want to keep home, but is reaching out hands dripping with the blood of innocent children and defenseless women sent to an untimely death by the barbarous method of submarine warfare, which is out of harmony with all of the laws of humanity and fair play and is a violation of all of the principle of civilized warfare.

The German Kaiser is seemingly attempting to gather to himself all nations and to rule all peoples. Not satisfied with the rape of Belgium, he has overthrown the governments of Romania and Montenegro, and through hypocrisy and deceit he betrayed Russia into a disgraceful peace.

Woe to him that coveteth an evil covetousness to his house that he may set his nest on high; that he may be delivered from the power of evil.

Thou has consulted shame to thy house by cutting off many people, and hast sinned against thy soul.

He [Bishop Mason] declared if anyone is building hopes on the victories of the Kaiser in the present war, their hopes are in vain. Although he may conquer nations and devastate cities, in the end he has to meet God, and that the remnant of the Germans and all peoples saved out of the slaughter will rise up against him and cry. Woe unto thee because thou hast spoiled many nations; the people shall spoil thee.

Jesus Christ came to bring immortality and eternal life to light, to bind up the broken hearted and bring the glad tidings of salvation from sin and death to a lost and ruined world.

The devilish spirit of the Kaiser causes women to be ravished, infants to be dashed to pieces and prisoners of war to be tortured and put to death by methods only equaled by the Spanish Inquisition and the persecutions of the Christians under Nero.

He [Bishop Mason] compared this spirit of the Kaiser to the spirit of the Lord Jesus Christ, and declared that the Kaiser could not be of God, for the Scriptures declared, if any man have not the spirit of Christ he is none of his (Romans 8:9).

Quoting from the gospel of Luke 9:54: "And when his disciples James and John saw this they said, Lord, will thou that we command fire to come down from heaven and consume them, even as Elias did? But, He turned and rebuked them, and said. Ye know not what manner of the spirit ye are of." The disciples spoke as they thought men would do, or should do.

He [Bishop Mason] then quoted the master's answer (Luke 9:56): "The Son of Man is not come to destroy men's lives, but to save them."

Future events showed, before he would kill, he offered up himself, and by his death came peace, and if the Kaiser had been willing to die rather than shed the blood of his fellow men, we would now have peace.

I cannot understand, after preaching the gospel for twenty years and exhorting men to peace and righteousness, how I could be accused of fellowshipping with the anti-Christ of the Kaiser.

[Secretary Holt noted] Answering the question that has been asked him many times, namely: Is it right to buy Liberty Bonds? His reply was, yes! Yes! And he proceeded to define the Liberty Bonds.

[Bishop Mason said] What does it mean to buy Liberty Bonds?

It means to lend your country a certain amount of money.

What says the Scriptures? Matthew 5:42: Give to him that asketh thee, and from them that borrow of thee turn not away.

Brethren we are living by every word of God (Matthew 4:4). Our government is asking us for a loan, and we are in no violation of God's word in granting it, and not only to loan, hoping for nothing to gain (Luke 6:35).

I have loaned the government, and have succeeded in raising for the help of the government more than three thousand dollars, in taking out bonds, as far as I am concerned, the spiritual injunction stands. I have loaned, hoping for nothing in return.

He [Bishop Mason] prayed for the time to come when the German hordes should be driven back across the Rhine, the independence of Belgium restored and victory of allied armies restoring peace to a war-torn world—especially for the coming of the Prince of Peace and the day when men would beat their swords into plowshares and men would learn to war no more.

## NOTES

*Sermon source: History and Formative Years of the Church of God in Christ: with excerpts from the life and works of its founder Bishop C.H. Mason* (1969), edited by Bishop J.O. Patterson Sr., Rev. German R. Ross, and Mrs. Julia Mason Atkins.

Courtesy of Dr. David Hall Sr. and the Church of God in Christ Publishing House, Memphis, Tennessee.

1. Charles Mason, *A Brief Historical: and Doctrinal Statement and Rules for Government of the Church of God in Christ*. Compiled by Williams B. Holt circa 1917–18 (Memphis: Church of God in Christ Publishing House), 10.

2. The German Kaiser referred to here is Wilhelm II King of Prussia. *The World War I Biographical Dictionary* describes him: "Wilhelm symbolized his era and the nouveaux riche aspects of the German empire. The Kaiser suffered from a birth defect that left his left arm withered and useless. He overcame this handicap, but the effort to do so left its mark, and despite efforts of his parents to give him a liberal education, the prince became overly interested with religious mysticism, militarism, anti-Semitism, and the glorification of power politics. Some have claimed that he displayed elements of a narcissistic personality disorder. Bombastic, vain, insensitive, and possessed with grandiose notions of divine right rule, his personality traits paralleled those of the new Germany: strong, but off balance; vain, but insecure; intelligent, but narrow; self-centered yet longing for acceptance."

### *Bibliographical Sources*

Clemmons, Ithiel C. "Charles Harrison Mason," in *Dictionary of Pentecostal and Charismatic Movements*, ed. Stanley M. Burgess and Gary B. McGee. Grand Rapids, MI: Zondervan Press, 1988.

Daniels, David D. "They Had a Dream: Racial Harmony Broke Down, but the Hope Did Not." *Christian History* 17, no. 2, issue 58 (Spring 1998).

Herwig, Holger H., and Neil M. Heyman, eds. *The World War I Biographical Dictionary*. Westport, CT: Greenwood Press, 1982.

Hill, Samuel S., and Samuel Hill "Charles Harrison Mason," in *Encyclopedia of Religion in the South*. Reprint, Macon, GA: Mercer University Press, 1998.

Nelson, Douglas. "The Black Face of Church Renewal: The Meaning of a Charismatic Explosion (1901–1985)," in *Faces of Renewal: Studies in Honor of Stanley M. Horton*, ed. Paul Elber. Peabody, MA: Hendrickson Publishers, 1998.

Robeck, Cecil M., Jr. "The Past: Historical Roots of Racial Unity and Division in American Pentecostalism." Paper presented at "Pentecostal Partners: A Reconciliation Strategy for a 21st-Century Ministry," October 17–24, 1994, Memphis, TN.

Tinney, James. "William J. Seymour: Father of Modern Day Pentecostalism," in *The Journal of the Interdenominational Theological Seminary* 14, no. 1 (1976).

## A.W. NIX

*(ca. 1876–1943)*

Very little is known of A.W. Nix's early life, other than that he was born in Alabama around 1876. It has been suggested that he was a miner and piano player who was called to preach shortly before World War I. Nix was a plainspoken folk preacher, but showed that he had engaged in formal study by his use of historical figures, including Alexander, Xenophon, and Hannibal, in his sermon "The Matchless King."

Nix was a magnetic singer and a whooper. More than fifteen of his sermons have been reissued in the twenty-first century. Having disappeared from national view by 1940, Nix's name was reintroduced when the life story of Thomas Dorsey, the father of gospel music, was told by Michael Harris in his book *The Rise of the Gospel Blues*. Apparently, Dorsey underwent a conversion experience under the influence of Nix's preaching.[1]

In the 1920s, U.S. record companies discovered a market in the black community for recordings by black preachers. Within the three-minute limit imposed by the 78 rpm record, the preacher and a few members of his congregation would attempt to condense the experience of a thirty-minute church service, including a short sermon and often some music.

Through his primary record label, Vocalion, Nix recorded sermons in the late 1920s and early 30s. On most of these records he also sang. The only black preacher who produced more recordings during this period was J.M. Gates of Atlanta (see his biography and sermons earlier in this section). It is clear that the record labels for which Nix and Gates recorded kept a close eye on one another. Some of the recording techniques and sermon focus points that show up in recordings by Gates later show up in recordings by Nix, and vice versa. Some of their sermons had similar titles. Gates recorded "Where Will You Be Christmas Day?" "Will the Coffin Be Your Santa Claus?" and "Death Might be Your Santa Claus." Nix recorded "Death Might Be Your Christmas Gift," "That Little Thing May Kill You Yet" (which was a Christmas sermon), and "How Will You Spend Christmas?" In 1927, Gates recorded "Hell Bound Express Train" and a song titled "Death's Black Train is Coming." In that same year, Nix recorded the sermon for which he became best known, "The Black Diamond Express to Hell." In total, Nix appears to have made six 78 rpm recordings under this title, each a continuation of the previous. Like Gates in his sermons, in the later versions of "The Black Diamond Express to Hell," Nix begins to feature congregation members who have speaking roles during the sermon.

• • •

*Nix's most famous sermon concerns one metaphor—a train. Use of the train as a metaphor in sermons was common during this period. Train songs were also prevalent in the 1920s and 1930s. The preacher skill-*

*fully uses this metaphor to grab the attention of listeners and to make the sermon come alive. As Nix pulls the train into each station, one can easily see that this is a train that no one wants to ride. The majority of each sermon in the series is preached with cadence and continuous rhythm, making them even more electrifying.*

*Nix names various stops that a train takes on the way to hell. Stops include Liars Avenue, Drunkardsville, and Gambling Tower. Before each stop, Nix intones and thunders the phrase, "Next station!" At each stop, he gives the characteristics of the types of people likely to board the Black Diamond Express—gossipers, liars, gamblers, and more—and urges all of them to get off the train before it's too late. To maintain the interest of those who purchased his sermons, Nix added new stops on each recording. In the later recordings, aware that he now has many record listeners and in imitation of the successful recording style of J.M. Gates, members of Nix's recording congregations act out the roles of sinners who Nix is trying to persuade to get off the train. The most noted of these was Miz Hard-boiled, who shows up in parts 5 and 6. She is played by Nina Mae McKinney, a noted black singer-actress of the time. McKinney was not known for her church recordings, and the love she declares for Nix at the end of the sermon has a strange, carnal ring to it. The comments of Miz Hard-boiled and those of others from the congregation are provided in parentheses.*

## The Black Diamond Express to Hell, Parts 1–6 (1927)

### Part I

My text is Matthew the seventh chapter and the thirteenth verse: "Enter ye in at the strait gate: for wide is the gate, and broad is the way, that leadeth to destruction, and many there be which go in thereat."

This train is known as the Black Diamond Express Train to Hell. Sin is the engineer. Pleasure is the headlight and the devil is the conductor. I see the Black Diamond as she starts off for hell. The bell is ringing, hell bound, hell bound. The devil cries out, "All aboard for hell." First station is Drunkardsville. Stop there and let all the drunkards get on board. I have a big crowd down there at drinking junk city. Some drinking gin, some drinking moonshine, some drinking white mule and red horse. All you drunkards, you got to go to hell on the Black Diamond Train.

Black Diamond starts off for hell now. Next station is Liars Avenue.

Wait there and let all the liars get on board. I have a big crowd of liars down there. Have some smooth liars, some unreasonable liars, some professional liars, some bare-face liars, some ungodly liars, some big liars, some little liars, some go to bed lyin', get up lyin', lie all day, lie on you and lie on me. A big crowd of liars, you gotta go to hell on the Black Diamond Train.

Next station is Deceiversville. Wait there and let all the deceivers get on board. Some of you been deceivin' one another ever since you been in the world. Friends deceivin' friends, husbands deceivin' wives, wives deceivin' husbands. But, they got to go to hell on the Black Diamond Train.

Next station is Conjuration Station. Wait there and let all the conjurers get on board. I have a big crowd of Louisiana counjurers down there. They got to go to hell on the Black Diamond Train. They always takin' bits of dust and brass pins and matchheads and making little things to sell to one another. But they got to go to hell on the Black Diamond Train.

Next station is Confusion Junction. Wait there and let all the confusion makers get on. Some of you raise confusion in your home, confusion in the streets, confusion in the church, confusion everywhere you go. But you gotta go to hell on the Black Diamond Train.

Next station is Fight Town. Wait theeeeeere and let alllllllll the church fighters get on board. I have a big crowd of church fighters down there that never go to prayer meeting. That never go to Sunday School. That never go to morning service. They always stay way from morning church until they hear about the business meeting and they come runnin' up out of battle's bottom to put up a big fight in God's church. But allllllllll you church fighters, you gotta go to hell on the Black Diamond Train.

And now the Black Diamond Train will stop just a minute to pick up brimstone from hell.

## Part II

Black Diamond has taken on a fresh supply of brimstone and now she's ready to pull out for hell. Sin is the engineer and pleasure is the headlight and the devil is the conductor. Next station is Dancin' Hall Depot. Wait there. I have a large crowd of church members to get on down there. Some of you think you can sing in the choir on Sunday and Charleston on the ballroom floor on Monday. But you gotta go to hell on the Black Diamond Train. The Black Diamond pulls off now for hell.

Next station is Gambler's Tower. Wait theeerrrre and let alllllllll the gamblers get on board. Have a big crowd of gamblers and crap shooters and card players and bootleggers got to ride the Black Diamond Train to Hell. They all gets on the Black Diamond Train she starts out for hell now. She's almost into hell.

Next station is Stealin' Town. Wait there and let allllllllllllllll the church thieves get on board. (Preach Elder.) I have a big crowd of members in the church always been stealin' ever since they been in the church. Some always beggin' money for their church and never turn it in. Always givin' church suppers and then steal half the money. (Oh, my goodness.) Allllllll you church thieves you got to go to hell on the Black Diamond Train.

Next Station is Plotters Gap. Stop there and let all the church plotters get on. Have a big plot always plottin' against the church, always plottin' against the preacher, always plottin' against the deacons, plottin' against the church program. Always gettin' behind closed doors plottin' against me. All you church fighters, you got to go to hell on the Black Diamond Train.

Next station is Little, No Harm Park. I got a big crowd always down at the park parkin' all the time. They never can come to church on Sunday. Always parkin' all the time. I know that the devil soon to dispatch the engineer and tell him to pull his throttle wide open and hit the damnation switch in the black of midnight and tell him to make a fast run for hell. Oh gambler get off the Black Diamond Train. Oh midnight rambler, get off the Black Diamond Train. Ohhhhhhh, backslider get off the Black Diamond Train.

Children aren't you glad, you got off the Black Diamond Train a long time ago. I'm so glad I got off a loooooong time ago. Ever since I got off I've been singing: "All of my sins been takin' away. Well, all of my sins, been takin' away. Well, all of my sins been taken away, well glory hallelujah glory land, all of my sins have been taken away. Children aren't you glad you got off a long time ago. I'm glad I got off a long time ago." Amen.

## Part III

The second session of Black Diamond Express Train is now pulling out for hell. Sin is the engineer. Pleasure is the headlight and the devil is the conductor. (Right.) So many people are going to hell until the first session could not carry them all. The Devil has been busy day and night (Yes.) getting his crowd ready for the Black Diamond. (Right.) He has a fine personality. He is a sheep of sheep. The Black Diamond is now ready to pull out for hell. (Yes.) The devil cries out, all aboard for hell. (Alright.)

First station is Murder's Row. Got a big crowd of murderers down there. Old murderers and young murderers. They'll murder your feelings and destroy your reputation. (Yes.) But they got to go to hell on the Black Diamond. (Yes.)

Next station is Immoral Place. (Yes.) That's where young women lose their womanhood and virtue. (Yes.) Poor girls from good families are led astray by bad women and no count men, but they got to go to hell on the Black Diamond Train. (Yeah.)

Next station is Gossiping Town. A big crowd of tattlers and gossipers down there always goin' from door to door (Yes.) always talkin' about everything and everybody. But they got to go to hell on the Black Diamond Train. (Yes.)

Next station is Knockersville. A big crowd of knockers down there. Always knockin' on the preacher and knockin' on the church and knockin' on the Lord too. They're knockin' on heaven and they're knockin' on hell. You may knock the Black Diamond, but you got to go to hell on the Black Diamond Train. (Preach.)

Next station is Cheating Town. A big crowd down there are tryin' to get up in the world by cheatin' everybody. At some of these grocery stores you can never get full weight. At some of these meat markets, when the butcher weighs your meat, he'll weigh his hands with it. (Yes.) At some of these business stores, if you don't get a receipt when you pay your bill, they'll make you pay it over again. (Right.) And they got to go to hell on the Black Diamond Train.

Next station is Dishonest Camp. There's a big crowd down there that won't do right to save their lives. They'll borrow money from you and never pay you back. They owe everybody in the neighborhood. (Right.) And if you ask them for it, they'll get mad with yah and stop speakin' to you. They always buyin' on credit and never pay their bills. They move every month to keep from payin' their rent. But, they got to go to hell on the Black Diamond Train.

Next station is Hypocrite Drag. A big crowd of hypocrites in the church down there. They'll pray and shout all day Sunday and raise hell all day Monday. They claim to be your friends, but they're runnin' with your enemies. (Yes.) But, they got to go to hell on the Black Diamond Train. (Right.)

And now the Black Diamond will stop just a minute to see if there's anybody that would like to get off. Amen.

### PART IV

A motherless girl who promised to meet her mother in heaven and has just stepped off the Black Diamond. And now the Black Diamond will continue its trip on to hell. Next station is Fussin' Town. A big crowd of women down there who'd rather fuss than to eat. Some go to bed fussin' and get up fussin'. They'll go to work fussin' and come home fussin' and they'll raise a fuss anywhere. If it was possible, they'd raise a fuss in heaven. But, they got to go to hell on the Black Diamond Train. (Alright.)

Next station is the Twentieth-Century Style Shop. This is where the women get the latest styles of modern dress. (Alright.) The dresses the women are wearing these days are almost a knockout. Some of them wear Stacy sashes and Georgetta and you can see clear through them. (Yes.) Some are wearing satin beaded dresses with low necks and no backs. And all of them are wearing short, tight, skirts cut off above their knees, big shoes and window-pane stockings and socks and some no socks at all. With painted lips and powdered faces, they will charm you and then talk to you with their eyes. I tell you, this modern dress today is mighty hard on the men. You can find these women in large numbers on Hasting Street in Detroit and on Forty-seventh Street and South Parkway in Chicago and on Market Street in St. Louis and on Eighteenth Street in Kansas City, on Lenox Avenue in New York, on Beale Street in Memphis, on South Grand Park in New Orleans, and on Decatur Street in Atlanta, Georgia. And when these women ride on the train with their legs all crossed, the men will almost have to close their eyes. (Yes.) And the thing that looks so bad, now, old women have cut off their dresses above their knees tryin' to look giddy and gay. But the Black Diamond will give them a path right on down to hell.

And when the Black Diamond will hit the main line and make a fast run for hell, she'll land in hell while the hell fire is burnin' and while the hell hounds are howlin'. (Amen. Yes.) And when the devil will pull out for the pit of damnation and the lake of fire and brimstone, the devil will unload in hell.

Oh, mother's son, get off the Black Diamond Train. Oh, midnight rambler, get off the Black Diamond Train. Every since I got off the Black Diamond Train my soul has been singing, "Well, oh poor sinner, when the world is on fire, when the world starts burnin, don't be no gambler. Oh hide me over in the Rock of Ages. Rock of Ages cleff for me." If you don't get off the Black Diamond Train, it'll land you in hell just as sure as you are born. Amen.

### PART V

NIX: Brothers and sisters, the Black Diamond Express train is going to make another trip to hell. The first and second sections of the

Black Diamond Express Train carried a large crowd of high-class sinners and professional liars of all kinds and scientific gamblers and many women of high society who had plenty money to pay their way to hell on high-class accommodations. And now the devil is running a reduced rate for this train to hell. Come on here, all you cheapskates, you alley rats, you midnight ramblers, you little cheap streetwalkers. You all got to go to hell on the Black Diamond reduced-rate train, where you will burn in hell-fire and brimstone forever and forever in a lake of fire where they'll be wailing and gnashing of teeth. Get on here, all you hell-bound sinners.

MIZ HARD-BOILED: Hah, hah, hah. Listen at that old preacher. He's tryin' to scare somebody talkin' about goin' to hell. Say, you can't scare me and make me cry like you done all those old people. I ain't stuttin' about you and your old hell-bound train.

NIX: This train is leaving for eternal hell right now. All aboard to hell.

SINNER SEEKING GOD: Mr. Preacher what can I do to keep from going to hell?

NIX: You must come up right up here now to the altar and bow down and repent of your sins.

MIZ HARD-BOILED: Just look at all those old crazy fools up there bowin' down prayin'. You can't make me pray. Everybody calls me hard-boiled.

NIX: Yes, but you must give up the world and call on God and be saved now or else you will land in hell in the black shade of midnight. This is your last opportunity to get off the Black Diamond Train. I plead with you to get off the Black Diamond. I urge you to get off the Black Diamond before it be too late.

SINNER REPENTING: Now, I'll give up my sinful life and get off this hell-bound train.

NIX: Amen. Amen. Glory. Glory. Will you give up sister? And give your heart to God right now?

SINNER REPENTING: Oh Lord. Have mercy upon my poor soul. Yes Elder. I'll give up. I'll give up. I'll get off this hell-bound train.

NIX: Amen. Glory hallelujah. Another soul born into the Kingdom of God. Let us all sing. "Free at last. Free at last. Thank God Amighty, I'm free at last. Free at last, free at last, thank God Amighty, I'm free at last."

MIZ HARD-BOILED: Hah, hah, hah. If that ain't a mess. Say preacher, why don't you try to make me pray and cry. You know better. You know I won't fall for that kinda' stuff. You'll have to come after me some other way. My name is hard-boiled and believe me, I'm a hard nut for you to crack.

NIX: I'm bound for glory not eternal damnation and the upward road leads to eternal joy and happiness and whosoever will can come now. Choose ye this day which road you will take. The broad road leads to hell and the narrow road leads to glory and while the Black Diamond waits for a few minutes, make up your mind which road you gonna' take.

## PART VI

NIX: The train will stop just a few minutes at Farewell Station just long enough for everyone on board to bid the world farewell. In this world the white clouds and the Black Diamond Train will separate. Mothers will bid farewell to their children. Bid mother farewell. Farewell. Farewell. Farewell you hard-boiled sinners. The Black Diamond Express train will hit damnation switch and make a fast run for hell. Every child of God will rise above the clouds and bid farewell to every fear and wipe their weeping eyes. In hell in the black shade of midnight, in hell, with all the demons crying, in hell, with all the hell hounds hounding, the hobnobs of hell will be coming for your soul. You may not bow now, but you will bow in hell. You may not cry now, but you will cry in hell. Listen, I can hear some mother's daughter cryin'.

MOTHER'S DAUGHTER: Oh, Oh, Oh, Lord.

NIX: All the stubborn-hearted men and women will be in hell. All you hard-hearted sinners who turned down God and turned down the church and turned down the Gospel, will be in hell. I bid you hard-boiled sinners farewell, goodbye. We never will see you no more.

SINNER BEING LEFT BEHIND: Oh, don't leave me. Please don't leave me.

NIX: As we start off for heaven and immortal glory, I can hear the children of God singing, as they goin' up higher. (Preacher and congregation sing.) "There is joy in that land. There is joy in that land. There is joy in that land, where I'm bound, where I'm bound. Well, there is joy in that land, there is joy in that land, there is joy in that land, where I'm bound." Farewell. Goodbye. We're leaving you now.

MIZ HARD-BOILED: Ahhh, don't leave me. Please don't leave me. I don't wanna' go to hell. I'll pray and be good. Oh Lord, have mercy.

NIX: Yes my daughter. I'm glad to see you come over on the Lord's side.

MIZ HARD-BOILED: I will give my heart to the Lord and serve him as long as I live.

NIX: God bless you my dear child. God bless you.

MIZ HARD-BOILED: Elder, I'll do anything you want me to do. Elder will you please help me?

NIX: Huh, what did you say? Do you really mean that? My dear, "I'll do anything you want me to do." The Elder will comfort you now in this hour.

MIZ HARD-BOILED: I will join the church and I will be baptized. I will sing in the choir. I'll lead prayer meeting. I will do anything. I wanna meet the Lord in peace. Oh Lord have mercy on my poor soul.

NIX: This is the best step you ever did take my dear in this hour. The Lord is with you. The Lord is in you. You are one of the Lord's little lambs.

MIZ HARD-BOILED: Oh I love the Lord and I love all of his people and Elder above everything, I sure love you. You know I love you.

NIX: My dear little one you sure will meet the Lord in peace now.

MIZ HARD-BOILED: I'm so happy. Oh, I'm so happy. I'm glad I got off that hell bound train.

NIX: Yes my dear little lamb. Oh, you love everybody and we all love you. Amen.

## *NOTES*

*Sermon source: Rev. A.W. Nix and Rev. Emmett Dixon*, Vol. 2 (1928–1931), Document Records, 1996.

1. Some have confused the Reverend A.W. Nix who recorded sermons with the singer who is listed in the 1923 *Gospel Pearls* song book produced by the National Baptist Convention. The two were not the same.

## *BIBLIOGRAPHICAL SOURCES*

*Big Road Blues Show 3/29/09: The Year 1927*, pt. 1. http://sundayblues.org/index.php?s=vocalion (accessed April 5, 2008).

Harris, Michael W. *The Rise of Gospel Blues: The Music of Thomas Andrew Dorsey in the Urban Church*. New York: Oxford University Press, 1992.

O'Neal, Jim, and Amy van Singel. *Classic Interviews from Magazine*. New York: Routledge, 2001, 31.

Walton, Jonathan C. *Watch This: The Ethics and Aesthetics of Black Televangelism*. New York: New York University Press, 2009, 34.

# REVERDY CASSIUS RANSOM

*(1861–1959)*

Reverdy C. Ransom was born in Flushing, Ohio, in 1861 to Harriet Johnson. His father's name is not known. His mother eventually married George Warner Ransom, whose last name Reverdy took. From early childhood, Ransom attended schools operated by the African Methodist Episcopal Church. He married Leanna Watkins in 1881. The couple had one son, George.

Ransom attended Wilberforce University. While there he joined the AME Church. He transferred from Wilberforce to Oberlin, where he was expelled for protesting the mistreatment of black women students. He then returned to Wilberforce. He was licensed to preach in 1883, and pastored his first church in 1885. A year later he divorced his wife and in 1887 married Emma S. Conner, with whom he also had a son, Reverdy Ransom Jr.

From 1885 to 1896, Ransom pastored several churches in Pennsylvania and Ohio; he was ordained an elder in the AME Church in 1888. In 1896 he became the pastor of Bethel AME in Chicago. It was from this pastorate that he gained renown as an orator, civil rights leader, social worker, and pastor. He then pastored in Massachusetts and became a founding member of the Niagara Movement, which was started by W.E.B. DuBois and others. At the second annual meeting of the group Ransom delivered a speech titled "The Spirit of John Brown," which forever marked him as a brilliant and fiery orator with a burning concern for the plight of American blacks.

Ransom next pastored in New York, where he gained a national reputation for establishing a mission and working with the poor. During this period he also became the editor of the *AME Review.* While serving in this role Ransom became known as an editor who was an unapologetic and militant activist for the rights of blacks. The *AME Review* took on a tone it had never previously held.

In 1918 he unsuccessfully ran for Congress, and in 1924 was elected as the forty-eighth bishop of the AME Church. His second wife died in 1941, and he married Georgia Myrtle Teal in 1943. Ransom was a member of the board of trustees of Wilberforce and a member of the executive committee of the Federal (now National) Council of Churches. From 1948 to 1956, Ransom served as the historiographer for the AME Church.

In 1950 he published his autobiography, *The Pilgrimage of Harriet Ransom's Son*, and retired as a bishop in 1952.

• • •

*Ransom displayed the militant traditions of his church as well as the extemporaneous power and fluency of nineteenth-century oratory. In the following sermon, delivered on Thanksgiving Day at the Bethel AME Church in New York, Ransom uses the biblical story in Genesis 11 of the Tower of Babel, in which God confused the languages of those arrogantly attempting to erect a tower that would lead to heaven. The text is selected to make the point that the same confusion concerning the lack of mental acumen and moral rectitude of blacks in America has resulted from the arrogance of whites. Ransom asserts that this is an evil that blacks must make clear to the nation.*

## The American Tower of Babel; or, Confusion of Tongues Over the Negro (1909)

> *Therefore is the name of it called Babel; because the Lord did there confound the language of all the Earth.* —Genesis 11:9

The fruits of the field and the vine, the products of forest, quarry, and mine, the rains of heaven, freedom from pestilence and disease, lie in a realm in which the power of man does not enter. They are the gifts of God.

It is a long-established custom in this country, when the harvests have been garnered and all the bounties gathered from the lap of nature have been safely laid by, to call a solemn assembly to return thanks to the Giver of all these benefits.

It is also a time of reunion, when children who have gone forth from the family root tree, some to be wife and mother, others to make their way in the great world, return and, around the family fireside and the well-provided family board, rehearse old memories and revive the affections of the years gone by.

We are assembled here this morning to join with our fellow countrymen in thanks to God Almighty, for these and innumerable blessings that have come to us.

During the year our nation has enjoyed peace and prosperity. Speaking broadly, labor has been generally employed and capital has received its just reward. We have had peace with all the world; no pestilence or great catastrophe of nature of appalling proportions has visited our shores. It is our prayer that this nation may more and more seek to stand so firmly upon the foundations of justice and righteousness that it will merit a continuance of the blessings of God.

Turning from this phase of those considerations which give its chief emphasis to this day, I, in common with the large majority of clergymen in this country, have chosen to take up for discussion a phase or phenomenon of our national life; to discuss a question which is national in its aspects and vital in its relation to peace and the future well-being of this nation.

I have chosen for my theme "The American Tower of Babel; or, Confusion of Tongues over the Negro."

The Negro and the Negro question have passed through many phases, dating back nearly three hundred years ago when he first set foot upon this soil. The Negro question first came up for discussion at the time the foundations of the government were laid. For in the Constitutional Convention there were friends of freedom, some of whom were slaveholders. As a compromise measure over the adoption of that instrument, it was agreed that the slave trade should be prohibited after the year 1808. The question next appears in the discussion over the boundary lines of slavery, that is, as to whether slavery should be confined to the territory south of the Mason and Dixon line and as to whether within such territory, new states might be formed as slaveholding states, and finally as to whether new territory north of the Mason and Dixon line might be admitted into the Union as a slaveholding state.

Along with the discussion of these questions comes the Fugitive Slave Law, involving the right of the master to take his slave even from the boundaries of the free state and carry him into slavery. Another and by all odds the most momentous and burning discussion of this question arose over the subject of emancipation. Over this the tides of battle ebbed and flowed for more than a generation. The best statesmanship of the nation, ministers of religion of the highest standing, reformers, poets, writers, and thinkers of every school brought their contribution to this discussion. It caused great religious bodies to divide asunder; it separated families; it severed the ties of friendship, and finally brought on one of the greatest wars of modern times, until more than a million men stood in the field of battle in the awful carnage of war, until in the red streams of the blood of the slain the question of freedom triumphed. Abraham Lincoln's immortal Proclamation of Emancipation has been signed and sealed by none more enduring and omnipotent than the superscription and seal of Almighty God.

While there was much division, yet speaking in general terms, the nation was of one speech in the adoption of the Thirteenth, Fourteenth, and Fifteenth Amendments to the Constitution. It was felt that these great amendments had fixed forever the place of the Negro in this nation, that the awful cost of treasure and blood was not too great a price to pay for equal freedom and liberty to all men under our flag.

The South, devastated, impoverished, defeated, was for a time helpless yet sullen and in a sense defiant and unrepentant. The North was busy with its work of reconstructing the nation after the awful ravages of four years of bloody war. There was a brief lull after the conflict and then confusion began to arise, first over the question of the Negro's civil rights. Charles Sumner's Civil Rights Bill was an attempt to settle this matter finally, but the enemies of the Negro were again active, and this bulwark for his protection was ruthlessly set aside by the Supreme Court of the United States declaring it unconstitutional. This was the entering wedge, to be followed by all the tides of indecencies, injustices, humiliations, degradations, insults, and outrage that have come in under that form of legislation known as the Jim Crow laws. There are no Jim Crow laws in northern states, yet so powerful does this react that the Negro meets, at almost every place of public entertainment and in all those phases of conduct which in the line of business and duty must bring men together, the spirit of the same proscription which animates the Jim Crow laws of the South.

From this point and around this point the confusion of tongues has been increased and multiplied for the last thirty years; it has concerned itself in the discussion of his place socially. In the South the Negro's place socially is always interpreted to mean social equality. I have never believed that the South was sincere in its pretended fear of social equality, and so far as the Negro is concerned we are quite sure that it is a question which gives him no concern. He only asks to be permitted, like other men, to walk unhindered in the path of men.

The confusion has gathered volume and increasing virulence around the question of the Negro's sphere industrially and as to the kind of education he should receive. Some of his opponents justify their attitude by appealing to Heaven, on the ground that God himself has decreed that the Negro's place is one of inferiority and that only in the capacity of a menial should he be permitted to make his contribution to our industrial life. The trade unions have largely adopted this view by debarring Negro artisans from membership and excluding them from employment wherever possible, so that it has come to be that the millions of Negro toilers in this land have less protection and receive less incentive to produce, up to the limits of their capacity, at just reward, than any class of toilers in this country or enlightened nations of Europe.

The question of Negro education is one which for twenty years has divided even the friends of his advancement. So persistently and so skillfully has the view that a special brand of education should be prescribed for the Negro been propagated that willing ears in the North, as well as in the South, have accepted it as just. This view holds that he is to be trained to constitute a great black peasantry in this land; while there are others who hold to the view that the Negro, being a citizen and a man, should be educated just as the children of the Irish, the German, the Italian, and the Jew are educated, to qualify him to take his place in any phase of the nation's life, side by side with his fellow countrymen, and make the best contribution of which he is capable, according to his capacity and his powers.

While these are the great vital questions around which the voices of men are divided, there is still another and persistent note which seriously vibrates, on the question of deportation or immigration of the Negro to Africa, or to some other country outside the boundaries of the United States. Not having the courage to meet and face this question on the ground of justice and right, white men have adopted this view; not having the courage to stand up and fight, to suffer and endure, Negroes of prominence have acquiesced, but up to now they have received no sign from Heaven that Jehovah is crying aloud to the American people to let the Negro go, as He did in the case of Israel in Egypt in the day of Pharaoh.

The Negro was able to maintain himself for more than two hundred and fifty years in slavery here. For more than forty years of freedom he has increased, multiplied, prospered, in the face of obstacles and opposition discouraging and at times almost insuperable. The agitation of this question has not ceased and may not for a long time, but in the midst of it all, the Negro will continue to root and entrench himself so firmly in the nation that he cannot be uprooted without overturning the nation to its very foundation. He is here to stay.

The confusion of tongues over the Negro question in this country is illustrated by the attitude of the most intelligent and progressive Negroes. We have on the one hand Dr. Booker T. Washington and his adherents; on the other hand Dr. W.E.B. DuBois and his adherents; while outside of these there is a great unclassified host. Now the adherents of Dr. Washington speak one language and the adherents of Dr. DuBois speak another; neither can understand the other. Therefore, like the confused tower builders of the plains of Shinar, they go into different camps and take their separate ways, while the unclassified host to which I have referred stands hesitant and halting between the two conflicting bodies of opinions.

Mr. Washington says, "Eschew politics," and Mr. Du Bois says, "Vote." Mr. Washington places largest emphasis upon vocational training which shall be chiefly industrial, while Mr. DuBois insists upon no special brand but the largest opportunity for that which is highest and most liberal.

The attitude of these two champions may be best illustrated by referring to the National Negro Business League, of which Dr. Washington is president; and to the Niagara Movement, of which Dr. DuBois is president; or by considering the contents of Dr. Washington's chief book, *Up from Slavery,* and of Dr. DuBois's chief book, *The Souls of Black Folk.*

If we turn to the government itself, the Constitution of the United States speaks one tongue and the Unites States Supreme Court another. In each instance, thus far whenever the vital interests of the Negro have come up before this body, it has seemed to be unable to understand or to rightly interpret the express mandates of the Constitution. Or we may turn to former president Roosevelt and the present occupant of the White House, Mr. Taft. President Roosevelt, whatever may be our attitude as to his conduct with reference to the Brownsville affair, stood unequivocally for a square deal, for the open door of opportunity, and for an equal chance for all men, while on the other hand, the present occupant of the White House has gone out of his way to make public proclamation of his intention to appoint no Negroes as federal officers in communications where such appointments were displeasing to the white people of that community. His attitude in the matter of the taking of the census, now about to be underway, would seem to indicate that for the first time since our enfranchisement we are to be practically eliminated from this important service.

If we turn to the domain of science we find the same confusion here. We would expect that here there would be nothing but unbiased search for truth and for pure deductions of logic, the collection of data and the classification of facts without regard to where they lead, but not so. Science on the one hand is lending its high authority to the doctrine of Negro inferiority, by seeking to prove that because of the shape of the skull, the convolutions, weight, and size of the brain, the Negro is naturally inferior and that therefore treating him as an inferior is treating him according to nature and setting him in his proper place. But on the other hand science declares that the shape of the skull, the convolutions and the weight of the brain have nothing to do with intellectual capacity—that the Negro's brain is no smaller than that of the Swiss, Italian, and others, and that his cranial capacity is no less, that there is absolutely no difference between the brain of the Negro and that of any other man.

If we turn to the halls of legislation, the confusion increases. Georgia, Mississippi, and South Carolina advocate one set of laws; New York, Massachusetts, and Ohio another. Senator Tillman speaks one tongue and Senator Foraker quite another.

In literature confusion reigns. In the editorial rooms of the great newspapers and magazines there is no agreement of opinion.

If we turn to the realm of religion the confusion increases. When the pulpit is not hesitant or incoherent, it is absolutely dumb. What has religion to say to lynchers, to the disfranchisers, the despoilers of womanhood when it is black, and to the degradation of manhood by humiliation and ostracisms? There is no speech or language which is common to the different denominations, or even to various pulpits of the same denomination.

At the tower of Babel those who spoke the same language traveled in the same path as they took their way. So today those who hold the same views on the Negro question camp together.

But admittedly, the number of those who differ over the Negro question is growing less and less. There is forming in this country a large body of opinion unfriendly to the Negro; the various groups are more and more coming to a better understanding.

The lynching of Negroes or their burning at the stake no longer fills the country with horror; now great crowds of women participate in this human holocaust. There are no protests in Congress against disenfranchisement. The Supreme Court of the United States, as in the case of Berea College, may declare that the state has a right to prohibit white and colored youth from being educated in the same school, and, as Justice Harlan declares, that according to this opinion, they have the right to prohibit them from going to the public market at the same hour, or from walking upon the same side of the street.

The North, if we are to take the recreant Senator Cullom as authority, is coming over to the view that we are to acquiesce in the complete nullification of the Fifteenth Amendment, in order that the financial interest of the South and the tenure of power to the Republican Party may find a basis of union, and be it remembered that Senator Cullom resembles Abraham Lincoln in features, that he comes from the home of Lincoln, and was the friend of Lincoln.

Nothing could be more disastrous to the Negro at this time than the harmonizing of the divergent and conflicting views in regard to his status, if thereby his manhood is compromised or his citizenship circumscribed.

Amid the Babel of tongues over the Negro question in this country, the latest comes from an article in a recent number of *Leslie's Weekly*, in which the writer claims to quote from a man who was a government official under former president Roosevelt and who claims to have been in Mr. Roosevelt's confidence.

He says that the real object of Mr. Roosevelt's trip to Africa is not to hunt lions or to gather specimens for the Smithsonian Institute, but to find what he believes to be the true and only solution to the Negro problem. He quotes Mr. Roosevelt as saying that he has been convinced ever since he lunched with Dr. Booker Washington at the White House that no amount of education or other qualification could lift the Negro high enough in this country to cause him to be recognized as an equal, and that after thinking long and deeply over this question, the president had gone to Africa in an effort to work out a solution there. He said the president took a large quantity of trinkets with him to be distributed among the native tribes in the heart of Africa, in order to get on friendly terms with them, and that the president hopes to be able to get permission to take over a large section of the northern Sudan, east of the German sphere of influence, as this is one of the largest and most desirable portions of Africa not yet seized upon as a sphere of influence by the nations of Europe. When Mr. Roosevelt bursts from the heart of Africa next April he will declare his solution to the world. His plan will be, as an entering wedge, to persuade this country to repeal the Fifteenth Amendment; then he will propose that the states issue bonds, which are to be guaranteed by the national government, and that these bonds are to be used to pay the Negroes for the property they own in this country and to pay the cost of deportation to Africa, giving them 160 acres of land and all the necessary tools of industry. He claims that with the Fifteenth Amendment repealed, the property of Negroes may be taken, just as the land of the Indians was taken, and as the Indians were pushed back, so the property of the Negroes may be thus taken and the Negroes deported to Africa. The Negro in Africa, with the flag of this country over him, would furnish a check to further aggression of Germany and other European nations and also give the United States greater power as a factor in the partition of Africa, aside from settling for all time our race problem.

The thing which perhaps, more than any other, is undermining the foundations of individual and national character is America's double standard of morals. It has one moral standard for the white people and another moral standard for the colored people. This is aptly illustrated in the case of Senator Stone of Missouri, who not long ago assaulted a colored waiter on a dining car. In court Senator Stone pleaded in justification of his act that "he did not strike a man, he only slapped a nigger."

When a Negro is accused of a crime, the presumption is always in favor of guilt, thus reversing the very fundamental principle of our legal structure, that a man is presumed to be innocent until he is proven guilty. Severe sentences for misdemeanors visited upon Negroes in the South are far more excessive than those which would be imposed upon a white man who had actually been proven guilty of a crime.

Or take the question of the division of the school funds in the southern states, with perhaps two or three exceptions. They will apportion anywhere from 60 percent to 90 percent per capita more for the education of the white children than for the black.

But the application of the double standard of morals for the two races accomplishes its most destructive and degrading work in the relations of white men to colored women and of colored men to white women. If a colored man is accused or even suspected of a crime against a white woman, the vengeance with which he is put to death, without the process of law, reaches the height of madness and ferocity. If a colored man and a white woman are suspected or known to have relations which are entirely mutual, the very best that the Negro may hope is to be permitted to leave the community on pain of death.

In the South, if a colored girl is seduced by a white man, she has no redress at law; even if they were willing, they could not legitimatize their offspring, because it is a penitentiary offense for the two races to marry. She could not sue him for support, because this would be both against the law and public sentiment.

The white people of the South acquiesce in the immoral relations between young white men and colored girls, on the ground that it is a protection of the young white women of the South.

It is in this relation that the whole fabric of southern chivalry falls to the ground, their boasted reverence for womanhood, for virtue; yet they regard with absolute indifference and contempt all womanhood, except in the person of their fair sister, and make it a boast that the virtue of their black sister is their legitimate and proper prey.

Our confusion will grow more confusing until we as a nation comprehend the fact that the ethics of Jesus, as set down in the New Testament, is not an iridescent dream; that foundation stones of this nation have their last resting place upon the ethics of Jesus Christ, that of brotherhood based upon the fatherhood of God. Out of this, through all the struggles of our national life, we have been seeking to realize liberty, fraternity, and equality.

America is based not only upon the ethics of Jesus, but upon democracy, as set forth in the spirit of the Declaration of Independence. This means all men should be permitted here to achieve the highest possibilities of which they are capable.

The American Negro does not ask his white brother to take him on faith but on sight, and to recognize his worth as it is proven—his manhood, his industry, his skill, his patriotism, his ability, as they are demonstrated day by day right before his eyes.

The Negro himself can perhaps do more than any other to silence confusion by proving for himself and for the blacks throughout the world that he is capable of attaining to the very highest and best within this civilization. For the Negro here is the only Negro on the face of the earth in vital daily contact with the white man within the same government on terms of equality. If he fails through ignorance, incapacity, laziness, shiftlessness, courage, in a sense the black race throughout the world has failed.

We are to prove that the difference of color which divides us is only superficial and entirely nonessential. We are here to prove our common humanity and manhood. From the shores of this country the Negro and the white man should go forth, hand in hand, to teach Russia, Japan, England, India, Europe, and Africa how men of different races may live together upon terms of equality, of fraternity, and of peace.

I see, as from the tower of Babel, the scattered groups returning from the confusion that has so long kept them separated and divided. They have learned that despite all differences of speech, they have at all times had one word in common—that word is *man*. Now we learned to articulate in unison another word—that word is *brother*. Now standing face-to-face they say—"*man and brother*." The recognition is instant. Barriers are broken down, the confusion is silenced, and in brotherly cooperation they set themselves the task of building their civilization a tower of strength, because all men who toil and strive, who hope and aspire, are animated by a common purpose that is peace, happiness, and the common good of all.

## *Note*

*Sermon source:* This sermon is located in the Schomburg Center for Research in Black Culture in New York. It is contained in Ransom's *The Spirit of Freedom and Justice: Orations and Speeches*.

## *Bibliographical Sources*

Gomez-Jefferson, Annetta Louise. *The Sage of Tawawa: Reverdy Cassius Ransom, 1861–1959*. Kent, OH: Kent State University Press, 2002.

Morris, Calvin S. *Reverdy Ransom: Black Advocate of the Social Gospel*. Lanham, MD: University Press of America, 1990.

Pinn, Anthony, ed. *Making the Gospel Plain: The Writings of Bishop Reverdy C. Ransom*. Harrisburg, PA: Trinity Press International, 1999.

Ransom, Reverdy. *The Pilgrimage of Harriet Ransom's Son*. Nashville, TN: AME Sunday School Union, 1949.

———. *The Spirit of Freedom and Justice: Oration and Speeches*. Nashville, TN: AME Sunday School Union, 1926.

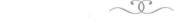

# LIZZIE WOODS ROBINSON

*(1860–1946)*

Lizzie Woods Robinson (also called Roberson) was born a slave on April 5, 1860, in Phillips County, Arkansas, to Mose Smith and Elizabeth Jackson.[1] At the end of the Civil War, Robinson, her mother, and four siblings were left without a husband and father. Although her mother never learned to read, she sent her children to the missionary schools, and by age eight Robinson was reading the Bible to her mother, who died when Robinson was fifteen years old. In 1881, she converted to the Baptist faith.

Eleven years later, she joined a black Baptist church in Pine Bluff, Arkansas. After embracing sanctification, she became the matron of the Baptist Academy in Dermott, Arkansas. Through the powerful preaching of Elder D.W. Welk, Robinson became attracted to the Church of God in Christ (COGIC), and in 1911 while Bishop Mason was running a revival, she received the baptism of the Holy Ghost. She then left the Baptist Academy and, later that same year during the Holy Convocation, Bishop Mason appointed Mother Robinson the first African American woman to serve as supervisor of COGIC's women's work. She has been described as a "pioneering foremother" of the COGIC church.[2]

In 1916, Mother Robinson and her husband, Elder Edward D. Robinson, moved to Omaha, Nebraska, where they and their daughter, Ida, established the first COGIC church there, which was eventually named for them. Robinson Memorial still conducts weekly services, and it has been placed in Nebraska's National Register of Historic Places. In 1946, after helping raise the money to build the historic Mason Temple and to purchase the church's neon-lighted sign, Mother Robinson passed away, ending the tenure of one of the greatest organizers among Christian women.

Women in ministry in the COGIC are not called preachers, nor does the denomination use the title Reverend when referring to these women. Instead, titles such as evangelist, revivalist, Mother, and missionary are used. Whatever title is applied, Lizzie Wood Robinson was indeed a preacher.

• • •

*Although Mother Robinson, with her tough dress code and uncompromising rules governing female behavior, has been described as a strict leader of the early women of COGIC, her ultimate aim was the uplift of the African American community, which included raising money to build churches and other institutions. Her holiness "code of ethics" was used as a social resistance strategy against the racism, sexism, and classism that plagued early twentieth-century America. Many black women who became sanctified Pentecostals during that time espoused a pro-black consciousness, had unflinching self-respect, and saw the high moral standards of sanctification as a means for African American improvement. As sociologist Cheryl T. Gilkes explains: "In order to counter the stereotypes used as rationales for the abuse of black women, Sanctified church women were encouraged to dress as becometh holiness."[3] We present an excerpt and sample of Mother Robinson's "code of ethics."*

## Personal Purity: Advice to Young People and Mothers, Secrets Kept from Children, Facts for Boys and Girls 12 to 20 Years (date unknown)

MOTHER

The mother in her office, holds the key
Of the soul; and she it is who stamps the coin
Of character, and makes the being who would be a savage
But for her gentle cares, a Christian man!
Then crown her queen of the world.

Mother: What other word awakens such tender emotions in our breasts? What other word has such power over the strong and the weak alike? What other word carries with it such a world of memories, ideality, love? Mother, whoever and wherever you are, do you know that you are the strongest, most convincing and most beloved personality in the world? Do you know that in your hands lies the vitality of the race, the strength of the nation, and the success of the commercial and social life of the land? You stand back appalled. You cannot believe it. You had never thought yourself of so much importance. You did not know the world had its eyes on you hopefully and fearfully. You thought the walls of your home shut you in, that it was simple duty to keep the house, rear the children—Stop! That is it—rearing the children, the great and wonderful mission of the noble woman's life. On that depends the welfare of the state. Your sturdy little boy, sitting placidly by your side, may be one of the builders of the nation in twenty years. He will have life's serious responsibilities on his shoulders. How are you going to fit him for that time? Have you ever realized the immense importance of the trust imposed upon you?

## The Most Holy of Vocations

That boy's future is in your hands: His manly vigor depends on the care his little body receives in childhood. Do you know how to take care of your child's health? His strength of character, his ability to stand the knocks of the world, depend on the principles you instill into his little brain. Are you prepared to teach him? Have you been taught how to be a successful Mother? If you have you are very fortunate. We have training schools and colleges filled with expensive apparatus to fit women for the other walks of life. We have schools for teachers, stenographers, dressmakers, milliners, and even doctors and lawyers, but we have no school in which to train women for the most serious, most real, most holy vocation of their lives—*motherhood*.

## Facing the Facts of Life

The sacred institution of marriage is entered into thoughtlessly or frivolously or shyly. A false modesty if not ignorance, on the part of both mother and daughter, prevents the maid from facing the facts of life until they are forced upon her by circumstances, and how, then, is she prepared to meet them? She is not prepared. Instinct enables her to go through her duties with indifferent success. A little forethought, consideration and knowledge would save her much of the mental and physical suffering that she has come to look upon as a part of her estate. The young mother, however, is not "the greatest sufferer from this ignorance of the principles of life." The helpless offspring is the chief claimant for our sympathy and concern. Too frequently, the child is brought into the world, feeble in body, weak in mind, and helpless in spirit. It grows up, alike unable to command its lawful heritage of health, knowledge, and power. How are we to prevent continuance of such conditions? How can you, a Mother, produce vigorous, intelligent, forceful children, and having produced them, bring them up, vigorous, intelligent, forceful, to the period of their manhood and their womanhood? Do you know how to care for your child in sickness and in health, how to develop its mind and body, how to create an environment that will best promote in mental and physical growth?

If not, dear Mother, it is time you bent your energies to the discovery. Study. Find out. It is not too late. The whole field of child-training is full of stumbling blocks, full of problems that must be solved.

Did you ever consider how much more motherhood is than merely the state of being a mother, or that of a Woman who has borne a child? The birds of the forests, the beasts of the field, all the animal world, in fact, perform that function of reproduction and their young are born in accordance with the laws of nature.

## The Instinct of Motherhood

Nature has given mere animals the instinct to protect and feed their young and it is well known that they will fight to the death for their offspring. They will deprive themselves of food that their young may be saved from starvation, and they will suffer exposure of every kind to keep them warm and sheltered. This is mere animal instinct with which the human mother is also provided, but as the Creator has endowed humanity with more exquisite faculties and a spark of divinity, and so has He given us much more responsibility. We are endowed with a mental and spiritual being the ordinary animal does not possess.

The human mother must answer to her Creator and give an accounting of her stewardship. It is not only her duty to know the anatomy of her child and use of every principal physical organ that she may guard its bodily health, but to study its mental make-up and care for its spiritual welfare.

The young bird is hatched and in a few weeks takes wing to care for itself. The young colt or calf can stand on its wobbly legs the first day or two and soon learns to care for itself. Not so with the human child who, intended for a longer life, more mental and spiritual, is naturally of slower development and practically helpless for nearly the first three years of its life.

Do you know how wonderfully God has made your child?

Are you aware of the functions performed by the different organs?

Do you know by what process the food is digested in its little stomach?

Do you know how the blood is pumped through its little heart?

How the air is filtered through the lungs?

Do you understand how poisons are thrown off through the millions of little pores in the skin?

The work of the kidneys?

The action of the liver?

The construction and expansion of its muscles?

What do you know of its nervous system, that can so easily cause the child to cry or laugh or sleep, etc., etc.?

These are only a few simple and quite ordinary questions but there are many more.

If a friend gave you an ordinary present you would examine it carefully to see how it was made and would give it close inspection, would you not?

## A Human Soul

God has given you the greatest gift in the world, a child; He has placed in your keeping not only a human body, but *a human soul*!

It is a sacred trust to be sacredly fulfilled, and the thought of this trust brings comfort to the mother—to be of such value to the world. As a mother, you attain your highest rank—the maker of mankind.

All progress of the human race toward better living; all moral and refining agencies have depended upon the mothers of humanity. She it is, through her suffering, her constant self-denials and her privations, brings into the world the future rulers of coming generations and the mothers of these rulers.

Our noble-hearted president, Abraham Lincoln, owed everything to the teachings of a true Christian mother. Hers was a life of poverty and privation, but through it all she taught her little "Abe" the lessons of truth and honor which have ever endeared him to the hearts of his countrymen.

## A Good Mother

"Show me a good man and I will show you a good mother," rings true in almost every case. It is because the mother, far more than the father, influences the action and conduct of the child, that her good example is of so much greater importance in the home. It is easy to understand why this should be so. The home is the woman's domain—her kingdom, where she exercises entire control. Her power over the little subjects she rules there is, or should be, absolute. The directing influence which every mother exercises over her children throughout life never ceases. When launched into the world, each to take part in its labors, anxieties and trials, they still turn to their mother for consolation, if not for counsel, in their times of trouble and difficulties. The pure and good thoughts she has implanted in their minds when children continue to develop and induce the performance of good acts long after she is dead. When there is nothing but a memory of her left, her children rise up and call her blessed.

Not all the days of the mother will be full of bliss. At times her life will be full of brightness and joyousness. Again, she sinks to the depths of despondency over the consciousness of the task regarding her dear ones. And, to attempt to trace the responsibility through all the life that lies before her is overwhelming if she had not learned to feel that "as her day so shall her strength be."

These words are a most inspiring promise and to most mothers it is fulfilled with constant reassurance. The strength is given her, and the reward with it.

## The Sweetest Sound to Woman

An earnest and devoted mother will always be proud of the babe God sees fit to give her. Be it the first or the tenth, that gurgle which means life is the sweetest sound that ever falls on a woman's ear. It means that she is the possessor of a jewel far more precious than rubies. A story is told of a woman who was the wife of a Roman by the name of Gracchus. One morning an acquaintance dropped in for a formal call. She had many beautiful and valuable jewels on her person, of which she was very proud. After showing them to this good wife, and praising their lustre, the visitor asked if she had not jewels, too? "Yes," said the wife of Gracchus, "I have," and, leaving the room, quickly returned, leading by the hands her little sons. "These," she said, "are my jewels."

## The Richest of Joys

Mother! You may also possess a little jewel, your little one whom you fondly clasp to your breast; who must still cling to you for its very existence. Or perhaps your child has grown into the bright-eyed romping school-boy or school-girl. Perchance your children have left the home where their childhood was spent and are now taking their places in the world with their fellow-beings. Whichever case it may be, *be thankful.*

There is no richer joy than lives in that home of yours. Don't fret if it is not pretentious. Don't grieve if your children do not wear the best grade of clothes. Just be thankful and rejoice that you still have them living; that you can still implant a kiss on their warm lips; that you can still entwine your arms around their necks and that you still can take them by the hand and call them by the fond name of son or daughter.

If a mother would only have this thought when stormy days arrive and say to herself: "These children certainly do weary me at times, but they are still with me; what would life be without them?" Let me say, tender mother, your life would be nothing without them. You would be robbed of your greatness and your blessing. You would put in an existence of a dull and aching void.

Do you happen to know a childless couple? If so, take a peep into their home. The surroundings may be very beautiful and comfortable, but the true comfort, the love of a little child, is sadly wanting there. Can you not recognize the soul's hunger? Can you not scent the heartfelt longings? They are to be pitied: the woman more than the man.

There is no denying the fact that a woman gets her greatest joy in "motherhood." It brings out all the highest emotions latent within her. It elevates and ennobles her and gives to her that supreme content which only those who have been mothers can experience. Nothing can be compared to the love of a child. Never, to a woman, can this thought come too often. Let each day find you thankful that God thought you fit to be the mother of another little life, on whose soul your thoughts and aims will leave their impress. Not one particle of this sweet power should you hold lightly or misuse.

And all the foregoing pages are only messengers of the reverence and esteem in which you *are* held, both by your children and your friends. You may not think it, but you stand next to God himself. God is the creator, you the producer of mankind, and in His supreme judgment He made you a mother—"the holiest thing alive." No human being can approach nearer Divinity than the mother. That is the reason you love your child with such never-dying love which lasts throughout this life and far beyond—into eternity.

## NOTES

*Sermon source:* Mother Lizzie Robinson, *Personal Purity: Advice to Young People and Mothers, Secrets Kept from Children, Facts for Boys and Girls 12 to 20 Years*, compiled by Alberta McKenzie (Birmingham, AL: Forniss Printing Company, n.d.).

1. Glenda Goodson sheds light on Mother Robinson's surname: "In early documents dated in the 1920s Mother Robinson's name is spelled Roberson. In documents dated in the 1940s her name is spelled Robinson. The International Women's Department has determined that the correct spelling is Robinson." (Personal correspondence, February 2005, and biographical information from Glenda W. Goodson on Mother Robinson.) Goodson, *Bishop Charles Harrison Mason and Those Sanctified Women.*
2. Ibid.
3. Gilkes, "Together and in Harness: Women's Traditions in the Sanctified Church."

### *Bibliographical Sources*

Gilkes, Cheryl Townsend. "Together and in Harness: Women's Traditions in the Sanctified Church," in *Signs: Journal of Women in Culture and Society* 10, no. 4 (Summer 1985): 685.

Goodson, Glenda W. *Bishop Charles Harrison Mason and Those Sanctified Women*, 2nd ed. Lancaster, TX: HCM Publishing, 2002.

# CHARLES ALBERT TINDLEY

*(ca. 1851–1933)*

Songwriter, preacher, and composer Charles Albert Tindley was born around 1851 in Berlin, Maryland, the son of a slave, Albert Tindley, and a free woman, Hester Miller Tindley. Although Tindley was freeborn, once he became old enough, he was hired out to work with slaves. He never received formal schooling during his childhood, but taught himself to read and write. He married Daisy Henry around the age of seventeen, then moved to Philadelphia to make a better life for both of them. In Philadelphia, Tindley worked as a janitor in Calvary Methodist Church. He wanted to become a minister but lacked a formal education. He began taking correspondence courses from Boston School of Theology, which enabled him to keep his job, support his family, and follow his dreams. Along with his courses, Tindley studied New Testament Greek and found a Jewish rabbi to tutor him in Hebrew.

After finishing his studies in 1902, Tindley was asked to become the minister of Calvary Methodist Church, the same church he had served as a janitor years earlier. He was minister for more than thirty years. Starting with two hundred members, Tindley used his soaring oratory, intellectual gifts, and talent for song writing to gain a congregation of more than ten thousand. During this time, he helped people who were migrating from the South to the North to get settled in the city, and composed hymns still contained in the songbooks of every Christian denomination. His more than fifty hymns include "I'll Overcome Someday" (which is popularly known as "We Shall Overcome," the anthem of the civil rights movement), "We'll Understand It Better By and By," and "Stand By Me." Tindley's songs and sermons tell of joy, hope, and salvation, but most of all the love of God. Because of Tindley's successful leadership, his Philadelphia church was renamed Tindley Temple Methodist Episcopal Church in 1924. He died in 1933, from gangrene resulting from a foot injury.

• • •

*Though well known for his music, an overflowing crowd of thousands came to hear Tindley preach each Sunday. With a booming voice and a six-foot-five-inch stature, Tindley preached profound messages of God's love and grace. One of Tindley's best-known sermons, "Heaven's Christmas Tree," depicts the fruits of the Holy Spirit as ornaments. Thousands looked forward to this sermon each year.*[1]

## Heaven's Christmas Tree
## (ca. 1913)

*In the midst of the street of it, and on either side of the river was the tree of life.* —Revelation 22:2

Some years ago, when I was serving as pastor in Washington, Delaware, I had an occasion to visit this city on Christmas Day. While passing along a certain street, I saw a large church with front doors open and many people, young and old, moving in and out. Out of curiosity, I crossed over so as to find out what the occasion was. In the lecture room of the church was a large tree, beautifully trimmed and laden with many packages. A young man was standing upon a stepladder and by means of a rod was lifting the packages from the limbs of the tree and calling out the names that were written on them. As he would call a name some hand would go up, indicating the person it belonged to. The happy recipients were passing in groups from the church, smiling and congratulating each other upon the favors received. I stood there until the tree was stripped of packages and all the people, except a very few, had passed out into the street. I noticed a little boy, who sauntered from the building almost, if not the last, with scanty clothing and pinched features. He wore a sickly mechanical smile, as though it was an unavoidable reflection from the numerous faces that surrounded him. His eyes were filled with tears, his lips moved as though his little soul was forcing audible expressions of its sad disappointment. He moved off down the street, kicking the bits of paper here and there as if to satisfy his empty feelings. I followed him until he turned into a little court and stood on the doorstep of one of the little dwellings.

After glancing this way and that for a minute, as though he dreaded to leave the street empty-handed and cheerless, he turned the doorknob and entered what I imagined was a poor, cheerless home. Until then, I was unconscious of a tear that was rolling down my face and dropping on my bosom. With a sigh, I turned away with the question: Will there ever be a time when the spirit of Christ shall so fill and control the lives of people that everybody, young and old, rich and poor, will receive some token of love on Christmas Day?

My query was directed more heavenward than earthward. I seemed to be asking the Christ of Christmas rather than anyone else. The answer must have come directly from him, for it was in the very language of my text. It was a happy thought, and I felt like saying thank God right out loud. Then my mind began to reflect and search for some good reasons for this happy thought, "Is Christ a tree? Is he a Christmas tree?" And, if so, are there any packages on this tree? And for whom? Yes! He is the Tree of Life. He was brought to this world and set up in Bethlehem Judea's manger more than nineteen hundred years ago. He bears a package of rare blessings for every human being in all this world. That Christ is called a tree in the Bible is proven by such sayings as: "If they do these things in the green tree, what shall be done in the dry?"[2] "I will give to eat of the tree of life."[3] "The leaves of the tree were for the healing of the nation."[4]

These passages of Scripture furnish good reasons for calling Christ a tree. When I read that this Tree of Life yields its fruit every month and that its leaves were good for the healing of nations, I have a right to think that there are packages on it for human beings. I call it a Christmas tree because it came to earth on Christmas Eve night. You are to imagine now that I am speaking of Christ Jesus in the light of a great Christmas tree set up in this world, bearing a package for every single creature that he has made. Yes, a package with your name on it is hanging on the limb of heaven's great Christmas tree.

I am going to have you see by faith heaven's Christmas tree, whose top reaches the ceiling and whose limbs touch all the walls of this building. It is sagging with packages fixed by fingers of love. On one of them is your name. I am going to call them off, and the Holy Spirit is going to take them to everyone that is in this building, for there is one for each of you. Here is Hope for the Hopeless. This package hangs on a limb that almost touches the ground. It is the lowest limb on the tree, and is the easiest package to reach. It shines with light and glitter of all the promises of God to sinners and to those who are discouraged and hopeless amid life's conflicts. It is for the struggling youth who is striving for an education with little or no help, who has had to leave school because of the want of funds to pay the bills. It is for aged parents, young brothers or sisters, or relatives. It is for that I am speaking to someone tonight who is at the point of despair concerning the accomplishment of his or her aim in life. You have experienced the loss of courage and ambition to further try to become anything like you hoped to be. I say to you tonight that there is a package on heaven's Christmas tree that holds a fit remedy for your case. It is set to the music of a beautiful song, a verse of that reads:

*Courage, brother, do not stumble,*
*Tho' your path be dark as night,*
*There's a star that guides the humble;*
*Trust in God, and do the right.*

I may be speaking to some parents who have come here hopeless of ever making anything worthwhile out of their son or daughter, or ever having their children become what they had hoped and prayed that they might be. I have a song for you too:

*Tho' the cloud may hide your sun,*
*Ere your battle has been won,*
*If you still will watch and pray,*
*Soon will come a brighter day.*

I may be speaking to someone who has tried to live a good life but has failed. The devil has told you that you are one of those who are doomed by your Creator to misery here and hell hereafter. You may have almost decided to quit and give up trying. I am going to beg of you a favor tonight, and that is reach up with all the strength you have left and take from heaven's Christmas tree this low-limbed package, hope. It is so low that you can reach it from the gutter, from the gambling den, from the barroom, and from the lowest places on earth. I beseech you, in God's name, take this package, Hope and try again.

I point to another package on another limb higher up. It is marked Forgiveness for the Guilty. It shines with the brightness of the Redeemer's face and is stained with the blood of Calvary. It is set in a frame carved out of the love of God and is dazzling with a chandelier of a thousand promises, whose jets flow with the breath of the Man of Sorrow and of many stripes. It is the most costly package on this tree. Those fingerprints you see on it were left there by the nail-pierced hand of the Man of Galilee. He tied it there in the darkness and earthquakes of that Friday afternoon when the dead woke up before the morning of the resurrection and the rocks broke their silence.

There are many of you in this building tonight, who as I do, need this package. Nobody can say that they have never sinned against God; nobody has had their sins canceled by their own deeds or deserving. Everybody, therefore, who is not now guilty of sin has been forgiven through the merits of Jesus Christ. It was the gift of God, for the sake of Jesus. Just as others have been forgiven, so everyone present and everybody in this whole world can, and may be, forgiven of all their sins. You know when God forgives you he remembers your sins against you no more forever. I like that word forever when it is on the side of heaven and happiness; I am afraid of it when on the side of misery and hell. But, I want you to know that "forever" means just as long a time in hell as it does in heaven and just as long a time in heaven as it does in hell. How many of you who are guilty of sin will take this package tonight?

I see another package on another limb higher up still; on it is written the words Help for the Weak. I have always thanked God for the numerous promises of help in the Bible. I don't know what Adam's strength was before the fall, but I do know that since that time human nature has not been equal in strength to the force of this world. The lust of the flesh, the lust of the eye, and the pride of life are mighty armies under the management of the devil for the downfall of everything that is good in the human being. I have never known but one man on this whole earth who, from his birth to his death, could stand against the forces of this world. I need not tell you that man is Jesus Christ. He not only conquered the world, the flesh, and the devil for himself, but also for every believer throughout all time.

It is this man, Christ Jesus, who promises help to everyone who wants to live for God. My belief is that there are hundreds who are in sin and on the way to hell who don't want to be there. They wish that in some way they could change their lives but are too weak to do so. I want you to see the mighty arm that reaches down over this package of which I am speaking, out to every helpless soul who wants to leave the devil. It is that mighty strong arm that upholds the world, weights the hills, and measures the waters. It is that great arm that destroyed Egypt, leveled the walls of Jericho, flung Babylon's glory in the dust, and plucked the Caesars from their thrones. He says, as he looks over the sea of faces tonight, I will help thee.

I see another package on a limb higher. It is marked Friendship for the Friendless. Do you know the value of friendship? If not, it is because you have never been friendless in this world. No matter how strong you are physically, mentally, or financially, you need a friend. Perhaps the most unhappy people in this building are not those who are poor in the things of this world but who are friendless. Nothing can get on very well alone. The slender pedestals on which earth's friendship sits are so easily knocked over that one is afraid to move. If you have money, fine clothes, a beautiful home, popular relations, or great ability, you may have friends and admirers; but when these are gone your brightest day may fade into a dark and dismal night.

I am reminded of an old gentleman who owned a little farm, in Maryland. His two boys were sent away to school, one to study medicine and the other agriculture and business. About the time they graduated, their mother died, which left their father a widower. He proposed to the farmer son that he should take the farm, and all he asked of him was that he be cared for in his own home until he died. When his will was made and the property all turned over to the two boys, the wife of the son who had charge of the farm began to complain of the old gentleman. She complained of his style of dress and of his habits of life in general; his hands were palsied and he would shake the coffee cup on the clean tablecloth; his teeth were gone and he couldn't eat the hard bread which she gave him. She wanted him to sleep in the attic, and he couldn't climb the stairs well because of rheumatism. Oh, many things she complained of, until the son suggested that the old man be taken to the poorhouse. The old saint agreed to go rather than remain in the way and to the discomfort of his son and daughter-in-law. He begged for the family Bible, which was covered with a piece of his own mother's dress sewn by the hand of his departed wife. This and other cherished momentos were all placed in an ox cart with him. When the cart had passed through the road gate and turned in the direction of the poorhouse, the old man, after swallowing lumps that came up in his throat and wiping with his old red handkerchief the tears that were falling on his gray beard, he said to his son: "I go as a load of dirt to the poorhouse, and were it not for one friend whom I came to know when I was eleven years old, I would be most miserable today. That friend is the Lord Jesus Christ, who is as tenderly near me today as when I first found him. He is going to the poorhouse with me and will remain with me until it pleases him to take my spirit to his beautiful home on high. I fear, son," said he, "that you and your wife will occupy a house more fit to be called a poorhouse than the one you are taking me to, for where parents are not honored there is poverty indeed." The young man stopped his oxen and with face covered with his hand for a moment said, "Father, I am going to take you back home to stay there until you die, or I will stay in the poorhouse with you."

I see another package higher still; it is marked Peace for the Troubled Soul. When I mention this, I know I start the spring of joy and the earnest longings from a thousand souls within this building. Only God knows the number of troubled and unhappy souls in this world. Some will tell you that the grace of God in your soul will do away with all trouble and anxiety concerning things on this earth; I don't believe it, neither do you. I have only to quote the words of Jesus Christ to prove that Christianity was never intended to take all the briars out of the field and the thorns from the thorn hedges of the world. Jesus said: "In this world ye shall have tribulations."[5] There are many kindred terms, but this one word tribulation is a pouch big enough to hold all the kinds of troubles and trials that one can ever have in this world. It is foolish as well as precarious to plan to go through this world without trouble.

The apostles all suffered great afflictions and most of them martyrdom. Oh, no, my friends, just because you have religion does not mean that you are going to heaven on flowery beds of ease, but I am happy to tell you that there is promise of sweet peace to all the children of God. What peace we have in this world is not instead of things, but in spite of things. I say to all of you who are troubled, there is coming a day of absolute and glorious peace, a peace that will take away all the gray hairs from your head, all the wrinkles from your face, all the tears from your eyes, and all the pangs of sorrow from your heart. When these heavy burdens and tight straps shall have been taken off your heart and from your soul, you will shout in the vigor of the new morning and with life and joy of happy childhood in the land that knows no sorrow.

There is just one more package that I wish to mention tonight. It hangs on the top limb of heaven's Christmas tree. It is too far away from this world and is lighted by a sunlight too bright for the endurance of that natural sight. You will have to see it with the eyes of faith, for it is spiritually discerned. I am going to get the Holy Spirit to read the name, for every time I look that way I hear someone saying, "Eyes have not seen, ears have not heard, neither has it entered into the heart the things that

God has for them that love him."[6] But, thank God, the Spirit has revealed them. On this top-limbed package are the words Home for the Homeless. I know you orphaned children, you widowed women, and you widower fathers are scarcely able to remain quiet under the sound of such happy news as this. As I speak to you, you are thinking of your own sweet homes of just a little while ago; sweet music and patter of happy children come to you tonight like an echo. The joy of those days seems like a dream whose glories fade with the waking and die at the opening of day. That dreaded monster death has carried your loved ones to the grave; your homes are broken up and you are homeless wanderers. Some of you mothers are with your children. This is a sweet and gracious providence if these children are good to you; it is an earthly torment if they are not. Some of you are living with strangers whose treatment of you is according to the money you pay. Some of you have scarcely a home in this world. I want you to fix your eyes toward the top limb of the package which is near enough to the homeland of the soul to catch the light of that eternal sun, oh sing with me

*My heavenly home is bright and fair;*
*Nor pain nor death shall enter there;*
*Its glittering towers the sun outshine,*
*that heavenly mansion shall be mine.*

I rejoice with you in the prospect of that great homecoming in the sweet by and by, where no children will mourn the loss of mothers, no funeral dirges are sung, no farewell tears are shed, and nobody will ever say good-bye.

I bid you in God's name and in the light of yon heavenly dome and within hearing distance of the songs of the redeemed and the hallelujahs of the ransomed, bear your crosses and endure your pains a little longer, for

*Beyond the smiling and weeping*
*we shall be soon;*
*Beyond the walking and the sleeping*
*we shall be soon . . .*

## NOTES

*Sermon source: The African American Pulpit* 5, no. 1 (Great Revivalists I; Winter 2001–2002), 50–55.

1. Special thanks to Geraldine D. Moser, church historian, Tindley Temple of Philadelphia, for her assistance in obtaining this material.
2. Luke 23:31 (King James Version).
3. Revelation 2:7 (KJV).
4. Revelation 22:2 (KJV).
5. John 16:33 (KJV).
6. 1 Corinthians 2:9 (KJV).

### *Bibliographical Sources*

"Charles Tindley's Faith Set Him Singing," in *Christian History Institute* (July 7, 1951).

Henson, Joyce. "Charles Albert Tindley, African American Hymn Writer." http://templeumc.org/archives/Charles_Tindley.html (accessed April 12, 2007).

Salzman, Jack, David Smith, and Cornel Smith, eds. *Encyclopedia of African-American Culture*. New York: Macmillan, 1996.

Spencer, Michael Jon. *Black Hymnody: A Hymnological History of the African-American Church*. Knoxville: University of Tennessee Press, 1992.

Williams, Michael, ed. *African American Encyclopedia*. New York: Marshall Cavendish, 1993.

## LACEY KIRK WILLIAMS

*(1871–1940)*

Lacey Kirk Williams was born in Barbour County, Alabama, on July 11, 1871. Convinced that there was greater opportunity for advancement in the West, his father, Levi, and mother, Elizabeth, moved the family to Burleson County, Texas. Lacey Kirk attended the River Lane public school in Pitt Bridge, Texas, and at sixteen he left home to work in Belton and in Waco, Texas.

After receiving a teaching certificate, Lacey Kirk taught in rural schools and served as the principal of River Lane School during the 1890s. Williams was ordained a Baptist minister in 1894 and assumed his first pastorate in a local church near Bryan, Texas. That year he also married Georgia Lewis, with whom he would have two sons. He was soon appointed pastor of the Thankful Baptist Church, which his parents founded in Brazos Bottom, Texas, and where he had been baptized ten years earlier. Williams moved on quickly to pastor four churches. In 1902 he enrolled in Bishop College in Marshall, Texas, and graduated many years later while pastoring full time.

From the start of his remarkable career as a Baptist preacher Williams was involved in the governance of the convention. Affiliated with the Baptist Missionary and Educational Convention, Williams served as the convention's president until he left Texas in 1916, when he was named pastor of Chicago's four-thousand-member Olivet Baptist Church, succeeding Elijah John Fisher. During his leadership, the church's membership not only grew to more than ten thousand but Olivet became a positive force in the life of Chicago's African American community. During the Great Migration, Williams sent members of the church to greet the flood of poor migrants from the South and direct them to the many educational, recreational, and social services Olivet provided. Olivet soon gained a reputation as a church that would offer assistance to those migrating from the South to the North and the numbers were legion.

Throughout the 1920s Williams lectured at the divinity schools of the University of Chicago, Northwestern University, and the Northern Baptist Theological Seminary. He achieved prominence when he became president of the National Baptist Convention in 1922 and as vice president of the Baptist World Alliance. In 1928, he received a national award—the Harmon Foundation prize for distinguished religious service. Lacey Kirk Williams was killed in a plane crash in 1940.

• • •

*L.K. Williams is one of the great masters of preaching. This sermon is indicative of his ability to appeal to the educated and folk classes, what Cayton and Drake called "mixed-type" preaching. Williams mixed quoting the Old Testament, classical literature, and the like with imagery that increasing numbers of migrants from the South could identify with, such as the text for the sermon "The Lord that Doth Go before Thee." The text and sermon have strong migrant themes of God's comfort in the midst of travel, transition, and change.*[1]

## God Ahead for 1926 (January 1926)

*And the Lord, He it is that doth go before thee.*

—Deuteronomy 31:8

*A Happy Prosperous New Year* is first my wish for and salutation to you this morning. I am unable to give you this, but I can offer some suggestions as to how it can be obtained. There is an inspiration in and a strange fascination about a New Year. You have come up from the Old Year tired, wearied; and you are glad, I know, to get rid of its monotony, uncertainties, foes and galling tasks. As we approach the close of the Old Year, we were inclined to be retrospective and to discover our gains, losses and failures. We have now a fresh sense of them. We find that many old acquaintances are gone; many old intimacies are dissolved; and many old chords of love are broken and will not vibrate. We find the vacant chairs and fail to hear the voices that are hushed forever, and we feel like tuning in with Tennyson when he said:

*But oh, for the touch of a vanished hand,*
*and the sound of a voice that is still.*

You are thinking, with the coming of the New Year, of the death of the past and the coming of something new in the future. Now, the disappointments and failures of last year are momentarily swept into oblivion by the thrill and promises of the New Year. No one can escape the shooting contagion of the maiden days of the New Year. It promises much. It paints the coming horizon with alluring colors of success and victory. It persuades you to believe that within its grasp are brighter days, the rifted clouds, and that during its span you will realize your hope. The promises of the New Year, if not a deception, are certainly an illusion. We do not have to go far before we find it is, in what it gives, as compared with what it offers, a bitter satire and touching ridicule. In Hebrews 11:8–10, Abraham expected much. "By faith Abraham, when he was called to go out into a place which he should after receive for an inheritance, obeyed; and he went out, not knowing whither he went. By faith he sojourned in the land of promise as in a strange country, dwelling in tabernacles with Isaac and Jacob, the heirs with him of the same promise. For he looked for a city which hath foundations, whose builder and maker is God." But Acts 7:5 shows what he got:

"And he gave him none inheritance in it, not so much as to set his foot on: yet he promised that he would give it to him for a possession, and to his seed after him, when as yet he had no child." This appears to be a pinching parody. God's promises are fulfilled in His own way. But what Abraham expected his heirs got. Of the patriarchs it is said:

"They all died without having received the promise." Canaan, with all that Israel needed, was promised, but forty years afterward they had only the wilderness with its horrors and perils. Korah, Dathan, Abiram and thousands were gone. The Ninetieth Psalm registers the sad musings and the vicissitudes of the pilgrimages of Israel. Hear them crying—No home, no Palestine—and then they cried: "We are consumed," all lost, nothing gained.

The New Year has a new number, but it shall be very much like the old. The same old sunshine shall characterize it. The same old winds shall fret, calm and frequent it; and in it the same dews shall distill; and upon it shall descend the same old rains. It shall have the same seasons: spring, unbosoming itself to man and God, while all nature will chant songs of gratitude to the Creator. We shall have the same summer, with dust, heat and toil. The autumn, with mournful colors; and, finally, winter with heavy mists, shorter days, dimmer suns, longer nights, repose, and times of serious reflection. It shall have the same number of days and months found in former years. You will have new almanacs, new calendars, but it is the old with a new name, an astounding equivocation. Since we shall have the same order and sequences in the physical world, we should not expect an entirely new order in the religious world, simply because we are receiving and hanging up new calendars. The old year is dead, but an invisible hand has transferred to the new the tasks, obligations, opportunities, problems, perils and foes of the old. In it we shall find our old temptations, desires, ambitions, hopes and longings. We shall find ourselves motivated by the same old prejudices, passions and affections. This being true, the New Year is wrongly labeled, and we are deceived and disappointed. Besides this, it is a voyage and a period of uncertainties as was last year. We realize it will try our faith, tax our energy, and we hesitate to start and wonder if we shall have the Happy New Year with which we are greeted and which we very much desire.

First, we need to know what constitutes happiness and prosperity. So much depends upon ourselves—our faith in God—and our determination, and not alone upon tangible things. For this period of halting perplexities, the death of the Old and the birth of the New Year, our text offers a way, consolation and inspiration. "The Lord, He it is that goeth before thee."[2] This is a sure and settled thing, an unknown way, but a known guide and God. Nothing is in it between us and the future that the Lord of Love and power has not anticipated. Social service workers talk much about the power and influence of environments, but the Bible stresses God as the most formidable environment. It deals with our past, a treacherous, tormenting environment, and announces the comforting truth: "God is your reward," gathering up the fragments, and that He has beset you from the rear. God is our environment. There was much in the past year and in our lives that will haunt us with a tormenting dread. But God has beset us from behind. The hostilities cannot subdue us by tormenting fears, for between us and all enemies in the past is God.

How we have grieved somebody, even God's spirit and God. Spurgeon, one of the greatest preachers, it is said, thought he would feel guilty and even ashamed in Heaven, if it were possible, because he had once sinned against and rejected Jesus. But all is well. You talk about family backgrounds, but God is the best one. He has beset us from the rear, and for the present He says: "My presence will go with thee." "I will take you over." Behind us and with us is the unseen, loving, powerful God.

There are foes of today for each of you, but you are not required to meet them alone, single-handed and unaided. The Spirit's presence aided David and Samson in the hour of their deepest need. During the New Year foes will come up from beneath you, but go forward with the assurance that "underneath are the everlasting arms." And maybe there will be powers of the air assaulting you from above, but be assured that the Everlasting God has encompassed you, and under the shadow of the Almighty you can hide and be protected. But my text speaks especially of God going before you—the God of the future, as he is of the past and present. Nineteen hundred and twenty-six and the future are unknown factors, and these always disturb and disquiet most. Upon the student, physician, experimentalist and theologian, they have the same effect. All now know what 1925 brought, for to some it was a bundle of surprises, new ventures, temptations, crushing sorrows, pinching griefs and new and unusual disappointments. Now we are wondering what will 1926 be to us and what will it bring. For the bewilderment of this moment, our text offers a balm and a solution: "The Lord, He it is that goeth before thee."[3] The meaning here is that we have an unknown way and future, but we have a constant God going on ahead of us. It means that your paths for 1926, by Divine hands, are already prepared. Why shouldn't we believe this? Adam and the human race found a prepared world. In a special sense, for your childhood, youth, manhood, all the needed preparations were already made. The child craves food; it was prepared for it. The fields, rains, sunshine, heat and dew labored together to furnish it. The eye is made for beauty, and beauty is here in lakes, clouds, skies, landscapes and in the flower in "crannied walls." The heart longs for love, and it can find it in homes and society. The home is more than a house and an enclosure; it is the fold, the harbor, the fortress, the sanctuary and the hall of Heaven. In it we learn the value of love and being loved. It is the reflection of Heaven on earth. In religion He has gone on ahead of us, planned, finished and now executes and offers a salvation that will save to the uttermost. I hear Him now pleading: "Come, for all things are ready." You found a prepared Book—the Bible. This morning I read of twenty-five of the best books published in 1925. In twenty-five years I think that most of them will be forgotten, but even then, and on forever, the Bible will stand. It is old, but modern. It yet meets man's needs. As a guide, no book is its equal. Because this is true, and because He has gone before in the past, and because He now pledges His continued aid and presence, I am constrained to preach as I am now doing today. You are not orphans, you are not left alone, you will not have to go through 1926 unaided, for the Eternal One will go before you. The ancients delighted to exclaim: "The Lord shall keep thy going out and thy coming in."[4] It is a fine and consoling thing to start the New Year with that motto, to start it announcing: "God is ahead of me for 1926." And every day shout to the world: "God is ahead of me today." Foes that chased and haunted you in 1925, you hear now; there will be death and decay, but God is ahead, anticipating and forstalling them. It is said that the presence of the Duke of Wellington was more helpful and inspiring to his army than a whole brigade. God, going before, is worth all to you, for He conquers and defeats your every enemy. The psalmist said: "He has beset me before."[5] It means God is between you and all future dangers, and there are many old and new ones ambushed in the unfolding cycles of 1926 and the future. I call attention to what it means to be thus assured. It should banish all your fears and discomforting feelings; for you are safe. Nineteen hundred and twenty-six may be your hardest year, but for you it is a prepared season and stretch of time. In it you will have pressing duties and burdens, but likewise a sustaining grace. This should lead you to be courageous and faithful; for the outcome is assured. The way of 1926 is a tried and tested way. Napoleon had once a war armament made, but before accepting or using it, he insisted that its maker should be willing to have it tested under shot and shell upon himself. God goes before testing and planning the way of His saints and nothing uncertain or unknown to Him can enter that way, and all that enter are His subjects and agencies.

Christ prayed for your safety. This should invite and deepen your faith and dependence upon God. It should check your haste, confusion and restlessness and make you satisfied with His daily provisions and providences. This should lead you to know that you are not a creature of chance or fate but the child of God and the heir of a pleasing heritage. If He permits or sends hardships, He will give upholding, enduring grace. Paul loathed his handicaps and prayed for their removal, but God's answer was, "My grace is sufficient for thee."[6] This is the thing that kindles and maintains hope and leads to victory. Surely we have here no uncertain way or doubtful results. For through Him we are conquerors, yea, more than conquerors.[7]

*Love celestial, whose prevenient aid abide*
*approaching ills.*[8]

Thank God! as He prepares the way, He prepares you for it. Paul was moved by this fact and resolved that nothing could separate him from the love of God. That in all things he was established. He was sometimes troubled but never fearful or cast down. God is concerned about us, knows our way and is actively interested in us.

A marvelous story is told of Napoleon. It is said, that when he was climbing the Alps, an avalanche carried before it a drummer boy to a lower level. He held on to his drum and began to beat a distress signal, but Napoleon commanded his soldiers to march on, for he was not touched by the distress of this boy. Then the drummer boy began to beat a death signal. Strong-hearted soldiers who remembered their own children at home wept over this lad as they were being rushed by this cold-hearted general to perish in the snows of Russia. Not so with our General and our God. He knows and is interested in us. He goes ahead in tender sympathy, direction and protection, and He will stop all to hear and aid His own.

Happiness and prosperity for 1926 are offered you. The recipe is plain and free, but for good effects, you must use it. There is no happiness for you this year, and never, unless you believe in, trust and submit yourselves to God; unless you see the resources which He offers. "The prevenient God" and this heritage of "prevenient grace" can be appropriated only by the New Man in the New Year; by the new creation; for him it is prepared.

The text is a portion of Moses' valedictory address to his people. He would be soon gathered to his fathers, and he wanted them to know one is removed, but God is not. He could not, but they must make it to Palestine. He had been for years lured by the charms of Palestine. He had followed the pathway of a leading, anticipating God. But now it appears that he will only see and not realize his hopes. He had toiled in faith, but now he must die without having obtained the promise. Can you say that his hopes were a mockery and his quest a tantalizing mirage? I think not, yea, I know not. Right dreams come true, but in God's way and time. If all were given in your own way, you would grow inactive and too complacent. So there is here discipline and training. Many of you have for years been in quest of the intangible and the unforeseen, but you have not realized your hopes; you did not last year. At first you will hesitate to start again where you have very often failed, but then the Spirit whispers, "The Master is come, and calleth for thee." And at once you find yourself on the way following Him who goes before you.

Rapidly, you are coming to the close of all your years. I have had telegrams this week announcing the home-going of three of our most useful ministers. Just now a moment's glance revealed to me the eternal absence from here of some good and faithful members who were here one year ago. Soon the Old Year of Time will pass into the numberless years of Eternity. Soon your pilgrimage between two eternities will be ended. The transition for every one of us will be a trying experience. But your existence and truer life will not end. The cravings of your heart say so.

*It must be so—Pilate thou reasonest well!—*
*Else whence this pleasing hope, this fond desire,*
*This longing after immortality?*
*Or whence this secret dread, and inward horror,*
*Of falling into naught? Why shrinks the soul*
*Back on herself, and startles at destruction?*
*Tis the divinity that stirs within us;*
*Tis heaven itself, that points out an hereafter,*
*And intimates eternity to man.*
*The stars shall fade away, the sun himself*
*Grow dim with age, and nature sink in years,*
*But thou shalt flourish in immortal youth,*
*Unhurt amidst the war of elements,*
*The wreck of matter, and the crash of worlds.*

—Addison[9]

This thing worried the ancients, and Job voiced their musings when he said (Job 19:25–27):

*But as for me I know that my Redeemer liveth*
*And at last he will stand upon the earth:*
*And after my skin, even this body, is destroyed,*
*Then without my flesh shall I see God;*
*Whom I, even I, shall see, on my side;*
*And mine eyes shall behold, and not as a stranger.*

It is a reality and a kind, wise, mysterious providence who has partly veiled and partly revealed it, giving such a sweet foretaste thereof that life's illusions and contradictions have ever fed your undying hope of a better day and a more satisfying order of things. They have been unto you a faithful schoolmaster. The failure of the years to grant the deeper quests of your soul has not extinguished that hope but added fuel thereto. Jacob wrestled to know the Unseen. Oh, the lure of God ahead! Mary wanted to touch her risen Lord, but He forbade her. It is so here. Changing Time for Eternity is a crucial hour, but if we have been faithful in life to a constant God, we shall have learned our first lessons in how to "meet our Pilot" and how to cross the bar. We shall find that His leadings were a training process—an education.

In the Twenty-third Psalm the psalmist said, when contemplating the passing, "Thou art with me." Up to that time he had been talking about his Shepherd, but in this difficult hour he talks to Him. The Shepherd has been going on ahead, but now it seems that He drops back and is in beautiful companionship with the believer. He shall guide you through the valley of the shadow of death and go before you to Heaven and Eternity. Bunyan's great heart knew all the way. Christ knew life. He knows Eternity and all of its immensities. Bless God, He knows you if you are His. He will own before God your worthless names. He said on leaving: ". . . I go to prepare a place for you."[10] For you who are tired, footsore and depressed; for you lonely ones not remembered with a gift by anyone at Christmas; for you who are homeless; for you who have been looking upward the past years through blinding tears; for you who have the bitter memory of sweet homes dissolved by the cruel blows of death; for you who trust Him, He is fitting up your mansions. And you shall get them, you shall win, shall conquer, for "The Lord, He it is that goeth before thee."[11]

## *Notes*

*Sermon source:* L.K. Williams, *Lord! Lord! Special Sermons and Addresses of Dr. L.K. Williams* (Detroit: Harlo Press, 1965), 44–53.

1. Horace R. Cayton, St. Clair Drake, and William Julius Wilson, *Black Metropolis: A Study of Negro Life in a Northern City* (Chicago: University of Chicago Press, 1993).
2. See Deuteronomy 31:8.
3. Ibid.
4. See Acts 9:28.
5. See Psalms 139:5.
6. 2 Corinthians 12:9 (King James Version).
7. See Romans 8:37.
8. This line is paraphrased from the poem "Amintor and Theodora" by David Mallett.

9. Joseph Addison, *Cato: A Tragedy* (Whitefish, MT: Kessinger Publishing, 1964).
10. John 14:2 (KJV).
11. See Deuteronomy 31:8.

### *Bibliographical Sources*

Appiah, Kwame Anthony, and Henry Louis Gates Jr., eds. *Africana: The Encyclopedia of the African and African American Experience*, 5 vols. New York: Oxford University Press, 2005.

Booth, H. Venchael, and Lillian B. Horace. *Crowned with Glory and Honor: The Life of Reverend Lacey Kirk Williams*. New York: Exposition Press, 1978.

Sernett, Milton. *Bound for the Promised Land: African American Religion and the Great Migration*. Durham, NC: Duke University Press, 1997.

Montgomery, William E. "Lacey Kirk Williams," in *The Handbook of Texas Online*. Texas State Historical Association. http://www.tsha.utexas.edu/handbook/online/articles/WW/fwiag.html (accessed June 19, 2005).

# 5

# CIVIL RIGHTS AND DIRECT ACTION: *1951–1968*

# INTRODUCTION

African American soldiers who had fought to liberate Europe from Fascism returned to an America besieged by white racism. In the early 1950s, the social segregation of the races codified in Jim Crow laws had also become the cultural code throughout the southern portion of the United States. Some whites enforced this code with ruthless intimidation and brutal violence, and even in the North, African Americans were subject to overt discrimination and racist practices. It was in this period, from 1951–68, that opposition to Jim Crow crystallized, and broad and sweeping social change was forced upon America in the North and South.

The struggle for African American civil rights existed from the inception of slavery. Over the centuries, countless freedom fighters, abolitionists, ministers, church leaders, politicians, artists, and educators had protested the injustices suffered by African Americans. In the 1950s, civil rights proponents combined a barrage of tactics, including legal action, economic boycotts, non-violent demonstrations, and student protests to combat racism. Of course, direct mass action to remedy social ills was not new; in the early 1940s, A. Phillip Randolph had threatened to organize a massive march on Washington until President Roosevelt issued an executive order assuring blacks jobs in war industries. Nonviolence also was not new; in the 1940s and early 1950s the Congress of Racial Equality (CORE) adopted a limited strategy of nonviolent protest. But during this period the sustained efforts of nonviolent direct action propelled the civil rights movement to new levels of influence and effectiveness.

In the landmark 1954 Supreme Court case *Brown v. Board of Education of Topeka,* a legal team led by Thurgood Marshall, chief attorney for the NAACP, persuaded the Supreme Court of the unconstitutionality of government-sponsored segregation in education. While historians rightly celebrate Thurgood Marshall's role in this legal victory, Marshall credited the victory to his judicial mentor, Charles H. Houston, the famed civil rights attorney.[1] Unfortunately, Houston died four years earlier, but his pioneering legal work had provided much of the expertise and momentum for the *Brown* decision.

In 1955, protesters in Montgomery, Alabama, took another stride toward freedom and the dismantling of legalized segregation. Civil rights activists in Montgomery had been waiting for the opportune moment to challenge segregation on the city's buses. On December 1, 1955, the moment arrived. Rosa Parks, a seamstress and civil rights activist, boarded a bus and refused to relinquish her seat at the demand of a white passenger. Her refusal, which was an unthinkable breach of the Jim Crow code, led to her arrest, which galvanized Montgomery's civil rights activists to boycott the city's buses.

The Montgomery Improvement Association, a newly formed civil rights organization, supervised the boycott. The group elected the Reverend Martin Luther King Jr., the new pastor of Montgomery's Dexter Avenue Baptist Church, as its president. The boycott endured for 381 days. The moral tenacity of the protesters, coupled with King's charismatic leadership and oratory, prompted the Alabama Supreme Court to integrate buses.

This legal and moral victory catapulted King onto a national stage. From that stage he, along with other civil rights activists, including A. Phillip Randolph, Roy Wilkins, Fannie Lou Hamer, Dorothy Cotton, Andrew Young, and Dorothy Height, would valiantly mount a nonviolent offensive against the unjust laws and discriminatory practices throughout the country. King articulated his "dream" for the nation during the 1963 march on Washington, won international acclaim as a recipient of the 1964 Nobel Peace Prize, and spoke passionately against the United States' escalating involvement in the Vietnam War.

In the midst of his political activism, King never forgot the mainstay of his power, the black church. Above all, King was a preacher, and some of his closest aides—Ralph Abernathy, Walter Fauntroy, John Lewis, Fred Shuttlesworth, Wyatt T. Walker, Jesse Jackson, and Andrew Young—were also preachers. Furthermore, black churches across the country functioned as incubators for justice. These churches provided meeting space for civil rights strategy sessions, drew upon their congregations to attend marches and engage in boycotts, and strengthened the resolve of black freedom fighters with soul-stirring worship, preaching, and singing.

No assessment of the modern civil rights movement is complete without a discussion of student involvement. From the integration of Central High School in Little Rock, Arkansas, in 1957, to the student sit-ins at lunch counters in the 1960s, to the pioneering work of the Student Nonviolent Coordinating Committee (SNCC), African American students occupied the vanguard of the movement. Compelled by moral suasion, many white students also joined the movement, risking life and limb alongside their black compatriots.

Considering integration as a treatment for and not a cure of white racism, some black students began infusing into the movement a more radical theme of black empowerment and self-determination. In the mid and late 1960s, many black youth chanted "Black power" and "Black is beautiful" instead of singing traditional civil rights hymns such as "We Shall Overcome." The Nation of Islam and Malcolm X provided the motivation and message for many of these young revolutionaries.

As in other eras, bloodshed was all too common. The roll call of lives taken by violence included Emmett Till, Denise McNair, Carole Robertson, Cynthia Wesley, Addie Mae Collins, Medgar Evers, James Chaney, Andrew Goodman, Michael Schwerner, and Martin Luther King Jr. Whether burning down buildings in rage in northern ghettoes, or burning draft cards in protest against the Vietnam War, the flames of cultural controversy engulfed the late 1960s.

## PREACHING FORMS, 1951–1968

Martin Luther King Jr. was a major force in the preaching of this period. King's social gospel preaching legitimized black aspirations for freedom in the eyes of many whites by investing the social and political struggle for freedom and equality with moral and spiritual authority. This legitimization was important, because King believed that freedom could never be won with violence and weapons, but only with moral suasion, including nonviolent direct action and the power of the spoken word, particularly preaching oratory. King opened up black preaching to a national white audience, and subsequently a global audience as well. After King, white America began to pay attention to African American preaching as never before. The scholar Mervyn A. Warren says, "the increased visibility and respectability of black preaching in America can be split into two eras, B.K. and A.K.—Before King and After King."[2] Warren argues that it was not happenstance that only in the early or middle 1970s did African American preaching begin to receive attention in white homiletic and academic hallways. It was the influence of King's oratory that redefined the perception of black preaching in white America.

### *J.H. Jackson and "Suffering Servant" Preaching*

While King was the most prominent preaching voice, the civil rights movement also brought to light the diversity of voices that spoke in the various tongues of black preaching. Reverend Joseph H. Jackson, longtime president of the National Baptist Convention, questioned the scriptural claims of "civil rights" preaching. Jackson's preaching cast the Negro in the biblical "suffering servant" image of the prophet Isaiah. His preaching insisted on protest against unjust laws, but not by means of what he saw as civil disobedience, the method preached by King and his colleagues. According to Jackson:

> Our forefathers were cross-bearers. They believed in it. You can't build a great church preaching hate, envy, and revenge, and sending the people out on the street after the sermon mad at the world. No matter how non-violent, civil disobedience lays the ground for civil hatred and the desire to destroy. They took from the civil rights struggle the religious faith that went with it.[3]

Others did not embrace nonviolent civil disobedience either, not even some of the preachers within the Southern Christian Leadership Conference (SCLC), which King helped to found. Studying the Birmingham civil rights campaign, SCLC executive director Wyatt Walker estimated that as many as 90 percent of black ministers shunned the activities of the SCLC altogether.[4] It is too often assumed that the creed of nonviolence was propagated by all in the Christian fold, but even as it lay at the heart of King's direct action advocacy, civil disobedience was perceived by many as radically defeatist before the crushing violence of a white supremist state. Some felt that violence was necessary, others that integration was a false hope, and yet others that even nonviolence was too extreme a method. King's ethic of nonviolence and the language in which he preached it appealed to segments of white America, but King fought, and eventually lost, an increasingly uphill battle in the 1960s to maintain the viability of nonviolence to the wider African American community.

### The Preaching of Black Nationalism

As the perception of the viability of nonviolence diminished within the black community, and many questioned the suffering servant motif, some turned to black nationalist faith traditions. Elijah Muhammad's *Message to the Blackman in America* (1965) came as a liberation song to many. Malcolm X, the son of a Baptist preacher, converted to Muhammad's Nation of Islam. With his charisma and fiery oratory, Malcolm X propelled himself to national prominence. He hurled unrelenting assaults on white people and white supremacy. In the nationalist tradition of Marcus Garvey, Malcolm X's sermons opposed the integrationist ideal and taught that blacks were heirs to a superior culture and civilization. Blacks were therefore to separate and seek control of the political and economic resources in their own communities. Malcolm's theology was born in the North's urban centers, where despite the absence of Jim Crow laws and proclamations of equality by generations of white liberals, economic and social conditions for blacks had not improved. The Nation of Islam, and the Black Power movement that followed, ministered to growing insecurity in black communities faced with violent suppression of the nonviolent civil rights protest and deepening economic insecurity.

In the face of intransigent racism and continued reduced circumstances, Malcolm criticized various civil rights organizations, considering them too accommodating to the white power structure. Although government officials and some moderate civil rights activists considered him a dangerous radical, Malcolm's sharp intellect, fearless posture toward white authority, and religious devotion enticed a generation of black youth who were disenchanted with the measured gains of integration. Even so, after a pilgrimage to Mecca toward the end of his life, Malcolm disavowed some of his earlier separatist teachings and embraced a more inclusive doctrine of racial cooperation and economic empowerment.

### Contemplative Preaching

While the debate raged between social gospel, suffering servant preaching, and black nationalism, another traditional form of preaching, contemplative preaching, continued to cut a deep channel in the practice of African American preaching. Contemplative preaching, as a genre and as a method, is influenced to a considerable extent by philosophical reasoning and mystical theology. The words "contemplation" and "contemplative" are associated with thoughtful observation, viewing or reflecting on an object or idea with continued attentiveness. These two words are often associated in religion with aspects of the monastic life, such as seclusion of the self for disciplined prayer and spiritual exercises in prolonged silence, in keeping with some traditions of meditation.

Arguably, the ablest and most renowned African American practitioner of contemplative preaching was Howard Thurman, a man who was one of the high peaks in a range of Christian mystics who served in strategic pulpits. Thurman was a master of the contemplative sermonic form in the way he wedded substance and style in his preaching.[5] Typical of responses to his contemplative preaching was this comment by a student who heard him, "Some men talk about God, which is of value if it inspires devotion to him. But, when Howard Thurman speaks, you somehow experience God. He seems to take God with him; or, rather, he seems propelled by God."[6]

Theologian J. Deotis Roberts has noted Thurman's contribution to African American religious thought as that of a mystic and religious philosopher, writing, "In this category, Howard Thurman has no rival and no second among his black brothers [and sisters]. He is, indeed, one of the great mystics of all times. His mysticism is not 'introverted,' nor is it a mysticism of withdrawal from human problems. His mysticism is practical and urges us toward involvement and engagement in the real world where social and ethical issues are at stake."[7] Historian Martin E. Marty paid Thurman a high posthumous tribute when he wrote, "He, at least, has shown us how the path of holiness and enlightenment is not merely parallel to but it links up with the path of community and action."[8] Preachers such as Mordecai Wyatt Johnson, John Malcus Ellison, Thea Bowman, Martin Luther King Jr., and Benjamin Mays all demonstrate the effectiveness of contemplative preaching and the fact that African American preaching can contain "intricate historical, political analyses, while at the same time feeding the flock mystical and theological insights."[9] Indeed, mystical and theological insights did inspire social activism.

## THE SERMONETTE-SONG AND WOMEN PREACHERS

African American faith communities have historically been hostile to women preachers. However, African American women have always stood up. In the 1960s women preachers, still fighting the conservative tenor of the times and being asked to wait until the battles of racism were fought before women's issues were addressed, were always industrious and found ways to declare the gospel amid the disdain shown for their God-given gifts by their own faith communities and the larger society.

One device that they used to proclaim the gospel and fulfill their callings was the sermonette-song. In the sermonette-song, preaching and singing are variously combined. Typically singers deliver a five- or ten-minute sermon before, during, or after a song. However, this act is rarely referred to as preaching, although that is clearly what it is. The sermons are brief, but indeed sermons. This device was and continues to be used by male gospel singers and groups. Gospel singing is one of the few arenas in the African American faith community where women are as popular and in some instances more popular than men.

The sermonette-song allowed women to carve out their own preaching and singing circuits without being focused upon as women preachers. They were also not first and foremost viewed as women preachers because many used the title *evangelist* at some point in their ministries. While male evangelists are considered preachers and are automatically also given the title Reverend, historically, women were viewed as a step below these men by the church and not easily accorded the additional clergy credentials or titles given to men. While many female gospel singers were preachers, more often than not, they used the sermonette-song rather than sermons alone as they went about delivering their messages.

One of the early users of the sermonette-song was one of the mothers of gospel music, Reverend Willie Mae Ford Smith (1904–94). Born in Rolling Fork, Mississippi, Ford was the seventh of fourteen children born to Mary (Williams) and Clarence Ford. Like Thomas Dorsey, Smith sang gospel music that was infused with blues. In 1922 her father formed the Ford Sisters Quartet and Smith led the group. In 1932 she met Dorsey and joined the gospel music movement being shepherded by Sallie Martin and Dorsey. Smith began as an evangelist and became an ordained preacher in the Lively Stone Apostolic Church in St. Louis, an affiliate of the Pentecostal Assemblies of the World. At one time she was also a Baptist and was comfortable singing before Baptist audiences, which aided in her work with Thomas Dorsey as he developed choirs and singers around the country for the gospel music movement.

Smith had a booming contralto voice. She could have been an opera singer. Her sermonette-songs were often all that were needed to raise an audience to its feet. Although Smith enjoyed a great deal of success, she did not enjoy the recording success of Mahalia Jackson and Roberta Martin; this allowed Smith to concentrate on singing and preaching at revivals.

Following Smith was Madam Edna Gallmon Cooke (1917–67). Cooke heard Willie Mae Ford Smith sing in 1938 and adopted much of her style. Cooke began recording in the 1950s and specialized in the sermonette-song. Her most famous recordings include "Amen" and "Evening Sun." She sang most often with the support of a male quartet. Horace Boyer, in *How Sweet the Sound: The Golden Age of Gospel*, describes a part of the sermonette from one of Cooke's most famous sermonette-songs, "Stop Gambler." It was delivered in cadence, as is the case with all sermonette-songs.

> *I can see the first gambler as he throws down the deuce, the two spot—representing Paul and Silas bound in jail. They didn't do any wrong, and God delivered them.*
>
> *The next gambler throws down the trey, the three-spot—representing Shadrach, Meshach, and Abednego. God delivered them from a fiery furnace.*
>
> *Look at the next gambler, he is throwing down the four spot now—representing the four gospel writers, Matthew, Mark, Luke and John.*
>
> *The next gambler is throwing down the five spot—now representing the fifth commandment: honor thy father and thy mother.*
>
> *The next one is throwing down the six spot—representing the six days God worked to create the earth.*
>
> Cooke addresses each card in the deck with the same kind of biblical reference. By the time she arrives at the ace, representing the Father, Son and Holy Ghost, her audience would be standing and waving, clapping their hands, and generally acting as if they were at the sports event that she had created through her oration, which was always accompanied by soft organ music.[10]

Cooke inspired Dorothy Norwood (1936– ). Norwood claimed the title "the Best Known Storyteller"; her 1998 album bore the same title. Born in Atlanta, Norwood began singing and touring with her family at age eight. In 1956 she moved to Chicago, and was soon singing with such notables as Mahalia Jackson, the Caravans, and Reverend James Cleveland. Norwood launched her solo career in 1964 and recorded her first album, which went gold. She followed it up with the stirring *Denied Mother*, which also went gold. In her four decades in the gospel music industry, Norwood has recorded more than 40 albums—five of which went gold. She has also received five Grammy nominations.

The most famous of all the sermonette-song singers is Shirley Caesar (1938– ). Caesar was born in Durham, North Carolina, the tenth of twelve children. She began singing early to help earn money to assist with taking care of her mother. Caesar's father died when she was a child. Like Reverend Willie Mae Ford Smith, she held the title evangelist in her early twenties, before becoming an ordained minister. She received the call to preach at age nineteen. However, most of the performance venues which made her famous would not have welcomed a woman using the title Reverend in the 1960s or 1970s. She became a professional singer when she joined the Caravans, led by Albertina Walker. After leaving the Caravans, she started her own group, the Shirley Caesar Singers. In 1976, as a solo act, she signed a one-million-dollar contract with Roadshow Records.

Caesar took the sermonizing-singing of Reverend Willie Mae Ford Smith to a new level and best epitomizes use of the sermonette-song. Though a great gospel singer (she holds more Grammy Awards than any gospel singer), a large part of her appeal are the sermonettes that precede many of her songs. Reverend Caesar is particularly well known for three sermonette-songs. Two involve mothers: "No Charge" and "Don't Drive Your Mother Away." The third is "Hold My Mule/Shoutin' John." In "No Charge" a little boy presents a list and requests payment from his mother for chores that he has performed. His mother responds by presenting her own list of tasks that she has performed as his mother and declares "No charge." Her work, of course includes carrying him for nine months, taking care of him when he was sick, and praying for him. "Hold My Mule/Shoutin' John" and "Don't Drive Your Mother Away" address how false pretensions associated with social class can limit spirituality and destroy family ties.

"Don't Drive Your Mother Away" is a classic sermonette-song. Caesar delivers this sermonette with cadence and tunes as if she is preparing to go into a full-fledged whoop. This and other sermonette-songs by Caesar even feature the historic call-and-response of the Protestant African American faith community. Following is an abbreviated version of "Don't Drive Your Mother Away." The audience response has been included in parentheses. The audience response helps establishes the cadence and speed of the sermonette. Part of the response is also provided by the singers who accompany Caesar.

> *There was a mother that had two sons. One of the sons was interested in himself. That son loved his mama so much. He said, Mama one day I'm gonna grow up, (Oh Yeahh) I'm going to college. (Yeahhh) I wanna' be somebody. (Yeahhhhhh) I wanna' take care of you, like you been taking care of me. (Oh Yeahhh, followed by hand clapping) That other brother was not conscientious about himself. (Well) He was no good. Stayed in trouble all the time. That mother had to always go to court (Oh yeah. Yesssss.) to get that son out of trouble. The other son said, "Mother I'm not gonna' worry your patience. I'm gonna be a good son for you." (Yesssss)*
>
> *I'm told tonight that those boys grew up. One went to college (Yeahhhh) and that no-good son left home. Ohhhhhhh Lord. (Ohhhhh Lord) That mama worked her fingers to the bones, and sent that son to school. She got on her knees and scrubbed floors, (Ohhhhhhh, yeahhhhhh) she climbed ladders and washed windows (Ohhhh, yeahhhhhhh, followed by hand clapping), hung out clothes, working her fingers to the bone. I want my son to be somebody. (Yeaaaaaah)*
>
> *After about eight long years, that son came home. He said, "Mama I am a doctor now. I've got MD behind my name. I want you to meet my wife. I met her while I was in college. She's a schoolteacher." Yeahhhhhhhhh. I'm told tonight they told that mama, "We want you to come and live with us. Help us take care of our children."*
>
> *As the years went on by and their children grew up, I'm told tonight, even though they were at school age, that schoolteacher went to her husband and said, "Honey, huh, your mama's in the way now. (Loooord) I think you ought to get rid of her, we can get somebody else to do this job. There are young girls in college, huh, they can work their way through school on this very job. Your mama uses bad English. She uses dis and dat and ain't and ises. I'm trying to teach my children to use good language." Yeahhhhhhhh, oh hallelujah.*

As the sermonette-song continues the well-to-do son is found driving his mother down the road in a limousine to an old-folks home. On their way there, the mother spies a beat-up automobile containing her no-account son. This son learns that his brother is about to place their mother in a nursing home. He explains that he "lives in a rented apartment and eats beans out of a can," but she is welcomed to go home with him. The mother gets into the car with the no-account son. Then Caesar ends the sermonette and breaks fully into song, ultimately saying, "God gave you your mother, don't drive her away!"[11]

## NOTES

1. Henry Louis Gates Jr. and Cornel West, *The African American Century: How Black Americans Have Shaped Our Century* (New York: The Free Press, 2000), 129.
2. Mervyn A. Warren, *King Came Preaching: The Pulpit Power of Martin Luther King, Jr.* (Downers Grove, IL: InterVarsity Press, 2001), 52.
3. "The Black Church: Three Views," in *ChickenBones: A Journal for Literary & Artistic African-American Themes*, excerpts from *Time* essay published on April 6, 1970, found at http://www.nathanielturner.com/blackchurch.htm (accessed March 20, 2005).
4. Allison Calhoun-Brown, "Upon This Rock: The Black Church, Non-Violence, and the Civil Rights Movement," http://www.apsanet.org/PS/june00/calhoun.fcm (accessed December 13, 2004).
5. See James Earl Massey, "Thurman's Preaching: Substance and Style," in *God and Human Freedom: A Festschrift in Honor of Howard Thurman*, ed. Henry J. Young (Richmond, IN: Friends United Press, 1983), 110–21.
6. See Mary Jennes, *Twelve Negro Americans* (New York: Friendship Press, 1936), 153; see Elizabeth Yates, *Howard Thurman: Portrait of a Practical Dreamer* (New York: The John Day Co., 1964), 185–86.
7. J. Deotis Roberts, "The American Negro's Contribution to Religious Thought" in *The Negro Impact on Western Civilization*, ed. Joseph S. Roucek and Thomas Kiernan (New York: Philosophical Library, 1970), 86–87.
8. See Martin E. Marty, "Mysticism and the Religious Quest for Freedom," in *God and Human Freedom*, 9; see Martin E. Marty's foreword to *Strange Freedom: The Best of Howard Thurman on Religious Experience and Public Life*, ed. Walter Earl Fluker and Catherine Tumber (Boston: Beacon Press, 1998), xxii, where Marty lauded Thurman for "the mixture of passion and reflection that he brought to the pulpit and rostrum."
9. William B. McClain, "African American Preaching," in *The Renewal of Worship*, vol. 3, ed. Robert E. Webber (Nashville, TN: Star Song Publishing Group, 1993), 317.
10. Horace Clarence Boyer, *How Sweet the Sound: The Golden Age of Gospel* (Washington, DC: Elliott and Clark, 1995), 238.
11. Cheryl Townsend Gilkes, "Shirley Caesar and the Souls of Black Folk Gospel Music as Cultural Narrative and Critique," *The African American Pulpit* 6, no. 2 (Spring 2003), 12–16.

# WILLIAM HOLMES BORDERS

*(1905–1993)*

William Holmes Borders was born in Macon, Georgia, on February 24, 1905. His father, James Buchanan Borders, was a Baptist minister, and at age eight Borders felt the call to follow in his father's footsteps. His mother died when he was twelve, and soon his father began to suffer ailments that prevented regular work. After graduating high school, Borders got a job as a mail carrier, earning barely enough money to support the family. He went on to earn a bachelor of arts degree from Morehouse College in Atlanta; a bachelor of divinity and master of arts from Garrett Theological Seminary, and was awarded numerous honorary doctoral degrees from Wilberforce University, Atlanta University, Howard University, and others.

While in seminary, Borders took his first pastorate at the Second Baptist Church in Evanston, Illinois. He eventually left Second Baptist and taught at Morehouse College. In 1937 he became pastor of Wheat Street Baptist Church in Atlanta, where he remained for five decades. "The Prophet of Wheat Street," as he came to be known, led the congregation into a comprehensive program of service in the community. Preachers who would become famous pastors and political leaders all came to hear Borders speak. In fact, on many a Sunday, when Daddy King did not see Martin Luther King Jr. in church, it was known that the young King was at Wheat Street.

By the 1950s the Wheat Street congregation had grown to four thousand members. Borders gained a national reputation as a leader in the fight for civil rights. He helped integrate Atlanta's police department and directed a campaign to attain decent hospital care and jobs for African Americans. In the early 1960s he chaired the committee that oversaw the integration of Atlanta's hotels, restaurants, and other facilities.

Borders died on November 23, 1993.

• • •

*A William Holmes Borders sermon provides an excellent example of the ability of African American preaching to combine intellectual and academic acumen with the fire and emotion typical of the folk preacher. Borders also combines the zeal of the social gospel preacher who is concerned with the economic and political plight of his people with the piety of the evangelist who is concerned with saving souls from the fires of hell. Borders's preaching ministry waged war against ignorance, poverty, unemployment, and sin. The following sermon is one of Borders's most popular.*

## Handicapped Lives
## (1972)

The other day at Tuskegee Institute, I visited the cemetery. I came to a tombstone. It read: "GEORGE WASHINGTON CARVER—Died in Tuskegee, Alabama, January 5, 1943. A Life that stood out as a gospel of Self-Forgetful Service. He could have added Fortune to Fame, but caring for neither, he found happiness and honour in being helpful to the world."

The center of his world was the South where he was born in slavery some years ago, and in the South, he did his work as a creative scientist. I reread the inscription as I removed my hat. I said to myself, "Not only was Carver a creative scientist but a blessed saint." I thought of his sickly body. I thought of how he was expected to die. I thought of how he was stolen and later swapped for a horse. I thought of how he made a garage laundry more popular than the college president's office. I thought of how he earned a master's degree at Iowa. I thought of Booker T. Washington bringing him to Tuskegee. I thought of the first time I met Carver. He wore greasy, ragged clothes. I thought of how he painted beautiful pictures with the ends of his fingers. I thought of how with those same fingers he played a piano. I thought of how he surmounted every obstacle in his path, climbing higher and higher until his recognition reached international proportions. I said to myself, as I left that cemetery, "A handicap can be a blessing."

My host whizzed me to the art department of the Institute. One of the students asked that I describe the aid that "art" could be to religion. At the close, I was told of an artist who had been sick for twenty-five years. I insisted that I be taken to his home. His wife was energetic, immaculate, and orderly. He had been flat on his back a quarter of a century, unable even to brush his teeth. The secret of his personality was revealed in his eyes. They sparkled more brilliantly than stars. He told his story. He reads all day. He has an improvised rack. The book is clinched with clothespins, so are the pages. His wife turns the pages and pins them for him. He reads while she does other things in the house. His granddaughter is his secretary. His body is dead. He writes poetry with his head. I came out of that home thanking God for its consecration and devotion. "A handicap can be a blessing."

My mind raced from Tuskegee to Atlanta. I remembered Charles Moseley in his blindness. His wife and three daughters rallied around his infirmity. The ends of his fingers developed eyes. He saw through blinded eyes how to build a house. Neighbors once called the police to make him come down off the roof where he had climbed to repair a leak. In my mind, I pitied him once. Then it dawned on me that he had a pocketbook full of money, that he repaired his house, that he collected his rent, that he was independent, that he supported his family, that he had done better blind than I had with eyes. Yes, it dawned on me that he did not need any pity. His blindness was the source of his power. Through his weakness, God had made him strong.

My mind moved from Moseley to a blind paper boy on the west side. I came across him one Sunday morning when I was late for my broadcast. He was on Hunter Street. I pulled up in my car and called, "Hey, here!" He stopped. This paper boy wore white slacks and a flopped hat. He said, "Who is this who knows me?" I said, "This is Reverend Borders." "Yes, I hear you all the time. I know you!" he replied. I asked, "How long have you been carrying papers?" "Nearly twenty-three years," he answered. "What's your name?" "Kelley." "How do you know where these houses are?" I asked. "I know how many steps I take. I can tell the feel of the pavement." "How do you know when to cross the street?" "I can see with my ears." "Are you married?" "I've been married." "Have you got any children?" "One boy, five years old—that is, he was five when my wife got her divorce." "So your wife got a divorce?" "Yes, and took all I had." "How much did you have?" "About two thousand dollars. I oughta give her another thousand!" "For what?" "It was worth an extra thousand to get rid of her," he concluded. I pulled away saying, "I'll see you." "All right, Reverend Borders."

My cup was already full—this ran it over. Everybody has an infirmity. Everybody has a weakness. Everybody has a defect. Everybody has a disease. Everybody has a problem. Everybody has an obstacle. Everybody has a difficulty. It may be cancer. It may be mental frustration. It may be spiritual inequity. It may be an unbalanced complex. Maybe you want to curse the moral order because you are Negro. Loneliness may be knocking at your door. Old age may be creeping up on you. Whatever it is, face it as a fact. Work within that limitation. That limitation is where your strength ends. It is where God's power begins. God says, "You are the creature. I am the Creator. You are finite. I am infinite. You have power. I have all power." In your weakness you are made strong. The limitation caused by your weakness is God's chance to prove his power. The uncured disease of a woman gave God's power through Jesus a chance.

Lazarus's death was Jesus' opportunity to prove himself master over the grave. The cross gave Jesus the best chance he had to pray. Joseph's tomb gave Jesus his best chance to conquer the world with all human odds against him.

One day I stopped by the home of Paul Laurence Dunbar; he gave one verse:

*A crust of bread and a corner to sleep in,*
*A minute to smile and an hour to weep in,*
*A pint of joy to a peck of trouble,*
*And never a laugh but the moans come double:*
*And that is life!*[1]

I remembered that he was tubercular and was dead before he was thirty-five.

Another day I opened my Bible to the Book of Daniel. In spirit, I was dragged from Jerusalem to the Babylonian captivity. Slavery had cut the hearts of some Jews into a thousand pieces. Babylonian slave music was brought up-to-date in Psalm 137:1, "By the rivers of Babylon we sat down. Yea, we wept when we remembered Zion." We yearned for home. We wanted fellowship and union with our sisters and brothers. The empty loneliness of Babylon brought sorrow to our hearts and tears to our eyes. "There they that carried us away captive required of us song. And, they that wasted us required of us mirth, saying, 'Sing us one of the songs of Zion.' How can we sing the Lord's song in a strange land?"[2] How can slaves shout for joy? How can we be happy chained in slavery? How can the clink of iron chains be converted into musical harmony? How can your heart sing when your body sags under fetters of iron? How can a mocking bird sing with a broken wing? How can a rabbit run with a broken leg? How can we sing—miles from home with a dagger in our hearts? Some do best under a handicap.

Bermuda grass grows best when you try to kill it. A certain kind of apple tree, gashed, yields its best fruit. Negro spirituals were born in dark days of bondage when trials were hard. Beethoven, who was deaf, composed eternal harmonies for other people's ears. A pearl is the result of disease in an oyster. John Milton peeped into paradise through blinded eyes. Moses was on his way when he chose "rather to suffer affliction with the people of God, than to enjoy the pleasures of sin for a season."[3] As the blaze leaped about her body, singeing her hair, Joan of Arc declared, "I have heard the voice of God; His voice must be obeyed." Shadrach, Meshach, and Abednego, dumped into the fire by Nebuchadnezzar, refused to bow. Adversity carried Job's casket to his bedside—obnoxious, diseased, bankrupt, wounded by death, discouraged by his wife, forsaken and forgotten by friends, this ancient saint's heart forced his lips to utter, "When he hath tried me, I shall come forth as gold."[4] On land, Paul's best prayer was in jail. On sea, Paul's best prayer was in a storm. Deacon Stephen's best prayer was in a ditch with stones bouncing off his skull. Jesus prayed best with his hands and feet spiked to a cross. Banished on the Isle of Patmos, John said, "I was in the Spirit on the Lord's day . . ."[5] David was at his best, not sitting on a throne, wearing robes of purple and gold, but rather in the Twenty-third Psalm, passing through the valley and shadow of death. He cried out, "I will fear no evil: for thou art with me; thy rod and thy staff they comfort me. Thou preparest a table before me in the presence of mine enemies."[6] When Herod severed John the Baptist's head from his body, that dead head rolled and preached God's word with greater power.

Suffering in Babylon, the Jew bounced back: "If I forget thee, O Jerusalem, let my right hand forget her cunning . . . let my tongue cleave to the roof of my mouth; if I prefer not Jerusalem above my chief joy."[7] Let me remember that God can give me *joy in sorrow, victory in defeat, light in darkness,* and *success in failure*. Paul declared to the Corinthians: "I glory in my infirmity. I have a thorn in the flesh."[8] It pricked deep. It twisted around in the muscle. It pained. It ached. It irked. It hurt until my whole body was a ceaseless wave of torture. My mind could not function. My soul was wounded by this thorn reaching through the flesh. My existence was impaired. This thorn in the flesh reduced me to a couch. I tossed and tumbled. I tried remedy after remedy without relief. This thorn in the flesh handled me roughly. It was gnawing my life away. It baffled medical skill. It had my body. It was disturbing my mind. It was mixing poison for my spirit."[9]

Curable disease is bad enough. Incurable disease is a torture. Physically curable diseases are handled by doctors. Incurables are handled by God. "Earth has no sorrow that heaven cannot heal." Somebody here now is an incurable. God has an absolute prescription. When the spirit strikes fire, it will be a signal that the perfect universal Doctor is waiting and willing to cure all diseases. Sick women! Diseased men! Take your case to God.

Paul did it. Diseased, pained, uncured, baffled—Paul sought the Lord. Said he: "I sought the Lord once." No answer came. "I sought the Lord twice. My weakness remained. I sought the Lord thrice." I imagine Paul spread himself before God saying, "I am your servant; you are my God. I am tortured and pained without end. I have done all I know. I have preached 'prayer.' I have preached 'power.' I have preached 'ability.' Now I am caught with a thorn in the flesh, which I can't master. I prayed once. I prayed twice. This is a third time. I need a personal answer. When it stormed, you sent an angel. When I was in Philippi, you rocked the jail. When I was trapped, you let me down over the Macedonian wall. When I was headed for Damascus to raise hell, you blocked the traffic. When I was stoned, you saved me. I need a personal answer to my plea. You made my body. A master mechanic knows his product. I have the faith in God, and you have the power."

Paul expected God to come by land, and he came by sea. God does not always answer prayer the way we want, or expect, but rather his way. God answered Elijah with a raven. God answered Moses with manna from on high. God answered Jesus by increasing a fish sandwich to a supermarket in the wilderness. God answered Joshua at Jericho with tumbling walls. God answered our slave parents with Sherman's march from Atlanta to the sea. God answered Gideon with three hundred who lapped water. God answered Elijah by fire. God answered Isaiah with fire. God answered Noah in the flood with an ark. God answered Paul on a stormy sea with an angel. God answered Jesus on the stormy Sea of Galilee with personal power when Jesus said, "Peace be still."[10] God answered Stephen in a ditch being stoned to death. God answered Gandhi enabling him to give the Hindu salute of forgiveness as bullets of death killed his body. God answered Jesus as murderers ripped his body. God answers not always the way you want or expect. Paul declares that after a third prayer God told him, "My grace is sufficient . . ."[11]

Paul moved on to write fourteen of the twenty-seven books in the New Testament. Scholars differ. Proof and disproof multiply Paul's greatness. He produced perhaps the greatest ode on love. He wrote a treatise on faith. His three major missionary journeys qualify him as one of the greatest. His prayers are religiously disturbing. His organizing of churches is gripping. His use of time behind iron bars writing solutions to church problems upset magistrates. His fiery gospel upset rulers. His easy use of several languages made *him* ready. In spite of handicaps of flesh, travel, jails, and persecution, Paul was second only to Jesus.

## NOTES

*Sermon source:* William M. Philpot, *Best Black Sermons* (Valley Forge, PA: Judson Press, 1983), 18–24.

1. See Paul Laurence Dunbar, "Life (1896)," in *The Complete Poems of Paul Laurence Dunbar* (New York: Dodd Mead and Company, 1993).

2. See Psalm 137:1, 3, 4 (King James Version).
3. Hebrews 11:25 (KJV).
4. Job 23:10 (KJV).
5. Revelation 1:10 (KJV).
6. Psalm 23:4–5 (KJV).
7. Psalm 137:5–6 (KJV).
8. See 2 Corinthians 12:5, 7 (KJV).
9. See 2 Corinthians 12.
10. Mark 4:39 (KJV).
11. 2 Corinthians 12:9 (KJV).

### *Bibliographical Sources*

Appiah, Kwame Anthony, and Henry L. Gates Jr., eds. *Africana: The Encyclopedia of the African and African American Experience*, 5 vols. New York: Oxford University Press, 2005.

Benson, Juel Pate Borders. "Victory Over Defeat: Eulogy of William H. Holmes Borders Sr." *The African American Pulpit* 4, no. 1 (Winter 2000–2001).

Borders, William Holmes. *45th Pastoral Anniversary: Rev. William Holmes Borders, 1937–1982*. Atlanta: Josten's American Yearbook Company, 1982.

———. *Trial By Fire and 25 Other Sermons*. Atlanta: Wheat Street Church, 1977.

———. *World Unity and Nineteen Other Sermons*. Atlanta: Morris Brown College Press, 1990.

English, James W. *Handyman of the Lord: The Life and Ministry of the Reverend William Holmes Borders*. New York: Meredith Press, 1967.

———. *The Prophet of Wheat Street: The story of William Holmes Borders, a Man who Refused to Fail*. Elgin, Illinois: Cook Publishing, 1973.

Young, Henry J., ed. *Preaching the Gospel*. Philadelphia: Fortress, 1976.

# TIMOTHY MOSES CHAMBERS

*(1895–1977)*

Timothy Moses Chambers was born in 1895 in Mount Pleasant, Texas, the son of Cicero Clarence and Jerreline Wade Chambers. He graduated from Fort I and M College and received a Bachelor of Theology from Bishop College, which produced so many noted black preachers, including one of Chambers's roommates, Manuel Scott Sr. Chambers married Hazel Thomas and they had five children.

Chambers also pastored Good Street Baptist Church in Dallas, Texas, which was later made famous by C.A.W. Clark, who succeeded Chambers. Additionally, he served as president of the Baptist Missionary and Educational Convention of Texas for several years.

After leaving Good Street, Chambers moved to Los Angeles where he became the pastor of Zion Hill Baptist Church. Chambers hosted a celebrated radio program in Los Angeles, *The Sweet Hour of Prayer*, for fifteen years. Having attained notoriety in the National Baptist Convention, U.S.A., Inc., because of his radio program, his leadership, and his preaching skills, Chambers was elected the first president of the Progressive National Baptist Convention, formed when a fracture occurred among National Baptists over tenure for the president and the direction in which Martin Luther King Jr. and others wanted to lead the group on civil rights. The new group also included revered African American preachers such as King and Gardner C. Taylor. Chambers served as president of the PNBC from 1961 to 1966. His leadership stabilized the group, which provided support for King during the civil rights movement. In 1966 Chambers left Zion Hill and started a new church, Roger Williams True Love Baptist Church. He remained at this church until his death in 1977.

• • •

*Chambers's popular sermons were often used by others. His simplicity and directness, his ability to speak to the common man and put him at ease, were evident in his sermons. He said a great deal with few words. Listeners also loved his use of tonality. In this sermon Chambers plainly discusses how a man should be measured. As with most of his preaching, his ultimate aim is to point people to Christ. This sermon was self-published by Chambers along with six others in a pamphlet he prepared in 1949 to provide clergy examples of different types of sermons.*

## The Measure of a Man (1949)

> *Till we all come in the unity of the faith, and of the knowledge of the Son of God, unto a perfect man, unto the measure of the stature of the fullness of Christ.* —Ephesians 4:13

In this age of classification and standardization of things, when tall pine and hardwood trees are yielding to the stroke of the stockman to put to humming the ceaseless wheels of industry; and the hills, plains and valleys are bedecked with stately mansions, skyscrapers, barn tops and bungalow cottages; when every brick and every stone in every building must be molded or hewn out by a gauge; when every thread in every garment must be woven true to form; when we realize that we are living on a tailor-made earth, measured by a tapeline of Divine scrutiny, let us agree that man, too, if he is to fill his place and serve the lofty purpose for which he was created, must be measured by a gauge.

As there are so many faint and false ideas in the field of human speculation, I shall endeavor first to regulate your thinking by presenting the negative side of the picture, or by reminding you of some things by which *man should not be measured*:

1. A man should not be measured exclusively by his knowledge of books. It is good to learn the literature of the nations of the earth, of course, but I wish to declare to you that we do not get it all from books. Remember that to the logically observant and those of inquiring minds, there is nothing insignificant and nothing little. Every object that steps in human gaze holds a lesson for mankind.

**A Match Head:** Wrapped in a little ignition point known as a match head, may be the destruction of a city, if trusted in careless hands; but if handled by careful or constructive hands, it may become the warmth or comfort of a city.

**A Mustard Seed:** In an illustration of a grain of mustard seed, the smallest seed in the vegetable kingdom, was described the beginning, growth and progress of the greatest kingdom known to mankind.

**The Earthworm:** The earthworm is not only used for fish bait, but its perpetual motion makes it an invisible plow hand, pulverizing and opening the pores of the earth for the sun rays to deposit oxygen for the vegetation to transmit it into the bodies of man and beast.

**Death on the Point of a Tack:** The careful eye discerns death on the point of a little tack, therefore, removes it by sweeping the driveway from the garage to the street, thus, preventing the death of a family from a blowout on the highway.

**A Little Pebble:** A little pebble, from the hand of a little baby thrown into the sea, may form a little circle on the water, a tempestuous wind may lift the circle of water into a tide, push it out to meet a ship and cause its mast pole to kiss the bosom of the water. Thus, you can see that the field for great lessons from even little objects, is almost unlimited.

2. *Not by his physical stature.* There is such thing as *much brawn but little brain.* Let that statement be sufficient.

3. *Not by the size of one's bank account,* as so many have proven by their unwise use of their wealth. Let that too be sufficient.

4. *Not by the color of the skin.* Far too many people are suffering these days from skin troubles. If others choose to remain ignorant of the facts or to cultivate false ideas on this point, I would have you know that there is an all out effort being put forth to convince the dark skin people that superiority or inferiority is not a matter of pigmentation. And real manhood is not measured by the color of the skin or the grade of the hair. Hence, I declared in my original poem that "The Negro Is a Man." I also declare it through my life.

## By What Then Should He Be Measured?

1. *By the depth of his knowledge.* I do not mean the mere scratching of the surface in agriculture, or the moisture that supports the roots of the plant life, nor should we stop with the strata of the rock, or the needle of the geologist, who punctures the veins of the earth, causing it to heave up petroleum, mineral and ore, but we should go deep enough in knowledge to find the name of the proper one on the cornerstone of creation. In the light of the Bible account of the creation of all things, that name is God.

2. *Man should be measured by the breadth of his interest,* which represents an unselfish program and spirit of love, broad enough to include everybody everywhere. Selfishness is littleness. The man who prayed, "Oh! my God! (as if he owned a whole God to himself) Bless me, my wife, our son Joe, his wife, we four and no more, Amen," is a narrow man, praying a narrow prayer, be he white or black.

3. *By the height of his ideal.* It is alright to emulate the traits of great earthly characters, but we must not place our standards too low. The tallest man on earth is still short when measured by the sky. We have had our attention focused on the ink trails of many noble characters and named our children for certain earthly heroes for they represent the height of our ambition. Some of my friends who heard my message in the Baptist World Alliance in Europe and the National Convention message which I delivered in Kansas City, Missouri, the same year, said to me, thereafter, "Chambers, you are my ideal." I appreciate the compliment, but it is rather risky to make me or anyone else on earth the height of your ideal. When I was elected president of our State Convention, some said, "It is our hope that you will be the second L.K. Williams in our state, our nation and our world." I appreciate this and regard L.K. as a worthy example, but I do not want to be the world's second anybody. I want to be God's first and only T.M. Chambers, making my contribution in an effort to reach the record of the highest.

## My Ideal

When sin had become science and vice was consecrated as a part of religion, rebellion had struck its roots deeply into the hearts of men and the hostility of man was vile against heaven. It was evident that apart from God, humanity could not be uplifted and a new element of power had to be imparted by Him, who made the world. The un-fallen worlds were waiting and watching to see Jehovah arise and sweep them into oblivion. The fast westerly sun was lingering on nature's treetops; angels were bubbling over to avert the doom of a guilty citizenry. The Angel of Mercy was folding up her wings to step down from the golden throne and make space for justice and swift coming judgment, but *my ideal* deferred the Council of the Holy Trinity and organized an angelic host to furnish music while the glory of His father flooded the hills of Bethlehem. He stepped on a heavenly made airplane and rode down into the low ground of sorrow, leaped into Virgin Mary and was born one day in the city of David, wrapped in swaddling clothes and laid in a manger.

Would you like to know His name? People are so forgetful, I would rather write it. Not on the ground, because the winds might blow trash on it or men walk over it without noticing it. I would not write it in the sky, because some people are not upward looking, they would walk beneath it face downward and never see it. I would not write it on the walls of a ruler's palace, because only the world's great ones could be admitted to see it. I would not write it on pearls, for the scarcity of pearls has so increased their value that none could have it but millionaires. I would not write in on money, for the rich would live and the poor would die, jobs often being scarce. I would not write it on paper, because grandmama did not go to school and the children are living too fast to stop and read it to her.

I tell you what I would do: I would rock people to sleep with a spiritual anesthetic, perform an operation on the left bosom with a sharp sword of God and lay bare the heart. Then I would dip my pen in a fountain of blood drawn from Emanuel's veins, I mean blood shed forth for man on Calvary, and I would write it down in the heart where people could read it at midnight and even when shut in by distress or imprisoned by circumstances. What would I write? *That name is Jesus.*

Moses and Elias were great characters on the Mount of Transfiguration, but after Peter, James and John were dazed by heaven's majesty, they lifted up their eyes and saw no man save "*Jesus only.*" Oh, do you know him?

### *Note*

*Sermon source:* Pamphlet by T.M. Chambers, "Educational Sermons, Addresses, and Subjects for Baccalaureate Commencement and Other Occasions," self-published by T.M. Chambers, copyrighted August 4, 1949, by T.M. Chambers.

### *Bibliographical Sources*


Booth, William D. *Call to Greatness: The Story of the Founding of the Progressive National Baptist Convention.* Lawrenceville, VA: Brunswick Publishing, 2001.

Kilgore, Thomas, Jr., and Jini Kilgore Ross. *A Servant's Journey: The Life and Work of Thomas Kilgore.* Valley Forge, PA: Judson Press, 1998.

McMickle, Marvin. *An Encyclopedia of African American Christian Heritage.* Valley Forge, PA: Judson Press, 2002.

# C.L. (CLARENCE LAVAUGHN) FRANKLIN

*(1915–1984)*

Reverend C.L. Franklin, pulpiteer, soul preacher extraordinaire, lovingly called "the learned one" and "the Rabbi," helped take the tradition of black preaching to new heights as he whooped his often extemporaneous sermons. According to Jesse Jackson Sr., "There's a little C.L. Franklin in our throats, if we have that talent, or in our hearts if we are possessed with the urge to preach."[1] Franklin was the most popular preacher of his generation. He is likely the most imitated African American preacher in history.

Franklin was born in 1915 in Sunflower County, a rural area in Mississippi. He grew up in a community of sharecroppers and listened to blues records, finding no conflict between the church and the blues because both settings included black cultural heritage. Franklin had his conversion experience when he was nine or ten years old, giving his testimony. He accepted his call to ministry at age twelve or thirteen, in the Baptist tradition. After doing migrant work, Franklin was ordained when he was seventeen or eighteen. After preaching on the circuit for several years and attending Greenville Industrial College, Franklin got married, moved to Memphis, and entered LeMoyne College. Subsequently, Franklin pastored in Memphis, Buffalo, and then the New Bethel Baptist Church in Detroit, where he served from 1946 until his death from a fatal beating in

1984. Franklin had a radio broadcast program where he preached and led in singing, beginning in 1951. In 1953, he began a relationship with Chess Records, who recorded his sermons and his singing. Following in the footsteps of recording preachers such as J.M. Gates, he toured with singers like the Dixie Hummingbirds and the Ward Singers. They all would sing and he would close with a sermon. Later he toured on his own with world-renowned daughter Aretha as a soloist. Franklin was also active in the civil rights movement, working with Dr. Martin Luther King Jr., the Southern Christian Leadership Conference, and PUSH (People United to Save Humanity). Franklin believed in a transcendent and immanent God of love.

Though Franklin's sermons are extemporaneous, he selected a pericope, consulted commentaries, did his exegesis, thought his notes through, and then developed a topical outline. His delivery involved spoken oration, then he went into his whoop, first tapping the intellect, then stroking the emotions. Some of his classic sermons, "The Eagle Stirreth Her Nest" (reprinted here), "Dry Bones in the Valley," "The Preacher Who Got Drunk," and "Give Me This Mountain," are sold on tapes and CDs, repreached, and imitated to this day.

• • •

*"The Eagle Stirreth Her Nest" (Deuteronomy 32:11–12) had been in the corpus of the black preaching canon for more than one hundred years by the time that Franklin developed this version.*[2] *Franklin, as well as other black preachers, knew and preached popular sermons from the canon. Franklin preaches that the eagle symbolizes God's concern and care for God's people. One day the eagle hears other eagles, and realizing it has grown too big to be in a cage, it flies away. In this portion of the sermon Franklin whoops: he sings and chants in free poetic verse. Franklin equates the eagles with his own soul, caged in his body, given by God. Like the eagle, one day his soul will fly away, and it will be at rest. While he does not whoop a standard hymn, gospel, or spiritual, his whooping accomplishes many of the things that music does in a sermon: it illustrates and heightens themes and ideas included or implied in the spoken text. Franklin's use of whooping heightens the experience for the listener. The lyrical drama moves one from listener to participant. Franklin knew the power of the known canon and preached this sermon at least once a year, beginning at age twenty-six and ultimately recording it in 1953. The sermon has been arranged in a format designed to capture as best possible its orality.*

## The Eagle Stirreth Her Nest (ca. 1941)

The eagle stirreth her nest. The eagle here is used to symbolize God's care and God's concern for his people. Many things have been used as symbolic expressions to give us a picture of God or some characteristics or one of his attributes. The ocean with her turbulent majesty, the mountains, the lions. Many things have been employed as pictures of either God's strength, or God's power, or God's love, or God's mercy. And, the psalmist has said that "the heavens declare the glory of God and the firmament shows forth his handiwork."[3] So, the eagle, here, is used as a symbol of God.

Now, in picturing God as an eagle stirring her nest, I believe history has been one big nest that God has been eternally stirring to make man better and to help us achieve world brotherhood. Some of the things that have gone on in your own experiences have merely been God stirring the nest of your circumstances. Now, the Civil War, for example, and the struggle in connection with it, was merely the prompting of providence to march man to a point of being brotherly to all men. In fact, all of the wars that we have gone through, we have come out with new outlooks and new views and better people. So, that throughout history, God has been stirring the various nests of circumstances surrounding us so that he could discipline us to first love ourselves and to help us to love one another and to help us hasten on the inauguration of the kingdom of God.

The eagle symbolizes God because there is something about an eagle that is a fixed symbol of things about God. In the first place, the eagle is the king of fowl. It is a regal or kingly bird. In that majesty, he represents the kingship of God or symbolizes the kingship of God. Listen, if you please. So, God is not merely a king. He is the king. Somebody hath said that he is the king of kings. For you see these little kings that we know, they've got to have a king over them. They've got to account to somebody for the deeds done in their bodies. But God is the king, and if the eagle is a kingly bird, in that way, he symbolizes the regalness and kingliness of our God.

In the second place, the eagle is strong. Somebody has said that as the eagle goes winging his way through the air, he can look down over a young lamb grazing by a mountainside and can fly down and just with the strength of his claws, pick up this young lamb and fly away to yonder cliff because he is strong. If the eagle is strong, then in that he is a symbol of God, for our God is strong. Our God is strong. Somebody has called him a fortress. So that when the enemy is pursuing me, I can run behind him. Somebody has called him a citadel of protection and redemption. Somebody else has said that he is so strong until they call him a leaning post that thousands can lean on him and he'll never give way. People have been leaning ever since time began in the Lord. Abraham leaned on him. Isaac and Jacob leaned on him. Moses and the prophets leaned on him. All of the early Christians leaned on him. People are leaning on him all over the world today, and he's never given way. He's strong.

In the second place he is swift. The eagle is swift. And, it is said that he can fly with such terrific speed that his wings can be heard roaring in the air. He's swift. And if he's swift in that way, he's a symbol of our God. For our God is swift. I said he's swift. Sometimes he'll answer you while you are calling him. He's swift. Daniel was thrown in a lion's den. And, Daniel knew him on the way to the lion's den. And, having met him, God had dispatched an angel from heaven and by the time Daniel got to the lion's den, the angel had changed the nature of the lions and made them lay down and act like lambs. He's swift. Swift. One night Peter was put in jail and the church went down on its knees to pray for him. And while the church was praying, Peter knocked on the door. God was so swift in answering prayer. So then, if the eagle is a swift bird, in that way, he represents or symbolizes the fact that God is swift. He's swift. If you get honest tonight and tell him about your troubles, he's swift to hear you. All you need is a little faith and ask him in grace.

Another thing about the eagle is that he has extraordinary sight. Extraordinary sight. Somebody said that he can rise to a lofty height in the air and look in the distance and see a storm hours away. That's extraordinary sight. And sometimes he can stand and gaze right into the sun because he has extraordinary sight. I want to tell you, my God has extraordinary sight. He can see every ditch that you have dug for me and guides me around it. God has extraordinary sight. He can look behind that smile on your face and see that frown in your heart. God has extraordinary sight.

Then, it is said, that an eagle builds a nest that is unusual. It is said, that the eagle selects rough material, basically, for the construction of her nest. And then, as the nest graduates towards a close or a finish, the material becomes finer and softer down at the end. And then, she goes about to set up residence in that nest. And, when the little eaglets are born, she goes out and brings in food to feed them. But, when they get to the point where they are old enough to be out on their own, the eagle will begin to pull out some of that fluff and let some of those thorns come through so that the nest won't be—you know—so comfortable. And, when they get to lounging around and roaming around, the thorns prick them here and there. Pray with me, if you please.

I believe God has to do that for us sometimes. Things are going so well and we are so satisfied that we just lounge around and forget to pray. You walk around all day and enjoy God's life, God's health, and God's strength and then go climb in the bed without saying, Thank you, Lord, for another day's journey. We'll do that. God has to pull out a little of the plush from around us, a little of the comfort around us and let a few thorns of trials and tribulations stick through the nest to make us pray sometimes. Isn't it so? For most of us forget God when things are going well with us. Most of us forget him.

It is said, that there was a man who had a poultry farm and that he raised chickens for the market. And, one day in one of his broods, he discovered a strange-looking bird that was very much unlike the other chickens on the yard. The man didn't pay too much attention, but he noticed as time went on that this strange-looking bird was unusual. He outgrew the other little chickens. His habits were strange and different. But, he let him grow on and mingle with the other chickens.

And then, one day a man who knew eagles when he saw them came along and saw that little eagle walking in the yard. And, he said to his friend, "Did you know that you have an eagle here?" The man said, "Well, I didn't really know it, but I knew he was different from the other chickens. I knew that his ways were different and I knew that his habits were different. And, he didn't act like the other chickens. But, I didn't know that he was an eagle." But the man said, "Yes, you have an eagle here on your yard. What you ought to do is build a cage because after awhile when he's a little older, he's going to get tired of the ground, and he's going to rise up on the pinion of his wings. And as he grows, you can change the cage and make it a little larger as he grows older and grows larger."

The man went out and built a cage and every day he would go in and feed the eagle. But, he grew a little older and a little older. His wings began to scrape on the sides of the cage and he had to build another cage and open the door of the other cage and let him into a larger cage. Oh, Lord. And, after awhile, he outgrew that one and he had to build another cage.

So, one day when the eagle had gotten grown, and his wings were twelve feet from tip to tip, he began to get restless in the cage. Yes he did. Well, he began to walk around and be uneasy. After a while, he heard noises in the air. A flock of eagles flew over and he heard their voices. Though he had never been around eagles, there was something about their voices that he heard that moved down in him and made him dissatisfied.

And, the man watched him as he walked around uneasy. He said, "Lord, my heart goes out to him. I believe I'll go and open the door and set the eagle free." He went there and opened the door. Yes. The eagle walked out, spread his wings and flapped them up and down. The eagle walked around a little longer and he flew up a little higher and into the barnyard. And, he sat there for a while. He moved up a little higher and flew into yonder tree. And then, he went on up a little higher and flew beyond a mountain.

One of these days my soul is going to move to a place that the Lord has made for me. My soul is caged in this old body. And, one of these days the man who made the cage will open the door and let my soul go home. You ought to be able to see me take the wings of my soul. I will fly away and be at rest. One of these old days when troubles and trials will be over, toil and tears are ended, one of these days my soul will take wings. My soul will take wings . . . in a few more days.

### *Notes*

*Sermon source: The African American Pulpit* 5, no. 1 (Winter 2001).
1. Jeff Todd Titon, *Give Me This Mountain, Rev. C.L. Franklin: Life History and Selected Sermons* (Urbana: University of Illinois Press, 1989), viii.
2. For information on the early preaching of "The Eagle Stirreth Its Nest," see Charles Lyell's *A Second Visit to North America*, vol. 1, 3rd ed. (London: Spottiswoodes and Shaw, New-Street-Square, 1855), especially chapter 2.
3. Psalm 19:1 (King James Version).

### *Bibliographical Source*

Salvatore, Nick. *Singing in a Strange Land: C.L. Franklin, the Black Church, and the Transformation of America.* New York: Little Brown & Company, 2005.

## MARTIN LUTHER KING JR.

*(1929–1968)*

Martin Luther King Jr. was born January 15, 1929, to Martin Luther King Sr., a pastor, and Alberta King, a schoolteacher. King was at the center of the civil rights movement during its decade of extraordinary achievement, between 1958 and 1968. He attended segregated public schools in Georgia, graduating from high school at the age of fifteen. In 1948, he received his bachelor's degree from Morehouse College in Atlanta. His encounter with Dr. Benjamin Mays, the distinguished pastor-scholar and president of Morehouse College, convinced the young King that a religious career could also be intellectually satisfying.

After three years of study at Crozer Theological Seminary in Pennsylvania, where he was elected president of the senior class, King won a fellowship for graduate studies at Boston University. In 1953 he married Coretta Scott and they had four children (Yolanda, Martin Luther King III, Dexter, and Bernice). King received his doctoral degree from Boston University in 1955. A year before receiving the doctorate, King returned to the South to become pastor of the Dexter Avenue Baptist Church in Montgomery, where he followed civil rights activist Rev. Vernon Johns. King also followed Johns in leading a nonviolent bus boycott protesting the mistreatment of African Americans. The boycott lasted for over a year, during which time King's home was bombed, his life threatened, and the African American protesters who joined King were met with state-sponsored brute force, but King and the protesters remained steadfast. By the time the boycott ended King was a national figure.

King was a preacher who spoke in biblical cadences perfect for leading a movement toward political and economic freedom that found its inspiration in Christianity and its operational tactics from Mahatma Gandhi. In 1957, King was elected president of the Southern Christian Leadership Conference, an organization created to lead the newly energized civil rights movement. In the next decade, King traveled and spoke widely, protesting wherever there was injustice; meanwhile he wrote five books, including *Stride Toward Freedom* (1958), *Strength to Love* (1963), and *Where Do We Go from Here?* (1967).

In these years, King also led a massive protest in Alabama that inspired his "Letter from a Birmingham Jail" (1963). In August 1963, King led more than a quarter million people at the March on Washington for Jobs and Freedom, where he delivered his famous speech, now known as the "I Have a Dream" speech. In 1964, *Time* magazine named King Man of the Year. King was regularly consulted by President John Kennedy and other political leaders. After the voter registration drive King led in Selma, Alabama, during which he called for fifteen hundred ministers to participate and they did, black and white alike, and many were beaten, President Lyndon Johnson signed the Voting Rights Act. King emerged not only as a leader of African Americans, but also of an internationally renowned movement for justice. At the age of thirty-five, he became the youngest man to receive the Nobel Peace Prize.

On April 4, 1968, while standing on the balcony of his motel room in Memphis, Tennessee, where he went to lead a protest march in support of striking city sanitation workers, King was assassinated. In 1986 Dr. King's birthday became a federal holiday, making King the only non-president or explorer and African American to be so honored.

• • •

*King had traveled to Memphis, Tennessee, to lead a march by and in support of striking sanitation workers. In preparation for the march, King spoke on April 3, 1968, at the Mason Temple Church of God in Christ. Earlier in the evening, King had asked his friend and ally in the civil rights movement, Reverend Ralph David Abernathy, to speak because King did not feel well. After arriving at the church and seeing the audience, Abernathy phoned King and told him he had to come and at least give brief remarks. Abernathy gave an extended and lengthy introduction of King. King followed and gave the following sermon without notes. It would be his last.*

*He was assassinated the next day. The audience response, which is typical of the black church, has been retained and placed in parentheses.*

## I'VE BEEN TO THE MOUNTAINTOP (APRIL 3, 1968)

Thank you very kindly, my friends. As I listened to Ralph Abernathy and his eloquent and generous introduction and then thought about myself, I wondered who he was talking about. (Laughter.) It's always good to have your closest friend and associate to say something good about you, and Ralph Abernathy is the best friend that I have in the world.

I'm delighted to see each of you here tonight in spite of a storm warning. You reveal that you are determined (Right.) to go on anyhow. (Yeah. Alright.) Something is happening in Memphis; something is happening in our world. And you know, if I were standing at the beginning of time, with the possibility of taking a kind of general and panoramic view of the whole of human history up to now, and the Almighty said to me, "Martin Luther King, which age would you like to live in?" I would take my mental flight by Egypt (Yeah.) and I would watch God's children in their magnificent trek from the dark dungeons of Egypt through, or rather across the Red Sea, through the wilderness on toward the Promised Land. And, in spite of its magnificence, I wouldn't stop there. (Alright.)

I would move on by Greece, and take my mind to Mount Olympus. And I would see Plato, Aristotle, Socrates, Euripides and Aristophanes assembled around the Parthenon (Applause.) and, I would watch them around the Parthenon as they discussed the great and eternal issues of reality. But I wouldn't stop there. (Oh yeah.)

I would go on, even to the great heyday of the Roman Empire (Yes.) and I would see developments around there, through various emperors and leaders. But I wouldn't stop there. (Keep on.)

I would even come up to the day of the Renaissance and get a quick picture of all that the Renaissance did for the cultural and aesthetic life of man. But I wouldn't stop there. (Yeah.) I would even go by the way that the man for whom I'm named had his habitat and I would watch Martin Luther as he tacks his ninety-five theses on the door at the church in Wittenberg. But I wouldn't stop there. (Alright.)

I would come on up even to 1863 and watch a vacillating president by the name of Abraham Lincoln finally come to the conclusion that he had to sign the Emancipation Proclamation. But I wouldn't stop there. (Yeah.) (Applause.)

I would even come up to the early thirties and see a man grappling with the problems of the bankruptcy of his nation, and come with an eloquent cry that "We have nothing to fear but fear itself." But I wouldn't stop there. (Alright.)

Strangely enough, I would turn to the Almighty, and say, "If you allow me to live just a few years in the second half of the twentieth century, I will be happy." (Applause.) Now that's a strange statement to make, because the world is all messed up. The nation is sick. Trouble is in the land; confusion all around. That's a strange statement. But I know, somehow, that only when it is dark enough can you see the stars. (Alright, yes.) And I see God working in this period of the twentieth century in a way that men, in some strange way, are responding—something is happening in our world. (Yeah.) The masses of people are rising up. And wherever they are assembled today, whether they are in Johannesburg, South Africa; Nairobi, Kenya; Accra, Ghana; New York City; Atlanta, Georgia; Jackson, Mississippi; or Memphis, Tennessee—the cry is always the same—"We want to be free." (Applause.)

And, another reason that I'm happy to live in this period is that we have been forced to a point where we're going to have to grapple with the problems that men have been trying to grapple with through history, but the demands didn't force them to do it. Survival demands that we grapple with them. (Yes.) Men, for years now, have been talking about war and peace. But now, no longer can they just talk about it. It is no longer a choice between violence and nonviolence in this world; it's nonviolence or nonexistence. That is where we are today. (Applause.)

And also, in the human rights revolution, if something isn't done, and done in a hurry, to bring the colored peoples of the world out of their long years of poverty, their long years of hurt and neglect, the whole world is doomed. (Alright.) (Applause.) Now, I'm just happy that God has allowed me to live in this period, to see what is unfolding. And, I'm happy that He's allowed me to be in Memphis. (Oh yeah.) (Applause.)

I can remember (Applause.) I can remember when Negroes were just going around as Ralph has said, so often, scratching where they didn't itch, and laughing when they were not tickled. (Laughter, applause.) But that day is all over. (Yeah.) (Applause.) We mean business now, and we are determined to gain our rightful place in God's world. (Yeah.) (Applause.) And that's all this whole thing is about. We aren't engaged in any negative protest and in any negative arguments with anybody. We are saying that we are determined to be men. We are determined to be people. (Yeah.) We are saying that we are God's children. (Yeah.) (Applause.) And if we are God's children, that we don't have to live like we are forced to live.

Now, what does all of this mean in this great period of history? It means that we've got to stay together. (Yeah.) We've got to stay together and maintain unity. You know, whenever Pharaoh wanted to prolong the period of slavery in Egypt, he had a favorite, favorite formula for doing it. What was that? He kept the slaves fighting among themselves. (Applause.) But whenever the slaves get together, something happens in Pharaoh's court, and he cannot hold the slaves in slavery. When the slaves get together, that's the beginning of getting out of slavery. (Applause.) Now let us maintain unity.

Secondly, let us keep the issues where they are. (Right.) The issue is injustice. The issue is the refusal of Memphis to be fair and honest in its dealings with its public servants, who happen to be sanitation workers. Now, we've got to keep attention on that. (That's right.) That's always the problem with a little violence. You know what happened the other day, and the press dealt only with the window-breaking.[1] (That's right.) I read the articles. They very seldom got around to mentioning the fact that one thousand, three hundred sanitation workers were on strike, and that Memphis is not being fair to them, and that Mayor Loeb is in dire need of a doctor. They didn't get around to that. (Yeah.) (Applause.)

Now we're going to march again, and we've got to march again, (Yeah.) in order to put the issue where it is supposed to be (Yeah.)

(Applause.)—and force everybody to see that there are thirteen hundred of God's children here suffering, (That's right.) sometimes going hungry, going through dark and dreary nights wondering how this thing is going to come out. That's the issue. (That's right.) And, we've got to say to the nation: we know how it's coming out. For when people get caught up with that which is right and they are willing to sacrifice for it, there is no stopping point short of victory. (Applause.)

We aren't going to let any mace stop us. We are masters in our nonviolent movement in disarming police forces; they don't know what to do, I've seen them so often. I remember in Birmingham, Alabama, when we were in that majestic struggle there, we would move out of the Sixteenth Street Baptist Church day after day. By the hundreds we would move out, and Bull Connor would tell them to send the dogs forth, and they did come; but we just went before the dogs singing, "Ain't gonna let nobody turn me around." (Applause.) Bull Connor next would say, "Turn the fire hoses on." And, as I said to you the other night, Bull Connor didn't know history. He knew a kind of physics that somehow didn't relate to the transphysics that we knew about. And that was the fact that there was a certain kind of fire that no water could put out. (Applause.) And we went before the fire hoses. (Yeah.) We had known water. (Alright.) If we were Baptist or some other denomination, we had been immersed. If we were Methodist, and some others, we had been sprinkled, but we knew water. That couldn't stop us. (Applause.)

And we just went on before the dogs and we would look at them; and we'd go on before the water hoses and we would look at it, and we'd just go on singing, "Over my head I see freedom in the air." (Yeah.) (Applause.) And then, we would be thrown in the paddy wagons, and sometimes we were stacked in there like sardines in a can. And they would throw us in, and old Bull would say, "Take 'em off," and they did and we would just go in the paddy wagon singing, "We Shall Overcome." (Yeah.) And every now and then we'd get in the jail, and we'd see the jailers looking through the windows being moved by our prayers (Yeah.) and being moved by our words and our songs. (Yeah.) And there was a power there which Bull Connor couldn't adjust to (Alright.) and so we ended up transforming Bull into a steer, and we won our struggle in Birmingham. (Applause.)

Now we've got to go on in Memphis just like that. I call upon you to be with us when we go out on Monday. (Yes.) Now about injunctions: We have an injunction and we're going into court tomorrow morning (Go ahead.) to fight this illegal, unconstitutional injunction. All we say to America is, "Be true to what you said on paper." (Oh yes.) (Applause.) If I lived in China or even Russia, or any totalitarian country, maybe I could understand the denial of certain basic First Amendment privileges, because they hadn't committed themselves to that over there. But somewhere I read of the freedom of assembly. Somewhere I read (Yes.) of the freedom of speech. (Yes.) Somewhere I read (Yes.) of the freedom of the press. Somewhere I read (Yes.) that the greatness of America is the right to protest for rights. (Applause.) And so, just as I say, we aren't going to let any dogs or water hoses turn us around; we aren't going to let any injunction turn us around. (Applause.) We are going on. We need all of you.

And you know what's beautiful to me, is to see all of these ministers of the Gospel. (Amen.) It's a marvelous picture. (Yes.) Who is it that is supposed to articulate the longings and aspirations of the people more than the preacher? Somehow the preacher must have a kind of fire shut up in his bones, (Yes.) and whenever injustice is around he must tell it. (Yeah.) Somehow the preacher must be an Amos, who said, "When God speaks, who can but prophesy?" (Yes.) Again with Amos, "Let justice roll down like waters and righteousness like a mighty stream."[2] (Yes.) Somehow, the preacher must say with Jesus, "The spirit of the Lord is upon me, (Yes.) because he hath anointed me to deal with the problems of the poor."[3] (Go ahead.)

And I want to commend the preachers, under the leadership of these noble men: James Lawson, one who has been in this struggle for many years. He's been to jail for struggling; he's been kicked out of Vanderbilt University for this struggling; but he's still going on, fighting for the rights of his people. (Applause.) Reverend Ralph Jackson, Billy Kyles; I could just go right on down the list, but time will not permit. But, I want to thank all of them and I want you to thank them, because so often, preachers aren't concerned about anything but themselves. (Applause.) And, I'm always happy to see a relevant ministry. It's all right to talk about "long white robes over yonder," in all of its symbolism. But ultimately, people want some suits and dresses and shoes to wear down here. (Applause.) It's all right to talk about streets flowing with milk and honey, but God has commanded us to be concerned about the slums down here, and his children who can't eat three square meals a day. (Applause.) It's all right to talk about the new Jerusalem, but one day, God's preachers must talk about the new New York, the new Atlanta, the new Philadelphia, the new Los Angeles, the new Memphis, Tennessee. (Yes.) (Applause.) This is what we have to do.

Now the other thing we'll have to do is this: always anchor our external direct action with the power of economic withdrawal. Now, we are poor people. Individually, we are poor when you compare us with white society in America. We are poor. Never stop and forget that collectively—that means all of us together—collectively we are richer than all the nations in the world, with the exception of nine. Did you ever think about that? After you leave the United States, Soviet Russia, Great Britain, West Germany, France, and I could name the others, the American Negro collectively is richer than most nations of the world. We have an annual income of more than thirty billion dollars a year, which is more than all of the exports of the United States, and more than the national budget of Canada. Did you know that? That's power right there, if we know how to pool it. (Yeah.) (Applause.)

We don't have to argue with anybody. We don't have to curse and go around acting bad with our words. We don't need any bricks and bottles. We don't need any Molotov cocktails. (Yes.) We just need to go around to these stores, (Yes, sir.) and to these massive industries in our country, (Amen.) and say, "God sent us by here, (Alright.) to say to you that you're not treating his children right. (That's right.) And we've come by here to ask you to make the first item on your agenda fair treatment, where God's children are concerned. Now, if you are not prepared to do that, we do have an agenda that we must follow. (Alright.) And our agenda calls for withdrawing economic support from you." (Applause.)

And so, as a result of this, we are asking you tonight, (Amen.) to go out and tell your neighbors not to buy Coca-Cola in Memphis. (Yeah.) (Applause.) Go by and tell them not to buy Sealtest milk. (Yeah.) (Applause.) Tell them not to buy—what is the other bread?—Wonder Bread. (Yes.) (Applause.) And, what is the other bread company, Jesse? Tell them not to buy Hart's bread. (Applause.) As Jesse Jackson has said, up to now, only the garbage men have been feeling pain; now we must kind of redistribute the pain. (Applause.) We are choosing these companies because they haven't been fair in their hiring policies and we are choosing them because they can begin the process of saying they are going to support the needs and the rights of these men who are on strike. And then, they can move on downtown and tell Mayor Loeb to do what is right. (That's right. Speak.) (Applause.)

But, not only that, we've got to strengthen black institutions. (That's right. Yeah.) I call upon you to take your money out of the banks downtown and deposit your money in Tri-State Bank. (Yeah.) (Applause.) We want a "bank-in" movement in Memphis. (Yes.) So go by the savings and loan association. I'm not asking you something we don't do ourselves at SCLC. Judge Hooks and others will tell you that we have an account here in the savings and loan association from the Southern Christian Leadership Conference. We're just telling you to follow what we're doing. Put your money there. (Applause.) You have six or seven black insurance companies in Memphis. Take out your insurance there. We want to have an "insurance-in." (Applause.) Now these are some practical things we can do. We begin the process of building a greater economic base. And at the same time, we are putting pressure where it really hurts. (There you go.) I ask you to follow through here. (Applause.)

Now, let me say as I move to my conclusion that we've got to give ourselves to this struggle until the end. (Amen.) Nothing would be more tragic than to stop at this point in Memphis. We've got to see it through. (Applause.) And when we have our march, you need to be there. If it means leaving work, if it means leaving school, be there. (Amen.) (Applause.) Be concerned about your brother. You may not be on strike (Yeah.) but either we go up together, or we go down together. (Applause.) Let us develop a kind of dangerous unselfishness.

One day a man came to Jesus; and he wanted to raise some questions about some vital matters in life. At points, he wanted to trick Jesus, (That's right.) and show him that he knew a little more than Jesus knew, and through this, throw him off base. [Recording interrupted] Now that question could have easily ended up in a philosophical and theological debate. But Jesus immediately pulled that question from mid-air, and placed it on a dangerous curve between Jerusalem and Jericho. (Yeah.) And he talked about a certain man, who fell among thieves. (Sure.) You remember that a Levite (Sure.) and a priest passed by on the other side; they didn't stop to help him. And finally, a man of another race came by. (Yes, sir.) He got down from his beast, decided not to be compassionate by proxy. But, he got down with him, administered first aid, and helped the man in need. Jesus ended up saying, this was the good man, this was the great man, because he had the capacity to project the "I" into the "thou," and to be concerned about his brother.

Now you know, we use our imagination a great deal to try to determine why the priest and the Levite didn't stop. At times we say they were busy going to church meetings—an ecclesiastical gathering—and they had to get on down to Jerusalem so they wouldn't be late for their meeting. (Yeah.) At other times, we would speculate that there was a religious law that one who was engaged in religious ceremonials was not to touch a human body twenty-four hours before the ceremony. (Alright.) And every now and then we begin to wonder whether maybe they were not going down to Jerusalem, or down to Jericho, rather to organize a Jericho Road Improvement Association. (Laughter.) That's a possibility. Maybe they felt that it was better to deal with the problem from the causal root, rather than to get bogged down with an individual effort. (Laughter.)

But, I'm going to tell you what my imagination tells me. It's possible that these men were afraid. You see, the Jericho road is a dangerous road. (That's right.) I remember when Mrs. King and I were first in Jerusalem. We rented a car and drove from Jerusalem down to Jericho. (Yeah.) And as soon as we got on that road, I said to my wife, "I can see why Jesus used this as a setting for his parable." It's a winding, meandering road. (Yes.) It's really conducive for ambushing. You start out in Jerusalem, which is about twelve hundred miles, or rather twelve hundred feet above sea level. And by the time you get down to Jericho, fifteen or twenty minutes later, you're about twenty-two hundred feet below sea level. That's a dangerous road. (Yeah.) In the days of Jesus it came to be known as the "Bloody Pass." And you know, it's possible that the priest and the Levite looked over that man on the ground and wondered if the robbers were still around. (Go ahead.) Or, it's possible that they felt that the man on the ground was merely faking. (Yeah.) And, he was acting like he had been robbed and hurt, in order to seize them over there, lure them there for quick and easy seizure. (Oh yeah.) And so, the first question that the priest asked—the first question that the Levite asked was, "If I stop to help this man, what will happen to me?"

But then the Good Samaritan came by and he reversed the question: "If I do not stop to help this man, what will happen to him?" (Yeah.) That's the question before you tonight. (Yes.) Not, "If I stop to help the sanitation workers, what will happen to my job?" Not, "If I stop to help the sanitation workers what will happen to all of the hours that I usually spend in my office every day and every week as a pastor?" (Yes.) The question is not, "If I stop to help this man in need, what will happen to me?" The question is, "If I do not stop to help the sanitation workers, what will happen to them?" That's the question. (Applause.)

Let us rise up tonight with a greater readiness. Let us stand with a greater determination. And let us move on in these powerful days, these days of challenge to make America what it ought to be. We have an opportunity to make America a better nation. (Amen.)

And I want to thank God, once more, for allowing me to be here with you. (Yes sir.) You know, several years ago, I was in New York City autographing the first book that I had written. And, while sitting there autographing books, a demented black woman came up. The only question I heard from her was, "Are you Martin Luther King?" And, I was looking down writing, and I said yes. And, the next minute I felt something beating on my chest. Before I knew it I had been stabbed by this demented woman. I was rushed to Harlem Hospital. It was a dark Saturday afternoon. And, that blade had gone through, and the X-rays revealed that the tip of the blade was on the edge of my aorta, the main artery. And once that's punctured, you're drowned in your own blood; that's the end of you. (Yes sir.)

It came out in the *New York Times* the next morning, that if I had merely sneezed, I would have died. Well, about four days later, they allowed me, after the operation, after my chest had been opened, and the blade had been taken out, to move around in the wheelchair in the hospital. They allowed me to read some of the mail that came in, and from all over the states, and the world, kind letters came in. I read a few, but one of them I will never forget. I had received one from the president and the vice president. I've forgotten what those telegrams said. I'd received a visit and a letter from the governor of New York, but I've forgotten what that letter said. (Yes.) But, there was another letter (Alright.) that came from a little girl, a young girl who was a student at the White Plains High School. And I looked at that letter, and I'll never forget it. It said simply, "Dear Dr. King: I am a ninth-grade student at the White Plains High School." And she said, "While it should not matter, I would like to mention that I'm a white girl. I read in the paper of your misfortune and of your suffering. And I read that if you had sneezed, you would have died. And I'm simply writing you to say that I'm so happy that you didn't sneeze." (Yes.) (Applause.)

And I want to say tonight, (Applause.) I want to say tonight that I too am happy that I didn't sneeze. Because if I had sneezed, (Alright.) I wouldn't have been around here in 1960, (Well.) when students all over the South started sitting in at lunch counters. And, I knew that as they were sitting in, they were really standing up (Yes sir.) for the best in the American dream, and taking the whole nation back to those great wells of democracy which were dug deep by the founding fathers in the Declaration of Independence and the Constitution. If I had sneezed, (Yes.) I wouldn't have been around here in 1961, when we decided to take a ride for freedom and ended segregation in interstate travel. (Alright.) If I had sneezed, (Yes.) I wouldn't have been around here in 1962, when Negroes in Albany, Georgia, decided to straighten their backs up. And whenever men and women straighten their backs up, they are going somewhere, because a man can't ride your back unless it is bent. If I had sneezed, (Applause.) if I had sneezed I wouldn't have been here in 1963, (Alright.) when the black people of Birmingham, Alabama, aroused the conscience of this nation, and brought into being the Civil Rights Bill. If I had sneezed, I wouldn't have a chance later that year, in August, to try to tell America about a dream that I had had. (Yes.) If I had sneezed, I wouldn't have been down in Selma, Alabama, to see the great movement there. If I had sneezed, I wouldn't have been in Memphis to see a community rally around those brothers and sisters who are suffering. (Yes.) I'm so happy that I didn't sneeze. (Yes.)

And they were telling me. (Applause.) Now it doesn't matter now. (Go ahead.) It really doesn't matter what happens now. I left Atlanta this morning, and as we got started on the plane, there were six of us, the pilot said over the public address system, "We are sorry for the delay, but we have Dr. Martin Luther King on the plane. And to be sure that all of the bags were checked, and to be sure that nothing would be wrong with the plane, we had to check out everything carefully. And we've had the plane protected and guarded all night." And then, I got into Memphis. And some began to say the threats, or talk about the threats that were out (Yeah.) or what would happen to me from some of our sick white brothers.

Well, I don't know what will happen now. We've got some difficult days ahead. (Amen.) But it doesn't matter with me now. Because I've been to the mountaintop. (Yeah.) (Applause.) and I don't mind. (Applause continues.) Like anybody, I would like to live a long life. Longevity has its place. But I'm not concerned about that now. I just want to do God's will. (Yeah.) And He's allowed me to go up to the mountain. (Go ahead.) And I've looked over. (Yes sir.) And I've seen the Promised Land. (Go ahead.) I may not get there with you. (Go ahead.) But I want you to know tonight, (Yeaahhh.) that we, as a people, will get to the Promised Land! (Applause.) (Go ahead.) And so I'm happy, tonight. I'm not worried about anything. I'm not fearing any man! Mine eyes have seen the glory of the coming of the Lord! (Extended applause.)

## *Notes*

*Sermon source:* Martin Luther King, Jr., Research and Education Center, Papers Project, http://stanford.edu/group/King/speeches/pub/I%27ve_been_to_the_mountaintop.html (accessed June 4, 2008).

1. On March 28, 1968, King led a protest march in Memphis that ended with violence and led to King returning to Memphis on April 3, 1968, to lead a nonviolent march, the occasion of this speech.
2. See Amos 5:24.
3. See Luke 4:18.

## *Bibliographical Sources*

Dyson, Michael Eric. *I May Not Get There With You: The True Martin Luther King Jr.* New York: Free Press, 2000.

Garrow, David. *Bearing the Cross: Martin Luther King and the Southern Christian Leadership Conference.* New York: Quill, 1986.

King, Coretta Scott. *My Life with Martin Luther King Jr.* New York: Henry Holt, 1993.

King, Martin Luther, Jr. *The Papers of Martin Luther King Jr.*, ed. Clayborne Carson, Ralph E. Luker, and Penny A. Russell. Berkeley: University of California Press, 1992.

———. *Strength to Love.* New York: Harper & Row, 1963.

———. *Stride Toward Freedom: The Montgomery Story.* New York: Harper & Row, 1968.

———. *Where Do We Go from Here: Chaos or Community?* New York: Harper & Row, 1967.

Washington, James, ed. *A Testament of Hope: The Essential Writings and Speeches of Martin Luther King, Jr.* San Francisco: HarperCollins, 1986.

# MALCOLM X (EL HAJJ MALIK EL-SHABAZZ)

*(1925–1965)*

In 1925 Malcolm Little (later known as Malcolm X and El Hajj Malik El-Shabazz) was born in Omaha, Nebraska, to Earl Little, a Baptist preacher from Georgia, and Louise Norton. Malcolm was Earl's seventh child (he had three by a previous marriage) and Louise's fourth. A year later the family moved to Milwaukee. In 1927 the Littles had another child. The following year they moved to Lansing, Michigan, where their home was burned to the ground about four months later. In 1931 Malcolm's father was killed by a streetcar. It is rumored that he was murdered by a white supremacist group. In 1938 Malcolm was placed with a foster family, and in 1939 his mother was declared legally insane and institutionalized. She remained in a Michigan mental hospital for twenty-six years, released in 1963. After his mother was institutionalized, Malcolm was placed in a juvenile home. A year later he was placed in a series of foster homes. In 1941 he moved to Boston and stayed with his half-sister.

From 1941 to 1946 Malcolm held a variety of jobs, including lounge performer. During this period he also sold drugs, stole, and was charged with breaking and entering. Eventually he was arrested, and with poor legal counsel and due to unequal sentences for blacks, he received a stiff sentence. After entering prison he was introduced to the Nation of Islam (NOI) by his brother Reginald. He gave up foul language, drug use, and tobacco and began to educate himself by reading anything he could while in prison.

In 1952 he was paroled from Massachusetts State Prison after serving seven years of his ten-year sentence. By 1953 he began attending NOI meetings, moving to Chicago and living with Elijah Muhammad while studying to become an NOI minister. He became the minister of the Boston Temple No. 11 and eventually of a temple in New York and one in Philadelphia.

In 1957 Malcolm gained notoriety for urging NOI member Hinton Johnson to sue police officers who beat him, and eventually the suit was settled in Johnson's favor. In 1958, Malcolm married Betty Sanders (also called Betty X and later Betty Shabazz); their first daughter was born the same year. In 1959 Malcolm began to speak for the NOI throughout the country. He published articles and appeared at universities, colleges, and on local and national television programs. Many were attracted to his message, although the white press often branded him as a hate monger. In 1960 a second daughter was born and in 1962 a third. In 1963 he delivered one of his most famous speeches, "A Message to the Grass Roots," at a conference in Detroit.

Malcolm wanted NOI to become more involved in political activities and began to question Elijah Muhammad's morality after hearing that Elijah was engaged in adulterous affairs. During this period Malcolm was silenced for ninety days by Minister Muhammad for saying about the assassination of John F. Kennedy that "chickens had come home to roost." After twelve years Malcolm left the NOI and established his own mosque and the Organization of Afro-American Unity. After a lawsuit, NOI ordered Malcolm to relinquish his home and car, both of which were owned by NOI.

In 1964 Malcolm took a second trip to the Middle East, where he was warmly received and able to see Islam practiced by persons of various races. He returned to America and renounced the brand of Islam that preached hate toward anyone and began practicing as a Sunni Muslim. His fourth daughter was also born in 1964. He began working with civil rights leaders. He was under constant surveillance by government entities, especially the FBI. In 1965 his New York home was bombed. Fourteen days later he was assassinated in the Audubon Ballroom, and three members of the NOI were indicted for his murder. Thirty thousand mourners filed through the Unity Funeral Home to view his body. His funeral was held in Harlem and led by playwright-actor Ossie Davis. Several months after her husband's assassination, Betty Shabazz gave birth to twin girls. She was a widow with six children (Attalah, Qubilah,

Ilyasah, Gamilah, Malaak, and Malikah), but nevertheless quietly continued her husband's legacy of speaking against injustice until her death in 1997 at age sixty-one.

• • •

*The following message, one of Malcolm X's most famous, was given at the Cory Methodist Church in Cleveland, Ohio. The meeting, sponsored by the Cleveland chapter of the Congress of Racial Equality, took the form of a symposium entitled, "The Negro Revolt—What Comes Next?" The speech represents an articulate and masterful performance of oratorical rage in the public space. Malcolm X's rhetoric functioned to raise the esteem and dignity of African American people.*

## The Ballot or the Bullet (April 3, 1964)

Mr. Moderator, Brother Lomax, brothers and sisters, friends and enemies: I just can't believe everyone in here is a friend, and I don't want to leave anybody out. The question tonight, as I understand it, is "The Negro Revolt, and Where Do We Go From Here? or What Next?" In my little humble way of understanding it, it points toward either the ballot or the bullet.

Before we try and explain what is meant by the ballot or the bullet, I would like to clarify something concerning myself. I'm still a Muslim; my religion is still Islam. That's my personal belief. Just as Adam Clayton Powell is a Christian minister who heads the Abyssinian Baptist Church in New York, but at the same time takes part in the political struggles to try and bring about rights to the black people in this country; and Dr. Martin Luther King is a Christian minister down in Atlanta, Georgia, who heads another organization fighting for the civil rights of black people in this country; and Reverend Galamison, I guess you've heard of him, is another Christian minister in New York who has been deeply involved in the school boycotts to eliminate segregated education; well, I myself am a minister, not a Christian minister, but a Muslim minister; and I believe in action on all fronts by whatever means necessary.

Although I'm still a Muslim, I'm not here tonight to discuss my religion. I'm not here to try and change your religion. I'm not here to argue or discuss anything that we differ about, because it's time for us to submerge our differences and realize that it is best for us to first see that we have the same problem, a common problem, a problem that will make you catch hell whether you're a Baptist, or a Methodist, or a Muslim, or a nationalist. Whether you're educated or illiterate, whether you live on the boulevard or in the alley, you're going to catch hell just like I am. We're all in the same boat and we all are going to catch the same hell from the same man. He just happens to be a white man. All of us have suffered here, in this country, political oppression at the hands of the white man, economic exploitation at the hands of the white man, and social degradation at the hands of the white man.

Now in speaking like this, it doesn't mean that we're anti-white, but it does mean we're anti-exploitation, we're anti-degradation, we're anti-oppression. And if the white man doesn't want us to be anti-him, let him stop oppressing and exploiting and degrading us. Whether we are Christians, or Muslims, or nationalists, or agnostics, or atheists, we must first learn to forget our differences. If we have differences, let us differ in the closet; when we come out in front, let us not have anything to argue about until we get finished arguing with the man. If the late President Kennedy could get together with Khrushchev and exchange some wheat, we certainly have more in common with each other than Kennedy and Khrushchev had with each other. If we don't do something real soon, I think you'll have to agree that we're going to be forced either to use the ballot or the bullet. It's one or the other in 1964. It isn't that time is running out—time has run out!

Nineteen sixty-four threatens to be the most explosive year America has ever witnessed. The most explosive year. Why? It's also a political year. It's the year when all of the white politicians will be back in the so-called Negro community jiving you and me for some votes. The year when all of the white political crooks will be right back in your and my community with their false promises, building up our hopes for a letdown, with their trickery and their treachery, with their false promises which they don't intend to keep. As they nourish these dissatisfactions, it can only lead to one thing, an explosion; and now we have the type of black man on the scene in America today—I'm sorry, Brother Lomax—who just doesn't intend to turn the other cheek any longer.

Don't let anybody tell you anything about the odds are against you. If they draft you, they send you to Korea and make you face eight hundred million Chinese. If you can be brave over there, you can be brave right here. These odds aren't as great as those odds. And if you fight here, you will at least know what you're fighting for.

I'm not a politician, not even a student of politics; in fact, I'm not a student of much of anything. I'm not a Democrat. I'm not a Republican, and I don't even consider myself an American. If you and I were Americans, there'd be no problem. Those Honkies that just got off the boat, they're already Americans; Polacks are already Americans; the Italian refugees are already Americans. Everything that came out of Europe, every blue-eyed thing, is already an American. And, as long as you and I have been over here, we aren't Americans yet.

Well, I am one who doesn't believe in deluding myself. I'm not going to sit at your table and watch you eat, with nothing on my plate, and call myself a diner. Sitting at the table doesn't make you a diner, unless you eat some of what's on that plate. Being here in America doesn't make you an American. Being born here in America doesn't make you an American. Why, if birth made you American, you wouldn't need any legislation; you wouldn't need any amendments to the Constitution; you wouldn't be faced with civil-rights filibustering in Washington, D.C., right now. They don't have to pass civil-rights legislation to make a Polack an American.

No, I'm not an American. I'm one of the twenty-two million black people who are the victims of Americanism. One of the twenty-two million black people who are the victims of democracy, nothing but disguised hypocrisy. So, I'm not standing here speaking to you as an American, or a patriot, or a flag-saluter, or a flag-waver—no, not I. I'm speaking as a victim of this American system. And I see America through the eyes of the victim. I don't see any American dream; I see an American nightmare.

These twenty-two million victims are waking up. Their eyes are coming open. They're beginning to see what they used to only look at. They're becoming politically mature. They are realizing that there are new political trends from coast to coast. As they see these new political trends, it's possible for them to see that every time there's an election the races are so close that they have to have a recount. They had to recount in Massachusetts to see who was going to be governor, it was so close. It was the same way in Rhode Island, in Minnesota, and in many other parts of the country. And the same with Kennedy and Nixon when they ran for president. It was so close they had to count all over again. Well, what does this mean? It means that when white people are evenly divided, and black people have a bloc of votes of their own, it is left up to them to determine who's going to sit in the White House and who's going to be in the dog house.

It was the black man's vote that put the present administration in Washington, D.C. Your vote, your dumb vote, your ignorant vote, your wasted vote put in an administration in Washington, D.C., that has seen fit to pass every kind of legislation imaginable, saving you until last, then filibustering on top of that. And your and my leaders have the audacity to run around clapping their hands and talk about how much progress we're making. And what a good president we have. If he wasn't good in Texas, he sure can't be good in Washington, D.C. Because Texas is a lynch state. It is in the same breath as Mississippi, no different; only they lynch you in Texas with a Texas accent and lynch you in Mississippi with a Mississippi accent. And these Negro leaders have the audacity to go and have some coffee in the White House with a Texan, a Southern cracker—that's all he is—and then come out and tell you and me that he's going to be better for us because, since he's from the South, he knows how to deal with the Southerners. What kind of logic is that? Let Eastland be president, he's from the South too. He should be better able to deal with them than Johnson.

In this present administration, they have in the House of Representatives 257 Democrats to only 177 Republicans. They control two-thirds of the House vote. Why can't they pass something that will help you and me? In the Senate, there are 67 senators who are of the Democratic Party. Only 33 of them are Republicans. Why, the Democrats have got the government sewed up, and you're the one who sewed it up for them. And what have they given you for it? Four years in office, and just now getting around to some civil-rights legislation. Just now, after everything else is gone, out of the way, they're going to sit down now and play with you all summer long—the same old giant con game that they call filibuster. All those are in cahoots together. Don't you ever think they're not in cahoots together, for the man that is heading the civil rights filibuster is a man from Georgia named Richard Russell. When Johnson became president, the first man he asked for when he got back to Washington, D.C., was "Dicky"—that's how tight they are. That's his boy, that's his pal, that's his buddy. But they're playing that old con game. One of them makes believe he's for you, and he's got it fixed where the other one is so tight against you, he never has to keep his promise.

So, it's time in 1964 to wake up. And when you see them coming up with that kind of conspiracy, let them know your eyes are open. And let them know you—something else that's wide open too. It's got to be the ballot or the bullet. The ballot or the bullet. If you're afraid to use an expression like that, you should get on out of the country; you should get back in the cotton patch; you should get back in the alley. They get all the Negro vote, and after they get it, the Negro gets nothing in return. All they did when they got to Washington was give a few big Negroes big jobs. Those big Negroes didn't need big jobs, they already had jobs. That's camouflage, that's trickery, that's treachery, window-dressing. I'm not trying to knock out the Democrats for the Republicans. We'll get to them in a minute. But, it is true; you put the Democrats first and the Democrats put you last.

Look at it the way it is. What alibis do they use, since they control Congress and the Senate? What alibi do they use when you and I ask, "Well, when are you going to keep your promise?" They blame the Dixiecrats. What is a Dixiecrat? A Democrat. A Dixiecrat is nothing but a Democrat in disguise. The titular head of the Democrats is also the head of the Dixiecrats, because the Dixiecrats are a part of the Democratic Party. The Democrats have never kicked the Dixiecrats out of the party. The Dixiecrats bolted themselves once, but the Democrats didn't put them out. I imagine these lowdown Southern segregationists put the Northern Democrats down. But, the Northern Democrats have never put the Dixiecrats down. No, look at that thing the way it is. They have got a con game going on, a political con game, and you and I are in the middle. It's time for you and me to wake up and start looking at it like it is, and trying to understand it like it is; and then we can deal with it like it is.

The Dixiecrats in Washington, D.C., control the key committees that run the government. The only reason the Dixiecrats control these committees is because they have seniority. The only reason they have seniority is because they come from states where Negroes can't vote. This is not even a government that's based on democracy. It is not a government that is made up of representatives of the people. Half of the people in the South can't even vote. Eastland is not even supposed to be in Washington. Half of the senators and congressmen who occupy these key positions in Washington, D.C., are there illegally, are there unconstitutionally.

I was in Washington, D.C., a week ago Thursday, when they were debating whether or not they should let the bill come onto the floor. And in the back of the room where the Senate meets, there's a huge map of the United States, and on that map it shows the location of Negroes throughout the country. And it shows that the Southern section of the country, the states that are most heavily concentrated with Negroes, are the ones that have senators and congressmen standing up filibustering and doing all other kinds of trickery to keep the Negro from being able to vote. This is pitiful. But it's not pitiful for us any longer; it's actually pitiful for the white man, because soon now, as the Negro awakens a little more and sees the vise that he's in, sees the bag that he's in, sees the real game that he's in, then the Negro's going to develop a new tactic.

These senators and congressmen actually violate the constitutional amendments that guarantee the people of that particular state or county the right to vote. And the Constitution itself has within it the machinery to expel any representative from a state where the voting rights of the people are violated. You don't even need new legislation. Any person in Congress right now, who is there from a state or a district where the voting rights of the people are violated, that particular person should be expelled from Congress. And when you expel him, you've removed one of the obstacles in the path of any real meaningful legislation in this country. In fact, when you expel them, you don't need new legislation, because they will be replaced by black representatives from counties and districts where the black man is in the majority, not in the minority.

If the black man in these Southern states had his full voting rights, the key Dixiecrats in Washington, D.C., which means the key Democrats in Washington, D.C., would lose their seats. The Democratic Party itself would lose its power. It would cease to be powerful as a party. When you see the amount of power that would be lost by the Democratic Party if it were to lose the Dixiecrat wing, or branch, or element, you can see where it's against the interests of the Democrats to give voting rights to Negroes in states where the Democrats have been in complete power and authority ever since the Civil War. You just can't belong to that Party without analyzing it.

I say again, I'm not anti-Democrat, I'm not anti-Republican, I'm not anti-anything. I'm just questioning their sincerity, and some of the strategy that they've been using on our people by promising them promises that they don't intend to keep. When you keep the Democrats in power, you're keeping the Dixiecrats in power. I doubt that my good Brother Lomax will deny that. A vote for a Democrat is a vote for a Dixiecrat. That's why, in 1964, it's time now for you and me to become more politically mature and realize what the ballot is for; what we're supposed to get when we cast a ballot; and that if we don't cast a ballot, it's going to end up in a situation where we're going to have to cast a bullet. It's either a ballot or a bullet.

In the North, they do it a different way. They have a system that's known as gerrymandering, whatever that means. It means when Negroes become too heavily concentrated in a certain area, and begin to gain too much political power, the white man comes along and changes the district lines. You may say, "Why do you keep saying white man?" Because it's the white man who does it. I haven't ever seen any Negro changing any lines. They don't let him get near the line. It's the white man who does this. And usually, it's the white man who grins at you the most, and pats you on the back, and is supposed to be your friend. He may be friendly, but he's not your friend.

So, what I'm trying to impress upon you, in essence, is this: You and I in America are faced not with a segregationist conspiracy, we're faced with a government conspiracy. Everyone who's filibustering is a senator—that's the government. Everyone who's finagling in Washington, D.C., is a congressman—that's the government. You don't have anybody putting blocks in your path but people who are a part of the government. The same government that you go abroad to fight for and die for is the government that is in a conspiracy to deprive you of your voting rights, deprive you of your economic opportunities, deprive you of decent housing, deprive you of decent education. You don't need to go to the employer alone, it is the government itself, the government of America, that is responsible for the oppression and exploitation and degradation of black people in this country. And you should drop it in their lap. This government has failed the Negro. This so-called democracy has failed the Negro. And, all these white liberals have definitely failed the Negro.

So, where do we go from here? First, we need some friends. We need some new allies. The entire civil-rights struggle needs a new interpretation, a broader interpretation. We need to look at this civil-rights thing from another angle—from the inside as well as from the outside. To those of us whose philosophy is black nationalism, the only way you can get involved in the civil-rights struggle is give it a new interpretation. That old interpretation excluded us. It kept us out. So, we're giving a new interpretation to the civil-rights struggle, an interpretation that will enable us to come into it, take part in it. And these handkerchief-heads who have been dillydallying and pussy footing and compromising—we don't intend to let them pussyfoot and dillydally and compromise any longer.

How can you thank a man for giving you what's already yours? How then can you thank him for giving you only part of what's already yours? You haven't even made progress, if what's being given to you, you should have had already. That's not progress. And I love my Brother Lomax, the way he pointed out we're right back where we were in 1954. We're not even as far up as we were in 1954. We're behind where we were in 1954. There's more segregation now than there was in 1954. There's more racial animosity, more racial hatred, more racial violence today in 1964, than there was in 1954. Where is the progress?

And now you're facing a situation where the young Negro's coming up. They don't want to hear that "turn-the-other-cheek" stuff, no. In Jacksonville, those were teenagers, they were throwing Molotov cocktails. Negroes have never done that before. But, it shows you there's a new deal coming in. There's new thinking coming in. There's new strategy coming in. It'll be Molotov cocktails this month, hand grenades next month, and something else next month. It'll be ballots, or it'll be bullets. It'll be liberty, or it will be death. The only difference about this kind of death—it'll be reciprocal. You know what is meant by "reciprocal"? That's one of Brother Lomax's words. I stole it from him. I don't usually deal with those big words because I don't usually deal with big people. I deal with small people. I find you can get a whole lot of small people and whip the hell out of a whole lot of big people. They haven't got anything to lose, and they've got everything to gain. And they'll let you know in a minute: "It takes two to tango; when I go, you go."

The black nationalists, those whose philosophy is black nationalism, in bringing about this new interpretation of the entire meaning of civil rights, look upon it as meaning, as Brother Lomax has pointed out, equality of opportunity. Well, we're justified in seeking civil rights, if it means equality of opportunity, because all we're doing there is trying to collect for our investment. Our mothers and fathers invested sweat and blood. Three hundred and ten years we worked in this country without a dime in return—I mean without a dime in return. You let the white man walk around here talking about how rich this country is, but you never stop to think how it got rich so quick. It got rich because you made it rich.

You take the people who are in this audience right now. They're poor. We're all poor as individuals. Our weekly salary individually amounts to hardly anything. But, if you take the salary of everyone in here collectively, it'll fill up a whole lot of baskets. It's a lot of wealth. If you can collect the wages of just these people right here for a year, you'll be rich—richer than rich. When you look at it like that, think how rich Uncle Sam had to become, not with this handful, but millions of black people. Your and my mother and father, who didn't work an eight-hour shift, but worked from "can't see" in the morning until "can't see" at night, and worked for nothing, making the white man rich, making Uncle Sam rich. This is our investment. This is our contribution, our blood.

Not only did we give of our free labor, we gave of our blood. Every time he had a call to arms, we were the first ones in uniform. We died on every battlefield the white man had. We have made a greater sacrifice than anybody who's standing up in America today. We have made a greater contribution and have collected less. Civil rights, for those of us whose philosophy is black nationalism, means: "Give it to us now. Don't wait for next year. Give it to us yesterday, and that's not fast enough."

I might stop right here to point out one thing. Whenever you're going after something that belongs to you, anyone who's depriving you of the right to have it is a criminal. Understand that. Whenever you are going after something that is yours, you are within your legal rights to lay claim to it. And anyone who puts forth any effort to deprive you of that which is yours, is breaking the law, is a criminal. And this was pointed out by the Supreme Court decision. It outlawed segregation.

Which means segregation is against the law. Which means a segregationist is breaking the law. A segregationist is a criminal. You can't label him as anything other than that. And when you demonstrate against segregation, the law is on your side. The Supreme Court is on your side.

Now, who is it that opposes you in carrying out the law? The police department itself. With police dogs and clubs. Whenever you demonstrate against segregation, whether it is segregated education, segregated housing, or anything else, the law is on your side, and anyone who stands in the way is not the law any longer. They are breaking the law; they are not representatives of the law. Any time you demonstrate against segregation and a man has the audacity to put a police dog on you, kill that dog, kill him, I'm telling you, kill that dog. I say it, if they put me in jail tomorrow, kill that dog. Then you'll put a stop to it. Now, if these white people in here don't want to see that kind of action, get down and tell the mayor to tell the police department to pull the dogs in. That's all you have to do. If you don't do it, someone else will.

If you don't take this kind of stand, your little children will grow up and look at you and think "shame." If you don't take an uncompromising stand, I don't mean go out and get violent; but at the same time you should never be nonviolent unless you run into some nonviolence. I'm nonviolent with those who are nonviolent with me. But when you drop that violence on me, then you've made me go insane, and I'm not responsible for what I do. And that's the way every Negro should get. Any time you know you're within the law, within your legal rights, within your moral rights, in accord with justice, then die for what you believe in. But don't die alone. Let your dying be reciprocal. This is what is meant by equality. What's good for the goose is good for the gander.

When we begin to get in this area, we need new friends, we need new allies. We need to expand the civil-rights struggle to a higher level—to the level of human rights. Whenever you are in a civil-rights struggle, whether you know it or not, you are confining yourself to the jurisdiction of Uncle Sam. No one from the outside world can speak out in your behalf as long as your struggle is a civil-rights struggle. Civil rights comes within the domestic affairs of this country. All of our African brothers and our Asian brothers and our Latin-American brothers cannot open their mouths and interfere in the domestic affairs of the United States. And as long as it's civil rights, this comes under the jurisdiction of Uncle Sam.

But the United Nations has what's known as the charter of human rights; it has a committee that deals in human rights. You may wonder why all of the atrocities that have been committed in Africa and in Hungary and in Asia, and in Latin America are brought before the UN, and the Negro problem is never brought before the UN. This is part of the conspiracy. This old, tricky blue-eyed liberal who is supposed to be your and my friend, supposed to be in our corner, supposed to be subsidizing our struggle, and supposed to be acting in the capacity of an adviser, never tells you anything about human rights. They keep you wrapped up in civil rights. And you spend so much time barking up the civil-rights tree, you don't even know there's a human-rights tree on the same floor.

When you expand the civil-rights struggle to the level of human rights, you can then take the case of the black man in this country before the nations in the UN. You can take it before the General Assembly. You can take Uncle Sam before a world court. But the only level you can do it on is the level of human rights. Civil rights keeps you under his restrictions, under his jurisdiction. Civil rights keeps you in his pocket. Civil rights means you're asking Uncle Sam to treat you right. Human rights are something you were born with. Human rights are your God-given rights. Human rights are the rights that are recognized by all nations of this earth. And any time any one violates your human rights, you can take them to the world court.

Uncle Sam's hands are dripping with blood, dripping with the blood of the black man in this country. He's the earth's number-one hypocrite. He has the audacity—yes, he has—imagine him posing as the leader of the free world. The free world! And you over here singing "We Shall Overcome." Expand the civil-rights struggle to the level of human rights. Take it into the United Nations, where our African brothers can throw their weight on our side, where our Asian brothers can throw their weight on our side, where our Latin-American brothers can throw their weight on our side, and where eight hundred million Chinamen are sitting there waiting to throw their weight on our side. Let the world know how bloody his hands are. Let the world know the hypocrisy that's practiced over here. Let it be the ballot or the bullet. Let him know that it must be the ballot or the bullet.

When you take your case to Washington, D.C., you're taking it to the criminal who's responsible; it's like running from the wolf to the fox. They're all in cahoots together. They all work political chicanery and make you look like a chump before the eyes of the world. Here you are walking around in America, getting ready to be drafted and sent abroad, like a tin soldier, and when you get over there, people ask you what are you fighting for, and you have to stick your tongue in your cheek. No, take Uncle Sam to court, take him before the world.

By ballot I only mean freedom. Don't you know—I disagree with Lomax on this issue—that the ballot is more important than the dollar?

Can I prove it? Yes. Look in the UN. There are poor nations in the UN; yet those poor nations can get together with their voting power and keep the rich nations from making a move. They have one nation—one vote, everyone has an equal vote. And when those brothers from Asia, and Africa and the darker parts of this earth get together, their voting power is sufficient to hold Sam in check. Or Russia in check. Or some other section of the earth in check. So, the ballot is most important.

Right now, in this country, if you and I, twenty-two million African Americans—that's what we are—Africans who are in America. You're nothing but Africans. Nothing but Africans. In fact, you'd get farther calling yourself African instead of Negro. Africans don't catch hell. You're the only one catching hell. They don't have to pass civil-rights bills for Africans. An African can go anywhere he wants right now. All you've got to do is tie your head up. That's right, go anywhere you want. Just stop being a Negro. Change your name to Hoogagagooba. That'll show you how silly the white man is. You're dealing with a silly man. A friend of mine who's very dark put a turban on his head and went into a restaurant in Atlanta before they called themselves desegregated. He went into a white restaurant, he sat down, they served him, and he said, "What would happen if a Negro came in here?" And there he's sitting, black as night, but because he had his head wrapped up the waitress looked back at him and says, "Why, there wouldn't no nigger dare come in here."

So, you're dealing with a man whose bias and prejudice are making him lose his mind, his intelligence, every day. He's frightened. He looks around and sees what's taking place on this earth, and he sees that the pendulum of time is swinging in your direction. The dark people are waking up. They're losing their fear of the white man. No place where he's fighting right now is he winning. Everywhere he's fighting, he's fighting someone your and my complexion. And they're beating him. He can't win any more. He's won his last battle. He failed to win the Korean War. He couldn't win it. He had to sign a truce. That's a loss.

Any time Uncle Sam, with all his machinery for warfare, is held to a draw by some rice eaters, he's lost the battle. He had to sign a truce. America's not supposed to sign a truce. She's supposed to be bad. But she's not bad any more. She's bad as long as she can use her hydrogen bomb, but she can't use hers for fear Russia might use hers. Russia can't use hers, for fear that Sam might use his. So, both of them are weaponless. They can't use the weapon because each's weapon nullifies the other's. So, the only place where action can take place is on the ground. And the white man can't win another war fighting on the ground. Those days are over. The black man knows it, the brown man knows it, the red man knows it, and the yellow man knows it. So, they engage him in guerrilla warfare. That's not his style. You've got to have heart to be a guerrilla warrior, and he hasn't got any heart. I'm telling you now.

I just want to give you a little briefing on guerrilla warfare because, before you know it, before you know it. It takes heart to be a guerrilla warrior because you're on your own. In conventional warfare you have tanks and a whole lot of other people with you to back you up—planes over your head and all that kind of stuff. But a guerrilla is on his own. All you have is a rifle, some sneakers and a bowl of rice, and that's all you need—and a lot of heart. The Japanese on some of those islands in the Pacific, when the American soldiers landed, one Japanese sometimes could hold the whole army off. He'd just wait until the sun went down, and when the sun went down they were all equal. He would take his little blade and slip from bush to bush, and from American to American. The white soldiers couldn't cope with that. Whenever you see a white soldier that fought in the Pacific, he has the shakes, he has a nervous condition, because they scared him to death.

The same thing happened to the French up in French Indochina. People who just a few years previously were rice farmers got together and ran the heavily mechanized French army out of Indochina. You don't need it—modern warfare today won't work. This is the day of the guerrilla. They did the same thing in Algeria. Algerians, who were nothing but Bedouins, took a rifle and sneaked off to the hills, and de Gaulle and all of his highfalutin' war machinery couldn't defeat those guerrillas. Nowhere on this earth does the white man win in a guerrilla warfare. It's not his speed. Just as guerrilla warfare is prevailing in Asia and in parts of Africa and in parts of Latin America, you've got to be mighty naive, or you've got to play the black man cheap, if you don't think some day he's going to wake up and find that it's got to be the ballot or the bullet.

I would like to say, in closing, a few things concerning the Muslim Mosque, Inc., which we established recently in New York City. It's true we're Muslims and our religion is Islam, but we don't mix our religion with our politics and our economics and our social and civil activities—not any more. We keep our religion in our mosque. After our religious services are over, then as Muslims we become involved in political action, economic action and social and civic action. We become involved with anybody, anywhere, any time and in any manner that's designed to eliminate the evils, the political, economic and social evils that are afflicting the people of our community.

The political philosophy of black nationalism means that the black man should control the politics and the politicians in his own community;

no more. The black man in the black community has to be re-educated into the science of politics so he will know what politics is supposed to bring him in return. Don't be throwing out any ballots. A ballot is like a bullet. You don't throw your ballots until you see a target, and if that target is not within your reach, keep your ballot in your pocket.

The political philosophy of black nationalism is being taught in the Christian church. It's being taught in the NAACP. It's being taught in CORE [Congress of Racial Equality] meetings. It's being taught in SNCC Student Nonviolent Coordinating Committee meetings. It's being taught in Muslim meetings. It's being taught where nothing but atheists and agnostics come together. It's being taught everywhere. Black people are fed up with the dillydallying, pussyfooting, compromising approach that we've been using toward getting our freedom. We want freedom now, but we're not going to get it saying "We Shall Overcome." We've got to fight until we overcome.

The economic philosophy of black nationalism is pure and simple. It only means that we should control the economy of our community. Why should white people be running all the stores in our community? Why should white people be running the banks of our community? Why should the economy of our community be in the hands of the white man? Why? If a black man can't move his store into a white community, you tell me why a white man should move his store into a black community. The philosophy of black nationalism involves a re-education program in the black community in regards to economics. Our people have to be made to see that any time you take your dollar out of your community and spend it in a community where you don't live, the community where you live will get poorer and poorer, and the community where you spend your money will get richer and richer.

Then you wonder why where you live is always a ghetto or a slum area. And where you and I are concerned, not only do we lose it when we spend it out of the community, but the white man has got all our stores in the community tied up; so that though we spend it in the community, at sundown the man who runs the store takes it over across town somewhere. He's got us in a vise.

So the economic philosophy of black nationalism means in every church, in every civic organization, in every fraternal order, it's time now for our people to become conscious of the importance of controlling the economy of our community. If we own the stores, if we operate the businesses, if we try and establish some industry in our own community, then we're developing to the position where we are creating employment for our own kind. Once you gain control of the economy of your own community, then you don't have to picket and boycott and beg some cracker downtown for a job in his business.

The social philosophy of black nationalism only means that we have to get together and remove the evils, the vices, alcoholism, drug addiction, and other evils that are destroying the moral fiber of our community. We ourselves have to lift the level of our community, the standard of our community to a higher level, make our own society beautiful so that we will be satisfied in our own social circles and won't be running around here trying to knock our way into a social circle where we're not wanted. So I say, in spreading a gospel such as black nationalism, it is not designed to make the black man re-evaluate the white man—you know him already—but to make the black man re-evaluate himself. Don't change the white man's mind—you can't change his mind, and that whole thing about appealing to the moral conscience of America—America's conscience is bankrupt. She lost all conscience a long time ago. Uncle Sam has no conscience.

They don't know what morals are. They don't try and eliminate an evil because it's evil, or because it's illegal, or because it's immoral; they eliminate it only when it threatens their existence. So you're wasting your time appealing to the moral conscience of a bankrupt man like Uncle Sam. If he had a conscience, he'd straighten this thing out with no more pressure being put upon him. So it is not necessary to change the white man's mind. We have to change our own mind. You can't change his mind about us. We've got to change our own minds about each other. We have to see each other with new eyes. We have to see each other as brothers and sisters. We have to come together with warmth so we can develop unity and harmony that's necessary to get this problem solved ourselves. How can we do this? How can we avoid jealousy? How can we avoid the suspicion and the divisions that exist in the community? I'll tell you how.

I have watched how Billy Graham comes into a city, spreading what he calls the gospel of Christ, which is only white nationalism. That's what he is. Billy Graham is a white nationalist; I'm a black nationalist. But since it's the natural tendency for leaders to be jealous and look upon a powerful figure like Graham with suspicion and envy, how is it possible for him to come into a city and get all the cooperation of the church leaders? Don't think because they're church leaders that they don't have weaknesses that make them envious and jealous—no, everybody's got it. It's not an accident that when they want to choose a cardinal, as Pope I over there in Rome, they get in a closet so you can't hear them cussing and fighting and carrying on.

Billy Graham comes in preaching the gospel of Christ. He evangelizes the gospel. He stirs everybody up, but he never tries to start a church. If he came in trying to start a church, all the churches would be against him. So, he just comes in talking about Christ and tells everybody who gets Christ to go to any church where Christ is; and in this way the church cooperates with him. So we're going to take a page from his book.

Our gospel is black nationalism. We're not trying to threaten the existence of any organization, but we're spreading the gospel of black nationalism. Anywhere there's a church that is also preaching and practicing the gospel of black nationalism, join that church. If the NAACP is preaching and practicing the gospel of black nationalism, join the NAACP. If CORE is spreading and practicing the gospel of black nationalism, join CORE. Join any organization that has a gospel that's for the uplift of the black man. And when you get into it and see them pussyfooting or compromising, pull out of it because that's not black nationalism. We'll find another one.

And in this manner, the organizations will increase in number and in quantity and in quality, and by August, it is then our intention to have a black nationalist convention which will consist of delegates from all over the country who are interested in the political, economic and social philosophy of black nationalism. After these delegates convene, we will hold a seminar; we will hold discussions; we will listen to everyone. We want to hear new ideas and new solutions and new answers. And, at that time, if we see fit then to form a black nationalist party, we'll form a black nationalist party. If it's necessary to form a black nationalist army, we'll form a black nationalist army. It'll be the ballot or the bullet. It'll be liberty or it'll be death.

It's time for you and me to stop sitting in this country, letting some cracker senators, Northern crackers and Southern crackers, sit there in Washington, D.C., and come to a conclusion in their mind that you and I are supposed to have civil rights. There's no white man going to tell me anything about my rights. Brothers and sisters, always remember, if it doesn't take senators and congressmen and presidential proclamations to give freedom to the white man, it is not necessary for legislation or proclamation or Supreme Court decisions to give freedom to the black man. You let that white man know, if this is a country of freedom, let it be a country of freedom; and if it's not a country of freedom, change it.

We will work with anybody, anywhere, at any time, who is genuinely interested in tackling the problem head-on, nonviolently as long as the enemy is nonviolent, but violent when the enemy gets violent. We'll work with you on the voter-registration drive, we'll work with you on rent strikes, we'll work with you on school boycotts; I don't believe in any kind of integration; I'm not even worried about it, because I know you're not going to get it anyway; you're not going to get it because you're afraid to die; you've got to be ready to die if you try and force yourself on the white man, because he'll get just as violent as those crackers in Mississippi, right here in Cleveland. But we will still work with you on the school boycotts because we're against a segregated school system. A segregated school system produces children who, when they graduate, graduate with crippled minds. But this does not mean that a school is segregated because it's all black. A segregated school means a school that is controlled by people who have no real interest in it whatsoever.

•Let me explain what I mean. A segregated district or community is a community in which people live, but outsiders control the politics and the economy of that community. They never refer to the white section as a segregated community. It's the all-Negro section that's a segregated community. Why? The white man controls his own school, his own bank, his own economy, his own politics, his own everything, his own community; but he also controls yours. When you're under someone else's control, you're segregated. They'll always give you the lowest or the worst that there is to offer, but it doesn't mean you're segregated just because you have your own. You've got to control your own. Just like the white man has control of his, you need to control yours.

You know the best way to get rid of segregation? The white man is more afraid of separation than he is of integration. Segregation means that he puts you away from him, but not far enough for you to be out of his jurisdiction; separation means you're gone. And the white man will integrate faster than he'll let you separate. So we will work with you against the segregated school system because it's criminal, because it is absolutely destructive, in every way imaginable, to the minds of the children who have to be exposed to that type of crippling education.

Last but not least, I must say this concerning the great controversy over rifles and shotguns. The only thing that I've ever said is that in areas where the government has proven itself either unwilling or unable to defend the lives and the property of Negroes, it's time for Negroes to defend themselves. Article number two of the constitutional amendments provides you and me the right to own a rifle or a shotgun. It is constitutionally legal to own a shotgun or a rifle. This doesn't mean you're going to get a rifle and form battalions and go out looking for white folks, although you'd be within your rights—I mean, you'd be justified; but that would be illegal and we don't do anything illegal. If the white man doesn't want the black man buying rifles and shotguns, then let the government do its job.

That's all. And don't let the white man come to you and ask you what you think about what Malcolm says—why, you old Uncle Tom. He would never ask you if he thought you were going to say, "Amen! No, he is making a Tom out of you." So, this doesn't mean forming rifle clubs and going out looking for people, but it is time, in 1964, if you are a man, to let that man know.

If he's not going to do his job in running the government and providing you and me with the protection that our taxes are supposed to be for, since he spends all those billions for his defense budget, he certainly can't begrudge you and me spending $12 or $15 for a single-shot, or double-action. I hope you understand. Don't go out shooting people, but any time—brothers and sisters, and especially the men in this audience; some of you wearing Congressional Medals of Honor, with shoulders this wide, chests this big, muscles that big—any time you and I sit around and read where they bomb a church and murder in cold blood, not some grownups, but four little girls while they were praying to the same God the white man taught them to pray to, and you and I see the government go down and can't find who did it.

Why, this man—he can find Eichmann hiding down in Argentina somewhere. Let two or three American soldiers, who are minding somebody else's business way over in South Vietnam, get killed, and he'll send battleships, sticking his nose in their business. He wanted to send troops down to Cuba and make them have what he calls free elections—this old cracker who doesn't have free elections in his own country.

No, if you never see me another time in your life, if I die in the morning, I'll die saying one thing: the ballot or the bullet, the ballot or the bullet.

If a Negro in 1964 has to sit around and wait for some cracker senator to filibuster when it comes to the rights of black people, why, you and I should hang our heads in shame. You talk about a march on Washington in 1963, you haven't seen anything. There's some more going down in '64.

And this time they're not going like they went last year. They're not going singing "We Shall Overcome." They're not going with white friends. They're not going with placards already painted for them. They're not going with round-trip tickets. They're going with one-way tickets. And if they don't want that non-nonviolent army going down there, tell them to bring the filibuster to a halt.

The black nationalists aren't going to wait. Lyndon B. Johnson is the head of the Democratic Party. If he's for civil rights, let him go into the Senate next week and declare himself. Let him go in there right now and declare himself. Let him go in there and denounce the Southern branch of his party. Let him go in there right now and take a moral stand—right now, not later. Tell him, don't wait until election time. If he waits too long, brothers and sisters, he will be responsible for letting a condition develop in this country, which will create a climate that will bring seeds up out of the ground with vegetation on the end of them looking like something these people never dreamed of. In 1964, it's the ballot or the bullet.

Thank you.

### *Notes*

*Sermon source:* George Breitman, ed., *Malcolm X Speaks* (New York: Grove Weidenfeld, 1965), 23–44.

1. The first speaker was journalist Louis E. Lomax; Malcolm X followed him. See Louis E. Lomax, *The Negro Revolt* (New York: Signet, 1972).

### *Bibliographical Sources*

Breitman, George. *The Last Year of Malcolm X: The Evolution of a Revolutionary.* New York: Pathfinder, 1967.

———. *Malcolm X Speaks.* New York: Grove Weidenfield, 1965.

Breitman, George, and Herman Porter. *The Assassination of Malcolm X.* New York: Pathfinder, 1976.

Goldman, Peter. *The Death and Life of Malcolm X.* Urbana: University of Illinois Press, 1979.

Haley, Alex. *The Autobiography of Malcolm X.* New York: Ballantine Books, 1964.

Magida, Arthur J. *Prophet of Rage: The Life of Louis Farrakhan and His Nation.* New York: Basic Books, 1996.

Mullane, Deidre. *Crossing the Danger Water: Three Hundred Years of African-American Writing.* New York: Doubleday, 1993.

## JOSEPH HARRISON JACKSON

*(1900–1990)*

Joseph Harrison Jackson was born on September 11, 1900, to Henry and Emily Johnson Jackson in Rudyard, Mississippi. Jackson spent his childhood in Mississippi, was ordained to the Baptist ministry at age twenty-two, and shortly afterward pastored in Macomb, Mississippi. He was educated at Jackson College in Mississippi, marrying Maude Alexander the same year he graduated. They had one daughter, Kinney. Jackson went on to attend Creighton University in Omaha, Nebraska, while pastoring in the city. He received a master's degree from Creighton in 1933.

In 1934 he became the executive secretary of the Foreign Mission Board of the National Baptist Convention, U.S.A., Inc., maintaining that position for nineteen years. In 1941 he followed L.K. Williams as pastor of the prestigious Olivet Baptist Church, where he would remain for the majority of his religious career. It was at Olivet that Jackson's exceptional preaching skills came to light.

In 1953 he became the president of the National Baptist Convention, U.S.A., Inc., the fourth largest denomination in America and for many years the largest African American denomination in the world. He led the convention for almost three decades. In the 1960s Jackson's leadership faced a serious challenge when Martin Luther King Jr. and others sought both Jackson's and the Convention's support for their strategies to bolster the civil rights movement and to change the Convention's tenure rules. When the challengers obtained neither, they broke away and formed the Progressive National Baptist Convention. Jackson supported the civil rights movement but disagreed with the strategy of nonviolent civil disobedience, believing that it would strain relations between blacks and whites, contrary to the Christian gospel. He insisted that African Americans should instead use the courts as an instrument of change. His statements were often taken out of context and used by right-wing groups in attempts to divide the African American community against King. Despite the schism, the National Baptist Convention grew from five million members to eight million during Jackson's tenure. Much of his longevity was due to his shrewdness as president and to his dynamic preaching ability. His presidential addresses have become famous in the annals of black preaching. Jackson authored *A Voyage to West Africa* (1936), *Some Reflections on Modern Mission* (1936), *Stars in the Night* (1950), and *A Story of Christian Activism: The History of the National Baptist Convention, U.S.A., Inc.* (1980), a 790-page retrospective of his leadership of the convention.

Jackson died on August 18, 1990.

• • •

*Jackson's sermons illustrate his enormous intellectual capacity, consummate grasp of Scripture, and keen use of folk culture, and made him one of the most sought-after preachers of his generation. This sermon, indicative of his great preaching ability, was preached before the closing meeting of the Southern Baptist Convention at the Chicago Stadium before an audience of twenty-two thousand.*

## Great God Our King (May 12, 1950)

Allow me to read to you two passages of Scriptures, one from the Old Testament and the other from the New.

> *For the Kingdom is the Lord's; and He is the governor among the nations.* —Psalms 22:28 (King James Version)

> *And behold, I come quickly, and my reward is with me, to give every man according as his works shall be. I am Alpha and Omega, the beginning, and the end, the first and the last.*
> —Revelation 22:12–13 (KJV)

Human beings are imperfect creatures. They are infected with an ignorance that is insurmountable and limitations of knowledge and wisdom that force them to guess about the future and to build much that seems creative and constructive on assumptions which they have not had the time or ability to prove. Modern science, as complete and matter-of-fact as it seems to be, begins with an assumption. It assumes that there is order in this vast universe and that for every cause there is an effect that follows. It assumes that the scientist has the ability to discover and know many of the laws of the universe and by them and out of the raw materials of the cosmic structure they may build that which is new, serviceable, and creative.

There can be no philosophy without a hypothesis on the basis of which syllogisms are built on whose scaffoldings we may climb to the golden summit of truth. There is no wisdom which does not assume the existence of that which antedates the speculation of the learned and the reasoning of the wise.

What we have said of science and philosophy is supremely true in the field of religion. Religion at its best begins with a Given, with the invincible surmise of the soul, and with an unfettered leap of faith. The first business of religion is never analysis, explanation and proofs. It does not begin with test tubes, logical propositions, and demonstrable proofs. It begins with a Given. Many critical minds today have rejected the Book of Genesis as being pseudo-science and folklore of a primitive people, but

Genesis meets the test of good religion in the first four words of the first chapter: "In the beginning God . . ." In many things, centuries of progress have carried us a long way from much for which the book of Genesis stands. We have arrived at a different concept of the cosmic order—maybe a more advanced anthropology, a higher ethical standard, and a more inclusive astronomy. The best astronomers need not start with the book of Genesis. They may begin with the latest revelations made possible by the seeing eye of our most modern telescope. But the best theologians and the more spiritual churches, and the most enlightened saints of the present and future, must begin where Genesis began, "In the beginning God . . ." For those who are sure of themselves and have arrived at an unimpeachable certainty and have found a human or earthly rock on which to stand and in which they may trust, this beginning may not be essential. They may wish to venture into the midnight void of a vast unknown and climb the slimy hills of human speculation, and seek by fleeting fancy and imagination to people this vast unknown with images and emissaries to their liking and satisfaction. But for men of faith, the beginning of Genesis is our beginning. The Christian Church is divided into many denominations and groups. They differ according to their respective emphasis and beliefs. Some believe in much water, others believe in a little, and some believe in no water. Still others desire that the Gospel be served with much heat and find their greatest inspiration for righteousness in the fear of a lake, not of water, but of *Fire*. It matters not how varied our rituals and our systems of thought, the Christian Religion at its best, begins with "God."

The mystery of the universe is not essentially our problem. The nature of time and the movement of the ages is not our primary concern. How time got its beginning in the womb of eternity, and how something was constructed out of nothing gives us little real worry. The truth is, while we are desirous of knowing all that we can about the world in which we live, we are satisfied to leave the unsolved mysteries in the hands of Him who created worlds and brought order out of chaos and put on-going life in the place where there was static death.

The writer of the Fourth Gospel was a learned scholar. He had been exposed to the best in Greek thought and culture. Yet, when he pens his great message about the Religion and works of Jesus, he begins with God. Says he:

> *In the beginning, was the Word and the Word was with God, and the Word was God. All things were made by him; and without him was not anything made that was made. In Him was life; and the*

*life was the light of men. And the light shineth in darkness and the darkness comprehended it not.*[1]

The Gospel of John is a rich religious book and much that it contains escapes human understanding and yields not to the logic of men. Because of this, it has often been misunderstood. The winds of doubt have blown against it, the storms of skepticism have beaten upon it, and the floods of hate and evil have surged against it, but it has stood because its foundation is laid in and on the eternal Rock of Ages. The message begins with God.

In 1948, in Amsterdam, Holland, I sought and was granted an audience with one of Europe's greatest theologians of today, Karl Barth. I was working on a manuscript on which I wanted his critical judgment. I read to him the first chapter. He listened for a while. Then he interrupted me with these words: "My friend, you have begun with philosophy. You must not so begin. You must begin with God." I say to conventions, nations and men, we must begin with God.

The Christian Church and the whole missionary enterprise begins with the great God that Jesus Christ revealed. He is a God of power and justice, a God of holiness, and a God of peace and love. He is an approachable Father and a trustworthy Saviour. He is our Lord and Master, our Great God and our King.

Jesus often referred to God as Father, but He also ascribed to Him a Kingdom and hence, apparently considered Him as a King. Dean Shailer Matthews, formerly of the University of Chicago, once discussed theology from the standpoint of social patterns. He pointed out that throughout history we can find evidence of man's concept of God being greatly influenced by the social patterns under which he lived. Those who lived in the days of feudal lords and absolute monarchies, thought of God in similar terms. There are those among us today who would advocate an idea of God, based on a personal conception of democracy. This may have some value, but it is difficult for us to think of God exclusively in democratic terms. While we believe in a God who wills our freedom and who leaves much to our decision and our effort, we must not go to the extreme of thinking that the universe has the ability to vote God in or out of power. God is King because His dominion is unquestioned, His powers unimpeachable. He is the same yesterday, today and as long as the world shall stand. Nations may reject Him, empires may deny Him, civilizations may revolt against His will; but He remains the God of power. In spite of the sins of the earth and the insults of hell itself, God is our King.

*Faith in and commitment to God is of little or no practical value to us unless by means of it, new and abundant energy is released to aid us in our present struggles of life.*

Religion would be an eternal detriment to the children of men, and faith in God, the greatest possible curse to the human spirit if, by means of it, human creatures were led to live below the highest possible standard of human excellency.

Religion has value only if it helps us to live better or to attain a richer life in this present world as well as in the hereafter. We ought to do all that we can do to help ourselves by our own initiative and effort. But, when we reach our wits end, we ought to have a higher power on which to depend. When thy heart is overburdened, there ought to be a higher rock to which thy soul may go.

In God, we find a Heavenly reason for earthly excellence and splendor. Of course, we will accept every constructive reason that the earth can give for the justification of every human good. But having done that, a believer in God may find still better reasons for this valuable experience. Faith in God and devotion to Him is a fruitless gesture if by it, our present lives are not made better and the world of men, not made more rich in moral and spiritual values. A religion that gazes always at God, and sees not the world about; a religion that is concerned exclusively about the other world, and the glories of the Heavenly climes that are yet to come, at the expense of seeing the needs in our present human situation, may indeed truly be called the opiate of the people, an enemy to human progress, and a dark night for the souls of men.

The preacher, in First John was a tender-hearted disciple of Christ, and his speech was seasoned with the ideals of love and he was not in the habit of using hard words, and stern speech but so stirred was he over those who seemed to find an excuse for their human failure of hate, that he called all men liars, who confessed to concentrate all their affections on God, to the neglect of their fellow men. Hence, he said: *"If any man says, I love God, and hateth his brother he is a liar; for if he loveth not his brother whom he hath seen, how can he love God whom he hath not seen? And this commandment have we from him, that he who loveth God, loveth his brother also."*[2]

What our Preacher seems to be saying is this, that religion, that faith or that devotion to God that stops with God, is false and far from the truth. That upward look that is not accompanied with a downward concern, is a deception and a curse to the spirit of men. The religion that blesses the souls of men, and gives light to a world of social and moral darkness is a religion that always links the well-being of man to faith in God. The only true and creative love for God is that which embraces my brother also.

The one fact that keeps religion from becoming meaningless speculation, an enemy to the spiritual life of man, and a means of darkening the mind and an excuse for our inner failures is the fact of the "*human also*" that is inseparable from faith in God.

The truth is, that church, that denomination, and that theological system, that does not bear constructive and creative fruits among the children of men, is a dying cause and a dead issue. "By their fruits, ye shall know them."[3] I believe the words of the Apostle James when he says: "*Faith without works is dead*."[4]

Any man who sits in a swivel chair and spends most of his time cloistered in a little room, engaged in the business of analyzing God into knowable elements, and dealing with the divine in the abstract, may last for a long time if he is salaried by endowments and gifts from the dead. But the days of any pastor or religious teacher are numbered, whose message does not break through the narrow confines of his studies to find and live with the people in their struggle for help and salvation.

I was born and reared on a forty-acre farm in the state of Mississippi, and learned something of the behavior pattern of successful farmers. We rose early and finished the chores about the house, had breakfast and by daybreak we were in the field; we worked until the noon and then at the sound of the bell or the taps on the old plow point, hung by wire on a post for that purpose, we stopped for dinner. Then we returned and worked until sunset. The sun was our clock and our guide, but we paid little attention to it directly. We did not gaze at it very long, once it was up, because it tended to blind the eyes and we could not see the row to distinguish the cotton from the grass. And a blind man is not much good with a hoe or behind a plow. We did not spend much time at night worrying about the sun, whether it would rise on tomorrow or not. We accepted that fact. We did not spend too much time trying to find out what phase of the sun rays caused the cotton and corn to grow and what part made the stalks turn green and ripen for harvest. Believing that all of these things were present, we planted the crops and tilled the soil. We made use of the light of the sun as farmers but did not go blind gazing at it. Men can go God-blind and miss the purpose of their existence. A church is God-blind that sees God only as the object of its love. A preacher is God-blind who thinks he can serve God and have no regard for the suffering and afflictions of the world. A theologian is God-blind who becomes so lost in making God conform to his notions that he fails to use the things that God has given him by faith, for the work of salvation and world redemption. Religious people may gaze at the profound beauties of heaven so long that they lose patience for the long struggles through which they must pass before they reach their spiritual land of promise. It is possible to be so obsessed with the fear of hell fire that we die spiritually from a hell stroke and never know the beauties of planting the fields and reaping some of the harvest in this present world. A religious vision is of much good when it helps man in his struggles here and now. The enlightening experience of John on the isle of Patmos is of great value because what he sees in the spirit on the Lord's Day can be sent to the seven Churches of Asia Minor for their help and comfort. A vision of the New Jerusalem, coming down from above, is empty ecstasy if it fades away before it tabernacles among the children of men long enough to make a new earth; lifting the valleys of moral depression and leveling the hills of pride and lust and making straight in the wilderness of confusion, a highway of peace and love.

Hence, we as believers are delighted to worship God, and to proclaim Him as our King, because in so doing, we see new relationships and it helps us in our present struggle.

Our faith in God commits us to many duties and places upon us some exacting responsibilities and gives us outlooks on life peculiar to Christians. Time will permit us to deal with only three things that grow out of our commitment to God as King.

## I. Since God is our King, we must hold a most exalted view of the world in which we live and have a most sacred regard for all of God's human creatures.

God's world is sacred and all that He has made is worthy of admiration and respect. We must hold in reverence every creature, every plant and every sprig of grass as products of the mind and will of God. We cannot think of the world as being the abode of evil alone, and the result of the work of unkind forces of corruption. This is God's world and as such it demands of us a spirit of worship and a sense of deep reverence.

As subjects of this great God, our King, all human beings have a peculiar dignity and worth. If we believe the words of Jesus, all human creatures are children of God and every man is an end within himself. The dignity of man from our Christian point of view is derived from the fact that he is the object of God's creation, he is made in the image of God. In him is the breath of the creator, the image of his maker, and the spirit of the eternal Father. It is the unique doctrine of the Christian Church and the profound message of Jesus of Nazareth that the worth of man is arrived at from the mental, moral and spiritual endowment that has been given to him by his creator.

Peter was indeed a great preacher. He had learned to follow Christ when he was a simple fisherman. He had recovered from the shock of the death of Jesus through his experiences at Pentecost, and the man who was once too weak to own Jesus as his Lord and Master in the presence of a little girl, now stands before a great multitude and preaches the gospel of the spirit, with power. The result of this sermon was the conversion of more than three thousand people. But Peter still lacked the great insight regarding the dignity and the worth of all men. Being wedded to the tradition of the elders and somewhat limited by the accepted notions of his own nation, Peter was yet to learn that the gospel which he preached belonged to all nations, to all men and all people, because they were the children of a common Father. When Cornelius, a centurion, sent for Peter to come to him, this was more than Peter had expected. He was not ready to preach the gospel to the Gentiles. God had to prepare him for this new duty, for this new responsibility. Hence he appeared to Peter in a vision and taught him that all men are eligible for the gospel of Christ because they have been brought into existence by a great God and a creative Father. God showed to Peter a new law that transcended the narrow concepts of his own nation. God showed him that all men were evaluated by the same standard. Hence when Peter met Cornelius, Cornelius having an inferiority complex, fell down at his feet and worshipped him. Having learned his lesson well, Peter took Cornelius by the hand and lifted him up saying: "Stand up; I, myself also am a man."[5] And as he talked with him, he went in and found many that were come together. And he said unto them, "ye know how that it is an *unlawful* thing for a man that is a Jew to keep company or come into one of another nation; but God hath shewed me that we should not call any men common or unclean."[6]

In the presence of Christ and under the spell of divine direction, we see deeper than national traditions and circumscribed philosophy. We see a new anthropology, a new psychology, and a new social order. In the opinion of Peter, there was nothing to justify this new venture in preaching the gospel to Gentiles, there was nothing to lead him to accept all men as men in the sight of God, but this lofty vision that had been given to him on the housetop. We today in our world outreach and in our missionary endeavor, find ourselves transcending the narrow limits of country and nationality and embracing all human creatures in the family of God, because God hath shewed us that we should not call any man common or unclean. International politics have divided the world into camps of the lesser and stronger nations; and into mother countries and colonial outposts, but *God hath shewed* us that all men are of one great family. If there is a dividing line it is based on the content of character, the attitude of the mind and the disposition of the soul. There are two groups in the world; one group rejects the word, the truth and the divine command, while the other accepts the way of God and strives to walk in His path. Like Peter, we have perceived that God is no respecter of persons, but in every nation he that feareth God and worketh righteousness is accepted with Him.

This Christian idea of the worth and dignity of man leads us to the conclusion that freedom is the common lot of all. Freedom's light is a holy light. When it grows dim or is blown out, men suffer the most terrifying mental anguish, society decays, nations fall into disrepute, and civilizations go down to the hell of ruins. Liberty is God's gift to the children of men. It is His will that all men be free. When we hear men groan for freedom and see them paying the most expensive price for liberty, and observe their heroic efforts to snap their fetters and break their chains, we must remember that they are acting according to their basic nature. Our great God has so made us all that we hunger and thirst for freedom at its best. Samuel F. Smith tells us that our great God is the author of liberty. We delight to sing to Him and adore His great name because of this precious gift to the children of men.

*Our Fathers' God to Thee, Author of Liberty*
*To Thee we sing.*
*Long may our land be bright, with freedom's holy light,*
*Protect us by Thy might. Great God our King.*[7]

In spite of the many wars of history, there are more slaves abroad in the world today than the last war whose freedom seems still far away, there are great nations who have enslaved the souls of their citizens by reducing men as subjects and slaves of the state. As we observe our economic order in our own country and note the change in the complexion of our nation due to the mastery of the machine, it seems that the whole of Western civilization is all but enslaved by the mechanical inventions of this modern day and generation. Few statesmen and no nations today as a whole, believe in war as a solution to our international problems, and yet like slaves of fear and victims of boundless greed, we seem to be driven towards another world conflict which can mean only devastation, ruin, and maybe the total destruction of modern civilization. In this day of confusion, the world needs an emancipator and a liberator to break its chains. It seems that this is the challenge for the church. The light of freedom must not go out. But if it is to last, the flickering flames of liberty must be protected by the might of our great God and our King, and He has elected the church to help in this task. Those who seem unprepared for freedom, and constant sinners against liberty, must not be given up. It is the task of the Christian Church to seek the lost and preach the gospel of freedom that will break chains and set the captives free. As Christians, we are not allowed to exempt any man or any set of men from the claims and the call of the gospel. All men must receive the life-giving words of God; for no nation can be free until freedom's holy light shines in every village and hamlet and every schoolhouse and church, and in every home and every human heart.

If the God of Jesus Christ be our King, then we must proclaim the sacredness of our world, the supreme dignity of man, and work for the preservation and the growth of freedom everywhere.

## II. God Is Our King, therefore the government of the world is in His hands.

International law is possible, because there is a Cosmic law of justice and truth. This law is the same in principle for all peoples whether they live in America or Europe, in Asia or Africa. It stands for the good of mankind. The best laws that men have written have been for the good of mankind. Hence, all the law makers of history have simply tried to set down on parchment or paper the ideals and principles of life as given to them by the oughtness of their own conscience. This law of justice and truth, God has written in every human soul, but only a few have been blessed with the rare genius to reveal and interpret this law for the good of human society.

When some wanted to criticize Paul for his doctrine of the inexcusableness of all men, they turned to the notion, that all men had not received the light of the law of righteousness and hence should be excused from its claims. But Paul's answer was to the effect that God had planted His truth in every human heart and hence, no man could go wrong or draw up a code of evil until he first broke the law within and changed the existing truth of God into a lie. Every lie is truth changed to the wrong direction, and established facts set to the wrong purpose. Said Paul in Romans 1:18–25.

> For the wrath of God is revealed from Heaven against all ungodliness and unrighteousness of men, who hold the truth in unrighteousness;
>
> Because that which may be known of God is manifest in them; for God hath shewed it unto them.

> For the invisible things of him from the creation of the world are clearly seen, being understood by the things that are made, even his eternal power and Godhead; so that they are without excuse:
>
> Because that, when they knew God, they glorified him not as God, neither were thankful; but became vain in their imaginations, and their foolish heart was darkened.
>
> Professing themselves to be wise, they became fools.
>
> And changed the glory of the uncorruptible God into an image made like to corruptible man, and to birds, and four-footed beasts, and creeping things.
>
> Wherefore God also gave them up to uncleanness through the lusts of their own hearts, to dishonor their own bodies between themselves.
>
> Who changed the truth of God into a lie, and worshipped and served the creature more than the Creator, who is blessed for ever. Amen.

This Cosmic law of justice and truth is really the law of righteousness (for whatever is true and just is righteous). And this law is also written in the hearts of men. We may also call it the Moral law.

It seems that God from time to time gives nations a chance to record the principles of their law for the aid and guidance of mankind. If they do not write well, God will, with His own finger of Providence, erase what they have penned and pass the scroll to another. Greece, Rome, Egypt, and Babylon wrote their share, did some good and made some mistakes and then passed the incompleted parchment to others, who came after them.

It seems that today, America's opportunity has come to help to write down or copy for the good of her nation and the nations of the world, God's Cosmic law of righteousness for this hour in history. If we do not write well the pen will be snatched from our hands and the scroll passed to another.

It is our task as Christians to tell Americans and the world that this business of making laws for human beings is serious business and ought to be approached as a Divine undertaking.

The story of how Moses got the law may not be accepted as good philosophy of jurisprudence, but it is good religion. Moses went up on the mountain and brought back a copy of what God had given him. He does not take credit for the lofty ethical concepts of the ten Commandments, for Moses thought they were given by the hand of God for the people who were enroute to the land of Promise.

Western civilization, in fact the civilizations of the world, are headed for a new land of human relationships, but they cannot enter until they have new laws to teach them how to behave once they reach that land.

Let us tell the parliaments of the world, the Congress of the United States that this generation awaits new laws. Laws that will guarantee the human rights of all the people of the earth, and we cannot go much further until we get our new codes. Baptists of America, Christians everywhere, let us tell our Congressmen and our Senators that theirs is a righteous responsibility and spiritual task. The day for power politics has passed and the hour has long since struck for God directed politics. It is not too late yet to even tell the members of this Eighty-first Congress the law of universal righteousness has already been drawn up and given by the will of God and the decree of our King. Tell them it would help to forget what their voters might think, what their party leaders might do, and spend each day some moments of quiet in the presence of God seeking to see and know what God wants recorded of His cosmic laws of justice and truth on the statute books of America.

Be well advised that Congress may delay but cannot defeat God's law of righteousness. For no man can eternally curse whom God has blessed, and no state or nation can eternally put down whom God has lifted up. And no League of Nations or Assembly of Nations can repeal the moral law of the world. "The Kingdom is the Lord's and He is the Governor among the nations."[8]

By His patience, long suffering and boundless mercy, God may permit the wrong to reign on thrones of power for a season, and will bless the undeserving, give the light of the sun to the wretched and the weak, and cause the rain to fall on the just and the unjust, but do not mistake patience for poverty of strength and wisdom. God still holds the government of the world in His hand. Dictators may endure for decades, the masters of conflict may reign for years, and the lords of war may wear their well plumed crowns of victory, but only for a while. For at His appointed time, God will send judgment against the unjust and wreak Divine vengeance on the wicked oppressors of truth and righteousness.

Divine judgment then, becomes a serious and dangerous fact. Justice cannot and will not be eternally destroyed, if God is our King. The biased decision of a bribed judge is not the last word. The verdict of unjust juries will not always stand, for there is a Supreme Court of Eternal Righteousness to which every weary soul may take its appeal. For it is written that, "The Judge of all the earth will be right."[9] Look abroad on the wide field of human history and you will see signs of the judgment of Truth, of Righteousness and of God.

Modern Germany was indeed one of the great nations of the past. But today she is a broken, dejected and prostrate people. Not because she did not have great scientists. Some of the greatest scientists of all times have been found on German soil, and some of the world's greatest thinkers were nurtured in the soil of this historic nation. Germany fell, not because she did not have a great army and strong willed soldiers in the field, but Germany fell because she embarked whole heartedly on an unjust, Godless and narrow scheme of oppression and persecution with the mistaken notion that she was by nature superior to all the other people of the world. Her ruthless leaders led the people to believe that might makes right, and force was the only key to national security and progress. But the righteous plan of God overturned the wicked plots of men, and today, this great nation lies in the cruel chains of an unwelcomed slavery.

What has happened to modern Germany and all the other nations that resorted to military power and bloodshed awaits every nation on the face of the globe that will not repent and turn to God.

He who opposed justice, and tries to crush truth, and regards not the souls of men, fights against God, and it is a dangerous thing to fight against God.

### III. If God Is Our King, those who struggle for righteousness and truth, struggle on the side of the victorious forces of the universe.

Notwithstanding the fact of our faith in God, we know that evil is abroad in the world. The struggle for truth is grave; the battle for the right sways to the right and the left and up to the present time there has been no conclusive or complete victory of the good over the bad by human effort. Yet, we believe that we are fighting a winning battle when we fight for truth and righteousness. Such a faith gives meaning, hope, and encouragement to those who struggle for the coming of the Kingdom of God. Those who talk most and with the greatest certainty about the warless world and the day of eternal peace are those who have faith in God. The prophets of God and not the political leaders of the past, saw most clearly that a new day of hope was sure to come. Note the victorious word of the Prophet Isaiah:

> And it shall come to pass in the last days, that the mountain of the Lord's house shall be established in the top of the mountains, and shall be exalted above the hills; and all nations shall flow unto it.
>
> And many people shall go and say, Come ye, and let us go up

> to the mountain of the Lord, to the house of the God of Jacob; and he will teach us of his ways, and we will walk in his paths: for out of Zion shall go forth the law, and the word of the Lord from Jerusalem.
>
> And he shall judge among the nations, and shall rebuke many people; and they shall beat their swords into ploughshares, and their spears into pruning hooks: nation shall not lift up sword against nation, neither shall they learn war anymore.[10]

The same prophet sees the final day when peace shall be established and war a thing of the past.

> The wolf also shall dwell with the lamb, and the leopard shall lie down with the kid; and the calf and the young lion and the fatling together; and a little child shall lead them.
>
> And the cow and the bear shall feed; their young ones shall lie down together: and the lion shall eat straw like the ox.
>
> And the sucking child shall play on the hole of the asp, and the weaned child shall put his hand on the cockatrice' den.
>
> They shall not hurt nor destroy in all my holy mountain: for the earth shall be full of knowledge of the Lord, as the waters cover the sea."[11]

One of the most disturbing notions of human experience is the notion of defeat at the end of our struggle. This is supremely true in our personal lives. Many of us have lost confidence in the victory of the right because we have known serious failures within our own lives and inner motives. Countless numbers have given up the Ghost and ceased to struggle because victory did not come as soon as they expected.

Some months ago a young student from India came to America and matriculated in one of the outstanding universities of our city, The University of Chicago. He came to America and to our University, seeking light of mind and understanding of heart, but he did not solve his problems as quickly as he had expected. His goal was not reached as readily as he desired: and on April thirtieth of this year he penned these lines:

> *Here lies one who messed up his life,*
> *He found that he could not live in such mental strife,*
> *So he decided that the best and the only sensible way,*
> *Was to make quite sure that this was, indeed, the last day,*
> *For the attention of those who care for him:*

*Do not feel sad because he's glad,*
*And happy to go to his Creator.*

This note was found on the body of our young Indian friend after he had ended his life by throwing himself in front of an elevated train at Randolph Street and Wabash Avenue. How unfortunate for Nadir H. Dastur, for most of us in some form or another have soiled or messed up our lives. Most of us have passed through and are still passing through some type of mental strife and strain. But we have decided that utter defeat is not the best and only sensible way out. As Christians we have found a WAY—a Way of Hope for the despondent and the despairing—a Way of strength for the weak—a Way of cleansing for the unclean—and a Way of Redemption for the guilty—and a Way of Peace for the confused of heart. To us, Jesus Christ is that WAY—for He brings to us the all sufficiency of His Grace. He admonished us all to continue the struggle, cease not to fight against the limitations of the flesh and He always says that "My Grace Is Sufficient For Thee."[12] How to be completely successful in living the Life of Christ, no human being of himself has known or experienced. How to withstand the tempter's plot, we know only in part, and how to realize a good life here and now, we cannot of ourselves grasp or comprehend. Our victory lies in the power, the guidance, and the help that comes to us from the Cross of Christ. In Him is victory, and through Him, deliverance.

Why the long struggle between right and wrong? I cannot tell; and why God has adopted the method of gradualness in building His Kingdom I do not know, but my faith tells me whatever He does is for the best and every struggle for the good will be crowned with everlasting victory. We fight not alone, we fight with Him.

The Pharaoh of ancient Egypt for awhile made slaves of the helpless Hebrews, made their loads heavy, their burdens almost unbearable, and bound them with chains of oppression. For awhile, Pharaoh withstood the kind invitation of Moses to "let God's people go."[13]

Pharaoh was cruel, full of pride, and boasted of his power; for with him was the master's lash, a standing army, and soldiers ready for battle. He withstood the orders of God, but only for a season. On the side of the helpless Hebrews was a blazing star to guide them by night, and a pillar of cloud to lead them by day. The waters of the Red Sea allowed them passage while the armies of Egypt were wrecked and destroyed, and Israel eventually reached the Land of Promise.

The Church believes that our struggle is victorious and that the gates of hell cannot prevail against us, and even death itself cannot eternally hinder the onward March of Divine Truth.

Men made sport of Jesus on the Cross and had begun to write failure against everything He did and said; but after three days, the Resurrection Faith told a new story and flashed forth a new hope. For He came forth victorious over the grave and Master of death and hell, and He shouted aloud, "All Power is in My Hands."[14] The Church was sent forth not to weep because of the death of a bare-footed preacher; the Church was sent forth not to utter words of revenge against Pilate and the cruel soldiers who nailed Jesus to the Cross and put a spear in His Side; the Church was sent forth not to lament the fact that so good a Man as Jesus had been maltreated and crucified by those whom He came to save—the Church was sent forth to announce the victorious struggle of The Sons of God. The Church was sent forth to tell both saints and sinners that the cross was not a losing battle, but a victorious effort; for Jesus does not say to us—"Go Into All The World" before He announces, "All Power Is In My Hands."[15] It is the Easter Sunday Morning that gives us hope while we preach, consolation while we struggle, and succor and comfort to die for the noble cause of The Kingdom of God that is sure to come. Being obsessed with this faith, we see victory and the call of God in the most discouraging circumstance.

When the slaves faced discouragement and lived on the brink of despair, they found their answer in a living faith, in a God of love and mercy. They used to sing in the quiet moments of the night—"Steal Away, Steal Away to Jesus, I Ain't Got Long to Stay Here." Thunder and lightning were usually considered as signs of distress and indications of the anger of God and the repulsive threats of eternal damnation; but these humble slaves saw new meaning in bursting thunders and jagged forks of lightning that flooded the ebony bosom of troubled skies. They sang:

*My Lord Calls Me, He Calls Me By*
*The Thunder,*
*My Lord Calls Me, He Calls Me By*
*The Lightning,*
*The Trumpet Sounds Within My Soul,*
*I Ain't Got Long To Stay Here.*[16]

The souls of men blessed by the music of hope and made active and alive by the trumpet of God within can hear the Voice of God in the storms and see the light of His Promise in the darkest night and be certain of an immortal victory in the face of chilly death and in the presence of a gruesome grave.

### NOTES

*Sermon source:* Joseph Harrison Jackson, "Great God Our King," Folder 2 (2000. 196), Chicago Historical Society, Olivet Baptist Church, Box 1.
1. St. John 1:1, 3–5 (King James Version).
2. 1 John 4:20–21 (KJV).
3. See Matthew 7:16.
4. James 2:20 (KJV).
5. Acts 10:26 (KJV).
6. Acts 10:26–28 (KJV).
7. Samuel Francis Smith, "My Country, 'Tis of Thee," *The New National Baptist Hymnal* (Nashville, TN: National Baptist Publishing Board, 1983), number 474, verse 4.
8. Psalm 22:23 (KJV).
9. See Genesis 18:25.
10. Isaiah 2:2–4 (KJV).
11. Isaiah 11:6–9
12. 2 Corinthians 12:9 (KJV).
13. See Exodus 5:1.
14. See Matthew 28:18.
15. See Matthew 28:18–19.
16. "Steal Away to Jesus," *African American Heritage Hymnal* (Chicago: GIA Publications, 2001), number 546.

### BIBLIOGRAPHICAL SOURCES

Faison, Bernilee. "The King is Dead: Long Live the King: The Eulogy of Joseph Harrison (J.H.) Jackson," *The African American Pulpit*, Spring 2005.

Hitchmough, Sam. "Missions of Patriotism: Joseph Jackson and Martin Luther King American Studies in Britain," *The British Association of American Studies Newsletter*, issue 84 (Spring/Summer 2001).

Jackson, Joseph Harrison. *A Story of Christian Activism: The History of the National Baptist Convention, U.S.A., Inc.* West Berlin, NJ: Townsend Press, 1980.

———. *Religious Leaders of America*, 2nd ed. Detroit: Gale Research, 1991.

## BENJAMIN ELIJAH MAYS

*(1894–1984)*

Benjamin Elijah Mays was born August 1, 1894, in Ninety Six, South Carolina, to former slaves S. Hezekiah and Louvenia Mays. He graduated valedictorian from the high school department of the South Carolina State College in Orangeburg in 1916. Because he often had to abbreviate his school years in order to assist his parents with farming, Mays was older than most high school graduates. For his undergraduate work, Mays matriculated at Bates College in Lewiston, Maine. At Bates, he was active on the debate and football teams. Mays completed his bachelor's degree there in 1920.

Mays began graduate study at the University of Chicago, but at the invitation of Morehouse College president John Hope, Mays left Chicago and traveled to Morehouse in 1921, where he taught math, psychology, and religion for three years. In 1924, Mays resumed his graduate study at the University of Chicago Divinity School and in 1925 he completed a master of arts degree. His first wife, Ellen Harvin, whom he married in 1920, died in 1923. In 1926, he married Sadie Gray.

Mays taught briefly at South Carolina State College, worked for a stint at the Urban League in Tampa, Florida, and also served as the student secretary for the National YMCA. In 1934, Mays was appointed dean of Howard University's School of Religion; in 1935 he received his doctorate from the University of Chicago. His dissertation, which would later be published under the title *The Negro's God: As Reflected in His Literature*, was a progenitor of Black Theology, the systematic effort to assess the meaning of God and human experience from the black perspective.

In the summer of 1940, Mays became the sixth president of Morehouse College, the first to hold a Ph.D. As a college president, Mays was frugal, earning him the nickname "Buck Benny," because he could do so much with a dollar. Mays raised Morehouse's financial and intellectual stature. More importantly, he is credited with creating the pride and mystique associated with "the Morehouse Man." Every Tuesday during his twenty-seven-year presidency, Mays would deliver mesmerizing addresses to the Morehouse students at chapel service.

Although Mays influenced countless Morehouse men, one student in particular would emerge as Mays' most celebrated protégé—Martin Luther King Jr. King began his study at Morehouse in 1944 when Mays was in his fourth year as president. King often cited Mays as his intellectual and spiritual mentor. Mays, who introduced Gandhi's nonviolent philosophy to King, remained supportive of and loyal to King throughout his student's ministry, and Mays preached King's eulogy.

Mays was also a prolific author. He wrote and edited nine books and more than one thousand articles, and delivered more than eight hundred public addresses. He received fifty-six honorary doctorates. Additionally, Mays was deeply involved in political affairs. He served as the president of the United Negro College Fund, vice president of the NAACP, and was the first black vice president of the Federal Council of Churches (now called the National Council of Churches). Dr. Mays died March 28, 1984.

• • •

*Below is Mays' eulogy delivered at Martin Luther King Jr.'s funeral. The world watched as Mays, King's mentor and friend, stood at the rostrum to eulogize his student, a fellow preacher and the nonviolent voice for the poor and downtrodden. Mays begins the eulogy by expressing his personal sadness at the loss of King and then gives voice to the grief of millions. At the core of Mays's sermon are his words: "Too bad, you say, that Martin Luther King Jr. died so young. I feel that way too. But, as I have said many times before, it isn't how long one lives, but how well. It's what one accomplishes for mankind that matters."*

## EULOGY FOR DR. MARTIN LUTHER KING JR. (APRIL 9, 1968)

To be honored by being requested to give the eulogy at the funeral of Dr. Martin Luther King Jr. is like being asked to eulogize a deceased son—so close and so precious was he to me. Our friendship goes back to his student days at Morehouse College. It is not an easy task; nevertheless, I accept it with a sad heart and with full knowledge of my inadequacy to do justice to this man. It was my desire that if I predeceased Dr. King, he would pay tribute to me on my final day. It was his wish that if he predeceased me, I would deliver the homily at his funeral. Fate has decreed that I eulogize him. I wish it might have been otherwise, for, after all, I am three score years and ten, and Martin Luther is dead at thirty-nine.

Although there are some who rejoice in his death, there are millions across the length and breadth of this world who are smitten with grief that this friend of mankind—all mankind—has been cut down in the flower of his youth. So multitudes here and in foreign lands, queens, kings, heads of government, the clergy of the world, and the common man everywhere are praying that God will be with the family, the American people, and the president of the United States in this tragic hour. We hope that this universal concern will bring comfort to the family—for grief is like a heavy load—when shared it is easier to bear. We come today to help the family carry the heavy load.

We are assembled here from every section of this great nation and from other parts of the world to give thanks to God that he gave to America, at this moment in history, Martin Luther King Jr. Truly, God is no respecter of persons. How strange! God called the grandson of a slave on his father's side, and the grandson of a man born during the Civil War on his mother's side, and said to him: "Martin Luther, speak to America about war and peace, about social justice and racial discrimination; about its obligation to the poor, and about nonviolence as a way of perfecting social change in a world of brutality and war."

Here was a man who believed with all his might that the pursuit of violence at any time is ethically and morally wrong; that God and the moral weight of the universe are against it; that violence is self-defeating; and that only love and forgiveness can break the vicious circle of revenge. He believed that nonviolence would prove effective in the abolition of injustice in politics, in economics, in education, and in race relations. He was convinced also that people could not be moved to abolish voluntarily the inhumanity of man to man by mere persuasion and pleading, but they could be moved to do so by dramatizing the evil through massive nonviolent victories won in the federal courts. He believed that the nonviolent approach to solving social problems would ultimately prove to be redemptive.

Out of this conviction, history records the marches of Montgomery, Birmingham, Selma, Chicago, and other cities. He gave people an ethical and moral way to engage in activities to perfect social change without bloodshed and violence, and when violence did erupt, it was that which is potential in any protest which aims to uproot deeply entrenched wrongs. No reasonable person would deny that the activities and the personality of Martin Luther King Jr. contributed largely to the success of the student sit-in movements in abolishing segregation in downtown establishments, and that his activities contributed mightily to the passage of the civil rights legislation of 1964 and 1965.

Martin Luther King Jr. believed in a united America. He believed that the walls of separation brought on by legal and de facto segregation and discrimination based on race and color could be eradicated. As he said in his Washington Monument address: "I have a dream."

He had faith in his country. He died striving to desegregate and integrate America, to the end, that this great nation of ours, born in revolution and blood, conceived in liberty, and dedicated to the proposition that all men are created free and equal, will truly become the lighthouse of freedom: where none will be denied because his skin is black and none favored because his eyes are blue; where our nation will be militarily strong but perpetually at peace, economically secure but just, learned but wise; where the poorest—the garbage collectors—will have bread enough and to spare; where no one will be poorly housed, each educated up to his capacity; and where the richest will understand the meaning of empathy. This was his dream and the end toward which he strove. As he and his followers so often sang: "We shall overcome someday; black and white together."

Let it be thoroughly understood that our deceased brother did not embrace nonviolence out of fear or cowardice. Moral courage was one of his noblest virtues. As Mahatma Gandhi challenged the British Empire without a sword and won, Martin Luther King Jr. challenged the interracial wrongs of the country without a gun. And he had the faith to believe that he would win the battle for social justice. It took more courage for King to practice nonviolence than it took the assassin to fire the fatal shot. The assassin is a coward; he committed his dastardly deed and fled. When Martin Luther disobeyed an unjust law, he accepted the consequences of his actions. He never ran away, and he never begged for mercy. He returned to the Birmingham jail to serve his time.

Perhaps he was more courageous than soldiers who fight and die on the battlefield. There is an element of compulsion in their dying. But when Martin Luther faced death again and again, and finally embraced it, there was no pressure. He was acting on an inner compulsion that drove him on. He was more courageous than those who advocate violence as a way out, for they carry weapons of destruction for defense. But, Martin Luther faced the dogs, the police, jail, heavy criticism, and finally death, and he never carried a gun, not even a knife, to defend himself. He had only his faith in a just God to rely on and the belief that "thrice is he armed that hath his quarrel just." This is the faith that Browning writes about when he said: "One who never turned his back but marched breast forward, / Never doubted clouds would break, / Never dreamed, though right were worsted, wrong would triumph, / Held we fall to rise, are baffled to fight better, / Sleep to wake."[1]

Coupled with moral courage was Martin Luther King Jr.'s capacity to love people. Though deeply committed to a program of freedom for Negroes, he had love and concern for all kinds of people. He drew no distinction between the high and the low, none between the rich and the poor. He believed especially that he was sent to champion the cause of the man farthest down. He would probably say that if death had to come, he was sure there was no greater cause to die for than fighting to get a just wage for garbage collectors. He was supra-class and supra-culture. He belonged to the world and to mankind. Now he belongs to posterity.

But there is a dichotomy in all this, this man loved by some and hated by others—if any man knew the meaning of suffering, King knew. House bombed, living day by day for thirteen years under constant threat of death, maliciously accused of being a communist, falsely accused of being insincere and seeking the limelight for his own glory, stabbed by a member of his own race, slugged in a hotel lobby, jailed thirty times, occasionally deeply hurt because friends betrayed him—and yet this man had no bitterness in his heart, no rancor in his soul, no revenge in his mind, and he went up and down the length and breadth of this world preaching nonviolence and the redemptive power of love. He believed with all his heart, mind, and soul that the way to peace and brotherhood is through nonviolence, love, and suffering. He was severely criticized for his opposition to the war in Vietnam. It must be said, however, that one could hardly expect a prophet of Dr. King's commitments to advocate nonviolence at home and violence in Vietnam. Nonviolence to King was a total commitment, not only in solving the problems of race in the United States, but in solving the problems of the world.

Surely, this man was called of God to do this work. If Amos and Micah were prophets in the eighth century B.C., Martin Luther King Jr. was a prophet in the twentieth century. If Isaiah was called of God to prophesy in his day, Martin Luther King Jr. was called to prophesy in his day. If Hosea was sent to preach love and forgiveness centuries ago, Martin Luther was sent to expound the doctrine of nonviolence and forgiveness in the third quarter of the twentieth century. If Jesus was called to preach the Gospel to the poor, Martin Luther King Jr. fits that designation. If a prophet is one who does not seek popular causes to espouse, but rather the causes he thinks are right, Martin Luther qualifies on that score.

No! He was not ahead of his time. No man is ahead of his time. Each man is within his star, each in his time. Each man must respond to the call of God in his lifetime and not in somebody else's time. Jesus had to respond to the call of God in the first century A.D. and not in the twentieth century. He had but one life to live. He couldn't wait. How long do you think Jesus would have to wait for the constituted authorities to accept him? Twenty-five years? A hundred years? A thousand? He died at thirty-three. He couldn't wait. Paul, Galileo, Copernicus, Martin Luther—the Protestant reformer—Gandhi and Nehru couldn't wait for another time. They had to act in their lifetimes. No man is ahead of his time. Abraham, leaving the country in obedience to God's call; Moses, leading a rebellious people to the Promised Land; Jesus, dying on the cross; Galileo, on his knees recanting; Lincoln, dying of an assassin's bullet; Woodrow Wilson, crusading for a League of Nations; Martin Luther King Jr. dying fighting for justice for garbage collectors—none of these men were ahead of their time. With them, the time was always ripe to do that which was right and which needed to be done.

Too bad, you say, that Martin Luther King Jr. died so young. I feel that way too. But, as I have said many times before, it isn't how long one lives, but how well. It's what one accomplishes for mankind that matters. Jesus died at thirty-three; Joan of Arc at nineteen; Byron and Burns at thirty-six; Keats at twenty-six; Marlowe at twenty-nine; Shelley at thirty; Dunbar before thirty-five; John Fitzgerald Kennedy at forty-six; William Rainey Harper at forty-nine; and Martin Luther King Jr. at thirty-nine.

We will pray that the assassin will be apprehended and brought to justice. But make no mistake, the American people are in part responsible for Martin Luther King Jr.'s death. The assassin heard enough condemnation of King and of Negroes to feel that he had public support. He knew that millions hated King.

The Memphis officials must bear some of the guilt for Martin Luther's assassination. The strike could have been settled several weeks ago. The lowest paid men in our society should not have to strike for a more just wage. A century after emancipation, and after the enactment of the Thirteenth, Fourteenth, and Fifteenth Amendments, it should have not been necessary for Martin Luther King Jr. to stage marches in Montgomery, Birmingham, and Selma, and to go to jail thirty times trying to achieve for his people those rights which people of a lighter hue get by virtue of their being born white. We, too, are guilty of murder. It is time for the American people to repent and make democracy equally applicable to all Americans. What can we do? We, not the assassin, represent America at its best. We have the power—not the prejudiced, not the assassin—to do things right.

If we love Martin Luther King Jr. and respect him, as this surely testifies, let us see to it that he did not die in vain; let us see that we do not dishonor his name by trying to solve our problems through rioting in the streets. Violence was foreign to his nature. He warned that continued riots could produce a fascist state. But let us see to it conditions that cause riots are promptly removed, as the president of the United States is trying to get us to do. Let black and white alike look in their hearts; and if there be prejudice in our hearts against any group, let us exterminate it and let us pray, as Martin Luther King Jr. would pray if he could: "Father, forgive them for they know not what they do."[2] If we do this, Martin Luther King Jr. will have died a redemptive death from which all mankind will benefit.

I close by saying to you what Martin Luther King Jr. believed: if physical death was the price he had to pay to rid America of prejudice and injustice, nothing could be more redemptive. And to paraphrase the words of the immortal John Fitzgerald Kennedy, Martin Luther King Jr.'s unfinished work on earth must truly be our own.

### *Notes*

*Sermon source:* Freddie C. Colston, ed., *Dr. Benjamin E. Mays Speaks: Representative Speeches of a Great American Orator* (Lanham, MD: University Press of America, 2002), 247–53.

1. For the quoted text in context, see Robert Browning, *Asolando: Fancies and Facts* (New York: Houghton, Mifflin and Company, 1982), 113.
2. Luke 23:24 (King James Version).

### *Bibliographical Sources*

Carter, Lawrence Edward, Sr., ed. *Walking Integrity: Benjamin Elijah Mays, Mentor to Martin Luther King, Jr.* Macon, GA: Mercer University Press, 1998.

Mays, Benjamin. *Benjamin E. Mays Speaks: Representative Speeches of a Great American Orator*, ed. Freddie C. Colston. New York: University Press of America, 2002.

———. *Born to Rebel: An Autobiography*. New York: Scribner, 1971.

# JESSE JAI McNEIL

*(1913–1965)*

One of the most venerated scholars, educators, and clergymen in Baptist history, Jesse Jai McNeil was born in North Little Rock, Arkansas, on February 24, 1913, to Henry and Servelier (Edwards) McNeil. He began preaching at age thirteen. He began his post–high school education at Shurtleff College and then went to Virginia Union, where he received his bachelor of divinity. He next attended Columbia University in New York City, from which he received a master's and a doctorate of education. He married Pearl Lee Walker, with whom he had four children.

McNeil taught at Bishop College in Marshall, Texas, where his genius as a Christian educator gained him national prominence and made him a mentor to future generations of famous preachers. In 1944 he became the dean of the School of Religion at Bishop. In the 1940s he also became a writer for the Sunday School Publishing Board of the National Baptist Convention, U.S.A., Inc. McNeil's writings challenged the National Baptist leadership to improve education in schools that catered to the vocational needs of persons seeking careers in the ministry. Believing that it was not enough that preachers be called by God, McNeil insisted that preachers also needed a sound theological education to prepare for their missions in "mass society." He urged "preacher-prophets" to seek the training necessary to enliven their ministries so that they would be able to speak out on behalf of justice as well as tell of the joy and salvation to be found in living the Christian gospel.

McNeil was equally active in international religious education work. A graduate of the Ecumenical Institute in Céligny, Switzerland, McNeil returned to Europe in the late 1940s to lead discussions in the Third World Congress of Young Baptists. In 1950, he served as a Bible leader for the World Convention on Christian Education in Toronto. Among his pastorates were the prestigious Spruce Street Baptist Church of Nashville, Tennessee, and Tabernacle Baptist Church of Detroit, Michigan, where he served from 1947–1961. Within the Detroit community McNeil stewarded his talents as a preacher-prophet by serving as the vice president of the Mayor's Interracial Commission, whose mandate was to build bridges between African American and white communities in the city. Among his books are *As Thy Days, So Thy Strength* (1960), *The Preacher-Prophet in Mass Society* (1961), and *Mission in the Metropolis* (1965). McNeil died at age fifty-two. His death was mourned by millions who were National Baptist and by many others who were not.

• • •

*McNeil wrote "Days of Waiting" as a meditation, combining biblical mysticism with everyday life to deliver profound messages that reached the core of people's lives. In his typical schoolteacher fashion, McNeil instructs us on how to properly wait on God in each situation, even those that try our faith and attempt to diminish our hope.*

## Days of Waiting
## (1960)

*To everything there is a season, and a time to every purpose under heaven.* —Ecclesiastes 3:1 (King James Version)

*I had fainted, unless I had believed to see the goodness of the Lord in the land of the Living. Wait on the Lord: be of good courage, and he shall strengthen thine heart: wait, I say on the Lord.*
—Psalm 27:13–14 (KJV)

*But if we hope for that we see not, then do we with patience wait for it.*
—Romans 8:25 (KJV)

There is an economy of God in which man figures prominently, according to the Book of Ecclesiastes. All of its periods and operations are given, but man may work with them, through them, and according to them. There are only two periods and operations, listed in the first eight verses of the third chapter of Ecclesiastes, which are left more generally to the disposal of God than to man: "A time to be born, and a time to die."[1] But in all else man has a considerable degree of control over the others. He may work with the seasons which require the expenditure of his energy and the application of his effort. He may cooperate with the seasons which require him to wait upon the operation of certain processes. "A time to plant, and a time to pluck up that which is planted" is an instance of the former requirement and "a time to be born" and "a time to heal" are instances of the latter.[2]

Not only must man wait upon and cooperate with processes which are not generally left to his disposal, but he must also learn the discipline and grace of waiting for results in those periods and operations in which his effort is an important factor. Man may plant, but before he may reap he must wait upon other processes, generally out of his hand to give the increase. Man may possess desires which motivate him to action and which sustain him in the pursuit of envisioned ends but he must wait upon their fulfillment, which is not left altogether to him.

In this economy of God three things must be recognized as essentials: the governance of nature, which is the agent of God, in the natural world; the governance of God through Christ in the moral world, and the aspirations, discipline, and work of man in both. God's governance in both the natural and the moral worlds indicates that some things are *given* in man's earthly existence, and he may disregard them only at distress and peril to himself. A significant part of his problem of waiting with its attending distress at times is his negligence, due to ignorance or indolence, in getting some things started in time. And the results for which he waits do not materialize because the time or the season has run out for them. Or the opposite of this may be the case. Man's problems of waiting may be due to his eagerness to get some things started too soon.

Some seed must be planted early in the spring if the crop is to do well because a long season is required for it to mature. On the other hand, some plants cannot be set out in the spring because they are not hardy as a spring crop, and consequently will not do well. But whether a plant makes a hardy spring, summer, or fall crop, it must be set out and given time to mature *in its season.* Otherwise its season may run out before it reaches maturity and its promise of a good crop will be destroyed. So many of the disappointments we have and a good deal of the distress we suffer in waiting are the results of our own doing—not nature's, not God's, but ours.

Someone may point to the problem of timing in getting things started too soon or too late. We must admit that such a problem may exist, especially in the moral world. But it is not a problem to which we have no answers—perhaps, not absolutely correct answers, but approximately correct ones which, if accepted and appropriated, do bring us to the best solutions at a given time. The answers, however, that we have at our disposal are not back of the book answers. They are answers which require constant engagement in study and instruction, our use of observation and experience—the enjoyment of our best knowledge and skills, our highest disciplines and deepest faith.

Waiting may become a distressing problem to us because we try to meet its demands with depleted interior resources. Dr. T.G. Dunning tells in his little book, *The Altar of Youth*, of a forced march in which natives of the Amazon were engaged. For two days their leader led them without incident. On the third day, however, the natives stopped. They would go no farther. The leader asked for an explanation. They explained that "they were waiting for their souls to catch up with their bodies." How illustrative of what we so often need! Waiting under many and difficult circumstances may be taken in our stride, cheerfully and expectantly. But at other times, when having to wait for the fulfillment of some desire or the results of some effort we react with a distress and impatience which are all out of proportion to the importance or the urgency of the thing for which we wait. This is a danger signal. It warns us that our inner resources are decreasing, if not already depleted. Our souls need to catch up with our bodies.

When we are spiritually anchored with "hope that we see not" we may wait with patience for its fulfillment. For one thing, it means to look patiently and expectantly toward the Lord. There was once a small boy who would stand at the front gate of his home each afternoon, looking through the pickets toward the direction from which his father would soon be coming home. Nothing could move him from that gate. Nothing disturbed nor distracted him. He simply stood with his hands on the pickets looking through them for his father. He knew that his father would soon be in sight. He had waited there on many other afternoons, and his waiting was not in vain. Presently he would see his father walking slowly down the dusty road, coming home and bringing joy to his young son. This is waiting with patience.

Waiting with patience also means to look toward the fulfillment of our hope in a state of mind characterized by steadfastness and endurance—a steadfastness and endurance which keeps us busy doing what is at hand or what is possible to do, until our hope is fulfilled. During Ulysses' long absence from Ithaca in the Trojan War, his wife, Penelope was beset by suitors tempting her to give up any further hope of her husband's return. But she continued in faithfulness to him, waiting patiently and hopefully for the day when he would come home from the war. She contrived to postpone giving a decision to her suitors and to remain steadfast in her hope that Ulysses would return with the weaving of a funeral pall for her father-in-law which she never finished. Each night she would unravel what she had woven during the day. This she continued until Ulysses returned home and drove her unwelcomed suitors away.

Whenever we become weary of waiting upon the fulfillment of a hope which is God's promise to us and are tempted to fall away from the Lord, we may drag upon our confidence in the faithfulness of God and trust Him to do what He has promised. This is a confidence and trust born of many past experiences of God's faithfulness to us and to all those who have put their trust in Him. These past experiences teach us not only that God does come to us in time, fulfilling His promises to us, but that we may endure our periods of waiting more cheerfully and easily if we keep busy doing the things that our hands may find to do—and doing them with all our mind and strength. Thus the Psalmist could say to us out of his own past experiences: "Trust in the Lord, and do good; so shalt thou dwell in the land, and verily thou shalt be fed. Delight thyself also in the Lord; and he shall give thee the desires of thine heart . . . Rest in the Lord, and wait patiently for him."[3]

## PRAYER

Grant me the grace, O Heavenly Father, to wait patiently upon the fulfillment of Thy promises for me. Make me too confident in Thy faithfulness to doubt Thy loving care for all those who put their trust in Thee; through Jesus Christ our Lord. Amen.

## *NOTES*

*Sermon source:* Jesse Jai McNeil, *As Thy Days, So Thy Strength* (Grand Rapids, MI: Eerdmans, 1960), 161–64.

1. Ecclesiastes 3:2 (King James Version).
2. Ecclesiastes 3:2–3 (KJV).
3. Psalm 37:3–4 (KJV).

### *Bibliographical Sources*

Jones, Amos, Jr., ed. *The Preacher-Prophet in Mass Society.* Nashville, TN: Townsend Press, 1994.

McNeil, Jesse Jai, Sr. *Men in the Local Church.* Nashville, TN: Townsend Press, 1960.

———. *The Ministers Service Book for Pulpit and Parish.* Grand Rapids, MI: William B. Eerdmans Publishing, 1961.

———. *Mission in the Metropolis.* Grand Rapids, MI: William B. Eerdmans Publishing, 1965.

———. *Moments in His Presence.* Grand Rapids, MI: William B. Eerdmans Publishing, 1961.

# HOWARD THURMAN

*(1899–1981)*

Howard Thurman was a Baptist clergyman, chapel dean, educator, religious philosopher, and writer. Born in Daytona Beach, Florida, he was the third child and only son of Saul Solomon Thurman and Alice Ambrose Thurman. Thurman's father died when Howard was a young boy. Thurman was licensed to preach at nineteen and distinguished himself as a student at Morehouse College, graduating in 1923 as class valedictorian. In 1926, Thurman received his seminary degree from Colgate-Rochester Theological Seminary, and a year before graduation was ordained a Baptist minister. He also studied at Haverford College with noted mystic Rufus Jones. His marriage to Katie Kelley followed graduation; they had one daughter. After this he became pastor of the Mount Zion Baptist Church in Oberlin, Ohio.

Due to his wife's failing health, he returned to the South, where, during her prolonged illness, he taught religious studies and directed religious life in Atlanta at Morehouse College and nearby Spelman College. A chapel, meditation room, and a memorial in the shape of an obelisk on the Morehouse campus honor Thurman.

Thurman remained with the Atlanta colleges for two years after Katie died, but left in 1932, answering the call from President Mordecai W. Johnson to join the religion faculty at Howard University in Washington, D.C. There he taught theology and chaired the university committee on religious life. He was appointed dean of Howard's Andrew Rankin Chapel in 1936, which brought him increased distinction on a national and international level. In 1932, he married author and social activist Sue Bailey. Bailey was also the founder and editor of the *Afra-American Women's Journal*, the first published organ of the National Council of Negro Women, from 1940–44. Howard and Sue had one daughter.

After Thurman visited India and met with Mohandas K. Gandhi, among others, he returned to America stirred by a vision to establish and lead a truly interracial church that would apply the teachings of Jesus regarding human relations to the problem of segregation in church and society. His developed statements regarding Jesus' love ethic was published in the now-classic book, *Jesus and the Disinherited* (1949). Thurman left Howard University in 1944 to become co-pastor (with Alfred G. Fisk) of a newly formed religious fellowship in San Francisco. Within nine years, the Church for the Fellowship of All Peoples, as it was named, had increased in numbers from fewer than forty to more than three hundred, with African Americans, Asians, and whites sharing in a common commitment of worship, life, and witness—with an additional one thousand members-at-large, persons beyond San Francisco who shared the dream of interracial, intercultural, and international fellowship—one of the first of its kind.

Howard Thurman remained with Fellowship Church until 1953, when he left to become dean of Marsh Chapel and professor of Spiritual Disciplines and Resources at Boston University—the first black full-time professor in that university's history. Over the next decade, Thurman's star continued to rise, and his witness was increasingly recognized and valued. The April 6, 1953, issue of *Life* magazine identified him as one of the nation's twelve greatest preachers. Two of the twenty-one books Thurman wrote preserve sermons from his regular pulpit ministry at Marsh Chapel: *The Growing Edge* (1956), which was a Pulpit Book Club selection, and *Temptations of Jesus* (1962). Thurman left Boston University in 1965 after repeated negative encounters with some of the school's leaders.

In addition to writing and speaking as a respected spiritual leader, Howard Thurman served as director of the Howard Thurman Educational Trust, which provided scholarships to needy students, schools, and community programs. Many students and professionals were known to visit this mystical saint in San Francisco prior to his death in 1981.

• • •

*The experience of hearing Thurman preach was often an experience of a sense of presence, due in part to his contagious attitude as a worshipper and also to his preferred method of shaping the mood for listening by prefacing his sermon with a focused meditational reading. Thurman's preaching was not primarily textual but thematic, with a concentration on philosophical and religious aspects of a text or of some experience in correspondence to biblical truths. Aided by training in rhetoric, a gift for imagery, apt illustrations, deliberate timing, a rich baritone voice, and a transparent sincerity, Howard Thurman did not usually follow the classical sermon style in which several points are discussed as aspects of an idea, nor did he follow the traditional black preaching style, which involves reiteration, rhythmic tonality, upbeat cadences, and celebration. Yet, as seen in this example, his sermons were celebratory and gripping, the soul-stirring concern being the insight regarding God and God's relation to our lives, which he explored and expounded and applied with graphic words, arresting expressions, strategic silence, pregnant pauses, poetic passages, and the insinuated tension of guided listening. For Howard Thurman, sermon substance and sermon style were two sides of the coin of preaching, and these were at one with the passion of his own soul.*

## Lord, Teach Us to Pray (1956)

> *And it came to pass, that, as he was praying in a certain place, when he ceased, one of his disciples said unto him, Lord, teach us to pray, as John also taught his disciples.* —Luke 11:1 (King James Version)

It is of very great significance to me that the only specific request the disciples of Jesus made of him for themselves was the request concerning prayer. "Lord, teach us to pray." This is important because it suggests that it was in the area of his religious experience, in the area of his experience with God, that Jesus was most utterly compelling. So compelling was he that with unerring insight his disciples put their hands on this key to the meaning of his life, the accent, the flavor of his power and contagion.

The basic proposition underlying our need for prayer is this: We wish never to be left, literally, to our own resources. Again and again, we discover that our own resources are not equal to the demands of our living.

We are made to realize this in many ways. We know that we are not self-contained. We know how utterly dependent we are upon so many things around us. Our dependence upon those we know, and upon many whom we do not know, is evident. How contingent our present life is upon life that has gone before! In the simplest aspects of our living, we see this demonstrated. Consider the words we use—yes, even our alphabet. How long it must have taken our forebears, somewhere, in some way, to fashion simple things like the alphabets out of which words are made. And the words we use? What a story they have to tell about the involvement of hundreds of thousands of minds and spirits, in successes and failures, in heartaches and trepidations, before at last, language, the miracle of communication, became possible. Thus, it is obvious that, in literal truth, we cannot be left entirely to our own resources. We do not often, however, apply our sense of dependence to our personal relationships to God. What is the most dramatic utterance that we make when pressure bears down upon us? We cry out Something to Somebody. Sometimes we do it in conventional ways, and sometimes in ways that are not quite conventional. But, in dire necessity we always recognize the poverty of our little lives. We feel that we can't go on alone if left to our little resources, however powerful we may seem to be at other times.

Now prayer is one of the most searching, and I think one of the most comprehensive, methods for tapping resources that are beyond ourselves. We tap such resources: in behalf of our own needs, and to banish the shadows that cross our paths. We tap such resources in behalf of the needs of others. Again and again, men may find themselves unable to ask for help in their own behalf, but, at the same time, they do not hesitate to ask it in behalf of the objects of their affection, or the objects of their concern. Often a man who will not pray for himself, who will not seek to relate himself to some source that can confirm and renew and revitalize his own life, will be most humble and most abject in his effort to pray for his loved one, if his loved one is threatened.

It is possible to draw upon resources beyond ourselves. You will recall the man to whom Jesus said, "This can be done, if you have faith." And the man replied, "I have faith, help my lack of faith."[1] It is as part of the awareness of faith itself that the sense of the lack of faith arises. The resource that is within us is the clue to the resource that is beyond ourselves, and this we tap in the experience of prayer. Some years ago, Irwin Edman wrote a book called *Richard Kane Looks at Life*. It is a series of letters between a philosophy professor and a rather precocious student. The student was conscious of some inner insecurity and tried in various ways to find the meaning of life. At length he wrote to the professor saying that in spite of his efforts to solve his problems, the quest was still going on; he had not been able to find what he sought. Perhaps, he said, it was God he was seeking, after all. The professor in his reply suggested that the hunger itself was God. The thing within me is also that which is without. I tap the resource that is beyond me by making conscious contact with the resource that is within me. "The beyond is within" is the way Plotinus puts it.

Now, if this presents a true picture, then some preparation is very much in order. It takes time to learn how to tap the resources that are beyond ourselves. And we are all in a hurry. Our lives are moving at a rapid rate. We cannot reach for the support we need if we do not take time to "ready" our spirits, to prepare ourselves. We must have time for quiet and some place where we can have an atmosphere of quiet outside, before what is outside begins to move inside our consciousness.

In my first church, there was a certain lady who sat about four rows from the front each Sunday morning. She always went to sleep. She would manage to stay awake until after the hymn before the offering and the doxology. Then she settled down and slept until the benediction. I went to call on her husband who was ill. On my way out of the house, she walked with me to the door. As I was about to go down the steps she said to me: "I know you wonder why I sleep every Sunday during your sermon. There are two reasons. The first is that it takes you so long to say what you want to say, and I simply give up; I find it too exhausting to listen to you. And the second reason is that I am so tired." As I listened, I took in her situation and said, "Now that I have visited your home and seen the kind of turmoil in which you live six and a half or seven days a week, I feel that the greatest contribution the church can make to you is to provide a quiet place, once a week, in which you can sit down and go to sleep in peace."

It is important to recognize that we cannot prescribe the rules by which spiritual power is available to us. Who are we, with our little conceits, with our little arrogances, with our little madnesses, to lay down the conditions upon which we will accept the resources of life that sustain and confirm the integrity of our being? No, we must learn how to be quiet; and this takes discipline. We must find, each of us for himself, the kind of rhythmic pattern which will control our stubborn and unyielding and recalcitrant nervous systems, and nourish our spiritual concerns and our growth in grace.

Prayer: *Teach me to pray, O God, my Father, that I may find the rhythmic pattern of my own spirit, which will lead me to the source of all life, lest my soul perish.*

## NOTES

*Sermon source:* Howard Thurman, *The Growing Edge*, 32–36.

1. See Mark 9:24.

## BIBLIOGRAPHICAL SOURCES

Boulware, Marcus. *The Oratory of Negro Leaders: 1900–1968*. Westport, CT: Negro Universities Press, 1969.

Fluker, Walter Earl, and Catherine Tumber, eds. *A Strange Freedom: The Best of Howard Thurman on Religious Experience and Public Life*. Boston: Beacon Press, 1998.

Massey, James Earl. "Thurman's Preaching: Substance and Style," in *God and Human Freedom: A Festschrift in Honor of Howard Thurman*, ed. Henry J. Young. Richmond, IN: Friends United Press, 1983.

Smith, Luther, Jr. *The Mystic as Prophet*. Richmond, IN: Friends United Press, 1991.

Thurman, Ann. *For the Inward Journey: The Writings of Howard Thurman*. New York: Harcourt Brace Jovanovich, 1984.

Thurman, Howard. *Deep Is the Hunger*. New York: Harper and Brothers, 1951.

———. *Deep River and the Negro Spiritual Speaks of Life and Death*. Richmond, IN: Friends United Press, 1975.

———. *Disciplines of the Spirit*. Richmond, IN: Friends United Press, 1963.

———. *The Growing Edge*. New York: Harper & Row, 1956.

———. *Jesus and the Disinherited*. New York: Abingdon-Cokesbury, 1949.

———. *Temptations of Jesus: Five Sermons given by Dean Howard Thurman in Marsh Chapel, Boston University*. San Francisco: Lawton Kennedy Production, 1962.

———. *With Head and Heart: The Autobiography of Howard Thurman*. New York: Harcourt Brace Jovanovitch, 1979.

Williams, Robert C. "Worship and Anti-Structure in Thurman's Vision of the Sacred," in *The Journal of the Interdenominational Theological Center* 14 (Fall 1986 / Spring 1987).

Yates, Elizabeth. *Howard Thurman: Portrait of A Practical Dreamer*. New York: John Day Co., 1964.

Young, Henry J. *Major Black Religious Leaders Since 1940*. Nashville, TN: Abingdon Press, 1979, 46–54.

# 6

# FROM BLACK TO AFRICAN AMERICAN AND BEYOND: *1969 to the Present*

# INTRODUCTION

ON JULY 20, 1969, AMERICANS CELEBRATED AS THREE U.S. ASTRONAUTS—Neil Armstrong, Michael Collins, and Edwin Aldrin—completed history's first manned lunar landing. Their mission fulfilled the dream of slain President John Kennedy, who had predicted in the early 1960s that America would place people on the moon by the end of the decade. While the first manned lunar mission was accomplished, the goal of victory in Southeast Asia was much more elusive.

The war in Vietnam was a painful issue confronting a divided America in the early 1970s. The costs of the war, both in terms of the wounded and dead and underfunded social programs, fueled an aggressive end-the-war movement. Upon leaving Vietnam, it was not clear that victory had been achieved. On the heels of Vietnam, the cost of living in America rose to exorbitant levels. The rate of inflation soared, and an energy crisis created fuel shortages. Long lines of motorists waiting for gasoline became commonplace.

In 1969, Shirley Chisholm, the social activist and New York politician, became the first African American woman to serve in the Congress. As one of the founders of the National Organization for Women and a contender for the 1972 presidential election, Chisholm also distinguished herself as a vigilant advocate for women's rights. This period also witnessed an influx of other African American elected officials who occupied seats in Congress or presided over the nation's major cities as mayors. For example, in 1972, Barbara Jordan, an attorney from Texas, became the first African American woman from the South to serve in Congress. Jordan provided political and moral leadership to the country during the infamous political scandal Watergate, serving on the House Judiciary Committee that conducted the 1974 Watergate hearings, and saying these words now etched in the memory of the American psyche: "My faith in the Constitution is whole, it is complete, it is total. I am not going to sit here and be an idle spectator to the diminution, the subversion, the destruction of the Constitution." While Nixon vigorously denied his involvement, tapes surfaced that implicated him in fraudulent activities. In August 1974, President Nixon resigned from office.

In the late 1970s, the United States elected Jimmy Carter to the presidency; his term in office lasted from 1977 to 1981. Carter appointed several blacks to key cabinet positions. For instance, he elevated Andrew Young, a minister, civil rights activist, and politician, to the position of Ambassador to the United Nations.[1] Nevertheless, foreign policy dilemmas hampered Carter's presidency.

During the 1980s, President Ronald Reagan galvanized much of the nation with his aggressive foreign policy, especially toward the Soviet Union, the United States' Cold War adversary. Domestically, during the eight years of Reagan's presidency, a climate of political conservatism seized the country. Reagan's disproportionate military expenditures often decreased the funding and political will available for civil rights and social justice initiatives.

The income gap between the wealthy and the poor widened considerably during the 1980s, and many advocates for justice feared the erosion of hard-won civil rights gains. In the face of this conservatism, Jesse Jackson Sr., a minister and civil rights activist, mounted substantial national support in two failed bids for the presidency in 1984 and 1988. Jackson's campaigns made him a national and international leader.

Military conflict opened the last decade of the twentieth century. In 1990, Saddam Hussein, the president of Iraq, invaded Kuwait. In response, President George H.W. Bush led the United States into the Gulf War and the U.S. won a quick and decisive victory. However, Hussein was able to retain power. This victory did not obscure the growing domestic dissatisfaction with a flagging American economy. Furthermore, the Los Angeles riots in April 1992, prompted by the acquittal of police officers caught on video assaulting a black man, Rodney King, revealed an ever-widening racial divide in the country. American voters registered their discontent by electing Bill Clinton to the presidency in 1992.

During the two-term Clinton presidency, the economy surged, and

African Americans such as Ron Brown and Hazel O'Leary received high-ranking cabinet positions. The growing popularity of the personal computer, along with the development of the Internet and the World Wide Web, contributed to a financial resurgence and created a new epoch in the world economy, the Information Age. Despite the financial largesse enjoyed by wealthy and middle-class persons, crack, a new more addictive form of cocaine, and HIV/AIDS continued to ravage poor, urban communities. In response to the ills bedeviling the black community, and especially black men, Louis Farrakhan, the controversial black Muslim leader, called for a Million Man March in October 1995 to demonstrate solidarity among black men. While many considered the march a success, its attendance estimated at 650,000 to 1.1 million men, others questioned its lack of a practical political and social agenda, and some questioned its exclusion of black women.[2]

As the country prepared itself for the conclusion of the century, presidential scandals involving financial dealings and marital infidelity abounded in the Clinton White House. A scandal also caused national upheaval in the 2000 election, which featured Republican candidate George W. Bush and Democratic candidate Albert Gore. Discrepancies with voters' ballots created ambiguity concerning the election's outcome. Eventually, the Supreme Court intervened. Despite losing the national popular vote, Bush, the son of former president George H.W. Bush, was selected as the country's new leader.

Less than a year into Bush's presidency, a terrorist attack at the World Trade Centers in New York and the Pentagon in Washington on September 11, 2001, shook the very foundation of the country. In response to those attacks, the United States engaged in a far-reaching War on Terror that led to military involvement in Afghanistan and Iraq. The expense of this military involvement soared into the billions and continues. More tragically, one can never quantify the real toll of these wars—the precious loss of thousands of lives. Beginning in 2000, the number of African Americans enlisting in most branches of the U.S. military began to decrease, and by 2008 had declined more than fifty percent.[3] During these early moments of the twenty-first century, the military might of the United States remains. However, the defeat of international terrorism is a challenge that clearly cannot be overcome with military options alone. By the end of George W. Bush's second term it was clear that the world wanted the United States to commit to moral leadership, the eradication of poverty, the empowerment of socially oppressed groups, and creative diplomacy for world peace.

## THE RISE OF THE BLACK MIDDLE CLASS

Built upon the civil rights movement and the progressive legislation of the 1960s and 1970s, new inroads were created for African Americans into the middle class. This resulted in an exodus from the inner city to the safer streets, single-family homes, and white picket fences of the suburbs. Without question, the hallmark of the 1970s for blacks was the rise of a large number in the middle class.

There had always been a black middle class in America; historically, there had always been some black educators, artisans, shopkeepers, college professors, athletes, and entertainers, to mention a few careers. Yet, as Cornel West points out in *Race Matters*, until the civil rights period of the 1960s this group of middle-class blacks never constituted more than 5 percent of the total black population. But from 1969 to 2005, the black middle class jumped to well over 25 percent of the black population in America.[4]

Despite these economic gains, there was and still is a wide disparity between middle class blacks and chronically poor blacks; one third of African Americans and half of all black children still live below the poverty line. The hundreds of thousands caught in abject poverty bear the brunt of significant challenges to black personal and social life: illiteracy, undereducation, drugs, violence, incarceration, poor health, joblessness, and teenage pregnancy.

Abetted by joblessness, the concentration of drugs in poverty-stricken urban areas and the opportunity to secure large sums of money quickly by selling drugs formed a major crisis in the black community. First, and most tragically, hundreds of young black males were killed or wounded in widespread drug-related violence. Many of the victims were members of gangs that fought for turf rights to secure more customers and profits. Hundreds of others were innocent victims, caught in the crossfire. An important by-product of this violence was that thousands of grandmothers and grandfathers had to rear grandchildren.[5]

Due in part to stricter prison sentences enacted to curtail drug trafficking and, in part, to an unjust criminal justice system, the disproportionate incarceration of African American males and females was another social challenge which sorely affected African American economic, political, and social life. According to the Bureau of Justice Statistics, at the beginning of President Reagan's administration in 1980 there were 501,886 people in prisons and jails throughout the United States. By June 2002, the prison population stood at 2,014,500. Nearly 44 percent were black males, while the total black population stands at a little more than 12 percent of the U.S. population.[6]

The other enormous social challenge to African American life in the 1980s and 1990s was the unprecedented escalation of teenage pregnancies. The reality of unmarried "babies having babies" sent emotional, economic, and moral shock waves throughout the African American community. Teenage mothers are more likely to be poor and receive welfare, are less educated, and are less likely to be married. Their children lag in the standards of early childhood development. The consequences of teenage families placed enormous burdens on the black community. Though the rate of teenage pregnancies has fallen, according to 2005 data, African Americans still comprise about 50 percent of teenage mothers ages fifteen to nineteen.[7]

Along with the challenges posed by drugs, violence, and teenage pregnancies, the African American community witnessed the rise of new art forms that soon developed their own rhetoric, philosophy, and cultural influence. Rap music and hip-hop culture became outlets for youths, their musical, psychological, and emotional expression. Initially characterized by lyrics that emphasized the reality of poor black urban life and resistance to police and political oppression, rap evolved into a culture that at its best espoused and displayed honesty, diversity, and creativity, and at its worst advocated violence, misogyny, and excessive materialism. Although some cultural critics predicted the quick demise of rap music, it swiftly gained crossover appeal among white and Latino audiences. The proliferation of cable television and music videos greatly facilitated rap's ascendancy as well as other musical styles, including contemporary gospel and modern country-and-western music. Cable television stations such as Black Entertainment Television (BET) and Music Television (MTV) enabled large audiences to see, as well as hear, popular musical performers.

In addition to drugs, violence, incarceration, and teenage pregnancy, the black community continued to wrestle with the perennial nemesis of racism. The high-profile court case involving policemen who brutally beat Rodney King and the controversial trial of former football star O.J. Simpson reminded the nation and the world that race and racism were still open wounds in America's body politic. During this time, racial rhetoric and politics were influential factors in the rollback of two social initiatives that had touched black life at its core: affirmative action and welfare. Hurricane Katrina, in the fall of 2005, brought poverty and racism back to the forefront of the national consciousness. The fact that the overwhelming majority of those left stranded in New Orleans were African American served as a reminder of the work that is yet to be done in the areas of racial, political, and economic equality.

Only one thing could have put race on the front pages more than Hurricane Katrina—the election of American's first black president, Barack Hussein Obama. On November 4, 2008, Mr. Obama, age forty-seven, was elected the forty-fourth president of the United States. His victory stunned many given America's fraught racial history and the fact that he was a first-term, little-known senator when his presidential campaign began. For many, his election represented the achievement of much of what Dr. Martin Luther King Jr. dreamed and for which so many blacks and others died.

President Obama was born in Hawaii. His father, Barack Obama Sr., was Kenyan and his mother, Stanley Ann Dunham of Kansas, was white. His parents divorced when he was two. Obama graduated from Columbia University and later served as the first African American president of the Harvard Law Review. In 1992 he married Michelle Robinson and continued his work as a community organizer in Chicago. He then went to work at a civil rights law firm and taught constitutional law at the University of Chicago. He was elected to the Illinois State Senate in 1996. In 2000 he was soundly defeated by Bobby Rush in the Democratic primary for Illinois' first Congressional district. In 2004 he was elected to U.S. Senate and became the fifth African American senator in the country's history. His keynote address at the 2005 Democratic Convention introduced him to a national audience as a man of outstanding oratorical ability and great intellect. Although Obama claimed the presidency as the United States was embroiled in two wars and faced great financial instability, his election represented for many a new period of hope for African Americans and all Americans.

## PREACHING SHIFTS

Following within the general parameters of the tradition of African American preaching, there were several shifts that helped preachers respond to the new realities of African American life during this period. These changes are reflected in new denominations, Afrocentric preaching, empowerment preaching, word preaching, prosperity preaching, and womanist preaching.

### *A New Denomination and New Voices*

As this brief survey of 1969–2009 indicates, the period saw vast changes in American culture and life. A major change in the African American faith community occurred with the rise of preachers, many of whom had been reared in historically African American denominations, who received notoriety after beginning their own denominations or starting nondenominational churches. Paul Morton began the Full Gospel Baptist Church Fellowship International, whose purpose was to lead believers, primarily Baptists, into the fullness of the Holy Spirit while maintaining Jesus Christ as their foundation. Other founding leaders of this group included Eddie Long, Kenneth Ulmer, and Robert Blake, each of whom pastored churches with memberships of more than ten thousand. As with most new denominations, fractures occurred and some left this movement. After Hurricane Katrina destroyed the two churches pastored by Morton in New Orleans, some doubted the future of the Full Gospel movement. Despite Morton's reduced television presence, however, the denomination continued to gain adherents. Morton rebuilt a church in New Orleans and expanded and opened a church in Atlanta.

The shift away from historic African American denominations and the meteoric rise of television ministries aided the promotion of many individual preachers, instead of the promotion of churches. Although the African American faith community has always had figures who were better known than the churches they led (Richard Allen, John Jasper, Charles Tindley, Daddy Grace, Father Divine, C.L. Franklin, Gardner Taylor, and Johnnie Colemon, for example), in the 1990s and early part of the twenty-first century it became commonplace to see the names of individual preachers standing alone, or the names of the churches coupled in a minor way with that of the preacher. For instance, the leader of the Potter's House, T.D. Jakes, has better name recognition than the church he pastors. Paul Morton, Eddie Long, Johnnie Colemon, Fred Price, Noel Jones, Keith Butler, Frederick Haynes III, and James Meeks are all better known than their churches. This change has been wrought by several things, not the least of which is that during the 1990s preachers began establishing ministries and media presence through television, tapes, CDs, videos, DVDs, books, conferences, and the Internet in their own names, typically separate from their churches. The trend was also evident in non–African American churches.

During this period the mechanics of African American preaching changed, and, in much of the African American faith community, worship reverted to a more charismatic form. Relative to the mechanics, the speed of preaching increased significantly. This was not surprising, since the preachers who came of age between 1975 and 2005 did so while immersed in a quick-paced hip-hop culture. Elements of that culture found expression in the preaching styles of a new generation of African American preachers. The quicker pace, though familiar and comfortable to the ears and tastes of the young, in the infancy days of this preaching change left some older adults unable to fully comprehend this new style of preaching. Yet by 2009 a faster style of preaching had become commonplace.

With this change in sermonic speed came another fundamental shift in black preaching—the historic "call and response" of the black church to the preached word was replaced by a preacher-directed response. For example, no longer were parishioners starting or finishing the sentences of preachers due to their shared storehouse of worship jargon—instead, preachers were now prompting worshipers to "touch two people," "give the Lord a hand-clap of praise," "high-five a friend," "touch a neighbor," or repeat something else as instructed by the preacher.

An additional common practice in African American preaching during the latter half of the twentieth century and the first decade of the twenty-first century was the use of multiple crescendo moments in sermons. Many preachers no longer waited until the end of a sermon to soar to a high moment of sermonic intensity. Instead, through inflection, speed, and force, high moments of sermonic intensity were strewn throughout their sermons. This sustained preaching intensity often caused many worshipers to stand and/or applaud throughout the sermon rather than just at the end of the message.

As worship reverted to a more charismatic style, ecstatic worship became commonplace and phrases such as "praise and worship" entered the worship vernacular of African American churches. Praise dancers, praise and worship ensembles/teams, and even mime dancers became the norm. Also, the attire of preachers changed. Many preachers removed their robes and opted for suits and other less formal attire. In some churches, handheld and stationary microphones were replaced by lapel microphones and sound systems that gave preachers unconstrained mobility. These new sound systems were typically part of worship services that were either on television, streamed via the Web, or both. Churches also joined the technological revolution through the use of church Web sites, e-giving (allowing people to contribute financially to churches via the Internet), and e-blasts (messages sent to parishioners via e-mail and cell phones).

African American preaching still fell mainly within the four basic classifications set forth earlier—social activist preaching, black identity preaching, cultural survival preaching, and empowerment preaching. But during this period, based upon the new religious and cultural realities of African American life, several subsets of African American preaching emerged or reemerged: Afrocentric preaching (a subarea of social activist and black identity preaching), word preaching (which does not proceed from and is not a subarea of the four basic classifications), prosperity preaching (arguably a subarea of empowerment preaching), and womanist preaching (a subarea of each of the four basic classifications).

### *Afrocentric Preaching*

Portions of the African American church community have always focused on African heritage. In the 1970s several churches, including Trinity United Church of Christ of Chicago and its then-pastor, Jeremiah A. Wright Jr., became known for its Afrocentrism. The Trinity motto, "Unapologetically black and unashamedly Christian," was adopted by several churches as a mantra for a Christian church that joined black pride, the black liberation struggle, the Bible, and Africa. Afrocentric preaching lifts the history, heritage, and positive values of African American culture without appealing to Europe and white America for validation. Afrocentric preachers are not willing to accept white theologians and white biblical scholars and preachers as the main arbiters of religious truth. Their liberation theology focuses heavily on Africa as the point of departure, with heroes such as Malcolm X, Bishop Henry McNeal Turner, Sojourner Truth, Nat Turner, and Harriet Tubman. While Afrocentric preaching was a presence, in general, the presence of prophetic preaching declined.

### *Word Preaching*

Television evangelists such as Frederick K. Price don't preach the word as much as they teach it, meaning that they use few of the historical African American homiletical approaches. Their style of delivery has come to be called "word preaching." Word preaching first gained notoriety in the 1980s, primarily through white word preachers who had extensive media presence. The style places heavy emphasis on scriptural recitation and exposition, often with a word-by-word or line-by-line exegesis of texts. There is more emphasis on the didactic elements of the preaching process. Many familiar with the African American church would view such an approach as more of a Bible study than the proclamation of a sermon. Also, listeners are expected to take notes during the sermon.

The reasons for the shift to word preaching in African American churches include the congregants' desire for more scriptural support for everyday living, a belief that this type of preaching enhances biblical literacy, and the desire to balance the historically strong emotive experience of black preaching with the cognitive dimensions of preaching by those who saw the two as diametrically opposed. In the 1990s many churches experienced unprecedented growth in midweek Bible study and in Sunday attendance as a result of word preaching. While it continues in numerous religious circles, the advent in some churches, and the return in others, to more emotionally charged worship had lessened the popularity of word preaching by the end of the first decade of the twenty-first century.

### *Prosperity Preaching*

Prosperity preaching provides an unequivocal message of wealth and success. Individuals find liberation in changing their consciousness rather than in movements of social reform. Prosperity preaching downplays social critique and focuses instead on an empowering, individualistic strategy of success and acquisition of material possessions. Personal responsibility for advancement and wealth is a major tenet of prosperity preaching.

In prosperity preaching there is a change in emphasis from spiritual to practical dimensions of living, from prophetic to therapeutic preaching. God is seen as a life coach. Some labeled prosperity preachers would argue that they are simply accentuating the self-help and therapeutic aspects of empowerment preaching. Congregants of prosperity churches are more likely to hear a sermon about managing relationships, managing finances, and the favor of God than a prophetic critique of social injustice, poverty, and racism. As more African Americans entered the middle class, prosperity preaching went from the fringe in the African American church to become more mainstream. The prevalence of prosperity preaching on television and the Internet also helped it become a major force in black religious life. The viability of its prominence remains to be seen as the global economy expands and retracts.

### *Womanist Preaching and Theology*

Another important trend during this period was the vast increase in the number and recognition of the work and skills of African American female preachers. For most of its existence the African American church insisted on the subordination of women in ministry roles, forbidding the ordination of women as preachers and refusing to select them as pastors. Some provided an alternative arrangement, allowing women to preach and lead revivals under the title *evangelist*. Even as early as the 1700s, some women overcame these restrictions and claimed their roles as preachers and religious leaders. But beginning in the 1980s denominational leaders, preachers, pastors, and bishops such as Pauli Murray, Yvonne Delk, Prathia Hall, Vashti McKenzie, Barbara Harris, Johnnie Colemon, and others blazed a trail that has led to a paradigm shift in the black church.

Women scholars also helped cause this sea change. Katie Cannon, Emilie Townes, Jacqueline Grant, Delores Williams, and Renita Weems were leaders in shaping what is now known as womanist theology and womanist preaching. They led in fashioning theological positions that advocated uplift and equality for black women in the black church, in the white halls of academia, in theological texts, and in society. Womanist preaching intentionally advocates for women. It deconstructs theologies and hermeneutics that frame the church and the world as primarily male provinces. It does not advocate against anyone except those who perpetuate misogyny and second-class treatment of women, girls, and the poor and oppressed.

The number of black women in seminary classes now often equals that of men. Yet while gains have been made, it is important to hear Cheryl Townsend Gilkes when she says, "Preaching is the most masculine aspect of black religious rights. Despite the progress of women in ministry, preaching remains overwhelmingly a form of male discourse."[9] The black church has yet to open its major pulpits and denominational offices to women. In 2009 no women clergy hold offices that affect change in the largest black denominations, the Church of God in Christ and the National Baptist Convention, U.S.A., Inc. The African Methodist Episcopal Church appointed its first female bishop in 213 years, Vashti McKenzie, and three others, but women clergy are still not granted the pulpits or salaries that would lead to major female clergy empowerment in this denomination. During this period African American women did become bishops in the United Methodist, Episcopalian, and Anglican churches, which are not majority or historically African American denominations.

## NOTES

1. James Oliver Horton and Lois E. Horton, *Hard Road to Freedom: The Story of African America* (New Brunswick, NJ: Rutgers University Press, 2001), 334.
2. "Million Man March," *Wikipedia: The Free Encyclopedia.* http://en.wikipedia.org/wiki/million_man_march#crowd_size_controversy (accessed June 23, 2007).
3. "Military Sees Big Decline in Black Enlistees," *Boston Globe,* October 7, 2007, http://www.boston.com/news/nation/washington/articles/2007/10/07/military_sees_big_decline (accessed December 8, 2008).
4. Cornel West, *Race Matters* (New York: Vintage Books, 2001), 54.

5. *The Journals of Gerontology Series B: Psychological Sciences and Social Sciences* 60 (2005), S82–S92.
6. Paige M. Harrison and Jennifer C. Karberg, "Bureau of Justice Statistics Bulletin: Prison and Jail Inmates at Midyear 2002" (U.S. Department of Justice, April 2003), available at http://www.csdp.org/research/pjim02.pdf (accessed June 23, 2007).
7. The Guttmacher Institute, "U.S. Teenage Pregnancy Statistics: Overall Trends, Trends by Race and Ethnicity and State-by-State Information" (April 2009).
8. A review by Martha Simmons of more than eight hundred sermons submitted for the period 1997–2009 by African American clergy to *The African American Pulpit*, a homiletics publication specifically for African American clergy, revealed that less than 20 percent of the sermons that had been published in the journal for this period would be considered as belonging to the historic prophetic preaching tradition of the African American church. Marvin McMickle in his 2006 book, *Where Have All the Prophets Gone*, also makes the claim that the prophetic tradition in the African American church has declined over the last twenty-five years. Additionally, this claim has continually been made at African American teaching/preaching conferences during the past fifteen years.
9. Cheryl Townsend Gilkes, *If It Wasn't for the Women: Black Women's Experience and Womanist Culture in Church Community* (Maryknoll, NY: Orbis, 2001), 129.

# CHARLES GILCHRIST ADAMS

*(1936– )*

Charles Gilchrist Adams is the son of Charles Nathaniel Adams and Clifton Gilchrist Adams, born December 13, 1936, in Detroit, Michigan. Adams was named one of *Ebony*'s fifteen greatest black preachers and their top one hundred most influential African Americans. A past president of the Progressive National Baptist Convention, Adams has served as Conference Preacher for the Hampton University Ministers' Musicians' Organists' Choir Directors' Guild Conference.

Adams pastored the historic Concord Baptist Church in Boston, Massachusetts, from 1962 to 1969. Since 1969, he has been pastor of Hartford Memorial Baptist Church in Detroit. He was appointed the Harvard Divinity School's Professor of the Practice of Ethics and Ministry in 2007 and has taught theological courses at Boston University, Andover Newton School of Theology, Central Baptist Seminary in Kansas City, Iliff School of Theology in Denver, and Ecumenical Theological Seminary in Detroit. He was instrumental in the development of the Harvard Divinity School Summer Leadership Institute, which engages ministers from around the country in economic and community development. Adams is past president of the Detroit NAACP and serves on numerous boards, including those of the National Council of Churches and Morehouse College.

A minister who addresses national and internationally relevant issues of our time, Adams spoke before the United Nations in 1989 to call for an end to the apartheid regime in South Africa, and in Seoul, Korea, before the Baptist World Alliance. In 1991 he was elected to the World Council of Churches' Central Committee, where he advocated that the World Council of Churches use its resources to counter the effects of racism. In 1994, he accompanied President Bill Clinton to Jordan to witness the signing of the peace accord between Jordan and Israel.

• • •

*Charles Adams is known for his poetic, dramatic, and engaging sermonizing. Simultaneously biblical and contemporary, he joins scriptural texts with morning headlines, connecting heavenly inspiration with earthly realities. Hallmarks of his preaching include repetitiveness, long lists, and alliteration, each of which builds in a crescendo. Through repetition, voice inflection, rhythm, and call-and-response communication from the congregation, Adams sings his sermon to the finish line with fiery abandon. His method of preaching has earned him the title, "the Harvard Whooper." "Chaos or Creation" is an example of his unique preaching style.*

## Chaos or Creation (1987)

> *In the beginning when God created the heavens and the earth, the earth was a formless void and darkness covered the face of the waters. Then God said, "Let there be light"; and there was light.*
>
> —Genesis 1:1–3 (New Revised Standard Version)

There are two ways of looking at the creation of people and things; two theological ways of understanding how the world came to be. First, there is the Western philosophic tradition, which is defined under the Latin term *creatio ex nihilo*, which means "creation out of nothing." The Greek and Latin theological fathers and scholars who, reflecting philosophically upon the creation, made a clear distinction between something and nothing, between being and nonbeing. They said: God created the universe out of nothing. That doctrine of the creation of everything by God out of nothing is an abstract theological declaration and spiritual witness that simply asserts that there is no matter, no energy, no reality, no time, no being, no person, no place, no thing that God did not create. If God did not create it, it does not exist. Plain and simple!

Nothing that exists is independent of God's sovereign will and creative action. Nothing stands on its own. Nobody stands alone. All being derives existence from God. All beings owe their life to God. Nothing else is eternal. Everything and everybody *but* God is derived *from* God. There is no other God before God, with God, in God, besides God, but God. No matter how terrible and terrorizing may be the forces of evil in the world, no matter how overwhelming may be the destructive force of the split atom, no matter how captivating may be the addictive tenacity of crack cocaine, or nicotine, or caffeine, or any other substance, these threats are powerful, but they are not supreme. They are not God and they are not in charge. These powers are devastating, but they are helpless to prevent the realization of God's creative intention and redemptive purpose. Nothing that people or demons or things can do can destroy being itself or life itself.

This doctrine of creation out of nothing is the desacralization of nature and the world. If God created, not generated, the universe out of nothing, then only God is supreme and not nature. If God created the universe out of nothing, the universe, which was once nothingness, is not to be feared nor worshipped; but examined, understood, enjoyed, developed, utilized, shared and enhanced . . . but not exploited. We don't have to worship the sun, moon, stars, earth, sky or sea, as some ancients did, because the faith of the Hebrew Bible taught us that all these things are exactly that: things in nature created by God. We don't have to check the horoscope or astrology to know our origin or destiny. Everything that has happened, is happening or will happen has been fixed and arranged by God's own power, authority, creativity and love.

The doctrine of creation out of nothing desacrilized and secularized the natural order so that it was made accessible to unlimited scientific inquiry, empirical analysis and technological development. Thus, theology became the founder of science, and faith became the mother of understanding. St. Anselm said, "*Fides quaerens intellectum.*" That means, "Faith ever searches for understanding." The doctrine of creation by God out of nothing is thus a valuable, Western theological statement that helped produce science, technology and capitalism.

The doctrine of creation out of nothing is the theology of Eurocentric scholars and Western church fathers. But, that is not the only way of looking at creation. There is an alternative doctrine of creation. It is the oriental option of Asian and African political and poetic consciousness and symbolism. The Bible was not written by Europeans. The Bible was written by Africans and Asians. The Bible is a product of Asian and African religion. In the ancient Asian and African worldview, of which the Bible is an expression, there is no such thing as a philosophical split or dichotomy between being and non-being, between somethingness and nothingness.

Those who wrote the Bible talked about not being versus nothingness, but they also talked about order versus disorder,

creation versus chaos,
or community versus disintegration,
or nonviolence versus mutually assured destruction,
or co-existence versus non-existence.

The Bible does not speak about a clean category of sheer nothingness that existed before the creation of the universe. The Bible does not describe for us a state or a condition of absolute nothingness. Nothingness is hard to understand. Nothingness is very difficult to conceptualize. You can only conceptualize something that can be defined and named and described as discreet, knowable and communicable. If it's conceivable, it's something, and if it is somethingness, it cannot be nothingness. The Bible is not so abstract and out-of-touch to speak about a clear, clean category of sheer and absolute nothingness. But the Bible in Genesis 1 describes for us a state of chaos, disaster, disintegration and dislocation. Chaos is described as active, churning, oppositional chaos that preceded the birth of creation, life and hope.

Genesis 1:1 is a temporal or relative clause. The correct translation should be, not "In the beginning God created the heavens and the earth—period." But, it should be rendered, "In the beginning *when* God created the heavens and the earth—comma." Then the writer goes on to talk about, not nothingness, but the pre-creational chaos, out of which God produced order, organization, and continuity. The pre-creational chaos had three parts:

1. The earth was a formless void—a shapeless, clueless, hopeless absurdity;
2. Darkness covered the face of the deep—the darkness was infinitely and intolerably lightless and hopeless;
3. The Spirit of God moved—the Absolute Source of life,<br>radically<br>reflexively

intensively
vigorously
destructively

upon the waters. The Spirit of God, being hope, was intimately active on the surface of uncontrolled, unmitigated and unlimited chaos. There was more going on than the groaning, churning and crunching of the abysmal chaos. There was more going on than the oppositional thickness, toughness and impenetrability of the darkness. There was more going on than the helplessness, hopelessness and cluelessness of chaotic, unlimited darkness and the undifferentiated water of tragic, lifeless chaos. God also was there, actively, forcefully, determinatively present on top of the surface of the vicious and violent chaos. Before there was a when or a where, a now or a then, a this or a that, God was there as the "Ruach Elohim," the Spirit of the Living God planting life and hope in hopeless, hellish chaos. The Spirit of God was not discouraged, disabled or defeated by the chaos! The indomitable spirit of Almighty God moved radically, intensively, reflexibly, decisively, incisively, transformatively, mightily and masterfully upon the face of the water, and the darkness of hopeless chaos. The Spirit of God is present at the beginning of life and possibility in order to coax creation out of chaos. In the beginning when God . . . ! Chaos was chaos, but it was helpless to defy God, deny God or prevent God from creating the cosmos out of the chaos. The threat of primordial chaos was only an empty dare against the power of our eternal, glorious, victorious and omnipotent God.

Notice, in this world, every threat you face is nothing but an idle bluff, an empty dare and a futile sound. God already has your back, your front, your bottom, your top, and all around you. Don't worry about total darkness, danger, death, hate, non-support, sea monsters, dragons, demons, devils and all the conflicts and confusions that swirl, yawn, groan, growl and lash out at you on every side. There is a God who is strong enough and mighty enough to bring all chaos under God's control. There is deep darkness, but there is also God. There is the deep, dark river of death, but there is also God. There is the threat of total annihilation, devastation and extinction, but there is also God who can defeat all chaos, penetrate all darkness and transform all opposition.

If God was *there*, we know God is *here*. If God was present when chaos seemed to be having its way, and prevented all plants from growing, all animals from existing and nothing was able to live or breathe or exist in the vicious, violent, unlighted swirl of bestial chaos, we know God is here. We know God is real and we know God is able. Psalm 24:1 says,

"The earth is the Lord's and all that is in it, the world and those who live in it, for he has founded it upon the seas and established it on the rivers."

The miracle of creation is not making something out of nothing, but it is the mightier miracle of making some order and some sense and some mercy and some meaning out of the mess that we already have on our hands. The miracle *is* to create order out of confusion, and to form human community out of dark and daunting difficulty. The miracle of creation is taking the wreck, waste, violence and cruelty of jungle chaos and turning it into something that is beautiful, sane, saved and safe.

Now tell me, brother Charles, why did the African-Asian mind of the Bible deal with *chaos* rather than nothingness? A good question. Glad you asked. This answer is: *Because they knew something about chaos*. They knew nothing about nothingness. *You can't* know *something* about *nothing*. Nothingness is a meaningless category, in that it can neither be conceived, or imagined, or experienced. You can't imagine total nothingness, total emptiness and total lack of being. You can only speculate on that. You can't point to it, remember it, or relate it to anything. You will not ever have to face total nothingness, not even when you die. There will always be something—something before death, and life after death. Even on earth after you die, something will be left behind: a body, a funeral, a grave, some ashes thrown in the wind, scattered in every direction, some memories and influences that will last for generations, and some people left who will remember you for about seventy years after you die; but not nothingness. Ah! but the chaos is there. We do know something about chaos, disorder, displacement, disruption, dislocation, disaster, discrimination, despair, lack of order, mass confusion, unmitigated mess.

The Africans and Asians knew much about the chaos of the Sea, which they conceptualized as Leviathan, Behemoth or Tiamat in the mythologies of the Ancient Near East. That's the dreaded sea dragon. They also knew about the chaos of the desert, the awful beast of the political oppression of the Roman Empire symbolized in Revelation 13. The African writers of the Bible knew much about the chaos of slavery, injustice, war, strife, interracial conflict, international hostility, violence, meanness, horror, greed and terror. They were ex-slaves, remember? These were the chosen people—ex-slaves and their descendants, whom God had met in the churning waters of the Red Sea and delivered from racism, injustice, fear, slavery and worry. When they had come through the chaos of the sea and of the wilderness, they remembered their suffering and they sang the songs of their deliverance by the strong arm of Almighty God.

It's much more difficult to take a mess and fix it than to take nothing and make something out of it. It's much harder to start from something and transform it than to start from nothing and make a new creation. If you start with nothing, your way is clear. You can take nothingness and shape it and fill it with anything you may desire. But, when you come to a mess and find yourself in a mess that you did not create, then much more is required of you than if you had no mess, tragedy or chaos going on in your life. That's a hard gospel to preach. It's much cheaper to build something from nothing than to take a wreck and make it beautiful. That's what God, the Supreme Cosmetologist, is working with. It is not emptiness and nothingness. It is chaos, tragedy, sin and death. The chaos that tragic human sin has made is the material out of which Almighty God is creating a new heaven and a new earth.

Everyone that lives in this world more than five minutes will learn something about chaos. We know something about it, because we have absorbed it, sucked it up, suffered it to be, struggled against it, fought against it. That's what we dealt with all our lives, chaos. When you have suffered oppression, you know something about chaos. If you are disliked for no reason, you know something about chaos. When you are lied on, talked about and scandalized irrationally and untruthfully, you know something about chaos. When you are hauled into court for doing nothing wrong. When you're thrown in jail, even when you are innocent. When you get a bad decision from a judge who fell asleep during your testimony, you know something about chaos. Everybody in here has had a date with the devil and a bout with chaos. If you haven't had it, get ready. It's coming soon. If you live in this world, you will have chaos. You will have

Disorder
Displacement
Disruption
Dislocation
Disaster
Disappointment
Discrimination
Disparagement
Disorganization
Disorientation
Disfranchisement
Disinheritance
Disapproval
Dispossession

Disrespect
Disbelief
Disgust
Dismissal
Discouragement . . . just
Dissedness!

Everybody in here must face the unmitigated mess of a sinful world. And whenever the world tries to alienate itself from God, separate itself from God and isolate itself from people, look out for chaos. The African Hebrews of the Hebrew Bible knew a whole lot about chaos because they had met chaos face to face in their experiences with chaos in the form of racial hatred, the rejection of nature, wars, strife, interethnic conflict, international hostility, violence, meanness, horror and terror.

The African Hebrews had been damaged by people, but delivered by God. They had been crucified by Gentiles, but resurrected by God, who claimed them, possessed them, empowered them and prospered them. The African Hebrews were God's claimed, called and chosen people. These were the people who wrote about chaos because they were willing to take some responsibility for changing chaos and twisting chaos into a new creation.

Only the oppressor and not the oppressed can talk innocently and piously about "*Creatio ex Nihilo*," Creation out of Nothing. That is nonthreatening, nonpolitical, trans-historical, noncontroversial and ultimately irrelevant. Henry Hitt Crane, an anointed, prophetic, fiery white preacher, was pastor of Central United Methodist Church, downtown Detroit, from 1938 to 1958. He always talked about two primary and stubborn evils in every sermon he preached, and had the only truly integrated church in the city. The two evils he never neglected to mention were racial injustice and war. Martin Luther King Jr. added another absurdity to Crane's twins, and that was poverty. In every sermon he preached or speech he gave, Martin Luther King Jr. addressed the issues of racism, war and poverty. Poverty is not God's will. Poverty is also not necessary. Poverty is caused by the deliberate, structured, intended, legalized maldistribution of resources and opportunities, and these avoidable causes of poverty should be condemned. They didn't kill King until he condemned war and poverty. The biggest crime in America is for green money to be in Black hands.

We are dealing with a whole lot of chaos today. There's chaos in our personal lives. There's chaos in our communal life, the exploitation of nature, the despoiling of the ecosystem, and the depletion of the soil.

There is the raping of the earth by strip mining and cash crop monopolies, the production of atomic and biological weapons of mass destruction, the demonic idolatries of race, class, religion and nature, cruel denials of truth and justice, systematic deprivations of opportunity and hope. The whole urban community is being attacked viciously and violently by chaos, abandoned by economic withdrawal on one hand and the invasion and implosion of illicit drugs on the other hand, leaving the dark ghettos drained of appreciated history, appropriated opportunity and apprehended destiny. We see trouble everywhere. That's why I love the Bible. It doesn't ignore the reality of the chaos we all have to deal with. It does not bypass chaos, but it faces it squarely. It says, "the earth was a formless void, darkness was upon the face of the deep," but chaos is not supreme.[1]

In the midst of all that unformed chaos, watery chaos, vicious chaos, endless chaos, above all of that mess, on top of all of that senseless absurdity, the Bible shouts that the Spirit of God, the Ruach Elohim was moving, radically and intensively and reflexively on all that chaos. God does not run from chaos, but jumps in the middle of chaos, leaps up and down on top of chaos, bringing life out of death and hope out of hell, meaning out of misery and creation out of chaos! God Almighty, the Holy Spirit, worked on top of chaos, until darkness gathered its sable skirts and fled, until light appeared, until order arrived, until the day made a debut, until light and life were brightly revealed and upheld. The good news is that chaos is terrible, mean and powerful; but chaos is not supreme. Chaos is not God! Only God is God! Don't worry about the chaos. There's going to be a whole lot of drama and chaos in your life and my life; but there is a God, working on top of chaos, covering every inch of it. You don't have to run from chaos. You can reach for God's hand in all the chaos and drama of this deluded world.

God's Hand will hold you.
God's Light will guide you.
God's Love will lift you.
God's Spirit will build you up.
God's Presence will bless you.
God's Wind will move you.
God's Joy will strengthen you.
God's Fire will empower you.

Don't get too upset when folks lie on you and tear down your good name. God is still God. God is still working with all the chaotic, castigating distortion of truth, in order to reveal in you the whole truth that will set you free. Don't be defeated by racism and sexism on your job. Don't let that mess drive you out of your job and out of your mind, because God is still real, God is still there and God is still good. God will bring out of occupational chaos your creativity as a worker, your ability as a thinker and your victory as a child of God.

Don't play dead before the chaos of alcohol, food, sex or any other addictive force, because God is walking, leaping and working on top of your stormy sea of chemical dependency and other dependencies to make you independent of everything and everybody but God. Don't let the chaos of an ugly divorce mess up your mind or ruin your life. God is still God, even in your most embarrassing loss of security and companionship, and God will surely bring you out of your most painful times. God will give you

your dignity as a woman,
your might as a man,
your character as a Christian,
your power as a person and
your penitent self-improvement as a child of God.

Don't let injustices in the courts or in the elections wreck your soul because God is on top of that too. God can take the injustice of dirty politics and the failure of jurisprudence and turn all that big time chaos into your resurrection of

courage,
conscience,
competence,
creativity,
community,
compassion and hope.

God will meet you in the chaos of tragedy, calamity and adversity to show you

how great God is,
how good God is,
how wonderful God is,
how creative God is and
how mighty God is!

Never give up. Never cop out. Never cave in. There is a God who can lead you, bless you, fix you, deliver you in all the chaos and monstrosities that you must face. There is a God who is able to keep you from falling and present you faultless before God's presence with exceeding joy. How do I know? I know because of Jesus. I know because of Calvary. I know because of a hill of chaos, shaped like a bony skull. I know because of one Friday afternoon when Jesus was dying on an old rugged cross, the super chaos of death, the devil and hell tried to take Jesus out: the sun burnt out like a cinder. That's chaos. The moon turned red like blood. That's chaos. The stars dispersed and fell down in a purple streak. That's chaos. The earth went reeling and rocking like a drunken universe. That's chaos. The whole world was tossed into a tizzy of tragic convulsions. That's chaos. The land vomited up its righteous dead. That's chaos. Darkness covered the earth like a thick blanket of impenetrable gloom. That's chaos. Right was on the scaffold: Chaos. Wrong was on the Emperor's throne: Chaos. Jesus was nailed to the cross: Chaos. Innocence was crucified. Death was glorified. Love was slain. Hate was strutting. Darkness was ruling. Light was retreating. Evil was reigning. Justice was being denied. That's chaos on top of chaos. But, look again and see what God did with all that chaos. God took all that maddening meanness to create your salvation and my salvation. God took chaos and fixed it, finished and furnished my salvation and yours. God took chaos and:

Verified Descartes' intuition;
Magnified Hegel's hope;
Clarified Plato's idea;
Satisfied Socrates' question;
Purified Kant's categories;
Justified Abraham's faith;
Gratified Amos' justice;
Fortified Hosea's love;
Sanctified Micah's mercy;
Beautified Ezekiel's vision;
Edified Job's confidence;
Dignified the Whole Creation;
Glorified the Whole Church;
Rectified the Whole World; and
Qualified the Whole Human Race.
Hallelujah it's done!
Hallelujah you're saved!
Hallelujah you're blessed!

Hallelujah you're free!
Hallelujah you're sanctified!
Hallelujah you're justified!
Hallelujah you're a child of God!!

### *Notes*

*Sermon source:* The text for this sermon was provided to the editors by the author.

1. See Genesis 1:2.

### *Bibliographical Sources*

"Charles G. Adams," Hartford Memorial Baptist Church. http://www.hartfordchurchdetroit.org/html/pastor/pastor.html (accessed April 5, 2008).

"Charles G. Adams," in *Who's Who Among African Americans*, 18th ed. Detroit: Gale Publishing Group, 2005, 5.

LaRue, Cleophus J. *Power in the Pulpit: How America's Most Effective Black Preachers Prepare Their Sermons*. Louisville, KY: Westminster John Knox Press, 2002.

## CHARLES E. BOOTH

*(1947– )*

Charles Edward Booth was born in Baltimore, Maryland, in 1947, the son of William and Hazel Booth. After attending Baltimore's public schools, Booth went on to graduate from Howard University, Eastern Baptist Theological Seminary, and United Theological Seminary. Booth was mentored by three legendary preachers and African American pastor-scholars: J. Pious Barbour in the 1970s, Harold A. Carter in the 1980s and Samuel DeWitt Proctor in the 1990s. Booth co mentored several groups of doctoral students with Proctor at United Theological Seminary from 1992 to 1995 and served as a "senior mentor" of the doctoral program at United after Proctor's death.

A preacher since the age of seventeen, Booth has become one of the most distinguished and sought-after revival preachers in the United States. On several occasions he has served as the guest lecturer and morning and evening preacher for Hampton University's Ministers' Musicians' Choir Directors' Guild Conference, the premiere gathering of African American preachers in the country. He has been a speaker at numerous colleges, universities, and seminaries, as well as denominational and civic gatherings. He served as adjunct professor of preaching at United Theological Seminary in Dayton, Ohio, from 1987 to 1994 and currently serves as professor of preaching at Trinity Lutheran Seminary in Columbus.

Booth served as pastor of the Calvary Baptist Church of Chester, Pennsylvania, and since 1978 has been the senior pastor of the Mount Olivet Baptist Church in Columbus. In 1993, *Ebony* magazine placed him on its honor roll of great preachers. He is author of *Bridging the Breach: Evangelical Thought and Liberation in the African American Preaching Tradition* (2000).

• • •

*An ardent student of preaching, Booth adopted and perfected Samuel DeWitt Proctor's Hegelian preaching method of thesis, antithesis, and synthesis. While mastering the fundamentals of homiletic technique, Booth added the flair and freedom of the African American homiletical artist, resulting in his imitation by many preachers. The following sermon is illustrative of his preaching style and theology.*

## An Uneven Hand
## (June 2001)

> *Then the man who had received the one talent came. Master, he said, I knew that you are a hard man; harvesting where you have not sown and gathering where have you have not scattered. So I was afraid and went out and hid your talent in the ground. See, here is what belongs to you. His master replied, you wicked, lazy servant. So you knew that I harvested where I have not sown scattered seed. Well then, you should have put my money on deposit with the bankers so that when I returned, I would have received back with interest. Take the talent from him and give it to the one who has the ten talents.*
>
> —Matthew 25:19–28 (New International Version)

Is God fair? No. God isn't fair. I say it undeniably. I say it indisputably. Nowhere in the Bible does God ever say God is fair. He says, "I'm all-powerful." He says, "I know all things." He says, "I'm everywhere at once; I am love; I am grace; I am mercy; I am holy." But he never says, "I'm fair." Look at the distribution of the talents: to one he gave five, and to another, two, and to the third, one. That is unfair or unequal distribution. There's no way of getting around it, God is not fair.

Now, of course, the classical argument is that God gives to us what we can handle. And you are absolutely right. But if we were standing in line today and the person next to us got five, the other person got two, and God gave us one—many of us would look at God and say, "What's wrong with me? How come I don't rank to get five? How come I don't rank to get two?"

There are people who have come to this conference every year who are properly prepared and who are tremendously gifted. And in your mind, male or female, you ask yourself, "Why don't I have a certain kind of church? Why don't I get invited to preach or teach at the Hampton Ministers' Conference? My stuff is as good as his. In fact, I'm better than he or she." Come on and tell the truth and shame the devil. But the bottom line, my brothers and sisters, is that all of us have in our hand an uneven hand.

You know one of the things I've discovered about saved people is that we want to believe that we have totally forgotten all of our past. But some of you haven't forgot your pinochle days. You ain't forgot your five hundred gin rummy days. You ain't forgot your bid whist days. You know that when you're dealt cards, the first thing you do is size up your hand. Nine times out of ten you are dealt an uneven hand. But, you've got to stay in the game and pluck cards from the deck. With every new card your hand has the possibility of changing. A whole lot of us started out with an uneven hand, but across the journey, I've gotten some more cards and things are beginning now to even up. In other words, it doesn't look as bleak as it use to look.

You see, what we have to understand is: God wants us to acknowledge the hand dealt us. You have got to admit that you have the hand. You might not like the hand. You might not be happy with the hand; but for now, it's the best hand you have.

Now, you also have to hold your cards close to your chest so that nobody else can see your hand. But a whole lot of us reveal our hands by constantly and chronically complaining about everything that ain't right in our lives. Learn how to play your cards close to your chest. If you've got five; fine. If you've got two; fine. If you've got one; fine. What you must do is acknowledge the hand that you have.

Now, when Jesus tells this parable, Jesus does not pick or make any bones about the fact that there is an unequal distribution. I don't care how you exegete the text. I don't care how you interpret it. I don't care what kind of hermeneutic you apply to it. Jesus never offers an apology for the text, nor does he ever answer the question of why he unequally distributes. But he does say that you have to accept or acknowledge what is in your grasp.

Everybody here does not have the same gift. Everybody in here does not have the same ability. Look at the kind of hand Jesus was dealt—the King of Glory; the Lord of Lords; tiptoed through the back door of human history; dropped from the loins of a virgin on a bed of straw in a manger in Bethlehem; born to a disadvantaged people called the disinherited. Somewhere between his twelfth and thirtieth year, his father dies and he assumes the responsibility of taking care of his mother, his brothers, and his sisters—an uneven hand. When he is baptized in Jordan and makes his way into the wilderness, he is tempted on three different occasions. In forty days, he comes out and he begins doing good. The blind receive their sight. The deaf get their hearing. The dumb, their speech. The lame, their limbs. He even raises dead folk from their slumbering couches. The more good he did, the more his enemies got on his trail. No friend of the Pharisees. No friend to the Scribes. No friend to the Sadducees. No friend to the Herodians. Look at the hand that was dealt him. He selected twelve men. And every one of them, save the Internal Revenue Service agent, Matthew, was a blue-collar worker. Not one academician; not one educator; not one economist; not one engineer; not one architect; not one social activist. And, in the end, everyone turned on him—an uneven hand.

Even his family did not really grasp who he was. One day when his mama, his brothers, and his sisters came to interrupt him, he raised the question, "Who is my mother? Who is my father? Who are my brothers and my sisters?"[1] And he asked his father in Gethsemane to let him out of the salvation contract; not once; not twice, but three times. "Father, if it be possible, let this cup pass." Then he said, "Nevertheless, not mine, but thy will be done."[2] But that was not the end of the problem. Because if it were the end of the problem, why on Calvary would he ask God, "Why have you forsaken me?"[3] And then in the end, the most horrendous thing of all—crucified on a hill called Calvary—not between two candlesticks on an altar. Not in the sanctuary, but out at the place of the skull, he died. I'm trying to drive home one point. And the point is: Jesus had to live with the uneven hand he was dealt—not complaining, not feeling sorry for himself.

Acknowledging my hand does not mean that I'm resigned to my hand. In other words, these are the cards in my hand now. But the longer I stay in the game, the more apt my hand is to change. Now, while you're waiting for your hand to change, don't get drunk. Don't get high. Don't slip out to the hotel room when the session is over and get a little gin and tonic, rum and coke. Don't puff on a little weed. Don't snort on some crack. And don't y'all act like it just happens out there in the pew. We've got a lot of that junk going on right here in the pulpit. All this stuff that we see taking place in the body of Christ is not just out there in the pew. A lot of us who call ourselves anointed; a lot of us who call ourselves walking by faith and not by sight, have succumbed to the illusions of support that we claim surround us.

No, I'm not resigned to the hand that I have. Because I am not resigned to the acknowledged hand, I'm going to believe that God is somehow going to change my condition. God is going to rectify my circumstance. I may be down tonight, but about eight o'clock tomorrow morning, I'm going to be back up on my feet again. Because if I keep calling on God long enough, God's going to hear me when I cry. How many people have called upon the Lord and you may have had to wait, but God heard your cry? I thank God today that I'm not so Baptist that I can't be Christian. When I think about the goodness of Jesus and all he's done for me—I am not resigned.

Last year, most of us in the African American community got very delighted that there came to the big screen *Amistad*. I learned about *Amistad* back in 1965 when I entered as a freshman at Howard University in Washington, D.C. It is the story of fifty-three West Africans taken captive and held hostage and put on a vessel. But they mutinied around the tip of Cuba in 1839 because even though they acknowledged their plight, they were never resigned to their plight. And there was something there that was deep in their breasts that said something about freedom; that said something about emancipation; that said something about liberation, and the record is that they mutinied.

Now watch where I'm going. My mother taught me that if you would take one step, God would take two. And the theology of that statement is this: If you show some initiative; if you make an effort to come out of your chronic condition, instead of always complaining about your condition; if you'd just stop pouting, and take one step; God will invade your circumstance and make a way when it looks like there ain't no way. Is there anybody here that has ever been between a rock and a hard place? Has anybody here ever had your back up against the wall? Has anybody here ever been between the devil and the deep blue sea, but just when you thought you were about to lose it; just when you thought you were about to sink beneath the water line, when you put forth an effort, God inserted himself in your condition and did the impossible?

Fifty-three West African slaves mutinied in 1839. They were brought before a judiciary body in New England, and God raised up some folk to help them along the way. They were black and white fighting together for the release of these fifty-three Africans back in 1839. Are you listening? And some of you want to know how bad God is; how awesome God is. Somebody put it in the minds of Baldwin and Gilpin to go and talk to a United States congressman who had been the sixth president of our Republic, John Quincy Adams. And even though John Quincy Adams did not want to get in the fray, they reminded him that his record declared—that even though he was not willing to declare—his record declared that he was an abolitionist. God used the former sixth president of the United States of America, now a congressman, to stand before the Supreme Court of the United States and argue the case of fifty-three African slaves who were not resigned to their uneven hand. Don't you tell me what God can't do! God can make a way out of no way. God can open doors that no man can shut. God can put joy in the midst of your sorrow. God can reduce your mountains to valleys and your mountains to molehills if you trust and never doubt. God will—not God might, not there's a possibility—but God will bring you out. You don't have to be resigned to your plight. You don't have to be confined to your situation. God will bring you out.

Acknowledge the hand; don't be resigned to it. Look at what happens in the text. When the landowner comes back—show time! "You—I gave you five; what did you do with it?" The servant replies, "I multiplied it and got five more." "Well done!" "You—I gave you two, what did you do with it?" The servant replies, "I multiplied it, got two more." "Well done!" "You—yeah you over there in the corner. Yeah—you trying to duck down—come on. I gave you one." Now comes the excuse. The servant says, "Well, you're unfair and I knew you weren't fair. You gave him five and gave him two and only gave me one. And I've got a B.A. degree and I went to Virginia Union School of Theology and I studied under Jones and John Kinney and I got a M.Div. and I went up the road to Howard and got in that program and I was taught by Cartwright Davis and Clyde Newsome and I have a D.Min. and you only gave me one talent? I mean nobody puts words together like me. Nobody has elocutionary skills like me. Nobody has articulation and oratorical excellence like me and yet you only gave me one?" I mean the brother doesn't say it with any sense of timidity. He's bold, doggone it: "I'll tell you what I did with it. I took your one talent; the scrawny talent that you gave me. I took that measly little talent and I buried it."

What the brother with one talent did not understand and what many of us have to understand is, an uneven hand is better than no hand at all. One talent is better than no talent. God might not have given you five and he might not have given you two, but he gave you one. And whatever he gave you with one, you ought to be able to use. You ought to polish that one. You ought to embellish that one. You ought to hone that one with such a fine edge that somebody ought to say, "He's only got one, she's only got one, but my God, what he does with that one talent."

When I was a little boy, I lost my left eye. I can remember people were always laughing at me and calling me horrible names. When I got in high school, young ladies did not want to date me because one eye looked bigger than the other. I remember one night falling on my knees and my mother overheard me praying. And I said, "God, you gave everybody else two eyes, why didn't you give me two?" God said, "Sit down, shut up. I may have only given you one eye, but you don't need two eyes to preach. What I took out of your head, I put in your heart. You may not be able to see with two eyes, but I gave you a voice and I want you to tell everybody what I can do with only one talent." I've got only one eye but I thank God that one day I heard the voice of Jesus saying, "Come unto me and rest. Lay down thy weary one; lay down thy head upon my breast."[4] I came to Jesus just as I was, weary, worn and sad. I found in him a resting place and he has made me glad.

I'm glad that I'm a one-eyed preacher. I'm glad that I've got joy bells in my soul. I'm glad I've got a promise that no weapon formed against me shall prosper. I've got a promise that they that wait upon the Lord shall renew their strength. I've got a promise that—lo, I'll be with you always, even until the end of the world.[5] I've got a promise that he'll make a way when I need a way.

Can I tell you why I've got a promise? I've got a promise because I've got a name. Whether you've got five or whether you've got two or whether you've got one, you ought to be able to tell somebody that through many dangers, toils and snares, I have already come. It may be an uneven hand, but I thank God it's the hand God gave me and I'm going to wait until my change come. Because by and by and after a while, my change is going to come. And when he evens out my uneven hand, I ain't going to sit there with my arms folded and my legs crossed. But I am going to thank him for evening up my hand.

## NOTES

*Sermon source: The African American Pulpit* 5, no. 2 (Spring 2002), 135–38.

1. See Matthew 12:48.
2. See Matthew 26:39.
3. Matthew 27:46 (King James Version).
4. See Matthew 11:28.
5. See Matthew 28:20.

### *Bibliographical Sources*

"An Interview with Charles E. Booth." *The African American Pulpit* 4, no. 1 (Winter 2000–2001): 92–94.

LaRue, Cleophus J., ed. *Power in the Pulpit: How America's Most Effective Black Preachers Prepare Their Sermons*. Louisville, KY: Westminster John Knox Press, 2002.

"Welcome to Our New Advisory Board Members." *The African American Pulpit* 4, no. 1 (Winter 2000–2001): 6.

## THEA BOWMAN

*(1937–1990)*

Sister Thea Bowman was a nationally known speaker, teacher, and champion for intercultural relations and racial understanding. The founder of the Institute of Black Catholic Studies at Xavier University, Bowman was a trailblazer in merging African American culture with Catholic spirituality. Bowman united black theology with the creative arts to produce powerful expressions of preaching, teaching, and liturgy in worship.

Born Bertha Bowman to Mary Esther and Theon Edward Bowman of Yazoo City, Mississippi, she was baptized an Episcopalian, then was Methodist, and at age nine became a Catholic. By age sixteen, she entered Rose Convent in LaCrosse, Wisconsin, becoming the first African American sister in the order of the Franciscan Sisters for Perpetual Adoration. At age nineteen, she began her novitiate years and changed her name to Thea, which means "of God," and commenced her teaching career. She received a doctorate in English from the Catholic University of America in Washington, D.C., in 1972, where she explored the oral tradition of African American culture and music as a means of preserving and communicating history and culture. She became chair of the English department at Viterbo College in LaCrosse and served on the faculty at the Catholic University.

Returning to Mississippi in 1978 to care for her parents, Bowman became consultant to the Office of Intercultural Awareness for the diocese of Jackson, Mississippi, where she began to speak widely on the richness of African American and Native American heritage in that state. She emerged as a sought-after speaker, incorporating a deep and inspiring presence with singing, dancing, drama, poetry, and the Gospel message. She made more than one hundred public appearances each year and traveled to Canada, the Virgin Islands, and countries in Africa and Europe.

Until the time of her death in 1990 at age fifty-two, she continued speaking to audiences and pursuing her mission of racial justice, inclusion, and cultural celebration. Diagnosed with breast cancer in 1984, she prayed "to live until I die." She continued to serve in ministry from a wheelchair. In her life, she received numerous honors, including the Harriet Tubman Award and the Pope John XXIII Award. In 1989 she received a Doctorate of Religion from Boston College. She is the author of *Families: Black and Catholic, Catholic and Black* and is being considered for sainthood by the Catholic church.

• • •

*Sister Thea Bowman's preaching reflects both a commitment to black spirituality, what might be called Afrocentric, and inclusiveness of the richness of all cultures. Her sermons are centered on family and church, confidence in the essential good in all human nature, and living despite adversities such as cancer. In 1989, the U.S. bishops invited her to be a key speaker at their conference on black Catholics. The following message is that address.*

## Being a Black Catholic (June 1989)

### Our History

Our history includes the services of Simon of Cyrene, the search of the Ethiopian eunuch, the contributions of black Egypt in art and mathematics and monasticism and politics, the art and architecture of Zimbabwe, the scholarship of Timbuktu, the dignity and serenity of textile and gold and religion in Ghana, the pervasive spirituality and vitality of Nigeria, [and] the political and social systems of Zaire.

Our history includes enslavements, oppression and exploitation. As Malcolm X said, "My folks, most of them, didn't come over here on the Mayflower; they came over here on slave ships, in chains." Proud, strong men and women, artists, teachers, healers, warriors and dream makers, inventors and builders, administrators like yourselves, politicians, and priests. They came to these shores in the slave trade. Those who survived the indignity of the middle passage came to the American continents bringing treasures of African heritage, African spiritual and cultural gifts, wisdom, faith and faithfulness, art and drama. Here in an alien land; African people clung to African ways of thinking, of perceiving, of understanding values, of celebrating life, of walking and talking and healing and learning and singing and praying . . . African ways of laughing and being together and loving: That's culture.

To the Americas our people brought the secret memory of Africa, the celebration of life values in an African way and style: in song and instrumentation, in story and drum, in verse and anecdote, the memory of the survival mechanisms of Africa, the memory of color and texture, of culinary arts that translated even when we ate chitlins and other folks' leftovers.

African people here became African Americans. Expressing faith in the God who loves and saves, they embodied and celebrated their own lives and their own values, their goals, their dreams, their relationships. Our history includes the island experience—the Virgin Islands, Haiti, Cuba; our Hispanic experience in Central and South America; our Native experience, where African blood commingled with Choctaw and Chickasaw and Cherokee, with people of Asian and Asian-Pacific origin, with Europeans from France and Germany. You want to know how come some of us look like we do?

African people of the diaspora, we are here in this land, and this is our land. That's part of our history too.

Our people, black people, helped to build this nation in cotton and grain and beans and vegetables, in brick and mortar.

They cleared the land and cooked the food that they grew.

They cleaned houses and built churches, some of them Catholic churches. They built railroads and bridges and national monuments.

Black people defended this country as soldiers and sailors. Black people taught and molded and raised the children—and I'm not just talking about the black children . . .

You know what I'm talking about, church? I mean, are you walking with me, church?

Surviving our history, physically, mentally, emotionally, morally, spiritually, faithfully and joyfully, our people developed a culture that was African and American, that was formed and enriched by all that we experienced. And despite all this, despite the civil rights movement of the sixties and the socio-educational gains of the seventies, blacks in the eighties are still struggling, still scratching and clawing as the old folks said, still trying to find home in the homeland and home in the church, still struggling to gain access to equal opportunity.

A disproportionate number of black people are poor. Poverty, deprivation, discrimination, stunted physical, intellectual and spiritual growth—

I don't need to tell you this, but I want to remind you, more than a third of the black people that live in the United States live in poverty, the kind of poverty that lacks basic necessities.

I'm talking about old people who have worked hard all their lives and don't have money for adequate food or shelter or medical care.

I'm talking about children who can never have equal access and equal opportunity because poverty doomed them to low birth weight and retardation and unequal opportunity for education.

More than 55 percent of black babies are born to single mothers. About 41 percent of black families are single-parent families headed by women. The divorce rate for blacks is twice as high as for whites.

Black children are twice as likely as white children to be born prematurely, to suffer from low birth weight, to live in substandard housing, to have no parent employed.

Unemployment and underemployment among us are endemic. And many of us don't have the social and political contacts that put us where the jobs are when jobs are being passed out. One of every twenty-one black males is murdered. A disproportionate number of our men are dying of suicide and AIDS and drug abuse and low self-esteem.

## Black and Catholic

What does it mean to be black and Catholic? For many of us it means having been evangelized, having been educated, having been given a chance through the work of the Catholic Church, through the Josephites or the Divine Word Fathers or the Holy Ghost Fathers or the Franciscans or the Edmundites or the Sisters of the Blessed Sacrament.

I'm from Mississippi. The first schools in Mississippi were started in the cathedral basement by diocesan priests and a group of lay women. For so many of us, being black and Catholic means having come into the church because education opened the door to evangelization. It means, in an age when black men and black women were systematically kept out of the priesthood and out of most religious communities, there were those who cared and who came and who worked with and for us and among us and helped us to help ourselves.

And now our black American bishops, in the name of the church universal, have publicly declared that we as a people of faith, as a Catholic people of God, have come of age. And it is time for us to be evangelizers of ourselves.

What does it mean to be black and Catholic? It means that I come to my church fully functioning. That doesn't frighten you, does it? I come to my church fully functioning. I bring myself, my black self, all that I am, all that I have, all that I hope to become, I bring my whole history, my traditions, my experience, my culture, my African American song and dance and gesture and movement and teaching and preaching and healing and responsibility as gifts to the church.

I bring a . . . spirituality [that] is contemplative and biblical and holistic, bringing to religion a totality of mind and imagination, of memory, of feeling and passion and emotion and intensity, of faith that is embodied, incarnate praise, . . . a spirituality that is communal, that tries to walk and talk and work and pray and play together—even with the bishops. You know, when our bishop is around, we want him to be where we can find him, where we can reach out and touch him, where we can talk to him. Don't be too busy, you-all.

A spirituality that in the middle of your Mass or in the middle of your sermon just might have to shout out and say, "Amen, hallelujah, thank you Jesus." A faith that attempts to be Spirit-filled. The old ladies say that if you love the Lord your God with your whole heart, [with] your whole soul and your whole mind and all your strength, then you praise the Lord with your whole heart and soul and mind and strength.

If you get enough fully functioning black Catholics in your diocese, they are going to hold up the priest and they are going to hold up the bishop. We love our bishops, you-all. We love you-all too. But see, these bishops are our own, ordained for the church universal, ordained for the service of God's people, but they are ours; we raised them; they came from our community and in a unique way they can speak for us and to us. And that's what the church is talking about. Indigenous leadership. The leaders are supposed to look like their folks, ain't that what the church says?

To be black and Catholic means to realize that the work of the ordained ministers is not a threat to me and I'm no threat to that. The work of the ordained minister, of the professional minister, is to enable the people of God to do the work of the church. To feed us sacramentally, to enable us to preach and to teach, and I ain't necessarily talking about preaching in the pulpit.

You know as well as I do that some of the best preaching does not go on in the pulpit, but as a Catholic Christian I have a responsibility to preach and to teach, to worship and to pray. Black folk can't just come into church and depend on the preacher and say, "Let Father do it." And, if Father doesn't do it right, then they walk out and they complain, you know, "That liturgy didn't do anything for me."

The question that we raise is, What did you do for the liturgy? And the church is calling us to be participatory and to be involved. The church is calling us to feed and to clothe and to shelter and to teach. Your job is to enable me, to enable God's people, black people, white people, brown people, all the people, to do the work of the church in the modern world. Teaching, preaching, witnessing, worshipping, serving, healing and reconciling in black, because we are wedded to the lived experience, to the history and the heritage of black people.

Getting in touch. To be black and Catholic means to get in touch with the world church, with my brothers and sisters in Rome, with my brothers and sisters in China, with my brothers and sisters in Europe and Asia and Latin America, with the church of Africa. Do your folk realize that there are more Catholic Christians in Africa than in North America, and then they run around talking about the minority? In Africa right now three hundred people become Christian every day, and 75 percent of them are becoming Roman Catholics.

The Vatican central office reports that in Africa the number of students for the priesthood increased by 88 percent between 1970 and 1988, while in North America the number dropped by 43 percent.

To be black and Catholic means to be intensely aware of the changing complexion of the College of Cardinals. I picked up your Catholic newspaper and I saw the picture church, world church, and a lot of folk look like me. We've got to get the word out. To be black and Catholic still, though, often feels like being a second- or third-class citizen of the holy city.

## Black Leadership in the Church

You know, Bishop Jim Lyke said a long time ago that black Catholic Christians will be second-class citizens of the church until they take their places in leadership beside their brothers and sisters of whatever race or national origin . . .

The majority of priests, religious and lay ministers who serve the black community in the United States still are not from the black community, and many of those people who attempt to serve among us . . . do not feel an obligation to learn or understand black history or spirituality or culture or life, black tradition or ritual. They work for the people, but they have not learned to share life and love and laughter with the people. They somehow insulate themselves from the real lives of the people because they don't feel comfortable with black people.

I travel all over the country, and I see it: black people within the church, black priests, sometimes even black bishops, who are invisible. And when I say that, I mean they are not consulted. They are not included. Sometimes decisions are made that affect the black community for generations, and they are made in rooms by white people behind closed doors.

Some of us are poor. Some of us have not had the advantages of education. But how can people still have a voice and a role in the work of the church? Isn't that what the church is calling us all to?

I see people who are well educated and experienced and willing to work. Sometimes they're religious; sometimes they're lay. They are not included in the initial stages of planning. They are not included in the decision making. Now, I know you are bishops and I'm not talking about somebody coming into your diocese and trying to tell you what to do. I'm talking about the normal, church-authorized consultative processes that attempt to enable the people of God to be about the work of the Catholic Church. If you know what I'm talking about, say Amen.

See, you-all talk about what you have to do if you want to be a multicultural church: Sometimes I do things your way; sometimes you do things mine . . .

Black people who are still victims within the church of paternalism, of a patronizing attitude, black people who within the church have developed a mission mentality—they don't feel called, they don't feel responsible, they don't do anything. Let Father do it, let the sisters do it, let the friends and benefactors from outside do it. That's the mission mentality. And it kills us and it kills our churches. And so, within the church, how can we work together so that all of us have equal access to input, equal access to opportunity, equal access to participation?

Go into a room and look around and see who's missing and send some of your folks out to call them in so that the church can be what she claims to be, truly catholic.

They still talk about black folk in the church. You hear it, you know, you hear it over on the sidelines. They say we're lazy. They say we're loud. They say we're irresponsible. They say we lower the standards. So often we've been denied the opportunities to learn and to practice. You learned by trial and error; ain't that how you learned? . . .

Some black people don't approve of black religious expression in Catholic liturgy. They've been told that it's not properly Catholic. They've been told that it's not appropriately serious or dignified or solemn or controlled, that the European way is necessarily the better way.

How can we teach all the people what it means to be black and Catholic? The *National Catechetical Directory* says that all catechesis is supposed to be multicultural, but how little of it is. When we attempt to bring our black gifts to the church, people who do not know us say we're being non-Catholic or separatists or just plain uncouth.

## Catholic Education

I've got to say one more thing. You-all ain't going to like this but that's all right. Catholic schools have been a primary instrument of evangelization within the black community. The church has repeatedly asked black folk, What do you want? What can the church do for you? And black folk all over the country are saying, "Help us to education. We need education. The way out of poverty is through education."

We can't be the church without education, because ignorance cripples us and kills us. Black people are still asking the Catholic Church for education. Now, sometimes we don't have the money. Are we finding alternative ways to speak to the black community in a language that they understand? Bishop Brunini said a lot of Catholics spend time ministering to the saved and go out there and work with the church folks. A lot of black people out there are unchurched.

## We Shall Overcome

We have come a long way in faith. Just look where we have come from. We as black people find ourselves at the threshold of a new age. And as I look about the room I know that many of you have walked and talked and worked and prayed and stood with us in society and in the church. And in the name of all black folk, I thank you.

Today we're called to walk together in a new way toward that land of promise and to celebrate who we are and whose we are. If we as church walk together, don't let nobody separate you. That's one thing black folk can teach you. Don't let folk divide you or put the lay folk over here and the clergy over here, put the bishops in one room and the clergy in the other room, put the women over here and the men over here.

The church teaches us that the church is a family. It is a family of families and the family got to stay together. We know that if we do stay together, if we walk and talk and work and play and stand together in Jesus' name, we'll be who we say we are, truly Catholic; and we shall overcome—overcome the poverty, overcome the loneliness, overcome the alienation and build together a holy city, a new Jerusalem, a city set apart where they'll know we are his because we love one another.

*We shall overcome (You all get up!)*
*We shall overcome*
*We shall overcome*
*We shall overcome someday*

*Oh, deep in my heart,*
*Deep in my heart I know,*
*I do believe we shall overcome someday.*[1]

Now, bishops I'm going to ask you-all to do something. Cross your right hand over your left hand. You've got to move together to do that. All right now, walk with me. See, in the old days, you had to tighten up so that when the bullets would come, so that when the tear gas would come, so that when the dogs would come, so that when the horses would come, so that when the tanks would come brothers and sisters would not be separated from one another.

And you remember what they did with the clergy and the bishops in those old days, where they'd put them? Right up in front, to lead the people in solidarity with our brothers and sisters in the church who suffer in South Africa, who suffer in Poland, who suffer in Ireland, who suffer in Nicaragua, in Guatemala, in Northern Ireland, all over this world. We shall live in love.

*We shall live in love*
*We shall live in love*
*We shall live in love today*
*Deep in my heart,*
*Deep in my heart I know I do believe,*
*We shall live in love.*[2]

That's all we've got to do: love the Lord, to love our neighbor. Amen. Amen. Amen. Amen.

## Notes

*Sermon source:* Thea Bowman, *Sister Thea Bowman Shooting Star: Selected Writings and Speeches*, ed. Celestine Cepress (Winona, MN: St. Mary's Press, 1993).
1. See "We Shall Overcome," *The New National Baptist Hymnal*, 16th ed. (Nashville, TN: National Baptist Publishing Board, 1977), number 372.
2. Ibid.

## Bibliographical Sources

Dyer, Ervin. "Black Nun Examined for Sainthood." *Pittsburgh Post-Gazette*, November 28, 2003. http://www.postgazette.com/localnews/20031128TheaBowman1128p4.asp (accessed November 20, 2009).

Franciscan Sisters of Perpetual Adoration. "Sister Thea Bowman." http://www.fspa.org/fspanews/thea_bowman.asp (accessed August 19, 2005).

Nutt, Maurice. *Thea Bowman: In My Own Words.* Liguori, MO: Liguori Publications, 2009.
"Sister Thea Bowman (1937–1990): A Tribute." Boston College. http://www.bc.edu/offices/ahana/about/history/bowman.html (accessed July 13, 2007).

# KATIE GENEVA CANNON

*(1950– )*

Best known as one of the mothers of womanist theology within the American Academy of Religion, Katie Cannon was the first African American woman to be ordained in the United Presbyterian Church. In 1983, Cannon earned a doctorate in Philosophy from Union Theological Seminary in New York, again becoming the first African American woman to reach that milestone. Born in 1950, daughter of Esau Cannon and Corine Lytle Cannon, in Kannapolis, North Carolina, during the depths of segregation, Cannon looked to theology for answers to the racist cruelties she suffered growing up as a black person. Cannon developed tenets of womanist theology to reflect the experience of African American women in religion and society. Cannon states that most traditional theology pretends that "who we are in our bodies does not affect the way in which we see God or the way in which we experience God in our lives." Employing Alice Walker's definition of womanism from Walker's book *In Search of Our Mother's Garden*, Cannon asserts throughout her writings and in her preaching that black women are challenging the patterns and systems of their suppressed role in the African American church, community, family, and larger society by asserting the rights, authority, power, beauty, and wonder of the black woman's voice.[1]

Cannon has taught at Temple University and at the Episcopal Divinity School in Cambridge, Massachusetts. She is currently the Annie Scales Rogers Professor of Christian Ethics at Union Theological Seminary and Presbyterian School of Christian Education in Richmond, Virginia. She is the author of *Black Womanist Ethics, Katie's Canon: Womanism and the Soul of the Black Community, Righteous Content: Black Women Speak of Church and Faith* and *Teaching Preaching: Isaac Rufus Clark and Black Sacred Rhetoric.* Her essays have appeared in more than fifty additional books.

• • •

*Womanist preaching cannot be easily defined or identified. It is a mixture of a variety of historical movements, including the movement of the African American preaching tradition. Womanist preaching occurs when a black female preacher discerns for herself what it means to be made in the image of God, when the point of departure is a world that says being black, female, and likely poor is a liability. The womanist preacher claims equal space in the dialogue of the human family and speaks from the experience of black women about God's mind, will, and purpose for the world. The following sermon is one representation of womanist preaching. It also contains strands of empowerment, black identity, and cultural survival preaching.*[2]

## Prophets for a New Day
## (1998)

> *So the prophet picked up the body of the man of God, laid it on a donkey, and brought it back to his own city to mourn for him and bury him. Then he laid the body in his own tomb, and they mourned over him and said, "Oh, my brother!"*
>
> —1 Kings 13:29–30 (New International Version)

One day King Jeroboam, the king of Israel, went to the city of Bethel to prepare for a special feast. The king wanted to make things ready for a high and holy day so that he could celebrate his kingdom in all of its splendor and all its wonder. Just when King Jeroboam started to burn the incense on the altar, one of God's prophets from Judah arrived on the scene. The prophet from Judah was a man of God who had entered into a covenant with God the Creator and Sustainer, the same kind of covenant that God-fearing women and men, and girls and boys, have made down through the ages. The prophet of Judah wanted to be obedient to the word of God wherein God called the prophet to go forth and prophesy against the sacrificial altars and idol worship of King Jeroboam. The prophet predicted desecration, pronounced doom, and declared death and destruction because King Jeroboam was causing the people to turn away from following the true and living God. Doers of justice today need to ask ourselves the question, Who are the Jeroboams in our churches and our communities who embody spiritual wickedness in high places? Who are the Jeroboams in our national public arenas burning incense at the altar who are causing the people of God to fall into apostasy, to bow down and worship idol gods?

Now, the prophet from Judah was quite aware of the awesomeness of his call, the treacherousness of his mission, and the seriousness of his special assignment. The prophet knew that a person like King Jeroboam would not eagerly, and with outstretched arms, embrace God's message of repentance.

The king did become very angry with the message of the prophet. His rage started to bubble and boil over so much so that the king stretched out his hand to seize the prophet. But, in that very moment, in the twinkle of an eye, God caused the king's hand to become paralyzed. King Jeroboam proceeded to plead with the prophet to restore his hand, to put life back into his arm, to heal him. The prophet prayed to almighty God, and King Jeroboam's hand was healed. The king was so grateful that he invited the prophet to the kingdom to receive his just reward. The prophet refused the offer, responding that he would not go home with the king if granted half the kingdom. Furthermore, the prophet told the king that he was under divine orders not to eat or drink and not to return by the same road on which he had arrived.

The news of the happenings between the king and the prophet spread like wildfire. An old man, a self-proclaimed prophet, enters the story. When the old man heard about the prophet from Judah, he ordered his sons to saddle a mule so that he could go and search for the prophet. He found him resting under an old oak tree and invited him back to Bethel for refreshment. The prophet from Judah gave the same reply to the old man that he had given to the king: he was under orders not to eat, drink, or return home by the same road.

Upon hearing this, the old man told the prophet that he too was a prophet and that God had told him to invite the prophet from Judah to his home. Convinced, the prophet from Judah went to share a meal with the old man. While they were sitting at the dinner table, the old man turned to his unsuspecting guest and pronounced that he would die for disobeying the original commands of the Lord not to eat, drink, or return by the same road on which he had arrived.

Not long after he had set out again, the prophet from Judah was killed by a lion. When the old man heard the news, he went and retrieved the body, brought it back to Bethel, and buried the prophet in his own ancestral grave. The story concludes with a request by the old man to his sons to be buried with the prophet from Judah because he believed that the dead prophet's words would, indeed, come to pass.

Sisters and brothers, just like the prophet from Judah, we have a tendency to yield, time and time again, to temptation whenever we are baited by persons who purport to be just like us. We hear things like "Why, we were born under the same zodiac sign." "We have the same alma mater." "We do the same kind of work." "Our children were born in the same hospital." And the biggest bait of all: "We are all Christians, and we serve the same God." The problem with being pulled hook, line, and sinker by this so-called sameness is that far too often we end up easing the true and living God out of our lives. More than ever before we need true prophets, prophetic women and prophetic men, prophetic youth and prophetic adults, who will be God's people—and no other's—morning by morning and day by day. We need prophets who will not be baited by the attraction of sameness and compromise.

How do we become prophets for a new day? First, we need to take a spiritual inventory. Each of us needs to get away from the hustle and bustle of daily life and discover exactly what it is that God is calling us to do. We need to go to the quiet corners, the private gardens, to our praying places, and ask God as humbly as we know how, What is my mission at this particular point and time in my life? As we look again at the biblical story, we find that the prophet from Judah was satisfied with his spiritual inventory. Before the king, he stood firm and held forth. He did not quiver or quake in his face-to-face confrontation with the king, the most powerful ruler in Israel. He was clear about his mission and free from ambiguity about his ministry. The prophet knew beyond a shadow of a doubt exactly what the Lord was calling him to do. The same can be true for each of us today. I believe that if we are to resist temptation, be free from self-destructive enticements, receive liberation from death-dealing seduction, and follow Christ in all that we say and do, we must take a spiritual inventory.

The second thing that we need to do in order to become prophets for a new day is obey the will of God. This means, among other things, that we must accept the findings of our spiritual inventory. The spiritual inventory may mean that God is calling us to be more loving in our homes. We may need to cut out the fussing and cussing. We may need to stop the fighting and nagging. We may need to eliminate the pouting and the mood swings. We may need to seek recovery from all kinds of substance abuse and addictive behavior that make our homes feel more like war zones instead of places where peace, love, and justice begin.

Others of us may feel that our homes are already grounded in faith, hope, and love. Obedience for us may mean engaging in strategic action and reflection about the social crisis around us involving our children and teenagers. As Jonathan Kozol documents in his book *Savage Inequalities: Children in America's School,* there are public schools (primarily populated by African American and Hispanic children) where teachers are forced to set up classes in coatrooms.[2] Some classes are held in storage bins and bathrooms. There are schools without libraries; books are lying on top of each other, piled on floors in corners. Obedience in the face of this gross systemic neglect and abuse may mean making the conscious connections between children in public schools and those youth and adults in the church and community who are added to the illiterate population at the rate of 2.3 million every year.

And still, one or two of us may discover that obedience means that we become full-time doers of justice. This means that we refuse to run and hide in the face of the formidable ethical issues of our time. Some of us will need to be on the front line against domestic abuse. Others of us need to be part of the vanguard for comprehensive AIDS education. And still others of us need to be about the business of developing recycling programs that will stop the destruction of the rain forest and other nonrenewable resources. Tens of thousands of persons die each year as a result of environmentally induced cancer, and the vast majority of those are people of color.

Each of us could go on naming the various forms of obedience needed in our lives. It is true that no one outside of us can dictate to us what it is that God is laying on our hearts to do. Moreover, we should remember that obedience does not mean trying to climb the highest mountain or trying to swim the deepest ocean; obedience is surrendering our lives and our will to the care of God each day.

The third and final thing we need to do in order to become prophets for a new day is give praise and honor to almighty God. In the story, the old man gains entry to the prophet from Judah through the latter's idle moment. In the story, he is sitting under a tree doing nothing when the tempter comes. While nothing can be good to do sometimes, I interpret the prophet's nothing, not just in terms of a laxity toward the word of God as revealed to the prophet, but in terms of the worship of God as required of us all. What I mean here is an attitude of gratitude that keeps us in spiritual shape and strengthens us to stand against temptation. Maybe the prophet would have been able to resist temptation if only he had possessed the conviction of the Negro spiritual: "We keep so busy praising the Lord Jesus. We keep so busy praising the Lord Jesus. We keep so busy praising the Lord Jesus we ain't got time to die."[3] Calling: Prophets for a new day.

Needed: Prophets who will take a spiritual inventory, prophets who will obey God's will, and prophets who will display an attitude of gratitude to the ends of both the praise and power of God.

### *Notes*

*Sermon source: The African American Pulpit* 1, no. 2 (Spring 1998), 13–18.

1. Alice Walker, *In Search of Our Mother's Garden* (San Diego: Harcourt Brace Jovanich, 1983).
2. Jonathan Kozol, *Savage Inequalities: Children in America's Schools* (New York: Crown Publishers, 1991).
3. Hall Johnson, "Ain't Got Time to Die," available at http://www.negrospirituals.com/news_song/ain_t_got_time_to_die.htm (accessed June 23, 2007).

### *Bibliographical Sources*

Lawrence-Lightfoot, Sara. *I've Known Rivers: Lives of Loss and Liberation.* Reading, MA: Addison-Wesley Publishing, 1994.

Theide, Barbara. "From the Margin to the Ministry," *The Charlotte Observer*, April 16, 2005.

Union Theological Seminary and Presbyterian School of Christian Education. "Katie Geneva Cannon." http://www.union-psce.edu/community/faculty/fulltime/cannon.shtml (accessed June 23, 2007).

Wade, Jennifer. "Hearing the Voice of the Most Marginalized in Theology and Ethics: A Conversation with Rev. Dr. Katie Cannon," *The Bulletin, Voice of the Washington Theological Consortium,* February/March 2004, http://www.washtheocon.org/feb2004.pdf (accessed June 23, 2007).

## CAESAR ARTHUR WALKER CLARK SR.

*(1914–2008)*

C.A.W. Clark served as the venerated pastor of Good Street Baptist Church in Dallas for more than fifty years. Born in 1914 in Shreveport, Louisiana, Clark could not continue school past the seventh grade because his help was too valuable to the family farm. He ultimately educated himself during his teenage years and earned admittance to Bishop College, from which he graduated in 1946. Clark began preaching at age fourteen in April 1929 and was ordained four years later in 1933. His first pastorate, at age nineteen, was the Israelite Baptist Church in Longstreet, Louisiana.

In 1950, Clark became the pastor of Good Street Baptist Church. Clark played an active role in our nation's civil rights struggle. He was responsible for bringing Martin Luther King Jr. to Dallas in 1958 for the first of his many speeches there, and continued work in the civil rights struggle in Dallas. He served as president of the Missionary Baptist Association of

Texas and as vice president of the National Baptist Convention, U.S.A., Inc. He also held the prestigious position of editor of the *National Baptist Voice* for many years starting in the 1950s. For more than forty years, Clark was one of the top five African American revivalists, averaging thirty weeklong revivals a year.

Clark, a nationally renowned humanitarian and respected leader, was twice named by *Ebony* magazine as one of the fifteen outstanding black preachers in America. He served his parishioners, community, and fellow clergy with such distinct wisdom and humility that he gained the overflowing esteem due a great elder and father figure.

• • •

*Clark was one of the most imitated preachers in the history of the African American Church and a master folk preacher. The* Encyclopedia of African American Christian Heritage *locates Clark at the very depths of the tradition of African American preaching: "If any one preacher could be called the modern preserver and practitioner of the black folk tradition of preaching that dates back to the slave era, it would be Caesar Clark."*[1] *He excelled at the use of stories, metaphors, repetition, alliteration, and scriptural exegesis. His signature rhythmic and melodious intonation, or whooping, is one of many reasons why Clark's preaching was so popular to so many. The following sermon is one of his classic messages and illustrates his preaching prowess. As few preachers can, Clark provides in entertaining, riveting, commentary-like fashion the story of one of the most famous families in the annals of Judeo-Christian history, the Herods. Toward the conclusion, the recorders attempt to bring the orality of the sermon to the written page in a format designed to capture and maintain the dialect and tonality of a whooping preacher. Clark is by far one of the best whoopers that the African American faith community has produced.*

## The Worms Got Him
## (1979)

In the twelfth chapter of the Acts of the Holy Spirit through the Apostles, we have these words: "He was eaten of worms and gave up the ghost, but the word of God grew and multiplied."[2] This text is all the more striking and impressive because of what immediately precedes it. Come with me to view the burial place of the family of Herod. This Herod family was a bad lot. Both the name Herod and the sound of it suggests the law which in modern time is known as heredity but which was declared ages ago when God gave the commandment to Moses. In the second commandment, God says that he is a jealous God, visiting the iniquities of the fathers upon the children unto the third and fourth generations.

These Idumean descendants of Esau came to power in the century before Christ. All of the Herods show evil and dangerous traits. In the burial ground of the Herod family, the most famous of them is Herod the Great, who slew the innocents when Christ was born. This Herod also murdered his three sons. He drowned his brother-in-law, Aristobulus, and had his beautiful queen, Marianne, whom he sincerely loved, strangled to death. When Herod the Great lay dying in his ivory palace at Jericho knowing that people would rejoice rather than sorrow when they heard that he was dead, he had the representatives of the chief families shut up in the hippodrome, where they were to be put to death the moment the breath left his body. Thus, he made sure that there would be mourning in the land when he was dead. Even though the mourning would not be for him, there would nevertheless be mourning in the land.

Next to Herod the Great lies his son, Archelaus, banished by Augustus after nine years of misrule. There is another Herod, Herod Antipas, also known as the tetrarch. Herod Antipas was the Herod who, to please his wicked wife Herodias, beheaded John the Baptist. On the grave of Herod Antipas is that brief epithet—that fox—written by Christ himself.

And then move over a little, and there is the grave of Herod Agrippa II, the one before whom Paul preached, and this is his epithet written by himself: "Almost thou persuadest me to be a Christian."[3] And then move over a little ways, and you come to the grave of the bloodthirsty and beautiful Herodias and her dancing daughter. And then here is the grave of Bernice, the beautiful and wicked sister of Herod Agrippa. And by her side her sister, Drusilla, who married that Felix, who trembled when Paul preached but did not repent. It is not enough to tremble at hearing the Word; you have to repent also. A bad lot all of them, the family of Herod as they are called in the Acts of the Holy Spirit through the Apostles.

Herod Agrippa I was no exception in this family of degenerates and murderers. On the grave of this Herod is written this epithet, "He was eaten of worms and gave up the ghost, but the word of God grew and multiplied." Herod Agrippa I was the grandson of Herod the Great. As a young man, he had spent much time in Rome and had been led into wild excesses by Drusus, the son of the emperor Tiberius. A favorite of the emperor Caligula, then of Claudius, this Herod was given sovereignty under the Romans in Palestine. In order to please the Jews, Herod Agrippa I instituted persecution against the Christians. He killed James, the brother of John, with a sword. The mother of James and John had once asked Jesus that they might sit the one on his right hand and the other at his left when he came into his glory.[4] When Jesus asked them if they were able to drink of his cup and be baptized with his baptism, they said, "We are able."[5] Now James knows what that means, though he was not the first of the martyrs, for that distinction belongs to Stephen. But James was second of the twelve apostles to drink of the martyr's cup.

When Herod Agrippa I saw the history of the people, he sought to ingratiate himself further with them by laying his murderous hands upon an even more notable prisoner by the name of Peter. Luke says that when he saw that it pleased the Jews, he proceeded further to seize Peter also. The first act of sin always suggests and sometimes demands a second and a third act of sin. When all hope had been given up and Peter's death seemed inevitable, the angel of the Lord awakened him and released him from prison. The cruel Herod, when he could not find Peter, had all the soldiers who guarded him put to death.

Then Herod went down to Caesarea. The people of Tyre and Sidon had in some way displeased him, but having bribed Blastus, the king's treasurer, they managed to secure peace with the king. Probably Blastus had told the people of Tyre and Sidon that Herod was very sensitive to flattery, and they proceeded to flatter him after his own taste. The narrative in the Book of Acts is supplemented by the graphic stories of Josephus in his Antiquities of the Jews. Kings and shows were being celebrated at Caesarea in connection with the victories of the emperor. A great crowd had gathered on the second day of these spectacles, and Herod came to the theater early in the morning arrayed in a gorgeous garment made wholly of silk. As he stood before the people in the light of the morning sun, his garments shone with dazzling splendor. As they looked upon him and listened to his voice as he made them an oration, the people shouted, saying, "It is the voice of a god, and not of a man."[6] Immediately he was stricken with a fatal disease. As the people gathered around him he was heard to say, "I who you call a god am commanded presently to depart this life. My providence thus disproves the lying words you just said to me. I who was by you called immortal am immediately to be hurried away by death." The Bible narrative, while not conflicting with that of Josephus, sums up the end of this Herod in a much more concise and dramatic sentence, "And immediately the angel of the Lord smote him, because he gave not God the glory: and he was eaten of worms and gave up the ghost. But the word of God grew and multiplied."[7]

The first thing that this text shows us is that there is a law of justice and of retribution at work in the world. I said that the first thing that this text shows us is that there is a law of justice and retribution in the world. We cannot always see the working of the Lord. Now and then God lets us see the flashing of the sword of his judgment. The history of the world is the judgment of the world. It always pays to read this chapter from beginning to end. If one had only read the beginning of this chapter one would have seen Herod on his throne a corrupt and irresistible tyrant, but when one reads to the end of the chapter, he sees Herod prostrate in the dust and eaten of worms while the truth of God spreads and prospers.

Slowly wrote the historian, the hand had crawled along at a dire pace, slowly as if the event would never come and Rome would keep on rolling, and oppression cried, and it seemed as if no ear had heard its voice. The dimension of wickedness was at length fulfilled. The finger touched the hour, and as the stroke of the great hammer rang out above the nation, in an instant the whole fabric of iniquity was shivered to ruin. That hour had now struck forever, and the hour of judgment will strike for every doer of iniquity. The hour of judgment will strike for every wrongdoer. The hour of iniquity will strike for every unrepentant sinner. The hour of judgment will strike for everyone whose heart is not right with God. It doesn't matter how long the wicked prosper; the hour of judgment will strike for yah' if you keep on walking in sin. It doesn't matter how looooong you live in sin, nor how secure you think you are. I remind you, if you keep on living in rebellion against God, the hour of judgment will strike.

Then the second thing that this text tells us is that right will finally prevail over wrong and the kingdom of Christ will finally prevail over the kingdom of Satan. An-ah' because the right thing will finally win out, I would rather be identified with the persecuted than to be allied with the persecutors. Because the right thing will win out, I'd rather have wrong done to me than to do wrong to others. Because the right thing will win out, I'd rather be a black man having dogs set on me than to be a white man setting dogs on somebody else.

The incarnate monarch of materialism and paganism and animalism and an ever-increasing multitude shouts beneath the voice of God, but we remember this Herod who was smitten by the angel of the Lord. We remember his grandfather, who slaughtered children but sought in vain to slay Jesus. In the end, Herod died, but Jesus lived. In the end, the wicked will die and the righteous will live. We remember the Pharaoh who sought in vain to destroy the destiny of God's people. Pharaoh died, and God confirmed for himself a remnant, because God never leaves himself without a witness. We remember Haman, who persuaded the Persian despot to issue a decree for the destruction of the Jews but who himself perished on the gallows at execution time that he had built for another man. He who sows a pit for his brother shall fall therein. The righteous will finally triumph. Whatever is right will finally prevail. The kingdom of Christ will finally win out over the kingdom of Satan.

Yeahhhh, Lord. I'm glad to be on the Lord's side, because the Lord's side is the winning side. I'm glad to be on the Lord's side, because it doesn't matter how long it takes, in the end the right thing will succeed. I know it is so because God is God, and right is right, and right today will win. I know that the wicked prosper, but don't be uneasy about it; ahhhh, in the end whatever is right will win out.

Another thing that's here is that the angel of the Lord strikes. In this one-chapter history of Herod the king there is one of those tremendous contrasts of which the Bible alone is capable. When Peter was in Herod's prison chained to two soldiers and guarded by sixteen more, suddenly the prison was filled with light. Now Peter didn't have a lawyer to plead his case. Peter didn't have money to pay his bond. And the church didn't have the means to secure legal assistance for him. But the women got together an-ah' had a prayer meeting. Oh, Lord. The church is a living organism. The church is not a human institution, but it is a divine institution. An-ah' when things go wrong, the church just ought to pray. Too many church people, ah, resort to shrewdness. Too many church people resort to trickery. Too many church people resort to trying to outsmart each other. But when there is a difficulty in the church, instead of trying to outsmart one another, instead of trying to defeat each other, we ought to go down on our knees in prayer, for the Lawwwd will hear and answer prayer. I know the Lord will hear and answer prayer. That's the reason I can say, "I love the Lord; he heard my cry and pitied every groan. Long as I live and trouble rise, I'll hasten to his throne."[8] Yes, Lord.

A few women got together; methinks I hear them talking among themselves saying, "They already killed brother James, and Peter's in jail, and they intend to kill him after Easter Sunday. We don't have any influence with the men who put him in there. We don't have any money to get a lawyer to plead his case. But I tell you what we can do, we'll have a prayer meeting." Ahhhhhh, Lord, the women got down and began to talk to the Lawd. Methinks, I think I hear them saying, "Laaaaaawd, Lawd, we don't have any money to hire a lawyer. Laawwwwd, we don't have any money to go Peter's bond. Laaawwwwd, they already killed James. Laawwwwd, they intend to kill Peter after Easter Sunday. Laaawwd, we don't have any means of getting him out of jail. Two soldiers are guarding him; he's chained to one on the right and the other on the left, and sixteen others are standing around. And the inner door is locked, and the outer gate is made of iron. Laaaaaawd, Laaaaaawd, hear our prayer. In thine own way, moooooove in our behalf."

While the women were talking on earth, ah, Lawd, you know heaven is concerned about what goes on on the earth. You see, heaven is the roof of man, and this earth is a colony of the father's land. Ahhh, Lawd, wellll, you know heaven is concerned. Remember when Jacob laid down to sleep, he had a dream. He said, "I saw a ladder. One end of it reached to the throne of God. The other end rested on the earth. And I saw angels coming down and going up." Ahhhhh, Lawd, I tell you that the father's land is concerned about what goes on on the earth. And the reason I know it is, I hear Jesus saying, "When one sinner repents, there's joy in heaven." You don't have to say amen, but evvvery time a sinner turns to Christ, there's jooooy on high. You don't have to make noise about it, but evvvery time a sinner comes to Christ, there's joooooy in heaven. Ahhhh, Lawd. Yes, Lord.

While the women were talking to the Lord, God heard them, and he answered while they were still praying. Methinks I hear him saying, "Come here, angel. I want you now to take two wings to veil your face, two wings to cover your feet, two wings to fly from here." And the angel stood in the presence of God and then left the shining coast of glory quicker than right now and sooner than at once. He came down; he didn't ask anybody directions to the jail. He had the directions before he ever left heaven. Ahhhh, Laawd, he walked right by the jailers. The jailers didn't see him. He went on through the door. Ohhh, when he got through the inner prison, he found Peter, sleeping between two soldiers. He just walked over and laid his hand on him. When he laid his hands on him, chaaains, aaaaaah, Lawd. The angel said to Peter, "Follow me, ahhhhhhh, follow me." Ah, Lawd. Peter followed the angel on through the door. Then it looks like I hear Peter saying, "We are not out of danger yet, for there's an iron gate yonder. And you don't have a key to unlock the gate." It looks like I hear the angel saying, "Don't worry about it, Peter, come on. Come on. Ahhhhhhhh, come on." The angel walked up to the gate; the iron gate flew open. Ah, Lawd, Peter went on up to where the prayer meeting was going on.

But now there's another side of it. The same angel that smote Peter and delivered him smote King Herod. Now one smiting meant deliverance, the other smiting meant destruction. One smiting meant life, and the other smiting meant death. One smiting meant rejoicing, the other smiting meant mourning. Ahhhhhh, Lawd. The same angel that touched Peter touched Herod. The worms started working, ahhhhh, Lawd. You'd better not fight the Lawd. If you try to fight the Lawd, the worms will get yah'.

Ahhhhhh, Lawwwwwd. If you rebel against Gawd, the worms will get yah'. If you go around trying to destroy other people, the worms will get yah'. If you go around digging pits for other people, the worms will get yah'. If you keep on walking in sin, the worms will get yah'. If you keep on using what Gawd gave you in the service of the devil, the worms will get yah'. Ahhhhhhh, Lawd.

Well . . . . . . , ahhhhhhhah. You know Gawd has a whole lot of things at work for him. You know down yonder in Egypt, when Pharaoh rebelled against Gawd, Gawd had all the lice working for him, and then he had all the flies working for him. Well . . . . . . God mooooves in a mysterious way his wonders to perform. He plants his footsteps upon the sea and rides upon the storm.

Now the angel here is a type of the gospel. The angel smote Peter, and he was delivered. The angel smote Herod, and the worms got him. If you obey the gospel, the gospel will deliver you. But if you resist the gospel, the same gospel that delivers one man will condemn the other man. The same gospel that saves one man will damn another man. The same gospel that blesses one man will curse another man.

I'mmmmmmm gllllllaad I responded to the gospel a looooooong time ago; the angel of the gospel touched this soul of mine. A loooooong time ago, it snatched me from the branch of the burning. A looooooong time ago, a new name was written down. A loooooong time ago, my sooooul was set on fire. A looooooong time ago, I heard the voice of Jesus saying, "Come unto me and rest. Lay down, thou weary one, lay down thy head upon my breast. I came to Jesus, I came to Jesus, I came to Jesus, as I was, weary, worn, and sad. I found in him, I found in him a resting place, and he has made me glad." I know he's a wonderful Savior. I can tell you that. I . . . . . . know that my redeemer lives. I knnnnnnnnnow that my soul has got a hidin' place, beyond the grave. The angel smote brother Herod and the worms got him, but one of these mornins' or one of these evenins', when my work is done and the great Gawd of heaven shall command the angel of death to touch this frame of mine, I tell you what I'll do. I'll drop this mantle of dress and step out of time into eternity. I'll bid farewell to sickness and sorrow. I'll hear him say, "Servant, sssssservant, ssservant, job well done. Rest from thy labor. The battle is fought, the victory is won, enter thy Master's joy." I'll praise great Gawd Almighty, and doooooown, dooooooown, by the riverside, I'm gonna lay my burdens down, dooooooown by the riverside. I . . . . . . will stick my sword in the sands of time. Ahhhhhhhhhhh. One of these mornings when my work is ended, I'll go home, oooooooooh, I know I'll go home. I know it's all right. And just as soon as my labor is ended, I . . . . . . know I'll go home. I know that the Lord will wipe all my tears away.

### *Notes*

*Sermon source: The African American Pulpit* 6, no. 2 (Spring 2003), 35–40.
1. *An Encyclopedia of African American Christian Heritage,* 54–55.
2. Acts 12:23–24 (King James Version).
3. Acts 26:28 (KJV).
4. See Matthew 20:20–21.
5. Matthew 20:22 (KJV).
6. See Acts 12:22.
7. See Acts 12:23–24.
8. Richard Smallwood, "I Love the Lord," http://www.music-lyrics-gospel.com/gospel_music_lyrics/i_love_the_Lord_249.asp (accessed April 9, 2009).

### *Bibliographical Sources*

"America's Fifteen Greatest Black Preachers," *Ebony* (September 1984): 27–33.
McMickle, Marvin A., ed. *An Encyclopedia of African American Christian Heritage.* Valley Forge, PA: Judson Press, 2002, 54–55.
Murphy , Larry G., J. Gordon Melton, and Gary L. Ward, eds. *Encyclopedia of African American Religions.* New York: Garland Publishing, Inc., 1993, 178.

# JOHNNIE COLEMON

*(ca. 1922– )*

Johnnie Colemon was born in Columbus, Mississippi, from what available public information indicates, a little more than eighty years ago. She is the founder and now-retired pastor of Christ Universal Temple in Chicago, one of the largest churches in the Windy City and the largest in the country solely pastored by an African American woman. The only child of John Haley and Lula Parker Haley, Colemon was named after her father, who had wanted a son.

She graduated from Union Academy High School in Columbus, Mississippi, as class valedictorian and went on to receive her bachelor of arts from Wiley College in Marshall, Texas, where she excelled not only in academics but also in sports. After teaching for several years in Mississippi, she moved to Illinois and taught in Chicago's public schools. In

1952, physicians told her that she had an incurable disease and that she had only six months to live. With her mother's encouragement, Colemon enrolled in the Union School of Practical Christianity in Lee's Summit, Missouri, where she became an ordained minister. Colemon was drawn by Unity's "positive thought" philosophy, which now echoes in her teachings. In two years, all signs of her disease had vanished and she began her ministry in a local YWCA building in Chicago.

Twelve years later, Colemon became the first black president of the Association of Unity Churches. Allegedly because of racism, some member churches withdrew their support from the association under her leadership. Colemon withdrew as well, and renamed her congregation Christ Universal Temple in 1956. She also established the Universal Foundation for Better Living, an international association of New Thought Christian churches and study groups dedicated to better living through positive thought and speech. Colemon saw her ministry grow to nearly twenty thousand members and occupy a thirty-two-acre multicomplex.

Colemon has been widowed twice. She has no children of her own, but parishioners' children are often called "Johnnie Colemon babies" because they were brought up in her church. On May 1, 1977, Colemon received an honorary Doctor of Divinity degree from Wiley College.

• • •

*The following sermon typifies Colemon's preaching and teaching ministry, in particular her New Thought teaching, which is based on five principles. The first principle is the omnipresence of God: Everything that exists, or ever will exist is pressed out of the body of God (God-substance); so, there can be no evil in reality. The second principle is the divinity of man: Man is made in the image of God. The third principle is the value and power of thought: It is through thinking that people form that which they have in life. The fourth principle is practicing the presence, accomplished through abiding in the presence of God, prayer (communication with God), and meditation, conscious thought on aspects of God. The fifth principle is the law of demonstration, the results that follow from the practice of the first four principles. The responsibility of men and women as sons of daughters of God is right thinking, right words, right feelings, right actions, and right reactions. She coined the phrase, "It works if you work it." This sermon provides an example of Colemon's application of Scripture to daily living.*

## Dear Enemy, I Love You (February 10, 2002)

Over two thousand years ago, there was a city called Athens. And Athens was the intellectual center of the world. But, there was another city called Corinth, and Corinth was the *love center* of the world. Now, Corinth is in trouble. They did whatever they wanted to do, however they wanted to do it. No rules, no regulations, no laws, no nothing—just everybody go for yourself. Very much like our world today. Paul was in Athens, the intellectual center, and got the message from God: "Go to Corinth, Paul; they need help. I want you, Paul, to withdraw from Athens. You have served your purpose. You've learned your lessons intellectually. Now, I want you to go to the Corinthians and help my children understand who and what they are and why they are here." And Paul listened. He heard and he obeyed.

And when he got to Corinth, Paul, as you know, wrote an essay that we call First Corinthians and sent this message: "Even though you may speak in beautiful and impressive languages, but if your words are not prompted by love, they will not reach the hearts of men and women."[1] Paul meant that even though you may speak intellectually in beautiful words, if they are not based in love, then people don't even understand what you're saying, and it does not matter. Paul said that if I give everything I have to poor people, and if I were burned alive for preaching, but did not love others, it would be of no value whatever. Paul reports that after he got to Corinth and discovered the true meaning of love, he went to that love center within himself and the power called love was awakened within him. Paul says, "And I made a great discovery and that discovery was just to say—*I love you.*" For Paul, love was more than a bunch of words easily stated. Paul discovered that there are elements to love. And Paul listed several elements involved in love or what some people will call the spectrum of love in First Corinthians 13. I do not have time to list them all, but I will list several.

The very first element in love involves patience.[2] You've got to be patient—even patient with yourself. Remember that the demonstrations of patience don't come sometimes easily or just like that. Love makes us wait on demonstration knowing that God is the demonstration; but God is also the demonstrator. Be patient. Don't be disturbed with the seeming faults of others. Love covers a multitude of faults. If we but love, which is God, there will be no faults.

Patience; be patient with yourself. Wherever you are at this particular time, you didn't get there overnight. Do you understand what I'm saying? It means work. It means the daily changing of your feelings, your thoughts. And the thoughts are not going to go away and leave you alone just because you've made a decision. But, when you're ready for patience, every time impatience gets ready to challenge you, you're ready. I'm patient and I'm going to do it *now*. Keep putting the word *now* in it.

The next element is generosity. Generosity is saying—*love does not envy.*[3] Why should I envy you when you've got the same thing I've got? Why should I envy you when God is no respecter of persons? All of us are His children. He is our Father. He has provided for all of us. If you are not making the demonstration, if you're not being what God created you to be, it is *not* God's fault! It is our fault because we won't go to the places wherever that is and I'm not talking to CUT [Christ Universal Temple]. Wherever it is that your soul feels good and happy. Wherever you can go and the next morning when you wake up and see your friends and they say, "Did you go to church yesterday?" And you say—"Oh yeah! I went to church yesterday." What was church like? "Oh, I don't know, honey, we just had a good time." I think it's possible to have a good time, but also leave church not the way you came. Go home a different way!

Another element is humility; what is the text saying? *Love is not puffed up.*[4] Love does not do to receive, but to accomplish—this is wonderful! To accomplish and forget the doing! When I do it from the center of love, whatever I do for you I do it because I love it. When I love doing *it*, then I'm not waiting to see—Do you remember what I did last month, yesterday or this morning? Humility explains itself.

Another element is good temper; love is not provoked.[5] Good temper. And when you go through a test again, remember that you love so nobody can make you angry. Next, love takes no account of evil.[6] Next, sincerity; love rejoices with the truth.[7] These are but a few from the thirteenth chapter of First Corinthians, but practice them daily. Languages may change, but the language of love and its elements are always the same and can always be understood.

That is why we can and I can speak these words: *Dear enemy, I love you*. Take your bulletin in your hand if you please and let's look at love in action through scriptures. I want to say— "Dear enemy, I love you," not because I want to, but because I have to! Not for your sake, but for my own sake. I love you, enemy, because to hate, to harbor resentment, is what I call spiritual suicide. Hate ain't killing nobody but yourself. Somebody's always telling me: I didn't see that in the scripture; is it in the scriptures?

We read in First John 4, verses 7 and 8 in the King James Version: Let us practice loving each other for love comes from God. Those who are loving and kind show that they are children of God and that they are getting to know Him better. However, if a person isn't loving and kind, it shows that he does not know God for God is love. And we read in John 14:21, "The one who obeys me is the one who loves me and because he loves me, my Father will love him and I will, too, and I will reveal myself to him." And finally in Proverbs 19:8, "He who loves wisdom loves his own best interest and will be a success."

Now, if I wrestle with you, I only give you and the negative further life and power. The only existence hate or resentment has is that which you give it by temporarily giving it your thoughts. You are what you think! I am what I think because thoughts are things. And I am a thinker that thinks a thought and makes the thing. I am the thinker. There are no enemies where love reigns. You got it?

I want to ask you a question. Do you want an abundance of prosperity? Do you want loving relationships in your family or on your job? Do you want to be healed? Your lungs, breasts and chest are affected if you allow hurt feelings, selfish love, anger and intense depression to remain in the love center. Where is the love center? —In back of the heart. Spend time each today quietly forgiving everything and everybody.

You know I think I said this to you last week. I've been doing some special prayer work and I've been talking to God and I've been saying to Him: "Now God, we don't have it somewhere. Something we are missing, God." And God said—"Why are you saying that?" And I'm saying to God, "Because we're showing everything but health, prosperity, joy, and peace! We are missing the mark somewhere!" What is it! All I can ever get—and that's why I'm back to this lesson that I'm doing today—all I can get is *forgiveness*. That we have not forgiven. I don't know when it happened to you, but that's why I practice not remembering nothing. I don't remember your name and don't be insulted with hurt feelings because I don't know who you are. I practice forgiving and for me when I forgive, I forget. Work on that.

Here you are walking around with some old mess that happened nine hundred years ago and brag about it, "I'll never forget what they did." You'd better forget what they called themselves doing to you. They're not worth it! And what do we say here? You don't hurt them. They're gone on somewhere hurting somebody else while you're walking around [saying] "I'll never forget them. I'll never forgive them." Well, they don't care.

Spend some time every day quietly forgiving everything and forgiving everybody. Love and forgiveness will dissolve gallstones, cancers, tumors and other so-called incurables. Not saying a thing against the doctors; we have to have them but they know that they can just go so far. I'm real excited. Somebody mailed me from the hospital a doctor's report that he gave to one of his patients. And on it surprisingly was about eight affirmations and he called them affirmations. And he said to the patient: "Take time and affirm these statements if you really want to be healed." And I thought—my, my, my, my, my! Love has been described as the physician of the universe. Love is the affirmation medicine that heals all diseases. And you really don't have to take my word for it. Just try it. The question may be: "How do I forgive others?" You can say: "Dear enemy, I love you."

Let's review the word *forgiveness*. You've heard it a million times here in classes, and you need to hear it a million more times. Forgiveness means to *give for*. Forgiveness means the giving up of something. It means to give love for hate. It means to give understanding for misunderstanding. It means to give joy for sadness. What do you need to give up? Can't nobody answer that for you but you. What did Jesus Christ say about it? Jesus Christ said, "Father, forgive them for they know not what they do."[8] Now, that's what Jesus said. Can you live according to the teachings of Jesus Christ? Can you follow His example? Jesus was above all hatred, all animosity, and all thoughts of revenge. He proved it that day at Calvary. Visualize with me if you will the scene. See the crowds? You know how we are when something's happening. When you ought to be at home, everybody's there coming out of curiosity to see what it is like. So there were people from everywhere; crowds and crowds of people. We're at the scene now. Hear the shouts. And you know what kind of crowd it was. Feel the pressure of the thorns on His head. Taste and smell the agonies of pain and death. Jesus' first request on the cross was not for Himself. His cry was, "Father, forgive them for they know not what they do."

He did not call for angels to come and rescue Him. And, personally, the kind of power that Jesus had grown into, the kind of changes that Jesus made from the human to the spiritual, I really believe that Jesus could have called for anything and anybody to stop what was going on if he had wanted to. Do you believe he had that kind of power? He had that kind of power. He did not have to go through what we read about he went through. He prayed for the Roman soldiers who had nailed Him to the cross. Now that's heavy. He prayed for the chief priest rulers who had incited the people to riot. He prayed for the crowd who had mercilessly demanded his death through all He had done for them and all that he had done was good. Jesus could have ruined the day on that outstanding day by striking back at these people who had hurt and who were now killing Him. But, he reached down into the innermost part of His being and said, "Father, forgive them."

Many of them never responded, but the important thing was that he responded. He forgave. Question: Can you respond? I'm asking you. Can you forgive? That's what I'm asking you. Can you forgive and turn within and ask yourself these questions? I don't care how dirty and low down and mean seemingly it was, forgive them for they know not. *Dear enemy, I love you.*

Oh, I use that statement so often and I have to use it often: *Dear enemy, I love you.* Opportunity presents itself all the time being a *Johnnie Colemon*—being accused of everything. I don't even know what they're talking about sometimes, but I just pray—Father, forgive them for they know not. But, I'm working for Johnnie Colemon. Do you understand? Get selfish in this part of your life, your world and your affairs. Get down in there and see what's stuck back in the corners of your subconscious phase of your being. Do whatever it is you have to do in order to become what God created you to be. He did not create us to be sick! He didn't even create us to die. He did not create us to be broke and poor and just can make it from one payday to the other when He's put all the money and everything you ever will need here for you! But, because you dislike somebody that did something to you and you don't even know if those people are living now. They may be gone on to wherever it is they have to go and you're walking around saying, "I can't forget it?" Not worth it! Nobody is! *Dear enemy, I love you.* I love you in spite of your enfoldment and your growth wherever you are at this particular time.

When you say, *Father forgive me*, metaphysically you're saying that all negative beliefs of resentment, bitterness, hatred, ill will and you name all the rest of it, are to be crossed out by an act of forgiveness. Sometimes we have a tendency to rationalize claiming that we had a legitimate reason or the right to be whatever and won't forgive. But, all you're doing is keeping yourself in bondage. Freedom is found only through forgiveness.

Now hear me. I'm talking about you this morning and I'm talking about me. I'm talking about all of us. I'm talking about a person's enemies are those of his own household; those of his own consciousness. The enemies are within our own households. Now, you can sit there and look cute if you want to. You are just the one I'm talking about! One writer said, "There is a destiny that makes us brothers. None goes his way alone. All that we send into the lives of others comes back into our own."[9]

According to First John 4:20 in the King James Version, "If a man says I love God and hates his brother, he is a liar, for he that loveth not his brother whom he has seen cannot love God whom he has not seen." When you hold resentment against anyone, you are bound to that person by a cosmic link. I'm going to say it again. When you hold resentment against anyone, you are bound to that person by a cosmic link.

What am I going to do about it, Johnnie? I put it on the back of your bulletin. I'm going to saw off all of these beliefs out of my mind, out of my life, out of my affairs. It begins with forgiveness and forgiveness has healing power. All these negative beliefs, and if I didn't name the ones that you need to saw off, add it to the list yourself. All these beliefs have to be sawed off. If you have accused anyone of injustice, what are you going to do? Saw it off. If you have discussed—do you know what discuss means? If somebody calls you up later tonight, which they will and you remember your Sunday lesson and you're going to say to yourself, I'm not supposed to discuss this. But, you say to the other person: "Now I'm not going to discuss it but I'm listening." You want to hear the good dirty dirt whatever it is and you just say, "Uh huh, oh yeah." But, you're still listening and probably going to call them up tomorrow so you can hear it all over again.

If you have discussed anyone unkindly, saw it off. If you have criticized or gossiped about anyone, you've got to saw that belief off. Don't keep waiting until you get worse than you are now. Don't wait until things happen to you. If you have had a falling out with friends or relatives, saw it off. And, you add any other thing that you need to put under that last one. Again, you know more about whom you're not speaking to. When you hold resentment against anyone, you are bound to that person by a cosmic link. You are tied by a cosmic link. Tied to the thing you hate. Love your enemies. Bless them that curse you. Do good to them that hate you and pray for them that despitefully use you and persecute you.[10] I love you. I love you. I love everybody in here because I don't want to be tied to you. *Dear enemy, I love you.*

## Notes

*Sermon source:* This unpublished sermon was submitted to the editors by Johnnie Colemon.

1. Quotation based on 1 Corinthians 13:1 (KJV).
2. 1 Corinthians 13:4 (KJV).
3. Ibid.
4. Ibid.

5. 1 Corinthians 13:5 (KJV).
6. 1 Corinthians 13:6 (KJV).
7. Ibid.
8. Luke 23:24 (KJV).
9. Edwin Markham, "A Creed," lines 1–4, in David L. George, ed., *The Family of Best Loved Poems* (New York: Doubleday & Company, 1952).
10. Matthew 5:24 (KJV).

### *Bibliographical Sources*

Baer, Hans, and Merrill Singer. *African-American Religion in the Twentieth Century*. Knoxville: University of Tennessee Press, 1992.

Harrison, Milmon F. *Righteous Riches: The Word of Faith in Contemporary African American Religion*. New York: Oxford University Press, 2005.

Kinnon, Joy Bennett. "Pastor: Johnnie Colemon—The Many-Splendored Faces of Today's Black Woman." *Ebony*, March 1997.

Melton, J. Gordon, ed. *The Encyclopedia of American Religions*, vol. 2. New York: Triumph Books, 1991.

Smith, Jessie Carney, ed. *Notable Black American Women, Book II*. Detroit: Gale Group, 1996.

# CLAUDETTE A. COPELAND

*(1952– )*

Claudette Anderson Copeland was born on August 17, 1952, to E. Juanita Anderson Day and Charles A. Anderson in Buffalo, New York. She was licensed as an evangelist at age eighteen in the Church of God in Christ. After earning her bachelor of arts in psychology from the University of Connecticut, she went on to obtain a master of divinity in pastoral care and counseling from the Interdenominational Theological Center in Atlanta, and a doctorate of ministry from United Theological Seminary in Dayton, Ohio. She was ordained in 1979, and in 1980 became a commissioned officer in the U.S. Air Force Chaplaincy. She and her husband, David M. Copeland, were the first African American clergy couple in the history of the U.S. military chaplaincy program, where they served with distinction before returning to the civilian pastorate.

The Copelands have served as pastors and cofounders of the New Creation Christian Fellowship of San Antonio, Texas, for more than twenty years. Claudette gives much of her attention to mission field preaching, teaching, and lecturing in many national and international venues. For more than fifteen years she has been hailed as one of the outstanding women preachers in America. Her passionate approach to preaching, her gifts as a teacher, and her ability to sing, have gained her the label "triple threat." *Ebony* magazine named her as one of the top fifteen women preachers in the country in 1997.

Rev. Copeland is the founder of C.O.P.E. Professional Services, a consulting agency for personal effectiveness training in the public sector, and of Destiny Ministries, a national empowerment group for women. Her work has been published in *The African American Pulpit*, and she is the author of *Coming Through the Darkness: Cancer and One Woman's Journey to Wholeness* and *Stories from Inner Space: Confessions of a Preacher Woman and Other Tales.*

• • •

*Copeland's preaching is widely recognized because of her ability to apply biblical insights to the complexity of the human condition. She is able to combine depth of intellectual thought with the freedom and emotion of the African American preaching moment for a sermonic tour de force. "Why Are You Here?" is an excellent example of Copeland's empowerment preaching. It was preached at a conference for women preachers in Los Angeles. Copeland uses women's everyday struggles to convince and convert clergywomen to a different way of thinking. In the true style of the African American preaching tradition, this sermon promotes the uplift of a people, in this case black women.*

## "Why Are You Here?"
## (2000)

> *So he got up and ate and drank. Strengthened by that food, he traveled forty days and forty nights until he reached Horeb, the mountain of God. There, he went into a cave and spent the night. And the word of the Lord came to him saying, "What are you doing here, Elijah?"* —1 Kings 19:8–9 (New International Version)

Every relationship needs questions. In spite of the assumptions and presumptions therein, every relationship needs questions—questions to air it out, questions to refresh the stagnation of the assumptions. For every relationship to remain vital and living and reproductive, I said every relationship. Questions serve a myriad of purposes. Questions come to comfort and to assure—"Is there anything too hard for God?"[1] Questions come to bring conviction, to bring you into full awareness of your condition and to locate you in your reality—"Adam, where are you?"[2] Other questions come to clarify, to arrest, to indict—"Peter, do you love me?"[3] Every relationship needs questions.

The inaugural question posed in this lesson is pertinent to every preaching woman who has ever found herself alone and at the front door of a wilderness, depleted of emotional resources and spiritual reserves. It is the nature of our profession as professional helpers, as purveyors of divine revelation, as peddlers of hope that sooner or later you're going to end up Scripture quoting, Bible toting, but find that you have been just going through the motions.

Listen! There is a secret legacy of depression among women who preach. It's acted out in private moments when we cry alone. It tells on us in public opportunities as we try to outrun and out-perform and out-succeed and obscure our personal sorrows. We make extravagant demands on our congregations so they can buy us bigger toys and bigger things, so we can feel like we're loved because of what "our peoples" did for us. Or we make extravagant demands on our personal lovers. You know—the man you're with or the woman you're with or the drug you use. You make demands in private so you can feel better to make another public appearance. "What are you doing here?" We're here because nobody ever told us how not to get here.

Elijah, tonight, is the tutor for our lesson. Elijah teaches us that the cumulative effects of doing ministry without being ministered *to* is to be sitting up in the cave sucking your thumb, twirling your weave, and looking crazy. You may not want to hear about this, but I came by just to help somebody because I'm a survivor of crazy. I came by to tell you that I know what it's like to turn on the switch and flick the "on" button and come before the people with your Holy-Ghost, Pentecostal persona and then cry at night before I get back to my room. I know what it's like to be able to lay hands on other people and they get well, and I'm sick in my body, wondering if I'm going to live or die. I tell you, I'm a survivor of crazy! And, if you're there tonight—and you know if you're there—I came by to ask you, "What you doing there?"

"What you doing here, Elijah?"[4] God asked. Elijah said, "Well, there's a couple of things that got me here." And, as we are preaching women and pastors, there are a couple of things I want you to watch out for so you don't end up crazy.

The first thing I see in the life of Elijah in 1 Kings 17–19 is that you've got to watch the issue of your sacrifice. Elijah said, "At my word, there will be no rain or no dew for three years upon the earth." He has the power of God in his mouth, and what he speaks comes to pass. If you have the power of God in your life that makes a difference in the earthly realm, then it is because you have sacrificed somewhere behind the scenes. The moment Elijah makes this decree, the moment that he begins to move in his ministry and begins to get results, God said, "What you're going to have to do, Elijah, is to get down to the brook of Cherith, and you're going to have to get down there awhile and let the ravens feed you."[5]

There are seasons in your life and in your ministry where you have to live in sacrificial positions . . . There is a time of going without and doing without. I don't know about you, but there have been times in my life when I had to wait on the raven to bring me a sandwich—that period of being at the mercy of the board, at the mercy of the committee, the denomination, and sometimes at the mercy of a man—the period of having to ask. There have been times in my life when I had to wait on the goodwill of the widow woman to give me an offering. But, if you're not careful, your time of sacrifice will make you bitter. You've got to be careful how you handle your seasons of sacrificial going through. Because if you don't handle your sacrifice right, you'll get on the other end of it, and you'll think somebody owes you something. If you don't handle your seasons of sacrifice right, you will begin to covet and resent the blessings of those who have already gone before you and made a way. You will begin to get a little crazy. You'll begin to get a little off. Your attitude will begin to get a little funky.

The second lesson that Elijah teaches is that we must be careful how we manage a season of silence. In the eighteenth chapter, it says that the word of the Lord came to Elijah—after three years. Women of God, you've got to be real careful because sometimes in your ministry there are seasons of prolonged silence. You can go too long without a word for yourself. Oh yeah, you've got a word for the conference, for the congregation, and for your Sunday morning people. But, how many of you know that there is a difference in the anointing that is on you for other folk and the anointing that is within you for yourself? And if you're not wise, you'll begin to equate the anointing that is *on* you with the thing that is *in* you. And I want you to know, baby, the last thing to go is your preaching. The last thing to go is your ministry. You can be operating in the gift, but there could be silence in your spirit about your life. There can be marvelous manifestations of power on you, and emptiness in you.

Elijah shows that if you're not going to land up in the place of spiritual depression and depletion, you've got to be really wise about your season of silence. I tell you what: there comes a time in the life of every preaching woman—if you're honest about it—where you find yourself giving away stuff that you really need to keep for yourself. Times when people come up to you, "Prophet, is there a word for me? What are you seeing about my life?" Look here, I'm not looking for nothing about your life, I'm trying to hear something for myself. Be careful of the silence, because other people don't know that even though God is speaking to them through you, you ain't heard nothing for yourself. Giving away encouragement when you need to be encouraged. Giving away direction when you need some direction for yourself. Teaching how to walk when you don't even know where to put your foot. Having to lead folk when actually you don't know where you're going. You've got to be careful how you manage the times of silence. Silence from God has to be taken seriously. That's the reason I wouldn't give a quarter for a preaching woman who is too grand to go to Sunday school—because you need to hear something. You can't only come to church when you're preaching. You need a word for yourself or else life will become silent.

The third lesson for tonight is that Elijah says, "I'm here because of my success." Elijah meets the prophets of Baal on Mt. Carmel, daring and defiant. Public demonstration is enough to make one heavy. You've got the crowds now. You've got the degrees now. Not just some master of divinity, but you've got a little Ph.D. Oh, you've got all of the stuff. You've got the Holy Ghost's manifestations. You've got success. You've got the reputation. You've got the promotion. You've got the title. You've got success, and people love success. People gravitate toward success. People attach themselves to success. People come around you when you're succeeding. But I want you to know, baby, success is a dangerous illusion. People love success. But, women of God, they hate successful people. You've got to learn how to manage your success, you see, because success pulls up resentment. You've got to be careful how you manage success because people hate successful people.

Success is the thing that makes you powerfully attractive to men of God. I'm talking to you, preaching women. And, they'll invite you in the door and bring you to the conferences. But you've got to be real careful that you don't get success confused with attraction. Y'all don't know—the kind of woman that he would never marry, but he would have an affair with because your gifts are so admirable. You've got to learn how to manage your success because people love success, but they hate successful people.

Elijah cried, "I'm the only one left! They done killed all the rest of the prophets and I'm the only one left."[6] Success will make you overly responsible. It'll make you think you're the only one. I want you to know, baby, before you ever showed up it was someone. When you go off the picture, it's going to be some more. We're glad for you and you're important, but you're not the end all and be all. Don't be confused, honey, about your momentary success. You're just a part of the picture.

How did you get here, depleted, depressed, in a corner, sucking your thumb and twirling your weave? Because success has become a kind of cycle of endorsed and induced highs and it puts you on an addictive cycle and you just keep going and going and going like the Energizer Bunny and you don't have a clue about how to turn off and sit down, rest and take Sabbath time. Go home and make love to your husband. Go home and comb your kid's head. Take a vacation because the currency with which we get paid is the admiration of people. We have got to be careful about our success.

Fourth, Elijah ends up depleted and depressed and in the corner needing psychiatric assistance because he has become stalked by seasons of terror and fleeing. Jezebel put him on the run. Jezebel is the spirit of intimidation—the spirit that says, "I'm going to take your life."[7] The season of terror and fleeing—you run when you should stand. It is the time when you are stalked by demonic retribution on the heels of spiritual victory. It is the threat which says to your mind, "Oh yeah, you got by on that one, but I'm going to get you on the next one." That thing in your mind that says, "You looked good in that battle, but I'm going to expose you in the next one." The tormentor that threatens to get back at you for what you have done for God. It makes you afraid, and so you run and you run and you run back to a familiar comfort. And you run back to a thing that everybody else thinks you're delivered from. Jezebel gets after you and begins to threaten you and begins to intimidate you and push you up into a corner, and you back off and start to run.

I want you to know, baby, it always takes more energy to run than it does to stand! Some of us have run from denominations and we have run from conflicts and we've run from troubles and we've run from marriages and we've run from schools because it was too hard. But I want to tell you today, if you stop running, God will give you strength to stand!

Finally then, it says, "Elijah came to Beersheba."[8] Beersheba means "the well of the oath." Elijah came to Beersheba and the Bible says: "And he left his servant there, went into the wilderness—a day's journey—by himself."[9] The last thing you've got to be careful of is the shame that causes isolation. This passage reminds me that everybody needs isolation sometimes, but you've got to be careful that your shame does not make you isolate yourself from the very accountability and feedback that will keep you healthy.

Elijah leaves his servant and goes into the wilderness by himself. The time you *need* your servant is when you've got to go into the wilderness. But when we are preaching women, we want to be real careful that don't nobody know our business. We want to be real packaged. So you become untouchable. The intercessors have to discern your needs because you're too proud to tell them. You think you're the only one that's ever had a raggedy marriage, and you allow shame to back you off. You think you're the only one whose child has ever got on crack cocaine and went to jail while you were preaching on an evangelistic crusade, and you allow shame to make you shrink. You isolate yourself by yourself and you find yourself like Elijah saying, "I've had enough! Take my life. I'm no better than my ancestors."[10]

When you get by yourself, the only voice you can hear is yourself. You'd better come on out the corner, baby, and let somebody encourage you! "Why are you here?" You're here because you're ashamed to let somebody know you've had trouble and struggle. But I've got news for you. You are not any place where the rest of us have not already been. You need a girlfriend, honey. You need a prayer partner, honey. You need a pastor, honey. You need somebody who knows your stuff, baby. You need somebody who knows you when your makeup ain't on. You need somebody who knows you when your wig ain't on. You need somebody who knows you're in the wilderness. Come on here. You need somebody to know the real you. You need somebody to know the life you came out of so they can hold on to you when you're tempted to go back in it. Quit being 'shame. What are you doing here, Elijah, suicidal?

But I found out something—that no matter how deep in the dark, in the back, in the corner, detached and defective you might become, you're so depressed you want to quit—but for the gifts and the callings of God. You got mad with God because he married her and jilted you. With your jilted, single, mad self, the gifts and the callings of God are without repentance. They are irrevocable. God will never change his mind about you. You can be mad if you want to, but you're going to have to get up after awhile. You can be disgusted if you want to, but you're going to have to get undisgusted after awhile.

Go back to the bar stool, honey, sit up, and order you a drink. Cross your leg and flirt with the bartender. God's going to send somebody on the bar stool next to you and say, "What you doing here? You don't belong here. You look like a holy woman." Get mad and leave your husband if you want to and meet your boyfriend at the Holiday Inn. Get yourself a room on the seventh floor. Slide up under the covers with somebody who ain't your husband. God will send a room-service man and say, "Excuse me.

Somebody's out here to see you." Because the gift and the calling of God is without repentance. Touch your friend and say, "What you doing here?"

### *Notes*

*Sermon source: The African American Pulpit* 8, no. 4 (Fall 2005), 33–37.

1. See Jeremiah 32:7.
2. See Genesis 3:9.
3. See John 21:15–17.
4. 1 Kings 19:8–9 (New International Version).
5. See 1 Kings 17:3–4.
6. See 1 Kings 18:22.
7. See 1 Kings 19:2.
8. 1 Kings 19:3 (NIV).
9. See 1 Kings 19:3–4.
10. See 1 Kings 19:4.

### *Bibliographical Sources*

Destiny Ministries public relations materials. http://www.destinyministries.org (accessed July 12, 2005).

LaRue, Cleophus, ed. *This Is My Story: Testimonies and Sermons of Black Women in Ministry.* Louisville, KY: Westminster John Knox Press, 2005.

Simmons, Martha. "An Interview with Claudette Copeland." *The African American Pulpit* 4, no. 1 (Winter 2001–2002).

# FREDERICK JOSEPH EIKERENKOETTER

*(1935–2009)*

Reverend Ike was born Frederick Joseph Eikerenkoetter II on June 1, 1935, in Ridgeland, South Carolina, to Frederick Joseph Eikerenkoetter Sr., a Baptist minister, and Rema Matthews Eikerenkoetter, a teacher. The young Frederick was raised on the fundamentalist theology of the Bible Way Church, where he became an assistant minister at the age of fourteen. He earned a bachelor of arts in theology from the American Bible College in Chicago in 1956, and served as chaplain in the U.S. Air Force. In 1962, he began to use the name "Reverend Ike" and established the United Christian Evangelical Association (UCEA).

At his peak in the 1970s, Reverend Ike was one of the first African American ministers with a broadcast show; his weekly sermons were aired from New York by some seventeen hundred television and radio stations across America. Reverend Ike preached that happiness and fulfillment come from financial prosperity and that it is the lack of money, not the love of it, that is the root of all evil. He often said to his flock, "the best thing you can do for the poor is not be one of them." Reverend Ike was not one of them. In acknowledgement of donations, the flamboyant Reverend Ike sent Blessing Plans, which he claimed would guarantee the purchaser's material success. The response to his gospel of prosperity was so overwhelming that in 1969 the congregation purchased the historic Palace Auditorium on 175th Street in Harlem. He claimed over one million followers in 1972, and over seven million by 1982.

Critics called him a charlatan who robbed the poor, and many argued that his belief in personal success distorted the Christian Gospel and undermined African American community advancement. Reverend Ike's showmanship, flashy attire, and opulent lifestyle prevented many observers from recognizing the appeal of his theology to African Americans who wanted a greater share of the American dream.

Reverend Ike passed on July 28, 2009, at the age of seventy-five.

• • •

*The appeal of Reverend Ike was his charisma and innovation. His teaching packaged and popularized a new gospel of positive thinking within the African American church. Reverend Ike marketed new thought principles based on offering ways to wealth and prosperity for the poor who wanted a greater share of American prosperity, and in so doing was one of the earliest African American prosperity preachers. The following message is indicative of the gospel according to Reverend Ike.*

## Curse Not the Rich (January 1976)

*Curse not the rich.* —Ecclesiastes 10:20 (King James Version)

### A Science of Living Principle

Your attitude toward money and all good determines the extent to which good enters your life. Never begrudge anyone the blessings he is receiving. Don't moan and complain and feel sorry for yourself and your conditions. Improve your conditions by changing your attitude toward those who are succeeding and prospering, and by changing your attitude toward the good you desire.

I was invited to Atlanta, Georgia, not long ago, to speak to students at Morris Brown College and to several groups of professional people. And since I was to spend a week there, for my convenience, I directed that two of the church's Rolls Royces be sent there. Some people who saw those Rolls Royces asked, "What kind of preacher is this?" And they said to each other, "The Bible says that Jesus rode on a borrowed ass. What kind of preacher is this, coming into town with two Rolls Royces, one following the other one!"[1]

Many people look at the rich and say, "Look at that rich so-and-so." They curse the rich!—by "cursing" I mean they have negative thoughts toward the rich. They have resentment toward those who are succeeding and prospering.

The Bible says, "Curse not the rich."[2] And this means that as long as you curse the rich, you will never be one of them. As long as you say negative things about someone who is prospering, you will never prosper.

## Rejoice in the Prosperity of Others

If you do not have the correct self-awareness to be rich, you can never know any of the riches of life. You cannot have health, happiness, love, success, prosperity, and money, without the proper consciousness for these good things. When you curse the rich, when you have negative thoughts and say things about the riches someone else is experiencing, you are sending out negative vibrations, and the riches of life cannot come into your experience. That is why it is important, if you want to prosper, to cleanse your mind of resentment and envy toward those who are prospering. When you see someone with a new car, a new home, or newfound love and happiness, bless them. Always think positive thoughts and rejoice in the happiness and prosperity of others.

One night after my speaking engagement at Morris Brown College in Georgia, I was getting into one of the Rolls Royces. And there was a wonderful young man—a student—who said to me, "I'm glad to see you prospering like this." And he told the other students, "Isn't it wonderful to see a preacher with a car like that!"

I said to the people who were with me, "Now you see that young man? He has the kind of attitude that draws prosperity to him!" *Whenever you see people experiencing health, happiness, love, success, and prosperity, be glad for them. Bless them and send them your good vibrations.* Never curse the rich! Remember: If you curse the rich, you'll never be one of them. You cannot draw success, prosperity, and money to you, if you do not have the correct consciousness for these riches. When you curse the rich, your subconscious mind is receiving the idea that you don't like riches. And whatever idea you give to your subconscious mind, that will be your experience. So if you want to be rich, never, *never* curse the rich.

### Identify Yourself with Success and Prosperity

I remember when I first came to New York and sometimes didn't have subway fare to get to school and back. I used to see those people in their big cars and Rolls Royces riding up to Saks Fifth Avenue and the ritzy part of town. And instead of resenting those people, instead of cursing them, I blessed them. I was glad to see such wonderful success and prosperity! I was glad to see people enjoying their fine cars. And I identified with the success and prosperity that I saw around me. I identified with the riches I saw around me, and I saw myself as rich. I saw myself being, doing, and having all the good I desired.

There were other times, too, while working my way through Bible school, that I would pass by the Edwardian Room at the Plaza Hotel in New York. But I didn't identify myself as the hungry little boy passing by the Plaza window. I identified myself with those people who were eating inside. I saw myself staying at the Plaza. And now I can stay at the Plaza any time I want. I've stayed there only once though—not because I needed to, but because I had to fulfill my dream.

Whenever you see people experiencing success and prosperity, identify yourself with them. See yourself experiencing that same success and prosperity. And you will magnetize yourself for a greater experience of success and prosperity. Identify yourself with the good you want, and you will experience that good. I always identify myself with success and prosperity. I never curse the rich. And I AM succeeding and prospering—so I know that what I am teaching you works.

### Quotes to Remember

"Assume a virtue, if you have it not." —Shakespeare

"People often begrudge others what they cannot enjoy themselves." —Aesop

"As long as you curse the rich you will never be one of them." —
Reverend Ike

### Affirmative Treatment

I AM glad to see the success and prosperity of others.

I eliminate every envious, negative thought about the rich from my mind.

My positive thoughts toward everyone and everything are bringing good into my life, right here and right now.

Thank you, God-in-me!

#### *Notes*

*Sermon source: Science of Living Study Guide* 6, no. 2 (December 1975–February 1976), 22–25.

1. See Matthew 21:2–7.
2. Ecclesiastes 10:20 (King James Version).

#### *Bibliographical Sources*

Fay, Robert. "Reverend Ike," in *Africana: The Encyclopedia of the African and African American Experience*, ed. Kwame Anthony Appiah and Henry L. Gates Jr. New York: Oxford University Press, 2005.

Gallatin, Martin V. "Reverend Ike's Ministry: A Sociological Investigation of Religious Innovation." Ph.D. diss., New York University, 1979.

Levy, Sholomo B. "Reverend Ike," in *African American Lives,* ed. Henry L. Gates Jr. and Evelyn Higginbotham. New York: Oxford University Press, 2004.

McGrory, Brian. "Reverend Ike and His Empire." *Boston Globe,* January 22, 1999.

## LOUIS FARRAKHAN

*(1933– )*

Electrifying speaker and leader of a segment of the Nation of Islam since 1975, Louis Farrakhan preaches a message of self-reliance and personal responsibility that resonates among many young, urban, African American males. Followers see him as a courageous leader willing to confront a racist society. Some of his inflammatory remarks have caused critics to claim that he appeals to racism and anti-Semitism to promote his views.

Born Louis Eugene Walcott in New York City, Louis Farrakhan grew up in Boston, Massachusetts. Raised by his mother, a native of St. Kitts, he and his brother, Alvan, learned early the value of work, responsibility, and intellectual development. Having a strong sensitivity to the plight of black people, his mother engaged her sons in conversations about the struggle for freedom, justice, and equality. She also exposed them to progressive material, such as *Crisis* magazine, published by the NAACP. He was an excellent student in school, and began taking violin classes at the age of five. Walcott became a Calypso singer known in Boston's musical circuits as "The Charmer." But in 1955, his life changed dramatically. After hearing the leader of the Nation of Islam (NOI), Elijah Muhammad, speak in Chicago, Walcott cast his lot with the group and changed his name to Louis Farrakhan.

When Malcolm X broke with the NOI in 1964, Farrakhan sided with Elijah Muhammad. When Malcolm X was assassinated in 1965, Farrakhan was appointed minister in charge of Harlem's Temple No. 7, and spokesperson for Elijah Muhammad. After Elijah Muhammad died in 1975, his son Wallace Muhammad steered the Nation of Islam toward mainstream Islam. Farrakhan became the leader of a separate group within the organization that revitalized Elijah Muhammad's original teachings, which emphasized black nationalism.

Farrakhan's public profile soared throughout the 1980s as he established new mosques and reached out to mainstream African Americans. In January 1996, Farrakhan embarked on a "world friendship tour" that included stops in Iran, Libya, and Iraq, countries then regarded as rogue states by the U.S. government. Farrakhan openly criticized the U.S. government on this tour, provoking condemnation from U.S. officials. Often critical of domestic and international politics, economics, and policies of the U.S. government, Farrakhan gives voice to the latent frustrations, pain, and anger of many black Americans. A hate-monger to his critics, Farrakhan draws large crowds to hear his messages. Establishing his legitimacy as a leader of masses of African American people, Farrakhan issued a call for men to come to Washington for purposes of atonement and reconciliation in 1995. More than one million men answered the call and confirmed Farrakhan's leadership position within the African American community.

• • •

*Following the legacy of Elijah Muhammad and Malcolm X, in 1995 Minister Farrakhan continued the tradition of the performance of African American rage in the public space at the Million Man March. The speech, which was almost two hours long, asked black men to go through an eight-stage process, of which atonement was the fifth. According to Farrakhan, completion of all stages would lead to "perfect union with God" and "perfect union" with each other.*

*Farrakhan uses language that is familiar to Christians, quoting Judeo-Christian scriptures, as well as to Muslims, ending the speech with a prayer in Arabic. His employment of the same language that was used in the U.S. Constitution—"a more perfect union"—is not an accident, but an oratorical and political strategy. Given the space limits of this anthology, we condensed the speech while attempting to maintain the essence of Farrakhan's message.*

## Toward a More Perfect Union (October 17, 1995)

In the name of Allah, the beneficent, the merciful. We thank Him for his prophets, and the scriptures which they brought. We thank him for Moses and the Torah. We thank him for Jesus and the Gospel. We thank him for Muhammad and the Koran. Peace be upon these worthy servants of Allah. I am so grateful to Allah for his intervention in our affairs in the person of Master Farad Muhammad the Great Madi, who came among us and raised from among us a divine leader, teacher, and guide, his messenger to us the Most Honorable Elijah Muhammad. I greet all of you, my dear and wonderful brothers, with the greeting words of peace. We say it in the Arabic language, *Asalam Eleecum.*

I would like to thank all of those known and unknown persons who worked to make this day of atonement and reconciliation a reality. My thanks and my extreme gratitude to the Reverend Benjamin Chavis and to all of the members of the national organizing committees. To all of the local organizing committees, to Dr. Dorothy Height and the National Council of Negro Women, and all of the sisters who were involved in the planning of the Million Man March. Of course, if I named all those persons whom I know helped to make this event a reality, it would take a tremendous amount of time. But, suffice it to say that we are grateful to all who made this day possible. . . .

And so, our brief subject today is taken from the American Constitution. In these words, Toward a more perfect union. Toward a more perfect union.

Now, when you use the word *more* with *perfect* [editors' italics], that which is perfect is that which has been brought to completion. So, when you use *more perfect* [editors' italics], you're saying that what you call perfect is perfect for that stage of its development but not yet complete. When Jefferson said, "toward a more perfect union," he was admitting that the union was not perfect, that it was not finished, that work had to be done. And so we are gathered here today not to bash somebody else. We're not gathered here to say, all of the evils of this nation. But we are gathered here to collect ourselves for a responsibility that God is placing on our shoulders to move this nation toward a more perfect union. Now, when you look at the word toward, toward, it means in the direction of, in furtherance or partial fulfillment of, with the view to obtaining or having shortly before coming soon, eminent, going on in progress. Well, that's right. We're in progress toward a perfect union. Union means bringing elements or components into unity.

It is something formed by uniting two or more things. It is a number of persons, states, etcetera, which are joined or associated together for some common purpose. We're not here to tear down America. America is tearing itself down. We are here to rebuild the wasted cities. What we have in the word toward is motion. The honorable Elijah Muhammad taught us that motion is the first law of the universe. This motion which takes us from one point to another shows that we are evolving and we are a part of a universe that is ever evolving.

We are on an evolutionary course that will bring us to perfect or completion of the process toward a perfect union with God. In the word toward there is a law and that law is everything that is created is in harmony with the law of evolution, change. Nothing is standing still. It is either moving toward perfection or moving toward disintegration. Or under certain circumstances doing both things at the same time. The word for this evolutionary changing affecting stage after stage until we reach perfection. In Arabic it is called Rhab. And from the word Rhab you get the Rhaby, or teacher, one who nourishes a people from one stage and brings them to another stage. Well, if we are in motion and we are, motion toward perfection and we are, there can be no motion toward perfection without the Lord, who created the law of evolution and is the master of the changes. Our first motion then must be toward the God, who created the law of the evolution of our being. And if our motion toward him is right and proper, then our motion toward a perfect union with each other and government and with the peoples of the world will be perfected. So, let us start with a process leading to that perfect union; it must first be seen. Now, brothers and sisters, the day of atonement is established by God to help us achieve a closer tie with the source of wisdom, knowledge, understanding, and power.

For it is only through a closer union or tie with him, who created us all, with him who has power over all things that we can draw power, knowledge, wisdom, and understanding from him, that we may be enabled to change the realities of our life. A perfect union with God is the idea at the base of atonement. Now, atonement demands of us eight steps, in fact, atonement is the fifth step in an eight-stage process.

Look at our division, not here, out there. We are a people, who have been fractured, divided, and destroyed because of our division now must move toward a perfect union. But let's look at a speech delivered by a White slaveholder on the banks of the James River in 1712. Sixty-eight years before our former slave masters permitted us to join the Christian faith. Listen to what he said. He said, "In my bag I have a foolproof method of controlling black slaves. I guarantee everyone of you, if installed correctly, it will control the slaves for at least three hundred years. My method is simple. Any member of your family or your overseer can use it. I have outlined a number of differences among the slaves and I take these differences and I make them bigger. I use fear, distrust, and envy for control purposes."[1]

I want you to listen. What are those three things? Fear, envy, distrust. For what purpose? Control. To control who? The slave. Who is the slave? Us. Listen, he said:

> These methods have worked on my modest plantation in the West Indies and they will work throughout the South. Now, take this simple little list and think about it. On the top of my list is age. But it's only there because it starts with an A. And the second is color or shade. There's intelligence, sex, size of plantation, status of plantation, attitude of owners, whether the slaves live in the valley or on a hill, north, east, south, or west, have fine hair or coarse hair, or is tall or short. Now that you have a list of differences I shall give you an outline of action. But before that, I shall assure you that distrust is stronger than trust. And envy is stronger than adulation, respect, or admiration. The black slave after receiving this indoctrination shall carry it on and will become self-refueling and self-generating for hundreds of years. Maybe thousands of years. Now don't forget, you must pitch the old black male against the young black male. And the young black male against the old black male. You must

> use the female against the male. And you must use the male against the female. You must use the dark-skinned slave against the light-skinned slave. And the light-skinned slave against the dark-skinned slave. You must also have your white servants and overseers distrust all blacks. But it is necessary that your slaves trust and depend on us. They must love, respect, and trust only us. Gentlemen, these keys are your keys to control. Use them. Never miss an opportunity. And if used intensely for one year, the slaves themselves will remain perpetually distrustful. Thank you, gentlemen.

End of quote. So spoke Willie Lynch 283 years ago.

And so, as a consequence, we as a people now have been fractured, divided, and destroyed, filled with fear, distrust, and envy. Therefore, because of fear, envy, and distrust of one another, many of us as leaders, teachers, educators, pastors, and persons are still under the control mechanism of our former slave masters and their children. And now, in spite of all that division, in spite of all that divisiveness, we responded to a call and look at what is present here today. We have here those brothers with means and those who have no means. Those who are light and those who are dark. Those who are educated, those who are uneducated. Those who are business people, those who don't know anything about business. Those who are young, those who are old. Those who are scientific, those who know nothing of science. Those who are religious and those who are irreligious. Those who are Christian, those who are Muslim, those who are Baptist, those who are Methodist, those who are Episcopalian, those of traditional African religion. We've got them all here today.

And why did we come? We came because we want to move toward a more perfect union. And if you notice, the press triggered every one of those divisions. You shouldn't come, you're a Christian. That's a Muslim thing. You shouldn't come, you're too intelligent to follow hate! You shouldn't come, look at what they did, they excluded women, you see? They played all the cards, they pulled all the strings. Oh, but you better look again, Willie. There's a new Black man in America today. A new Black woman in America today.

Now brothers, there's a social benefit of our gathering here today. That is, that from this day forward, we can never again see ourselves through the narrow eyes of the limitation of the boundaries of our own fraternal, civic, political, religious, street organization or professional organization. We are forced by the magnitude of what we see here today, that whenever you return to your cities and you see a Black man, a Black woman, don't ask him what is your social, political, or religious affiliation, or what is your status. Know that he is your brother.

You must live beyond the narrow restrictions of the divisions that have been imposed upon us. Well, some of us are here because it's history making. Some of us are here because it's a march through which we can express anger and rage with America for what she has and is doing to us. So, we're here for many reasons but the basic reason while this was called was for atonement and reconciliation. So, it is necessary for me in as short of time as possible to give as full an explanation of atonement as possible.

As I said earlier, atonement is the fifth stage in an eight-stage process. So, let's go back to the first stage of the process that brings us into perfect union with God. And the first stage is the most difficult of all because when we are wrong, and we are not aware of it, someone has to point out the wrong. I want to, I want to say this again, but I want to say it slowly. And I really want each one of these points to sink in. How many of us in this audience, at some time or another, have been wrong? Would we just raise our hands? Okay. Now, when we are wrong, Lord knows we want to be right. The most difficult thing is when somebody points it out do we accept it, do we reject it, do we hate the person who pointed out our wrong? How do we treat the person who points out our wrong? Now, I want you to follow me. When you go to a doctor, you're not feeling well, the doctor says, what's wrong? Well, I don't know, doc. Well, where is the pain? Tell me something about the symptoms. You want the doctor to make a correct diagnosis. You don't smack the doctor when he points out what's wrong.

You don't hate the doctor when he points out what's wrong. You say, thank you, doctor. What's my prescription for healing? We alright? Now, look, whoever is entrusted with the task of pointing out wrong, depending on the nature of the circumstances is not always loved. In fact, more than likely, that person is going to be hated and misunderstood. Such persons are generally hated because no one wants to be shown as being wrong. Particularly when you're dealing with governments, with principalities, with powers, with rulers, with administrations. When you're dealing with forces which have become entrenched in their evil, intractable, and unyielding their power produces an arrogance. And their arrogance produces a blindness. And out of that evil state of mind, they will do all manner of evil to the person who points out their wrong. Even though you're doing good for them by pointing out where America went wrong.

Now, Martin Luther King Jr. was probably the most patriotic American. More patriotic than George Washington. More patriotic than Thomas Jefferson. More patriotic than many of the presidents because he had the courage to point out what was wrong in the society. And because he pointed out what was wrong, he was ill spoken of, vilified, maligned, hated, and eventually, murdered. Brother Malcolm had that same road to travel. He pointed out what was wrong in the society and he had to suffer for pointing out what was wrong and he ultimately died on the altar for pointing out what was wrong. Inside the Nation, outside the Nation, to the greater nation and to the smaller nation. We talking about moving toward a perfect union. Well, pointing out fault, pointing out our wrongs is the first step.

The second step is to acknowledge. Oh, thank you. Oh, man, I'm wrong. To acknowledge means to admit the existence, the reality or the truth of some reality. It is to recognize as being valid. Or having force and power. It is to express thanks, appreciation, or gratitude. So in this context, the word *acknowledgment* [editors' italics] to be in a state of recognition of the truth of the fact that we have been wrong. This is the second step.

Well, the third step is that after you know you're wrong and you acknowledge it to yourself, who else knows it except you confess it. You say, well, yeah, all right. But who should I confess to? And why should I confess? The Bible says confession is good for the soul. Now, brothers I know, I don't have a lot of time, but the soul is the essence of a person's being. And when the soul is covered with guilt from sin and wrongdoing, the mind and the actions of the person reflect the condition of the soul. So, to free the soul or the essence of man from its burden, one must acknowledge one's wrong, but then one must confess. The Holy Koran says it like this: I've been greatly unjust to myself, and I confess my faults. So grant me protection against all my faults, for none grants protection against faults but Thee. It is only through confession that we can be granted protection from the consequences of our faults.

For every deed has a consequence. And we can never be granted protection against the faults that we refuse to acknowledge or that we are unwilling to confess. So, look. Who should you confess to? I don't want to confess. Who should you confess to? Who should I confess to? Who should we confess to? First, you confess to God. And everyone of us that are here today, that knows that we have done wrong. We have to go to God and speak to Him in the privacy of our rooms and confess. He already knows, but when you confess, you're relieving your soul of the burden that it bears.

But, then, the hardest part is to go to the person or persons whom your faults have ill affected and confess to them. That's hard. That's hard. But, if we want a perfect union, we have to confess the fault. Well, what happens after confession? There must be repentance. When you repent, you feel remorse or contrition or shame for the past conduct which was and is wrong and sinful. It means to feel contrition or self-reproach for what one has done or failed to do.

And, it is the experiencing of such regret for past conduct that involves the changing of our mind toward that sin. So, until we repent and feel sick, sorry over what we have done, we can never, never change our minds toward that thing. And if you don't repent, you'll do it over and over and over again. But to stop it where it is, and Black men, we got to stop what we're doing where it is. We cannot continue the destruction of our lives and the destruction of our community. But that change can't come until we feel sorry.

I heard my brother from the West Coast say today, I atone to the mothers for the death of the babies caused by our senseless slaughter of one another. See, when he feels sorry deep down inside, he's going to make a change. That man has a change in his mind. That man has a change in his heart. His soul has been unburdened and released from the pain of that sin, but you got to go one step further, because after you've acknowledged it, confessed it, repented, you've come to the fifth stage. Now, you've got to do something about it.

Now, look brothers, sisters. Some people don't mind confessing. Some people don't mind making some slight repentance. But, when it comes to doing something about the evil that we've done we fall short. But atonement means satisfaction or reparation for a wrong or injury. It means to make amends. It means penance, expiation, compensation, and recompense made or done for an injury or wrong. So atonement means we must be willing to do something in expiation of our sins so we can't just have a good time today, and say we made history in Washington. We've got to resolve today that we're going back home to do something about what's going on in our lives and in our families and in our communities. . . .

Now, we alright? Can you hang with me a few more? Now, brothers and sisters, if we make atonement it leads to the sixth stage. And the sixth stage is forgiveness. Now, so many of us want forgiveness, but we don't want to go through the process that leads to it. And so, when we say we forgive, we forgive from our lips, but we have never pardoned in the heart. So, the injury still remains. My dear family. My dear brothers. We need forgiveness. God is always ready to forgive us for our sins. Forgiveness means to grant pardon for, or remission of, an offense or sin. It is to absolve, to clear, to exonerate and to liberate. Boy, that's something!

See, you're not liberated until you can forgive. You're not liberated from the evil effect of our own sin until we can ask God for forgiveness and then forgive others, and this is why in the Lord's Prayer you say, "Forgive us our trespasses as we forgive those who trespass against us."[2] So, it means to cease to feel offense and resentment against another for the harm done by an offender. It means to wipe the slate clean.

And then, that leads to the seventh stage. You know, I like to liken this to music. Because in music, the seventh note is called a leading tone. Do, re, me, fa, so, la, te . . . You can't stop there. Te. It leaves you hung up, te. What you got to get back to? Do. So, whatever you started with when you reach the eighth note, you're back to where you started only at a higher vibration. Now, look, at this. The seventh tone, the leading tone that leads to the perfect union with God is reconciliation and restoration because after forgiveness, now, we are going to be restored to what? To our original position. To restore, to reconcile means to become friendly, peaceable again, to put hostile persons into a state of agreement or harmony, to make compatible or to compose or settle what it was that made for division.

It means to resolve differences. It can mean to establish or re-establish a close relationship between previously hostile persons. So, restoration means the act of returning something to an original or unimpaired condition. Now, when you're backed to an impaired position, you have reached the eighth stage, which is perfect union. And when we go through all these steps, there is no difference between us that we can't heal. There's a balm in Gilead to heal the sin sick soul. There is a balm in Gilead to make the wounded whole.

We are a wounded people but we're being healed, but President Clinton, America is also wounded. And there's hostility now in the great divide between the people. Socially the fabric of America is being torn apart and it's black against black, black against white, white against white, white against black, yellow against brown, brown against yellow. We are being torn apart. And we can't gloss it over with nice speeches, my dear, Mr. President.

Sir, with all due respect, that was a great speech you made today. And you praised the marchers and they're worthy of praise. You honored the marchers and they are worthy of honor. But of course, you spoke ill indirectly of me, as a purveyor of malice and hatred. I must hasten to tell you, Mr. President, that I'm not a malicious person, and I'm not filled with malice. But I must tell you that I come in the tradition of the doctor who has to point out, with truth, what's wrong. And the pain is that power has made America arrogant. Power and wealth has made America spiritually blind and the power and the arrogance of America makes you refuse to hear a child of your slaves pointing out the wrong in your society.

But I think if you could clear the scales from your eyes, sir, and give ear to what we say, perhaps, oh perhaps, what these great speakers who spoke before me said, and my great and wonderful brother, the Reverend Jesse Jackson said, and perhaps, just perhaps from the children of slaves might come a solution to this Pharaoh and this Egypt as it was with Joseph when they had to get him out of prison and wash him up and clean him up because Pharaoh had some troubling dreams that he didn't have any answer to. And he called his soothsayers and he called the people that read the stars and he called all his advisors, but nobody could help him to solve the problem. But he had to go to the children of slaves, because he heard that there was one in prison who knew the interpretation of dreams. And he said bring him, bring him and let me hear what he has to say.[3] God has put it for you in the scriptures, Mr. President. Belshazzar and Nebuchadnezzar couldn't read the handwriting on the wall. But Daniel had to read the handwriting for him. Your kingdom has been weighed in the balance and has been found wanting. Do you want a solution to the dilemma that America faces? Then, don't look at our skin color, because racism will cause you to reject salvation if it comes in the skin of a black person. Don't look at the kinkiness of our hair and the broadness of our nose and the thickness of our lips, but listen to the beat of our hearts and the pulsating rhythm of the truth. Perhaps, perhaps, you might be as wise as that Pharaoh and save this great nation.

And so, the eighth stage is perfect union with god. And in the Koran, it reads, "Oh soul that is at rest, well pleased with thy lord and well pleasing." Oh, brothers, brothers, brothers, you don't know what it's like to be free. Freedom can't come from white folks. Freedom can't come from staying here and petitioning this great government. We're here to make a statement to the great government, but not to beg them. Freedom cannot come from no one but the God who can liberate the soul from the burden of sin. And this is why Jesus said "come unto me," not some who are heavy laden, "but all that are heavy laden, and I will give you rest."[4]

But listen, all of these eight steps take place in a process called time. And whenever a nation is involved in sin to the point that God intends to judge and destroy that nation, he always sends someone to make that nation or people know their sins, to reflect on it, to acknowledge, to confess, to repent, and to atone that they might find forgiveness with God. America, oh America. This great city of Washington is like Jerusalem. And the Bible says "Jerusalem, oh Jerusalem, you that stoneth and killeth the prophets of God."[5] Right from this beautiful Capitol and from the beautiful White House have come commands to kill the prophets. David's trouble came from this house. Martin Luther King's trouble came from this house. Malcolm's trouble came from this house. W.E.B. DuBois' trouble came from this house. And from this house, you stoned and killed the prophets of God that would have liberated Black people, liberated America.

But I stand here today knowing, knowing that you are angry. That my people have validated me. I don't need you to validate me. I don't need to be in any mainstream. I want to wash in the river of Jordan and the river that you see and the sea that is before us and behind us and around us. It's validation. That's the mainstream. You're out of touch with reality. A few of you in a few smoke-filled rooms, calling that the mainstream while the masses of the people, White and Black, Red, Yellow, and Brown, poor and vulnerable are suffering in this nation.

Well, America, great America. Like Jerusalem that stoned and killed the prophets of God. That a work has been done in you today unlike any work that's ever been done in this great city. I wonder what you'll say tomorrow? I wonder what you'll write in your newspapers and magazines, tomorrow. Will you give God the glory? Will you give God the glory? Will you respect the beauty of this day? All of these black men that the world sees as savage, maniacal, and bestial. Look at them. A sea of peace. A sea of tranquility. A sea of men ready to come back to God. Settle their differences and go back home to turn our communities into decent and safe places to live. America. America, the beautiful. There's no country like this on the earth. And certainly if I lived in another country, I might never have had the opportunity to speak as I speak today. I probably would have been shot outright and so would my brother, Jesse, and so would Maulana Ron Karenga and so would Dr. Ben Chavis and Reverend Al Sampson and the wonderful people that are here.

But because this is America you allow me to speak even though you don't like what I may say. Because this is America, that provision in the Constitution for freedom of speech and freedom of assembly and freedom of religion, that is your saving grace. Because what you're under right now is grace. And grace is the expression of divine love and protection which God bestows freely on people.

God is angry, America. He's angry, but His mercy is still present. Brothers and sisters, look at the inflictions that have come upon us in the Black community. Do you know why we're being afflicted? God wants us to humble ourselves to the message that will make us atone and come back to Him and make ourselves whole again. But why is God afflicting America? Why is God afflicting the world? Why did Jesus say there would be wars and rumors of wars, and earthquakes in diverse places and pestilence and famine, and why did He say that these were just the beginning of sorrows?

In the last ten years America has experienced more calamities than at any other time period in American history. Why America? God is angry. He's not angry because you're right. He's angry because you're wrong and you want to stone and kill the people who want to make you see you're wrong. And so the Bible says Elijah must first come. Why should Elijah come? Elijah has the job of turning the hearts of the children back to their fathers, and the father's heart back to the children. Elijah becomes an axis upon which people turn back to God and God turns back to the people. And that's why it said Elijah must first come. And so, here we are, four hundred years, fulfilling Abraham's prophecy. Some of our friends in the religious community have said, "Why should you make atonement? That was for the children of Israel." I say yes, it was. But atonement for the children of Israel prefigured our suffering here in America. Israel was in bondage to Pharaoh four hundred years. We've been in America four hundred and forty years. They were under affliction. We're under affliction. They're under oppression. We're under oppression. God said that nation which they shall serve, I will judge. Judgment means God is making a decision against systems, against institutions, against principalities and powers. And that's why Paul said, "We war not against flesh and blood, but against principalities and powers, and the rulers of the darkness of this world and spiritual wickedness in high places." God is sending his decision. I can't help it. If I've got to make the decision known. You don't understand me. My people love me. . . .

We want Willie Lynch to die a natural death. And the only way we can kill the idea of Willie Lynch, we have to build trust in each other . . . Now, brothers, I want you to take this pledge. When I say I, I want you to say I, and say your name. I know that there's so many names, but I want you to shout your name out so that the ancestors can hear it. Take this pledge with me. Say with me please, I, say your name, pledge that from this day forward I will strive to love my brother as I love myself. I, say your name, from this day forward will strive to improve myself spiritually, morally, mentally, socially, politically, and economically for the benefit of myself, my family, and my people. I, say your name, pledge that I will strive to build businesses, build houses, build hospitals, build factories, and then to enter international trade for the good of myself, my family, and my people. I, say your name, pledge that from this day forward I will never raise my hand with a knife or a gun to beat, cut, or shoot any member of my family or any human being, except in self-defense. I, say your name, pledge from this day forward I will never abuse my wife by striking her, disrespecting her, for she is the mother of my children and the producer of my future. I, say your name, pledge that from this day forward I will never engage in the abuse of children, little boys or little girls, for sexual gratification. But I will let them grow in peace to be strong men and women for the future of our people. I, say your name, will never again use the B-word to describe my female, but particularly my own Black sister. I, say your name, pledge from this day forward that I will not poison my body with drugs or that which is destructive to my health and my well-being. I, say your name, pledge from this day forward, I will support Black newspapers, Black radio, Black television. I will support Black artists, who clean up their acts to show respect for themselves and respect for their people, and respect for the ears of the human family. I, say your name, will do all of this so help me God. . . .

In the name of Allah the beneficent, the merciful, praise be to Allah the Lord of the world, the beneficent, the merciful master of the day of requital. Thee do we worship. Thine aid we seek. Guide us on the right path. The path of those upon whom you have bestowed favors, not the path of those upon whom wrath is brought down. Nor those who go astray. Oh, Allah. We thank you for this holy day of atonement and reconciliation. We thank you for putting your spirit and your calm in Washington, D.C., and over the heads of this nearly two million of your servants. We thank you for letting us set a new example, not only for our people but for America and the world. We thank you, oh, Allah, for bringing us safely over the highways and we beg you to bring us safely back to our wives and our children and our loved ones, who saw us off earlier or a few days ago. And as we leave this place, let us be resolved to go home to work out this atonement and make our communities a decent, whole, and safe place to live. And oh, Allah, we beg your blessings on all who participated, all who came that presented their bodies as a living sacrifice, wholly and acceptable as their reasonable service. Now, let us not be conformed to this world, but let us go home transformed by the renewing of our minds and let the idea of atonement ring throughout America. That America may see that the slave has come up with power. The slave has been restored, delivered, and redeemed. And now call this nation to repentance. To acknowledge her wrongs. To confess, not in secret documents, called classified, but to come before the world and the American people as the Japanese prime minister did and confess her faults before the world because her sins have affected the whole world. And perhaps, she may do some act of atonement, that you may forgive and those ill affected may forgive, that reconciliation and restoration may lead us to the perfect union with thee and with each other. We ask all of this in your Holy and Righteous Name. [The speech was concluded with a prayer in Arabic.]

### NOTES

*Sermon source:* "Minister Farrakhan Challenges Black Men: Transcript from Minister Louis Farrakhan's Remarks at the Million Man March," available at http://www.cnn.com/us/9510/megamarch/10-16/transcript/index.html (accessed June 27, 2007).

1. Willie Lynch, *The Willie Lynch Letters and the Making of a Slave* (Chicago: Lushena Books, 1999).
2. See Luke 11:4.
3. See Genesis 41:14–15.
4. See Matthew 11:28.
5. See Matthew 23:37.

### BIBLIOGRAPHICAL SOURCES

Gardell, Mattias. *In the Name of Elijah Muhammad: Louis Farrakhan and the Nation of Islam*. Durham, NC: Duke University Press, 1996.

Magid, J. *Prophet of Rage: The Life of Louis Farrakhan and His Nation*. New York: Basic Books, 1996.

*Microsoft Encarta Online Encyclopedia 2005*, s.v. "Farrakhan, Louis," http://encarta.msn.com (accessed June 27, 2007).

Nation of Islam. "Bio Sketch of the Honorable Minister Louis Farrakhan." http://www.noi.org/mlf-bio.html (accessed May 4, 2005).

Nelson, William E. "Black Church Politics and the Million Man March," in *Black Religious Leadership from the Slave Community to the Million Man March: Flames of Fire*, ed. Felton Best. Lewiston, NY: Edwin Mellen Press, 1998.

Taylor, Clarence. "The Evolving Spiritual and Political Leadership of Louis Farrakhan: From Allah's Masculine Warrior to Ecumenical Sage," in *Black Religious Intellectuals*. New York: Routledge, 2002.

# JAMES ALEXANDER FORBES JR.

*(1935– )*

James Alexander Forbes was born in 1935 in Burgaw, North Carolina, the second of eight children of James Alexander Forbes Sr. and Mabel Clemons Forbes. His father was a pastor and evangelist in the United Holy Church, and retired in 1986 as president and presiding bishop of the Original United Holy Church.

Forbes went north to pursue his education, first at Howard University in Washington, D.C., where he earned a bachelor of science in chemistry in 1957; next, a master's of divinity from Union Theological Seminary in New York City in 1962; and finally a doctorate in ministry from Colgate-Rochester Divinity School in Rochester, New York, in 1975. In addition, he has been awarded thirteen honorary degrees.

Forbes is an ordained minister through the American Baptist Churches and the Original United Holy Church of America. He learned to preach and pastor at the United Holy Church congregations he served in North Carolina and Virginia from 1960 to 1973. From 1968 until 1970 he also worked as campus minister for Virginia Union University in Richmond, Virginia. Forbes served from 1976 until 1985 as the Brown-Sockman Associate Professor of Preaching, and from 1985 until 1989 as Union Theological Seminary's first Joe R. Engle Professor of Preaching. On June 1, 1989, Forbes was installed as the fifth senior minister of the Riverside Church in New York, an interdenominational, interracial, and international church, affiliated with the American Baptist Churches and the United Church of Christ. Forbes retired from the Riverside Church in June 2007.

In their March 4, 1996, issue, *Newsweek* recognized Forbes as one of the twelve most effective preachers in the English-speaking world. He was twice designated as one of America's greatest black preachers by *Ebony*, in 1984 and again in 1993. A well-known preacher and lecturer in the United States and abroad, in 1986, Dr. Forbes gave the Lyman Beecher Lecture at Yale University. The lectures in this series were published in 1989 in his book, *The Holy Spirit and Preaching*. He is married to Bettye Frank Forbes, and they have one son, James A. Forbes III.

• • •

*James Forbes weds the very best of the emotional freedom of the Pentecostal preacher with the disciplined logic of an academician and pastor who is also a prophet. He combines the demands of social justice with the appeal to spiritual conversion with fervor. Ever mindful of the need to stand as prophet and priest in this moment, he reminds listeners of the biblical dictates concerning the poor and what our response must be given these dictates. As he does this, he reveals his homiletical sensitivity and creativity. He takes one of the gravest tragedies in America, the attack of September 11, 2001, and with the skill of a caring pastor who is also a prophet shows how we can all end up destitute given the right circumstances. At the same time, he denounces the United States' rush to war. Finally, he closes the sermon by pointing to our personal responsibility and ultimately to the good news of the Christian Gospel.*

## Spiritual Renewal: Good News for the Poor (May 24, 2004)

> *When the day of Pentecost had come, they were all together in one place. And suddenly, a sound came from heaven like the rush of a mighty wind, and it filled all the house where they were sitting. And there appeared on them tongues as of fire, distributed and resting on each one of them. And they were all filled with the Holy Spirit and began to speak in other tongues, as the Spirit gave them utterance.*
> —Acts 2:1–4 (New International Version)

During the time when welfare as we had come to know it was changing, a conversation took place in the City Hall of New York City. It was not a public meeting, it was one of the backroom meetings, but a report was made. The discussion was about the fact that New York City's benefits for poor people were so favorable that people were coming from poorer and less-generous states to tap into New York's resources for the poor. As the conversation went on somebody in the room said, "We've got to stop this influx of poor people from other areas and the best way to do it is to so drastically reduce the benefits given in New York City that poor people will not come to New York. In fact, many of the poor people who are in New York will find it necessary to leave as we begin cutting." When I heard that reported through a newspaper reporter, I became indignant. The very idea that somebody wants to reduce our response to the needs of the poor so that the poor would be driven out of New York City! I was so upset that I was on the verge of righteous indignation. But I tried to use that in a positive way. So I sat down and wrote this reflection when I thought about things getting so bad for all of the poor that they'd just be leaving New York City. This is what I wrote:

> And I saw a great exodus from New York City—all the bridges, tunnels, and piers were jammed with the departing poor. As they walked or limped along they pushed their carts of precious little things. After the poor had all departed, God looked around and saw them. They who remained in the city now breathed a sigh of relief. They could enjoy their precious little things in peace without the burden of care for the destitute and the poor. Then God, in deep

> sorrow and tender compassion, began to gather God's precious little things so God could journey with those who had been cast from the city. And it came to pass that when God had gathered up the sunlight and rain, the seed-bearing fruit and the light and the air, God wept over the city and departed, pushing God's own cart of precious little things. And New York City was no more.

This reflection was picked up by a magazine. When they put it together, they put this reflection and then drew the New York skyline at the bottom. It was 9/11 when what had been a vision of the poor departing became reality as I watched on television—people were walking—black and white and rich and poor and immigrants and longtime inhabitants of the land were now covered with ash but they were leaving New York City across the Brooklyn Bridge.

In that context they were *all* poor. Many of whom did not know whether they would reach their homes, or whether the workers who had been beside them just a moment or so ago, whether they had escaped. There were people who were riding bicycles and cars were going and in this moment of total impoverishment for everybody there was no distinction. People picked up strangers they did not know. People opened their doors for folks they did not know. Schoolchildren were invited to stay overnight until the parents could be notified. It was as if the parable of utter impoverishment had now become a reality, only it was not a matter of class or race or nationality or previous condition of servitude. That was a strange moment, indeed.

I am so sorry that that moment of radical experience of poverty that we all had so quickly was mobilized for war. For if our experience of poverty had given rise to conversations about what poverty means, and who we are and how we ought to live as sons and daughters of heavenly parents; if we had paused before the rush into war, we might have thought not only about our vulnerability, we might have paid attention to the fact that what we suffered—citizens around the world have grown accustomed to—in poverty, in war, refugee camps where the only means of survival is to act like we're all brothers and sisters together. Oh, if only we had not rushed to war. If only we had waited long enough to see what it was like to be poor, it might have affected the way we responded even to Al Qaeda. It might have steeled us against the humiliation visited upon others, especially in the case of war and the ravages thereof, all the abuses that happened. If we had waited and had paid attention to what it feels like to be poor, perhaps, perhaps we would be at a different place as the source of power in the world today.

So very shortly after the article appeared, I wrote again, this time not about the poor leaving New York, but that something would have happened so that we could return to live together in a gorgeous mosaic. So I wrote this, and this is what I want to talk about—how I contrast that parable of utter impoverishment with this new look about things and what would it take to make this latter description more the reality not only in New York but across our nation. This is what I said when I was trying to be hopeful, when I was trying to believe that God had not abandoned us, when I was confident that "God will hear us, God will hear us." And this is what will happen then:

> I detected coming up from the subways and across the bridges of all the boroughs were citizens of every language, creed, and color hastening from places of work, learning, recreation, entertainment, family outings, sightseeing, and worship. Though different in a thousand ways, they did not seem like strangers, for they knew they were safe and secure in the city of neighborly strength and care. Proudly they walked the streets of challenging opportunity and climbed the steps of fair and just striving. Visitors marveled at the spirit of vitality which filled the air and the pulsing energy which quickened their pace and sparked their imaginations. They luxuriated in symphony of sound, of sidewalk entertainers, the hum of traffic, schoolchildren at play, and feisty lovers ventilating their disappointments for unrighteous affections. And there were no homeless or jobless among them, nor any who begged around the trash heap in search of food. For the spirit of New York had released a grand new mentality, a partnership of the passion and commitment that made a bold declaration: "A city where everybody counts is a city where everyone contributes, and a city where everyone contributes is richer by far than the ancient kingdom where some are locked out."

The parable of living together, affirming one another across the infinite number of expressions of divine creativity. Which one will it be? Which one will it be across our nation?

Well, if Pentecost this year could become something other than ancient history, if Pentecost could become this coming Sunday's current event, then those of you who know the story, don't need to even read it. The first part is about the wonderful experience of the disciples being up in the upper room, on one accord, and suddenly there was the sound of a rushing mighty wind and it filled the house where they were seated. Tongues of fire sat upon their heads and they began to speak in other tongues as the Spirit gave them utterance. And although they were there from all over the Diaspora they understood each other though they spake in different languages. And Peter, who formerly had been a coward, now stands up and says, "These folks are not drunk as you think they are. This is what Joel said was going to happen, in the last days I will pour out my Spirit upon all flesh."[1] So that's the first part.

I hope you'll like this point in Acts chapter two, part two. Because, it's not just the speaking in tongues that suggests that the Spirit has come, it is what happened as a result of the presence of the Spirit. When the Spirit descended upon the church they said that these people represented many different walks of life, experiencing themselves coming together from house to house continuing in the Apostles' doctrine, which is to say, discussing what is it that he said and what are the signs by which we would know that he has come and what were the marks of our being faithful to our Father. They had a chance to talk about it, to talk about how he said, "Listen, when you see the poor, you see me. When you give them something to eat, you're feeding me. When you visit them in prison, you are visiting me. When you look into their desperate situation and do something about it, you are visiting me." They had a chance to talk about it.

I think I'm valid in this. Some folks have Pentecostal experiences without continuing in the Apostles' doctrine. They get religion and then they haul off and try to change the world without getting in the Apostles' doctrine to see what Christianity really looked like. They don't take time to read Isaiah 65, where God talks about a time when brothers and sisters, if they didn't make it to a hundred years old, because of the health-care advances, they'd say, "something's wrong with this person." Children would not die in infancy, food would be plentiful, clothing for everybody, housing for families, and a quality of joy that made Jerusalem a delight in the presence of God. Oh, Pentecost doesn't come just because you have a heart that's strangely warmed. It's because you have a heart that's transformed whereas there's no isolation. When Pentecost comes, they had all things in common. Folks began to sell what they had so that if anybody lacked anything they would be provided with what they needed.

What would happen in the United States of America this summer if the Holy Spirit, like it came at Pentecost, would come to our churches? Oh, what would happen if the Holy Spirit were to descend right in this place of hymns, in this family and the wind of the Spirit would just blow a little south and head down to 1600 Pennsylvania Avenue. And then it would blow to the judiciary and down to the legislature and up to New York and down to the country where you come from. Wouldn't that be a wonderful thing? I'm telling you it might be. I'm feeling it now. I'm feeling it.

I have the feeling, my brother, that we are here because God knows that some promises have been made, that there has been eschatological vision that's been put off much too long. And that God has said, "I'll be your Provider in the time of need."[2]

And I think that Isaiah said in the ninth chapter sometimes God gets a zeal. I like that word. That means that morally we have no choice. I got to get something done here. There are people who are intentional. There are people who are working two and three jobs and still don't have a living wage. There are people who are really doing the best they can to take care of their health but they don't have health-care coverage. And God has promised "I'll be with you" and even David used to say, "I've never seen the righteous forsaken or their seed begging bread."[3] But I have. And God is disappointed in us and I feel it. I feel that liberals and evangelicals, Baptists, Methodists, Salvation Army, Moravians, Mennonites, folks that can spend all night long fussing about where we don't agree, can be asked to put down that issue for just a little while because God sees the poor. Oh, I'm so happy. It is my privilege to be here on this occasion. I would pay to be here.

Well, brothers and sisters, if the Holy Spirit comes this coming Sunday and blows across this land the poor will know about it. But let me stop right now and ask, how eager are you for the Spirit to blow that way? Are there any poor people in here tonight? Do you know any poor people? Sometimes we bypass them. We preach about them. We talk about them. I know something about poverty. Some of it out of experience, some of it I've read. But I just want to make sure that you know what I'm talking about. I know something about growing up in a family where there was not always enough to eat. Some of you northerners don't know anything about grits, do you? Have you ever heard of R.C. grits? That's what Mama called it when the next day there was nothing to eat, she called it R.C. grits, meaning reconditioned grits. I know something about living in a house where when children are born there was no bassinet for the baby. My sisters were placed in a bureau drawer. You know about that? A little pillow, nice little blanket, but no bassinet. I know something about when it was that we had managed to sound like we were not at home when the bill collectors came by. "Just be real quiet children. Don't say anything because there's no money to pay the bill." I know what it's like to have that long thing that they use to turn the water off. Have any of you ever been there? I know what it's like to have the man find the meter and cut the electricity off because the bill had not been paid. I know what it's like to go down to the health department or sometimes at school to a big truck that's got cabbage that's old and thrown away, and the kids are encouraged to pick it up and take it home. I know what it's like to have Mama take that stinking cabbage, peel the rotten parts off, wash off the core, and sprinkle some stuff in it and I remember sometimes not feeling like saying that verse to the Lord, "I thank you for what I'm about to receive," because I know where it came from.

Poverty is a weapon of mass destruction. Something's got to be done about it. Therefore, brothers and sisters, I close tonight by telling you maybe what we've got to do and people don't understand why we are so excited about this vision, why we feel the way we do about it. Is this the best that you can do to loosen bonds of injustice, to undo the bond of the yoke, to let the oppressed go free and break every yoke? Is this your answer, to share your bread with the hungry and bring the homeless poor into your house; when you see the naked, to cover them, and not to hide from your own kinfolk? Then, I'll show up, then I'll come. Then the light shall break forth like the dawn, and your healing shall spring up quickly. Don't come worshiping in my court, if you have not cared for the poor, don't even show up. If you do, the doors of my heart may be closed even though the doors of the sanctuary are open.

Well, I've preached longer than I was allotted—that happens to me sometimes. And with this I'm ready to close up, to say to you that:

*I looked around the other day and saw*
*How truly blessed this life of mine has been.*
*I have life and health abundantly,*
*Peace and joy within,*
*Special care in times of desperation,*
*A helping hand when friends are few.*
*So I asked the Lord what can I do*
*To return some thanks to you?*
*I expected mission impossible.*
*A depth of service all the way.*
*But instead, it's just an assignment God sends to us each day.*
*Love my children.*
*That's all I ask of you.*
*Love my children.*
*That's the least that you can do.*
*If you love them and I love them*
*We shall see them safely through.*
*Love yourself, love me, too,*
*And whatever else you do,*
*Love my children.*

Let's make a deal. Lord, Lord, if you would come by and touch us in the impoverishment of our spirits, then, even though we're not going to feed all, we will make sure that our church and our tithes and offerings will be offered with compassion. If you would show up, Lord, we promise that we will ask our governmental authorities to stop canceling the programs for the poor just because of the war. If you would show up, God, we promise you that we will make sure that there is housing, and we promise you that we will ask every politico that wants our vote how he stands on poverty. While you show up, you can count on us. Like Isaiah of old we say, "Did you want us to do it? Yea, God. Send me. I'll be there." And this year Pentecost will be good news for the poor.

### *Notes*

*Sermon source:* Transcript of a sermon preached by James A. Forbes at Washington National Cathedral in Washington, D.C., at a service of Unity to Overcome Poverty sponsored by Call to Renewal on May 24, 2004. Transcript provided by Dr. James Forbes.

1. Acts 2:15.
2. See Genesis 22:14.
3. See Psalm 37:25.

### *Bibliographical Sources*

"James A. Forbes," Wikipedia entry, available at http://en.wikipedia.org/wiki/James_A._Forbes (accessed June 27, 2007).

"James A. Forbes: Senior Minister Emeritus, The Riverside Church, New York City," available at http://www.theRiversidechurchny.org/about/?minister-emeritus (accessed June 27, 2007).

"Reverend James Forbes and the Riverside Church," available at http://www.pbs.org/now/society/Forbes.html (accessed June 27, 2007).

## PETER J. GOMES

*(1942– )*

Born in Boston, Massachusetts, in 1942, Peter J. Gomes is widely regarded as one of America's most compelling preachers. The grandson of a Baptist minister, Gomes, an only child, was always expected to become a man of the cloth. On Sunday afternoons he would play church, repeating that morning's sermon while standing behind a pulpit made from cranberry boxes. Gomes's mother, Orissa Josephine White, came from a family that was a pillar of Boston's aristocracy and was a graduate of the New England Conservatory of Music. She played organ and directed the choir at the mainly white Baptist church. Then, in the evening, the Gomeses attended the Bethel AME Church, along with the few other blacks who lived in his community. His father, Peter Lobo Gomes, was born in the Cape Verde islands and attended a Catholic monastery as a youth and teen before moving to United States to become a cranberry farmer.

Gomes obtained a bachelor of arts from Bates College in 1965 and bachelor of sacred theology from Harvard Divinity School in 1968. After teaching and serving as director of freshman studies at Alabama's Tuskegee Institute in the late 1960s, he went to Harvard in 1970 as assistant minister in the Memorial Church. He became the minister of the Memorial Church in 1974 and was appointed Plummer Professor of Christian Morals at Harvard College. He is also a member of the faculty of Arts and Sciences and of the School of Divinity of Harvard University. In 2001 Harvard presented him with the Phi Beta Kappa Teaching Award. In 1998, Gomes presented the Lyman Beecher Lectures at Yale Divinity School. In 1998 he was also named Clergy of the Year by Religion in American Life.

Gomes has several *New York Times* best-selling books, including *The Good Book: Reading the Bible with Mind and Heart* (1996) and *Sermons: Biblical Wisdom for Daily Living* (1998). His other titles include *The Good Life: Truths That Last in Times of Need* (2002), *Strength for the Journey: Biblical Wisdom for Daily Living* (2003), and *The Backward Glance and the Forward Look* (2005). He has also published ten volumes of sermons as well as numerous articles and papers.

In *The Good Book*, Gomes opposes the use and abuse of the Bible to alienate others from Christ. Explaining his theology, Gomes writes, "I want black people, women, and homosexuals, among others, to see and to hear that the Bible is both for them and with them. I want them to know that the Bible is theirs by right and intention." In 1991 Gomes announced that he was gay after a member of a student group at Harvard published a lengthy paper denouncing homosexuality. Gomes proclaimed from the steps of the Memorial Church, "I am a Christian who happens as well to be gay." This surprised some, given that Gomes is considered by many to be a conservative evangelical. Following this announcement, Gomes was attacked from numerous camps. However, he was supported by the majority of Harvard faculty, administration, and students and remains at Harvard.

• • •

*This sermon was delivered in the Memorial Chapel at Harvard in response to September 11, 2001. The sermon received national attention as a response to the tragedy. In the sermon Gomes joins the best exegetical scholarship with the depths of contemplative piety and devotion to yield a Bible that is relevant and alive in a post-9/11, postmodern world. Gomes's preaching is a feast for the theological mind and for those who earnestly seek to know the Christian God at more than a surface level. In this message he uses every tool in his homiletical arsenal: scripture, history, theology, poetry, film, a book from the* New York Times *bestseller list, literature, humor, song, stories, and testimonies to reach his listeners.*

*This sermon has produced a now often-used quote: "The question is not where God is when disaster strikes; the real and interesting question is where you were before disaster struck? Where were you two weeks ago? Three weeks ago? Where will you be three weeks from now, or four weeks from now? God has not forgotten you, but is it not reasonable to suggest that before September 11, many of us had forgotten God? God is where God always is and has always been; it is we who have to account for our absence."*

## Outer Turmoil, Inner Strength (September 23, 2001)

> *Set a straight course and keep to it, and do not be dismayed in the face of adversity.* —Ecclesiasticus 2:2 (Revised English Bible)

Let me begin with an observation, one might say, of comparative religion. I understand that in the traditions and liturgies of the Greek Orthodox Church, our brethren in the East, when a child is baptized—and by "child" I mean an infant, not a squalling seven-year-old but a real infant, literally still damp—in that church, after the baptism has been performed, the minister or priest or bishop takes his very large pectoral cross (twice the size of mine) and forcefully strikes the little child on its breast. Strikes it so hard that it leaves a mark, and so hard that it hurts the child and the child screams. In the West, we give the child roses. What is the difference here?

The symbolism of the Eastern baptism is clear, indicating that the child who has been baptized into Christ must bear the cross, and that the cross is a sign not of ease or of victory or of prosperity or of success, but of sorrow, suffering, pain, and death. And by it, those things are overcome. It is important to remember that. The symbol of our Christian faith is this very cross that you see on that holy table, carved in that choir screen, worn around the necks of many of us, and held in honor and esteemed by all of us. And it stands to remind us of the troubles of the world that placed our Savior upon it for sins that he did not commit. We Christians, therefore, like those Greek Orthodox babies, ought to expect trouble, turmoil, and tribulation as the normal course of life. We don't, however, because we have been seduced by a false and phony version of the Christian faith which suggests that by our faith we are immune to trouble.

Because we have been nice to God, our thinking goes, then God should be nice to us. Because you have interrupted your normal routine and come here today, God should somehow take note of it, mark it down in the book, and spare you any trouble, tribulation, turmoil, or difficulty. Tribulation, we know, happens only to bad people. Should it, therefore, be happening in spades to all those people who are not here this morning but just getting up out of bed, recovering from a night of pleasure and satiety? Tribulation happens only to the nonobservant and the bad people, and when, as Rabbi Kushner so famously and quite profitably noted, bad things happen to good people, we feel that something has gone terribly wrong. God is not supposed to behave that way, we think, for that is not part of the deal. And we ask, "Where is God?"

Now, let me hasten to say that the answer to that conundrum is not a false conception of God. The issue has nothing whatsoever to do with the so-called death of God, and everything to do with the life and the faith of the believer. It is not the death of God that should concern us; it is the questionable state of the life of the believer. God does not spare us from turmoil. Even the most casual observance of the Scriptures tells us that God strengthens us for turmoil. It is a shabby faith that suggests that God is to do all the heavy lifting and that you and I are to do none. The whole record of Scripture from Genesis to Revelation and the whole experience of the people of God from Good Friday down to and beyond Tuesday, September 11, suggest that faith is forged on the anvil of human adversity. No adversity, no faith.

Consider the lessons we heard this morning. The first lesson, read for us from one of the ancient books of the Jews, the Book of Ecclesiasticus in the Apocrypha, could it be put any plainer? "My son, if thou comest to serve the Lord, prepare thy soul for temptation. Set thy heart aright, and constantly endure, and do not make haste in time of calamity." You don't need a degree in Hebrew Bible or exegesis to figure out what that is saying. What is the context for these words? Trouble, turmoil, tribulation, and temptation: that's the given, that's the context. What is the response for calamity? Endurance. Don't rush, don't panic. What are we to do in calamitous times? We are to slow down. We are to inquire. We are to endure. Tribulation does not invite haste; it invites contemplation, reflection, perseverance, endurance.

Where may we turn for examples of what I am trying to say that the Scriptures say to us? We are in the middle of the great "Days of Awe," with the beginning of the Jewish New Year and the Day of Atonement. And when the Jewish people celebrate these Days of Awe and begin their new year and atone for their sins, they always remember two things. First, they remember the troubles and the tribulations through which they have been, and they recite the history, not of their victories, but of their sorrows and their troubles. They remind themselves and everybody else how they have been formed and forged through the experience of trial and tribulation. They remember those things.

The second thing they remember is how the Lord delivered them out of those troubles and helped them to endure and eventually overcome them. They are reminded of that, and they remind themselves of it over and over and over again. And, when it is said that "It is not the Jew who keeps the law, but the law which keeps the Jew," it is to this process of remembrance, endurance, and deliverance that the aphorism speaks. Again, it says in the Book of Ecclesiasticus, "Look at the generations of old, and see. Whoever did put his trust in the Lord, and was ashamed? Or who did abide in his fear, and was forsaken? Or who did call upon him, and he despised him?" The history of the Jews in the world is not a history of escape from trouble. Would that it were, but it is not! It is the record of endurance through tribulation, an endurance which would have been impossible without God. If any people had the right to claim that "God was dead," or at least on sabbatical, it was the Jews, but they never have said it, and they never will, for they know better. They do not worship a metaphor or a simile or a theological construct. They worship the one who stands beside them and who has been with them from Egypt to Auschwitz and beyond, and who enables them to stand up to all that a world of tribulation can throw at them. If we want to know about outer turmoil and inner strength we need look no farther than to our neighbors the Jews. Remember, they wrote the book on the subject.

We may also look a little closer to home. We may look to the authentic witness of the Christian faith to which we bear, in this church, unambiguous allegiance. We do not just believe in God in general, or in a spiritual hope: we believe in Jesus Christ, who is all that we can fully know about God. So, we look at this tradition for inner strength in the midst of outer turmoil.

Consider St. Paul, a Jew and a Christian, and consider his view of things in a less than agreeable world. I hope you heard that second lesson read this morning in J.B. Phillips's pungent prose. Listen to what St. Paul says: "We are handicapped on all sides"—a very fashionable translation of the word, but apt—"but we are never frustrated. We are puzzled," he says, "but never in despair. We are persecuted, but we never have to stand it alone, and"—this fourth part is the part I like the most—"we may be knocked down, but we are never knocked out."[1]

Now Paul is not an abstract theologian, like so many of my colleagues. Paul speaks from the experience of a frustrated but not defeated believer. This is not the sort of "How to be Leaders and Win" sort of stuff that he writes; this is not the kind of CEO book that they trot out in the business school and in motivational seminars. No. Paul writes out of failure, frustration, and conflict, but never out of despair. If you are looking for something to read in these troublesome times, do not turn to books of cheap inspiration and handy-dandy aphorisms; do not look for feel-good and no-stress and a lot-of-gain-and-no-pain kinds of books. They're all out there and you will be sorely tempted, but if you want to read something useful during these times, my brothers and sisters in Christ, read the letters of Paul. Read them and weep! Read them and rejoice! Read them and understand that neither you nor I are the first people in the world ever to face sorrow, death, frustration, or terror: we are not the first, and there is a record of coping here that is not merely of coping but of overcoming. If you do not wish to succumb to the tidal wave of despair and temptation and angst that surrounds us on every hand, you will go back to the roots of our faith, which are stronger than any form of patriotism. *I don't despise patriotism—don't misunderstand me—but there is no salvation in love of country. There is salvation only in love of Jesus Christ, and if you confuse the two, the greatest defeat will have been achieved.* Remember that. Read the letters of Paul.

When you look at that fourth chapter in 2 Corinthians, you will discover that this is not a faith of evasion, a faith of success, or a faith of unambiguous pleasure and delight. It is reality, a reality that believers have always been forced to face. "In the world," says the apostle John, "we shall have tribulation." Jesus says, "Be of good cheer; I have overcome the world." Well, that's all very right and good for Jesus, who in fact has overcome the world, and good for him, I say again; but for us who have not yet overcome the world, John's Gospel is as true as ever it was. In the world we shall have tribulation, and anyone who promises you otherwise is either uninformed or lying, and perhaps both; and owes no allegiance to the gospel. When we face the world as believers, we face it with tribulation on every hand.

From this very pulpit my venerable predecessor Willard Sperry often quoted his friend and colleague George Tyrell, who was one of the famous Catholic modernists of the first third of the twentieth century, and in a time when World War I was still fresh and World War II was clearly on the horizon, Sperry preached week after week to congregations like this—to your grandparents, three generations removed. One of his favorite quotations of Father Tyrell's was Tyrell's definition of Christianity, and this is what Tyrell said, what Sperry quoted, and what I now quote again: "Christianity is an ultimate optimism founded upon a provisional pessimism." In this world we shall have tribulation.

So, a reasonable person—and we're all reasonable persons here, are we not? That's why we're here and not in some other church—might ask, "From where has this notion come, that Christians are entitled to a free 'get-out-of-jail' card, an exemption to the world of turmoil and tribulation?" This misreading of the Christian faith (for that is exactly what it is) comes from the fashionable, cultural faith with which we have so often confused the Christian faith. Most of us aspire to be believers in the Christian faith, but all of us to one degree or another, alas, ascribe to the cultural faith. And that cultural religion in times of prosperity is often easy and always dangerous. Be suspicious of religion in times of prosperity and ease. Why is it dangerous? It is dangerous because prosperity itself can become a terribly tempting false god and a substitute for religion, and in the name of the religion of prosperity, success, and control, most of us will do anything and almost everything—and we have.

In times of prosperity either we make prosperity our religion, or we imagine that we can do without religion altogether. Who needs it? When turmoil happens to others we can be mildly empathetic, perhaps even sympathetic, and maybe we can even utter that famous aphorism, "There but for the grace of God go I"; but when turmoil hits us, when we are knocked flat, when all of our securities and our cherished illusions are challenged to the breaking point, and break, then comes the great question we must both ask and answer, "What is left when everything we have is taken from us?"

What is left when everything you have is taken from you? For the last decade I have asked on commencement morning, in my sermons to the seniors about to leave this college, questions like this: "How will you live after the fall?" I don't mean autumn; I mean the Fall. "How will you manage when trouble comes? How will you manage when you are tested and fail the test? How will you cope with frustration and fear and failure and anxiety?" Many of them have thought those to be quaint and even rude questions, perhaps the kind of rhetorical excess that preachers engage in around commencement time, a kind of raining on their parade.

Since September 11, however, these are no longer abstract, philosophical, or theoretical questions, and people have gravitated in astonishing numbers to the places where such questions are taken seriously. Every rabbi, minister, priest, imam, and spiritual leader of whom I know or have heard reports, as can I, of the incredible turn toward faith in this time of our current crisis. Probably not since the Second World War has there been such a conspicuous turn to the faith in our country, and both our ordinary and our extraordinary services here in the last ten days bear profound witness to this. On Tuesday afternoon, September 11, the day of the terrorist attacks on the World Trade Center and the Pentagon, and the downing of the plane in Pennsylvania, we saw thousands here in the Yard in an ecumenical witness, and on Friday of that same week, we saw almost as many here at a service of prayer and remembrance, on a day especially designated as a national day of prayer and remembrance. Last Sunday's service was like Easter day, and this one is very close to it. The daily service of morning prayers in Appleton Chapel is nearly standing-room only, and this past week the president of this university asked if he could come and speak at morning prayers on Friday, thus proving beyond all shadow of a doubt that there is a God. With his opening words from our lectern he said that this was the last place he expected to find himself so early in his administration. This is from a secular man who, by the standards of this secular place, is as close to God as many aspire to reach.

These are extraordinary times, this is an extraordinary moment, we are witnessing extraordinary things, and I ask you this: Is it not an incredible irony that in the face of the most terrible and tangible facts available to us, the destruction of those monuments to material success—the brutally physical, worldly reality with the violence before our very eyes—that men and women instinctively turn to the very things that cannot be seen? They turn not to the reality of the visible but to the reality of the invisible which, when compared to what can be seen, ultimately endures. Seeking faith amidst the ruins is the subtext of these days. There's a terrible parable there, that as the very temple to which we offered our secular worship is destroyed before us we seek the God who precedes and who follows these temples made and destroyed by human hands. People are seeking inner strength beyond the outer turmoil. That is what I see and that is what I hear on every hand, in every paper, in every magazine, on every talk show, and on everybody's lips.

In light of this, the question, "Where is God?" seems almost irrelevant. This was the question of the day for the religion editor of the *Boston Globe* last weekend, and a host of my clerical colleagues attempted an answer or two. I was not asked—another proof of the existence of God—but had I been, I would have said what I now say to you, which is that it was the wrong question. The question is not where God is when disaster strikes; the real and interesting question is where you were before disaster struck? Where were you two weeks ago? Three weeks ago? Where will you be three weeks from now, or four weeks from now? God has not forgotten you, but is it not reasonable to suggest that before September 11, many of us had forgotten God? God is where God always is and has always been; it is we who have to account for our absence.

Be certain of one thing, however. We should not be embarrassed that now in adversity we seek the God whom we had forgotten in prosperity, for what is God for if he is not to be there when we seek him? We should not be embarrassed that in trouble we have remembered one profound theological truth, that God is to be found where God is most needed—in trouble, sorrow, sickness, adversity, and even in death itself. Over and over and over again the Psalms make this point, as we sang in the sermon hymn, in paraphrase of Psalm 46: "God is our refuge and strength; a very present help in trouble." Isn't this Luther's point in his great hymn "A Mighty Fortress Is Our God"?

*Let goods and kindred go,*
*This mortal life also;*
*The body they may kill;*
*God's truth abideth still,*
*His kingdom is forever.*[2]

You don't have to be a Lutheran to know the truth of that. That hymn wasn't written yesterday. It was not written by someone who did not know turmoil. It was written by someone who in the midst of outer turmoil had inner strength.

This last week, as I've thought about this morning and my obligations toward you, two images have flashed in my mind. One was the indelible image of those burning towers and those terrible encounters with the airplanes, a kind of conflict of our own magnificent technologies coming together in a horrible parody of our skills and our strengths. That was one image. The other goes back to one of my favorite movies, which will identify all of my phobias and predilections and will also give away my age. Between Dunkirk and Pearl Harbor there was produced one great film, *Mrs. Miniver.*[3] Those of you who know it know that I'm referring to that last scene in the bombed-out church on a Sunday morning, where, with the window destroyed and the cross standing in the broken window and the people of the congregation ripped apart by Hitler's bombing of their little village, yet still they sing, "Children of the heavenly King, as we journey sweetly sing." I know it was a great propaganda film. I know it was designed to rouse the souls and the spirits of the British people. I know it was the British version of Hollywood, with Walter Pidgeon and Greer Garson. I know all of that, and I believe it! So did the British people, and so do you need to believe that in that destruction somewhere rests that image of the God who was with us at the most terrible moment of our time. The answer to the question, "Where is God?" is that God is where God is always—by the side of those who need him. He is not in front to lead, not behind to push, not above to protect, but beside us to get us through: "Beside us to guide us, our God with us joining."

I cannot imagine those heroic firefighters and police officers and workers and volunteers, amidst the rubble of Ground Zero in New York, indulging in the luxurious theological speculation about where God might or might not be. They *know* where God is; he is right there with them, enabling them, empowering them, strengthening them, even when hope itself has died. If you want to know where God is, do not ask the prosperous. Ask the suffering. Ask the sorrowing. Ask those who are acquainted with grief.

In the Book of Common Prayer there is a collect which begins, "God of all comfort . . ." To some who don't know any better, that sounds like mere consolation, something soothing, inadequate words in troubled times of turmoil and tribulation, a kind of Band-Aid on cancer, if you will, like the "comfortable words" in the old Book of Common Prayer, which were not very comforting to a church and a culture that had grown too comfortable. Do you know the proper meaning of the word "comfort"? It means to "fortify," to "strengthen," to "give courage," even "empower," and not mere consolation. The God of all comfort is the one who supplies what we most lack when we most need it. As Paul puts it, he gives us sufficient capacity that when we are knocked down we are not knocked out. The God of all comfort is not the god who fights like Superman or Rambo or Clint Eastwood or any of our conventional cultural heroes. The God of all comfort is the one who gives inner power and strength to those who would be easily outnumbered, outmaneuvered, outpowered by the conventional forces and the conventional wisdom. Inner strength is what is required when in the midst of turmoil we do not know what to do with our outward power and our outward might.

Let us also not forget one powerful fact that we are tempted to forget, which is that the world has always been a dangerous and precarious place. The fact that we have just discovered this terrible fact for ourselves does not make it any less true, or any less dangerous. Outer turmoil is no longer the fate that falls to others: the shrinking world that has allowed us to export technology abroad has now, alas, permitted terror to be imported to us. The great question now is how we stand and how we manage in a world now less brave, now less new than it ever was.

Inner strength, I believe, comes from the sure conviction that God has placed us in the world to do the work of life, and not of death. This is what Paul says in 2 Corinthians: "We are always facing death," he writes, "but this means that we know more and more of life" (2 Corinthians 4:11). Faith is not the opposite either of doubt or of death but the means whereby we face and endure doubt and death, and overcome our fear of them. Our inner faith as believers comes from the sure conviction that neither death nor doubt nor fear is the last word. This is not a policy statement for the nation; this is a sure conviction for Christian believers. Therefore, because we believe that, and because that belief is testified to by the experience of our ancestors in the faith and our contemporaries who labor beside us and for God in the rubble, we are able to endure. We are able to go through the worst for the best, come what may. Endurance is what it takes when you have nothing left. Phillips Brooks once said that we do not pray for lighter loads but for greater strength to bear the loads we are given. Heavy loads have been placed upon us in these days, and even greater burdens and sacrifices are to come: of that there can be no doubt. And, like Jesus in the garden, we would be less than human if we did not pray that this cup might pass us by—but it won't. The real issue for us then, as it was for Jesus, is, how do we manage?

Inner strength in the midst of turmoil, I suggest, is not simply stoic endurance and perseverance, important as they are, especially in tough, demanding times. Nor is inner strength simply a form of mind over matter, a kind of moral escapism that says that you may have captured my body but my mind is free. It's not either of those. When I tried to think of what it was, I remembered a story told by old Dr. Ernest Gordon, for many years dean of the chapel at Princeton, who was more famous because of his book about his captivity on the River Kwai during World War II. In that Japanese prison camp, Ernest Gordon said that he and his fellow British who were captives were initially very religious, reading their Bibles, praying, singing hymns, witnessing, and testifying to their faith, and hoping and expecting that God would reward them and fortify them for their faith by freeing them or at least mitigating their captivity. God didn't deliver, however, and the men became both disillusioned and angry, and some even faithless. They gave up on the outward display of their faith, but after a while, Gordon says, the men, responding to the needs of their fellows—caring for them, protecting the weaker ones, and in some cases dying for one another—began to discern something of a spirit of God in their midst. It was not a revival of religion in the conventional sense, but rather the discovery that religion was not what you believed but what you did for others when it seemed that you could do nothing at all. It was compassion that gave them their inner strength, and it was from their inner strength that their compassion came. (I owe this insight to Dr. A. Leonard Griffiths, from *Illusions of our Culture*.)[4]

Could it be that amidst the cries of vengeance and violence and warfare, and the turmoil that is attempting to sweep us all up in the calamity of these days, the inner strength we so desperately seek is the strength that comes from compassion, from hearing and heeding the cry of the other? In one of Theodore Parker Ferris's books I found underlined these words about strength:

> Some people's strength is all drawn from themselves. They are like isolated pools with limited reserves. Others are more like rivers. They do not produce or contain the power, but it flows through them, like blood through the body. The more they give, the more they are able to draw in. That strength is not their own.[5]

Then the author says, in words that I wish were mine:

> The strength that God gives is available to those who care for others, for they are showing the spirit of Jesus. The power of God's spirit fortifies them.[6]

Can it be that inner strength is not simply the capacity to endure, but to give? Can it be that compassion is superior to power? Can it be that amid the turmoil of that violent crowd on Good Friday, from his inner strength Jesus showed compassion? He forgave his enemies, he reunited his friends, and he redeemed the criminal.

When in the midst of turmoil and calamity you seek the inner strength that helps you not only to endure but to overcome, do not look for what you can get. Look rather for what you have been given, and for what you can give. We begin with calamity, but we end with compassion. Remember the quotation that Theodore Ferris had underlined: "The strength that God gives is available for those who care for others . . ."

### *Notes*

*Sermon source: 9.11.01: African American Leaders Respond to an American Tragedy*, ed. Martha Simmons and Frank A. Thomas (Valley Forge, PA: Judson Press, 2001), 150–61.

1. See 2 Corinthians 4:8.
2. See "A Mighty Fortress Is Our God," *The National Baptist Hymnal* (National Baptist Publishing Board, 1977), number 15.
3. William Wyler and Sidney Franklin (producers), *Mrs. Miniver* (release date June 4, 1942).
4. Leonard Griffiths, *Illusions of our Culture* (London: Hodder & Stoughton, 1969).
5. Actually, Ferris quotes Hugh Martin, *The Beatitudes* (New York: Harper & Brothers, 1953), 39.
6. Ibid., 39.

### *Bibliographical Sources*

Boynton, Robert. "God and Harvard: A Profile of Peter Gomes." *The New Yorker*, November 11, 1996.

Gomes, Peter J. *The Good Book: Reading the Bible with Mind and Heart.* San Francisco: HarperSanFrancisco, 2002.

———. "Patriotism is Not Enough." *Sojourners Magazine* 32, no. 1 (January–February 2003): 20–25.

## PRATHIA L. HALL

*(1940–2002)*

Prathia Laura Ann Hall was born in 1940 in Philadelphia, Pennsylvania, one of four children of Berkeley and Ruby Hall. She was licensed and ordained for ministry by her father. Her interest in the civil rights movement led her, after college, to join the Student Nonviolent Coordinating Committee (SNCC) and to become one of the first women field leaders for SNCC in southwest Georgia. Hall was married and divorced and was the mother of a son and a daughter. Her daughter died at age twenty-three due to a stroke.

Hall held a master of divinity and a doctoral degree from Princeton Theological Seminary. She specialized in womanist theology, ethics, and African American church history. She was an ordained American Baptist minister and also an officer with the Progressive National Baptist Convention. She was a pioneering woman in ministry. In 1978 she became the pastor of Rose of Sharon Baptist Church of Philadelphia, formerly pastored by her father. In 1982 she was the first woman received into membership of the Baptist Ministers' Conference of Philadelphia and Vicinity. She later was associate dean of spiritual and community life, director of the Harriet L. Miller Women's Center, and dean of African American ministries at United Theological Seminary in Dayton, Ohio. She also served as a visiting professor at the Interdenominational Theological Center in Atlanta, Georgia.

When *Ebony* magazine presented its only list of the Outstanding African American Women Preachers in America in 1997, Prathia Hall was listed first. She was among the first group of women preachers in the twentieth century, of any race, who achieved national notoriety. Hall was a revivalist, which as late as 2002, was still a rare achievement for women preachers. Hall had several serious health conditions, which ultimately cut short her life. A little less than two years before her death, she served as an associate professor at Boston University School of Theology, holding the Martin Luther King Jr. Chair in Social Ethics.

The height of compliment was paid to Hall's preaching when Martin Luther King Jr. said: "Prathia Hall is one platform speaker, I would prefer not to follow."[1] Some believe that King incorporated the phrase "I have a dream" in his speeches after hearing it from Prathia Hall.[2]

• • •

*"Between the Wilderness and a Cliff" is one of Prathia L. Hall's best-known sermons. This version of the sermon was preached at the Hampton University Ministers' Conference Choir Directors' Organists' Guild Workshop and was foundational in establishing that women had the preaching prowess to stand in male-dominated national African American preaching venues. A great part of the sermon's power and of Hall's preaching was that she knew how to take the Gospel, her own experiences, and her theological maturity to present timeless messages. Having stood in the midst of the hostile fields of the civil rights movement in the South, losing a young daughter to a stroke, and enduring church patriarchy long before there was a women's movement in the church, along with health issues and divorce, she knew what it meant to be a Christian and practice ministry between the wilderness and a cliff.*

## Between the Wilderness and a Cliff (June 1992)

*Then Jesus, filled with the power of the Spirit, returned to Galilee, and a report about him spread through all the surrounding country. He began to teach in their synagogues and was praised by everyone . . . The eyes of all in the synagogue were fixed on him. Then he began to say to them, "Today this Scripture has been fulfilled in your hearing." . . . When they heard this, all in the synagogue were filled with rage. They got up, drove him out of the town, and led him to the brow of the hill on which their town was built, so that they might hurl him off the cliff. But he passed through the midst of them and went on his way.*

—Luke 4:14–15, 20, 28–30 (New Revised Standard Version)

I want to talk this afternoon about the context of Christian ministry between the wilderness and the cliff. We are very familiar with this text. It is our Lord's inaugural sermon as he begins his earthly ministry. There had been some preliminary acts of ministry, but it is here that Jesus formally announces his mission.

The words of his announcement have comprised a Christian manifesto, a summary assertion of the Christian witness: The Spirit of the Lord is upon me, because the Lord has anointed me to preach good news to the poor, the Lord has sent me to proclaim release to the captives, the recovery of sight to the blind, to let those who are oppressed go free, and to declare that right now is God's time to do it.[3]

What a ministry. What a mission. What a message. That land, as well as this land, cries out for good news to the poor, deliverance to captives, sight for the blind, freedom for the oppressed. This is, indeed, the greatest sermon ever preached, the greatest sermon we can ever preach. Indeed, if what we do in the pulpit is not good news to the poor, deliverance to the captives, sight to the blind, healing for the broken, and freedom for the oppressed, it may be sweet, it may be eloquent, it may even be deep, but it ain't preaching.

However, I am struck not only by the text but also by the context of the text. The context, the situation which surrounds the text, is the reason that we can't take one verse, one line, one phrase and run with it; the context, that which precedes and succeeds the text; the context of the text. This sermon proceeds from the preparation of our Lord for his ministry. The thirty years before he made his announcement would suggest a long period of preparation and study and prayer. And if our Lord had to prepare for ministry, then my God, so must we. I do not say that we must each have the same preparation. But if we can give the school system of a state department a four-year bachelor's and then two more years for a master's degree, we can give God's ministry three more years for seminary preparation. Jesus goes through an intense and profound period of preparation.

There he is at the Jordan, going down into the waters of baptism. And when he comes up, the heavens are open, and we hear heaven making an announcement: "This is mine. This is my beloved Son. Hear him."[4] The divine voice announced, "You are mine. I'm well pleased with you." The living God presents him to the dying world. "This is my Son. Hear him." He is presented, and his identity is confirmed by the Spirit.

And then, full of the Spirit, he returns from the Jordan and is led by the Spirit into the wilderness. The Spirit is the orchestrator, the conductor of the preparation process. Indeed, Mark says that he was driven by the Spirit into the wilderness. Luke says he was led in the wilderness. But one does not preclude the other. If you're driven by the Spirit into the wilderness, then you best be led by the Spirit when you get there.

The wilderness is a critical context. The Spirit is the only acceptable guide. And so this inaugural sermon is preached by our Lord. The text is preceded by a sojourn in the desert for forty days. A long time. But, when the sermon has been preached, Luke tells us that the hearers were so filled with rage that they got up, drove him out of town, and led him to the brow of the hill on which the town was built so that they might hurl him off the cliff.

And so we see that the initial sermon of our Lord takes place between the wilderness and the cliff. This is the context of Christian ministry. It is the context of our Lord's ministry. It is the context of Christian life. It is the context of African American life and struggle. It is the context of gospel preaching, and God in heaven knows it is the context of the ministry of women. We preach, pray, teach, heal, help, bless between the wilderness and then the cliff!

Now, we are not strangers to the wilderness, and the wilderness is no stranger to us. Our sainted fathers and mothers called the wilderness a low ground of sorrow. We know about the wilderness. We know we've been wandering through the wilderness. Indeed, one of the problems of our children is that although we came through the wilderness, we raised them for the Promised Land, and we are yet a wilderness people. So here they are in the wilderness, and racism is slapping them silly, and they don't know how to struggle.

My friends, there are no shortcuts through the wilderness. The only way out of the wilderness is through the wilderness. What happens in the wilderness? We learn from Israel's sojourn something about the perils of the wilderness. Amnesia about God is a peril of the wilderness. Just beyond the deliverance at the sea, they had already forgotten the God who delivered them through the sea and had started to murmur and complain.

Fear of freedom is a peril of the wilderness. We don't know what the wilderness holds. "Moses, you brought us out here to kill us in this wilderness?"[5] How utterly stupid. Why would Moses or the living God deliver them just to kill them? But fear of freedom causes us to do stupid things. It makes us back up just when we're on the threshold of victory. It makes us back up and start fighting among ourselves, arguing with each other, black folk and women, and then tearing our leaders down. Fear of freedom makes us do stupid things.

We know about the wilderness. There is perpetual peril in the wilderness. And now from our Lord, we learn about the temptation of the wilderness, for in the wilderness, our sainted Lord does battle with ultimate temptation. Satan offers to him a deal, and this is the deal, it can be summed up in one sentence: Jesus, surrender your identity, Jesus, if you are the Son of God, if you are who you supposed to be. Twice Satan frames the proposition with "If you are the Son of God, do a stunt, perform a trick, prove that you are who you say you are."

But the issue is not really with Jesus. Jesus has not said, "I am heaven's Son. In me, heaven is well pleased." Heaven has spoken on its own behalf. The living God has said, "This is my Son, my beloved. Hear him." But you see, if Satan can get you to surrender your identity, then Satan will have won. Why is our identity so important? Because identity determines activity. What we do is determined by who we are. If we will only convince our children of who they are, of whose they are, that they are the very handiwork of God, rare and lovely, then they will know that they are too precious to God and too vital to us, our only hope of a future, to destroy their lives with dope and dehumanizing existence. If only we will tell them who they are.

The identity question is critical, because Satan knows that once Jesus surrenders his identity, he will then voluntarily sabotage the divine project. "Just fall down and worship me. Jesus, jump down, spin around, make a fool out of yourself and God, and I'll give you power and prizes and prosperity and pleasure, and all of it without pain." That's the deal. Prizes without pain.

Preacher, if you are really God's anointed woman, just let me name you, let me form you, let me get you to dance to my tune, let me get you to jump at my command, let me get you to do my tricks. Preaching woman, let me tell you who you are, where you belong, when and where you can preach. You can make a pretty good reputation just doing Women's Days. You'll be all right. Just stay in a woman's place. Stay in the woman's slot. Stay in the female box. Because if you will surrender your identity to me, I won't have to worry about God getting the glory out of your ministry. I won't have to worry about you fulfilling the dangerous mission to which God has called you. Bow down to me and sabotage the divine project, prove who you are.

My sisters and my brothers, surrendered identity is deadly. It is more deadly than lost identity. Surrendered identity means that you intentionally relinquished who you are, and you voluntarily sell out God's divine ministry.

How many of us have been seduced by the temptation to prove who we are? But Jesus, our blessed Lord, overcame it. He looked Satan in the face: "Don't you quote the Word to me. I am the living Word, and I know what I am about." So Satan departed until a more opportune moment. But don't you fool yourself. Jesus was not out of Satan's sight or off Satan's mind; he was just waiting until a more opportune time.

And now, filled with the Spirit, with the power of the Spirit, Jesus returns to Galilee and announces, "The Spirit of the Lord is upon me." He has been anointed not as kings and priests are anointed, with oil, but he has been anointed by the power of the Spirit of the living God.

How did they hear him? They should have heard him gladly. They were poor. They were captive. They were oppressed. God knows they were blind. He brought good news. And at first, it sounded mighty good. But remember that good news to some is also bad news to somebody else. Good news to the poor is bad news to the rich who keep folk poor. Deliverance to captives is judgment to those who hold them captive. Sight to the blind is disaster to those who exploit their blindness.

Jesus did not just deliver the short version, but he walked down their street, stopped at their door, came into their house, and put his feet under their table. Here he is: he has moved from the wilderness to the cliff at the edge of the wilderness, between the wilderness and the cliff. This place is worse than between a rock and a hard place. It's worse than between the devil and the deep blue sea. He is between the devil in the wilderness and the devil in devilish people at the cliff.

They laid hostile hands on him to hurl him off the cliff. But thanks be to God, the Spirit who led him into the wilderness and into the town did not leave him at the cliff. At the cliff, escape was viable. At the cliff. But I want you to note that the path of escape was not up, up, and away; it was neither under them nor around them; the path of escape was through their midst.

My friends, the context of our ministries is between the wilderness and the cliff, but we are able to escape the cliff. We can escape the cliff, but we can't escape the crowd. He escaped through their midst. We escape the people, but only through the very people who would hurl us over the cliff, for these are the people whom God has called us to serve. These are the people whom God will save through our ministries. The temptation at the cliff is contempt for the crowd. But don't you surrender to contempt. Your escape is not in their hands.

Follow our Lord's example, for the next time we see him, he is among the crowd, healing a man of unclean spirit, preaching and teaching in the synagogues, calling disciples, cleansing a leper, healing a paralytic. The path of ministry is through the midst of the people. It's in the ministry to which we are called and for which we have been consecrated. So wherever the people are, that's the preaching place, the teaching place, and we have just one sermon: Good news to the poor, deliverance to the captives, sight to the blind, healing for the broken, and freedom for the oppressed.

Well, the day came when they did lay hostile hands on him out on the cliff of Calvary. They led him up the hill. Out there, even out there, he paused to tell them, "You got your hands on me, but I am not in your hands. Nobody, nobody takes my life from me. I lay it down."[6] Well, they hung him high, and as the old saints used to say, they stretched him wide. And when they took him down, Satan tasted victory. Satan said, "Uh-huh, you would not fall down at my feet, you would not jump down at my command, but look at you now. I got you. I got you." And they took him down from the cross and laid him in a borrowed grave. Well, it was all right for him to borrow a grave. He wasn't going to need it very long anyhow. He would soon return to Joseph just a slightly used tomb.

Satan tasted victory. It was sweet in his mouth. But it soon got bitter in his gut. Because that's when your Lord and mine went to work. It didn't taste like victory. Satan felt a burning in his gut. That's when heaven's joy and earth's hope went to work. He took on the wilderness and the cliff. Every briar, every thorn, every thistle, every rock, every quagmire, every desert, every deadly deed, every death-dealing temptation: dope, disease, disappointment, despair, and finally the big one, finally the last enemy, finally, death itself.

They laid hostile hands on him, hey, hey, hey, hey. But he laid holy, holy, holy hands on them, until a cry went up, "Oooh, death, where, where is thy sting? Oooh, grave, where, where, where is your victory?"[7]

Death to the grave said, "We had it, but you got it." Well, now it's getting-up time. And so up, the one who would not fold, the one who would not jump down, the one they laid down is now rising up, up, up, up, up from the grave. He arose. Hey, hey, hey. And he didn't come up empty-handed, but he cried, "All power, all power in heaven, in earth, under the earth, all power is in my hands."[8] And now this, this is the best part, "And lo, I am with you always, even to the end of the age."[9]

So preachers, teachers, servants of God, don't you get tangled up between the wilderness and the cliff. Don't you surrender your identity. Sister preacher, whether they believe you or not, you better know who you are. The God who has called us is the God who has consecrated us, is the God who is right now, right now anointing us. And that God is with us, with us, with us. So go, preach, pray, heal, bless, hold, help, and in this desert, in this wilderness, prepare ye the way of the Lord, for every valley shall be exalted, every mountain and hill shall be brought low, every rough place is being made smooth.[10] Hey, hey, hey. Crooked places and crooked people are being straightened out. And all flesh, male and female, all flesh, black, white, brown, yellow, red, all flesh oppressed, repressed, depressed, suppressed, I said all flesh shall see it together, for the mouth of the Lord, the mouth of the Lord, the anointed one, the mouth of the Lord, the sovereign God, the only one who has any right to talk about who gets called and who doesn't, the mouth of the Lord, the everlasting present tense, the mouth of the Lord,[11] the "I Am." The mouth of the Lord has spoken it, glory, glory, glory, glory, glory, glory, glory, glory, hallelujah, hallelujah, hallelujah.

## *Notes*

*Sermon source: The African American Pulpit* 5, no. 2 (Spring 2002), 116–20.

1. "Prathia Hall," *This Far by Faith: African American Spiritual Journeys,* PBS, available at http://pbs.org/thisfarbyfaith/people/Prathia_Hall.html (accessed June 25, 2007).

2. "Inaugural Events Dedicated to the Late BU Theology Prof. Prathia Hall." News release, The Center for African American Religious Research and Education, October 2, 2003, http://www.bu.edu/sth/news/archive/caarre-hall.htm (accessed July 13, 2007).

3. Luke 4:18–19 (New Revised Standard Version).

4. Luke 3:22 (NRSV).

5. Exodus 14:11–12 (NRSV).

6. John 10:18 (NRSV).

7. 1 Corinthians 15:15 (NRSV).

8. Matthew 28:28 (NRSV).
9. Matthew 28:20 (NRSV).
10. Isaiah 40:4 (NRSV).
11. Isaiah 40:5 (NRSV).

### *Bibliographical Sources*

"Inaugural Events Dedicated to the Late BU Theology Prof. Prathia Hall." News release, The Center for African American Religious Research and Education, October 2, 2003, http://www.bu.edu/sth/news/archive/caarre-hall.html (accessed June 27, 2007).

"Prathia Hall." *This Far by Faith: African American Spiritual Journeys.* PBS, available at http://www.pbs.org/thisfarbyfaith/people/Prathia_Hall.html (accessed June 25, 2007).

"Prathia Hall, Pioneering Woman in Ministry, Dies." American Baptist News Service Press Release, http://www.wfn.org/2002/08/msgoo114.htm (accessed June 25, 2007).

## BARBARA C. HARRIS

*(1930– )*

Barbara C. Harris is a native of Philadelphia, Pennsylvania. She attended Villanova University and studied at the Urban Theology Unit in Sheffield, England. She is also a graduate of the Pennsylvania Foundation for Pastoral Counseling and the Charles Morris Price School of Advertising and Journalism. Harris's journey to the priesthood started with public relations work in the corporate world from 1949 to 1978, where she rose to become senior staff consultant at the Sun Company.

As a young woman, Harris was active in the civil rights struggle, participating in freedom rides and voter registration campaigns, as well as marching with Martin Luther King Jr. in Selma, Alabama. In 1974, Harris continued to work for justice as she publicly supported a group of Episcopal bishops who defied a ban on the ordination of women priests. Her deep involvement in justice issues led to her ordination to the diaconate in September 1979 and ordination as an Episcopal priest in 1980.

In her ministry she joined her corporate journalism and public relations experience with her call to the priesthood and prophetic witness. She served as priest in charge of St. Augustine of Hippo Church in Norristown, Pennsylvania, from 1980 to 1984, and then became chaplain to the Philadelphia County prisons and counselor to industrial corporations for public policy issues and concerns. In 1984 she was named executive director of the Episcopal Church Publishing Company and publisher of *The Witness* magazine. In 1988 she was elected suffragan (assisting) bishop of the Diocese of Massachusetts. On February 11, 1989, she was elected and consecrated as bishop, the first woman to be ordained to the episcopate in the worldwide Anglican communion.

All were not pleased with her election as bishop, and protests were launched. Several priests broke ties with the Anglican church completely, and several top leaders in England refused to acknowledge female bishops. Because of their opposition to female priests, ecumenical ties with the Roman Catholic Church were strained. Harris stood strong and forthrightly confronted any challenges to her election. Years later, many of her critics attest to the quality of her ministry and life and the value of her service. She was a passionate advocate for justice, diversity, and the inclusion of women as full partners in the church.

She is a member of the Episcopal Church's Standing Commission on Anglican and International Peace with Justice Concerns and is a member of the board of trustees of Episcopal Divinity School in Cambridge, Massachusetts. Harris has received honorary degrees from numerous colleges, universities, and theological schools, including Yale University and the Church Divinity School of the Pacific. She retired in 2002.

• • •

*Barbara C. Harris stands in the contemplative preaching tradition. She is a gifted storyteller with quick wit, a finely honed imagination, and a deep love for people. She is a celebrated preacher nationwide and an outspoken advocate for, in her words, "the least, the lost, and the left out." This sermon is typical of Harris's use of the Gospel to address the thorny issues of the day and to advocate for the "least of these."*

## A Circle of Concern
## (2004)

> *John said to Jesus, "Teacher, we saw someone casting out demons in your name, and we tried to stop him, because he was not following us." But Jesus said, "Do not stop him; for no one who does a deed of power in my name will be able soon afterward to speak evil of me. Whoever is not against us is for us."*
>
> —Mark 9:38–40 (New Revised Standard Version)

These brief verses from this morning's Gospel speak to three continuing and almost universal troubles—in both church and society today—elitism, egotism, and exclusivity.

It was a very human and a very natural feeling that prompted the disciples to order this strange, unknown, and unattached person to cease and desist from acting as an exorcist and casting out demonic spirits or healing in Jesus' name. I am sure they might have said things such as, Who are you? Where did you come from? What do you think you are doing? Who gave you the right to do what we are supposed to do? You can't do this because you're not one of us, so out!

John perhaps was feeling rather good about what they had done as he reported to Jesus. In essence he said, "We nipped that stuff right in the bud and told that guy to quit it. Hang it up." What John was expressing was not hard and narrow bigotry or meanness. It probably sprang from some very good sources—from loyalty to Jesus; from some confidence in the truth that Jesus proclaimed; from a desire to keep the truth uncorrupted. He might have been motivated by a strong sense of the need for unity in their small, struggling community of disciples. Not bad things in and of themselves. They are not unlike the kinds of sentiments that we often express and that move us to wittingly or unwittingly shut people out of the faith community of which we are a part.

I remember as a child my friends and I used to play in a circle. There was The Farmer in the Dell, some game called Oh King Glory of the Valley, and another called Little Sally Ann, Sitting in the Sand. You know—dumb stuff, but fun for kids. Some of you may have played variations of these or similar circle games in which, invariably, some people were chosen to be in the circles while others were left out. Some were included, and some were excluded. Depending on how you felt on a given day, you chose one friend or another to be in the circle. But some people were never chosen.

The games children play often reflect deeper things about a culture or a community and its prevailing trends and values. The children in war-torn countries, for example, often play war games. And they play them with a vengeance. Here at home young people play computer and video games that often are highly competitive contests of skill with the emphasis on beating the odds and winning, and they too can be violent. These games reflect current trends, just as the simple circle games I mentioned reflected my generation's circular lifestyle. And it is a lifestyle that still is so much a part of our thinking, we are scarcely aware of it.

Who is inside and outside the circle of concern? It is a question to which we need to give some thought. Who is in and who is outside our personal circles of concern? One way to measure the boundaries of our circle of concern is to look at our prayer life. Who do you pray for? What do you wish for? What do you long for? What do you ask God for? What are your concerns? Are they narrowed to personal needs and interests or perhaps to those of your family and close friends? Who is in your circle of concern?

I am sure many of you consciously pray and do it often. Some of you are deeply spiritual. But we all need a broader expression of individual spirituality. We need to move beyond the "me and my God" kind of spirituality that makes religion a very private and personal kind of thing that you guard like your toothbrush. That kind of spirituality does not give us a sense of community in which were are called by God to live with each other in this vain world that is no friend to grace.

Sometimes during the prayers of the people, we hear people express aloud a concern for something other than the health of their friends and acquaintances. Sometimes we hear concern expressed for our brothers and sisters in Central America or those who are starving in the sub-Sahara, persons living with AIDS, the homeless or the hungry, or the refugees of Rwanda. That is good. But we also need to put some flesh on our prayers. In other words, it is not enough just to pray. We also must act! That's when we really mean it.

Sometimes our prayers are like the resolutions or statements adopted at gatherings such as a general convention of our church. Everybody goes home feeling good because they gave some attention to a particular hot issue, but then they have no further responsibility in the matter. That is an inadequate response to our Lord's words: "I give you a new commandment, that you love one another. Just as I have loved you, you also should love one another."[1] Jesus not only loved, Jesus worked to change things and to make conditions better for all whom he loved. He meant it.

If as we pray, we let God speak to us about God's concerns for the world, gradually we can come to develop the mind of Christ—to see things as our Lord sees them in this world around us. We then can make a connection between our prayer and our involvement in the world in which we live. We then can recognize who is in and who is outside the circle of concern. And we can stop acting like those anxious disciples—trying to deny those who are doing what we are supposed to be doing because they do not belong to our group.

It often is said that prayer changes things. It is perhaps more accurate to say that prayer changes people to *do* things. Prayer can change the way we see other people. Prayer can change the way we see ourselves, especially in relationship to and with other people. Prayer can change the way we view the world.

I am suggesting that prayer should move us outward from ourselves, not inward. When prayer moves outward, beyond ourselves, our circle of concern widens. Our circle of concern can widen to include those beyond our small group—a small group even the size of this congregation—as we begin to share the concern and love of God for all of God's people.

Who is in and who is outside the church's circle of concern? Unfortunately, many who should be in, many for whom we offer words of prayer, are outside. We pray, and at the same time we make judgments about why people are in the condition they are. We all have heard people say that the poor are poor because they are lazy, or that homeless people want to be on the streets rather than accept responsibility, or that people on welfare don't want to hold jobs.

Author Jonathan Kozol, who wrote among other books *Amazing Grace*, concerning an Episcopal church that serves the poor community of Mott Haven in New York City, a few years ago told a group of Episcopal church people who do social work something that is true of many in our church and society today. He said, "You vote against social justice programs that would help solve some of our problems. Then when the problem gets bad enough, you run to the homeless shelter with your cupcakes and feel you have done something." He challenged them, as I would ask you—to be not only caring people but also people who will work for change in a society that is abandoning its poor.

The modern church is in conflict with the kind of community God intended—where everyone is respected, where the worth of each individual is acknowledged and valued, and where the watchword is *love*. The modern church is very much concerned with its own institutional life and with serving its own interests. But, as we heard in last Sunday's Gospel, Jesus said, "He who wishes to be great among you must be your servant."[2]

Jesus' commandment to love one another was not entirely new. The Jewish community to which Jesus came already knew about living for others. They already had the commandments given to Moses, which included "thou shalt love thy neighbor as thyself."[3] But the commandment to love one another as given by Jesus was new in purpose. It was a much broader interpretation of love. It said love your neighbor more than you love yourself. Love your neighbor as God loves you. Good gracious.

Too often our love is based on what we can get in return. The love of which Jesus spoke, love freely given to all, offers no guarantees of return or reward. It may even bring us into contact with people like the man the disciples tried to stop from healing in Jesus' name because he was not one of them. Yet it is the kind of love we are called upon to demonstrate.

Our circle of concern must enlarge itself over and over and over again to include all of God's people—especially those who seem hard to love. For when we love those who seem hard to love, we may be loving ourselves as well. Let us then be careful whom we might be tempted to forbid in Jesus' name, because, as he said, "Whoever is not for us is against us."[4]

### *Notes*

*Sermon source: The African American Pulpit* 7, no. 2 (Spring 2004), 31–33.

1. John 13:31 (New Revised Standard Version).
2. See Matthew 23:11.
3. Matthew 19:19 (King James Version).
4. Mark 9:40 (NRSV).

### *Bibliographical Sources*

"Barbara Harris, A Spiritual First," African American Registry, http://www.aaregistry.com/african_american_history/1196/Barbara_Harris_a_spiritual_first (accessed June 27, 2007).

"Biography of Barbara C. Harris," Episcopal Diocese of Washington, http://www.edow.org/diocese/bishops/harris_bio.html (accessed June 27, 2007).

McMickle, Marvin A. "Barbara Harris," in *An Encyclopedia of African American Christian Hertiage.* Valley Forge, PA: Judson Press, 2002.

## EDWARD VICTOR HILL

*(1933–2003)*

Edward Victor (E.V.) Hill was one of five children born in Texas to a single mother during the Great Depression. His mother was so poor that she allowed Hill to be reared in a rural log cabin by one of the mothers of the church. As a boy, this same woman prophesied that he would graduate from high school and college. At the time African Americans rarely had the opportunity to proceed beyond the tenth grade. Hill went on to study at Prairie View A&M University in Texas on a four-year scholarship. He answered the call to ministry in 1951, and in the same year became the president of the Youth Auxiliary of the National Baptist Convention, U.S.A., Inc., where he grew into an influential figure during various administrations, eventually rising to the level of vice-president of the convention.

A gifted preacher, Hill was known as "a common man's theologian" and a compassionate minister to both the poor of spirit and those poor in worldly goods. He is said to have mentored more than one thousand preachers. Hill preached an extremely conservative, no-nonsense, back-to-basics type of Christianity, which held individuals accountable for their lives. His first pastorate was in Austin, Texas, at the Friendly Will Missionary Baptist Church. Soon after that, at age twenty-one, he became pastor of Mount Corinth Baptist Church in Houston. While there, Hill helped establish the Southern Christian Leadership Conference and nominated Martin Luther King Jr. to serve as president. The conference was to become central to the civil rights movement.

In 1961, Hill became pastor of Mount Zion Missionary Baptist Church of Los Angeles, where he remained until his death. Under his leadership, the congregation became the hub of political and social activism. Mount Zion built a kitchen for the homeless, the "Lord's Kitchen," where, at the time of Hill's death, more than two million meals had been served. The church also operated a credit union and senior citizen housing and Hill had become one of the best known pastors and revivalists in America.

Hill was an enigma to many observers because of the varied political and theological circles in which he traveled. As the most prominent African American Republican clergy of his time, he gave one of the inaugural prayers for President Richard Nixon, and twice led the Clergy for Reagan Committee. Hill also served on the board of the Los Angeles NAACP. Within the African American community, his connections to certain preachers with ties to the evangelical right, particularly Kenneth Hagin, Jerry Falwell, and Oral Roberts, made him even more controversial. Hill was opposed to women being preachers and pastors.

Pastor Hill died on February 24, 2003. He wrote two books, *A Savior Worth Having*, a collection of some of his best-known sermons, and *Victory in Jesus: Running the Race You Are Meant to Win.*

• • •

*Despite controversy around his conservative politics and theology, there was no disputing that Edward Victor Hill mastered the folk preaching style. At a skill level matched by few others, he could tell a story, use biblical imagery, and convey emotion in the preaching process. The following sermon is one of Hill's most famous and is indicative of his plain-spoken, evangelical approach to preaching and his abiding belief in Jesus Christ as the solution for all of humanity's problems. In it he also addresses his own battles with racism and what he has suffered at the hands of his own people for some of his positions.*

*The entire sermon could not be obtained, but all aspects of it as provided by Moody Press are included here.*

## What You Have When You Have Jesus (February 1980)

I was in Kansas City, Missouri, and I was preaching at a real good, juicy revival. Folk were being saved, and we were having a good time shouting—just a good group of "Negroes" who really loved the Lord. At the close of the service, a girl came up to me and she said, "Pastor, I have a sister who has joined the Black Panther Party, and she is a very militant part of it. I want you to pray for her." I said, "Why don't you see if she will come to church." "Oh, she would never do that." I said, "Well let's pray about it and ask her anyway." On the closing night just before I got up to preach I saw a girl come in and sit on the back row and act very hostile. Somehow or another I was just led to believe that was her. And, after I got through preaching, she got in line with all the other people. She got up to me and said, "Now, because of my sister I came and I've listened to you now for over an hour and a half. I want you to know you said nothing relevant. You said nothing that would bring deliverance to my people. I think you are a fraud. I think you are someone who needs to be done away with."

The other folk were trying to shake my hand so I said to her, "Why don't you just stand aside a moment and let me get some more kisses and hugs. I'll deal with you later." I said, "Come in the room here," and we got on this one-to-one relationship and she began to berate me and damn the church and damn our cause. I just listened to her and prayed and sometimes that's all you can do.

And then, the Lord opened a wide door. She said, "By the way, you tried to get me to accept Christ. You kept beckoning for me and asking me to accept Christ. I saw you." I said, "Yes, I had you in mind." She said, "I want to ask you a question. If I had accepted Jesus, what would I have now?" That's the door wide open. She said, "If I had gotten up and accepted Christ and been born again and filled with the Spirit—in other words, preacher, what do you have when you have Jesus?"

I said, "Now, you asked me and you must let me answer in all fairness." She said, "Alright, tell me." Then she proceeded and tried to help me. "Will I have my bills all paid? Will I have a split-level home? Will I have two cars in every garage? Will I have mink stoles? Will whitey get up off my neck?" I said, "Well now, I don't know too many of us who have Jesus who have all of that. We don't have houses and land, silver and gold where I come from."

One of the words that I want to give today is that accepting Jesus Christ is no immunization against the problems of this world in the area of economics, in the area of paying those bills other than that He gives us wisdom and patience and faith as we struggle with the normal problems of living. The fact that you do have a split-level home, the fact that you do have several cars, is no indication you are closer to the Lord than the one who rides RTD. That's Rapid Transit in Los Angeles. Nor even the one who doesn't have the money to ride Rapid Transit. And those who are busy across our nation suggesting God came into this world to give us this world's goods, must take another look at the one who came into this world who had nowhere to lay His head. That God has something better than houses and land, silver, and gold. That God has something infinitely greater in satisfaction than mink stoles and alligator shoes. He plans to bring something greater than this world's goods.

So, I said, "I can't promise all of that." She said, "Well then, alright is He going to deliver us from our burdens and oppressions of the white man?" "I can't promise that because He moves in strange and mysterious ways. I know, I understand, and I share your feeling. Nobody hated white people more than I did until I was a freshman in college. I could have taught Ralph Brown and Stokely Carmichael how to do it because I was in Texas. I was born amidst hatred and discrimination. I saw all of the evils and I grew up not only hating white people, but I hated them with what I felt was the sanction of the Holy Ghost. And when somebody kills you in the name of Jesus, you're dead. I really can't ever remember when I stopped hating white people. All I do is I tell you I don't anymore because I have a great love that has come—a miraculous birth in Christ."

She said, "Well now rush and tell me." I said I have a bunch of them and I want you to write them down. I have twelve that I want to deal with this morning and I'll get to as many as I can. She said, "I'm ready." When you have Jesus, the first thing according to the Book of Romans: "Therefore, being justified by faith, we have peace with God through our Lord Jesus Christ."[1]

Now, that's the first statement, that when you have Jesus, you have peace with God in light of the fact that He was raised again from the dead. In light of the fact that He did die; in light of the fact He was buried; in light of the fact that He was raised again for our justification we have something and that something . . . there is, therefore, now peace with God for those who accept Jesus Christ. Now, that is so mind blowing. That is so wonderful. That is outstanding that God and I are alright.

Now there are a whole lot of other places I'm glad I have peace with. I remember when I bought my first home. I went down to the bank and I told them that I was the pastor of a church now, the pastor of the second oldest church in Houston, and it was a distinguished church, and I was a promising and potential pastor, and I wanted to borrow some money. And, he looked at my credit rating and said, "Uh-uh." I had no peace at that bank whatsoever. He wouldn't accept me, and I didn't like him. And so, a deacon of our church, I told him I'm about to get married and I always promised that I was going to have my own home. I lived in housing projects and city projects and there's nothing wrong with that. Great times in those projects, but I decided I wanted to have my own home.

He said, "Well, pastor, I think you should have your own home." But I went down to this bank and they won't let me have any money. "Well, now," he said, "that's my bank. How much do you need?" Seven hundred and fifty dollars to pay down. "How much do you have?" "Ten." And, he went down and he said, "Mr. President, I want my pastor to have a thousand dollars." "Of course, Brother Douglas"—I thought he'd taken another look at my credit rating—"*and*," he said, "because of you, we will be glad to give it." He had me to sign and he said, "But," he said, "Brother Douglas, you sign too."

I signed my name; I signed it plain. *But*, he said, *Brother Douglas, you sign*. I thought my name, Edward Victor Hill, was sufficient. He said, *Brother Douglas, you sign*. And it was the signing of Brother Douglas that released unto me a thousand dollars. I've been gone from Houston nineteen years, and I can go back to that bank. I have peace with that bank, and I can now sign without Brother Douglas, and that's marvelous. I have peace with my wife. But oh, wait a minute. More than with a bank, more than with the board of deacons where I pastor, more than with my wife, more than with my secretary, I have peace with God! God and I are talking. God is smiling on me.

And, there are a lot of you here who have economic peace, you have political peace, you have all kinds of peace. But, there are some of you under my voice today who do not have the certainty that you have peace with God. That's who you ought to try to get together with. He's got the whole world in His hand. You'd better get together with Him. He's got you and me in His hand. He's got everything—potential and past. He's got your voice, your breath, your future, your everything in His hand. You'd better have peace with God!

I turned to this hostile young lady and I said now did you write that down? And I said now wouldn't you really want to have peace with God?

She said, "If I thought there was a God and, if I thought I would one day meet him, I would like to be at peace with Him." I said write it down and incidentally, as you write it down, knock out all the "ifs." He *is*, and you *will* meet Him.

"Number two," I said, "Now not only will you have peace with God, but once you get this transcending peace with God who is high, holy, lifted up, exalted above—then something else comes down." And, in the Book of Philippians it's called the peace of God. But then Paul, in his letter to the Philippians, said the peace of God is received once you have peace with God.[2] That comes down and first of all it gets all in your head and mind. It gets all in your understanding, and all of a sudden, things that were cloudy and difficult and hard to believe and understand, you begin to say, yes Lord, because you're beginning now to receive the peace of God.

It doesn't stop in your head, and it's mighty good that I say this here at this school. It gets all down in here because it says it not only keeps your mind, it works on the heart—to keep your heart. And not only does it get in your heart, it gets all over you so that it surpasses all understanding. And you can get so peaceful in the midst of conflict and in the midst of tragedies and trials until folk who don't know God will claim you're nutty!

The peace of God is my mama serving a ho-cake and molasses and fat meat bowing her head saying, "Father, we thank you for the blessing we're about to receive." The peace of God passes all understanding. The Apostle in jail praying—peace of God; Daniel in a lion's den resting away—peace of God; Shadrach, Meshach, and Abednego saying, "Throw us in." The peace of God. The apostle Paul on a ship sinking saying, "Have some food." The peace of God it surpasses all understanding. You can't understand it; you can't explain it; you can't write it out. No psychiatrist knows the answer to it. No sociologist can understand it. It's just something that comes in your heart when you have Jesus.

I said to this young lady when you have Jesus, number two is you're not only at peace with Him, but you have the peace that He gives to your mind and your heart and your being, which surpasses all understanding, so that we do not live in a world absent from storms. We do not live in a world absent from problems, we do not live in a world absent of headaches and conflicts, but we live in a world with storms, with conflicts, with problems and just like a king who stays on a throne, we're never left alone.

Somebody called me about ten years ago late at night—a friend of mine—and said to me, "Hill, I hear you're having trouble." Thirty-five years too late; I've been having trouble ever since I've been in this world. I have never known a calm day. I have never known a day where the thunder didn't roar and the lightning didn't flash. I had to be guarded when I was in the South by my deacons and trustees with shotguns to preserve my life from the Ku Klux Klan. And I had to be guarded in Los Angeles last year even in my church by policemen to preserve my life from black militants. I have never had a cloudy day that I didn't have the peace of God, which passes all understanding. I have slept with crosses burning. I have turned over and snored. When I've gotten calls that a group was on its way out to blow up my house, I've turned over and went to sleep. It surpasses all understanding. You can't figure it out.

I said to her, "Do you have any peace?" She said, "How can you have peace in a world like this?" I said, "Aren't you really troubled?" She said, "I'm troubled on every side. I drink myself to sleep. I take pills to go to sleep. I take pills to wake up. I take pills to pep up." She said, "Because this world won't let me be peaceful." I said, "You can have it! And, when you have it, it doesn't mean that you withdraw from the battle! You don't withdraw from the conflict! You rest in the midst of it."

Number three and this is my favorite one. When you have Jesus you become subject—and you don't always receive it. Let me be different from the reverends that are on radio and television who say that you always get it. No, you don't always get it, but you're subject to getting it. You're a candidate for it. It's very likely and more possible that you're going to get it. And that is . . . when you have Jesus, not only do you have peace with God and the peace of God, but you are subject to receiving at any moment fantastic, unbelievable, divine supplement. And by that I mean that nobody in this room, none of us are sufficient within our own selves, Ph.D.s or no Ds. All of us come to a point where we can only go so far, we can tiptoe so far, just so far and no farther and you need somebody who is able to put a little rope on the end of your grasp. You can't do it yourself. You're not able. No student, no preacher, no anybody—you need somebody every now and then to just reach out and say, here! And, you don't deserve it and it's not a result of whether or not you prayed all night or whether you have more faith than that one has faith. It's not a result of this or that. It doesn't mean that He loves you more. It means that every now and then in God's own sovereign will and in His own way and His own time, He just says, here! It doesn't mean that you're better qualified. Doesn't mean that because you have your Ph.D., you're going to get it quicker. He may even say to a student who has no degree, there! He's able to do it.

I said to her don't you need help sometime? She said, "Oh, preacher, you know I do. I have a child. I'm out of wedlock. Problems are so great." I said, "I don't want to promise you if you come to Jesus all of that is going to clear up and the father is going to come back and own his child. You may not ever see him no more. But I do promise you that He has done it before! He has run into some awful messes in His life. He's run into some awful wrecks. He's had some awful fellows on his hand—Samson, Solomon, David, and all the rest of them. And, somehow or another when they were at their weakest, He just reached out and said here, boy!"

Mama made two statements that made Sweet Home, the little country town where I was brought up in—not in town but out from town. She made two statements that made the whole community laugh. I was not reared by my mother, I was reared by Mama. Mother had five children, and it was during the Depression, and we had no welfare and no Aid to Dependent Children. We had no monthly checks and so my Mama—who was no kin to me, no relationship—was just a lady who saw me playing in the yard one day and she said to my mother, "I live in the country; can I take this boy out in the country and feed him and let him run around and play with horses, give him some milk, pecans and hick-o-nuts?" She said: "I would appreciate it. I don't have quite enough food to go around."

And so Mama got me to take me out to feed me. I was only four then, and I never went back to live with my mother; I stayed in the country. Mama only had a two-room log cabin, and I finished high school in a log cabin. One announcement she made when I was about in the ninth grade, she said, "Ed's going to finish high school." Everybody laughed. They said, "Ella, that boy's big enough to quit school and work and help you." She said, "Nah, nah, nah, that boy's going to school." Mama shucked peanuts right along with me and picked cotton, and we killed rabbits, and raised a hog so I could stay in school. And then on my graduation, and when they finished laughing, I was the only graduate of that school that year out in thc country.

She made another announcement that everybody laughed about. She said, "Ed's going to college." And they said, "Now wait a minute. We've suffered with you through one ordeal, but, Ella, you're now sixty-something years old. You can't shuck no more peanuts. You can't pick no more cotton. You've got him through high school now let him go to work and help you." Mama said, "He's going to college!"

Mama took me down to the Trailways bus, and had my suitcase, and tied it with a rope. She bought my ticket and gave me five dollars, and then she said, "Now, go on to Prairie View and Mama is going to be praying for you." I didn't know much about prayer, but I knew Mama did. I got on that bus and I went to Prairie View and I bought a hamburger and a bowl of chili on the way. When I got to Prairie View, I had a dollar and ninety cents in my pocket. When I went in the bursar's office, the financial office, it said eighty dollars in cash, money order, or cashier's check, and I had a dollar and ninety cents and Mama was at home. I didn't know nobody, but I got in line. The devil said, "Now wait a minute. You're worse than your Mama getting in line. Don't you understand it's not a dollar and ninety cents, not eighty cents, but eighty dollars!"

I got in line, and soon there were four before me. I stood in line, and the devil said to get out of line, but as I attempted to get out of line I heard Mama saying in my ear, "I'll be praying for you." I stood in line on Mama's prayer. Soon there was one before me and I begin to get nervous, but I stayed in line. She took her time and she paid her bill, and then she took her time to fold up her change from her bill, and to put it away, and then it was to be me and the cashier. Just about the time she got all of her stuff and turned away, Dr. Drew touched me on the shoulder and he said, "Are you Ed Hill?" I said, "Yes." "Are you Ed Hill from Sweet Home?" "Yes." "Was your principal R.V. Arnold?" "Yes." "Have you paid yet?" "Not quite." "We've been looking for you all this morning and we were hoping we would get you before you paid so we wouldn't have to go through the ordeal of refunding you." I said, "Well what do [you] want with me?" "We have a four-year scholarship that will pay your room and board, your tuition and give you thirty-five dollars a month to spend." And I heard Mama say, "I will be praying for you!"

Every now and then when you have Jesus, when you've done all you can do and God knows your heart and He knows that you have tried, just every now and then when you're stepping out on faith and you're not even able to see where you're stepping, every now and then He'll say, "Here!" I said, "Don't you need somebody to supplement you, somebody to reach down sometime? Then, here, bring a wounded heart. Earth has no sorrow that heaven cannot heal when you have Jesus." What do you have, preacher, when you have Jesus? You have peace with God. You have the peace of God. . . .

## *Notes*

*Sermon source:* E.V. Hill, *A Savior Worth Having* (Chicago: Moody Press, 2002), audio CD.

1. Romans 5:1 (New International Version).
2. See Philippians 4:7.

### *Bibliographical Sources*

Blake, Charles E. "Is Anything Forever? Eulogy for Edward Victor (E.V.) Hill." *The African American Pulpit* 8, no. 2 (Spring 2005).

Curry, Erin. "E.V. Hill Remembered as Conservative African American Pastor, Civil Rights Leader." *Baptist Press*, February 26, 2003. http://www.bpnews.net/asp?id=15322 (accessed on July 4, 2005).

"A Memorial Assembly in Loving Memory of Edward Victor Hill." Mount Zion Missionary Baptist Church, Los Angeles, California, March 7, 2003.

Profile of Dr. E.V. Hill, available at http://www.zoominfo.com/search/PersonDetail.aspx?PersonID=20454116 (accessed July 7, 2007).

# JESSE LOUIS JACKSON

*(1941– )*

Jesse Louis Jackson was born on October 8, 1941, in Greenville, South Carolina, to Helen Burns, an unwed teenager. Jesse took the name of his stepfather, Charles H. Jackson, who formally adopted him in 1957. At Sterling High School, Jackson was elected president of his class, the honor society, and the student council. In 1959, he left the South to attend the University of Illinois on an athletic scholarship. Met with searing racism on campus and on the football team, Jackson decided to return south to North Carolina's Agricultural and Technical (A&T) College in Greensboro, a predominantly African American institution. There he fulfilled his leadership and athletic potential, serving as quarterback and as president of the student body. It was also while in college that he became involved in the civil rights movement, organizing sit-ins in "whites only" institutions and protest marches.

After receiving his bachelor of arts degree in sociology in 1964, Jackson attended the Chicago Theological Seminary, and began to organize through the Southern Christian Leadership Conference (SCLC) under the influence of Martin Luther King Jr. He found success and fame in the 1970s as the man who pressured several large Chicago organizations into hiring more African Americans. Jackson broke from SCLC and eventually founded two groups to promote racial and economic justice in the United States: Operation PUSH (People United to Serve Humanity) and the National Rainbow Coalition. In 1984 and 1988, Jackson campaigned as a candidate for the Democratic presidential nomination.

In the decade following the 1988 election, Jackson resumed the non-aligned diplomacy he had begun in the late 1970s. His intervention, in 1991, secured the release of American hostages held by Iraqi president Saddam Hussein. In 1999, Jackson once again assumed the role of roving ambassador and succeeded in securing from Slobadan Milosevic the release of three American soldiers taken prisoner during the NATO-led war. A year later, he was awarded the U.S. Presidential Medal of Freedom, the nation's highest civilian honor.

In terms of homiletical style, Jackson has become known around the world for his use of alliteration and rhyme and his rhetorical cadence. He does not just speak sermonic lines, he rhythmically rolls lines across his tongue and punctuates them with a folksy tone. His sermons are often filled with statistics or current cultural facts that are of relevance to his listeners.

Though not without his detractors for some of his political stances, approaches to achieving economic and social justice, and what some have called overexposure, to many, Jackson remains a relevant voice in the African American pulpit and on the American and national stage.

• • •

*This address is an excerpt from the historic speech delivered at the Omni Coliseum in Atlanta, Georgia, before the 1988 Democratic National Convention, following Jackson's bid for the United States presidency. Although titled a speech, this message is remembered because those who understand the African American preaching tradition could clearly tell when Jackson (in the historic style of African American preacher-politicians) stopped giving a speech and began preaching. He uses scripture, history, poetry, and the headlines of the day to press home his message. Although he failed to win the nomination, Jackson's presidential run was significant because it galvanized disadvantaged people to participate in the political process, register, and vote; placed important social and racial issues on the national agenda; and seriously introduced the possibility that an African American could win the nation's highest office.*

## Keep Hope Alive
## (July 19, 1988)

Twenty-four years ago, the late Fannie Lou Hamer and Aaron Henry—who sits here tonight from Mississippi—were locked out onto the streets in Atlantic City by the head of the Mississippi Freedom Democratic Party.

But tonight, a Black and White delegation from Mississippi is headed by Ed Cole, a Black man from Mississippi; twenty-four years later.

Many were lost in the struggle for the right to vote: Jimmy Lee Jackson, a young student, gave his life; Viola Liuzzo, a white mother from Detroit, called "nigger lover," and brains blown out at point blank range; [Michael] Schwerner, [Andrew] Goodman and [James] Chaney—two Jews and a Black—found in a common grave, bodies riddled with bullets in Mississippi; the four darling little girls in a church in Birmingham, Alabama. They died that we might have a right to live.

Dr. Martin Luther King Jr. lies only a few miles from us tonight. Tonight he must feel good as he looks down upon us. We sit here together, a rainbow, a coalition—the sons and daughters of slavemasters and the sons and daughters of slaves, sitting together around a common table, to decide the direction of our party and our country. His heart would be full tonight.

As a testament to the struggles of those who have gone before; as a legacy for those who will come after; as a tribute to the endurance, the patience, the courage of our forefathers and mothers; as an assurance that their prayers are being answered, that their work has not been in vain, and, that hope is eternal, tomorrow night my name will go into nomination for the presidency of the United States of America.

We meet tonight at the crossroads, a point of decision. Shall we expand, be inclusive, find unity and power; or suffer division and impotence?

We've come to Atlanta, the cradle of the Old South, the crucible of the New South. Tonight, there is a sense of celebration, because we are moved, fundamentally moved from racial battlegrounds by law, to economic common ground. Tomorrow we'll challenge to move to higher ground. Common ground. Think of Jerusalem, the intersection where many trails met. A small village that became the birthplace for three great religions—Judaism, Christianity, and Islam. Why was this village so blessed? Because it provided a crossroads where different people met, different cultures, different civilizations could meet and find common ground. When people come together, flowers always flourish—the air is rich with the aroma of a new spring.

Take New York, the dynamic metropolis. What makes New York so special? It's the invitation at the Statue of Liberty, "Give me your tired, your poor, your huddled masses who yearn to breathe free." Not restricted to English only. Many people, many cultures, many languages with one thing in common: They yearn to breathe free. Common ground.

Tonight in Atlanta, for the first time in this century, we convene in the South; a state where governors once stood in schoolhouse doors;

where Julian Bond was denied a seat in the state legislature because of his conscientious objection to the Vietnam War; a city that, through its five Black universities, has graduated more black students than any city in the world. Atlanta, now a modern intersection of the New South. Common ground. That's the challenge of our party tonight—left wing, right wing.

Progress will not come through boundless liberalism nor static conservatism, but at the critical mass of mutual survival—liberalism nor static conservatism, but at the critical mass of mutual survival. It takes two wings to fly. Whether you're a hawk or a dove, you're just a bird living in the same environment, in the same world.

The Bible teaches that when lions and lambs lie down together, none will be afraid, and there will be peace in the valley. It sounds impossible. Lions eat lambs. Lambs sensibly flee from lions. Yet even lions and lambs find common ground. Why? Because neither lions nor lambs want the forest to catch on fire. Neither lions nor lambs want acid rain to fall. Neither lions nor lambs can survive nuclear war. If lions and lambs can find common ground, surely we can as well—as civilized people.

The only time that we win is when we come together. In 1960, John Kennedy, the late John Kennedy, beat Richard Nixon by only 112,000 votes—less than one vote per precinct. He won by the margin of our hope. He brought us together. He reached out. He had the courage to defy his advisors and inquire about Dr. King's jailing in Albany, Georgia. We won by the margin of our hope, inspired by courageous leadership. In 1964, Lyndon Johnson brought both wings together—the thesis, the antithesis, and the creative synthesis—and together we won. In 1976, Jimmy Carter unified us again, and we won. When we do not come together, we never win. In 1968, the vision and despair in July led to our defeat in November. In 1980, rancor in the spring and the summer led to Reagan in the fall. When we divide, we cannot win. We must find common ground as the basis for survival and development and change and growth.

Today when we debated, differed, deliberated, agreed to agree, agreed to disagree, when we had the good judgment to argue a case and then not self-destruct, George Bush was just a little further away from the White House and a little closer to private life.

Tonight, I salute Governor Michael Dukakis. He has run—he has run a well-managed and a dignified campaign. No matter how tired or how tried, he always resisted the temptation to stoop to demagoguery. I've watched a good mind fast at work, with steel nerves, guiding his campaign out of the crowded field without appeal to the worst in us. I've watched his perspective grow as his environment has expanded. I've seen his toughness and tenacity close up. I know his commitment to public service. Mike Dukakis's parents were a doctor and a teacher; my parents a maid, a beautician, and a janitor. There's a great gap between Brookline, Massachusetts, and Haney Street in the Fieldcrest Village housing projects in Greenville, South Carolina. He studied law; I studied theology. There are differences of religion, region, and race; differences in experiences and perspectives. But the genius of America is that out of the many we become one. Providence has enabled our paths to intersect. His foreparents came to America on immigrant ships; my foreparents came to America on slave ships. But whatever the original ships, we're in the same boat tonight.

Our ships could pass in the night—if we have a false sense of independence—or they could collide and crash. We would lose our passengers. We can seek a high reality and a greater good. Apart, we can drift on the broken pieces of Reaganomics, satisfy our baser instincts, and exploit the fears of our people. At our highest, we can call upon noble instincts and navigate this vessel to safety. The greater good is the common good.

As Jesus said, "Not My will, but Thine be done."[1] It was his way of saying there's a higher good beyond personal comfort or position. The good of our nation is at stake. It's commitment to working men and women, to the poor and the vulnerable, to the many in the world. With so many guided missiles, and so much misguided leadership, the stakes are exceedingly high. Our choice? Full participation in a democratic government, or more abandonment and neglect. And so this night, we choose not a false sense of independence, not our capacity to survive and endure. Tonight we choose interdependency, and our capacity to act and unite for the greater good.

Common good is finding commitment to new priorities to expansion and inclusion. A commitment to expanded participation in the Democratic Party at every level. A commitment to a shared national campaign strategy and involvement at every level. A commitment to new priorities that insure that hope will be kept alive. A common ground commitment to a legislative agenda for empowerment, for the John Conyers bill—universal, on-site, same-day registration everywhere. A commitment to D.C. statehood and empowerment—D.C. deserves statehood. A commitment to economic set-asides, commitment to the Dellums bill for comprehensive sanctions against South Africa. A shared commitment to a common direction. Common ground.

Easier said than done. Where do you find common ground? At the point of challenge. This campaign has shown that politics need not be marketed by politicians, packaged by pollsters and pundits. Politics can be a moral arena where people come together to find common ground.

We find common ground at the plant gate that closes on workers without notice. We find common ground at the farm auction, where a good farmer loses his or her land to bad loans or diminishing markets. Common ground at the school yard where teachers cannot get adequate pay, and students cannot get a scholarship, and can't make a loan. Common ground at the hospital admitting room, where somebody tonight is dying because they cannot afford to go upstairs to a bed that's empty waiting for someone with insurance to get sick. We are a better nation than that. We must do better. Common ground.

What is leadership if not present help in a time of crisis? And so I met you at the point of challenge. In Jay, Maine, where paper workers were striking for fair wages; in Greenville, Iowa, where family farmers struggle for a fair price; in Cleveland, Ohio, where working women seek comparable worth; in McFarland, California, where the children of Hispanic farm workers may be dying from poisoned land, dying in clusters with cancer; in an AIDS hospice in Houston, Texas, where the sick support one another, too often rejected by their own parents and friends. Common ground.

America is not a blanket woven from one thread, one color, one cloth. When I was a child growing up in Greenville, South Carolina, and grandmama could not afford a blanket, she didn't complain and we did not freeze. Instead she took pieces of old cloth—patches, wool, silk, gabardine, crockersack—only patches, barely good enough to wipe off your shoes with. But they didn't stay that way very long. With sturdy hands and a strong cord, she sewed them together into a quilt, a thing of beauty and power and culture. Now, Democrats, we must build such a quilt.

Farmers, you seek fair prices and you are right—but you cannot stand alone. Your patch is not big enough. Workers, you fight for fair wages, you are right—but your patch labor is not big enough. Women, you seek comparable worth and pay equity, you are right—but your patch is not big enough. Women, mothers, who seek Head Start, and day care and prenatal care on the front side of life, relevant jail care and welfare on the back side of life, you are right—but your patch is not big enough. Students, you seek scholarships, you are right—but your patch is not big enough. Blacks and Hispanics, when we fight for civil rights, we are right—but our patch is not big enough. Gays and lesbians, when you fight against discrimination and a cure for AIDS, you are right—but your patch is not big enough. Conservatives and progressives, when you fight for what you believe, right wing, left wing, hawk, dove, you are right from your point of view, but your point of view is not enough. But don't despair. Be as wise as my grandmama. Pull the patches and the pieces together, bound by a common thread. When we form a great quilt of unity and common ground, we'll have the power to bring about health care and housing and jobs and education and hope to our nation.

We, the people, can win. We stand at the end of a long dark night of reaction. We stand tonight united in the commitment to a new direction. For almost eight years we've been led by those who view social good coming from private interest, who view public life as a means to increase private wealth. They have been prepared to sacrifice the common good of the many to satisfy the private interests and the wealth of a few. We believe in a government that's a tool of our democracy in service to the public, not an instrument of the aristocracy in search of private wealth. We believe in government with the consent of the governed, "of, for and by the people." We must now emerge into a new day with a new direction.

Reaganomics: Based on the belief that the rich had too little money and the poor had too much. That's classic Reaganomics. They believe that the poor had too much money and the rich had too little money, so they engaged in reverse Robin Hood, took from the poor, gave to the rich, paid for by the middle class. We cannot stand four more years of Reaganomics in any version, in any disguise.

How do I document that case? Seven years later, the richest 1 percent of our society pays 20 percent less in taxes. The poorest 10 percent pay 20 percent more: Reaganomics. Reagan gave the rich and the powerful a multibillion-dollar party. Now the party is over. He expects the people to pay for the damage. I take this principal position, convention, let us not raise taxes on the poor and the middle class, but those who had the party, the rich and the powerful, must pay for the party.

I just want to take common sense to high places. We're spending one hundred and fifty billion dollars a year defending Europe and Japan forty-three years after the war is over. We have more troops in Europe tonight than we had seven years ago. Yet the threat of war is ever more remote. Germany and Japan are now creditor nations; that means they've got a surplus. We are a debtor nation—means we are in debt. Let them share more of the burden of their own defense. Use some of that money to build decent housing. Use some of that money to educate our children. Use some of that money for long-term health care. Use some of that money to wipe out these slums and put America back to work!

I just want to take common sense to high places. If we can bail out Europe and Japan; if we can bail out Continental Bank and Chrysler—and Mr. Iacocca, make [*sic*] eight thousand dollars an hour—we can bail out the family farmer.

I just want to make common sense. It does not make sense to close down six hundred and fifty thousand family farms in this country while importing food from abroad subsidized by the U.S. Government. Let's make sense.

It does not make sense to be escorting all our tankers up and down the Persian Gulf paying two dollars and fifty cents for every one dollar worth of oil we bring out, while oil wells are capped in Texas, Oklahoma, and Louisiana. I just want to make sense.

Leadership must meet the moral challenge of its day. What's the moral challenge of our day? We have public accommodations. We have the right to vote. We have open housing. What's the fundamental challenge of our day? It is to end economic violence. Plant closings without notice—economic violence. Even the greedy do not profit long from greed—economic violence.

Most poor people are not lazy. They are not black. They are not brown. They are mostly white and female and young. But whether White, Black or Brown, a hungry baby's belly turned inside out is the same color—color it pain; color it hurt; color it agony. Most poor people are not on welfare. Some of them are illiterate and can't read the want-ad sections. And when they can, they can't find a job that matches the address. They work hard every day. I know. I live amongst them. I'm one of them. I know they work. I'm a witness. They catch the early bus. They work every day. They raise other people's children. They work every day. They clean the streets. They work every day. They drive dangerous cabs. They work every day. They change the beds you slept in in these hotels last night and can't get a union contract. They work every day.

No, no, they are not lazy! Someone must defend them because it's right, and they cannot speak for themselves. They work in hospitals. I know they do. They wipe the bodies of those who are sick with fever and pain. They empty their bedpans. They clean out their commodes. No job is beneath them, and yet when they get sick they cannot lie in the bed they made up every day. America, that is not right. We are a better nation than that. We are a better nation than that.

We need a real war on drugs. You can't "just say no." It's deeper than that. You can't just get a palm reader or an astrologer. It's more profound than that. We are spending a hundred and fifty billion dollars on drugs a year. We've gone from ignoring it to focusing on the children. Children cannot buy a hundred and fifty billion dollars worth of drugs a year; a few high-profile athletes—athletes are not laundering a hundred and fifty billion dollars a year—bankers are.

I met the children in Watts, who, unfortunately, in their despair, their grapes of hope have become raisins of despair, and they're turning on each other and they're self-destructing. But I stayed with them all night long. I wanted to hear their case. They said, "Jesse Jackson, as you challenge us to say no to drugs, you're right; and to not sell them, you're right; and not use these guns, you're right." (And by the way, the promise of CETA [Comprehensive Employment and Training Act]; they displaced CETA—they did not replace CETA.) "We have neither jobs nor houses nor services nor training—no way out. Some of us take drugs as anesthesia for our pain. Some take drugs as a way of pleasure, good short-term pleasure and long-term pain. Some sell drugs to make money. It's wrong, we know, but you need to know that we know. We can go and buy the drugs by the boxes at the port. If we can buy the drugs at the port, don't you believe the federal government can stop it if they want to?" They say, "We don't have Saturday night specials anymore." They say, "We buy AK-47s and Uzis, the latest make of weapons. We buy them along these boulevards." You cannot fight a war on drugs unless and until you're going to challenge the bankers and the gun sellers and those who grow them. Don't just focus on the children; let's stop drugs at the level of supply and demand. We must end the scourge on the American culture.

Leadership. What difference will we make? Leadership. Cannot just go along to get along. We must do more than change presidents. We must change direction. Leadership must face the moral challenge of our day. The nuclear war buildup is irrational. Strong leadership cannot desire to look tough and let that stand in the way of the pursuit of peace. Leadership must reverse the arms race. At least we should pledge no first use. Why? Because first use begets first retaliation. And that's mutual annihilation. That's not a rational way out. No use at all. Let's think it out and not fight it out because it's an unwinnable fight. Why hold a card that you can never drop? Let's give peace a chance.

Leadership. We now have this marvelous opportunity to have a breakthrough with the Soviets. Last year two hundred thousand Americans visited the Soviet Union. There's a chance for joint ventures into space—not Star Wars and arms war escalation but a space defense initiative. Let's build in space together and demilitarize the heavens. There's a way out.

America, let us expand. When Mr. Reagan and Mr. Gorbachev met, there was a big meeting. They represented together one-eighth of the human race. Seven-eighths of the human race was locked out of that room. Most people in the world tonight—half are Asian, one half of them are Chinese. There are twenty-two nations in the Middle East. There's Europe; forty million Latin Americans next door to us; the Caribbean; Africa—a half-billion people. Most people in the world today are Yellow or Brown or Black, non-Christian, poor, female, young, and don't speak English in the real world.

This generation must offer leadership to the real world. We're losing ground in Latin America, [the] Middle East, South Africa because we're not focusing on the real world. That's the real world. We must use basic principles—support international law. We stand the most to gain from it. Support human rights—we believe in that. Support self-determination—we're built on that. Support economic development—you know it's right. Be consistent and gain our moral authority in the world. I challenge you tonight, my friends, let's be bigger and better as a nation and as a party.

We have basic challenges—freedom in South Africa. We've already agreed as Democrats to declare South Africa to be a terrorist state. But don't just stop there. Get South Africa out of Angola, free Namibia, support the front-line states. We must have a new humane human rights consistent policy in Africa.

I'm often asked, "Jesse, why do you take on these tough issues? They're not very political. We can't win that way." If an issue is morally right, it will eventually be political. It may be political and never be right. Fannie Lou Hamer didn't have the most votes in Atlantic City, but her principles have outlasted every delegate who voted to lock her out. Rosa Parks did not have the most votes, but she was morally right. Dr. King didn't have the most votes about the Vietnam War, but he was morally right. If we are principled first, our politics will fall in place.

"Jesse, why do you take these big bold initiatives?" A poem by an unknown author went something like this: "We mastered the air, we conquered the sea, annihilated distance and prolonged life, but we're not wise enough to live on this earth without war and without hate."

As for Jesse Jackson: "I'm tired of sailing my little boat, far inside the harbor bar. I want to go out where the big ships float, out on the deep where the great ones are. And should my frail craft prove too slight for waves that sweep those billows o'er, I'd rather go down in the stirring fight than drowse to death at the sheltered shore." We've got to go out, my friends, where the big boats are.

And then for our children. Young America, hold your head high now. We can win. We must not lose you to drugs and violence, premature pregnancy, suicide, cynicism, pessimism, and despair. We can win. Wherever you are tonight, I challenge you to hope and to dream. Don't submerge your dreams. Exercise above all else, even on drugs, dream of the day you are drug free. Even in the gutter, dream of the day that you will be up on your feet again. You must never stop dreaming. Face reality, yes, but don't stop with the way things are. Dream of things as they ought to be. Dream. Face pain, but love, hope, faith, and dreams will help you rise above the pain. Use hope and imagination as weapons of survival and progress, but you keep on dreaming, young America. Dream of peace. Peace is rational and reasonable. War is irrational in this age, and unwinnable.

Dream of teachers who teach for life and not for a living. Dream of doctors who are concerned more about public health than private wealth. Dream of lawyers more concerned about justice than a judgeship. Dream of preachers who are concerned more about prophecy than profiteering. Dream on the high road with sound values.

And then America, as we go forth to September, October, November, and then beyond, America must never surrender to a high moral challenge. Do not surrender to drugs. The best drug policy is a "no first use." Don't surrender with needles and cynicism. Let's have "no first use" on the one hand, or clinics on the other. Never surrender, young America. Go forward.

America must never surrender to malnutrition. We can feed the hungry and clothe the naked. We must never surrender. We must go forward. We must never surrender to illiteracy. Invest in our children. Never surrender; and go forward. We must never surrender to inequality. Women cannot compromise ERA or comparable worth. Women are making sixty cents on the dollar to what a man makes. Women cannot buy meat cheaper. Women cannot buy bread cheaper. Women cannot buy milk cheaper. Women deserve to get paid for the work that you do. It's right! And it's fair. Don't surrender, my friends. Those who have AIDS tonight, you deserve our compassion. Even with AIDS you must not surrender.

But even in your wheelchairs. I see you sitting here tonight in those wheelchairs. I've stayed with you. I've reached out to you across our nation. And don't you give up. I know it's tough sometimes. People look down on you. It took you a little more effort to get here tonight. And no one should look down on you, but sometimes mean people do. The only justification we have for looking down on someone is that we're going to stop and pick them up. But even in your wheelchairs, don't you give up. We cannot forget fifty years ago when our backs were against the wall, Roosevelt was in a wheelchair. I would rather have Roosevelt in a wheelchair than Reagan and Bush on a horse. Don't you surrender and don't you give up. Don't surrender and don't give up!

Why can I challenge you this way? "Jesse Jackson, you don't understand my situation. You're on television. You don't understand. I see you with the big people. You don't understand my situation." I understand. You see me on TV, but you don't know the me that makes me, me. They wonder, "Why does Jesse run?" because they see me running for the White House. They don't see the house I'm running from. I have a story. I wasn't always on television. Writers were not always outside my door.

When I was born late one afternoon, October eighth, in Greenville, South Carolina, no writers asked my mother her name. Nobody chose to write down our address. My mama was not supposed to make it, and I was not supposed to make it. You see, I was born of a teenage mother, who was born of a teenage mother. I understand. I know abandonment, and people being mean to you, and saying you're nothing and nobody and can never be anything. I understand.

Jesse Jackson is my third name. I'm adopted. When I had no name, my grandmother gave me her name. My name was Jesse Burns 'til I was twelve. So I wouldn't have a blank space, she gave me a name to hold me over. I understand when nobody knows your name. I understand when you have no name.

I understand. I wasn't born in the hospital. Mama didn't have insurance. I was born in the bed at [the] house. I really do understand. Born in a three-room house, bathroom in the backyard, slop jar by the bed, no hot and cold running water. I understand. Wallpaper used for decoration? No. For a windbreaker. I understand. I'm a working person's person. That's why I understand you whether you're Black or White. I understand work. I was not born with a silver spoon in my mouth. I had a shovel programmed for my hand. My mother, a working woman. So many of the days she went to work early, with runs in her stockings. She knew better, but she wore runs in her stockings so that my brother and I could have matching socks and not be laughed at at school. I understand.

At three o'clock on Thanksgiving Day, we couldn't eat turkey because Momma was preparing somebody else's turkey at three o'clock. We had to play football to entertain ourselves. And then around six o'clock she would get off the Alta Vista bus and we would bring up the leftovers and eat our turkey—leftovers, the carcass, the cranberries—around eight o'clock at night. I really do understand.

Every one of these funny labels they put on you, those of you who are watching this broadcast tonight in the projects, on the corners, I understand. Call you outcast, low down, you can't make it, you're nothing, you're nobody, subclass, underclass; when you see Jesse Jackson, when my name goes in nomination, your name goes in nomination.

I was born in the slum, but the slum was not born in me. And it wasn't born in you, and you can make it. Wherever you are tonight, you can make it. Hold your head high; stick your chest out. You can make it. It gets dark sometimes, but the morning comes. Don't you surrender! Suffering breeds character, character breeds faith. In the end faith will not disappoint. You must not surrender! You may or may not get there but just know that you're qualified! And you hold on, and hold out! We must never surrender! America will get better and better. Keep hope alive. Keep hope alive! Keep hope alive! On tomorrow night and beyond, keep hope alive!

I love you very much. I love you very much.

### NOTES

*Sermon source:* "Keep Hope Alive," reprinted from www.americanrhetoric.com/speeches/jessejackson1988dnc.htm (accessed June 28, 2007).

1. Luke 22:42 (King James Version).

### BIBLIOGRAPHICAL SOURCES

Abernathy, Ralph David. *And the Walls Came Tumbling Down: An Autobiography.* New York: Harper & Row, 1989.

Appiah, Kwame Anthony, and Henry L. Gates Jr., eds. *Africana: The Encyclopedia of the African and African American Experience.* New York: Oxford University Press, 2005.

Colton, Elizabeth. *The Jackson Phenomenon: The Man, the Power, the Message.* New York: Doubleday, 1989.

*Microsoft Encarta Online Encyclopedia*, s.v. "Jackson, Jesse (Louis)" (by Paul Finkelman), http://encarta.msn.com (accessed June 28, 2007).

Henderson, Ashyia, ed. "Jesse Jackson," in *Contemporary Black Biography*, vol. 27. Detroit: Gale Group, 2001.

Reynolds, Barbara. *Jessie Jackson: America's David.* Washington, DC: JFJ Associates, 1985.

# THOMAS DEXTER (T.D.) JAKES

(1957– )

Few pastors have become better known as quickly as T.D. Jakes, a preacher, entrepreneur, musician, playwright, and author born in South Charleston, West Virginia, on June 9, 1957. His mother was a teacher; his father owned a successful janitorial company. It was a churchgoing family. Jakes, also known to some as the "shepherd of the shattered," is no stranger to the healing and empowerment he preaches. When he was ten, his father developed kidney disease, and for the next six years until his death, Jakes and his mother, Odith, cared for Ernest. Entering adulthood in the shadow of emergency rooms and a kidney machine, Jakes briefly studied psychology.

Jakes was raised Baptist and became a Pentecostal at Greater Emmanuel Apostolic Church, where he was later ordained a bishop. He resigned from that denomination and began to fellowship with Higher Ground Always Abounding Assemblies. In 1979, he began fulfilling his call to the ministry by pastoring a small congregation of ten members while working days at a local plant. After he married Serita Jamison in 1981 and the couple had twin boys, the plant shut down. The couple later had three more children.

In 1993, Jakes self-published *Woman, Thou Art Loosed*, a book about women facing abuse and depression. It sold almost two million copies. Television programs and conferences that grew out of that success helped Jakes further expand his ministry. Two years later, he moved his church and fifty families to Dallas and renamed the church The Potter's House. The Potter's House had a membership that approached twenty thousand by 2009. The church beams its Sunday services to several continents, and Jakes is known as a global entrepreneur. The Potter's House operates more than fifty ministries, including a grade school (Clay Academy); an offender re-entry program; ministries for youth, those desiring to be business entrepreneurs, the homeless, and drug addicts; and ministries that provide aid to African countries.

The success of Jakes is the result of at least three factors. First, he ushered in a new emphasis on success and wealth by accentuating the therapeutic and self-help aspects of his messages. Second, he blended expositional preaching with narrative and Pentecostal-flavored preaching, which many who were new to the church may have experienced as a new hearing of the Gospel message. Third, masterfully using media, unlike any black preacher before him, he built an entrepreneurial empire that includes books, conferences, plays, CDs (one of which received a Grammy Award in 2004), and movies.

In early 2001, Jakes founded an interdenominational network of some 250 churches. He serves as CEO of the alliance, its senior minister, and mentor, providing leadership for pastors from Presbyterian to Baptist to Pentecostal faiths. He has been featured on the cover of *Time* magazine and numerous religious magazines and journals. Reverend Jakes, called by most Bishop Jakes, has now also become well known for his Man-Power and Woman Thou Art Loosed conferences, which were merged into his MegaFest Conference in 2004. Jakes has sold out venues as large as the Georgia Dome for his conferences. A regular visitor to the White House during the presidency of George W. Bush, he also participates on stages with well-known white preachers, including Joyce Meyers, Benny Hinn, and Rod Parsley. He has raised the ire of some who have labeled his preaching empowerment language that sneaks in prosperity gospel and have complained that his extravagant lifestyle, including a bowling alley inside of one of his homes, does not comport with the Gospel of Jesus and making the poor a priority.

Some of the other books written by T.D. Jakes include *Maximize the Moment* (2000); *The Lady, Her Lover and Her Lord* (2000); *Help I'm Raising My Children Alone* (2001); *Maximize the Moment: God's Action Plan for Your Life* (2001); *Lay Aside the Weight: Take Control of It Before It Takes Control of You* (2002); *God's Leading Ladies: Out of the Shadow and into the Light* (2002); *The Great Investment: Balancing Faith, Family and Finance to Build a Rich Spiritual Life* (2002); *He-Motions: Even Strong Men Struggle* (2004); *Promises From God for Single Women* (2005); and *Reposition Yourself* (2007).

• • •

*The following sermon demonstrates that Jakes's genius lies in his ability to join and master two traditions within the African American folk preaching tradition: the Baptist whoop and neo-Pentecostal freedom in the Holy Spirit. This combination results in dramatic, spontaneous, and emotional eruptions from the congregation, which have become a trademark of his services. Closely aligned with and part of this emotive effect is Jakes's masterful use of the new call-and-response in the African American church, also now used in white churches, in which the preacher instructs the congregation to repeat phrases to further emphasize what the preacher has said and exponentially increase audience participation. Jakes has mastered the delivery of the African American preaching style to mass audiences through the medium of television and marketing.*

*Following the tragedy of September 11, 2001, many watched Jakes on television the next Sunday as he preached the message reprinted here.*

## The Gathering of America
## (September 16, 2001)

We are cognizant of the huge responsibility that rests upon this nation and its leadership and even upon this church to do what we can in some small way to encourage people who are going through adversity. There are many, many people in this church who knew someone or were related to someone who was in the World Trade Centers or Washington, D.C., when the planes crashed and knew somebody who was on the plane that crashed in Pennsylvania. Hardly any American in this country and few of the friends of Americans around the world have been untouched in some way by the magnitude of the travesty that has occurred before us. I want to talk to you a little bit about that today.

In the Gospel of St. Matthew, chapter thirteen, beginning with verse twenty-four (King James Version), let us read from the Word of God:

> Another parable put he forth unto them, saying, The kingdom of heaven is likened unto a man which sowed good seed in his field: But while men slept, his enemy came and sowed tares among the wheat, and went his way. But when the blade was sprung up, and brought forth fruit, then appeared the tares also. So the servants of the householder came and said unto him, Sir, didst not thou sow good seed in thy field? From whence then hath it tares? He said unto them, "An enemy hath done this." The servants said unto him, "Wilt thou then that we go and gather them up?" But he said, "Nay; lest while ye gather up the tares, ye root up also the wheat with them. Let both grow together until the harvest: and in the time of harvest I will say to the reapers, Gather ye together first the tares, and bind them in bundles to burn them: but gather the wheat into my barn."

Verse thirty says, "Let both grow together until the harvest: and in the time of harvest I will say to the reapers, Gather ye together first the tares, and bind them in bundles to burn them: but gather the wheat . . ." Repeat it: But gather the wheat, but gather the wheat into my barn.

I want to talk about the Gathering of America.

I stand before you today with mixed emotions. I certainly am, on one hand, glad to be back home and glad to be at the helm of this church to do what God has called me to do. So, it's good to be home. And yet there is a certain sobriety, a certain seriousness, a certain weightiness, that I feel at this moment. I'm weighted not only with the tragedies that have riveted this nation. I'm also weighted with the responsibility of Christian leadership to be used of God to answer questions and to give direction. Significant issues are challenging us. I've been amazed by what has happened in the last few days, not only in terms of what has happened in New York and in Washington, at the Pentagon and what the enemy wanted to do to Air Force One, but also amazed at the open entree that God has given us to be able to discuss with the nation—through secular media—the impact that these events are having on the nation and the possible medicinal influences that are about in the country when we looked to God for our strength and for our shelter. While we normally have a very, very good crowd, the crowd is stronger than normal today, and I think that alone reflects your concern and your understanding for the challenges before us.

I want to open by telling you that I have never in the forty-four years of my life seen anything as disturbing as what we've been riveted by in this country at this particular time. Yes, we've had some skirmishes and we've had some Desert Storms and we've gone into Kosovo, and we've thrown some weight around and we've even lost some lives in the process of doing what we thought was appropriate to do, but never in my life, including Vietnam, have I seen anything that is as disturbing as what I'm seeing occur right now. And if you're taking it seriously, you're a very smart person. If you don't take it seriously, you are very, very foolish. There is a tremendous concern facing this country.

Our prayers strongly go out to President Bush. Strongly, strongly. Emphatically. Without question, we're deeply praying for him. And I don't want you to get caught in the trap of you voted for him, you didn't vote for him, you're Republican, you're Democrat, you don't like how the election went. It makes no difference how the election went now. He is the president of the United States of America. Let's be clear. I believe [President Bush] deserves our whole support, our complete prayer, and our consecration because we have never been threatened like we are being threatened right now. You're hearing words like *campaign;* they're launching a campaign, which is basically just a nice word for war. And they're launching a war strategy specifically to protect and defend this country. You're hearing terminology like *a new war.* And one of the reasons that I think we need to bombard the president with prayer is that he's hardly unpacked his office supplies in the Oval Office. He's hardly gotten used to the atmosphere in Washington, D.C. And now he's confronting one of the most serious conflicts in the history of this nation. A conflict that, by the way, is unprecedented. We have nothing to compare it to. Although you've heard a lot of things said about Pearl Harbor, Pearl Harbor is a poor comparison to what we are facing today. More people died in that World Trade Center alone than in all the death and destruction of Pearl Harbor. With one fatal swoop this—this enemy—this evil and wicked, vile person who has moved against us—has turned our own aircraft into bombs that exploded and ignited thousands of lives. The last report I had was 4,972 people have been listed as missing.[1] The numbers are mounting while we're talking. Out of all of that, 152 bodies have been recovered. Ninety-two of them have been identified. Most of the bodies in that rubble are not even recognizable. They are now asking people to bring toothbrushes of their loved ones so that they can test the DNA to be able to identify the bodies that are not recognizable. This is horrendous.

The media has been very tactful and very tasteful in its coverage of this event. They've spared us the gory details. They have not given us close-ups of bodies diving out of windows. They've not given us close-ups of body parts. That's all they've been able to find of people. They have not talked of people who have been set afire and burned. They have not talked about what the heat of jet fuel igniting would do—that it was so strong that it melted steel, that steel lost its strength. The heat force was so strong that people chose to dive out of a window from one hundred and four floors up rather than to face that heat.

Whatever you think this is, it is worse than what you think. But, I think you understand the magnitude of this problem. It's very difficult for me to watch it and see thousands and thousands of people standing up in Manhattan where I had just left a few days before. Walking down the same streets that I had just happened to be on a few days before. Traveling the same airway that I had just happened to travel a few days before. Holding up pictures of loved ones in the hopes that they might find them. Searching the morgues. Searching the hospitals. Desperately waiting. Every time the phone rings, leaping to their feet. Hoping against hope that it might be a call from a loved one. Listening and hoping that some tap or some sound beneath the concrete might be their wives or their mothers or their husbands or their brothers.

This nation is riveted like I have never seen it before. So here we are—in America, from which we have often gone to rescue other countries from these tragedies. It has come home to roost. And we are concerned, we're deeply concerned, and we ought to be concerned. But, the reality is, we can't even begin the comforting process because we've not truly entered into grief yet, because many of us haven't even recognized the magnitude of what happened. And, as that begins to hit this nation and the reality that many of those pictures are going to end up being memorials to people who did not escape . . .

It is just gut-wrenchingly painful to think of what has happened. There's not a home, an intelligent home in this country that hasn't been riveted by the possibility, that hasn't thought in the back of their mind, that could have been me. That could have happened to us. There's not an intelligent person anywhere in the world who shouldn't understand the vulnerability that has been announced to this country, that everyone is suspect. If you've read any papers, you recognize that this is a part of a master and grand scheme that the enemy has unleashed against us, and if anybody ought to be concerned, we ought to be concerned because part of that networking was right here in Fort Worth. So, if you're not going to get concerned with that in your backyard, I don't know who is going to be concerned. If that doesn't drive you to your knees, if that doesn't put you in the position of prayer, shame on you. Because we're not just talking about going somewhere to battle, we're talking about the battle coming to us.

Are you hearing what I'm saying? And so I'm weighted by that! I'm deeply concerned about that and I challenge you to be concerned as well. When I pray, I ask God to give me some words of encouragement and, particularly, of direction, and so I'm going to seize this text [in Matthew 13] and I'm going to, not so much exegete the complexities of the text itself, but I'm going to use it as a canvas on which to paint the current contemporary issues that are facing our society today.

This text is a parable in which Jesus talks about what the kingdom of heaven is like. And when he begins to talk about it, he compares it to a man who sowed good seed in his field. "But while men slept, his enemy came and sowed tares among the wheat, and went his way." While men slept. You need to understand that this country in many, many ways has been in a state of sleep. We've been asleep. We've been asleep spiritually. We've been asleep to the fact that we could be threatened. We've been asleep to the fact that we could be attacked at any moment. And while we were engrossed in the sleepiness and the boredom of our frivolous thinking, while we were asleep debating political issues arguing amongst Democrats and Republicans, while we were asleep pitting one race against the other, one culture against the another, while we were asleep arguing over church and state and whether you can pray at a football game or whether you can pray at a graduation ceremony—while we were asleep, America, the enemy was slipping in and creeping in and strategically planting tares amongst the wheat.

While we were asleep, busy digging through the trash can of our leaders. While we were asleep, turning our government into the *Jerry Springer Show*, becoming voyeurs of each other's private and sexual lives. While we were asleep, spending millions of dollars on Hollywood entertainment so we could make war games and play video games of war games, and spending millions of dollars in technology to simulate war so that we could go to movies and watch people play war. While we were asleep, using war as a cliché and talking about the war on crime and the war on drugs and the war on this and the war on that, because we have been so long without a real war that we have forgotten what war is. While we were asleep in the absence of war, we've become each other's voyeurs. Talk shows have taken over the country. We've become gossipers; we've become preoccupied with digging down in the trash cans of each other's lives for entertainment. We've traded in TV for "real TV," for using people in different situations for entertainment. While we were sleeping, arguing about percentages and interests and stock markets and investments and annuities, the enemy was stealthily creeping in our backdoor, building networks, setting up structures.

Do you hear what I'm saying? You must understand that this is deeper than one man. This is not just the workings of one man. It is far deeper than that. It goes far more intensely than anything Osama bin Laden would do. It is deeper than that. Yes, if it were one person you could easily take him out. But while we were sleeping in this country, the enemy was busy setting up networks all across this country and around the world, which has put us in a dilemma where this war will not be like any other war that we have ever had to fight. In times past, we were fighting against a country in a particular geographical location. But this enemy has sowed his tares everywhere. And when the president talks about it being a "new war," it will be a new war because the enemy is literally everywhere and our leaders are trying to trace all of his sites and all of his locations.

While we were asleep. Do you hear me? The enemy has come and planted tares amongst the wheat! I hope you hear me today, 'cause I didn't come to play patty-cake with you this morning. I came to sound an alarm in Zion. And I came to serve notice on you. Yes, America has been asleep, but she's awake now. She's awake right now. Do you hear what I said? She is alive and awake right now.

Now, imagine with me. They have shut off all the boroughs around Manhattan. Completely closed down. Everything is in a state of emergency. All the police are focused on the remains and the rubble of the buildings. The firefighters who haven't been killed in it are fighting for it. Volunteers are all centered around what was the World Trade Center and yet, there were no reports for days of any lootings, of any robberies. America is awake. That's not natural. That's not normal. Nobody's bothering anything or taking anything.

Imagine with me. The president has gone to Congress and he asked for twenty billion dollars. They gave him forty billion. No arguments, no fighting, no political junk, and no arguing between Democrats and Republicans. Imagine with me. Who would have thought, after the bitter fight that existed for the presidency, that Al Gore and George Bush would be sitting up in church together with Bill Clinton singing songs and praying prayers. America is awake. We may have been asleep, baby, but we're not asleep now. America is wide awake.

According to the most recent polls, there is no difference between how African Americans feel and how Caucasian Americans feel about this. There is no difference in how Hispanics feel about this. The polls are coming in conclusively that all Americans are on the same page about this. So, if the devil thought that while we were sleeping that we wouldn't wake up, I came to serve notice on him!

Now, let's put this into perspective. The enemy has sowed tares. When you sow tares, you sow them strategically, and there's been a strategy released. When Colin Powell begins to talk about launching a campaign, he's talking about a rigorous campaign, because the enemy has stealthily crept in and planted various things in various places in an attempt to overthrow what God would have us to have. That is freedom. Not only freedom for America, but for all of the free countries of the world is being jeopardized. The prime ministers and presidents from all over the world are calling in their support. You need to pray, right there, that all the communities, the global community, would get on the same page with us. Because the president has said that America (and I'm glad that we've lost enough arrogance to admit we need some help), America cannot win this war by herself. So we're going to need favor. (Somebody needs to send Osama bin Laden my tape, "Favor Ain't Fair.") We need favor, because we do not intend to fight fair. I said, We don't intend to fight fair.

And you must understand, my brothers and sisters, this is not about retaliation, though there are many people that are using that word *retaliation*. We don't have the luxury of retaliation. We don't have the luxury of arguing about vengeance and revenge and the theology that centers around whether we should seek revenge. This isn't about seeking revenge; this is about self-defense. It's about self-defense, because they are coming and they are coming back again. We have a short time to turn this around. And I don't mean to alarm you, but I do mean to wake you up out of your sleep. We cannot say to our young people, If you stay at home, we can spare your life. If we don't send troops in there to fight, there won't be a home for young people to stay at. A friend of mine called me and he said that walking around the streets of New York, he thought he was in Beirut. If we don't fight, you could look outside your back door tomorrow and swear *you* were in Beirut. Bullets zinging around your windows, blowing up our grandparents in their beds, destroying high-rise homes for senior citizens. Everything that we have has been threatened.

I was interviewed on CNN the other morning. Right in the middle of the interview, they stopped me and said, "Would you just pray?" On

CNN. I didn't say TBN, I said CNN. "Pray for the nation." And I found myself praying for the nation on CNN. Nobody is arguing about prayer in the schools. Nobody's talking about the separation of church and state. Nobody's saying, "That prayer offended me." Nobody's offended now. Everybody wants some prayer up in here. I have been telling you for a long time that it was the vision of this church for blacks and whites and browns to come together in one place and worship God. I have been beating the pulpit telling you that it has never been God's will for there to be such things as white churches and black churches and Hispanic churches. It's rubbish, it's ridiculous. When Osama bin Laden, or whoever it was behind this treacherous act, sent those planes toward the World Trade Centers, he didn't send them after black folks, he didn't send them after white folks, he didn't send them after Hispanics or Jews. He sent them after America. America. Somewhere in the red, white, and blue, there is you.

Now admittedly, this country has had its share of problems and it's had its share of challenges and it hasn't been right about everything, and historically we've bickered like children in the sandboxes, arguing about the issues of life. But, we bickered because there was a sandbox. Now they're about to blow up the sandbox. We've got to stop arguing about what's going on in the box, and fight for the box. Because if we don't fight for the box, they're going to come in from the outside and blow up the box, and it won't just be black folks or white folks or brown folks. It's going to be American folks.

I was in a foreign country just a couple of years ago, and they were treating me kind of funny and I couldn't figure out why. I'd never been looked at quite like that. I could tell it wasn't a friendly look; it was a little hostile look, but it was a different look than what I was accustomed to. I couldn't understand it. Some Africans were in the same country, and [the natives] treated them very nicely. So I ruled out my first thought; being raised in this country, I thought it was a color issue. But when they treated the Africans, who happened to be darker than me, better than me, suddenly, I realized it wasn't color. I was all the way back home before I realized they hated me for being American. I'm used to being hated for being black. I've kinda gotten used to that. But now when I'm out of the country, I'm hated for being American. Something about being hated for being American suddenly drove home the fact that, regardless of the color of my skin, I am very much American.

These people that are coming against us are coming against our country, not our color. They're coming against our country, not our politics. They're coming against our country, not our lifestyle, and we had better come together, "one nation, under God, indivisible, with liberty and justice for all." You don't hear what I'm saying to you. I want to sound the alarm this morning. I want to blow the trumpet in your ears. It's high time for you to wake out of your sleep. And yes, we're hurt. And yes, we're weeping. And yes, we're angry. And don't tell me that just because I'm a Christian I shouldn't be angry. Jesus was angry and cleared the temple. The Bible said, "Be angry and sin not."[2] Sometimes you're going to need anger. You're going to need fire to drive you, but you don't want to be reckless with the anger. This is a significant point. You must understand that Osama bin Laden and all of his activities do not represent the Muslim theology. And so you've got to be careful because there are millions of Arab Americans who love this country like we do. So you can't start harassing people because they look different or because they worship differently. They are still Americans. Do you hear what I'm saying? I am a Christian. I'm unashamedly a Christian. And I'm proud to be a Christian. And I don't agree with the theology of the Muslims. But, I do defend their right to believe what they believe. I defend their right to worship the way they want to worship. And, I defend my right to disagree with how they worship. But that is what America is all about—the freedom to worship. Don't allow people to push you into going out at random and picking people who look like Osama bin Laden and attacking them, because if anybody ought to understand racial profiling! Come on, come on. It's time for you to stand up. So, we've got to be angry, but we can't be reckless. We can't be sinful and we can't be disrespectful. What we need is a cold, calculated, God-given strategy.

So, there's a debate going on. From whence cometh these tares? From whence did they come? What happened? We just woke up and all of a sudden our buildings are blowing up. And everybody is trying to find out, why did this happen? So everybody's looking at our foreign policy. They're looking at our government's posture. They're looking at how things were done. The preachers are all standing up. And all of them are trying to say, Why did this happen? We're trying to explain God. God doesn't need an explanation. We don't need to try to explain the mind of God; we need to teach people the mercy of God. Who can know the mind of God? God said, "My thoughts are above your thoughts, my ways above your ways."[3] We don't need to explain God. And so, people are trying to say, "Well God did it." Not mine! Not mine! Maybe yours, not mine. The God that I've been worshipping all of these years is not a God that would send a 747 into the World Trade Centers and kill at random innocent, praying, godly people—not my God. Not the one I lift my hands to and worship. No, I do not believe it! And you cannot make me believe it. The Bible said clearly, "An enemy has done this."[4] Don't you put that on God! Don't you get deep and spiritual and condescending and self-righteous and act like God is judging America. If God has been merciful to the world, I believe that that same God would be merciful to America. This is not the workings of God; this is the workings of an enemy. The Bible said, "An enemy has done this."[5] Don't let anybody tell you this is God. And you don't even have to fight over it. Just stand on the fact that our God is a just God. He's a holy God. He's a loving God. He's a merciful God.

God knows how to capitalize on what the enemy did. For the Bible said, "For all things work together for the good of them who love the Lord."[6] Maybe the devil did do it, but God's going to take that which the devil meant for evil and make it turn out for good because America is gathering together. We're coming together. We're praying together. We're worshipping together. We're uniting our forces together, and I want to serve notice on the devil: *You ain't seen nothing yet.* Clap your hands like you understand what I'm saying.

There must be a separation in our understanding between government and church. We must understand that the Bible said that the powers that be, talking about the government, are ordained of God. Don't allow people to overwhelm you with "If you were really a Christian you should not be interested in revenge." First of all, it's not revenge, nor is it retaliation; it's self-defense. Second thing you need to understand is the decision to go to war is not going to come from the pulpit. It is not coming from the pulpit; it is coming from the White House. And according to the Scriptures, we are supposed to support those who are in positions of power. We cannot weigh them down this time with our religious rhetoric. We need to be on our knees praying. And if Osama bin Laden or whoever was involved behind him and with him and the countries who supported him are laughing today because they have knocked America to their knees, let me explain that when America gets on her knees, it's not because she's defeated, baby. It's because she's getting ready to fight. My war position is on my knees. I'll knock you out from my knees! I'll overcome my enemies on my knees. If I've been knocked to my knees, I'm going to fight on my knees.

Touch three people and say, "Let's get together." Black folk, white folk, red folk, brown folk, rich folk, poor folk, educated, illiterate: Let's get together. No bickering, no complaining, no murmuring, no fighting. Let's stand together. Together we stand, divided we fall. Let's get together. And so my brothers and sisters, when you pray, ask God to give our president, our commander in chief and all of his advisors, to give them divine strategies, supernatural wisdom, agility of wit, articulation of speech. Ask God to make the president cunning. Right now we need somebody cunning. We don't need anybody cute. We don't need a mamby-pamby, soft-baked, freeze-dried president. We need somebody that's shrewd, and the public doesn't need to know everything. You can't fight this kind of enemy if your strategies are going to be all over CNN. And so God says in the parable, God says to them, he says, Don't you move quickly and try to separate the wheat from the tares, lest in the process of getting the tares, you destroy the wheat.

And the issue before us now, since these networks, these cells, are set up all over our country and other countries—is how to get in and pull out the tares with the most minimal amount of damage to the wheat. It's not like they're all in one place. We need a shrewd God-given strategy, tip-toeing up stealthily on this enemy.

But this enemy has got to go. If we have to go get some boys from the hood, he's got to come out of here now. He's got to go. He's got to go. This is not optional. This is not optional. It wasn't my country when I got here, but it is now. My ancestors' blood is running down into the soils of this country. You're not going to run me up out of here. Nah, nah, nah. If slavery didn't run me out, if the civil rights movement didn't run me out, if being beat with a water hose didn't run me out, if the trouble you went through didn't run you out, if people came here from all walks of life and they endured hardships and overcame the Depression and withstood the second World War and stood here, then no terrorist group is going to run us out of here. Not without the fight of your life. And I believe to my soul, if we fight and if we pray, we'll win.

Let me quickly caution you that this will not be easy. Congress has approved forty billion dollars to fight, but the real cost will not be dollars; it will be lives. It will be body bags. It will be our sons and daughters. This is not a cliché of war. This is real war, and this is not the kind of war that President Bush can confer with other presidents about and figure out how they did it because this is a new kind of war. So, the churches need to pray everywhere.

The question arises, How do we talk to our children? Some have said, just comfort the children and tell them everything is going to be okay. That's not going to work. You cannot teach your children this Santa Claus, ice-cream-cone mentality that we've had the luxury of enjoying while we were asleep. You have got to educate your children as to what is happening and what it means, not to terrorize them but to train them. Baby doll, if you look out there and you see a strange man drop a suitcase in a strange place, then you've got to get out of there quickly. You cannot train children if you have lulled them to sleep in a false sense of security. Not while *their* children are carrying M-16s up and down the street. America has got to grow up, and we've only got this weekend to get it done. Whether you realize it or not, our sons and daughters, black, white, and brown, have already got their papers. The military is already starting to move them into positions. Some of them have already left. This is real. The urgency in Colin Powell's voice is staggering.

As I talk to major news commentators across the country, news commentators who have covered some of the greatest atrocities of our age are breaking into tears. This is a critical issue. This is no joke. I have a rule when I fly on a plane that when the plane hits an air pocket and it scares me, I always look to the flight attendant, and if the flight attendant is still smiling, I go back to reading the paper. But if I turn to her and her skin looks scaly and her eyes are bucked and her skin is unusually white, I put my book up and get my prayer cloth out. And, when I look at this nation's leaders and I see their lips trembling, when I see them holding hands and praying with people who they were arguing with last week, when I see news commentators getting choked up in the middle of what would normally have been a professional dissertation, I know it's some real trouble up in here.

The Lord said, "In the time of harvest, I will come in and I will gather the tares into bundles."[6] So, I want you to pray that God would expose the enemy. Expose him. Everywhere. Anywhere. Expose his devices. Pray that God exposes his tactics. Expose him on foreign soils. Expose him if he's got spies in our government. Expose him because they've broken our codes and they've entered into our computer systems. Expose him on technology. You've got to put your King James English up and start praying up to date. We're not fighting no two-thousand-year-old demon. This is a 2001 contemporary, twenty-first-century devil who is hacking into our computer systems. We have to pray against hackers. You gotta start praying in tongues and praying in the Holy Ghost, and watch and pray and believe God. And God said, "In the time of harvest."[7] Tell Osama bin Laden, "It's harvest time." Tell the demonic forces behind him, "It's harvest time." Tell every country that's harboring these enemies, "It's harvest time." God said, "In the time of harvest, I will bind the tares into bundles to burn them."[8] See, it's not "Am I going to fight?" It's not "Is the country going to fight?" The only thing that the devil needs to know is that God is going to fight. And if God be for us, *who?* Shake somebody's hand and tell them, "The Lord is on my side." Don't you turn on me because the Lord is on my side! And when it's all said and done—we're going to win!

I'm going to hasten to a close, but I want to tell you quickly, all that stuff you've been singing about and all the things you've been praying about and all the things we've been rehearsing, have been getting us ready. And while America has been asleep, the church has been preparing for spiritual warfare for a long time. See, we got to fight like Moses fought. The Bible said that Moses got up on the mountain and lifted up his hands, and while he lifted up his hands, Joshua fought in the valley.[9] And the church has got to assume the position of Moses and lift up holy hands before God and begin to call upon the name of the Lord. Let Colin Powell be the Joshua that goes down in the valley and begins to fight. But let the preachers and the leaders of the religious institutions lift up holy hands and call on the name of our God. And the God who hears in secret will reward you openly. And, no weapon—*no weapon*—formed against you shall prosper, and every tongue that rises against you, God will condemn. "In the time of harvest, I will bind the tares into bundles to burn them."[10] See, it's not "Am I going to fight?" It's not "Is the country going to fight?" The only thing that the devil needs to know is that God is going to fight. And if God be for us, *who?* Shake somebody's hand and tell them, "The Lord is on my side." Don't you turn on me because the Lord is on my side! And when it's all said and done—we're going to win!

## NOTES

*Sermon source:* Martha Simmons and Frank A. Thomas, eds., *9.11.01: African American Leaders Respond to an American Tragedy* (Valley Forge, PA: Judson Press, 2001), 19–32.

1. The actual deaths were 2,603 at the World Trade Center, 125 at the Pentagon, and 246 on four planes for a total of 2,974. http://en.wikipedia.org/wiki/September_11,_2001_attacks#fatalities (accessed June 27, 2007).
2. Ephesians 4:26.
3. See Isaiah 55:8.
4. See Matthew 13:28.
5. Ibid.
6. Ibid.
7. Ibid.
8. Ibid.
9. See Exodus 17:8–11.
10. See Matthew 13:30.

## BIBLIOGRAPHICAL SOURCES

Copeland, Libby. "With Gifts from God." *Washington Post*, March 25, 2001. Available at http://www.trinityfi.org/press/tdjakes01.html (accessed June 27, 2007).

"Is This Man the Next Billy Graham?" *Time*, September 17, 2001.

Lee, Shayne. *America's New Preacher: T. D. Jakes*. New York: New York University Press, 2006.

Starling, Kelly. "Why People, Especially Black Women, Are Talking about Bishop T.D. Jakes." *Ebony*, January 2001.

# MILES JEROME JONES

*(1925–2003)*

Miles Jerome Jones was a preacher's preacher. For more than twenty-five years, Jones taught preaching at Virginia Union Seminary (now the Samuel DeWitt Proctor School of Theology at Virginia Union) in Richmond, Virginia. The students and colleagues who were witness to his gifts as an instructor and preacher are legion. Miles Jones, one of five children of Ethel and John Jones, was born in Suffolk, Virginia. When he was a child the family moved to New York, where he attended elementary and completed high school. He then entered the air force and served during World War II. Upon returning to New York, he joined Cornerstone Baptist Church, pastored by Sandy F. Ray, who mentored Jones and convinced him to pursue ministerial studies. Jones married Marion Nanton in 1947, and they had one son, Keith Timothy.

In 1955 Jones entered Virginia Union College and then Virginia Union Seminary. He also obtained a master's degree from Union Presbyterian Seminary in Richmond. In 1963, after pastoring two other churches part-time, Jones became the full-time pastor of Providence Baptist Church in Richmond, where he served for thirty years.

Miles Jones became a fixture in Richmond and part of the group of preachers who were known as "The Richmond Magnificent Seven": James Forbes, Samuel DeWitt Proctor, David Shannon, Wyatt Walker, Walter Fauntroy, and J.M. Ellison.

Jones was a master teacher in and out of the pulpit and a pulpit theologian. He taught and preached about the issues that most affected the African American community. Hundreds of preachers who are now spread across the nation sat in rapt attention in Dr. Jones's classes as he instructed them in the principles of preaching. Jones was an early liberation theologian and was among the National Committee of Black Churchmen, who in 1968 took out a full-page ad in the *New York Times* to protest ill treatment of blacks in America. While in Richmond, he also served on the school board. The city would honor him by naming an elementary school after him. His death in 2003 marked the passing of a majestic preacher and teacher.

• • •

*This sermon was preached for a Men's Day service at First Baptist Church West in Charlotte, North Carolina. In it Jones defines faith and what one needs to do to be a disciple of Christ.*

## Dealing with Disciples (June 1996)

> *Now when the eleven disciples went to Galilee to the mountain where Jesus had directed them and when they saw him they worshipped him but some doubted. And Jesus came and said to them, "All authority in heaven and on earth has been given to me. Go therefore and make disciples of all nations, baptizing them in the name of Father and of the Son and of the Holy Spirit, teaching them to observe all things I have commanded you. And lo I am with you always to the close of the age."*
>
> —Matthew 28:16–20 (New Revised Standard Version)

This theme of discipleship today leads me to come again to this text that you have chosen for your responsive reading in this twenty-eighth chapter of Matthew's Gospel. It's very often considered to be a declaration of a commission and usually when one deals with it, it is dealt with under the rubric of The Commission, The Divine Commission, the commandment that was left for disciples. And yet I want to approach it today from another vantage point. Not so much as a commandment, as an ordinance, or even as a requirement. But I want to suggest that it manifests a way of the Divine in dealing with disciples. And if I were to entitle this sermon, I would call it Dealing with Disciples. For my presumption is that the men of this congregation want to deepen their discipleship and so they have chosen this as their theme for today. They want to deepen their commitment to the eternal and become better servants. And this scripture, I think, might shed some light upon the doing of that deed.

It's a post-resurrection scripture. As a matter of fact, many believe that it was a product of the early Church and that it came as a consequence of the Church's desire to establish a baptismal formula—in the name of the Father and of the Son and of the Holy Spirit. And there are those who contend that this was a later addition to the canon. It was believed to have been put there for the convenience of the later church and for their development of the baptismal formula. However, I think we can profitably view this scripture today as including ingredients—ingredients for indicating discipleship awareness.

Hear the words again. "Now when the eleven disciples went to Galilee to the mountain where Jesus had directed them and when they saw him they worshipped him but some doubted. And Jesus came and said to them, 'All authority in heaven and on earth has been given to me. Go therefore and make disciples of all nations, baptizing them in the name of Father and of the Son and of the Holy Spirit, teaching them to observe all things I have commanded you. And lo I am with you always to the close of the age.'"

I submit that that's a Divine dealing with disciples. And those of us who really want to be learners of our Lord, followers of the Master, sharers of the pilgrimage, participants in that which is ever unfolding before us, I think we can be guided by these words in several ways. The fact that our concern is for discipleship would underscore the fact that all of us would seek to become better learners about our Lord. For that's what a disciple is, one who learns about the Master—one who takes his cue from the one who leads.

Significantly enough, the section opens with the observation that now the *eleven* disciples went to Galilee. These persons are following the direction that has been given to them by those who first beheld the risen Lord. He had given them directions to go to Galilee. "There you will find me," he said. Following the resurrection he did not tarry around Jerusalem but rather he instructed those who had seen him to go to Galilee and tell my disciples to meet me in Galilee.

It's interesting to note that we now have eleven and not twelve. The scripture is indicative of the fact that something is missing in this entourage that goes forth. The complete number is not here. There is a gap, if you please. There is a kind of diminishing of that which formerly obtained. Disciples, even as they begin the trek that leads them to Galilee, even as we start out on the journey that would inform us of the resurrected presence, we can be made aware that there is a shortcoming. There is a diminution of numbers, if you please. There is a significant lessening of that which obtained earlier.

At most, at most, even in our deepest desire to become disciples with our most fervent interest in becoming participants in the enterprise, we are elevenish, if you please. There's something about our numbers, our ability, even our worthiness, that keeps us just being elevenish. There oughta be twelve. There should have been twelve. It was designed to be twelve. He called twelve. Twelve were with him. But when it comes to understanding the significance of this turn of events, now, there are eleven. It is as though the writer wants us to understand that at our best, at our strongest, at our most significantly strengthened moment, we are as it were, elevenish. There's something yet missing. There's something undone. And we need not be too elated because we have been selected as disciples, for as those who shall pursue him or see him, or share his message or his ministry; there is still a shortcoming. And when we come to the high hills of our Galilees, we need to be aware that we're still just elevenish. And when we are highly touted or even medaled, if you please, be aware that we're still elevenish. Oh, how that can keep us humble; how that can burst our bubble; how that can keep us grounded in the reality of our discipleship. We would be prone to pride, perhaps, if we always had twelve. How close to arrogance would we come if the number always stayed the same and we never lost anything? But were reminded that at our best, we're elevenish.

Now, you need not, however, be cast down, because discipleship is a consequence of God's doing and God's design and God's desire. And so the word is, "tell them to meet me there." And so these *eleven* disciples went to Galilee. They were not deterred because there were not twelve. They took the number that was available unto them and went as they had been directed. They did not mind the fact that they did not have the previous number. It's significant that they went without all that they had previously had. I think discipleship begins there. True discipleship begins with the recognition that we are not all that we ought to be. We don't have all that we ought to have or would like to have, but that need not be a deterrent to following the directions of the Divine.

The direction of the Divine is to "meet me." Go where I direct you. Following the directions of the Divine need not necessarily mean that you are fully equipped to do the job or that you are really ready. It means recognizing that at your best you are elevenish. And yet you can still proceed. You can find yourself on the path to progress, on the path to discipleship, on route to the eternal, even with eleven. So, I want to encourage you today. I want to begin with encouragement. Even though you might have brought less to the sanctuary than you had intended, it's still possible. Even though you do not have all the men you'd like to have gathered with you, it's still possible. Even though you might feel a deep sense of shortcoming, it's still possible. We are elevenish, elevenish.

But I thank God for the eleven. If you worry about the twelve, then you'll overlook the eleven. And the word is clear, isn't it, the eleven went. They followed the direction of the Divine. And so, the enterprise can get underway, the trek can begin. We can start participating now with that which the Divine has to do with disciples, if we go with the eleven. I don't know how many there are here today. I haven't counted the number who are present. But, there're still some who ought to be here who are not. You know them better than I. I don't know them, but you know them. You know that there are some who really should be here to participate in this splendid event of celebration led by the men, but they're not here. But that need not deter those who are here. It need not make Chairman Chisholm unhappy. Thank God for all who are here. They reflect the fruit of his endeavors and the calls of his wife. (Laughter.)

We can be thankful for those who participate in the celebration of men's time in this congregational cycle. Thank God. Praise his name; give him glory for those who are here sharing the enterprise of witnessing today and encouraging the congregational presence as it seeks to make its witness effective in the community. Thank God for that. Thank God for the men of the congregation who seek to put their feet in the path of discipleship and make their witness meaningful from this place. Not all we should have, not all we'd like to have. But thank God for the ones who are here, eleven, if you please.

And then, the text continues, when they saw him, when they got there, when they realized that the risen Lord's words were true, and that they could follow the direction that had been given to them about meeting him in Galilee; when they got there it says they worshipped him. When they saw him, they worshipped him. But some doubted. But some doubted; you don't want to overlook the doubters. There are doubters among disciples and they are to be expected. Doubters make up the group as well. Now, let me say a word about those doubters. Let me say a word about the significance of their being included in this. The Bible is so significant for us because it includes even that which might be detracting. Perhaps if I were writing this, I'd leave out the doubters. I wouldn't include them because they would tend to detract from the narrative and most of us just want pleasant things. Most of us just want positive indications. But, the text includes the fact that some of them were doubters.

Why, I wonder. Why would they be included, even identified? I want to suggest that even among disciples and would-be disciples, there are doubters. Part of the reason, I submit to you, is that even in our following our Lord and becoming disciples and proclaimers of his truth, this matter of resurrection is such a phenomenal event, it's really hard to believe. To be truthful about it, this matter of Jesus having been raised from among the dead is so phenomenal, the wonder is that you don't have more doubters. This blows consciousness. One almost feels that one has to be super gullible to appropriate this unto one's self. It is as though doubt would really be the posture of faith and I submit to you that it is!

*Doubt is the avenue to discipleship* and it might very well be a part of our faithfulness. We tend very often to make doubt the opposite of faith. When, in fact, that isn't the case at all. But that's what we've been taught. The opposite of faith is not doubt. The opposite of faith is certainty. Doubt participates in faith. If one is certain, then one doesn't need faith. If I know for sure, absolutely, positively, unequivocally am certain, what need have I for faith? *The opposite of faith is not doubt, but rather certainty.*

Certainty kills faith. Certainty obliterates faith. Certainty wipes faith right off the slate. And so, I walk by sight then; I walk by what I know. I walk by what I can trust under my feet or in my hands. Seeing is believing then. And we don't give doubt its proper place in the construction of a faithful regard. So, this text helps us appreciate that one of the ingredients of our faithful response to the Eternal might be a question. Can I really believe this? Can I really buy this? I'm going on. They're there. That's the important thing. The important thing is that they're there. They're there with their doubts. The important thing is to show up even if you have a doubt. To participate with one's doubt is a matter of moving on to faith.

So the writer includes them because they may be very, very, instructive for us in our pilgrimage as well. It's certainly instructive for us as we begin to identify disciples. For disciples who have never had doubt, may not be strong or worthy. Disciples who've never had doubts, who've never raised a question, who've always been certain from day one, one wonders about that kind of certainty and faithfulness. For this resurrection, this matter of having been raised from the dead, the belief that this one who just a few days ago, according to this text, had been captured by the enemy, crucified by those persons who were his detractors, buried and the largest stone that they could find had been rolled in front of the cave, and then they put soldiers there to make sure that he never got out. Then you tell me that he's in Galilee! I saw them crucify him. I saw them put him in the grave. I saw them roll the stone there. I saw the soldiers standing guard. Now you tell me he's in Galilee? I'm going; I'm going but . . . I'm going because he said I should go. But, I should tell you, I've got some real questions about this thing. But I'm going. That's the important thing; I'm going. But, I've got some questions.

Now be honest with me this morning, First Baptist, don't you sometimes feel like that? You're called upon to participate, but so much of the evidence is against the enterprise. You go but, you really wonder whether it's worthwhile. The record is so stacked against the possibility of success, that you have a question about the outcome. And you stand before the Eternal, you know God is able; you believe in the depths of your soul that it can be, but, but. But the evidence is so overwhelming that you have to wrestle with the inner conflict because the data is marshaled against the deed. All that is there would suggests otherwise and if one would come to faith, then one must overcome the nevertheless. And the way one comes to faith therefore, is to overcome the nevertheless. That's the real path of faith. The path of faith, the path down which we come to faith is an OVERCOMING and when you overcome something to come to faith, then you can stand there as a disciple sho' nuff. I've overcome to come. If you come just dry long so, as we used to say down in the country, just dry long so, if you come without any kind of opposition, if you come without any incredulous overcoming, then it's almost like getting it with a silver spoon. It's almost getting it on your terms. The phenomenon has not gripped you. The matter of its improbability has not grabbed your life.

But these persons, these disciples, that's what I want to call them, they're on their way to becoming disciples, that's why the theme is so significant for this men's day. For I dare say that probably what keeps most men from becoming ardent and avid disciples of the Divine, is that they've got to overcome the incredulity of it all. They're so rational in their consciousness. They're so precise in the way they think through things. They're so mathematically inclined and intellectually oriented that they are kept from becoming *real* faithful followers. They often dismiss this as women's stuff. I'll go because she wants me to go, but I haven't been gripped by it myself. I don't think there's much to it, but I'll go, because I want to keep peace in the house. That's why this is an excellent theme for men. Most of the brothers say, "I doubt that there's anything that's gonna happen, I really doubt that any benefit is going to be derived, but I'll go."

And that's what happens and here we have the significant fact in this narrative, that the path to discipleship may include doubters. And here, first we're elevenish; we haven't got all we need and now we have doubters and it proceeds to the next step and here is where it gets interesting—he comes, he comes. And Jesus came; here it comes, and Jesus came and Jesus came! The story doesn't get good until he comes. Our little bitty eleven and our doubts, but here it starts to get good and Jesus came.

What does that mean and he came? He had been there all the while. And Jesus came and said to them, that is he showed himself differently now. In this post-resurrection pronouncement, he came and Jesus came. Well, here is the manifestation of the Eternal in a new way and Jesus came and said to them, "All authority in heaven and in earth has been given to me." "All authority in heaven and in earth has been given to me." Here is now a pronouncement of power that they had not heard nor had before. Here is now an utterance of the Eternal that they had not heard before. Here comes now a declaration about the Divine and the possibilities for discipleship that they had not heard before. He came and spoke to them about the nature of authority that he now makes manifest in their midst. And he came and said to them, "All authority in heaven and in earth is given to me."

You brought some authority with you when you came. You brought the authority of your own personhood and your own presence. But I want you to understand that *all* authority, leaving out nothing now, "all authority, in heaven and in earth, is given to me." Suspend your feeble doubts. Overcome that which was somehow inadequate in your midst. The fact that it's just eleven of you or the fact that you brought doubts, forget that. All authority, the inclusiveness of the eternal is now made manifest in your midst. All authority, not some, not a little bit, all authority and when you say all, there's nothing excluded. All authority, any kind of authority you wanna talk about, I've got that now. Any dimension of authority you think about, that's mine. Human authority, divine authority, would-be authority, gonna-be authority, whatever it is, I've got that. All authority, I've got that; everything, everything is now under my control. Everything, your manhood is under my control. You can't do anything unless I say you can do it. I got the authority; it belongs to me, it's in my hand. All authority is given to me!

Now, the pronouncement of the Eternal becomes significant you see; it changes everything. And you know how we tend to do, particularly males, we tend to strut and think we're in charge of something. We tend to walk like we're in charge. All authority, can you imagine what this includes? There is no dimension, a human or divine dimension, that is not included in what he has said. I am in charge. How can he say it? What is it that makes it possible? Because he has defied the most negative aspect of life—death. There is nothing now that can control him. When he got up, when he was raised, he became the one in charge of everything. You and I must ultimately fall down and sleep. We're going the way of all flesh, after a while we will be no more and our place might be marked by those who succeed us. After while, we're going. But there is no going for him now. He has overcome life's most negative expression—death. Death has now been dealt with. The sting of death is gone. The fact of death is dealt with. Death has become subject to life again and he stands there now as a victor over death, a representative of life, and that's why he can say, "all authority." "All authority is given to me"; death can't do you no harm. I've got death; I've dealt with death and I'll deal with life and that's what he's saying now. You can walk with me now.

So, disciples now can walk in him, not in your own strength. And what he is saying is I've got all authority and what he does now is most important. Hear this word: after he says to them, "All authority in heaven and in earth has been given to me," here it is, he says to them, "Go therefore," for disciples are to depart after all is said and done. But how are they to depart? Depart, therefore. They go as a consequence of his having come. That's a therefore going. "Go, therefore." That little word "therefore" is so important, it's so significant, it's so hooked up with the reason we go and the power in which we go. "Go, therefore." That means you go based upon what has happened previously. The previous action determines your going now. You go, therefore. Things have happened, things have been said, now you can go. If you appropriate unto yourself that which has just transpired, you can go. It's the stepping stone for going forward. You stand now and go therefore. That going therefore is the way disciples are to depart. Go therefore and teach. "Go therefore and make disciples of all nations; baptize them in the name of Father and of the Son and of the Holy Spirit, teaching them to observe all things of which I have commanded you and lo I am with you always to the close of the age."

Now, disciples depart on the basis of that which has been provided for them. They depart not in spite of, they depart therefore. We go because he has come before us and he has given us our task, to make disciples, to teach all persons now. Teaching them displays that we have confidence in his accompanying presence. You will go now and tell them what you have learned about me. You will go now and share the witness to my presence and my being. You will go now and become representatives of the Eternal in a special way. You will go now because you've been to Galilee. You will go now and I will be with you, not for a limited period of time, you will go now, and I will be with you, always.

That's significant because just like he had all power, he's now talking about always. Everything is included now in the declaration for discipleship. You will go because I have all power and you will go because I will be with you always. There is no way you can go now once you become a disciple that I'm not with you. There is no place you can go that I will not be, because I'm with you.

All the time and all the way. What more do we need? All the time and all the way. There is nothing else to have. If he's gonna go with us all the time and he's got all the power, what more do we need? What are we waiting for? That's all the all there is. There is no more all. He is all. He is all in all. When you have Him, you have all there is to have. And now you can break out and go all the way all the time because he is with us, all the time and all the way. You can afford to be disciples. Men can go in his name; women can go in his name. The Church can go forth in his name. We can afford to be his disciples because we go with him, and he goes all the way, not half the way. When you're up, he's with you. When you go down, he's with you. Whatever way you go, he's with you and when life comes to its bitter end, he's with you. I am with you always, every way you go. I'm with you every way you don't go; I'm with you. I go before you, I go around you, I go instead of you, I go with you.

He goes with us and I'm glad about that. Because it strengthens us as disciples for the way we have to go. Because, sometimes we go by way of a hospital bed, but, we go anyhow. Sometimes we go after we close a loved one's grave, but we go anyhow; and sometimes we go by way of joy, but we go anyhow. And sometimes bitter disappointment clouds our path, but we go anyhow. And sometimes we get old and tired, but we've got to go anyhow. But remember, he's with you always. I'm glad about that and I encourage you to take this design of discipleship and go with it just as you are. Just as you are with your elevenish self, just as you are with your doubts, he goes with you and so I urge you to go with him. I urge you today, if you're here, this can be your moment, your time, for God is saying just as you are, you can come, just as you are. I end by encouraging you to go and may you learn more about him until at last he says, well done!

### *Note*

*Sermon source:* This sermon was provided by Professor Nathan Dell of the Samuel DeWitt Proctor School of Theology at Virginia Union Seminary. Professor Dell also eulogized Miles Jones.

### *Bibliographical Sources*

Jones, Miles. "A Prince and a Great Man: Eulogy of Miles Jerome Jones." *The African American Pulpit* 8, no. 2 (The Eulogy Issue; Spring 2005): 72–79.

Walker, Wyatt T. *The Preaching Papers: The Hampton and Virginia Union Lectures of Miles Jerome Jones.* New York: Martin Luther King Fellows Press, 1995.

# WILLIAM AUGUSTUS JONES JR.

*(1934–2006)*

William Augustus Jones Jr. was the son and grandson of Baptist ministers and one of six siblings. He was born February 24, 1934, in Louisville, Kentucky, and graduated from the University of Kentucky and Crozier Theological Seminary. Jones earned a doctorate from Colgate Rochester Divinity School, and pursued special studies in West Africa at the University of Lagos, Nigeria, and the University of Ghana.

A dedicated activist, he was for many years a leader in the struggle for human rights and social justice. Jones served as national chairman of the Southern Christian Leadership Conference's Operation Breadbasket, an organization dedicated to improving the economic well-being of the African American community. Jones was president of the Progressive National Baptist Convention. During his tenure he came under fire for not supporting women in ministry, although past presidents of the denomination had already established this precedent. He was the founder of the National Black Pastor's Conference, and he served as a member of the General Council of the Baptist World Alliance. For his religious and civic accomplishments, he received the New York Urban League's Frederick Douglass Award in 1972 and was cited as the Dean of New York's Great Preachers by the New York *Daily News*.

Jones was married to Natalie Barkley Brown Jones, and to this union four children were born: William Augustus III, Elsa, Leslie, and Jennifer. They later divorced.

Jones held honorary doctorates from six universities, including a doctor of humanities from the University of Kentucky in 1993. Jones worked as visiting professor at various seminaries, including Princeton Theological Seminary and Union Theological Seminary. His published writings include *God in the Ghetto* (1979) and *The African-American Church: Past, Present, and Future*. He became pastor of Bethany Baptist Church in New York in 1962, where he remained until 2005 when he retired due to illness. Jones died in February 2006.

• • •

*William Augustus Jones preached Afro-centric, empowerment gospel in a booming baritone, demanding justice for the oppressed and offering hope. The following sermon was one of Jones' most popu-*

*lar, one of several sermons that highlighted different characters in the prodigal son story. This particular version focuses on the forgiveness of the father for the son, and symbolically the forgiveness of God for us. Jones, in the best sense of the word, "argues" with great insight, precision, and spiritual depth the absolute necessity of forgiveness in human life and the awesome mercy and grace of God who makes forgiveness possible. Jones concludes his argument with a whoop. We have tried to capture the orality of the whoop on the written page by extending the vowels and endings where the preacher extends them, such as Yesssssssssssss, or Graaaaaaaace. Jones's booming voice clothed with the inspiration of the Wisdom of the Ages, skilled in the genius of the African American preaching tradition, makes an undeniable clarion call for grace, mercy, and forgiveness in human life. This unique set of preaching gifts and graces made Jones a preacher who influenced several generations.*

## AN ANATOMY OF FORGIVENESS (1986)

> *And he arose, and came to his father. But when he was yet a great way off, his father saw him, and had compassion, and ran, and fell on his neck, and kissed him.* —Luke 15:20 (King James Version)

This fifteenth chapter of the Gospel of Luke is in a real sense the lost and found column of the New Testament. It lifts up for us to clearly see the high level to which human concern is capable of rising when something of great value has managed to get away from us. This lost and found column is a threefold response on the part of the Master to a charge regularly leveled against him by his chief critics. Jesus, the personification of divine love and mercy, was possessed of tremendous pulling power, especially with regard to the struggling masses—those who were up against it, those who belonged to the ranks of the culturally despised. Wherever he went, such crowds collected in mass. And it wouldn't be long before his detractors, his enemies showed up also. They followed him unrelentingly; they hounded him; they pounded him. They sought desperately to discredit him. And the declarations that make up this lost and found column were the verbal responses of Jesus to the murmurings of some scribes and Pharisees who followed him.

One day in a public place in the city of Jerusalem, a great host of publicans and sinners gathered to hear the field preacher from Galilee. It was a mammoth host. Luke, the meticulous physician, describes the setting by saying, "Then drew near unto him all the publicans and sinners for to hear him."[1] All the publicans and sinners. All the hated tax collectors and all the social and religious castaways. And somewhere on the edges, somewhat away from Jesus, but within hearing distance, there stood some scribes and Pharisees who were present not to profit but to protest. Their complaint, their charge was plain and pointed. This man receiveth sinners and eateth with them. He is devoid of moral purity. He is without ethical sanctity. He fellowships with the wrong people. And in response to their self-righteous remarks, Jesus established this lost and found column. He put before them three parables to demonstrate God's love and his mercy. He gave to them three shining examples of the meaning of recovery and restoration. He outlines for all people, for all times, an anatomy of forgiveness.

And I want us to see today the anatomy for purposes of analysis. There were three entries in the Master's lost and found column—a sheep that was lost and then found, a coin that was lost and then found, and a son who was lost and then found. One animate object that was not human, one inanimate object, and one animate object that was thoroughly human. It is the latter that I want us to focus upon. I want us to see this son. See him in his self-centeredness, see him in his self-assertiveness, see his self-destruction. See him in his self-discovery and see him in his self-fulfillment. The kind of fulfillment that comes only by the restitution of right relationship.

Now across the years of my preaching pilgrimage, I've preached several different and hopefully altogether distinct sermons on this boy, this prodigal, this profligate, this unthinking, ungrateful philanderer. That's the kind of bad light I've sometimes put him in. And then on other occasions, when my own heart was a little softer, I've found it easy to sympathize with his wanderlust spirit. Perhaps home wasn't right. We know that the sibling relationship was terribly strained. At times I've dwelt on the young man's humble journey back to his father's house.

But today, I want to focus our attention on forgiveness. That which took place when youthful rebellion and licentious living and the long walk home were all behind him, when he stood in his father's presence, in his father's house. Man to man, head to head, heart to heart, eye to eye. I believe that the behavior of father and son alike accord us, to some helpful degree, an anatomy of forgiveness.

See again the scenario. Listen if you will to the beat of the music. It moves to the cadence of two heartbeats. Feel the good vibrations that make reunion full and festive. Listen if you will. And when he came to himself he said, "How many hired servants of my father have bread enough and to spare and I perish with hunger? I know what I'll do. I will arise and go to my father. And when I get there I will say to him, 'Father, I have sinned against heaven and before thee and am no more worthy to be called thy son. Make me as one of thy hired servants.' "[2] And he arose and came to his father. But, when he was yet a great way off, his father saw him and had compassion and ran and fell on his neck and kissed him. And the son said, "Father, I have sinned against heaven and in thy sight and am no more worthy to be called thy son." But the father said to his servants, "Bring forth the best robe and put it on him and put a ring on his hand and shoes on his feet. And bring hither the fatted calf and let us eat and make merry. For this my son was dead and is alive again. He was lost and is found," and they began to celebrate![3]

Now it is the father's house and the father's honor that were offended by the son. But something far deeper was torn and shattered and wounded, almost mortally so. Not just house and honor, but also heart. The father's heart had borne for a long time the terrible pain of precipitous parting. The agony of not knowing and the thought of what at times appeared to be utterly hopeless. You know nothing can break the heart like unresponsive and unrequited love. Have you ever been in love? I hope you have. Love will break your heart. Parting has been labeled "such sweet sorrow." And the label is a pretty good one. But there are times when it is simply sorrow. Sorrow with no trace of sweetness at all. The sweetness is obviated or obscured by the sorrow. It happens when trust is betrayed. It happens when a child goes astray. When a parent sees a son or a daughter take leave and move headlong in the direction of the lost column. How many times have I heard the plea, "Preacher, please pray for my boy." Or, "Preacher, when you talk to God, please remember my daughter." It's no easy thing to stand almost paralyzed and watch your child rush toward the low road. Something on the inside starts talking. Something way down deep says, "That's me out there; my genes and my chromosomes are out yonder. Bone of my bone, flesh of my flesh, blood of my blood. That's me out yonder! I can't be passive and unconcerned about me. In spite of my child's independence, there is a lot of me in my child. In a real sense, he is me and I can't ignore the me that is he. I have to acknowledge the me in what's mine. I can't forsake or give up on anybody who looks like me, and walks like me, and talks like me and acts like me. To fail to forgive him is to fail me. For that's me out there. Wherever he is, there's some me there."

Now of course that's really what salvation and incarnation are all about. God made us in his image, and our sin not withstanding, God had to come to seek and to save that which was lost. God said in effect, there's too much of me in man for me to abandon man. I can't forsake the me in man, therefore I'm sending me, the second part of myself to rescue and deliver and restore the me in man.

Ours is a time of widespread abandonment. A lot of children all over this land and beyond, I've seen them on Forty-second Street, I've seen them on Dam Square in Amsterdam. I've seen them all over this world, a lot of children have been physically, psychologically, and spiritually abandoned. There are lost sons and daughters all over the land. And many parents have said to their children, "I'm through with you. I give up as far as you're concerned. Later for you." Well, anybody who talks like that has really given up on self. Y'all better hear me today. I'm blessed with four children, and if I'm through with any of them, I'm through with me. For I've denied self. I've died without dying. I can't do that to me. I think too much of me. God's done too much with me and for me and in spite of me, for me to be through with the me in each of the offspring he's given me!

And there's something about this me connection that has magnetic pull. When the son started for home, home was already out there looking for the son. That's magnetism, love's magnetism at work. That's what I call the "magnetic me" in operation. Listen to Jesus again. "And he arose and came to his father, but when was yet a great way off his father saw him and had compassion and ran and fell on his neck and kissed him."[4]

That's really what the world needs—an awareness of the magnetic me. If we could recognize it in ourselves and our children, perhaps we could see it in blacks and whites, in Arabs and Jews, and in all of God's children and as a consequence beat our swords into plowshares, our spears into pruning hooks, and study war no more. It is the magnetic me that makes forgiveness possible. The son came to himself. He saw the father in himself. "I will arise and go to my father." The father saw himself in his son. "When he was yet a great way off his father saw him and had compassion and ran to him."[5]

Now if you will, permit me to deal with a certain myth in this anatomy of forgiveness. All of your life you've heard people say, "Let's forgive and forget." You've also heard people say, "I forgive, but I'll never forget." And for some reason the idea has been promoted that forgiveness is not finished or completed until the forgiver forgets. Well, I tell you without any fear of successful contradiction that that's wrong. That's pure myth. That's bunk. That's poppycock. That's hogwash. Let such error be permanently eliminated from your thinking. To forgive is not to forget. I repeat, to forgive is not to forget. I reiterate, to forgive is not to forget! I'd better say it again. To forgive is not to forget, and I'll tell you why. You have to remember in order to know that you have forgiven. If you don't remember what you've forgiven, then you don't know that you've forgiven. You don't forget it, you drop it!

There's a Methodist preacher, a friend of mine, Robert Klink in Philadelphia, who has rightly remarked, "Forgiveness means that you don't owe anything anymore." The father forgave. He didn't forget. "My son was dead." That's remembrance. "Is alive again," that's forgiveness. "Was lost," that's remembrance. "Is found," that's forgiveness! You don't forget it, you drop it. "Forgiveness means that you don't owe anything anymore." That boy felt that he owed so much to his daddy for the error of his ways, he not only felt that he owed him an apology, he felt that he owed him some service as a hired servant.

Come on back to the pigpen. Look at this boy as he rises from alllllll of the dirt and grime of the pigpen predicament. When he came to himself, he composed a little speech. A speech to be delivered as soon as he gets home. I will arise and go to my father and when I get there, I will say to him, "Father, I have sinned against heaven and before thee and am no more worthy to be called thy son. Make me as one of thy hired servants."[6]

That was his prepared speech and I am confident that he rehearsed it all the way home. I can see him moving up the dusty trail and as he goes along, he keeps reciting this speech. "Father, I have sinned against heaven and before thee and am no more worthy to be called thy son. Make me as one of thy hired servants." All the way home he keeps rehearsing it. And then that encounter of the best kind. When he got home he started his speech, "Father, I have sinned against heaven and before thee and am no more worthy to be called thy son."[7] He didn't get a chance to deliver the complete speech. He didn't get a chance to deliver the hired servant section of the speech—"Father, I have sinned against heaven and before thee and am no more worthy to be called thy son . . ."

But then the father broke in! The father interrupted. The father said by implication, son you don't owe anything anymore! I don't need more servants; I need a son. I have no servant shortage, I'm short on sons. Son, you don't owe anything anymore. My what renewal and what a reunion, runnin', huggin', kissing, full forgiveness. Absolute acceptance, a royal reception! Come here servants. Come quickly; bring forth the best robe and put it on him. Servants put a ringgggggg on his finger. Servants, put shoes on his feet. You servants over there, go out there to the barnyard and kill the fatted calf, let us eat and be merry. It's celebration time. It's time to have a good time. "For this my son was dead and is now alive. He was lost and is now found!"[8]

And says Jesus, "That's the way God does it." Love spells mercy, and mercy spells forgiveness. Grace is God's unmerited favor extended to us in spite of our utter unworthiness. And you know that grace and mercy came via Jesus Christ. At Calvary, mercy was great and so grace was freed. And ever since Calvary the word's been out—if we confess our sins, he is faithful and just to forgive us our sins and cleanse us of all unrighteousness. Thank God for his grace. Thank him for his mercy. Thank him for forgiveness full and free. I have to thank him, for you see I found it when I needed it. In fact I still need it and you need it too. So,

*Come ye disconsolate, wherever ye languish.*
*Come to the mercy seat, fervently kneel.*
*Here bring your wounded hearts, here tell your anguish*
*for earth hath no sorrow that heaven cannot heal.*

*Joy of the desolate, light of the straying,*
*hope of the penitent, fadeless and pure.*
*Here speaks the Comforter tenderly saying,*
*"Earth hath no sorrow that heaven cannot cure."*[9]

I have to thank him, because you see I'm a member of the forgiven crowd. You see, I've fallen short. I've missed the mark. I've failed my father. I've mistreated his mercy. But I heard him say, "I forgive you." Yesssssss. "I came to Jesus just as I was, weary, worn, and sad. I found in him a resting place, and he has made me glad."[10] I don't owe anything anymore. The debt's been paid. Jesus paid it. He paid it all. All my sins have been washed in the blood of the lamb. I'm all right now. I stand confident in him. Somebody here ought to know what I'm talkin' about. He will fix you. Fix you for living. Fix you for dyin'. Yessssssss Lord. Hallelujah. Hallelujah.

Whatever you do, don't you give up on anybody. God can lift anybody, anytime, from any place. Yessssssssss. Yes. Old folk down in my native Kentucky used to put it this way, "He can lift you from a dead level to a living perpendicular." God can fix you up and straighten you out and make you look better than you ever looked before. He can make ugly folks pretty. He can make crooked folk straight. Do I have a witness, yessssssss. Yesssssss.

And when he was a great way off, his father saw him and ran and fell on his neck and kissed him and declared this my son wassssss dead, but is now alive. Waaaaaaaas lost, but is now found. He moved from was to is, and God can work with what was and bring you into a state of "isness." That abrogates, that cancels, that wipes out everything in your "wasness." Yesssssssss.

It is the miracle of grace, wonderful grace, amazing grace, yesssssssss, that makes you declare, "I looked at my hands and my hands looked new.

I looked at my feet and they did too." Graaaaaace. You don't know what I'm talkin' bout. Graaaaaaace, graaaaaaace. Mercy finds me, but grace restores me. Mercy locates me, but grace takes me home. Graaaaaaace. Was lost, but is found!

### *Notes*

*Sermon source: The African American Pulpit* 5, no. 1 (Winter 2001–2002), 82–87.

1. See Luke 15:1.
2. Luke 15:17–19 (King James Version).
3. Luke 15:22–24 (KJV).
4. Luke 15:20 (KJV).
5. Ibid.
6. Luke 15:19 (KJV).
7. Luke 15:21 (KJV).
8. See Luke 15:24.
9. "Come Ye Disconsolate," *The National Baptist Standard Hymnal* (Nashville, TN: Sunday School Publishing Board, National Baptist Convention, U.S.A., Inc., 1924), number 196.
10. "He Took My Sins Away," by Mrs. M.J. Harris; lyrics available at http://jemaf.free.fr/carmen-surrender.pdf (accessed June 28, 2007).

### *Bibliographical Sources*

Bailey, E.K., and Warren Wiersbe. *Preaching in Black & White: What We Can Learn from Each Other.* Grand Rapids, MI: Zondervan, 2003.

"Dr. William Augustus Jones, Jr." 2003 Pace Warren Lectures. Available at http://www.2preslex.org/PACE03.HTM (accessed July 21, 2005).

# VASHTI MURPHY McKENZIE

*(1947– )*

Vashti Murphy McKenzie shattered the "stained glass ceiling" in 2000 when she was consecrated the first female bishop in the more than two-hundred-year history of the African Methodist Episcopal (AME) Church. She was born May 28, 1947, into the Murphy clan, a prominent family with a history in publishing, politics, and black social advancement. Her great-grandfather John H. Murphy started the *Afro-American Newspaper* in 1892; her grandfather Carl H. Murphy succeeded his father as publisher and editor, and her grandmother Vashti Turly Murphy was a founding member of Delta Sigma Theta, a Christian African American college sorority that currently has a national membership of more than a quarter million. She attended the University of Maryland and after a brief career in journalism, earned a master's of divinity from Howard University in Washington, D.C., and a doctor of ministry from United Theological Seminary in Dayton, Ohio. McKenzie was assigned a small congregation in Chesapeake City, but it was her 1990 call to Payne Memorial AME's pulpit that triggered her meteoric rise to bishop.

Under McKenzie's leadership, the Payne congregation transformed Baltimore's inner city through a variety of community empowerment projects: job service programs, a summer school program, a food pantry, and a senior care center. As bishop, her community-focused spirituality again came to light. During a tour of duty in southern Africa, she helped start parental-support systems for AIDS orphans and numerous educational projects. McKenzie is currently presiding prelate of the Thirteenth Episcopal District and president of the AME's Council of Bishops. She is author of *Not Without a Struggle* (1996), *Strength in the Struggle* (1998), and *Journey to the Well* (2002). In 1997, she was named one of *Ebony* magazine's fifteen greatest African American female preachers. She is married to Stan McKenzie, and they have three children: Jon-Mikael, Vashti-Jasmine, and Joi-Marie.

• • •

*Based upon her preaching gifts and abilities and her major role as the first female bishop in the AME Church, Vashti M. McKenzie is one of the most sought-after and recognized preachers in America. McKenzie matches mother wit with folk religion and a high level of passion to deliver a relevant preaching word to the masses. The following sermon was preached at the first Samuel DeWitt Proctor Pastors Conference in Atlanta, Georgia, in February 2004. It is intended for preachers, addressing some of the pressures they face and what they must do to faithfully meet the challenges of ministry in the twenty-first century.*

## Keep the Pressure On
## (February 2004)

*And so, John came baptizing in the desert region and preaching a baptism of repentance for the forgiveness of sin. The whole Judean countryside and all of the people of Jerusalem went out to hear him. Confessing their sins they were baptized by him in the Jordan River.*

> *John wore clothing made of camel hair with a leather belt around his waist. He ate locust and wild honey and this was his message: "After me will come one more powerful than I, the thongs of whose sandals I am not worthy to stoop down and untie. I baptize you with water, but he will baptize you with the Holy Spirit."*
>
> —Mark 1:4–8 (New International Version)

One of the culinary memories of my childhood is waiting for the delicacies that would come out of my mama's pressure cooker on the stove. It could be anything from pot roast to pig feet, chili or neck bones. And so, I waited with tiptoe anticipation—waiting in the doorway of the kitchen because I had learned listening to the tales of the elder women in my family that it could be dangerous for children who stood too close to a pressure cooker on the stove.

The pressure cooker was a unique utensil in my mama's arsenal of pots and pans. It allowed its contents to cook quickly with an intense high temperature that produced steam in such a volume that it placed pressure upon its contents.

You see pressure, beloved, is caused when weight above or around an object exerts a force and that force can be called pressure. There are gaskets in the pressure cooker—these are rubber seals around the edge of the pot that seal the force inside. And there's a tube that's in the middle of the pot—a steam vent—that allows just the right amount of steam to escape because there is a small weight in a gauge on top of the steam vent that jiggles and does a happy dance to allow the steam to escape.

Now, this pressure cooker is also a dangerous utensil because if the pressure gauge is not set properly, the pot could explode, the contents exploding all over the kitchen, potentially causing bodily harm and certainly a waste of food. If the elements are not properly balanced, then the food, the pot, and the kitchen could be destroyed. Thus, one wisely stands in the door of the kitchen waiting for the food to be done. But, when the gauge is balanced, then the pressure is controlled, and the food cooks quickly.

Beloved, so it is with the pressure of our profession. Outside of this room there are those who believe what we do is a walk in the park. Outside of this room they think what we do is an easy thing; that our workweek is nothing but prayer and playing around. Out of this room, they believe that we just study and sit around waiting for the next service to start. Outside of this room, they are oblivious to what we do and what we have to go through to get it done. They think that we are just pampered pontificators on pedestals who are waiting to be served rather than serving.

Beloved, they are oblivious to all of us living in a pressure cooker in the kingdom. Pressure is the weight of something that bears down. Remember the definition—upon something, around something that exerts a force—that is called pressure. And so, when God's will bears down on your will, that's pressure. When your way of life fails to intersect with God's Word—that's pressure. When the ministry to the flock conflicts with the ministry to the family—that's pressure. When decisions are made in fear rather than faith—that's pressure. When what you pray for is not what you get, it asserts pressure. When you carry the cross, but want to hold the crown—it's pressure. When the blessings of the call meet the burden of preparation for the call—that's pressure. When the expectations of others combined with your own personal expectations and what you believe God expects of you, that's pressure.

What pressure? There is the pressure of perfection. We must live perfect lives, have perfect families, live in perfect houses, have perfect wardrobes, with perfect appointment books and perfect lifestyles. We must be God's Exhibit A—God's role model—preacher, pastor and servant.

If it's not the pressure of perfection, it is the pressure of originality. Everyone who sits under your preaching and teaching expects it to be brand new even though we're working from the same reference book, the same material. Yet, you must be an original every time no matter how many commentaries you need to read.

There is the pressure of relevance—taking what was written to ancient people in an agricultural age and retooling it for the twenty-first century; coding it in a relevant delivery system so that it is received without sacrificing truth.

What pressure? The pressure of performance—we are in a let-me-entertain-you age where church can't happen without staging and video screens and sound bites. Let's push the altar aside, remove the cross. It is a let-me-entertain-you time. No! You can't stand behind the pulpit anymore, you've got to come out. You've got to jump a bit. You've got to dance a bit. You've got to prance a bit. It's the pressure of performance. What I like about this conference is the diversity of style. Each one came with their own gifts not being pressured to go outside of their way and perform in another style.

What pressure? Then there is the privacy. You have none. And the pressure of our humanity—we are under pressure of the same social conditions, the same temptations. We are as vulnerable as the ones we preach to. And then there's the pressure between your house and the house of God. I've got pressure. You've got pressure. All God's children got pressure.

We need someone to help us with this issue of pressure. And so, the lot falls to John the Baptist who seems to be one who has handled the pressure of the perfection before the pressure handled him and then he kept the pressure on in his community. What kind of pressure did John have? Well, he was perhaps under pressure to be just like everybody else. Can you imagine life for this young man? Oh, he couldn't play ball like all the rest of the young men; could not hang out at the mall; couldn't sneak a cigarette outside of school buildings; couldn't dance the night away at the club for he was an ordained Nazarite. And can you imagine him not being under pressure?

John is a good example because he was pressured to produce with few resources. Look at the text. It says that he was assigned to the wilderness AME-Baptist-Pentecostal-Apostolic-Presbyterian-Church of Christ of the Church of God in Christ. He was assigned to the west side of the Dead Sea in a wild, wilderness area where very few people lived. And so he was assigned to do the work of the Lord where there were very few people.

And then there was the pressure of potential. John had a special birth announced and foretold by an angel to a womb believed barren. And the potential was great. There was the expectation that this son—the only son in this priesthood family—was going to be somebody. Pressure to do something; to make his mark and impact upon religious life and impact upon the community. For it had been a long time before there was an authentic word from the Lord. And, yet, Mark says there was crying in the wilderness.

Now, this is a homily and not a sermon and so therefore it means I have no time to exegete the text. (Laughter.) And so since there is not time to exegete the text, I say that just so that you'll know that I understand that you ought to exegete the text when you stand and say something for the Lord. And so, I won't tell you that Mark abruptly began his gathering of sayings of the story of Christ with a proclamation of the divinity of Jesus being the Son of God. I won't tell you that Mark seemed not to spend a lot of time with the Old Testament prophecies and yet in some instances explained Jewish customs and words, perhaps because his audience was Gentile. Since I don't have time to exegete the text, I won't tell you that Mark's gospel was peppered with words like *immediately* and *quickly* because he seemed to be pressing forward, concentrating on the Galilean ministry and the passion narrative. If I had time I would tell you that Mark introduced his subject by spending a moment on the forerunner of the Christ—that is John the Baptist.

And so this prophet who was under pressure kept pressure on in his community. He, in this esthetic lifestyle and who ate honey and locust kept the pressure on. John did not do power lunches and pass the salad and fried chicken and greens and sweet potatoes. This one was a little weird and different than all the others. You may call him a geek and his résumé was not encouraging. For some scholars say that John had a no-nonsense approach to his call. In other words he needed to work on his people skills. He was not affected by title or heritage. But in spite of the negatives that could be launched on John's side, in the fifth verse it says, "All of Jerusalem came out to John and he heard their confession and they repented and were baptized." "All of the people came out to Jerusalem." That makes a good text, illustrating that when people's needs are met, they will go where their needs are met. And so although John didn't look like the rest of the boys, and he had a church on the other side of town, and he did not participate in the ministerial alliance, and he was subject to all of the pressures of the profession, John was still able to apply the pressure on those who were around him.

So then how did John do it? This is how he did it, and this is where you write it down. John was focused. When we leave here, we have to work on our focused agenda. All John did—his diet, his demands, his actions—was all centered upon his purpose and mission. He was not sidetracked. He was not distracted. He preached an unbroken record, "Repent and be baptized and the Messiah is coming."

I had a seminary professor who said we preach one sermon all of our lives. It matters not the text; it matters not the exegesis; but we're all simply preaching the same sermon again and again and again. John was able to apply pressure in his community because everything he did was focused to accomplish the mission and goal. He didn't water it down. It was a tough call. It was a tough message. John remained strong and the testimony is—the people followed and came to the west side of the Dead Sea.

But, more than that he was more concerned about being heard than he was about anything else. So, when we leave here we don't have to be weird to be holy. We just have to be focused on living right. When we leave here, speak the truth in love. Act like a neighbor. Do your work; get your job done; pay your bills; be faithful to the spouse you have; take care of your responsibility. If you mess up, then clean up. If you make a mistake, then say you're sorry. Do your part. Carry your weight. Shoulder your load. Speak words that are of God. And, as Paul wrote to the church of Thessalonica; take care of your own business. Do your own work and watch . . . the people will go great distances to hear.

How was he able to survive the pressures of the profession and yet maintain pressure on the community? He didn't become a part of the crowd to get a crowd to change the crowd. John didn't lower his standards at all. He wasn't trying to fit in to get in; to go along to get along. He didn't become a part of the world, but he wanted to have an impact on it. He wasn't trying to be a chameleon changing color on a whim and each changing fad. But John maintained his standards and love of an awesome God.

People may not love you because you maintain high standards; you may not win a lot of friends because you stand on the high standards of God; but, baby, they may not love you, but they will respect you for where you stand. John is our example who survived the pressure of his profession and applied pressure in his community because he wasn't afraid to stand alone. There was one voice crying in the wilderness. There was no other support. You may be the only watchman in the tower. You may be the only one on the wall. You may be the only voice crying in the wilderness but you've got to keep your C-Count [courage count] up. Be brave and bold and speak up for God. Otherwise the pressure of politics will overwhelm you. You'll spend more time wondering, "What should I say? Should I say it now? Who do I need to be friends with? Who do I need to stand with? They're in trouble. I've got to get away from them. They're rising up. I've got to stay with them. When do I announce which presidential candidate I'm supporting? Do I wade in now or do I wade in later?" No, John didn't go through all of those things. He was willing to stand alone. For if you stand alone, God will never leave you nor forsake you.

Lastly, look at the example John set as he navigated the pressures of the profession, and kept the pressure on his community, practiced what he preached, and matched what he said with what he did. If John had preached repentance and lived immorally; if John had called for holiness and had a dishonest reputation; if his word had not matched his life; everybody would have stayed home and no one would have come to the west side of the Dead Sea. The people are more interested sometimes in what we do rather than what we say. They are watching us every day—examining us closely in our personal life and in our congregational life. They want to know how you are applying scripture to your personal life.

And the text said when he did all of that, the people came flocking out of Jerusalem, and it remains the same for us as we prepare to leave this place. Pressure can wear you out. Pressure can make your heart feeble. Pressure can make you restless in spirit. Pressure can drain your resources. Pressure can bankrupt you spiritually. Pressure can break the best of us, and depress the rest of us. But John understood the right balance of pressure. He was focused on what God had called him to do. He wasn't focused on anybody else's ministry except for what God had called him to do. He didn't become a part of the crowd to get a crowd or to change a crowd. He wasn't afraid to stand alone. He understood his relationship with Christ. He wasn't the Christ but the forerunner. He was to handle water and Jesus was to handle fire, and he practiced what he preached.

And so now as we go out into the wilderness to do the work that God has for us to do, we cannot fall under pressure of our profession, but like John we must keep up the pressure in our community. We must keep the pressure on. We must keep the pressure on a nation that can find billions of dollars to rebuild Afghanistan and Iraq, but cannot find enough money to rebuild our educational institutions. We have got to keep the pressure on when millions are trying to live without health care and the prescriptions cost more than the Social Security. We have got to keep the pressure on when we live in a country where a war hero like Shoshana Johnson has to fight for 30 percent disability when they give Jessica Lynch 80 percent disability.[2] We have to keep the pressure on when we live in a place where a white detective can conduct an undercover sting operation in Texas and the only folk who are arrested are black, married to blacks, dating black, or black high school athletic stars. We have got to remain focused, not to attempt to become a part of the crowd, not to be afraid to stand alone, and, what we preach we've got to live.

The pressure of our profession—we must make sure that it doesn't handle us; that we handle it. And at the same time keep the pressure on where we live.

## *Notes*

*Sermon source: The African American Pulpit* 7, no. 4 (Fall 2004), 62–67.

1. Shoshana Johnson (an African American) and Jessica Lynch (a Caucasian) were both soldiers in the Iraq War and were part of a group of American soldiers who were ambushed in March 2003. Johnson and Lynch were both injured and then rescued. Lynch received a book deal, a movie deal, and a larger disability pension than Johnson.

## *Bibliographical Sources*

"Bishop Vashti Murphy McKenzie Invested as First Female President of the AME's Bishop's Council." *Tennessee Tribune*, December 9, 2004.

Christian Century Foundation. "African Methodist Episcopal Church Elects Vashti McKenzie Bishop." *Christian Century*, July 19, 2000.

McDowell, Wendy. "Bishop in a Pick-up Truck: First Woman AME Bishop Describes Her Work in Africa." *Harvard Gazette*, October 16, 2003.

McGill, Jennifer. "Reverend Dr. Vashti Murphy McKenzie: First Woman Bishop in the AME Church." *ChickenBones: A Journal for Literary & Artistic*

*African-American Themes*. http://www.nathanielturner.com/vashtimckenzie.htm (accessed on May 2, 2005).

Saunders, Shellie M. "Vashti M. McKenzie." in *Contemporary Black Biography*, vol. 29. Detroit: Gale Group, 1992.

## ELLA MURIEL PEARSON MITCHELL

*(1917–2008)*

Ella Muriel Pearson Mitchell, whose name was usually linked with that of her husband Henry H. Mitchell (married in 1944) because of their teamwork in classrooms and pulpits, was born in Charleston, South Carolina, in 1917, the daughter of a Presbyterian minister and his wife. She was graduated from Avery Institute, Talladega College in 1939; Union Theological Seminary in New York, Columbia University in 1943, and furthered her studies at Fresno State, UCLA, and the University of Massachusetts, before completing a doctorate at the School of Theology at Claremont in California in 1974. In addition to serving churches in New York City and Los Angeles as minister of church education, her career involved service as a public school teacher in Fresno and Claremont, California; teacher for the Oakland-Berkeley Council of Churches in their Released Time Program; Berkeley Baptist Divinity School (now named American Baptist Seminary of the West); Compton College; Claremont School of Theology; and, after her ordination to ministry in 1978, as associate professor of Christian education and director of continuing education at the Proctor School of Theology of Virginia Union University in Richmond (1982–1986).

Her background experience and pulpit prowess were honored in 1986 when she was appointed dean of Sisters Chapel at Spelman College in Atlanta, Georgia. Shortly afterward, she and her husband Henry began team-teaching homiletics as visiting professors at the Interdenominational Theological Center in Atlanta, and later, both taught in the doctor of ministry program at United Theological Seminary, in Dayton, Ohio.

Ella Mitchell has been credited with helping many African American women find their voices, frame their thoughts, focus their messages, and convincingly speak their words in a profession historically dominated by men. In 1997 *Ebony* magazine listed her as one of the top fifteen black women preachers in America.

She edited all four volumes of *Those Preachin' Women*, and also edited

*Women: To Preach, or Not to Preach*; *Twenty-One Outstanding Black Preachers Say Yes!* Published works with her husband, Henry Mitchell, include *Together For Good: Lessons from Fifty-five Years of Marriage.* Ella Mitchell died in 2008.

• • •

*As an ordained minister for twenty-nine years and as a preacher for more than forty, Ella Mitchell brought an unparalleled depth of life experience and creativity to the pulpit. The chief characteristic of her preaching is her imagination and her ability to fluctuate her voice to varying levels to indicate mood and nuance buried deep within the text. In this sermon Mitchell shrewdly argues in a conversation with God for the right to preach for women, those without formal theological training, those born under difficult circumstances, and all flesh as God decides.*

## All Flesh is Eligible!<br>(January 1999)

> *And it shall come to pass afterward, that I will pour out my Spirit on all flesh, and your sons and your daughters shall prophecy.*
>
> —Joel 2:28 (King James Version)

As a woman, I have greatly enjoyed the prophet Joel's famous words about God pouring out the Spirit on *all* flesh. Recently, however, I have sensed a scope of meaning here that is startling to say the least. So I entered into a kind of prayerful meditation/conversation with God about this "all flesh." I invite you to turn up your spiritual imagination and listen in on the flow, as it were:

> Ella: O gracious, almighty Creator, I am humbly seeking to know what you meant when you told Brother Joel that you would pour out your blessed, powerful Holy Spirit on *all* flesh. That was a broad and sweeping promise. Please pardon me for being so presumptuous as to ask.

The Lord made it plain that questions are always welcome and in order. Indeed, we should never be so fearful or presumptuous as to wonder if our questions ever threaten God. Questions are a way of loving our Lord with our minds, as well as our hearts. Then came an answer that stretched my mind.

GOD: Now, dear Ella, that "*all* flesh" is the hope of *all* the people of the world, though first delivered, of course, to Israel. It goes far beyond the "daughters" that I c*all* to prophecy. That word *all* includes everybody you can think of in every possible human category: genders and social classes that Joel mentioned. I mean levels of education, and even ethnic groupings and *all* religious affiliations.

ELLA: It sounded impressive but I still wondered. Surely not "*all*," when you consider *all* the people we would norm*all*y exclude from the prophesying role—the pulpit. So I just asked God point blank, "Will you actu*all*y pour out your Spirit without regard to formal training—folk whose backgrounds are very limited? I ask this especi*all*y since there are so many printed Bibles and other resources. No excuse for ignorance."

GOD: My beloved Ella, I delight in the way my Word is circulated in print. But have you ever considered the fact that the disciples who launched the worldwide church were likely *all* nonreaders, except for Matthew the tax collector? Are you aware that, as recently as the 1700s and early 1800s, these United States were amazingly revived in two Great Awakenings, most of whose preachers did not have nearly the level of the training you have? If the western U.S.A. had had to wait for everybody to go to college and seminary, it might *never* have been won to Christ.

Listen carefully as I list some of the people on whom I poured out my Spirit. Remember that famous overseer, Francis Asbury, whom Wesley sent over, and who was later consecrated bishop? He came origin*all*y as a layman! And don't you know that I poured out my Spirit on his coachman, known as Black Harry, said to be the better preacher of the two. Since neither was trained as a preacher, did you ever wonder why Harry was the better preacher?

ELLA: I didn't have a clue. "No, Lord. I never re*all*y dug into that."

GOD: Well, you see, I pour out my spirit on *all* flesh, and both Asbury and Black Harry received it. But Black Harry had cultural gifts that Asbury didn't have. Asbury no doubt had gifts in administration from England, and the Spirit used those. But Harry had storytelling gifts from Africa, and with those you can make the Bible re*all*y come alive. The Spirit needs educational and cultural equipment to kindle the flame.

ELLA: Are you suggesting that you give *no* particular recognition to the fact that some preachers go to the very best of schools? Like Yale and Princeton, Howard and Virginia Union and ITC?

GOD: No, dear, but remember that I pour out my Spirit on *all* flesh. Schools do not make good preachers, automatic*ally*. It's like it is with a piano. It does not matter how much training and practice the preacher has if the cultural system of communication is poor. But when a well-trained preacher with cultural gifts is used by the Spirit, I have the best of both worlds with which to communicate.

Look at Priscilla. She studied theology by oral tradition, with no books or scrolls whatever. She learned while she and her husband mended tents with the apostle Paul. When the fledgling Apollos came up short on theology, she was used by My Spirit to correct his deficiencies. Then Apollos could re*all*y preach.

And no preacher dare ask Me to reveal things to him or her that are easily available at the seminary. *All* flesh is given the gift of my Spirit only *after* they have done their best with what is already available. For young men and women today, that means striving step by step until they have at least finished basic theological training.

ELLA: Thank you, Lord for clearing that up. Please tell me about family backgrounds. It is a brutal fact that "*all* flesh" does not have "proper" parentage. Lord, we have a lot of broken homes, single-parent families, and teenage mothers with no marriage even considered. The children from these homes cause a lot of problems. How could offspring from such dysfunctional families be capable of being re*all*y used by an outpouring of your Spirit?

I knew that the wisdom of God is true and righteous altogether, but I was utterly amazed at how God's Spirit is distributed.

GOD: (a new variety of voice came forth, a tiny bit harsh) Did it ever dawn on you that My own Son's earthly family tree included a number of women with less than supposedly "proper" histories? The first few verses of Matthew reveal Rahab, an ex-street-person, as David's great-grandma. That didn't stop David from receiving the anointing. And *all* through the intervening years I have poured out my Spirit on saints, many of whom had an unfortunate family background. In your day and age, you may happen to find a number of preacher friends who have come out of one-parent homes. But did you notice these preachers are at the *top* of the list, not the bottom?"

ELLA: It was true. One night my husband did a lecture-sermon, preceding the main revival sermon. He talked about manger babies, and Jesus' family tree. The main revival preacher rose to preach and said, "I'm one of those babies who never knew a father." This giant of a preacher had been born of an unwed mother, in an unheard of village, but God had poured out more of the Spirit on him than almost anybody. The same was true of other preachers. No matter who your parents were or were not, *all* are eligible to have the Spirit poured out on them. It's been decreed from God Almighty!

But I had one more wonderment about those on whom God pours out the Spirit. I said, "Lord, what about the wannabe preacher-prophets whose morality is open to serious question? What about the host of preacher-men who, as they say, harass women? Lord, they are not included in the *all* flesh, or are they?"

God's answer this time was re*all*y shocking.

GOD: "You know very well that I pour out my Spirit, at times, on those whom you *call* grand rascals. You've seen it countless times, but Ella, you keep forgetting that I said *all* flesh is eligible. If I were to wait to pour out my Spirit on perfect people only, I'd never give away a drop. I know you rightly assume that you yourself don't go to the extremes to which some may go, but could I give any of the Spirit to you, if I demanded perfect purity?

ELLA: I was wiped out. I wanted to cry, or hang up the phone, or do something. But my *all*-knowing Maker and Creator and Redeemer read my mind and saw one last question, even though I was scared to ask it out loud: "Lord, don't you even care about those grand rascals who are so popular on TV?"

GOD: Be not deceived, my child. I am not mocked. Those grand rascals reap what they sow, and don't you ever forget it. But *all* flesh is still eligible, and I reserve the right to pour out my spirit on *all* grades of sinners.

ELLA: The more I think about it, the more I realize that the eligibility of *all* flesh has been in effect ever since the f*all* of humanity in the Garden of Eden. Scan three of the greatest biblical characters: Moses, David, and Paul. God's Spirit was poured out in abundance on *all* three, and yet *all* of them could be convicted of first degree murder, directly or by conspiracy. All of us are sinners. But *all* of them and us are still in that sweeping category c*all*ed *all* flesh. And *all* flesh is eligible!

*Lord, I hear of showers of blessing;*
*Thou art scattering full and free;*

*Showers the thirsty soul refreshing;*
*Let some drops now fall on me.*
*Even me, Lord, even me!*
*Let some drops now;*
*Fall on me.*[1]

### Notes

*Sermon source: 30 Good Minutes*, Chicago Sunday Evening Club, January 17, 1999, Program #4215, available at http://www.csec.org/csec/sermon/mitchell_4215.htm (accessed June 27, 2007).

1. "Even Me," arr. Roberta Martin, *New National Baptist Hymnal* (Nashville, TN: National Baptist Publishing Board, 1977), 131.

### Bibliographical Sources

McMickle, Marvin A. *An Encyclopedia of African American Christian Heritage.* Valley Forge, PA: Judson Press, 2002.

Mitchell, Ella P., and Henry H. Mitchell. *Together For Good: Lessons from Fifty-five Years of Marriage.* Kansas City: Andrews McMeel Publishing, 1999.

Roberts, Samuel K., ed. *Born to Preach: Essays in Honor of the Ministry of Henry and Ella Mitchell.* Valley Forge, PA: Judson Press, 2000.

## PAUL S. MORTON SR.

*(1950– )*

Paul Sylvester Morton Sr. is a gifted musician, preacher, ministry-builder, and founder of the Full Gospel Baptist Movement. Morton was born in Windsor, Ontario, on July 30, 1950, into a preaching family; his mother, father, sisters, and brothers were all called to ministry. Morton left Canada after receiving God's direction to go to New Orleans, where he became pastor of Greater St. Stephen Missionary Baptist Church in 1975. Under his leadership, the church grew from six hundred and forty-seven members to more than fifteen thousand. His wife, Elder Debra B. Morton, serves with him as co-pastor. In 1997 the community purchased a military base, renamed it St. Stephen City, and built affordable housing for seventy-five families, an apartment complex, and "seasoned citizens" housing for the elderly. Over the years, Greater St. Stephen planted five additional ministries in areas surrounding New Orleans. In 2005, when Hurricane Katrina devastated the Gulf Coast, the Greater St. Stephen community lost nearly everything, but became "One Church in Two States" with services in New Orleans and in Atlanta each Sunday.

In the early 1990s, Morton began the Full Gospel Baptist Church Fellowship, which seeks to teach the people of God, especially Baptists, how to operate fully in the gifts and doctrine of the Holy Spirit according to the Bible, remaining rooted in the foundation of Jesus Christ. In 1993 Morton was consecrated to the office of International Presiding Bishop, and Greater St. Stephen Baptist Church changed its name to Greater St. Stephen Full Gospel Baptist Church.

Morton is an anointed preacher and singer who ministers worldwide through his preaching and music ministry. Some of his musical projects include *Crescent City Fire*, *We Offer Christ*, *Healing Hands*, *As for Me and My House*, and *Let it Rain*. Morton hosts "Changing a Generation," a daily radio and television broadcast, and is the author of several books, including *Why Kingdoms Fall*. Morton serves on many boards, among them the One Church, One Addict organization. He is the president of the Paul S. Morton Sr. Scholarship Foundation and of the Paul S. Morton Bible College and School of Ministry.

• • •

*Joining Pentecostal emotion and exuberance with the basics of African American folk preaching (story, imagination, and biblical imagery), Paul Morton has influenced many preachers and congregations all over the world. In addition, Morton's musical gifts have made him a master communicator. He is especially admired for his ability to conclude a sermon, often with a whoop. "The Enemy Inside Your Mind" was a part of a series that Morton developed in 2001. Given that he has suffered severe depression and what he refers to as a mental breakdown, Morton decided to use his experience to assure listeners that they could overcome any obstacle.*

## The Enemy Inside Your Mind (2001)

> *Casting down imaginations, and every high thing that exalteth itself against the knowledge of God, and bringing into captivity every thought to the obedience of Christ.*
>
> —2 Corinthians 10:5 (King James Version)

I just believe as we face a new year that there is no need in trying to face a new year with the same old problems. I'm stilllllll having trouble. I'm stilllll broke. I'm stilllllll in pain. The cycle goes around and around and around. And the problem is I don't know where the enemy is, and this is what's really getting me down. I really don't know. I think I know, but I don't know where the enemy is.

People of God—we go through a lot of things year after year because we are attacking the wrong enemy. You're looking at someone and you're saying, He messed my life up. She messed my life up. My job messed my life up. My environment messed my life up. My circumstances messed my life up. But I'm here to tell somebody tonight—wrong enemy.

The Bible says we wrestle *not* against flesh and blood.[1] Who has flesh and blood? People. We wrestle not against people. People are not your problem. You are going to have to deal with this enemy because I really want you to have a good year and you've got to realize where this enemy is. It's not people. It's not flesh and blood. It's about powers and principalities that take over our mind. I let the enemy inside my mind because the enemy is inside their mind. Instead of letting the enemy stay in their mind and take authority over what's in their mind—what do I do? I let the enemy get in my mind, and it messes me up over and over and over again. You have to know, people of God—it's important for us to see that the enemy is inside your mind.

When I look at Matthew, the fourth chapter, and I focus in on verse 1, I read what happened to Jesus. The Bible says in Matthew 4:1, "Then was Jesus led up of the Spirit." The devil didn't take him here, but he was led up of the Spirit into the wilderness to be tempted of the devil. The devil met him in the wilderness. Now, when I really understood this wilderness experience, my mind became aware of how the enemy really wants to get in. How many of you know that the devil really has a way of deceiving you? And that's what he will do, because for many, many years I really thought that this wilderness experience that Jesus was going through was just dealing with the geographical location—the place where he was. That the devil was tempting him and bothering him in the place where he was—the wilderness.

But then, as I began to look at God's Word, I realized that it was not just this geographical location that was a wilderness, but there was a wilderness in his mind. Hear me, good people of God. Jesus was in a human body, and because he was in a human body, he followed the laws of humans. So then if he was to follow the law of human beings, he did not hop from place to place or snap his finger like a genie or twitch his nose like Samantha on *Bewitched*. So, when the devil was trying him, what the devil did was take him from place to place in his mind.

You see, when you look at Matthew 4:5, the Bible says, "Then the devil taketh him up into the holy city and setteth him on a pinnacle of the temple." Listen—the devil taketh him up into the holy city and setteth him on a pinnacle of the temple? Well, people of God, there was no temple in the wilderness. Jesus saw the temple in his mind. Satan drew the picture. I can do this for you. And while he was talking, Jesus could see the temple. He could see the pinnacle of the temple. But he decided—no, no, no, no, no, you're not going to come in my mind like that. You don't tempt the Lord thy God. You've got to know what to say when the devil attacks your mind. You've got to know how to deal with this enemy when he attacks your mind. So I look in verse 5 and I realize—no, he wasn't in Jerusalem; he wasn't in the holy city; he was in the wilderness. The devil attacked him in his mind.

Come down to Matthew 4:8, and the Bible says, "Again, the devil taketh him up into an exceeding high mountain, and showeth him all the kingdoms of the world." Now how many of you know—I don't care how high the mountain is, you can't see all the kingdoms of the world. He was in the wilderness, but you see the picture was seen in his mind. This is what Satan was saying: I can give you all the kingdoms of the world. That's what the devil will do. He will mess with your mind.

I told you the devil attacks the mind to see who will control your reality. You're going to have to decide as you face your new year who will be more real to you. I don't care what kind of mind you came here with tonight; I want to let you know he is able to renew your mind. I mean he will transform your mind. You may have come in here tonight with negative thinking, but before you leave here tonight, you are going to be so transformed because what you're getting ready to do is identify the enemy. I thought it was you, I thought it was you, but I found out—it's in here [points to his head], baby, and if I can control what is in here and give it to Jesus as it relates to what's in here, you can't bother me out there. The only way you can bother me out there is if I let you in here. And so I've decided tonight, you ain't getting in here. Roll your eyes at me; cuss me out; talk about me like a dog, but you ain't getting in, because, Satan, I know where you want to go. You want to control my reality. You want me to believe that this pain that I'm experiencing is more powerful than the joy of the healing that God can bring. You want me to think that my trouble is the ultimate when he's already told me that whatever you need, I will supply your every need. So I'm not going to allow you to attack my mind.

You see, the enemy attacks us, and the strongholds that attack us the most are not random thoughts or occasional sins. But the strongholds that affect us the most are those things that are so hidden in our thinking patterns that we do not recognize them or identify them as being evil. Let me tell you, people of God, you can have some stuff so deep inside of you. It can be so deep inside of you that you don't even think it's evil anymore. Let me tell you—cussing can be so deep inside of you that when you cuss you don't even realize you cussed. Somebody can say, Oh, please don't do that in public. What did I say?

There are some things, people of God, that can get so deep inside of you, and that's what the devil wants. He wants to deal with those things hidden in your thinking patterns that you do not even identify as being evil. So, because you don't identify it as being evil, you blame it on something else. Because if I don't know what's in here, I've got to blame it on something else. It has got to be my circumstances. It has got to be that this was passed down from my momma or my daddy. It's got to be in my blood. It's got to be in my genes because I'm dealing with all of these problems. So, if Satan can hide stuff from you, if Satan can hide evil from you, then that's how he achieves the victory.

That's why when I look at Matthew, the twelfth chapter and verse 43, I hear Jesus speaking to us, and Jesus gives a word as it relates to unclean spirits. And this is what he says in Matthew 12:43; he says, "When the unclean spirit is gone out of a man, he walketh through dry places, seeking rest, and findeth none."

See, that's why you've got to watch out tonight, because demons that are going to be cast out of you, they are looking for a dry place. They're looking for depressed people. Demons are looking for people who are down and who feel like there's no answer and there is no way out. I mean, I had it rough last year, and I'm going to have it rough this year. I just came tonight because I'm just supposed to be here, but I don't believe nothing is going to happen. And then, what happens is the demon's antenna goes up and says—uh huh, I've found the dry place. Yeah, before you leave here tonight—you see, somebody is going to be delivered, and those demons have got to find someone else to possess. They've got to get into somebody. So what the demon says to his next victim is, I'm going to attack your mind, and I'm going to get in your mind, because he looks for a dry place so that he can rest!

Demons don't like confusion. Demons really love rest. You see, unclean spirits are seeking rest. The sense of rest they seek originates from being in harmony with the environment that they're used to. They want harmony in their environment so when the devil acts up and it don't bother you, he likes that. Oh, I done found me a new home. He likes folks that like to shout on Sunday but feel comfortable with living with the devil on Monday. The devil likes that. He likes to rest. He don't want nobody talking about I bind you in the name of Jesus. You've got to go! Get on out of my mind, devil! I'm taking authority! No, no! Demons don't like that. They like rest. So they look for harmony in their environment. In other words, when our thought life is in agreement with unbelief, the devil likes that. He likes people who don't believe what the Bible says. You've settled for the doctor's report. The doctor says it's a terminal disease. The devil wants to get in your mind to bring unbelief. My momma died with this. My granddaddy died with this, and I'm just going to have to accept it. I'm going to die with this. Or, you can say, he was wounded for my transgression. He was bruised for my iniquity. The chastisement of our peace was upon him, and with his stripes I am healed.[2]

Because the enemy is inside your mind, and unbelief is what he's attacking many of you with, you will go into your new year with the same problem and with unbelief, and you'll wonder why everybody else is being blessed and you're still going through. You're going to have to take authority tonight over your unbelief. Devil, get on out of here! I believe God's Word! I may not have what I want to have right now, but it's on the way because my trust is in God and I need you to help my unbelief.

The devil likes unbelief, and he likes our thought life to be in agreement with fear. That's all he wants you to do is have fear, fear, fear. You walk around in fear. But you do understand that God has not given us the spirit of fear, but he has given us power. He has given us love. He has given us a sound mind.[3] But if the devil can make you fearful—put fear throughout your mind, he's got you! Some of you can't even travel anymore. Fear! I ain't getting on no more airplanes. And you're just going bumpity, bump—let Greyhound do the driving for us, and you're all sore when you get to your destination. Fear will mess you up.

Let me tell you something, people of God, bin Laden really doesn't have to do another thing. Because you know what has happened in America? Fear has taken over our minds, and because fear has taken over our minds—that's why the economy is all messed up. Stock market is down. I mean, fear is crazy. You go to the airport, and they don't care who they stop. Eighty-year-old woman—now what is she going to have on her? Can hardly move; can hardly walk. Fear! This is what the devil does. Bin Laden can just stand back and laugh and say, I don't have to do anything. I've got them now. But you've got to take authority. Oh, I wish I had some witnesses in this place. You have to take authority over fear. The devil will bind you in your new year with fear, but you've got to tell that devil, No, you've got to go! You're not going to hold me down with fear. It didn't come from God, and anything that does not come from God, I don't want it. And God has made it clear in a letter to you. He's telling you I did not give you that spirit of fear, so cast it out of your mind. Get it on out of your mind.

Next, you've got to take authority, people of God, over habitual sins! And the devil will make you do stuff over and over and over and over again. And the devil likes that, because when you do it over and over and over and over again, he just rests. I've got you, now I can take it easy. Now, I've got to work on some other folk, but I ain't got to work on you no more; you've got it down. When you go out to service on Sunday, just make sure you lift your hands so nobody else will know. They won't know although your hands are lifted, your mind is bogged down by fear.

If Satan can get inside your mind, that's all he wants to do. Some folks believe—you can't get ahead because of your race—because of the color of your skin, because in your mind, you have this concept that if I'm black, I've got to step back. And as long as you keep that concept in your mind, the devil will never allow you to get to the next level in your life.

Some of you—your family tree is holding you back. I don't care if your momma didn't make it. I don't care if your granddaddy wasn't successful. You've got to tell the devil that the buck stops here, and I'm here to tell you get on out of my mind! Don't remind me about the bad people in my family. I'm not worried about the bad people in my family. Look at me, devil! I'm the good one! And you'd better get used to that. Look at me right in my face—all up in my face. I've come to let you know that I've come to make a difference. You've got to cast the devil out of your mind.

The Bible says, "casting down imaginations."[4] Now, the devil will make you imagine stuff. He'll have your mind all messed up. That's all he wants is your imagination. He doesn't have to do anything to you, but once he gets your imagination and starts you imagining stuff, then he's got you where he wants you. But I come to prophesy to somebody tonight—to tell you that we're getting ready to put every bad thought in prison tonight. I've come to give those bad thoughts a life sentence. Don't you mess with me no more. In fact, I think it's good right through here—I don't know about you as it relates to your bad thoughts—I think capital punishment is good. Kill 'em; kill 'em. Kill those bad thoughts, because if you put them in jail, they may break out again. Kill 'em.

Let me move on. People of God, I want you to see something tonight because it is important. It is significant that the process of deliverance quite often involves a season of inner conflict and turmoil. See, some of you think that that inner conflict is not good, that the turmoil is not good.

But I come to tell you it's good because the demons can't rest. Because I'm fighting this thing. Oh, I know that every time I go to do good, evil is right there, but I'm not resting. Devil, I'm fighting this thing. You're not going to win this battle. Oh, I know sometimes we fail and sometimes we fall, but I want you to know you've got to stop worrying about the turmoil and the inner conflict. It's a good sign signifying the individual's will—desire to be free. In other words—Satan, I'm tired of you messing with my mind. I'm tired of you bothering me. You've got to get sick of that devil, y'all. I'm not talking about getting sick of people. Get sick of what's in here [points to his head] that keeps you up all night long having you hate somebody, being jealous of somebody. Get rid of what's in here. You get restless, get tired of that, and say, no, you ain't going to mess with me, devil. You've got to go, and I'm taking authority in the name of Jesus.

Oh, people of God, I'm here to tell you—you've got the authority to take authority over the devil. Do you know what the Bible says? When you resist the devil, he will flee. He's going to run from you! Resist the devil in your mind, and he can't get in. He hates it. He hates it. He hates it. You see, he's got to get in your mind to take control. But if you don't let him in, baby, you've got the victory. In the name of Jesus, block him out.

So, what happens now? This is where you get scared. You get scared because the devil now gets mad. He's mad because you resisted him. Now, you really have to understand that. It's been awhile ago—I was walking out of my hotel room and down the hall and one of the maids saw me and said, "Um, you look good." And I said, "No, I don't play that; you've got the wrong person." And I just walked on. And as I walked off, you know what she said? "I didn't want no short man no how." Mad!

You see, you've got to know, people of God, and hear me good tonight—whenever you resist the devil, he's going to get mad. Some of you are wondering why he's attacking you when you decide to tithe. Because in your mind he's been messing with you. Don't tithe because you ain't got enough for your ends to meet. Don't be no fool. Don't be crazy. But then you hear the Word of God and say, No, I'm going to tithe. I'm going to give to God because he says do it. Don't you think the devil is going to just stand back and say, Well now, let me back off. Baby, he will attack your finances. He'll attack your home. He'll attack your job. You've got to know how to tell that devil, I don't care if you are mad; I'm going to win this. I may have some winners in this house. I just may have some winners here tonight because you are breaking your agreement with the devil, who will fight for you to remain in the life that he has for you.

Oh, you see, while we may find comfort in being Christians, being Christians has not made us perfect. Ain't no need of you sitting up in here acting like you're all perfect. There's a war that's still going on. In fact, it is rare for a Christian not to be limited by at least one of the following thoughts in our minds. There's somebody in here that at some point in your life it was unbelief. For somebody in here it may have been cold love—acting like you loved someone but it was so cold. For somebody maybe it is time you dealt with fear. For somebody it's been pride. Somebody in here it's been unforgiveness. I can forgive everybody else, but I can't forgive you. You hurt me too bad. Don't look at me like I'm crazy. Some of you are on this list tonight. Maybe I ain't got to you yet. It may be lust. It may be greed. It may be jealousy or any combination of these. It may be all of these or some other things, but I'm here to tell you—all of us have sinned and come short of the glory of God. Because it is the devil's job to attack our minds. He's always trying to bother us.

Because we excuse ourselves so readily, it is difficult to discern the areas of oppression in our lives. After all, these are my thoughts. Nobody told me this. This is my thought. This is my attitude. This is my perception. This is how I perceive things. This is how I look at things. And somebody can say I didn't do that or I didn't say that. Well now, I know you did. I can tell you did. But we justify and defend our thoughts with the same degree of intensity with which we justify and defend ourselves. And you know how you defend yourself. When somebody just comes straight up and says to you, Are you mad? Are you upset with me? No. Well, it looks like you're mad. I told you I wasn't mad! We will defend ourselves. But let me tell you something, people of God, as a man thinketh—that's why I'm working on this tonight. Because ain't no need of you trying to go through no year with all of these thoughts that have you all messed up. We've come to speak deliverance in this place, and ain't no need of you trying to get stuff straight out there until you get stuff straight in your mind. And I come tonight to get some stuff straight in here. Can I preach in this place tonight? I come to get some stuff straight in my mind so that I can see what God has for me. And that's why the old folks used to say, Devil, we cast you out of our minds. I'm casting you out of my mind. I'm here to tell you, people of God, when you speak deliverance into your life, something is going to happen. Speak it into your life. Say, create in me a clean heart and renew a right spirit within me. I'm here to tell somebody tonight: throw it down. I believe that God is bringing deliverance right now!

Let me read it one more time. Though we walk in the flesh we do not war after the flesh, for the weapons of our warfare are not carnal but mighty through God. "Casting down imaginations and every high thing."[5] If it ain't of God it's too high. "Every high thing that exalteth itself against the knowledge of God, and bringing into captivity every thought to the obedience of Christ."[6] Since I know where the enemy is, I'm casting him out of my mind. I dare you to scream it tonight—go! You've got to go! You've got to go!

### *Notes*

*Sermon source: The African American Pulpit* 7, no. 2 (Spring 2004), 68–74.

1. See Ephesians 6:12.
2. See Isaiah 53:5.
3. See 2 Timothy 1:7.
4. See 2 Corinthians 10:5.
5. Ibid.
6. Ibid.

### *Bibliographical Sources*

"About Bishop," at http://www.paulmorton.org (accessed June 27, 2007).
"Guest Bio Bishop Paul S. Morton," CBN.com, http://www.cbn.com/700club/guests/bios/bishop_morton_042104.aspx (accessed June 27, 2007).

## OTIS MOSS JR.

*(1935– )*

Preacher, theologian, pastor, and civic leader Otis Moss Jr. has long been one of America's most influential religious leaders and most highly sought-after preachers. He was born in LaGrange, Georgia, on February 26, 1935, to Magnolia and Otis Moss Sr., who was a sharecropper. Otis is one of five siblings. He learned early about difficulty and perseverance. His mother died when he was four and his father died when Otis was only sixteen.

Otis attended Morehouse College where he was mentored by the distinguished Dr. Benjamin Mays and earned a bachelor of arts in 1956; he received a master of divinity from Morehouse School of Religion/Interdenominational Theological Center in 1959 and gained his doctor of ministry from United Theological Seminary in Dayton, Ohio in 1990. He was also a member of the adjunct faculty at United.

From 1954 to 1975 Moss pastored several churches. In the early days of his ministry, he also worked with Dr. Martin Luther King Jr. in the Southern Christian Leadership Conference (SCLC), and years later briefly co-pastored Ebenezer Baptist Church in Atlanta with Martin Luther King Sr. Moss married Sharon JoAnn Howell in 1959; Dr. Martin Luther King Jr. presided over the wedding ceremony along with Dr. Samuel Williams. To this union one child, Daphne (now deceased) was born. Unfortunately, Moss's wife died in 1964 of cardiac arrest following surgery due to pregnancy complications. In 1966 Moss married Edwina Hudson Smith and Dr. King again presided over the ceremony along with Dr. Samuel Proctor. To this union one son, Otis III, was born. Edwina also had a son, Kevin, from a previous marriage.

Moss was a founding member of Operation PUSH (People United to Serve Humanity), the economic justice organization that emerged out of SCLC's Operation Breadbasket. In 1975 he moved to Cleveland to pastor Olivet Institutional Baptist Church.

His Christian social ethic rests on a conviction that the role of the church is salvation, liberation, and reconciliation. Moss teaches that salvation through faith in Jesus is fundamental, but salvation without liberation is not salvation at all. Religion must have an impact on a person's economic, social, and political standing. In keeping with these theological beliefs, Moss led Olivet Institutional in developing programs of spiritual and social renewal. Olivet provides educational programs and services to the Cleveland community and offers health-care services through the Otis Moss Jr. University Hospital Medical Center, which is a partnership between the church and University Hospital of Cleveland. Along with his pastoral duties, Moss served on the board of the Martin Luther King Jr. Center for Nonviolent Social Change, and is currently a member of the board of Morehouse School of Religion, and the board of directors of Morehouse College.

His ministry also extends to the political sphere: President Carter often consulted Moss on moral and social issues facing America, and in 1994, President Clinton invited him to Camp David to witness the signing of the peace treaty between Israel and Jordan. Hailed as one of the greatest preachers of the twentieth and twenty-first century, Moss was invited to deliver the Lyman Beecher Lectures at Yale University in 2004. He was also named one of the top fifteen preachers by *Ebony* in 1993. He has received honorary degrees from Myers University, Lagrange College, Cleveland State University, Shorter College, Morehouse, and Temple Bible College. He retired in 2008.

• • •

*Otis Moss Jr. has been called a regal preacher because of his continuous posture of calmness under fire, including while working in the trenches as an activist. He also exudes quiet fire as he meticulously moves through each sermon. His sermons make the text primary but never fail to signify his keen understanding of the history of his people and the weightiness of theological and social matters. With humor, stories, and impeccable, passionate delivery, Moss consistently brings crowds to their feet. The following sermon, which was preached at the 2004 Samuel DeWitt Proctor Pastors Conference, concerns a subject of which he has personal knowledge—being prophetic when it is not popular.*

*In this sermon Moss reminisces on his work with King and details how badly King was treated by whites and by his own people. He moves from these reminiscences to prod the audience to gain more courage and do the work of God in difficult times.*

## A Prophetic Witness in an Anti-Prophetic Age (February 2004)

> *The Spirit of the Lord is upon me; because the Lord hath anointed me to preach good tidings unto the meek; He hath sent me to bind up the brokenhearted, to proclaim liberty to the captives, and the opening of the prison to them that are bound.*
>
> —Isaiah 61:1 (King James Version)

It is amazing that Jesus, after being protected in Africa among people who looked like him, came back to Nazareth, and decided to go to a normal gathering, an ordinary gathering, and brought to it an extraordinary, unexpected prophetic word. They simply gave him a document. The King James translation version says, "They gave him a book," but we know that's not true. They gave him a scroll out of the prophetic tradition, what we now call the sixty-first chapter of Isaiah and told him to read it. He started reading it and then preached a sermon shorter than the text. "This day is this scripture fulfilled in your hearing."[1] And the record said he sat down. What a sermon! Have you ever preached a sermon shorter than your text? And then they engaged in a brief dialogue. I think it was after the sermon. And he started talking about some things. And before the dialogue was over, we would call it a fellowship, he almost got killed just talking about the sermon.

How often have our lives, as representatives of the gospel of Jesus

Christ, been threatened for having dialogue about the sermon we had just delivered? We are not in particular danger because we have too often adjusted to this anti-prophetic age. There is no danger in the sermons we preach, no challenge, and no threat to anybody in particular.

But Jesus almost got killed on his first public sermon—perhaps, his first public sermon. And let me say, we ought to remember that the community, the world does not like prophets, and neither does the church. The world does not like prophets. Prophets disturb us. They shake us out of our dogmatic slumber. So we prefer comfort to commitment. The world does not like prophets. Prophets override our creeds and our half-truths. Prophets expose our injustices and our contradictions and put to shame our mediocrity. The world does not like prophets and the church often refuses to celebrate them.

We all have Dr. King's photograph on our walls. But I was there when his own denomination excommunicated him and, in the words of Gardner Taylor, denied him a home address. In his own denomination, he was vice president of the National Baptist Sunday School and BTU Congress, now the Christian Education Congress. But by tyrannical acts of a few people, he was removed without a vote from that position and made unwelcome. I stood after that with tears in my eyes, and I heard not a member of the Ku Klux Klan, but I heard a brother who looks like us say: "He's got everything; on the cover page of *Time* magazine. Every time I open the newspaper he's in it. Every time I turn on the television he's on it. Give us something." And that was the size and the depth and the height and the width of his ministry.

We don't like prophets. Let me tell you something you might not have heard before. Dr. King gave his final message to the Progressive National Baptist Convention against the war in Vietnam. In less than a year he would be assassinated. I was an original representative of the Southern Christian Leadership Conference and Dr. Abernathy called me and said: "Otis, here's what we want you to do. Go out and get five thousand leaflets printed and put on it the time that Dr. King is going to speak to the Convention and give the subject: *The War in Vietnam and the Christian Conscience.*" Put that on the leaflet and distribute that throughout the Convention and the Cincinnati community. I said, "Yes," but before I could get to the printer I got a telephone call that I did not return because the Spirit told me that it was a call that I wanted to get afterwards.

So I had all of the leaflets printed up and got some young people from our congregation to help distribute them and then I took the call. The call came from a high official in our convention—I'm talking about the Progressive National Convention—called me and said: "You have a relationship with Dr. King. Please tell him not to speak on Vietnam." Some of the brethren won't like it. Well, by that time I had already sent out the leaflets. I said: "Well, I'll tell you, I can't talk to him because I don't know where he is. He's on his way here and the leaflets are already out. Why don't we just pray?"

On that occasion Dr. King spoke, and the Progressive National Baptist Convention after he spoke unanimously endorsed or adopted a resolution that we had written in his hotel room against the war in Vietnam. It was the last time he spoke to the Progressive National Baptist Convention, but there were a handful of ministers who left before he spoke. He was not wanted in Atlanta.

Now listen to me carefully. I was here when the announcement went out that Martin Luther King Jr. was moving from Montgomery, Alabama, to Atlanta, Georgia. The governor of Georgia, whose name at that time was Ernest Vandover, he called a press conference in the state capitol and said that Martin Luther King Jr. is not welcome in Georgia. Now he [King] was born here. And then a black reporter from *Atlanta Daily World*, a black newspaper, went throughout the community interviewing—not white folk—but black folk. He said: "What do you think about Dr. King's coming to Atlanta?" Leader number one: "No comment." Scholar number two: "I don't want to get into that controversy." Leader number three: "We've already got enough leaders in Atlanta." He was not wanted in his own hometown. So, bombed in Montgomery; jailed in Birmingham, Albany, and St. Augustine; stoned in Chicago; invited out of town in Cleveland; and unwanted in Atlanta.

But the Spirit of the Lord was upon him. And, if I could rephrase it I would say, he was wounded for his nation's transgressions, bruised for America's iniquities, and the burdens of black people and white people and all people were upon his shoulders. And because he was a prophet, everybody here, and those who are not here can stand a little taller; walk the earth with a little more dignity. He gave teachers more to teach and preachers more to preach. He made newspapers worth reading, and television worth watching. Why? Because the spirit of the Lord was upon him. God told him to proclaim the good news.

Now, if I was going to be here for a week, I would deal with this whole text; but time is running out. If you go down—"the Spirit of the Lord is upon me . . . God has anointed me"—that has to be theological. "To proclaim good news to the poor"—I believe that's economics. "God told me to get release to the captives"—that must be political. To "recover the sight of the blind"—that's educational and sociological. "To let the oppressed go free"—that's liberation theology. And then, "to proclaim the year of Jubilee; to proclaim the acceptable year of the Lord"—that's theological.[2]

So, at the top of the text is theology. And in between is economics, politics, and sociology. In between it's all of the social public policy. And then at the bottom it's theology. At the top—theology—and all the rest in between. So, if you are preaching a gospel that has nothing about politics, nothing about economics, nothing about sociology, it's an empty gospel with a cap and some shoes and no body to it. It might be popular, but it's not powerful. It might be expedient, but it's not saving. Let me put it another way: it might be safe, but it's not saving. God told me to tell you that we need prophets in this age where prophets are not liked. We need prophets of peace—I didn't say peaceful prophets. Prophets of peace understand why we could have taken medicine to Iraq and not bombs.

Now let me back up just a moment and say that the church has allowed generals of the army to become more prophetic than we are. That's a bold statement. Let me defend myself. After World War I, Field Marshal Haig said: "It's the business of the church to make my business as a soldier impossible." I'm quoting not Amos and Hosea and Micah, now. I'm quoting generals of the army. General H.H. Arnold said: "We won the last war"—talking about World War II—"and it is the last war we will ever win. For in a nuclear age victory is no longer possible. War itself is defeat." General Omar Bradley, who was not even a registered voter, said: "We have too many men of science and too few men of God. We know more about killing than we know about living. We know more about making war than we know about making peace. We live in an age of nuclear giants and ethical infants." I'm still quoting the generals. I haven't gotten to the prophet yet. And, General Douglas MacArthur, who was perhaps at the bottom of his being a racist, said: "War should be outlawed." General Sherman is reported to have said—we're not sure that he said it—but allegedly said: "War is hell." And it is.

And the prophet said they shall beat their swords into ploughshares and the spears into pruning hooks. Nation shall not lift up sword against nation. Neither shall they learn war anymore. We need prophets of peace. Let me tell you I know where the weapons of mass destruction are. I know where they are and you know where they are! According to statistics, AIDS is a weapon of mass destruction. Mis-education and no education are weapons of mass destruction. Forty-four million people without Medicare—a weapon of mass destruction. Children with good minds and no money to go to school are weapons of mass destruction. People who have done no wrong living outdoors and under bridges this morning are weapons of mass destruction. And the prophet said, "Come unto me all ye that labor and are heavy laden and I will give you rest."[3]

Let me close with a country illustration. You can see something and hear something and feel something and say something and do something that appears to be strange to other folks because if you have a mountain moving faith and a mountain climbing faith and a mountain claiming faith—you can develop that, too.

I come from the country and I have country illustrations. There was a young woman who was working in a restaurant and one day when she went to work they were expecting a large turnout because it was a day before a holiday. They cooked an extraordinary supply of chicken, but the expected company and customer base didn't come. So, towards the end of the day when she had already worked overtime, the proprietor of the restaurant told her to take some of the chicken home. But by this time she had missed her last bus and had to walk home in the dark. As she walked home with this big bag of chicken in the dark, somebody moved out of a dark alley and put a choke hold around her neck and dragged her down the alley. And she said a strange thing: "While the attacker was dragging me, I heard a voice that said, take out a piece of chicken and eat it." Being dragged down an alley by an attacker and a voice says take out a piece of chicken and eat it. And strangely enough she obeyed the voice and while she was taking out the chicken, there were two hungry alley dogs down the alley fighting a garbage can. But when she pulled the chicken out of the bag, the aroma got caught up on the wings of angels and moved down the alley and captured the attention and the appetite of the hungry dogs. They came charging down the alley, growling and ready to fight and the attacker turned her loose and ran away. And she gave a little chicken to the dogs. And then for the rest of her journey as she walked home, she would take a little piece of the chicken out of the bag and give it to these alley dogs.

You know the Lord is my shepherd.[4] Yeah though I walk through the valley, but drop the "v" and say; yeah though I walk through the alley of the shadow of death, I will fear no evil because God can take alley dogs and make them guardian angels. For God's prophet, proclaim the year of jubilee!

## NOTES

*Sermon source: The African American Pulpit* 7, no. 4 (Fall 2004), 68–72.

1. Luke 4:21 (King James Version).
2. See Isaiah 61:1.

3. Matthew 11:28 (KJV).
4. See Psalm 23.

### *Bibliographical Sources*

Olivet Institutional Baptist Church Web site, http://www.oibc.org (accessed July 26, 2005).

*Who's Who Among African Americans*, 18th ed. Detroit: Gale Publishing Group, 2005.

# ANNA PAULI MURRAY

*(1910–1985)*

Anna Pauli Murray, born Anna Pauline Murray in Baltimore, Maryland, in 1910, was an Episcopal priest, educator, and attorney. She lost her parents as a child and was reared by her maternal grandparents and aunts. She was a freedom rider in the early 1940s and was arrested for protesting segregated seating on interstate buses. She wrote in one of her memoirs, *Proud Shoes: The Story of an American Family,* that among the characteristics expected of her as a member of her family were "honor and courage in all things."

Honor and courage in all things allowed her many firsts. She was the only woman in the June 1944 class at Howard University Law School, where she graduated first in her class. She was the first African American to be awarded a doctor of juridical science degree from the Yale University Law School, the first African American to serve as a deputy attorney general of the State of California, and the first African American woman to publish a lead article in a law review of an American law school (the *University of California Law Review*). Additionally, she wrote the amendment that provided for the inclusion of women in Title VII of the Civil Rights Acts of 1964, which prohibited discrimination in employment. Murray also authored the legal brief for *White v. Crook*, which ended state laws that denied women the right to serve on juries.

It was also Murray who found in Washington, D.C., the nineteenth-century city ordinance prohibiting discrimination in public accommodations. This was provided to Mary Church Terrell, who used it in a 1953 Supreme Court case to challenge the legality of segregation in the District of Columbia. She wrote *States' Laws on Color and Race*, which was published in 1951. Thurgood Marshall lauded this book, and it became a bible for civil rights lawyers working against segregation. She practiced law in New York City, was Distinguished Professor of Law and Politics at Brandeis University, and vice president of Benedict College in South Carolina. She was named Woman of the Year by the National Council of Negro Women in 1946 and by *Mademoiselle* magazine in 1947. She was one of the founders of the National Organization for Women (NOW) in 1966.

Deeply saddened that she could not give last rites to a close, devout Episcopalian friend, Murray decided to devote her life to the church and entered seminary at age sixty-two. She graduated with a master of divinity degree from General Theological Seminary in New York City in 1976 and was ordained in the National Cathedral in Washington, D.C., on January 8, 1977, the first ordination of an African American woman as an Episcopal priest. She served at two parishes, one in Washington, D.C., and later the Church of the Holy Nativity in Baltimore, before retiring in 1984. She lived in California, New York City, Massachusetts, Sweden, and Ghana. She wrote many articles; a book of poetry; four other books on law, family, and Ghanaian government; and her autobiography, *Song in a Weary Throat* (published posthumously in 1987). She died on July 1, 1985, of pancreatic cancer, in Pittsburgh, Pennsylvania.

• • •

*Pauli Murray taught that the Christian tradition entitled the oppressed—and especially women—to claim their full humanity and overcome their historical subordination even in the church. This sermon expresses Murray's belief that when people are emancipated everyone will live fully in God's image—social imbalance will cease to exist.*

## Male and Female He Created Them (May 21, 1978)

*So God created man in his own image. In his image he created him; male and female he created them.*

—Genesis 1:27 (King James Version)

Here in the poetry of ancient Hebrew literature, we have the glorious story of creation . . . ending with the creation of Man. Let us also hear this story in the words of James Weldon Johnson, one of our own twentieth-century poets in his poem "The Creation":

*Then God walked around,*
*And God looked around*
*On all that He had made . . .*
*He looked on His world*
*With all its living things,*
*And God said: I'm lonely still.*
*Then God sat down—*
*On the side of a hill where He could think;*
*By a deep, wide river He sat down;*
*With His head in His hands,*
*God thought and thought,*
*Till He thought: I'll make me a man!*
*Up from the bed of the river*
*God scooped the clay;*
*And by the bank of the river*
*He kneeled Him down;*
*And there the Great God Almighty,*
*Who lit the sun and fixed it in the sky,*
*Who flung the stars to the most far corner of the night,*
*Who rounded the earth in the middle of His hand;*
*This Great God,*
*Like a mammy bending over her baby,*
*Kneeled down in the dust*
*Toiling over a lump of clay*
*Till he shaped it in His own image;*
*Then into it He blew the breath of life,*
*And man became a living soul.*
*Amen. Amen.*[1]

In the very beginning of Holy Scripture is expressed the most liberating idea known to humanity—Man is made in the image of God, and Man here means male *and* female. *They*, not *he*, are to have dominion over the earth. This theme is repeated in Genesis 1:27 "When God created man, he made him in the likeness of God. Male and female he created them, and he blessed them and named them Man when they were created."

Despite the clarity of this language that male and female both share the reflection of their Creator at the creaturely level and both share equally in the dominion over the earth, what has in fact happened is that sexism—the dominance of a patriarchal male-oriented society—is the oldest and most stubborn form of human oppression and has served as a model for other forms of human exploitation and alienation.

Nowhere is this more apparent than in the language, symbolisms and structures of organized religion. As Casey Miller and Kate Swift have pointed out in their perceptive study, *Women and Language*:

> Since the major Western religions all originate in patriarchal societies and continue to defend a patriarchal world view, the metaphors used to express their insights are by tradition and habit overwhelmingly male-oriented. As apologists of these religions have insisted for tens of centuries, the symbolization of a male God must not be taken to mean that God really *is* male. In fact, it must be understood that God has no sex at all. But inevitably, when words like *father* and *king* are used to evoke the image of a personal God, at some level of consciousness it is a male image that takes hold. And since the same symbols are used of male human beings—from whom, out of the need for analogy, the images of God have been drawn—female human beings become less Godlike, less perfect, different, "the other." We are indebted to contemporary women scholars and theologians for a critical reexamination of the Biblical myths which lie at the foundation of the [Judeo]-Christian tradition, and who call attention to their misinterpretation over thousands of years.[2]

Miller and Swift continue their analysis:

> From antiquity, people have recognized the connection between *naming* and *power* (*Roots*; Kunta Kinte).[3] The master-subject relationship, which corrupts the master and degrades the subject, is foreshadowed in one of the biblical creation myths when the primal male assumes the right to name his equal, the primal female. The notion that *the sexes were created equal and at the same time* is not widely accepted.[4]

Here they are referring to the second and older version of the Creation story found in Genesis 2:4 and following; the myth of Adam and Eve. In the second chapter of Genesis "God formed man of the dust of the ground" and later made woman out of one of his ribs. In this version, the man said:

> This at last is bone of my bones and flesh of my flesh, she shall be called Woman, because she was taken out of Man (Genesis 2:23).

From this kind of Biblical anthropology comes the notion [that] Man is the head of woman, the confusion of the generic term *man* with the generic term *male* and the biblical justification for the dominance of males over females. Dr. Phyllis Trible, associate professor at Andover Newton Theological School, has examined this story in the original Hebrew and finds that much of its meaning has been distorted in the English translation. She points out that the "man" formed out of the dust of the ground is *'adham,* a generic term in ancient Hebrew which means, not male, but humankind.

This original being was sexually undifferentiated, having the potentiality of both sexes. The term used to describe such a being is *androgynos* "being both male and female." The King James Version continues, ". . . the Lord God said, It is not good that the man should be alone; I make him an *help meet* for him." The Revised Standard Version uses term: "a fit helper." The New English Bible uses the word "partner."

Until God performs surgery upon the sleeping *'adham,* this androgynous creature containing the potentiality of both sexes is given the power to name the animals and assert authority over them, but they are *'adham*'s equals. Professor Trible notes that it is only *after* the rib surgery that the generic term *'adham* is now accompanied by two additional terms: the Hebrew words specifying the human male, *'ish,* and the human female, *'ishshah.* " *'Adham,* whose flesh and bones have now been sexually identified as female and male, speaks of the two sexes in the third person. 'She shall be called woman' (*'ishshah*), because she was *differentiated from* man (*'ish*) provides a valid alternative for the Hebrew term usually rendered 'taken out of.' "

Thus, according to Trible, "She shall be called woman" is not an act of naming. Only later, after God has already judged the couple but has not yet expelled them from the Garden of Eden, does the man, "invoking the same formula used in naming the animals and asserting supremacy over them, 'called his wife's name Eve.' Trible concludes, 'The naming itself faults the man for corrupting a relationship of mutuality and equality,' and then God evicts the primal couple from Eden."

Following up on Professor Trible's analysis, Miller and Swift observe:

> The recorder of that early human effort to understand the nature and meaning of existence speaks across the millenniums of patriarchy. The story is far different from the male-oriented interpretation of creation that has embedded itself in our conscious understanding and our less conscious use of language. In English the once truly generic word *man* has come to mean *male,* so that males are seen as representing the species in a way females are not. Humanity, divided against itself, become the norm and the deviation, the namer and the named.[6]

Here we have the genesis of the theological subordination of women, the arguments against the change of the status and role of women, the opposition to women in the priesthood, particularly in the liturgical communions of the Christian Church and the Orthodox Hebrew faith. Recently, I met a conductor on the Metroliner [train] between Washington and New York. He saw my clerical collar and we got to talking. It turned out that he was an Episcopalian who has left the Church and says he is going to become an Orthodox Hebrew, his reason being that not in his lifetime will *that* particular faith admit women to an ordained ministry.

As patriarchy has distorted the role and function of women (and men), so it has distorted our perceptions of God. And, as one feminist theologian [Phyllis Bird] has pointed out, "the Old Testament is a man's 'book' . . . a collection of writings by males from a society dominated by males. These writings portray a man's world. They speak of events and activities engaged in primarily or exclusively by males (war, cult and government) and of a jealously singular God, who is described and addressed in terms normally used for males."[7]

And while we say in theory that God has no sex—in fact, the images of God handed down to us from our Christian tradition are almost exclusively male: "God the Father," for example. It is here that James Weldon Johnson's poetry on the Creation has a special significance for women. The image:

*This Great God,*
*Like a mammy bending over her baby,*
*Kneeled in the dust Toiling over a*
*lump of clay.*[8]

The female imagery of the Divine Being has been ignored or suppressed, so much so that a brilliant theologian from the Roman Catholic tradition like my friend and colleague, Mary Daly, has felt impelled to call herself a post-Christian and to write a book called *Beyond God the Father.* But the female imagery is there—in the Wisdom literature, in Jesus of Nazareth brooding over Jerusalem like a Mother Hen, in the eleventh-century English bishop, theologian, and monk St. Anselm of Canterbury, who refers to Jesus as "Our Mother" in his prayers, and sees Christ, according to Eleanor McLaughlin, "as our caring mother who comforts, gentles, revives, consoles." Divine motherhood is also depicted by the fourteenth-century mystic and anchoress, Dame Julian of Norwich, England, who experienced God in a feminine way and also referred to Christ as our Mother. She wrote:

> The human mother will suckle her child with her own milk, but our beloved Mother, Jesus, feeds us with himself, and, with the most tender courtesy, does it by means of the Blessed Sacrament. . . . The human mother may put her child tenderly to her breast, but our tender Mother Jesus simply leads us into his blessed breast through his open side, and there gives us a glimpse of the Godhead and heavenly joy—the inner certainty of eternal bliss.[9]

If I have come down hard on patriarchal religion, it is because both men and women are imprisoned in rigid roles dominated by a male-oriented hierarchy. All one has to do is to look at CBS television news each night or listen to Agronsky's panel to see *who* dominates the world and *in what terms*—males depicting and analyzing wars and terrorism and cynical politics, all instigated and carried out by other males for the most part. The world society is in dangerous imbalance, and the cultural patterns developed by males, as Erik Erikson and others point out, "have about reached their limit of value, utility and rationality, unless society is considerably modified by feminine input."[10] "This framework even—or perhaps, especially—infects the perception of God, so that 'the Ultimate is invoked to substantiate a destructively masculine world,' "[11] says theologian Patricia Martin Doyle. With Erikson, she agrees that "Such a gigantic one-sidedness, . . . has brought us to our current appalling situation in which the traditional feminine values of realism in householding, responsibility in upbringing, resourcefulness in keeping and making the peace, devotion to healing, creativity in fostering life, hitherto ignored, must find a new emphasis and input into our cultural life."[12] When this happens, and we are free to be wholly human, there will be no need for special Women's Day services in the Christian Church. Every service will be Women's Day, Men's Day, and Children's Day in which all participate in worship according to our individual gifts to the glory of God, our Father and Mother, who created us in the Divine image. *Amen.*

## NOTES

*Sermon source:* Collier-Thomas, *Daughters of Thunder,* 234–39.

1. James Weldon Johnson, *God's Trombones: Seven Negro Sermons in Verse* (New York: Viking Press, 1955), 19–20.
2. Casey Miller and Kate Swift, *Words and Women* (New York: Anchor Books, 1976), 71–72.
3. Murray's mention of Kunta Kinte, a central character in Alex Haley's *Roots,* is to illustrate the connection between naming and power. Kunta Kinte's master beat him until he agreed to take the name Toby, a name chosen by his master.

4. *Words and Women,* 16 (emphasis and parenthetical notation added by Murray).
5. Ibid., 16–17.
6. Ibid.
7. Phyllis Bird, "The Image of Women in the Old Testament," typescript, Temple University, 1972 (the brackets are Murray's).
8. *God's Trombones*, 20.
9. Julian of Norwich, *The Revelation of Divine Love in Sixteen Showings Made to Dame Julian of Norwich*, trans. M.L. Del Mastro (Liguori, MO: Triumph Books, 1994), 168.
10. On the liberation of males and females, see Erik Erikson, *Dimensions of a New Identity* (New York: W. W. Norton, 1979), 115–18.
11. Patricia Martin Doyle, "An Educator's Perspective about God," *Consultation on Language about God*, sound recording, October 3–4, 1977, United Presbyterian Church, U.S.A., and Louisville Theological Seminary (Louisville, KY: Louisville Presbyterian Theological Seminary, 1977).
12. Ibid.

### *Bibliographical Sources*

Collier-Thomas, Bettye. *Daughters of Thunder: Black Women Preachers and their Sermons, 1850–1979.* San Francisco: Jossey-Bass Publishers, 1998.
Murphy, Larry G., J. Gordon Melton, and Gary L. Ward, eds. *The Encyclopedia of African American Religions.* New York: Garland Publishing, 1993.
Murray, Pauli. *Pauli Murray: The Autobiography of a Black Activist, Feminist, Lawyer, Priest and Poet.* Knoxville: University of Tennessee Press, 1989.
"Pauli Murray," available at http://oasis.harvard.edu/html/schooo67.html (accessed July 8, 2007).
Pinn, Anthony B. *Pauli Murray: Selected Writings and Sermons.* Maryknoll, NY: Orbis Books, 2006.
"Rev. Dr. Pauli Murray." *Ebony* 34 (September 1979): 107–12.

## GILBERT E. PATTERSON

*(1939–2007)*

Gilbert Earl Patterson was born September 22, 1939, to Bishop and Mrs. W.A. Patterson Sr. and Mary Louise Patterson in Humboldt, Tennessee. Patterson lived in Memphis until his family moved to Detroit in 1952. Patterson accepted his call at age seventeen and preached his first sermon. He was ordained as an elder in the Church of God in Christ (COGIC) in 1957 by Bishop J.S. Bailey in Detroit. He attended Lemoyne-Owen College in Memphis, the Detroit Bible Institute, and obtained an honorary doctorate from Oral Roberts University. Patterson returned to Memphis in 1961 to become co-pastor with his father at Holy Temple COGIC. On May 27, 1967, Patterson married Louise Dowdy; they were married for forty years.

In 1975 Patterson left COGIC and founded Temple of Deliverance, the Cathedral of Bountiful Blessings. In 1988 COGIC bishops approved Patterson's return to the church. In May 1999, Patterson and the Temple of Deliverance Church of God in Christ entered their new Worship Center, which cost approximately thirteen million dollars to build and seats five thousand. In 2007 the church had more than fifteen thousand members.

Patterson was the founder and president of *Bountiful Blessings Ministries,* viewed worldwide on cable networks and on a variety of local television stations throughout the country. His television broadcast gave wide exposure to his preaching ministry and many regarded him as one of the best preachers in the world. He edited and published *Bountiful Blessings* magazine, with a distribution list of over one hundred thousand individuals. He was the president and general manager of WBBP Radio, a five-thousand-watt, full-time gospel radio station, and president of Podium Records, a record label whose first project, *Bishop G.E. Patterson Presents Rance Allen and the Soul Winners' Conference Choir,* was nominated for a 1999 Grammy Award. In 2008 Podium Records released the hit CD *Bishop G.E. Patterson and Congregation Singing the Old Time Way.* He is the author of *Here Comes the Judge: Finding Freedom in the Promised Land* (2002).

On November 14, 2000, Bishop Patterson was elected presiding bishop of the Church of God in Christ, Inc., claiming six and a half million members in fifty-eight countries. He was reelected unanimously in November 2004. In his office as the presiding bishop, he served as the chairman of the general board and president of the Church Corporation. He continued to be one of the most sought-after speakers in the country until his death on March 20, 2007.

• • •

*Gilbert E. Patterson is representative of the historic Pentecostal preaching style. He was a master of story, imagination, biblical application to real life, and whooping. Patterson had several signature sermons that could have been included, but we chose the following, because it highlights the issue of racism in both the church and society at large. This sermon also briefly addresses the racial history of Pentecostalism. At several points, the aurality of the sermon is maintained by the inclusion of audience response. The audience response is placed in brackets.*

## God's Cure for Racism and Loneliness (June 1998)

*And when the day of Pentecost was fully come, they were all with one accord in one place. . . . And they were all filled with the Holy Ghost.* —Acts 2:1, 4 (King James Version)

I want to talk to you about God's cure for loneliness and racism, for these seem to be two overwhelming problems that we are experiencing in our society. Well has it been said that God will be to you whatever you will let Him be, whatever you will allow Him to be. When you have the medicine for your illness, it doesn't make any sense for you to go on crying and complaining about the illness when all you have to do is take the medicine. God has given us the medicine that will cure all our ills. But in every generation it seems as though we humans have a tendency to believe that we are smarter than God. We'll find that so many of the problems that plague us today will not plague us if we understand that we already have the remedy.

But today people who claim to be members of the body of Christ—saved, sanctified, filled with the Holy Ghost—are constantly out of one relationship and into another. And I'll tell you something, even though I'm looking forward to my sixtieth birthday next year, I haven't always been in the middle-age realm, on the border of senior citizenship. So I know that when a person feels that he or she is in love with an individual and something happens that causes that relationship to be broken, if that person turns to another trying to get instant consolation from the heartbreaking relationship that just ended, that person will become more involved in the next relationship and be twice as broken when that one ends. So we live in a world where people go from one relationship to another. And all they're doing is trying to find somebody to console them. And I wish sometimes that I could just cry out and say, "Stop!"

You don't need to get involved in another carnal, human, physical relationship. You need to sit down and say, "All relationships are off while I form a greater relationship with God." Turn your Bibles to John, chapter 14. Look at verses 14–18. Let's read them:

> If ye shall ask any thing in my name, I will do it. If you love me, keep my commandments. And I will pray the Father, and he shall give you another Comforter, that he may abide with you for ever, Even the Spirit of Truth; whom the world cannot receive, because it seeth him not, neither knoweth him: but ye know him; for he dwell-

eth with you, and shall be in you. I will not leave you comfortless: I will come to you.

Jesus here is in the upper room on the night in which he was betrayed. A few minutes after uttering these words, Jesus is going to conclude the activities of the Passover. Knowing that a soon-to-be sequence of events will lead to his crucifixion on Calvary the next day, which will lead to his death, which will lead to his burial, which will lead to his resurrection, which will lead to his ascension, Jesus says, "I'm not going to continually be with you in the flesh. I am going to leave you. While being with you, I have been your companion. I have been your source of solace. I have been your comforter, but I'm getting ready to go. But I want you to know that I will pray the Father, and he will give your another comforter!"[1]

And look at what Jesus says in verse 16: "And he shall give you another Comforter that he may" . . . Do what? "Abide." Abide. That word abide means "stay." In other words, the Comforter is not just going to come in and stay for a little while. Jesus says that he will abide. Touch somebody and tell them that the Spirit abides. *[The Spirit abides.]* Which means "He will stay." *[He will stay.]* He will remain. *[He will remain.]* How long will he remain? He will abide with you foreverrrr!!

So how in the world can you talk about being bored to death? "I'm so lonesome I've got to just get out of here and find me somebody." "Been six months since I was in a relationship; I've just got to have me somebody." If you've got the Holy Ghost, you've got somebody. You've got somebody that doesn't wait to call you once a week to go out to dinner. You've got somebody that sleeps with you. You've got somebody that wakes you up in the morning. You've got somebody that sits at the breakfast table with you. You've got somebody that goes to the job with you. You've got somebody that even when the enemy is trying to destroy you, lying on you, digging ditches, throwing stumbling blocks in your way, while the devil looks to see you give up and throw in the towel, you just start "Hah, hah, hah" laughing 'cause you know who has the victory. Come on, tell three people, "If you've got the Holy Ghost, you've got God and some." *[If you've got the Holy Ghost, you've got God and some!]*

When I was filled with the Holy Ghost in 1956, September 16 to be exact, in Detroit, Michigan, at age seventeen and ordained at eighteen, there were those folks who said, "You know, you got to be thinking about getting a wife. You know you got to be married; you can't live this way." And I wanted to know, "What in the world are you talking about?" Because I found out that if you can't live it single, you won't live it married. There's only one that can really keep you. Hello somebody!

But what we really need to understand is that God, like the master architect, when he created us, he created a place within us that neither the opposite sex nor the same sex can fill. He created in us a place that hobbies won't fill. Because God said, "I designed that inner chamber for myself alone." And you will always be lonely and looking here and looking there and wandering until you get that inner place filled. Nobody can fill it. No thing can fill it. God said, "That's my spot. That's the inner chamber. I reserved it for myself."

And then once God moves in, you must let him do his work! Well, preacher what do you mean, "Let him do his work?" Paul said on one occasion, "Quench not the Spirit."[2] What he meant was, "Don't try to confine the Spirit; don't try to hinder the Spirit from doing his work." Now there are people that are filled with the Spirit of God, but have allowed the gift of the Holy Ghost within them to take a dormant place. I guess the best way to explain this is through the story of the night that Jesus told his disciples, "Let us go over to the other side."[3] So he got on a ship tired. And what did he do? He went down into the hinder part of the ship and put his head on a pillow and went to sleep. And when the storm arose, out there on that Sea of Galilee, they were battling the waves, trying to get the ship to the other side, and they couldn't do so. And after a while Peter got disgusted and said, "I'm going down here and wake up Jesus." When he woke him up, Jesus spoke, "Peace," and the storm was over.[4] Touch somebody and tell them, "If the Holy Ghost is dormant in your life *[If the Holy Ghost is dormant in your life]*, allow him to do his work. *[Allow him to do his work.]* Wake him up!" *[Wake him up!]*

What do you mean, Preacher? Well, let me say it this way. When I was a youngster, we had an old-fashioned open fireplace. It was an open fireplace, and we didn't want to go out and come back and find the house burned down. So my father or my brother would take a little shovel and scoop up the ashes and sprinkle those ashes over that fire, and before you knew it, instead of that flaming fire, you would see nothing but all of those ashes. When we'd come back home, the house would be ice-cold. And you would look into the fireplace, and you didn't see a spark. They would take a poker iron and stick it into that fireplace and just start stirring it and the ashes would fall down through the grate onto the hearth beneath. And then you'd start seeing little flickers. So they would take some little light kindling wood and put that on it. Then maybe they'd take a little piece of paper and light that kindling wood, and then what you thought was a dead fire would be blazing all over again.

I'm trying to tell you that there are persons who have allowed the ashes of gossip, the ashes of doctrines that are contrary to the Word of God, the ashes of hate, to put the fire down so low that you wonder whether they still have it there. And I'm here to tell you that if you ever had the fire alllllllll you neeeeed is to be stirred again! Somebody oughta say, "Lord, stir me up again!" *[Lord, stir me up again!]*

The Holy Ghost is God's cure for loneliness in the body of Christ. But let me move on. Not only is the Holy Ghost God's cure for loneliness, but we have in this country a reoccurring, a reverberating, racial problem. The sad thing is, it's not just in the world, it's in the church. The great thing about the Azusa Street Revival in 1907—when our founder, the late Bishop Charles Harrison Mason, was filled with the Holy Ghost and so many others came out of that with a Holy Ghost experience—was that the man that God used as the evangelist in charge was a black man named W.J. Seymour. And everybody knew that it had to be a move of God anytime that people came from all over the world, all different types of ethnic groups, to hear a black man. Hello somebody?

Bishop Mason led a church that was 50 percent white and 50 percent black from 1907 to 1914. But the racial attitudes in the South in 1914 caused those white elders that he had ordained to go to Hot Springs, Arkansas, and set up the first general assembly of the Assemblies of God. And when we went to the church where Pastor Andrew Jackson is now, it was an Assemblies of God church. The pastor there then said, "Oh yeah, you're from the Church of God in Christ, our sister church." I said, "No, your mother church!" Honesty will help racism.

Racism caused that thing to happen like it did! And we have talked, blacks and whites who are together in the Pentecostal experience. And we've asked ourselves the question, What would have happened if those white elders who started with Bishop Mason had remained fervent in spite of the racism in the country? If the white and black tongue speakers had stayed together, this whole country would be different. It wouldn't be as far behind as it is now.

President Clinton has talked about racism and how it is still threatening to blow us up. But even the president can't make the right thing happen. The Supreme Court can't make it happen. Congress can't make it happen. There is nothing that any man can do in order to put love in the heart of one ethnic community toward another.

And something is happening in our country now that a lot of folk don't understand. As long as it was black boys and girls getting high on crack, in drive-by shootings . . . Y'all don't hear what I'm saying. As long as we had more black young men in jail than in college, as long as in our community we were scared to sleep, you didn't hear much of an outcry. But when you allow demons to function, after a while demons run wild! And now it's no longer just the demons in the ghetto or urban America. The demons have attacked young whites, and they're bored and drug crazy, so now they're shooting their parents and they're shooting their teachers and they're shooting up their classmates because the devil wants them to know that his demon will work in white or black. And God is saying, "My power will work on white or black!" (Musician strikes chord and begins to play in unison with the preacher.)

On the day of Pentecost, as I get ready to go to my seat, the Bible says, "When the day of Pentecost . . ."[5] Touch somebody and say, One day, *[One day.]* When the day was fully come, they were all together in one place. Can I hear somebody say, "One day in one place?" *[One day in one place.]* They were all on one accord, of one mind. Come on and turn to somebody and say, "It was one day," *[One day]* "and they were in one place and on one accord." *[One place and one accord.]* And suddennnnnnlay there came a sound—somebody oughta say, "One sound" *[One sound.]*—a sooooound from heaven as of a russshin' mighty wind, and there appeared unto them cloven tongues.

So it was on one day, in one place. But out of one place, on one day, with one sound, those with one mind received one tongue. But when God got through with one tongue representing many people, the end result was unity in the body of Christ. And God is saying to the body of Christ today, "Quit looking at color." And I'm saying to you when you go out to witness, don't just witness to black faces. Witness to white faces. Witness to the Chinese faces. Witness to the Hispanics because God has one gospel for the whole world. He has one Holy Ghost for the whole body of Christ, and the Holy Ghost makes us one. And God doesn't have a black Holy Ghost or a white Holy Ghost. He only has the Holy Ghost from heaven. And the Holy Ghost is for yoooooou; it's for your childrennnnnnn; it's for all who will follllooow!

I shall never forget when I was at the World Conference of Pentecostal Churches in Toronto, Canada, and they had Pentecostal believers from around the world. You would have one person speaking. Standing to the right of that person would be an interpreter. And if the person on the podium was speaking in German, the interpreter would interpret it in your language. And all around that coliseum there were groups, and the Word would go forth. But it did not matter who the speaker was. When God confused the languages at the Tower of Babel, he didn't leave but one ecstatic praise word that is the same in every language. When they would be praising and preaching, every once in a while the main speaker would get carried away and say, "Hallelujah," and the interpreters didn't say anything! Because in German it was "Hallelujah." In French it was

"Hallelujah." In Chinese it was "Hallelujah." In Spanish it was "Hallelujah." In Russian it was "Hallelujah." Hallelujah. Hallelujah. When you've got the Holy Ghost, you've got to say, "Hallelujah."

### NOTES

*Sermon source: The African American Pulpit* 3, no. 4 (Fall 2000), 84–89.

1. John 14:16 (King James Version).
2. 1 Thessalonians 5:19 (KJV).
3. See Matthew 8:8.
4. See Mark 4:39.
5. Act 2:1 (KJV).

### BIBLIOGRAPHICAL SOURCES

"Biography of Bishop Gilbert E. Patterson," Office of Presiding Bishop, Church of God in Christ, Inc., Memphis, TN.

Dowd, James. "God's Calling, Bishop G.E. Patterson: September 22, 1939–March 20, 2007." *Memphis Commercial Appeal*, April 1, 2007, 61–64.

"Gilbert Earl Patterson," Bountiful Blessing Church, available at http://bbless.org/cogic.ge-patterson-history-pb.htm (accessed July 2, 2007).

## FREDERICK K.C. PRICE

*(1932– )*

Frederick K.C. Price was born January 9, 1932, in Santa Monica, California, to Winifred and Fred Price. The husband of Betty Price for more than fifty years, Fred K.C. Price is the founder of Crenshaw Christian Center (CCC) in Inglewood, California. In 1973 CCC began with three hundred members from the West Washington Community Church in Los Angeles, where Price was pastor for eight years. CCC currently has a membership of more than eighteen thousand and worships in the FaithDome, a ten-thousand-seat sanctuary. Ever-Increasing Faith, CCC's multimedia outreach ministry, at one point aired on one hundred and sixteen television and forty-two radio stations and reached thirty-three million homes in twenty-three U.S. markets and around the world. In 2001 CCC established a church in New York City and has recently established Spanish services at the Inglewood location.

Price's ministry journey began with restlessness and spiritual hunger.

Between 1955 and 1965 he served in Baptist, African Methodist Episcopal, Presbyterian, and the Christian and Missionary Alliance churches. Price was inspired by Kathryn Kuhlman's book *God Can Do It Again.* He wrote, "It stirred my soul. This was the missing dimension—the demonstration of the power of the Spirit of God, or what the Bible terms 'the gifts of the Spirit.'" On February 28, 1970, Price experienced a baptism of the Holy Spirit and "the evidence of speaking in tongues" which he attributes to the beginning of his global ministry.

In 1990 Price founded the Fellowship of Inner-City Word of Faith Ministries (FICWFM), an international fellowship of nondenominational urban ministries. Through conferences and regional gatherings members share ideas and best practices for effective urban ministry. Price is committed to engage churches applying biblical practices to address the challenges of inner-city life. Establishing schools, drug and alcohol recovery programs, and other outreach ministries, Price sponsors economic empowerment and financial development initiatives to build up the surrounding communities.

Considered a prophet of prosperity by some, Price ignited a firestorm in 1997 when he began a yearlong series on racism in America. The series followed the comments of Kenneth Hagin Jr., who indicated that he did not believe blacks and whites should intermarry. Price had been a friend of the Hagin family and had been mentored by Kenneth Hagin Sr. Price subsequently published *Religion & Racism, Volume 1: A Bold Encounter with Racism in the Church*; *Volume 2: Perverting the Gospel to Subjugate a People*; and *Volume 3: Jesus, Christianity and Islam.* While many radio and television stations canceled his show and several ministers disassociated with him, Price received the Horatio Alger Award and the Kelly Miller Smith Interfaith Award from the Southern Christian Leadership Conferences, presented by Martin Luther King III.

• • •

*Price is a chief practitioner of word preaching and the sermon reprinted here illustrates that style vividly. Word preaching is conversational and gained prominence among a small segment of the African American community in the 1980s. Not known for preaching messages concerning race and racism in the early years of the CCC, Price began steadily preaching on race in 1997. In this sermon he mentions that the Dake Bible, although it contained many racist comments, was widely read by Pentecostals when it was first published in 1963. Price used it to show how the church has historically supported racism. Finnis Dake's children actually sent a letter to Price upon hearing about his series, apologizing for any harm that the Dake Bible may have caused and indicating that their father was not a racist. Price responded to their letter and indicated that he accepted their apology, but that they had not gone far enough to fix offensive and racist statements in the Bible. The following sermon is taken from the series on racism.*

## How God Sees the Races
## (2002)

Having disproved Dake's first reason for segregating the races, we will now look at his second reason:

> God made everything to reproduce "after his own kind" (Genesis 1:11–12, 21–25; 6:20; 7:14). Kind means type and color, or he would have kept them all alike to begin with.

When Dake adds the explanatory statement, "*Kind* means type or color," he grossly misses the mark. In the book of Genesis, the word *kind* appears eighteen times. The eighteen passages where the word *kind* is used tell us that it means something very different from Dake's supposed definition. Let's read these passages carefully to see what the Bible means by *kind*.

Genesis 1:11–12 (King James Version) states: Then God said, "Let the earth bring forth grass, the herb that yields seed, and the fruit tree that yields fruit according to its *kind* [all italics mine], whose seed is in itself, on the earth"; and it was so. And the earth brought forth grass, the herb that yields seed according to its *kind*, and the tree that yields fruit, whose seed is in itself according to its *kind*. And God saw that it was good.

Genesis 1:21–25 (KJV) tells us: So God created great sea creatures and every living thing that moves, with which the waters abounded, according to their *kind*, and every winged bird according to its *kind*. And God saw that it was good. And God blessed them saying, "Be fruitful and multiply, and fill the waters in the seas, and let birds multiply on the earth." So the evening and the morning were the fifth day. Then God said, "Let the earth bring forth the living creature according to its *kind*: cattle and creeping thing and beast of the earth, each according to its *kind*"; And it was so. And God made the beast of the earth according to its *kind*, cattle according to its *kind*, and everything that creeps on the earth according to its *kind*. And God saw that it was good.

According to Genesis 6:20 (KJV):"Of the birds after their *kind*, of animals after their *kind*, and of every creeping thing of the earth after its *kind*, two of every *kind* will come to you to keep them alive."

Genesis 7:14 (KJV) tells us: they and every beast after its *kind*, all cattle after their *kind*, every creeping thing that creeps on the earth after its *kind*, and every bird after its *kind*, every bird of every sort.

Dake says that "kind means type and color." However, as we can see from the above Scriptures, in the book of Genesis, the word *kind*, generally means "species" and *never* means "color." With all due respect to Dake, "type and color" is not an accurate definition of *min* (also spelled *meen* or *miyn*), the Hebrew word for *kind. The New Strong's Exhaustive Concordance of the Bible* translates *min* as: "From an unused root meaning to portion our; a sort, i.e. species:—kind."[2] *The Analytical Concordance to the Bible* by Robert Young, who, like James Strong, was a distinguished Hebrew and Greek scholar, also translates the word *kind* from the Hebrew word *min* to mean *species*, as do both *The New Wilson's Old Testament Word Studies* and *The New Brown-Driver-Briggs-Gesenius Hebrew-English Lexicon.*[3]

*The Theological Wordbook of the Old Testament* by Harris, Archer, and Waltke provides a broader and fuller explanation of the term:

> God created the basic forms of life called *min*, which can be classified according to modern biologists and zoologists as sometimes species, sometimes genus, sometimes family or order.[4]

In his attempt to offer another reason for segregating the races, Dake translates *kind* as "type and color" so that each ethnic and racial group would be defined as a different *kind*. All of the other scholars I've quoted agree that, in fact, *kind* means "species" or sometimes "genus, . . . family or order." We can see this borne out in the Scriptures we've examined—the very Scriptures Dake cites to support his false ideas. Grass is a different *kind* from fruit, winged birds are a different *kind* from cattle, cattle are a different *kind* from creeping things. But human beings of all ethnic and racial groups and skin color are all of one *kind*, the species *Homo sapiens.*

First Corinthians 15:39 sums it up: "All flesh is not the same flesh, but there is one kind of flesh of men, another flesh of animals, another of fish, and another of birds."

Since God clearly states that there is one kind of flesh of men—only one—there is no credibility to Dake's second reason for segregating the races. Black people are not a different "kind" from white people—or from people of any other color. We are all humankind.

### Notes

*Sermon source:* Frederick K.C. Price, *Race, Religion & Racism, Vol. 2: Perverting the Gospel to Subjugate a People* (Los Angeles: Faith One, 2001), 30–33.

1. Finnis J. Dake's *The Dake Annotated Reference Bible* (Lawrenceville, GA: Dake Publishing, 2001); see http://www.dake.com.
2. James Strong, *The New Strong's Exhaustive Concordance of the Bible* (Nashville, TN: Thomas Nelson Publishers, 1995).
3. Robert Young, *The Analytical Concordance to the Bible* (Peabody, MA: Hendrickson Publishers, 1984); see Wiliam Wilson, *The New Wilson's Old Testament Word Studies* (Peabody, MA: Hendrickson Publishers, 1990); see Francis Brown, Edward Robinson, S.R. Driver, and Charles A. Briggs, eds., *The New Brown-Driver-Briggs-Gesenius Hebrew-English Lexicon* (Peabody, MA: Hendrickson Publishers, 1995).
4. R. Laird Harris, Glenson L. Archer, and Bruce K. Waltke, eds., *The Theological Wordbook of the Old Testament* (Chicago: Moody Publishers, 2000).

### Bibliographical Sources

Crenshaw Christian Center, "Frederick K.C. Price," available at http://www.crenshawchristiancenter.net (accessed June 28, 2007).

The Horatio Alger Association of Distinguished Americans, "Frederick K. C. Price," available at http://www.horatioalger.com/members/member_info.cfm?memberid=PR198 (accessed July 2, 2007).

# SAMUEL DEWITT PROCTOR

*(1921–1997)*

Samuel DeWitt Proctor was born in Norfolk, Virginia, in 1921. His paternal grandmother and maternal grandfather had been slaves. His father, Herbert Proctor, and his mother, Velma Gladys Hughes, instilled deep religious devotion in Proctor and his five siblings.

Proctor graduated from Norfolk's Booker T. Washington High School in 1937. For two years he matriculated at Virginia State College in Petersburg, where he was an accomplished clarinet and saxophone player. After acknowledging his call to the ministry in 1940, he transferred to Virginia Union University in Richmond. Upon completing his bachelor of arts at Virginia Union in 1942, he entered Crozer Theological Seminary in Pennsylvania in the fall of 1942. In 1944 Proctor married Bessie Louise Tate, and to this union four sons were born. In 1945 he graduated from Crozer Seminary.

Proctor began his doctoral studies in social ethics at Yale University and served as pastor of the Pond Street Baptist Church in Providence, Rhode Island, during his doctoral work. He eventually transferred to Boston University. While finishing his doctoral work at Boston University, Proctor began teaching at his alma mater, Virginia Union, at the invitation of his mentor, John Ellison, the distinguished clergyman and Virginia Union president. Proctor received his doctor of theology from Boston University in 1950.

Proctor assumed the presidency of Virginia Union in 1955, holding that position until 1960, when he became the president of North Carolina Agricultural and Technical State University in Greensboro. His stint there was interrupted when President John F. Kennedy invited him to serve as the director of the first full Peace Corps unit in Nigeria. After resigning from the North Carolina A & T presidency in 1964, Proctor worked for the Peace Corps and also for the National Council of Churches and the Office of Economic Opportunity.

In 1969 Proctor was appointed Martin Luther King Memorial Professor at Rutgers University in New Brunswick, New Jersey. While holding his professorship at Rutgers, he began serving as pastor of the historic Abyssinian Baptist Church in Harlem in 1972.

During his illustrious career, Proctor received more than forty honorary doctorates and delivered the Lyman Beecher preaching lectures at Yale Divinity School in 1990. He also served as a mentor to notable leaders such as Martin Luther King Jr., Jesse Jackson, Medgar Evers, and Douglas Wilder, America's first black governor. After Proctor's retirement in 1989, he held several distinguished visiting professorships. He died on May 29, 1997.

His books include *Sermons for the Black Pulpit*, *Preaching About Crisis in the Community*, *We Have This Ministry: The Heart of the Pastor's Vocation*, and *The Substance of Things Hoped For.*

• • •

*Samuel DeWitt Proctor mentored a generation of pastors and public orators through his unique preaching and teaching style and his role as an educator. Proctor was most widely known for preaching about social crisis in the black community. For Proctor, as the following sermon illustrates, if a preacher is not concerned about the real needs of flesh and blood humanity and their social concerns, then he or she was irrelevant at best, and not preaching the gospel at worst. Proctor taught and utilized a preaching method influenced by the Hegelian method of thesis-antithesis-synthesis, demonstrated in this sermon. First the thesis: Jesus taught that we should be concerned about the ones who are strangers, hungry, thirsty, imprisoned, and so forth. Second, the antithesis: the contemporary church is not as concerned as it should be about these things. Finally, the synthesis: Jesus says, "As you have done it to the least of these you have done it to me." Combining academic insights with folk story and narrative, Proctor influenced a generation of preachers to adopt his style and method.*

## THE BOTTOM LINE
## (1984)

In Matthew 25:31–46, Jesus is summarizing what he has been teaching and preaching for three years. The time is getting short. The cross is two days away, and he does not have much opportunity left to make things any plainer to his followers. As he often did, he folded it all up in one vivid, succinct, unambiguous parable that a child could understand.

He said that when the Son of man comes to judge the nations, he will separate them like a shepherd divides the sheep from the goats. And he would say to the sheep on his right hand, ". . . I was hungry, and ye gave me meat: I was thirsty, and ye gave me drink: I was a stranger, and ye took me in: Naked and ye clothed me: I was sick, and ye visited me: I was in prison, and ye came unto me." And the sheep will ask when had they seen him hungry, or thirsty, or a stranger, or naked, or sick, or in prison. And the King shall answer and say unto them, "Verily I say unto you, Inasmuch as ye have done it unto one of the least of these my brethren, ye have done it unto me."[1] Then he will say to the goats on his left that he was hungry and they gave him no meat, thirsty and they gave him no drink, a stranger and they would not take him in, naked and they did not clothe him, sick and in prison and they would not visit him. And the goats will ask when they had seen him hungry, thirsty, a stranger, naked, sick in prison. And he will reply, "Inasmuch as ye did not to one of the least of these, ye did it not to me."[2] And he will send them away "into everlasting punishment: but the righteous into life eternal."[3]

It is embarrassing to see how straightforward Jesus was in setting out the basic requirements of God for his people and how confusing and complicated we have made it. We have seen Europe soaked in blood over religious wars, fighting for thirty years at a time, a hundred years, burning scholars on the stake, beheading so-called heretics, imprisoning Bible translators, and driving millions of people to exile. And yet Jesus, in simple clarity, gave us the bottom line: "I was an hungred and ye gave me meat; I was thirsty, and ye gave me drink: I was a stranger, and ye took me in: Naked, and ye clothed me: I was sick, and ye visited me: I was in prison, and ye came unto me."[4] That's the very bottom line.

We have written millions of books about Jesus. We have fought over how much water we need in order to baptize in his name. We have broken up churches on how to remember him with simple bread and wine and created two hundred fifty religious denominations in the United States alone, in his name.

I recall taking a church history examination in seminary on which I was asked to explain the difference between *consubstantiation* and *transubstantiation,* between *homo-ousios* and *homoi-ousios.* One question asked me to describe *antidisestablishmentarianism*! And Jesus said, "I was hungry and you gave me meat."[5] *That* is the bottom line. If the Master saw those examination questions, he would never have believed that they had anything to do with himself! But Christians, for centuries, with long, serious faces, wearing heavy gowns, and shut away from the real world, have spent their lives on such questions.

One of the obvious problems here is that most of us are not close enough to the hungry, the thirsty, the naked, the stranger, the sick, or the prison bound. Our life's chances were so much better than theirs that we have outdistanced them and we don't even know their names and addresses. We have no one-on-one access to these "losers" in our society. And, as a matter of fact, some of us are not that sure about our own station in life, and we don't want to get too close to "the least of these" and risk being taken for one of them!

Recently, I asked a leading Christian minister from India what changes had taken place in the condition of the "untouchables," the outcasts, those who live beneath the lowest caste in Hindu society, in the last twenty years. He replied that he had not noticed any change, except that they had migrated into the cities in larger numbers and that they were protesting more vigorously against their economic plight.

But he did not stop there. He said that they had no advocates, even though 90 percent of India's nineteen million Christians came from the untouchables themselves. Those Christians have outdistanced "the least of these." Yet, Jesus said that in the final judgment the sheep will be those who have fed the hungry, given drink to the thirsty, clothed the naked, taken in the stranger, and visited the sick and the prison bound. Our priorities notwithstanding, this *is* the bottom line.

It is true, however, that it could get to be rather clumsy if all of us tried to volunteer to take care of the world's neediest on a purely spontaneous, personal, charitable basis. A curious suggestion was made recently by the mayor of New York City when asking churches to take care of New York's homeless victims. This is clearly a task that ought not be shoved off on the uneven and unreliable, spontaneous goodwill of a few people of modest means while a million others shrug it off. Obviously, it was not a serious suggestion. Yet President Reagan has given hints that the churches should divide the poor families among them; again, a suggestion that had to be purely impromptu, for the number of poor families left would remain a staggering problem.

We are too far from the early frontier days for such small-scale, primitive, responses to national needs. It is almost like asking every family to install its own water purification plant and to vaccinate its own children. Reverting to such private efforts, without "big" government programs, we would run the risk of having smallpox and diphtheria return. Some would even give up public schools and risk massive ignorance as a national experiment!

No. Our care of the hungry, the thirsty, the naked, and the prison bound is still largely a public obligation; but we are not finished when we say that. The obligation requires caring Christians to stay on the case, to participate in the political arena, to be involved in public policy making so that *we all* don't end up as "goats" on the left hand of the righteous judge.

Some things that we have heard recently from high places tell us that not everyone agrees that the hungry *should* be fed or that the naked *should* be clothed. Some people are more interested in blaming the victims, holding them responsible for their own condition. A gross ignorance is abroad in the land on how the poor became poor, on how deeply entrenched job discrimination has been, on how inadequate some education has been, and on how much hatred and rank hostility many people have had to endure while trying to hold on to a little dignity.

How easy it is for those who have arrived to forget! And, not many have earned the good fortune that they inherited. I once heard an old preacher say, "If you ever see a turtle on a tree stump, you know it didn't get there by itself!" Too many of us are turtles on tree stumps who forgot how we got there!

We have not begun to examine our institutions closely enough with that objective, cool, intense, long-term persistence of which we are so capable or to find a way to offer everyone an ample opportunity to overcome marginal existence.

Yet, having acknowledged the problems of a one-on-one response to "the least of these"—a purely voluntary, spontaneous outpouring of goodwill—it is true that more often than we care to recall, we have stood face to face with a need and with a clear, unambiguous chance to do something that would make a difference, and we have rationalized our way around it.

One day when I was a young college president, a student came by to tell me that his money had run out and that he had to leave school. In those days presidents knew students by name and knew much about their personal circumstances. But this student gave me some details about himself that I had not known. He said that he was a "country orphan." That is a child who gets passed around from one willing family to another with no legal papers signed by anyone. The last family to have him had died, and he needed to get out and "regroup." His immediate need was for someone to drive him some fifty miles into the country to get an old trunk and some fragments of furniture and household items that he cherished and thought he needed.

My first response was to brush it off, officially, as something beyond my office and let luck take care of his need. I tried that, and I even told myself that it was beneath a college president to take a school van or truck and drive a country orphan fifty miles into the woods to pick up scraps of junk. I had *almost* sold myself on that idea except for *one* thing: I had read too much, sung too much, prayed too long, and preached too often,

> Take my life and let it be Consecrated, Lord, to thee; Take my hands, and let them move At the impulse of thy love. . . .
>
> Take my will and make it Thine; It shall be no longer mine; Take my heart, it is thine own! It shall be Thy royal throne . . .[6]

The next thing I knew, I had gotten the school's pickup truck, changed my clothes, and the student and I had headed out for the country to get a country orphan's leavings. And the trip went fast because we sang and talked about the life of a country orphan all the way. That old truck seemed like the upper room where the Spirit descended or the temple where Isaiah saw the Lord. It was a benchmark for me, and brief moments like that have been spread over my years, and they have blessed me.

"Lord, when saw we thee a stranger, or naked, or hungry . . ." "Inasmuch as ye did it to the least of these my brethren, ye did it unto me."[7] The bottom line.

One other problem is that we allow no room, no space, no time in our lives for this kind of activity, this concern. "Our programs are crowded, and we are in a big hurry, Jesus. We understand *you,* but you don't understand *us*. We live in the real world, we protest, and this simple idealism has no place here." We are caught up in an urbanized, technological culture that is marked by competitiveness, and we are taught to be predatory, greedy, cunning, and ambitious. The side effect is that we have become hedonists, devoted to our personal delights, and narcissistic, lovers of ourselves before everyone else. It is a new idolatry, self-worship! So we have no time for the "least of these."

This creeps into our institutions, and we forget why they exist. A very large church in one of our major cities was sending over one hundred thousand dollars a year to Nigeria to convert and educate Yorubas in the Christian faith. Many Nigerians benefited from this generous effort; several achieved doctor's degrees in some of America's finest universities. But one Sunday morning a small group of Nigerians appeared and sought to worship in that magnificent church. And officers of the church, prominent businessmen, fraternal leaders, and persons of high standing in town, stood on the marble steps of that massive colonial building and denied those young Yorubas, with tribal marks on their cheeks and with an education provided by funds from that *very* church, *denied* them a chance to worship in the name of the One who said, ". . . I was a stranger and ye took me not in."[8]

One wonders what was said around the Lord's table when the decision was made to do such a thing, even in the 1950s. How did this action relate to the Christ whose praises the church members sang with such zest? Of course, many Christians have a strange view of their religion; they think that it only prepares them for death and heaven and that concern for the hungry, the hurt, the dispossessed, the alienated is some kind of liberalism or social gospel. By giving it such a label, they think they have gotten rid of the concern. But it was no "liberal" or "social gospel" propagandist who said, "Inasmuch as you did it not unto the least of these, ye did it not to me . . . go away into everlasting punishment."[9]

It appears that one sure way to go to hell is to ignore the so-called "social gospel"! The gospel, by its very nature, is social. If persons suffer in groups, that is "social." If groups *cause* the suffering, that makes it "social" also. "Social" refers only to how many persons are affected, and "the least of these my brethren" is more than one, single person. It is a cheap cop-out to use loaded labels in dealing with human suffering. If we are not prepared for discipleship, we should confess our weakness and ask for God's help. It is insincere to pretend that we do not understand what Jesus meant.

Clarence Jordan, the late director of the experimental farm called Koinonia in Americus, Georgia, was one of the finest preachers of the claims of Christ that we have had in our country. Once he was preaching to ministers at a Baptist conference in Green Lake, Wisconsin, when a preacher asked him straightforwardly, "Dr. Jordan, how can a modern, urban pastor preach the Sermon on the Mount and be a success?" Jordan replied, "Jesus did not give the Sermon on the Mount to successful, modern, urban pastors. He gave it to his disciples. You have to choose which you want to be if there is a conflict." This is the bottom line.

Thank God, every now and then we find a witness who helps us to understand what Jesus meant when he said, "I was a stranger and you took me in."[10] Ed Tuller and his late wife, Rose, had a fine ministry at the American Church in Paris. One Sunday morning, they noticed a black child in church, a member of a refugee family from Uganda, with massive cataracts practically blinding both eyes. The Lord laid this on their hearts, and within weeks it happened that a worldwide ophthalmology conference on eye diseases was held in Paris. When they spoke of this child's ailment, they found that a Jewish specialist, who lived near them back in New Jersey, and who attended that conference, volunteered to help the little girl to get surgery in New York. Rose and Ed spent an entire leave period shuttling back and forth between New Jersey and New York and attending to the needs of the Ugandan child whom they met in Paris. Later, a Hispanic surgeon operated and saved her sight in one eye. White Protestants, a New Jersey Jew, a Latin American, and a little girl from Uganda were caught up in living out what the Master meant when he said, "was a stranger and ye took me in."[11] The bottom line.

It is not too late for Christians to reclaim the power and authority of the Good News. God revealed to us in Christ his love and his expectation for the human family. He used a human life, a person with human dimensions like our own. Following him, we find the power, the authority, and the right to become the children of God. No one of us may ever do this to perfection, but by the grace of God, this is the direction in which we should be headed. This is the road we should be traveling; this is how life takes on joy and purpose. "I was hungry and you gave me meat . . . I was a stranger and you took me in."[12]

Finally, it gets clearer all the time how far God went to reach us. Even though God revealed himself to us in nature, in history, in logic, in music, and in mathematics, ultimately he deliberately chose the son of a poor Galilean carpenter's family. God passed over the mighty and the powerful and came to us in a life close to the heartache, the pain, and the estrangement in the world; a life lived in an occupied land, among people living in a police state, under a cold, indifferent expatriate governor and a puppet king; a life begun in a barn in Bethlehem. Everywhere a person turned, there was somebody in trouble. And this was the point at which the God of wisdom and love chose to enter time out of eternity, in the very midst of the human struggle.

In the third chapter of Luke is a clue to God's purpose, which has been marvelously illuminated in a recorded sermon by Gardner C. Taylor. Luke is telling us who the important people were when Jesus was born: Tiberius was emperor; Pilate was governor; Herod was king, a tetrarch, ruler over one fourth of the realm; Phillip was a tetrarch; and Lysanias was still another tetrarch; Annas was a high priest, and so was Caiaphas. But the word of God came to *John*—and not to any of the above!—the son of Zacharias, in the wilderness. He had no title at all. He wore a loincloth and ate locusts and honey. And the *Word* passed over all of those titled subjects and came to *John*; it passed by the palaces and the "most holy" places and found *John* in the wilderness. This almost says to us that if we really want to find God, we have to look for him somewhere other than around wealth and power, for somehow these thrive best where God is *not,* where God is excluded.

Preaching and witnessing for Christ will always be timeless and relevant, for each new generation has to be told the message again and again, in its own language and idiom. No one can inherit this message. The experience of finding God is more precious than finding a career, a spouse, or a lifetime job, for these things are all burdens without God. Yet isn't it strange how we tend to be naturally attracted to evil, rather than to God?

In my boyhood in Huntersville, a dusty hollow of Norfolk in those days, we had a familiar sight in our streets, a woman whose mind was defective and who pushed a cart constantly, picking up crepe paper, medicine bottles, coat hangers, broken toys, and you-name-it. She wore whatever she felt like wearing, winter clothes in hot summer weather, an evening gown that someone had thrown away, an abandoned fur coat—anything.

And the boys and girls, who had the nerve, would holler at her calling her "Crazy Ida!" Sometimes she would chase them or throw a bottle or a stick at them. Funny, I wanted to call her Crazy Ida too, but I couldn't find the nerve to do it.

Well, one day she rolled her cart slowly toward my end of the street, and I was alone, I thought. I checked all around to be sure, and then took my place in the lane beside our house, behind a bush. And just as she passed, I took in a deep breath and let the devil use me. "Crazy Ida," I shouted and ran like a thief.

But before I could get out of the back end of the lane, my mother had opened a side window that we never used. I could have dug a hole and crawled in. One gets embarrassed like that only two or three times in a full life span. She said, "Did you call her Crazy Ida?"

No reply. Just plain humiliation and shame. I had learned enough about Jesus to know better than to do what I did, but that awful, primordial, atavistic drag! Sin! It was so tempting to heap more pain on one already wounded deeply.

"Crazy Ida," Mamma said softly, which was not her style. "Don't call her that. She hasn't always been like she is today. We were girls together. She used to sing in choruses and recite poems like the rest of us, but she had a terrible marriage, and she broke under the strain. They took her children from her and sent her away. When she came back, her mind was gone. Don't add to her suffering."

She said more, but the impression has lasted for more than fifty years! I was so wrong. This is the bottom line: "Inasmuch as you did it to the least of these, you did it to me," Jesus said.[13]

Good religion meets life right where it is and deals with it. And I fear that the Christian faith will have to get closer to the real issues of life before it can become relevant to these times. I see a generation out there, raised on television violence, who do not know Martin Luther King, Adam Clayton Powell, John F. Kennedy, or Rosa Parks except by reputation, who have only heard of the Great Depression, and who have not had to work for their spending money. Our generation has been preoccupied with alcohol, divorce, materialism, military expansion, racism, pornography, and making money. So no wonder this generation finds it hard to believe in God!

But if *we* followed Jesus more closely, the people of this generation would see God in the Christ *we* serve and love. If *we* would lift him up in our own lives, they would say like the Greek visitors to the disciples, "Sir, we would see Jesus." They haven't met anyone like Jesus. They have not confronted any personality so compelling as Christ. They had not had their hearts touched like Jesus can touch them. They have not loved like Jesus can teach them to love. Their lives have never been changed like Jesus will change them, and nobody can take their talent, their strength, their fine abilities and harness them for good like Jesus can. Nobody can satisfy their curiosity, satiate their hunger, quench their thirst or revive their souls like Jesus can. We used to sing in church,

*I heard the voice of Jesus say,*
*"Behold I freely give*
*The living water; thirsty one,*
*Stoop down and drink, and live."*[14]

People don't need to get high. They don't need to shoot up. They don't need to sniff coke, smoke pot, or pop pills. They don't need to drink themselves into oblivion or soak their brains with one chemical after another. All they need is to open their hearts to Christ!

*I came to Jesus, and I drank*
*Of that life-giving stream;*
*My thirst was quenched, my soul revived,*
*And now I live in him.*

I'll never forget the image of Jesus that intrigued my mind so much so that I could not turn down his claim on my life. In Matthew 26:6 it is about halfway between Palm Sunday and Good Friday, Wednesday, and Jesus is in Bethany, at the house of Simon the Leper, having dinner. In Matthew 21:17 we read, "And he left them, and went out of the city into Bethany; and he lodged there." He took a room in Bethany on Palm Sunday night, and Wednesday he was still in Bethany at Simon's house. Of all the places for Jesus to be staying this last week on earth, the week before Calvary! He was lodging with a leper, a man with deep pits in his face, joints missing from his fingers and toes, a man who was too much of an embarrassment, too unclean, to be allowed to live with his family or friends. (The entire thirteenth and fourteenth chapters of Leviticus explain how a leper is to be handled from the time the disease is found until he is declared cleansed. It is one long round of humiliation, ostracism, and separation from everybody!) And people must have asked Simon, "Does Jesus know you? Are you from Galilee, too, Simon? Why is he staying at your house?"

Why did Jesus sleep in Simon's house and eat at his table and fellowship with one whom everyone sought to avoid? I could understand if Jesus had stopped there. But Jesus lodged there; the Son of God, living with a brokenhearted, lonely leper! He was there because he is a loving Jesus and a saving Jesus. He said, "I was sick and you visited me. I was a stranger and you took me in. Inasmuch as you did to the least of these my brethren, you did it to me."[15] This is the bottom line.

## NOTES

*Sermon source:* Samuel D. Proctor and William D. Watley, *Sermons from the Black Pulpit* (Valley Forge, PA: Judson Press, 1984), 87–91.

1. Matthew 25:40 (King James Version).
2. Ibid.
3. Matthew 25:46 (KJV).
4. Matthew 25:35–36 (KJV).

5. See Matthew 25:35.
6. Frances R. Havergal, "Take my Life and Let It Be" (1874), available at http://www.cyberhymnal.org/htm/t/m/tmlalib.htm.htm (accessed June 20, 2007).
7. Matthew 25:40 (KJV).
8. See Matthew 25:35.
9. See Matthew 25:40.
10. See Matthew 25:35.
11. Ibid.
12. Ibid.
13. See Matthew 25:40.
14. Horatio Bonar, "I Heard the Voice of Jesus Say" (1846), available at http://www.oremus.org/hymnal/i/io66html (accessed June 20, 2007).
15. Ibid.

### *Bibliographical Sources*

"Preachers Turn Out to Honor Samuel Proctor." *New York Times*, May 31, 1997.
Proctor, Samuel DeWitt. *The Substance of Things Hoped For: A Memoir of African-American Faith.* New York: G.P. Putnam's Sons, 1995.
Williams, Audrey. "Samuel D. Proctor," in Jessie Carney Smith, ed., *Notable Black American Men.* Detroit: Gale, 1999, 971–73.

# SANDY F. RAY

*(1898–1979)*

Sandy F. Ray was born in a rural farming community near Marlin, Texas, on February 3, 1898. He was one of ten children born to Sandy and Fannie Ray, migrant workers—hardworking, uneducated, and deeply religious. He attended Arkansas Baptist College and later Morehouse College in Atlanta, Georgia. His family moved to Ohio, and in the late 1930s Ray organized voting drives in Columbus. In 1942 Ray became the first black from Franklin County to be elected to the Ohio legislature.

In 1944 he became the pastor of Cornerstone Baptist Church in Brooklyn, New York, where he served until his death in 1979. Ray was a preacher's preacher and an activist. He believed in the reverse proclamation of the gospel and its practical implementation. As early as the 1950s, Cornerstone operated a day care center and a credit union. In 1964 the church built a one-million-dollar educational facility.

He was president of the Empire State Convention (New York State Baptist Convention) from 1954 until his death. He also was a first vice president in the National Baptist Convention, U.S.A., Inc., from 1968 until his death.

• • •

*Ray was known to many as a gentle preaching giant with a laugh and smile that put everyone at ease. It has been said of many preachers, "He's good, but he can't say it like Sandy Ray." Ray was best known for seeing in Scripture what few saw but wished they did. In this sermon Ray uses a towel, of all things, to talk about the importance of those who are treated as unimportant. He was able to join the commonplace images of life and experience with profound, deep spiritual insight that refreshed the many thousands that listened to him.*

## The Testimony of a Towel (1979)

> *He riseth from supper, and laid aside his garments; and took a towel, and girded himself.* —John 13:4 (King James Version)

He was approaching the end of his earthly life. His disciples were hopeful that Jesus would assert his power and take over the leadership of the religious and political systems of the nation. They felt certain that this young hero who had performed so many miracles and had gathered such a following could master the cruel Roman Empire and the arrogant church leaders.

They had started angling for positions in the prospective empire. They had been disputing along the way as to who would be the greatest in the kingdom. A lovely lady had approached him with a request that one of her sons would have a seat on the left and the other on the right. She assumed that both of them would be in his cabinet.

Jesus did not wish to leave the kingdom's redemption program in the hands of leaders whose sights were set on seats only. He did a most dramatic thing. The record says, "He stood up and laid his garments; and took a towel and girded himself." His disciples were stunned, shocked, bewildered. They were thinking of him appearing with a scepter, crown, throne, servants, and sword. Girded in a towel was a strange appearance for the king they had envisioned. How does he hope to control an empire girded in the attire of a slave?

In their humiliation, only Simon Peter would hazard a verbal protest. It was another impetuous and characteristic outburst. The very same Peter who drew a sword in Gethsemane and fled, who went to the palace of the high priest, and then denied his Lord. The same Peter who rushed into the water and then cried, "Lord, save me, I perish."[1] Who suggested on the Mount of Transfiguration, "Let us build three tabernacles."[2] And when our Lord spoke on his cross said, "This shall not be done unto thee."[3]

Peter said, "No, Master, not this. You are our revered leader. This is embarrassing to our fellowship. You should be taking a royal posture and regal charisma. This act is beneath your status. I am sorry, but I cannot permit you to wash my feet."

Jesus said, "Peter, if you refuse this, you will have no portion in common inheritance of the kingdom of God. You will miss the entire concept and purpose of the kingdom. If you miss this, you will be excluded from my unfolding dream. If you miss this, you will cancel your reservation to an inspiring spiritual pilgrimage." Peter said, "if it means this, 'Not only my feet, but my hands and head.' "[4]

Jesus was not merely washing the dust from the Judaic deserts from their feet; he was washing shackling fetters of tradition from their minds. He was washing the ancient cobwebs of customs and crippling concepts from their souls. Their feet were not as dusty as their hearts and attitudes. Their hearts and minds were dusty with selfish ambitions.

Jesus was not embarrassed to be girded in a towel because he knew that he was the only one in the fellowship who was tall enough to take a towel. The disciples walked on tiptoes seeking high seats; the Master took a towel. Jesus knew who he was, and he did not need any external pomp or regalia to prove who he was. He could have had angels serve him. He knew that he was a king in exile.

Jesus knew how to manage power. His disciples felt that he did not use his powers wisely. On one occasion they urged him to "call down fire" on people. Power is terribly dangerous in the hands of irresponsible people. Jesus was never power-drunk.

## What Is the Testimony of a Towel?

Jesus is saying that the kingdom of Heaven is not to be modeled after the Roman Empire and existing church. It is not to be a place for prestige, position, titles, and rank. The towel represents the royalty of service. Real royalty is wrapped in a towel, not a title. Humility is the watchword in the kingdom of heaven. "When you pray, use humility."[5] Do not use vain repetition . . . do not stand at a street corner and pray aloud to be heard by passersby. Closet yourself. "When you do alms," do not call the press or get on radio or TV. The Christian church is not a place for showmanship and exhibition.

Jesus said you have been conditioned in the old system that is rank- and racket-ridden. The greatest in my kingdom shall be the towel takers. In my kingdom, seats will be won by service. Crowns are made of towels. If there are no towel takers, the spiritual operation will be greatly impaired. Organized religion has an overabundance of rank-happy seat and status seekers.

There are degree mills all over this nation to satisfy people who feel that a degree will enhance their seating status. Many preachers feel that a degree will give them a seat in the higher category of the clergy fraternity. There are others who have girded themselves in the gospel towel and have humbly dedicated themselves to preaching the Word of God.

## The Towel Is the Symbol of True Greatness

We hear and read a great deal of the *greatest* in all circles of society. One wonders about their criterion for determining greatness. How does mankind measure greatness? In the clergy we hear a great deal of the greatest. We think of the size of the congregation, the staff, budget, eloquence, popularity, et cetera. We are living in a period of arrogance. It runs from individuals to nations. It is in our government, industries, labor unions, social agencies, intellectual circles, and religious circles. The tale of the towel is not popular in our world of pushing and pride.

Matthew 7:21–23: "Not every one that saith unto me, Lord, Lord, shall enter into the Kingdom of Heaven; . . . Many will say to me in that day, Lord, Lord, have we not prophesied in thy name? And in thy name have cast out devils? And in thy name done many wonderful works? And then will I profess unto them, I never knew you."

While the arrogant, disappointed group wanders in outer darkness, a humble, dedicated group on the right hand hears the joyful words, "Come, ye blessed of my Father, inherit the kingdom prepared for you from the foundation of the world."[6] In your credentials you do not have reference to casting out devils, prophesying, or any wonderful works, but you were sensitive to the needs of suffering people. The towel is the test of true greatness.

If we remove the towels from our culture, it would collapse. The titles would perish if there were no towels. The towel brigade on farms, in factories, sanitation, firemen, policemen, in kitchens, laundries, office workers, truck drivers, plumbers, electricians, and many other unheralded and non-titled keep our society moving.

A towel team is the hope of our arrogant, domineering, pompous, haughty world. The Lord is trying to say something to us, girded in a towel. He is trying to speak to organized religion, with all of its complicated machinery, formalities, theological dialogues, arguments, and theories split up by race, class, and clime. If we could meet our Lord, girded in a towel, most of our differences would be resolved, and we could exclaim like Thomas, "My Lord, and my God."[7]

Many executives in industry send their sons and daughters into factories to study the practical operation of the plant or factory. Later they move them into the front office where they might become vice president—later president. God sent his Son into this world, not with a scepter or a crown, but a towel. The record says that he laid aside his royalty and took a towel for his redemptive task. He met all types of arrogance, pride, egotism, jealousy, hatred, and bitterness.

His humility was tested in his ministry. It was tested in his arrest. He walked through a mob, girded in a towel of humility. Humility dominated his trial. At the church trial, the high priest and his cohorts could not deal with his poise and calmness. Pilate became terribly upset when Jesus looked into his frightened eyes. He attempted to wash what he saw in that humble man from his hands, but the humility of Jesus had penetrated his heart.

Jesus' humility was tested on the cross. I heard an old minister say many years ago that Death pounced upon Jesus on the cross to rush the dying process. Jesus told Death that he was giving up his life—no one could take it, and that he had several things to do during his crucifixion.

His humility was tested in his resurrection. When he arose from the tomb, he did not have a ticker-tape parade through Jerusalem. He did not call the press for an announcement. He spoke calmly to his disciples and said, "I am he who was dead, but behold I am alive forevermore."[8]

The headlines now read: "He endured the cross, despised the shame, and now he sits on the right hand of God the Father." Angels fall at his feet and cry, "Holy, worthy is the lamb who was slain from the foundation of the world. To him be power and dominion, and majesty and glory, and riches and wisdom and strength and blessing forever . . . And he shall reign forever and ever."[9]

If we would be great in the kingdom of God, we must take a towel. A towel is the route to glory. The real joy in religion is associated with a towel. The happiest people in this world are those who are satisfied to take a towel. Saints with towels build the kingdom of heaven. The towel brigade build and maintain our churches. When Jesus returns, he will not be seeking titles; he will be checking towels.

It was a towel crusade that followed Jesus into Jerusalem on the Palm Sunday demonstration. Someone said that the towel crew was entirely too noisy. They had come from the rural areas, villages, fisheries, farms, and were acquainted with the formalities of the capital city. Jesus said, "If we silence this towel talk, the rocks will cry out." Our arrogant, title, rank-happy culture desperately needs the warm, poised, calm seasoning of true humility. This should emerge from people who claim Jesus as their Lord.

### *Notes*

*Sermon source:* Sandy F. Ray, *Journeying through a Jungle* (Nashville, TN: Broadman Press, 1979), 31–38.

1. See Matthew 14:30.
2. See Luke 9:33.
3. Matthew 16:22 (King James Version).
4. See Matthew 18:8.
5. Matthew 6:5 (and just below, verse 2).
6. Matthew 25:34–40.
7. John 20:28 (KJV).
8. See Revelations 1:18.
9. See Revelations 5:12.

### *Bibliographical Sources*

"Ohio's African American Legislators," available at http://www.georgewashington-williams.org/text/rayS.html (accessed on July 4, 2005).

Taylor, Gardner C. "A President of Preaching: Eulogy of Sandy F. Ray." *The African American Pulpit* 4, no. 1 (Winter 2000–2001).

# FREDERICK G. SAMPSON II

*(1928–2001)*

Frederick George Sampson II was born in 1928 in Port Arthur, Texas, to Fredrick G. Sampson Sr. and Florence Frisco Sampson. A gifted athlete and also passionate for academics and scholarship, he graduated from Bishop College, Howard University, and the University of Louisville, culminating his formal education with a doctoral degree from the Virginia Theological Seminary. A lifelong learner, he continued with advanced studies at Columbus University, the University of Kentucky, and the Episcopal Theological Seminary of Virginia. One could not hear Sampson preach and not appreciate insights based in his love of knowledge and learning.

Seeking to bring his broad education to serve the needs of the community, Sampson served as the senior pastor of Mt. Lebanon Baptist Church in Louisville, Kentucky, from 1961 to 1970. He actively challenged the injustice of segregation and voter discrimination as he joined Martin Luther King Jr. and others in the 1965 protest in Selma, Alabama. Subsequently, he led hundreds of young people in a demonstration, attempting to integrate the downtown restaurants and movie theaters of Louisville, and because of his leadership role, he was arrested.

On June 10, 1950, Sampson married Earlene Zane Harrison. To this union of forty-seven years was born two children, Frederick G. III and Freda GeLene.

For thirty years, from 1971 to 2001, Sampson pastored the Tabernacle Baptist Church of Detroit, Michigan. Under his leadership the church developed outreach programs and ministries that served the needs of the community and received national attention. He was also preacher and pastor to the entire city of Detroit, and upon his death on October 10, 2001, the city mourned a great loss and paid respect to his distinguished service to the entire city.

Joining his intellectual passion with tremendous gifts in preaching, Sampson's ministry extended worldwide, including Germany, Rome, the Netherlands, five countries in Africa, Israel, and the Bahamas and other Caribbean islands. Sampson was a frequent lecturer at colleges and universities throughout the United States, and he served as annual keynote speaker for various congresses, fellowships, conventions, councils, community programs, and coalitions. Sampson was honored by *The African American Pulpit* as one of the "Great Revivalists" in America in its Winter 2001–2002 issue. Sampson was also recognized twice by *Ebony* magazine as one of the fifteen greatest black preachers in America.

• • •

*During fifty years of ministry, Sampson traveled across America and the world preaching, teaching, inspiring, loving, correcting, and helping audiences ponder the profound mysteries of God. Combining intellectual depth with the passion and emotional freedom of the African American preaching tradition, he presented a model of preaching that thousands emulated. He is most remembered for his unique ability to use philosophy, medicine, science, poetry, imagery, stories, and nature to make his sermons come alive. "The Death of Hope" is one of Sampson's most beloved sermons and is indicative of his preaching prowess.*

## The Death of Hope (May 1982)

*And they stood still, looking sad. One of them, named Cleopas, answered and said to Him, "Are You the only one visiting Jerusalem and unaware of the things which have happened here in these days?" And He said to them, "What things?" And they said to Him, "The things about Jesus the Nazarene, who was a prophet mighty in deed and word in the sight of God and all the people, and how the chief priests and our rulers delivered Him up to the sentence of death, and crucified Him. But we were hoping that it was He that was going to redeem Israel. Indeed, besides all this, it is the third day since these things happened."* —Luke 24:17–21 (New American Standard Bible)

There is not a person here who hasn't had similar experiences that these men are having on their way to Emmaus. They are having an Egypt experience. Egypt is not a matter of geography, just as Eden cannot be geographically fixed, or the land of Nod necessarily located. Egypt can be everybody's experience. If you've lived at least a few years, you've had an experience with Egypt. Come on now. And if you haven't, just keep on going to bed and keep on waking up. If you don't go to Egypt, Egypt is going to locate itself in you.

Egypt is that point in life when we experience the death of hope. Come on. It's when we experience the going down of the sun of joy, when the dark sky covers the ability to see. When the harmonious sounds of life run into discord, and you can't make sense out of life's nonsense. It's that point in life when we thought we were free, then we experience the gravity of enslavement. When in all of our decisions we discover we no longer can keep what we promised. We can't do what we said, we can't reach where we were headed, and we can't stand as tall as we told folk we would stand. That's Egypt.

Egypt is that point where a fellow bragged about doing things that he wanted to do and others knew he was wrong. But he declared, "I can stop when I want to." It's when habitual habits become compulsive forces and compulsion runs into repulsion. Come on now. It's when a drinking man brags about how he can hold his whiskey and then his whiskey starts holding him. It's when a young man walks away from his daddy and declares, "you lived your life, now I'm going to live mine" and living for him becomes nothing but a lift from a sidewalk. And when the sun goes down it drops him at a one-way street, and he loses the map to take him into tomorrow, and all of his days become nothing but yesterdays.

Egypt is that day when that young woman looks at her mamma and says, "I'm tired of your foolishness. I didn't ask to be born. I'm on my way to live my own life." And because she looks good and boys tell her that she makes them feel good, she thinks life is good. But then she wakes up one day and discovers there are better bodies being made every day, she's in Egypt. The saddest sight in the world is to see a woman who depended upon her physical beauty and her talents and age begins to take both of them from her. Come on now. And the same folks she used to look down on she's got to go and lean on. What do you do when hope dies?

What do you do with life when you've been giving most of your time to a job and you discover it's not the source of your joy? How do you handle life when you've moved from where you were and try to walk where you're going without Jesus, who brought you to discover where you've gotten is worse than what you thought it was gon' be? And then the powers that you thought you could control begin to overpower you. Come on. How do you handle your life when the sun of joy goes down beyond the western hills of happiness?

A loss of hope will dismantle your dreams. A loss of hope will diminish your expectation, and a loss of hope will disintegrate your dedication. And you don't have to be a black in the ghetto to experience the death of hope. And I tell young folks to stop lying, stop going around here saying, "I would have been something if my daddy . . ." No, don't tell me what your daddy didn't do. What have you done for you lately? The ghetto ain't the problem. The house in which we were born is not the problem. I say to professors, you be careful just because you got some smarts in your head doesn't mean you got some sense in your heart. Come on now. Because all you've got in your head can't handle your heart when it breaks. You better hear me. When hope dies you need something else.

Let's pick up three people or groups close to Jesus—the women, these men on the road to Emmaus, and the disciples—and watch them when their hope dies. First, those women came to the tomb, but look what they came with. They didn't come with singing. They didn't come with shouting. They didn't come to get their dreams fulfilled. They came with oil, frankincense, and myrrh. They came to embalm a dead hero, not to welcome a resurrected savior. And even when he showed up they didn't know him. Oh come on now, because Mary said, "They have taken away my Lord, and I do not know where they have laid him."[1]

Second, these two men on the road to Emmaus were going from the tomb. The action was at the tomb. Now, I don't care what kind of noise you find in the church. I don't care how they hurt your heart at the church. I don't care how the preacher won't come see you at the church.

You better not walk away from the church because your hope is in the church. These men were walking away from the tomb and that's where the power was and they were going to the west. Come on now. The west is sundown. The east is sunrise! Whenever you walk away from the church, you're on your way to sundown. I don't care how much money you make, you're on your way to sundown. I don't care how big your house is, you're on your way to sundown, and finally life is gon' put you down! Be careful how you walk away from the church.

Third, the apostles were above the tomb hopeless because they were trying to recapture yesterday. Jesus had already been resurrected. They had already seen him and Peter still said, "I'm going fishing." And the others said, "I'm going with you."[2] They had seen the resurrection and still they did not believe. They were trying to recapture yesterday. Baby, I don't care how happy you were at courtship, it can't help you in marriage. I don't care how you loved your other pastor, you better try to love the one you got now. Come on now because yesterday can't be revisited. Yesterday can't be relived, and yesterday can't be revised. You got a lot of church members who are not as loyal as they used to be. They used to tithe. They don't tithe anymore because they see folk not living for Jesus. They find deacons doing wrong, teachers doing wrong, preachers doing wrong, and then they say, "I'm not going to do right." The Bible says, "Fret not thyself because of evildoers, neither be thou envious against the workers of iniquity. For they shall soon be cut down like the grass, and wither like the green herb."[3] The Bible says, "Lean not unto thine own understanding . . . Commit thy way unto the Lord . . . and He shall direct thy path."[4] Now the thing that bothers me about all three of them was that it was on the third day. Oh, you don't hear me. I said it was on the third day that their hope died. They forgot. Jesus said that the son of man must be delivered. The son of man must suffer.[5] The men on the road were talking about all that happened, but Jesus told them it was going to happen. He said it was going to happen on the third day, and on the third day it happened.

But they wanted it to happen the way they wanted it to happen. You can't make Jesus do what you want him to do. And Jesus is not going to do it at the time you want him to do it. But his delays are not his denial. Come on now. I asked him for water, he gave me a shovel and told me to dig. I asked him for shelter, he gave me a forest and told me to build. I asked him for food, he gave me some seeds and told me to plant. I asked him for courage and hope, he gave me some enemies and put me in the darkness and told me to struggle.

But my word tonight is that Canaan is always available. If you find yourself in Egypt, Canaan is always available. If your hope dies, all you've got to do is let Jesus relocate in your heart. Oh, my God. And whenever Jesus shows up, that is the resurrection of hope. And the good thing is that if you've got Jesus as your Savior and your hopes die, you don't have to send for him. For the Bible said, as they were walking and discussing the things that killed their hope, Jesus himself walked in. What I like about Jesus is he walks into the scene of your misery. He catches up with you. I dare you to worship him. I dare you to be loyal to him. When you fall down, you don't have to come to church. It's good to have a pastor, but you don't have to call your preacher when the world knocks you down. That's a good position from which to get in touch with heaven. Jesus himself will show up.

Look at what Jesus did for these men of the road to Emmaus and ultimately for the women, the disciples, and us. He enlightened their minds, enriched their hearts, and endowed their souls. Come on now. God doesn't have to kill your enemies. He doesn't have to put the darkness away. God can let you walk into the teeth of the storm, and all you will need is an enlightened mind. He could let your enemies come all around you and all you will need is an enriched heart. He could let folk knock you down, talk about you, lie on you, let your husband walk away, let your wife love somebody else, let your children disobey, and with an enlightened mind, enriched heart, and endowed soul, you'll stand up anyhow. You'll become like that little toy man I brought my son when he was a little boy. You've seen one of those rubber men. It's big at the bottom and my little boy used to knock it down. Bam. It stood back up. Bam, it stood back up again. And all of a sudden he knocked it down and got on top of it. He rolled around with it and stayed down with it. But the moment he let it go, it stood up again. He said, "Daddy, I can't beat it." I said, "I know, son. You're attacking it from the outside, but what makes it stand up is on the inside." Oh, you don't hear me.

You let the world knock you down. You let loneliness knock you down. You let heartache knock you down. Let a lost job knock you down. Let hopelessness knock you down, but I dare you to have Jesus on the inside. Any time they knock you down, you'll stand up again with an enlightened mind, an enriched heart, and an endowed soul.

I am on my way somewhere. I don't know about you, but I'm on my way somewhere. Jesus is all the world to me, my light, my joy, and my all. He gives me strength from day to day and without him I would fall. Somebody said, "You're getting old and yet you just keep on plowing. What keeps you going?" Leaning on the everlasting arms. Oh how bright the path grows from day to day leaning. I said, "Leaning on the everlasting arms."[6] I heard, I said I heard, I heard somebody say, that when troubles rise I'll hasten to his throne. Jesus, I said Jesus is all you'll need. Jesus will walk by your side. Jesus will come when you need him. Jesus will be there every time. When you've wiped your pillow with your midnight tears, Jesus will walk with you. Your enemies might be all around you. But don't worry. Don't worry. Don't worry. Jesus will prepare a table before you in the presence of your enemy.[7] He's alright. I said he's alright. Is he alright? Is he alright? Jesus. I said Jesus. When Hope dies, Jesus can resurrect it. Is he alright?

### *Notes*

*Sermon source: The African American Pulpit* 5, no. 1 (Winter 2001–2002), 104–7.

1. John 20:13 (New American Standard Bible).
2. John 21:3 (NASB).
3. Psalm 37:1–2 (King James Version).
4. Proverbs 3:5, Psalm 37:5, Proverbs 3:6.
5. Mark 8:31 (NASB).
6. "Leaning on the Everlasting Lord," Sing to the Lord Hymnal (Kansas City: Lillenas Publishing, 1993), number 596.
7. See Psalm 23:5.

### *Bibliographical Sources*

"Celebrating a Life of Love." *Detroit Free Press*, October 18, 2001, B1.

"Celebrating the Life, the Legacy, and the Love of Reverend Dr. Frederick G. Sampson II." Funeral program, Tabernacle Missionary Baptist Church, October 17, 2001.

"The Legacy of a Leader." *Michigan Chronicle*, October 17–23, 2001, A1.

"The Reverend Frederick Sampson II." *Detroit News*, November 7, 2001, S125.

## MANUEL L. SCOTT SR.

*(1926–2002)*

Eminent pastor, theologian, and educator Manuel Lee Scott Sr. retired from full-time pastoral ministry on March 5, 1995, after more than fifty years of faithful service to the church. Scott pastored Calvary Baptist Church in Los Angeles for three decades before settling, in 1982, in Dallas, Texas, where he ministered to the congregation of St. John Missionary Baptist Church. Under Scott's guidance, the St. John church experienced an exceptionally vibrant period of growth in numbers and community service.

Born on November 11, 1926, to Opal Williams and Thomas Busy Scott in Waco, Texas, Rev. Scott graduated from Bishop College with a bachelor of arts degree before receiving a doctor of divinity degree from Texas College. In 1947 he married Thelma Jean (Joe) and they had six children: Sherilyn, Rev. Manuel Scott Jr., Ronald, Paula, Gregg, and Jackie. Manuel Scott Jr. became a great preacher in his own right and was one of the leading African American Youth Revival evangelists of the 1970s and '80s.

Manuel Scott Sr. was well regarded for the poetic brilliance of his sermons, his masterful delivery, his biblical knowledge, his capacity to simplify scripture and make it relevant, and for preaching timeless sermons. This preaching made him a leading revivalist for thirty-plus years.

All of the great African American preachers are known for producing homiletical offspring, and Scott was a part of this tradition. As a regular lecturer at Bishop College in Dallas, he left an indelible impression on the African American homiletical training landscape. In its heyday, the now defunct college served as a major place of training for African American clergy. Many of the Bishop preachers trained in the 1960s, '70s, and '80s were known for having some of the Scott style in their delivery.

Scott served as president of the Western Baptist State Convention of California and conducted notable lectures for the National Baptist Congress of Christian Education, the Southwestern Baptist Theological Seminary, Monrovia Baptist Seminary in Liberia, and Boston University, among others. Scott was also well known for his evangelism work and served as secretary of the board of evangelism for the National Baptist Convention of America, U.S.A., Inc. He was also active in the International Congress for World Evangelism in Switzerland.

Morehouse College in Atlanta inducted him into the Martin Luther King Jr. International College of Preachers in 1994. He wrote two books: *From a Black Brother* (1971) and *The Gospel for the Ghetto* (1973). Manuel Scott Sr. was honored by *Ebony* magazine as one of the fifteen greatest black preachers in America in November 1993.

• • •

*This sermon is an example of Scott's impeccable ability to make the Gospel plain, relevant, and timeless. Though preached in the 1970s, it speaks to Christians of any age. It is sprinkled with metaphors and highlights Scott's use of quotes from learned writers. It is evangelical in tone, and in step with the leanings of much of the African American Baptist Church.*

## Heavenly Grace and Human Response (ca. 1970s)

*What shall I render unto the Lord for all his benefits toward me?*
—Psalm 116:12 (King James Version)

The person who is wise and well-meaning yearns to do something for those who have done something for him or her. If you are a well-meaning person and if you are wise, you hunger and thirst to do something for the people who are nice to you. With that idea in the foreground and background, I want to talk today about "Heavenly Grace and Human Response."

I turn to the Old Testament to designate a text for this talk. We should keep in mind that while the Old Testament is not as full and systematic in formulating the concept of grace, it does record the experience of grace. And so, it is to the Old Testament, Psalm 116:12, that I turn for the text of the morning.

The psalmist asks, "What shall I render unto the Lord for all of his benefits toward me?" Since God has been so kind to me, what shall I give God back? Heavenly grace and human response.

One Sunday I talked about amazing grace—an interpretation. I put the spotlight on heavenly grace. Robert Louis Stevenson once said that all is grace. We breathe grace. We walk on it. We live and die by grace. Grace, it has been said time and again, grace is God's unmerited favors and undeserved benefits. Grace is the good we have that we didn't even ask for. All of us are beneficiaries of divine grace.

Grace, says Wineman, is that concrete good in every situation that we did not place there. Grace is the leftover from our lost paradise. Grace is that equipment for existence that did not expire with the endemic expunging. God did put humankind out of the garden, but some good things were left. Grace is the ambassador and attendant of life. Grace meets us on our arrival, and grace follows us until the journey is over.

You hear people say, "You know, I've never had any good thing." But, oh yes, you have! The moment you entered the time space drama, good things met you. Things you didn't ask for, things you couldn't make—like the sun, the moon, the wind, and the stars. Heavenly grace—we did not put it here. It was all here when we got here. You're talking about,

"I'm a self-made man." Nah, you're not. Nobody is self-made. If God had not put the earth here, you would not be here. Grace is all over the place—heavenly grace.

Grace is the sum total of all that God has done for us in Jesus Christ, and through Jesus Christ, and that's why we celebrate every Lord's day. We celebrate Jesus because through Jesus Christ, we have forgiveness for our sins. We have the demands of the law met. We have reconciliation with God Almighty. We are liberated from the curse of a broken law. We have a ticket out of hell and a passport to paradise. That's why I get happy sometimes—because through Jesus Christ, great grace has visited me. Christ is the good Samaritan who picks me up time and again after I've been wounded and beaten, stripped down. Jesus comes along and picks me up.

Christ is like a mother hen. Time and again, he gathers us like chickens under his wings and hides us, shelters and protects us. Heavenly grace. Many of us wouldn't be here if he had not sheltered us, had not hidden us from the dangers of this life. Heavenly grace. And, since God's grace is all about us; since we couldn't make a day—maybe you don't have any religion, but I want to tell you—you couldn't make it a day without heavenly grace. In fact, there isn't anyone among us who could make it a day. If you think you're smart, try to make a day. If you think our technology and our science have somehow or another moved us into being gods, let one of us try to make a day or keep night from coming on. Heavenly grace. Listen, you ought to do something about that. You ought not just shout about it and sing about it. You ought to respond, because heavenly grace just hangs over our destiny. Heavenly grace.

Maybe you heard about that man who joined one of those sophisticated, silk stockings churches. And, of course, he said amen and he shouted. And, a lot of the sophisticates complained about his hallelujah/hosanna-type religion. And so, they sent a committee to see him. The committee was to tell him that this church is a very sophisticated church, and we don't shout, and we don't say amen. We're intellectuals, and we've got our religion invisible and incomprehensible. And we would like for you, next time when you come to church, just to be quiet. When the committee arrived at his home, he was plowing using his mules—working on the farm he owned. And they told him what the church desired. And he said, "Thank you for coming. But, I want to tell you something. You see that little house on the hill? The Lord gave it to me. See this land, this little farm of ours? I didn't get it by myself; the Lord gave it to me, and it's paid for. You see this body of mine that I am plowing this field with? I didn't make me; the Lord made me. See my wife over there, and my children? The Lord gave all that to me. So, I'll tell you what you do. Since you don't want me to shout in your church, hold my mules. Just thinking about it all makes me want to shout right here!"

If you think about it this morning, you'd feel like shouting, too. Because whatever you have, the Lord gave it to you. Heavenly grace. I think the reason history is not renewed and society not reconstructed is because we have celebrated God's grace, but most of us haven't done anything about it. We haven't responded to it. We talk about it being amazing grace, but then what is our response?

Since God's grace has brought us thus far, what shall we do? Francis Schaeffer, moving in the same thought vein, raises the question, How then shall we live? Since grace saved us, how then shall we live? How shall I say thank you for all the things that you've done for me?[1] You know what he's asking? He's asking: Since God is so good, what should be my response? How shall I say thank you?

Saints of God, he let me get up and go to work and rear my children and keep making it night and day, and he keeps sending the seasons—then how shall I say thank you? What shall I render unto God? I just hope I can send somebody away from here wanting to do something. You see, the preacher is not an actor, nor is he simply an artist. The gospel preacher is a proctor and a provoker, and you people are not just spectators and theatergoers. It's time you came to church and acted like the people who heard John preach on the Jordan. You ought to be asking, "Preacher, what must I do? What shall I do? Since grace has picked me up and given me great salvation, what shall I render back to God for all of his benefits?"

Well now, listen, what shall I do? You must not take the grace of God in vain. The apostle Paul said, "By the grace of God I am what I am. . . ."[2] Now that's true of every one of us. You can't sing like you sing, and I can't either without God's grace. Whatever we are, we are that by God's grace. Then how shall we say thank you? Well now, for one thing, since you know God's grace has helped you to make it and that without it you just couldn't be, the first thing I would do is respond—have you ever done something for people and they do nothing for you? Some of you parents know about it. You know what it is to rear children who just act like you're dead. They never do nothing for you. Some of you wives know about it. You are always giving, and he never does nothing for you. How shall we respond?

So let me tell you—for one thing, you know what you ought to do? You ought to live as good as you can. Now none of us can live perfectly, but we can practice goodness and do the best we can. And, the more I look around, the more I ache from the fact that the reason our planet, our world, is in such a mess is not simply a lack of intelligence but a lack of integrity. A lot of people don't intend to do what's good. It isn't that they don't know. They just don't intend to. We're in misery on this planet also not simply because of ignorance but because of the presence of meanness. Some folk are just mean. They get a kick out of messing with other folk's peace. They get a joy out of needling other folk. They are just downright mean. They'd rather lie than tell the truth. They'd rather make you cry than to see you smile. That's just downright meanness. They'd rather give you a frown than to give you a smile. Just downright meanness.

And, not only that, many people are not just weak; they are wicked. There is a difference, you know. That brother with the bottle in his mouth may just be weak. That's right. That brother with that needle in his arm might just be weak. But when you plot pain for other folk, when you scheme and strategize so you can bleed other folk, then you're not weak; you're wicked. I tell you what you do—since God has been so good, live as good as you can. If you can't make a hundred, keep pressing up toward the mark, because goodness will surely win out. Live as good as you can. I want to tell you something. Nothing has happened in the New Testament to invalidate, "Blessed is the man that walketh not in the counsel of the ungodly, nor standeth in the way of sinners, nor sitteth in the seat of the scornful."[3] That man is blessed. And, it goes on to say, "He shall be like a tree planted by the rivers of water . . . his leaf also shall not wither; and whatsoever he doeth shall prosper."[4] Since God by his grace has been so nice to you, you ought to live as good as you can. Don't just struggle along caring nothing about how you live. Shame on you! God loves good living.

Well now, that's one way to respond, but then there's a second way. I'm talking about human response to heavenly grace. Since the grace of God has blessed you so, then you ought to be as generous as you can. Since amazing grace is all over the place, then I'll tell you what you ought to do. You ought to be as gracious, as generous as you can. I hate to see a stingy saint. Don't you hate to see people who talk about Jesus has saved them and they are niggardly cheap; won't give a cripple man a crutch. Since God is so gracious, then each of us who knows that grace ought to be as generous as we can. It is still true. It is more blessed to give than to receive. It is still true. Cast your bread upon the waters and wait for it. After many days, God will send it back again. Some see certain folk and say, "They're not going to ever have anything." Whoever gives has. Jesus has decreed that he who would save his life must lose it, and he who would gain his life must give it.[5] I get so sick of folk telling me, "You don't have no sense, just giving." But, ah, you can't beat God giving. If he doesn't give me anything else, he's already given me so much of his grace. I could die today and it would be all right. The grace of God has blessed me. The only way this world will get straight is we've got to raise up more generous folk. Some folk who won't bank everything, but somehow or another will share it with people who don't have it. That's the only way this world will get straight.

Since God's grace has saved me, it makes me generous, generous. You can't live unless you give; you'd die. And then you ought to give until it hurts. That's the way God gave. He gave Jesus until it hurt God. It hurt God to see his Son born in a barn in a manger. That hurt. It hurt God to see Jesus walking in poverty among the rest of humanity. It hurt God. And then, to see him betrayed and denied, that hurt God. And then, to see him hang there on an old rugged cross—that hurt God. The old preacher said that God turned his back on the world and said that if my Son groans one more time, I'll grasp the world out of existence. It hurt God when he was giving, and you have to give until it hurts. And don't give it because people will give back to you. Do it because God has already given.

Well now, let me close. One more time, heavenly grace. I'll tell you what it makes me do. It makes me live as good as I can, and it makes me be as generous as I can. But then, it also makes me graceful. Listen, since God's grace has done all this for me, then God makes me a dispenser and distributor of grace. Since amazing grace has come into my life and since amazing grace makes up my environment; since amazing grace is a dominant reality in the universe; since amazing grace is the ultimate cosmic good, since amazing grace is a many-splendored thing; since amazing grace saved a wretch like me, then I ought to be a dispenser of grace.

Listen, a lot of people look at me, and they think I'm soft. But do you know it takes more courage to be compassionate? It takes more courage to dispense grace than it takes to put your foot down. I just keep hearing somebody say, "Put your foot down." God Almighty, if God had put his foot down, I wouldn't have been here this morning. If God had put his foot down, you wouldn't have been here. Grace makes me a dispenser of grace. That's right. A real, mature Christian is abundant in mercy.

And you know what grace did for you and me? Grace clothed me with a righteousness I don't have. And that's the way I'll do you. I look at you and I know that you're not altogether right. You've got some imperfections and shortcomings in you. But when I look at you, I do what God's grace did for me. I put righteousness on you that you don't have. I look at you and know you're not a perfect saint, but I put on you righteousness that you don't have.

Amazing grace let me off the hook. And, since it let me off, then I have to let you off, because that's what he did for me. And then, amazing grace sought me out, looked for me, tried to find me. And, since it did that for me, somehow or another I have to seek for you. And then, through many dangers, toils, and snares, I have already come. Grace brought me. Grace sustained me safe thus far, and grace will lead me on. Since grace sustained me, then when I look at you and you don't feel like going on, since grace gave me a push, I'll give you a push. That's the way this world will get right. Somebody here this morning ought to raise that question—what shall I render since God has been so good to me, what shall I render unto him?

### *Notes*

*Sermon source: The African American Pulpit* 7, no. 1 (Winter 2003–2004), 84–88.

1. See "My Tribute," *African American Heritage Hymnal*, number 11 (Chicago: GIA Publishing, 2001).
2. 1 Corinthians 15:10 (King James Version).
3. Psalm 1:1 (KJV).
4. See Psalm 1:3.
5. See Mark 8:35.

### *Bibliographical Sources*

Scott, Manuel Lee, Sr. *From a Black Brother.* Nashville, TN: Broadman Press, 1971.

———. *The Gospel for the Ghetto: Sermons from a Black Pulpit.* Nashville, TN: Broadman Press, 1973.

Texas Legislature Online. "Texas House of Representatives, Resolution No. 437," in *Texas Legislature.* http://www.capitolstate.tx.us/tlo/74R/billtext/HR004371.htm (accessed January 19, 2005).

# GARDNER CALVIN TAYLOR

*(1918– )*

Gardner Calvin Taylor was born in Baton Rouge, Louisiana, the only child of the Rev. Washington Monroe Taylor and Selina Taylor. Gardner Taylor grew up in a home committed to Christian concerns and racial uplift, influenced by the wisdom and lore of the black church tradition. Though without formal education, his father was one of the leading preachers of his day. He died when Gardner was thirteen.

Although originally intent on pursuing law, after graduation from Leland College in 1937 he entered Oberlin Graduate School of Theology in Ohio. He attended Oberlin in answer to the call he sensed from God after surviving an automobile accident in which two white men died and only he and two white men witnessed the accident.

While in seminary at Oberlin, Taylor served as student pastor of Bethany Baptist Church in nearby Elyria, Ohio. After graduating in 1940 he married Laura Scott; to this union one daughter, Martha, was born. He then returned to his home state to pastor Beulah Baptist Church in New Orleans. In 1943 he was called back to Baton Rouge to pastor Mt. Zion Baptist Church, where his father had served. Five years later, in 1948 at thirty years of age, Taylor accepted the call to pastor Concord Baptist Church of Christ in Brooklyn, New York. He remained at Concord until he retired in 1990 after forty-two fruitful years. During Taylor's tenure Concord Baptist became New York City's largest Protestant congregation and one of the largest churches in America.

Taylor's voice has been heard from the pulpit or platform at several meetings of the World Baptist Alliance, the American Baptist Convention, the Progressive National Baptist Convention; the National Baptist Convention, U.S.A., Inc. and the Protestant Council of Churches of New York City, to name a few places. His sermons as guest preacher on the NBC-sponsored *National Radio Vespers Hour* and on *The Art of Living* were heard by millions throughout America from 1959 to 1970. In his sermons one sees the excellence of his craftsmanship and the spiritual depths of their content. Taylor has received numerous testimonies to his gifts and genius. Taylor was described by Michael Eric Dyson in a cover story for *The Christian Century* (January 4–11, 1995) as "poet laureate of the pulpit" and by Edward Gilbreath in *Christianity Today* (December 11, 1995) as "The Pulpit King." *Christian Century* also named him the "Poet Laureate of American Protestantism." Laura Scott Gardner died in 1995, and in late 1996 Taylor married Phillis Strong.

In 2000 he received from President Bill Clinton the Presidential Medal of Freedom, America's highest civilian honor. *Ebony* magazine has consistently listed him as an outstanding African American preacher, and he has also been honored by *Time* and *Newsweek*. He has written *How Shall They Preach?* (1977) as well as other books. *The Words of Gardner C. Taylor* is a six-volume collection that spans five decades of sermons, lectures, essays, and interviews.

• • •

*A consummate pulpiteer, in Taylor's sermons, as in the one presented here, one always sees his poetic flair and high Christology. The depth and breadth of his erudition, his admirable ability to depict and express meaning vividly, and his ability to inspire combine to make each Taylor sermon a road map toward greater understanding and appropriation of the Christian faith. There have been few preachers who can show the lights and shadows of Scripture by such ready adjectives, pictorial phrases, and the traditional grand manner of euphony and resonance. In this particular contemplative sermon, Taylor shows his deep devotion to Scripture and to his Lord and helps listeners to see and experience the length and breadth of human depravity, then lifts them to the heavenly realm to experience and see the saving life and activity of Jesus Christ. "His Own Clothes" was preached during the 1982 Hampton University Ministers' Conference.*

## His Own Clothes
## (1982)

> *And when they had mocked him, they took off the purple from him, and put his own clothes on him, and led him out to crucify him.*
> —Mark 15:20 (King James Version)

Short of the cross, and the awful sting of the betrayal by a friend, the encounter our Lord had that night in the barracks with the soldiers represents to me the most humiliating aspect of all that he passed through in your interest and in my interest. We may suffer a very great deal and we may bear it, and may bear it nobly, if we have left to us our dignity. But when our sense of personhood is assaulted, when our humanity is pushed off and becomes the target of the jibes and sneers of those around us, and we are pictured and characterized as other than and less than human, this represents the nadir, the bottom-most pit of humiliation.

Black people in this country have endured a great number of things. But I think the most sinister indication of pain that we have known occurred in the long record of the attempt to push us out of the human family, to deny us our standing as human beings, to caricature how we looked. The old, long idea that ran through so much of our pain in this country had much to do with the image of course, the image was done partly on the part of the oppressor trying to salvage some of his humanity by denying to the oppressed its humanity. But the caricature of the thick white lips, the wide-eyed terror, the foot shuffling, the head scratching, the wide-tooth showing, grinning darky, was an attempt to deny us our humanity. The Stepin Fetchit caricature was aimed at denuding us of our dignity—stripping us of our participation in the human family. And one of the greatest flights of the human spirit is represented on this continent that we (you and I) are gathered here as the children and grandchildren and the descendants of those who would not be denied their humanity.

If someone says that the caricature of Stepin Fetchit had its counterpart in the Laurel and Hardy comics, in the slapstick comics, the Marx Brothers, they were comic relief. They had also Clark Gable and Myrna Loy. We had only Stepin Fetchit.

More than the ridicule and the scorn which were visited upon us was the outrage visited upon our Lord, Jesus. Do you ever ponder in the quietness and stillness of your own reflection what the Lord went through for you? Does it ever ring your heart, the humiliation which he endured? It was a descent into the most profound shame the human spirit has ever been called upon to bear. It started on that Thursday evening in the inner-agony of Gethsemane. It followed with a sting of the betrayal by a friend. There was the submission to the chains of hands that had raised themselves against nobody, except to touch eyes that were blinded.

Then there was the trial; they spat on your Lord that night and then blindfolded him and in challenge and defiance of his holy son-ship, they taunted him with words, as the stinging sound of the slap rang against his cheek. "Prophesy who struck you."[1] And then they scourged him probably on the same platform where the accused prisoners stood; they took a leather whip with bits of metal and slices of bone studding the whip. Every lash of the whip on his naked back where they had stripped him down to his waist for you and yes, for me. And with his hands tied to a pillar, every stroke of the lash drew its own canal of blood and the bits of lead and the pieces of bone gouged out pieces of flesh. Men were known to die under that lash and others emerged from that ordeal in raving madness. The Lord Jesus took it all for you and for me.

Does it touch your heart? Do you sometimes in the solitude of your own reflection weep a silent tear as the words of that hymn come to you, "Was it for crimes that I have done, / he groaned upon the tree. / Amazing pity, grace unknown / and love beyond degree. / Alas and did my savior bleed / and did my sovereign die. / Would he devote *that* sacred head / for a sinner such as I? / Well might the sun in darkness hide / and shut his glory in, / when Christ the mighty maker died, / for man the creature's sin."[2]

Then, when sentence had been passed, they turned him over to the soldiers. Let me tell you about these men. They were hard-bitten, tough, professional legionaries already chaffing at having drawn this assignment in that hot, dry-ridden country with its dust and its barrenness and among a strange and offensive people whom they could never understand and among whom there were always the ripples of rebellion. A Roman soldier cursed his fate that he was assigned to this outpost of civilization. They found little pleasure in Palestine and they took their sport where they could find it. One of their pleasures, a wicked and terrible pleasure it was, but these men were not in a position to choose their pastime. One of their pleasures was having turned over to them a convicted criminal that he might be taunted and become the butt of their jokes and the target of their sport and the object of their barrack humor to suffer all of the vulgarity of their stored-up obscenity, serving in that outpost of civilization, far off the beaten path of history.

And so they took him and led him off. The Praetorian Guard (Pilate's military detachment), they carried him over to the barracks with no supervising authority to keep restraint upon them. And there he became game for them, for whatever brand of humor, for whatever obscenity, for whatever outrage of his personhood they chose to visit upon him. Now, a thread of rumor had rung through the barracks from those who were stationed at the trial that the charge was that he claimed to be a king. So they decided that kingship would be the theme of their mockery and they would caricature him as king. So one of the fellas ran out and got a cane, a reed, and stuck it in his hands. And they stripped him of his own clothes and one of them went and got an old cloak, a faded, purple cloak, which was a part of the uniform of the Roman soldier on dress parade. But this was an old, tattered, faded, purple cloak. "A king?" "A king?" "A king, he says." So they flung, having taken off his own clothes, they flung the old cloak around his shoulders and one fella more daring than the others went outside and along the walls of the barracks, found a thorn bush, cut it with his sword, platted it into a crown, and came back and jammed it on the head of the Savior until rivulets of blood began running down his brow. And then, in mock worship, mock worship, they bowed down before him and said, "We hail you, king." And then, gales of laughter, wicked, scornful, laughter rang and reverberated through the barracks, beat against the walls, and echoed back.

It was not the last time that the Savior was deprived of his own clothes. There are still those who give to him a mock respect. I hear them sometimes in the fashionable drawing rooms of my own city. They speak with a kind of patronizing respect about the Savior of the world. They say, "Jesus was a good man. I respect his teachings." And some of them will say, "His Golden Rule is what I live by." And then, as if they have delivered themselves of some profound comment, they go on to say, "But as for his church," talking now about the church for which he died—"I have no place for it. It's alright for those who need it, but all of the other stuff that goes with this religion, forget it." And when they say that to me, I feel like saying and sometimes I do—that I had a Doberman pinscher, a bloodied dog, once, he never went to church either. I had that dog for twelve years. He never expressed any interest in going to church. And I feel like saying to them, I know why he didn't go. He was a dog. Now, why is it you don't go?

I was talking with a man the other day, who said to me, "I'm not religious" as if he had declared himself one of the chief intellectuals of Athens. He said, "but I follow the Ten Commandments." And I said to him, Well where did they come from, if not from a smoking mountain, trembling under the impact of the presence of Jehovah or so Moses reported when he came down from the smoking summit bearing the tablets of the Law?

There are others who take the Lord's own clothes off him and mock him with a kind of superficial loyalty and worship but their hearts are far from him. They mouth his name, but they do not love him. Some of them call themselves Christian, but they do not love the Lord, Jesus. They do not love him, because they do not love his people. Some of them say that they are pro-life people, but they are more interested in life before birth, than they are in life after birth. They broadcast from various states including the great dominion of Virginia and they speak constantly of being born-again Christians. But they ganged up to drive the only avowed, born-again Christian president out of the White House the nation has had in living memory. The only president who carried his Bible publicly instead of riding boots, and who taught Sunday School every Sunday instead of spending his weekends in the wilds of Maryland. They mock the Lord Jesus by calling his name. Their hearts do not belong to Jesus Christ. I blush. I blush at black preachers and black Christians who capitulate to that kind of mockery and to these workers of sinister evil who clothe themselves as angels of light—*Shame! Shame! Shame!*

And when they had finished and they had tired of their sport, their humor had worn thin, they put his own clothes back on him. They took the mock, regal robe of the soldier's dress-uniform cloak off and put his own clothes back on him and led him out to crucify him. Thanks be to God, in his own clothes, he died. In his own clothes, he climbed the hill at Golgotha. In his own clothes, he asserted his role as redeemer. In his own clothes, he declared himself the Savior of the world.

And when we see the Savior, not in this mock garment, but in his own clothes, a great desire to be better crosses our hearts. When we see him in the clothes of his saviorhood, in his clothes as the captain of our salvation, in his clothes as the redeemer of the world, in his clothes as our Passover, in his own clothes, as our precious price at the gates of hell, a great desire crosses the heart, and a desire and prayer for forgiveness. "If I have wounded one soul today, / If I have caused one foot to go astray. / If I have walked in my own willful way, / dear Lord, please forgive."[3] And when you see him in his own clothes, do you not desire to do better?

Dr. Donald Shelby, the California United Methodist preacher, has told of an awful storm which broke out on Lake Michigan. A young Northwestern student named Edmon Spencer went out on the water, a ship was wrecked, a boat, and he went out and back, out and back until seventeen people were rescued. And when they dragged him out of the water, faded, almost exhausted, and carried him to his room, the only question he asked was, "Did I do my best?" Well, when I see the Savior, in his own clothes, I cannot help asking every time I come out of a pulpit—do you in the secret places of your own heart? Do you say, Lord, did I do my best? Choir member, did I do my best? And when the sun goes down each day and you are alone with your own soul, do you ask yourself, did I do my best? Did I walk in the name of the Lord? Did I try the best I could? If I failed, did I try?

To see him marching up to Calvary, in his own clothes, draws forth from our hearts the question that was on the lips of that lyrical poet, Isaiah, "Who is this that cometh out of Edom with blood-dyed garments from Bozra, traveling with his glorious apparel. Wherefore art thy garments red, like one that treadeth in the wine fat."[4] In his own clothes, he paid the price. In his own clothes, he lifted up every valley and brought down every mountain, made the crooked way straight, the rough places plain, pulled down the barrier, opened a highway from earth to bright Glory! Called, the prisoner, made the prisoner free, called the Prodigal home, restored the exile to his citizenship. In his own clothes, he fixed it and it's alright, now! It's alright, now! It's alright, now!

I told you last night that I want to see him. But what will I see? I will see him in his own clothes. No longer with that royal, old, faded cloak around his shoulders. No longer with the handcuffs and chains on his wrist. No longer with the crown of thorns on his brow. No longer with the pain lining his face. No longer with the hurt of the world upon his heart. No longer . . .

But I'll see him in the glory of his son-ship. We shall see him in the beauty of his holiness and in the holiness of his beauty, with the ten thousand, times ten thousand, angels all around him singing, "Worthy is the Lamb to receive blessings, and honor and wisdom and power and thanksgiving."[5] And the great orchestra of heaven and the choirs of heaven singing his praises and the great organ of heaven, in demi pausa notes, singing his praise and all of our voices together as the angels announce the marriage supper of the Lamb is come. And we shall be there to see him and to cry, thank you! Thank you! Thank you, Jesus. Thank you, Lord. Thank you for every tear. Thank you every sorrow. Thank you for every ache. Thank you for every heartbreak. Thank you for every climb. Thank you! Thank you!

## *Notes*

*Sermon source:* The sermon was transcribed from disc one of the *Essential Taylor CD.* (Valley Forge, PA: Judson Press, 2001).

1. Luke 22:64.
2. "Alas! And Did My Savior Bleed," *The Baptist Standard Hymnal with Responsive Readings: A New Book for all Services* (Nashville, TN: Sunday School Publishing Board, National Baptist Convention, U.S.A., 1924), 83.
3. "An Evening Prayer," C. Maude Battersby, 1911, available at http://www.cyberhymnal.org/htm/e/v/evprayer.htm (accessed June 27, 2007).
4. See Isaiah 63:1–2.
5. Revelation 5:12.

## *Bibliographical Sources*

"America's 15 Greatest Black Preachers." *Ebony*, September 1984: 27–33.

"The Dean of Black Preachers: He Didn't Want to Be a Preacher," in *The Irresistible Urge to Preach: A Collection of African American "Call" Stories*, ed. William H. Myers. Atlanta, GA: Aaron Press, 1992.

Dyson, Michael Eric. "Gardner Taylor: Poet Laureate of the Pulpit." *The Christian Century*, January 4–11, 1995: 12–16.

Farmer, David Albert. "Pulpit Laureate and Presidential Favorite: An Interview with Gardner Taylor." *Pulpit Digest*, September/October 1996: 97–101.

Gilbreath, Edward. "The Pulpit King," *Christianity Today*, December 11, 1995: 25–28.

Lischer, Richard. "Gardner C. Taylor," in *Concise Encyclopedia of Preaching*, ed. William H. Willimon and Richard Lischer. Louisville, KY: Westminster John Knox Press, 1995.

Taylor, Gardner C. *The Words of Gardner C. Taylor.* Compiled by Edward L. Taylor. 6 vols. Valley Forge, PA: Judson Press, 1999–2001.

Taylor, Gardner C., and Samuel D. Proctor. *We Have This Ministry: The Heart of the Pastor's Vocation.* Valley Forge, PA: Judson Press, 1996.

# RENITA WEEMS

*(1954– )*

Renita Weems grew up in Nashville, Tennessee, and remembers her stepmother unexpectedly telling her at age fifteen, "Neetie, God's got His hand on your life." It took two decades for her to understand her stepmother's words as a call to minister to "thinking women of faith." She wrote later, "Sometimes it takes the mind and body years to catch up to what the soul knows already."

In the meantime, after studying at Wellesley College, where she earned a bachelor's degree in economics, Weems began working as a stockbroker in New York City. She received a doctorate in biblical studies, specializing in Hebrew Bible at Princeton Theological Seminary in 1989, and began fulfilling her vocation as an elder in the African Methodist Episcopal Church and, for fifteen years, from 1987 to 2004, as a professor of Hebrew Bible in the Divinity School at Vanderbilt University. *Ebony* magazine celebrated Weems as one of America's top fifteen women preachers.

In 1987, Weems wrote *Just A Sister Away: A Womanist Vision of Women's Relationships*. Weems's writings and sermons explore women's spirituality, relationships, and wholeness. She is also the author of *I Asked for Intimacy*; *Showing Mary: How Women Can Share Prayers, Wisdom, and the Blessings of God*; and *What Matters Most. Listening for God: A Minister's Journey through Silence and Doubt* won the Religion Communicators Council Wilbur Award for excellence in communicating religious values to the secular media. She was formerly the William and Camille Cosby Visiting Professor of Humanities at Spelman College in Atlanta, Georgia, and presently co-pastors Ray of Hope Community Church in Nashville with her husband, Rev. Martin Espinosa. They have one daughter, Savanah Nia.

• • •

*Renita Weems has developed a preaching style that marries the best of African American folk religion with the best of the critical biblical scholarship methods to appeal to what she calls "thinking women of faith." In the following sermon, Weems gives perceptive biblical exegesis, setting the text in its appropriate first-century historical and social context, then draws insightful parallels to the present, giving the bib-*

*lical text a fresh sense of relevancy and aliveness. She preaches and teaches from the perspective that women are full partners and participants in the divine human drama revealed in Scripture, with no need to justify, explain, or defend her position. In the best of the African American folk tradition, she concludes the sermon with celebration, centering upon the "hall of fame" in Hebrews 11, and leaving the listener encouraged in the truth of Scripture and ready to act based upon that truth. Her genius at combining African American folk preaching tradition with biblical scholarship makes her in great demand nationally and internationally as preacher and lecturer.*

## NOT . . . YET
## (FEBRUARY 2004)

*These all died in faith not having received what was promised.*
—Hebrews 11:13 (New King James Version)

When I think back on this journey to this fine place so far from home, I was reminded while preparing this sermon that it was, in fact, the book of Hebrews that created the opening through which I first encountered my vocation. This year will celebrate for me twenty-five years in ministry. And twenty-five years ago it was a particular verse in the book of Hebrews that arrested my imagination and me, and filled me with longing to know more about God and to study religion, the Bible, faith, and the history of people with similar longings and whose journey was from a struggle and through a struggle and to a struggle.

It was the very opening verse of Hebrews, chapter 1 and verse 1, and I only knew it then and I still vaguely remember now:

> God, who at sundry times and in divers manners spake in time past unto the fathers by the prophets, Hath in these last days spoken unto us by his Son, whom he hath appointed heir of all things, by whom also he made the worlds; Who being the brightness of his glory, and the express image of his person, and upholding all things by the word of his power, when he had by himself purged our sins, sat down on the right hand of the Majesty on high.

This particular verse arrested me. It gave me a glimpse of what I might become. It was the verse that led me into the systematic study of Scripture, of religion, and of the word of God and faith. It was this particular verse.

But now, twenty-five years later, education has killed something. For all of the privileges that come with education and all of the doors that it opens, it makes you unfit and ill-suited for some things. While it makes you question the motives of others, it also makes you suspicious of your own motives. Education can paralyze you. Because now I catch myself, twenty-five years later, with all these degrees and all that stuff you read on the résumé—I always tell myself that there's a résumé and then there's the truth. I catch myself wondering now—was that really you, God? Or was that my fascination with the grandiloquent phraseology of sixteenth-century Elizabethan English? "God who at sundry times and in divers manners . . ." All I knew at the time was that one verse contained the scope, the depth, the mystery, the rationale for the Christian faith . . . its historical origin, its theological origin, its literary origin.

It was written in the last third of the first century when the early church found itself struggling to survive amidst a changing political, religious, and economic environment, frustrated with having to live with delayed promises. Delayed promises are the best way to describe and characterize the small Christian congregation that stands behind the book of Hebrews. A small, persecuted congregation struggling to hold fast to their belief in a crucified Judean carpenter as the risen Savior, faced as they were with the dissonance of living and worshiping in the midst of a half-Jewish, half-pagan, and entirely hostile society.

Years, perhaps decades, had passed since they first heard the good news of the kingdom of God with all of its attending promises. And now they had to ask themselves, "Did I really hear right? Did I misunderstand some things? Are we sure that the gospel is of God? Is this really the right path I'm supposed to be taking? Did I hear right about who Jesus Christ was?" And so, in the midst of a hostile, half-pagan, half-Jewish culture, this Jewish Christian audience was now looking at ten, maybe twenty, maybe even thirty years since the last time they had heard from God and the next time they would hear from God—those delayed promises.

Deep disagreements have cropped up in the church. Considerable differences of opinion over doctrine, dogmatic theology, and church history have arisen in the church, leaving the congregation dismayed, disheartened, disgusted, disappointed, and divided. Instead of having a social element to the ministry, instead of going out and preaching good news to the captives and setting the oppressed free, they are arguing over whether homosexuals really ought to belong to the church and they are arguing over whether to have a woman bishop or not. Quibbling over doctrine while the homeless are on the street and teenagers are becoming pregnant with the third child. While we're going to Iraq, we're arguing about whether we should have bishops and archbishops in the Baptist church. Delayed promises can distract you. They make you major in minor things . . . tearing up the church over doctrine.

Most scholars say it's unlikely that Paul actually wrote the book of Hebrews. Clement insisted that it was Paul. Tertullian thought it was perhaps Barnabas. Luther argued that it was Apollos. But it's unlikely that it was either one of the three. The fact that the book is the only book in the New Testament that opens without the normal kind of introductory boasting of one's place in the ministry . . . boasting that one had seen Jesus himself: "Paul, an apostle, (not of men, neither by man, but by Jesus Christ and God the Father . . .)"[1] Well, that leads Arnold Harnack, the German philosopher, to say that a woman probably wrote the book of Hebrews, because she didn't have to get up and talk about her credentials because they were not going to impress anybody anyway. And then, it's also one of the few books where women are commended for their faith, and Paul doesn't tend to major in commending women.

And so it speaks of somebody with sharp understanding and astute theological insight. It had to be Priscilla. It just had to be Priscilla, a thinking woman of faith. A woman with insight who knew how to cut through the bull and get to the real issue at hand. Priscilla, a teacher; Priscilla, a theologian; Priscilla, a leader; Priscilla, married to a man of substance; Priscilla, married to a man who didn't mind being paired up with a strong woman; hallelujah, hallelujah for Priscilla! She gets straight to the point.

Time has passed and the very thing that Jesus has promised has not yet come to pass: "Lo, I am with you always, even unto the end of the world."[2] And lo, this thing had not yet come to pass. Paul had promised, "Behold, I show you a mystery; We shall not all sleep, but we shall all be changed, In a moment, in the twinkling of an eye . . ." in a moment we shall see him.[3]

Oh, time has passed now and what do you do? What do you do when you know you heard God tell you something and time passes on? It took David twenty years between the time he heard God anoint him as king and when he finally got his appointment papers. What a hard word for those of you who are here and who just heard from God day before yesterday and now you want to pastor the big church. I know that's a hard word for those of you who just learned John 3:16 last week, and already you've got the biggest Bible and the biggest cross and us gon' pastor the people of God. I know that's a hard word because I teach the seminarians who just come for credentials. They don't come to learn; they just come for credentials. "Don't touch my Jesus; don't touch my faith; don't touch my tradition; I just came to get the credentials. I don't want to learn nothing. I don't want to understand nothing. I don't want to read nothing. Do I have to read all those books?" Come to graduate school, got a pager, got a cell phone, got a Lexus, but ain't got no computer—handing me handwritten papers with arrows going all over the paper.

You just want to put the Bible under your arm, and you just want to go out and do "thus saith the Lord." When you start preaching, you just believe that you won't stop preaching until everybody gets saved. Then you turn thirty, and you're happy if half the congregation gets saved. Then you turn fifty, and you're happy if about four of them get saved. Then you turn sixty, and you are just glad if one person knows what you said. Your expectations start shrinking. You're not as excited and confident as you once were. You're not quite sure anymore if it really matters whether you spend time with a manuscript working out what you should say. You turn on the television, and there's somebody walking across the platform, back and forth and mimicking black women. And you say, my God, why did I spend all this time if all I had to say was, "Get ready, get ready, get ready!"?

And I'm really not trying to put anybody down, but the world has changed. The preaching has changed. I just looked around and things were gone. Things had changed. The things that I worked so hard on in my lifetime had changed. My devotion to words and language and thinking a thought through just changed. My laboring over the Word of God and trying to hear from God . . . and things have changed. Nobody wants to think anymore. They don't want to go deep in the faith anymore. They don't want to delve into the mysteries, the contradictions. That's what drew me to ministry. It was not just the promises; it was the journey of faith.

And so, this congregation understood themselves to be living with delayed promises and were not quite sure what to believe anymore. They asked, "Is this thing real? Do I walk away from it?" The congregation asked, "Why? How long?" These are the questions that break the back of the faithful. These are the questions that separate the old saints from the new converts . . . questions that make a mature Christian out of you. And so, a whole generation of second-generation Christians had begun to defect and leave the Christian ministry because it was too hard; it was too difficult, and they were not getting the results they were expecting. And so, there were those who were beginning to reach back to what was safe and conventional, to what they had grown up on and what had always gotten a shout and a hallelujah, instead of doing the hard work. . . .

And so you've got factions in this local church. You've got the conservatives who were saying, "We're going back to the old tradition. We're giving up on Jesus Christ and this Christian faith. We're going back to the law and to the angels and to the belief in sacrifices and the priesthood." And then, you've got the moderates. Well, the moderates are saying, "If we just syncretize this thing—let's get a little bit of this over here and a little bit of that over there. So, let's do hip-hop and 'O For a Thousand Tongues to Sing.' All right, well, let's try the drums and then say Ashéa rather than Amen. Let's do a little African religion and a little Pentecostal laying on of hands." And so, you've got the moderates in the midst: "If this doesn't work then maybe this will work. If that doesn't work, let's try this." They are inconsistent.

Then you've got the liberals who want to tear away from everything from the past and just say, "Let's reinvent ourselves. Let's do something brand-radical-new. Let's do something nobody else is doing. Let's just become a brand new religion. We ain't named it yet, but let's just do what us wants to do."

How are you going to live between the last time you heard from God and the next time you hear from God? It ain't going to be believing in angels; it ain't going to be believing in prophets; it ain't going to be believing in priests. Ah, but, "Faith is the substance of things hoped for and the evidence of things not seen."[4] You don't need a prophet; you need faith. You don't need angels and crystals; you need faith. You don't need a hundred dollar line and a fifty dollar line; you need faith. You don't need a jet and you don't need a limousine; you need faith.

Faith is the roux in the gumbo. You can't make the gumbo unless you can make that roux, baby! The gumbo falls and rises on the roux. You've got to get the faith issue. "Now faith is the substance of things hoped for and the evidence of things . . ." If you're going to walk with God—because without faith, it is impossible to please God—you're going to have to preach to five as though it's five thousand. You're going to have to study even when the registrar says that the check didn't come. You're going to have to pastor through a broken heart. You're going to have to lead your mama into the sanctuary with her Alzheimer's and watch her eating crackers while you preach that God is a healer. You're going to have to preach "God is a way maker" even though they're getting ready to repossess everything you've got. You're going to have to preach that he's a mother to the motherless and she's a father to the fatherless, even though you never met your father and your mother walked away. You're going to have to preach it because it's true, and not necessarily because you've experienced it.

That's what nobody tells you when you first start out in this journey. When you come into this journey, mesmerized by the success stories, nobody tells you about the failures. That's why I'm nervous around people who want me to mentor them, because what they really want are my successes. Folks looking for a mentor really don't want to know about your failures, because the moment they discover your failures, your weaknesses, your warts—they walk away. "I thought she was something" or "She ain't nothing." They want to hear about the grand times when you stood at the Samuel Proctor conference and you preached until sweat poured down. Ah, they don't want to hear about when you got up to preach at another event and you didn't know the first part of the sermon and you couldn't figure out the second part of the sermon and you sure didn't have the end of the sermon. . . . They don't want to hear about when you stood up and you were getting ready to preach and, the truth of the matter is, you sho'nuff, flat-out flopped, baby. You should have stayed upstairs in your hotel room.

There's the résumé and there's the truth. The résumé says you graduated; it doesn't say barely. It says you used to work on Wall Street; it doesn't say you left right before they were ready to fire you. It says you're the first African American woman with a Ph.D. in Old Testament, but it doesn't tell you that the whole school said, "We'll never give her a Ph.D." It says that you are "the Reverend Doctor," but it doesn't say that a prophet is without honor in her own country.

Let me go through the hall of fame. By faith, Abel offered God a better sacrifice than Cain.[5] By faith, Enoch forgot to die and was translated from this life to the life to come.[6] Ah, by faith—by faith—Noah, when warned of things to come, began to build an ark.[7] By faith, Abraham, when called to go from this place and that he would later receive his inheritance—he obeyed and went on to do great things.[8] Ah, by faith, Abraham decided to sacrifice his son Isaac. But, God saw that he was a good man and sent a ram in the bush.[9] By faith, Sarah—way past the age of having babies—received from God the delight of her soul.[10]

Now, all these died in faith, but when history was written it said, ". . . not having received what was promised." They had the faith, but they didn't have the fulfillment. They had the promises of God, but [without the fulfillment], they were failures . . . every one of them.

These all died in faith, but not having received what was promised. When my own time is over and I have taught at as many seminaries as I care to talk about and as they write my name across the pages of history—there will nevertheless be a voice in the background saying, "She died in faith, not having received what was promised." I'm talking about the failure that dogs your success. I'm talking about those weaknesses that nip away at your possibilities. I'm talking about that stuff that's half success and half failure.

I'm talking about those successes that feel like failures, but those failures are redeemed by faith. "These all died in faith not having received what was promised." Faith—learning how to live between a promise and its fulfillment. Faith—having to learn how to live between a vision and its reality. Faith—learning how to live between the last time you heard from God and the next time you hear from God. Faith—learning how to live with the silence of God. Learning how to live on nothing but the memory that you think you heard from God. Faith—learning how to live on your memory. Faith—learning how to live in the meantime. Faith—learning how to live in that amorphous, unspecified, unspecific time in history when it's the now, and at the same time, it's the not yet.

The signature on the promissory note says Jesus. Each generation passes the baton to the next generation. If it were left up to me, I would have been angry and left the ministry a long time ago. But, I have no right to leave the ministry, because Nannie Helen Burroughs wanted to be a minister and they would never allow her to be a minister. So, every time I stand, I stand on the shoulders of Nannie Helen Burroughs. I'm telling you, Jarena Lee wanted to be a minister. So, when I take my text, I think of Jarena Lee. Ella Baker was never going to be as well known as Martin Luther King, but every time I stand, I'm standing on the shoulders of Ella Baker. And one day, I'm going to decrease and the next generation of little girls are going to increase, and they are going to stand on my shoulders—not having received what was promised.

Therefore, "seeing that we are surrounded by so great a cloud of witnesses. . . ."[11] When I want to give up, I'm surrounded. When I want to cuss everybody out, I'm surrounded by so great a cloud of witnesses. Can't you see they're in the room right now? Can't you feel their presence right now? Can't you hear them saying, "Come on, children, don't you get weary. There's a better camp meeting on the other side." Can't you hear our ancestors saying, "We have come this far by faith, leaning on the Lord"?

Right now, this race is not about me and you. It's about generations who are coming after us. It's about little girls and boys in our churches. It's about the little one with the little nappy hair whose mama is on drugs and whose daddy is in jail. And she sees us standing here preaching, and she comes up to us and we say a word of encouragement, just like the old ladies in the Pentecostal church who said a little word of encouragement to me. Me, who grew up with a mama who was on alcohol and a daddy who was violent over my mama. But, it's because of those little church ladies who went down in the bosom and gave me a little bit of money and said, "Baby, God is going to make a way out of no way. You just keep your hand in God's hand." I know I am where I am right now because I am standing, and you are standing, on the shoulders of people who died in faith. There they are right now, looking down on you and me, saying, "Don't get weary. There's a better camp meeting on the other side."

### *Notes*

*Sermon source: The African American Pulpit* 7, no. 4 (Fall 2004), 79–84.

1. Galatians 1:1 (King James Version).
2. Matthew 28:20 (New American Standard Bible).
3. 1 Corinthians 15:51–52 (NASB).
4. Hebrews 11:1 (KJV).
5. Hebrews 11:4 (NASB).
6. Hebrews 11:5 (NASB).
7. See Hebrews 11:7.
8. See Hebrews 11:8.
9. See Hebrews 11:17.
10. See Hebrews 11:11–12.
11. See Hebrews 12:1.

### *Bibliographical Sources*

"Dr. Renita Weems Biography." http://www.somethingwithin.com/weems.htm (accessed on May 2, 2005).

Weems, Renita J. *Showing Mary: How Women Can Share Prayers, Wisdom, and the Blessing of God.* West Bloomfield, MI: Walk Worthy Press, 2002, 31–33.

———. *What Matters Most: Ten Lessons in Living Passionately from the Song of Solomon.* New York: Warner Books, 2004.

## JASPER WILLIAMS JR.

*(1943– )*

Jasper Williams Jr. is the pastor of Salem Bible Church in Atlanta, Georgia, where he has ministered for forty-plus years. Although a pastor, Williams is best known as an evangelist. Under the tutelage of C.L. Franklin, Williams traveled the country in the ministry of the Gospel of Jesus Christ and was one of the leading African American revivalists in America for more than two decades.

Born in Memphis, Tennessee, on July 22, 1943, to Rev. Jasper Williams Sr. and Alice Stewart Williams, Jasper Williams Jr. grew up in a preaching and ministry family. His father and his uncle, Alton Roosevelt Williams, were known throughout the country for their powerful revivals and preaching prowess. By the time Williams graduated from Morehouse College with a major in sociology and a minor in religion, he was expected to return to Memphis to serve as associate pastor of his father's Lane Avenue Baptist Church. However, on Easter Sunday 1963, at age nineteen, Williams was the guest preacher at Salem Baptist Church in Atlanta. He was subsequently invited to serve as Salem Baptist's pastor and accepted the call in November. Under Williams' leadership, Salem has been one of the key churches in the Baptist network. The church has instituted community outreach programs, including free psychological counseling programs and a children's day-care center. Williams' mission for ministry is "expansion through evangelism."

Williams is widely known for his magnetic preaching style and explosive sermon delivery. From 1965 to 1985 he offered whooping classes, and preachers from across the country filled them. He continues to offer preaching conferences. He has emerged as one of the most influential preachers of his generation, and many have imitated his style.

Williams has served on a number of service organization boards and was the National Baptist Convention's chair of the Evangelistic Committee's Late Night Services for ten years. He has received many awards and honors, including the Rev. C.L. Franklin Masters Award, the NAACP Award, and the Gospel Music Workshop's Award of Excellence. He holds two honorary Doctor of Divinity degrees from Miller University and Temple Bible College and Seminary. He is the father of two sons who are also preachers: Jasper Williams III and Joseph L. Williams.

• • •

*For more than three decades Jasper Williams Jr. has been considered a master whooper and folk preacher. "God at the Midnight Ball" is one of his signature sermons. In the sermon, he shows why his preaching has aroused the imagination and senses of many who have heard him. First, his descriptions are so vivid that as he takes you into the court of King Belshazzar you believe that he is there and that he is giving an eyewitness account, also referred to in African American preaching as "telling the story." In so doing, you too become an eyewitness. Second, as an eyewitness you experience all of the emotions appropriate to the drama that is unfolding before you. The listener feels King Belshazzar's fear, terror, and dread, as well as his or her own, because the listener knows of places in his or her conscience where he or she is as guilty as the king. Thirdly, Williams masterfully shows us the way out of King Belshazzar's predicament and offers us hope. Williams places the hope in the musical-preaching drama known as whooping, and the listener experiences complete resolution and victory. Unfortunately, the written text can never do justice to the oral nature of whooping.*

## God at the Midnight Ball
## (1960s)

> *In that same hour came forth fingers of a man's hand, and wrote over against the candlestick upon the plaster of the wall of the king's palace: and the king saw the part of the hand that wrote.*
>
> —Daniel 5:5 (King James Version)

Daniel 5 begins by saying, "Belshazzar the king made a great feast to a thousand of his lords." According to Josephus's Antiquities, the banquet hall was most definitely in keeping with the grandeur and splendor of a world-class kingdom. The floor of the banquet hall was made of white, red, black, and blue marble, and the walls were hung with tapestries on which were traced the winged symbols of Babylonian power. Green, yellow, and white curtains entwined the marbled pillars, and Persian rugs with their mystic designs were spread out on the floor. Chandeliers wrought in far-off Damascus swung from the ceilings and gave illumination, and golden candlesticks glowed with soft radiance on the tables. At the windows were iron-girt balconies, where the guests could lean over the rail and look down upon the broad, flowing Euphrates. In the center of the hall, gushing fountains flung up their silver spray, while strange fish splashed in the water and rare birds sang their songs in the cages along the walls. Innumerable pipes with pleasant intoxicants filled the hall with sweet incense.

The text deals with an unusual episode that took place on the last night of King Belshazzar, the last king of Babylon. Babylon was one of the most notable, renowned, and splendid cities in the world at that time. It was located on an immense plain called the fertile crescent of Mesopotamia. There were about a hundred gates adorned in brass that surrounded the city and, coupled with Nebuchadnezzar's hanging gardens, made it one of the most beautiful and attractive cities of that day. The walls of Babylon were 350 feet tall, 87 feet across, and about 60 miles around. The gates and walls of Babylon were surrounded by a deep, broad moat, which made it almost impregnable and invincible. No military device at that time could breach those walls, and no army could storm those gates. Right through the middle of the city flowed the Euphrates River, and Babylon therefore grew its own produce and had water in great abundance. It was therefore made a city of riches and prosperity because of its great accessibility for trade.

But Belshazzar, the king of Babylon, was a worthless wretch. Belshazzar was a wicked, ruthless, and godless king. As a matter of fact, Belshazzar is the only king in the Bible that the Bible has nothing good to say about. King Saul, filled with jealousy and rage over a shepherd boy's popularity, took his own life in the heat of the battle. But it could be said of Saul that he was a great warrior, and through his leadership, he took a ragged group of tribes and began the process of making them a great nation. Yes, King David had a multiplicity of faults, for he took another man's wife, and then maliciously had the other man killed. But it could be said that David was a man after God's own heart, and that he was a man of prayer and meditation. King Solomon was marred by his love of things and his lust (the Queen of Sheba, seven hundred wives, three hundred concubines). But it was said that he made a good king in that he carried Israel into the construction of a magnificent temple to the glory of God. But the Bible has not even one good thing to say about King Belshazzar. And you know, church, it's bad when you live a whole life and are gone and nobody has one good thing to say about you. You know, in our world today, you have a lot of people who live and that's all they do, just live. The Bible records Methuselah as having lived for 969 years. But in all of those years, all the Bible says is that he died.

Nothing good could be said of Belshazzar. He profaned the sacred. The Lord's house is sacred. In church, the seats upon which you sit, sacred. The instruments which you play, sacred. The lights that are burning, sacred. Certain things ought not to be done in and around them; they're sacred. The water fountain in the Lord's house is sacred. Belshazzar brought sacred vessels that belonged in the Lord's house to his banquet hall. Yes, Belshazzar and his guests desecrated, profaned, and unhallowed that which was sacred, holy, and divine.

The Bible says that when Belshazzar had those holy vessels brought into his banquet hall, they filled them with wine, gave a toast, drank to, and sang praises to six gods. They drank to the god of wood, the god of stone, the god of bronze; they drank to the god of iron, gold, and silver. And nowhere in their praise was there any mention of the Lord God Jehovah, the God of Abraham, Isaac, and Jacob. There was no mention of the one true and living God. And you know, anything that's going on and God ain't in it, it's best that you get out of it. Belshazzar left God out. God can give you a whole lot, and you think you are something, and God is nothing. And this is what's wrong with the world today: in too many instances, in too many things, and on too many occasions, we have left God out. You don't have to be no religious freak—always praise the Lord, thank you, Lord, et cetera—but don't leave God out.

A few years ago, the Supreme Court of these United States handed down a decision that no longer could there be prayer in schools. And nowadays our young people graduate from school not knowing how to read, write, and count. Instead of them coming out of high school as graduates, they come out hoodlums, thugs, junkies, and drug addicts. How come? Because our school systems have left God out. Many marriages today end up on the rocks and couples are consequently filing for divorces. Children are having to be reared in broken homes. How come? Because when couples get married, they make the mistake of leaving God out. Too many couples just got together—God didn't put them together.

But wait a minute. While they wined and dined, cussed and fussed, as they joked and jested, when the party was at its peak and everybody was high, all of a sudden the music stopped playing; the noise died down. Feet that had been shuffling across the ballroom floor stood still. Plates started cracking. Wine bottles started falling. All of a sudden, the peacocks stopped strutting. All of a sudden, the laughter ceased, joke-telling stopped, fingers stopped popping. For the Bible says, "In that same hour came forth fingers of a man's hand, and wrote over against . . . the plaster of the wall of the king's palace."[1] In that same hour.

You know, there are certain hours in your life when you must be ever so careful. In that same hour, there came forth the fingers, the fingers, the fingers of a man's hand. In that same hour. You know, God will always have the last word. Wherever you find sin, wherever you find national decay, you do not need a prophet to point out the handwriting on the wall. For the deeper the sin, the closer the judgment. In the case of Belshazzar, we see the sin and the judgment side by side, back to back. "In that same hour came forth fingers of a man's hand."

Yes, this is the way it was with old Belshazzar; however, it is not always this way with us. God does not always intrude upon us like he did with Belshazzar. He doesn't always crash our parties or interrupt our frequent get-down celebrations of eating, drinking, and being merry. For sometimes he lets the party go on for years. But judgment is always going on, and the verdict examines us every day. Like Belshazzar, we are observed without our even knowing it. Without our being aware of it, the cosmic court is trying our case every day.

While Belshazzar partied, "in that same hour came forth fingers of a man's hand." Yes, this was a most unusual sight to behold. For they all had probably seen a hand without fingers, but never had they seen fingers without a hand. In that same hour, nothing but fingers. There was no Bic and no Paper Mate, just fingers. No Parker pen, just fingers. No chalk and no paintbrush, just fingers. No hand, no wrist, and no arm, just fingers. No shoulder, no head, and no body, just the fingers of a man's hand.

Yes, God the great party stopper with his fingers crashed Belshazzar's ball. God did not come to Belshazzar's ball in the flash of zigzag lightning. He did not come in the sound of an erupting volcano, the pealing of thunder, or the trembling of an earthquake. But he came across the purple mountain of eternity with a long, powerful arm, turned old Belshazzar's wall into stationery and his fingers into a writing pen, and began to write a telegram on the wall.

When Belshazzar saw the handwriting on the wall, his countenance was changed. His mind got confused. Belshazzar's face was blank. His slobbering lips trembled. His knees started knocking. And that holy vessel that he held in his defiling hand fell with a loud crash on the marble tile.

The question that arises here in my mind is, Why is it that Belshazzar became so terrified and so alarmed? He could not read the writing, so he did not know what it meant. Since he was a worshiper of the gods of wood, stone, bronze, iron, gold, and silver, why couldn't the handwriting on the wall have been some favorable message of good tidings from the gods in whom he believed? But Belshazzar did not entertain such thoughts. Instead a horrible dread took hold of him. Terror and trembling seized his flesh. I wonder why? Why was he so perplexed and distressed? Why?

The reason Belshazzar was so frightened at the sight of the handwriting on the wall was because of that little God-given monitor in all of us called a conscience. Belshazzar had a guilty conscience. And you know, a guilty conscience has a way of making a coward out of you. And whenever a person is in sin, he or she is afraid of anything that he or she doesn't understand. Conscience is the ghost that writes upon all our walls. Conscience is a ghost that none of us can shut out. Brothers and sisters, when you do somebody wrong, nobody has to tell you. You are the first one to know. Won't your conscience bother you? So when Belshazzar saw the handwriting on the wall, it was obviously his guilty conscience that caused him to be frightened. He knew he had done something wrong.

And after a while, when King Belshazzar partly regained his composure, still being startled, baffled, and puzzled, he became concerned about what the handwriting on the wall meant. Belshazzar, none of his lords, none of his wives or concubines knew what the handwriting on the wall meant. Belshazzar called in all of his astrologers and said to them, "Can you read the handwriting on the wall?" The astrologers looked at the writing and said, "Your Majesty, we're sorry, but we cannot read the handwriting on the wall. If it had been a star on the wall, we could tell you what it means. If it had been one of the signs of the zodiac, if it had been something about Jupiter or Mars, we could tell you what it means. But, O king, to our regret, we cannot read the handwriting on the wall."[2]

Belshazzar said, "Whoever shall read for me the handwriting on the wall, I will clothe him in clothes of scarlet. I will put a gold chain around his neck, and I'll make him the third ruler of my kingdom."[3] He brought in the Chaldeans and said to them, "Can you read the handwriting on the wall?" The soothsayers and none of the Babylonian wise men could read the handwriting on the wall. Now one school of thought suggests that as it related to the handwriting on the wall, the mysterious thing about it is not that they did not know what the words were saying. The astrologers, the Chaldeans, the soothsayers, and the wise men of Babylon could all decipher the strange words, but none of them could give meaning or interpretation. In other words, when they said that they could not read the writing, it meant that they could not read it with understanding. God had written to them in their own language, but they could not make sense of four apparently unrelated terms: "Mene, Mene, Tekel, Upharsin." What could that mean? "Numbered, numbered, weighed, divided"? No wonder Belshazzar was almost delirious, demanding, "Who can read the handwriting on the wall?"[4]

Belshazzar asked again and again, "Who will and who can read for me the handwriting on the wall?" The queen, who some schools of thought say was Belshazzar's grandmother, said to Belshazzar, "Son, there is a man in your kingdom who can read the writing on the wall. There is a man by the name of Daniel, who during the lifetime of your grandfather interpreted many of his mysterious dreams. And I'm pretty sure that if you get him, he'll read for you this mysterious writing on the wall."[5]

When they found Daniel, he was no doubt old now. Belshazzar had Daniel brought in and asked him if he could read the writing on the wall. "Daniel, if you read the writing on the wall, I'll give you clothes of scarlet, I'll put a gold chain around your neck, and I'll make you the third ruler of my kingdom. Now tell me, Daniel, can you read the handwriting on the wall?" Daniel said, "Yes, king, I can read the writing on the wall, for it is not strange language to me because it is my Father's writing." And every child knows his father's handwriting. He said, "King, I don't want your gold chain. I don't want your clothes of scarlet, and I don't want to be the third ruler of your kingdom. You see, king, I'm God's man, and I don't have to be bought or bribed to tell you the truth, the whole truth, and nothing but the truth."[6]

Daniel went on to tell Belshazzar, "King, God is tired of your evil, wicked, and godless ways. You, king, have worshiped, given praise and glory to the gods of silver, gold, brass, wood, stone, and iron. And the God in whose hand is thy breath, thou hast thou not glorified."

And you know, Salem, we are guilty of the same thing. Like Belshazzar, we separate ourselves from God, and we live as though there is not a God, as if God does not exist. We talk as if God does not hear us. We do dirt as if God does not see us. We live as though we are not dependent upon God, and whenever he gets ready, he can snap from us our lives without a moment's notice. For we live, we move, and have our being in God. So Daniel said, "O king, the Lord is telling you in this handwriting on the wall that the day of reckoning is at hand."

Oh, I'm afraid today that as we stop and see the signs of the times, we must attest to the fact that the handwriting is on the wall. Stop and view our economy, and see how inflation and unemployment are going up and down like a seesaw. This tells me that the handwriting is on the wall. As we look at how the natural resources of our world are running out and the experts predict that in a few years we won't be able to sustain the way we live, the handwriting is on the wall. Astounding world events—the handwriting is on the wall, and the day of reckoning is at hand!

So Daniel said to Belshazzar, "Yes, I can read for you the handwriting on the wall. Mene, Mene, Tekel, Upharsin. O king, the days of thy kingdom and the days of thy life have been numbered. Thou hath been weighed in the balances of God and found wanting. Thy kingdom will be divided and will be given to the Medes and the Persians."[7] And that same night, Babylon fell and Belshazzar lost his life.

I've got to close here now. Yes, God examines us all, and every day of our lives, we are being weighed in the balances of God. And I'm afraid that many of us are going to be found wanting. You're not tall enough. You don't weigh enough. I mean you're mighty puny on the commandments. You're anemic on love. You're short on your concern for one another. Some of you are weak on your commitment to the church. You are sick on stewardship; you have been weighed in the balances of God and found wanting. Choir members, you're singing all right, but don't be found wanting; ushers, mothers, deacons, and preachers . . . I'm going to stand before God and be weighed. You can't weigh fifty, ninety-nine won't do. But you've got to make a hundred. That day, when we all must stand before God, every knee has to bow and every tongue must confess. Can you say, "I did my best, Lord. I tried"? You better get ready.

I don't know what happened when Daniel read the handwriting on the wall. But if that had been him telling me that I had fallen short of the glory of God, if it had been me getting a message like that from God, I would have ignored the king. I would have ignored the queen and bowed right there in the middle of the banquet hall and told the Lord, "Lord! Lord! Lord! If I have been found wanting, fix me! And while you're fixing me, search me! Try me! Fill me through and through! Turn the light from heaven on my soul. If you find anything that shouldn't be, Lord, take it out and strengthen me. For I want to do right, I want to be saved, I've got to be whole. Search me! Search me! Search me, and Lord, write on. Write until we love one another. Write on until we treat each other right. Write on. Write on." God at the Midnight Ball.

### *Notes*

*Sermon source: The African American Pulpit* 6, no. 2 (Spring 2003), 97–102.

1. See Daniel 5:5.
2. Daniel 5:8.
3. Daniel 5:7.
4. Ibid.
5. Daniel 5:10–11.
6. Daniel 5:17.
7. Daniel 5:25–28

### *Bibliographical Sources*

Jasper Williams Jr. biography at Salem Bible Church Web site: http://www.salembiblechurch.org/index.cfm/PageID/325/index.html (accessed June 26, 2007).

"Jasper Williams Jr.," http://Thepreachingnetwork.com (accessed July 13, 2007).

## JEREMIAH A. WRIGHT JR.

*(1941– )*

Born on September 22, 1941, in Philadelphia, Pennsylvania, Jeremiah A. Wright Jr. became one of the preeminent preachers in America. After his education at Virginia Union University, Wright enlisted in the military, graduating as valedictorian from the Great Lakes Naval Training Center in 1963. He attended Howard University and the University of Chicago Divinity School. Concluding his formal education, Wright earned a doctor of ministry degree in black sacred music from United Theological Seminary in Dayton, Ohio.

In 1972, at the age of thirty-one, he became pastor of a small United Church of Christ congregation in the inner city of Chicago, Trinity United Church of Christ. His congregation has not only grown into the largest United Church of Christ body in the United States, with over ten thousand active members, but also now engages in a vast array of community empowerment programs. Joining his Christian faith with pride in African American history and heritage has led Wright to create an Afrocentric ministry with the motto: "Unashamedly Black and unapologetically Christian." His sermons, preached in the best of the African American prophetic tradition, marry biblical hope with an active commitment to social and political renewal.

Wright has used his gifts as a preacher to oppose U.S. involvement in wars and to raise such previously taboo subjects as AIDS and homosexuality from the pulpit. Radical to some and outspoken, Wright has received death threats for some of his stances.

Wright is married to Rev. Ramah Wright. He has four daughters, Janet Marie Moore, Jeri Lynne Wright, Nikol D. Reed, and Jamila Nandi Wright, and one son, Nathan D. Reed. Wright is equally an accomplished author and a musical composer; he is featured on Wynton Marsalis's album *The Majesty of the Blues*, where he recites a spoken word piece written by Stanley Crouch. His books include *Africans Who Shaped Our Faith* (1995), *Good News! Sermons of Hope for Today's Families* (1995), and *What Makes You So Strong? Sermons of Joy and Strength from Jeremiah A. Wright Jr.* (1993). He has preached and taught around the world, received more than eight honorary degrees, and helped found the Samuel DeWitt Proctor Conference, a forum in which African American clergy share social, theological, and political concerns and engage in social justice advocacy. He retired as pastor of Trinity United Church of Christ in 2008 and continues to preach and lecture around the country and abroad.

• • •

*A good example of Afrocentric and prophetic preaching is the sermon below by Jeremiah A. Wright Jr., preached the Sunday following September 11, 2001. The sermon combines a prophetic critique of America—reminiscent of critiques of their culture given by Old Testament prophets—with hope, which Wright says in this message can be found in a return to God, family, and community. Portions of this sermon were at the center of a media firestorm during the 2008 presidential campaign. When sound bites from the sermon were first aired Wright had been the pastor of then–presidential candidate Barack Obama for twenty years. ABC's* Good Morning America *aired four brief video clips of what they characterized as controversial comments from the sermon. This was followed by continuous loops of sound bites from this sermon and others by Wright that some considered incendiary.*[1] *Journalists questioned whether candidate Obama agreed with and condoned Wright's comments. When asked about the comments, candidate Obama initially stood by his longtime pastor and referred to him as "family." However, after additional comments by Wright at the National Press Club on April 28, 2008, Obama resigned his membership from Trinity United Church of Christ. Wright was supported by many for his candor in the sermon, and his long-standing support of justice issues, especially African American clergy who saw the attacks on Wright as attacks on the prophetic tradition of the African American church.*

## THE DAY OF JERUSALEM'S FALL (SEPTEMBER 2001)

> *Remember, Oh Lord against the Edomites, the day of Jerusalem's fall.* —Psalm 137:7 (New Revised Standard Version)

Psalm 137 has inspired anthems, spirituals, poems and sermons. Psalm 137 has inspired the hearts of millions as they have reflected on the beauty and splendor of the city of God. Jerusalem. "If I forget you Oh Jerusalem, let my right hand forget her skill," the text says in Psalm 137:5. It means may my right hand become useless if I forget Jerusalem. The text goes further to say in verse six, "Let my right hand, my strength just wither away, let my tongue, designed to sing praises, cling to the roof of my mouth, if I do not remember you, Oh Jerusalem, if I do not sense Jerusalem, above my highest joy."

Now in our class sessions on our church study trips, I have lifted up these verses to help our church members understand much of what it is they feel as they have stood in the slave castles in West Africa, as they have stood among the poverty in Ethiopia, stood in the townships of South Africa and stared at the prevails in El Salvador, in Rio de Janeiro, and in Brazil. African Americans have a surge of emotions as they see the color of poverty in a world of wealth and begin to understand that it is no accident that the world's poor are one color, and the world's rich are another color. When they tie together the pieces of five hundred years of colonialism, racism, and slavery with what they see in 2001, a surge of emotions hits them and the last three verses of Psalm 137 help them to understand what it is they are feeling. I have treated these verses in a classroom setting and on the study tours that our congregation has taken, but I have never touched them in a sermon. I was licensed to preach in May of 1959. I was ordained in January of 1967, and I became a pastor in March of 1972, but in all of my years of preaching, I have never preached a sermon which dealt with these difficult verses, these last three verses in Psalm 137. These verses are brutally honest and express what the people of faith really feel after a day of devastation and senseless death.

Today I was telling Freddie Haynes that the spirit of God has nudged me to touch them and to treat them prayerfully as many of us try to sort out what it is we are really feeling, and why it is we are feeling what we feel after the trauma and the tragedy of the attacks on the World Trade Center and the Pentagon, symbols of who America is, the money, and the military. Some of the feelings we have as people of faith in the twenty-first century are similar to the feelings the people of faith had in the sixth century, B.C., and when you read and study this Psalm in its entirety the parallel between those feelings becomes almost eerily clear. That's why I didn't want you to stop at the famous and familiar, verse six, I wanted you to read, to hear, and to experience all nine versus of Psalm 137 to get the full scope of this Psalm.

Turn in your Bibles to II Kings, the twenty-fifth chapter. In that chapter, there is a graphic description of the carnage and the killings that took place on the day of Jerusalem's fall. The king of Judah with all of his army fled. Verse four, they tried to run but the army of the Chaldeans pursued the King, captured the King, and literally committed murder. Verse seven, they slaughtered and did senseless killings; they slaughtered the sons of Zedekiah, and made the King watch. Then they put out his eyes so that would be the last thing he had any visual image of, like a commercial airliner passenger plane slamming into an office building, two office buildings killing thousands, for no reason other than hatred. The psalmist back in 137 says, "Remember Oh Lord the Edomites, the Day of Jerusalem's fall."

Verse eight of Second Kings 25 says, "Nebuzaradan, captain of the guard, in the service of the Nebchudnezzar, King of Babylon, came to Jerusalem, and burned." Now get this image clear. Burned. Get it in your mind. He burned the house of the Lord. He burned the King's house.

He burned all the houses of Jerusalem, and every great house he burned down. Remember Oh Lord, again the Edomites, the Day of Jerusalem's fall. All the army of Chaldeans, who were with the captain of the guard, broke down the walls of Jerusalem.

Now you've got to remember the real and the symbolic significance of the walls of Jerusalem. Our choir sings Psalm 48, "Great is the Lord and greatly to be praised in the city of our God." Jerusalem. "Let Mount Zion rejoice." Jerusalem. "Let the daughters of Jerusalem be glad. Walk around Zion." That's Jerusalem. "Go around about her, count her towers, tell the towers, tell the towers thereof." The towers of Jerusalem were a visible symbol of her greatness, her power, and her invincibility. "Mark ye well, her bulwarks and consider her palaces." There is Jerusalem, invulnerable Jerusalem, invincible Jerusalem, and the city where God dwells. Jerusalem. The Chaldeans smashed and shattered that sense of security and invincibility when "A breach was made in the invincible walls." One side of the Pentagon was wiped out and the people who were in there, like the people who defended Jerusalem on that wall, were wiped out.

First there was a breach in the wall in verse four, and then verse ten it says they broke down all the walls of Jerusalem. They burned everything they could burn and took most of the people into exile. "Remember Oh Lord against the Edomites, the day of Jerusalem's fall." The symbol of power was gone. The substance of their military and monetary power was gone. The towers of Jerusalem were gone. It took eight years to build the World Trade Center. It took Solomon seven years to build a temple in Jerusalem with its towers and within eight hours, it was gone. It took Solomon fourteen years to build his palace, the symbol of wealth, the symbol of magnificence, might, majesty, and within eight hours it also was gone.

The day of Jerusalem's fall was a day that changed their lives forever. When you read this Psalm of remembrance you can understand, "By the waters of Babylon we sat down and wept when we remembered Jerusalem."[2] When you read the song of remembrance, you see the people of God make three distinct moves. They move first of all from reverence, a thought of Jerusalem, the memories of Jerusalem are memories of reverence. Jerusalem is where the house of God was. Reverence. Jerusalem is where the temple of Solomon was. Reverence. March about Zion, and go 'round about her. Reverence. The Lord is in His holy temple. Reverence. Isaiah said in the year that King of Zion died I saw also the Lord sitting on a throne high and lifted up and the train of his garment of the hem of his robe filled the temple.[3] Reverence. The seraphim were in attendance above the Lord, each had six wings. That's in Isaiah 6:2. They covered their face with two, they covered their feet, and with the other two, they flew and called out one to the other "Holy, Holy, Holy is the Lord of hosts, the earth is full the whole earth is full of His glory."[4] Reverence. Jerusalem means reverence when Solomon prayed and asked God's blessing on temple in Jerusalem. You know the story, fire came down from heaven in Second Chronicles 7, and the glory of the Lord filled the temple. The priests could not go in and the people fell down and worshipped. Reverence. The thoughts of Jerusalem in Psalm 137 are thoughts of reverence. If I forget you, Oh Jerusalem, let my right hand forget her cunning reverence. Let my tongue cleave to the roof of my mouth if I do not remember you Jerusalem—reverence.

But keep on reading. The people of faith move from reverence in verses four to six to revenge. In verses eight and nine, they want revenge. They want somebody to destroy those who devastated them. In fact they want God to get even with those who did evil. "*Remember Oh Lord against these Edomites. Remember Oh Lord the day of Jerusalem's fall.*" The first move is when the people of faith moved from reverence to revenge.

The second move in this text is a move from worship to war. Jerusalem is where they worshipped. Now they have declared war. Let me put it another way. The second move is a move from the thoughts of paying tithes. The second move now in Psalm 137, there's a move from the thoughts of paying tithes to the thoughts of paying back. Oh daughter of Babylon you devastator. Happy blessed shall they be, who pay you back for what you did to us. That's payback. The big payback.

Every public service of worship I have heard about so far, in the wake of American tragedy, has had sympathy and compassion for those who were killed and their families, and God's guidance upon the "selected" president and our war machines as they do what they do and what they "gotta do." Payback. There's a move in Psalm 137, from thoughts of paying tithes to thoughts of payback. A move if you will, from worship to war. A move in other words from the worship of the God of creation to war against those whom God created.

And I want you to notice very carefully the next move. One of the reasons Psalm 137 is rarely read in its entirety is because it spotlights the insanity of the cycle of violence and the cycle of hatred. Look at verse nine. "Happy shall they be who take your little ones and dash them against the rocks." The people of faith have moved from the hatred of armed enemies, these soldiers who capture the king, those soldiers who slaughtered his sons and put his eyes out, the soldiers who sacked the city, burned their town, burned their temple, and burned their towers. They moved from the hatred for armed enemies to the hatred of unarmed innocence. The babies. The babies. "Blessed are they who dash your babies' brains against a rock," and that my beloved is a dangerous place to be. Yet that is where the people of faith are, in 551 B.C. and that is where far too many people of faith are in 2001 A.D. We have moved from the hatred of armed enemies to the hatred of unarmed innocence. We want revenge, we want paybacks, and we don't care who gets hurt in the process.

Now, I asked the Lord, what should our response be in light of such an unthinkable act? But before I share with you what the Lord showed me I want to give you one of my little faith footnotes. Visitors, I often give faith footnotes so that our members don't lose sight of the big picture. Let me give you a little faith footnote. Turn to your neighbor and say, "faith footnote." I heard Ambassador Peck on an interview yesterday. Did anybody else see him or hear him? He was on Fox News. This is a white man and he was upsetting the Fox News commentators to no end. He pointed out what Malcolm X said when he got silenced by Elijah Muhammad was in fact true, "America's chickens are coming home to roost."

We took this country by terror, away from the Sioux, the Apache, the Comanche, and the Navaho. Terrorism. We took Africans from their country to build our way of ease and kept them enslaved and living in fear. Terrorism. We bombed Grenada, killed innocent civilians, babies, nonmilitary personnel. We bombed the black civilian community of Panama with Stealth bombers, and killed unarmed teenagers, and toddlers, pregnant mothers, and hard-working fathers. We bombed Khadafi's home and killed his child. "Blessed are they who bash your children's heads against the rock." We bombed Iraq—we killed unarmed civilians trying to make a living. We bombed a plant in Sudan to payback for an attack on our embassy, killed hundreds of hard-working people, mothers and fathers who left home to go that day, not knowing they'd never get back. We bombed Hiroshima. We bombed Nagasaki and we nuked far more than the thousands in New York and the Pentagon and we never batted an eye. Kids playing in the playground, mothers picking up children after school, civilians not soldiers; people just trying to make it day by day. We have supported state terrorism against the Palestinians and black South Africans and now we are indignant because the stuff we have done overseas is now brought right back into our own front yards. "America's chickens are coming home to roost."

Violence begets violence. Hatred begets hatred, and terrorism begets terrorism. A white ambassador said that, not a black minister, not a reverend who preaches about racism, but an ambassador whose eyes are wide open and who's trying to get us to wake up and move away from this dangerous precipice upon which we are now poised. The ambassador said the people overseas are wounded, but don't have the military capability. We have superior military might, but they have individuals who are willing to die to take thousands with them, and we need to come to grips with that. Let me stop my faith footnote right there, and ask you to think about that over the next few weeks if God grants us that many days. Turn back to your neighbor say, "Faith footnote note is over."

Now, now come on back to my question to the Lord, "What should our response be right now in light of such an unthinkable act?" I asked the Lord that question: "What should our response be?" I saw pictures of the incredible. People jumping from 110 floors. People jumping from the roof because the stairwells and elevators above the eighty-ninth floor were gone. Black people jumping to a certain death. People holding hands jumping. People on fire jumping, and I asked the Lord, "What should our response be?" I read what the people of faith felt in 551 B.C., but this is a different time; this is a different enemy; this is a different world; this is a different terror. This is a different reality. What should our response be?

The Lord showed me three things. Let me share them with you quickly, and I'm going to leave you alone to think about the faith footnote. Number one, the Lord showed me that this is a time for self-examination. As I sat nine hundred miles away from my family and my community of faith, two months after my own father's death, God showed me that this is a time for me to examine my relationship with God, my own relationship with God, my personal relationship with God. I submit to you it is the same for you. Folks flocked to the church in New Jersey last week. You know that foxhole religion syndrome kicked in, that little red box you see, pull in case of emergency, it showed up full force. Folks who ain't thought about church in years were in church last week. I heard that midweek prayer services all over this country, which are poorly attended fifty-one weeks a year, were jam-packed all over the nation. But the Lord said, "This ain't the time for you to be examining other folks' relationships; this is the time of self-examination." The Lord said to me, "How is our relationship doing Jeremiah? How often do you talk to me personally? How often do you let me talk to you privately? How much time do you spend trying to get right with me, or do you spend all your time trying to get other folk right?" This is a time for me to examine my own relationship with God. Is it real or is it fake? Is it forever or is it for show? Is it something that you do for the sake of the public, or is it something that you do for the sake of eternity? This is a time to examine my own and a time for you to examine your own relationship with God. Self-examination. Then this is a time in light of the unbelievable tragedies, this is a time to examine my relationship with my family. Self-examination.

As soon as the first plane hit the World Trade Center, I called home, and I called my mother. Ramah [wife] was taking Jamila [daughter] to the schoolbus, my mother's phone was busy, and the thought hit me, "Suppose you could never talk to her again? Suppose you never see your family—Jamila, Janet, Jerry, Stevie, Jazzy, Jay, and Ramah—ever again?" What is the quality of the relationship between you and your family? The soul station in New York kept playing Stevie Wonder's song "These Three Words." When is the last time you took the time to say to your family, "Honey, I love you," and then that family thought led me to my extended family and my church family. We fight, we disagree, we fall out, we have diametrically opposed views on some critical issues, but I still love you. When is the last time you said that to your church family—when your daddy died? Well that was two months ago Reverend, you need to say that every chance you get. So let me just say that to you now I love y'all. I love you. I love you. Listen. Listen. Don't clap. Turn to the person sitting next to you worshipping next to you and say it while you have the chance say I love you. Listen. Listen. This past week was a grim reminder of the fact that I might not have the chance to say that next week. So say it now, I love you.

I had two deacons, two deacons when they realized I could not fly home, Dedrick wanted to be anonymous, Dedrick Roberts and Deacon Reggie Crenshaw, they got in a car and drove twelve straight hours, put my bags in the trunk, put me in the backseat, turned right around, and drove back twelve hours because they loved me. I want them to know, I love you man. I love you. I love you. I thank God for you. Turn back and tell your neighbor one more time, "I love you." This is what a church family is, the beloved community, a community of love. Fights? Yes. Disagreements? Yes. Falling outs? Yes. Different viewpoints? Yes. Doctrinal disputes? Yes. But love that is of God and given by God who loved us so much that while we were yet sinners, God gave God's son rather than give up on us. This is the time of self-examination, a time to examine our personal relationships with God. A time to examine our personal relationships with our family, and a time to examine our personal relationships with our extended family, the family of God.

Then the Lord showed me this is not only a time for self-examination, this is also a time for social transformation. This is going to be the hardest step we have to take. But now is the time for social transformation. We have got to change the way we have been doing things. We have got to change the way we have been doing things as a society. Social transformation. We have got to change the way we have been doing things as a country, social transformation. We have got to change the way we have been doing things as an arrogant racist military superpower. Social transformation. We just can't keep messing over people and thinking that, "Can't nobody do nothing about it." They have shown us that they can and that they will, and let me suggest to you that rather than figure out who we gonna declare war on, maybe we need to declare war on racism. Maybe we need to declare war on injustice. Maybe we need to declare war on greed. Those same lawmakers you saw gathered at the Capitol praying are the same lawmakers who just passed a 1.3 trillion dollar gift for the rich. Maybe we need to rethink the way we do politics and declare war on greed. Maybe we need to declare war on AIDS. In five minutes the congress found forty billion dollars to rebuild New York and the families of those who died in sudden deaths. Do you think we could find the money to make medicine available for people who are dying a slow death? We need to declare war on the health care system that leaves the nation's poor with no health coverage. Maybe we need to declare war on the mishandled educational system and provide quality education for everybody, every citizen based on their ability to learn, not their ability to pay. This is a time for social transformation. We can't go back to doing business as usual and treating the rest of the world like we have been treating them. This is the time for self-examination. This is the time for social transformation.

But then ultimately as I looked around and saw that God had given me another chance, to try to be the man that God wants me to be, another chance to try to be the person that God meant for me to be. Another chance to try to be the parent that God knows I should be. Another chance to try to make a positive difference in a world full of hate. Another chance to teach somebody the difference between our God's awesomeness and our nation's arrogance. When I looked around and saw that for whatever the reason God had let me see another day, I realized that the Lord was showing me that this is not only a time for self-examination, this is not only a time for social transformation, but this is also a time for spiritual adoration. In other words, this is a time to say, "Thank you Lord." This is the day that the Lord has made. I will rejoice and be glad in it. I may not have tomorrow, so I'm going to take this time on this day to say, "Thank you Lord, thank you for my life." You didn't have to let me live. Thank you for my blessings, I could have been on one of those airplanes. I could have been in downtown New York or a few blocks from the Pentagon, but for whatever the reason you let me be here. So while I am here I'm going to take the opportunity to adore you, and to say, "Thank you Lord." Thank you for the lives of those who were lost. Thank you for the way in which they touched our lives and the way in which they blessed other lives. Thank you Lord. Thank you for the love we have experienced, for love in itself is an inexpressible gift, and thank you Lord for the gift of our lives because when I look around and realize that my life itself is a gift that God has given me, and so I say thank you. Thank you Lord. While I have another chance, thank you. Just say it, thank you Lord for my friends and my family. Thank you Lord for this opportunity. Thank you for another chance to say thank you. If you mean that from your heart throw your head back and adore him this morning. Say thank you Lord. Thank you Lord for another chance. Another chance to say thank you. It's time for spiritual adoration.

## NOTES

*Sermon source:* Martha Simmons and Frank A. Thomas, eds., *9.11.01: African American Leaders Respond to an American Tragedy* (Valley Forge, PA: Judson Press, 2001), 81–93.

1. Brian Ross and Rehah E-Brui, "Obama's Pastor: God damn America, U.S. to blame for 9/11," *Good Morning America*, ABC Television, March 13, 2008. Also see Edward S. Herman and David Peterson, "Jeremiah Wright in the Propaganda System," *Monthly Review*, September 2008, for additional information on Jeremiah Wright and the American media.
2. Psalm 137:1 (New Revised Standard Version).
3. See Isaiah 6:1.
4. See Isaiah 6:3.

## BIBLIOGRAPHICAL SOURCES

"Reverend Dr. Jeremiah Wright Jr." http://www.festivalofhomiletics.com/speaker.html (accessed May 23, 2005).

"Reverend Dr. Jeremiah Wright Jr." http://www.tucc.org/pastor/wright2004.html (accessed May 23, 2005).

Wright, Jeremiah A., Jr. "Doing Black Theology in the Black Church," in *Living Stones in the Household of God: The Legacy and Future of Black Theology*, ed. Linda E. Thomas. Minneapolis: Fortress Press, 2003.

———. "Here I Am, Send Me," in *Awakened to a Calling: Reflections on the Vocation of Ministry*, ed. Ann M. Svennungsen and Melissa Wiginton. Nashville, TN: Abingdon Press, 2005.

———. "Music as Cultural Expression in Black Church Theology and Worship." *Journal of Black Sacred Music* 3, no. 1 (Spring 1989).

# WHOOPING: THE MUSICALITY OF AFRICAN AMERICAN PREACHING PAST AND PRESENT

## *Martha Simmons*

AFRICAN AMERICANS HAVE PRODUCED A UNIQUE FORM OF PREACHING whose signature is tonality. Referred to as whooping (sometimes spelled incorrectly as hooping, which is a sports term), it has other names, including squalling, pulling it, intoning, humming, and zooming, Those who are not steeped in the idiom have incorrectly referred to it as chanting.[1]

Pre-1970s styles of whooping are often discussed as "the old-fashioned Negro style of preaching," "old fashioned Black preaching," and "folk preaching."[2] Often in the literature all preaching done by African Americans is called folk preaching. This is a manifest error. Additionally, when used in reference to whoopers, the term "folk preaching" is often not meant as a term of genuine respect and admiration. Unfortunately, when those who are spectators of whooping discuss it, whether they are African American or not, they sometimes reduce it to just a debased art form or a style of preaching done by ignorant folk. Not all folk preachers are whoopers, and certainly not all African American preachers are whoopers, though I highly suspect that most would whoop it if they could, if only every now and then.

This style of preaching is awesomely powerful and beautiful when performed by persons naturally fluent in the idiom. It remains dearly loved and sought after in a large proportion of African American churches. Even among those African Americans who have been acculturated away from whooping, it is hard not to be moved by whooping at its best.

## THE NATURE OF WHOOPING

The phenomenon called whooping is seen and described in various ways; one takes risks in any simple attempt to narrowly define it. While most who are familiar with it have trouble defining it, they know whooping when they hear it. Whooping can be thought of as parallel to great opera. The tonality enhances the beauty as well as the depth of impact. The hearer is more readily caught up in the sermon, as one may be caught up in the dramatic power of an opera, because of the combined impact of tone and word. What is whooping? In the introduction to *Sacred Symphony: The Chanted Sermon of the Black Preacher*, homiletician William Turner of Duke Divinity School writes: "That which is variously referred to as whooping, intoning, chanting, moaning or tuning is essentially melody. This particular style of melody is definable as a series of cohesive pitches which have continuity, tonality, quasi-metrical phraseology and formulary cadence."[3]

Whooping is first melody, one that can be identified by the fact that its pitches are logically connected and have prescribed, punctuated rhythms that require certain modulations of the voice, and is often delineated by quasi-metrical phrasings. Charles Adams, about whom more will be said later, undoubtedly referring to pre-1970s styles, says of whooping:

> That the line between singing and preaching is very thin is boldly illustrated in the Black American slave preacher's practice of a form of proclamation that transformed declarative and didactic speech into dramatic and celebratory song. That is what the Black preacher's vaunted whoop is all about.[4]

However, whooping should not be confused with tuning. Tuning may best be defined as a slight preparatory melody attached to the spoken word, and it may or may not lead to whooping. Preachers who are not whoopers may tune; even laity may tune when praying. Laity, primarily deacons and older women in the church (typically called mothers of the church and deaconesses of the church), are known to excel in tuned prayers. These older women and older deacons are the laity most often called upon to pray, because their fervor pours forth in holy, poetic, well-known phrases powerfully tuned. Just as it is common in the African American church to request laity who can tune to pray, there is a common African American prayer, parts of which are often tuned. The most common aspects of the prayer are:

*Lord here we are again;*
*knee bent and body bowed.*
*Lord we wanna' thank yah*
*for watching over us last night*
*as we slumbered and slept.*
*We wannna' thank yah*
*that the kiver [or cloth] we covered with*
*last night was not our winding sheet,*
*and the bed we lied on*
*was not our cooling board*
*and the four walls of our room*
*were not the fall walls of our grave.*
*And when we woke this morning,*
*and looked around at the family,*
*we saw that the circle still hadn't been broken.*
*So we wanna' stop right now,*
*to say much obliged.*

The most often tuned aspects of the prayer are:

*Now Lawd, in few more risin's and settins' of the sun,*
*when all my battles have been fought and victories won.*
*When my tongue has cleaved to the roof of our mouth,*
*my feet are cold and my hands are folded across my breast,*
*my eyes have been shut by old chilly death,*
*please give me a restin' place some where around your throne.*
*Anywhere will do, just some where around your throne.*
*And we'll be careful not to take the credit, but to give it all to you.*

Slight variations and extensions of this prayer have traveled throughout African American culture from state to state and denomination to denomination for centuries. Much of its remains intact in prayers heard today, especially in the South and in smaller and storefront churches.

Tuning is often an acknowledgment that one has an understanding of the culture's adoration of whooping. So, although one may not produce a full-fledged whoop, he or she knows that the congregation will appreciate the beginning melody, even when it stops short of a complete whoop. Those who cannot tune use cadence, sometimes accompanied by rhymes. Martin Luther King Jr. used slight cadence. Jessie Louis Jackson Sr. uses cadence with rhyme. Whether they are tuning or using cadence, when black preachers are in historically black denomination churches and settings (and sometimes even when elsewhere, as with the speech given by Jesse Jackson at the 1988 Democratic Convention) this is their way of saying, "By the use of these particular oratorical devices, I may not be a whooper, but I understand its power and its deep roots in black culture and with it, I too am at home."

One typically does not need singing ability to tune. Whoopers often have singing ability, but this is less true among post-1970s whoopers. Also, in spite of the sexism in the Protestant African American church, tuning is even acceptable from women, especially older women. However, whooping, especially in its pre-1970s forms, has been seen as much more acceptable coming from men.

## TONALITY IN THE ROOT CULTURE OF AFRICA AND IN WESTERN CULTURE

One of the most prevalent misconceptions concerning tonal preaching is that of its origins. This discussion is but one aspect of the larger debate over the origins of many African American traditions, and whether African culture was rooted out of African Americans who were enslaved in the Americas. It must be fully understood that African culture was not totally stripped from those in bondage during the Middle Passage, nor in the early years of the so-called "breaking in" of enslaved African Americans. Ethnomusicologist Joyce Marie Jackson speaks to how enslaved African preachers in America continued in the tradition of their ancestors, the griots:

> The Black folk preacher in the United States emerged during the period of slavery as a panegyric or praise poet, in the tradition of his cultural predecessor, the West African griot. Both griot and preacher deal with heroic material and draw upon a particular wellspring of imagery, which is usually fitted into a metrical pattern.[5]

In examining parallels seen in the griot and the African American folk preaching tradition, such as training function, content, mode, and style of performance, it can be seen how the black folk preacher who whooped manifested African traditions, traditions that were strong enough to hold their own when they came into contact with white culture and religious customs. Jackson goes on to say:

> In as much as Africans came to the New World in great numbers and carried a deep-rooted tradition of religion and music, it would be astonishing if no vestige of their background religious traditions were retained. It also seems reasonable to believe that everything cultural which the Black man brought with him from Africa could not have been eradicated from his heritage, despite the several centuries of development outside of Africa, the thousands of miles which have separated him from the ancestral homeland, and the eroding influence of an overwhelming and inescapably dominating culture.[6]

In addition to the cultural, soul-ensconced, musical reverberations that could not be erased, the Middle Passage experience unleashed, like never before, the moans of those coffled like beasts and led away from their homeland. Professor of African American religion James Noel discusses it in this fashion:

> The moan became the first vocalization of a new spiritual vocabulary—terrible and wonderful, it was a cry, a critique, a prayer, a hymn, a sermon, all at once . . . The moan expressed loneliness, pain, and the inchoate hope which would later fuse with biblical imagery. Its rhythm was not so much the syncopated beat of the West African drum as the rock and sway of the sea-faring vessel which contained their bodies.[7]

It was not until after the American revolution that large numbers of African Americans became converts and joined Methodist and Baptist churches.[8] Noted author and scholar Dr. W.E.B. DuBois indicates how long it took African Americans to affiliate in significant numbers with the Euro-American Christian Church.

> It [the Negro church] was not at first by any means a Christian Church, but a mere adaptation of those heathen [foreign to Americans] rites which we roughly designate by the term Obe Worship, or "Voodoism." Association and missionary effort soon gave these rites a veneer of Christianity, and gradually, *after two centuries* [emphasis mine], the [Black] Church became Christian . . . , but with many of the old customs still clinging to the services. It is this historic fact that the Negro Church of today bases itself upon the sole surviving social institution of the African fatherland that accounts for its extraordinary growth and vitality.[9]

So, for more than 150 years in America, Africans had only their African religious heritage and their plaintive moans and cries on which to depend.

After 1789, blacks did not simply replace older, African values, but adapted new patterns onto older ones. Consequently, blacks were not converted to the white Christian God; they converted their God(s) to fit into English language. African religious sensibilities were the starting point, with European religious concepts selectively adapted to the specialized needs of African Americans.

Whooping provides perhaps one of the clearest examples of the convergence of West African and Euro-American cultural streams. Within the context of North American slavery, African American preachers carefully selected, personalized, and presented biblical texts in accord with the needs and aesthetic preferences of their people. In North America, Christian themes merged with preexistent African methods of worship to create a unique folkloric genre.

The most convincing evidence of this happens to be tonality. The whoop evolved by adaptation, from tonally rich African speech. Indeed, it would have been strange if African tonality had disappeared, given that it was inherent in most West African languages, and that most Africans brought to North America came from West Africa. Tonality was part of the signal system in the spoken language, and it was advanced by the playing of various instruments, such as drums.[10]

When slaves preached to other slaves with tonality, the vast majority were simply using the cultural tools they came with in their sincere efforts to heal and empower their hearers. Their African background provided no other way to communicate what was considered holy or wise. It was not a decision to whoop or not whoop. It was a matter of speaking or not speaking with remnants of the tongues they brought from home. As African musician and author Francis Bebey writes in *African Music: A People's Art*:

> The music is clearly an integral part of the life of every African from the moment of his birth. The musical games played by children are never gratuitous; they are a form of musical training which prepares them to participate in all areas of adult activity: fishing, hunting, farming, grinding maize, attending weddings, funerals, dances, and by necessity even fleeing wild animals.
>
> . . . This intimate union between man and art is rare outside of Africa. It amounts to a total communion that is shared by the whole community . . . The art of music is so inherent in man that it

> is superfluous to have a particular name for it . . . In fact, African music which is an "impure" art form in that it is nearly always coupled with some other art, such as poetry or dance, is without doubt one of the most revealing forms of expression of the Black soul.[11]

Bebey's explanation of the role of music in Africa, regardless of one's location or clan, indicates that it was and is an inherent part of all of life, including worship. Although enslaved Africans were not permitted to use African languages, they kept music as a part of who they had always been and would remain. It was soul deep at the core of their being. Words and word systems may be confined to geographic boundaries over time, but tone knows no such bounds. The power of music (tonality) transcends geographic limits.

## EARLY TONAL PREACHING: BLACK AND WHITE

While New Englander Jonathan Edwards (1703–1758) was the major name in the great American religious revival called the First Great Awakening, the most traveled and widely heard preacher was George Whitefield (1714–1770), a white young itinerant from England. His power as a preacher was such that the huge audiences were forced to gather outdoors to hear him. The crowds who came to hear him in downtown Philadelphia were estimated to be larger than the actual population of the city itself.[12] During a forty-five-day period in 1740, Whitefield delivered more than 175 sermons to thousands of people, in addition to exhorting frequently in private.[13]

Whitefield's novel dramatizations stemmed from his habit of speaking extemporaneously. This method had not been practiced before by Congregational ministers and had not been taught in colleges. Of all his innovations, it attracted the most comments from blacks. Throughout his journeys, Whitefield urged ministers and aspiring ministers to preach without notes, and he criticized written-out sermons as "deficient of faith." Whitefield said, "Though they are not to be condemned who use notes, yet it is a symptom of the decay of the religion, when reading sermons becomes fashionable."[14]

Not only did Whitefield's vivid portrayals correspond to the rich African heritage of delivering narrative imagery (storytelling), but his sonorous delivery, perhaps adopted to reach thousands without technical help, also appealed irresistibly to those with tonal language roots. Perhaps most importantly, black preachers heard what Whitefield did without notes, and they knew immediately that they had the cultural tools to preach as rousingly as Whitefield did. It was safer and more acceptable for blacks to use their unique form of tonality now that whites had a form of preaching akin to it. Whitefield's preaching without notes also appealed to the enslaved because it was typically against the law for them to read and write. In some states, blacks could be killed for attempting to learn to read and write. Since writing was not necessary, enslaved preachers were free to speak from memory and through metaphor and story in panoramic color with fiery tones that were so unforgettable to their audience.

While no one would give Whitefield credit for teaching slaves to whoop, what he did was to legitimize tonality among whites and to begin to extricate the Christian faith from the rise of rationalism and the reduction of worship to opening exercises. He made extemporaneous preaching with tonality attractive to blacks. One can track Whitefield's tonality as it flowed into what was called in Georgia the "holy whine."[15] And one can trace whooping by some of the first black Baptist preachers in Georgia to the fact that they learned the faith as well as the craft of American preaching in the same Kiokee, Georgia, church that was the mother of all the white Baptists.[16] The Whitefield influence reached the black American church of the Deep South quite directly. Tonal preaching (whether called whooping or holy whine) has survived far better in black circles than in white, but it remains, to some extent, among both.

## STYLES OF WHOOPING

Whooping by blacks is rightly divided into four approximate periods (given that we do not have a record of much of black preaching before 1800): 1700–1899, when the influence of African Traditional Religion was heaviest and blacks intersected with EuroAmerican culture; 1915–1950s, the Gates era; 1955–1975, the Franklin era; and 1980–present, the Adams era, in which the speed of whooping shifts, and cadence or naked tone, rather than melody, is pervasive.

Jon Michael Spencer writes in *Sacred Symphony*:

> The principal melodic mode employed by black preachers in their whooping is the pentatonic, a scale common to African folk song and traditional black spirituals. From the tonic, the ascending intervals of this scale are a minor third, two major seconds, and another

> minor third . . . Even further embellishment of the pentatonic is possible by means of such customary vocal inflections as the lowering, the bending, scooping and wavering of pitches . . . [T]he music of black preaching can be understood as a sort of "singing in the spirit," for there is a surplus (glossa) expressed in music which accompanies the rational content (logos) enunciated in words. The logical portion is contained in the structure of the sermon . . . For the glossa portion, the preacher becomes an instrument of musical afflatus: a flute through which divine air is blown, a harp upon which eternal strings vibrate . . . This melodious declamation is delineated into quasi-metrical phrases with formulaic cadence.[17]

Whooping is not a narrowly defined genre; the tonal approaches of whoopers vary, thus allowing for a variety of styles. The embellishment of the pentatonic leads to a range from a soft growl (Caesar Clark, discussed below, was an exemplar of this style) to a hack or guttural gasp, which resembles and may be a gasping for breath, to whoops that are so melodious that they are called "sweet whoops."

Because it could be done by almost anyone, the hack was a prominent type of whooping in the late 1800s and early-to-mid 1900s. It takes less breath control to whoop and hack. One of the best examples of a preacher using a hack was recorded by Zora Neale Hurston (1901–1960) in *The Sanctified Church.* The sermon was preached by Rev. C.C. Lovelace in Eau Gallie, Florida, in 1929 (see page 392). Hurston recorded the hack or guttural-gasp as Ha!, the sound that comes forth when a preacher does this kind of whooping. The Reverend Mary M. Nelson (of whom very little is known), a Pentecostal preacher from Memphis, had a slight guttural gasp that it is said became a growling whoop that had melody. Recorded in the 1920s, Nelson also had a powerful singing voice, and a few of her songs can still be purchased. Her song "Judgment" (1927) and her only published sermon, "The Royal Telephone" (1928), are required listening for those who love whooping or want to learn about it. Perhaps the most famous modern whooper, Jasper Williams Jr. of Atlanta, at one point had a guttural gasp, moved to a melodious whoop, and by 2000 had become primarily a squaller (see page 845). Williams, a major revivalist from the 1960s to the 1980s, gained attention after delivering the eulogy for the well-known preacher C.L. Franklin, and he produced several recordings. By the 1990s Williams had gained such a following that he began offering Whoopology classes and selling instructional material.

J.M. Gates (1884–1945) of Atlanta is an unheralded whooper. It was Gates whom the king of the melodious sweet whoop (C.L. Franklin) recalled when asked whom he listened to while growing up.[18] It was Gates to whom Malcolm X's father, a Baptist preacher, was also said to have listened. Gate's recordings were unique. The sheer number is still unparalleled: two hundred recordings between 1926 and 1941. Gates recorded one quarter of all the sermons released in the country up to 1943. When his "Death's Black Train Is Coming" was released in 1926, more than thirty-five thousand copies were sold. On some occasions, Gates preached his way through sermons and made no attempt to whoop, but when he decided to let go, his whoop was fiery and melodic. One can not be certain if it was whooping alone that made Gates so popular. It was likely also his practices of including the voices of his four-person traveling congregation and engaging in back-and-forth dialogue with them on the recordings. This had not been done before.

The most admired whoopers were those who had melodious, smooth whoops, minus the gasp or hack. The ultimate melodic whooper was Clarence LaVaughn (C.L.) Franklin (1915–1984). Franklin (affectionately called Frank by many) stands as the best-known whooper of the twentieth century, as well as one of the most imitated. Many young preachers from the 1950s to the '70s wanted to whoop like Frank.[19] Franklin, father of soul singer Aretha Franklin, produced seventy-six albums, and his sermons continue to be sold in record stores, on the Internet, and at various religious conferences and denominational conventions. When preaching, he moved seamlessly into a whoop. This is not often done. His voice was explosive and filled with a river of music. So many have tried to imitate his whoop that Franklin has likely cloned more whoopers than any preacher of the twentieth century. But not only could he whoop, his sermons were interesting, substantive, theologically strong, and relevant, and he was a master at using metaphors.

Another style of whoop begins as almost a grumble, slowly drags toward a growl, and is punctuated by an African American southern drawl. It is most clearly seen in the preaching of Caesar A.W. Clark of Dallas (1914–2008), and was once common in parts of Louisiana and surrounding areas. Clark is among the most beloved whoopers of the twentieth century and one of the most prolific revivalists from 1960 to 1985. Donald Parson (1947– ) of Chicago is known for having a whoop that stays in tune for an unbelievably long time. When a preacher whoops at the end of a sermon, the whoop typically lasts five to ten minutes. Parson has been known to whoop sections of his sermons (in pre-1970s melodic fashion) for more than twenty minutes!

Yet another type of whooping is typified by Gilbert Earl Patterson (1939–2007), once a presiding bishop of the Church of God in Christ. It was melodic and continued longer than most whoops, and the shift from word to whoop was easily tracked. Despite his whooping not being seamless, the tracking heightens the preaching experience. It is not unusual for COGIC preachers to whoop throughout sermons. Patterson's whoop was fluid, robust, and yet quite melodic; in his later preaching life, he began to whoop mainly at the conclusion of his messages rather than throughout.

Interestingly, Holiness-Pentecostal preachers have long been criticized for whooping throughout sermons. However, in the late 1980s and beyond, Baptist, Methodist, and nondenominational preachers have begun to use the newer form of whooping throughout sermons.

Yet another type of whoop is the squall, which some consider an incomplete whoop, although this is not true. While it is not as robust and is only mildly melodic, when used skillfully it has great impact. It is not atypical to hear women whoopers referred to as squallers.

## WHOOPING POST-1970S— EVERYTHING MUST CHANGE

Notwithstanding its history and power, some believed that by the 1970s the great folk art treasure of whooping was fading. It was thought that the tides of attrition, the ever-infiltrating influence of the majority culture, educational gains by African Americans, and pollution of the craft by lazy, insincere, and manipulative practitioners all had taken a major toll. However, just as the spirituals are no longer in their original folk art state, by the late 1970s neither was whooping. Whooping was not fading; it was transitioning. The process here parallels that of the blues transitioning and evolving and spinning off other genres from classical (or pre-) jazz to rhythm and blues, to rock-and-roll, to hard rock, to rap, and so on.

The first noticeable transition that occurred in whooping in more than two-hundred-plus years was marked by the preaching of Rev. Charles Gilchrist Adams (1936– ). Although a preacher long before the 1970s, Adams became a revivalist and academic lecturer of national note in the late 1970s. African American audiences could hear that his preaching was different. It was filled with multiple alliterative lists; it could contain four or five crescendo moments that were as high as the typical sermon celebration/conclusion of most whoopers. It had cadence, but almost no melody. Listeners knew that it was not a typical form of whooping. The Adams style was much more subtle than those who hacked and the melodic whoopers, but it was still whooping. Because Adams, a Harvard graduate, was considered erudite, he turned on their heads all of the traditional notions of whoopers as persons with little formal education or with substandard education. Nevertheless, listeners knew that he was whooping, and he was dubbed the "Harvard Whooper."

Adams uses cadence throughout his sermons as a vehicle of modulation and to help him modulate his continuous production of long, alliterative lists (also referred to as producing runs and riffs), a hallmark of his preaching. Those who stand in the Adams lineage, such as Frederick Haynes III (1959– ) of Dallas, Texas, and Carolyn Knight (1956– ) of Atlanta, Georgia, also use cadence as a vehicle to modulate their production throughout their sermons. The preaching of Haynes and Knight contains few pauses; when they first appeared on the national stage, listeners often wondered if they ever took a breath. The whooping of Adams, Haynes, and Knight contains almost no melody, with Knight retaining the most melody. The preaching of Haynes and Knight is much quicker than that of Adams, probably because they are much younger, and preaching quickly with continual cadence is physically exhausting. Haynes and Knight typically leave pulpits with drenched clothing and are two of the busiest revivalists on the national preaching circuit.

In the late 1980s and 1990s African American churches changed: small pulpit areas that contained six chairs and wooden lecterns became long, wide, carpeted stages with transparent lecterns, a process that many African Americans believe began with the ministry of Frederick Price (1932– ) of Crenshaw Christian Center in south-central Los Angeles. Almost no whooping was heard in these churches. For several years, Price and other so-named Word preachers gained prominence. T.D. Jakes (1957– ) of the Potter's House in Dallas used a transparent lectern on a long stage, but although aspects of his approach resembled the Word preachers, he knew how to whoop and how to use cadence. Along with Jakes (who introduced her to national audiences at one of his conferences) came Juanita Bynum (1956– ). Her preaching speed is much quicker than that of Jakes, and her sermons are filled with Adams-like cadence. For a variety of reasons, not the least of which was whooping, Jakes and Bynum became much larger figures on the preaching landscape than Price did.

The post-1970s forms of whooping are much less melodic and filled with fewer pauses. They require a quick speech pace, and they contain numerous crescendo moments and continuous cadence. Much of the preaching of even non-whoopers post-1980 has sped up. Accordingly, the traditional form of call-and-response (the back-and-forth recitation of phrases by the preacher, and then the congregation in response, or vice versa) are lessened, and so is the repeating of stock phrases that have been historically known throughout the African American Protestant community. Such phrases include: "He picked me up and turned me around and placed my feet on solid ground"; "He died all night Friday. Died all night Saturday, but early, early Sunday morning, he got up with all power in his hands"; and, "I was too mean to live and wasn't fit to die, but the Lord saved me anyhow." While audience participation is lessened in some ways, it may be heightened in others, especially with preaching by those whoopers who tend to place several crescendo moments within their sermons, as opposed to one crescendo moment at the conclusion. Also, with the modern use of rhetorical devices that preachers use, such as "turn and tell your neighbor" or "give someone a high five" or "tell three people . . . ," audience response is maintained, perhaps even enhanced. However, unlike in the past, this newer type of call-and-response is only led by the preacher, not by the congregation. If overused, the modern call-and-response devices have been shown to be distracting and can hurt the flow of a sermon.

The placement or timing of pre-1970s whooping in a sermon reflects a determination made by the preacher (and in some instances the hearers) that it is time to conclude the sermon. Most African American preachers and the few white preachers who whoop or understand whooping primarily still view whooping as a kind of climactic utterance. When the message has progressed in emotional impact and reached its zenith or finale, the preacher celebrates the conclusion of the sermon with appropriate tonality and sits down. The hearer understands the whoop to mean that the Helper (the Holy Spirit) has come and overpowered the preacher. In preaching post-1970, the preacher and hearer may end up celebrating four or five times during the sermonic moment, and yet even more powerfully at the end of the sermon.

## IS IT LEARNED OR SHUT UP IN ONE'S BONES?

Is whooping learned, or is it something one is born with the ability to do? It seems to be a combination of both. One can be born and reared in a cultural context that gives one the predisposition to whoop, but the skill still has to be honed, and that honing is learned from others. The white folklorist Bruce Rosenberg, author of *Can These Bones Live?: The Art of the American Folk Preacher*, identifies three stages in the development of a whooper, whom he calls chanters.

> At first as a young child, the preacher sits in church . . . and learns the stories of the Bible, the popular sermon topics, the melody and rhythm of . . . songs and more importantly the melody and rhythm of his pastor's chanted sermons, and however unconsciously, many of the phrases which will later become formulas . . . The second stage [in the preacher's development] often comes when the apprentice involves himself with church work so that he attends services more frequently . . . The final stage begins when the preacher takes his own church; at this point he must feel that his repertoire is sufficient to sustain the congregation week after week . . . He then becomes an active part of his tradition: he has mastered certain aspects of language and certain rhythms and pitch patterns which he knows are sure to elicit a predictable response.[20]

Rosenberg is correct and incorrect; this is not just the process by which whoopers learn to whoop. It is the process by which most preachers, not just African American clergy, learn to preach. As preachers begin their preaching careers emulating those from whom they first learned to preach, whoopers also must master certain rhythms and pitch patterns from others.

Interestingly, in its pre-1970s forms, whooping was communal. Apprentices were not just learning the stock phrases of their pastor, they were learning the stock phrases that belonged to the entire African American Protestant community. This is why the responses of historically African American congregations were so uniformly predictable before the 1990s. Worshippers had grown up hearing the phrases and could teach them to new preachers. While a young preacher may have entered ministry having only been a part of the church for a brief time, the older members could teach all of the stock phrases that the preacher would need to learn. If a preacher said, "They hung him high," the members knew and sometimes would shout out the responding line "They stretched him wide." When a preacher reached the line "Early, early, on Sunday morning," the congregation was ready with "He got up, with all power in his hands." This call-and-response occurs most often with pre-1970s styles of whooping, which are slow enough to allow audiences to infuse their stored call-and-response knowledge into the preaching moment.

Also, while a preacher may in fact learn to preach and mimic their pastor or parent in the ministry, whoopers always practice by listening to the most popular whoopers. C.L. Franklin listened to J.M. Gates. Although Franklin has been dead for more than twenty years, preachers continue to listen to his recordings. Caesar Clark's tapes are still purchased at national conferences and conventions, though Clark, who died in 2008, was no longer in the pulpit by 2001. Along with the old-school preachers, younger preachers are now listening to Charles Adams, Frederick Haynes III, and Carolyn Knight for a whoop with speed and cadence.

But there is so much more that must be learned in order to be a credible whooper. Most importantly, preachers must have something substantive to say, or he or she will become known as a preacher with "just a whoop"—a major insult in African American culture. Authentic whoopers have whooping shut up in their bones. Through communal experiences, this fire is heightened and unleashed, and the preacher becomes a contributor to a grand tradition, and hopefully, enhances the viability of the tradition. While it is acceptable to begin one's preaching career by emulating other whoopers, eventually one must find one's own style.

## THE CULTURE'S RECEPTION TO WHOOPING

In the African American church, the reception to whooping ranges from rigid intolerance, to occasional tolerance, to joyous acceptance of it as a signal of the ultimate celebrative moment in preaching. Many a young preacher, especially women (who may have been born with the ability to whoop, but have had few role models to help them refine this gift), have missed being called to a church because a far-less-trained and less-substantive preacher has come forth with a sweet whoop.

Although as of 2009 most of the socially influential African American churches in America are not pastored by whoopers, it is quite noteworthy that these same churches still bring in whoopers for revivals and special occasions in the life of their churches, and these pastors still attend conferences and denominational conventions and go to hear the whoopers. Whoopers, especially pre-1970s-style whoopers, still hold sway during the national gatherings of the two largest African American denominations: the Church of God in Christ and the National Baptist Convention, U.S.A., Inc. What is known as "Late Night" at the National Baptist Convention, U.S.A., Inc., is famed for the mainly pre-1970s-style whoopers featured each year.

Even if one is not a whooper, to succeed long-term in the historically African American denominations and churches one must at least have an understanding of the esteem in which whooping is held in the culture. At a minimum preachers understand that theirs will be a frosty reception if they cannot celebrate (conclude their sermon) with a high level of intensity and some tonality or cadence. Even if they can only tune, that will be welcomed. The importance of musicality in preaching in African American culture is immense. William Turner of Duke goes so far as to say that in some venues inside the culture it is a criterion for preaching:

> To those who are part of the tradition where musical delivery is customary, such a form often emerges as the criterion for preaching. This valuation categorizes other styles of delivery as a speech, address, or lecture, but hardly as preaching. In the vernacular of the culture, preaching of this type must start low, go slow, climb higher, and strike fire. If this does not occur, the speaker is often thanked for a "talk" as a means of communicating the judgment that preaching, per se, has not taken place. *Although few credible preachers and hardly any homileticians would make musical delivery a measure for preaching*, it remains a highly treasured aspect of the culture [emphasis mine]. *It spans the gamut from the "cornfield preacher," to the "Harvard Whooper," from the "No D" to the "Ph.D." and every D in between.*[21]

Those who have spent their lives in the Protestant African American church and those who professionally or casually study its preaching will affirm Turner's view of how the African American church feels about tonality in preaching. While agreeing with Turner that tonality in delivery should not be made a "measure" for preaching, and if so, only a minor measure, there is no disputing that this type of preaching has been the most widely celebrated in African American culture.

## WHAT WHOOPING OFFERS

Why is whooping so celebrated? For African Americans whooping symbolizes the freedom to be "who I culturally am" as a person in a society where we were once not free to express love of our culture and where such expression continues to take courage to display without reservation. It also symbolizes freedom to exhibit one's African American identity with the expectation that it will be affirmed. Whites who whoop may also feel some sense of affirmation in worship services where listeners affirm their use of this style.

Another function of whooping is that it signals that the preacher, continuing in the Spirit, has reached a pinnacle moment, and thus is able to communicate from her or his innermost depths without inhibition or restraint. The hearer gains the same liberty of expression by identification with the preacher and may show that identification by hand clapping or tuning lines of the sermon as the preacher proceeds. Sometimes listeners tune before the preacher gives a well-known line. Foot patting and call-and-response are other ways in which listeners may show their identification with the preacher.

Whooping is a soul's free expression in the very presence of God and a means of self-affirmation that has healed and blessed ever since the days when African Americans were physically enslaved in the Americas. Rev. J. Alfred Smith Sr., a past president of the Progressive Baptist Convention and a homiletics professor, says of whooping:

> In seminary, they taught us that the word *Selah* was never to be read when found in scripture. It meant pause or a moment of reflection or silence. I think that in preaching, when the whoop is released, that is the Selah moment. One has said all they can say in their conversational everyday voice, and then there is the Selah moment, a musical, spiritual, healing, volcanic eruption that blesses, not burns.[22]

Two other reasons for the powerful appeal of whooping are its symbolic function as a signal of identity and roots, and its function as psychological nourishment. Early on African Americans saw whooping as an adaptation of the tonal languages from which they had come. Tears flowed when they listened to tonal preaching, although it was not in their native languages. This tonal affirmation of their identity came to be interpreted as a distinct moment of encounter with the Spirit of God during the preaching moment, which gave whooping not only the appeal of nostalgia but also the soul-stirring role of being a bridge to communing with the all-powerful Creator of the universe in a way that was familiar. To powerless persons in chains, this was an invaluable affirmation of group and individual identity. How nourishing to the soul and psyche of slaves to have a tie to Africa binding them that slavery could not destroy.

Whooping also has the capacity to communicate on its own as an alternative language. The changes in volume and variations in tone and phrasing all say something beyond the bare significance of the words themselves. The vocal nuances, undertones, and overtones all communicate directly, not by hint or innuendo. Whooping provides a different wavelength on which to offer the saving Gospel—an additional, simultaneous channel on which to supplement communication.

## WHOOPING AND WOMEN

Whooping is not an art form that has yet become prevalent among women preachers. This is understandable, given that African American women only began to receive ordination in significant numbers in the late 1980s. Moreover, as late as 2009, the governing bodies of the two largest African American denominations (the Church of God in Christ and the National Baptist Convention, U.S.A., Inc.) did not officially recognize the ordination of women as preachers, although individual churches in these denominations have ordained women clergy. Additionally, women are rarely named as church pastors unless they are called to or placed in small or struggling churches. This means that women who are born whoopers will have fewer opportunities to hone this gift, and congregations will not have the opportunity to become comfortable with them. Thus, the notion of whooping being "manly" will continue unless women begin using the post-1970s styles. The preaching of post-1970s whooper Carolyn Knight has done much to establish a model to and of women whoopers.

## THE NEGATIVE SIDE OF WHOOPING

As is the case with anything that is powerful, whooping can be used for good or for harm. Sometimes it is used for less-than-admirable purposes. There are occasions when it is used to cover a sermon's weaknesses and the fact that it has been inadequately prepared. Tonal power is for such preachers a handy substitute for homiletical substance. Having little or nothing relevant and substantive to say from the Gospel, they lean on black culture's conditioned response to whooping to carry the load and satisfy the audience.

Whooping has historically come under great criticism from academic circles and by black preachers who are not whoopers.[23] Those within and without the culture have spared no pains in painting whooping as showmanship and a circuslike performance done to please the crowd. Some intimate and others outright declare that whooping shows blatant disrespect for the pulpit and the Gospel. They criticize preachers who are caught up by whooping as preachers who will whoop anything, from a welcome to visitors during a church service, to the benediction, to the alphabet. The critics are also quick to express their annoyance at parishioners who only endure the rest of the sermon while they wait for the whoop. They believe that some congregations will mindlessly respond to whooping, unaware or not caring whether there is any spiritual nourishment included in the sermon.

Another common criticism heaped upon whoopers is that they give credence to the Amos and Andy caricature of buffoonery that the dominant culture has stamped on the black pulpit.[24] Some have expressed great anger that black preachers do not understand that those who whoop, flail their arms, and make guttural sounds are doing a disservice to those who are working hard to keep the black pulpit respectable and a societal force with which to be reckoned.[25]

Perhaps the main criticism commonly leveled against whoopers is that they lack scholarly and theological depth. A common phrase used during these instances is "we need more theology and less whoopology." Even today, many years after slavery, large numbers of whoopers have only a limited amount of formal theological and homiletical training. Whoopers have also been accused of perpetuating the belief that they can preach their way out of any circumstance. Perhaps the darkest side of whooping is the use of this powerful gift as a way out when the preacher morally fails the church. There is still a prevalent notion that if preachers are outstanding whoopers, that despite committing almost any wrongdoing, they will still be allowed to pastor their church. There is evidence that this is slowly changing. As larger segments of the population are becoming educated, larger numbers of congregants are reading the Scriptures for themselves and attending seminaries and Bible colleges to gain greater biblical knowledge. They are demanding substantive sermons. It is also changing because the church is no longer the primary venue of activity in the African American community on Sundays.

## STILL A POWERFUL ART FORM

Although whooping has a negative side, it does not alter the fact that it is a powerful and highly celebrated art form in African American culture. Those who are aware of its power have not thrown out the baby with the murky bathwater. As for the matter of whooping operating as an enemy of the intelligent, whooping operates beneath the common structures of communication. However, this is not to suggest it is an enemy of intelligence, or just window dressing tacked on by African American preachers to make sermons more entertaining. Nor is whooping an art form performed by African American preachers whose limited education would make them more inclined to whoop than not. Even many educated preachers appreciate having whooping as part of their arsenal. Just as those who lean on whooping because they have prepared inadequately are to be criticized, famous whoopers such as John Jasper, C.L. Franklin, Caesar Clark, Charles Adams, and Carolyn Knight should be saluted and studied for their theological depth, homiletical imagination, mastery of metaphors, and ability to make the Word come alive, as well as their mastery of whooping.

Whooping stands as a powerful art form, partly because of its ability to reach those spaces where words alone cannot go, and partly because of its African roots. Tonal communication may well be one of the areas to which the African American and even other faith communities turn for future homiletical insights. Whooping should never be regarded as incidental or ornamental. With its deep appeal, it should always be used when one is engaged in serious communication of the sermon, not in entertainment. One also can imagine what whooping meant for the enslaved Africans. Whooping satisfied the cultural nostalgia of the enslaved, providing for healing, affirmation, and empowerment. This was and will always be whooping at its best, regardless of the form it takes.

## *Notes*

1. See Bruce Rosenberg, *Can These Bones Live? The Art of the American Folk Preacher* (Urbana: University of Illinois Press, 1970); Gerald L. Davis, *I Got the Word in Me and I Can Sing It, You Know* (Philadelphia: University of Pennsylvania Press, 1985).
2. See *Can These Bones Live?*, *I Got the Word*, and William Pipes, *Say Amen, Brother! Old-Time Negro Preaching: A Study in American Frustration* (Westport, CT: Negro University Press, 1951).
3. Jon Michael Spencer, *Sacred Symphony: The Chanted Sermon of the Black Preacher* (New York: Greenwood Press, 1987), 9.
4. Charles G. Adams, "The Sermon as Song," unpublished lecture given for the William Belden Nobel Lecture at Harvard University, Cambridge, MA, October 1995.
5. Joyce Marie Jackson, *Discourse in Ethnomusicology II: A Tribute to Alan P. Merriam* (Bloomington: Ethnomusicology Publication Group, Indiana University, 1981), 219.
6. Ibid., 220.
7. James A. Noel, "Call and Response: The Meaning of the Moan and Significance of the Shout in Black Worship," *Reformed Liturgy and Music* 28, no. 2 (Spring 1994), 72–76.
8. Cheryl Ann Cody, "There Was No Absalom on the Ball Plantations: Slave Naming Practices in South Carolina Low Country 1720–1865," *American Historical Review* (1992), 573, 580–81, 588.
9. W.E.B. DuBois, *The Negro Church*, Atlanta University Publications, no. 8 (Atlanta: Atlanta University Press, 1903), 5.

10. Henry H. Mitchell, "Preaching and the Preacher in African American Religion," in *The Encyclopedia of African American Religions*, ed. Larry G. Murphy, J. Gordon Melton and Gary L. Ward (New York: Garland Publishing, Inc. 1993), 607–8.
11. Francis Bebey, *African Music: A People's Art,* trans. Josephine Bennett (New York: Lawrence Hill, 1975), 22–23.
12. Harry S. Stout, *The New England Soul: Preaching and Religious Culture in Colonial New England* (New York: Oxford University Press, 1986), 190–92.
13. Ibid., 189.
14. Ibid., 223.
15. Henry H. Mitchell, *Black Church Beginnings: The Long-Hidden Realities of the First Years* (Grand Rapids, MI: Eerdmans, 2004), 39. See also "Preaching and the Preacher in African American Religion," 608.
16. *Black Church Beginnings*, 43.
17. *Sacred Symphony*, 13.
18. Craig Werner, *Higher Ground: Stevie Wonder, Aretha Franklin, Curtis Mayfield and the Rise and Fall of American Soul* (New York: Crown Publishers, 2004), 17.
19 C.L. Franklin, *Give Me This Mountain: Life History and Selected Sermons of C.L. Franklin*, ed. Jeff Todd Titon (Urbana: University of Illinois Press, 1989), foreword.
20. *Can These Bones Live?*, 31.
21. *Sacred Symphony*, xxi.
22. Interview with Reverend J. Alfred Smith Sr., July 2003, Oakland, California.
23. See Richard Allen, *The Life, Experience and Gospel Labors of the Rt. Rev. Richard Allen* (Philadelphia: Lee and Yeocum, 1888), 64; and Virgil Woods, et al. *The African American Jubilee Edition Bible* (New York: American Bible Society, 2000), 29.
24. *Amos and Andy* was a radio and television show that was produced by Freeman Gosden and Charles Correll in the 1940s. Gosden and Correll starred in the radio version. In 1951, when the show moved to television, all of the characters were black. The show featured blacks as shiftless, conniving, and unintelligent. It ran for two years on CBS and another approximately ten years in reruns.
25. For more on historic aspersions cast against whooping and similar styles of preaching see *A History of the African Methodist Episcopal Church: Being a Volume Supplemental to a History of the African Methodist Episcopal Church by Daniel Alexander Payne chronicling the principal events in the advancement of African Methodist Episcopal Church from 1856 to 1922* (Philadelphia: Book Concern of the A.M.E. Church, 1922; reprint, New York: Johnson Reprint Corp., 1968), vol. 2, 126–27; and Albert Raboteau, *Slave Religion: The Invisible Institution in the Antebellum South* (New York: Oxford University Press, 1978), 66–69.

# OTHER NOTABLE PREACHERS

| Name | Place of Birth | Date of Birth–Date of Death | Denomination or Faith Affiliation |
|---|---|---|---|
| Marie Ackey | *Unknown* | *(?–1938)* | *Pure Holiness Church of God* |

Marie Ackey is most noted for her missionary efforts and for establishing two churches in Liberia.

| | | | |
|---|---|---|---|
| Henry Adams | *Franklin County, Georgia* | *(1802–1872)* | *Baptist* |

Reverend Adams served as the first moderator of the General Association of Colored Baptists in Kentucky. He was instrumental in the founding of the State University in Lexington, now Simmons College of Kentucky.

| | | | |
|---|---|---|---|
| John H. Adams | *Columbia, South Carolina* | *(1929– )* | *AME* |

Reverend Adams was the eighty-seventh elected bishop of the African Methodist Episcopal Church. He was named one of the top fifteen black preachers in America by *Ebony* magazine in 1984. He retired in 2004.

| | | | |
|---|---|---|---|
| William Amiger | *Culpepper, Virginia* | *(1870–1930)* | *Baptist* |

Reverend Amiger was the president of State University in Louisville, Kentucky. He wrote several books, including *Deductive Hebrew Lessons*, *Studies in Anthropology*, and *The Hands of Jesus.*

| **Name** | **Place of Birth** | **Date of Birth–Date of Death** | **Denomination or Faith Affiliation** |
|---|---|---|---|

**Barbara Amos** *Portsmouth, Virginia* *(1955– )* *Mount Sinai Holy Church of America*

Bishop Amos founded Faith Deliverance Christian Center, Inc., in Norfolk, Virginia, in 1986. She is the overseer of the North Carolina region of the Mount Sinai Holy Church of America and a member of the executive council of Pentecostal and Charismatic Churches of North America.

**Ida Mae Anderson** *Gloster, Mississippi* *(1898–1984)* *COGIC*

Mother Anderson was an early pioneer of the Church of God in Christ (COGIC). She founded the Ladies Youth Council at Anderson Memorial COGIC in Detroit, was the wife of the late Bishop C.L. Anderson Sr., and the mother of Bishop C.L. Anderson Jr.

**Moses Anderson** *Selma, Alabama* *(1928– )* *Catholic*

In 1982, Reverend Anderson was chosen as Auxiliary Bishop of Detroit. He was one of the central figures in remaking the Catholic Church's image and bettering its treatment of blacks. Bishop Anderson retired in 2001.

**Anne P. Bailey** *Temple, Texas* *(1894–1975)* *COGIC*

Evangelist Bailey organized the COGIC Business and Professional League and the National Sunday School Representative unit. She also served as the Third National Supervisor of the Women's Department of the COGIC from 1964 to 1975.

**J.W. Bailey** *Wiley, Texas* *(ca. 1870–?)* *Southern Baptist*

Reverend J.W. Bailey was the superintendent of missions for the state of Texas and then served as an evangelist for the Southern Baptist Convention.

**Russell C. Barbour** *Nashville, Tennessee* *(1897–1944)* *National Baptist Convention, U.S.A., Inc.*

Reverend Russell Barbour was the pastor of First Baptist Church (Capitol Hill) and the editor of the *National Baptist Voice*. He was also a civil rights leader and a theology professor at the American Baptist Theological Seminary.

**William Bell** *Memphis, Tennessee* *(1887–1962)* *CME*

Bishop William Yancy Bell was elected the twentieth Colored Methodist Episcopal bishop at the 1938 General Conference and elected senior bishop in 1958. He also founded Williams Institutional CME Church in Harlem.

**Amos G. Beman** *Colchester, Connecticut* *(ca. 1812–1874)* *Congregationalist*

Reverend Beman (last name also variously spelled Beaman and Beamon) was the first licensed, full-time black preacher in Connecticut. He pastored Temple Street African

Congregational Church in New Haven, the first black Congregational church in the country, and later the Abyssinian Congregational Church in Portland, Maine. He was an abolitionist and also served as chaplain of the Connecticut Senate in 1872.

**JEHIEL C. BEMAN** *Chatham, Connecticut* *(1789–1858)* *AMEZ*

Reverend Jehiel C. Beman, father of Amos G. Beman, established the Middletown Anti-Slavery Society and other chapters of the American Anti-Slavery Society. He was the pastor of Cross Street AMEZ Church in Middletown and later led an AMEZ Church in Boston, now the Columbus Avenue AME Zion Church.

**EMILY BRAM BIBBY** *Dallas, Texas* *(1916–2008)* *COGIC*

Mother Bibby was an evangelist, one of the leading preachers in the COGIC, and an elder among male and female preachers of the denomination. In addition to being a dynamic preacher, she was also a stirring singer. She concluded her career in ministry at Shiloh COGIC in Kansas City.

**SHELTON BISHOP** *New York, New York* *(1889–1962)* *Episcopal Church*

Reverend Shelton Bishop was the first black to serve on a diocesan standing committee in U.S. Episcopal history. Bishop was also named one of the ten best black preachers in America by *Ebony* magazine in 1954.

**CHARLES E. BLAKE** *Little Rock, Arkansas* *(1940– )* *COGIC*

Bishop Blake was appointed bishop of the First Jurisdiction of Southern California of the COGIC in 1985. He was listed in *Ebony* magazine in 1984 as one of America's fifteen greatest black preachers. He is the senior pastor of the ten-thousand-member West Angeles Church of God in Christ in Los Angeles, and in 2007 was elected presiding bishop of the COGIC.

**CHARLES BODDIE** *New Rochelle, New York* *(1911–1997)* *Baptist*

Reverend Boddie was the president of the American Baptist College and Seminary in Nashville. He also helped establish the United Negro College Fund and wrote *A Giant in the Earth,* which concerned his father Jacob, and *God's Bad Boys*, in 1972.

**JACOB B. BODDIE** *Rocky Mount, North Carolina* *(1872–1936)* *Baptist*

Reverend Boddie pastored Bethesda Baptist Church in New Rochelle, New York, for more than thirty years. His biography, *A Giant in the Earth*, was written by his son.

**JAMES BOWEN JR.** *Baltimore, Maryland* *(1889–1962)* *Methodist Episcopal Church*

Reverend Bowen was the ninth African American bishop of the Methodist Episcopal Church. He edited the *Central Christian Advocate* from 1944–1948.

| **Name** | **Place of Birth** | **Date of Birth–Date of Death** | **Denomination or Faith Affiliation** |
|---|---|---|---|
| **John Bowen Sr.** | *New Orleans, Louisiana* | *(1855–1933)* | *Methodist Episcopal Church* |

John Bowen was the first African American to serve as a full-time professor at Gammon Theological Seminary. He pastored Centennial Methodist Episcopal church in Baltimore.

| | | | |
|---|---|---|---|
| **Richard Boyd** | *Noxubee County, Mississippi* | *(1846–1922)* | *National Baptist Convention, U.S.A., Inc.* |

Reverend Boyd is one of the most famous names in black Baptist history: He founded the National Baptist Publishing Board, organized the first African American Baptist Association in Texas and wrote *What Baptists Believe and Practice* (1902), and played a major role in the publication of the 1903 National Baptist hymnal. He eventually split from the National Baptist Convention, U.S.A., Inc., over who actually owned the National Baptist Publishing Board.

| | | | |
|---|---|---|---|
| **Edward M. Brawley** | *Charleston, South Carolina* | *(1851–1923)* | *American National Baptist Convention* |

Reverend Brawley was instrumental in the publication of *The Negro Baptist Pulpit* (1890) and a key figure in the establishment of the American National Baptist Convention (he also served as president). Brawley also served as president of Selma University, Alabama Normal and Theological School, and Morris College in South Carolina.

| | | | |
|---|---|---|---|
| **Benjamin H. Broadie** | *Not known* | *(ca. 1902–1965)* | *Nondenominational* |

Elder Broadie, known as "The World's Wonder Radio Preacher," was named by *Ebony* as a top radio preacher in July 1949. His radio program was broadcast nationally from the Gospel Tabernacle Church in Newark, New Jersey.

| | | | |
|---|---|---|---|
| **Audrey Bronson** | *Deland, Florida* | *(1930– )* | *Nondenominational* |

Reverend Bronson is the senior bishop of the International Fellowship of Churches. She also served as the dean of the Urban Education Institute of Black Clergy in Philadelphia and is the pastor of the Sanctuary Church of the Open Door in Philadelphia.

| | | | |
|---|---|---|---|
| **John M. Brown** | *Odessa, Delaware* | *(1817–1893)* | *AME* |

Bishop Brown was elected the eleventh bishop at the 1868 General AME Conference. As a result of his dedication and hard work, at least twenty-nine churches have been named in his honor.

| | | | |
|---|---|---|---|
| **Morris Brown** | *Charleston, South Carolina* | *(1770–1849)* | *AME* |

Morris Brown was elected the second bishop of the AME Church in 1825. Morris Brown College in Atlanta, Georgia, is named in his honor, as are several churches.

**William C. Brown** *Chowan County, North Carolina* *(1877–1964)* *AMEZ*

Reverend Brown pastored churches in Virginia, North Carolina, and Connecticut before being called to First Church (Fleet Street) in Brooklyn, New York. He led the urban league in New York and was consecrated an AMEZ Bishop in 1936.

**Andrew Bryan** *Goose Creek, South Carolina* *(1737–1812)* *Baptist*

Reverend Bryan was a pioneer Baptist preacher and founder of the Colored Baptist Church in Georgia. After growing that church, he helped start two more Georgia churches: the Second Colored Baptist Church (1799), which he turned over to another preacher; he did the same for the Ogeechee Colored Baptist Church.

**John R. Bryant** *Baltimore, Maryland* *(1943– )* *AME*

Bishop Bryant was elected the 106th bishop of the AME Church at the 1988 AME General Conference.

**Peter J. Bryant** *Sylvania, Georgia* *(1870–1929)* *Baptist*

Reverend Bryant organized the Atlanta Benevolent and Protective Association, a small insurance society, which became Atlanta Life Insurance Company. Bryant also pastored the renowned Wheat Street Baptist Church in Atlanta.

**Calvin O. Butts III** *Bridgeport, Connecticut* *(1949– )* *American Baptist*

Calvin O. Butts III became the pastor of Abyssinian Baptist Church in New York in 1989. In 1999 he became the President of the State University of New York College at Old Westbury.

**Josiah S. Caldwell** *Charlotte, North Carolina* *(1862–1935)* *AME*

Josiah Samuel Caldwell was elected the thirtieth bishop at the 1904 AME General Conference.

**Jabez P. Campbell** *Slaughter Neck, Delaware* *(1815–1891)* *AME*

In 1864, Jabez Pitt Campbell was elected the eighth bishop of the AME Church. Campbell College in Jackson, Mississippi, and numerous churches bear his name.

**Matthew Campbell** *Madison County, Kentucky* *(1823–1896)* *Colored Baptist*

Reverend Matthew, also referred to as Madison Campbell, pastored in Kentucky. He believed in developing churches for others to lead and so organized a church at New Liberty in 1869, and the Mount Pleasant Church in 1873, as well as churches in Otter Creek and Mount Nebo. He was the first pastor of the First Baptist Church in Richmond, baptizing thousands and officiating at the wedding of many more. See *Autobiography of Eld. Madison Campbell: Pastor of the United Colored Baptist Church, Richmond, Kentucky*, for more information about Campbell.

| NAME | PLACE OF BIRTH | DATE OF BIRTH–DATE OF DEATH | DENOMINATION OR FAITH AFFILIATION |
|---|---|---|---|
| MACK KING CARTER | *Ocala, Florida* | *(1947– )* | *National Baptist Convention, U.S.A., Inc.* |

Reverend Carter is among the leading revivalists of the twentieth and twenty-first centuries. He began pastoring the New Mount Olive Baptist Church in Fort Lauderdale Florida in 1981. By 2005, he had written *Catechism for Baptists*; *Interpreting the Will of God: Principles for Unlocking the Mystery*; and *A Quest for Freedom: An African American Odyssey.*

| | | | |
|---|---|---|---|
| ARLENE H. CHURN | *Philadelphia, Pennsylvania* | *(1937– )* | *National Baptist Convention, U.S.A., Inc.* |

Beginning as a child preacher, Reverend Churn has preached throughout America and pastored for seventeen years in Philadelphia. She was inducted into the Board of Distinguished Preachers at Morehouse University and named one of America's foremost female ministers by *Ebony* magazine in 1997.

| | | | |
|---|---|---|---|
| ELMER ELIJAH CLEVELAND | *Oklahoma* | *(1901–ca. 1992)* | *COGIC* |

Bishop E.E. Cleveland was a bishop in the Church of God in Christ, a noted revivalist, and pastor of Ephesians Church of God in Christ in Berkeley, California, until 1990.

| | | | |
|---|---|---|---|
| JOSEPH JACKSON CLINTON | *Philadelphia, Pennsylvania* | *(1823–1881)* | *AMEZ* |

Elected in 1856 at the age of thirty-two, Joseph Clinton was the youngest elected AMEZ bishop up to that time. As the first AMEZ bishop of the South, Clinton oversaw tremendous expansion for the denomination, including the establishment of thirteen annual conferences.

| | | | |
|---|---|---|---|
| HELENA B. COBB | *Monroe County, Georgia* | *(1870–1915)* | *CME* |

Helena Brown Cobb was president of the Conference Mission Society and Inter-Conference Missionary Movement. She also founded the Helena B. Cobb Industrial Institute for Girls, the only CME school for girls.

| | | | |
|---|---|---|---|
| CLARENCE H. COBBS | *Memphis, Tennessee* | *(1907–1979)* | *Metropolitan Spiritual Churches of Christ* |

Reverend Cobbs, affectionately known as "Preacher," was president of the Metropolitan Spiritual Churches of Christ from 1945 until his death. He pastored the First Church of Deliverance in Chicago from age sixteen until his death. His Sunday evening radio program, which lasted more than thirty years, was heard by as many as a million listeners per day.

**Daniel Coker** *Baltimore County, Delaware* *(ca. 1780–ca. 1846)* *AME*

Reverend Coker was one of the founders of the AME church, and he founded the West African Methodist Church. Although he resigned before he was consecrated, Coker was elected the first bishop of the AME church on April 9, 1816.

**Mattie E. Coleman** *Gallatin, Tennessee* *(1870–1942)* *CME*

Mattie Elizabeth Coleman was the first president of the Woman's Missionary Council of the CMEs. Her position and ability as a speaker enabled her to become the most visible and influential woman in the CME church in the early 1900s. A church in Knoxville is named in her honor.

**Suzan D. Johnson Cook** *New York, New York* *(1957– )* *American Baptist*

Suzan D. Johnson Cook is the pastor of Bronx Christian Fellowship in Bronx, New York, and formerly pastored Mariners' Temple Baptist Church in New York. She served as the first female president of the Hampton University Ministers' Conference, is the author of more than seven books, and has worked in various capacities with several presidential administrations.

**Philip R. Cousin** *Pittsburgh, Pennsylvania* *(1933– )* *AME*

Philip Robert Cousin was elected the ninety-sixth AME bishop in 1976. He is also a former president of the National Council of Churches.

**Emma Crouch** *Dangerfield, Texas* *(1911–1997)* *COGIC*

Mother Crouch founded the Christian Women's Council of the COGIC and served it in many capacities, including International Supervisor, Jurisdictional Sunshine Band President, National Usher Board President, and member of the National Board of Trustees.

**W. Leo Daniels** *Center, Texas* *(1938–1977)* *National Baptist Convention, U.S.A., Inc.*

Reverend Daniels was the pastor of Greater Jerusalem Missionary Baptist Church in Houston and a popular revivalist. He was also a successful recording artist with such sermons as "Build Your Own Fire," "What in Hell Do You Want," "Put Down that Whiskey Bottle," "Common-Law Marriage," and "Let's Make A Deal." He produced more than twenty recordings through multiple record labels, including Jewel Records and Peacock Records.

**Daniel W. Davis** *Richmond, Virginia* *(1862–1913)* *Baptist*

Reverend Davis was a civic leader, pastor, and a widely published poet. His poems include "Weh Down Souf" and "Idle Moments."

| NAME | PLACE OF BIRTH | DATE OF BIRTH–DATE OF DEATH | DENOMINATION OR FAITH AFFILIATION |
|---|---|---|---|
| WILLIAM NELSON DEBERRY | *Nashville, Tennessee* | *(1870–1948)* | *Congregationalist* |

DeBerry was an 1899 graduate of Oberlin Seminary and pastored the St. John Congregational Church in Springfield, Massachusetts. He was a trustee of Fisk University. He also served as an assistant moderator of the National Council of Congregational Churches in America.

| | | | |
|---|---|---|---|
| WILLIAM DERRICK | *Antigua, West Indies* | *(1843–1913)* | *AME* |

William Benjamin Derrick was elected bishop at the 1896 AME General Conference. He is also one of the founders of Campbell College and the founder of the Lillian Derrick Institute, now Wilberforce Institute.

| | | | |
|---|---|---|---|
| ERNESTINE CLEVELAND REEMS DICKERSON | *Okmulgee, Oklahoma* | *(1929– )* | *Pentecostal* |

Reverend Dickerson was the longtime pastor and founder of the Center of Hope Community Church in Oakland, California. She has been honored for civic and social work, including leading in the building of a senior citizens' facility and a charter school for children grades K–8. She was consecrated as a bishop in the Monument International Church Assemblies in 2000.

| | | | |
|---|---|---|---|
| ALFRED G. DUNSTON JR. | *Coinjock, North Carolina* | *(1915– )* | *AMEZ* |

Alfred Gilbert Dunston Jr. was elected bishop at the 1963 AMEZ General Conference. He is the author of *Black Man in the Old Testament and Its World*. A chaplain in World War II, he was named one of America's top fifteen black preachers in 1984 by *Ebony* magazine. He retired in 1992.

| | | | |
|---|---|---|---|
| GEORGE W. DUPEE | *Gallatin County, Kentucky* | *(1826–1897)* | *Baptist* |

George Washington Dupee pastored in Paducah and Pleasant Green, Kentucky. He was the second moderator of the General Association of Colored Baptists of Kentucky and the founding editor of the *Baptist Herald*. He was known for carrying a hickory stick into the pulpit.

| | | | |
|---|---|---|---|
| JOHN MALCUS ELLISON | *Northumberland County, Virginia* | *(1889–1979)* | *Baptist* |

Reverend Ellison was the first African American president of Virginia Union University, Richmond, VA. He wrote *They Who Preach*, *The Art of Friendship*, *Tensions and Destiny*, and *They Stand through the Crisis*.

| | | | |
|---|---|---|---|
| ERNEST ESTELL | *Decherd, Tennessee* | *(1894–1964)* | *National Baptist Convention, U.S.A., Inc.* |

Reverend Estell served as vice president of the National Baptist Sunday School and

Training Union Congress. He led the development of a three-million dollar complex, Estell Village, and is featured in the book *God's Bad Boys*.

HENRY EVANS *Stokes County, Virginia* *(1740–1810)* *AMEZ*

Reverend Evans was a pioneer Methodist Episcopal Church preacher. He established Evans Metropolitan AME Zion Church, the first Methodist church in Fayetteville, North Carolina.

J.B. FIELDS *Prairieville, Missouri* *(1850–ca. 1916)* *Baptist*

Reverend Julius Fields pastored Zion Baptist Church in Denver as well as other churches. He was a popular lecturer who traveled widely and publicly opposed the rise of agnosticism as promulgated by other leading preachers of his time.

FLOYD FLAKE *Houston, Texas* *(1945– )* *AME*

Reverend Flake is the Senior Pastor of Greater Allen AME Cathedral. The church is one of the largest nonprofit corporations in the country and the second largest African-American employer in New York City as of 2005. He also served as a U.S. Representative from 1986–1997.

LOUIS FORD SR. *Clarksdale, Mississippi* *(1914–1995)* *COGIC*

Louis Henry Ford Sr. was a presiding bishop of the COGIC (1990–1995). A freeway in Chicago bears his name. He pastored in Chicago and was known for numerous social ministries.

DAVID GEORGE *Essex County, Virginia* *(1742–1810)* *Baptist*

Reverend George is considered to be the pastor of the first black Baptist church in America, probably the first black church of any denomination. He also established the first African Baptist Church in Freetown, Sierra Leone.

JONATHAN GIBBS *Philadelphia, Pennsylvania* *(ca. 1821–1874)* *AME and Presbyterian*

Reverend Gibbs served as Florida's first African American cabinet member when he was appointed secretary of state in 1868. He also served as its first black superintendent of Public Instruction. Several high schools, a junior college, and a hall on the campus of Florida Agriculture and Mechanical University bear his name.

JOHN GLOUCESTER *eastern Tennessee* *(1776–1822)* *Presbyterian*

Reverend Gloucester, pastor and educator, was the founder of the First African Presbyterian Church in Philadelphia. Gloucester was also a noted abolitionist who worked for the uplift of blacks.

MORRIS E. GOLDER *Indianapolis, Indiana* *(1913–2000)* *Pentecostal Assemblies of the World*

Bishop Golder pastored an integrated church in St. Louis in the 1930s. In 1953 he founded Grace Apostolic Church. He wrote *The Principles of Our Doctrine*, *Confes-*

| **Name** | **Place of Birth** | **Date of Birth–Date of Death** | **Denomination or Faith Affiliation** |
|---|---|---|---|

*sions of Sins,* and *The History of the Pentecostal Assemblies of the World and the Bishops*. In 1972 he was elevated to the board of bishops of the Pentecostal Assemblies of the World.

David A. Graham *Princeton, Indiana* *(1861–1936)* *AME*
Reverend Graham pastored Bethel Church in Chicago, and First AME Church in Seattle from 1916 to 1920. He was also one of the earliest AME ministers to serve as a missionary in Liberia. His daughter, Shirley, married W.E.B. DuBois in 1951.

Leonard A. Grimes *Leesburg, Virginia* *(1815–1873)* *American Baptist*
Reverend Grimes served as president of the American Baptist Missionary Convention and of the Consolidated Baptist Convention. He was also a prominent member of the Underground Railroad.

Cynthia L. Hale *Roanoke, Virginia* *(1952– )* *Disciples of Christ*
Cynthia L. Hale is the founding pastor of Ray of Hope Christian Church (Disciples of Christ) in Decatur, Georgia. She has served in this capacity since 1986, and the church now has more than five thousand members. She is one of the leading voices in the Protestant Church and the only female officer of the historic Hampton University Ministers' Conference, and since 2005 has held a national conference specifically to equip African American women in ministry.

Shelvin Hall *Yoakum, Texas* *(1916–2007)* *National Baptist Convention, U.S.A., Inc.*
Reverend Hall was the long time pastor of Friendship Baptist Church in Chicago and president of The One Church/One Child national adoption program for several years. He had a lengthy tenure as the president of the Baptist General State Convention of Illinois.

Gordon Blaine Hancock *Ninety Six, South Carolina* *(1884–1970)* *Baptist*
Reverend Hancock attended Benedict College and received his master's degree from Harvard in 1921. He was the pastor of Moore Street Baptist Church in Richmond, Virginia, from 1925 to 1963 and professor of economics and sociology at Virginia Union University. He wrote a newspaper column, *Between the Lines*, which was syndicated in more than one hundred black newspapers from 1928 to 1965. He organized the first school of race relations, the Torrance School, in 1931.

William R. Haney *Cataula, Georgia* *(1906–1985)* *National Baptist Convention, U.S.A., Inc.*
Reverend Haney pastored Dexter Avenue Baptist Church in Detroit and served as the president of the Wolverine State Missionary Baptist Convention.

**EUGENE HATCHER** *Eufala, Alabama* *(1902–1969)* *AME*

Eugene Clifford Hatcher was elected seventy-third AME bishop in 1952. He also served on the General Board of the National Council of Churches.

**FREDERICK DOUGLASS HAYNES** *Barbour County, West Virginia* *(1901–1971)* *National Baptist Convention, U.S.A., Inc.*

Reverend Haynes pastored Third Baptist Church of San Francisco from 1932 to 1971, leading the church in growth from fifty members to more than twenty-five hundred by the time of his death. He was succeeded by his son, Frederick D. Haynes II. His grandson, Frederick D. Haynes III, is one of the leading pastors and revivalists of the late twentieth and early twenty-first centuries.

**J. RAYMOND HENDERSON** *Charlottesville, Virginia* *(1898–ca. 1967)* *National Baptist Convention, U.S.A., Inc., and the Progressive National Baptist Convention*

Reverend Henderson pastored Wheat Street Baptist Church in Atlanta from 1930 to 1937, then Betheseda Baptist Church of New Rochelle, New York, and finally Second Baptist Church of Los Angeles from 1941 to 1963. A friend to Dr. Martin Luther King Jr., best man in the wedding of Vernon Johns, Henderson was an ardent civil rights activist. He also presided at the formation meeting for the Progressive National Baptist Convention.

**RICHARD D. HENTON** *Chicago, Illinois* *(1933– )* *Monument Church Association*

Apostle Henton is the founder of Monument of Faith Evangelistic Church and Logos Bible College. He is also the leader of the Monument Church Association.

**H. BEECHER HICKS JR.** *Baton Rouge, Louisiana* *(1943– )* *Progressive Baptist Convention & American Baptist Churches U.S.A., Inc.*

H. Beecher Hicks Jr. has served as the pastor of the historic Metropolitan Baptist Church in Washington, DC, since 1977. He is the author of six books, most notably *Preaching Through a Storm*. He has been one of the leading preachers and pastors in America for more than thirty years, and in 1993 *Ebony* magazine named him one of the "fifteen greatest African American preachers."

**JAMES HOLMES** *King and Queen County, Virginia* *(1826–1900)* *Baptist*

Reverend Holmes was the first black pastor of the First African Baptist Church in Richmond, where he pastored for thirty-four years. He is said to have married fourteen hundred couples and baptized fifty-eight hundred persons.

**ZAN HOLMES** *San Angelo, Texas* *(1935– )* *UMC*

Reverend Holmes pastored St. Luke Community UMC in Dallas for twenty-eight years. He retired in 2002 after increasing the membership of the church from fifty to

| **Name** | **Place of Birth** | **Date of Birth–Date of Death** | **Denomination or Faith Affiliation** |
|---|---|---|---|

five thousand. He served two terms in the Texas state legislature and was an associate professor of preaching at Perkins Seminary for twenty-four years. He wrote *Encountering Jesus*, as well as other books.

THOMAS HOYT JR. *Fayetteville, Alabama* *(1941– )* *CME*
Bishop Hoyt is the forty-eighth presiding bishop of the CME Church. He is also a former president of the National Council of Churches and has served as a professor at the Interdenominational Center of Howard Divinity School and Hartford Seminary. He earned a doctorate in religion from Duke University in 1975 and delivered the Yale Lyman Beecher Lecture in 1993. Bishop Hoyt has written several books.

WILLIAM IMES *Memphis, Tennessee* *(1889–1986)* *Presbyterian*
Reverend Imes helped found and was president of Harlem's Own Cooperative, Inc. He published several books, including *Integrity: Meditations of the Book of Job*; *The Way of Worship in Everyday life: A Course of Studies in Devotion*; and *The Black Pastor: Essays and Sermons.*

JESSICA INGRAM *College Station, Arkansas* *(1947– )* *AME*
Jessica Ingram is Supervisor of Women for the AME Tenth Episcopal District. She was named one of the fifteen top African American female preachers by *Ebony* magazine in 1997. She received her doctor of ministry from United Theological Seminary, Dayton, Ohio, and is the author of *Still on the Journey.*

UNCLE JACK *Unknown, Africa* *(ca. 1746–1843)* *Baptist*
Uncle Jack was deemed the best preacher, black or white, by the judges in Beardstown County, Virginia. The book *The African Preacher: An Authentic Narrative*, written by William Spotswood white in 1849 and available online through the University of Carolina Chapel Hill's Documenting the American South, provides his life story.

PETER JOHNSON *Augusta, Georgia* *(1802–1881)* *Baptist*
Reverend Johnson is one of the earliest African American Baptists in Georgia and South Carolina. He founded the Central Baptist Church in Augusta, and for several decades served Storm Branch and Spirit Creek Baptist churches near Augusta.

CHARLES O. JONES *Pike County, Georgia* *(1830–?)* *Baptist*
An Atlanta pastor, Reverend Jones helped organize the New Hope Baptist Association in Rome, Georgia, and served several congregations in Polk County, including Pleasant Grove Baptist Church.

HARVEY JONES *near Pittsburgh, Pennsylvania* *(1821–1901)* *Congregationalist*
Reverend Jones helped organize First Church of Christ in Wabaunsee, Pennsylvania. He was a student at Oberlin College, graduating in 1852. In 1864 he became the pas-

tor of the Congregational Church in Geneva, Pennsylvania. He also served as Superintendent of Home Missions for the state of Kansas.

JOSEPH ENDOM JONES *Lynchburg, Virginia* *(1850–1923)* *Baptist*

Professor Jones held the chair of homiletics and Greek at the Richmond Theological Seminary. He served as corresponding secretary of the Baptist Foreign Mission Convention, editor of the *Baptist Companion* of Virginia, and was president of the Virginia Baptist Sunday School Convention for six years.

NOEL JONES *Spanish Town, Jamaica* *(1948– )* *Nondenominational*

Reverend Jones is the founder of Noel Jones Ministries and pastors City of Refuge Church in Gardena, California. He is also a leading revivalist and has written several books.

OZRO T. JONES SR. *Fort Smith, Arkansas* *(1891–1972)* *COGIC*

Ozro Thurston Jones Sr. was the second presiding bishop of the COGIC. He also founded the International Youth Congress of the COGIC.

SINGLETON T. JONES *Wrightsville, Pennsylvania* *(1825–1891)* *AMEZ*

Singleton Thomas Jones was elected the sixteenth bishop of the AMEZ Church in 1868. He was also one of the founders and editors of *Zion's Standard and Weekly Review.*

THOMAS KILGORE JR. *Woodruff, South Carolina* *(1913–1998)* *American Baptist and Progressive Baptist Convention*

Reverend Kilgore was elected the first black president of the American Baptist Churches in the United States and was president of the Progressive Baptist Convention. *Ebony* magazine named him one of the top fifteen black preachers in America in 1984. He held several long-term pastorates, including Second Baptist Church of Los Angeles, and was also a civil rights activist.

DEARINE EDWIN KING *LaGrange, Kentucky* *(1910–1993)* *National Baptist Convention, U.S.A., Inc., and Progressive Baptist*

D.E. King pastored Monumental Baptist Church in Chicago for more than thirty years. He is listed in Philpot's *Best Black Sermon*, and wrote *Preaching to Preachers.*

JOHN KINNEY *Wheeling, West Virginia* *(1947– )* *National Baptist Convention, U.S.A., Inc.*

John Kinney is a well-respected and admired systematic theologian and preacher, and the longtime dean of the Samuel DeWitt Proctor School of Theology at Virginia

| **Name** | **Place of Birth** | **Date of Birth–Date of Death** | **Denomination or Faith Affiliation** |
|---|---|---|---|

Union University in Richmond, Virginia. He also serves as the pastor of Ebenezer Baptist Church in Beaverdam, Virginia.

| **Laura Adorkor Kofey** | *Ghana* | *(1893–1928)* | *African Universal Church* |
|---|---|---|---|

Reverend Kofey (also spelled Kofi and Koffey) arrived in America in the early 1920s from Ghana. She was part of the Garvey movement and one of its most forceful preachers. In 1927 Garvey denounced her. She formed a splinter group of Garvey's UNIA Movement and began holding revival services. Throngs went to the Masonic Temple in Jacksonville, Florida, to hear her. She founded the African Universal Church and Commercial League. Its aim was to repatriate blacks back to West Africa. She taught her followers Bantu, an African language, along with the Bible. She was assassinated in March 1928 while in the pulpit.

| **Samuel "Billy" Kyles** | *Shelby, Mississippi* | *(1934– )* | *Progressive Baptist Convention* |
|---|---|---|---|

A long time leader in the civil rights movement, Kyles was one of only two men who were present with Dr. Martin Luther King before he was assassinated in Memphis. Kyles has been the pastor of Monumental Baptist Church in Memphis, Tennessee since 1959.

| **Marie Laveau** | *Santo Domingo* | *(1794–1881)* | *Voodoo/Catholic* |
|---|---|---|---|

Marie Laveau was the queen of voodoo in New Orleans. She was famous for performing spells and incantations for those who came to see her. Her daughter, whose name was also Marie, followed in her mother's footsteps. For additional information on the life of Laveau see *Voodoo in New Orleans*, by Robert Tallant, and *Mysterious Marie Laveau, Voodoo Queen*, by Raymond J. Martinez.

| **Robert Clarence Lawson** | *New Iberia, Louisiana* | *(1883–1961)* | *Church of Our Lord Jesus Christ of the Apostolic Faith* |
|---|---|---|---|

Robert Lawson founded the Church of Our Lord Jesus Christ of the Apostolic Faith, opening the mother church of this denomination in New York. He also had a widely heard radio broadcast. At the time of Lawson's death, the denomination claimed seventy thousand members in the United States, Africa, the Dominican Republic, the West Indies, and London.

| **William A. Lawson** | *St. Louis, Missouri* | *(1928– )* | *National Baptist Convention, U.S.A., Inc.* |
|---|---|---|---|

William Lawson was the founding pastor of Wheeler Avenue Baptist Church in Houston. Lawson grew the church from a small number of families to more than five thousand by his retirement in 2004. Lawson is also a staunch civil rights activist.

**George W. Lee** *Edwards, Mississippi* *(1904–1955)* *National Baptist Convention, U.S.A., Inc.*

Reverend Lee pastored in Belzoni, Mississippi, and was the vice president of the Regional Council of Negro Leadership. A leader in the NAACP, he was assassinated in 1955.

**Reuben Lee** *Georgetown, Kentucky* *(1825–1876)* *Baptist*

Reverend Lee was the pastor of First Baptist Church of Georgetown. For fourteen years he pastored both Second Baptist Church of Versailles, Kentucky, and Georgetown Baptist Church.

**Jermain Wesley Loguen** *Davidson County, Tennessee* *(ca. 1813–1872)* *AMEZ*

Reverend Loguen was the founder of numerous AMEZ churches in central New York and, the Loguen Temple in Knoxville, Tennessee. He was the thirteenth bishop of the AMEZ Church.

**Joseph Lowery** *Huntsville, Alabama* *(1921– )* *United Methodist*

Considered one of the deans of the civil rights movement, Lowery, along with Dr. Martin Luther King Jr., founded the Southern Christian Leadership Conference, serving as its president from 1977 to 1998. He was a long-term pastor, and *Ebony* magazine twice named him one of the fifteen greatest black preachers. He delivered the benediction for the inauguration of President Barack Obama.

**James D. Lynch** *Baltimore, Maryland* *(1839–1872)* *Presbyterian and AME*

Reverend Lynch was the first black Mississippian elected to a statewide office. He was also a presiding elder in the Mississippi Mission Conference.

**Anderson Major Martin** *Mississippi* *(1903–1960)* *National Baptist Convention, U.S.A., Inc.*

Reverend Martin was the longtime pastor of New Light Baptist Church in Detroit, Michigan.

**Elliot Mason** *Toledo, Ohio* *(1922– )* *American Baptist National Baptist Convention, U.S.A., Inc.*

Reverend Mason pastored Trinity Baptist Church in Los Angeles from 1962 to 1985. He is best known for his mystic-like approach to preaching and lecturing.

**Lena Doolin Mason** *Quincy, Illinois* *(1864–ca. 1926)* *AME*

Reverend Mason, called to preach at age twelve, entered ministry at age twenty-three and spent her first three years preaching to mainly white congregations before joining the AME Church. She was also affiliated with the CME Church for part of her time

| **Name** | **Place of Birth** | **Date of Birth–Date of Death** | **Denomination or Faith Affiliation** |
|---|---|---|---|

in ministry. She preached in numerous locations. She wrote the poem "A Negro In It" as well as at least one song.

| **Madison Charles Butler Mason** | *Houma, Louisiana* | *1859–1915)* | *Methodist Episcopal* |
|---|---|---|---|

Reverend Mason was the assistant secretary of the Freedmen's Aid and Southern Education Society and editor of *The Christian Educator*. He was a graduate of Gammon Seminary and considered one of the leading orators of his day.

| **Ford Washington McGee** | *Winchester, Tennessee* | *(1890–1971)* | *COGIC* |
|---|---|---|---|

McGee recorded at least forty-six sermons and or songs on LP between 1927 and 1930. His sermon "With His Stripes We Are Healed" is purported to have sold more than eighty thousand copies. His combination singing and preaching contributed to his ability to sell records. McGee also sang with the Jubilee Singers quartet. He was a revivalist and made the COGIC better known in Kansas and Iowa through tent revivals. He pastored in Oklahoma City and finally in Chicago.

| **Theodore D. Miller** | *New York, New York* | *(1835–1897)* | *Baptist* |
|---|---|---|---|

Reverend Theodore Doughty Miller was the pastor of First African Baptist Church in Philadelphia, corresponding secretary of the American Baptist Missionary convention, and recording secretary of the New England Baptist Missionary convention. A sketch of his life can be found in the *Biographical Sketches of Our Pulpit,* by E.R. Carter, and *Men of Mark,* by William J. Simmons.

| **Emerson Moore** | *New York, New York* | *(1938–1995)* | *Catholic* |
|---|---|---|---|

Bishop Emerson John Moore was appointed Auxiliary Bishop of New York and Titular Bishop of Curubis in 1982. He served as a priest for thirty-one years and as a bishop for thirteen. He founded the Office for Black Ministry for the Archdiocese of New York. In 1990, he was the only bishop in the country to sign a full-page newspaper advertisement calling for major changes in the Catholic Church. Those changes included ordaining women, pursuing the idea of married priests, and rethinking the church's teaching on sexuality.

| **John J. Moore** | *Martinsburg, Virginia* | *(ca. 1804–1893)* | *AMEZ* |
|---|---|---|---|

John Jamison Moore was elected AMEZ bishop in 1868. He organized black schools in California and the Pacific Coast. He was considered one of the greatest preachers in the AMEZ denomination. He wrote *The History of the AMEZ Church in America* in 1884.

**CHARLES SATCHELL MORRIS SR.** *Louisville, Kentucky* *(1865–ca. 1931)* *National Baptist*

Reverend Morris was a missionary in Liberia and South Africa. He pastored Abyssinian Baptist Church in New York City from 1902 to 1908 and Bank Street Baptist Church in Norfolk, Virginia from 1911 to 1916. He received national notoriety for his 1899 Boston speech concerning the 1898 Wilmington Massacre, in which several blacks were killed by rioting whites.

**WILLLIAM H. MOSES** *Charlotte County, Virginia* *(1872–?)* *National Baptist Convention, U.S.A., Inc.*

Reverend Moses was the corresponding secretary of the Virginia Baptist State Convention and editor of the *Baptist Statesman*. He wrote *Life of Christ*. He was a candidate for the presidency of the National Baptist Convention and an ardent supporter of the Garvey Movement.

**LOUIS NARCISSE** *New Orleans, Louisiana* *(1921–1989)* *Spiritual Church of the West*

Louis Narcisse, also known as "His Grace, the King of the Spiritual Church of the West Coast" was the founder of the Mount Zion Spiritual Temple. He also hosted the radio program *Moments of Meditation*.

**JAMES O. PATTERSON SR.** *Derma, Michigan* *(1912–1989)* *COGIC*

James Oglethorpe Patterson Sr. was the third presiding bishop of the COGIC. In 1984 he was named one of the one hundred most influential black Americans by *Ebony* magazine.

**THOMAS PAUL SR.** *Exeter, New Hampshire* *(1773–1831)* *Baptist*

Reverend Paul helped found Abyssinian Baptist Church in New York City. Paul also took over as the leader of the African Masonic Lodge after its founder, Prince Hall, died.

**CHRISTOPHER PAYNE** *Monroe County, Virginia* *(1848–1925)* *American Baptist*

Reverend Payne was the first black state legislator in West Virginia. He also organized and was the first president of the West Virginia Baptist State Convention.

**JAMES PERKINS** *Williamson, West Virginia* *(1951– )* *The Progressive National Baptist Convention*

James Perkins is the longtime pastor of Greater Christ Baptist Church in Detroit. Reverend Perkins is a leading revivalist, author, and officer for the Progressive Baptist Convention.

| **Name** | **Place of Birth** | **Date of Birth–Date of Death** | **Denomination or Faith Affiliation** |
|---|---|---|---|

RUFUS LEWIS PERRY | *Smith County, Tennessee* | *(1834–1895)* | *AMEZ*

Reverend Perry was a minister, journalist, editor, ethnologist, essayist, logician, and a scholar in Greek, Latin, and Hebrew. His most comprehensive work, *The Cushite*, was published in 1893.

ERNEST L. PETERSEN | *Virgin Islands* | *(1896–1959)* | *American Catholic Church*

Reverend Petersen founded the American Catholic Church (Syro-Antiochian). He was also named one of the top radio ministers by *Ebony* magazine in July 1949.

CHARLES H. PHILLIPS | *Milledgeville, Georgia* | *(1858–1951)* | *CME*

Charles Henry Phillips was elected the eighth bishop of the CME church in 1902 and published the *History of the Colored Methodist Episcopal Church in America*.

JAMES POINDEXTER | *Richmond, Virginia* | *(1819–1907)* | *Baptist*

Reverend Poindexter pastored the Second Baptist Church of Columbus, Ohio. An activist and politician, he served on the city council and board of education in Columbus.

ADAM C. POWELL JR. | *New Haven, Connecticut* | *(1908–1972)* | *Baptist*

Adam Clayton Powell Jr. was named one of the top black preachers in America by *Ebony* in 1954. He was also a longtime U.S. Congressman and author of *Adam by Adam: The Autobiography of Adam Clayton Powell, Jr.* He served as pastor of Abyssinian Baptist Church in New York, as did his father before him.

WILLIAM P. QUINN | *Calcutta, India* | *(ca. 1788–1873)* | *AME*

William Paul Quinn was consecrated the fourth bishop of the AME church and later succeeded Morris Brown as senior bishop in 1849, a position he held for nearly twenty-five years. Paul Quinn College and churches in fifteen states bear his name.

FLORENCE RANDOLPH | *Charleston, South Carolina* | *(1866–1951)* | *AMEZ*

Reverend Randolph founded and served as president of the New Jersey State Federation of Colored Women's Clubs. She was also national president of the AMEZ Women's Home and Foreign Missionary Society from 1916 to 1920.

D.C. RICE | *Barbour County, Alabama* | *(ca. 1888–1973)* | *Pentecostal*

Reverend Rice released some thirty recordings between 1928 and 1930; his singing is notable, and he provided a rarely heard mix of singing and preaching in the late twenties and thirties. He became known for preaching while being accompanied by an eight- and sometimes nine-piece band.

LIEUTENANT M.T. ROBERSON *Columbia, South Carolina* *(1840–1914)* *Baptist*

Reverend Roberson was a member of the executive board of the Georgia State Baptist Convention. He pastored Cotton Avenue Baptist Church in Macon, one of the largest churches in the state at the time, and later Antioch Baptist Church in Atlanta.

IDA B. ROBINSON *Hazelhurst, Georgia* *(1891–1946)* *Mt. Sinai Holy Church of America*

Pastor Robinson founded the Mount Sinai Holy Church of America. She was also a leading revivalist. More information concerning her life can be found in *Daughters of Thunder,* by Bettye Collier-Thomas.

LEORA ROSS *Unknown* *(1900–ca. 1982)* *Chicago's Church of the Living God*

Reverend Ross released at least eight songs from 1926 to 1928 and at least five sermons. She was one of the first black female preachers to record a sermon. Her sermons were recorded on Okeh Race Records.

CHRISTOPHER RUSH *Cravens County, North Carolina* *(1777–1873)* *AMEZ*

Christopher Rush was the second bishop of the AMEZ church. In 1852 he published *A Short Account of the Rise and Progress of the AME Church in America.*

CLAYTON D. RUSSELL *Unknown* *(ca. 1911–ca. 1980)* *Church of Christ*

Reverend Russell was named as one of the top radio ministers by *Ebony* in 1949. He pastored People's Independent Church of Christ in Los Angeles, one of the largest churches in the United States at the time; it claimed to have had eleven thousand members.

ALFRED C. SHARPTON *Brooklyn, New York* *(1954– )* *COGIC*

Reverend Al Sharpton is the founder of the National Action Network and is active in many civil rights related groups. He has been a candidate for the U.S. Senate and for president of the United States.

WILLIAM J. SIMMONS *Charleston, North Carolina* *(1849–1890)* *American National Baptist Convention, U.S.A., Inc.*

Reverend Simmons founded the American National Baptist Convention, which is now the National Baptist Convention, U.S.A., Inc. He published *Men of Mark.* He taught at the Normal and Theological Institute at Louisville, Kentucky, which is now Simmons University.

| **Name** | **Place of Birth** | **Date of Birth–Date of Death** | **Denomination or Faith Affiliation** |
|---|---|---|---|
| C.B.T. Smith | *La Vernia, Texas* | *(1917–2009)* | *National Baptist Convention, U.S.A., Inc.* |

Clarence Booker Taliaferro Smith was the pastor of Golden Gate Missionary Baptist Church in Dallas for forty-five years. He was a leading revivalist.

| | | | |
|---|---|---|---|
| Kelly M. Smith | *Mount Bayou, Mississippi* | *(1920–1984)* | *National Baptist Convention U.S.A., Inc.* |

Reverend Smith became pastor of Nashville's First Baptist Church in 1951 and remained at the church until his death. He was named one of the top ten African American preachers by *Ebony* in 1954. Smith served on the faculties of Natchez College, Alcorn College, and American Baptist Theological Seminary. In 1969 he was appointed assistant dean of Vanderbilt University's Divinity School. In 1983 Dr. Smith delivered the prestigious Lyman Beecher Lecture at Yale University. In 1984 he published *Social Crisis Preaching*.

| | | | |
|---|---|---|---|
| Lucy Smith | *Athens, Georgia* | *(1874–1952)* | *Pentecostal* |

Elder Smith was the pastor of the four-thousand-member All Nations Pentecostal Church in Chicago. Smith was nationally recognized for her popular radio broadcasts, *The Glorious Church of the Air*, and for her healing ministry. She also provided food and clothing for the poor, built two churches, and started a Pentecostal Conference with three other churches in Alabama, Nebraska, and Florida.

| | | | |
|---|---|---|---|
| Nelson H. Smith | *Brewton, Alabama* | *(1930–2006)* | *National Baptist Convention, U.S.A., Inc.* |

Nelson Smith was the longtime pastor of New Pilgrim Baptist Church in Birmingham, an ardent civil rights activist, and a well-known revivalist.

| | | | |
|---|---|---|---|
| Utah Smith | *Shreveport, Louisiana* | *(1906–1965)* | *COGIC* |

Reverend Smith was a renowned preacher, traveling evangelist, and guitarist. His recordings can be found on *Slide Guitar Gospel: The Complete Recordings of Rev. Utah Smith*.

| | | | |
|---|---|---|---|
| Wallace C. Smith | *Philadelphia, Pennsylvania* | *(1948– )* | *American Baptist Churches and the Progressive National Baptist Convention* |

Reverend Smith served as the vice president of the Baptist World Alliance and as the first African American president of Palmer Theological Seminary. He pastored First Baptist Church in Nashville and became the pastor of Shiloh Baptist Church in Washington, D.C., in 1991. He is author of *The Church in the Life of the Black Family*.

**WILLIE MAE FORD SMITH** *Rolling Fork, Mississippi* *(1904–1994)* *Pentecostal Assemblies of the World*

Reverend Smith, also known as Mother Smith, was a famed gospel singer during the 1940s and 1950s. She was ordained by the AMEZ church and later joined a church that was part of the Pentecostal Assemblies of the World. Two of her best-known songs are "Give Me Wings" and "The Life Boat Is Coming." She mentored numerous gospel singers, including Mahalia Jackson.

**STEPHEN G. SPOTTSWOOD** *Boston, Massachusetts* *(1897–1974)* *AMEZ*

Stephen Gill Spottswood was consecrated the fifty-eighth bishop of the AMEZ in 1952. He was also president of the national board of the NAACP and a noted civil rights leader.

**MARSHALL ALEXANDER TALLEY** *Concord, North Carolina* *(1877–ca. 1949)* *National Baptist Convention, U.S.A., Inc.*

Reverend Talley pastored First Baptist Church in Wilson, North Carolina; First Baptist Church in Selma, Alabama; Clark Memorial Baptist Church in Homestead, Pennsylvania; Mount Zion Baptist Church in Indianapolis, Indiana; and Northside New Era Baptist Church, also in Indianapolis. He was elected to the Indiana state legislature in 1935 and was the dean of the National Baptist Sunday School Congress from 1933–1949.

**WALTER S. THOMAS SR.** *Baltimore, Maryland* *(1950– )* *Baptist*

Bishop Thomas is the president of the Kingdom Association of Covenant Pastors. Thomas served as the president of the Hampton University Ministers' Conference and since 1975 has pastored New Psalmist Baptist Church in Baltimore, with a membership of more than six thousand.

**STEPHEN J. THURSTON** *Chicago, Illinois* *(1952– )* *National Baptist Convention of America, Inc.*

Stephen John Thurston began serving as president of the National Baptist Convention of America in 2003 and is the youngest president in the history of the denomination. He is a leading revivalist and the longtime pastor of New Covenant Ministry Baptist Church in Chicago, where his father and grandfather previously served as pastor.

**AUGUSTUS TOLTON** *Ralls County, Missouri* *(1854–1897)* *Catholic*

Father Tolton was ordained a priest in Rome in 1886, and although he died at age forty-three, he became a symbol for those seeking to integrate the Catholic Church and gain more black priests and greater power for blacks. Although James Healy was the first black priest and became a bishop, Healy had the ability to pass for white,

| **Name** | **Place of Birth** | **Date of Birth–Date of Death** | **Denomination or Faith Affiliation** |
|---|---|---|---|

and a history of acknowledging Tolton as the first undeniably black priest has only recently emerged.

| TRUDIE TRIMM | *Spearsville, Louisiana* | *(ca. 1915–1984)* | *National Baptist Convention, U.S.A., Inc.* |
|---|---|---|---|

Reverend Trimm was the first woman minister recognized as an ordained female clergy by the National Baptist Convention, U.S.A., Inc. She pastored the New Testament Missionary Baptist Church in Chicago for nineteen years.

| KENNETH ULMER | *East St. Louis, Illinois* | *(1948– )* | *Nondenominational* |
|---|---|---|---|

Kenneth Ulmer is the pastor of Faithful Central Bible Church, located in the seventeen-thousand-seat Great Western Forum in Inglewood, California. In 2005 he was also a board member of King's College and Seminary, and he is the author of several books.

| RICHARD H. VANDERHORST | *Georgetown, South Carolina* | *(1813–1872)* | *CME* |
|---|---|---|---|

Bishop Vanderhorst was elected as the second bishop of the CME Church at the CME General Conference in 1870.

| PETER VINEGAR | *Midway, Kentucky* | *(ca. 1842–1905)* | *Baptist* |
|---|---|---|---|

Reverend Vinegar served at Main Street Colored Baptist Church in Lexington for twenty years, after which he led well-attended revivals throughout the region.

| WYATT T. WALKER | *Brockton, Massachusetts* | *(1929– )* | *The Progressive National Baptist Convention* |
|---|---|---|---|

Wyatt Tee Walker was the vice president and executive director of the Southern Christian Leadership Conference and worked closely with Dr. Martin Luther King Jr. He also served as the pastor of Canaan Baptist Church in New York for thirty-seven years until his retirement in 2004, and he was written numerous books, including *Spirits that Dwell in Deep Woods* (1987).

| WILLIAMS J. WALLS | *Chimney Rock, North Carolina* | *(1885–1975)* | *AMEZ* |
|---|---|---|---|

Bishop Walls was elected forty-second bishop at the 1924 AMEZ General Conference and later became the senior bishop. He wrote *The African Methodist Episcopal Zion Church*.

| ANDREW WARNER | *Washington, Kentucky* | *(1850–1920)* | *AMEZ* |
|---|---|---|---|

Bishop Warner was consecrated thirty-third bishop at the 1908 AMEZ General Conference. He was nominated for Congress in the first Alabama district and was twice chosen presidential elector. He also ran for governor of Alabama in 1896.

**F.D. WASHINGTON** *Dermott, Arkansas* *(1913–1988)* *COGIC*
Bishop Washington was a popular minister at Brooklyn, New York's Washington Temple Church of God in Christ. He became a bishop in the COGIC in 1955.

**WILLIAM WATLEY** *St. Louis, Missouri* *(1948– )* *AME*
Reverend Watley is the pastor of St. James AME Church in Newark, New Jersey. He served as chief executive officer and secretary of the New Jersey Commerce & Economic Growth Commission. He is also the author of several books.

**RALPH D. WEST** *Houston, Texas* *(1959– )* *National Baptist Convention, U.S.A., Inc.*
Ralph Douglas West is the pastor of Brookhollow Baptist Church (The Church Without Walls), which he formed in 1987; it is one church with three locations in Houston, Texas. The church has a membership of more than ten thousand. Reverend West is a leading revivalist and has regularly been named a preacher for the historic Hampton University Ministers' Conference; he is also the author of two books.

**ELLA EUGENE WHITFIELD** *Tolberton, Georgia* *(Unknown)* *National Baptist Convention, U.S.A., Inc.*
Preacher and missionary Reverend Whitfield was the field secretary for the Woman's Convention Auxiliary of the National Baptist Convention.

**C.S. WILKINS** *Jefferson County, Georgia* *(1859–?)* *Baptist*
A graduate of the Atlanta Baptist Seminary, Reverend Wilkins served several pastorates in Alabama, most notably Friendship Baptist Church in LaFayette. One biographer notes that he was known in LaFayette as "Cicero" and the "Silver-Tongued Orator."

**CECIL WILLIAMS** *San Angelo, Texas* *(1929– )* *United Methodist*
Cecil Williams was the longtime pastor of the six-thousand-member Glide Memorial United Methodist Church in San Francisco. He is best known for his programs to feed the hungry, provide low-income housing, and for opening his church to persons regardless of their sexual orientation, race, or class.

**H.M. WILLIAMS** *northern area of Louisiana* *(1863–ca. 1934)* *National Baptist Convention, U.S.A., Inc.*
Reverend Williams was the statistician of the General Baptist Convention of Texas, superintendent of the Texas state mission work for the General Baptist State Convention, and moderator of the Lincoln Association. He pastored the Avenue L Missionary Baptist Church in Galveston from 1904 to 1933.

| **Name** | **Place of Birth** | **Date of Birth–Date of Death** | **Denomination or Faith Affiliation** |
|---|---|---|---|
| **Henry Williams** | *Washington, Georgia* | *(1843–ca. 1885)* | *Baptist* |

Reverend Williams traveled as an evangelist in central Georgia, doing so even at the expense of violent beatings. He served as the pastor of the First Baptist Church of Macon.

| | | | |
|---|---|---|---|
| **Riley Williams** | *St. Francisville, Louisiana* | *(1897–1952)* | *COGIC* |

Bishop Williams was one of the first five bishops chosen by COGIC founder C.H. Mason. He was also building commissioner of Mason Temple, then the largest building constructed and owned by an African American religious group.

| | | | |
|---|---|---|---|
| **Smallwood E. Williams** | *Lynchburgh, Virginia* | *(1907–1991)* | *Pentecostal* |

Reverend Williams was the pastor of the Bible Way Church of the Lord Jesus Christ. He formed the Bible Way Church of Our Lord Jesus Christ World-Wide, Inc. (an organization of African American Pentecostal churches) in 1957. He pastored a five-thousand-member church and had a popular radio broadcast. *Ebony* magazine named him one of the top radio preachers in the country in 1949.

| | | | |
|---|---|---|---|
| **Joseph Willis** | *Baldwin County, North Carolina* | *(ca. 1758–1854)* | *Baptist* |

Reverend Willis was one of the first black Baptist preachers west of the Mississippi River. He helped found the Louisiana Baptist Association at Cheneyville, Louisiana.

| | | | |
|---|---|---|---|
| **Elisah Arlington Wilson** | *Garland City, Arkansas* | *(1876–ca. 1943)* | *National Baptist Convention, U.S.A., Inc.* |

Elisha Wilson was considered one of the leading orators of his day. He was also one of the most educated, earning three degrees including a law degree from Houston College. Wilson served as the recording secretary of the National Baptist Convention, U.S.A., Inc. He pastored in Kansas City, but is best known for being the pastor of Macedonia Baptist Church in Dallas from 1919 to 1933. Macedonia later became the Good Street Baptist Church.

| | | | |
|---|---|---|---|
| **Robert H. Wilson** | *Columbia, South Carolina* | *(1924– )* | *National Baptist Convention, U.S.A., Inc.* |

Robert Henry Wilson is a former chief executive officer of the National Baptist Convention of America's Foreign Mission Board. He also founded the Bethlehem Foundation in Dallas, a social service organization. He was the longtime pastor of Cornerstone Baptist Church in Dallas.

THEODORE S. WRIGHT | *Providence, Rhode Island* | *(1797–1847)* | *Presbyterian*

Reverend Wright pastored the first Colored Presbyterian Church in New York for twenty years, succeeding Samuel Cornish. He was mentor to Henry Highland Garnett, who followed him. Wright is believed to be the first or second black American to graduate from an American theological seminary (Princeton, 1828), but he received private tutoring at the school and official records are unclear regarding his date of graduation. He was also a leading abolitionist, member of the American Anti-Slavery Society, and organizer of the Phoenix Literary Society.

JOHNNY RAY YOUNGBLOOD | *New Orleans, Louisiana* | *(1948– )* | *The Progressive National Baptist Convention*

Reverend Youngblood served as the pastor of the six-thousand-member St. Paul Community Baptist Church in Brooklyn, New York, for more than thirty years, retiring in 2008. He was featured in *New York* magazine as one of the ten most influential people in New York in 2004. In 1995 Youngblood began *The Commemoration of the Maafa through a Church Production, The Maafa Suite: A Healing Journey.* This production is now emulated in numerous churches. His work as pastor and the ministries of St. Paul are chronicled in the book in *Upon This Rock: The Miracles of a Black Church.*

## *BIBLIOGRAPHICAL SOURCES*


Bacote, Samuel William, ed. *Who's Who among the Colored Baptists of the United States.* Kansas City: Franklin Hudson Publishing, 1913.

Branch, Taylor. *Pillar of Fire: America in the King Years, 1963–5.* New York: Touchstone, 1998.

Burgess, Stanley M., and Edward M. Vander Maas, eds. *The New International Dictionary of Pentecostal and Charismatic Movements.* Grand Rapids, MI: Zondervan, 2001.

Carter, E.R. (1888) *Biographical Sketches of Our Pulpit.* Reprint ed. Chicago: Afro-Am Press, 1969.

Collier-Thomas, Bettye. *Daughters of Thunder: Black Women Preachers and Their Sermons, 1850–1979.* San Francisco: Jossey-Bass Publishers, 1998.

DuPree, Sherry Sherrod, ed. *Biographical Dictionary of African-American, Holiness-Pentecostals.* Washington, DC: Middle Atlantic Regional Press, 1989.

Harley, Sharon. *The Timetables of African-American History.* New York: Touchstone, 1995.

Murphy, Larry G., J. Gordon Melton, and Gary L. Ward, eds. *Encyclopedia of African American Religions.* New York: Garland Publishing, 1993.

Sernett, Milton C., ed. *African American Religious History: A Documentary Witness,* C. Eric Lincoln Series on the Black Experience. Durham, NC: Duke University Press, 1999.

Simmons, William J. *Men of Mark: Eminent, Progressive and Rising.* New York: George M. Rewell & Co, 1870. Reprint, Chicago: Johnson Publishing Co., 1970.

Warner, Robert A. "Amos Gerry Beman, 1812–1874: A Memoir on a Forgotten Leader." *Journal of Negro History* (1937): 200–221.

Williams, Ethel L. *Biographical Directory of Negro Ministers*. New York: Scarecrow Press, 1965.

Wright, Richard Robert. *Centennial Encyclopedia of the African Methodist Episcopal Church*. Philadelphia: Book Concern of the AME Church, 1916

# BIBLIOGRAPHY

## *Books*


Alexander, Glennie. *Sermons Preached on Plantations*. Freeport, NY: Books for Libraries Press, 1971.

Angell, Stephen W. *Black Methodist Preachers in the South Carolina Upcountry, 1840–1866: Isaac (Counts) Cook, James Porter, and Henry McNeal Turner.* Columbia: University of South Carolina Press, 1996.

Bacon, Thomas. *Sermons Addressed to Masters and Servants and Published in the Year 1743*. Winchester, VA: John Heiskell Publisher, 1813.

Bailey, E.K., and Warren W. Wiersbe. *Preaching in Black and White: What We Can Learn from Each Other.* Grand Rapids, MI: Zondervan, 2003.

Beale, Lawrence L. *Towards a Black Homiletic*. New York: Vantage Press, 1979.

Blount, Brian K., and Gary W. Charles. *Preaching Mark in Two Voices*. Louisville, KY: Westminster John Knox Press, 2002.

Bond, L. Susan. *Contemporary African American Preaching: Diversity in Theory and Style*. St. Louis, MO: Chalice Press, 2003.

Borders, William Holmes. *Forty-fifth Pastoral Anniversary, 1937–1982*. Atlanta: Josten's American Yearbook Company, 1982.

———. *Trial By Fire and 25 Other Full Length Sermons*. Atlanta: Wheat Street Church, 1977.

———. *World Unity and 19 Other Sermons*. Atlanta: Morris Brown College Press, 1990.

Boulware, Marcus H. *The Oratory of Negro Leaders: 1900–1968*. Westport, CT: Negro Universities Press, 1969.

Bowen, John Wesley. *What Shall The Harvest Be? A National Sermon: or A Series of*

*Plain Talks to the Colored People of America on their Problems*. Washington, DC: Press of the Stafford Printing Company, 1892.

Bowman, Thea. *Sister Thea Bowman, Shooting Star: Selected Writings and Speeches*, ed. Celestine Cepress. Winona, MN: St. Mary's Press, 1993.

Brawley, E.M. *The Negro Baptist Pulpit: A Collection of Sermons and Papers on Baptist Doctrine and Missionary and Educational Work by Colored Baptist Ministers*. Philadelphia: American Baptist Publication Society, 1890. Reprint, Freeport, NY: Books for Libraries Press, 1971.

Braxton, Brad. *Preaching Paul*. Nashville, TN: Abingdon Press, 2004.

Cannon, Katie Geneva. *Teaching Preaching: Isaac Rufus Clark and Black Sacred Rhetoric*. New York: Continuum International Publishing Group, 2002.

Carter, Edward R. *Biographical Sketches of Our Pulpit*. 1888. Reprint, Chicago: Afro-Am Press, 1969.

Chavis-Othow, Helen. *John Chavis: African American Patriot, Preacher, Teacher and Mentor, 1763–1838*. Jefferson, NC: McFarland Press, 2001.

Collier-Thomas, Bettye. *Daughters of Thunder: Black Women Preachers and Their Sermons, 1850–1979*. San Francisco: Jossey-Bass Publishers, 1998.

Colston, Freddie C., ed. *Dr. Benjamin E. Mays Speaks: Representative Speeches of a Great American Orator*. Lanham, MD: University Press of America, 2002.

Crawford, Evans E., and Thomas H. Troeger. *The Hum: Call and Response in African American Preaching*. Nashville, TN: Abingdon Press, 1995.

Daughtry, Herbert. *My Beloved Community: Sermons, Lectures and Speeches of Rev. Daughtry*. Trenton: Africa World Press, 2001.

Davis, Gerald L. *I Got the Word in Me and I Can Sing It, You Know: A Study of the Performed African-American Sermon*. Philadelphia: University of Pennsylvania Press, 1985. Reprint, Trenton: Africa World Press, 2001.

Diamond, John C., and Joseph E. Troutman, eds. *Perspectives on Womanist Theology*. Atlanta: ITC Press, 1995.

Ellison, John Malcus. *They Who Preach*. 1892. Reprint, Nashville, TN: Broadman Press, 1956.

Forbes, James A. *The Holy Spirit and Preaching*. Nashville, TN: Abingdon Press, 1989.

Fry Brown, Teresa L. *Delivering the Sermon: Voice, Body, and Animation in Proclamation*. Minneapolis, MN: Fortress Press, 2008.

———. *Weary Throats and New Songs: Black Women Proclaiming God's Word*. Nashville, TN: Abingdon Press, 2003.

Grimke, Francis. *The Work of Francis James Grimke*, ed. Carter G. Woodson. Washington, DC: The Associated Publishers, 1942.

Hamilton, Charles V. *The Black Preacher in America*. New York: Morrow, 1972.

Harris, James H. *Preaching Liberation*. Minneapolis, MN: Fortress Press, 1995.

———. *The Word Made Plain: The Power and Promise of Preaching*. Minneapolis, MN: Fortress Press, 2004.

Haskins, James. *Keeping the Faith: African American Sermons of Liberation*. New York: Welcome Rain Publishers, 2002.

Hatcher, William E. *John Jasper: The Unmatched Negro Philosopher and Preacher*. Chicago: Fleming H. Revell Co., 1908. Reprint, New York: Negro Universities Press, 1969.

Haynes, Lemuel. *A Sermon, Delivered at Rutland West-Parish in the Year 1805*. Troy, NY: Ryer Schermerhorn, 1807.

Hicks, H. Beecher. *Preaching through a Storm*. Grand Rapids, MI: Zondervan, 1987.

Hill, Edward Victor. *A Savior Worth Having*. Chicago: Moody Press, 2002.

Hood, James Walker. *The Negro in the Christian Pulpit, or The Two Characters and Two Destinies as Delineated in Twenty-One Practical Sermons*. Raleigh, NC: Edwards, Broughton, 1884.

Horace, Lillian B. *Crowned with Glory and Honor: The Life of Rev. Lacey Kirk Williams*, ed. Venchael L. Booth. Hicksville, NY: Exposition Press, 1978.

Hubbard, Dolan. *The Sermon and the African American Literary Imagination*. Columbia: University of Missouri Press, 1994.

Jea, John, and George White. *Black Itinerants of the Gospel: The Narratives of John Jea and George White*, ed. Graham Russell Hodges. Madison: Madison House, 1993. Reprint 2002.

Johnson, James Weldon. *God's Trombones: Seven Negro Sermons in Verse*. New York: Viking Press, 1927.

Johnson, Joseph Andrew. *The Soul of the Black Preacher*. Cleveland, OH: Pilgrim Press, 1971.

Johnson-Smith, Robert, II. *Wisdom of the Ages: The Mystique of the African American Preacher*. Valley Forge, PA: Judson Press, 1995.

Jones, Amos. *As You Go Preach! Dynamics of Sermon Building and Preaching in the Black Church*. Nashville, TN: Bethlehem Book, 1996.

Jones, Edward, and Ephraim H. McKissack. *The Cayugan Baptist: Sermons, Rock-Ribbed Fundamentals, Facts and Truths and Brief Biographies of Eminent Preachers*. Chicago: A. Lindell & Co., 1922.

Jones, Kirk Byron. *The Jazz of Preaching: How to Preach with Great Freedom and Joy*. Nashville, TN: Abingdon Press, 2004.

Jones, Miles Jerome. *Preaching Papers: The Hampton & Virginia Union Lectures*. New York: Martin Luther King Press, 1995.

Jones, Ralph H. *Charles Albert Tindley: Prince of Preachers*. Nashville, TN: Abingdon Press, 1982.

Kienzie, Beverly Mayne, and Pamela J. Walker. *Women Preachers and Prophets through Two Millennia of Christianity*. Berkeley: University of California Press, 1998.

LaRue, Cleophus. *The Heart of Black Preaching*. Louisville, KY: Westminster John Knox, 2000.

———, ed. *Power in the Pulpit: How America's Most Effective Black Preachers Prepare Their Sermons*. Louisville, KY: Westminster John Knox, 2002.

Lassiter, Valentino. *Martin Luther King in the African American Preaching Tradition*. Cleveland, OH: Pilgrim Press, 2001.

Liburd, Ronald N. *Textual Harrassment? A Hermeneutical Perspective on African American Preaching*. Boston: Brill, 2003.

Lischer, Richard. *The Preacher King: Martin Luther King, Jr. and the Word That Moved America*. New York: Oxford University Press, 1997.

Marable, Manning, and Leith Mullings. *Let Nobody Turn Us Around, Voices of Resistance, Reform, and Renewal: An African American Anthology*. Lanham, MD: Rowman & Littlefield, 2000.

Marrant, John. *A Narrative of the Lord's Wonderful Dealings with John Marrant, a Black (A Preacher of the Gospel in Nova-Scotia) Born in New York, then North America.* London: R. Hawse, 1785. Reprint, Yarmouth, ME: J. Barnes, 1824.

Massey, James Earl. *The Burdensome Joy of Preaching.* Nashville, TN: Abingdon Press 1996.

———. *Designing the Sermon.* Nashville, TN: Abingdon, 1980.

———. *The Responsible Pulpit.* Anderson, IN: Warner Press, 1974.

———. *Sharing Heaven's Music: The Heart of Christian Preaching: Essays in Honor of James Earl Massey.* Nashville, TN: Abingdon Press, 1995.

Mays, Benjamin E. *Born to Rebel: An Autobiography.* New York: Scribner, 1971.

———. *Dr. Benjamin E. Mays Speaks: Representative Speeches of a Great American Orator*, ed. Freddie C. Colston. Lanham, MD: University Press of America, 2002.

McMickle, Marvin A. *Preaching to the Black Middle Class: Words of Challenge, Words of Hope.* Valley Forge, PA: Judson Press, 2000.

———. *Shaping the Claim: Moving from Text to Sermon.* Minneapolis, MN: Fortress Press, 2008.

McNeil, Jesse Jai, and Amos Jones. *As Thy Days, so Thy Strength.* Grand Rapids, MI: Eerdmans, 1960.

———. *The Preacher-Prophet in Mass Society.* Nashville, TN: Townsend Press, 1994.

McReynolds, James Evans. *Black Preaching: Burden of a People.* Nashville, TN: Warren Press, 1970.

Mitchell, Ella Pearson. *Those Preaching Women.* 3 vols. Valley Forge, PA: Judson Press, 1985.

———. *Women: To Preach or Not To Preach? 21 Outstanding Black Preachers Say Yes!* Valley Forge, PA: Judson Press, 1991.

Mitchell, Henry H. *Black Preaching: The Recovery of a Powerful Art.* Philadelphia: J. B. Lippincott Company, 1970. Reprint, Nashville, TN: Abingdon Press, 1990.

———. *Celebration and Experience in Preaching.* Nashville, TN: Abingdon Press, 1990.

———. *The Recovery of Preaching.* New York: Harper & Row, 1977.

Mitchell, Henry H., and Ella Pearson Mitchell. *Fire in the Well: Sermons by Ella and Henry Mitchell.* Valley Forge, PA: Judson Press, 2003.

Mitchell, Henry H., and Emil Thomas. *Preaching for Black Self-Esteem.* Nashville, TN: Abingdon Press, 1995.

Mitchell, Henry H., and Martha J. Simmons. *A Workbook to Accompany Celebration and Experience in Preaching.* Nashville, TN: Abingdon, 1995.

Morris, Calvin S. *Reverdy C. Ransom: Black Advocate of the Social Gospel.* Lanham, MD: University Press of America, 1990.

Mountford, Roxane. *The Gendered Pulpit: Preaching in American Protestant Spaces.* Carbondale: Southern Illinois University Press, 2003.

Moyd, Olin P. *Preaching and Practical Theology: An African American Perspective.* Nashville, TN: Townsend Press, 1994.

———. *The Sacred Art: Preaching & Theology in the African American Tradition.* Valley Forge, PA: Judson Press, 1995.

Mullane, Deirdre. *Crossing the Danger Water: Three Hundred Years of African-American Writing*. New York: Doubleday, 1993.

Newbold, Robert T., ed. *Black Preaching: Select Sermons in the Presbyterian Tradition*. Louisville, KY: Westminster John Knox, 1977.

Norris, Frederick W. "The Catholicity of Great Black Preaching," in *Sharing Heaven's Music: The Heart of Christian Preaching: Essays in Honor of James Earl Massey*, ed. Barry Callen. Nashville, TN: Abingdon Press, 1995.

Offley, Greensbury Washington. *A Narrative of the Life and Labors of the Rev. G.W. Offley, a Colored Man and Local Preacher*. Hartford: n.p., 1860.

Parker, Theodore S.W. *The Slave History of the Life of Rev. Ebenezer Bird and His Work as a Preacher*. n.p., 1875.

Philpot, William M. *Best Black Sermons*. Valley Forge, PA: Judson Press, 1972.

Pinn, Anthony B. *Pauli Murray: Selected Writings and Sermons*. Maryknoll, NY: Orbis Books, 2006.

Pipes, William H. *Say Amen, Brother! Old-Time Negro Preaching: A Study in American Frustration*. Westport, CT: Negro University Press, 1951.

Pitts, Walter F. *Old Ship of Zion: The Afro-Baptist Ritual in the African Diaspora*. New York: Oxford University Press, 1996.

Ponder, Rhinold, and Michele Tuck-Ponder, eds. *The Wisdom of the Word Love: Great African American Sermons*. New York: Crown Publishers, 1997.

Proctor, Samuel D. *The Certain Sound of the Trumpet: Crafting a Sermon of Authority*. Valley Forge, PA: Judson Press, 1994.

———. *"How Shall They Hear?" Effective Preaching for Vital Faith*. Valley Forge, PA: Judson Press, 1992.

———. *Preaching About Crisis in the Community*. Philadelphia: Westminster Press, 1988.

———. *Substance of Things Hoped For: A Memoir of African American Faith*. Valley Forge, PA: Judson Press, 1999.

Proctor, Samuel D., and Gardner C. Taylor. *We Have This Ministry: The Heart of the Pastor's Vocation*. Valley Forge, PA: Judson Press, 1996.

Proctor, Samuel D., and William D. Watley. *Sermons from the Black Pulpit*. Valley Forge, PA: Judson Press, 1984.

Ransom, Reverdy C. *Making the Gospel Plain: The Writings of Bishop Reverdy C. Ransom*, ed. Anthony B. Pinn. Harrisburg, PA: Trinity Press International, 1999.

———. *The Pilgrimage of Harriet Ransom's Son*. Nashville, TN: AME Sunday School Union, 1949.

———. *The Spirit of Freedom and Justice: Orations and Speeches*. Nashville, TN: AME Sunday School Union, 1926.

Ray, Sandy F. *Journeying through a Jungle*. Nashville, TN: Broadman Press, 1979.

Roberts, Samuel K., ed. *Born to Preach: Essays in Honor of the Ministry of Henry and Ella Mitchell*. Valley Forge, PA: Judson Press, 2000.

Robinson, James H. *Adventurous Preaching*. Great Neck, NY: Channel Press, 1956.

Rosenberg, Bruce A. *The Art of the American Folk Preacher*. Rev. ed. New York: Oxford University Press, 1970.

———. *Can These Bones Live? The Art of the American Folk Preacher*. Urbana: University of Illinois Press, 1988.

Salvatore, Nick. *C.L. Franklin, the Black Church, and the Transformation of America.* New York: Little, Brown, and Company, 2005.

*Seven Black Preachers Tell: What Jesus Means to Me.* Nashville, TN: Broadman Press, 1971.

Simmons, Martha J., ed. *Preaching on the Brink: The Future of Homiletics, in Honor of Henry H. Mitchell.* Nashville, TN: Abingdon, 1996.

Simmons, Martha J., and Frank A. Thomas, eds. *9.11.01: African American Leaders Respond to an American Tragedy.* Valley Forge, PA: Judson Press, 2001.

Simpson, Gary V. *Preaching by Punctuation: Moving from Texts and Ideas to Sermons That Live with Passion.* Boston: Beacon Press, 1999.

Smith, C.S. *Sermons Delivered by Bishop Daniel A. Payne.* Nashville, TN: Publishing House of the AME Sunday School Union, 1888.

Smith, J. Alfred. *Preach On! A Concise Handbook of the Elements of Style in Preaching.* Nashville, TN: Broadman Press, 1984.

———, ed. *No Other Help I Know: Sermons on Prayer and Spirituality.* Valley Forge, PA: Judson Press, 1996.

———, ed. *Outstanding Black Sermons.* Valley Forge, PA: Judson Press, 1976.

Smith, Kelly Miller. *Social Crisis Preaching.* Macon, GA: Mercer University Press, 1984.

Southern, Eileen, and Josephine Wright, eds. *African-American Traditions in Song, Sermon, Tale, and Dance 1600s–1920: An Annotated Bibliography of Literature, Collections, and Artworks.* Westport, CT: Greenwood Press, 1990.

Spencer, Jon Michael. *Sacred Symphony: The Chanted Sermon of the Black Preacher.* Westport, CT: Greenwood Press, 1987.

Spillers, Hortense J. *Martin Luther King and the Style of the Black Sermon.* Garden City, NY: Anchor Press/Doubleday, 1974.

Stewart, Carlyle Fielding. *Joy Songs, Trumpet Blasts, and Hallelujah Shouts: Sermons in the African-American Preaching Tradition.* Lima, OH: C.S.S. Publishing Company, 1997.

Stewart, Warren H. Sr., *Interpreting God's Word in Black Preaching.* Valley Forge, PA: Judson Press, 1984.

Sunnemark, Fredrik. *Ring Out Freedom!: The Voice of Martin Luther King, Jr. and the Making of the Civil Rights Movement.* Bloomington: Indiana University Press, 2004.

Taylor, Gardner C. *How Shall They Preach?* Elgin, IL: Progressive Baptist Publishing House, 1977.

———. *The Words of Gardner Taylor.* 6 vols. Compiled by Edward L. Taylor. Valley Forge, PA: Judson Press, 1999.

Taylor, Mark V.C. *What Can We Say to These Things? The Sermon as a Moment of Spiritual Combat in the African American Church Tradition.* Boston: Beacon Press, 1999.

Terrill, Robert. *Malcolm X: Reinventing Radical Judgment.* East Lansing: Michigan State University Press, 2004.

Thomas, Frank A. *The Lord's Prayer in Times Like These.* St. Louis, MO: Chalice Press, 2002.

———. *They Like to Never Quit Praisin' God: The Role of Celebration in Preaching.* Cleveland, OH: United Church Press, 1997.

Thomas, Gerald Lamont. *African American Preaching: The Contribution of Dr. Gardner C. Taylor.* New York: Peter Lang Publishing, Inc., 2004.

Thomas, Walter, et al. *Outstanding Black Sermons.* Valley Forge, PA: Judson Press, 2001.

Thurman, Howard. *The Growing Edge.* New York: Harper & Row, 1956.

Thurman, Michael, ed. *Voices from the Dexter Pulpit.* Montgomery, AL: NewSouth Books, 2001.

Titon, Jeff Todd. *Give Me This Mountain: Life, History and Selected Sermons of Reverend C.L. Franklin.* Urbana: University of Illinois Press, 1989.

Turner, Mary Donovan, and Mary Lin Hudson. *Saved from Silence: Finding Women's Voice in Preaching.* St. Louis, MO: Chalice Press, 1999.

Turner, William Clair, Jr. *Preaching that Makes the Word Plain: Doing Theology in the Crucible of Life.* Eugene, OR: Cascade Books, 2008.

Voipio, Aarni. *Sleeping Preachers: A Study in Ecstatic Religiosity.* Helsinki: Annales Academiae Scientiarum Fennicae, 1951.

Walker, David. *David Walker's Appeal: To the Coloured Citizens of the World, But in Particular, and Very Expressly, to Those of the United States of America.* Rev. ed. with an introduction by Sean Wilentz. New York: Hill and Wang, Inc., 1995.

Walker, Robbie Jean, ed. *The Rhetoric of Struggle: Public Address by African American Women: Critical Studies on Black Life and Culture*, vol. 20. New York: Garland, 1992.

Walker, Wyatt Tee. *The Soul of Black Worship, A Trilogy: Praying, Preaching, Singing.* New York: Martin Luther King Fellows Press, 1984.

Warren, Mervyn A. *Black Preaching: Truth and Soul.* Washington, DC: University Press of America, 1977.

———. *King Came Preaching: The Pulpit Power of Dr. Martin Luther King, Jr.* Downers Grove, IL: InterVarsity Press, 2001.

Waters, Kenneth L., Sr. *Afrocentric Sermons: The Beauty of Blackness in the Bible.* Valley Forge, PA: Judson Press, 1994.

Watley, William D. *Bring the Full Tithe: Sermons on the Grace of Giving.* Valley Forge, PA: Judson Press, 1995.

———. *From Mess to Miracle and Other Sermons.* Valley Forge, PA: Judson Press, 1989.

———. *Sermons on Special Days Preaching Through the Year In the Black Church.* Valley Forge, PA: Judson Press, 2001.

———. *You Have To Face It to Fix It: Sermons on the Challenges of Life.* Valley Forge, PA: Judson Press, 1997.

White, Daniel. *When Black Preachers Preach: Leading Black Preachers Give Direction and Encouragement to a Nation that Has Lost Its Way.* Atlanta: Torch Publications, 1994.

Williams, Delores S. *Sisters in the Wilderness: The Challenge of Womanist God-Talk.* Maryknoll, NY: Orbis Books, 1993.

Williams, L.K. *Lord! Lord! Special Occasion Sermons and Addresses of Dr. L.K. Williams.* Detroi, MI: Harlo Press, 1965.

Williams, Stacy. *The New Revised History of the Black Preacher and the Black Church.* Detroit, MI: Peace Baptist Church of Detroit, 1985.

Woodbey, George Washington. *Black Socialist Preacher: The Teachings of Reverend George Washington Woodbey and His Disciple, Revered G. W. Slater, Jr.*, ed. Philip S. Foner. San Francisco: Synthesis Publication, 1983.

Woodson, Carter G., ed. *Negro Orators and Their Orations*. Washington, DC: Associated Publishers, 1925.

Wright, Jeremiah A., Jr. *Good News! Sermons of Hope for Today's Families*. Valley Forge, PA: Judson Press, 1995.

———. *What Makes You So Strong? Sermons of Joy and Strengths*. Valley Forge, PA: Judson Press, 1993.

Young, Henry J., and William Holmes Borders. *Preaching the Gospel*. Philadelphia: Fortress Press, 1976.

Young, Henry J., ed. *Preaching On Suffering and a God of Love*. Philadelphia: Fortress Press, 1977.

## *Articles and Journals*

Alvarez, Alexandra. "Martin Luther King's 'I Have a Dream': the Speech Event as Metaphor." *Journal of Black Studies* 18 (1987): 337–57.

American Rhetoric. "Malcolm X Speech, The Ballot or the Bullet." *American Rhetoric*. http://www.americanrhetoric.com/speeches/malcolmxballot.htm (accessed on July 29, 2007).

"America's Fifteen Greatest Black Preachers." *Ebony* (September 1984).

Anderson, Fred. "Slave Preacher." *Baptist History and Heritage* 32 (July–October 1997): 58.

Anderson-Larson, Virginia. "Ordinary Letter: The Ministry of Preaching," in *Ordinary Ministry: Extraordinary Challenge: Women and the Role of Ministry*, ed. Norma Cook Everist, 85–90. Nashville, TN: Abingdon Press, 2000.

Andrews, Dale P. "Ecclesiology, Preaching, and Pastoral Care in the African American Church Tradition," in *Papers of the Annual Meeting, Academy of Homiletics*, 22–45. Oakland, CA: Academy of Homiletics, 1997.

Andrews, William L. "Frederick Douglass, Preacher." *American Literature* 54 (1982): 592–97.

Baai, G.S. "Dynamic Complementarity: A Study of the Relationship Between Scripture and Culture in Black Preaching." *Journal of Theology for South Africa* 83 (June 1993): 58–64.

Baldwin, Lewis V. "The Minister as Preacher, Pastor, and Prophet: The Thinking of Martin Luther King, Jr." *American Baptist Quarterly* 7 (June 1988): 79–97.

Battle, Michael A. "The Kerygmatic Ministry of Black Song and Sermon." *Journal of Black Sacred Music* 1 (Fall 1987): 17–20.

Bell, Marty G. "Fire in My Bones: The Prophetic Preaching of Martin Luther King, Jr." *Baptist History and Heritage* 34 (Winter 1999): 7–20.

Bengston, Dale R. "The Eagle Stirreth Her Nest: Notes on an Afro-American Shamanistic Event." *Journal of Religious Thought* 33 (Spring–Summer 1976): 76–86.

Bennett, John. "A Revival Sermon at Little St. John's." *Atlantic Monthly* 98 (August 1906): 256–68.

Benson, Juel Pate Borders. "Victory Over Defeat: Eulogy of William Holmes Borders Sr." *The African American Pulpit* 4, no. 1 (Winter 2000–2001): 34–39.

Blackwell, John A. "Black Preaching." *Princeton Seminary Bulletin* 65 (July 1972): 37–42.

Blake, Charles E. "Is Anything Forever?: Eulogy for Edward Victor (E.V.) Hill." *The African American Pulpit* 8, no. 2 (Spring 2005).

Blount, Marcellus. "The Preacherly Text: African American Poetry and Vernacular Performance." *Proceedings of the Modern Language Association* 107 (1992): 582–93.

Booth, Charles Edward. "An Uneven Hand." *The African American Pulpit* 5, no. 2 (Spring 2002): 135–38.

Booth, William D. "The Open Door for Women Preachers: Acts 2:17, 18; Romans 10:15; Ephesians 4:11." *Journal of Religious Thought* 50 (Fall–Spring 1993–1994): 108–15.

Boynton, Robert. "God and Harvard: A Profile of Peter Gomes." *The New Yorker*, November 11, 1996: 64.

Brooks, Joanna. "John Marrant's Journal: Providence and Prophesy in the Eighteenth-Century Black Atlantic." *North Star: A Journal of African American Religious History,* 1999.

Brownlow, Paul C. "The Pulpit and Black America: 1865–1877." *Quarterly Journal of Speech* 58 (1972): 431–40.

Burkle, Horst. "Patterns of Sermons from Various Parts of Africa," in *African Initiatives in Religion,* ed. David B. Barrett, 222–31. Nairobi, Kenya: East African Publishing House, 1971.

Butler, Lee H. "Sermon on the Mall: A Pastoral Theological Look at the Million Man March," in *Black Religion after the Million Man March,* ed. Garth Kasimu Baker-Fletcher, 91–101. Maryknoll, NY: Orbis Books, 1998.

Callender, Christine, and Deborah Cameron. "Responsive Listening as a Part of Religious Rhetoric: The Case of Black Pentecostal Preaching," in *Reception and Response: Hearer Creativity and the Analysis of Spoken and Written Texts,* ed. Graham McGregor and R. S. White, 160–78. London: Routledge, 1990.

Calloway-Thomas, Carolyn, and John Louis Lucaites. "Introduction," in *Martin Luther King Jr., and the Sermonic Power of Public Discourse*, ed. Carolyn Calloway-Thomas and John Louis Lucaites, 1–17. Tuscaloosa: University of Alabama Press, 1993.

Cannon, Katie Geneva. "Prophets for a New Day." *The African American Pulpit* 1, no. 2 (Spring 1998): 13–17.

———."Womanist Interpretation and Preaching in the Black Church," in *Searching the Scriptures,* ed. Elisabeth Schüssler Fiorenza, 326–37. New York: Crossroad, 1993.

"Charles Albert Tindley's Faith Set Him Singing." Christian History Timeline, Christianity Today International, July 2007. http://www.christianhistorytimeline.com/DAILYF/2003/07/daily-07-07-2003.shtml.

Chism, Keith A. "Christian Perfection Among Nineteenth-Century African-American Preaching Women." *Wesleyan Theological Journal* 35, no. 2. (Fall 2000): 179–93.

Christian Century Foundation. "African Methodist Episcopal Church Elects Vashti McKenzie Bishop." *Christian Century* (July 19, 2000).

Clark, Caesar, "The Worms Got Him." *The African American Pulpit* 6, no. 2 (Spring 2000).

Clemmons, Ithiel. "True Koinonia: Pentecostal Hopes and Historical Realities." *Pneuma: The Journal for the Society of Pentecostal Studies* 4 (Spring 1982): 46–56.

Coleman, Will. "Rap and Preaching." *Journal for Preachers* 21, no. 2 (1998): 15–19.

Conduit, Celeste Michelle, and John Louis Lucaites. "Malcolm X and the Rhetoric of Revolutionary Dissent." *Journal of Black Studies* 23 (1992): 291–313.

Conwill, Giles A. "Black Preaching and Catholicism," in *The Black-Christian Experience*, ed. Emmanuel L. McCall, 31–42. Nashville, TN: Broadman Press, 1972; reprinted in *Ministry Among Black Americans,* 31–43. Indianapolis, IN: Lilly Endowment, Inc., 1980.

Cooney, Patrick L., and Henry W. Powell. "The Life and Times of the Prophet Vernon Johns: Father of the Civil Rights Movement." http://www.vernonjohns.org/tcal001/vjtofc.html (accessed on July 27, 2007).

Cooper, Grace C. "Black Preaching Style in James Weldon Johnson's God's Trombones." *MAWA Review* 4, no. 1 (June 1989): 13–16.

Copeland, Claudette. "Why Are You Here?" *The African American Pulpit* 8, no. 4 (Fall 2005).

Cox, J. Robert. "The Fulfillment of Time: King's 'I Have a Dream' Speech (August 28, 1963)," in *Texts in Context: Critical Dialogues on Significant Episodes in American Political Rhetoric*, ed. Michael C. Leff and Fred J. Kauffeld, 181–204. Davis, CA: Hermagoras Press, 1989.

Curry, Erin. "E.V. Hill Remembered as Conservative African American Pastor, Civil Rights Leader." *Baptist Press*, February 26, 2003.

Dagenais, Julia. "Frontier Preaching as Formulaic Poetry." *Mid-America Folklore* 19 (1991): 118–26.

Daniels, David D. "They Had a Dream: Racial Harmony Broke Down, but the Hope Did Not." *Christian Century* 17, no. 2 (Spring 1998).

Davis, John W. "George Liele and Andrew Bryan, Pioneer Negro Baptist Preachers." *Journal of Negro History* 3 (1918): 119–27.

Dietz, Diane. "Faithful Hear the Preacher's Call to Vote." *Register Guard Newspaper*, Eugene, OR, June 29, 2004.

Dionisopoulos, George A., Victoria J. Gallagher, Steven R. Goldzwig, and David Zarefsky. "Martin Luther King, the American Dream, and Vietnam: A Collision of Rhetorical Trajectories." *Western Journal of Communications* 56 (1992): 91–107.

Dodson, Jualynne. "Nineteenth-Century AME Preaching Women: Cutting Edge of Women's Inclusion in Church Polity," in *Women in New Worlds: Historical Perspectives on the Wesleyan Tradition,* vol. 1, ed. Hilah F. Thomas and Rosemary Skinner Keller, 276–89. Nashville, TN: Abingdon Press, 1981; reprinted in *Black Women in American History*, vol. 1, ed. Darlene Clark Hine, 333–49. Brooklyn, NY: Carlson Publishing Inc., 1990.

Dowd, James. "God's Calling, Bishop G.E. Patterson: September 22, 1939–March 20, 2007." *Memphis Commercial Appeal*, April 1, 2007.

Dowd, Jerome. "Sermon of an Ante-Bellum Negro Preacher." *Southern Workman* 30, no. 11 (November 1901): 655–58; reprinted in *Strange Ways and Sweet Dreams: Afro-American Folklore from the Hampton Institute,* ed. Donald J. Waters, 352–55. Boston: G. K. Hall & Co., 1983.

Dunbar, Paul Laurence. "An Ante-Bellum Sermon," in *Lyrics of Lowly Life*. New York: Dodd, Mead, and Company, 1988: 26–30.

Dyer, Ervin. "Black Nun Examined for Sainthood." *Pittsburgh Post-Gazette*, November 28, 2003.

Dyson, Michael Eric. "Gardner Taylor: Poet Laureate of the Pulpit." *Christian Century* 112 (1994): 12–16.

Eikerenkoetter, Frederick Joseph. "Curse Not the Rich." *Science of Living Study Guide* 6, no. 2 (December 1975–February 1976).

An Englishwoman's journal. "Slave Preaching." *Living Age* 65, no. 832 (May 12, 1860): 326–29.

Estes, David C. "Preaching in an Afro-American Spiritual Church: Archbishop Lydia Gilford and the Traditional Chanted Sermon." *Cultural Perspectives on the American South* 5 (1991): 79–102.

Farmer, David Albert. "Pulpit Laureate and Presidential Favorite: An Interview with Gardner Taylor." *Pulpit Digest* (September–October 1996).

Fasion, Bernilee. "The King Is Dead; Long Live the King: The Eulogy of Joseph Harrison Jackson (J.H.) Jackson." *The African American Pulpit* 8, no. 2 (Spring 2005).

Franklin, C.L. "The Eagle Stirreth Her Nest." *The African American Pulpit* 5, no. 1 (Winter 2001–2002): 78–81.

Franklin, Robert Michael. "Beyond Preaching: Unchurched Black Men," in *Preaching on the Brink: The Future of Homiletics,* ed. Martha J. Simmons, 44–53. Nashville, TN: Abingdon Press, 1996.

Fry Brown, Teresa L. "An African American Woman's Perspective: Renovating Sorrow's Kitchen," in *Preaching Justice: Ethnic and Cultural Perspectives,* ed. Christine Marie Smith, 43–61. Cleveland, OH: United Church Press, 1998.

Genovese, Eugene D. "Black Plantation Preachers in the Slave South." *Louisiana Studies* 11 (1972): 188–214. Reprinted in *Southern Studies*, n.s., 2 (1991): 203–29.

Gertel, Elliott B. "The Sermons of the Rev. Martin Luther King, Jr.: A Jewish Response." *Conservative Judaism* 48, no. 3 (Spring 1996): 26–32.

Gilbreath, Edward. "The Pulpit King: The Passion and Eloquence of Gardner Taylor, A Legend Among Preachers." *Christianity Today* 39 (December 11, 1995): 25–28.

Gilkes, Cheryl Townsend. "Shirley Caesar and the Souls of Black Folk: Gospel Music as Cultural Narrative and Critique." *The African American Pulpit* 6, no. 2 (Spring 2003): 12–16.

Goatley, David Emmanuel. "The Hum: Call and Response in African American Preaching." *Memphis Theological Seminary Journal* 34 (Spring 1996): 55–56.

Goodwin, W.T. "Easter Sunrise Sermon," transcribed by Peter Gold. *Alcheringa: Ethnopoetics* (Autumn 1972): 1–14.

Graessle, Isabelle. "An Ecclesiology in Transition: From Homiletical Rhetoric to Feminist Preaching." *Women Magazine* 49 (June 1998): 43–44.

Griesinger, Emily. "Why Baby Suggs, Holy, Quit Preaching the Word: Redemption and Holiness in Toni Morrison's Beloved." *Christianity and Literature* 50, no. 4. (Summer 2001): 689–702.

Hall, Prathia. "Between the Wilderness and a Cliff." *The African American Pulpit* 5, no. 2 (Spring 2002): 116–20.

Hamlet, Janice Denise. "Religious Discourse as Cultural Narrative: A Critical Analysis of African American Sermons." *Western Journal of Black Studies* 18 (1994): 11–17.

Hammon, Jupiter. "An Address to the Negroes in the State of New York." (microform), New York: W. Abbatt, 1925.

Hardman-Cromwell, Youtha C. "'Freedom From:' *Negro Preaching of the 19th Century.*" *American Transcendental Quarterly* 14, no. 4 (2000): 277–95.

Hariman, Robert. "Time and the Reconstitution of Gradualism in King's Address: A Response to Cox," in *Texts in Context: Critical Dialogues on Significant Episodes in American Political Rhetoric*, ed. Michael C. Leff and Fred J. Kauffeld, 205–18. Davis, CA: Hermagoras Press, 1989.

Harris, Barbara C. "A Circle of Concern." *The African American Pulpit* 7, no. 2 (Spring 2004): 31–33.

Harris, James Henry. "Preaching Liberation: The Afro-American Sermon and the Quest for Social Change." *Journal of Religious Thought* 46 (Winter–Spring 1989–1990): 72–89.

Harrison, Robert D., and Linda K. Harrison. "The Call from the Mountaintop: Call-Response and the Oratory of Martin Luther King, Jr.," in *Martin Luther King, Jr., and the Sermonic Power of Public Discourse,* ed. Carolyn Calloway-Thomas and John Louis Lucaites, 162–78. Tuscaloosa: University of Alabama Press, 1993.

Hatch, Gary Layne. "Logic in the Black Folk Sermon: The Sermons of Rev. C.L. Franklin." *Journal of Black Studies* 26 (1995–96): 227–44.

Hayden, J. Carleton. "Black Episcopal Preaching in the Nineteenth Century: Intellect and Will." *Journal of Religious Thought* 39 (Spring–Summer 1982): 12–20.

Haynes, Lemuel. "Ye Shall Not Surely Die: A Short Sermon by Lemuel Haynes." *American Tract Society*, 1805.

Haywood, Chanta M. "Prophesying Daughters: Nineteenth-Century Black Religious Women, the Bible, and Black Literary History," in *African American and the Bible: Sacred Text and Social Texture,* ed. Vincent Wimbush, 355–66. New York: Continuum, 2001.

Herman, Edward S., and David Peterson. "Jeremiah Wright in the Propaganda System." *Monthly Review*, September 2008. Available at http://www.monthlyreview.org/080901herman-peterson.php (accessed December 8, 2008).

Hitchmough, Sam. "Missions of Patriotism: Joseph Jackson and Martin Luther King American Studies in Britain." *The British Association of American Studies Newsletter* 84 (Spring/Summer 2001).

Holt, Grace. "Stylin' Outta the Black Pulpit," in *Rappin' and Stylin' Out: Communication in Urban Black America,* ed. Thomas Kochman, 189–204. Urbana: University of Illinois Press, 1972.

Honan, William Holmes. "John Jasper and the Sermon that Moved the Sun." *Speech Monographs* 23 (1956): 255–61.

Hong, Lawrence K., and Marion V. Dearman. "The Streetcorner Preacher: Sowing Good Seeds by the Wayside." *Urban Life* 6 (1977): 56–57.

Hoots, Allegra S. "Prophetic Voices: Black Preachers Speak on Behalf of Children." Washington, DC: *Black Community Crusade for Children*, coordinated by the Children's Defense Fund, 1993.

Howard, Robert R. "Additions to Black Preaching Bibliography." *Homiletic* 26, no. 1 (Summer 2001): 1–4.

Howard, Robert R. "African-American Preaching: A Bibliography Part 2." *Homiletic* 25, no. 1 (Summer 2000): 25–30.

Hubbard, Dolan. "The Black Preacher Tale as Cultural Biography." *College Language Association Journal* 30 (1987): 328–42.

Illo, John. "The Rhetoric of Malcolm X." *Columbia University Forum* 9, no. 22 (Spring 1966): 5–12; reprinted in *Language, Communication, and Rhetoric in Black America*, ed. Arthur L. Smith, 158–75. New York: Harper & Row, Publishers, 1972.

"Is This Man the Next Billy Graham?" *Time*, September 17, 2001.

Jackson, Jesse Louis. "Keep Hope Alive." American Rhetoric, http://www.americanrhetoric.com/speeches/jessejackson1988dnc.htm (accessed June 28, 2007).

Jackson, Joyce M. "The Black American Folk Preacher and the Chanted Sermon: Parallels with a West African Tradition," in *Discourse in Ethnomusicology II: A Tribute to Alan Merriam*, ed. Caroline Card, et al., 205–22. Bloomington, IN: Ethnomusicology Publishing Group, 1981.

Jasper, John. "The Sun Does Move." *Fundamentalist Journal* 5, no. 2 (Fall 1986): 35–36.

Jea, John. "The African Preacher, 1773–1816." *Journal of American Studies* (Great Britain) 33, no. 3 (1999): 473–90.

Jelks, Randal. "The Character and Work of a Spiritual Watchman Described: The Preaching of Lemuel Haynes and the Quest for Personal Freedom." *Fides et historia* 26 (Winter–Spring 1994): 126–33.

Johnson, Joseph. "The Moral and Spiritual Requisites of the Black Preacher." *AME Zion Quarterly Review* 106 (April 1994): 9–18.

Jones, Absalom. "A Thanksgiving Sermon," in *Black Gospel/White Church*, ed. John M. Burgess. New York: Seabury, 1982.

Jones, Darryl L. "The Sermon as 'Art' of Resistance: A Comparative Analysis of the Rhetorics of the African-American Slave Preacher and the Preacher to the Hebrews." *Semeia*, no.79 (1997): 11–26.

Jones, Kirk Byron. "An Interview with Charles E. Booth." *The African American Pulpit* 4, no. 1 (Winter 2000–2001): 92–95.

———. "An Interview with E.V. Hill and H. Beecher Hicks, Jr." *The African American Pulpit* 3, no. 2 (Spring 2000): 121–27.

———. "An Interview with Jeremiah A. Wright, Jr. *The African-American Pulpit* 2, no. 2 (Spring 1999): 90–94.

———. "An Interview with Vashti M. McKenzie." *The African-American Pulpit* 3, no. 1 (Winter 1999): 88–93.

Jones, William Augustus. "An Anatomy of Forgiveness." *The African American Pulpit* 5, no. 1 (Winter 2001–2002): 82–87.

Kealing, H.T. "The Colored Ministers of the South—Their Preaching and Peculiarities." *AME Church Review* 1 (1884): 139–44.

Kelly, Leontine T.C. "Preaching in the Black Tradition," in *Women Ministries*, ed. Judith L. Weidman, 67–76. San Francisco: Harper & Row, 1985.

Kilgore, Thomas. "Preaching in the Black Church." *Christian Ministry* 19 (March–April 1988): 19–20.

King, Martin Luther, Jr. "I Have a Dream," in *American Rhetoric.* http://www.americanrhetoric.com/speeches/Ihaveadream.htm (accessed December 5, 2005).

Kinnon, Joy Bennett. "Pastor: Johnnie Colemon—The Many-Splendored Faces of Today's Black Woman." *Ebony,* March 1997.

Knight, Carolyn Ann. "Linking Texts with Contexts: The Biblical Sermon as Social Commentary," in *The Courage to Hope: From Black Suffering to Human Redemption,* ed. Quinton Dixie and Cornell West. Boston: Beacon Press, 1999.

Kyle, Sharon. "Truly, Madly, Deeply: Women's Experience of Preaching." *Anvil: An Anglican Evangelical Journal for Theology and Mission* 14 (1997): 254–61.

Lacewell, Melissa Harris. "Black Churches Liberation or Prosperity?" in *Sightings,* Martin Marty Center at the University of Chicago Divinity School, October 14, 2004.

"The Legacy of a Leader." *Michigan Chronicle,* October 17–23, 2001.

Lincoln, C. Eric, and Lawrence H. Mamiya. "The Performed Word and the Black Church," in *Readings in African American Church Music and Worship,* compiled and ed. by James Abbington, 39, 41. Chicago: GIA Publications, 2001.

Lischer, Richard. "The Word That Moves: The Preaching of Martin Luther King, Jr." *Theology Today* 46 (July 1989): 169–82.

Love, Emanuel K. "Emancipation Oration: Delivered by Rev. E.K. Love," in Savannah, Georgia, at the Emancipation Celebration at Augusta, Georgia, January 1, 1891, with introduction by Judson W. Lyons, Esq. Available at http://memory.loc.gov/CBI-Bin/Query/R?Ammem/murray:efield(DocidteLit(LCRBMRPTOBO8Dival) (accessed July 7, 2007).

———. "Mission of the Gospel Church: A Dedication Sermon by Rev. E.K. Love." Baltimore: J.F. Weishampel, Jr., 1880.

———. "A Sermon on Lynch Law and Raping Preached by Rev. E.K. Love," at First African Baptist Church, Savannah, Ga., of which he is pastor, November 5, 1893; Augusta: Georgia Baptist Print, 1894.

Luker, Ralph E. "Murder and Biblical Memory: The Legend of Vernon Johns." *Virginia Magazine of History and Biography* 112, no. 4.

Marrant, John. "A Journal of the Rev. John Marrant from August 18, 1785 to the 16th of March, 1790," to which are added two sermons; one preached on Ragged Island on Sabbath Day, the 27th Day of October, 1787; the other at Boston, in New England, on Thursday, the 24th Day of June, 1789. London: J. Taylor, 1790. Found at office of Commonwealth Library: The Bureau of the State of Pennsylvania.

Mason, Michael. "Captive and Client Labor and the Economy of the Bida Emirate, 1857–1901." *Journal of African American History* 14, no. 3: 459–60.

Massey, James Earl. "Thurman's Preaching: Substance and Style," in *God and Human Freedom: A Festschrift in Honor of Howard Thurman,* ed. Henry J. Young, 110–21. Richmond, VA: Friends United Press, 1983.

McClain, William B. "African American Preaching and the Bible: Biblical Authority or Biblical Literalism." *Journal of Religious Thought* 51 (Winter–Spring 1994–1995): 111–16.

———. "African American Preaching," in *The Renewal of Sunday Worship,* vol. 3, ed. Robert E. Webber, 317. Nashville, TN: Star Song Publishing Group, 1993.

———. "The 'Mystic Harmonies' of African-American Preaching." *Sewanee Theological Review* 39 (Easter 1996): 185–90.

McDowell, Wendy. "Bishop in a Pick-up Truck: First Woman AME Bishop Describes Her Work in Africa." *Harvard Gazette*, October 16, 2003. Available at http://news.harvard.edu/gazette/.

McGill, Jennifer. "Reverend Dr. Vashti Murphy McKenzie: First Woman Bishop in the AME Church." *ChickenBones: A Journal for Literary & Artistic African-American Themes*, http://www.nathanielturner.com/vashtimckenzie.htm (accessed May 2, 2005).

McGrory, Brian. "Rev. Ike and His Empire." *Boston Globe*, January 22, 1999.

McKenzie, Vashti Murphy. "Keep the Pressure On." *The African American Pulpit* 7, no. 4 (Fall 2004): 62–66.

Merriam, Alan P., and Caroline Card Wendt, eds. "The Black Sermon and the Communication of Innovation," in *Discourse in Ethnomusicology II: A Tribute to Alan Merriam*, 173–204. Bloomington, IN: Ethnomusicology Publishing Group, 1981.

"Military Sees Big Decline in Black Enlistees." *Boston Globe*, October 7, 2007.

Miller, Keith D. "Martin Luther King, Jr., and the Black Folk Pulpit." *Journal of American History* 78 (June 1991): 120–23.

Mitchell, Henry H. "African-American Preaching: The Future of a Rich Tradition." *Interpretation* 51, no. 4 (October 1997): 371–83.

———. "Black Preaching." *Review & Expositor* 70 (Summer 1973): 331–40.

———. "The 'New' Phenomenon of Black Preaching." *Homiletic* 4 (1979): 6–10.

Morris, E.C. "Sermons, Addresses and Reminiscences and Important Correspondence, with a Picture Gallery of Eminent Ministers and Scholars." Nashville, TN: National Baptist Publishing Board, 1901.

Moss, Otis, Jr. "A Prophetic Witness in an Anti-Prophetic Age." *The African American Pulpit* 7, no. 4 (Fall 2004): 68–72.

Moyd, Olin P. "Elements in Black Preaching." *Journal of Religious Thought* 30, no. 1 (1973): 52–62.

Newman, Richard, ed. " 'The Presence of the Lord': An Unpublished Sermon by Lemuel Haynes." Boston: *Bulletin of the Congregational Library* 32 (Fall 1980): 4–13.

Niles, Lyndrey A. "Rhetorical Characteristics of Traditional Black Preaching." *Journal of Black Studies* 15, no. 1 (September 1984): 41–52.

O'Neal, Eddie S. "An Embarrassed Stammering." *The African-American Pulpit* 3, no. 1 (Winter 1999): 83–87.

"Patriotism Is Not Enough." *Sojourners Magazine* 32, no. 1 (January–February 2003): 20–25.

Patterson, Gilbert Earl. "God's Cure for Racism and Loneliness." *The African American Pulpit* 3, no. 4 (Fall 2000).

Perry, Dwight. "Preaching in the Black Church," in *Breaking Down Barriers: A Black Evangelical Explains the Black Church*, 95–101. Grand Rapids, MI: Baker Books, 1998.

Pitts, Walter F. "West African Poetics in Black Preaching Style." *American Speech* 64, no. 2 (1989): 137–49.

"Preachers Turn Out to Honor Samuel Proctor." *New York Times*, May 31, 1997.

Rawick, George P., ed. "The American Slave: A Composite Autobiography." Westport: Greenwood Publishing Company, 1972: 36–38; reprint of 1941 edition. (Section of a narrative from a former slave then living in Kentucky, quoting a sermon found in a scrapbook dated 1839, recorded by the Federal Writers' Project of the Works Progress Administration in the 1930s).

"Rev. Dr. Pauli Murray." *Ebony* (September 1979).

"The Reverend Frederick Sampson, II." *Detroit News* (MI), November 7, 2001, section S.

Richards, Phillip M. "Nationalist Themes in the Preaching of Jupiter Hammon." *Early American Literature* 25, no. 2. (1990): 123–38.

Sampson, Frederick G., II. "The Death of Hope." *The African American Pulpit* 5, no. 1 (Winter 2001–2002): 104–7.

Sanders, Cheryl J. "The Woman as Preacher." *Journal of Religious Thought* 43, no. 1 (Spring–Summer 1986): 6–23.

Sandidge, O'Neal Cleaven. "The Uniqueness of Black Preaching." *Journal of Religious Thought* 49 (Summer–Fall 1992): 91–97.

Schier, Tracy, ed. "A Conversation with Bettye Collier-Thomas." *Initiatives in Religion* 7, no. 2 (Spring 1998): 3–7.

Schneider, Gilbert. "Daniel Emmett's Negro Sermons and Hymns: An Inventory." *Ohio History* 85, no. 1 (1976): 67–83.

Scott, Manuel L., Sr. "Heavenly Grace and Human Response." *The African American Pulpit* 7, no. 1 (Winter 2003–2004).

"Sermons and Preaching," in *The Oxford Companion to African American Literature,* ed. William L. Andrews, Frances Smith Foster, and Trudier Harris, 648–52. New York: Oxford University Press, 1997.

Sevitch, Benjamin. "When Black Gods Preached on Earth: The Heavenly Appeals of Prophet Cherry, Daddy Grace, and Father Divine." *Journal of Communication and Religion* 19, no. 1 (March 1996): 26–36.

Seymour, William J. "Receive Ye the Holy Ghost." *The Apostolic Faith* 1, no. 5 (January 1907).

Shannon, David T. "'An Ante-Bellum Sermon': A Resource for an African American Hermeneutic," in *Stony the Road We Trod*, ed. Cain Hope Felder, 98–123. Minneapolis, MN: Fortress Press, 1991.

Simmons, Martha. "An Interview with Claudette Copeland." *The African American Pulpit* 4, no. 1 (Winter 2001–2002): 177–122.

———. "Sermon Help: Focus, Focus, Focus." *African American Pulpit* 3, no. 2 (Spring 2000): 129–32.

Spencer, Jon Michael. *Protest and Praise: Sacred Music of Black Religions*. Minneapolis, MN: Fortress Press, 1990.

Starling, Kelly. "Why People, Especially Black Women, Are Talking about Bishop T.D. Jakes." *Ebony*, January 2001.

Stewart, Maria. "Mrs. Stewart's Farewell Address to Her Friends in the City of Boston," in *African American Religious History: A Documentary Witness,* ed. Milton C. Sernett, 203. Durham: Duke University Press, 1999.

Taylor, Gardner C. "Preaching and the Power of Words: An Interview." *Preaching* (January–February 1994): 2–8.

———. "A President of Preaching: Eulogy of Sandy F. Ray." *The African American Pulpit* 4, no. 1 (Winter 2000–2001): 80–84.

Theide, Barbara. "From the Margin to the Ministry." *Charlotte Observer* (NC), April 16, 2005.

Tilmon, L. "A Brief Miscellaneous Narrative of the More Early Part of the Life of L. Tilmon, Pastor of a Colored Methodist Congregational Church in the City of New York, Written by Himself." Jersey City: W.W. & L.A. Pratt, 1853, 30–39.

Tindley, Charles. "Heaven's Christmas Tree." *The African American Pulpit* 5, no. 1 (Great Revivalists I; Winter 2001–2002): 50–55.

Tinney, James S. "Miracle of Black Preaching." *Christianity Today* 20 (January 30, 1976): 14–16.

Trulear, Harold Dean, and Russell E. Richey. "Two Sermons by Brother Carper: 'The Eloquent Negro Preacher.'" *American Baptist Quarterly* 6, no. 1 (March 1987): 3–16.

Turnbull, Ralph G. *A History of Preaching: From the Close of the Nineteenth Century to the Middle of the Twentieth Century*. Grand Rapids, MI: Baker Book House, 1974: 201–9.

Turner, William C. "The Musicality of Black Preaching: A Phenomenology." *Journal of Black Sacred Music* 2 (Spring 1988): 21–34.

Wade, Jennifer. "Hearing the Voice of the Most Marginalized in Theology and Ethics: A Conversation with Rev. Dr. Katie Cannon." *The Bulletin, Voice of the Washington Theological Consortium*, February/March 2004, http://www.washtheocon.org/feb2004.pdf.

Walker, James Perry. "Rev. Louis Cole, Black Baptist Circuit Preacher, 1901–1981." *Southern Quarterly* 23, no. 3 (Spring 1985): 49–69.

Warner, Robert A. "Amos Gerry Beman—1812–1874, a Memoir on a Forgotten Leader." *Journal of Negro History* 22, no. 2 (April 1937): 200–221.

Warren, Timothy S. "The Hum: Call and Response in African American Preaching." *Bibliotheca Sacra* 155 (April–June 1998): 251–52.

Weems, Renita. "Not . . . Yet." *The African American Pulpit* 7, no. 4 (Fall 2004): 79–84.

Williams, Jasper, Jr. "God at the Midnight Ball." *The African American Pulpit* 6, no. 2 (Spring 2003): 97–102.

Williams, Jeane. "Loose the Woman and Let Her Go! Pennsylvania's African American Women Preachers." *Pennsylvania Heritage Society* 22, no. 1 (1996): 4–9.

Williams, Robert C. "Worship and Anti-Structure in Thurman's Vision of the Sacred." *Journal of the Interdenominational Theological Center* 14 (Fall 1986/Spring 1987).

"A Working Man's Remarks on a Sermon Written by a Clergyman, Entitled: The Rights of Women to Preach: Considered in the Light of Nature, History, and Religion." Author unknown. Newcastle-upon-Tyne: printed by Thomas Fordyce, 1800.

Yoder, Don. "Trance-Preaching in the United States." *Pennsylvania Folklore* 18, no. 2 (1968): 12–18.

## *General Works*

Abarry, Abu Shardow. "Mpai: Liberation Oratory," in *The African Aesthetic: Keeper of the Traditions,* ed. Kariamu Welsh-Asante, 85–101. Westport, CT: Praeger, 1994.

Abbington, James, ed. *Readings in African American Church Music and Worship.* Chicago: GIA Publications, Inc., 2001.

Abernathy, Ralph David. *And the Walls Came Tumbling Down: An Autobiography.* New York: Harper & Row, 1989.

Abrahams, Roger D. "Patterns of Performance in the British West Indies," in *Afro-American Anthropology: Contemporary Perspectives,* ed. Norman E. Whitten Jr. and John Szwed, 163–80. New York: Free Press, 1970. Reprinted in Roger D. Abrahams, *The Man-of-Words in the West Indies: Performance and the Emergence of Creole Culture,* 1–20. Baltimore: Johns Hopkins Press, 1983.

———. "Traditions of Eloquence in the West Indies." *Journal of Inter-American Studies and World Affairs* 12 (1970): 505–27. Reprinted in Roger D. Abrahams, *The Man-of-Words in the West Indies: Performance and the Emergence of Creole Culture,* 21–39. Baltimore: Johns Hopkins Press, 1983.

"Adams, Charles G.," in *Who's Who among African Americans,* 18th ed. Detroit: Gale Group, 2005.

Albert, Ethel M. "'Rhetoric,' 'Logic,' and 'Poetics' in Burundi Culture Patterning of Speech Behavior." *American Anthropologist* 66 (October 1964): 35–54.

Allen, William Francis, Charles Pickard Ware, and Lucy McKim Garrison, eds. *Slave Songs of the United States,* 1867. Reprint, New York: Dover Publications, 1995.

Anderson, Rich. "The United States Army in World War II: Manpower, Replacements, and the Segregated Army," in *Military History Online,* http://www.militaryhistoryonline.com/wwii/usarmy/manpower.aspx (accessed July 27, 2007).

Andrews, Dale. *Practical Theology for Black Churches: Bridging Black Theology and African American Folk Religion.* Louisville, KY: Westminster John Knox Press, 2002.

Andrews, William A. *To Tell a Free Story: The First Century of Afro-American Autobiography, 1760–1865.* Urbana: University of Illinois Press, 1986.

Andrews, William L. *Sisters of the Spirit: Three Black Women's Autobiographies of the Nineteenth Century.* Bloomington: Indiana University Press, 1986.

———, ed. Oxford *Companion to African American Literature.* London: Oxford University Press, 1997.

Appiah, Kwame Anthony and Henry Louis Gates Jr. *Africana: The Encyclopedia of the African and African American Experience.* 5 vols. New York: Oxford University Press, 2005.

Atwater, Deborah F. "A Dilemma of Black Communication Scholars: The Challenge of Finding New Rhetorical Tools." *Journal of Black Studies* 15 (1984): 5–16.

Austin, Allan. "Islamic Identities in Africans in North America in the Days of Slavery, 1731–1865." *Islam et Sociétés au Sud du Sahara,* France (1993): 205–19.

Austin, Deborah A. "In the Middle of Everyday Life: The Spaces Black Clergywomen Create," in *Perspectives on Womanist Theology,* ed. Jacquelyn Grant. Atlanta: Interdenominational Theological Press, 1995.

"Azusa Street Revival," in *Dictionary of Pentecostal and Charismatic Movements,* ed.

Stanley M. Burgess and Gary B. McGee. Grand Rapids, MI: Zondervan Publishing House, 1988, 36.

Bacote, Samuel William, ed. *Who's Who Among the Colored Baptists of the United States.* Kansas City: Franklin Hudson Publishing, 1913.

Baer, Hans, and Merrill Singer. *African-American Religion in the Twentieth Century.* Knoxville: University of Tennessee Press, 1992.

Baldwin, James. "Go Tell It on the Mountain," in *James Baldwin: Early Novels and Stories.* New York: Knopf, 1953. Reprint, New York: Library of America, 1998: 1–216.

Baldwin, Lewis V. "Festivity and Celebration in a Black Methodist Tradition, 1813–1981." *Methodist History* 20 (July 1982): 183–91.

———. "'Invisible' Strands in African Methodism: African Union Methodist Protestant and Union American Methodist Episcopal Churches, 1805–1980." Metuchen, NJ: Scarecrow Press, 1983.

"Barbara Harris," in *An Encyclopedia of African American Christian Heritage,* ed. Marvin A. McMickle. Valley Forge, PA: Judson Press, 2002.

Barrett, Leonard. *Soul Force: African Heritage in Afro-American Religion.* Garden City, NY: Anchor Books, 1974.

Basker, James G. *Amazing Grace: An Anthology of Poems about Slavery, 1660–1810.* New Haven, CT: Yale University Press, 2002.

Berry, Mary Frances, and John W. Blassingame. "Family and Church: Enduring Institutions," in *Long Memory: The Black Experience in America.* New York: Oxford University Press, 1982, 70–113.

Bethel, Elizabeth Rauh. *The Roots of African-American Identity: Memory and History in Free Antebellum Communities.* New York: St. Martin's, 1997.

Bibb, Stephanie F., ed. *Women's Liberation Jesus Style: Messages of Spirituality and Wisdom.* Downers Grove, IL: InterVarsity Press, 2002.

Billingsley, Andrew. *Mighty Like a River: The Black Church and Social Reform.* New York: Oxford University Press, 1999.

Blassingame, John. *The Slave Community: Plantation Life in the Antebellum South,* rev. ed. New York: Oxford University Press, 1979.

Booth, William D. *Call to Greatness: The Story of the Founding of the Progressive National Baptist Convention.* Lawrenceville, VA: Brunswick Publishing, 2001.

Borden, Karen Wells. "Black Rhetoric in the 1960s: Socio-historical Perspectives." *Journal of Black Studies* 3 (1973): 423–31.

Bowen, Nancy R. "The Daughters of Your People: Female Prophets in Ezekiel 13:17–23." *Journal of Biblical Literature* 118 (1999): 417–33.

Boyer, Horace Clarence. *How Sweet the Sound: The Golden Age of Gospel.* Washington, DC: Elliot and Clark, 1995.

———. "Shirley Caesar," in *Black Women in American: A Historical Encyclopedia,* ed. Darlene Hine, Elsa Brown, Rosalyn Terbory-Penn. Indianapolis: Indiana University Press, 1993, 214.

Branch, Taylor. *Parting the Waters: America in the King Years, 1954–1963.* New York: Simon & Schuster, 1988.

———. *Pillar of Fire: America in the King Years, 1963–1965.* New York: Simon & Schuster, 1998.

Brawley, Benjamin. *Negro Builders and Heroes*. Chapel Hill: University of North Carolina Press, 1937.

Breitman, George. *The Last Year of Malcolm X: The Evolution of a Revolutionary*. New York: Pathfinder, 1976.

———. *Malcolm X Speaks: Selected Speeches and Statements*. New York: Grove Weidenfeld, 1965.

Breitman, George, Herman Porter, and Baxter Smith. *The Assassination of Malcolm X*. New York: Pathfinder, 1976.

Browning, Robert. *Asolando; Fancies and Facts*. Boston: Houghton, Mifflin and Company, 1982.

Brunner, Marta L., and Roxanne Mountford. "Tropes of Conversion: American Religious Discourse in the Feminist Imaginary," http://www.u.arizona.edu/~roxanne/RhetAnalysis/tropes3.html (accessed September 1, 2005).

Burgess, Stanley M., and Edward M. Vander Maas, eds. *The New International Dictionary of Pentecostal and Charismatic Movements*. Grand Rapids, MI: Zondervan, 2001.

Burgess, Stanley M., and Gary B. McGee, eds. *Dictionary of Pentecostal and Charismatic Movements*. Grand Rapids, MI: Regency Reference Library, 1988.

Burkett, Randall K. "The Baptist Church in the Years of Crisis: J.C. Austin and Pilgrim Baptist Church, 1926–1950," in *African-American Christianity: Essays in History*, ed. Paul E. Johnson. Berkeley: University of California Press, 1994, 134–58.

Burnam, Kenneth. *God Comes to America: Father Divine*. Boston: Lambeth Press, 1979.

Burnstine, Lyn. *Anita Trueman Pickett: New Thought Preacher*. Boston: Skinner House Books, 2000.

Burroughs, Nannie H. "Report of the Work of Baptist Women," in *African American Religious History: A Documentary Witness*, ed. Milton C. Sernett. Durham, NC: Duke University Press, 1999, 376–402.

Butler, Jon. "Africans' Religions in British America, 1650–1840." *Church History* 68, no. 1 (1999): 118–27.

Calhoon, Robert M. "The African Heritage, Slavery and Evangelical Christianity Among American Blacks, 1700–1870." *Fides et Historia* 21, no. 2 (1989): 61–66.

Calhoun-Brown, Allison. "No Respect of Persons, Religion, Churches and Gender Issues in the African American community." *Women and Politics* 20, no. 3 (Summer 1999): 27–44.

Carretta, Vincent, ed. *Unchained Voices: An Anthology of Black Authors in the English-Speaking World of the Eighteenth Century*. Lexington: University Press of Kentucky, 1996.

Carson, Clayborne. "Martin Luther King, Jr., and the African-American Social Gospel," in *African-American Christianity: Essays in History*, ed. Paul E. Johnson. Berkeley: University of California Press, 1994, 159–77.

Carter, Lawrence Edward, Sr., ed. *Walking Integrity: Benjamin Elijah Mays, Mentor to Martin Luther King, Jr.* Macon, GA: Mercer University Press, 1998.

Cayton, Horace A., and St. Clair Drake. *Black Metropolis: A Study of Negro Life in a Northern City*, 4th ed. Chicago: University of Chicago Press, 1993.

Chambers, T.M. "Educational Sermons, Addresses, and Subjects for Baccalaureate Commencement and Other Occasions." Self-published, 1949.

Chenu, Bruno. *The Trouble I've Seen: The Big Book of Negro Spirituals*. Valley Forge, PA: Judson Press, 2003.

Childs, Lydia Maria. "Letters from New York." *National Anti-Slavery Standard* 2, no. 13 (December 9, 1841): 107.

Chireau, Yvonne Patricia. "The Bible and African American Folklore," in *African American and the Bible: Sacred Text and Social Textures*, ed. Vincent Wimbush. New York: Continuum, 2000, 673–81.

Clarke, Erskine. *Wrestlin' Jacob: A Portrait of Religion in the Old South*. Atlanta: John Knox Press, 1979.

Clarkson, Thomas. *The History of the Rise, Progress and Accomplishment of the Abolition of the African Slave Trade by the British Parliament*. 2 vols. Reprint, London: Frank Cass, 1968.

Clemmons, I.C. "Charles Harrison Mason," in *Dictionary of Pentecostal and Charismatic Movements*, ed. Stanley M. Burgess and Gary B. McGee. Grand Rapids, MI: Zondervan, 1988.

Clifton, Catherine. *Harriet Tubman: The Road to Freedom*. New York: Little, Brown, 2004.

Clinton, George Wylie. "Third Paper: To What Extent is the Negro Pulpit Uplifting the Race?" in *Twentieth Century Negro Literature, or A Cyclopedia of Thought on the Vital Topics Relating to the American Negro by One Hundred of America's Greatest Negroes*, ed. Daniel W. Culp. Atlanta: J. L. Nichols, 1902. Reprint, New York: Arno Press, 1969, 115–20.

Coates, Simon. "Regendering Radeund? Fortunatus, Baudonivia and the Problem of Female Sanctity in Merovingian Gaul," in *Gender and Christian Religion: Studies in Church History*, vol. 34., ed. R.N. Swanson. Suffolk, Great Britain: Boydell Press, 1988, 37–50.

Cobbins, Otha B. *History of the Church of Christ (Holiness) USA, 1895–1965*. New York: Vantage Press, 1996.

Cocke, Sarah Johnson. "The Rooster and the Washpot." *Saturday Evening Post* 179 (June 2, 1917): 77, 81.

Colledge, Edmund, et al. *Julian of Norwich: The Classics of Western Spirituality*. New York: Paulist Press, 1978.

Colton, Elizabeth. *The Jackson Phenomenon: The Man, the Power, the Message*. New York: Doubleday, 1989.

Cone, James H. "Black Theology, Black Churches, and Black Women," in *Out of the Revolution: The Development of Africana Studies*, ed. Delores P. Aldridge and Carlene Young. Lanham, MD: Lexington Books, 2000.

———. *Martin & Malcolm & America: A Dream or a Nightmare*. Maryknoll, NY: Orbis Books, 2002.

Coppin, Levi Jenkins. *Unwritten History*. Philadelphia: AME Book Concern, 1919. Reprint. New York: Negro Universities Press, 1968.

Coquet, Cécile. "My God Is a Time-God: How African American Folk Oratory Speaks of Time," in *African Americans and the Bible*. New York: Continuum, 2000, 514–36.

Costanzo, Angelo. *Surprising Narrative: Olaudah Equiano and the Beginnings of Black Autobiography*. New York: Greenwood Press, 1987.

Coulter, Merton. "Henry M. Turner: A Georgia Negro, Preacher-Politician." *Georgia Historical Quarterly* 48, no. 4 (1964): 371–410.

Cowman, Krista, "'We Intend to Show What Our Lord Has Done for Women': The Liverpool League for Women's Suffrage, 1914–18," in *Gender and Christian Religion*, ed. R.N. Swanson, 475–86; *Studies in Church History*, vol. 34. Great Britain: Boydell Press, 1998. (See esp. page 485, "Woman's Church" in Wallasey, England, 1914.)

Cromwell, John W. "The Earlier Churches and Preachers," in *The Negro Church: Report of a Social Study Made Under the Direction of Atlanta University*, ed. W. E. Burghardt DuBois. Atlanta: Atlanta University Press, 1903, 30–35.

Crowther, Edward R. "Charles Octavius Boothe: An Alabama Apostle of Uplift." *Journal of Negro History* 78, no. 2 (1993): 110–16.

Cummings, Melbourne S. "Problems of Researching Black Rhetoric." *Journal of Black Studies* 2 (1971): 503–8.

Cummings, Melbourne S., and Jack L. Daniel. "The Study of African American Rhetoric," in *The Rhetoric of Western Thought*, ed. James L. Golden, Goodwin F. Berquist, and William E. Coleman, 6th ed. Dubuque: Kendall/Hunt Publishing Co., 1997, 360–85.

Curtin, Phillip D. *The Atlantic Slave Trade: A Census*. Madison: University of Wisconsin Press, 1969.

Curtis, Edward E., IV. *Islam in Black America: Identity, Liberation, and Difference in African-American Islamic Thought*. Albany: State University of New York Press, 2002.

Dake, Finis J. *The Dake Annotated Reference Bible*. Lawrenceville, GA: Dake Publishing, 2001.

Dance, Daryl Cumber. *400 Years of African American Folklore*. New York: W. W. Norton & Company, 2002.

Daniel, Jack L., and Geneva Smitherman. "How I Got Over: Communication Dynamics in the Black Community." *Quarterly Journal of Speech* 62 (February 1976): 26–39.

Davenport, Frederick Morgan. *Primitive Traits in Religious Revivals: A Study in Mental and Social Evolution*. New York: Macmillan Company, 1905. Reprint, New York: AMS Press, 1972.

———. "The Religion of the American Negro." *Contemporary Review* 88 (September 1905): 369–75.

Davis, Charles T., and Henry Louis Gates Jr. *The Slave's Narrative*. Oxford: Oxford University Press, 1985.

Davis, I.D. "Fourth Paper: To What Extent is the Negro Pulpit Uplifting the Race?" in *Twentieth Century Negro Literature, or a Cyclopedia of Thought on the Vital Topics Relating to the American Negro by One Hundred of America's Greatest Negroes*, ed. Daniel W. Culp. Atlanta, GA: J. L. Nichols, 1902. Reprint, New York: Arno Press, 1969, 124.

Davis, Ruby I. *And He Called a Young Woman to Preach*. New York: Carlton, 1976.

Davis, Sidney Fant. *Mississippi Negro Lore.* Jackson, TN: McCowat-Mercer, 1914, 35.

"The Dean of Black Preachers: He Didn't Want to Be a Preacher," in *The Irresistible Urge to Preach: A Collection of African American Call Stories*, ed. William H. Myers. Atlanta, GA: Aaron Press, 1992.

"Divine, Father." *Columbia Electronic Encyclopedia*, 6th ed. Columbia University Press, 2005. Available at http://infoplease.com/ce6/people/A0815667.html.

DuBois, William Edward Burghardt. *The Negro.* New York: Henry Holt Company, 1915. Reprint, New York: Oxford University Press, 1970, 254.

———, ed. *The Negro Church: Report of a Social Study Made under the Direction of Atlanta University; Together with the Proceedings of the Eighth Conference for the Study of Negro Problems held at Atlanta University May 26, 1903.* Atlanta University Publications 8. Atlanta: Atlanta University Press, 1903. Reprint, New York: Arno Press and *New York Times,* 1968, 212. Available at http://www.h-net.mus.edu/reviews/showrev.cgi?path=204761094326026.

———. "One Christmas at Shiloh." *The Heart of Happy Hollow.* New York: Dodd, Mead & Company, 1904, 309. Reprint, Freeport, NY: Books for Libraries Press, 1970.

———. "The Religion of the American Negro." *New World: A Quarterly Review of Religion, Ethics, and Theology* 9 (December 1900): 614–25.

Dunbar, Paul Laurence. *The Collected Poetry of Paul Laurence Dunbar*, ed. Joanne M. Braxton. Charlottesville: University Press of Virginia, 1993.

———. *The Complete Poems of Paul Laurence Dunbar.* New York: Dodd Mead and Company, 1993.

———. "The Fruitful Sleeping of the Rev. Elisha Edwards." *The Strength of Gideon, and other Stories.* New York: Dodd, Mead & Company, 1900: 362. Reprint, New York: Arno Press and *New York Times,* 1969.

DuPree, Sherry Sherrod. *Biographical Dictionary of African-American Holiness: Pentecostals, 1880–1990.* Washington, DC: Middle Atlantic Regional Press, 1989.

Dyson, Michael Eric. *I May Not Get There with You: The True Martin Luther King, Jr.* New York: Free Press, 2000.

Earl, Riggins R. "The Black Church, Black Women, and the Call." *Liturgy* 7, no. 4 (Spring 1989): 87–95.

Eisen, Ute E. "Apostles" and "Prophets," in *Women Officeholders in Early Christianity: Epigraphical and Literary Studies*, trans. Linda M. Maloney. Collegeville: Liturgical Press, 2000: 47–87.

Elaw, Zilpha. *Memoirs of the Life, Religious Experience, Ministerial Travels and Labours of Mrs. Zilpha Elaw, an American Female of Colour; Together with Some Account of the Great Religious Revivals in America (Written by Herself).* London: by the Authoress, 1846. Reprinted in *Sisters of the Spirit: Three Black Women's Autobiographies of the Nineteenth Century*, ed. William L. Andrews, *Religion in North America* series. Bloomington: Indiana University Press, 1986, 49–160.

Embree, Edwin R. *13 Against the Odds.* New York: Viking Press, 1944.

English, James W. *Handyman of the Lord: The Life and Ministry of the Reverend William Holmes Borders.* New York: Meredith Press, 1967.

———. *The Prophet of Wheat Street: The Story of William Holmes Borders, a Man Who Refused to Fail*. Elgin, IL: Cook Publishing, 1973.

Erikson, Erik. *Dimensions of a New Identity*. New York: W. W. Norton & Company, 1979.

Essien-Udom, Essien Udosen. *Black Nationalism: A Search for An Identity in America*. Chicago: University of Chicago Press, 1995.

Estes, Phoebe Beckner. "The Reverend Peter Vinegar." *Southern Folklore Quarterly* 23, no. 4 (December 1959): 239–52.

Faduma, Orishatukeh. "The Defects of the Negro Church: Occasional Paper No. 10." *The American Negro Academy Occasional Papers*, 1–22. Washington, DC: Published by the Academy, 1904. Reprint, New York: Arno Press and *New York Times*, 1969.

Farrakhan, Louis. "Minister Farrakhan Challenges Black Men: Transcript from Minister Louis Farrakhan's Remarks at the Million Man March," CNN, October 17, 1995. http://www-cgi.cnn.com/US/9510/megamarch/10-16/transcript/index.html.

Fauset, Arthur Huff. *Black Gods of the Metropolis: Negro Religious Cults in the Urban North*. Philadelphia: University of Pennsylvania Press, 1971.

Ferris, William H. "A Historical and Psychological Account of the Genesis and Development of the Negro's Religion." *AME Church Review* 20 (1904): 343–53.

———. "The Old Time and the New Time Negroes." *American Missionary Magazine*, n.s., 62 (October 1908): 359–60.

Fish, Beverly Ann. "Sojourner Truth: Crusader for Women's Rights," in *Black Women in American History*, vol. 2, ed. Darlene Clark Hine. Brooklyn, NY: Carlson Publishing, Inc., 1990, 386–94.

Fisher, Miles Mark. *The Master's Slave: Elijah John Fisher: A Biography by His Son, Miles Mark Fisher*. Philadelphia: Judson Press, 1922. Reprint, microfiche, Chicago: Library Resources, 1971.

Fletcher, Anthony. "Beyond the Church: Women's Spiritual Experience at Home and in the Community, 1600–1900," in *Gender and Christian Religion*, ed. R.N. Swanson, 187–203; *Studies in Church History*, vol. 34. Suffolk, Great Britain: Boydell Press, 1998. (See esp. 201–3, Sarah Wight and Anna Trapnel.)

Fluker, Walter Earl, and Catherine Tumber, eds. *A Strange Freedom: The Best of Howard Thurman on Religious Experience and Public Life*. Boston: Beacon Press, 1998.

Foley, Albert S., "Healy, Patrick Francis," in *Dictionary of American Negro Biography*, ed. Rayford W. Logan and Michael R. Winston. New York: W. W. Norton & Company, 1982, 304–5.

Foner, Philip S. *From Slavery to Socialism: George Washington Woodbey, Black Socialist Preacher*. Westport, CT: Greenwood Press, 1998: 65–92.

Foner, Philip S., and Robert James Branham, eds. *Lift Every Voice: African American Oratory, 1787–1900*. Tuscaloosa: University of Alabama Press, 1998.

Franklin, John Hope, and Alfred A. Moss Jr. *From Slavery to Freedom: A History of Negro Americans*, 6th ed. New York: Alfred A. Knopf, 1988.

Franklin, Robert Michael. "The Safest Place on Earth: The Culture of Black Congregations," in *American Congregations*, ed. James P. Wind and James W. Lewis, 257–97. Chicago: University of Chicago Press, 1994. (See esp. 264–75.)

Frey, Sylvia R., and Betty Wood. "Come Shouting to Zion: African American Protestantism," in *American South and British Caribbean to 1830.* Chapel Hill: University of North Carolina Press, 1998.

Fry Brown, Teresa L. *God Don't Like Ugly: African-American Women Handing on Spiritual Values.* Nashville, TN: Abingdon Press, 2000.

Frye, Nancy Kettering. *An Uncommon Woman: The Life and Times of Sarah Righter Major.* Elgin, IL: Brethren Press, 1997.

Fullinwider, S.P. *The Mind and Mood of Black America Twentieth-Century Thought.* Homewood, IL: Dorsey Press, 1969.

Gardell, Mattias. *In the Name of Elijah Muhammad: Louis Farrakhan and the Nation of Islam.* Durham, NC: Duke University Press, 1996.

Garrow, David J. *Bearing the Cross: Martin Luther King, Jr., and the Southern Christian Leadership Conference.* New York: Quill, 1986.

Gates, Henry Louis, Jr., and Cornel West. *The African American Century: How Black Americans Have Shaped Our Century.* New York: Free Press, 2000.

Gates, Henry Louis, Jr., and E. Higginbotham. *African-American Lives.* New York: Oxford University Press, 2004.

Gates, Henry Louis, Jr., and Nellie Y. McKay, eds. *The Norton Anthology of African-American Literature.* New York: W. W. Norton & Company, 1997.

Gaustaud, Edwin Scott. *A Religious History of America*, rev. ed. San Francisco: HarperSan Francisco, 1990.

Genovese, Eugene. *Roll, Jordan, Roll: The World the Slaves Made.* New York: Vintage, 1972.

George, Carol V.R. *Segregated Sabbaths: Richard Allen and the Emergence of Independent Black Churches, 1760–1840.* New York: Oxford University Press, 1973.

Gilkes, Cheryl Townsend. *If It Wasn't for the Women—: Black Women's Experience and Womanist Culture in Church Community.* Maryknoll, NY: Orbis, 2001.

———. "The Politics of 'Silence': Dual-Sex Political Systems and Women's Traditions of Conflict in African-American Religion," in *African-American Christianity Essays in History*, ed. Paul E. Johnson. Berkeley: University of California Press, 1994, 80–110.

———. " 'Some Mother's Son and Some Father's Daughter': Gender and Biblical Language in Afro-Christian Worship Tradition," in *Shaping New Vision: Gender and Values in American Culture*, ed. Clarissa Atkinson, Constance H. Buchanan, and Margaret R. Miles. Harvard Women's Studies in Religion. Ann Arbor: University of Michigan Institute Research Press, 1987, 73–99.

———. "Together and in Harness: Women's Traditions in the Sanctified Church," in *Signs, Communities of Women* 10, no. 4 (Summer 1985): 685.

Gilyard, Keith, and Anissa Wardi, eds. *African American Literature.* New York: Pearson and Longman, 2004.

Goldman, Peter. *The Death and Life of Malcolm X.* Urbana: University of Illinois Press, 1979.

Goldsborough, Edmund K. *Ole Mars An' Ole Miss.* Washington, DC: National Publishing Company, 1900. Reprint, Freeport, NY: Books for Libraries Press, 1972.

Goldstein, Walter. "The Natural Harmonic and Rhythmic Sense of the Negro." *Music Teacher's National Association Proceedings,* Series 12 (1918): 29–30.

Gomes, Peter J. *The Good Book: Reading the Bible with Mind and Heart.* San Francisco: Harper San Francisco, 2002.

———. "Outer Turmoil, Inner Strength," in *9.11.01: African American Leaders Respond to an American Tragedy*, ed. Martha Simmons and Frank A. Thomas. Valley Forge, PA: Judson Press, 2001.

Gomez, Michael A. *Black Crescent: The Experience and Legacy of African Muslims in the Americas.* Cambridge: Cambridge University Press, 2005.

———. *Exchanging Our Country Marks: The Transformation of African Identities in the Colonial and Antebellum South.* Chapel Hill: University of North Carolina Press, 1998: 280–81.

Gomez-Jefferson, Annetta Louise. *The Sage of Tawawa: Reverdy Cassius Ransom, 1861–1859.* Kent, OH: Kent State University Press, 2002.

Goodson, Glenda. *Bishop Charles Harrison Mason and Those Sanctified Women.* Lancaster, TX: HCM Publishing, 2002.

Grant, Jacquelyn. "Black Theology and the Black Woman," in *Words of Fire: An Anthology of African-American Feminist Thought*, ed. Beverly Guy-Sheftall. New York: New Press, 1995; originally published in *Black Theology: A Documentary History, 1966–1979*, ed. S. Welmore and J. Cone. Maryknoll, NY: Orbis, 1979.

———, ed. *Perspectives on Womanist Theology.* Atlanta: ITC Press, 1995.

Green, Teresa. "The African-American Church Experience in Black and White Denominations: A Historical Profile of Political Differences." *Michigan Academician* 32, no. 4 (2000): 385–410.

Gregory, Jeremy. "Gender and the Clerical Profession in England, 1660–1850," in *Gender and Christian Religion,* ed. R.N. Swanson, 235–71; *Studies in Church History*, vol. 34. Suffolk, Great Britain: Boydell Press, 1998.

Griffiths, Leonard. *Illusions of Our Culture.* London: Hodder & Stoughton, 1969.

Hale, Thomas A. *Griots and Griottes: Masters of Words and Music.* Bloomington: Indiana University Press, 1998.

Haley, Alex. *The Autobiography of Malcolm X.* New York: Ballantine Books, 1964.

Haley, James T., comp., and Booker T. Washington. *Afro-American Encyclopedia: Thoughts, Doings, and Sayings of the Race.* Nashville, TN: Winston-Derek Publishers, 1992.

Harlan, Antonio. *From Slavery to Salvation.* Bloomington, IN: First Books Library, 2002.

Harley, Sharon. *The Timetables of African American History.* New York: Touchstone, 1995.

Harris, Michael. *The Rise of Gospel Blues: The Music of Thomas Andrew Dorsey in the Urban Church.* New York: Oxford University Press, 1992.

Harris, R. Laird, Gleason L. Archer, and Bruce K. Waltke, eds. *Theological Wordbook of the Old Testament.* Chicago: Moody Publishers, 2000.

Harrison, Daniel W. "Southern Protestantism and the Negro, 1860–1865." *North Carolina Historical Review* 41, no. 3 (1964): 338–59.

Harrison, Milmon F. *Righteous Riches: The Word of Faith Movement in Contemporary African American Religion.* New York: Oxford University Press, 2005.

Harrison, Paige M., and Jennifer C. Karberg. "Bureau of Justice Statistics Bulletin:

Prison and Jail Inmates at Midyear 2002." U.S. Department of Justice, April 2003. http://www.csdp.org/research/pjim02.pdf.

Harrison, William P., ed. *When the Spider Danced: The Gospel Among the Slaves.* Nashville, TN: Alland, 1893.

Haynes, Lemuel. *Black Preacher to White America: The Collected Writings of Lemuel Haynes, 1774–1832*, ed. Richard Newman. Brooklyn, NY: Carlson, 1990.

Heeney, Brian. *The Women's Movement in the Church of England, 1850–1930.* New York: Oxford University Press, 1988. (See esp. 89–92, 120–26, Maude Royden, Edith Picton-Tuberville.)

Heilbut, Anthony. "The Gospel Sound, 238, Shirley Caesar: Putting the Gospel Truth into Politics." *Ebony* (December 1988): 66–67, 70.

Heinze, Lee. "Charles A. Tindley: Preacher, Pastor, Hymnwriter." *Fundamentalist Journal* 4, no. 11 (December 1985): 40–41.

Hempton, David. *The Religion of the People: Methodism and Popular Religion, 1750–1900.* London: Routledge, 1996. (See esp. 183–86.)

Henson, Joyce. "Charles Albert Tindley, African American Hymn Writer." Temple United Methodist Church. http://templeumc.org/archives/charles_tindley.html.

Herskovits, Melville J. *The Myth of the Negro Past.* New York: Harper & Row Publishers, 1941.

Herwig, Holger H., and Neil M. Heyman, eds. *The World War I Biographical Dictionary.* Westport, CT: Greenwood Press, 1982.

Hicks, H. Beecher, Jr. "Challenge to the African American Church: Problems and Perspectives for the Third Millennium." *Journal of Religious Thought* 51 (Summer 1994): 81–97.

Hicks, William. *History of Louisiana Negro Baptists from 1804–1914.* Nashville, TN: National Baptist Publishing Board, 1914.

Hill, Samuel S., and Charles S. Lippy, eds. *Encyclopedia of Religion in the South.* Reprint, Macon, GA: Mercer University Press, 1998.

Hinks, P. Peter. *To Awaken My Afflicted Brethren: David Walker and the Problem of Antebellum Slave Resistance.* University Park: Pennsylvania State University Press, 1996.

Hinson, Glenn. *Fire in My Bones: Transcendence and the Holy Spirit in African American Gospel: In Collaboration with Saints from a Host of Churches.* Philadelphia: University of Pennsylvania Press, 2000.

Holloway, Houston Hartsfield. "Autobiography of Houston Hartsfield Holloway, Put into This Package by His Eldest Son, J. W. Holloway, September 6, 1932, Nashville, Tenn." Manuscript, 204. Washington, DC: Library of Congress, Manuscript Division, Miscellaneous Collections.

Holmes, Zan W. "Encountering Jesus in Worship," in *Readings in African American Church Music and Worship*, compiled and ed. by James Abbington. Chicago: GIA, 2001.

Hood, James Walker. *One Hundred Years of the African Methodist Episcopal Zion Church; or The Centennial of African Methodism.* New York: AME Zion Book Concern, 1895.

Horton, James Oliver and Lois E. Horton. *Hard Road to Freedom: The Story of*

*African America*. Vol. 1, *From African Roots to the Civil War*. New Brunswick: Rutgers University Press, 2001.

Hubbard, Dolan, and Bernard H. Sullivan Jr. "'Let My People Go': A Spiritually Charged Mascon of Hope and Liberation." *African Methodist Episcopal Zion Quarterly Review* 97, no. 2 (October 1985): 18–28.

Hubert, Susan J. "Testimony and Prophesy in the Life and Religious Experience of Jarena Lee. *Journal of Religious Thought* 54, no. 2 (1998): 2–12; 55, no. 1: 45–52.

Hughes, Louis. "Religious Meetings of the Slaves," in *Thirty Years a Slave: From Bondage to Freedom: The Institution of Slavery as Seen on the Plantation and in the Home of the Planter: Autobiography of Louis Hughes*. Milwaukee: South Side Printing Company, 1897, 52–54.

Humez, Jean McMahon. "'My Spirit Eye': Some Functions of Spiritual and Visionary Experience in the Lives of Five Black Women Preachers, 1810–1880," in *Women and the Structure of Society: Selected Research from the Fifth Berkshire Conference on the History of Women*, ed. Barbara Harris and JoAnn McNamara. Durham, NC: Duke University Press, 1984, 129–43.

Hurston, Zora Neale. *The Sanctified Church*. Berkeley, CA: Turtle Island Press, 1981.

Idowu, E. Bolaji. *Olodumare: God in Yoruba Belief*. London: Longman Group, 1962.

"Inaugural Events Dedicated to the Late BU Theology Prof. Prathia Hall." News release, The Center for African American Religious Research and Education, October 2, 2003. http://www.bu.edu/sth/news/archive/caarre-hall.html (accessed June 27, 2007).

Irvin, Dale T. "Charles Price Jones: Image of Holiness," in *Portraits of a Generation: Early Pentecostal Leaders*, ed. James R. Goff, Jr., and Grant Wacker. Fayetteville: University of Arkansas, 2002.

Isichei, Elizabeth. *A History of Christianity in Africa from Antiquity to the Present*. London: SPECK, 1955.

Jackson, Joseph Harrison. *A Story of Christian Activism: The History of the National Baptist Convention, U.S.A., Inc*. West Berlin, NJ: Townsend Press, 1980.

———. *Religious Leaders of America*, 2nd ed. Detroit: Gale Research, 1991.

———. "Great God Our King." Folder 2 (2000. 196), Chicago Historical Society, Olivet Baptist Church, Box 1.

Jakes, Thomas Dexter. "The Gathering of America," in *9.11.01: African American Leaders Respond to an American Tragedy*, ed. Martha Simmons and Frank A. Thomas. Valley Forge, PA: Judson Press, 2001.

"James A. Forbes: Senior Minister Emeritus." The Riverside Church, New York City, http://www.theRiversidechurchny.org/about/?minister-emeritus.

Jennes, Mary. *Twelve Negro Americans*. New York: Friendship Press, 1936.

"Jesse Jackson," in *Contemporary Black Biography*, ed. Ashyia Henderson. Detroit: Gale Group, 2001, 27.

Johannesen, Richard L. "The Ethics of Plagiarism Reconsidered: The Oratory of Martin Luther King, Jr." *Southern Communication Journal* 60 (1994): 185–94.

Johns, Vernon. "Transfigured Moments." *Best Sermons*, http://www.bestsermons.net/1926/Transfigured_Moments.html (accessed June 1, 2007).

Johnson, Alonzo. *Ain't Gonna Lay My 'Ligion Down: African American Religion in the South*. Columbia: University of South Carolina Press, 1996.

Johnson, Clifton H., ed. *God Struck Me Dead: Religious Conversion Experiences and Autobiographies of Ex-Slaves*. Cleveland, OH: Pilgrim Press, 1993.

Johnson, Robert B. "From Slavery to Servanthood: John Jasper Sang the Praises of Jesus." *Fundamentalist Journal* 5, no. 2. (Fall 1986): 32–34.

Johnson-Bey, Susan D. "Noble Drew Ali and the M.S.T. of A.," 3rd ed. Moorish Science Temple of America, 1999.

Johnstone, Ronald L. "Negro Preachers Take Sides." *Review of Religious Research* 11 (1969): 81–89.

Jones, Charles Edwin. *Black Holiness: A Guide to the Study of Black Participation in Wesleyan Perfectionist and Glossolalic Pentecostal Movements*. Metuchen, NJ: American Theological Library Association / Scarecrow Press, 1987.

Jones, E.A. *A Candle in the Dark: A History of Morehouse College*. Valley Forge, PA: Judson Press, 1967.

Jordan, A.C. "Tale, Teller and Audience in African Spoken Narrative," in *Proceedings of a Conference on African Languages and Literatures Held at Northwestern University April 28–30, 1966*, ed. Jack Berry, Robert Plant Armstrong, and John Povey, 33–44. Evanston, IL: Northwestern University, 1966.

Joyner, Charles. "'Believer I Know': The Emergence of African-American Christianity," in *African-American Christianity: Essays in History*, ed. Paul E. Johnson. Berkeley: University of California Press, 1994, 18–46; esp. 25–27.

Julian of Norwich. *The Revelation of the Divine Love in Sixteen Showings to Dame Julian of Norwich*, trans. M.L. del Mastro. Liguori, MO: Triumph Books, 1994.

Kealing, H.T. "A Race Rich in Spiritual Content." *Southern Workman* 32 (January 1904): 41–44.

Kearney, Belle. *A Slaveholder's Daughter*. London: Abbey Press, 1900. Reprint, New York: Negro Universities Press, 1969.

Kilgore, Thomas, Jr., and Jini Kilgore Ross. *A Servant's Journey: The Life and Work of Thomas Kilgore*. Valley Forge, PA: Judson Press, 1998.

King, Coretta Scott. *My Life With Martin Luther King, Jr.* New York: Henry Holt, 1993.

King, Martin Luther, Jr. "I've Been to the Mountaintop." Martin Luther King, Jr., Research and Education Center, Papers Project, http://stanford.edu/group/King/speeches/pub/I%27ve_been_to_the_mountaintop.html (accessed June 4, 2008).

———. *The Papers of Martin Luther King, Jr.*, ed. Clayborne Carson, Ralph E. Luker, and Penny A. Russell. Berkeley: University of California Press, 1992.

———. *Strength to Love*. New York: Harper & Row, 1963.

———. *Stride Toward Freedom: The Montgomery Story*. New York: Harper & Row, 1968.

———. *Where Do We Go From Here: Chaos or Community?* New York: Harper & Row, 1967.

Kinzer, Stephen. "Interest Surges in Voodoo." *New York Times*, November 30, 2003.

Kozol, Jonathan. *Amazing Grace*. New York: Crown Publishers, 1995.

———. *Savage Inequalities: Children in America's Schools*. New York: Crown Publishers, 1991.

Lamm, Alan K. *Five Black Preachers in Army Blue 1884–1901: The Buffalo Soldier Chaplains*. Lewiston, NY: Edwin Mellen Press, 1998.

LaRue, Cleophus, ed. *This Is My Story: Testimonies and Sermons of Black Women in Ministry.* Louisville, KY: Westminster John Knox Press, 2005.

Lawrence-Lightfoot, Sara. *I've Known Rivers: Lives of Loss and Liberation.* Reading, MA: Addison-Wesley Publishing, 1994.

Lee, Shayne. *America's New Preacher: T. D. Jakes.* New York: New York University Press, 2006.

Levine, Lawrence W. "Slave Songs and Slave Consciousness: An Exploration in Neglected Sources." *African-American Religion: Interpretive Essays in History and Culture,* ed. Timothy E. Fulop and Albert J. Raboteau. New York: Routledge, 1997.

———. *Black Culture and Black Consciousness: Afro-American Folk Thought from Slavery to Freedom.* New York: Oxford University Press, 1977.

Levy, Sholomo B. "Reverend Ike," in *African American Lives*, ed. Henry L. Gates Jr. and Evelyn Brooks Higginbotham. New York: Oxford University Press, 2004.

Lischer, Richard. "Gardner C. Taylor," in *Concise Encyclopedia of Preaching*, ed. William H. Willimon and Richard Lischer. Louisville, KY: Westminster John Knox Press, 1995.

Logan, Rayford W. and Michael R. Winston, eds. *Dictionary of Negro Biography.* New York: W. W. Norton & Company, 1982.

Lomax, Louis E. *The Negro Revolt.* New York: Signet, 1972.

Love, Emanuel K. *History of the First African Baptist Church, from its Organization January 20, 1788 to July 1, 1888*. Savannah, GA: Morning News Print, 1888.

Lovell, John, Jr. *Black Song: The Forge and the Flame—The Story of How the Afro-American Spiritual Was Hammered Out.* New York: Paragon House Publishers, 1972.

Lowery, Irving E. *Life on the Old Plantation in Ante-bellum Days.* Columbia: State Company, 1911.

Luker, Ralph E. "Johns the Baptist." http://ralphluker.com/vjohns/baptist.html (accessed July 29, 2007).

Lynch, Willie. *The Willie Lynch Letters and the Making of a Slave.* Chicago: Lushena Books, 1999.

Magida, Arthur J. *Prophet of Rage: The Life of Louis Farrakhan and His Nation.* New York: Basic Books, 1996.

Martin, Hugh. *The Beatitudes.* New York: Harper & Brothers, 1953.

Martin, Joan. "Church Women and the Women's Movement: Speaking Out From a Black Perspective." *The Church Woman* (November 1978): 11–13.

Marty, Martin E. Forword to *A Strange Freedom: The Best of Howard Thurman on Religious Experience and Public Life,* ed. Walter Earl Fluker and Catherine Tumber. Boston: Beacon Press, 1998.

———. "Mysticism and the Religious Quest for Freedom," in *God and Human Freedom: A Festschrift in Honor of Howard Thurman,* ed. Henry J. Young. Richmond, IN: Friends United Press, 1983.

Massey, James Earl. "Thurman's Preaching: Substance and Style," in *God and Human Freedom: A Festschrift in Honor of Howard Thurman*, ed. Henry J. Young. Richmond, IN: Friends United Press, 1983.

Maynard-Reid, Pedrito U. *Diverse Worship: African-American, Caribbean & Hispanic*

*Perspectives.* Downers Grove: InterVarsity Press (2000). See "The Spoken Word" (African-American), 86–98; "The Word & the Response" (Caribbean), 150–57.

Mays, Benjamin E. *Born to Rebel: An Autobiography.* New York: Charles Scribner's Sons, 1971.

———. *Disturbed about Man.* Richmond, VA: John Knox Press, 1969.

Mays, Benjamin E., and Joseph W. Nicholson. *The Negro's God as Reflected in His Literature.* Boston: Chapman & Grimes, 1938. Reprint, Westport, CT: Greenwood, 1969.

McAlister, Elizabeth. "The Madonna of 115th Street Revisited: Vodou and Haitian Catholicism in the Age of Transnationalism," in *African American Religious Thought*, ed. Cornel West and Eddie Glaude Jr. Louisville, KY: Westminster John Knox Press, 2003.

McGregor, David. "The Development and Distinctive Character of the Black Church in the South, From the Beginning of Slavery to the Reconstruction Era." *Flinders Journal of History and Politics* (Australia) 16 (1993): 27–37.

McKenzie, Vashti M. *Contemporary Black Biography*, ed. Shellie M. Saunders. Detroit: Gale Group, 1992, 29.

McKinney, Richard I. *Mordecai: The Man and His Message: The Story of Mordecai Wyatt Johnson.* Washington, DC: Howard University Press, 1997.

McMickle, Marvin A. *An Encyclopedia of African American Christian Heritage.* Valley Forge, PA: Judson Press, 2002.

McMickle, Marvin A., and Otis Moss. *From Pulpit to Politics: Reflections on the Separation of Church and State.* Euclid, OH: Williams Custom Printing, 1999.

McNeil, Jesse Jai. *Men in the Local Church.* Nashville, TN: Townsend Press, 1960.

———. *Moments in His Presence.* Grand Rapids, MI: William B. Eerdmans Publishing, 1961.

———. *Mission in the Metropolis.* Grand Rapids, MI: William B. Eerdmans Publishing, 1965.

Melton, Gordon, ed. *Encyclopedia of American Religions*, vol. 2. New York: Triumph Books, 1991.

*Microsoft Encarta Online Encyclopedia*, s.v. "Jackson, Jesse (Louis)" (by Paul Finkelman), http://encarta.msn.com (accessed June 28, 2007).

Miller, Casey, and Kate Swift. *Words and Women: New Language in New Times.* New York: Doubleday, 1976.

Miller, Rebecca. "Female Improvement." *Christian Palladium* 10, no. 2 (May 15, 1841): 35–36; reprinted in *Outreach and Diversity,* ed. Margaret Lamberts Bendroth, Lawrence N. Jones, and Robert A. Schneider. New Haven, CT: Yale University Press, 1996: 129–31; *The Living Theological Heritage of the United Church of Christ*, vol. 5, ed. Bendroth, Margaret Lamberts, Lawrence Jones, Robert A. Schneider and Barbara Brown Zikmund. Cleveland, OH: Pilgrim Press, 2000.

Mitchell, Ella Pearson. "All Flesh Is Eligible." *30 Good Minutes*, Chicago Sunday Evening Club, January 17, 1999, Program #4215. http://www.csec.org/csec/sermon/mitchell_4215.htm (accessed June 27, 2007).

Mitchell, Ella Pearson, and Henry H. Mitchell. *Together For Good: Lessons from Fifty-five Years of Marriage.* Kansas City: Andrews McMeel Publishing, 1999.

Mitchell, Mozella G. "New Africa in America: The Blending of African and American Religious and Social Traditions among Black People in Meridian, Mississippi, and Surrounding Counties." *Martin Luther King, Jr. Memorial Studies in Religion, Culture, and Social Development*, vol. 5. New York: Peter Lang, 1994: 143–97.

Montgomery, William E. "Lacey Kirk Williams," in *The Handbook of Texas Online*. Texas State Historical Association. http://www.tshaonline.org/handbook/online/.

———. *Under Their Own Vine and Fig Tree: The African American Church in the South 1865–1900*. Baton Rouge: Louisiana State University Press, 1993: 307–32.

Moore, N. Webster. "John Berry Meachum (1789–1854): St. Louis Pioneer, Black Abolitionist, Educator, and Preacher." *Missouri Historical Society Bulletin* 29, no. 2 (1973): 96–103.

Morrison, Toni. *Beloved*. New York: Knopf, 1987, 87–89, 177 (sermon of Baby Suggs, Holy).

Murphy, Jeanette Robinson. *Southern Thoughts for Northern Thinkers and African Music in America*. New York: Bandanna Publishing Company, 1904.

Murphy, Larry G., J. Gordon Melton, and Gary L. Ward, eds. *Encyclopedia of African American Religions*. New York: Garland Publishing, Inc., 1993.

Murray, Ellen. "One of the Least: A Bit of Folklore." *Southern Workman* 31 (October 1902): 562–63.

Murray, Pauli. *Pauli Murray: The Autobiography of a Black Activist, Feminist, Lawyer, Priest and Poet*. Knoxville: University of Tennessee Press, 1989.

Myers, William H. *God's Yes Was Louder than My No: Rethinking the African American Call to Ministry*. Grand Rapids, MI: William B. Eerdmans Publishing Company, 1994.

———. *The Irresistible Urge to Preach: A Collection of African American "Call" Stories*. Atlanta: Aaron Press, 1991.

Nash, Gary B. "New Light on Richard Allen: The Early Years of Freedom." *William and Mary Quarterly* 46, no. 2 (1989): 332–40.

Nelson, Douglas. "The Black Face of Church Renewal: The Meaning of Charismatic Explosion (1901–1985)," in *Faces of Renewal: Studies in Honor of Stanley M. Horton*, ed. Paul Elbert. Peabody, MA: Hendrickson Publishers, 1998.

Nelson, William E. "Black Church Politics and the Million Man March," in *Black Religious Leadership from the Slave Community to the Million Man March: Flames of Fire*, ed. Felton Best. Lewiston, NY: Edwin Mellen Press, 1998.

Newman, Richard, Patrick Rael, and Philip Lapsansky, eds. *Pamphlets of Protest: An Anthology of Early African American Protest Literature*. New York: Routledge, 2001.

Noel, James A. "Call and Response: The Meaning of the Moan and Significance of the Shout in Black Worship." *Reformed Liturgy & Music* 28 (Spring 1994): 72–76.

Nutt, Maurice. *Thea Bowman: In My Own Words*. Liguori, MO: Liguori Publications, 2009.

Old, Elizabeth. *Memoir of Old Elizabeth, A Coloured Woman*. Philadelphia: Collins, 1863; reprinted in *Six Women's Slave Narratives*. The Schomburg Library of Nineteenth-Century Black Women Writers. New York: Oxford University Press, 1988.

Oliver, Paul. *Songsters and Saints: Vocal Traditions on Race Records*. New York: Cambridge University Press, 1984.

O'Neal, Jim, and Amy van Singel. *Classic Interviews from* Living *magazine.* New York: Routledge, 2001.

Opoku, Kofi Asare. *West African Traditional Religion.* Accra, Ghana: FEP International Private, 1979.

"Otis Moss, Jr." *Who's Who Among African Americans*, 18th ed. Detroit: Gale Group, 2005.

O'Toole, James M. *Passing for White: Race, Religion, and the Healy Family, 1820–1920.* Amherst: University of Massachusetts Press, 2002.

Painter, Nell Irvin. "Representing Truth: Sojourner Truth's Knowing and Becoming Known." *The Journal of American History* 81, no. 2 (September 1994): 465–71.

———. *Sojourner Truth: A Life, a Symbol.* New York: W. W. Norton & Company, 1996.

Patterson, Gilbert E. "Biography of Bishop Gilbert E. Patterson." Memphis, TN: Office of the Presiding Bishop, Church of God in Christ, Inc., 2006.

Patterson, J.O., German R. Ross, and Julia Mason Atkins. *History and Formative Years of the Church of God in Christ with Excerpts from the Life and Works of Its Founder—Bishop C. H. Mason.* Memphis, TN: Church of God in Christ Publishing House, 1969.

Patterson, Orlando. *Slavery and Social Death.* Cambridge, MA: Harvard University Press, 1982.

Payne, Daniel. *Men of Mark: Eminent, Progressive and Rising.* Chicago: Johnson Publishing Company, 1970.

Pentecostal Charismatic Churches of North America Web site. "Pentecostal Partners: A Reconciliation Strategy for a 21st Century Ministry" Conference. http://www.pccna.org/ (accessed August 2005).

Person, Mary Alice. "The Religion of the Negro." *Southern Workman* 32 (July 1904): 403–4.

Peters, Kate. "'Women's Speaking Justified': Women and Discipline in the Early Quaker Movement, 1652–1656," in *Gender and Christian Religion,* ed. R.N. Swanson, 205–34. *Studies in Church History,* vol. 34. Suffolk, Great Britain: Boydell Press, 1998.

Pierson, William D. *Black Legacy: America's Hidden Heritage.* Amherst: University of Massachusetts Press, 1993.

———. *Black Yankees: The Development of an Afro-American Subculture in Eighteenth-Century New England.* Amherst: University of Massachusetts Press, 1988.

Pinn, Anthony B. *Varieties of African American Religious Experience.* Minneapolis, MN: Fortress Press, 1998.

Pleasant-Bey, Elihu. *The Biography of Noble Drew Ali: The Exhuming of a Nation.* Charleston, SC: Booksurge Publishing, 2004.

Ponder, Rhinold, and Michele Tuck-Ponder. *The Wisdom of the Word Love: Great African American Sermons.* New York: Crown Publishers, 1997.

Porter, Dorothy. *Early Negro Writings, 1760–1837.* Boston: Beacon Press, 1971.

"Prathia Hall." *This Far by Faith: African-American Spiritual Journeys*, PBS. http://www.pbs.org/thisfarbyfaith/people/prathia_hall.html (accessed June 25, 2007).

Price, Frederick K.C. *Race, Religion & Racism*, vol. 1, *Perverting the Gospel to Subjugate a People.* Los Angeles: Faith One, 2001.

Raboteau, Albert J. *Slave Religion: The "Invisible Institution" in the Antebellum South.* Oxford: Oxford University Press, 1978.

Reagon, Bernice Johnson, ed. *We'll Understand It Better By and By: Pioneering African American Gospel Composers.* Washington, DC: Smithsonian Institution Press, 1993.

Reavis, Ralph, Sr. "Black Higher Education among American Baptists in Virginia: From the Slave Pen to the University." *American Baptist Quarterly* 11 (December 1992): 357ff.

Reed, Harry A. "Martin Luther King, Jr.: History and Memory, Reflections on Dreams and Silences." *Journal of Negro History* 84 (1999): 150–66.

"Reverend Dr. Jeremiah Wright, Jr." Festival of Homiletics. http://www.festivalofhomiletics.com/speaker.html (accessed May 23, 2005).

"Reverend James Forbes and the Riverside Church." *NOW*, PBS, December 26, 2003. Available at http://www.pbs.org/now/society/forbes.html (accessed June 27, 2007).

Reynolds, Barbara. *Jesse Jackson: America's David.* Washington, DC: JFJ Associates, 1985.

Richardson, Harry V. *Dark Glory: A Picture of the Church Among Negroes in the Rural South.* New York: Friendship Press, 1947.

Riggs, Marcia Y. *Can I Get a Witness? : Prophetic Religious Voices of African American Women: An Anthology.* Maryknoll, NY: Orbis Books, 1997.

———. *Plenty Good Room: Women Versus Male Power in the Black Church.* Cleveland, OH: Pilgrim Press, 2003.

Robeck, Cecil M., Jr. "The Past: Historical Roots of Racial Unity and Division in American Pentecostalism." Paper presented in Memphis, Tennessee, during October 17–24, 1994. *Cyberjournal for Pentecostal-Charismatic Research.* Available at http://www.pctii.org/cyberj/cyber14/robeck.html (accessed July 19, 2005).

Roberts, J. Deotis. "The American Negro's Contribution to Religious Thought," in *The Negro Impact on Western Civilization,* ed. Joseph S. Roucek and Thomas Kiernan. New York: Philosophical Library, 1970.

———. *Africentric Christianity: A Theological Appraisal for Ministry.* Valley Forge, PA: Judson Press, 2000.

Robinson, Lizzie. *Personal Purity: Advice to Young People and Mothers, Secrets Kept From Children, Facts for Boys and Girls 12 to 20 Years*, ed. Alberta McKenzie. Birmingham, AL: Forniss Printing Company, n.d.

Roediger, David R. "And Die in Dixie: Funerals, Death, & Heaven in the Slave Community, 1700–1865." *Massachusetts Review* 22 (1981): 163–83.

Ross, Kenneth R. "The Message of Mainstream Christianity in Malawi: An Analysis of Contemporary Preaching." Sources for the Study of Religion in Malawi. Zomba, Malawi: Department of Theology and Religious Studies. Chancellor College: University of Malawi, 1993.

Ryan, Judylyn S. "Spirituality and/as Ideology in Black Women's Literature: The Preaching of Maria W. Stewart and Baby Suggs, Holy," in *Women Preachers and Prophets through Two Millennia of Christianity*, ed. Beverly Mayne Kienzie and Pamela J. Walker. Berkeley: University of California Press, 1998, 267–87.

Saillant, John. "Traveling in Old and New Worlds with John Jea, the African Preacher, 1773–1816." *Journal of American Studies* 33 (December 1999): 473–90.

Salzman, Jack, David L. Smith, and Cornel West, eds. *Encyclopedia of African American Culture and History*. New York: Macmillan, 1996.

Sanders, Rufus G. *William Seymour: Black Father of 20th Century Pentecostal/Charismatic Movements*. Sandusky, OH: Alexandria Publications, 2001.

Sernett, Milton C. *Bound for the Promised Land: African American Religion and the Great Migration*. Durham, NC: Duke University Press, 1997.

———, ed. *African American Religious History: A Documentary Witness*, 2nd ed. Durham, NC: Duke University Press, 1999.

———. *Black Religion and American Evangelicalism: White Protestants, Plantation Missions, and the Flowering of Negro Christianity, 1787–1865*. Metuchen, NJ: Scarecrow Press, 1975.

Shorney, David. "'Women May Preach but Men Must Govern': Gender Roles in the Growth and Development of the Bible Christian Denomination," in *Gender and Christian Religion*, ed. R.N. Swanson. *Studies in Church History*, vol. 34. Suffolk, Great Britain: Boydell Press, 1998, 309–22.

Sidwell, Mark. *Free Indeed: Heroes of Black Christian History*. Greenville, NC: Bob Jones University Press, 2001.

Sieger, Hans, and Merrill Singer. "*Religious Diversification During the Era of Advanced Industrial Capitalism*," in *An Encyclopedia of African American Christian Heritage*, ed. Marvin A. McMickle. Valley Forge, PA: Judson Press, 2002.

Simmons, William J. *Men of Mark: Eminent, Progressive and Rising*. 1870. Reprint, Chicago: Johnson Publishing Company, 1970.

Sims, David. "The Negro Spiritual: Origins and Themes." *Journal of Negro Education* 35, no. 1 (1966): 35–41.

"Sister Thea Bowman (1937–1990): A Tribute." Boston College. http://www.bc.edu/offices/ahana/about/history/bowman.html.

Smith, Arthur L. "The Black Revolution: 1954–1973," in *America in Controversy: History of American Public Address*, ed. DeWitte Holland, 371–89. Dubuque, IA: Wm. C. Brown, 1973.

———, ed. *Language, Communication, and Rhetoric in Black America*. New York: Harper & Row, 1972.

Smith, Elizabeth J. "Biblical Interpretation and Preaching in Worship," in *Bearing Fruit in Due Season: A Feminist Hermeneutics and the Bible in Worship*. Collegeville, MN: Liturgical Press, 1999.

Smith, Jessie Carney, ed. *Notable Black American Women, Book II*. Detroit: Gale Group, 1996.

Smith, Luther, Jr. *The Mystic as Prophet*. Richmond, IN: Friends United Press, 1991.

Smith, Theophus H. *Conjuring Culture: Biblical Formations of Black America*. New York: Oxford University Press, 1994.

Sobel, Mechal. *Trabelin' On: The Slave Journal to an Afro-Baptist Faith: Contributions in Afro-American and African Studies*. Westport, CT: Greenwood Press, 1979.

Speaks, Ruben L. "The Kerygma and the Black Church." *AME Zion Quarterly Review* 110 (April 1998): 24–32.

Spencer, Jon Michael. *Black Hymnody: A Hymnological History of the African-American Church*. Knoxville: University of Tennessee Press, 1992.

———, ed. *Unsung Hymns by Black and Unknown Bards*. Durham, NC: Duke University Press, 1990.

Spillers, Hortense J. "Moving On Down the Line." *American Quarterly* 40, no. 1 (1988): 83–109.

Stallings, James O. *Telling the Story: Evangelism in Black Churches*. Valley Forge, PA: Judson Press, 1988.

Stevens, Abel. *Sketches and Incidents*. New York: G. Lane and P. P. Sandford, 1844.

Strong, Douglas M. "Julia A.J. Foote (1823–1900) Holiness Preacher: Overcoming Prejudice through Sanctification," in *They Walked in the Spirit: Personal Faith and Social Action in America*. Louisville, KY: Westminster John Knox Press, 1997.

Strong, James. *The New Strong's Exhaustive Concordance of the Bible*. Nashville, TN: Thomas Nelson Publishers, 1995.

Swartley, Mary, and Rhoda Keener, eds. *She Has Done a Good Thing: Mennonite Women Leaders Tell Their Stories*. Scottsdale, AZ: Herald Press, 1999.

Takon, Roland. *Should the Woman Preach? An Incisive Scriptural View of Women in the Ministry: Mainly for Women and Ministers*. Lagos, Nigeria: Frontline Services, 1998.

Taylor, Alrutheus Ambush. "The Impression the Church Made," in *The Negro in the Reconstruction of Virginia*. Washington, DC: The Association for the Study of Negro Life and History, 1926: 194–207.

Taylor, Clarence. "The Evolving Spiritual and Political Leadership of Louis Farrakhan: From Allah's Masculine Warrior to Ecumenical Sage," in *Black Religious Intellectuals*. New York: Routledge, 2002.

———. "The Formation and Development of Brooklyn's Black Churches from the 19th Century to the Early 20th Century." *Long Island Historical Journal* 5, no. 2 (1993): 209–28.

Thomas, Hugh. *The Slave Trade: The History of British Slavery*. London: Harper Collins, 1982.

Thomas, Latta R. "The American Baptist Churches' Contribution to Black Education in Southern America: Testimony from a Beneficiary." *American Baptist Quarterly* 11 (December 1992): 344–56.

Thomas, Walter S. *Spiritual Navigation for the 21st Century*. Valley Forge, PA: Judson Press, 2000.

Thompson, Charles. *Biography of a Slave: Being the Experiences of Rev. Charles Thompson, a Preacher of the United Brethren Church, While a Slave in the South*. Dayton, OH: United Brethren Publishing House, 1875.

Thurman, Ann. *For the Inward Journey: The Writings of Howard Thurman*. New York: Harcourt Brace Jovanovich, 1984.

Thurman, Howard. *Deep is the Hunger*. New York: Harper and Brothers, 1951.

———. *Deep River and the Negro Speaks of Life and Death*. Richmond, IN: Friends United Press, 1975.

———. *Disciplines of the Spirit*. Richmond, IN: Friends United Press, 1963.

———. *The Growing Edge*. New York: Harper & Row, 1956.

———. *Jesus and the Disinherited*. New York: Abingdon-Cokesbury, 1949.

———. *Temptations of Jesus: Five Sermons Given by Dean Howard Thurman in the Marsh Chapel, Boston University, 1962*. Richmond, IN: Friends United Press, 1978.

———. *With Head and Heart: The Autobiography of Howard Thurman*. New York: Harcourt Brace Jovanovich, 1984.

Tinney, James S. "William J. Seymour (1855–1920): Father of Modern-Day Pentecostalism." *Journal of the Interdenominational Theological Center* 4, no. 1 (Fall 1976): 34–44.

Tolbert, James A. *The Life and Times of Rev. James R. Rosemond: His Early Life as a Slave Preacher: A Complete Biography*. Greenville, SC: Shannon & Co., 1902.

Turner, William C., Jr. "Movements in the Spirit: A Review of African American Holiness/Pentecostals/Apostolics," in *Directory of African American Religious Bodies*, ed. Wardell Payne. Washington, DC: Howard University Press, 1991.

Wade, Richard C. "Beyond the Master's Eye," in *Slavery in the Cities: The South, 1820–1860*. New York: Oxford University Press, 1964: 143–79.

Walker, Alice. *In Search of Our Mother's Garden*. San Diego: Harcourt Brace Jovanich, 1983.

Walls, William J. *The African Methodist Episcopal Zion Church: Reality of the Black Church*. Charlotte, NC: AME Zion Publishing House, 1974.

Walton, Jonathan L. *Watch This: The Ethics and Aesthetics of Black Televangelism*. New York: New York University Press, 2009.

Washington, Booker T. "The Negro Preacher and the Negro Church," in *The Story of the Negro: The Rise of the Race from Slavery*, no. 1. New York: P. Smith, 1940: 251–78.

Washington, James Melvin. *Frustrated Fellowship: The Black Baptist Quest for Social Power*. Macon: Mercer University Press, 1985.

———, ed. *A Testament of Hope: The Essential Writings and Speeches of Martin Luther King, Jr*. San Francisco: HarperCollins, 1986.

Watley, William D. "The Tradition of Worship," in *Readings in African American Church Music and Worship*, compiled and ed. by James Abbington. Chicago: GIA, 2001, 282–93.

Watts, Jill. *God, Harlem U.S.A: The Father Divine Story*. Berkeley: University of California Press, 1992.

Webb, Stephen H. "Introducing Black Harry Hoosier: The History Behind Indiana's Namesake." *Indiana Magazine of History* 98, no. 1 (2002): 30–41.

Weems, Renita. *What Matters Most: Ten Lessons in Living Passionately from the Song of Solomon*. New York: Warner Books, 2004.

Weisbrot, Robert. *Father Divine and the Struggle for Racial Equality*. Urbana: University of Illinois Press, 1983.

Weisenfeld, Judith, and Richard Newman. *This Far by Faith: Readings in African-American Women's Religious Biography*. New York: Routledge, 1996.

Werner, Craig. *Higher Ground: Stevie Wonder, Aretha Franklin, and Curtis Mayfield and the Rise and Fall of American Soul*. New York: Crown Publishers, 2004.

Wesley, Charles H. *Richard Allen: Apostle of Freedom*. Washington, DC: Associated Publishers, 1969.

———. *Richard Allen: The Gospel Labors of Richard Allen*. Philadelphia: Martin and Boden, 1833.

West, Cornel. *Prophetic Fragments*. Grand Rapids, MI: William B. Eerdmans Publishing Company, 1988.

———. *Race Matters*. New York: Vintage Books, 2001.

Westerkamp, Marilyn J. "Gender, Revolution, and the Methodists" and "Voices and Silence: Women, the Spirit, and the Enlightenment," in *Women and Religion in Early America, 1600–1850: The Puritans and Evangelical Traditions*. London: Routledge, 1999.

Wheeler, Edward L. *Uplifting the Race: The Black Minister in the New South 1865–1902*. Lanham, NJ: University Press of America, 1986.

White, Shane, and Graham White. "At Intervals I Was Nearly Stunned by the Noise He Made: Listening to African-American Religious Sound in the Era of Slavery." *American Nineteenth Century History* (Great Britain) 1, no. 1 (2000): 34–61.

White, William S. *The African Preacher: An Authentic Narrative*. Philadelphia: Presbyterian Board of Publication, 1849. Reprint, New York: Books for Libraries Press, 1972.

"Who Is Gilbert Earl Patterson?" Bountiful Blessings. http://bbless.org/cogic.ge-patterson-history-pb.htm (accessed July 2, 2007).

Williams, Audrey. "Samuel D. Proctor," in *Notable Black American Men*, ed. Jessien Carney Smith. Detroit: Gale Group, 1999.

Williams, Ethel L. *Biographical Dictionary of Negro Ministers*. New York: Scarecrow Press, 1965.

Williams, Ethel, and Clifton Bround, eds. *Howard University Bibliography of African and Afro-American Religious Studies*. Wilmington, DE: Scholarly Resources, 1977.

Williams, James. "Narrative of James Williams: An American Slave Who Was for Several Years a Driver on a Cotton Plantation in Alabama." New York: American Anti-Slavery Society; Boston: Isaac Knapp, 1838: 25–27.

Williams, Juan, and Quinton Dixie. *This Far by Faith: Stories from the African American Religious Experience*. New York: Blackside Inc., 2003.

Williams, Michael, ed. *African American Encyclopedia*. New York: Marshall Cavendish, 1993.

Wills, David, and Richard Newman. *Black Apostles at Home and Abroad: Afro-Americans and the Christian Mission from the Revolution to Reconstruction*. Boston: G.K. Hall, 1982.

Woodson, Carter G. *The History of the Negro Church*. Washington, DC: Associated Publishers, 1921.

———. *Negro Orators and Their Orations*. Washington, DC: Associated Publishers, 1925.

Wright, Jeremiah A., Jr. "The Day of Jerusalem's Fall," in *9.11.01: African American Leaders Respond to an American Tragedy*, ed. Martha Simmons and Frank A. Thomas. Valley Forge, PA: Judson Press, 2001.

Wright, Richard Robert. *Centennial Encyclopedia of the African Methodist Episcopal Church*. Philadelphia: Book of Concern of the AME Church, 1916.

Yankah, Kwesi. "Speaking for the Chief: Okyeame and the Politics of Akan Royal Oratory," in *African Systems of Thought*. Bloomington: Indiana University Press, 1995, 6–24; "Okyeame: A Theoretical Framework," 45–67.

Yates, Elizabeth. *Howard Thurman: Portrait of a Practical Dreamer*. New York: The John Day Co., 1964.

Young, Henry J. *Major Black Religious Leaders Since 1940*. Nashville, TN: Abingdon Press, 1979.

Young, Robert. *The Analytical Concordance to the Bible*. Peabody, MA: Hendrickson Publishers, 1992.

Zink-Sawyer, Beverly. *Hidden Treasure: Women's Voices in the History of Preaching*. Richmond, VA: Baptist Theological Seminary at Richmond Center for Preaching and Worship, 1999.

## *Unpublished Works*

Asberry, Robert Lee. "A Rhetorical Analysis of the Preaching Style of Three African-American Preachers with Application for Black Homiletics." Thesis/diss., Dallas Theological Seminary, 2000.

Butler, Jennifer Bailey. "An Analysis of the Oral Rhetoric of Mordecai W. Johnson: A Study of the Concept of Presence." Ph.D. diss., Ohio State University, 1977.

Clark, Sandra Jean Stephens. "The Discourse of Birdie Smith: A Study of a Woman Preacher's Participation in the Church of God (Anderson, Indiana) Discourse Community." Ph.D. diss., Ball State University, 1995.

Cuff, Elliott. "Rediscovering the Power of the Redemptive Preaching Done in the Civil Rights Movement." Thesis/diss., United Theological Seminary, 1997.

Daniels, David Douglass, III. "The Cultural Renewal of Slave Religion: Charles Price Jones and the Emergence of the Holiness Movement in Mississippi." Ph.D. diss., Union Theological Seminary, 1992.

Flake, Margarett Elaine McCollins. "Preaching Healing to Hurting Women: A Womanist Hermeneutical and Homiletical Approach to Ministry with African American Women." A final document submitted to the Doctoral Studies Committee in partial fulfillment of the requirements for the degree of Doctor of Ministry. Dayton: United Theological Seminary, 1996.

Forney, Barbara White. "Rhetorical Structure and Personal Narrative: The African-American Oral Tradition in Sermons, Folktales, and Campus Ministry." Ed.D. diss., Widener University, 1997.

Franklin, Marion J. "The Relationship of Black Preaching to Black Gospel Music." Thesis/diss., Drew University, 1982.

Gallatin, Martin V. "Reverend Ike's Ministry: A Sociological Investigation of Religious Innovation." Ph.D. diss., New York University, 1979.

Goode, Gloria Davis. "Preachers of the Word and Singers of the Gospel: The Ministry of Women Among Nineteenth Century African Americans." Ph.D. diss., University of Pennsylvania, 1991.

Harris, James H. "How Shall We Preach Without a Song? A Model for African American Sacred Music." A final document submitted to the Doctoral Studies Committee in partial fulfillment of the requirements for the degree of Doctor of Ministry. Dayton: United Theological Seminary, 1996.

Haywood, Chanta M. "Prophesying Daughters: Nineteenth-Century Black Women Preachers, Religious Conviction and Resistance." Ph.D. diss., University of California, 1995.

Jones, Kirk Byron. "Let the Church Say, "Amen! The Role of Dialogue in Black Preaching." Thesis/diss., 1986.

Larkin, William Charles. "The Black Preacher as Educator from 1787 to 1909." Ed.D. diss., University of Massachusetts, 1979.

LaRue, Cleophus James. "What Makes Black Preaching Distinctive? An Investigation Based on Selected African-American Sermons from 1865–1915 in Relation to the Hermeneutical Discussion of David Kelsey." Ph.D. diss. Princeton Theological Seminary, 1996.

Lovett, Leonard. "Black Holiness-Pentecostalism: Implications for Ethics and Social Transformation." Ph.D. diss., Emory University, 1978.

Lucky, Crystal Jones. "Without Holiness: Free Black Women's Spiritual Narratives of the 19th Century." Ph.D. diss., University of Pennsylvania, 1999.

Mahlangu-Ngcobo, Mankekolo, and John Richard Bryant. "The Preaching of Bishop John R. Bryant." Submitted in partial fulfillment of the degree of Doctor of Ministry. Thesis/diss., United Theological Seminary, 1994.

May, Marvis P. "Didactic Preaching in the Black Church Tradition." Thesis/diss., United Theological Seminary, 1992.

McClendon, Howard A. "Postmodern Homiletics and Authority in the African American Preaching Tradition." Thesis/diss., Northern Baptist Theological Seminary, 1999.

McMickle, Marvin Andrew. "Film Portrayals of the Black Preacher from 1929 to the Present." Ph.D. diss., Case Western Reserve University, 1998.

Mitchell, Henry H. "The Genius of Negro Preaching: A Linguistic and Stylistic Examination of the Homiletical Twin Brother to the American Negro Spiritual, with Some Possible Implications of the Result for American Protestant 'White' Churches." Thesis/diss., Fresno State College, 1965.

Mitchell, Nevalon Jr. "Black Preaching and the Black Church: Traditions Viewed in the Context of Liberation Theology." Thesis/diss., Louisville Presbyterian Theological Seminary, 1984.

Moldovan, Russel John. "The Social Preaching of Martin Luther King, Jr." Thesis/diss., Emmanuel School of Religion, 1993.

Moss, Beverly Janine. "The Black Sermon as a Literacy Event." Thesis/diss., University of Illinois at Chicago, 1988.

Moyd, Olin P. "Black Preaching: The Style and Design of Dr. Sandy F. Ray." Thesis/diss., Howard University, 1972.

Napton, Dennis R. "Inclusive Preaching: One Preacher's Attention to Women's Issues in Preaching." D.Min. thesis, Lutheran School of Theology in Chicago, 1995.

Nelson, Douglas J. "For Such a Time as This: The Story of Bishop William J. Seymour and the Azusa Street Revival. A search for Pentecostal/Charismatic Roots." Ph.D. diss., University of Birmingham: Birmingham, England, 1981.

Nichols, M. Celeste. "The Rhetorical Structure of the Traditional Black Church." Thesis/diss., University of Louisville, 1991.

Peck, Catherine. "Your Daughters Shall Prophesy: Women in the Afro-American Preaching Tradition." M.A. thesis, University of North Carolina, 1983.

Rohde, Ted B. "The Oratory of Martin Luther King, Jr.: Rhetorical Analysis within an Historical Perspective." Thesis/diss., Lincoln Christian Seminary, 1991.

Sanders, Brian D. "Power and Sacrifice: The Transformation of Black Theology as Reflected in Black Preaching Since the Civil Rights Era." Thesis/diss., University of South Florida, 2002.

Savage, Gerald. "The Afro-American Speech-Singing Style." Thesis/diss., University of Pittsburgh, 1983.

Shaw, William J. "The Black Preacher and Black Biblical Interpretation." D.Min. thesis, Colgate Rochester Divinity School: Bexley Hall/Crozier Theological Seminary, 1975.

Simpson, Lacy Edward. "A Biblical Approach to the Inclusion of Women Preachers in the Progressive Tar River Missionary Baptist Association." D.Min. thesis, Dayton: United Theological Seminary, 1998.

Snowden, Bernard J. "A Rhetorical Analysis of the Preaching Style of Albert Louis Patterson, Jr. with Application for Black Homiletics." Thesis/diss., Dallas Theological Seminary, 2000.

Spencer, Raymond Bernard. "Imagery and Improvisation in African American Preaching Resources for Energizing the Protestant Pulpit." Thesis/diss., Southwestern Baptist Theological Seminary, 2001.

Spillers, Hortense J. "Fabrics of History: Essays on the Black Sermon." Ph.D. thesis, Brandeis University, 1974.

Stephens, Reginald Van. "The Preaching of Howard Thurman, William A. Jones, Jr., William Watley, and Jeremiah Wright, Jr.: A Comparison of Distinctive Styles in Black Preaching." A final document submitted to the Doctor of Ministry Program Committee of United Theological Seminary in partial fulfillment of the requirements for the degree of Doctor of Ministry. Dayton: United Theological Seminary, 1992.

Stewart, Warren H. "Hermeneutics in Black Preaching: An Essential Tool for Telling the Story. Thesis/diss., American Baptist Seminary of the West, 1982.

Stone, Sonja Haynes. "The Black Preacher as Teacher: An Exploratory Study." Ph.D. diss., Northwestern University, 1975.

Thomas, Frank Anthony. "Preaching as the Celebrative Moment: A Handbook on Celebration." Thesis/diss., United Theological Seminary, 1991.

Thomas, John L. "Voices in the Wilderness: A Socio-Theological Study of African-American Preaching." Thesis/diss., Phillips Graduate Seminary, 1991.

Thomas, Michael O. "Preaching to the Crises of Violence in Prince George's County, Maryland: A final document submitted to the Doctoral Studies Committee of United Theological Seminary, Dayton, Ohio in partial fulfillment of the requirements for the degree of Doctor of Ministry." Dayton: United Theological Seminary, 1994.

Townes, Emilie Maureen. "The Kingdom of God in Black Preaching: An Analysis and Critique of James H. Cone." Thesis/diss., University of Chicago, 1982.

Varner, William C. "To Preach or Not to Preach? A Biblical Study of Women in the Church." M.S.T. thesis, Biblical School of Theology, 1976.

Wesley, Howard-John. "Prescriptive Preaching to the Next Generation of Black Churchgoers." Thesis/diss., Northern Baptist Theological Seminary, 2003.

Wharry, Cheryl. "'I'm Gonna Preach It, Amen': Discourse Functions of Formulaic Expressions in African American Sermons." Thesis/diss., Oklahoma State University, 1996.

Widener, Gregory K. "The Interethnic Black Preaching Style of Cynthia L. Hale: An Exploratory Study." Ph.D. diss., University of Kentucky, 1998.

## *Media*

Cleveland, E.E., and Ernestine Cleveland Reems, et al. *The Performed Word.* The Anthropology Film Center Foundation Presents a Red Taurus Films Production; Producer: Gerald L. Davis; Directors: Ernest Shinagawa, Carlos de Jesus; Scriptwriters: Ernest Shinagawa, Gerald L. Davis, Santa Fe, New Mexico. Memphis: Center for Southern Folklore, 1982.

Cohn, Lawrence. Introduction to compact disc notes for J. M. Gates, *The Best of Reverend J. M. Gates.* Sony Music International, 2004.

Cooper, J. Jerome, and J.S. Campbell, et al. *Sermons of Black Preachers in the Presbyterian Church.* New York: Audio Visual Production Services, Presbyterian Church U.S.A., 1984.

Gates, J.M. "Reverend J.M. Gates Sermons with Responses, Assisted by His Congregation," vol. 1. Originally released 1927–1940. Sony Music International Inc. Columbia: Legacy and Okeh Electric, 2004.

Howard University. *Education for Freedom: A Documentary Tribute to Celebrate the Fiftieth Anniversary of the Election of Mordecai W. Johnson as President of Howard University.* Washington, DC: Howard University Archives, Moorland-Spingarn Research Center, 1976.

Johnson, James Weldon, and James Earl Jones. *God's Trombones: A Trilogy of African-American Poems.* New York: Billy Budd Films, 1994.

Martin, Patricia Doyle. "An Educator's Perspective About God," in *Consultation on Language About God* (sound recording) October 3–4, 1977, United Presbyterian Church, U.S.A., and Louisville Theological Seminary. Louisville, KY: Louisville Presbyterian Theological Seminary, 1977.

Nix, A.W., and Emmett Dickinson. *Rev. A.W. Nix & Rev. Emmett Dickinson: In Chronological Order, Vol. 2, 1928–1931.* Document Records, DOCD-5490. Vienna, Austria: 2000.

Taylor, Gardner C. *Essential Taylor.* Valley Forge, PA: Judson Press, 2000.

———. *Essential Taylor II.* Valley Forge, PA: Judson Press, 2001.

Weems, T.E., W.A. White, A. Wilson, and B.L. Wrightman. *Preachers and Congregations, Complete Recorded Works, Vol. 7, 1925–1928.* Document Records, DOCD-5547. Vienna, Austria: 1997.

# CREDITS

Adams, Charles G. "Chaos or Creation." Reprinted by permission of Charles G. Adams.

Ali, Noble Drew. *The Holy Koran: Moorish Science Temple of America*, (1927), "Know Thyself and Thy Father God Allah," from *The Holy Koran*, Chapter VI, "Life and Works of Jesus in India Among the Muslims," "The Divine Instructions," Chapter X, "Jesus Spake on the Unity of Allah and Man to the Hindus." Copyright © 1927. Reprinted by permission of Robert Jones-Bey, Grand Sheik, Moorish Science Temple of America, Inc.

Allen, Richard. "An Address to Those Who Keep Slaves and Approve the Practice." This sermon was taken from the University of North Carolina at Chapel Hill Digitization Project, *Documenting the American South*, 2001. Reprinted by permission of the University of North Carolina at Chapel Hill.

Booth, Charles E. "When God Deals an Uneven Hand," from *The African American Pulpit*, Spring 2002. Reprinted by permission of Charles E. Booth.

Borders, William Holmes. "Handicapped Lives," from *Best of Black Sermons*, edited by William M. Philpot. Copyright © 1972 by Judson Press. Used by permission of Judson Press, 800-4-JUDSON, www.judsonpress.com.

Bowman, Thea. "To Be Black and Catholic," Origins CNS Documentary Service. Copyright © 1989, Catholic News Service. Reprinted with permission of CNS.

Cannon, Katie G. "Prophets for a New Day." from *The African American Pulpit*, Spring 1998. Reprinted by permission of Katie G. Cannon.

Chambers, Timothy Moses. "The Measure of A Man." Copyright © 1949. Printed by permission of Wendell Keith Woods.

Chavis, John. "Letter Upon the Doctrine of the Extent of the Atonement of Christ." This sermon was taken from *John Chavis, African American Patriot, Preacher,*

*Teacher and Mentor (1763–1838)*. Reprinted by permission of Helen Chavis Othow.

Clark, Caesar A.W. "The Worms Got Him," from *The African American Pulpit*, Spring 2003. Reprinted by permission of Carolyn Clark.

Colemon, Johnnie. "Dear Enemy, I Love You" (2002). Reprinted by permission of Helen Carry for Johnnie Coleman.

Copeland, Claudette. "Why Are You Here," from *The African American Pulpit*, Fall 2005. Reprinted by permission of Claudette Copeland.

Derrick, William Benjamin. "Address to 23rd General Conference of the AME Church." This sermon was taken from the University of North Carolina at Chapel Hill Digitization Project, *Documenting the American South*, 2001. Reprinted by permission of the University of North Carolina at Chapel Hill.

Douglass, Frederick. "What, to the Slave, is Fourth of July?" This sermon was taken from *Lift Every Voice: African American Oratory, 1787–1900*. Reprinted by permission of The University of Alabama Press.

Eikerenkoetter, Frederick J. "Curse Not the Rich," from *Science of Living Study Guide*, vol. 6, no. 2. Copyright © December 1975, January, February 1976. Reprinted by permission of United Christian Evangelistic Association for Frederick J. Eikerenkoetter.

Elaw, Zilpha. "On Christian Marriage." This sermon was taken from *Sisters of the Spirit*. Reprinted by permission of University of Indiana Press.

Farrakhan, Louis. "The Million Man March." Copyright © October 16, 1995. Reprinted by permission of Louis Farrakhan.

Foote, Julia A.J. "A Threshing Sermon" (1851), "A Word to my Christian Sisters" (ca. 1861), "Women in the Gospel" (1887), and "Christian Perfection" (1894). These sermons and the message to the *Star* newspaper (1894) were taken from *Sisters of the Spirit*. Reprinted by permission of University of Indiana Press.

Forbes, James, Jr. "Spiritual Renewal: Good News for the Poor" (2004). Reprinted by permission of James Forbes, Jr.

Franklin, Clarence LaVaughn. "The Eagle Stirreth Her Nest," from *Give Me This Mountain: Life History and Selected Sermons*. Copyright © 1989 by the Board of Trustees of the University of Illinois. Reprinted by permission of the University of Illinois Press.

Gomes, Peter J. "Outer Turmoil, Inner Strength," from *9.11.01: African Americans Respond to an American Tragedy*. Copyright © 2001, Valley Forge, PA: Judson Press. Reprinted by permission of Peter J. Gomes.

Hall, Prathia. "Between the Wilderness and the Cliff," from *The African American Pulpit*, Spring 2002. Reprinted by permission of Dubois Wynn.

Harris, Barbara Clementine. "A Circle of Concern," from *The African American Pulpit*, Spring 2004. Reprinted by permission of Barbara Clementine Harris.

Haynes, Lemuel. "Universal Salvation: A very Eminent doctrine; with some Account of the Life and Character of its Author. A Sermon Delivered at Rutland, West Parish in the Year 1805." This sermon was taken from the University of North Carolina at Chapel Hill Digitization Project, *Documenting the American South*, 2001. Reprinted by permission of the University of North Carolina at Chapel Hill.

Hill, Edward Victor. "What You Have When You Have Jesus," Moody Founders Week, February 1980. Reprinted by permission of Edward V. Hill, II.

Hurston, Zora Neale. "The Wounds of Jesus," from *The Sanctified Church* (1988). Reprinted by permission of the Estate of Zora Neale Hurston.

Jackson, Jesse Louis. "Keep Hope Alive," July 19, 1988. Reprinted by permission of Jesse Louis Jackson, Sr.

Jakes, Thomas Dexter. "The Gathering of America," from *9.11.01: African Americans Respond to an American Tragedy*. Copyright © 2001, Valley Forge, PA: Judson Press. Reprinted by permission of Thomas Dexter Jakes.

Jea, John. Excerpts from sermons by John Jea. This material was taken from the electronic edition of *The Life, History, and Unparalleled Sufferings of John Jea, the African Preacher* in the University of North Carolina at Chapel Hill Digitization Project, *Documenting the American South*, 2001. Reprinted by permission of the University of North Carolina at Chapel Hill.

Johns, Vernon. "Transfigured Moments." Reprinted by permission of Elizabeth L. Johns.

Johnson, James Weldon. "The Creation," from *God's Trombones* by James Weldon Johnson. Copyright 1927 Viking Press, Inc., renewed © 1955 by Grace Nail Johnson. Used by permission of Viking Penguin, a division of Penguin Group (USA) Inc.

Johnson, Mordecai Wyatt. "Work, Business and Religion," from *Mordecai: The Man and His Message: The Story of Mordecai Wyatt Johnson*, edited by Richard I. McKinney. Copyright © 1997 by Richard I. McKinney. Reprinted with the permission of Howard University Press. All rights reserved.

Jones, Charles Price. "The Battle Royal: A Contention for the Faith Once Delivered to the Saints (Jude 25)." Reprinted by permission of Emory Lindsay, Church of Christ (Holiness) USA.

Jones, Miles. "Dealing with Disciples." Reprinted by permission of Marion Jones.

Jones, William Augustus. "An Anatomy of Forgiveness," from *The African American Pulpit*, Winter 2001–2002. Reprinted by permission of Jennifer Jones Austin.

Kinch, Emily Christmas. "Speech Delivered in Liberty Hall." This sermon was taken from *Black Redemption: Churchmen Speak for the Garvey Movement* by Randall Burkett. Reprinted by permission of Randall Burkett.

King, Martin Luther, Jr. "I've Been To The Mountaintop." Copyright 1968 the Estate of Martin Luther King Jr., copyright renewed 1996. Reprinted by arrangement with the Estate of Martin Luther King Jr., c/o Writers House as agent for the proprietor New York, NY.

Lee, Jarena. "Receiving the Call To Preach." This essay was reprinted from *Sisters of the Spirit*. Reprinted by permission of University of Indiana Press.

Mays, Benjamin E. "Eulogy for Dr. Martin Luther King, Jr., April 9, 1968." Reprinted by permission of Bernice Mays Perkins.

McKenzie, Vashti. "Keep the Pressure On," from *The African American Pulpit*, Fall 2004. Reprinted by permission of Vashti McKenzie.

McNeil, Jesse Jai. "Day of Waiting." Reprinted by permission of Jesse Jai McNeil, Jr.

Mitchell, Ella P. "All Flesh is Eligible." Reprinted by permission of Ella P. Mitchell.

Morris, Elias Camp. "1899 Presidential Address to the National Baptist Convention."

This sermon was taken from the University of North Carolina at Chapel Hill Digitization Project, *Documenting the American South*, 2001. Reprinted by permission of the University of North Carolina at Chapel Hill.

Morton, Paul S. "The Enemy Inside Your Mind," from *The African American Pulpit*, Spring 2004. Reprinted by permission of Paul S. Morton.

Moses, Henry William. "Understanding the Times and Knowing What to Do." This sermon was taken from *Black Redemption: Churchmen Speak for the Garvey Movement* by Randall Burkett. Reprinted by permission of Randall Burkett.

Moss, Otis, Jr. "A Prophetic Witness in an Anti-Prophetic Age," from *The African American Pulpit*, Fall 2004. Reprinted by permission of Otis Moss, Jr.

Patterson, Gilbert Earl. "God's Cure for Loneliness and Racism," from *The African American Pulpit*, Fall 2000. Reprinted by permission of Louise D. Patterson.

Price, Frederick K. "How God Sees the Races," from *Race, Religion, and Racism*, vol. 2, *Perverting the Gospel to Subjugate a People*, chapter 3, Frederick K. C. Price Ministries, 2003. Reprinted by permission of Angela Evans.

Proctor, Samuel D. "The Bottom Line," from *Sermons from the Black Pulpit* by Samuel D. Proctor and William D. Watley, Valley Forge, PA: Judson Press, 1984, pp. 87–97. Reprinted by permission of Judson Press.

Ransom, Reverdy Cassius. "The American Tower of Babel or Confusion of Tongues Over the Negro," from *The Spirit of Freedom and Justice: Orations and Speeches*, Nashville, TN: AME Sunday School Union, 1926. Reprinted by permission of Johnny Barbour, Jr.

Ray, Sandy F. "The Testimony of the Towel," from *Journeying Through a Jungle*, Nashville, TN: Broadman Press. Copyright © 1979. This material is used by permission of B&H Publishing Group, Nashville, TN.

Robinson, Lizzie Woods. "Personal Purity: Advice to Young People and Mothers, Secrets Kept from Children, Facts for Boys and Girls 12 to 20 Years." Forniss Printing Co., Birmingham. Reprinted by permission of Glenda Williams Goodson.

Sampson, Frederick G., II. "The Death of Hope," from *The African American Pulpit*, Winter 2000–2001. Reprinted by permission of Freeda Sampson.

Scott, Manuel L., Sr. "Heavenly Grace and Human Response," from *The African American Pulpit*, Spring 2002, Judson Press, Copyright © 2001. Reprinted by permission of Sherilyn Williams.

Tate, Mary Lena. "If We Work Six Days, the Seventh is the Sabbath." Reprinted by permission of the Lewis-Tate Foundation and Archives, Nashville, TN.

Taylor, Gardner C. "The Christian's Dearest Sight" and "Jesus Christ." Reprinted by permission of Gardner C. Taylor.

Thurman, Howard. "Lord, Teach Us to Pray," "The Grace of God," and "Not Peace—A Sword," from *The Growing Edge*, pp. 32–36, 73–76, and 97–99, respectively. From *The Growing Edge* by Howard Thurman, Friends United Press, 1980. Used by permission of Friends United Press.

Tindley, Charles Albert. "Heaven's Christmas Tree," from *The African American Pulpit*, Winter 2001–2002. Reprinted by permission of Hope For Life International, Inc.

Weems, Renita. "Not . . . Yet," from *The African American Pulpit*, Fall 2004. Reprinted by permission of Renita J. Weems.

Williams, Jasper, Jr. "God at the Midnight Ball," from *The African American Pulpit*, Spring 2003. Reprinted by permission of Jasper Williams, Jr.

Wright, Jeremiah A., Jr. "The Day of Jerusalem's Fall," from *9.11.01: African Americans Respond to an American Tragedy*, Valley Forge, PA: Judson Press, 2001. Reprinted by permission of Jeremiah A. Wright, Jr.

X, Malcolm. "The Ballot or the Bullet," from *Malcolm X Speaks*, pp. 36–58. Copyright © 1965, 1989 by Betty Shabazz and Pathfinder Press. Reprinted by permission of Pathfinder Press.

# ACKNOWLEDGMENTS

SPECIAL THANKS TO CYBIL MOSES AND THE STAFF OF THE LIBRARY OF Congress; the manager and all librarians at the Fulton County Auburn Avenue Research Library on African American Culture and History; the staff of the Special Collections Department at Emory University; the reference librarians at Emory University; Melanie Harris of Union Theological Seminary; Dr. Richard Wills for assistance in securing material concerning Vernon Johns; Meharry Lewis and the Lewis-Tate Foundation and Archives in Nashville, Tennessee, for use of material concerning Mary Lena Lewis Tate; Randall Burkett for use of material from *Black Redemption: Churchmen Speak for the Garvey Movement*; Milton Sernett for use of material from *African American Religious History: A Documentary Witness*; the University of Alabama Press for use of sermons from *Lift Every Voice: African American Oratory, 1787–1900*; Broadman Press; the Wilson Library of the University of North Carolina at Chapel Hill; Dr. Helen Chavis Othow; Dr. Jeremiah Wright Jr., Rev. Charles G. Adams, Bishop John Bryant, Bishop Vashti McKenzie, and Dr. Katie Cannon for reviewing lists of preachers for inclusion in this book; and Dr. Gardner Calvin Taylor for his invaluable wisdom, guidance, and assistance, and especially for the generous foreword. Additionally we thank Professor Nathan Dale, Mrs. Marion Jones, and Dr. William Turner for assistance in securing materials about Rev. Miles Jones.

Our appreciation goes to the following persons and institutions for permission to publish sermons or use photographs in advertising the anthology: the L. Douglas Wilder Library of Virginia Union University; Georgetown University Special Collections; the family of the late Rev. Vernon Johns; Bernice Mays Perkins; Dr. Richard McKinney; the West Virginia Regional History Collection of the West Virginia University Libraries; Howard University Press; the Moorland-Spingarn Research Center at Howard University; and Judson Press.

The following persons greatly assisted in research on the Holiness/ Pentecostal tradition: Dr. Beverly Bond, University of Memphis History Department; Dr. Janann Sherman, chair of University of Memphis History Department; Dr. Fredrick Knight, University of California, Riverside; Dr. Charles Crawford, director of oral history, University of Memphis History Department; Dr. Barbara Holmes, Memphis Theological Seminary; Dr. Anthea Butler, president of the Society for Pentecostal Studies; Dr. David Daniels, McCormick Theological Seminary, Chicago, Illinois; Dr. Odie and Nan Tolbert, COGIC archivist and retired University of Memphis librarian, respectively; Dr. David Tucker, University of Memphis History Department; Dr. Kenneth Goings, chair of the African American Studies Department, Ohio State University; Dr. Earline Allen, dean of Greater Emmanuel Bible Institute; Dr. Sherry S. DuPree, Santa Fe Community College; Dr. Vinson Synan, Regents University; Dr. Douglas Nelson, historian; Dr. Walter Hollenweger, University of Birmingham, England; Dr. Alan Anderson, University of Birmingham, England; Dr. Benjamin Hooks and the Hooks Brothers' historic photo collection; Dr. David Hall and the COGIC Publishing House; Dr. Johnson and the staff of the Memphis Shelby County Library's Memphis Room; Elder Raynard Smith and COGIC Scholars, Inc.; Elder Calvin Burns, editor of *The Whole Truth*; Bishop A. Z. Hall and the COGIC archive in Memphis, Tennessee; Gary R. Rosenberg and the Omaha and Douglas County Historical Society; Marlon Milner and the Afro-American Pentecostal List Serve; Otonya Eskridge, Sabrina Gates, and the Bountiful Blessings, Inc., Temple of Deliverance COGIC's Audio-visual Archive Department; Pastor Jack Hunt and Deliverance Temple COGIC, Memphis, Tennessee; Glen Ghor, Wayne Warner, and the Assemblies of God Archive; Ed Frank and the University of Memphis Special Collections Department; Glenda W. Goodson, specialist in COGIC women's history; Julia Mason Atkins, daughter of Bishop C. H. Mason; and Emma J. Clark, founder and director of the Dr. Mattie McGlothen Museum and Library Archive in Richmond, California.

Special thanks to the Communications Department at the University of Memphis, especially the late Michael Charles Leff, John A. Campbell, M. Allison Graham, Katherine G. Hendrix, Antonio Raul deVelasco,

Sandra Sarkela, and Amanda Young; and to Brad McAdon of the English Department at the University of Memphis.

Sincere appreciation to our research/editorial assistants: Ijeoma Nwachukwu and LaDonna M. Sanders Nkosi for the invaluable work on the biographies; Kim Patricia Johnson on proofing; Vera Banks for the tireless work in obtaining permissions to use materials; and Sallie Tipton for transcription services.

Special thanks to our editor, Amy Cherry; our agent, Djana Pearson-Morris; and Joyce, Tony, and Rachel Thomas for patience and encouragement every step of the way. Also, special appreciation is offered to Ralph Wheeler, Reginald Simmons, and Mary Simmons (mother of Martha Simmons).

We also acknowledge all PhD students who assisted with this project: Reginald Bell of the Communications Department, University of Memphis, for research, and Kimberly Johnson of the Communications Department, University of Memphis for proofing, editing, and formatting.

Most of all we give thanks to God for calling us to this "ministry of the scribe."

Martha Simmons<br>
Frank A. Thomas<br>
November 15, 2009